Japan
日本

Chris Rowthorn   **Andrew Bender**
John Ashburne   **Sara Benson**
David Atkinson   **Craig McLachlan**

LONELY PLANET PUBLICATIONS
Melbourne • Oakland • London • Paris

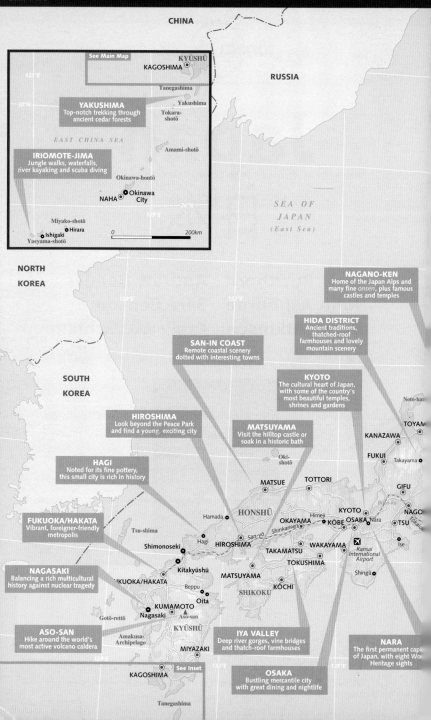

CHINA

RUSSIA

See Main Map

KAGOSHIMA

KYŪSHŪ

Tanegashima

YAKUSHIMA
Top-notch trekking through ancient cedar forests

Yakushima

Tokara-shotō

EAST CHINA SEA

IRIOMOTE-JIMA,
Jungle walks, waterfalls, river kayaking and scuba diving

Amami-shotō

Okinawa-hontō

NAHA

Okinawa City

Miyako-shotō

Hirara

Ishigaki

Yaeyama-shotō

0   200km

SEA OF JAPAN (East Sea)

NORTH KOREA

SOUTH KOREA

NAGANO-KEN
Home of the Japan Alps and many fine *onsen*, plus famous castles and temples

HIDA DISTRICT
Ancient traditions, thatched-roof farmhouses and lovely mountain scenery

SAN-IN COAST
Remote coastal scenery dotted with interesting towns

KYOTO
The cultural heart of Japan, with some of the country's most beautiful temples, shrines and gardens

Noto-han

TOYAM

KANAZAWA

FUKUI

HIROSHIMA
Look beyond the Peace Park and find a young, exciting city

MATSUYAMA
Visit the hilltop castle or soak in a historic bath

Oki-shotō

Takayama

GIFU

HAGI
Noted for its fine pottery, this small city is rich in history

MATSUE

TOTTORI

HONSHŪ

KYOTO

NAGO

FUKUOKA/HAKATA
Vibrant, foreigner-friendly metropolis

Tsu-shima

Hamada

Himeji

OKAYAMA

Nara

OSAKA

KŌBE

TSU

Biwa-ko

Hagi

San-yō

Shinkansen

Ise

NAGASAKI
Balancing a rich multicultural history against nuclear tragedy

Shimonoseki

'UKUOKA/HAKATA

HIROSHIMA

TAKAMATSU

WAKAYAMA

Kansai International Airport

Kitakyūshū

TOKUSHIMA

Shingū

Beppu

SHIKOKU

MATSUYAMA

KŌCHI

ASO-SAN
Hike around the world's most active volcano caldera

KUMAMOTO

Oita

Nagasaki

Aso-san

Gotō-rettō

KYŪSHŪ

IYA VALLEY
Deep river gorges, vine bridges and thatch-roof farmhouses

NARA
The first permanent capi of Japan, with eight Wo Heritage sights

Amakusa-Archipelago

MIYAZAKI

OSAKA
Bustling mercantile city with great dining and nightlife

KAGOSHIMA

See Inset

Tanegashima

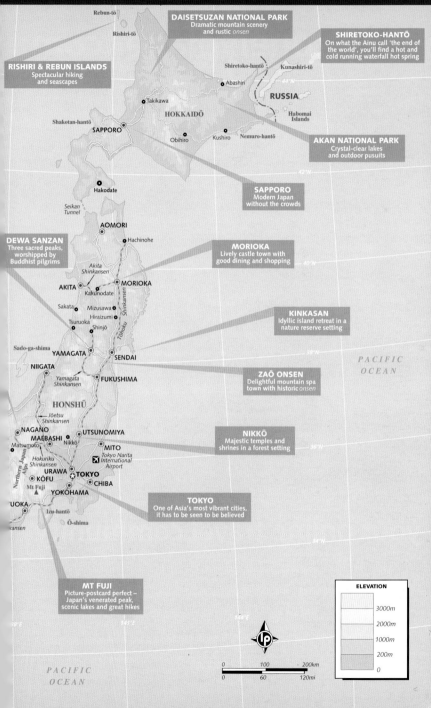

Rebun-tō

Rishiri-tō

DAISETSUZAN NATIONAL PARK
Dramatic mountain scenery
and rustic *onsen*

SHIRETOKO-HANTŌ
On what the Ainu call 'the end of
the world', you'll find a hot and
cold running waterfall hot spring

Shiretoko-hantō
Kunashiri-tō

RISHIRI & REBUN ISLANDS
Spectacular hiking
and seascapes

Abashiri

RUSSIA

Takikawa

HOKKAIDŌ

Habomai
Islands

Shakotan-hantō

SAPPORO

Obihiro
Kushiro
Nemuro-hantō

AKAN NATIONAL PARK
Crystal-clear lakes
and outdoor pusuits

SAPPORO
Modern Japan
without the crowds

Hakodate

Seikan
Tunnel

DEWA SANZAN
Three sacred peaks,
worshipped by
Buddhist pilgrims

AOMORI

Hachinohe

MORIOKA
Lively castle town with
good dining and shopping

Akita
Shinkansen

AKITA
MORIOKA

Kakunodate

Sakata
Mizusawa

KINKASAN
Idyllic island retreat in a
nature reserve setting

Tsuruoka
Hiraizumi

Shinjō

Sado-ga-shima

YAMAGATA
SENDAI

PACIFIC
OCEAN

NIIGATA
Yamagata
Shinkansen

FUKUSHIMA

ZAŌ ONSEN
Delightful mountain spa
town with historic *onsen*

HONSHŪ

Jōetsu
Shinkansen

NAGANO
UTSUNOMIYA

MAEBASHI
Nikkō

NIKKŌ
Majestic temples and
shrines in a forest setting

Matsumoto

MITO

Hokuriku
Shinkansen

Tokyo Narita
International
Airport

URAWA
TOKYO

Northern Japan Alps

KŌFU
CHIBA

Mt Fuji
YOKOHAMA

TOKYO
One of Asia's most vibrant cities,
it has to be seen to be believed

UOKA

Izu-hantō

kansen

Ō-shima

MT FUJI
Picture-postcard perfect –
Japan's venerated peak,
scenic lakes and great hikes

ELEVATION

3000m

2000m

1000m

200m

0

PACIFIC
OCEAN

0   100   200km
0   60   120mi

Contents – Text

2 Contents – Text

CENTRAL HONSHŪ

KANSAI

WESTERN HONSHŪ ...438

NORTHERN HONSHŪ ...491

Contents – Maps

The Authors

Chris Rowthorn
Chris was born in England and grew up in the USA. He has lived in Kyoto since 1992, where he worked first as a regional correspondent for the *Japan Times* before joining Lonely Planet. He's worked on 12 books for Lonely Planet, including *Hiking in Japan*; *Tokyo*; *Kyoto*; *Southeast Asia*; *Malaysia, Singapore & Brunei*; *Victoria*; and *Read This First: Asia & India*. Despite all this work-related travel, he still takes every opportunity to explore the world, in particular the Himalayas and Southeast Asia. When he's not on the road, he spends his time soaking away his cares in Japanese hot springs and searching out great restaurants.

John Ashburne
John Ashburne grew up in Yorkshire, flirted with English Literature and Education at Durham and Cambridge Universities, and worked as a private tutor in the Caribbean. Thereafter he attempted office work with Robert Maxwell's publishing company in Oxford, fleeing two seconds ahead of his dismissal notice, and ending up in the rural hinterlands of Japan. Sixteen years later he resides in Kyoto, where he roots out noodle restaurants, when he's not off to Vietnam, Cambodia or Italy – in search of more noodle restaurants. He is the author of several books on Japan, and twice winner of the Mazda International Photo Contest.

He wishes to be reincarnated as an Asakusa rāmen shop owner.

David Atkinson
David Atkinson is a London-based freelance travel writer and has previously both lived and worked in Japan. His travel stories have been published in various titles, including the *Sunday Times*, the *Guardian*, the *South China Morning Post* and *Time Asia Magazine*. He is a member of the British Guild of Travel Writers.

Andrew Bender
France was closed, so after college Andy left his native New England to work in Tokyo, not speaking a word of Japanese. It ended up being a life-changing journey, as visits to Japan often are. Since then he's learned the language, mastered chopsticks and worked with Japanese companies in Japan and his adopted home of Los Angeles. He also sometimes leads tours of Japan. Andy's been writing professionally – mostly about travel and food – since 1998, with articles published in *Travel & Leisure*, *Fortune*, *In Style* and in-flight magazines. Other LP titles include *Germany*, *Norway* and *Western Europe*. When not on the road, he bikes at the beach, enjoys the occasional margarita (no salt), coddles Elvis the cat and schemes over ways to spoil his niece and nephews.

8

Sara 'Sam' Benson

Years ago Sara Benson graduated with a futile liberal arts degree from the University of Chicago. Afterwards, she journeyed for a few years through the wilds of Asia, racking up thousands of kilometres on Japanese *shinkansen*, broken Chinese bicycles, rickety Laos buses and along all kinds of roads on foot.

At home and abroad, Sara ran through several jobs as an English teacher, journalist and corporate hack before signing on with Lonely Planet many moons ago. A traveller by passion and a writer by trade, she has worked on over a dozen titles for Lonely Planet.

Craig McLachlan

A wanderer at heart, Craig has put in a lot of footwork in Japan. He's walked from Kagoshima to Hokkaidō; climbed Japan's 100 Famous Mountains; hiked around the 88 Sacred Temples of Shikoku; walked from the Sea of Japan to the Pacific (climbing all Japan's 3000m peaks along the way); and journeyed around the 33 Temples of Kannon Pilgrimage. Three of Craig's books on his adventures have been published in Japan in both English and Japanese, and he coauthored Lonely Planet's *Hiking in Japan*. He splits his time between Queenstown, New Zealand, where he runs an outdoor adventure company, and Osaka, Japan – along with long-suffering wife Yuriko and boys Riki and Ben. Still wondering what to do when he grows up, Craig recently completed a Japan-focused MBA at the University of Hawaii.

FROM THE AUTHORS

Chris Rowthorn Chris would like to thank the following people: Anthony and Denise Weersing for their excellent restaurant picks, among many other things; Paul Carty for great restaurant info and much besides; Divyam for providing the perfect retreat; Neelu Kaur for her usual excellent Kōbe info; coauthors Sam Benson, John Ashburne, Craig McLachlan, Andy Bender and David Atkinson for their hard work; Michael Day for the support and excellent editorial advice; Kishimoto Yorihiku for his great Osaka restaurant picks; the folks at Nakazonoso for many dinners etc; the folks at the New York and Kyoto JNTO/TIC offices; Danny Diskin for the cool *izakaya* info; Tadg McLoughlin for his graciousness; Miho Miner and Ishiura Hisayo for the assistance; Isoda Norie for all sorts of good tips on Osaka; and all the readers of Lonely Planet *Japan* books who sent in letters and emails with information about Japan – your input really helps and I've tried to use as much of it as possible!

John Ashburne John would like to give infinite *arigatos* to Masami 'Onna no ko' Itoh, Aaron Berman, Hannayo Sakai, Micah Gampel, and the good souls who helped him on the road and off. Special thanks too to colleagues Chris Rowthorn and Michael Day.

David Atkinson Thanks: Akemi Fujimoto and Kylie Clark at the Japan National Tourist Organisation in London, Naoki Sato in Yamagata, Eiko Miura in Kakunodate, Yoko Fukushima and Kayo Yoshida in Sendai, Tatsuya & Yuri Sasaki in Tozawa-ko, Lou Coppard in Aomori and, most of all, Yuriko Sugawara in Morioka.

Thanks also to Lonely Planet readers Andreas Strohm, Bernd Kruyt and Dianne Boothroyd, Selene Koh, Paul Minza, Laurie Williams, Ned Milburn and Alexander Engelheardt for their useful input.

Sara Benson Enormous thanks to Justin Bales, who once again went above and beyond the call of duty in giving me a spare futon, enduring late-night phone calls from odd places and always making me laugh.

A shout-out to all the folks who showed me random kindness on the road, including: Chris Rowthorn; Hashii Kimihiro, my 18-kippu companion; Nobuko-san in Kirishima NP; the friendly innkeepers, chefs and bartenders of Karatsu, Kumamoto, Kagoshima and Yaku-shima; Ms Keiko Chinen and her daughters for a lift into Naha; Nippon Rent-a-Car on Miyako-jima; Amy-Lynn Fischer, who endured the mosquitoes, too; and the inimitable Tatsu-san & Co.

Andrew Bender First off, thanks to Daisuke Tonai, Yohko Scott and Carol Wang of the JNTO in Los Angeles for valuable pre-departure help, with assistance from Hiroshi Kato of the Hokkaidō government and Kei Kawaguchi of the Nagoya government, both in Los Angeles. Staff at tourist offices from Nagoya to Noboribetsu, Wajima to Wakkanai lavished me with more time and energy than I deserved, and special acknowledgement goes to Katsuhisa Miyasaka in Yudanaka, and Taka Fukushima at Zenkōji and Becky Marck of Shinshū University, both in Nagano. I always knew Japan was generous with visitors, and your welcome confirmed it. Finally, thanks to Chris Rowthorn and Michael Day for making this such a memorable job.

Craig McLachlan Most importantly, I must thank my living kanji dictionary and exceptionally beautiful wife, Yuriko, for all her help on this book. Thanks also to our boys Riki and Ben, especially for not messing up all the papers, brochures and photos that covered most of the floor of our house for weeks on end. Thanks to my parents-in-law for putting up with me, to Keizo for battling to get me computer literate, and to the guy who knocked me off my scooter in Tottori for not crushing my laptop. Gratitude also to Stirling Elmendorf, Jennie Gold, Nina Mai, Sharon Woon, Ruth Bassett, and the team at Wilderness Adventures in Queenstown for keeping the business going while I was away.

This Book

This 8th edition of *Japan* has been updated by a fantastic group of authors. Chris Rowthorn took the role of coordinating in his stride, and also updated the front chapters and the Kansai chapter. John Ashburne covered all things hip in and around Tokyo. Andrew Bender meticulously researched Central Honshū and Hokkaidō, while David Atkinson covered a lot of kilometres in Northern Honshū. Craig MacLachlan provided insight into Western Honshū and Shikoku and also contributed western Fukui-ken (Central Honshū) and Northern Kansai & the San-in Coast (Kansai). The busy Sam Benson covered Kyūshū and Okinawa & the Southwest Islands.

The first three editions of this book were written by Ian L McQueen. The 4th edition was rewritten by Chris Taylor, Robert Strauss and Tony Wheeler. Chris Taylor updated the 5th edition. The 6th edition was updated by Chris Taylor, Nicko Goncharoff, Mason Florence and Chris Rowthorn; and the 7th edition by Chris Rowthorn, John Ashburne, Sam Benson and Mason Florence.

FROM THE PUBLISHER

This 8th edition of *Japan* was produced in Lonely Planet's Melbourne office.

The unflappable Chris Tsismetzis coordinated the cartography with assistance from Barbara Benson, Daniel Fennessey, Laurie Mikkelsen, Jack Gavran, Hunor Csutoros, Sarah Sloane, Cris Gibcus and Csanád Csutoros.

Kyla Gillzan and Craig Kilburn tag-teamed the editing coordination with assistance from Stefanie Di Trocchio, Simon Sellars, Maryanne Netto, Hilary Ericksen, Kristen Odijk, Justin Flynn, Melissa Faulkner and Sally Steward.

Script-master Nick Stebbing guided the book safely through the challenges of layout, with Kyla Gillzan (editorial). Pablo Gastar, Sally Darmody and John Shippick (layout) and Julia Taylor (editorial) provided timely layout assistance.

Michael Day was the commissioning editor and oversaw development of this title in conjunction with regional publishing manager Virginia Maxwell. Project manager Chris Love ensured everything ran smoothly.

Quentin Frayne compiled the language chapter; Pepi Bluck organised the illustrations; Kusnander prepared the climate charts; and Nic Lehman designed the cover. Chizuru Fazio assisted with script checking. The images used in this book were supplied by LPI.

Thanks to managing editors Jane Thompson, Bruce Evans, Darren O'Connell and Martin Heng; managing cartographer Corie Waddell; and layout managers Adriana Mammarella and Kate McDonald for their assistance.

Big *arigatō gozaimasu* also to authors Chris, John, Andrew, Craig, David and Sam who have been fab to work with.

THANKS
Many thanks to the travellers who used the last edition and wrote to us with helpful hints, advice and interesting anecdotes. Your names appear in the back of this book.

11

Foreword

ABOUT LONELY PLANET GUIDEBOOKS

The story begins with a classic travel adventure: Tony and Maureen Wheeler's 1972 journey across Europe and Asia to Australia. There was no useful information about the overland trail then, so Tony and Maureen published the first Lonely Planet guidebook to meet a growing need.

From a kitchen table, Lonely Planet has grown to become the largest independent travel publisher in the world, with offices in Melbourne (Australia), Oakland (USA), London (UK) and Paris (France).

Today Lonely Planet guidebooks cover the globe. There is an ever-growing list of books and information in a variety of media. Some things haven't changed. The main aim is still to make it possible for adventurous travellers to get out there – to explore and better understand the world.

At Lonely Planet we believe travellers can make a positive contribution to the countries they visit – if they respect their host communities and spend their money wisely. Since 1986 a percentage of the income from each book has been donated to aid projects and human rights campaigns, and, more recently, to wildlife conservation.

> Although inclusion in a guidebook usually implies a recommendation we cannot list every good place. Exclusion does not necessarily imply criticism. In fact there are a number of reasons why we might exclude a place – sometimes it is simply inappropriate to encourage an influx of travellers.

UPDATES & READER FEEDBACK

Things change – prices go up, schedules change, good places go bad and bad places go bankrupt. Nothing stays the same. So, if you find things better or worse, recently opened or long-since closed, please tell us and help make the next edition even more accurate and useful.

Lonely Planet thoroughly updates each guidebook as often as possible – usually every two years, although for some destinations the gap can be longer. Between editions, up-to-date information is available in our free, monthly email bulletin *Comet* (Ⓦ www.lonelyplanet.com/ newsletters). You can also check out the *Thorn Tree* bulletin board and *Postcards* section of our website which carry unverified, but fascinating, reports from travellers.

Tell us about it! We genuinely value your feedback. A well-travelled team at Lonely Planet reads and acknowledges every email and letter we receive and ensures that every morsel of information finds its way to the relevant authors, editors and cartographers.

Everyone who writes to us will find their name listed in the next edition of the appropriate guidebook. The very best contributions will be rewarded with a free guidebook.

We may edit, reproduce and incorporate your comments in Lonely Planet products such as guidebooks, websites and digital products, so let us know if you don't want your comments reproduced or your name acknowledged.

How to contact Lonely Planet:
Online: Ⓔ talk2us@lonelyplanet.com.au, Ⓦ www.lonelyplanet.com
Australia: Locked Bag 1, Footscray, Victoria 3011
UK: 72-82 Rosebery Ave, London, EC1R 4RW
USA: 150 Linden St, Oakland, CA 94607

Introduction

Few countries make such conflicting claims on the imagination as Japan. The mere mention of the word Japan is enough to set off a cascade of contrary images: ancient temples and futuristic cities; mist-shrouded hills and lightning-fast bullet trains; kimono-clad geisha and suit-clad businessmen; quaint thatch-roofed villages and pulsating neon urban jungles.

Amazingly, all of these images are accurate. This peculiar synthesis of the modern and the traditional is one of the things that makes travel in Japan such a fascinating experience. It also ensures that no matter what your taste, you'll find a side of Japan that suits your interests.

If traditional culture is your thing, you can spend weeks in cities like Kyoto and Nara, gorging yourself on temples, shrines, kabuki, nō, tea ceremonies and museums packed with treasures from Japan's rich artistic heritage.

If modern culture and technology is your thing, you'll find Japan's cities an absolute wonderland – an easy peek into the future of the human race, complete with cool cafés and great restaurants!

Outside the cities, you'll find natural wonders the length and breadth of the archipelago. From the coral reefs of Okinawa to the snow-capped peaks of the Japan Alps, the giant cedar trees of Yaku-shima to the wide-open spaces of Hokkaidō, most visitors are pleasantly surprised to discover that Japan has more than enough natural wonders to compete with its cultural treasures.

But for many visitors, the real highlight of their visit to Japan is the gracious hospitality of the Japanese themselves. Indeed, a night in a good ryokan (traditional Japanese inn) may well put you off hotels for the rest of your life. From the deep bow of the hostess at the door, to the steaming *furo* (Japanese bath), to the thick futon laid out for you after you dine, you'll find the whole experience unforgettable.

Then there's Japanese food. No matter how much Japanese food you've eaten outside the country, nothing can prepare you for how delicious the genuine article is when served in its home country. Whether it's impossibly fresh sushi in Tokyo, perfectly battered tempura in Kyoto or a hearty bowl of *rāmen* in Osaka, if you like eating, you're going to love Japan!

Best of all, Japan is an incredibly easy and safe country in which to travel. The Japanese public transport system is one of the best in the world. From the sleek bullet trains to humble local buses and trams, you will find that getting around the country is an absolute breeze. And with an extensive network of information offices spread across the nation, figuring it all out is remarkably easy.

The fact is, whatever your image of Japan, it probably exists somewhere on the archipelago – and is just waiting for you to discover it. So what are you waiting for?

Facts about Japan

HISTORY
Prehistory

The origin of Japan's earliest inhabitants is obscure. There was certainly emigration that occured via land bridges that once connected Japan with Siberia and Korea, but it is also thought that seafaring migrants from Polynesia may have landed on Kyūshū and Okinawa. It is likely that the Japanese people are a result of emigration from Siberia in the north, China and Korea to the west and, perhaps, Polynesian stock from the south.

The first signs of civilisation in Japan are from the Neolithic period around 10,000 BC. This is called the Jōmon (Rope Mark) period after the discovery of pottery fragments with rope marks. The people at this time lived as fishers, hunters and food-gatherers.

This period was gradually superseded by the Yayoi era, which dates from around 300 BC and is named after the site near Tokyo where pottery fragments were found. The Yayoi people are considered to have had a strong connection with Korea and their most important developments were the wet cultivation of rice and the use of bronze and iron implements.

The period following the Yayoi era has been called the Kofun (Burial Mound) period by archaeologists who discovered thousands of grave mounds concentrated mostly in central and western Japan. Judging by their size and elaborate construction, these mounds must have required immense resources of labour. It seems likely that the custom of building these tombs was brought to an end by the arrival of Buddhism, which favoured cremation.

As more and more settlements banded together to defend their land, groups became larger until, by AD 300, the Yamato clan had loosely unified the nation through either conquest or alliance. The Yamato leaders claimed that they were descended from the sun goddess, Amaterasu, and introduced the title of *tennō* (emperor) around the 5th century. With the ascendancy of the Yamato emperors, Japan for the first time became a true nation, stretching from the islands south of Kyūshū to the northern wilds of Honshū.

Buddhism & Early Chinese Influence

In the mid-6th century, Buddhism was introduced from China via the Korean kingdom of Paekche. The decline of the Yamato court was halted by Prince Shōtoku (573–620), who set up a constitution and laid the guidelines for a centralised state headed by a single ruler. He also instituted Buddhism as a state religion. Despite family feuds and coups d'etat subsequent rulers continued to reform the country's administration and laws.

From the earliest days of the Yamato court, it was the custom to relocate the capital following the death of an emperor (presumably to free the capital from the taint of death). However, after the shift of the capital to Nara in 710, this long-held custom was altered as the capital remained there for the next 75 years, before moving to Nagaoka-kyō in 784.

During the Nara period (710–94) there was strong promotion of Buddhism particularly under Emperor Shōmu, who ordered the construction of Tōdai-ji and the casting of its Daibutsu (Great Buddha) as supreme guardian deity of the nation. Both the temple and Buddha image can still be seen in Nara.

Historical Periods

period	date
Jōmon	10,000–300 BC
Yayoi	300 BC–AD 300
Kofun	300–710
Nara	710–94
Heian	794–1185
Kamakura	1185–1333
Muromachi	1333–1576
Momoyama	1576–1600
Edo	1600–1868
Meiji	1868–1912
Taishō	1912–26
Shōwa	1926–89
Heisei	1989 to the present

Establishment of a Native Culture

By the end of the 8th century, the Buddhist clergy in Nara had become so politically meddlesome that Emperor Kammu decided to relocate the capital to insulate it against their growing influence. The site eventually chosen was Heian-kyō (modern-day Kyoto).

Like Nara, Heian-kyō was modelled on Chang-an (present-day Xi'an), the capital of the Tang dynasty in China, and it was to continue as the capital of Japan until 1868. The Heian period (794–1185) saw a great flourishing in the arts and important developments in religious thinking as Chinese ideas and institutions were imported and adapted to the needs of the Japanese.

Rivalry between Buddhism and Shintō, the traditional religion of Japan, was reduced by presenting Shintō deities as manifestations of Buddha. Religion was assigned a role separate from politics. Japanese monks returning from China established two new sects, Tendai and Shingon, which became the mainstays of Japanese Buddhism.

During the late Heian period, emperors began to devote more time to leisure and scholarly pursuit and less time to government. This created an opening for the Fujiwara, a noble family, to capture important court posts and become the chief power brokers, a role the clan was able to maintain for several centuries.

The Heian period is considered the apogee of Japanese courtly elegance, but out in the provinces a new power was on the rise, that of the samurai, or 'warrior class', which built up its own armed forces and readily turned to arms to defend its autonomy. Samurai families soon moved into the capital, where they muscled in on the court.

The corrupt Fujiwara were eventually eclipsed by the Taira clan, who ruled briefly before being ousted by the Minamoto family (also known as the Genji) at the battle of Dannoura (modern-day Shimonoseki) in 1185.

Domination through Military Rule

The Kamakura period (1185–1333) followed on from the Heian period. In 1192 Minamoto Yoritomo conquered the inhabitants of what is now Aomori-ken, thereby extending his rule to the tip of northern Honshū. For the first time in its history, all of Japan proper was now under unified rule. After assuming the title of shōgun (military leader), Minamoto set up his headquarters in Kamakura, while the emperor remained the nominal ruler in Kyoto. It was the beginning of a long period of feudal rule by successive samurai families. In fact, this feudal system was to linger on, in one form or another, until imperial power was restored in 1868.

Minamoto purged members of his own family who stood in his way, but following his death in 1199 after falling from a horse, his wife's family (the Hōjō) eliminated all of Minamoto's potential successors and became the true powers behind the figureheads of shōguns and warrior lords.

During this era, the popularity of Buddhism spread to all levels of society. From the late 12th century, Japanese monks returning from China introduced a new sect called Zen, the austerity of which offered a particular appeal to the samurai.

The Mongols, under their leader Kublai Khan, reached Korea in 1259 and sent envoys to Japan seeking Japanese submission. In response, the envoys were expelled. The Mongols reacted by sending an invasion fleet, which arrived near present-day Fukuoka in 1274. This first attack was only just repulsed with a little help from a typhoon. Further envoys sent by Kublai Khan were promptly beheaded.

In 1281 the Mongols dispatched a huge army of over 100,000 soldiers to Japan to make a second attempt at invasion. After initial success, the Mongol fleet was almost completely destroyed by yet another typhoon. Ever since, this lucky typhoon has been known to the Japanese as the kamikaze (divine wind) – a name later given to the suicide pilots of WWII.

Although the Kamakura government emerged victorious in battles with the Mongols, it was unable to pay its soldiers and lost the support of the samurai class. In an attempt to take advantage of popular discontent, Emperor Go-Daigo led an unsuccessful rebellion against the government and was exiled to Oki-shotō, the islands near Matsue in western Honshū, where he waited a year before trying again. The second attempt successfully toppled the government.

Country at War

This heralded the start of the Muromachi period (1333–1576). Emperor Go-Daigo refused to reward his warriors, favouring the aristocracy and priesthood instead. This led to the revolt of Ashikaga Takauji, who had previously changed sides to support Emperor Go-Daigo. Ashikaga defeated Go-Daigo at Kyoto, then installed a new emperor and appointed himself shōgun; the Ashikaga family later settled at Muromachi, an area of Kyoto. Go-Daigo escaped to set up a rival court at Yoshino, a mountainous region near Nara. Rivalry between the two courts continued for 60 years until the Ashikaga made a promise (which was not kept) that the imperial lines would alternate.

The Ashikaga ruled with gradually diminishing effectiveness in a land slipping steadily into civil war and chaos. Despite this, there was a flourishing of those arts now considered typically Japanese, such as landscape painting, classical nō (stylised dance-drama), ikebana (flower arranging) and *chanoyu* (tea ceremony). A number of Kyoto's famous gardens date from this period, as do such well-known monuments as Kinkaku-ji (Golden Temple) and Ginkaku-ji (Silver Temple). Formal trade was re-established with Ming-dynasty China and Korea, although Japanese piracy continued to strain these relationships.

The Ōnin War, which broke out in 1467, developed into a full-scale civil war and marked the rapid decline of the Ashikaga family. *Daimyō* (domain lords) and local leaders fought for power in bitter territorial disputes that were to last for a century. This period, from 1467 to around the start of the Momoyama period in 1576, is known as the Warring States period (Sengoku-jigai).

Politically, the Japan of the Warring States period resembled pre-Yamato Japan: the country was merely a collection of disparate groups vying for control of local areas without any centralised authority. It was up to the next generation of leaders to reverse this situation and bring the country under the control of a powerful centralised government once more.

Return to Unity

In 1568 Oda Nobunaga, the son of a *daimyō*, seized power from the imperial court in Kyoto and used his military genius to initiate a process of pacification and unification in central Japan. His efforts were cut short when he was betrayed by one of his own generals, Akechi Mitsuhide, in 1582. Under attack from Akechi and seeing all was lost, he disembowelled himself in Kyoto's Honnō-ji.

Oda was succeeded by his most able commander, Toyotomi Hideyoshi, who was reputedly the son of a farmer, although his origins are not clear. His diminutive size and pop-eyed features earned him the nickname of Saru-san (Mr Monkey). Toyotomi extended unification so that by 1590 the whole country was under his rule. He then became fascinated with grandiose schemes to invade China and Korea. The first invasion was repulsed in 1593 and the second was aborted on the death of Toyotomi in 1598.

The arts of the Momoyama period (1576–1600) are noted for their flamboyant use of colour and gold-leaf embellishment. There was also a vogue for building castles on an extravagant scale; the most impressive example is Osaka-jō, which reputedly required three years of labour by up to 100,000 men.

The Christian Century

In the mid-16th century, when the Europeans first made their appearance, foreign trade was little regulated by Japan's central government. The first Portuguese to be shipwrecked off southern Kyūshū in 1543 found an appreciative reception for their skills in firearm manufacture, skills which were soon adopted by the Japanese. The Jesuit missionary Francis Xavier arrived in Kagoshima in 1549 and was followed by more missionaries, who quickly converted local lords keen to profit from foreign trade and assistance with military supplies. The new religion spread rapidly, gaining several hundred thousand converts, particularly in Nagasaki.

At first Oda Nobunaga saw the advantage of trading with Europeans and tolerated the arrival of Christianity as a counterbalance to Buddhism. Once Toyotomi Hideyoshi had assumed power, however, this tolerance gradually gave way to a suspicion that an alien religion would subvert his rule. Edicts against Christianity were followed in 1597 by the crucifixion of 26 foreign priests and Japanese converts.

Veiled goth girl, Tokyo

Motorcycle riders, Tokyo

Trainee sumo wrestlers, Tokyo

Pigeon-covered man, Sensō-ji

Farmer, Muroto-misaki, Kōchi-ken

Maruyama-kōen, Kyoto, Kansai

Portrait of a *maiko* (apprentice geisha)

Maiko in a traditional Japanese garden, Kyoto, Kansai

Maiko under a cherry tree

Samurai

The prime duty of a samurai, a member of the warrior class, was to give faithful service to his domain lord or *daimyō*. In fact, the origin of the term samurai is closely linked to a word meaning 'to serve', and this overlap can be seen in the kanji used to write the word. Over the centuries, the samurai established a code of conduct that came to be known as *bushidō* (the way of the warrior). This code was drawn from Confucianism, Shintō and Buddhism.

Confucianism required a samurai to show absolute loyalty to his lord. Toward the oppressed a samurai was expected to show benevolence and exercise justice. Subterfuge was to be despised, as were all commercial and financial transactions. A real samurai had endless endurance and total self-control, spoke only the truth and displayed no emotion. Since his honour was his life, disgrace and shame were to be avoided above all else and all insults were to be avenged.

From Buddhism, the samurai learnt the lesson that life is impermanent – a handy reason to face death with serenity. Shintō provided the samurai with patriotic beliefs in the divine status both of the emperor and of Japan, the abode of the gods.

Seppuku (ritual suicide), also known as *hara-kiri*, was a practice to which Japanese Buddhism conveniently turned a blind eye and was an accepted means of avoiding dishonour. Seppuku required the samurai to ritually disembowel himself, watched by an aide, who then drew his own sword and lopped off the samurai's head. One reason for this ritual was the requirement that a samurai should never surrender but always go down fighting. Since surrender was considered a disgrace, prisoners received scant mercy. During WWII this attitude was reflected in the Japanese treatment of prisoners of war – still a source of bitter memories for those involved.

In quiet moments, a samurai dressed simply but was easily recognisable by his triangular *eboshi*, a hat made from rigid black cloth.

MARGARET JUNG

The samurai's standard battle dress or armour (usually made of leather or maybe lacquered steel) consisted of a breastplate, a similar covering for his back, a steel helmet with a visor and more body armour for his shoulders and lower body. Samurai weaponry – his pride and joy – included a bow and arrows (in a quiver), swords and a dagger; and he wasn't complete without his trusty steed.

Before entering the fray, a samurai was expected to be freshly washed and groomed. The classic samurai battle took the form of duelling between individuals rather than the clashing of massed armies.

Not all samurai were capable of adhering to their code of conduct – samurai indulging in double-crossing or subterfuge, or displaying outright cowardice, were popular themes in Japanese theatre.

Proscription and persecution of Christianity continued under the Tokugawa government until it reached its peak in 1637, with the ferocious quelling of the Christian-led Shimabara Rebellion. This brought the Christian century to an abrupt close, although the religion continued to be practised in secret until it was officially allowed to resurface at the end of the 19th century.

Peace & Seclusion

The supporters of Toyotomi Hideyoshi's young heir, Toyotomi Hideyori, were defeated in 1600 by Toyotomi's former ally, Tokugawa Ieyasu, at the battle of Sekigahara. Tokugawa set up his field headquarters

(*bakufu*) at Edo, now Tokyo, and assumed the title of shōgun. This marked the beginning of the Edo or Tokugawa period (1600–1868). The emperor and court continued to exercise purely nominal authority in Kyoto.

A strict political regime was introduced. The Tokugawa family, besides retaining large estates, also took control of major cities, ports and mines; the remainder of the country was allocated to autonomous *daimyō*. In descending order of importance, society consisted of the nobility, who had nominal power; the *daimyō* and their samurai; the farmers; and, at the bottom of the list, artisans and merchants. To ensure political security, the *daimyō* were required to make ceremonial visits to Edo every alternate year, and their wives and children were kept in permanent residence in Edo as virtual hostages of the government. The cost of this constant movement and the family ties in Edo made it difficult for the *daimyō* to remain anything but loyal. At the lower end of society, farmers were subject to a severe system of rules that dictated in minute detail their food, clothing and housing. Social mobility from one class to another was blocked as social standing was determined by birth.

Under Tokugawa rule, Japan entered a period of *sakoku* (national seclusion). Japanese were forbidden on pain of death to travel abroad or engage in trade with foreign countries. Only the Dutch, Chinese and Koreans were allowed to remain in Japan, and they were placed under strict supervision. The Dutch were confined to the island of Dejima, near Nagasaki, and their contacts restricted to merchants and prostitutes.

The rigid emphasis of these times on submitting unquestioningly to rules of obedience and loyalty has lasted to the present day. One effect of strict rule during the Tokugawa period was the creation of an atmosphere of relative peace and security in which the arts thrived. There were great advances, for example, in haiku (17-syllable poems), bunraku (classical puppet theatre) and kabuki (stylised Japanese theatre). Weaving, pottery, ceramics and lacquerware became widely appreciated by the privileged classes for their refined quality.

By the turn of the 19th century, the Tokugawa government was falling into stagnation and corruption. Famines and poverty among the peasants and samurai further weakened the system. Foreign ships started to challenge Japan's isolation with increasing insistence, and the Japanese soon realised that their outmoded defences were ineffectual. Russian contacts in the north were followed by British and American visits. In 1853 Commodore Matthew Perry of the US Navy arrived with a squadron of 'black ships' to demand the opening up of Japan to trade. Other countries moved in to demand the opening of treaty ports and the relaxation of restrictions on trade.

The arrival of foreigners proved to be the decisive blow to an already shaky Tokugawa regime. Upset by the shōgunate's handling of the foreign incursion, two large *daimyō* areas in western Japan, the Satsuma and the Chōshū, allied themselves with disenchanted samurai. They succeeded in capturing the emperor in 1868, declaring a restoration of imperial rule and an end to the power of the shōgun. A brief counterattack by Tokugawa guards in Kyoto in the same year failed. The ruling shōgun, Tokugawa Yoshinobu, resigned, and Emperor Meiji assumed control of state affairs.

Emergence from Isolation

The initial stages of the Meiji Restoration (1868–1912) were resisted in a state of virtual civil war. The abolition of the shōgunate was followed by the surrender of the *daimyō*, whose lands were divided into the prefectures that exist today. Edo became Japan's new capital and was renamed Tokyo (Eastern Capital). The government became centralised again and Western-style ministries were appointed for specific tasks. A series of revolts by the samurai against the erosion of their status culminated in the Saigō Uprising, where the samurai were finally defeated and stripped of their power.

Despite nationalist support for the emperor under the slogan of *sonnō-jōi* (Revere the emperor; repel the barbarians), the new government soon realised it would have to meet the West on its own terms. Under the slogan *fukoku kyōhei* (rich country; strong military), the economy underwent a crash course in Westernisation and industrialisation. An influx of Western experts was encouraged and Japanese students were sent abroad to acquire expertise in modern technologies. In 1889 Japan created a Western-style constitution which, like the military revival, owed much to Prussian influences.

By the 1890s government leaders were concerned by the spread of liberal Western ideas and encouraged a swing back to nationalism and traditional values.

Japan's growing confidence was demonstrated by the abolition of foreign treaty rights and by the ease with which it trounced China in the Sino-Japanese War (1894–95). The subsequent treaty recognised Korean independence and ceded Taiwan to Japan. Friction with Russia eventually led to the Russo-Japanese War (1904–05), in which the Japanese army attacked the Russians in Manchuria and Korea. The Japanese Navy stunned the Russians by inflicting a crushing defeat on their Baltic fleet at the battle of Tsu-shima. For the first time, the Japanese were able to believe that they had drawn level with the Western powers.

Industrialisation & Asian Dominance

On his death in 1912, Emperor Meiji was succeeded by his son, Yoshihito, who chose the name Taishō for his reign. His period of rule was named the Taishō era (1912–26). The later stages of his life were dogged by ill health that was probably attributable to meningitis.

When WWI broke out, Japan sided against Germany but did not become deeply involved in the conflict. While the Allies were occupied with war, Japan took the opportunity, through shipping and trade, to expand its economy at top speed. At the same time, Japan gained a strong foothold in China, thereby giving Japan the dominant position in Asia.

Social unrest led the government to pursue a more democratic, liberal line; the right to vote was extended, and Japan joined the League of Nations in 1920. Under the influence of the zaibatsu (financial cliques of industrialists and bankers), a moderate and pacific foreign policy was followed.

Nationalism & the Pursuit of Empire

The Shōwa era (1926–89) commenced when Emperor Hirohito ascended the throne in 1926. He had toured extensively in Europe, mixed with European nobility and developed quite a liking for the British lifestyle.

A rising tide of nationalism was quickened by the world economic depression that began in 1930. Popular unrest was marked by plots to overthrow the government and political assassinations. This led to a strong increase in the power of the militarists, who approved the invasion of Manchuria in 1931 and the installation there of a puppet regime controlled by the Japanese. In 1933 Japan withdrew from the League of Nations and in 1937 entered into full-scale hostilities against China.

As the leader of a new order for Asia, Japan signed a tripartite pact with Germany and Italy in 1940. The Japanese military leaders saw their main opponents to this new order for Asia, the so-called Greater East Asia Co-prosperity Sphere, in the USA.

World War II

When diplomatic attempts to gain US neutrality failed, Japan launched itself into WWII with a surprise attack on Pearl Harbor on 7 December 1941.

At first, Japan scored rapid successes, pushing its battle fronts across to India, down to the fringes of Australia and out into the mid-Pacific. The Battle of Midway opened the US counterattack, puncturing Japanese naval superiority and turning the tide of the war against Japan. By 1945, exhausted by submarine blockades and aerial bombing, Japan had been driven back on all fronts. In August of the same year, the declaration of war by the Soviet Union and the atomic bombs dropped by the USA on Hiroshima and Nagasaki proved to be the final straw: Emperor Hirohito announced unconditional surrender.

Having surrendered, Japan was then occupied by Allied forces under the command of General Douglas MacArthur. The chief aim of the USA was a thorough reform of Japanese government through demilitarisation, the trial of war criminals and the weeding out of militarists and ultranationalists from the government. A new constitution was introduced that dismantled the political power of the emperor, who completely stunned his subjects by publicly renouncing any claim to divine origins. This left him a mere figurehead.

The occupation was terminated in 1952, although the island of Okinawa was only returned to Japan in 1972. Okinawa is still home to American military bases.

Postwar Reconstruction

At the end of the war, the Japanese economy was in ruins and inflation was rampant. A programme of recovery provided loans, restricted imports and encouraged capital investment and personal saving.

By the late 1950s, trade was again flourishing, and the economy continued to expand rapidly. From textiles and the manufacture of labour-intensive goods, such as cameras, the Japanese 'economic miracle' spread into virtually every sector of economic activity. Economic recession and inflation surfaced in 1974 and again in 1980, mostly as a result of steep increases in the price of imported oil, on which Japan is dependent. But despite these setbacks, Japan became the world's most successful export economy, generating massive trade surpluses and dominating such fields as electronics, robotics, computer technology, car manufacturing and banking.

Recent History

For a long time, Japan seemed unstoppable. It appeared to be a nation of unassailable job security and endless economic growth. Then, in the early 1990s the so-called 'Bubble Economy' burst, and the old certainties vanished. Japan's legendary economic growth slowed to a standstill, and the economy actually started to contract.

Partially as a result of economic turmoil, in 1993, after 38 years at the helm, the conservative Liberal Democratic Party (LDP) was swept from power by an eight-party coalition of reformers. Then, in January 1995, a massive earthquake struck Kōbe; the government was confused and slow to react, and confidence in Japan's much vaunted earthquake preparedness was shattered. And to top it all off, just months later, a millennial cult with doomsday ambitions – the Aum Shinrikyō (Aum Supreme Truth Sect) – engineered a poison gas attack on the Tokyo subway system that killed 12 people and injured thousands.

The bad news continued apace in the late 1990s and early years of the new millennium, as Japan's economy continued to stagnate and politicians bickered about the best way to turn things around. In July 2000, the department store giant Sogō declared bankruptcy, followed by several other high-profile bankruptcies in 2001, including the Mycal supermarket chain and Aoki Construction.

As businesses large and small closed their doors, increasing numbers of Japanese workers found themselves out of work, and the unemployment rate topped 5% for the first time in 2001. Worse still, after almost 12 years of recession, the Japanese economy now faced the spectre of deflation, as prices of consumer goods decreased and personal and corporate assets declined in value.

In April 2001, LDP member Koizumi Junichiro assumed the role of prime minister, promising a raft of uncompromising economic reforms aimed at reviving Japan's economy. Ironically, Koizumi's major accomplishment to date has nothing to do with economic policy: in September 2002, Koizumi became the first Japanese prime minister to visit North Korea. As a result of his visit, the North Koreans admitted to having abducted 13 Japanese citizens in the 1970s and 1980s in order to train North Korean spies to operate in Japan. Koizumi was able to secure the release of five of the surviving abductees, who returned to Japan amid great fanfare (and anger about those who had died while on North Korean soil).

In October 2001, partially as a result of the terrorist attacks of 11 September 2001, Japan's politicians made a seemingly innocuous change to Japan's post-war constitution (under which anything but defensive military action was proscribed): the Diet voted to allow Japan's Jieitai (Self-Defence Force) to participate in a support capacity in military actions abroad. Critics both inside and outside Japan argued that this change opens the door for renewed Japanese militarism.

While Japanese had a lot to worry about in the early years of the millennium, there were also some occasions for joy. On 1 December 2001, Crown Princess Masako gave birth to a baby girl, whom she and Crown Prince Naruhito named Aiko. The birth of Aiko was a huge relief to the nation, since the royal couple had previously been childless, but it also rekindled an old debate as to whether a female can ascend to Japan's throne (the imperial family has been without a male child for 36 years).

The FIFA World Cup, held jointly by Japan and the Republic of Korea (South Korea) was another cause for celebration in Japan. The Japanese squad managed to crack the final 16 for the first time in their history, but it was the Brazilians who took top honours, defeating Germany 2-0 in Yokohama.

At the time of writing, the outlook for Japan is rather bleak. The economy remains mired in recession, the government appears unable to make any significant changes, the population is ageing at an alarming rate, and, as its economic competitors surge ahead, Japan confronts the reality of negative economic growth. If all this sounds incredibly depressing, it is worth pointing out that Japan has more than once come back from almost complete ruin to achieve astonishing success.

GEOGRAPHY & GEOLOGY

Japan is an island nation. Much of its cultural heritage has been drawn from nearby Asian countries, but it is this 'apartness' from the Asian mainland that is defining for many Japanese. Both China and Korea are close enough to have been decisive influences, but at the same time they are too distant to have dominated Japan.

Japan has not always been physically isolated. It was as recently as the end of the last ice age, around 10,000 years ago, that the level of the sea rose enough to flood a land bridge connecting Japan with the Asian continent. Today, Japan consists of a chain of islands that rides the back of a 3000km-long arc of mountains along the eastern rim of the continent. It stretches from around 25°N at the southern islands of Okinawa to 45°N at the northern end of Hokkaidō. Cities at comparable latitudes are Miami and Cairo in the south and Montreal and Milan in the north. Japan's total land area is 377,435 sq km, and more than 80% of it is mountainous.

Japan consists of some 3900 small islands and four major ones: Honshū (slightly larger than Britain), Hokkaidō, Kyūshū and Shikoku. Okinawa, the largest and most significant of Japan's many smaller islands, is about halfway along an archipelago that stretches from the western tip of Honshū almost all the way to Taiwan. It is far enough from the rest of Japan to have developed a culture that differs from that of the 'mainland' in many respects.

There are several disputed islands in the Japanese archipelago. The most important of these are the Kuril Islands, north of Hokkaidō. Seized by Russia at the close of WWII, they have been the source of tension between Japan and Russia ever since. While the Japanese have made some progress toward their return in recent years, they remain, for the time being, part of Russia.

If Japanese culture has been influenced by isolation, it has equally been shaped by the country's mountainous topography. A number of the mountains are volcanic, and more than 40 of these are active, many of them on the southern island of Kyūshū. On the plus side, all this geothermal activity is responsible for Japan's fabulous abundance of hot springs *(onsen)*.

In addition to all its volcanoes, Japan has the dubious distinction of being one of the most seismically active regions of the world. It has been estimated that Japan is hit by over 1000 earthquakes a year, most of which are, fortunately, too small to notice without sophisticated seismic equipment. This seismic activity is particularly concentrated in the Kantō region, in which Tokyo is situated. But earthquakes can strike just about any part of the archipelago, as the citizens of Kōbe discovered in the disastrous earthquake of January 1995, which killed more than 6000 people.

CLIMATE

The combination of Japan's mountainous territory and the length of the archipelago (covering about 20° of latitude) makes for a complex climate. Most of the country is located in the northern temperate zone, which yields four distinct seasons. In addition, there are significant climatic differences between Hokkaidō in the north, which has short summers and lengthy winters with heavy snowfalls, and the southern islands such as Okinawa in Nansei-shotō (Southwest Archipelago), which enjoy a subtropical climate.

In the winter months (December to February), cold, dry air masses from Siberia move down over Japan, where they meet warmer, moister air masses from the Pacific. The resulting precipitation causes huge snowfalls on the side of the country that faces the Sea of Japan. The Pacific Ocean side of Japan receives less snow but can still be very cold; Tokyo has colder average January temperatures than Reykjavík in Iceland, but snow, when it does fall on the capital, rarely lasts long.

The summer months (June to August) are dominated by warm, moist air currents from the Pacific, and produce high temperatures and humidity throughout most of Japan (with the blissful exception of Hokkaidō). In the early part of summer, usually mid-May to June, there is a rainy

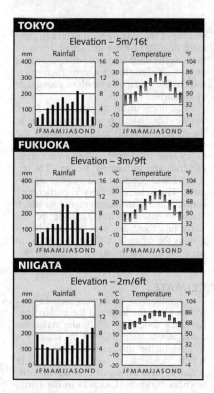

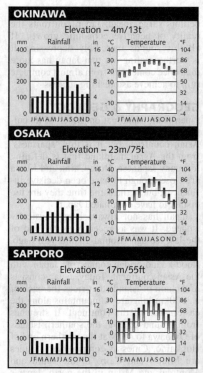

season lasting a few weeks that starts in the south and gradually works its way northwards. Although it can be inconvenient, this rainy season is not usually a significant barrier to travel. Further bad weather can occur in late summer when the country is visited by typhoons bringing torrential rains and strong winds that can have devastating effects, particularly on coastal regions.

In contrast to the extremes of summer and winter, spring (March to May) and autumn (September to November) in Japan are comparatively mild. Rainfall is relatively low and the days are often clear. These are, without a doubt, the very best times to visit the country.

ECOLOGY & ENVIRONMENT

Japan was the first Asian nation to industrialise. It has also been one of the most successful at cleaning up the resulting mess, though problems remain. In the early postwar years, when Japan was frantically

rebuilding its economy, there was widespread public ignorance of the problems of pollution, and the government did little to enlighten the public.

Industrial pollution was at its worst from the mid-1960s to the mid-1970s. But public awareness of the issue had already been awakened by an outbreak in 1953 of what came to be called Minamata disease (after the town of the same name), in which up to 6000 people were affected by mercury poisoning. It was not until 1968 that the government officially acknowledged the cause of the 'disease'.

By the late 1960s public consciousness of environmental problems had reached levels that the government could not ignore. Laws were passed to curb air and water pollution. These have been reasonably successful, though critics are quick to point out that while toxic matter has been mostly removed from Japanese waters, organic pollution remains a problem. Similarly, controls on air pollution have had mixed

What Happened to the Hills?

Visitors to Japan are often shocked at the state of the Japanese landscape. It seems that no matter where you look, the hills, rivers, coastline and fields bear the unmistakable imprint of human activity. Indeed, it is only in the highest, most remote mountains that one finds nature untouched by human hands. Why is this?

Undoubtedly, population density is the crucial factor here. With so many people packed into such a small space, it is only natural that the land should be worked to the hilt. However, it is not just simple population pressure that accounts for Japan's scarred and battered landscape; misguided land management policies and money-influenced politics also play a role.

Almost 70% of Japan's total land area is wooded. Of this area, almost 40% is planted, most of it with uniform rows of conifers, known as *sugi* (cryptomeria). Even national forests are not exempt from tree farming and these forests account for 33% of Japan's total lumber output. The end result of this widespread tree farming is a rather ugly patchwork effect over most of Japan's mountains – monotonous stands of *sugi* interspersed with occasional swaths of bare, clear-cut hillside.

To make matters worse, the planting of monoculture forests and clear cutting reduces the stability of mountain topsoil, resulting in frequent landslides. To combat this, land engineers erect unsightly concrete retaining walls over huge stretches of hillside, particularly along roadsides or near human habitations. These, combined with high-tension wire towers and patchwork forests, result in a landscape that is quite unlike anything elsewhere in the world.

As if this wasn't enough, it is estimated that only three of Japan's 30,000 rivers and streams are undammed. In addition to dams, concrete channels and embankments are built around even the most inaccessible mountain streams. Although some of this river work serves to prevent flooding downstream, much of it is clearly gratuitous and can only be understood as the unfortunate result of Japanese money-influenced politics.

In Japan, rural areas yield enormous power in national politics, as representation is determined more by area than by population. In order to ensure the support of their constituencies, rural politicians have little choice but to lobby hard for government spending on public work projects, as there is little other work available in these areas. Despite the negative effects this has on the Japanese landscape and economy, Japanese politicians seem unable to break this habit.

The upshot of all this is a landscape that looks, in many places, like a giant construction site. Perhaps the writer Alex Kerr put it best in his book *Lost Japan*: 'Japan has become a huge and terrifying machine, a Moloch tearing apart its own land with teeth of steel, and there is absolutely nothing anyone can do to stop it.' For the sake of the beauty that remains in Japan, let's hope he is wrong.

results: photochemical smog emerged as a problem in Tokyo in the early 1970s; it remains a problem and now affects other urban centres around Japan.

In 1972 the government passed the Nature Conservation Law, which aimed to protect the natural environment and provide recreational space for the public. National parks, quasi-national parks and prefectural parks were established, and it appears that such measures have been successful in increasing wildlife numbers.

More recently, Japan has been facing a new set of problems, including dioxin given off by waste incineration plants and a series of accidents at nuclear reactors and nuclear fuel processing facilities. The only up side

is that these accidents have forced the government to revise its safety guidelines for the nuclear power industry.

Of course, the news isn't all bleak. The governor of Kumamoto-ken announced in 2002 that the Arase Dam on Kuma-gawa would be removed, starting in 2010. In a country with a surplus of unnecessary dams (see the boxed text 'What Happened to the Hills' earlier), this is a major step in the right direction.

FLORA & FAUNA

The latitudinal spread of the islands of Japan makes for a wide diversity of flora and fauna. The Nansei and Ogasawara archipelagos in the far south are subtropical, and flora and fauna in this region are related to those found on the Malay Peninsula. Mainland Japan (Honshū, Kyūshū and Shikoku), on the other hand, shows more similarities with Korea and China, while subarctic northern and central Hokkaidō has its own distinct features.

Flora

The flora of Japan today is not what the Japanese saw hundreds of years ago. This is not just because much of Japan's natural landscape has succumbed to modern urban culture, but also because much of Japan's flora is imported. It is thought that some 200 to 500 plant species have been introduced to Japan since the Meiji period, mainly from Europe but also from North America. Japanese gardens laid out in the Edo period and earlier are good places to see native Japanese flora, even though you won't be seeing it as it might have flourished naturally.

Much of Japan was once heavily forested. The cool to temperate zones of central and northern Honshū and southern Hokkaidō were home to broad-leaf deciduous forests and still are to a certain extent. Nevertheless, large-scale deforestation is a feature of contemporary Japan. Pollution and acid rain have also taken their toll. Fortunately, the sheer inaccessibility of much of Japan's mountainous topography has preserved some areas of great natural beauty – in particular the alpine regions of central Honshū and the lovely national parks of Hokkaidō.

Fauna

Japan's land bridges to the Asian land mass allowed the migration of animals from Korea and China. The fauna of Japan has much in common with these regions, though there are species that are unique to Japan, such as the Japanese giant salamander and the Japanese macaque. In addition, Nansei-shotō, which has been separated from the mainland for longer than the rest of Japan, has a few examples of fauna (for example the Iriomote cat) that are classified by experts as 'living fossils'.

Japan's largest carnivorous mammals are its bears. Two species are found in Japan – the *higuma* (brown bear) of Hokkaidō and the *tsukinowaguma* (Asiatic brown bear) of Honshū, Shikoku and Kyūshū. The brown

bear can grow to a height of 2m and weigh up to 400kg. The Asiatic brown bear is smaller at an average height of 1.4m and a weight of 200kg.

Japanese macaques are medium-sized monkeys that are found in Honshū, Shikoku and Kyūshū. They average around 60cm in length and have short tails. The last survey of their numbers was taken in 1962, at which time there were some 30,000. They are found in groups of 20 to 150 members.

A survey carried out in 1986 by the Japanese government's Environment Agency found that 136 species of mammals were in need of protection and that 15 species were already extinct. Endangered species include the Iriomote cat, the Tsushima cat, Blakiston's fish owl and the Japanese river otter.

National Parks

Japan has 28 *kokuritsu kōen* (national parks) and 55 *kokutei kōen* (quasi-national parks). Ranging from the far south (Iriomote National Park) to the northern tip of Hokkaidō (Rishiri-Rebun-Sarobetsu National Park), the parks represent an effort to preserve as much as possible of Japan's natural environment.

When discussing Japan's national and quasi-national parks, it must be noted that these parks are quite different from national parks in most other countries. Few of the parks have facilities that you might expect in national parks (ranger stations, camping grounds, educational facilities etc). More importantly, national park status doesn't necessarily mean that the area in question is free from residential, commercial and even urban development. Indeed, in many of these parks, you'd have no idea that you were in a national or quasi-national park unless you looked on a map.

The highest concentration of national parks and quasi-national parks is in northern Honshū (Tōhoku) and Hokkaidō, where the population density is relatively low. But there are also national parks and quasi-national parks, such as Chichibu-Tama and Nikkō, within easy striking distance of Tokyo. The largest of Japan's national parks is the Seto-Nai-Kai Kokuritsu-kōen (Inland Sea National Park), which extends some 400km east to west, reaches a maximum width of 70km and encompasses almost 1000 islands of various size.

GOVERNMENT & POLITICS

Japan's governmental system is similar to the British parliamentary system. Just as the British parliament has two houses, so the Japanese governing body, known as the Diet, has the lower House of Representatives and the upper House of Councillors. The party that controls the majority of seats in the Diet is the ruling party and has the right to appoint the prime minister – usually the party's president. The prime minister then appoints his cabinet, which is usually constituted entirely of Diet members.

The members of Japan's Diet are elected by popular vote, making the country, in principle, a democracy. In fact, real power is wielded by powerful political cliques in conjunction with the country's dominant *keiretsu* (business cartels). Together, these two groups make almost all of the country's important policy decisions behind closed doors. Until quite recently, this seemed to suit Japanese voters just fine, but the present economic difficulties have given rise to calls for a more transparent and representative form of government.

Since its formation in 1955, the conservative Liberal Democratic Party, or LDP, has been almost continuously in power, shaking off scandal after scandal. Elections in 1993 pushed the LDP out into the cold for a brief spell, but it quickly recaptured political power under the leadership of Hashimoto Ryutaro. Since then, the LDP has remained in power, with a series of prime ministers, the most recent of whom is Koizumi Junichiro, who took the reins in April 2001. At the time of writing, Koizumi's inability to make good on his promises of reform make it likely that he will soon be joining the long list of ex-prime ministers.

Finally, in addition to the elected government, Japan retains its emperor, who holds a curious position within the nation. For centuries under the shōgunate, the role was purely symbolic, but during the Meiji Restoration the emperor was 'restored' to power. In fact, he was merely brought out of the closet, dusted off and given a new figurehead position. The close of WWII brought further changes when it was announced that the emperor was no longer divine; despite this, he is still a figure of enormous respect in Japan and criticism of the emperor is almost unheard of.

Geographical, Political & Administrative Divisions

Japan is divided into nine political regions and subdivided into 47 divisions. *Ken* (prefectures) make up 43 of these divisions, and their names are written as, for example, 'Okayama-ken' or 'Chiba-ken'. The remaining four divisions are Hokkaidō, which is a *dō* (district); Tokyo-to, which is a *to* (metropolis); and Osaka-fu and Kyoto-fu, which are *fu* (urban prefectures). Each of the three city areas incorporates the named city but is otherwise similar in land area to a *ken*.

Ken are subdivided into *gun* (county), *mura* (village) and *chō* (neighbourhood or village), while *to* and *fu* are subdivided into *shi* (city), *ku* (ward) and *chō*. Hokkaidō is the exception to all this, being subdivided into 14 *shichō*, which are prefecture-like 'districts'.

There are also traditional names for each region of the country. Thus, Chūgoku, or Western Honshū, consists of the San-in, or North Coast, region and the San-yō, or South Coast, region. Other traditional names that you may come across in tourist literature or in other sources include Hokuriku (Fukui, Ishikawa and Toyama prefectures), Sanriku (Aomori, Iwate and Miyagi), Shin-etsu (Nagano and Niigata) and Tokai (Aichi, Gifu, Mie and Shizuoka). In addition to these, the Tokyo area is often referred to as Kantō, while the area around Osaka and Kyoto is known as Kansai or Kinki.

ECONOMY

The Japanese economic phenomenon is a rags to riches story that has left commentators around the world searching for its whys and wherefores. In the space of just 50 or so years, Japan has gone from a defeated nation to the world's largest creditor nation.

The Japanese economy was devastated at the end of WWII. The MacArthur government of occupation restored the competitiveness of Japanese products by drastically devaluing the yen. From a prewar yen–dollar exchange rate of ¥4 to US$1, the yen plummeted to ¥360 to US$1. Before long, Japanese products were filling the 'cheap and nasty' bins of supermarkets and stores around the world.

It might have stayed that way except that Japanese industry reinvested profits into research and development, so that by the mid-1970s Japan was filing more patents than the USA. The Japanese began to make products that were cheap but also skilfully produced and of high quality. Even a potentially disastrous event, such as the unstable oil prices of the 1970s, which vastly increased the costs of Japan's imported energy needs, conspired to cooperate with Japanese export ambitions. It pushed the yen down, increasing the competitiveness of Japanese goods, and made Japanese fuel-efficient cars suddenly a lot more attractive than they had been before.

Until 1990, it looked as though the Japanese economic juggernaut was unstoppable. But there was trouble in paradise. During the 1980s, escalating property values, a bullish stock market and easy credit led to what is now known as the 'Bubble Economy'. With a seemingly endless supply of easy money on hand, developers and investors threw their money into one grand scheme after another, on the assumption that the Japanese stock prices and land values would continue rising indefinitely.

In January 1990, however, the Tokyo stock market began to slide. By October of the same year it had lost 48% of its value – the bubble was about to burst. In 1991, Japanese banks, hit by the fall in stock market values, could no longer afford to be so free with their money and raised their interest rates. In turn, land prices came crashing back to earth. The sudden economic slowdown led to the failure of many of the speculative development ventures initiated during the 1980s, leaving the country's banks with a mountain of bad loans. The repercussions were felt in every sector of the economy and the country plunged into a recession from which it has yet to recover.

At the time of writing, Japan's jobless rate stands at 5%, and some critics contend that the actual figure may be higher. Worse still, the economy has actually contracted in recent years, posting a negative 0.4% GDP growth rate in 2001. For the fiscal year ending March 2003, it is estimated that the figure will return to the black, but a growth rate of only 0.2% is hardly cause for celebration.

In an effort to stimulate the economy, the government has responded with a series of vast public works projects, most of them financed by borrowing, swelling an already huge government debt. While some critics hold that these pump-priming measures will eventually pay off, most argue that the only way for Japan to pull out of the current crisis is to radically reorder its economy. However, for the time being the government seems to lack the necessary resolve to do this.

POPULATION & PEOPLE

Japan has a population of approximately 127 million people (the ninth largest in the world) and, with 75% of it concentrated in urban centres, population density is extremely high. Areas such as the Tokyo-Kawasaki-Yokohama conurbation are so densely populated that they have almost ceased to be separate cities, running into each other and forming a vast coalescence that, if considered as a whole, would constitute the world's largest city.

One notable feature of Japan's population is its relative ethnic and cultural homogeneity. The main reason for this ethnic homogeneity is Japan's strict immigration laws, which have ensured that only a small number of foreigners settle in the country.

The largest non-Japanese group in the country is made up of 650,000 *zai-nichi kankoku-jin* (resident Koreans). For most outsiders, Koreans are an invisible minority. Indeed, even the Japanese themselves have no way of knowing that someone is of Korean descent if he or she adopts a Japanese name. Nevertheless, Japanese-born Koreans, who in some cases speak no language other than Japanese, were only very recently released from the obligation to carry thumbprinted ID cards at all times, and still face discrimination in the workplace and other aspects of their daily lives.

Aside from Koreans, most foreigners in Japan are temporary workers from China, Southeast Asia, South America and Western countries. Indigenous groups such as the Ainu have been reduced to very small numbers and are concentrated mostly in Hokkaidō.

Burakumin

The Burakumin are a mysterious minority. They are racially the same as other

Japanese, and yet history has made them an outcast class. Traditionally, the Burakumin belonged to communities whose work brought them into contact with the contamination of death – butchering, leatherworking and the disposing of corpses.

There are thought to be around three million hereditary Burakumin nowadays. While discrimination against Burakumin is now technically against the law, there continues to be significant discrimination against Burakumin in such important aspects of Japanese social life as work and marriage. It is common knowledge, though rarely alluded to, that information about any given individual's possible Burakumin origin is available to anyone (generally employers and prospective fathers-in-law) who is prepared to make certain discreet investigations. Many Japanese dislike discussing this topic with foreigners and, unless you are on very familiar terms with your hosts or in liberal company, it is probably bad taste to bring it up.

Ainu

The indigenous populations of Hokkaidō originally included a variety of ethnic groups, but the most dominant of these still residing on the island are the Ainu. In Ainu language, the word 'Ainu' means 'man' or 'human being'. There is a possible link between the Ainu and the people known in ancient records as the Ezo, who lived in Tōhoku. Other experts theorise that the Ainu are a Caucasian race who pushed into Japan from Siberia. Although the Ainu have more body hair and tend towards lighter skin colouring, the physical differences between Ainu and Japanese are slight. Intermarriage has further reduced these differences, and it's calculated that there are now probably less than 200 pure-blood Ainu left.

Estimates of the total Ainu population in Hokkaidō range from 24,000 to 77,000, with the largest communities of Ainu residing in Shiraoi, Asahikawa, the Hidaka district and Akan National Park. There are also a few thousand Ainu living on Honshū (mostly in Tokyo) and Russia's Sakhalin Island. The exact population figures are hard to pin down since many people choose not to identify themselves as Ainu for fear of social discrimination.

Culturally, the Ainu have suffered a historical experience similar to Native Americans in North America. As far back as the 7th century, Ainu were known to have inhabited northern Japan, Hokkaidō and Russia's Sakhalin and Kuril Islands. Over the centuries, Japanese traders, farmers and military expeditions made repeated incursions into southern Hokkaidō. In the 16th century, the Matsumae clan arrived in force and negotiated formal trading treaties with the Ainu, but by the end of the 19th century the Tokugawa shōgunate and the successive Meiji government had taken back direct control and accelerated the colonisation of Hokkaidō.

At that time, many Ainu customs, including women's tattoos and the burning of a house where a person had died, were outlawed. Land and hunting rights were severely curtailed in an attempt to force the Ainu, who were traditionally hunters and gatherers, into becoming settled agriculturists. The Japanese government did provide limited social welfare and public education, but this system fostered a disempowering reliance by Ainu communities, that continues to some extent today, on government aid.

Some Japanese still exercise racial discrimination against people of Ainu descent, though Ainu are usually only distinguishable from their Japanese neighbours when they choose to identify themselves. The Japanese Diet passed a new law in 1997 that mandated nationwide promotion of Ainu culture and traditions. This law also provided funds and increased support for Ainu research, private Ainu cultural associations and, most importantly, Ainu language classes, as only a few of the older generation are fluent and able to pass on the rich tradition of *yukar* (epic poems).

Most Japanese tourists seem comfortable with seeing Ainu culture only in the context of pseudo 'Ainu villages', with souvenir shops selling cheap replicas of traditional crafts. Ainu traditions are re-enacted by sometimes listless performers and these tourist circuses can be pretty depressing – they are often combined with caged bears in a debased imitation of the Ainu's sacred Iyomante (Bear) festival. It is worth keeping in mind, however, that these tourist sites were often created, and are still managed,

Urban Anthropology

Visitors to Japan expecting to find a nation of suit-wearing conformists are often shocked by the sheer variety of subcultures they discover. Indeed, in places like Tokyo's Shibuya or Osaka's Shinsaibashi, ordinary street traffic on a Friday night approaches a kind of gaudy street theatre, and people-watching is half the fun of being there. The following guide delineates some of the more common types that you're likely to encounter in the big cities.

Bosozoku These are motorcycle gangs, who dye their hair and wear bright, flashy clothes. Typically, they'll spend a night loudly revving their motorcycle engines and speeding off tailed by the police, who never catch them. Like *chimpira*, some of the wilder *bosozoku* go on to become *yakuza*.

Chimpira This is often a *yanqui* who has taken rebellion a step further and hopes to attract the attention of *yakuza* and be asked to join the gang as a junior yakuza.

Ko Gyaru *Ko* comes from either *kōkō*, the Japanese word for high school, or *ko*, the word for 'girl' or 'small', while *gyaru* comes from the English word 'girl' or 'gal'. This is a high-school girl who favours day-glo colours, miniskirts, towering high-heel boots, a dark suntan, blonde hair and, of course, a mobile phone. She is sometimes just called a *gyaru*.

Obattalion This word is derived from the Japanese word *obaasan* (grandmother) and the English word 'battalion'. Perhaps best translated as 'battle axe', an *obattalion* is an elderly woman known for shouldering her way onto trains and buses, terrorising shop clerks and generally getting her way in any situation.

Office Ladies Also known as OLs, these women may be secretaries, but may equally be women who do the same work as their male bosses for half the pay. OLs usually travel in small groups wearing matching uniforms of skirts, white blouses and vests.

---

by Ainu communities in which much of the profits are reinvested. For a long time, these sites were the only evidence of Ainu culture left in Japan. Many souvenir shops, if you look carefully, actually do sell good-quality woodcarving, as well as other traditional items, such as those made from sturdy woven elm-bark cloth.

If you want to see how the Ainu wish to portray themselves, make a point of visiting any of the several museums of Ainu culture in Hokkaidō, most notably at Biratori and Shiraoi. There are also several other smaller museums with exhibits on Ainu culture and the other indigenous peoples of Hokkaidō, the best of which are at Abashiri and Hakodate. For more information on Ainu cultural events and related reading, see the Hokkaidō chapter.

Ageing Japan

WWII left Japan with a very young population that, at the time, had a relatively short average lifespan compared with the average lifespan of people in advanced Western nations. Now, Japan's astonishingly low birth rate of 1.4 births per woman and Japanese people's extreme longevity are turning this

situation around. From being a nation of youngsters Japan is rapidly becoming a nation of oldsters. Taken together with Japan's strict rules on immigration, this will inevitably result in a shrinking population. Experts predict that the present population of 126 million will grow slightly until 2007, after which it will rapidly decline; to 100 million in 2050 and 67 million in 2100. Needless to say, such demographic change will have a major influence on the economy in coming decades.

EDUCATION

Japanese often describe their society as a *gaku-reki shakai*, a society in which a person's future is almost completely determined by their academic record. It is not surprising, then, that the Japanese take education very seriously. Indeed, it is fair to say that education is the defining force in Japanese society.

It all starts at a very young age: after a blissful two or three years of freedom in infancy, Japanese children are thrown into one of the most gruelling education systems in the world. Competition is fierce from the beginning, since getting into the

Urban Anthropology

Ojōsan This is a young woman, usually a college student or graduate, who is middle class and headed for marriage to a young
salaryman. An *ojōsan*'s dress is conservative, with the exception
of the occasional miniskirt.

Parasite Single These are single women who continue to live with
their parents well into their twenties and thirties, hence the
name 'parasite'. They are part of what is known in Japan as the
mukekkon sedai (non-marriage generation).

Salarymen These are just what you'd expect: businessmen, always
clad in suits, often in matching groups.

Yakuza These are the real thing. They used to stand out, with tight
'punch-perms' and loud suits, but modern *yakuza* are hardly no-
ticeable, except perhaps for their swagger and black Mercedes
with tinted windows.

MICHAEL TAYLOR

Yan-mama This word is formed from the English word 'young' or the Japanese *yanqui*, and *mama*
(mother). A *yan-mama* is a woman who has married and had children at a very young age (usually as a high-school student) and continues to dress in miniskirts and platform shoes, to the
great horror of conservative weekly magazines in Japan.

Yanqui Pronounced 'yankee', a member of this tribe prefers brown or blond hair, sports flashy
clothes and has a mobile phone permanently glued to one ear. Male *yanqui* often work in the
construction industry, where their penchant for loud clothes is expressed in the brightly coloured
nikka-bokka (from the English word 'knickerbockers') pants that they wear.

right school can mean an important head start when it comes to university exams. These exams, of legendary difficulty, are so demanding that any student preparing for them and getting more than four hours sleep a night is said to have no hope of passing.

To help coach students through the exams, *juku* (evening cram schools) teach students those things that they might have missed in their regular schools. Students who fail to gain entry to the university of their choice frequently spend one or two years repeating the final year of school and sitting the exams again. These students, known as *rōnin*, or 'masterless samurai', are in a kind of limbo between the school education system and the higher education system, the key to employment in Japan.

The intense pressure of this system derives in no small part from the fact that 12 years of education culminates in just two examinations that effectively determine whether or not the student will enter university. One exam is sat by all Japanese final-year high school students on the same day; the other exam is specific to the university the student wishes to attend

Once exams have been completed and a student gains a university place, it is time to let loose a little. University or college is considered a transitional stage between the worlds of education and employment, a stage in which one spends more time in drinking bouts with other students than in the halls of higher learning. In a sense, the university years, for those who make it, are a time to recover from the struggles of the previous 12 years.

It is also worth noting that male and female students often take different paths in the Japanese educational system. Not only do far more male students go on to the top-level universities, but the academic majors chosen by male and female students are often different: male students tend to major in economics or engineering, while female students tend to major in foreign languages or literature. As a result, Japanese female graduates are in the vanguard of the country's push toward internationalisation, accounting for the majority of interpreters, translators and bilingual workers, while the majority of male graduates go on to become 'salarymen' in the nation's large companies.

SOCIETY & CONDUCT

The Japanese are so convinced that they are different from everyone else that it's easy to find yourself agreeing with them. A complex mythology of uniqueness has grown up around the Japanese, and one of the challenges of discovering Japan for yourself is putting the myths straight. See also Social Graces in the Facts for the Visitor chapter.

The Group

One of the most cherished ideas about the Japanese is that the group is more important than the individual. It's easy to start seeing Japan's business-suited workers as members of a collectivised society that rigorously suppresses individual tendencies. But remember that the Japanese are no less individual than their Western counterparts: they experience the same frustrations and joys as Westerners do, and are just as likely to complain about their work conditions, the way their boss treats them and so on.

The tension between group and individual interests has been a rich source of inspiration for Japanese art. Traditional values emphasise conflict between *honne* (the individual's personal views) and *tatemae* (the views that are demanded by the individual's position in the group). The same conflict is expressed in the terms *ninjō* (human feelings) and *giri* (social obligations). Salaried workers who spend long hours at the office away from the families they love are giving priority to *giri* over *ninjō*.

All this is deeply rooted in Japanese history. Until very recently, almost all Japanese lived in small villages, many of them engaged in rice farming. In order to live in harmony and produce a successful harvest, a high degree of cooperation was vital – there was little room for free-thinking individualists. Perhaps more importantly, with so many people packed into so little space, the Japanese learned long ago that the only way to live together was to put the needs of the group before those of the individual.

Men & Women

Traditional Japanese society restricted the woman's role to the home, where as house-keeper she wielded considerable power, overseeing all financial matters, monitoring the children's education and, in some ways, acting as the head of the household. Even in the early Meiji period, however, the ideal was rarely matched by reality: labour shortfalls often resulted in women taking on factory work; even before that, women often worked side by side with men in the fields.

As might be expected, the contemporary situation is complex. There are some women who stick to established roles. They tend to opt for shorter college courses, often at women's colleges, and see education as an asset in the marriage market. Once married, they leave the role of breadwinner to their husbands.

Increasingly, however, Japanese women are choosing to forgo or delay marriage in favour of pursuing their own career ambitions. Of course, changing aspirations do not necessarily translate into changing realities, and Japanese women are still significantly under-represented in upper-management and political positions, but over-represented as office fodder, such as OLs (office ladies; see the boxed text 'Urban Anthropology' earlier). Part of the reason for this is the prevalence of gender discrimination and sexual harassment in Japanese companies. Societal expectations, however, also play a role: Japanese women are forced to choose between having a career and having a family. Not only do most companies refuse to hire women for career-track positions, the majority of Japanese men are simply not interested in having a career woman as a spouse. This makes it very intimidating for a Japanese woman to step out of her traditional gender role and follow a career path.

The Japanese & Gaijin

As a foreign visitor to Japan, you are a *gaijin*, literally, an 'outside person'. Some foreigners insist (correctly in fact) that the term *gaikokujin* (literally, 'outside country person') is more polite than the contraction *gaijin*, but the latter is so widely used that you will be knocking your head against a brick wall if you try to change it. And, it's worth noting that the word simply means 'foreigner', so there really is nothing to get upset about.

Away from the big cities it's not unusual to hear whispered exclamations of *gaijin da* (it's a foreigner!); even in suburban Tokyo, where *gaijin* are a dime a dozen, some school children are still unable to resist erupting into giggles at the sight of a foreign face.

Long-term visitors to Japan are prone to develop a love-hate relationship with the Japanese. After initially being overwhelmed by Japanese courtesy, many foreigners who feel that they have been in Japan long enough to deserve to be on a more intimate footing with their hosts come to the conclusion that Japanese politeness and helpfulness mask a morbid ethnocentricity.

Fortunately, most short-term visitors come away with miracle stories of Japanese courtesy. If you approach the Japanese with an open mind and a smile on your face, it's almost certain that you too will be the recipient of countless acts of spontaneous kindness, and this, more than anything else, is one of the great joys of travelling in Japan.

Meeting the Japanese

In general, it is quite easy to meet with the Japanese, at least on a superficial basis. You'll find that the Japanese are very curious about other countries and people and are keenly interested in how Japan is perceived by outsiders. By far the best place to meet the Japanese is in an *izakaya* (Japanese pub-eatery). Here, after a few drinks, you'll find people just about queuing up to talk to you. Indeed, you might even find the attention cloying after a while. If you prefer a more formal introduction, you can also try the Home Visit System (see later in this section).

Shyness The Japanese are a relatively shy lot, especially when it comes to dealing with foreigners. There are two main reasons for this. First, many Japanese tend to speak limited English at best, and are afraid of making mistakes when speaking the language. Second, most Japanese have had precious little interaction with foreigners and simply aren't sure how to handle the situation. Thus, when you deal with the Japanese you should always speak slowly and clearly and approach everyone with a smile on your face.

O-miyage Obligation

Gifts are the grease that keeps the wheels of Japanese society turning. A gift can serve as a token of appreciation, a sign of respect, a guarantee of continued favour or even a bribe (just think of Japanese politics).

Perhaps the most troublesome and time-consuming gift of all is *o-miyage* – a souvenir given to friends, family and colleagues upon return from travel. In most Japanese companies, leaving for a holiday naturally entails a sense of shame, of letting down the team. To make up for this betrayal, an armful of *o-miyage* is required. Of course, shopping for all these gifts can eat up an entire holiday (particularly a Japanese holiday, which usually lasts only a few days anyway).

Ever resourceful, the Japanese have come up with a unique solution to this problem – the train station regional speciality store. These stores are located in the passageways around major city train stations. In the space of a few hundred metres you can pick up crab from Hokkaidō, dolls from Kyūshū and pickled vegetables from Shikoku. Even if everybody knows that their souvenir was picked up at the local train station, the obligation is fulfilled and everybody is happy.

Recently, these stores have sprung up in airports as well, selling souvenir gifts from Japan's favourite international destinations: Hawaii, Disneyworld and Paris.

People have also thought of new ways to make use of gifts purchased at these stores. The story goes that they are commonly used as alibis: after a weekend spent at the local love hotel, a gift purchased at a regional speciality store is face-saving proof that a wayward salaryman was actually on a business trip.

You should also beware of a type of Japanese person who is anything but shy. These are 'serial English speakers' who approach any vaguely Western-looking foreigner in the hope of getting a free English conversation lesson. You should have little difficulty determining those who really want to communicate with you and those who merely want to practise their language skills. If you think your opposite party falls into the latter group, the easiest thing to do is simply declare that you are busy.

Visiting a Shrine

Entering a Japanese shrine can be a bewildering experience for travellers. In order to make the most of the experience, follow these guidelines and do as the Japanese do.

Just past the torii (shrine gate), you'll find a *chōzuya* (trough of water) with long-handled ladles perched on a *hishaku* (rack) above. This is for purifying yourself before entering the sacred precincts of the shrine. Some Japanese do forgo this ritual and head directly for the main hall. If you choose to purify yourself, however, take a ladle, fill it with fresh water from the spigot, pour some over one hand, transfer the spoon and pour water over the other hand, then pour a little water into a cupped hand and rinse your mouth, spitting the water onto the ground beside the trough, not into the trough.

Next, head to the *haiden* (hall of worship), which sits in front of the *honden* (main hall) enshrining the *kami* (god of the shrine). Here you'll find a thick rope hanging from a gong, in front of which is an offerings box. Toss a coin into the box, ring the gong by pulling on the rope (to summon the deity), pray, then clap your hands twice, bow and then back away from the shrine. Some Japanese believe that a ¥5 coin is the best for an offering at a temple or shrine, and that the luck engendered by the offering of a ¥10 coin will come further in the future (since 10 can be pronounced *tō* in Japanese, which can mean 'far').

If photography is forbidden at a shrine, it will be signposted as such; otherwise, it is permitted and you should simply use your discretion when taking photos.

Home Visit System The Home Visit System is publicised in JNTO (Japan National Tourist Organization) pamphlets and gives visitors to some of Japan's larger cities the opportunity to visit a Japanese family in their home. Visits take place in the evening and, while dinner is usually not served, the hosts will often provide tea and sweets. It is polite to bring a small gift with you when you visit to show your appreciation of your hosts' thoughtfulness and hospitality. Contact the nearest JNTO office for details (see Tourist Offices in the Facts for the Visitor chapter).

RELIGION

Westerners, who are used to the exclusivity of their patriarchal religions, often find Japanese religion confusing. This is because the Japanese, for the most part, are happy to practise the rituals of at least two, and sometimes three or even four, religions.

Shintō (the native 'religion' of Japan), Buddhism, Confucianism and even Christianity all play a role in contemporary Japanese social life, and are defining in some way of the Japanese world view. If you are sceptical of the inclusion of Christianity, you need only attend a Japanese wedding to find certain Christian elements mingling happily with more traditional practices.

Shintō and Buddhism, the major religions in Japan, have coexisted for many centuries in relative harmony. A notable break in this amicable relationship occurred during the Meiji period, when nationalist fervour introduced 'State Shintō' as the state religion. Severe restraints were placed on Buddhism, which came under attack from nationalist zealots. The balance was restored with the abolition of State Shintō after the Allied occupation in 1945.

Shintō

Shintō is an indigenous religion that acquired its name, 'the way of the gods', to distinguish it from Buddhism, a later import. It seems to have grown out of an awe for manifestations of nature that included the sun, water, rock formations, trees and even sounds. All such manifestations were felt to have their *kami* (god), a belief that led to a complex pantheon of gods and a rich mythology. In particularly sacred spots, shrines were erected. Important to Shintō is the concept of purification before entering such sacred domains.

Shintō is a religion without a founder and without a canon; indeed it is not a religion in the sense that you could conver

[Continued on page 65

FRANK CARTER

RICHARD I'ANSON

Title Page: Curtain with geisha design and traditional scenery (photograph by Frank Carter)

Top: Geisha perform in the Kamogawa Odori, Kyoto, Kansai

Bottom: Lead guitar, Yoyogi-kōen, Tokyo

Until the 19th century the major influences on Japanese art came from China and Korea. While Japan was still living in the Stone Age, China had a well-developed technological culture. It's hardly surprising, then, that when frequent contact was established that Japan would be hungry for whatever skills and knowledge the Chinese had to give. In borrowing many aspects of Chinese culture, Japan also absorbed influences from distant cultures, such as those of Persia, Afghanistan and even ancient Rome, as China had maintained an active trade along the Silk Road. Perhaps the most important influence of all came from India, via China, in the form of Buddhism, which entered Japan in the 6th century.

Looking beyond these outside influences, the Japanese always add something of their own to their arts. There is a fascination with the ephemeral, with the unadorned, with forms that echo the randomness of nature. A gift for caricature is also present, from early Zen ink paintings right up to the manga, or comics, of contemporary Japan. There also exists a wildness and passion that is less evident in the arts of China. An interest in the grotesque or bizarre is also often visible, from Buddhist scrolls depicting the horrors of hell to the stylised depictions of body parts in the ukiyo-e (wood-block prints) of the Edo period.

When asked to define their aesthetic principles, Japanese artists reach for words like *wabi*, *sabi* and *shibui*, words that have no real English-language equivalents. These concepts tend to overlap, and are often used more emotively than descriptively. Together they refer to a kind of rustic simplicity and a restrained, quiet and cultivated sense of beauty. These ideals can be found, for example, in the measured proceedings of the tea ceremony. They are by no means, though, the final summation of a long and vibrant artistic tradition, for this tradition actively seeks new inspirations and produces surprising new forms.

Bottom: Detail of the roof of Zōjō-ji, Tokyo, owing the chrysanthe-mum national emblem

CHRIS MELLOR

ART PERIODS

Heavily influenced by mainland culture, it is natural that the Japanese arts continuously reflect the state of relations between Japan, China and Korea. During periods of frequent contact, new ideas and techniques were rapidly assimilated, resulting in art that was sometimes indistinguishable from that of the mainland. During periods of isolation, native ideas and sensibilities were allowed to come to the fore and the Japanese arts developed their own distinctiveness.

Archaeologists have unearthed a range of artefacts from Japan's earliest historical periods. The Jōmon period (10,000–300 BC) takes its name from the decorative 'coiled rope' pottery produced by Japan's early hunters and gatherers. Similarly, the Yayoi period (300 BC–AD 300), which saw the introduction of wet-rice farming and bronze and iron use from the mainland, has left many examples of simple, refined earthenware pottery and clay figurines. The Kofun period (AD 300–710) is named after the *kofun* – the round or keyhole-shaped burial mounds of Japan's earliest emperors. *Haniwa* (clay ring) earthenware cylinders and sculptures, some as tall as 1.5m, surrounded these burial mounds.

The Asuka (552–645) and Hakuhō (645–710) periods mark an important turning point. The arrival of Mahayana, or Greater Vehicle, Buddhism introduced religious themes that would inspire the Japanese arts for more than 500 years. The earliest works of sculpture were produced by Korean artisans – notable examples can be seen at the temples Hōryū-ji in Nara and Kōryū-ji in Kyoto. However, by the Nara period (710–94) a golden age of Japanese sculpture had arrived. Japanese sculptors produced masterpieces, such as the Shō-Kannon statue and the Yakushi Triad (both on display at Yakushi-ji in southern Nara), as well as the Ganjin statue at Tōshōdai-ji. Also during this period, outstanding religious murals were painted, very much in the vein of Indian religious cave paintings.

It was difficult in these early days for Japan to shrug off the influence of China. However, by the early Heian period (794–1185), as Tang-dynasty China faltered and Japan distanced itself from its mainland neighbour, a truly native culture began to emerge. For the Japanese, this period is the apogee of elegant courtly life. The imperial capital moved from Nara to Heian (modern-day Kyoto), and the literary arts flourished. The break with Chinese tradition can be seen in the development of the 31-syllable *waka* poem, precursor to the 17-syllable haiku, and in narrative epics like *Genji Monogatari* (The Tale of Genji) by Murasaki Shikibu. In the visual arts, *yamato-e* (Japanese painting) broke with Chinese landscape tradition by depicting imperial court scenes on folding panels. The graceful lines of Kyoto's Byōdō-in, a temple that is one of the few remaining structures from this period, are also testament to the beauty of Heian architecture.

After a period of brutal internecine warfare, a military government was established in Kamakura. The early art of the Kamakura period (1185–1333) was filled with a wild energy, though later art of the period became more subdued under the influence of a military government that eschewed vibrancy in the arts for a more spartan aesthetic. During this period, Zen Buddhism became popular in Japan. Its disavowal of Buddha images gave rise to a new tradition of human portraits and statues, and marked the beginning of a secularisation of the arts that would gain momentum in the following centuries.

In 1336 the centre of power moved back to Kyoto. During the Muromachi period (1333–1576) Zen had an enormous impact on the arts in Japan, exemplified by the ink paintings of Sesshū, the tea ceremony of the master Sen-no-Rikyū and the garden of Ginkaku-ji in Kyoto. The period was marked by a spirit of contemplation. However, in 1467 the 11-year Ōnin War broke out, which essentially destroyed the country. This 'brush with the void' left a deep impact on Japan, and the idea of *wabi*, or stark simplicity, was born.

After another period of internal struggle, a powerful shōgun, Toyotomi Hideyoshi, took control and presided over an era of unprecedented grandeur and flamboyance in the arts. The new elite encouraged artists to produce elaborate works to decorate their palaces. The Momoyama period (1576–1600) was typified by huge gardens, gilded screen paintings and brilliant textile work. Also during this period, the first Westerners arrived, bringing with them technology and treasures unlike anything yet seen in Japan.

During the Edo period (1600–1867) of *sakoku*, or national seclusion, the Japanese arts coalesced into the forms we recognise today. With the rise of the merchant class, the arts were no longer the province of emperors and nobles and this had a tonic effect on Japanese artists, who could now sell their work to a much wider audience. The most important development during this time was ukiyo-e, or wood-block print, depicting the 'floating world' of Edo courtesans and kabuki (stylised theatre) performers. Ukiyo-e marks the end of a long progression in the Japanese arts, which began with depictions of the Buddha and ended with depictions of people in everyday situations.

Since the Meiji Restoration (1868–1912), the arts in Japan have been revolutionised by contact with the West. As was the case with early Chinese influences, Japanese artists have swiftly moved from imitation to innovation. From film to fashion, architecture to literature, Japanese artists have made and continue to make unique international contributions.

Bottom: Street art for sale, near Shibuya, Tokyo

LIZ THOMPSON

MUSIC

Traditional Music

Gagaku is 'elegant' classical music of the Japanese imperial court, which was derived from Chinese models. It flourished between the 8th and 12th centuries then declined for several centuries until a revival of interest in national traditions during the Meiji period. Court orchestras were divided into two sections, with formally prescribed functions: the orchestra of the 'right' played Korean music; the orchestra of the 'left' played Chinese, Indian or Japanese music. The repertoire of an orchestra included *kangen* (instrumental) pieces and *bugaku* (dance) pieces.

Today, a *gagaku* ensemble usually consists of 16 players performing on drums and kettledrums, string instruments such as the *biwa* (lute) and koto (plucked zither), and wind instruments such as the *hichiriki* (Japanese oboe) and various types of flute.

Traditional Instruments

Several traditional Japanese instruments continue to play a part in Japanese life, both publicly and privately. Some are used in orchestras or the theatre, while others are used for solo performances.

The *shamisen* is a three-stringed instrument resembling a banjo with an extended neck. It was very popular during the Edo period, particularly in the entertainment districts of Osaka and Edo. It is still used as formal accompaniment in kabuki and bunraku (classical puppet theatre), and the ability to perform on the *shamisen* remains one of the essential skills of a geisha.

The koto is a type of plucked zither with 13 strings. It was adapted from a Chinese instrument some time before the 8th century and the number of strings gradually increased from five to 13. A bass koto, with 17 strings, was created in the 20th century – leading to an even greater musical range for this ancient instrument.

The *biwa*, which resembles a lute and also derives from a Chinese instrument, appeared in Japan in the 8th century. It was played by travelling musicians, often blind, who recited Buddhist sutras (collections of dialogues and discourses) to the accompaniment of

FRANK CARTER

Bottom: Detail of a *taiko* (drum)

the instrument. During the Heian period, the *biwa* was used in court orchestras. In the succeeding Kamakura period, storytellers created a different style for the *biwa* to accompany tales from medieval war epics, the most famous of which are the Tales of Heike. Although *biwa* ballads were in vogue during the 16th century, the instrument later fell out of favour. More recently, the composer Takemitsu Tōru has found a new niche for the *biwa* in a Western orchestra.

The *shakuhachi* is a wind instrument imported from China in the 7th century. The *shakuhachi* was popularised by wandering Komusō monks in the 16th and 17th centuries, who played it as a means to enlightenment as they walked alone through the woods.

Taiko refers to any of a number of large Japanese drums often played at festivals or in parades. Perhaps most famous of all *taiko* music is performed during the Earth Celebration festival on Sado-ga-shima, near Niigata (see the boxed text 'Festive Sado' in the Northern Honshū chapter). The drummers who perform this music train year-round to endure the rigours of playing these enormous drums. Check with the Tourist Information Center (TIC) about an occasional special *taiko* festival held on the island.

Contemporary Music

Japan has a huge domestic market. More than any other nation in Asia, the Japanese have taken to Western music, and you can meet fans of every type of music from Bach to acid jazz. An overwhelming feature of the local music scene is the *aidoru* (idol singers). The popularity of idols is generated largely through media appearances and is centred on a cute, girl-next-door image.

The predominance of Western-style imitation is probably the main reason why few Japanese acts have had any popularity in the West. Notable exceptions are electronic music performers, such as Kitarō, whose oriental synthesised sounds have had considerable success, and Ryūichi Sakamoto, a former member of Yellow Magic Orchestra and composer of the score for *The Last Emperor* (for which he won an Oscar).

Punk-pop girl-bands Shonen Knife and the 5.6.7.8s gained international celebrity in the 1990s as Japan's answer (or would that be riposte?) to the Ramones.

A perhaps surprising musical export was Orqesta de la Luz, a salsa band composed entirely of Japanese musicians. The band regularly played to ecstatic Hispanic audiences at stadium-sized venues across the USA and Latin America in the 1990s. In 1993 they became the first group ever to receive an award for cultural achievement from the United Nations. Still, no Japanese act has as yet been able to match the success of one Sakamoto Kyū, who made it to the top of the American hit parade in 1963 singing 'Sukiyaki'.

In addition to his growing popularity in Japan, Okinawan music maverick Kina Shokichi has been a driving force in placing Okinawan music on the world circuit. He is one of the few Japanese musicians to develop a true following in the West (his fans include David Byrne and Ry Cooder). His electric-traditional crossovers make for fascinating, often haunting listening.

Denki Download

Japanese electronic music has been well received internationally. This may owe something to the Western view of Japan as a technology-obsessed nation, but is also probably due to the stress electronic music places on sounds, rather than lyrics. The trailblazing Yellow Magic Orchestra, which formed in 1978, is still cited as one of the seminal founders of ambient house.

Japanese electronica comes in many flavours. Denki Groove, Pizzicato Five, Kyoto Jazz Massive and Buffalo Daughter have gained international recognition by mixing traditional instruments and vocals with a decent serve of electronic noise.

Tokyo is the best place to sample contemporary electronic music. The Liquid Room in Shinjuku is an institution, featuring Japanese as well as international artists. Also check the listings in *Tokyo Classified* or *Tokyo Journal*. The Japanese music scene has a sizable Web presence – most musicians have official pages or fan sites, with details on new releases and appearances, and free downloadable music! A good place to start your search is **w** www.bento.com/obscure.html.

CINEMA

Japan has a vibrant film industry and proud, critically acclaimed cinematic and cinematographic traditions. Renewed international attention since the mid-1990s has reinforced interest in domestic films, which account for an estimated 40% of box-office receipts, nearly double the level in most European countries. Of course, this includes not only artistically important works, but also films in the science-fiction, horror and 'monster-stomps-Tokyo' genres for which Japan is also known.

At the time cinema was first developed in the West, Japan was in the throes of the Meiji Restoration and was enthusiastically embracing everything associated with modernity. Cinema was first introduced to Japan in 1896 and, in characteristic fashion, the Japanese were making their own films by 1899. Until the advent of talkies, dialogue and general explanations were provided by a *benshi*, or narrator. This was necessary for foreign films, but even with Japanese silent films the *benshi* quickly became as important a part of the cinematic experience as the film itself. It was the narrator who brought the characters to life for the audience, and in essence became the star of early Japanese cinema.

At first, Japanese films were merely cinematic versions of traditional theatrical performances, but in the 1920s, Japanese directors starting producing films in two distinct genres: *jidaigeki* (period films) and new *gendaigeki* films, which dealt with modern themes. The more realistic storylines of the new films soon reflected back on the traditional films with the introduction of *shin jidaigeki* (new period films). During this era, samurai themes became an enduring staple of Japanese cinema.

As the government became increasingly authoritarian in the years leading up to WWII, cinema was largely used for propaganda purposes.

After the war, feudal films, with their emphasis on blind loyalty and martial themes, were banned by the Allied authorities, but cinematic energy soon turned to new pursuits, including *anime* (animated films), monster movies and comedies.

The decade of the 1950s was the golden age of Japanese cinema, beginning with the release in 1950 of Kurosawa Akira's *Rashōmon*, winner of the Golden Lion at the 1951 Venice International Film Festival and an Oscar for best foreign film.

The increasing realism and high artistic standards of the period are evident in such landmark films as *Tōkyō Monogatari* (Tokyo Story, 1953), by the legendary Ōzu Yasujirō; Mizoguchi Kenji's classics *Ugetsu Monogatari* (Tales of Ugetsu, 1953), a winner at the 1953 Venice International Film Festival, and *Saikaku Ichidai Onna* (The Life of Oharu, 1952), best foreign film at Venice in 1952; and Kurosawa's 1954 masterpiece *Shichinin no Samurai* (Seven Samurai). Annual attendance at the country's cinemas reached 1.1 billion in 1958, and Kyoto, with its large film studios, such as Shōchiku, Daiei and Tōei, and its more than 60 cinemas, enjoyed a heyday as Japan's own Hollywood.

As it did elsewhere in the world, television spurred a rapid drop in the number of cinema-goers in Japan in the high-growth decades of the 1960s and 1970s. But despite falling attendance, Japanese cinema remained a major artistic force. These decades gave the world such landmark works as Ichikawa Kon's *Chushingura* (47 Samurai, 1962), and Kurosawa's *Yōjimbo* (1961).

The decline in cinema-going continued through the 1980s, reinforced by the popularisation of videos, with annual attendance at cinemas bottoming out at just over 100 million. Yet Japan's cinema was far from dead: Kurosawa garnered acclaim worldwide for *Kagemusha* (1980), which shared the Palme d'Or at Cannes, and *Ran* (1985). Imamura Shōhei's heartrending *Narayama Bushiko* (The Ballad of Narayama) won the Grand Prix at Cannes in 1983. Itami Jūzō became perhaps the most widely known Japanese director outside Japan after Kurosawa with such biting satires as *Osōshiki* (The Funeral, 1985), *Tampopo* (Dandelion, 1986) and *Marusa no Onna* (A Taxing Woman, 1988). Ōshima Nagisa, best known for controversial films such as *Ai no Corrida* (In the Realm of the Senses, 1976), scored a critical and popular success with *Senjo no Merry Christmas* (Merry Christmas, Mr Lawrence) in 1983.

In the 1990s popular interest in Japan seemed to catch up with international attention as attendance rates began to rise once again. In 1997 Japanese directors received top honours at two of the world's three most prestigious film festivals: *Unagi* (Eel), Imamura Shohei's black-humoured look at human nature's dark side won the Palme d'Or in Cannes – making him the only Japanese director to win this award twice; and 'Beat' Takeshi Kitano took the Golden Lion in Venice for *Hana-bi*, a tale of life and death, and the violence and honour that links them. The undisputed king of popular Japanese cinema, 'Beat' Takeshi Kitano is a true Renaissance man of media: he stars in and directs his films, and is a newspaper columnist, author and poet. He even does stand-up comedy, as one half of the *manzai* act The Two Beats. He got his start with the seminal *Sono Otoko, Kyobo ni Tsuki* (Violent Cop, 1989).

To carry on a proud tradition in cinema, a new generation of directors is emerging; it includes Koreeda Hirokazu, with *Maboroshi no Hikari* (Wonderful Life), Kurosawa Kiyoshi, with *Cure*, and Ichikawa Jun, winner of the Best Director's prize at the Montreal Film Festival in 1997 for *Tōkyō Yakyoku* (Tokyo Drugstore).

Anime

The term *anime*, a Japanese word derived from French and English, is used worldwide to refer to Japan's highly sophisticated animated films. Unlike its counterparts in other countries, *anime* occupies a position very near the forefront of the film industry in Japan. *Anime* films encompass all genres, from science fiction and action adventure to romance and historical drama, and while *anime* is supported by three key media –

television, original video animation and full-length feature films – it is the stunning animation of the latter that has brought *anime* critical acclaim worldwide.

Unlike its counterparts in many other countries, *anime* targets all age and social groups. *Anime* films include deep explorations of philosophical questions and social issues, humorous entertainment and bizarre fantasies. The films offer breathtakingly realistic visuals, exquisite attention to detail, complex and expressive characters and elaborate plots. Leading directors and voice actors are accorded fame and respect, while characters become popular idols.

Japan's most famous *anime* genius is Miyazaki Hayao, creative head of Studio Ghibli since 1984. Miyazaki's films include *Kaze no Tani no Nausicaa* (Nausicaa of the Valley of the Winds, 1984), *Tonari no Totoro* (My Neighbour Totoro, 1988) and *Majō no Takkyubin* (Kiki's Delivery Service, 1989). During 1997 Miyazaki's *Mononoke-hime* (The Princess Mononoke), a fantasy about a 14th-century princess who fights the destruction of the forests, opened at 250 theatres across Japan, the largest opening in Japanese cinema history. History was made again in 1998 when *Mononoke-hime* broke the Japanese box-office record set by *E.T.* in 1982. In 1998 the film opened to a tremendous reception in the United States after Disney signed an agreement to release subtitled and dubbed versions of Miyazaki's films. Miyazaki continued

BOTH ILLUSTRATIONS BY MICK WELDON

his winning streak with the fantastical *Sen to Chihiro no Kamikakushi* (Spirited Away, 2002), which has won a swag of local and international awards.

Other leading *anime* masters to have gained recognition worldwide include Ōishi Mamoru whose 1995 masterpiece *Ghost in the Shell* has become a cult classic in Japan and overseas, and Ōtomo Katsuhiro, creator of the science-fiction action adventure classic *Akira*.

Top & Bottom: Manga-style cartoons

PERFORMING ARTS
Classical Theatre

There are four principal forms of classical Japanese theatre, ranging from dance-drama to comedy and puppetry. Don't be intimidated by the 'classical' label. While prior study will help you understand the nitty-gritty, as with all good theatre there are elements that transcend language – just as well, considering that archaic Japanese (used particularly in kabuki and nō) is as difficult for modern Japanese to understand as Shakespeare is for modern English-speakers. The introduction of programmes and headphone guides in modern Japanese and English have made it easier for people to follow the proceedings on stage.

Nō Quite possibly, people will tell you that nō is boring. But if shōgun Ashikaga Yoshimitsu (1358–1408) were around, he'd probably ask you to make up your own mind. He was so impressed by the actor and playwright Kan'ami (1333–84) that he extended shōgunal patronage to him. Kan'ami went on to wow courtly audiences with an amalgamation of elements of popular song-and-dance forms, Shintō sacred dances and Zen Buddhist ideals. Kan'ami's son, Zeami (1363–1444), was responsible for the art's development into its current form, and is commonly considered the greatest of all nō dramatists. Nō was still going strong in the Edo period (1600–1867), when the Tokugawa shōgunate endorsed five schools of nō for the entertainment of the samurai class.

Nō is a hypnotic dance-drama that reflects the minimalist aesthetics of Zen. The movement is gloriously powerful, the chorus and music sonorous, and the expression subtle. A sparsely furnished cedar stage directs full attention to the performers, who include a chorus, drummers and a flautist. There are two principal characters: the *shite*, who is sometimes a living person but more often a demon, or a ghost whose soul cannot rest; and the *waki*, who leads the main character towards the play's climactic moment. Each nō school has its own repertoire, and the art form continues to evolve and develop. One of the many new plays performed over the last 30 years is *Takahime*, based on William Butler Yates' *At the Hawk's Well*.

Although nō is traditionally a family affair, unlike kabuki, it accepts performers from outside, on a more-or-less equal basis. Among the actors and musicians who have undertaken the years of training required to master technique are many amateur nō groups and practitioners, and even some Westerner practitioners. While often considered to be a pastime of the elite, nō continues to attract large audiences.

Kabuki The first performances of kabuki were staged early in the 17th century by a female troupe led by Ōkuni, a dancer consecrated to the shrine Izumo Taisha, who created and performed short plays interspersed with dances. The performances were erotic and attracted great support from the merchant classes. In true bureaucratic fashion, Tokugawa officials feared for the people's morality and banned women from the stage in 1629. Since that time, kabuki has been performed exclusively by men, giving rise to the institution of *onnagata*, or *ōyama*, male actors who specialise in female roles.

JOHN ASHBURNE

Over the course of several centuries, kabuki has developed a repertoire that's drawn on popular themes, such as famous historical accounts and stories of love-suicide, while also borrowing copiously from nō, *kyōgen* (comic vignettes) and bunraku. Most kabuki plays border on melodrama, although they vary in mood.

Formalised beauty and stylisation are the central aesthetic principles of kabuki; the acting is a combination of dancing and speaking in conventionalised intonation patterns, and each actor prepares for a role by studying and emulating the style perfected by his predecessors. Kabuki actors are born to the art form, and training begins in childhood – the leading families of modern kabuki go back generations. Actors today enjoy great social prestige, and their activities on and off the stage attract as much interest as those of popular film and television stars.

Some actors have recently pushed the traditional boundaries of kabuki. For example, Ichikawa Ennosuke's Super Kabuki are high-tech, larger-than-life kabuki spectaculars that use modern language. Although purists have accused him of debasing the art, Ichikawa has attracted thousands of spectators since his first Super Kabuki, in 1986.

Regular kabuki performances are held year-round at Kabuki-za Theatre and Japan's national theatre Kokuritsu Gekijō in Tokyo, the Minami-za in Kyoto and the Shin-Kabuki-za in Osaka.

Kyōgen The humorous aspect of *sarugaku* (monkey music), one of the song-and-dance forms from which nō was developed, evolved into what eventually came to be called *kyōgen*. These comic vignettes are highly physical; the characters are ordinary people – bumbling samurai, lecherous priests, unfaithful women and lazy servants – and the plays are performed in the vernacular. Performers are not masked, and a chorus often accompanies the action. *Kyōgen* was originally performed as light relief between nō plays, but today major nō theatres also present *kyōgen*-only programmes.

In addition to giving over hundreds of *kyōgen* performances a year, leading actors also appear in contemporary plays, movies, television dramas and advertisements. These performers have sparked a new *kyōgen* craze and are drawing a whole new group of fans.

Top: Replica of Nakamura-za Kabuki Theatre facade (1805) at Edo Museum, Ryogoku, Tokyo

Bunraku Japan's traditional puppet theatre developed at the same time as kabuki, when the *shamisen* (a three-stringed lute), imported from Okinawa, was combined with traditional puppetry techniques and *joruri* (narrative chanting). Bunraku, as it came to be known in the 19th century, addresses many of the same themes as kabuki, and in fact many of the most famous plays in the kabuki repertoire were originally written for the puppet theatre. Bunraku involves large puppets – nearly two-thirds life-size – manipulated by up to three black-robed puppeteers. The puppeteers do not speak; a seated narrator tells the story and provides the voices of the characters, expressing their feelings with smiles, weeping and starts of surprise and fear. The best places to see bunraku are Kokuritsu Gekijō in Tokyo and the National Bunraku Theatre in Osaka.

Rakugo

A traditional Japanese style of comic monologue, *rakugo* (literally, 'dropped word') dates back to the Edo period (1600–1867). The performer, usually in kimono, sits on a square cushion on a stage. Props are limited to a fan and hand towel. The monologue begins with a *makura* (prologue), which is followed by the story itself and, finally, the *ochi* (punch line, or 'drop', which is another pronunciation of the Chinese character for *raku* in *rakugo*). Many of the monologues in the traditional *rakugo* repertoire date back to the Edo and Meiji periods, and while well known, reflect a social milieu unknown to modern listeners. Accordingly, many practitioners today also write new monologues addressing issues relevant to contemporary life.

Manzai

Manzai is a comic dialogue, with its origins in the song-and-dance and comedy routines traditionally performed by itinerant entertainers during Shōgatsu (New Year's celebrations). It is a highly fluid art that continues to draw large audiences to hear snappy duos exchange clever witticisms on up-to-the-minute themes from everyday life. Although popular everywhere, *manzai* is identified particularly with the Kansai region.

Butoh

In many ways, *butoh* is Japan's most accessible and exciting dance form (there are no words except for the occasional grunt). It is also its newest dance form, dating only to 1959, when Hijikata Tatsumi (1928–86) performed the first *butoh* performance. *Butoh* was born out of a rejection of the excessive formalisation that characterises traditional forms of Japanese dance. It also has its roots in the desire to return to the ancient roots of the Japanese soul, and, as such, is also a rejection of Western influences that flooded Japan in the post-war years.

Butoh performances are best likened to performance art rather than traditional dance. During a *butoh* performance, one or more dancers use their naked or semi-naked bodies to express the most elemental and intense human emotions. Nothing is sacred in *butoh*, and performances often deal with taboo topics such as sexuality and death. For this reason, critics often describe *butoh* as scandalous, and *butoh* dancers delight in pushing the boundaries of what can be considered tasteful in artistic performance.

Butoh tends to be more underground than the more established forms of Japanese dance, and it is, consequently, difficult to catch a performance. The best way to find out if a performance is on while you are in town is to check with the local TIC or look for announcements of shows in the local English-language media.

Contemporary Theatre

The emergence of a distinct consumer culture during the late Taishō (1912–26) and Shōwa (1926–89) periods brought major challenges to popular entertainment. The evolution of new forms of popular theatre and music, and the adjustment of traditional forms, were more than a mere reflection of the times – they appear to have contributed to the transformation of Japanese society.

Most of Japan's major cities have large commercial theatres, although Tokyo remains the undisputed centre of contemporary theatre in Japan. Venues include such institutions as the Imperial Theatre and the Tokyo Takarazuka Theatre, as well as newer facilities such as New National Theatre, Tokyo Panasonic Globe Theatre and the Ginza Saison Theatre in Tokyo; and the Kintetsu Theatre in Osaka. Small, privately owned theatres also abound, including such Tokyo icons as The Suzunari, Theatre Tops, Ekimae Gekijō and Agora Gekijō.

Commercial Theatre In Japan today commercial theatre en-compasses classical and contemporary dramas and musicals, both home-grown and imported, staged by large entertainment companies and starring well-known actors, singers and other celebrities. So if, when you're in Japan, you happen to be struck by a sudden hankering for a Royal Shakespeare Company production of *Richard III*, or a Japanese-language performance of *Phantom of the Opera*, you might just be in luck.

FRANK CARTER

Bottom: Geisha perform in the Kamogawa Odori, Kyoto, Kansai

Tōhō Musical and the OSK Japan Revue and Gekidan Shiki are known for their splashy, long-running productions of leading musicals from London and New York. Each has its own theatre, and all three troupes tour extensively throughout the country.

The all-female Takarazuka troupe offers a musical experience unlike any other. Founded in 1913, partially as an inversion of the all-male kabuki theatre, Takarazuka combines Japanese traditional elements with Western music in a format aimed at audiences of all ages, from every social status and of both sexes. But truth be told, its most devoted admirers by far are young women, who, in a state of truly super-human suspension-of-disbelief, swoon with romantic abandon over the troupe's beautiful 'men'. Takarazuka adopted its present revue format in the late 1920s, and with the exception of the years of WWII – during which the troupe proved an ideal propaganda tool – has continued to perform musicals and revues set in exotic locations. You too can ogle the performers in the Takarazuka Theatre near Kōbe, or at the Tokyo Takarazuka Theatre.

Noncommercial Theatre Contemporary theatre productions not backed by the major entertainment companies have rather limited commercial viability. There is little public-sector support for theatre in Japan, and although this has begun to change in recent years, very few performing-arts organisations receive financial assistance. It's generally impossible for actors and directors to earn a living from the stage.

An entirely new concept at the time, *shingeki* (new theatre) began late in the Meiji period (1868–1912), establishing theatre troupes that performed Western works in translation. Tsukiji Shōgekijo, formed by the writer and director Osanai Kaoru in 1924, played an outstanding role in the development of this movement. Seinenza, established in 1954, started out by performing original productions, dramatising novels by authors such as Mishima Yukio and presenting works by young Japanese playwrights. It later expanded its focus to include musicals and Western works in translation.

Theatre the world over spent the 1960s redefining itself, and it was no different in Japan. The *shogekijō* (little theatre) movement, also called *angura* (underground), has given Japan many of its leading playwrights, directors and actors. It arose as a reaction to the realism and structure of *shingeki* and featured surrealistic plays that explored the relationship between human beings and the world. Like their counterparts in the West, these productions took place in any space available – in small theatres, tents, basements, open spaces and on street corners.

The first generation of *shogekijō* artists included directors Terayama Shūji, Ninagawa Yukio, Satō Makoto, Kara Jūro and Suzuki Tadashi, and troupes such as Black Tent Theatre (directed by Satō), Red Tent (Kara), Waseda Shogekijō (Suzuki) and Ninagawa Company (Ninagawa). In the 1970s the movement was dominated by director Tsuka Kōhei, leader of the Tsuka Kōhei Office, who added a comic element. But it was in the 1980s that *shogekijō* took off, led by playwrights such as Noda Hideki, Kokami Shōji and Kawamura Tadashi, who took movement in two key directions – speedy comedy using wordplay and images from popular culture to highlight the lunacy of modern life, and mind-game fantasy about nuclear war and its aftermath.

The past decade has brought a shift in the focus of *shogekijō* to more realistic and contemporary themes, such as modern Japanese history, war, environmental degradation and social oppression. Changing cultural perceptions have propelled the movement in new directions, notably towards socially and politically critical dramas (eg, those by Kaneshita Tatsuo and Sakate Yōji), psychological dramas (eg, by Iwamatsu Ryō, Suzue Toshirō and Hirata Oriza) and satirical portrayals of modern society (eg, by Nagai Ai and Makino Nozomi). Recent works are attracting considerable attention from overseas: a successful production of Sakate's *Epitaph for Whales* (1993) was held in London in 1998, while Hirata's *Tokyo Notes* was staged in four locations in France in early 2000. *Shogekijō* troupes that gained prominence in the 1990s include The Gazira (led by Kaneshita), Rinkō-gun (Sakate), Seinendan (Hirata) and MOP (Makino).

A number of developments begun in the 1990s are blurring Japan's modern theatrical boundaries. *Shingeki* troupes are increasingly producing original plays by Japanese playwrights, and no longer exist in parallel to *shogekijō*. New theatrical troupes sit comfortably in neither category, and one-off projects have emerged that combine elements of previously separate genres, such as Noda Hideki's NODA MAP productions featuring the leaders and principal actors from other troupes.

LITERATURE

Like its other arts, Japan's literature has always been heavily influenced by outside sources. For most of Japan's history, this influence came from China. Japan's first real literature, the *Kojiki* (Record of Ancient Matters) and *Nihon Shoki* (Chronicle of Japan), was written in the 8th century in emulation of Chinese accounts of the country's history. It was only during times of relative isolation from the mainland that Japanese literature developed its own voice.

Interestingly, much of Japan's early literature was written by women. One reason for this was that men wrote in kanji (imported Chinese characters), while women wrote in hiragana (Japanese script). Thus, while the men were busy copying Chinese styles and texts, the women of the country were producing the first authentic Japanese literature. Among these early female authors is Murasaki Shikibu, who wrote one of Japan's all-time classics, *Genji Monogatari* (The Tale of Genji). Now available in translation, this novel documents the intrigues and romances of early Japanese court life. Although it is perhaps Japan's most important work of literature, its extreme length probably limits its appeal to all but the most ardent Japanophile. *The Narrow Road to the Deep North* is a famous travel classic by the revered Japanese poet Matsuo Bashō.

Kokoro, by Natsume Sōseki, is a modern classic depicting the conflict between old and new Japan in the mind and heart of an aged scholar. The modern and the traditional also clash in the lives of two couples in *Some Prefer Nettles* by Tanizaki Junichirō. *The Makioka Sisters*, also by Tanizaki, is a famous family chronicle that has been likened to a modern-day *The Tale of Genji*. Ibuse Masuji's *Black Rain* is a response to Japan's defeat in WWII. (Although made into a film in Japan, the book bears no relation to the Hollywood movie of the same name.)

Manga – Japanese Comics

The Japanese are insatiable readers of manga – a catch-all word covering cartoons, magazine and newspaper comic strips, and the ubiquitous comic book. Even high-art ukiyo-e prints were once a form of *manga*, evolving with the *kibyōshi* (yellow cover) wood blocks that were used to create adult storybooks. The great ukiyo-e artist Hokusai actually coined the word *'manga'* by combining the characters for 'frivolous' and 'picture'.

The father of modern manga is Tezuka Osamu, who, in the late 1940s, began working cinematic effects based on European movies into his cartoons – pioneering multipanel movements, perspectives that brought the reader into the action, close-ups, curious angles and a host of movielike techniques. His adventurous stories quickly became movie-length comic strips – essentially films drawn on paper. What Tezuka started took off in a big way once weekly magazines realised that they could boost sales by including manga in their pages. As a result of Tezuka's innovations, Japanese comics are rarely slim affairs (weekly comics as thick as phone directories are not unusual). And with this popularity came recognition – Japanese comic-strip artists are often elevated to celebrity status, becoming as wealthy and well known as pop *idoru* (idols).

Many manga also spin off into popular, cutting-edge *anime* (animation films) that can make Disney creations look like goofy doodling (to say nothing of the soundtracks). Ōishi Mamoru's 1995 *anime* version of the Masamune Shiro manga *Ghost in the Shell* is a good example (see Cinema earlier in this section).

Manga text is in Japanese, but there's usually an English subtitle on the cover announcing whether it's a 'lady's comic', a 'comic for business boys' or even an 'exciting comic for men' ('exciting' is generally a euphemism for soft porn). Japanese censors may entertainingly blur the pubic hair in imported porn, but it's all on view in comic books. Manga isn't all 'frivolous', however. It also tackles straight subjects: *jitsuma* manga (practical comics) and *benkyō* manga (study comics) set out to teach everything from high-school subjects to ikebana and international finance.

Those interested in Japanese comics can join the crowds leafing through recent issues in bookshops. A good introduction to manga is *Dreamland Japan Writings on Modern Manga*, by Frederik Schodt (1996). If you're really keen, make a trip to the Hiroshima City Manga Library, which has a small Comic Museum.

Snow Country, by Kawabata Yasunari, is a famous story set in Japan's northern regions. Endō Shūsaku's *Silence* is a historical story of the plight of Japanese Christians following Tokugawa Ieyasu's unification of the country.

Mishima Yukio's *The Golden Pavilion* recounts the life of a novice monk who burned down Kyoto's famous golden temple, Kinkaku-ji, in 1950. Although Mishima is probably the most controversial of Japan's modern writers, and is considered unrepresentative of Japanese culture by many Japanese, his work still makes for very interesting reading. Abe Kōbō's *Woman of the Dunes* is a classic tale by one of Japan's more respected avant-garde writers.

Of course not all Japanese fiction can be classified as literature in high-brow terms. Murakami Ryū's *Almost Transparent Blue* is strictly sex and drugs, and was a blockbuster in the Japan of the 1970s. Murakami has written another provocative bestseller for the 1990s, *Coin Locker Babies*. Murakami Haruki is another bestselling author; titles of his widely available in English include *A Wild Sheep Chase* and *Dance, Dance, Dance* – both touch on sheep and Hokkaidō. Banana Yoshimoto has had surprising international success for her novel *Kitchen*.

Ōe Kenzaburō is Japan's Nobel laureate. Look out for *Pluck the Buds, Shoot the Kids* – which must rate alongside Mishima's *The Sailor Who Fell from Grace with the Sea* as one of the best titles in modern Japanese fiction. Ōe's semi-autobiographical *A Personal Matter* tells the story of how the birth of a brain-damaged child affects his father.

SCULPTURE

Fine art in Japan begins with the introduction of Mahayana Buddhism in the 6th century. At this time the nation turned its nascent artistic skills, already manifest in its production of fine pottery and metalwork, to the production of Buddhist images. Early works of this time are heavily continental in influence, many of them actually made by Korean or Chinese immigrants. These sculptors were brought over from the mainland to furnish Japan's new temples with Buddhist images. Later, when contacts with China evaporated during the late Heian era (794–1185), native sculpture techniques were allowed to flourish and a distinct Japanese style emerged.

A knowledge of the different types of Buddhist sculptures found in Japanese temples is a good step to understanding Buddhism itself. The images fall into four main groups, each of which represents a different level of being in the Buddhist cosmology. This cosmology, of course, comes to Japan from India, via China and Korea, and Japanese Buddhist art naturally reflects this rich inheritance.

JEFF CANTARUTTI

Bottom: Buddha statue at Nanzen-ji, Kyoto

At the head of Japanese Buddhism's hierarchy of deities are *nyorai*, or Buddhas. These are beings who have attained enlightenment and freed themselves from the cycle of rebirth. A *nyorai* image is most conspicuous by the simple robes, a weight of stone on the head that symbolises wisdom and a head of tight 'snail shell' curls.

The major *nyorai* are: Shaka (the Historical Buddha), recognisable by one hand raised in a preaching gesture; Yakushi (the Healing Buddha), with one hand also raised in a preaching gesture and the other hand clutching a vial of medicine; Amida (the Buddha of Western Paradise or Buddha of Light), usually seen sitting with knuckles together in a meditative posture; and Dainichi (the Cosmic Buddha), usually portrayed in princely attire, sitting with one hand clasped around a raised finger of the other hand (a sexual gesture indicating the unity of being). *Nyorai* are usually portrayed with two Bodhisattvas in a triad configuration.

The next most important beings are *bosatsu* (Bodhisattvas). These are beings who have put off their own personal entry into nirvana in order to help others attain enlightenment. Images of *bosatsu* are more human in appearance than *nyorai* and are most easily distinguished from the latter by a topknot of hair or a crowned headpiece, sometimes with smaller figures built into the crown. The most common *bosatsu* in Japanese temples is Kannon, the goddess of mercy. Also common, both in temples and scattered around the countryside, are images of Jizō, the Bodhisattva assigned to aid travellers and children. Jizō are often depicted carrying children in their arms.

The next group of beings are not native to Buddhism, but were borrowed from Hinduism to serve particular purposes in the Buddhist cosmology. These beings are called *ten* (heavenly beings or deva). While some appear as beastly ogres, others are human in appearance. The most common of these are *niō* (guardians), which are often found in the gates leading up to temples. The giant Kongō guardians at Nara's Toōdai-ji are perhaps the most famous of these images.

Finally, there are the *myō-ō* (kings of wisdom or light). These beings serve as protectors of Buddhism and were introduced to Japan along with esoteric Buddhism in the 9th century. The most common *myō-ō* image is Fudō Myō-ō, who is usually depicted as a wrathful being clutching an upright sword.

PAINTING

The techniques and materials used in the early stages of Japanese painting owe much to Chinese influence. By the end of the Heian period (794–1185), the emphasis on painting religious themes, following Chinese conventions, gave way to a purely Japanese style of painting. Known as *yamato-e*, this style covered local subjects and was frequently used in scroll paintings and on screens.

Ink paintings, known as *suiboku-ga* or *sumi-e*, by Chinese Zen artists were introduced to Japan during the Muromachi period (1333–1576) and were copied by Japanese artists, who produced *kakemono* (hanging pictures), *emaki* (scrolls) and decorated screens and sliding doors.

During the Momoyama period (1576–1600), Japan's *daimyō* (domain lords) flaunted their wealth and power by commissioning artists who painted in flamboyant colours and used copious gold-leaf embellishment. The most popular themes depicted Japanese nature, or characters from Chinese legends. The Kanō school was the most famous follower of these painting styles.

Western techniques of painting, including the use of oils, were introduced during the 16th century by the Jesuits. Japanese painters who combined Western and Japanese styles sometimes produced interesting results: portraits of Westerners thoughtfully included an incline to the eyes.

The Edo period (1600–1867) was marked by the enthusiastic patronage of a wide range of painting styles. The Kanō school continued to be in demand for the depiction of subjects connected with Confucianism, mythical Chinese creatures or scenes from nature. The Tosa school, the members of which followed the *yamato-e* style of painting, was kept busy with commissions from the nobility to paint scenes from ancient classics of Japanese literature.

The Rimpa school not only absorbed the style of other schools (Chinese, Kanō and Tosa) but progressed beyond these conventions to produce strikingly original decorative painting. The works of art produced by a trio of outstanding artists from this school – Tawaraya Sōtatsu, Hon'ami Kōetsu and Ogata Kōrin – rank among the finest of this period.

CALLIGRAPHY

Shodō (the way of writing) is one of Japan's most valued arts, cultivated by nobles, priests and samurai alike, and still studied by Japanese schoolchildren today as *shūji*. Like the characters of the Japanese language itself, the art of *shodō* was imported from China. In the Heian period (794–1185), a distinctly Japanese style of *shodō* evolved called *wayō*. This is more fluid and cursive than the purely Chinese style, which is referred to as *karayō*. The Chinese style remained popular in Japan among Zen priests and the literati, even after the Heian period.

In both Chinese and Japanese *shodō* there are three important types. Most common is *kaisho*, or block-style script. Due to its clarity, this style is favoured in the media and in applications where readability is a must. *Gyōsho*, or running hand, is semicursive, and often used in informal correspondence. *Sōsho*, or grass hand, is a truly cursive style. *Sōsho* abbreviates and links the characters together to create a flowing, graceful effect.

HAN-GA & UKIYO-E

If there is one art form that Westerners instantly associate with Japan, it is ukiyo-e, a type of *han-ga* (block print). Ukiyo-e (pictures of the floating world) comes from the term 'ukiyo' – a Buddhist metaphor for the transient world of fleeting pleasures. The subjects chosen by artists were characters and scenes from the 'floating world' of the entertainment quarters in Edo (modern-day Tokyo), Kyoto and Osaka.

The Decorated Skin

Japanese *irezumi* (tattooing) is widely considered the best of its kind. Usually completed in blue and red natural dyes, the tattoos often cover the whole body, with intricate designs featuring auspicious animals, flowers, Buddhist deities or folktale characters. In feudal times, the authorities tattooed criminals, thus stigmatising them as 'branded'. In due course, those who had been tattooed exhibited a defiant pride in these markings that set them apart from the rest of society. As a sop to foreign sensibilities, tattooing was banned during the Meiji era, but

was promptly reinstated after the Prince of Wales (later to become King George V) took a liking to the art and had a dragon tattooed on his arm in 1881. Today, the *yakuza*, or Japanese mafia, are the only ones to stand out with magnificent *irezumi*, though to have a chance to see their exquisite body art you may have to visit *sentō* (public baths) regularly!

The floating world, centred in pleasure districts like Edo's Yoshiwara, was a topsy-turvy kingdom, an inversion of all the usual social hierarchies that were held in place by the power of the Tokugawa shōgunate. Here, money counted for more than rank, actors and artists were the arbiters of style, and prostitutes elevated their art to such a level that their social and artistic accomplishments matched those of the ladies of noble families. Added to this was an element of spectacle. Both kabuki and sumō, with their ritualised visual opulence, found large popular audiences in this period.

The vivid colours, novel composition and flowing lines of ukiyo-e caused great excitement in the West, sparking a vogue that a French art critic dubbed 'Japonisme'. Ukiyo-e became a key influence on impressionists (for example, Toulouse-Lautrec, Manet and Degas) and post-impressionists. Among the Japanese the prints were hardly given more than passing consideration – millions were produced annually in Edo. They were cheap items, often thrown away or used as wrapping paper for pottery. For many years, the Japanese continued to be perplexed by the keen interest foreigners took in this art form, which they considered of ephemeral value.

The first ukiyo-e prints in the early 17th century were black and white; the technique for colour printing was only developed in the middle of the 18th century. The success of a print lay in the close cooperation between the artist, engraver and printer through all stages of production.

The first stage required the *eshi* (artist) to draw a design on transparent paper and indicate the colouring needed. The *horishi* (engraver) then pasted the design face down on a block of cherry wood and carved out the lines of the design in relief. The *surishi* (printer) inked the block and took a proof. Each colour required a separate block; it was up to the printer to use his skill to obtain accurate alignment and the subtle colour effects that depended on the colour mixture and pressure applied.

The reputed founder of ukiyo-e was Iwa Matabei. The genre was later developed by Hishikawa Moronobu, who rose to fame with his illustrations for erotic tales. His wood-block prints of scenes from the Yoshiwara entertainment district introduced the theme of *bijin-e* (paintings of beautiful women), which later became a standard subject. Early themes also covered scenes from the theatre (including the actors), and erotic pictures, or *shunga*. Kitagawa Utamarō is famed for his *bijin-e*, which emphasise the erotic and sensual beauty of his subjects. All that is known about Tōshūsai Sharaku, a painting prodigy whose life is a mystery, is that he produced 145 superb portraits of kabuki actors between 1794 and 1795.

Towards the end of the Edo period (1600–1867), two painters produced outstanding ukiyo-e works. Hokusai Katsushika was a prolific artist who observed his fellow inhabitants of Edo with a keen sense of humour. His most famous works include manga, *Fugaku Sanjūrokkei* (Thirty-Six Views of Mt Fuji) and *Fugaku Hyakkei* (One Hundred Views of Mt Fuji). As Hokusai approached the end of his life (he died at the age of 89) he delighted in signing his works with the pen name *gakyōrōjin* (literally, 'old man mad with painting'). Andō Hiroshige followed Hokusai, specialising in landscapes, although he also created splendid prints of plants and birds. His most celebrated works include *Tōkaidō Gojūsan-tsugi* (Fifty-three Stations of the Tōkaidō), *Meisho Edo Hyakukei* (One Hundred Views of Famous Places in Edo) and *Omi Hakkei* (Eight Views of Lake Omi) – Omi is now known as Biwa-ko.

IKEBANA

The art of flower arranging developed in the 15th century and can be grouped into four main styles: *rikka* (standing flowers), *nageire* (thrown-in flowers), *shōkai* (living flowers) and *moribana* (heaped flowers). There are several thousand different schools at present, the top three of which are Ikenobō, Ōhara and Sōgetsu, but they share one aim – to arrange flowers to represent heaven, earth and humanity. Ikebana displays were originally used as part of the tea ceremony but now can be found in private homes – in the *tokonoma* (display alcove) – and even in large hotels. Apart from its cultural associations, ikebana is also a lucrative business; today its schools have millions of students, including many young women who view proficiency in the art as a means to improve their marriage prospects.

TEA CEREMONY

Chanoyu, also known as *sadō*, or 'the way of tea', dates back to the Nara period (710–94), when meditating Buddhist monks used it to promote alertness. By the 14th century the tea ceremony had developed into a highly elaborate and expensive pursuit for the aristocracy.

In the 16th century, the tea master Sen no Rikyū (1522–91) established a new aesthetic in the tea ceremony, replacing the over-refined artifice then in vogue with a spartan aesthetic, using utensils that echoed the irregularities of the natural world. Other tea masters took different approaches, and today the tea ceremony can be divided into the three Senke schools (Ura, Omote and Mushakoji) and other influential schools such as Enshu, Yabunouchi and Sohen.

The traditional setting for the tea ceremony is a thatched teahouse in a landscaped garden. The preparation and drinking of the tea is conducted according to a highly stylised etiquette, and the mental discipline involved was once an essential part of the training of a samurai. Novices tend to find the proceedings fatiguing, and connoisseurs maintain that full appreciation of the art takes years of training and reflection.

For a demonstration of *chanoyu* in Tokyo or Kyoto ask for details at the TIC or check with the large hotels. A classic treatment of this subject, written with precision and devotion, is *The Book of Tea* by Okakura Kakuzō.

CERAMICS

The ceramic arts in Japan are usually considered to have started around the 13th century, with the introduction of Chinese ceramic techniques and the founding of a kiln in 1242 at Seto, in central Honshū, by Tōshirō. The Japanese term for pottery and porcelain, *setomono* (literally, 'things from Seto'), clearly derives from this still-thriving ceramics centre. During the 14th century another five kilns were established: Tokoname, Shigaraki, Bizen, Echizen and Tamba. Together with Seto, these were known as the 'Six Ancient Kilns' and acquired a reputation for high-quality stoneware.

The popularity of the tea ceremony in the 16th century stimulated further ceramic development. The great tea masters, Furuta Oribe and Sen no Rikyū, promoted the production of exquisite Oribe and Shino wares in Gifu. The powerful shōgun Toyotomi Hideyoshi, who thought nothing of plastering the walls of his tearoom with gold, encouraged the master potter Chōjiro to create works of art from clay found near Hideyoshi's palace. Chōjiro was allowed to embellish the tea bowls he created with the Chinese character 'raku' (enjoyment). This was the beginning of Kyoto's famous *raku-yaki* style of pottery. Tea bowls became prized objects, commanding inflated prices. Even today, connoisseurs of the tea ceremony are happy to pay as much as US$30,000 for a tea bowl.

Hideyoshi's invasion of Korea at the end of the 16th century was a military disaster, but it proved to be a boon to Japanese ceramics production when captured Korean potters introduced Japan to the art of manufacturing porcelain. In 1598 a Korean master potter, Ri Sampei, built the first porcelain kiln at Arita in Kyūshū. During the Edo period (1600–1867), many *daimyō* encouraged the founding of kilns and the production of superbly designed ceramics. The 'climbing kiln', or *noborigama*, was widely used. Constructed on a slope, the kiln had as many as 20 chambers and the capability to achieve temperatures as high as 1400°C.

During the Meiji period (1868–1912), ceramics waned in popularity, but were later included in a revival of interest in folk arts, or *mingei-*

hin, headed by Yanagi Sōetsu, who encouraged famous potters such as Kawai Kanjirō, Tomimoto Kenkichi and Hamada Shōji. English potter Bernard Leach studied in Japan under Hamada and contributed to the folk art revival. On his return to Cornwall, Leach maintained his interest in Japanese ceramics and promoted their appreciation in the West.

There are now over 100 pottery centres in Japan, with large numbers of artisans producing everything from exclusive tea utensils to souvenir folklore creatures. Department stores regularly organise exhibitions of ceramics. Master potters are highly revered and the government designates the finest as 'Living National Treasures'.

Famous Ceramic Centres

Arita-yaki porcelain is still produced in the town where the first Japanese porcelain was made – Arita in Kyūshū. In the mid-17th century, the Dutch East India Company exported these wares to Europe, where they were soon copied in ceramics factories such as those of the Germans (Meissen), the Dutch (Delft) and the English (Worcester). It is commonly known to Westerners as 'Imari', after the name of the port from which it was shipped. The Kakiemon style uses designs of birds and flowers in bright colours. Another popular style is executed in blue and white, and incorporates scenes from legends and daily life. In addition to Arita, some other famous ceramic centres include:

Satsuma-yaki The most common style of this porcelain, from Kagoshima in Kyūshū, has a cloudy white, crackled glaze enamelled with gold, red, green and blue.

Karatsu-yaki Karatsu, near Fukuoka in northern Kyūshū, produces tea ceremony utensils that are Korean in style and have a characteristic greyish, crackled glaze.

Hagi-yaki The town of Hagi in western Honshū is renowned for Hagi-yaki, a type of porcelain made with a pallid yellow or pinkish crackled glaze.

Bizen-yaki The ancient ceramics centre of Bizen in Okayama-ken, Honshū, is famed for its solid unglazed bowls, which turn red through oxidation. Bizen also produces roofing tiles.

Mashiko-yaki The town of Mashiko in Tochigi-ken, northern Honshū, is renowned as a folk craft centre, producing wares with a distinctive reddish glaze.

Mino-yaki From Toki, in Gifu-ken in central Honshū, come pieces executed in the Oribe style, which have a greenish glaze and are decorated with creatures and flowers. The Shino style, greatly prized by connoisseurs of tea ceremony utensils, employs a heavy white glaze.

Temmoku-yaki Seto city in Aichi-ken, central Honshū, has a long tradition as a ceramics centre. The standard product is ash-glazed, heavy stoneware, but Seto also produces special ceramic wares such as *temmoku*, an ancient Chinese style with a brown and black glaze.

Kiyomizu-yaki The approach road to the temple Kiyomizu-dera, in Kyoto, is lined with shops selling Kiyomizu-yaki, a style of pottery that can be enamelled, blue-painted or red-painted in appearance.

Kutani-yaki The porcelain from Ishikawa-ken, in central Honshū, is usually green or painted.

The TIC's useful *Ceramic Art & Crafts in Japan* leaflet is published by the Japan National Tourist Organization (JNTO) and provides full details of pottery centres, kilns and pottery fairs in Japan.

LACQUERWARE

The Japanese have been using lacquer to protect and enhance the beauty of wood since the Jōmon period (AD 10,000–300 BC). In the Meiji era (1868–1912), lacquerware became very popular abroad and it remains one of Japan's best-known products. Known in Japan as *shikki* or *nurimono*, lacquerware is made using the sap from the lacquer tree *(urushi)*. Raw lacquer is actually toxic and causes severe skin irritation in those who have not developed immunity. Once hardened, however, it becomes inert and extraordinarily durable.

The most common colour of lacquer is an amber or brown colour, but additives have been used to produce black, violet, blue, yellow and even white lacquer. In the better pieces, multiple layers of lacquer are painstakingly applied and left to dry, and finally polished to a luxurious shine.

Japanese artisans have devised various ways to further enhance the beauty of lacquer. The most common method is called *maki-e*, which was developed in the 8th century. Here, silver and gold powders are sprinkled onto the liquid lacquer to form a picture. After the lacquer dries, another coat of lacquer is applied to seal the picture. The final effect is often dazzling and some of the better pieces of lacquerware made using this method are now National Treasures.

WASHI

Traditional Japanese handmade paper, known as *washi*, was introduced from China in the 5th century. Its golden age was the Heian era (794–1185), when *washi* was highly prized by members of the Kyoto court for writing poetry and for diaries. Colours were added to produce patterns (silver and gold leaf was often applied), and sometimes paper was specially made to complement the mood of a particular poem. *Washi* continued to be made in large quantities until the introduction of Western paper in the 1870s. After that time, the number of families involved in papermaking plummeted to only 851 in 1973. Recently, *washi* has enjoyed something of a revival and a large variety of colourful, patterned paper is widely available.

TEXTILES

Textiles have always played an important role in Japanese society: the fabric used in a kimono was an indication of class status. Until the introduction of cotton to Japan in the 16th century, Japanese textiles were made mostly of bast fibres or silk. Of all Japanese textiles, intricately embroidered brocades have always been the most highly prized, but sumptuary laws imposed on the merchant class in the Edo period (1600–1867) prohibited the wearing of these kimono. To circumvent these laws, new techniques of kimono decoration were devised – the most important being the technique of *yūzen* dyeing.

In this technique, rice paste is applied to the fabric like a stencil to prevent a colour from bleeding onto other areas of the fabric. By repeatedly changing the pattern of the rice paste, very complex designs can be achieved.

At the other end of the spectrum, *aizome* (the technique of dyeing fabrics in vats of fermented indigo plants) gave Japan one of its most distinctive colours. Traditionally used in making hardy work clothes for the fields, Japan's beautiful indigo-blue can still be seen in many modern-day textile goods.

FURNITURE

If jade is the perfect medium for the expression of the Chinese artistic genius, then for the Japanese it is wood – perhaps nowhere in the world has the art of joinery been lifted to such high levels. This genius for joinery translates well to the art of cabinetmaking. Chests called *tansu* are particularly prized by collectors of Japanese antiques. Perhaps the most prized of all *tansu* is the *kaidan dansu*, so named because it resembles a flight of stairs (*kaidan* is the Japanese word for 'stairs'). These are becoming increasingly difficult to find, but determined hunting at flea markets and antique stores may still turn up the occasional good piece, but don't expect a bargain.

JAPANESE DOLLS

Dolls, or *ningyō*, have played a part in Japanese society from prehistoric times, when the rites of burial demanded that clay figures be buried along with the dead. During the Kofun period (300–710) of ancient Japan, burial mounds of emperors and nobles were usually surrounded by hundreds of *haniwa* clay figures, some in human form.

Today, dolls still figure prominently in two Japanese festivals: the Hina Matsuri (Doll Festival, 3 March), when girls display ornamental *hina-ningyō* on tiered platforms as part of the festivities; and on Kodomo-no-hi (Children's Day, 5 May), when both boys and girls display special dolls. Some of the more common dolls today are: *daruma*, which are based on the figure of Bodhidarma, who brought Buddhism to China from India; *gosho-ningyō*, chubby plaster dolls sometimes dressed as figures in nō dramas; *kyō-ningyō*, elaborate dolls made in Kyoto, dressed in fine brocade fabrics; *kiku-ningyō*, large dolls covered by real chrysanthemum flowers; and *ishō-ningyō*, which is a general term for elaborately costumed dolls, sometimes based on kabuki characters.

ARCHITECTURE
Traditional Secular Architecture

Houses With the exception of the northern island of Hokkaidō, traditional Japanese houses are built with the broiling heat of summer in mind. They are made of flimsy materials designed to take advantage of even the slightest breeze. The reasoning behind this is that it is easier to bundle up in winter than it is to cool down in summer. Before the advent of air-conditioning, this was certainly the case. Another reason behind the gossamer construction of Japanese houses is the relative frequency of earthquakes in the country, which precludes the use of heavier building materials such as stone or brick.

Principally very simple and refined, the typical house is constructed of post-and-beam timber, with sliding panels of wood or rice paper (for warmer weather) making up the exterior walls. Movable screens, or shoji, divide the interior of the house. There may be a separate area for the tea ceremony – the harmonious atmosphere of this space is of the utmost importance and is usually achieved through the use of natural materials and the careful arrangement of furniture and utensils.

A particularly traditional type of Japanese house is the *machiya* (townhouse) built by merchants in cities such as Kyoto and Tokyo. Until very recently, the older neighbourhoods of Kyoto and some areas of Tokyo were lined with neat, narrow rows of these houses, but most have fallen victim to the current frenzy of construction. These days, the best place to see *machiya* is in eastern Kyoto, near the temple Kiyomizu-dera. Takayama, as well as the post towns along the Kiso Valley, are also good spots to view traditional *machiya* architecture. The more elegant mansions of the noble classes and warriors, with their elaborate receiving rooms, sculptured gardens and teahouses, can also be viewed in places such as Kyoto, Nara and Kanazawa and in former feudal cities scattered around Japan.

Farmhouses The most distinctive type of Japanese farmhouse is the thatched-roof *gasshō-zukuri*, so named for the shape of the rafters, which resemble a pair of praying hands. While these farmhouses look cosy and romantic, bear in mind that they were often home for up to 40 people and occasionally farm animals as well. Furthermore, the black floorboards, soot-covered ceilings and lack of windows guaranteed a cavelike atmosphere. The only weapon against this darkness was a fire built in a central fireplace in the floor, known as an *irori*, which also provided warmth in the cooler months and hot coals for cooking. Multistorey farmhouses were also built to house silkworms for silk production (particularly prevalent during the Meiji era) in the airy upper gables.

Bottom: Traditional wooden house in the Higashi geisha district of Kanazawa

FRANK CARTER

ARTS & ARCHITECTURE

Storehouses Japan's traditional *kura* (storehouses) are instantly recognisable by their white plaster walls. The use of a thick coat of plaster was not merely decorative but was designed to protect the building and the valuables stored inside from the frequent fires that plagued Japanese cities. The plaster seems to have done its job, and many *kura* survive to this day in villages such as Imai-cho in Nara, Kurashiki in western Honshū and Kitakata in northern Honshū.

Castles Japan has an abundance of castles. Few of them are originals, however, and even the copies represent a small proportion of the number that once dotted the country. The first Japanese castles were simple mountain forts that relied more on natural terrain than on structural innovations for defence. The great disadvantage of these structures was that they were as inaccessible to the defenders as to the enemy.

The 'plains castle', or *hira-jiro*, the kind mostly seen in Japan today, evolved from the fortified residences of *daimyō*, which were built on flatter terrain. By the Momoyama period (1576–1600), castle architecture had reached a high level of sophistication, with such masterworks of impregnability and grace as Himeji-jō, Osaka-jō and Fushimi-jō. Defences became ever more elaborate, with the addition of stone walls, moats, earthworks and labyrinthine halls and tunnels within the castles. *Jōka-machi*, or castle towns, grew around the castles.

The central feature of the castle was the *donjon*, a tower or keep. The larger castles had several *donjon* ranging around the central one, and the various gates were also mounted with fortifications. The buildings atop stone ramparts were mostly built of wood, but the wood was covered with plaster to protect it against fire and firearms.

The wide-ranging wars of the 16th and 17th centuries left Japan with a huge number of castles. In 1615 the Edo government, seeking to rein in the power of local *daimyō*, ordered that there be only one castle to each domain. In the years of peace that followed, the castle fell into disuse. During the Meiji era (1868–1912) more castles were destroyed, leaving only 39 originals. By the end of WWII this number had further been reduced to 12. The 1960s saw an enormous spate of castle reconstructions, most built of concrete and steel, but these were all rebuilt like Hollywood movie sets – authentic-looking when viewed from a distance but distinctly modern in appearance when viewed from up close.

Some of the best castles to visit include Himeji-jō, which is often described as the most dramatic original castle still standing in Japan. Also known as White Egret Castle because of its white colour, it was situated on a major route to the western provinces and originally had

Bottom: Himeji-jō, near Kyoto

ADINA TOVY AMSEL

three moats, along with a five-storey *donjon* and three smaller *donjon*. Edo-jō, around which modern Tokyo has grown, was first built in 1457 by Ōta Dōkan. Soon after marching into Edo (as Tokyo was then known) in 1590, the shōgun Tokugawa Ieyasu gained control of the castle and began a massive rebuilding project – the main compound at one stage covered an amazing 357,000 sq metres. It was to remain the Tokugawa shōgunate's headquarters until 1868. The last of the surviving original castles is Matsuyama-jō, which was rebuilt in 1854 after a fire 70 years earlier. It was again restored in 1969, with many of the original structures, including the main *donjon* and three lesser *donjon*, now rebuilt.

Traditional Religious Architecture

Shintō Shrines The sacred buildings of Japan's indigenous religion, Shintō, are known in Japanese as *jinja* (shrines). Shintō translates in English as the 'Way of the Gods'. Japanese *kami* (gods) inhabit all natural phenomena – from towering volcanoes to curiously misshapen rocks – and the earliest Shintō shrines were simply sacred places marked off with a special plaited rope, called a *shimenawa*, and strips of *gohei*, or white paper. From this rope evolved fences and eventually the torii, or Shintō shrine gate, which is now one of the most obvious features of a shrine.

Shrine buildings come in many varieties, but the architecture of most probably evolved from the storehouses and dwellings of prehistoric Japan: many of their now ornamental features were once functional in nature. Pairs of stone lionlike creatures called *komainu* often flank the main path to a shrine; one usually has its mouth open in a roar and the other has its mouth closed. Further along the approach is a *chōzuya* (ablution basin) where visitors use the *hishaku* (ladle) to rinse both hands before pouring water into a cupped hand to rinse their mouths.

The shrine's main building is the *honden*, which enshrines the resident *kami*. The *honden* is off limits to layfolk, and only occasionally entered by Shintō priests. In front of the *honden* is the *haiden*, or hall of worship. In smaller shrines, these may share one roof. In front of the *haiden* is a *saisen-bako* (offering box), above which hang a gong and a long piece of rope. Visitors each throw a coin into the box, then sound the gong twice, make two deep bows, clap loudly twice, bow again twice (once deeply, once lightly) and then step back to the side.

The oldest Japanese shrines were built in a 'pure' native style. But with the introduction of Buddhism to Japan, shrine buildings started to incorporate elements of Chinese temple architecture. The 'pure' style is marked by features such as natural wood columns and walls (as opposed to red and white), *chigi* (horns) protruding over the ridge of the roof, and free-standing columns that support the ridge of the roof at either gabled end. Look, too, for *katsuogi* – short logs that lie horizontally across the ridge of the roof.

The three major Shintō shrine styles are the *shimmei, taisha* and *sumiyoshi*. The Naikū (Inner Shrine) – a pre-Buddhist, Japanese-style shrine that forms part of Ise-jingū at Ise in Mie-ken – is a stunning example of the *shimmei* style. Izumo Taisha, in Shimane-ken, is a notable example of the *taisha* style, and the eponymous Sumiyoshi-jinja, in Osaka, is a fine example of the *sumiyoshi* style.

As part of an ideal of renewal and purity, shrines were traditionally rebuilt on the same spot every 20 years. This practice is extremely lengthy and costly, and, as a result, Ise is the only shrine that is still regularly rebuilt. It has been rebuilt 60 times, the last time being in 1973, while Izumo Taisha has been rebuilt 25 times.

Buddhist Temples Along with Buddhism itself, Japan also imported the architectural styles of the Buddhist temples of China and Korea. China's temple architecture strongly influenced the Japanese until the 8th century, when a native Japanese style emerged. Temples are divided into three broad architectural categories: *wayō*, or Japanese style; *daibutsuyō*, or Great Buddha style; and *karayō*, or Chinese style.

One of the best ways to distinguish a Buddhist temple from a Shintō shrine is to examine the entrance. The main entrance of a shrine is customarily a torii (Shintō shrine gate), usually composed of two upright pillars, joined at the top by two horizontal cross-bars, the upper of which is normally slightly curved. Torii are often painted a bright vermillion, but some are left as bare wood. In contrast, the main entrance gate *(mon)* of a temple is often a much more substantial affair, constructed of several pillars or casements, joined at the top by a multitiered roof, around which there may even be walkways. Temple gates often contain guardian figures, usually *Niō* (deva kings). Keep in mind, though, that shrines and temples sometimes share the same precincts, and it is not always easy to tell where one begins and the other ends.

In early Japanese temples, the principal structure was the pagoda, a building that evolved from the Indian stupa (a reliquary for enshrining sacred remains of the Buddha). The Japanese variety, a graceful terraced structure of roofs capped with a spire, is Chinese-influenced. In time, the pagoda became just one of many buildings that could typically be found in a temple complex, with accessory structures including the drum tower and the holy font. Temples vary widely in their construction, depending on the type of school and the historical era of construction, although wood has always been a favourite material and the framing is generally of post-and-beam form.

Bottom: Yōmei-mon, the spectacular entrance gate of Tōshō-gū, Nikkō

UNBEATEN TRACKS IN JAPAN, JF BISHOP 1900

Buddhist temples can be found the length and breadth of Japan, but a selection of the finest Buddhist temples would include many in and around Kyoto, Nara and Kōya-san, as well as Eihei-ji near Fukui in Chūbu; Chūson-ji at Hiraizumi in northern Honshū; Zenkōji in Nagano; and, close to Tokyo, the temple complexes of Nikkō and Kamakura.

The Japanese Garden

Garden design is considered to be a form of high art in Japan, and Japanese gardens are considered by some to be among the most beautiful in the world. Japanese artists have long had an appreciation of abstract and minimalist forms. The ancient Chinese collected rocks that resembled mythical creatures or geographical features, such as dragons and mountains; the Japanese took this one step further, collecting rocks that looked like nothing, and so would succumb to a plethora of interpretations – a garden that could be meditated upon indefinitely.

Japanese gardens are epitomised by *kare sansui*, or gardens that set these ambiguously shaped rocks in raked gravel. The best known of these is Ryōan-ji in northwestern Kyoto, but this type of garden can be seen at other Zen Buddhist temples around Japan, and in other forms around the globe.

Although some Japanese gardens are very formal, and all are carefully arranged, the Japanese garden does not use straight lines or symmetry to achieve this formality. Instead, the gardens are a miniaturisation of the Japanese landscape, albeit a very refined version. *Tsukiyama* gardens, as these are called, often incorporate meandering paths that lead the viewer through a carefully controlled set of scenes. This control is achieved in ways such as slowing a viewer by placing stepping-stones or rough paving where a certain detail is in need of appreciation, or creating mystery by partially concealing garden features. Views will often include a 'borrowed' landscape, a common concept in Japanese garden design. Vistas of distant mountains and other features beyond the garden boundary are carefully framed, becoming an integral part of the garden.

Another basic type of garden is the tea garden, or *chaniwa*. This garden supports the traditional Japanese tea ceremony, both as a backdrop and as a functional facility. Water-features in *chaniwa*, for instance, are used for washing prior to entering the tea-ceremony pavilion.

Japanese gardens can also be categorised according to how they are viewed: *funa asobi* gardens, such as Byōdō-in in southern Kyoto, are set around a lake, and are best viewed from a boat; *shūyū* gardens, such as Ginkaku-ji in Kyoto, are revealed along a winding path; *kanshō* gardens are viewed from a single viewpoint (such as the *kare sansui* meditation gardens, where a walk in the garden might result in a confrontation with a rake-wielding Zen monk!); and *kaiyū* gardens, such as Katsura Rikyū Imperial Villa in western Kyoto, formed by many smaller gardens that are often set around a central pond and a teahouse.

Much contemporary landscape design follows some of the basic principles of the traditional ways. Variations mostly impose more obvious human intervention in the scene, reflecting contemporary Japanese society's technological slant. Abstract granite blocks are more likely to be carefully composed alongside a stainless-steel lightpost than a stone lantern. Raked gravel gardens abound, as they do throughout the world, but they rarely achieve anything like the standards set over 500 years ago.

Modern & Contemporary Architecture

Contemporary Japanese architecture is currently among the world's most exciting and influential. The traditional Japanese leaning towards simple, natural and harmonious spaces is still evident in the work of modern architects, but this style is now combined with high-tech materials and the building techniques of the West.

Tradition has always been of extreme importance to the Japanese, but this does not necessarily imply permanence. This attitude has allowed Japanese architecture to incorporate new influences without losing the essence of its origins. A unique set of circumstances, including strong economic growth and the devastation wrought on the landscape by WWII, has meant many chances to move in new directions, and the resulting changes to the urban fabric have been extreme.

Japan first opened its doors to Western architecture in 1868 with the Meiji Restoration. Japan's architects immediately responded to these new influences, combining traditional Japanese methods of wood construction with Western designs, but some 20 years later, a nationalistic push against the influence of the West saw a resurgence in the popularity of traditional Japanese building styles.

This ambivalence towards Western architecture continued until after WWI, when foreign architects, such as Frank Lloyd Wright and his assistant Antonin Raymond, came to build the Imperial Hotel in Tokyo. Lloyd Wright introduced the International Style, characterised by sleek lines, cubic forms and materials such as glass, steel and brick.

By WWII many Japanese architects were using Western techniques and materials and blending old styles with the new. Later, the aggressively sculptural work in concrete and stone of French architect Le Corbusier was to exert a strong influence on Japanese architects. By the mid-1960s Japanese architects had developed a unique style and were beginning to attract attention on the world stage.

Japan's most famous post-war architect Tange Kenzō was strongly influenced by Le Corbusier. Tange's buildings, including the Kagawa Prefectural Offices at Takamatsu (1958) and the National Gymnasium (completed 1964), fuse the sculptural influences and materials of Le Corbusier with traditional Japanese characteristics, such as post-and-beam construction and strong geometry. His Tokyo Metropolitan Government Offices (1991), located in Nishi-Shinjuku (west Shinjuku), is the tallest building in Tokyo. It may look a little sinister and has been criticised as totalitarian, but it is a remarkable achievement and pulls in around 6000 visitors daily. Those with an interest in Tange's work should also look out for the United Nations University, close to Omote-sando subway station in Tokyo.

In the 1960s architects such as Shinohara Kazuo, Kurokawa Kisho, Maki Fumihiko and Kikutake Kiyonori began a movement known as Metabolism, which promoted flexible spaces and functions at the expense of fixed forms in building. Shinohara finally came to design in a style he called Modern Next, incorporating both modern and postmodern design ideas combined with Japanese influences. This style can be seen in his Centennial Hall at Tokyo Institute of

MICHAEL TAYLOR

Technology, an elegant and uplifting synthesis of clashing forms in a shiny metal cladding. Kurokawa's architecture blends Buddhist building traditions with modern influences, while Maki, the master of minimalism, pursued design in a modernist style while still emphasising the elements of nature – like the roof of his Tokyo Metropolitan Gymnasium (nearby Sendagaya Station), which takes on the form of a sleek metal insect. Another Maki design, the Spiral Building, built in Aoyama in 1985, is a favourite with Tokyo residents and its interior is also a treat.

Isozaki Arata, an architect who originally worked under Tange Kenzō, also promoted the Metabolist style before later becoming interested in geometry and postmodernism. His work includes the Gunma Museum (1974) in Takasaki and the Cultural Centre in Mito (1990), which contains a striking geometrical snakelike tower clad in different metals. Situated about an hour's travelling time from Tokyo, the trip to Mito is a popular one for day-trippers and well worth the effort.

A contemporary of Isozaki's, Kikutake, went on to design the Edo-Tokyo Museum (1992) in Sumida-ku, which charts the history of the Edo period, and is arguably his best-known building. It is a truly enormous structure, encompassing almost 50,000 sq metres of built space and reaching 62.2m (the height of Edo-jō) at its peak. It has been likened in form to a crouching giant and it easily dwarfs its surroundings.

Top: Tokyo Big Sight (Tokyo International Exhibition Center)

Another influential architect of this generation is Hara Hiroshi. Hara's style defies definition, but the one constant theme is nature. His Umeda Sky building (1993), in Kita, Osaka, is a sleek, towering structure designed to resemble a garden in the sky. The Yamamoto International Building (1993) on the outskirts of Tokyo, is the headquarters of a textile factory. Both these buildings, though monumental in scale, dissolve down into many smaller units upon closer inspection – just like nature itself.

In the 1980s, a second generation of Japanese architects began to gain recognition within the international architecture scene, including Andō Tadao, Hasegawa Itsuko and Toyo Ito. This younger group has continued to explore both modernism and postmodernism, while incorporating the renewed interest in Japan's architectural heritage.

Andō's architecture in particular blends classical modern and native Japanese styles. His buildings often combine materials such concrete with the strong geometric patterns that have so regularly appeared in Japan's traditional architecture. Andō's restrained and sensitive use of materials often lends itself to the design of reflective or religious spaces.

[Continued from page 32]

to it. It encompasses myths of the origin of Japan and the Japanese people, beliefs and practices in local communities and the highly structured rituals associated with the imperial family. Shintō tradition held that the emperor himself was a *kami*, or divine being, until 1945, when the emperor was officially disabused of his divine status under the American occupation of Japan.

Japanese Myths The chief sources for Japanese myths are the Kojiki (Records of Ancient Matters), and the Nihon Shoki (Chronicle of Japan). The myths contained in these 8th-century works have much in common with those of neighbouring countries and the Southeast Asian and Mongolian areas.

Japan's creation is ascribed to Izanagi-no-Mikoto (creator god) and Izanami-no-Mikoto (creator goddess). Standing on the Floating Bridge of Heaven, they dipped the Heavenly Jewelled Spear into the ocean. Brine dripped from the spear and created the island of Onogoro-jima, where the two were married. Izanami gave birth to the islands of Japan and to its deities.

Izanami gave birth to 35 gods, but in giving birth to the fire deity she was burned and died. Izanagi ventured into the Land of the Dead (Yomi-no-Kuni). There he found Izanami, horribly transfigured by death, who joined with the Eighty Ugly Females to pursue her former mate. He escaped only by blocking the entry to Yomi with a huge boulder, thus separating the lands of the living and the dead. On his return to the Land of the Living, Izanagi purified himself in a stream. This act created more deities, the three most important being Amaterasu Ōmikami (the sun goddess, from whom the imperial family later claimed descent), Tsukuyomi-no-Mikoto (the moon god) and Susano-ō-no-Mikoto (the god of oceans).

According to the legend, Amaterasu ruled the High Plain of Heaven and Susano-ō was given charge of the oceans. Susano-ō missed his mother and stormed around causing general destruction for which he was exiled by his father. In a fit of pique, Susano-ō visited his sister, Amaterasu, and

they had such a quarrel that Amaterasu rushed off to hide in a cave, plunging the world into darkness. All the gods assembled round the cave entrance to find a way to make Amaterasu return.

Ame-no-Uzume-no-Mikoto (goddess of fertility) finally performed a ribald dance causing much laughter among the onlookers. Amaterasu, attracted by the commotion, peeped out of her cave and was quickly hauled out to restore light to the High Plain of Heaven. The site of these events is near Takachihō in Kyūshū. Susano-ō was deprived of his beard, toenails and fingernails and banished to earth, where he landed in Korea before heading to Izumo in Japan.

Okuninushi, a descendant of Susano-ō, took control of Japan but passed it on to Ninigi, a grandson of Amaterasu. Myth merges into history with Ninigi's grandson, Jimmu, who became the first emperor of Japan. Amaterasu is credited with having supplied the emperor with the Three Treasures (mirror, sword and beads) – symbols of the emperor's authority.

Shintō & Buddhism With the introduction of Buddhism in the 6th century, the Japanese formed a connection between the religions by considering Buddha a *kami* from neighbouring China. In the 8th century *kami* were included in Buddhist temples as protectors of the Buddhas. Assimilation progressed with the belief that *kami*, like huma n beings, were subject to the suffering of rebirth and similarly in need of Buddhist intercession to achieve liberation from this cycle. Buddhist temples were built close to Shintō shrines and Buddhist sutras were recited for *kami*. Later, *kami* were considered incarnations of Bodhisattvas (Buddhas who delay liberation to help others). Buddhist statues were included on Shintō altars or statues of *kami* were made to represent Buddhist priests.

State Shintō There had been something of a revival of interest in Shintō during the Edo period, particularly by neo-Confucian scholars interested in Japan's past. Some of them called for a return to imperial rule, with Shintō as the state religion. This is exactly what happened with the advent of the Meiji Restoration.

During the Meiji period, Shintō shrines were supported by the government, Shintō doctrines were taught in school and the religion became increasingly nationalistic. It was a relatively brief affair. After Japan's WWII defeat, the Allied forces dismantled the mechanisms of State Shintō and forced the emperor to refute his divine status, a principal tenet of Shintō.

The main training centres for priests are Kokugakuin University in Tokyo and Kōgakukan University in Ise. Priests are allowed to marry, and most of the posts are commonly patrilineal.

Shintō Rites & Festivals These events are important components of Japanese life. For newborn children the first shrine visit occurs on the 30th or 100th day after birth. On 15 November, the Shichigosan rite is celebrated by taking children aged *shichi* (seven), *go* (five) and *san* (three) to the shrine to be blessed. Seijin-no-hi, the day of adulthood, is celebrated on the second Sunday in January by young people who have reached the age of 20.

Virtually all marriages are performed according to Shintō ritual by taking a vow before the *kami*. Funerals, however, are almost always Buddhist. Both religions coexist in traditional Japanese homes, where there are two altars: a Shintō *kamidana* (a shelf shrine) and a Buddhist *butsudan* (Buddha stand).

Shintō also plays a role in professional and daily life. A new car can be blessed for accident-free driving, a purification rite is often held for a building site or the shell of a new building, and completed buildings are similarly blessed. One of the most common purification rites is *oharai*, when the priest waves a wand to which are attached thin strips of paper.

Amulets are popular purchases at Japan's shrines. Special talismans (*omamori*) are purchased at shrines to ensure good luck or ward off evil – taxi-drivers often have a 'traffic-safety' one dangling from the rearview mirror. Votive plaques (*ema*) made of wood with a picture on one side and a blank space on the other are also common. On the blank side visitors write a wish: a hope for success in exams, luck in finding a sweetheart or safe delivery of a healthy child. Dozens of these plaques can be seen attached to boards in the shrine precincts.

Fortunes (*omikuji*) are selected by drawing a bamboo stick at random from a box and picking out a fortune slip according to the number indicated on the stick. Luck is classified as *dai-kichi* (great good fortune), *kichi* (good fortune), *shō-kichi* (middling good fortune) and *kyō* (bad luck). If you like the fortune slip you've been given, you can take it home. If you've drawn bad luck, you can tie it to the branch of a tree in the shrine grounds – presumably some other force can then worry about it.

The *kannushi* (chief priest) of the shrine is responsible for religious rites and the administration of the shrine. The priests dress in blue and white; on special occasions they don more ornate clothes and wear an *eboshi*. The *miko* (shrine maidens) dress in red and white. The ceremonial *kagura* dances performed by the *miko* can be traced back to shamanistic trances.

Shintō *matsuri* (festivals) occur on an annual or occasional basis and are classed as grand, middle-size or minor. See the boxed text 'Matsuri Magic' in the Facts for the Visitor chapter.

Buddhism

Buddhism was introduced to Japan via Korea in the 6th century. Japanese Buddhism has evolved in a unique fashion with some decisive differences from other forms of the religion. Shōtoku Taishi, acknowledged as the 'father of Japanese Buddhism', drew heavily on Chinese culture to form a centralised state and gave official recognition to Buddhism by constructing temples in and around the capital. Horyū-ji, close to Nara, is the most celebrated temple in Japan from this period.

Nara Period The establishment of the first permanent capital at Heijō-kyō (present-day Nara) in AD 710 also marked the consolidation of Buddhism and Chinese culture in Japan.

In 741, Emperor Shōmu issued a decree for a network of state temples (*kokubun-ji*) to be established in each province. The centrepiece of this network was Tōdai-ji, with its gigantic Daibutsu.

Nara Buddhism revolved around six schools – Ritsu, Jōjitsu, Kusha, Sanron, Hossō and Kegon – which covered the whole range of Buddhist thought as re-

Zen Buddhism

Japan's most famous brand of Buddhism actually arose in China, though its origins lie in India. The word zen is the Japanese reading of the Chinese ch'an (from Sanskrit dhyana). Legend has it that Bodidharma, a 6th-century Indian monk, introduced Zen to China, but most historians credit this to Huineng (638–713), a Chinese monk.

It took another 200 years for Zen to take root in Japan. It did so in two major schools: Rinzai and Sōtō. The differences between the schools are not easily explained, but at a simple level the Sōtō school places more emphasis on zazen (seated meditation), and the Rinzai school on kōan (riddles). The object of meditative practice for both schools is satori (enlightenment).

The practice of zazen has its roots in Indian yoga. Its posture is the lotus position: the legs are crossed and tucked beneath the sitter, the back ramrod straight, the breathing rhythmical. The idea is to block out all sensation and empty the mind of thought – much harder than you might imagine.

A kōan is a riddle that lacks a rational answer. Most are set pieces that owe their existence to the early evolution of Zen Buddhism in China. In the course of meditating on an insoluble problem, the mind eventually returns to a form of primal consciousness. The most famous kōan was created by the Japanese monk Hakuin: 'What is the sound of one hand clapping?' Fans of The Simpsons will already know the answer to this one, and are already enlightened.

Although Zen emphasises the direct, intuitive approach to enlightenment rather than rational analysis, there are dozens of books available on the subject. Two favourites are Zen & Japanese Culture by DT Suzuki and Zen Flesh, Zen Bones compiled by Paul Reps.

---

ceived from China. Three of these schools have continued to this day: Kegon school, based at Tōdai-ji; Hossō school, based at Kōfuku-ji and Yakushi-ji; and Ritsu school, based at Tōshōdai-ji.

Heian Period In 794, the capital was moved from Nara to Heian-kyō (present-day Kyoto). During the Heian period, political power drifted away from centralised government into the hands of aristocrats and their clans, who became a major source of Buddhist support.

The new schools, which introduced Mikkyō (Esoteric Buddhism) from China, were founded by separate leaders on sacred mountains away from the orthodox pressures of the Nara schools.

The Tendai school (derived from a Chinese school on Mt Tiantai in China) was founded by Saichō (762–822), also known as Dengyō Daishi, who established a base at Enryaku-ji on Hiei-zan, near Kyoto.

Saichō travelled to Mt Tiantai in China, where he studied meditation and the Lotus Sutra. On his return, he expanded his studies to include Zen meditation and Tantric ritual. The Tendai school was only officially recognised a few days after his death, but Enryaku-ji developed into one of Japan's key Buddhist centres and was the

source of all the important schools (Pure Land, Zen and Nichiren) in the following Kamakura period.

The Shingon school (derived from the Chinese term for 'mantra') was established by Kūkai (714–835), often referred to as Kōbō Daishi. Kūkai established the mountain-top monastery of Kōya-san in Wakayama-ken (see the Kansai chapter) and performed a now-famous pilgrimage around the island of Shikoku (see the boxed text '88 Sacred Temples of Shikoku' in the Shikoku chapter).

Kūkai trained for government service but decided at the age of 18 to switch his studies from Confucianism and Taoism to Buddhism. He travelled as part of a mission to Chang-an (present-day Xi'an) in China, where he immersed himself in Mikkyō. On return, he made a broad impact on cultural life, spreading and sponsoring the study of Mikkyō, and compiling the first Chinese-Japanese dictionary and the hiragana syllabary, which made it easier for the Japanese to put their language into writing.

During this period, assimilation with Shintō continued. Many jingū-ji (shrine temples) were built for Buddhist rituals in the grounds of Shintō shrines. Theories were propounded that held the Shintō kami to be manifestations of Buddhas or

Japanese Gods & Mythical Creatures

Japan has a curious medley of folk gods. You might see representations of some of these in temples, shrines and artwork. Common ones include the following:

Benzaiten The goddess of art is skilled in eloquence, music, literature and wisdom. She holds a *biwa* (Japanese lute) and is often escorted by a sea snake.

Bishamon The god of war wears a helmet and a suit of armour and brandishes a spear. As a protector of Buddhism, he can be seen carrying a pagoda.

Daikoku The god of wealth has a bag full of treasures slung over his left shoulder and a lucky mallet in his right hand.

Ebisu The patron of seafarers and a symbol for prosperity in business, Ebisu carries a fishing rod with a large red sea bream dangling on the line and can be recognised by his beaming, bearded face.

Fukurokuju This god looks after wealth and longevity. He has a bald, dome-shaped head, and a dumpy body and wears long, flowing robes.

Jurojin This god also covers longevity. He sports a distinguished white beard and holds a cane to which is attached a scroll listing the life span of all living beings.

Hotei The god of happiness is instantly recognisable (in Japan and elsewhere in Asia) by his large paunch and Cheshire-cat grin. Originally a Chinese beggar-priest, he is the only god in this group whose antecedents can be traced to a human being. His bulging bag provides for the needy and is never empty.

Shichifuku-jin The Seven Gods of Luck are a happy band of well-wishers plucked from Indian, Chinese and Japanese sources. Their images are popular at New Year, when they are, more often than not, depicted as a group on a *takarabune* (treasure ship).

Bodhisattvas. The collapse of law and order during these times inspired a general feeling of pessimism in society and encouraged belief in the Mappō (End of the Law) theory, which predicted an age of darkness with a decline in Buddhist religion. This set the stage for subsequent Buddhist schools to introduce the notion of Buddhist saviour figures such as Amida.

Kamakura Period In this period, marked by savage clan warfare and the transfer of the capital to Kamakura, three schools emerged from Tendai tradition.

The Jōdo (Pure Land) school, founded by Hōnen (1133–1212), shunned scholasticism in favour of the Nembutsu, a simple prayer that required the believer to recite *namu amida butsu* (hail Amida Buddha), as a path to salvation. This 'no-frills' approach – easy to practise and easy to understand – was popular with the common folk.

Shinran (1173–1262), a disciple of Hōnen, took a more radical step with his master's teaching and broke away to form the Jōdo Shin (True Pure Land) school. The core belief of this school considered that Amida had *already* saved everyone and hence to recite the Nembutsu was an expression of gratitude, not a petition for salvation.

The Nichiren school bears the name of its founder, Nichiren (1222–82), a fiery character who spurned traditional teachings to embrace the Lotus Sutra as the 'right' teaching. Followers learned to recite '*namu myōhō rengekyō*' (hail the miraculous law of the Lotus Sutra). Nichiren's strident demands for religious reform of government caused antagonism all round and he was frequently booted into exile.

The Nichiren school increased its influence in later centuries; the now famous Hokke-ikki uprising in the 15th century was led by Nichiren adherents. Many of the new religious movements in present-day Japan – Sōka Gakkai, for example – can be linked to Nichiren.

Later Developments During the Tokugawa period, Buddhism was consolidated as a state institution. When the shōgunate banned Christianity, a parallel regulation rigidly required every Japanese to become a certified member of the local temple.

Japanese Gods & Mythical Creatures

A variety of fabulous creatures inhabit Japanese folklore and crop up regularly in shops, festivals and shrines:

Kappa These are amphibious creatures about the size of a 12- or 13-year-old child. They have webbed hands and feet. They have a reputation for mischief, such as dragging horses into rivers or stealing cucumbers. The source of their power is a depression on top of their heads that must always contain water. A crafty method to outwit a *kappa* is to bow to it. When the *kappa* – Japanese to the core – bows back, it empties the water from its head and loses its power. The alternatives are not pleasant. *Kappa* are said to enjoy ripping out their victim's liver through the anus!

Kitsune This creature is a fox, but for the Japanese it also has strong connections with the supernatural and is worshipped in Japan at over 30,000 Inari shrines as the messenger of the harvest god. Fushimi Inari Taisha, a shrine near Kyoto, is the largest of its kind and is crammed with fox statues.

Maneki-neko The Beckoning Cat is a very common sight outside shops or restaurants. The raised left paw attracts customers – and their money.

Tanuki This creature is often translated as 'badger', but bears a closer resemblance to a North American raccoon. Like the fox, the *tanuki* is thought of as a mischievous creature and is credited with supernatural powers, but it is more a figure of fun than the fox. Statues usually depict the *tanuki* in an upright position with straw headgear, clasping a bottle of sake.

Tengu The mountain goblin has a capricious nature – sometimes abducting children, sometimes returning those who were missing. Its unmistakable feature is a long nose, like that of a proboscis monkey.

During the Meiji period, Shintō was given priority and separated from Buddhism, which created a backlash of resentment. Today, Buddhism prospers in Japan both in the form of traditional schools and in a variety of new movements.

Buddhist Gods There are dozens of gods in the Japanese Buddhist pantheon. Images vary from temple to temple, depending on the religious schools or period of construction, but three of the most common images are those of Shaka (in Sanskrit 'Sakyamuni'), the Historical Buddha; Amida (in Sanskrit 'Amitabha'), the Buddha of the Western Paradise; and Miroku (in Sanskrit 'Maitreya'), the Buddha of the Future.

Kannon (in Sanskrit 'Avalokitesvara') is the 'one who hears their cries' and is available in no less than 33 different versions, including the goddess of mercy, a female form popular with expectant mothers. When Christianity was banned, Japanese believers ingeniously kept faith with the Holy Virgin by creating a clone 'Maria Kannon'.

Jizō is often depicted as a monk with a staff in one hand and a jewel in the other.

Pieces of clothing or red bibs draped around Jizō figures are an attempt to cover the souls of dead children. According to legend, this patron of travellers, children and expectant mothers helps the souls of dead children perform their task of building walls of pebbles on the banks of Sai-no-kawara, the river of the underworld. Believers place stones on or around Jizō statues as additional help.

For information on Buddhist temples see the Traditional Religious Architecture section in the 'Arts & Architecture' special section.

Shugendō

This somewhat offbeat Buddhist school incorporates ancient Shamanistic rites, Shintō beliefs and ascetic Buddhist traditions. The founder was En-no-Gyōja, to whom legendary powers of exorcism and magic are ascribed. He is credited with the enlightenment of *kami*, converting them to *gongen* (manifestations of Buddhas). Practitioners of Shugendō, called *yamabushi* (mountain priests), train both body and spirit with arduous exercises in the mountains.

Until the Meiji era, many of Japan's mountains were the domain of *yamabushi* who proved popular with the locals for their skills in sorcery and exorcism. During the Meiji era, Shintō was elevated to a state religion and Shugendō was barred as being culturally debased. Today, *yamabushi* are more common on tourist brochures than in the flesh, but Shugendō survives on mountains such as Dewa Sanzan in Yamagata-ken and Omine-san in Nara-ken.

Confucianism

Although Confucianism is essentially a code of ethics, it has exerted a strong enough influence to become part of Japanese religion. Confucianism entered Japan via Korea in the 5th century. To regulate social behaviour, Confucius took the family unit as his starting point and stressed the importance of the five human relationships: master and subject, father and son, elder brother and younger brother, husband and wife, friend and friend.

The strict observance of this social 'pecking order', radiating from individual families to encompass the whole of society, has evolved over centuries to become a core concept in Japanese life. The influence of Confucianism can be seen in such disparate examples as the absolute loyalty demanded in *bushidō* (the way of the warrior), the extreme allegiance to the emperor in WWII, the low status of women, and the hierarchical ties in modern Japanese companies.

Christianity

Portuguese missionaries introduced Christianity to Japan in the 16th century. In 1549 Francis Xavier landed at Kagoshima in Kyūshū. At first, the *daimyō*, with their subjects, seemed eager to conver. However, the motivation was probably less faith and more an interest in gaining trade advantages.

The initial tolerance shown by Oda Nobunaga was soon reversed by his successor, Toyotomi Hideyoshi, who considered the Jesuits a colonial threat. The religion was banned in 1587 and 26 Christians were crucified in Nagasaki 10 years later. After expelling the remaining missionaries in 1614, Japan closed itself off from the outside world for several centuries. During this time a small number of Christians kept their faith active as a type of 'back-room Buddhism'. Christian missions were allowed back at an early stage during the Meiji era to build churches and found hospitals and schools, many of which still exist.

Despite these efforts, Christianity has not met with wide acceptance among the Japanese, who tend to feel more at home with Shintō and Buddhism. There are very few Christians in Japan – possibly one million.

New Religions

A variety of new religions has taken root in Japan. They cover a wide range of beliefs, from cults to faith healing. Easily the largest of these new religions is Sōka Gakkai (Creative Education Society). Founded in the 1930s, this religion follows Nichiren's teachings and boasts over 20 million followers. (Kōmeito, which is now part of the ruling coalition in Japan, was founded in 1964 as a political offshoot of Sōka Gakkai, but now tends to play down the association).

Aum Shinrikyō drew attention to the existence of cults in Japan with its 1995 subway gas attack in downtown Tokyo. Another group, Hō-No-Hana (The Flower of the Way), made headlines in Japan by bilking millions of yen from a group of housewives by promising to deliver miracle cures for a variety of illnesses.

Facts for the Visitor

SUGGESTED ITINERARIES

Given the high cost of touring Japan, most travellers keep to fairly tight itineraries. Fortunately, with a little forethought this is easy to do: Japan's excellent road and rail network allows you to get around quickly, and public transport almost unfailingly runs to schedule. If you want to see a lot of Japan in a short time without spending a fortune, you'll need to organise a Japan Rail (JR) Pass before you go (see Japan Rail Pass under Train in the Getting Around chapter).

In this section we suggest some broad itineraries for touring the country. Be sure to see also the introductions to the individual chapters in this book, in which we give specific itineraries for each area we cover.

Tokyo–Kyoto

The Tokyo–Kyoto route is the classic Japan route and the best way to get a quick taste of Japan. For first-time visitors with only a week or so to look around, a few days in Tokyo sampling the modern Japanese experience and four or five days in the Kansai region exploring the historical sites of Kyoto and Nara is a recommended option. This allows you take in some of Japan's most famous attractions while not attempting to cover too much ground. The journey between Tokyo and Kyoto is best done by *shinkansen* (bullet train) to save valuable time.

Tokyo & Southwest

Travellers with more time to spend in Japan tend to head west and south before considering northern Honshū and Hokkaidō. The reason is that Kansai, western Honshū and Kyūshū are richer in sights than the northern regions of Japan. But if you're a nature buff, you should consider dropping these regions in favour of the **Japan Alps** and **northern Honshū** and **Hokkaidō**, where there is superb hiking.

Assuming you fly into **Tokyo**, spend a few days exploring the city before heading off to the **Kansai** area (notably **Kyoto** and **Nara**). A side trip en route would be to **Takayama** from Nagoya.

From Kansai, many Rail Pass travellers take the *shinkansen* straight down to **Fukuoka** in **Kyūshū**. Some of Kyūshū's highlights include **Nagasaki**, **Kumamoto**, natural wonders like **Aso-san**, and the hot-spring town of **Beppu**.

The fastest way to return from Kyūshū to Kansai or Tokyo is by *shinkansen* along the Inland Sea side of **western Honshū**. Possible stopovers include **Hiroshima** and **Himeji**, a famous castle town. From Okayama, the seldom visited island of **Shikoku** is easily accessible. The Japan Sea side of western Honshū is visited less frequently by tourists, and more rural – notable attractions are the shrine at **Izumo** and the small cities of **Matsue** and **Tottori**.

Tokyo/Kansai & Northern Japan

A good approach to northern Japan from either Tokyo or Kansai is via **Matsumōto** and **Nagano**, which are excellent bases for hikes in and around places like **Kamikōchi**. From Nagano, you might travel up to Niigata and from there to the island of **Sado-ga-shima**, famous for its *taiko* drummers and August Earth Celebration. On the other side of Honshū, the city of **Sendai** provides easy access to **Matsushima**, one of Japan's most celebrated scenic outlooks.

Highlights north of Sendai include peaceful **Kinkazan-jima**; **Tazawa-ko**, the deepest lake in Japan. **Morioka, Osorezan** and **Towada-Hachimantai National Park** are also worth a visit.

Travelling from northern Honshū to Hokkaidō by train involves a journey through the world's longest underwater tunnel, the Seikan Tunnel. If you're short on time, **Sapporo** is a good base, with relatively easy access to **Otaru, Shikotsu-Tōya National Park** and **Biei**. Sapporo is particularly lively during its Yuki Matsuri (Snow Festival) and Summer Festival (late July to late August). Rail travellers will arrive via the Seikan Tunnel and might consider a visit (including seafood meals) to the historic fishing port of **Hakodate**.

The real treasures of Hokkaidō are its national parks, which require either more time or your own transport. If you've only got three or four days, you might hit **Shiretoko** and **Akan National Parks**. If you've got at least a week, head to **Daisetsuzan National Park**. More distant but rewarding destinations include the scenic islands of **Rebun-tō** and **Rishiri-tō**.

PLANNING
When to Go
Without a doubt, the best times to visit Japan are the climatically stable seasons of spring (March to May) and autumn (September to November).

Spring is the time when Japan's famous cherry trees burst into bloom. Starting from Kyūshū sometime in March, the *sakura zensen* (cherry tree blossom line) advances northward, usually passing the main cities of Honshū in early April. Once the *sakura* bloom, their glory is brief, usually lasting only a week. Luckily, if you're travelling around Honshū at this time, you'll probably find *sakura* at *mankai* (peak of bloom) somewhere along your route.

Autumn is an equally good time to travel, with pleasant temperatures and soothing autumn colours. The autumn foliage pattern reverses that of the *sakura*, starting in the north sometime in October and peaking across most of Honshū sometime in November. And the autumn foliage season lasts significantly longer than the *sakura* bloom.

Travelling in either winter or summer is a mixed bag. Mid-winter (December to February) weather can be bitterly cold, particularly on the Japan Sea coast of Honshū and Hokkaidō, while the sticky summer months (June to August) can turn

Closed for New Year

Be warned that many businesses close down over the Shōgatsu period (29 December to 3 January). While public transport still operates during this period, most restaurants shut down completely, starting on the morning of 1 January, and don't reopen until 3 or 4 January. Some also close a few days earlier. If you aren't prepared for this, you may find yourself surviving on convenience store rations, as more than one Lonely Planet author has had to do in the past – we can assure you that a steady diet of instant *rāmen* (noodles) and rice balls quickly gets old!

even the briefest excursion out of an air-conditioned environment into a steam bath. June is also the month of Japan's brief rainy season, which in some years brings daily downpours and in other years can hardly be called a rainy season at all. It certainly isn't reason enough not to visit if this is the only time you can come (and the rainy season skips Hokkaidō entirely).

Also keep in mind that peak holiday seasons, particularly Golden Week, which falls in late April to early May, and the mid-August O-bon (Festival of the Dead) are extremely popular for domestic travel and can cause problems with reservations and crowds.

Likewise, everything in Japan basically shuts down during Shōgatsu (New Year period). See the boxed text 'Closed for New Year' below.

Maps
If you'd like to buy a map of Japan before arriving, both Nelles and Periplus produce reasonable maps of the whole country. If you want more detailed maps, it's better to buy them after you arrive in Japan.

The Japan National Tourist Organization's (JNTO) free *Tourist Map of Japan*, available at JNTO-operated tourist information centres inside the country and JNTO offices abroad, is a reasonable English-language map that is suitable for general route planning. If you'd like something a little more detailed, both Shobunsha and Kodansha (Japanese publishers) publish a series of bilingual fold-out maps with prices starting at around ¥700.

The *Japan Road Atlas* (Shobunsha) is a good choice for those planning to drive around the country. Those looking for something less bulky should pick up a copy of the *Bilingual Atlas of Japan* (Kodansha). Of course, if you can read a little Japanese, you'll do much better with one of the excellent *Super Mapple* road atlases published by Shobunsha.

What to Bring
The number one rule in Japan, as anywhere else, is travel light. Bulky luggage can be a hassle, as often the coin lockers at train stations are only large enough to hold a day-pack – not ideal if you wish to stop en route and go exploring.

Map Warning

Japan's streets are a maze of small alleys interconnected with wider streets. Many of the maps in this guide only *approximate* an area's actual layout: many small lanes or narrow streets have not been drawn. Keep this in mind when navigating your way around.

What clothing you bring will depend not only on the season, but also on where you are planning to go. Japan extends a long way from north to south: the north of Hokkaidō can be under deep snow at the same time Okinawa and Nansei-shotō (the Southwest Islands) are basking in tropical sunshine. If you're going anywhere near the mountains, or intent on climbing Mt Fuji, you'll need good cold-weather gear, even at the height of summer.

Have a good look at the Climate section of the Facts about Japan chapter, and the When to Go section earlier in this chapter, when deciding what clothes to bring to Japan. Rain is possible at any time of year in Japan, so you should consider bringing a folding umbrella and, perhaps, a light rain coat.

Unless you're in Japan on business, you won't need formal or even particularly dressy clothes. Men should keep in mind, however, that trousers are preferable to shorts, especially in restaurants. And both sexes should bring at least one outfit that is suitable for a nice restaurant, that is if you intend to visit one.

Choose your shoes carefully – you want shoes which are not only comfortable for walking but also easy to slip on and off for the frequent occasions where they must be removed. You'll find that slip-on shoes are more convenient than lace-ups. You'll also want to be sure that you have socks *without* holes in them, as they will be on display a good bit of the time.

Bring a towel – even in an expensive ryokan (traditional Japanese inn), a towel is not necessarily provided, or it may be of a size Westerners will equate with a washcloth.

Other than larger-sized shoes and clothes, you'll be able to buy whatever you need in Japan. Perhaps the only exception to this is English-language books, which are only available in big cities such as Tokyo, Osaka and Kyoto. If you're a voracious reader, you might want to stock up there or bring a few books from home.

See Health later in this chapter for advice on health-related items to bring with you.

TOURIST OFFICES

Japan's tourist information services are first rate. You will find information offices in most cities, towns and even some small villages. The best are those operated by the Japan National Tourist Organization (JNTO; see the following section). Others are operated by local tourism promotion boards etc.

A note on language difficulties: English speakers are usually available at tourist information offices in larger cities (and all JNTO-operated information offices). Away from the big cities and at non-JNTO offices, you'll find varying degrees of English-language ability. In rural areas and small towns you may find yourself relying more on one-word communication and hand signals. Nonetheless, with a little patience and a smile face you will usually get the information you need from even the smallest local tourist information office.

Japan National Tourist Organization (JNTO)

The Japan National Tourist Organization (JNTO; **w** www.jnto.go.jp) is the main English-language information service for foreign travellers to Japan. JNTO produces a great deal of useful literature, which is available from both its overseas offices and its Tourist Information Centers (TICs) inside the country. Most publications are available in English and, in some cases, other European and Asian languages. JNTO's website is very useful in planning your journey.

JNTO Tourist Information Centers (TICs) JNTO operates five main TICs:

Kansai (☎ 0724-56-6025) Kansai international airport, Passenger Terminal Bldg, 1st floor, Izumi-Sano, Osaka 549-0011. Open 9am to 9pm daily.
Kyoto (☎ 075-371-5649) 1st floor, Kyoto Tower Bldg, Higashi-Shiokoji-chō, Shimogyō-ku, Kyoto 600-8216. Open 9am to 5pm weekdays, 9am to noon Saturday, closed Sunday and national holidays.

Narita (☎ 0476-34-6251) New Tokyo international airport, Passenger Terminal 2, 1st floor, Narita airport, Chiba 282-0004. Open 9am to 8pm daily.
Branch office: (☎ 0476-30-3383) Passenger Terminal 1, 1st floor, Narita airport, Chiba 282-0004. Open 9am to 8pm daily.
Tokyo (☎ 03-3201-3331) 10th floor, Tokyo Kōtsu Kaikan Bldg, 2-10-1, Yurakuchō, Chiyoda-ku 100-006. Open 9am to 5pm weekdays, 9am to noon Saturday, closed Sunday and national holidays.

The Welcome Inn Reservation Center
Working closely with the JNTO, Welcome Inn Reservation Center staff at TICs can make reservations for you at member hotels and ryokan. TIC staff cannot make transport bookings; they can, however, direct you to agencies that can, such as the Japan Travel Bureau (JTB).

Tourist Information System
In addition to its main offices listed earlier, JNTO operates 111 English-language tourist information offices that are located throughout Japan. The centres are usually found in the main railway stations of major Japanese cities. Look for the red question mark with the word 'information' printed beneath it.

Tourist Offices Abroad
JNTO has a number of overseas offices including those in the following countries:

Australia (☎ 02-9232 4522) Level 33, The Chifley Tower, 2 Chifley Square, Sydney, NSW 2000
Canada (☎ 416-366 7140) 165 University Ave, Toronto, ON M5H 3B8
France (☎ 01 42 96 20 29) 4 rue de Ventadour, 75001 Paris
Germany (☎ 069-20353) Kaiserstrasse 11, 60311 Frankfurt am Main 1
UK (☎ 020-7734 9638) Heathcoat House, 20 Savile Row, London W1S 3PR
USA (☎ 312-222 0874) 401 North Michigan Ave, Suite 770, Chicago, IL 60611
Los Angeles: (☎ 213-623 1952) 515 South Figueroa St, Suite 1470, Los Angeles, CA 90071
New York: (☎ 212-757 5640) One Rockefeller Plaza, Suite 1250, New York, NY 10020
San Francisco: (☎ 415-292 5686) 1 Daniel Burnham Court, Suite 250C, San Francisco, CA 94109

Other Information Offices
There are tourist information offices (*kankō annai-sho* 歓光案内所) in almost all major railway stations, but the further you venture into outlying regions, the less chance you have of finding English-speaking staff. If you want a licensed, professional tourist guide, ask at a JNTO-operated TIC or a large travel agency such as JTB, or, alternatively, contact the **Japan Guide Association** (☎ 03-3213-2706; **W** www.jga21c.or.jp/f_introduction.html) in Tokyo.

Counselling & Advice If you're staying long-term, adjusting to life in Japan can be tough, but there are places to turn to for help. The **Foreign Residents Advisory Center** (☎ 03-5320-7744; open 9.30am-noon & 1pm-4pm Mon-Fri) is a useful service operated by the Tokyo metropolitan government. Otherwise, try the 24-hour **Japan Helpline** (☎ 0120-461-997). See also Emergencies later in this chapter.

VISAS & DOCUMENTS
Passport
A passport is essential. If yours is within a few months of expiry, get a new one now – you will not be issued a visa if your passport is due to expire before the visa.

Visas
Generally, visitors who are not planning to engage in income-producing activities while in Japan are exempt from obtaining visas and will be issued a *tanki-taizai visa* (temporary visitor visa) on arrival.

Stays of up to six months are permitted for citizens of Austria, Germany, Ireland, Mexico, Switzerland and the UK. Citizens of these countries will almost always be given a 90-day temporary visitor visa upon arrival, which can usually be extended for another 90 days at immigration bureaus inside Japan (see Visa Extensions later in this section).

Citizens of the USA, Australia and New Zealand are granted 90-day temporary visitor visas, while stays of up to three months are permitted for citizens of Argentina, Belgium, Canada, Denmark, Finland, France, Iceland, Israel, Italy, the Netherlands, Norway, Singapore, Spain, Sweden and a number of other countries.

For additional information on visas and regulations, contact the nearest Japanese embassy or consulate, or visit the website of the **Japan Ministry of Foreign Affairs** (**w** www.mofa.go.jp) where you can check out the Guide to Japanese Visas, read about working-holiday visas and find details on the Japan Exchange & Teaching (JET) programme, which sponsors native English- speakers to teach in the Japanese public school system.

Working-Holiday Visas Australians, Canadians and New Zealanders between the ages of 18 and 25 (the age limit can be pushed up to 30 in some cases) can apply for a working-holiday visa. This visa allows a six-month stay and two six-month extensions. It is designed to enable young people to travel extensively during their stay; although employment is supposed to be part-time or temporary, in practice many people work full time.

A working-holiday visa is much easier to obtain than a work visa and is popular with Japanese employers. Single applicants must have the equivalent of A$2500 (C$2005) of funds, a married couple must have A$5000 (C$4010), and all applicants must have an onward ticket from Japan. For details, inquire at the nearest Japanese embassy or consulate (see Embassies & Consulates later in this chapter).

Work Visas It is not as easy as it once was to get a visa to work in Japan. Ever-increasing demand has prompted much stricter work visa requirements. Arriving in Japan and looking for a job is quite a tough proposition these days, though people still do it. There are legal employment categories for foreigners that specify standards of experience and qualifications.

Once you find an employer in Japan who is willing to sponsor you, it is necessary to obtain a Certificate of Eligibility from the nearest immigration office. The same office can then issue you your work visa, which is valid for either one or three years. The whole procedure usually takes two to three months.

Visa Extensions With the exception of those nationals whose countries have reciprocal visa exemptions and can stay for six

months, the limit for most nationalities is 90 days or three months. To extend a temporary visitor visa beyond the standard 90 days or three months, apply at the nearest immigration office (see Information in the destination chapters). You must provide two copies of an Application for Extension of Stay (available at the immigration office), a letter stating the reasons for the extension, supporting documentation, as well as your passport. There is a processing fee of ¥4000.

Many long-term visitors to Japan get around the extension problem by briefly leaving the country, usually going to South Korea. Be warned, though, that immigration officials are wise to this practice and many 'tourist visa returnees' are turned back at the entry point.

Alien Registration Card Anyone, and this includes tourists, who stays for more than 90 days is required to obtain an Alien Registration Card (Gaikokujin Torokushō). This card can be obtained at the municipal office of the city, town or ward in which you're living, but moving to another area requires that you re-register within 14 days.

You must carry your Alien Registration Card at all times as the police can stop you and ask to see the card. If you don't have the card, you may be taken back to the station and will have to wait there until someone fetches it for you.

Onward Tickets

Japan requires that visitors to the country entering on a temporary visitor visa possess an ongoing air or sea ticket or evidence thereof. In practice, few travellers are asked to produce such documents, but to avoid surprises it pays to be on the safe side.

Travel Insurance

A travel insurance policy to cover theft, loss and medical problems is a good idea. Some policies specifically exclude 'dangerous activities', which can include scuba diving, motorcycling and even trekking; if you plan to engage in such activities, you'll want a policy that covers them.

You may prefer a policy which pays doctors or hospitals directly rather than have you pay on the spot and claim later. If you have to claim later, make sure you keep all documentation. Some policies ask you to call (reverse-charge) a centre in your home country where an immediate assessment of your problem is made. Check that the policy covers ambulances or an emergency flight home.

Some policies offer lower and higher medical-expense options; choose the high-cost option for Japan. Be sure to bring your insurance card or other certificate of insurance with you to Japan; Japanese hospitals have been known to refuse treatment to foreign patients with no proof of medical insurance.

Driving Licence
To drive in Japan, you will need an International Driving Permit backed up by your national licence. See Car in the Getting Around chapter for more details.

Hostel Cards
Youth hostel accommodation is plentiful in Japan. See Youth Hostels under Accommodation later in this chapter for information about obtaining a membership card.

Student & Youth Cards
Japan is one of the few places left in Asia where a student card can be useful, though some places only offer discounts to high school students and younger, not to university and graduate students. Officially, you should be carrying an International Student Identity Card (ISIC) to qualify for a discount, but you will often find that any youth or student card will do the trick.

Seniors Cards
There are a variety of discounts available in Japan for seniors over the age of 65. In almost all cases a passport will be sufficient proof of age, so seniors cards are rarely worth bringing.

International Health Certificate
Japan is scrupulous about trying to prevent international travellers bringing infectious diseases, like yellow fever or cholera, into the country. If you are arriving from a high-risk area, it would be a good idea to come prepared with an International Health Certificate that indicates you have had all the necessary jabs.

An example of Japan's vigilance can be seen in the comment below:

When travellers fill out the yellow quarantine forms on arrival, they should be careful with their answers. A friend arriving from Thailand admitted to stomach problems and after being sent for a medical checkup, was isolated in quarantine for 10 days without a translator or any appropriate food (she was a vegetarian).

Dennis Nielsen

Other Documents
Extra passport photographs are easy to get in Japan. Those hoping to obtain a work visa should take their original degree (not a copy), and documentation of work experience.

Copies
All important documents (passport data page and visa page, credit cards, travel insurance policy, air/bus/train tickets, driving licence etc) should be photocopied before you leave home. Leave one copy with someone at home and keep another with you, separate from the originals.

EMBASSIES & CONSULATES
Japanese Embassies & Consulates
Diplomatic representation abroad:

Australia (☎ 02-6273 3244, **W** www.japan .org.au) 112 Empire Circuit, Yarralumla, ACT 2600
  Consulate in Brisbane: (☎ 07-3221 5188)
  Consulate in Melbourne: (☎ 03-9639 3244)
  Consulate in Perth: (☎ 08-9480 1800)
  Consulate in Sydney: (☎ 02-9231 3455)
Canada (☎ 613-241 8541, **W** www.ca.emb-ja pan.go.jp) 255 Sussex Dr, Ottawa, ON K1N 9E6
  Consulate in Edmonton: (☎ 780-422 3752)
  Consulate in Montreal: (☎ 514-866 3429)
  Consulate in Toronto: (☎ 416-363 7038)
  Consulate in Vancouver: (☎ 604-684 5868)
France (☎ 01 48 88 62 00, **W** www.fr.emb-ja pan.go.jp) 7 Ave Hoche, 75008 Paris
Germany (☎ 30-21 09 40, **W** www.embjapan .de) Hiroshimastrasse 6, 10785, Berlin
Ireland (☎ 01-269 42 44, **W** www.ie.emb-ja pan.go.jp) Nutley Bldg, Merrion Centre, Nutley Lane, Dublin 4
The Netherlands (☎ 70-346 95 44, **W** www.nl .emb-japan.go.jp) Tobias Asserlaan 2, 2517 KC, The Hague

New Zealand (☎ 04-473 1540, W www.nz
.emb-japan.go.jp) Level 18, Majestic Centre,
100 Willis St, Wellington 1
Consulate in Auckland: (☎ 09-303-4106)
South Korea (☎ 822-2170 5200, W www.kr
.emb-japan.go.jp) 18-11, Jhoonghak-dong,
Jhongro-gu, Seoul
UK (☎ 020-7465 6500, W www.embjapan.org
.uk) 101-104 Piccadilly, London, W1J 7JT
USA (☎ 202-238 6700, W www.us.emb-japan
.go.jp) 2520 Massachusetts Ave, NW Wash-
ington DC 20008-2869
Consulate in Los Angeles: (☎ 213-617-6700)
Consulate in New York: (☎ 212-371-8222)
See website for other consulates in the USA.

Embassies & Consulates in Japan

Diplomatic representation in Japan:

Australia (☎ 03-5232-4111, W www.dfat
.gov.au/missions/countries/jp.html) 2-1-14
Mita, Minato-ku, Tokyo
Consulate in Fukuoka: (☎ 092-734-5055)
Tsurutakeyaki Bldg, 7F, 1-1-5 Akasaka,
Chuo-ku, Fukuoka
Consulate in Osaka: (☎ 06-6941-9271)
2-1-61 Shiromi, Chūō-ku, Osaka
Canada (☎ 03-5412-6200, W www.dfait-maeci
.gc.ca/ni-ka/tokyo-en.asp) 7-3-38 Akasaka,
Minato-ku, Tokyo
Consulate in Fukuoka: (☎ 092-752-6055) F.T.
Bldg, 7F, 4-8-28 Watanabe-dōri, Chuo-ku,
Fukuoka
Consulate in Osaka: (☎ 06-6212-4910) 2-2-3
Nishi Shinsaibashi, Chūō-ku, Osaka
France (☎ 03-5420-8800, W www.amba
france-jp.org) 4-11-44 Minami Azabu,
Minato-ku, Tokyo
Consulate in Osaka: (☎ 06-4790-1500)
1-2-27 Shiromi, Chūō-ku, Osaka
Germany (☎ 03-5791-7700, W www.german
embassy-japan.org) 4-5-10 Minami Azabu,
Minato-ku, Tokyo
Consulate in Osaka: (☎ 06-6440-5070)
1-1-88 Oyodonaka, Kita-ku, Osaka
Ireland (☎ 03-3263-0695, W www.embassy-av
enue.jp/ireland/index_eng.html) 2-10-7
Kojimachi, Chiyoda-ku, Tokyo
Consulate in Osaka: (☎ 06-6309-0055)
4-7-4 Nishinakajima, Yodogawa-ku, Osaka
The Netherlands (☎ 03-5401-0411, W www
.oranda.or.jp/index/english/index.html)
3-6-3 Shiba-kōen, Minato-ku, Tokyo
Consulate in Osaka: (☎ 06-6944-7272)
2-1-61 Shiromi, Chūō-ku, Osaka

New Zealand (☎ 03-3467-2271, W www.nz
embassy.com/home.cfm) 20-40 Kamiyama-
chō, Shibuya-ku, Tokyo
Consulate In Osaka: (☎ 06-6942-9016)
2-1-61 Shiromi, Chūō-ku, Osaka
South Korea (☎ 03-3452-7611) 1-2-5 Minami
Azabu, Minato-ku, Tokyo
Consulate in Fukuoka: (☎ 092-771-0461)
1-1-3 Jigyohama, Chuo-ku, Fukuoka
UK (☎ 03-3265-5511, W www.uknow
.or.jp/be_e) 1 Ichiban-chō, Chiyoda-ku,
Tokyo
Consulate in Fukuoka: (☎ 092-476-2525) c/o
Nishi Nippon Bank, Ltd, 1-3-6 Hakataekimae,
Hakata-ku, Fukuoka
Consulate in Osaka: (☎ 06-6281-1616) 3-5-1
Bakuromachi, Chūō-ku, Osaka
USA (☎ 03-3224-5000, W http://usembassy
.state.gov/tokyo) 1-10-5 Akasaka, Minato-
ku, Tokyo
Consulate in Fukuoka: (☎ 092-751-9331)
2-5-26 Ohori, Chuo-ku, Fukuoka
Consulate in Osaka: (☎ 06-6315-5900)
2-11-5 Nishitenma, Kita-ku, Osaka

CUSTOMS

Customs allowances include the usual tobacco products plus three 760mL bottles
of alcoholic beverages, 57g of perfume,
and gifts and souvenirs up to a value of
¥200,000 or its equivalent. You must be
over the age of 20 to qualify for these
allowances. The penalties for importing
drugs are very severe.

Although the Japanese are no longer cen-
soring pubic hair in domestically produced
pornography, customs officers will still
confiscate any pornographic materials in
which pubic hair is visible.

There are no limits on the importation
of foreign or Japanese currency. The export of foreign currency is also unlimited
but there is a ¥5 million export limit for
Japanese currency.

Visit Japan Customs (W www.customs
.go.jp) for more information on Japan's
customs regulations.

MONEY

Be warned that cold hard yen is the way
to pay in Japan. While credit cards are becoming more common, cash is still much
more widely used, and travellers cheques
are rarely accepted. *Do not* assume that
you can pay for things with a credit card.
Always carry sufficient cash. The only

places where you can count on paying by credit card are department stores and large hotels.

For those without credit cards, it would be a good idea to bring some travellers cheques as a back up. As in most other countries, the US dollar is still the currency of choice in terms of exchanging cash and cashing travellers cheques.

Currency

The currency in Japan is the yen (¥) and banknotes and coins are easily identifiable. There are ¥1, ¥5, ¥10, ¥50, ¥100 and ¥500 coins; and ¥1000, ¥2000, ¥5000 and ¥10,000 banknotes (the ¥2000 are very rarely seen). The ¥1 coin is an aluminium lightweight coin, the ¥5 and ¥50 coins have a punched hole in the middle (the former is coloured bronze and the latter silver). Note that some vending machines do not accept older ¥500 coins (a South Korean coin of much less value was often used in its place to rip off vending machines).

The Japanese pronounce yen as 'en', with no 'y' sound. The kanji for yen is: 円

Exchange Rates

When this book went to press, currency exchange rates were as follows.

country	unit		yen
Australia	A$1	=	¥76.89
Canada	C$1	=	¥85.29
Euro zone	€1	=	¥138.56
Hong Kong	HK$1	=	¥15.04
New Zealand	NZ$1	=	¥68.20
Singapore	S$1	=	¥68.13
South Korea	W100	=	¥9.80
Taiwan	NT1	=	¥3.37
United Kingdom	UK£1	=	¥192.38
United States	US$1	=	¥117.33

Exchange rates fluctuate; for the latest rates check the Oanda online currency converter (W www.oanda.com).

Exchanging Money

In theory, banks and post offices will change all major currencies. In practice, some banks refuse to exchange anything but US-dollar cash and travellers cheques. Note also that the currencies of neighbouring Taiwan (New Taiwan dollar) and Korea (won) are not easy to change, so you

should change these into yen or US dollars before arriving in Japan.

You can change cash or travellers cheques at an Authorised Foreign Exchange Bank (signs are always displayed in English), major post offices, some large hotels and most big department stores. These are easy to find in cities, but less common elsewhere.

Note that you receive a better exchange rate when withdrawing cash from ATMs than when exchanging cash or travellers cheques in Japan; just be aware that many banks place a limit on the amount of cash you can withdraw in any one day (often around US$400).

Banking Hours

Banks are open 9am to 3pm weekdays, and closed weekends and national holidays. Japan may be a hi-tech place, but to change money you have to show your passport, fill in forms and (sometimes) wait until your number is called, all of which can take up to half an hour. If you're caught without cash outside regular banking hours, try a large department store or a major hotel.

ATMs

Automated teller machines are almost as common as vending machines in Japan. Unfortunately, most of these do not accept foreign-issued cards. Even if they display Visa and MasterCard logos, most accept only Japan-issued versions of these cards.

Fortunately, you will find international ATMs in bigger cities like Tokyo, Osaka and Kyoto that do accept foreign-issued cards (see the Information sections in the destination chapters). Better still, the Japanese postal system has recently linked all of its ATMs to the international Cirrus and Plus cash networks (as well as some credit card networks), making life a breeze for travellers to Japan. You'll find postal ATMs in most large post offices. Most postal ATMs are open 9am to 5pm on weekdays, 9am to noon on Saturday, and are closed on Sunday and holidays. Press the button marked 'English Guidance' for English instructions when using these machines.

Credit Cards

Except for making cash withdrawals at banks and ATMs, it is best not to rely on credit cards in Japan. While department stores, top-end hotels and *some* restaurants do accept cards, most businesses in Japan do not. Cash-and-carry is still very much the rule. If you do decide to bring a credit card, you'll find Visa most useful, followed by MasterCard, American Express and Diners Club.

The main credit card offices are in Tokyo and their emergency numbers follow.

American Express (toll-free ☎ 0120-020-120, 24 hours) American Express Tower, 4-30-16 Ogikubo, Suginami-ku
MasterCard (☎ 03-5728-5200) Cerulean Tower, 16F, 26-1 Sakuragaoka-cho, Shibuya-ku
Visa (☎ 03-5251-0633, toll-free ☎ 0120-133-173) Nissho Bldg, 4F, 2-7-9 Kita-Aoyama, Minato-ku

International Transfers In order to make an international transfer you'll have to find a Japanese bank associated with the bank transferring the money. Start by asking at the central branch of any major Japanese bank. If they don't have a relationship with your bank, they can usually refer you to a bank that does. Once you find a related bank in Japan, you'll have to give your home bank the exact details of where to send the money: the bank, branch and location. A credit-card cash advance is a worthwhile alternative.

Bank & Post Office Accounts Opening a regular bank account is difficult for foreign visitors on a temporary visitor visa. Most banks ask to see an Alien Registration Card, and some may also require a name stamp (*hanko* or *inkan*, easily available at speciality stores in most towns). A much better option for long-term visitors or those who don't want to bother with changing money all the time is a postal savings account (*yūbin chokin*). You can open these accounts at any major post office in Japan. With a postal savings account you'll be issued a cash card that enables you to withdraw funds from any post office in Japan (and these are everywhere). You should be able to get things started by using the phrase: *yūbin chokin no kōza o hirakitai desu* (I would like to open a post office savings account).

Costs
Japan is generally considered a horrendously expensive country in which to travel. Certainly, this is the case if you opt to stay in top-end hotels, take a lot of taxis and eat all your meals in fancy restaurants. But Japan does not have to be expensive. Indeed, it can be cheaper than travelling in places like Europe and the United States if you are careful with your spending, and, in terms of what you get for your money, Japan is good value indeed.

The following are two sample daily budgets for travel in Japan. If you're on a tight budget, you can get by on slightly less than the sample low-end budget. Likewise, it's very easy to spend significantly more than our mid-range budget.

sample low-end daily budget	(yen) ¥
Youth hostel accommodation (per person)	2800
Two simple restaurant meals	2000
Train/bus transport	1500
One average temple/museum admission	500
Snacks, drinks, sundries	1000
Total	**7800**

sample mid-range daily budget	(yen) ¥
Business hotel accommodation (per person)	8000
Two mid-range restaurant meals	4000
Train/bus transport	1500
Two average temple/museum admissions	1000
Snacks, drinks, sundries	2000
Total	**16,500**

Saving Money Food costs can be kept down by ordering set meals (*setto*). A fixed 'morning service' breakfast (*mōningu sābisu* or *setto*) is available in most coffee shops for around ¥400. At lunch time there are set meals (*teishoku*) for about ¥700. Cheap noodle places, often found at stations or in department stores, charge around ¥400 for a filling bowl of noodles. For an evening meal, there's the option of a set course again or a single order – ¥700 to ¥900 should cover this. Average prices at youth hostels are ¥500 for breakfast and ¥900 for dinner.

Transport is a major expense, although there are ways to limit the damage. The

Japan Rail Pass and other regional rail passes are well worth the money if you intend to travel widely in a short space of time (see the Getting Around chapter). Overnight buses are cheaper than the train, and enable you to save on accommodation. Hitching is not only easy, it also puts you in touch with a cross section of Japanese society (see Hitching in the Getting Around chapter for warnings on solo hitchhiking and general information). If you want to avoid emptying your wallet at an alarming rate, you should only use taxis as a last resort. Most cities in Japan have fast, efficient public transport, so you rarely need to rely on taxis anyway.

Tipping & Bargaining

There is little of either in Japan. If you want to show your gratitude to someone, give them a gift rather than a tip. If you do choose to give someone a cash gift (a maid in a ryokan, for instance), place the money in an envelope first. Bargaining is largely restricted to flea markets (where anything goes) and discount electronics shops (where a polite request will often bring the price down by around 10%).

Taxes

Japan has a 5% consumer tax. If you eat at expensive restaurants and stay in top-end accommodation, you will encounter a service charge which varies from 10% to 15%. A local tax of 5% is added to restaurant bills exceeding ¥5000 and to hotel bills exceeding ¥10,000. This means it is sometimes cheaper to ask for separate bills. You can ask for separate bills by saying *betsu-betsu de onegaishimasu*, before your bill is tallied.

POST & COMMUNICATIONS

The Japanese postal system is reliable and efficient and, for regular postcards and airmail letters, not markedly more expensive than other developed countries.

Postal Rates

The airmail rate for postcards is ¥70 to any overseas destination; aerograms cost ¥90. Letters weighing less than 10g are ¥90 to

Addresses in Japan

In Japan, finding a place from its address can be a near impossibility, even for the Japanese. The problem is twofold: first, the address is given by an area rather than a street; and second, the numbers are not necessarily consecutive, as prior to the mid-1950s numbers were assigned by date of construction. During the US occupation after WWII, an attempt was made to bring some 'logic' to Japanese addresses, and many streets were assigned names, but the Japanese reverted to their own system as soon as the Americans left.

To find an address, the usual process is to ask directions – even taxi drivers often have to do this. The numerous local police boxes are there, in part, to give directions. Businesses often include a small map in their advertisements or on their business cards to show their location.

Starting from the largest area and working down to an individual address, first comes the *ken* (prefecture), as in Okayama-ken or Akita-ken. Four areas in Japan do not follow this rule – Tokyo-to, Kyoto-fu, Osaka-fu (those cities and the areas around them) and the island of Hokkaidō. After the prefecture comes the *shi* (city). Thus Okayama city in Okayama Prefecture is properly Okayama-shi, Okayama-ken. In country areas, there are also *gun*, which are like counties, and *mura* (villages).

Large cities are then subdivided first into *ku* (wards), then into *chō* or *machi* and then into *chōme*, an area of just a few blocks. The *chōme* is the smallest division, so an address like 4-4 3-*chōme* should locate the actual place you want. For the bewildered *gaijin* (foreigner), the system often seems to change without rhyme or reason, and an address like 2-4-8 Nishi Meguro can also be written 4-8 Nishi Meguro 2-chōme. The building number is either a single numeric or a hyphenated double numeric. When there are three hyphenated numerals the first one is the *chōme*, so 1-2-3 is building 2-3 in 1-chōme.

You can buy maps that show every building in every *chōme*, and there are often streetside signs indicating building locations, but they are very hard to interpret.

Highlights

People waiting to pray on New Year's Day, Kawasaki Daishi, south of Tokyo

MARTIN MOOS

Eniwa-dake, Shikotsu-Tōya National Park, Hokkaidō

MARTIN MOOS

Magnificent Himeji-jō, Himeji, Kansai

SIMON ROWE

Kyoto and Tokyo have to be considered the must-see attractions in Japan: Kyoto as a showcase of the country's rich cultural heritage and Tokyo as a showcase of its energetic present. Beyond these, whether or not you consider the things we recommend a must-see highlight in the country will depend very much on your interests. To this end, in this section we introduce some of the standouts.

Keep in mind that these lists are mere starting points and are by no means exhaustive. You'll find additional highlights by reading the introductions of the destination chapters of this book, as well as the highlights boxes contained therein. The colour map of Japan at the front of this book also identifies some of the country's finest attractions.

Scenery & Natural Attractions

Expressways, railways, factories, skyscrapers and a teeming population would scarcely seem to leave room for natural attractions. Yet, despite its population density, Japan is a mountainous country with many areas of great natural beauty.

Japan Alps Japan's most spectacular mountain scenery is found in Chūbu-Sangaku National Park (which straddles Nagano-ken as northern Gifu-ken) as well as around Takayama and the Shōkawa Valley, both in Gifu-ken.

Mt Fuji This much-climbed symbol of Japan can actually seem like Tokyo's busiest station at rush hour when you're climbing it, but from a distance it's as beautiful as it has ever been.

Hokkaidō The second-largest but least densely populated of Japan's main islands offers wonderful mountain scenery around the lake areas of Mashu-ko, in the Daisetsuzan National Park, and Tōya-ko and Shikotsu-ko in the west.

Okinawa & the Southwest Islands Yaku-shima's giant cedar trees are considered by some to be the most impressive natural wonder in Japan. Iriomote-jima is also worth a visit for its lush tropical jungle.

Castles & Imperial Villas

Japan has an abundance of castles, though few of them are originals. There are also several current and former imperial palaces and villas that rank among Japan's most impressive structures.

Himeji-jō (Kansai) Combining elegance and impregnability, this castle soars above the Himeji plain, earning it the name White Egret. It is generally considered the finest castle in all Japan.

Matsumoto-jō (Central Honshū) This is another fascinating castle that has withstood the march of time remarkably well.

Hikone-jō (Kansai) In Shiga-ken, near Kyoto, this is a lovely original castle with commanding views of nearby Biwa-ko, and an excellent adjoining garden.

Nijo-jō (Kansai) In Kyoto, this interesting former residence of the Tokugawa shōgunate contains some incredible artworks and is surrounded by lovely gardens.

Title Page: The red torii of Fushimi-Inari Taisha, Kyoto, Kansai (photograph by Izzet Keribar)

Gardens

Japan is famed for its beautiful gardens, whether they are the larger Edo 'stroll gardens' or the small contemplative Zen gardens. Without a doubt, Kyoto is the best place in the country to enjoy a wide variety of lovely gardens. Some of Japan's most impressive gardens:

Ryōan-ji (Kansai) You've probably already seen a picture of this classic Zen rock garden in Kyoto; now see the real thing.

Taizō-in (Kansai) Inside Myōshin-ji in northwest Kyoto, this is considered to be one of the finest gardens in Kyoto.

Tenryū-ji (Kansai) Another classic Kyoto Zen garden, this one dates to the 14th century.

Saihō-ji (Kansai) It's worth the trouble (an application is required) to visit this lush heart-shaped moss garden in Kyoto.

Koishikawa Kōraku-en (Tokyo) This Chinese-influenced stroll garden is an oasis of tranquility in otherwise hectic Tokyo.

Hamarikyū-teien (Tokyo) The size of this large garden makes it well worth a visit.

STUART WASSERMAN

14th-century gardens of Saihō-ji, Kyoto, Kansai

Historical Japan

While many of Japan's historical areas have been damaged over the centuries by fire, earthquake and war, some enchanting pockets of untouched buildings remain, and give the visitor a hint of what the Japan of old must have been like.

Kyoto (Kansai) Kyoto tops the list here, both because it was the imperial capital for centuries and because it escaped Allied bombing in WWII.

Takayama (Central Honshū) This mountain town has many fine old buildings and includes the farmhouses of Hida Folk Village, in the *gasshō-zukuri* (hands-in-prayer) style.

Kurashiki (Western Honshū) This pleasant city is famed for its canal district and old warehouses, many of which have been converted into museums.

Nara (Kansai) Like Kyoto, this city is filled with ancient temples and shrines. Also, like Kyoto it has some fine old *machiya* (traditional townhouses).

FRANK CARTER

Fierce wooden face, Nara National Museum, Kansai

Shrines

Some of Japan's most famous and dramatic Shintō shrines are listed here.

Ise-jingū (Kansai) Ise is the imperial shrine to Amaterasu, the mythical ancestor of the Japanese imperial line. It's also one of the most impressive and sacred shrines in Japan.

Nikkō (Around Tokyo) The various shrines of Nikkō are among Japan's most unforgettable sights.

Izumo Taisha (Western Honshū) With the largest and arguably oldest shrine hall in Japan, this shrine is well worth a visit if you're in this part of the country.

Meiji-jingū (Tokyo) The surrounding greenery here makes this shrine a welcome break in Tokyo.

Itsukushima-jinja (Western Honshū) You might want to visit this shrine in Miyajima to see its 'floating' torii (shrine gates).

Fushimi-Inari Taisha (Kansai) If you like gaudy torii, this is the place – there are more than you'd ever be able to count.

CHRIS MELLOR

Entrance to Meiji-jingū, Yoyogi-kōen, Tokyo

ADINA TOVY AMSEL

Pagoda overlooking the courtyard of Sensō-ji, Tokyo

MASON FLORENCE

Henro (pilgrim) walking the 88-temple circuit, Shikoku

ADINA TOVY AMSEL

Tokyo Metropolitan Government Offices

Temples

The most important temples in Japan are in Kyoto and Nara.

Nanzen-ji (Kansai) Though not as popular as some of Kyoto's other temples, this is our favourite in the city.

Ginkaku-ji (Kansai) This Zen temple is one of Kyoto's most visited, and for good reason: it's beautiful. Go early or battle the crowds.

Byōdō-in (Kansai) One of the few extant examples of Heian-period architecture, the main hall of this temple in Kyoto may be the country's most beautiful.

Tōdai-ji (Kansai) For sheer grandeur, you can't beat the vast main hall of Tōdai-ji, in Nara, and the giant Buddha contained therein.

Hōryū-ji (Kansai) This temple and its adjoining museum in Nara contains some of Japan's most important and revered Buddhist artwork.

Kōya-san (Kansai) This mountaintop Buddhist sanctuary in Wakayama has scores of separate temples; it's also the best place in Japan to try *shukubō* (temple lodging).

Sensō-ji (Tokyo) No-one would rank this among Japan's most beautiful temples, but it's much loved and is a good example of a 'working temple'.

Pilgrimages

Even in hyper-modern Japan, there are folks willing to drop it all and set off on a pilgrimage in search of enlightenment and merit. Some still do things the old way and walk the routes, while others take advantage of progress and use cars, buses and trains. If you choose to join them, you're likely to encounter a side of Japan that is hidden to most tourists.

One popular pilgrimage is the **88 Sacred Temples of Shikoku.** Ever since the great Japanese Buddhist saint Kōbōdaishi (AD 774–835) achieved enlightenment on the island of Shikoku, pilgrims have been following his path and walking the 1400km route around the island.

Modern Japan

Ancient temples and shrines, feudal castles and Zen gardens are all very well, but Japan is also the land of the future. A visit to some of Japan's main urban centres is a good and cheap way to get a glimpse into what the future holds for the human race. It's also a great way to sample some of the country's best restaurants, bars, clubs and shops.

Tokyo This may well be the world's most modern city. If you want to see the Japanese urban phenomenon in high gear, this is the place. It is, quite simply, a place everyone should see at least once in their lives.

Osaka (Kansai) Osaka rivals Tokyo as a showcase of modern Japanese urban culture. And, unlike Tokyo, it has one proper urban centre (as opposed to Tokyo's many subcentres). It's also got quite a different feeling from the capital.

Kōbe (Kansai) Much smaller than Tokyo and Osaka, this hip urban centre is known for its cosmopolitan air and scenic hillside location.

other countries within Asia, ¥110 to North America, Europe or Oceania (including Australia and New Zealand) and ¥130 to Africa and South America. One peculiarity of the Japanese postal system is that you will be charged extra if your writing runs over onto the address side (the right side) of a postcard.

Sending Mail

The symbol for post offices is a red T with a bar across the top on a white background (〒). District post offices (the main post office in a ward) are normally open from 9am to 7pm weekdays and 9am to 3pm Saturday, and are closed Sunday and public holidays. Local post offices are open 9am to 5pm weekdays, and are closed Saturday, Sunday and public holidays. Main post offices in the larger cities may have an after-hours window open 24 hours a day, seven days a week.

Mail can be sent to, from or within Japan when addressed in Roman script (romaji) but it should, of course, be written as clearly as possible.

Receiving Mail

Although any post office will hold mail for collection, the poste restante concept is not well known and can cause confusion in smaller places. It is probably better to have mail addressed to you at a larger central post office. Letters are usually only held for 30 days before being returned to sender. When inquiring about mail for collection ask for kyoku dome yūbin.

Telephone

Japanese telephone codes consist of an area code plus a local code and number. You do not dial the area code when making a call in that area. When dialling Japan from abroad, dial the country code ☎ 81, followed by the area code (drop the 0) and the number.

The Japanese public telephone system is very well developed; there are a great many public phones and they work almost 100% of the time. Local calls cost ¥10 for three minutes. Long-distance or overseas calls require a handful of coins, which are used up as the call progresses; unused ¥10 coins are returned after the call is completed, but no change is given on ¥100 coins.

Japan Area Codes

The country code for Japan is ☎ 81. When dialling from outside Japan, drop the zero from the area codes.

Fukuoka	☎ 092
Hiroshima	☎ 082
Kōbe	☎ 078
Kyoto	☎ 075
Matsuyama	☎ 0899
Nagasaki	☎ 0958
Nagoya	☎ 052
Nara	☎ 0742
Narita	☎ 0476
Osaka	☎ 06
Sapporo	☎ 011
Sendai	☎ 022
Tokyo	☎ 03
Yokohama	☎ 045

It is cheaper to make domestic calls by dialling outside the standard hours.

Most payphones will accept prepaid phonecards (terefon kādo), though probably not for international calls. It's much easier to buy one of these than worry about having enough coins. The cards are readily available from vending machines and convenience stores in ¥500 and ¥1000 denominations. The phone also displays the remaining value of your card when the card is inserted.

International Calls Due to the proliferation of counterfeit telephone cards, it is no longer possible to make international direct-dial calls from regular green pay phones.

Paid and reverse-charge (collect) overseas calls can be made from both grey ISDN phones and green phones that have a gold metal plate around the buttons. These are usually found in phone booths that are marked 'International & Domestic Card/Coin Phone'. Unfortunately, these are rare; try looking in the lobbies of top-end hotels and at airports.

Hotel lobbies also have KDD Credit Phones that allow you to make international calls with credit cards issued outside Japan. In some youth hostels and guesthouses, you will also find pink coin-only phones from which you *cannot* make international calls (though you can receive them).

If you do find a public phone that allows international calls, it's much more convenient to use a phonecard rather than coins. Calls are charged by the unit, each of which is six seconds, so if you don't have much to say you could phone home for just ¥100. You can save money by dialling late at night. Economy rates (20% off the normal rates) apply from 7pm to 11pm Monday to Friday, and from 8am to 11pm Saturday. Discount rates (40% off the normal rate) apply from 11pm to 8am Monday to Saturday and all day Sunday.

To place an international call through the operator, dial ☎ 0051 (international operators all seem to speak English). To make the call yourself, dial ☎ 001 (KDD), ☎ 0041 (ITJ) or ☎ 0061 (IDC) – there's very little difference in their rates – then the country code, the local code and the number.

Another option is to dial ☎ 0039 for home country direct, which takes you straight through to a local operator in the country dialled (your home country direct code can be found in phone books or by calling ☎ 0051). You can then make a reverse-charge call or a credit-card call with a telephone credit card valid in that country.

Another phonecard option is Lonely Planet's ekno phonecard (**w** www.ekno.lonelyplanet.com). It's aimed specifically at independent travellers and provides budget international calls (for local calls, you're usually better off with a local card), a range of message services, free email and travel information. Accessing its website is the easiest way to find out more or to join.

One more option for making international calls is prepaid phonecards, such as the KDD Superworld Card, which provides ¥3200 worth of calls for ¥3000. Unlike conventional phonecards, these operate via an access code that lasts as long as the charge remains on the card. There is no need to insert the card into a phone, and you can make international calls from any touch-tone phone. You can purchase these cards in hotels and ryokan that cater to foreigners; otherwise, try a convenience store.

Directory Assistance For local directory assistance dial ☎ 104. For international directory assistance dial ☎ 0057. To place a domestic collect call, dial ☎ 106. For orders and inquiries about phone installation, ring the **NTT English Service Section** (toll-free ☎ 0120-364-463).

The emergency telephone number for the police is ☎ 110, and for fire/ambulance emergency services it's ☎ 119.

Email & Internet Access

If you plan on bringing your laptop to Japan, first make sure that it is compatible with Japanese current (100V AC; 50Hz in eastern Japan and 60Hz in western Japan). Most laptops function just fine on Japanese current. Second, check to see if your plug will fit Japanese wall sockets (Japanese plugs are flat two pin, identical to most ungrounded North American plugs). Both transformers and plug adaptors are readily available in electronics districts like Tokyo's Akihabara or Osaka's Den Den Town.

Modems and phone jacks are similar to those used in the USA (RJ11 phone jacks). Conveniently, many of the grey IDD pay phones in Japan have a standard phone jack and an infrared port so that you can log on to the Internet just about anywhere in the country.

The major Internet service providers, such as AOL (**w** www.aol.com) and IBM (**w** www.ibm.net), have dial-ups in most big Japanese cities. It's best to download a list of these dial-up numbers before leaving home.

You'll find Internet cafés and other access points in most major Japanese cities. Rates vary, usually ranging from ¥200 to ¥700 per hour.

WEBSITES

The Web is a rich resource for travellers. You can research your trip, hunt down bargain air fares, make hotels reservations, check weather conditions or chat with locals and other travellers about the best places to visit (or avoid!).

There's no better place to start your Web explorations than the Lonely Planet website (**w** www.lonelyplanet.com). Here you'll find succinct summaries on travelling to most places on earth, postcards from other travellers and the Thorn Tree bulletin board, where you can ask questions before you go or dispense advice when you get back. You can also find travel news and updates to many of our most popular guidebooks, and the subWWWay section links you to the most useful travel resources elsewhere on the Web.

Other websites with useful Japan information and links:

Japan Ministry of Foreign Affairs (MOFA; W www.infojapan.org) Covers Japan's foreign policy and has useful links to embassies and consulates under 'MOFA info'.
Japan National Tourist Organization (JNTO; W www.jnto.go.jp) Great information on all aspects of travel in Japan.
Japan Rail (JR; W www.jreast.co.jp/e) Good information on rail travel in Japan with details on the Japan Rail Pass.

BOOKS

Most books are published in different editions by different publishers in different countries. As a result, a book might be a hardcover rarity in one country while it's readily available in paperback in another. Fortunately, bookshops and libraries search by title or author, so your local bookshop or library is best placed to advise you on the availability of the following recommendations. If you can't find these books at home, you should definitely be able to find them in Tokyo, Osaka or Kyoto. Outside these cities, however, you may have a hard time locating English-language books. For this reason, it's a good idea to stock up before heading out into the countryside.

Guidebooks

If you'd like to explore Tokyo or Kyoto in real depth, pick up a copy of Lonely Planet's *Tokyo* or *Kyoto* city guides. If you feel like taking the plunge into Japanese, Lonely Planet's *Japanese phrasebook* is a good place to start. This handy little book has phrases and vocabulary to cover most situations you're likely to encounter in Japan. *Hiking in Japan* is a must for anyone wishing to explore Japan's woods and mountains.

The best all-around guide to the wonders of Japanese cuisine is Robb Satterwhite's *What's What in Japanese Restaurants: A Guide to Ordering, Eating and Enjoying*. With detailed introductions to each major type of Japanese cuisine and extensive Japanese and English menus, Satterwhite 's book makes it possible for non-Japanese-speakers to enter any Japanese restaurant with confidence.

Travel

Travel books about Japan often end up turning into extended reflections on the eccentricities or uniqueness of the Japanese. One writer who did not fall prey to this temptation was Alan Booth. *The Roads to Sata* is the best of his writings about Japan, and traces a four-month journey on foot from the northern tip of Hokkaidō to Sata, the southern tip of Kyūshū. Booth's *Looking for the Lost – Journeys Through a Vanishing Japan* was his final book, and again recounts walks in rural Japan. A more recent account of a trek across the length of Japan is Craig McLachlan's enjoyable *Four Pairs of Boots*.

History

Several excellent books on Japanese history have come out in the last few years. These include Herbert Bix's *Hirohito and the Making of Modern Japan*, John Dower's *Embracing Defeat: Japan in the Wake of World War II*, and Donald Keene's *Meiji and His World, 1852–1912*. More general histories of Japan include Richard Storey's *A History of Modern Japan*, and *The Japanese Achievement* by Hugh Cortazzi, which spans early Japanese history to the present.

Religion

The role of religion in Japanese society is complex, but there are several good primers that are readily available in good Japanese bookshops. The best of these include *Japanese Religion: A Cultural Perspective* by Robert S Elwood & Richard Pilgrim, *Religions of Japan – Many Traditions Within One Sacred Way* by H Byron Earhart, and *Shintō: The Kami Way* by Ono Sokyo.

Probably the best introduction to Zen is *Zen & Japanese Culture* by Daisetsu T Suzuki.

Culture & Society

For an intimate look at Japan, pick up a copy of Alex Kerr's *Lost Japan* (Lonely Planet Journeys). Originally written in

Japanese, the book draws on the author's experiences in Japan over 30 years. Kerr explores the ritualised world of kabuki, retraces his initiation into Tokyo's board-rooms, and exposes the environmental and cultural destruction that is the other face of contemporary Japan. Kerr's new book *Dogs & Demons* continues where *Lost Japan* left off and is an unstinting and trenchant analysis of some of the problems facing modern Japan.

Although it's a little dated, Ruth Bene-dict's *The Chrysanthemum & the Sword* is considered by many to be the definitive study of Japanese culture and attitudes.

General

Among the more interesting books about Japan is Ian Buruma's *Wages of Guilt – Memories of War in Germany & Japan.* It explores the effects of Japan's (and Germany's) involvement in WWII on the contemporary psyche of the nation. Ian Buruma is also the author of one of the best introductions to Japan's sleazy 'water trade' and the overall cultural implications of what goes on there in *A Japanese Mirror.*

Foreign novelists have also tackled Japan in their writings, the most recent example being Arthur Golden's wildly successful *Memoirs of a Geisha.* Another interesting novel is Alan Brown's *Audrey Hepburn's Neck,* the story of a simple Hokkaidō lad. It's notable because it attempts to portray the Japanese as human beings instead of walking stereotypes.

NEWSPAPERS & MAGAZINES

There are three main English-language daily newspapers in Japan. In bigger cities, these are available at bookstores, conveni-ence stores, train station kiosks and some hotels. In the countryside, you may not be able to find them at all.

The Asahi Shimbun/The International Herald Tribune Published from Monday to Saturday, this paper combines Japanese news from the *Asahi Shimbun* and the *International Herald Tribune*, which itself consists of a number of articles from the *New York Times*, the *Washington Post* and its own writers. This paper is a good choice for those who want a broad picture of world news to go with their Japanese news.

The Daily Yomiuri Rating alongside the *Japan Times* in its coverage of local and international news, the *Daily Yomiuri* is particularly worth picking up on Saturday when a World Report from the *Los Angeles Times* is included, and on Sunday when it has an eight-page sup-plement, View From Europe, culled from the British *Independent*.

The Japan Times With its good international news section and unbiased coverage of local Japanese news, the *Japan Times* is read by most newcomers looking for work because of its employment section – the Monday edition has the most extensive listings.

Foreign magazines are available in the major bookshops in bigger cities, though they tend to be expensive. US magazines such as *Newsweek* and *Time* are popular and widely available.

Resident expats produce a number of interesting monthly magazines that pro-vide information on what's on, details about various cultural events, as well as classifieds for anything from marriage partners to used cars. See Information in the Tokyo, Osaka and Kyoto chapters for details on these.

RADIO

Recent years have seen an increase in the number of stations aimed specifically at Japan's foreign population. Many of these play surprisingly cosmopolitan music and give news updates in several languages, including English.

InterFM (76.1 FM) is a favourite of Tokyo's foreign population. The station broadcasts news and useful day-to-day information mainly in English, but also in seven other languages, including Spanish and Chinese.

The Kansai equivalent of InterFM is FM Cocolo (76.5 FM) which broadcasts in English and several other languages, including Portuguese, Thai, Chinese and Tagalog. In addition to useful news pro-grammes, the station plays a wide variety of multiethnic music.

TV

Some TVs have a bilingual function so you can watch certain English-language programmes and movies in either Japanese or English. The Japan Broadcasting Corpor-ation (NHK) has a nightly bilingual news report and on Sunday night you can catch fairly recent Hollywood movies with a simultaneous bilingual broadcast. Ask the owner of the place where you're staying if the TV has the bilingual feature. The more upmarket hotels also have English-language satellite services, including BBC and CNN.

Aside from bilingual broadcasts and satellite TV, you're going to have to content yourself with regular Japanese-language programming. While standard Japanese television fare is as inane as that found in most other countries, there are some blissful exceptions to this rule. NHK airs some excellent documentaries and variety shows, as well as insightful news shows. Of course, without a decent command of Japanese these may be of very little use to you but, even if you don't understand Japanese, it's worth turning on the TV to see what's on – it's a great window into the culture!

PHOTOGRAPHY
Film & Equipment
Japan is one of the best places in the world to buy film and camera equipment. You'll have no problem finding print film wherever you go, and high-quality slide film is widely available at camera shops in most cities. A 36-exposure roll of print film costs anywhere from ¥400 to ¥800. A 36-exposure roll of Kodachrome slide film costs about ¥950 without processing; Fuji slide film, such as Velvia and Provia, is similarly priced.

For more information on buying cameras and other photographic equipment, see the Shopping section later in this chapter.

Processing Film processing is fast and economical in Japan, standards are usually high, and shops offering this service are easy to find. A 36-exposure roll of print film typically costs around ¥600 to have developed. A 36-exposure roll of slide film usually costs around ¥900 to have developed and mounted, or ¥600 to have developed only.

TIME
Despite the distance between Japan's east and west, the country is all on the same time: nine hours ahead of Greenwich Mean Time (GMT). Sydney and Wellington are ahead of Japan (+1 and +3 hours, respectively), and most of the world's other big

Calendars & Dates

In 1873 the Japanese switched from the lunar calendar to the Gregorian calendar used in the West. As is the case throughout Asia, the result has been that official public holidays are dated according to the Gregorian calendar, while traditional festivals and events still follow the lunar calendar.

Years are counted in Japan according to two systems: Western and Imperial. The Western system sets the date from the birth of Christ. The Imperial system calculates the years from the accession of the emperor. The reign of each emperor is assigned a special name.

The reign of the previous emperor, Hirohito (1926–89), is known as the Shōwa (Enlightened Peace) era. Thus 1988 was Shōwa 63. The reign of the present emperor, Akihito, is in the Heisei era, so 2000 was Heisei 12, 2003 Heisei 15.

cities are behind Japan (New York -14, Los Angeles -17 and London -9).

Japan does not have daylight savings time (also known as summer time), so you must subtract one hour when calculating the time difference between Japan and a country using daylight savings time.

ELECTRICITY
Voltage & Cycles
The Japanese electric current is 100V AC, an odd voltage found almost nowhere else in the world. Furthermore, Tokyo and eastern Japan are on 50Hz, and western Japan, including Nagoya, Kyoto and Osaka, is on 60Hz. Most electrical items from other parts of the world will function reasonably well on Japanese current. If not, you can always buy a transformer at one of Japan's plentiful electronics shops.

Plugs & Sockets
Japanese plugs are the flat two-pin type, which are identical to North American plugs. If you have a three-pin plug, you'll have to buy an adaptor.

WEIGHTS & MEASURES
Japan uses the international metric system. One odd exception is the size of rooms, which is often given in tatami (tightly woven floor matting) measurements known as *jō*.

TOILETS

In Japan you will come across Western-style toilets and Asian squat toilets. When you are compelled to squat, the correct position is facing the hood, away from the door. This is the opposite to squat toilets in most other places in Asia. Make sure the contents of your pockets don't spill out! Toilet paper isn't always provided, so carry tissues with you. You may be given small packets of tissue on the street in Japan, a common form of advertising.

In many bathrooms in Japan, separate toilet slippers are often provided just inside the toilet door. These are for use in the toilet only, so remember to change out of them when you leave.

It's quite common to see men urinating in public – the unspoken rule is that it's acceptable at night time if you happen to be drunk. Public toilets are free in Japan. The katakana script for 'toilet' is トイレ, and the kanji script is お手洗い. You'll often also see these kanji:

Male 男   **Female** 女

HEALTH

Travel health depends on your predeparture preparations, your day-to-day health care while travelling and how you handle any medical problem or emergency that may develop. However, looking after your health in Japan should pose few problems as hygiene standards are high and medical facilities widely available.

Predeparture Preparations

Immunisations No immunisations are required for Japan. However, you should be aware that Japan scrupulously checks visitors who arrive from countries where there is a risk of yellow fever and other diseases. Vaccinations you should consider in consultation with your doctor include hepatitis A and E.

Health Insurance Make sure that you have adequate health insurance. See the Travel Insurance section under Visas & Documents earlier.

Travel Health Guides The most useful book on health and medicine in Japan is the *Japan Health Handbook* by Meredith

Maruyama, Louise Picon Shimizu & Nancy Smith Tsurumaki. Lonely Planet's *Healthy Travel Asia & India* is a handy pocket-size guide packed with useful information, including pre-trip planning, emergency first aid, immunisation and disease information, and what to do if you get sick on the road. *Travel with Children* from Lonely Planet also includes advice on travel health for younger children.

Other Preparations Make sure you're healthy before you start travelling. Dental treatment in Japan is expensive. If you're short-sighted, bring a spare pair of glasses and your prescription. If you require a particular medication, bring an adequate supply as it may not be available in Japan. Remember to bring the prescription as well – it may be illegal in Japan. If you think you will need a particular medicine in Japan, write down and bring the generic name of the drug as it may be marketed under a different brand name in Japan. If you're allergic to prescribed antibiotics such as penicillin, carry this information (eg, on a bracelet) when travelling.

Basic Rules

Care in what you eat and drink is the most important health rule; stomach upsets are the most likely travel health problem, but such problems are unusual in Japan.

Water Tap water is safe to drink all over Japan, but be cautious about drinking from mountain streams. On the island of Rebun-tō (Hokkaidō), travellers have been warned that the springs could be contaminated with fox faeces, which contain tapeworm cysts. There have been reports of the schistosomiasis parasite still lurking in rice paddies or stagnant water – avoid wading around barefoot in these places.

Food As a result of the high levels of hygiene in Japan, food almost never causes problems, but you should still avoid anything that looks obviously suspect (especially in the hot summer months). Most of the raw food can be eaten without health worries, although raw freshwater fish and raw wild boar meat should be avoided. The consumption of *fugu* (globefish) can famously result in death, but the dangers are absurdly exaggerated. (See the special section 'Japanese Cuisine' for more details.)

Medical Problems & Treatment

Self-diagnosis and treatment can be risky, so you should always seek medical help. An embassy, consulate or top-end hotel can usually recommend a local doctor or clinic. Although we do give drug dosages in this section, they are for emergency use only. Correct diagnosis is vital. In this section we have used the generic names for medications – check with a doctor for brands available locally.

Note that antibiotics should ideally be administered only under medical supervision. Take only the recommended dose at the prescribed intervals and complete the whole course, even if symptoms disappear. Stop immediately if there are any adverse reactions and don't use the antibiotic at all if you are unsure that you have the correct one. If you are allergic to prescribed antibiotics such as penicillin; carry this information (eg, on a bracelet) when travelling.

Medical Assistance JNTO-operated tourist information centers (see Tourist Offices earlier) have lists of English-speaking doctors and dentists, and of hospitals where English is spoken. Otherwise, see Medical Services under Information in the Tokyo chapter and the Kyoto section in the Kansai chapter. Dental care is widely available at steep prices. A peculiarity of the Japanese medical system is that most pharmaceuticals are supplied by hospital dispensaries, not pharmacies.

Environmental Hazards

Altitude Sickness It is possible that some people might develop altitude sickness when climbing Mt Fuji or some of the peaks in the Japan Alps. For this reason, we recommend that you familiarise yourself with the condition and how to prevent it before setting out on any climb over 2000 metres. Rick Curtis's *Outdoor Action Guide to High Altitude: Acclimatization and Illness* (w www.princeton.edu/~oa /safety/altitude.html) provides a comprehensive overview of altitude sickness and what can be done to prevent it.

Medical Kit Check List

Following is a list of items to consider including in your medical kit – consult your pharmacist for brands available in your country.

☐ **Aspirin or paracetamol (acetaminophen in the USA)** – for pain or fever

☐ **Antihistamine** – for allergies, eg, hay fever; to ease the itch from insect bites or stings; and to prevent motion sickness

☐ **Cold and flu tablets, throat lozenges and nasal decongestant**

☐ **Multivitamins** – consider these for long trips, when dietary vitamin intake may be inadequate

☐ **Loperamide or diphenoxylate** – 'blockers' for diarrhoea

☐ **Prochlorperazine or metaclopramide** – for nausea and vomiting

☐ **Insect repellent, sunscreen, lip balm and eye drops**

☐ **Antifungal cream or powder** – for fungal skin infections and thrush

☐ **Antiseptic (such as povidone-iodine)** – for cuts and grazes

☐ **Bandages, Band-Aids (plasters) and other wound dressings**

☐ **Scissors, tweezers and a thermometer** – note that mercury thermometers are prohibited by airlines

---

Hypothermia This occurs when the body loses heat faster than it can produce it and the core temperature of the body falls. It is surprisingly easy to progress from very cold to dangerously cold due to a combination of wind, wet clothing, fatigue and hunger, even if the air temperature is above freezing. It is best to dress in layers; silk, wool and some of the new artificial fibres are all good insulating materials. A hat is important, as a lot of heat is lost through the head. A strong, waterproof outer layer (and a 'space' blanket for emergencies) is essential. Carry basic supplies, including food containing simple sugars to generate heat quickly, and fluid to drink.

Symptoms of hypothermia are exhaustion, numb skin (particularly toes and fingers), shivering, slurred speech, irrational or violent behaviour, lethargy, stumbling, dizzy spells, muscle cramps and violent bursts of energy. Irrationality may take the form of sufferers claiming they are warm and trying to take off their clothes.

Warning! Medical Services in Japan

Foreign travellers to Japan should be warned that medical services in Japan may not be on par with those of other developed nations. Furthermore, as a non-Japanese-speaking foreigner, you may find it difficult to access the medical treatment you require or, worse still, you may suffer various forms of discrimination.

A recent study of new medical school graduates in Japan found that more than 80% lacked basic knowledge of cardiopulmonary resuscitation (CPR). Furthermore, there has been a rash of well-publicised deaths and injuries caused by medical malpractice in recent years in Japan. These facts, taken together with our own experiences with Japanese hospitals and doctors, lead us to conclude that you should approach Japanese medical services with a great deal of caution. For simple complaints, you should be fine; for emergencies, you may have no choice; but for elective procedures and anything else that can wait until you get home, we suggest that you do just that: wait until you get home.

As for discrimination, there are a couple of things you can do to ensure that you receive the treatment you require. First, you should try to bring a Japanese speaker with you whenever you visit a hospital (and have a Japanese speaker make the call if you need an appointment). Second, you should bring proof of your travel/health insurance that clearly indicates you are covered for any treatment you receive (one of the roots of discrimination against foreign patients is the fear that they cannot or will not pay for treatment). Third, insist that you receive the treatment you need.

For more information, see Medical Assistance in this section.

To treat mild hypothermia, first get the person out of the wind and/or rain, remove their clothing if it's wet and replace it with dry, warm clothing. Give them hot liquids – not alcohol, and some high-kilojoule, easily digestible food. Do not rub victims; instead, allow them to slowly warm themselves. This should be enough to treat the early stages of hypothermia. The early recognition and treatment of mild hypothermia is the only way to prevent severe hypothermia, which is a critical condition.

Infectious Diseases

Diarrhoea Simple things like a change of water, food or climate can all cause a mild bout of diarrhoea, and a few rushed toilet trips with no other symptoms does not indicate a major problem.

Dehydration, particularly as it can occur quite quickly in children or the elderly, is the main danger with diarrhoea. Under all circumstances fluid replacement (at least equal to the volume being lost) is the most important thing to remember. Weak black tea with a little sugar, soda water, or soft drinks allowed to go flat and diluted 50% with clean water are all good. Stick to a bland, fat-free diet as you recover. If the condition persists, see a doctor as soon as possible.

Fungal Infections Occurring with greater frequency in hot weather, fungal infections are most likely to affect the scalp, between the toes or fingers, the groin area and the body (ringworm). You get ringworm, which is a fungal infection not a worm, from infected animals or by walking on damp areas, like shower floors.

To prevent fungal infections, wear loose, comfortable clothes, avoid artificial fibres, wash frequently and dry carefully. If you do get an infection, wash the infected area daily with a disinfectant or medicated soap, and rinse and dry well. Apply an antifungal cream or powder like Tinaderm. Try to expose the infected area to air or sunlight as much as possible, and, as well as changing them often, wash all towels and underwear in hot water.

Hepatitis A common disease worldwide, hepatitis is a general term for inflammation of the liver. There are several different viruses that cause hepatitis, and they differ in the way that they are transmitted. The symptoms are similar in all forms of the illness, and include fever, chills, headache, fatigue, feelings of weakness, and aches and pains, followed by loss of appetite, nausea, vomiting, abdominal pain, dark urine, light-coloured faeces, jaundiced (yellow) skin and yellowing of the whites of the eyes. People who have had hepatitis should avoid alcohol for some time after the illness, as the liver needs time to recover.

Hepatitis A is transmitted by contaminated food and water. You should seek medical advice, but there is not much you can do apart from resting, drinking lots of fluids, eating lightly and avoiding fatty foods.

Hepatitis E is transmitted in the same way as hepatitis A; it can be particularly serious in pregnant women.

There are almost 300 million chronic carriers of **hepatitis B** in the world. It is spread through contact with infected blood, blood products or body fluids, for example through sexual contact, unsterilised needles, and blood transfusions, or contact with blood via small breaks in the skin. Other risk situations include having a shave, tattoo or body piercing with contaminated equipment. The symptoms of hepatitis B may be more severe than type A and the disease can lead to problems such as chronic liver damage, liver cancer or a long term carrier state.

Hepatitis C and D are spread in the same way as hepatitis B and can also lead to long-term complications.

There are vaccines against hepatitis A and B, but there are currently no vaccines against the other types of hepatitis. Following the basic rules about food and water (hepatitis A and E) and avoiding risky situations (hepatitis B, C and D) are important preventative measures.

Condoms

Condoms are widely available in Japan, but generally only locally produced varieties, which tend to be on the small side. If you think you're going to need them, it's a good idea to bring your own, since foreign-made condoms are all but impossible to find in Japan.

SOCIAL GRACES

One of the most enduring Western notions about Japan is that of Japanese courtesy and rigid social etiquette. However, with a little sensitivity, there is almost no chance of offending anyone, and the visitor to Japan should rest easy in the knowledge that the Japanese are very forgiving when it comes to the little slip-ups of foreign visitors.

Of course, there are certain situations where it is important to follow the Japanese example. Shoes *must* removed, for example, when entering a Japanese home or entering a tatami room of any kind, even a changing room – the Japanese will not make allowances for foreign customs in this case.

Bathing in Japan also conforms to fairly strict rules which you should follow. Whether it's a Japanese-style bath in a private home, a *sentō* (public bath) or an *onsen* (hot-spring bath), remember that body-washing takes place *before* entering the water. Showers or taps and plastic tubs are provided for this purpose. Baths and *onsen* are for soaking in *after* you have washed.

As in other parts of Asia, the respectful way to indicate that someone should approach you is to wave your fingers with the palm downwards.

The public use of handkerchiefs for blowing your nose is definitely frowned upon. The polite thing to do if you have a cold in public is to keep sniffing until you can get to a private place to have a good honk!

The Japanese don't eat food in the street unless there are seats provided for them to sit on while they do so. Ice-cream cones are an exception to this rule. It's up to you whether you want to abide by this custom: no-one's going to be particularly upset if they see you wandering down the street munching on a sandwich.

Sitting

When visiting a Japanese home or eating in certain types of restaurants, you will be expected to sit on the floor. In very formal situations, this is done by tucking your legs directly beneath you in what is known as the *seiza* position. However, in ordinary situations it is perfectly acceptable to sit in whatever manner is comfortable, as long as you don't point your feet at anyone. Indeed, the Japanese themselves are unlikely to sit in *seiza* pose for very long and are quick to adopt a more comfortable position. If you are unsure of what to do, simply emulate your Japanese hosts.

Bowing & Shaking Hands

There is a distinct etiquette to bowing. The general rule is that the deepness of a bow depends on the status (relative to oneself) of the person to whom one is bowing. Fortunately, no-one expects foreigners to understand this and the polite thing to do when meeting Japanese is to incline your head slightly and perhaps bow very slightly from the waist. Nowadays, of course, some Japanese are comfortable with a handshake. Since the practice is still a little unusual, it's probably better not to offer your hand – let the other party take the lead.

Business Cards

If you intend to find work in Japan, make sure you get some business cards printed. All introductions and meetings in Japan involve an exchange of business cards – handing out yours to the right people can make things happen. Cards should be exchanged and accepted with some ceremony, studied carefully and referred to often. It's polite to accept a card with two hands. Do not simply stuff a proffered card into your pocket, and never write anything on a card you are given.

Gift Giving

The exchange of gifts, the return of one kindness with another, is an important part of Japanese social life (see the boxed text 'O-miyage Obligation' in the Facts about Japan chapter). If you visit somebody at their home, you should bring them a gift. It needn't be anything big – chocolates, flowers or other items similar to those given as gifts in the West will do. Ideally, bring something from your own country. If money is given, it is presented in an envelope.

As a foreigner, it's quite likely that you will sometimes be given gifts 'for your travels'. You may not be able to reciprocate in these situations. The polite thing to do is to refuse a couple of times when the gift is offered. The other party will probably keep pushing as long as you keep refusing. A couple of refusals should be enough to ensure that you will not seem too grasping when you finally make off with the spoils.

Flattery

What passes for flattery in the West is often perceived as quite natural in Japan.

The foreigner who has made an effort to learn a few sentences of Japanese or to eat with chopsticks is likely to receive regular dollops of praise. The correct response to praise is to decline it with something like 'Not at all' (sono koto wa arimasen). Try to reciprocate if you can.

Directness

Japanese do not make a virtue of being direct. Indeed, directness is seen as vulgar. The Japanese prefer to feel their way through a situation when dealing with others. There is an expression for this that translates as 'stomach talk' – where both sides tentatively edge around an issue, feeling out the other's point of view until it is clear which direction negotiations can go. This can often result in what is, for many Westerners, an interminable toing and froing that only ever seems to yield ambiguous results. But don't be deceived: the Japanese can usually read the situation just as clearly as if both sides were clearly stating their interests.

Try to avoid direct statements that may be seen as confrontational. If someone ventures an opinion, however inaccurate it may seem, try not to crush it with a, 'No, I disagree completely', or something similar. And remember, silence has a very distinct meaning in Japan and it almost never signifies agreement.

WOMEN TRAVELLERS

Japan is one of the safest countries in which to travel – if you're a man. Japan is not as safe for women travellers. The primary dangers faced by women travellers to Japan are of a sexual nature: sexual harassment, molestation, attempted rape and rape.

Although some expats will assure you that it's safe to walk the streets of any Japanese city alone at night, ignore this *nonsense* and follow your common sense: keep to streets with heavier foot traffic, stay in groups etc. Western-looking women who are alone on foot are easy targets for verbal harassment, or worse, by passing male pedestrians, cyclists and motorists. Walking solo along roads in remote rural areas (even during broad daylight), and hitchhiking are definitely advised against. The risks simply aren't worth it.

It is the rare (or unusually lucky) woman who stays in Japan for any length of time without encountering some type of sexual harassment. Jam-packed trains or buses during rush hour, or late-hour services heaving with the inebriated masses, can bring out the worst in the Japanese male. When movement is impossible, the roving hands of *chikan* (men who feel up women and girls on packed trains) are sometimes at work. A loud complaint may shame the perpetrator into withdrawing his hand. Failing this, you may be able to push your way through to another part of even the most crowded train, especially if other passengers realise what is happening. Or, if possible, ride in the women-only train carriages that have recently been introduced in Japan (see Train in the Getting Around chapter for more information).

Keep your wits about you in traditional entertainment areas, where drunken men stumbling out of snack bars are often under the delusion that any female passerby will appreciate a quick squeeze or lewd remarks. Apparently some men find that words are not enough to express how they feel, as flashers and even more crude exhibitionists are not uncommon. These men target women in isolated situations (say, making a call from a phone box alone after dark) and may publicly expose themselves or even masturbate in front of you. They are, however, unlikely to be shamed into stopping by merely a stern look, or even yelling. The best thing you can do is quickly walk away. Other Japanese men engage in the all-too-common handshake scam, where a friendly man pretends to want to shake your hand Western-style, then fondles your breast at the same time. When in doubt, refuse to shake hands and bow instead.

Although statistics show low rates of violent crimes against women, many Japanese women's organisations and media attribute this to under-reporting. If you or someone you know is raped and you attempt to seek help, be forewarned that police and medical personnel can be quite unhelpful, even accusatory. Insist on receiving all necessary medical care (STD tests, antibiotic booster shot and, if you choose, the morning-after pill) and, as appropriate, filing a police report.

If you do have a problem and find the local police unhelpful, you can call the **Human Rights Center Information Line** (☎ 03-3581-2303) in Tokyo.

Finally, an excellent resource for any woman setting up in Japan is Caroline Pover's excellent book *Being A Broad in Japan*, which can be found in bookstores and ordered from her website at ⓦ www.being-a-broad.com.

GAY & LESBIAN TRAVELLERS

With the possible exception of Thailand, Japan is Asia's most enlightened nation with regard to the sexual preferences of foreigners. Tokyo, in particular, has an active gay scene, with clubs and support groups and a small but very lively gay quarter (Shinjuku-ni-chōme). Check *Tokyo Classified* or *Tokyo Journal* for listings of gay and lesbian clubs. Outside Tokyo, you will find it difficult to break into the local scene unless you spend considerable time in a place or have local contacts who can show you around.

Same-sex couples probably won't encounter too many problems travelling in Japan. However, some travellers have reported problems when checking into love hotels with a partner of the same sex; some have been turned away, others have been grossly overcharged. Apart from this, it's unlikely that you'll run into difficulties, but it does pay to be discreet in rural areas.

You may find **Gay Scene Japan** (ⓦ *http://members.tripod.co.jp/GSJ*) helpful when planning your trip. It's a fun and useful site with information specifically for gay and lesbian travellers.

DISABLED TRAVELLERS

On the plus side, many new buildings in Japan have access ramps, traffic lights have speakers playing melodies when it is safe to cross, train platforms have raised dots and lines to provide guidance and some ticket machines in Tokyo have Braille. Some attractions also offer free entry to disabled persons and one companion. On the negative side, many of Japan's cities are still rather difficult for disabled persons to negotiate.

If you are going to travel by train and need assistance, ask one of the station workers as you enter the station. Try asking: *karada no fujiyuū no kata no sharyō wa arimasu ka?* (Are there train carriages for disabled travellers?).

There are carriages on most lines that have areas set aside for people in wheelchairs. Those with other physical disabilities can use the seats set near the train exits, called *yūsen-zaseki*. You will also find these seats near the front of buses; usually they're a different colour from the regular seats.

The most useful information for disabled visitors is provided by the **Japanese Red Cross Language Service Volunteers** (☎ *03-3438-1311, fax 3432-5507;* **w** *http://accessible.jp.org; c/o Volunteers Division, Japanese Red Cross Society, 1-1-3 Shiba Daimon, Minato-ku, Tokyo 105-8521, Japan).* Its website has loads of useful information and it also produces an excellent guide called *Accessible Tokyo*, which can be requested by email, mail or telephone.

SENIOR TRAVELLERS

Japan is an excellent place for senior travellers. To qualify for widely available senior discounts, you have to be over 60 or 65, depending upon the place/company.

Japanese domestic airlines (JAS, JAL and ANA) offer senior discounts of about 25% on some flights. For more information, contact the airlines. JR offers a variety of discounts and special passes, including the Full Moon Green Pass, which is good for travel in Green Cars on *shinkansen*, regular JR trains and sleeper trains. The pass is available to couples whose combined age exceeds 88 years (passports can prove this). The pass costs ¥79,000, ¥98,000 or ¥122,000 per couple for five, seven or 12 consecutive days of travel respectively. They are available at major JR Stations within Japan from 1 September to 31 May and they are valid for travel between 1 October and 30 June (with the exception of 21 December to 6 January, 21 March to 5 April, and 27 April to 6 May).

Discounts are also available on entry fees to many temples, museums and cinemas.

TRAVEL WITH CHILDREN

Japan is a great place to travel with kids. It's safe and there's never a shortage of places to keep them amused – the only drawback is the expense. Look out for *Japan for Kids* by Diane Wiltshire Kanagawa & Jeane Huey Erickson, an excellent introduction to Japan's highlights from a child's perspective. In addition, Lonely Planet publishes *Travel with Children*, which gives the lowdown on getting out and about with your children.

DANGERS & ANNOYANCES
Theft

The low incidence of theft and crime in general in Japan is frequently commented on. Of course, theft does exist and its rarity is no reason for carelessness. It's sensible to take the normal precautions in airports and on the crowded Tokyo rail network, but there's definitely no need for paranoia.

Lost and found services do seem to work; if you leave something behind on a train or other mode of transport, it's always worth inquiring if it has been turned in.

Earthquakes

Japan is an earthquake-prone country, although most can only be detected by sensitive instruments. If you experience a strong earthquake, head for a doorway or supporting pillar. Small rooms, like a bathroom or cupboard, are often stronger than large rooms but even a table or desk can provide some protection from falling debris. If you're in an urban area, do not run outside as this could expose you to falling debris.

All Japanese hotels have maps indicating emergency exits, and local wards have emergency evacuation areas (fires frequently follow major earthquakes). In the event of a major earthquake, stay calm and follow the locals, who should be heading for a designated safe area.

In the event of a serious earthquake, the radio stations listed under Radio earlier will broadcast emergency information in English and several other languages.

Fire

Although modern hotels must comply with certain safety standards, traditional Japanese buildings with their wooden construction and tightly packed surroundings can be real firetraps. Fortunately, most old buildings are low-rise, but it's still wise to check fire exits and escape routes.

Beaches & Swimming

Few public beaches have lifeguards and summer weekends bring many drowning accidents. Watch for undertows or other dangers.

Noise

In Japanese cities the assault on the auditory senses can be overwhelming, so it's no wonder so many pedestrians are plugged in to Walkmans. Pedestrian crossings are serenaded by electronic playtime music, loudspeaker systems broadcast muzak or advertisements, bus passengers are bombarded with running commentaries in Mickey Mouse tones, and accommodation may include TVs turned up full volume in dining rooms or lounges. Earplugs can help, particularly when you're trying to sleep.

Size

Even medium-sized foreigners need to mind their heads in Japanese dwellings. The Western frame may make it hard to fit into some seats and those with long legs will often find themselves wedged tight. Toilets in cramped accommodation necessitate contortions and careful aim (be warned!). Bathtubs are also sometimes on the small side and require flexibility on the part of the bather.

EMERGENCIES

The emergency telephone number for the police is ☎ 110, and for fire/ambulance emergency services it's ☎ 119. You should be able to get your point across in simple English; however, if you do have problems communicating, ring the **Japan Helpline** (☎ 0120-461-997), an emergency number that operates 24 hours a day, seven days a week.

See Medical Problems & Treatment under Health earlier in this chapter for more information on dealing with a medical emergency.

LEGAL MATTERS

Japanese police have extraordinary powers compared with their Western counterparts. For starters, Japanese police have the right to detain a suspect without charging them for up to three days, after which a prosecutor can decide to extend this period for another 20 days. Police can also choose whether to allow a suspect to phone his or her embassy or lawyer, though if you find yourself in police custody you should insist that you will not cooperate in any way until allowed to make such a call. Your embassy is the first place you should call if given the chance.

Police will speak almost no English; insist that an interpreter *(tsuyakusha)* be summoned. Police are legally bound to provide one before proceeding with any questioning. Even if you do speak Japanese, it's best to deny it and stay with your native language.

For legal counselling in English and some other languages, call the **Human Rights Center Information Line** (☎ 03-3581-2302; operates noon-5pm Mon-Fri). **Gaikokujin Komarigoto Sōdan** (Foreigners' Crisis Consultation; ☎ 03-3503-8484) can provide telephone interpretation with police if necessary.

BUSINESS HOURS

Department stores usually open at 10am and close at 6.30pm or 7pm, seven days a week (with one or two days off each month). Smaller shops are open similar hours but may close on Sunday. Large companies usually work from 9am to 5pm Monday to Friday and some also operate on Saturday morning. (See Banking Hours under Money for banking hours, and the Post & Communications section for post office hours.)

PUBLIC HOLIDAYS & SPECIAL EVENTS

Japan has 14 national holidays. When a public holiday falls on a Sunday, the following Monday is taken as a holiday. You can expect travel and lodging to be fully booked during the New Year (29 December to 6 January), Golden Week (27 April to 6 May) and the mid-August O-Bon festival.

Japan's national holidays:

Ganjitsu (New Year's Day) 1 January
Seijin-no-hi (Coming-of-Age Day) Second Sunday in January
Kenkoku Kinem-bi (National Foundation Day) 11 February
Shumbun-no-hi (Spring Equinox) 20 or 21 March
Midori-no-hi (Green Day) 29 April
Kempō Kinem-bi (Constitution Day) 3 May
Kokumin-no-Saijitsu (Adjoining Holiday Between Two Holidays) 4 May

Kodomo-no-hi (Children's Day) 5 May

Umi-no-hi (Marine Day) 20 July

Keirō-no-hi (Respect-for-the-Aged Day) 15 September

Shūbun-no-hi (Autumn Equinox) 23 or 24 September

Taiiku-no-hi (Health-Sports Day) Second Monday in October

Bunka-no-hi (Culture Day) 3 November

Kinrō Kansha-no-hi (Labour Thanksgiving Day) 23 November

Tennō Tanjōbi (Emperor's Birthday) 23 December

Japan has a large number of *matsuri* (festivals). Some of Japan's best *matsuri* are listed in the 'Matsuri Magic' boxed text below. In addition to *matsuri*, there are several important annual events, which are often Buddhist imports from China or more recent imports from the West (eg, Valentine's Day). Some of the most important annual events:

January

Shōgatsu (New Year) The celebrations from 1 to 3 January include much eating and drinking, visits to shrines or temples and the paying of respects to relatives and business associates.

Seijin-no-hi (Coming-of-Age Day) Ceremonies are held for boys and girls who have reached the age of 20.

February–May

Setsubun (Last day of winter according to lunar calendar) 3 or 4 February. To celebrate the end of winter and drive out evil spirits, the Japanese indulge in setsubun (bean throwing) while chanting *fuku wa uchi oni wa soto* (In with good fortune, out with the devils).

Hanami (Blossom Viewing) The Japanese delight in the brief blossom-viewing season from February to April. The usual sequence is plum in February, peach in March and cherry in late March or early April.

Hina Matsuri (Doll Festival) 3 March. During this festival old dolls are displayed and young

Matsuri Magic

Witnessing a *matsuri*, a traditional festival, may be the high point of your trip to Japan, and offers a glimpse of the Japanese at their most uninhibited. A lively *matsuri* is a world unto itself – a vision of bright colours, hypnotic chanting, beating drums and swaying crowds. In addition to famous *matsuri*, such as Kyoto's Gion Matsuri, there are thousands of small, but spectacular local *matsuri* (see the boxed text 'Juhachiya Matsuri' in the Kyūshū chapter to gain some an idea of the visual feast in store for you).

True Shintō *matsuri* can be traced back to the sacred rites of Japan's rice farming peoples in the Yayoi (from 300 BC) and pre-Yayoi periods. These rites were performed to ensure a good rice harvest, to propitiate the gods and to pray for the health of the community. Although *matsuri* have evolved, their central meanings and patterns still reflect their agrarian roots.

In the Heian period (794–1185), Japan adopted a range of Buddhist and secular rites from China, adding these to native Shintō *matsuri* to form a full calendar of yearly events. These newer imports and other non-Shintō *matsuri* are properly referred to as *nenjō gyōji*. Of course, this distinction is largely academic, and these days almost any Japanese festival can be referred to as a *matsuri*, including modern creations, such as Sapporo Yuki Matsuri (Sapporo Snow Festival).

While *matsuri* vary tremendously in content and form, true Shintō *matsuri* do contain some common elements. The first element of a Shintō *matsuri* is called *monomi*. This is a period ranging from several days to a week in which the shrine priests ritually purify themselves in order to enter into communication with the *kami* (god) of the shrine. This is usually following by an offering to the *kami*. Typical offerings include rice, *mochi* (pounded rice cakes made of glutinous rice), sake or fruit and vegetables. Following this, there is ritual communication with the *kami* in which *matsuri* participants partake of these offerings, an act known as *nyorai*.

Of course, much of this happens behind closed doors, hence the most visible feature of any *matsuri* is a procession of *mikoshi* (or portable shrines) in which the *kami* is paraded around the neighbourhood on the backs of chanting young men (and, occasionally, women).

In some *matsuri*, the *mikoshi* may be carried down a mountainside, an act symbolic of bringing the Mountain God down to the rice fields to watch over the harvest. After the harvest is completed, another *matsuri* is performed in which the *kami* is returned to its mountaintop abode.

girls are presented with special dolls (hina) that represent ancient figures from the imperial court.

Golden Week 29 April–5 May. Golden Week takes in Green Day (29 April), Constitution Day (3 May) and Children's Day (5 May). This is definitely not a time to be on the move since transport and lodging in popular holiday areas can be booked solid.

Kodomo-no-hi (Children's Day) 5 May. This is a holiday dedicated to children, especially boys. Families fly paper streamers of carp (koi), which symbolise male strength.

July–August

Tanabata Matsuri (Star Festival) 7 July. The two stars Vega and Altair meet in the Milky Way on this night. According to a myth (originally Chinese), a princess and a peasant shepherd were forbidden to meet, and this was the only time in the year when the two star-crossed lovers could organise a tryst. Children copy out poems on streamers, and love poems are written on banners that are hung out on display. An especially ornate version of this festival is celebrated from 6 to 8 August in Sendai.

O-Bon (Festival of the Dead) 13–16 July and mid-August. According to Buddhist tradition, this is a time when ancestors return to earth. Lanterns are lit and floated on rivers, lakes or the sea to signify the return of the departed to the underworld. Since most Japanese try to return to their native village at this time of year, this is one of the most crowded times of year to travel or look for accommodation.

November

Shichi-Go-San (Seven-Five-Three Festival) 15 November. Traditionally, this is a festival in honour of girls who are aged three and seven and boys who are five. Children are dressed in their finest clothes and taken to shrines or temples, where prayers are offered for good fortune.

Matsuri Magic

Often accompanied by fire, these *matsuri* are among Japan's most spectacular; a good example being Nachi-no-Hi Matsuri (Nachi Fire Festival).

Other *matsuri* may include a tug-of-war, *kyūdō* (archery), horse-racing and sumō, all of which were originally used to divine the will of the shrine's *kami*. Still other *matsuri* involve *gagaku* (sacred music) and lion dances.

Japan's Best Matsuri

There are thousands of *matsuri* celebrated each year in Japan. While Kyoto, Nara and Tokyo are especially famous for their festivals, you can stumble across *matsuri* in every corner of Japan. For a real sensory overload, it's worth hitting one of the big ones.

Hatsumōde (First Shrine Visit) New Year's Eve, 1–2 January at any Shintō shrine in Japan
Yamayaki (Grass Burning Festival) 15 January in Nara, Kansai
Sapporo Yuki Matsuri (Sapporo Snow Festival) Early February in Sapporo, Hokkaidō
Kamakura Matsuri (Snow House Festival) 15 February, Yokote, Akita-ken, northern Honshū
Omizutori (Water-Drawing Ceremony) 12–13 March at Tōdai-ji, Nara, Kansai
Takayama Matsuri (Takayama Festival) 14–15 April at Hie-jinja, Takayama, Gifu-ken, central Honshū
Sanja Matsuri Third Friday, Saturday and Sunday of May, at Sensō-ji, Tokyo
Hana Taue (Rice Planting Festival) Mid-June, Hiroshima-ken, western Honshū
Nachi-no-Hi Matsuri (Nachi Fire Festival) 14 July at Kumano Nachi Taisha in Wakayama-ken, Kansai
Gion Matsuri (Gion Festival) 17 July, Kyoto, Kansai
Tenjin Matsuri 24–25 July, Osaka, Kansai
Kishiwada Danjiri Matsuri 14–15 September, Osaka, Kansai
Kurama-no-himatsuri (Kurama Fire Festival) 22 October, Kyoto (Kurama), Kansai

For more information on *matsuri*, see the Special Events sections in destination chapters, check with the JNTO or pick up a copy of its leaflet entitled *Annual Events in Japan*. If you do base a trip around festivals, remember that accommodation can be swamped by visitors from all over the country, so book well in advance.

ACTIVITIES
Cycling
Although much of Japan is mountainous, the coastal regions are popular with cyclists. See Bicycle in the Getting Around chapter for more information on cycling in Japan. See also Cycling Terminals under Accommodation later in this chapter for information on places to stay.

Diving
The Okinawan islands located in the far southwest of Japan and the Izu-shotō (Izu Seven Islands) south of Tokyo are popular among Japanese as diving destinations. Other dive sites in Japan include the waters around Sado-ga-shima, off northern Honshū; and the peninsula, Izu-hantō, southwest of Tokyo.

As you would expect, diving in Japan is expensive. Typical rates are ¥12,000 per day for two boat-dives and lunch. Courses for beginners are available in places such as Ishigaki and Iriomote islands, but starting costs are around ¥80,000. Instruction will usually be in Japanese. For these reasons, you're much better off learning to dive in a place like Thailand or Australia, if you've got the choice.

Hiking & Mountain Climbing
The Japanese are keen hikers, and many of the national parks of Japan have hiking routes. The popular hiking areas around Tokyo are Nikkō and Chichibu-Tama National Park. If you want to get away from it all, Gunma-ken offers hikes where you are very unlikely to happen across other foreigners. In the Kansai region, Nara, Shiga and Kyoto all have pleasant hikes.

Japan comes into its own as a hiking destination in the Central Alps, in northern Honshū and in Hokkaidō. In these less populated and mountainous regions of Japan, there may be the added incentive of an *onsen* soak at the end of a long day's walk. Hikers who trek into the mountains see a side of Japan that few foreigners ever experience.

While rudimentary English-language hiking maps may be available from local tourism authorities, it's better to seek out proper Japanese maps and decipher the kanji. Shobunsha's *Yama-to-Kōgen No Chizu* series covers all of Japan's most popular hiking areas in exquisite detail. The maps are available in all major bookshops in Japan.

Serious hikers will also want to pick up a copy of Lonely Planet's *Hiking in Japan*, which covers convenient one-day hikes near major cities and extended hikes in more remote areas.

Martial Arts
Japan is renowned for its martial arts, many of which filtered through from China and were then adapted by the Japanese. During feudal times, these arts were highly valued by ruling families as a means of buttressing their power.

After WWII martial arts were perceived as contributing to the aggressive stance which had led to hostilities, and teaching them was discouraged. Within a decade, however, they had returned to favour and are now popular both in Japan and abroad.

For more information contact the TIC or the associations listed under Tourist offices earlier. JNTO also publishes a leaflet entitled *Traditional Sports*, which covers this subject.

Kendō Meaning the 'way of the sword', Kendō is the oldest of the martial arts. It was favoured by the samurai to acquire skills in swordsmanship, as well as the development of mental poise. Today it is practised with a bamboo stave and protective body armour, gauntlets and a face mask. The winner of a bout succeeds in landing blows to the face, arms, upper body or throat of an opponent.

Karate The martial art karate (literally meaning 'empty hands') may have originated in India, but was refined in China and travelled from there to Okinawa, where it took hold. It began in the 14th century and spread to the rest of Japan in the first half of last century. For this reason it is not considered a traditional Japanese martial art.

The emphasis is on unarmed combat, as the name of the sport implies. Blows are delivered with the fists or feet. For optimum performance, all movements require intense discipline of the mind. There are two methods of practising karate. The first is *kumite*, when two or more people spar together. The second is *kata*, when one person performs formal exercises.

Aikidō The roots of this solely defensive art can be traced to the Minamoto clan in the 10th century, but the modern form of aikidō was started in the 1920s by Ueshiba Morihei.

Aikidō draws on many different techniques, including shintō, karate and kendō. Breathing and meditation form an integral part of aikidō training, as does the concentration on movement derived from classical Japanese dance, and the awareness of *ki* (life force or will) flowing from the fingertips.

Judō This is probably the best-known martial art; it has become a popular sport worldwide and regularly features in the Olympic Games. The origins of this art are found in *jūjutsu*, a means of self-defence favoured by the samurai, which was modernised into judō (the 'gentle way') by Kano Jigoro in 1882. The basic principles and subtle skills of the art lie in defeating opponents simply by redirecting the opponents' strength against themselves.

Studying Martial Arts in Japan Aikidō, judō, karate and kendō can be studied in Japan. Less popular disciplines, such as *kyūdō* (Japanese archery) and sumō, also attract devotees from overseas. Relevant addresses:

All-Japan Judō Federation (Zen Nihon Judo Renmei; ☎ 03-3818-4199, c/o Kodokan) 1-16-30 Kasuga, Bukyō-ku, Tokyo

Amateur Archery Federation of Japan (☎ 03- 3481-2387, W www.archery.or.jp) Kishi Memorial Hall, 4th floor, 1-1-1 Jinan, Shibuya-ku, Tokyo

International Aikidō Federation (☎ 03-3203-9236, W www.aikido-international.org) 17-18 Wakamatsu-chō, Shinjuku-ku, Tokyo

Japan Kendō Federation (☎ 03-3211-5804, W www.kendo.or.jp) c/o Nippon Budokan, 2-3 Kitanomaru-kōen, Chiyoda-ku, Tokyo

Nihon Sumō Kyōkai (☎ 03-3623-5111, W www.sumo.or.jp/eng/index.php) c/o Kokugikan Sumō Hall, 1-3-28 Yokoami, Sumida-ku, Tokyo

World Union of Karate-dō Organisation (☎ 03-3503-6640) 4th floor, Sempaku Shinkokaikan Bldg, 1-15-16 Toranomon, Minato-ku, Tokyo

Skiing

Skiing developed in Japan in the 1950s and there are now more than 300 ski resorts, many with high-standard runs and snow-making equipment. The majority of resorts are concentrated on the island of Honshū, where the crowds are huge, the vertical drops rarely more than 400m and all runs start at altitudes of less than 2000m. Snow cover in southern and eastern Honshū is generally adequate, but can be sparse and icy.

Skiers on Hokkaidō, however, can look forward to powder skiing that rivals anything in the European Alps or the Rockies in the USA. Niseko and Furano, two of Hokkaidō's best resorts, have excellent facilities (Niseko has 43 lifts) and neither suffers from extreme crowding.

JNTO's *Skiing in Japan* pamphlet covers 20 resorts on Honshū and Hokkaidō, and has travel information, ski season dates, accommodation details, resort facilities and costs.

Skiing is normally possible from December to April, though the season can be shorter in some of Honshū's lower-altitude resorts.

Resort accommodation ranges from hostels to expensive hotels but is heavily booked during the ski season. There are many resorts at hot springs that double as *onsen* or bathing spas. Avoid weekends and holidays, when lift lines are long and accommodation and transportation are heavily booked.

Lift passes cost ¥3000 to ¥4500 a day. Daily rental of skis, stocks and boots can cost up to ¥5000; finding larger-size ski boots may be difficult. Equipment can be rented at resorts and some ski shops in bigger cities.

As well as downhill skiing, Japan also offers good terrain for cross-country skiing and touring, especially in the Hakodate region of Hokkaidō – a good way to get away from the crowds.

For more information on skiing in Japan, you should pick up a copy of TR Reid's *Ski Japan*. Every winter, *Kansai Time Out* magazine also features articles on ski fields that are within easy reach of Kansai. For information on the Web have a look at **Snow Japan** (W www.skijapanguide.com /index.php).

COURSES

There are courses for almost every aspect of Japanese culture. JNTO has a wealth of printed information available. Cultural Activities visas require applicants to attend 20 class-hours per week. Those wishing to work while studying need to apply for permission to do so.

Japanese Language

There is no shortage of Japanese-language schools in Japan, most of them found in the bigger cities of Tokyo, Osaka, Nagoya, Kōbe and Kyoto. Some offer only part-time instruction, while others offer full-time and intensive courses and may sponsor you for a Cultural Visa, which will allow you to work up to 20 hours a week (after receiving permission) while you study. The best place to look for Japanese-language schools is in *Kansai Time Out* magazine and the various Tokyo English-language magazines. Schools also occasionally advertise in the three English-language newspapers. Alternatively, ask at any JNTO-operated tourist information office.

Costs at full-time private Japanese-language schools vary hugely depending on the school's status and facilities. There is usually an application fee of ¥5000 to ¥30,000, plus an administration charge of ¥50,000 to ¥100,000 and the annual tuition fees of ¥350,000 to ¥600,000. Add accommodation and food, and it is easy to see why it may be necessary to work while you study.

Traditional Arts

Many local cultural centres and tourist offices can arrange short courses in Japanese arts, such as ceramics, *washi* (Japanese papermaking), *aizome* (indigo dyeing), woodworking, calligraphy, ink painting and ikebana. The best place to pursue these interests is Kyoto, where the TIC or the **International Community House** (☎ 075-752-3010) can put you in touch with qualified teachers.

WORK

Finding work in Japan is possible but it's nowhere near as easy or as lucrative as it used to be. Teaching English is still the most common job for Westerners, but bartending, hostessing, modelling and various writing/editorial jobs are also possible.

Whatever line of work you choose, it's essential to look neat and tidy for interviews – appearances are *very* important in Japan. You'll also need to be determined, and you should have a sizeable sum of money to carry you through while you are looking for work, and possibly to get you out of the country if you don't find any (it happens). Foreigners who have set up in Japan over the last few years maintain that a figure of around US$5000 or more is necessary to make a go of it in Japan. People do it with less, but they run the risk of ending up penniless and homeless before they find a job.

English Teaching

Teaching English has always been the most popular job for native English speakers in Japan. While it's a fairly common option, competition for the good jobs is very tight since many schools have failed as a result of Japan's weakened economy. A university degree is an absolute essential as you cannot qualify for a work visa without one (be sure to bring the actual degree with you to Japan). Teaching qualifications and some teaching experience will be a huge plus when job hunting.

Consider lining up a job before arriving in Japan. Big schools, like Nova for example, now have recruitment programmes in the USA and the UK. One downside to the big 'factory schools' that recruit overseas is that working conditions are often pretty dire compared with smaller schools that recruit within Japan.

Australians, New Zealanders and Canadians, who can take advantage of the Japanese Working-Holiday Visa (see Visas earlier), are in a slightly better position. Schools are happier about taking on unqualified teachers if they don't have to bother with sponsoring a teacher for a work visa.

Private Schools The classifieds section of the Monday edition of the *Japan Times* is the best place to look for teaching positions. Some larger schools rely on direct inquiries from would-be teachers.

Tokyo is the easiest place to find teaching jobs; schools across Japan advertise or recruit in the capital. Heading straight to another of Japan's major population centres (say Osaka, Fukuoka, Hiroshima or Sapporo), where there are smaller numbers of competing foreigners, is also a good bet.

Check the fine print carefully once you have an offer. Find out how many hours you will teach, whether class preparation time is paid for and whether you receive sick leave and paid holidays. Find out also how and when you will be paid and if the school will sponsor your visa. It's worth checking conditions with other foreign staff. Ask whether your school is prepared to serve as a guarantor in the event that you rent an apartment.

Government Schools The programme run by **Japan Exchange & Teaching** (JET; W www.jetprogramme.org) provides 2000 teaching assistant positions for foreign teachers. The job operates on a yearly contract and must be organised in your home country. The programme gets very good reports from many of its teachers.

Teachers employed by the JET programme are known as Assistant Language Teachers (ALTs). Although you will have to apply in your home country in order to work as an ALT with JET, it's worth bearing in mind that many local governments in Japan are also employing ALTs for their schools. Such work can sometimes be arranged within Japan.

Visit the JET website or contact the nearest Japanese embassy or consulate for more details.

International Schools Major cities such as Tokyo and Yokohama, with large foreign populations, have a number of international schools for the children of foreign residents. Work is available for qualified, Western-trained teachers in all disciplines; the schools will usually organise your visa.

Proofreading & Editing

There is work, particularly in the Tokyo area, for editors, proofreaders and translators (Japanese to English and vice-versa). Needless to say, it is difficult for the casual visitor to simply waltz into these jobs – you'll need to have the proper qualifications and experience. And even for proofreading and editing, some Japanese-language ability is a huge plus, if only for

dealing with clients. If you think you've got what it takes, check the Monday edition of the *Japan Times* for openings.

Hostessing

A hostess is a woman who is paid to pour drinks for and chat with (usually) male customers in a so-called 'hostess bar'. Although hostessing does involve a lot of thinly veiled sexual innuendos and the occasional furtive grab at thighs or breasts, it is not a form of prostitution. However, at some of the seedier places, there may be some pressure to perform 'extracurricular activities'.

Hostessing involves late hours, frequent pressure to drink, and exposure to astonishing amounts of cigarette smoke. Hostesses should avoid being too casual about safety precautions if seeing clients outside working hours – there have been cases of foreign hostesses being raped and murdered by clients in Japan. See Women Travellers earlier for more information on safety issues.

Work visas are not issued for hostesses. Rates for Western women working as hostesses typically range from ¥3000 to ¥5000 per hour (plus tips), with bonuses for bringing customers to the club. An ability to speak Japanese is an asset, but not essential – many Japanese salarymen want to practise their English.

Bartending

Bartending does not qualify you for a work visa; most of the foreign bartenders in Japan are either working illegally or are on another kind of visa. Some bars in big Japanese cities hire foreign bartenders; most are strict about visas but others don't seem to care. The best places to look are 'gaijin bars', although a few Japanese-oriented places also employ foreign bartenders for 'ambiance'. The pay is barely enough to survive on – usually about ¥1000 per hour.

Modelling

Modelling jobs for foreigners are increasingly dominated by professional models; you will need a proper portfolio of photographs. Nonprofessionals are more likely to pick up casual work as extras in advertising or film.

ACCOMMODATION

Japan offers an interesting range of accommodation, from cheap guesthouses to first-class hotels, with almost everything in between. Although most options are more expensive than what you'd expect to pay in other Asian countries, you can still find some bargains.

JNTO offices abroad and TIC offices in Tokyo and Kyoto stock some useful materials such as the *Directory of Welcome Inns*, a very extensive listing of foreigner-friendly accommodation, and the Japanese Inn Group's (**w** www.jpinn.com) booklet, which has a number of ryokan (Japanese-style inn) throughout Japan that are used to dealing with foreigners.

Youth hostels are one of the cheapest options. The typical cost is ¥2400 to ¥3000. But staying only at youth hostels, will cut you off from an essential part of the Japan experience. Try to vary your accommodation with stays at a traditional ryokan, a *shukubō* (temple lodging) and a *minshuku* (Japanese B&B).

The best place to look for accommodation is around the main train station or bus terminal in any town. Here you'll usually find a mix of regular hotels and business hotels, with perhaps a few budget ryokan thrown in for good measure. Cheap guesthouses and youth hostels are usually some distance away from the town centre, but are almost always accessible by public transport. If you do find yourself without a place to stay and it's getting late, the best advice is to ask at the local *kōban* (police box) – they'll usually be able to point you in the right direction

Reservations & Checking In

It is quite feasible to look for a room after arriving in a new town, though it's always a good idea to make accommodation reservations a few days in advance if possible. During peak holiday seasons you should book as far ahead as possible, particularly if you have a special choice. Out of season, calling a day in advance is usually sufficient.

Tourist information offices at main train stations can usually help with reservations, and are often open until about 6.30pm or later. Even if you are travelling by car, the train station is a good first stop in town for information, reservations and cheap car parking. The Japanese run their accommodation according to an established rhythm that favours checkouts at around 10am and check-ins between 5pm and 7pm; unannounced early- or late-comers disturb this pattern.

Making phone reservations in English is usually possible in most major cities. Providing you speak clearly and simply, there will usually be someone around who can get the gist of what you want. There will also be occasions when hotel staff understand no English. If you really get stuck, try asking the desk staff at your current accommodation to phone your reservation through.

Welcome Inn Reservation Center

It is possible to make bookings at the **Welcome Inn Reservation Centers** (**w** www.itcj.or.jp) found in the TIC offices in Tokyo and Kyoto, and at Narita and Kansai airports (see JNTO Tourist Information Centers under Tourist Offices earlier). You can also make reservations online through its website (which is also an excellent source of information on member hotels and inns).

Hotels

You'll find a range of standard hotels in most Japanese cities and some resort areas. These range from typical mid-range hotels to first-class hotels that rank among the best in the world. Rates at standard mid-range hotels average ¥9000 for a single and ¥12,000 for a double or twin. Rates at first-class hotels average ¥15,000 for a single and ¥20,000 for a double or twin.

Like business hotels, you'll often find standard hotels near the main train station in a city. You can expect someone to speak English at the front desk, so making reservations and checking in shouldn't be the hassle it can be at other types of accommodation in Japan.

If you plan to stay in standard hotels during your stay in Japan, you might save some money by getting a package deal on transport and accommodation. Check with your airline or travel agency before you arrive.

Expect to pay 10% or more as a service charge plus a 5% consumer tax; add another 3% local tax if the bill exceeds ¥10,000. Asking for separate bills for meals can sometimes reduce the amount of tax charged.

Business Hotels These are economical and practical places geared to the single traveller, usually lesser-ranking business types who want to stay somewhere close to the station. Rooms are clean, Western style, just big enough for you to turn around in, and include a miniature bath/WC unit. A standard fitting for the stressed businessman is a coin-operated TV with a porno channel. Vending machines replace room service.

Cheap single rooms can sometimes be found for as low as ¥4500, though the aver-age rate is around ¥8000. Most business hotels also have twin and double rooms. They usually do not have a service charge.

Love Hotels As their name indicates, love hotels are used by Japanese couples for discreet trysts. You can use them for this purpose as well, but they're also per-fectly fine, if a little hokey, for overnight accommodation.

To find a love hotel on the street, just look for flamboyant facades with rococo-architecture, turrets, battlements and imi-tation statuary. Love hotels are designed for maximum privacy: entrances and exits are kept separate; keys are provided through a small opening without contact

---

Everything You Need to Know about Staying at a Ryokan

Note that the following describes a night at a mid-range or higher ryokan (traditional Japanese inn). Many ryokan in Japan that specialise in foreign guests may be much less formal and may not serve dinner or even breakfast.

On arrival at a ryokan, you leave your shoes at the entrance, don a pair of slippers, and are shown by a maid to your room, which has a tatami (reed mat) floor. Slippers are taken off before entering tatami rooms. Instead of using numbers, rooms are named after auspicious flowers, plants or trees.

The interior of the room will contain a *tokonoma* (alcove), probably decorated with a flower display or a calligraphy scroll. Do not step into or place any objects in the *tokonoma*. One side of the room will contain a cupboard with sliding doors for the bedding; the other side will have sliding screens covered with rice paper and, may perhaps, open onto a veranda with a garden view.

The room maid then serves tea, with a Japanese sweet, on a low table surrounded by *zabuton* (cushions) in the centre of the room. At the same time you are asked to sign the register. A tray is provided with a towel, *yukata* (cotton kimono) and *obi* (belt) which you put on before taking your bath. Remember to wrap the left side over the right – the reverse order is used for dressing the dead. In colder weather, there will also be a *tanzen* (outer jacket). Your clothes can be put away in a closet or left on a hanger.

Dressed in your *yukata*, you will be shown to the *o-furo* (bath). At some ryokan, there are rooms with private baths, but the communal ones are often designed with natural pools or a window looking out into a garden. Bathing is communal, but sexes are segregated. Make sure you can differentiate between the bathroom signs for men 男 and women 女, although ryokan used to catering for foreign-ers will often have signs in English. Many inns will have family bathrooms for couples or families.

Dressed in your *yukata* after your bath, you return to your room where the maid will have laid out dinner – in some ryokan, dinner is provided in a separate room but you still wear your *yukata* for dining. Depending on the price, meals at a ryokan can become flamboyant displays of local cuisine or refined arrangements of *kaiseki* (formal multicourse Japanese meal).

After dinner, while you potter around or go out for a stroll to admire the garden, the maid will clear the dishes and prepare your bedding. A futon is placed on the tatami floor and a quilt put on top. In colder weather, you can also add a *mōfu* (blanket).

In the morning, the maid will knock to make sure you are awake and then come in to put away the bedding before serving breakfast – sometimes this is served in a separate room.

Although ryokan etiquette can seem rather complicated at first, and some ryokan are a little wary of foreigners, once you grasp the basics you'll find yourself looking forward to the nights you spend in one. Truly, they are welcome havens for the weary traveller.

between desk clerk and guest; and photos of the rooms are displayed to make the choice easy for the customer. There's often a discreetly curtained parking area so your car cannot be seen once inside.

The rooms can fulfil most fantasies, with themes ranging from harem extravaganza to Tarzan-and-Jane jungle rooms. Choices can include vibrating beds, wall-to-wall mirrors, bondage equipment and video recorders to record the experience.

During the day, you can stay for a two- or three-hour 'rest' (*kyūkei* in Japanese) for about ¥4000 (rates are for the whole room, not per person). Love hotels are of more interest to foreign visitors after 10pm, when it's possible to stay the night for about ¥6500, but you should check out early enough in the morning to avoid a return to peak-hour rates. There will usually be a sign in Japanese (occasionally in English) outside the hotel, announcing its rates. Even if you can't read Japanese, you should be able to figure out which rate applies to a 'rest' and which applies to an overnight stay.

In theory, you can cram as many people as you like into a love hotel room; in practice you may be limited to two people and same-sex couples may be asked to pay more or may even be rejected outright.

Capsule Hotels One of Japan's most famous forms of accommodation is the *capseru hoteru*. As the name implies, the 'rooms' in a capsule hotel consist of banks of neat white capsules stacked in rows two or three high. The capsules themselves are about 2m by 1m by 1m – about the size of a spacious coffin. Inside is a bed, a TV, a reading light, a radio and an alarm clock. Personal belongings are kept in a locker room.

This type of hotel is common in major cities and often caters to workers who have partied too hard to make it home or have missed the last train. The majority are only for men but some also accept women; the women's quarters are usually in a separate part of the building. Most capsule hotels have the added attraction of a sauna and a large communal bath.

An average price is ¥3800 per night. You could try one as a novelty, but it's not an experience recommended to those who suffer from claustrophobia.

Ryokan

For a taste of traditional Japanese life, a stay at a ryokan is mandatory. Ryokan range from ultra-exclusive establishments to reasonably priced places with a homey atmosphere. Prices start at around ¥4000 (per person, per night) for a 'no-frills' ryokan without meals (*sudomari* is the Japanese term for 'no meals'). For a classier ryokan, expect prices to start at ¥8000. Exclusive establishments – Kyoto is a prime centre for these – charge ¥25,000 and often much more.

Ryokan owners prefer to charge on a room and board (breakfast and dinner) basis per person. If, like many foreigners, you find yourself overwhelmed by the unusual offerings of a Japanese breakfast, it should be possible to have dinner only but, in many ryokan, opting out of both meals is unacceptable. The bill is reduced by about 10% if you decline breakfast.

A service charge or consumption tax may be added to your bill in some establishments. Because this is not always the case and the amount may vary, it's best to ask when making reservations or checking in.

Ryokan Guides & Addresses Regional guides to ryokan and hotels that welcome foreigners are published by the **Welcome Inn Reservation Center** (see the entry on this under Tourist Offices earlier in this section). The *Directory of Welcome Inns* pamphlets are available at TICs, where bookings can be made. Prices quoted start from ¥4000.

JNTO publishes the *Japan Ryokan Guide*, a listing of government-registered members of the Japan Ryokan Association (JRA). Prices quoted start around ¥8000 and rise to astronomical heights.

Minshuku

A *minshuku* is usually a family-run private lodging, rather like a Western-style B&B. *Minshuku* can be found throughout Japan and offer an experience of daily Japanese life. The average price per person, per night is around ¥6000, with two meals. You are expected to lay out and put away your bedding, and provide your own towel.

Japan Minshuku Association (*☎ 03-3364-1855; Suegawa Bldg, 4-10-15, Takadanobaba,*

Shinjuku-ku, Tokyo 169-0075), has a leaflet in English describing the *minshuku* concept and providing advice on staying at one; a list of *minshuku* is also available. The **Nihon Minshuku Center** *(☎ 03-3216-6556; ⓦ www.minshuku.co.jp/english.html; Tokyo Kōtsū Kaikan Bldg, 2-10-1 Yūraku-chō, Chiyoda-ku, Tokyo 100-0006)*, can help with computer bookings; a similar office operates in Kyoto. Some of the places listed in the Japanese Inn Group's handy little booklet (see earlier) are really *minshuku* rather than ryokan. The line between the two accommodation categories can be fuzzy.

Guesthouses

Guesthouses are often old Japanese houses that have been converted into cheap inns, many expressly aimed at foreign travellers. Some also double as '*gaijin* houses' (see Long-Term Accommodation later in this section). Guesthouses are particularly common in Kyoto but you'll also find a few scattered about Tokyo. The advantage of guesthouses is that they offer youth hostel prices without the regimented routine. Of course, some guesthouses can be pretty run down, and it's well worth taking a look around before paying your money. Where possible, we list guesthouses in the appropriate Places to Stay sections; otherwise, the best way to find guesthouses is by looking in magazines like *Kansai Time Out*, or by word of mouth.

Pensions

Pensions are usually run by young couples offering Western-style accommodation based on the European pension concept, and many offer sports and leisure facilities. They are common in resort areas and around ski fields. Prices average ¥6000 per person per night or ¥8500 including two meals. Food is often excellent, typically a French dinner and an American breakfast.

Youth Hostels

For budget travellers, youth hostels are the best option, and it is quite feasible to plan an entire itinerary using them. The best source of information on youth hostels is the *Japan Youth Hostel Handbook*, which is available for ¥580 from the **Japan Youth Hostel Association** *(JYHA; ☎ 03-3288-1417; ⓦ www.jyh.or.jpenglishindex.html; Suido-bashi Nishi-guchi Kaikan, 2-20-7 Misaki-chō, Chiyoda-ku, Tokyo 101-0061)*. Many youth hostels in Japan sell this handbook.

The JYHA handbook is mostly in Japanese, though there is some English in the symbol key at the front and on the locater map keys. The hostels on each map are identified by name (in kanji) and given a page reference. Each hostel is accompanied by a mini-map, photo, address in Japanese, fax and phone details, a row of symbols, access instructions in Japanese, open dates, number of beds and prices for bed and meals.

Another good way to find hostels is the *Youth Hostel Map of Japan*, which has one-line entries on each hostel. It's available for free from JNTO and TICs in Japan.

The best way to find hostels is the JYHA website, which has details in English on all member hostels, and allows online reservations.

Youth hostels in Japan are usually comfortable, inexpensive by Japanese standards, and often good sources of information when used as a base for touring. They are also a good way to meet Japanese travellers and other foreigners. By carefully studying the JYHA handbook, you can select interesting places and weed out possible duds. Many hostels have superb sites: some are farms, remote temples, outstanding private homes or elegant inns.

However, some hostels have a routine strongly reminiscent of school, or perhaps even prison. In the high season, you are likely to encounter waves of school children and students. Finally, if you are reliant on public transport, access to some youth hostels is complicated and time-consuming.

Membership & Regulations You can stay at over 70 municipal hostels without a youth hostel membership card. Elsewhere, you will need a JYHA membership card or one from an affiliate of the International Youth Hostel Federation (IYHF), otherwise you must pay an extra charge. It is much simpler if you become a member in your own country, as JYHA registration requires members to have lived in Japan for a year, have an Alien Registration Card and pay a ¥2000 joining fee.

Nonmembers must pay an additional ¥600 per night for a 'welcome stamp'. Six welcome stamps plus a photograph entitles you to an IYHF International Guest Card valid worldwide for the rest of the year. If you purchase all six stamps at once, the price is reduced to ¥2800, a saving of ¥800.

Youth hostel membership has a minimum age limit of four years but no maximum age – you will meet plenty of Japanese seniors, and often a few foreign ones approaching their 70s.

Hostel charges currently average ¥2800 per night; some also add the 5% consumption tax. Private rooms are available in some hostels from ¥3500 per night. As a friendly gesture, some hostels have introduced a special reduction – sometimes as much as ¥500 per night – for foreign hostellers.

Average prices for meals are ¥500 for breakfast and ¥900 for dinner. Almost all hostels require that you use a regulation sleeping sheet, which you can rent for ¥100 if you do not have your own. Although official regulations state that you can only stay at one hostel for three consecutive nights, this is sometimes waived outside the high season.

Hostellers are expected to check in between 3pm and 8pm to 9pm. There is usually a curfew of 10pm or 11pm. Checkout is usually before 10am and dormitories are closed between 10am and 3pm. Bath time is usually between 5pm and 9pm, dinner is between 6pm and 7.30pm, and breakfast is between 7am and 8am.

Reservations Advance reservations are essential for the New Year holiday weeks, the late April/early May Golden Week period, and July and August. You should state the arrival date and time, number of nights' stay, number and sex of the people for whom beds are to be reserved, and which meals are required. The easiest way to reserve is via the JYHA website (**w** www.jyh.or.jp /english/index.html). Or, if you can muster enough Japanese, telephone bookings are the way to go. If you can't speak Japanese and can't get online, you can always ask a Japanese person (perhaps a fellow hosteller or a youth hostel owner) to make the call for you.

Out of season you can probably get away with booking a day or so in advance. Hostels definitely prefer you to phone, even if it's from across the street, rather than simply roll up without warning. If you arrive without warning, you shouldn't expect any meals.

Toho
The Toho network is a diverse collection of places that has banded loosely together to offer a more flexible alternative to youth hostels. Toho network inns ascribe to a common philosophy of informal hospitality at reasonable prices. Most of the network's 90 members are in Hokkaidō, although there are a few scattered around Honshū and other islands further south. The owners may not speak much (if any) English and you should *definitely* phone ahead to make reservations, even if it's just from a phone box down the street. The main drawback (or attraction for some travellers) of these places is that many of them are difficult to reach. Many owners, however, will provide a free pick-up service from the nearest train or bus station if you make arrangements in advance.

Prices average ¥4000, or ¥5000 with two meals for dormitory-style accommodation. Private rooms are sometimes available for about ¥1000 extra. A comprehensive Japanese-language Toho network guide (¥200) with detailed directions is available at bookshops in Hokkaidō or from Toho network inns. You can find information on the Toho network at **w** www.toho.net /english.htm. This site features a number of helpful links to individual member inn homepages.

Kokumin-shukusha
Kokumin-shukusha (people's lodges) are government-supported institutions offering affordable accommodation in scenic areas. Private Japanese-style rooms are the norm, though some places offer Western-style rooms. Prices average ¥5500 to ¥6500 per person per night including two meals. The best way to find *kokumin-shukusha* is to ask at local tourist offices or *kōban*.

Shukubō
Staying in a *shukubō* (temple lodging) is one way to experience another facet of

traditional Japan. Sometimes you are allocated a simple room in the temple precincts and left to your own devices. Other times, you may be asked to participate in prayers, services or *zazen* (sitting) meditation. At some temples, exquisite vegetarian meals *(shōjin ryōri)* are served.

The TICs in Tokyo and Kyoto both produce leaflets on temple lodgings in their regions. Kōya-san, a renowned religious centre in the Kansai region, includes over 50 *shukubō* and is one of the best places in Japan to try this type of accommodation.

Over 70 youth hostels are temples or shrines – look for the reverse swastika symbol in the JYHA handbook. The suffixes *-ji*, *-in* or *-dera* are also clues that the hostel is a temple.

Mountain Huts

Mountain huts *(yama-goya)* are common in many of Japan's hiking and mountain-climbing areas. While you'll occasionally find free emergency shelters, most huts are privately run and charge for accommodation. These places offer bed and board (two meals) at around ¥5000 to ¥8000 per person; if you prepare your own meal that figure drops to ¥3000 to ¥5000 per person. It's best to call ahead to reserve a spot (numbers are available in Japanese hiking guides and maps, and in Lonely Planet's *Hiking in Japan*), but you won't be turned away if you show up without a reservation.

Camping Grounds

Camping is the cheapest form of accommodation in Japan, but official camping grounds are often open only during the Japanese 'camping season' (July and August). Facilities range from bare essentials to deluxe. JNTO publishes *Camping in Japan*, a limited selection of camping grounds with details of prices and facilities.

In some restricted areas and national parks, wild camping is forbidden, but elsewhere, foreigners have reported consistent success. Even where there is no officially designated camping ground, campers are often directed to the nearest large patch of grass. Provided you set up camp late in the afternoon and leave early, nobody seems to mind, though it is common courtesy to ask permission first (assuming you can find the person responsible). Public toilets, usually spotless, and water taps are very common, even in remote parts of Japan.

The best areas for camping are Hokkaidō, the Japan Alps, Tōhoku and Okinawa.

Rider Houses

Catering mainly to touring motorcyclists, rider houses *(raidā hausu)* provide extremely basic shared accommodation from around ¥1000 per night. Some rider houses are attached to local *rāmen* shops or other eateries, and may offer discounted rates if you agree to eat there. You should bring your own sleeping bag or ask to rent bedding from the owner. For bathing facilities, you will often be directed to the local *sentō*. Although rider houses may not be the most comfortable places, they are generally safe for both sexes and are good places to meet alternative, independent Japanese travellers, including bicyclists, hitchhikers and other shoestring travellers.

There are innumerable rider houses throughout Hokkaidō, as well as a few in southern Japan, mainly Kyūshū and Okinawa. If you ask around town or at the local tourist information office for a *raidā hausu*, someone will probably point you in the right direction. Unfortunately, many rider houses are located out of town and are hard to reach on public transport. If you can read some Japanese, spiral-bound *Touring Mapple* maps, published by Shobunsha, mark almost all of the rider houses in a specific region, as well as cheap places to eat along the way. These maps are available at most Japanese bookshops.

Cycling Terminals

Cycling terminals *(saikuringu tāminaru)* provide low-priced accommodation of the bunk-bed or tatami-mat variety and are usually found in scenic areas suited to cycling. If you don't have your own bike, you can rent one at the terminal.

At around ¥2500 per person per night or ¥4000 including two meals, terminal prices compare favourably with those of a youth hostel. For more information contact the **Japan Bicycle Promotion Institute** (☎ 03-3583-5444; w *www.jbpi.or.jp/english*; *Nihon Jitensha Kaikan Bldg, 1-9-3 Akasaka, Minato-ku, Tokyo*).

Long-Term Accommodation

If you intend to stay longer in Japan, a job offer that appears lucrative may seem markedly less so when you work out your rent and other living costs. Ideally, you can avoid many hassles by negotiating decent accommodation as part of your work contract.

If at all possible, you should get a Japanese friend to help you with your search and negotiations, as Japanese landlords are notoriously wary of foreign tenants and often prefer to do business with a local go-between. If you are on good terms with a Japanese friend, this person may offer to act as a *hoshō-nin* (guarantor). This represents considerable commitment and the guarantor's *hanko* is usually required on your rental contract.

A pitfall, often overlooked, is that you may have to lay out the equivalent of several months' rent upfront. For starters, there's the equivalent of one to two months' rent payable as *reikin* (key money). This is a nonrefundable gift that goes into the pocket of the landlord. Then there's a *shikikin* (damage deposit) of one to three months' rent. This is refundable at a later date as long as both sides agree there's no damage. The *fudōsan-yasan* (real estate agent) will of course want *tesūryō* – the equivalent of one month's rent as a nonrefundable handling fee. Finally, you may have to pay *maekin,* which is equal to one month's rent in advance, and this may also be nonrefundable.

Of course, there are various ways around all these costs. If you get in with the local foreigners' scene in a particular city, you may get tipped off to open apartments and houses for which nothing more than monthly rent is required (this is particularly true outside Tokyo). If you can't afford to pay all the usual fees for an apartment or house in Japan, try looking a little bit harder and you might be able to find a special deal.

Where to Look There are several different methods to hunt for housing – it depends on what you want and how long you intend to stay.

Asking other foreigners at work or play in schools, clubs, bars and *gaijin* houses is one way of locating long-term accommo-dation. If you strike it lucky, you may find somebody leaving the country or moving on, who is willing to dump their job contacts, housing and effects in one friendly package.

Notice boards are another good source of information and are often found at tourist information offices, international clubs, conversation clubs etc. Even if there's nothing on the board, ask someone in charge for a few tips.

Regional and city magazines aimed at foreigners often have classified ads offering or seeking accommodation. In the Kansai area you should check out *Kansai Time Out*; in Tokyo check any of the numerous English-language publications available. There are plenty of magazines all over Japan with suitable ads. The TIC or the local tourist office should know which publications are best, particularly if you decide to live somewhere more remote, such as Hokkaidō or Okinawa.

Using a real estate agent is the most expensive option, and really only feasible if you intend to stay a long time and need to determine exactly the type and location of your housing. English-language magazines such as *Kansai Time Out* sometimes carry ads from estate agents specialising in accommodation for foreigners.

ENTERTAINMENT

Japan offers visitors a wealth of entertainment opportunities: including everything from kabuki to the latest in club music. Tokyo, Osaka and Kyoto are the best places for entertainment, but provincial cities and rural tourist destinations often turn up a surprise find.

The only complaint most visitors have with entertainment in Japan is the price. Cinema tickets, for example, range from ¥1800 to ¥2400, which probably makes Japan the most expensive place in the world to catch a movie. Live music prices are also high, ranging from around ¥1500 for a local act to ¥6000 and upwards for international performers.

The best way to find out what's on while you're in town is to check out the local English-language publications. TICs often have listings of upcoming events, and these are usually the best way to find out about traditional Japanese cultural events.

Izakaya

Izakaya are traditional pub-style restaurants where Japanese workers (mostly male) congregate to drink beer and sake. The drinks are usually accompanied by simple but hearty dishes like *niku jagga* (meat-and-potato stew) and plates of sashimi.

Izakaya are great places to meet the locals, and you'll find that a few glasses of sake breaks down language barriers faster than years of intensive language study. A meal and a few drinks in an *izakaya* will usually set you back around ¥3000. For more on *izakaya*, see the 'Japanese Cuisine' special section.

Bars

The range of bars in Japan is enormous: in cities like Tokyo and Osaka, you can rest assured that no matter what your musical, aesthetic and alcoholic tastes, you will find something right up your alley.

The most accessible bars for foreigners are known as *'gaijin* bars'. It's well worth calling into at least one of these bar while you're in Japan – like *izakaya*, they are great places to meet young Japanese and a few resident expats while you're at it.

Very few of the *gaijin* bars recommended in this book have entry charges, and where they do they are usually the price of a drink ticket, just to ensure that you do spend some money while you are there. Drink prices generally average ¥550 for a beer and ¥800 for spirits.

Another common form of bar in Japan is the hostess bar. Most of Japan's major cities have entire neighbourhoods devoted exclusively to hostess bars (when you see the buildings with hundreds of brightly coloured signs outside, you'll know it contains hostess bars). In these bars, young ladies (mostly Japanese, but there are foreign hostess bars) are paid to pour drinks for and chat up Japanese salarymen. Unless you fancy the idea of shelling out ¥10,000 for two drinks (assuming they'd let you in the first place), we recommend staying well clear of these spots.

Finally, if you want a civilised drink but don't fancy the idea of a *gaijin* bar, you should head to a top-end hotel. Most of these have elegant bars somewhere on their premises and they will have no problems with foreign customers. Best of all, if the hotel is a tall one, the bar will almost always be on or near the top floor, and you'll be able to enjoy the night view while you sip your drink.

Live Houses

A 'live house' is a uniquely Japanese expression for a small local club where independent bands and solo artists perform. These places can be a lot of fun but, as with such places anywhere in the world, the quality of the experience depends almost entirely on the quality of the act. The best way to find out who's playing is to check the local English-language publications or to ask local expats or Japanese.

Clubs & Discos

Most of Japan's big cities have various forms of clubs and discos where you can dance to a variety of music, from salsa to electronica to funk and rap. Bear in mind that most of these places have a ¥2000 to ¥5000 cover charge (this sometimes includes a few 'free' drinks). If you don't fancy shelling out for this, you can usually find free places to dance in big cities like Tokyo and Osaka. As usual, the local English-language publications and expats are your best source of information here.

Cinemas

If you are willing to fork out a fistful of yen (¥1800 to ¥2400) for your movie-going pleasure, Japan's major cities (in particular Tokyo) offer the opportunity to catch up with everything from the latest Hollywood blockbusters to rare art-house releases. Foreign movies are shown in their original language and subtitled in Japanese, which is a boon for foreign movie-goers. The English-language newspapers and magazines all have extensive movie listings.

Traditional Entertainment

Kabuki is one of the most popular traditional entertainments, and the best place to see it is in Tokyo. This is also true of nō (classical theatre), though tickets tend to sell out quickly and performance schedules vary – check with the TIC. Bunraku is an Osaka tradition. In Kyoto there are tourist performances that include a little of everything, such as *kyogen* (comic interludes) and *gagaku* (court orchestral music).

Geisha entertainment is too expensive for most travellers. Some operators offer 'geisha night tours' of Tokyo. The real thing will cost around ¥50,000 per head (or more) and will require an introduction by a well-connected Japanese person.

SPECTATOR SPORT
Sumō

Japanese wrestling is a simple sport; it's the ritual surrounding it that is complicated. The rules of the game are deceptively simple – the *higashi* (east) wrestler tries either to push his *nishi* (west) opponent out of the ring or unbalance him so that some part of his body other than his feet touch the ground. The 4.55m-diameter ring *(dohyō)* is on a raised platform, much like a boxing ring, but there the similarity ends. Sumō matches do not go 10 rounds: they are brief and often spectacular and the ritual and build up to the encounter is just as important as the clash itself.

There are no weight classes in sumō; they're all big, and in a nation of trim people, sumō wrestlers certainly stand out. Gargantuan bulk is the order of the day and sumō wrestlers achieve this through diet (or lack of it). Large quantities of a fattening stew called *chankonabe* are consumed, along with other fattening foods like *yaki-niku* (grilled meat). Would-be sumō wrestlers, usually 15-year-olds from rural areas, traditionally join one of the 28 *heya* (stables) of wrestlers, often run by retired fighters, and work their way up through the ranks.

Sumō still retains traces of its connections to Shintō rites, including the shrine-like roof which hangs over the ring and the *gyōji* (referee) in his wizard-like outfit. It is said that the dagger worn by the referee was to allow him to commit instant *seppuku* (ritual suicide) if he made a bad refereeing decision! The wrestlers wear a *mawashi* with a broad leather belt; it's rather like a *fundoshi* (the traditional loincloth drawn between the buttocks). A good grasp on the belt is a favourite hold but there are 48 recognised holds and throws.

The preliminaries often last far longer than the actual struggle, as the opponents first hurl salt into the *dohyō* to purify it and then put great effort into psyching each other out with malevolent looks and baleful stares. A series of false starts often follows before two immovable objects finally collide with an earth-shaking wallop. Sometimes that initial collision is enough to tip one wrestler out of the ring, but usually there's a brief interlude of pushing, shoving, lifting and tripping. Sometimes neither opponent is able to get a grip on the other and they stand there slapping at each other like two angry and very overweight infants.

The Tokyo sumō stables are in Ryōgoku, near the new Kokugikan sumō arena. Six major sumō *basho* (tournaments) are held each year: January (Tokyo – Kokugikan Stadium), March (Osaka – Furitsu Taiikukan Gymnasium), May (Tokyo – Kokugikan Stadium), July (Nagoya – Aichi Prefectural Gymnasium), September (Tokyo – Kokugikan Stadium) and November (Fukuoka – Kokusai Center).

Each tournament commences on the Sunday closest to the 10th of the month and lasts 15 days, during which each wrestler competes in one bout a day. The big crowds arrive in the late afternoon to watch the top-ranking wrestlers; the earlier part of the day is reserved for the lower-ranking fighters.

At a sumō tournament, prices start at ¥1000 for a bench seat at the back. If you can afford ¥7000 for a balcony seat, you will be both closer to the action and able to delve into the mysteries of the refreshment bag that comes with the ticket. Ringside seats are highly prized and virtually unobtainable unless you have inside contacts. Tune in to Far East Network (FEN) on 810kHz for simultaneous radio coverage of the action in English. TV coverage is extensive and most of the English-language newspapers devote a section to sumō.

If you want to see a sumō bout, but arrive in Japan at a time when no tournament is being held, you can visit one of the sumō stables to watch training. JNTO publishes the leaflet *Traditional Sports*, which has a sumō section with full details of tournaments, tickets purchase, visits to sumō stables and even a bibliography of books and magazines in English on the subject. Contact the TIC for more information.

For more information on sumō, check out the **Nihon Sumō Kyōkai** homepage (**W** www.sumo.or.jp/eng/index.php).

Baseball

Sumō may be the most Japanese of sporting activities, but baseball is Japan's number-one sport, both for spectators and participants. Baseball bounced into Japan in 1873 with the US teacher Horace Wilson, who taught at Tokyo University. There have been professional teams since the 1930s and, just as in the USA, there are little-league teams, school teams, work teams and 'bunch of friends in the local park' teams. At the professional level, however, baseball is big business and the nightly televised games draw huge audiences.

Despite the similarity to American baseball – even many of the terms are carried over without translation – baseball here has been cleverly altered to fit the Japanese culture. Read Robert Whiting's *You've Got to Have Wa* for the full story on baseball Japanese-style; even the Japanese emphasis on the group over the individual has played its part in fitting baseball into the Japanese mould – *wa* means something like 'team spirit'.

Japanese professional baseball is divided into two leagues: Central and Pacific. Each league has six teams, which are owned by large corporations. Each team is allowed two *gaijin* players, usually Americans past their prime or facing some sort of contractual difficulty in the USA. They often have trouble adapting to the Japanese requirements that they be just another member of the team, not rock the boat and definitely not show up the local stars!

The season lasts from April to October and is followed by the Japan Series, a seven-match contest between the top two teams. In Tokyo, the centre of the baseball universe is the Tokyo Dome next to Kōraku-en Amusement Park. Expect to pay around ¥1000 for a basic seat.

The All-Japan High School Baseball Championship Tournaments are taken very seriously in Japan. These are the major annual sporting events when the flower of youthful vitality goes on display. During August, when the summer tournament is in progress, baseball seems to be the only topic on anyone's mind.

For more information on Japanese baseball, check out the **Nippon Professional Baseball Organization of Japan** website (**w** www.npb-bis.com).

Soccer

Japan's interest in soccer was given a huge boost by the 2002 World Cup, which was held jointly in Japan and Korea. Japan's **J.League** (**w** www.j-league.or.jp/english _sitemap/index.html). professional soccer league comprises 16 teams. Excitement about the sport has died since the league's inaugural year of 1993, when it seemed that soccer was poised to sweep away all other sports and become a national obsession. The sport is still popular though, and the ruling that teams are allowed to employ up to five foreign players means that some of the world's best goal-scorers are lifting the standard of play. In Tokyo, matches are played at the National Stadium. For more on J.League, check out the official website.

SHOPPING

Although Japan is one of the world's most expensive countries, there are some good bargains out there, and you can certainly return home with a bag full of goodies without breaking the bank. As well as all the electronic gadgetry available in Japan, there is a wide range of traditional crafts to choose from, though for good stuff you really need to spend big money. It pays to shop around if you have anything particular in mind. The big department stores, which often have the best selections of Japanese gift items, can vary enormously in their prices from one store to another. In some shops, you are paying for extras such as the high level of service (a feature of all Japanese shops anyway), location and interior decor.

Tax-Free Shopping

Shopping tax-free in Japan is not necessarily the bargain that you might expect. Although tax-free shops enable foreigners to receive an exemption from the 5% consumption tax (*shōhi-zei*) levied on most items, these still may not be the cheapest places to shop. Shops that offer this exemption usually require that you pay the consumption tax and then go to a special counter to receive a refund. You will often need to show your passport to receive this refund. Tax-free shops will usually have a sign in English that announces their tax-free status.

Photographic Equipment

Tokyo is an excellent hunting ground for photographic equipment. As almost all of the big-name brands in camera equipment are locally produced, prices can be very competitive. The prices for accessories, such as motor drives and flash units, can even be compared to Singapore and Hong Kong. In addition, shopping in Japan presents the shopper with none of the rip-off risks that abound in other Asian discount capitals.

Be prepared to shop around. Tokyo's Shinjuku area is the best place for buying camera equipment, although Ginza too has a good selection of camera shops. Second-hand camera equipment is worth checking out. In Tokyo, both Shinjuku and Ginza have a fair number of second-hand shops where camera and lens quality is usually very good and prices are around half what you would pay for new equipment. In Osaka, the area just south of Osaka station has used-camera shops as well.

Electronics

Nowhere in the world will you find a better selection of electronics than in Tokyo's Akihabara district and Osaka's Den-Den Town. Keep in mind though that much of the electrical gadgetry on sale in Japan is designed for Japan's curious power supply (100V at 50 or 60Hz) and may require a transformer for use overseas. The safest bet is to go for export models – the prices may be slightly higher but, in the long run, you'll save the expense of converting the equipment to suit the conditions in your own country. Big electronics stores in Japan are about the only places where a little bargaining (don't get too carried away – this is not India!) will bring prices down around 10% or so. Just ask politely for a discount (this word is understood in Japan) and you'll probably receive one.

Computers

Computers, computer accessories and software are widely available. Unfortunately for the foreign traveller, most of what's out there – operating systems, keyboards and software – is in Japanese and not of any use unless you intend to work with the Japanese language. However, if you're after hardware like peripherals, chips and the like, where language isn't a factor, you will find lots to choose from, including second-hand goods at unbelievably low prices (check the Sofmap store in Osaka's Den-Den Town).

Music

When it comes to the recording arts, Japan could teach the West a thing or two. Japanese pressings are famed for their high fidelity, and there are stores devoted to every genre and subgenre of every style of music, especially in Tokyo. Prices range from ¥1500 to ¥2300. Local pressings are *more expensive* than imports – but you pay for quality.

Pearls

The Japanese firm Mikimoto developed the technique of producing cultured pearls by artificially introducing an irritant into the pearl oyster. Pearls and pearl jewellery are still popular buys for foreign visitors, but it would be wise to check prices in your own country. Size, quality and colour will all have a bearing on the price. Toba, in the Ise area (Kansai) is a centre for the production of cultured pearls.

Cars, Motorcycles & Bicycles

Information on purchasing cars, motorcycles and bicycles can be found in the Getting Around chapter.

Clothes

Japanese-made clothes and shoes are of excellent quality and needn't cost a fortune. It really is a matter of looking around and finding something that suits your budget, taste and – here's the hard part – your size! In upmarket and fashionable districts, many of the clothes shops are exclusive boutiques with exclusive prices, although there are always clusters of stores nearby that are more affordable. In less fashionable areas there are countless retail outlets for an industry providing economical, mass-produced versions of designer clothes. If you fit into the smaller sizes in your home country, you shouldn't have any problems finding clothes to fit (although pant/trouser length may cut it fine). Shoe size can also be a problem if your feet are anything bigger than what most Westerners would consider medium-sized.

Toys

Tokyo has some remarkable toy shops. See Kids' Stuff under Shopping in the Tokyo chapter for more information. Elsewhere, look out for some of the traditional wooden toys produced as regional specialities – they make good souvenirs for adults and children alike.

Japanese Arts & Crafts

As well as all the hi-tech knick-knacks produced by the Japanese, it is also possible to go home loaded with traditional Japanese arts and crafts. Anything from carp banners to kimono can make good souvenirs for the Japanophile.

Ningyō (Japanese Dolls) Not for playing with, Japanese dolls are usually intended for display. Often quite exquisite, with coiffured hair and dressed in kimono, they make excellent souvenirs or gifts. Also available are *gogatsu-ningyō*, dolls dressed in samurai suits used as gifts on Kodomo-no-hi (Children's Day). The most famous dolls are made in Kyoto and are known as *kyō-ningyō*.

Ningyō can be bought in tourist shops, department stores and special doll shops. In Tokyo, Edo-dōri in Asakusa is well known for its many doll shops (see Japanese Dolls under Shopping in the Tokyo chapter).

Kasa (Japanese Umbrellas) Another classic souvenir item, *kasa* (Japanese umbrellas) come in two forms: *higasa*, which are made of paper, cotton or silk and serve as a sunshade; and *bangasa*, which are made of oiled paper and keep the rain off. Again, department stores and tourist shops are your best bet for finding *kasa*.

Koinobori (Carp Banners) The lovely banners that you see waving in the breeze on Boy's Day in Japan (5 May) are called *koinobori*. The carp is much revered for its tenacity and perseverance, but you might like the banners for their simple elegance.

Katana (Japanese Swords) A fantastic souvenir – good *katana* (Japanese swords) are going to cost more than all your other travel expenses put together! The reason for their expense is both their mystique as the symbols of samurai power, and the great care that goes into making them. Sword shops that sell the real thing will also stock *tsuba* (sword guards), and complete sets of samurai armour. Department stores, on the other hand, stock realistic (to the untrained eye at least) imitations at affordable prices.

Shikki (Lacquerware) Another exquisite Japanese craft is lacquerware. The lacquerware-making process, involving as many as 15 layers of lacquer, is used to create objects as diverse as dishes and furniture. As you might expect, examples of good lacquerware cannot be had for a song, but smaller items can be bought at affordable prices from department stores. Popular, easily transportable items include bowls, trays and small boxes.

Washi (Japanese Paper) For more than 1000 years, Japanese paper has been famous as the finest handmade paper in the world. Special shops stock sheets of *washi* and products made from it, such as notebooks, wallets and so on. As they're generally inexpensive and light, *washi* products make excellent gifts and souvenirs. You'll find them in the big department stores. See Shopping under Kyoto in the Kansai chapter for suggestions on places to buy *washi*.

Pottery Numerous pottery villages still exist in Japan. Many of them feature pottery museums and working kilns that are open to the public. Of course, it is also possible to buy examples of stoneware and porcelain. Sources of different pottery styles abound: Mashiko, north of Tokyo (see the Around Tokyo chapter); Imbe, near Okayama in western Honshū, which is famed for its *bizen-yaki* pottery; and Koishiwara, Karatsu, Imari and Arita (in Kyūshū, the home of Japanese pottery).

Department stores are a surprisingly good place to look for Japanese pottery, and Takashimaya often has bargain bins where you can score some real deals. For even better prices try some of Japan's flea markets (see Shopping in the Kyoto and Tokyo chapters).

Ukiyo-e (Wood Block Prints) Originating in the 18th century as one of Japan's earliest manifestations of mass culture, wood block prints were used in advertising and posters. It was only later that ukiyo-e was considered an art form. The name (literally, 'pictures from the floating world') derives from a Buddhist term indicating the transient world of daily pleasures. Ukiyo-e uniquely depicts such things as street scenes, actors and courtesans.

Today, tourist shops in Japan stock modern reproductions of the work of famous ukiyo-e masters such as Hokusai, whose scenes of Fuji-san (Mt Fuji) are favourites. It is also possible to come across originals by lesser-known artists at prices ranging from ¥3000 to ¥40,000.

Kimono & Yukata Ceremonial occasions such as university graduations or weddings are when kimono are most commonly worn. For most non-Japanese, the cost of a kimono is prohibitively expensive. Prices start at around ¥60,000 and soar to ¥1 million or more. The best option for those interested in owning their own kimono is to head to a flea market or used-clothing shop. Used-clothing shops usually stock a variety of kimono ranging in price from ¥1500 to ¥9000, depending on quality.

For those not in the kimono league, another option might be to look for a *yukata* (the cotton bathrobes worn in ryokan and at summer festivals). They have a distinctively Japanese look and are not only affordable (from around ¥3500 up) but also highly usable. These are available from tourist shops and department stores in Japan.

Japanese Cuisine

JAPANESE CUISINE

OLIVER STREWE

JOHN HAY

Title Page: Eating a meal in a ryokan, Tokyo (photograph by Simon Rowe)

Top: Rows of giant tuna, Tsukiji Fish Market, Tokyo

Bottom: Fish on skewers, Tokyo

DINING OUT IN JAPAN

Those familiar with *nihon ryōri* (Japanese cuisine) know that eating is half the fun of travelling in Japan. Even if you've already tried some of Japan's better-known specialities in Japanese restaurants in your own country, you're likely to be surprised by how delicious the original is when served on its home turf. More importantly, the adventurous eater will be delighted to find that Japanese food is far more than just sushi, tempura or sukiyaki. Indeed, it is possible to spend a month in Japan and sample a different speciality restaurant every night.

Those in search of a truly Japanese experience will probably want to avoid Western-style fast food. Luckily this is quite easy to do, although some may baulk at charging into a restaurant where both the language and the menu are likely to be incomprehensible. The best way to get over this fear is to familiarise yourself with the main types of Japanese restaurants so that you have some idea of what's on offer and how to order it. Those timid of heart should take solace in the fact that the Japanese will go to extraordinary lengths to understand what you want, and will help you to order.

With the exception of *shokudō* (all-round restaurants) and *izakaya* (pub-style restaurants), most Japanese restaurants concentrate on a

Eating in a Japanese Restaurant

When you enter a restaurant, you'll be greeted with a hearty *irasshaimase!* (Welcome!). In all but the most casual places the waiter or waitress will next ask you, *nan-mei sama?* (How many people?). Indicate the answer with your fingers, which is what the Japanese do. You will then be led either to a table, or a place at the counter, or a tatami room.

At this point you will be given an *oshibori* (hot towel), a cup of tea and a menu. The *oshibori* is for wiping your hands and face. When you're done with it, just roll it up and leave it next to your place. Now comes the hard part: ordering. If you don't read Japanese, you can use the romanised translations in this section to help you, or direct the waiter's attention to the Japanese script. If this doesn't work, there are two phrases which may help: *o-susume wa nan desu ka?* (What do you recommend?) and *o-makase shimasu* (Please decide for me). If you're still having problems, you can try pointing at other diners' food or, if the restaurant has them, dragging the waiter outside to point at the plastic food displays in the window.

When you've finished eating, you can signal for the bill by crossing one index finger over the other to form an X. This is the standard sign for 'cheque please'. You can also say *o-kanjō kudasai*. Remember, there is no tipping in Japan and tea is free of charge. Usually you will be given a bill to take to the cashier at the front of the restaurant. At more upmarket places, the host of the party will discreetly ask to be excused and pay before the group leaves. One doesn't usually leave cash on the table by way of payment. Only the bigger and more international places take credit cards, so cash is always the surer option.

When leaving, it is polite to say to the restaurant staff *gochisō-sama deshita* (It was a real feast).

JAPANESE CUISINE

speciality cuisine. This naturally makes for delicious eating, but does limit your choice. Here we will introduce the main types of Japanese restaurants, along with a menu sample of some of the most common dishes served.

Where possible, we also list some of the best restaurants to sample each type of cuisine. For details on the restaurants that are listed in this section, see the Places to Eat sections of the relevant destination chapters.

Shokudō

A *shokudō* is the most common type of restaurant in Japan, and is found near train stations, tourist spots and just about any other place where people congregate. Easily distinguished by the presence of plastic food displays in the window, these inexpensive places usually serve a variety of *washoku* (Japanese) and *yoshoku* (Western) dishes.

At lunch, and sometimes dinner, the easiest meal to order at a *shokudō* is a *teishoku* (set-course meal), which is sometimes also called *ranchi setto* (lunch set), or *kōsu*. This usually includes a main dish of meat or fish, a bowl of rice, miso soup, shredded cabbage and some Japanese pickles *(tsukemono)*. In addition, most *shokudō* serve a fairly standard selection of *donburi-mono* (rice dishes) and *menrui* (noodle dishes). When you order noodles, you can choose between *soba* and *udon*, both of which are served with a variety of toppings. If you're at a loss as to what to order, simply say *kyō-no-ranchi* (Today's lunch), and they'll do the rest. Expect to spend from ¥800 to ¥1000 for a meal at a *shokudō*.

Some typical *shokudō* in Japan:

Eating House Hi-Lite Kyoto, Kansai (p369)
Kuishinbō-no-Mise Kyoto, Kansai (p369)
Kintoki Kōbe, Kansai (p403)

Rice Dishes

katsu-don	かつ丼	rice topped with a fried pork cutlet
niku-don	牛丼	rice topped with thin slices of cooked beef
oyako-don	親子丼	rice topped with egg and chicken
ten-don	天丼	rice topped with tempura shrimp and vegetables

Noodle Dishes

soba	そば	buckwheat noodles
udon	うどん	thick, white wheat noodles
kake	かけそば/うどん	*soba/udon* noodles in broth
kitsune	きつねそば/うどん	*soba/udon* noodles with fried tofu
tempura	てんぷらそば/うどん	*soba/udon* noodles with tempura shrimp
tsukimi	月見そば/うどん	*soba/udon* noodles with raw egg on top

Izakaya

An *izakaya* is the Japanese equivalent of a pub. It's a good place to visit when you want a casual meal, a wide selection of food, a hearty atmosphere and, of course, plenty of beer and sake. When you enter an *izakaya*, you are given the choice of sitting around the counter, at a table or on a tatami floor. You usually order a bit at a time, choosing from a selection of typical Japanese foods like *yakitori*, sashimi and grilled fish, as well as Japanese interpretations of Western foods like french fries and beef stew.

Izakaya can be identified by their rustic facades, and the red lanterns outside their doors bearing the kanji for *izakaya*. Since *izakaya* food is casual fare to go with drinking, it is usually fairly inexpensive. Depending on how much you drink, you can expect to get away with spending ¥2500 to ¥5000 per person. (See Yakitori later for more dishes available at *izakaya*).

Some of our favourite *izakaya* in Japan:

Domanin Kakunodate, northern Honshū (p531)
Youyake Koyake Yamagata, northern Honshū (p540)
Daizen Tottori, western Honshū (p489)
Kanaya Takamatsu, Shikoku (p637)

agedashi-dōfu	揚げだレ豆腐	deep fried tofu in a fish stock soup
jaga-batā	ジャカバター	baked potatoes with butter
niku-jaga	肉ジャテ	beef and potato stew
shio-yaki-zakana	塩焼力	a whole fish grilled with salt
yaki-onigiri	焼きおにぎり	a triangle of grilled rice with *yakitori* sauce
poteto furai	ポテトフライ	french fries
chiizu-age	チーズ揚げ	deep fried cheese
hiya-yakko	冷ややっこ	a cold block of tofu with soya sauce and scallions
tsuna sarada	ツナサラダ	tuna salad over cabbage
yaki-soba	焼き そば	fried noodles with meat and vegetables
kata yaki-soba	固焼きそば	hard fried noodles with meat and vegetables
sashimi mori-awase	刺身盛り合わせ	a selection of sliced sashimi

Okonomiyaki

The name means 'cook what you like', and an *okonomiyaki* restaurant provides you with an inexpensive opportunity to do just that. Sometimes described as Japanese pizza or pancake, the resemblance is in form only. At an *okonomiyaki* restaurant you sit around a *teppan* (iron hotplate), armed with a spatula and chopsticks to cook your choice of meat, seafood and vegetables in a cabbage and vegetable batter.

Some restaurants will do most of the cooking and bring the nearly finished product over to your hotplate for you to season with *katsuo bushi* (bonito flakes), *shōyu* (soya sauce), *ao-nori* (an ingredient similar to parsley), Japanese Worcestershire-style sauce and mayonnaise. Cheaper places, however, will simply hand you a bowl filled with the ingredients, and expect you to cook it for yourself. If this happens, don't panic. First, mix the batter and filling thoroughly, then place it on the hot grill, flattening it into a pancake shape. After five minutes or so, use the spatulas to flip it and cook for another five minutes. Then dig in.

Most *okonomiyaki* places also serve *yaki-soba* (fried noodles) and *yasai-itame* (stir-fried vegetables). All of this is washed down with mugs of draft beer.

One final word: don't worry too much about preparation of the food – as a foreigner you will be expected to be awkward, and the waiter will keep a sharp eye on you to make sure no real disasters occur.

Some good *okonomiyaki* places in Japan:

Chibou Sendai, northern Honshū (p502)
Okonomi-mura Hiroshima, western Honshū (p455)
Chabana Kyoto, Kansai (p368)

mikkusu okonomiyaki	ミックスお好み焼き	mixed fillings of seafood, meat and vegetables
modan-yaki	モダン焼き	*okonomiyaki* with *yaki soba* and a fried egg
ika okonomiyaki	いかお好み焼き	squid *okonomiyaki*
gyū okonomiyaki	牛お好み焼き	beef *okonomiyaki*
negi okonomiyaki	ネギお好み焼き	thin *okonomiyaki* with scallions

Yakitori

Yakitori (skewers of grilled chicken and vegetables) is a popular after-work meal. *Yakitori* is not so much a full meal as an accompaniment for beer and sake. At a *yakitori-ya* (*yakitori* restaurant) you sit

A World of Things to Eat

On the upper floors of most big department stores, in shopping malls and on the basement floors of some large office buildings, you'll find what the Japanese call *resutoran-gai* (restaurant towns). Within the space of a few hundred metres, these places contain almost every major type of Japanese restaurant, plus a variety of Western favourites like Italian, French and the inevitable fast-food joints.

At lunch and dinner most eateries in *resutoran-gai* display their specials outside for all to see; otherwise, most eateries will have the usual plastic food displays for you to choose from – all of which makes ordering a snap. So, when you find yourself at a loss for a place to eat in a Japanese city, you can always do what the locals do and head for a *resutoran-gai*.

around a counter with the other patrons and watch the chef grill your selections over charcoal. The best way to eat here is to order several varieties, then order seconds of the ones you really like. Ordering can be a little confusing since one serving often means two or three skewers (be careful – the price listed on the menu is usually that of a single skewer).

In summer, the beverage of choice at a *yakitori* restaurant is beer or cold sake, while in winter it's hot sake. A few drinks and enough skewers to fill you up should cost ¥3000 to ¥4000 per person. *Yakitori* restaurants are usually small places, often near train stations, and are best identified by a red lantern outside and the smell of grilling chicken.

For good *yakitori* in Tokyo, try **Tonton Honten** (*Yūraku-chō; p190*).

yakitori	やきとり	plain, grilled white meat
hasami/negima	はさみ・ねぎま	pieces of white meat alternating with leek
sasami	ささみ	skinless chicken-breast pieces
kawa	かわ	chicken skin
tsukune	つくね	chicken meat balls
gyū-niku	牛肉	pieces of beef
rebā	レバー	chicken livers
tebasaki	手羽先	chicken wings
shiitake	しいたけ	Japanese mushrooms
piiman	ピーマン	small green peppers
tama-negi	たまねぎ	round, white onions
yaki-onigiri	焼きおにぎり	a triangle of rice grilled with *yakitori* sauce

Sushi & Sashimi

Like *yakitori*, sushi is considered an accompaniment for beer and sake. Nonetheless, both the Japanese and foreigners often make a meal of it, and it's one of the healthiest meals around.

There are two main types of sushi: *nigiri-zushi* (served on a small bed of rice – the most common variety) and *maki-zushi* (served in a seaweed roll). Lesser-known varieties include *chirashi-zushi* (a layer of rice covered in egg and fish toppings), *oshi-zushi* (fish pressed in a mould over rice) and *inari-zushi* (rice in a pocket of sweet, fried tofu). Whatever kind of sushi you try, it will be served with lightly vinegared rice. In the case of *nigiri-zushi* and *maki-zushi*, it will contain a bit of *wasabi* (hot green horseradish).

Sushi is not difficult to order. If you sit at the counter of a sushi restaurant you can simply point at what you want, as most of the selections are visible in a refrigerated glass case between you and the sushi chef. You can also order à la carte from the menu. When ordering, you usually order *ichi-nin mae* (one portion), which usually means two pieces of sushi. Be careful, since the price on the menu will be that of only one piece. If ordering à la carte is too daunting, you can take care of your whole order with just one or two words by ordering *mori-awase*, an assortment plate of *nigiri-zushi*. These usually come in three grades: *futsū nigiri* (regular *nigiri*), *jō nigiri* (special *nigiri*) and *toku-jō nigiri* (extra-special *nigiri*). The difference is in the type of fish used. Most *mori-awase* contain six or seven pieces of sushi.

Be warned that meals in a good sushi restaurant can cost upwards of ¥10,000, while an average place can run from ¥3000 to ¥5000 per person. One way to sample the joy of sushi on the cheap is to try an automatic sushi place, usually called *kaiten-zushi*, where the sushi is served on a conveyor belt that runs along a counter. Here you simply reach up and grab whatever looks good (which certainly takes the pain out of ordering). You're charged by the number of plates of sushi you've eaten. Plates are colour-coded by their price and the cost is written either somewhere on the plate itself or on a sign on the wall. You can usually fill yourself up in one of these places for ¥1000 to ¥2000 per person.

Before popping the sushi into your mouth, dip it in *shōyu*, which you pour from a small decanter into a low dish specially provided for the purpose. If you're not good at using chopsticks, don't worry, sushi is one of the few foods in Japan that is perfectly acceptable to eat with your hands. Slices of *gari* (pickled ginger) will also be served to help refresh the palate. The beverage of choice with sushi is beer or sake (hot in the winter and cold in the summer), with a cup of green tea at the end of the meal.

Some of our favourite sushi and sashimi restaurants:

Fukuzushi Roppongi, Tokyo (p198)
Jiro Sushi Ginza, Tokyo (p191)
Kyubei Ginza, Tokyo (p191)
Tomi-zushi Kyoto, Kansai (p367)
Dai-sushi Osaka, Kansai (p396)
Janome Sushi Miyako, northern Honshū (p516)
Umai Sushikan Sendai, northern Honshū (p502)
Karato Ichiba fish markets Shimonoseki, western Honshū (p469)

ama-ebi	甘海老	sweet shrimp
awabi	あわび	abalone
ebi	海老	prawn or shrimp
hamachi	はまち	yellowtail
ika	いか	squid
ikura	イクラ	salmon roe
kai-bashira	貝柱	scallop
kani	かに	crab
katsuo	かつお	bonito
maguro	まぐろ	tuna
tai	鯛	sea bream
tamago	たまご	sweetened egg
toro	とろ	the choicest cut of fatty tuna belly
unagi	うなぎ	eel with a sweet sauce
uni	うに	sea urchin roe

Sukiyaki & Shabu-shabu Restaurants usually specialise in both these dishes. Popular in the West, sukiyaki is a favourite of most foreign visitors to Japan. Sukiyaki consists of thin slices of beef cooked in a broth of soya sauce, sugar and sake and is accompanied by a variety of vegetables and tofu. After cooking, all the ingredients are dipped in raw egg before being eaten. When made with high-quality beef, like Kōbe beef, it is a sublime experience.

Shabu-shabu consists of thin slices of beef and vegetables cooked by swirling the ingredients in a light broth, then dipping them in a variety of special sesame seed and citrus-based sauces. Both of these dishes are prepared in a pot over a fire at your private table; don't fret about preparation – the waiter or waitress will usually help you get started, and keep a close watch as you proceed. The key is to take your time, add the ingredients a little at a time and savour the flavours as you go.

Sukiyaki and shabu-shabu restaurants usually have traditional Japanese decor and sometimes a picture of a cow to help you identify them. Ordering is not difficult. Simply say sukiyaki or shabu-shabu and indicate how many people are dining. Expect to pay between ¥3000 to ¥10,000 per person.

Some good spots to try sukiyaki and shabu-shabu:

Asakusa Imahan Asakusa, Tokyo (p192)
Ibuki Shinjuku, Tokyo (p194)
Shabu-zen Osaka, Kansai (p396)

Tempura

Tempura consists of portions of fish, prawns and vegetables cooked in fluffy, non-greasy batter. When you sit down at a tempura restaurant, you will be given a small bowl of ten-tsuyu (a light brown sauce), and a plate of grated daikon (white radish) to mix into the sauce. Dip each piece of tempura into this sauce before eating it. Tempura is best when it's hot, so don't wait too long – use the sauce to cool each piece, and dig in.

While it's possible to order à la carte, most diners choose to order teishoku (full set), which includes rice, miso-shiru (miso soup) and Japanese pickles. Some tempura restaurants offer tempura courses that include different numbers of tempura pieces.

Expect to pay between ¥2000 and ¥10,000 for a full tempura meal. Finding these restaurants is tricky as they have no distinctive facade or decor: If you look through the window you'll see customers around the counter watching the chefs as they work over large woks filled with oil.

Three picks for good tempura in Japan:

Daikokuya Asakusa, Tokyo (p192)
Yoshikawa Kyoto, Kansai (p367)
Beni-e Nara, Kansai (p417)

tempura moriawase	てんぷら盛り合わせ	a selection of tempura
shōjin age	精進揚げ	vegetarian tempura
kaki age	かき揚げ	tempura with shredded vegetables or fish

Rāmen

The Japanese imported this dish from China and put their own spin on it to make what is one of the world's most delicious fast foods. *Rāmen* dishes are big bowls of noodles in a meat broth, served with a variety of toppings, such as sliced pork, bean sprouts and leeks. In some restaurants, particularly in Kansai, you may be asked if you'd prefer *kotteri* (thick) or *assari* (thin) soup. Other than this, ordering is simple: just sidle up to the counter and say *rāmen*, or ask for any of the other choices usually on offer (a list follows). Expect to pay between ¥500 and ¥900 for a bowl. Since *rāmen* is derived from Chinese cuisine, some *rāmen* restaurants also serve *chāhan* or *yaki-meshi* (fried rice), *gyōza* (dumplings) and *kara-age* (deep-fried chicken pieces).

Rāmen restaurants are easily distinguished by their long counters lined with customers hunched over steaming bowls. You can sometimes hear a *rāmen* shop as you wander by – it's considered polite to slurp the noodles and aficionados claim that slurping brings out the full flavour of the broth.

Some excellent places to try *rāmen*:

Ippūdō Rāmen Ebisu, Tokyo (p197)
Gojōgen Sapporo, Hokkaidō (p566)
Rāmen Yokochō Sapporo, Hokkaidō (p566)
Santōka Asahikawa, Hokkaidō (p581)
Genraiken Kitakata, northern Honshū (p495)
Charlie Matsuyama, Shikoku (p630)
Rāmen Stadium Fukuoka, Kyūshū (p649)
Riverside stalls Fukuoka, Kyūshū (p648)

rāmen	ラーメン	soup and noodles with a sprinkling of meat and vegetables
chāshū-men	チャーシュー麺	*rāmen* topped with slices of roasted pork
wantan-men	ワンタン麺	*rāmen* with meat dumplings
miso-rāmen	みそラーメン	*rāmen* with miso-flavoured broth
chānpon-men	ちゃんぽん麺	Nagasaki-style *rāmen*

Soba & Udon

Soba and *udon* are Japan's answer to Chinese-style *rāmen*. *Soba* are thin, brown, buckwheat noodles; *udon* are thick, white, wheat noodles. Most Japanese noodle shops serve both *soba* and *udon* in a variety of ways. Noodles are usually served in a bowl containing a light, bonito-flavoured broth, but you can also order them served cold and piled on a bamboo screen with a cold broth for dipping.

Top: The *bentō* (boxed lunch) serves as a handy, cheap and nutritious meal of rice, seafood, meat and vegetables

By far the most popular type of cold noodles is *zaru soba*, which is served with bits of *nori* (seaweed) on top. If you order these noodles, you'll receive a small plate of wasabi and sliced scallions – put these into the cup of broth and eat the noodles by dipping them in this mixture. At the end of your meal, the waiter will give you some hot broth to mix with the leftover sauce, which you drink like a kind of tea. As with *rāmen*, you should feel free to slurp as loudly as you please.

Soba and *udon* places are usually quite cheap (about ¥900 a dish), but some fancy places can be significantly more expensive (the decor is a good indication of the price). See Noodles Dishes under Shokudō, earlier, for more *soba* and *udon* dishes.

Some great spots for *soba* and *udon*:

Hinode Kyoto, Kansai (p367)
Misoka-an Kawamichi-ya Kyoto, Kansai (p367)
Omen Kyoto, Kansai (p369)
Tagoto Honten Kyoto, Kansai (p366)
Ebisuya Nagoya, central Honshū (p266)
Marusei Nagano, central Honshū (p303)
Nomugi Matsumoto, central Honshū (p297)
Uzuraya Togakushi, central Honshū (p304)
Azumaya Morioka, northern Honshū (p514)
Don Don Udonya Hagi, western Honshū (p476)
Tanuki-ya Kotohira, Shikoku (p634)
Wa-no-Ichi Naha, Okinawa (p719)
Shinzan Shokudō Nago, Okinawa-hontō, Okinawa (p723)

zaru soba	ざるそば	cold noodles with seaweed strips served on a bamboo tray

Unagi

Unagi (eel) is an expensive and popular delicacy in Japan. Even if you can't stand the creature, you owe it to yourself to try *unagi* at least once while in Japan. It's cooked over hot coals and brushed with a rich sauce of soy sauce and sake. Full *unagi* dinners can be expensive, but many *unagi* restaurants offer *unagi bentō* (boxed lunches) and lunch sets for around ¥1500. Most *unagi* restaurants display plastic models of their sets in their front windows, and may have barrels of live eels to entice passers-by.

If you'd like to try some eel while in Japan, consider:

Izu-ei Ueno, Tokyo (p191)
Kane-yo Kyoto, Kansai (p366)

unagi teishoku	うなぎ定食	full-set *unagi* meal with rice, grilled eel, eel-liver soup and pickles
unadon	うな丼	grilled eel over a bowl of rice
unajū	うな重	grilled eel over a flat tray of rice
kabayaki	蒲焼き	skewers of grilled eel without rice

Fugu

The deadly *fugu* (globefish) is eaten more for the thrill than the taste. It's actually rather bland – most people liken the taste to chicken – but is acclaimed for its fine texture. Nonetheless, if you have the money to lay out for a *fugu* dinner (around ¥10,000), it makes a good 'been there, done that' story back home.

Although the danger of *fugu* poisoning is negligible, some Japanese joke that you should always let your dining companion try the first piece of *fugu* – if they are still talking after five minutes, you can consider it safe and have some yourself. If you need a shot of liquid courage in order to get you started, try a glass of *hirezake* (toasted *fugu* tail in hot sake) – the traditional accompaniment to a *fugu* dinner.

Fugu is a seasonal delicacy best eaten in winter. *Fugu* restaurants usually serve only *fugu*, and can be identified by a picture of a *fugu* on the sign out the front.

Fugu is the speciality of western Honshū, and Shimonoseki is a good place to give it a try. Of course, you can also find *fugu* in other parts of Japan. Two of our favourite places:

Yabure-kabure Shimonoseki, western Honshū (p471)
Fugu Matsu Beppu, Kyūshū (p703)

fugu teishoku	ふぐ定食	a set course of *fugu* served several ways, plus rice and soup
fugu chiri	ふぐちり	a stew made from *fugu* and vegetables
fugu sashimi	ふぐ刺身	thinly sliced raw *fugu*
yaki fugu	焼きふぐ	*fugu* grilled on a hibachi at your table

Tonkatsu

Tonkatsu is a deep-fried breaded pork cutlet that is served with a special sauce, usually as part of a set meal *(tonkatsu teishoku)*. *Tonkatsu* is served both at speciality restaurants and at *shokudō*. Naturally, the best *tonkatsu* is to be found at the speciality places, where a full set will cost ¥1500 to ¥2500. When ordering *tonkatsu*, you are able to choose between *rōsu* (a fatter cut of pork) and *hire* (a leaner cut).

If you're in Tokyo, you might want to try the delicious *tonkatsu* at **Musashino** (Ueno; p191).

tonkatsu teishoku	とんかつ定食	a set meal of *tonkatsu*, rice, *miso shiru* and shredded cabbage
minchi katsu	ミンチカツ	minced pork cutlet
hire katsu	ヒレかつ	*tonkatsu* fillet
kushi katsu	串かつ	deep-fried pork and vegetables on skewers

Kushiage & Kushikatsu

Dieters beware: this is the fried food to beat all fried foods. *Kushiage* and *kushikatsu* are deep-fried skewers of meat, seafood and vegetables eaten as an accompaniment to beer. *Kushi* means 'skewer' and if food can be fit on one, it's probably on the menu. Cabbage is often eaten with the meal, a clever way to ease the guilt of eating all that grease.

You order *kushiage* and *kushikatsu* by the skewer (one skewer is *ippon*, but you can always use your fingers to indicate how many you want). Like *yakitori*, this food is popular with after-work salarymen and students and is therefore fairly inexpensive, though there are upmarket places. Expect to pay ¥2000 to ¥5000 for a full meal and a couple of beers. Not particularly distinctive in appearance, the best *kushiage* and *kushikatsu* places are found by asking a Japanese friend.

ebi	海老	shrimp
ika	いか	squid
renkon	レンコン	lotus root
tama-negi	たまねぎ	white onion
gyū-niku	牛肉	beef pieces
shiitake	しいたけ	Japanese mushrooms
ginnan	銀杏	ginkgo nuts
imo	いも	potato

Kaiseki

Kaiseki is the pinnacle of Japanese cuisine, where ingredients, preparation, setting and presentation come together to create a dining experience quite unlike any other. Born as an adjunct to the tea ceremony, *kaiseki* is a largely vegetarian affair (though fish is often served, meat never appears on the *kaiseki* menu). One usually eats *kaiseki* in the private room of a *ryōtei* (an especially elegant style of traditional restaurant), often overlooking a private, tranquil garden. The meal is served in several small courses, giving the diner an opportunity to admire the plates and bowls, which are carefully chosen to complement the food and season. Rice is eaten last (usually with an assortment of pickles) and the drink of choice is sake or beer.

All this comes at a steep price – a good *kaiseki* dinner costs upwards of ¥10,000 per person. A cheaper way to sample the delights of *kaiseki* is to visit a *kaiseki* restaurant for lunch. Most places offer a boxed lunch containing a sampling of their dinner fare for around ¥2500.

Unfortunately for foreigners, *kaiseki* restaurants can be intimidating places to enter. If possible, bring a Japanese friend or ask a Japanese friend to call ahead and make arrangements.

If you're ready to take the plunge into *kaiseki*, some of our picks:

Kisso Roppongi, Tokyo (p198)
Uzuki Kyoto, Kansai (p367)
Harishin Nara, Kansai (p416)
Kagetsu Nagasaki, Kyūshū (p666)

kaisekii	懐石	traditional, expensive Kyoto-style cuisine
ryōtei	料亭	a restaurant serving a variety of traditional Japanese dishes
bentō	弁当	boxed lunch
ume	梅	regular course
take	竹	special course
matsu	松	extra-special course

Sweets

Although most restaurants don't serve dessert (plates of sliced fruit are sometimes served at the end of a meal), there is no lack of sweets in Japan. Most sweets (known generically as *wagashi*) are sold in speciality stores for you to eat at home. Many of the more delicate-looking ones are made to balance the strong, bitter taste of the special *matcha* tea served during the tea ceremony.

Although pleasant to look at, some Westerners may find Japanese sweets unappealing – perhaps because many of them contain the unfamiliar sweet, red adzuki-bean paste called *anko*. This unusual filling turns up in even the most innocuous-looking pastries. But don't let anyone make up your mind for you: try a Japanese sweet for yourself.

With such a wide variety of sweets, it's impossible to list all the names. However, you'll probably find many variations on the anko-covered-by-glutinous-rice *(mochi)* theme.

Sweet shops are easy to spot; they usually have open fronts with their wares laid out in wooden trays to entice passers-by. Buying sweets is simple – just point at what you want and indicate with your fingers how many you'd like.

Some of our favourite sweet shops:

Gion Koishi Kyoto, Kansai (p370)
Kagizen Yoshifusa Kyoto, Kansai (p368)
Ōharameya Kyoto, Kansai (p368)
Donjiki Chaya Matsushima, northern Honshū (p504)

wagashi	和菓子	Japanese-style sweets
anko	あんこ	sweet paste or jam made from adzuki beans
mochi	もち	pounded rice cakes made of glutinous rice
yōkan	ようかん	sweet red bean jelly

DRINKING IN JAPAN

Drinking plays a big role in Japanese society, and there are few social occasions where beer or sake is not served. Alcohol (in this case sake) also plays a ceremonial role in various Shintō festivals and rites, including the marriage ceremony. As a visitor to Japan, you'll probably find yourself in lots of situations where you are invited to drink, and tipping back a few beers or glasses of sake is great way to get to know the locals. However, if you don't drink alcohol, it's no big deal. Simply order *oolong cha* (oolong tea) in place of beer or sake. While some folks might put pressure on you to drink alcohol, you can diffuse this pressure by saying *sake o nomimasen* (I don't drink alcohol).

What you pay for your drink depends on where you drink and, in the case of hostess bars, with whom you drink. Hostess bars are the most expensive places to drink (up to ¥10,000 per drink), followed by upmarket traditional Japanese bars, hotel bars, beer halls and casual pubs. If you are not sure about a place, ask about prices and cover charges before sitting down. As a rule, if you are served a small snack with your first round, you'll be paying a cover charge (usually a few hundred yen, but sometimes much more).

Izakaya and *yakitori-ya* are cheap places for beer, sake and food in a casual atmosphere resembling that of a pub. All Japanese cities, whether large or small, will have also a few informal bars with reasonable prices. Such places are popular with young Japanese and resident *gaijin*, who usually refer to such places as *gaijin* bars. In summer, many department stores open up beer gardens on the roof. Many of these places offer all-you-can-eat/drink specials for around ¥3000 per person.

izakaya	居酒屋	pub-style restaurant
yakitori-ya	焼鳥屋	*yakitori* restaurant

Alcoholic Drinks

Beer Introduced at the end of the 1800s, *biiru* (beer) is now the favourite tipple of the Japanese. The quality is generally excellent and the most popular type is light lager, although recently some breweries have been experimenting with darker brews. The major breweries are Kirin, Asahi, Sapporo and Suntory. Beer is dispensed everywhere, from vending machines to beer halls, and even in some temple lodgings. A standard can of beer from a vending machine is about ¥250, although some of the gigantic cans cost over ¥1000. At bars, a beer starts at ¥500 and the price climbs upwards, depending on the establishment. *Nama biiru* (draft beer) is widely available, as are imported beers.

biiru	ビール	beer
nama biiru	生ビール	draft beer

Sake Rice wine has been brewed for centuries in Japan. Once restricted to imperial brewers, it was later produced at temples and shrines across the country. In recent years, consumption of beer has overtaken that of sake, but it's still a standard item in homes, restaurants and drinking places. Large casks of sake are often seen piled up as offerings outside temples and shrines, and the drink plays an important part in most celebrations and festivals.

Most Westerners come to Japan with a bad image of sake, the result of having consumed low-grade brands overseas. Although it won't appeal to all palates, some of the higher grades are actually very good, and a trip to a restaurant specialising in sake is a great way to sample some of the better brews.

There are several major types of sake, including *nigori* (cloudy), *nama* (unrefined) and regular, clear sake. Of these, clear sake is by far the most common. Clear sake is usually divided into three grades: *tokkyū* (premium), *ikkyū* (first grade) and *nikyū* (second grade). *Nikyū* is the routine choice. Sake can be further divided into *karakuchi* (dry) and *amakuchi* (sweet). As well as the national brewing giants, there are thousands of provincial brewers producing local brews called *jizake*.

Sake is served *atsukan* (warm) and *reishu* (cold), with warm sake not surprisingly being more popular in winter. When you order sake, it will usually be served in a small flask called *tokkuri*. These come in two sizes, so you should specify whether you want *ichigō* (small) or *nigō* (large). From these flasks you pour the sake into small ceramic cups called *o-choko* or *sakazuki*. Another way to sample sake is to drink it from a small wooden box called *masu*, with a bit of salt on the rim.

However you drink it, with a 17% alcohol content, sake, particularly the warm stuff, is likely to go right to your head. After a few bouts with sake you'll come to understand why the Japanese drink it in such small cups. Particularly memorable is a real sake hangover born of too much cheap sake. The best advice is not to indulge the day before you have to get on a plane.

sake	酒	Japanese rice wine
nigori	にごり	cloudy sake
nama	なま	regular clear sake
tokkyū	特級	premium grade sake
ikkyū	一級	first grade sake
nikkyū	二級	second grade sake
karakuchi	辛口	dry sake
amakuchi	甘口	sweet sake
jizake	地酒	local brew
atsukan	あつかん	warm sake
reishu	冷酒	cold sake
o-choko	おちょこ	ceramic sake cup
sakazuki	さかづき	ceramic sake cup

Shōchū For those looking for a quick and cheap escape route from the sorrows of the world, *shōchū* is the answer. It's a distilled spirit, with an alcohol content of about 30%, and has been resurrected from its previous lowly status (it was used as a disinfectant in the Edo period) to become a trendy drink. You can drink it *oyu-wari* (with hot water) or *chūhai* (in a highball with soda and lemon). A 720mL bottle sells for about ¥600 which makes it a relatively cheap option compared to other spirits.

shōchū	焼酎	distilled grain liquor
oyu-wari	お湯割り	*shōchū* with hot water
chūhai	チューハイ	*shōchū* with soda and lemon

Wine, Imported Drinks & Whiskey Japanese wines are available from areas such as Yamanashi, Nagano, Tōhoku and Hokkaidō. Standard wines are often blended with imports from South America or Eastern Europe. The major producers are Suntory, Mann's and Mercian. Expect to pay at least ¥1000 for a bottle of something drinkable. Imported wines are often stocked by large liquor stores or department stores in the cities. Bargains are sometimes available at ¥600, but most of the quaffable imports cost considerably more.

Prices of imported spirits have been coming down in recent years and bargain liquor stores have been popping up in bigger cities. However, if you really like imported spirits, it is probably a good idea to pick up a duty-free bottle or two on your way through the airport. Whiskey is available at most drinking establishments and is usually drunk *mizu-wari* (with water and ice) or *onzarokku* (on the rocks). Local brands, such as Suntory and Nikka, are sensibly priced, and most measure up to foreign standards. Expensive foreign labels are popular as gifts.

Most other imported spirits are available at drinking establishments in Japan. Bars with a large foreign clientele, including hotel bars, can usually mix anything you request. If not, they will certainly tailor a drink to your specifications.

whiskey	ウィスキー	whiskey
mizu-wari	水割り	whiskey, ice and water
onzarokku	オンザロック	whiskey with ice

Nonalcoholic Drinks

Most of the drinks you're used to at home will be available in Japan, with a few colourfully named additions like Pocari Sweat and Calpis Water. One convenient aspect of Japan is the presence of drink machines on virtually every street corner, and at ¥120, refreshment is rarely more than a few steps away.

Coffee & Tea *Kōhii* (coffee) served in a *kisaten* (coffee shop) tends to be expensive in Japan, costing between ¥350 and ¥500 a cup, with some places charging up to ¥1000. A cheap alternative is one of the newer coffee-restaurant chains like Doutor or Pronto, or doughnut shops like Mr Donut (which offers free refills). An even cheaper alternative is a can of coffee, hot or cold, from a vending machine. Although unpleasantly sweet, at ¥120 the price is hard to beat.

When ordering coffee at a coffee shop in Japan, you'll be asked whether you like it *hotto* (hot) or *aisu* (cold). Black tea also comes hot or cold, with *miruku* (milk) or *remon* (lemon). A good way to start a day of sightseeing in Japan is with a *mōningu setto* (morning set) of tea or coffee, toast and eggs, which costs around ¥400.

kōhii	コーヒー	regular coffee
burendo kōhii	ブレンドコーヒー	blended coffee, fairly strong
american kōhii	アメリカンコーヒー	weak coffee
kōcha	紅茶	black, British-style tea
kafe ōre	カフェオレ	café au lait, hot or cold
orenji jūsu	オレンジジュース	orange juice

Japanese Tea Unlike black tea, which Westerners are familiar with, most Japanese tea is green and contains a lot of vitamin C and caffeine. The powdered form used in the tea ceremony is called *matcha* and is drunk after being whipped into a frothy consistency. The more common form, a leafy green tea, is simply called *o-cha*, and is drunk after being steeped in a pot. In addition to green tea, you'll probably drink a lot of a brownish tea called *bancha*, which restaurants serve for free. In summer a cold beverage called *mugicha* (roasted barley tea) is served in private homes.

o-cha	お茶	green tea
sencha	煎茶	medium grade green tea
matcha	抹茶	powdered green tea used in the tea ceremony
bancha	番茶	ordinary grade green tea, has a brownish colour
mugicha	麦茶	roasted barley tea

Top: Persimmons hanging from a length of bamboo, Kyoto, Kansai

Middle Left: Apricot pie, Tokyo

Middle Right: Prawn, cuttlefish and seaweed, Tokyo

Bottom: Riverside restaurant, Kibune, Kyoto, Kansai

ERIC WHEATER

JOHN HAY

JOHN HAY

LIZ THOMPSON

Japanese Cuisine

OLIVER STREWE

OLIVER STREWE

Top: Japanese sweets, Kyoto, Kansai

Bottom: Cold beer and a snack, Osaka, Kansai

Getting There & Away

While most people fly via Tokyo, there are several other ways of getting to/from Japan. For a start, there are many other airports in Japan, some of which make better entry points than Tokyo's somewhat inconvenient new Tokyo international airport (commonly known as Narita international airport). It's also possible to arrive in Japan by sea from a number of nearby countries, particularly South Korea.

AIR

There are flights to Japan from all over the world, usually to Tokyo but also to a number of other Japanese airports. Although Tokyo may seem the obvious arrival and departure point in Japan, for many visitors this may not be the case. If you plan on exploring western Japan or the Kansai region, it might be more convenient to fly into Kansai international airport (KIX) near Osaka.

Airports

There are international airports on the main island of Honshū (Nagoya, Niigata, Osaka/Kansai and Tokyo Narita), Kyūshū (Fukuoka, Kagoshima, Kumamoto and Nagasaki), Okinawa (Naha) and Hokkaidō (Sapporo).

Tokyo Narita International Airport With the exception of China Airlines, all international flights to Tokyo use the New Tokyo international airport, better known as Narita international airport (W www .narita-airport.or.jp/airport_e). Since Narita is the most popular arrival/departure point in Japan, flights via Narita are usually cheaper than those using other airports.

Of course, if you can get a cheap flight to another airport, particularly one close to your area of interest, then there's no reason not to use another airport.

Osaka/Kansai International Airport Almost all of Osaka's international flights now go via the new Kansai international airport (W www.kansai-airport.or.jp/english). It serves the key Kansai cities of Kyoto, Osaka and Kōbe. Airport transport to any of these cities is fast and reliable (though it can be expensive if you're going all the way to Kyoto).

Nagoya International Airport Conveniently located between Tokyo and Osaka is Nagoya international airport (W www.nagoya-airport-bldg.co.jp/index-e .html). From Nagoya, flights connect with Australia, Canada, China, Guam, Hong Kong, Indonesia, Malaysia, New Zealand, the Philippines, Saipan, Singapore, South Korea, Taiwan, Thailand and the USA.

Fukuoka International Airport Fukuoka, at the northern end of Kyūshū, is the main arrival point for western Japan. Fukuoka international airport, conveniently located near the city, has flights to/from Honolulu and a number of Asian destinations.

Naha (Okinawa) International Airport Located on Okinawa-hontō (the main island of Okinawa), Naha international airport has flights to/from Hong Kong, Seoul, Shanghai and Taiwan.

Niigata International Airport North of Tokyo, Niigata international airport has flights to/from Seoul, Shanghai, Harbin, Xian, Guam and Honolulu.

Other Airports On the island of Kyūshū, Kagoshima airport has flights to/from Hong Kong, Shanghai and Seoul, Kumamoto airport has flights to/from South Korea, and Nagasaki airport has flights to/from Shanghai and Seoul.

On Hokkaidō, Sapporo airport has connections with South Korea.

Departure Tax

Both Kansai and Tokyo Narita international airports charge a departure tax (¥2650 and ¥2040, respectively), but they are paid when you purchase your ticket, so you don't have to worry about paying them at the airport. Departure tax is not charged at the other international airports.

Travel Seasons

The price of your ticket will depend to a great extent on when you fly. High season prices are determined by two sets of holidays and popular travel times: those in the country you're flying from and those in Japan. Generally, high season for travel between Japan and Western countries is in late December (around Christmas and the New Year period), late April to early May (around Japan's Golden Week holiday), as well as July and August. If you must fly during these periods, book well in advance. And, obviously, you'll save a lot of money by flying outside these times.

Tickets

Japan In most of Japan's major cities there are travel agencies where English is spoken. For an idea of the latest prices in Tokyo check the travel ads in the various local English-language publications, and in Kansai check *Kansai Time Out*. In other parts of Japan check the *Japan Times*. For more details on travel agencies, see the Tokyo chapter and the Osaka and Kyoto sections of the Kansai chapter.

The USA Recent years have seen huge drops in prices for airline tickets between North America and Japan. From New York, in the low season you can find discount return fares for as low as US$650, sometimes even less. Some carriers to check include United Airlines, Northwest Airlines, Korean Air, Japan Airlines (JAL) and All Nippon Airways (ANA). From the US west coast, low season discount return fares start as low as US$450, while high-season discount fares will just about double these figures.

The *New York Times*, the *Los Angeles Times*, the *Chicago Tribune* and the *San Francisco Examiner* all produce weekly travel sections in which you will find a good number of travel agency ads.

Good student travel agencies in the USA are **Council Travel** (☎ 800-226-8624; W www.counciltravel.com) and **STA Travel** (☎ 800-781-4040; W www.statravel.com).

San Francisco's **Avia Travel** (☎ 800-950-2842, 510-558-2150; W www.aviatravel.com) is a favourite of Japan-based English teachers and can arrange tickets originating in Japan. **IACE Travel New York** (☎ 800-872-4223; W www.iace-usa.com/html/english.html) is a travel agency specialising in travel between the USA and Japan that can often dig up cheap fares.

Canada Return fares between Vancouver and Tokyo start at around C$900, while return fares between Toronto and Tokyo start at around C$1200. Carriers to check include JAL and ANA, and United, American, Delta and Northwest Airlines.

Travel CUTS (☎ 866-246-9762; W www .travelcuts.com) is a good student travel agency. You'll find more travel agencies listed in the *Globe & Mail*, the *Toronto Star*, the *Montreal Gazette* and the *Vancouver Sun*.

Australia Garuda, Malaysian Airlines and Cathay Pacific have some good deals for travel between Australia and Japan, but these fares often have a number of restrictions. Return fares start at around A$1200 with Garuda, which allows a stopover in Bali. Direct flights to Japan with airlines including Qantas and JAL are more expensive – expect to pay around A$1500 for a return fare.

The best place to look for cheap fares is in the travel sections of weekend newspapers, such as the *Age* in Melbourne and the *Sydney Morning Herald*. Two well-known agencies for cheap fares are **STA Travel** (☎ 1300 733 035 Australiawide; W www.statravel.com.au), which has offices in all major cities, and **Flight Centre** (☎ 133 133 Australiawide; W www.flightcentre.com.au), which has dozens of offices throughout Australia.

New Zealand Return fares between Auckland and Tokyo start at around NZ$1500. Airlines that fly this route include Malaysian Airlines, Thai International, Qantas and Air New Zealand. You'll save money by taking one of the Asian airlines via an Asian city rather than flying direct.

Flight Centre (☎ *0800 24 35 44;* W *www* *.flightcentre.co.nz)* has a large central office in Auckland at National Bank Towers (corner Queen and Darby Sts) and many branches. **STA Travel** (☎ *0508 782 872;* W *www.statravel.co.nz)* has its main office at 10 High St, Auckland with other offices in Auckland, Hamilton, Palmerston North, Wellington, Christchurch and Dunedin.

The UK Expect to pay from UK£500 to UK£600 for a return ticket with a good airline via a fast route. ANA and JAL offer direct flights between London and Japan. Air France is a reliable choice for flights to Japan (usually Tokyo), but you'll have to change in Paris. For a less convenient trans-Asian route, count on about UK£350.

Popular travel agencies in the UK include **STA Travel** (☎ *0870-1 600 599;* W *www.statravel.co.uk)*; **Trailfinders** (☎ *020- 7938 3939;* W *www.trailfinders.co.uk; 194 Kensington High St, London W8 7RG)*; and **Bridge the World** (☎ *0870-444 7474;* W *www.bridgetheworld.com; 4 Regent Place, London W1B 5EA)*.

Continental Europe Most direct flights between Europe and Japan fly into Tokyo but there are also some flights into Kansai. Typical low-season return fares from major European cities are Frankfurt–Tokyo €500, Rome–Tokyo €700 and Paris–Tokyo €580.

Recommended travel agencies in continental Europe include the following:

France
OTU Voyages (☎ 08 20 81 78 17, W www .otu.fr)
Nouvelles Frontières (☎ 08 25 00 07 47, W www.nouvelles-frontieres.fr)

Germany
STA Travel (☎ 01805 456 422, W www .statravel.de)

Italy
CTS Viaggi (☎ 840 50 11 50, W www.cts.it)

Spain
Usit Unlimited (☎ 902 25 25 75, W www.unlimited.es)

Switzerland
STA Travel (☎ 01 297 11 11, W www.ssr.ch)

The Netherlands
NBBS Reizen (☎ 0900 102 0300, W www .nbbs.nl)

South Korea Numerous flights link Seoul and Pusan with Japan. A Seoul–Tokyo flight purchased in Seoul costs around US$180/340 one way/return. From Tokyo, flights to Seoul are the cheapest way out of Japan. Low-season return fares start as low as ¥25,000.

In Seoul, **Joy Travel Service** (☎ *02-776 9871; 10th floor, 24-2 Mukyo-dong, Chung- gu)*, directly behind City Hall, offers good deals and has English-speaking staff. Cheap deals can also be found at the **Korean International Student Exchange Society** (*KISES;* ☎ *02-733 9494; 5th floor, YMCA building, Chongno 2-ga)*.

See the Sea section later in this chapter for information on sea-travel bargains between Korea and Japan.

China There are several daily flights between Japan and Hong Kong on Cathay Pacific, as well as on JAL, ANA and JAS (Japan Air System). Hong Kong–Tokyo return costs around US$900. Many travellers use the **Hong Kong Student Travel Bureau** (☎ *02-2730 3269; room 1021, 10th floor, Star House, Tsimshatsui)*. You might also try **Phoenix Services** (☎ *02-2722 7378; 7th floor, Milton Mansion, 96 Nathan Rd, Tsimshatsui)*.

There are also flights between Japan and Beijing, Shanghai, Guangzhou and Dalian on all the Japanese carriers as well as on Air China, China Eastern Airways and China Southern Air. Beijing–Tokyo costs around US$800 return.

Taiwan Return flights from Taipei to Tokyo start at around NT10,400. Flights also operate between Kaohsiung and Osaka or Tokyo.

A long-running agent is **Jenny Su Travel** (☎ *02-2506-6380; 4th floor, No 100, Section 1, Chungshiao W Rd, Taipei)*. In addition, **Wing On Travel** and **South-East Travel** have branches all over the island.

Other Asian Countries There are daily flights between Bangkok and Japan on Thai Airways International, ANA and Japan Airlines, with fares starting at about 17,000B return in the low season. From Singapore, return tickets cost about S$850; from Indonesia (Jakarta/Denpasar), a return flight costs around US$800.

From the Philippines (Manila) a return flight to Japan is around US$450 and from Malaysia (Kuala Lumpur) it's RM2500 return. From Vietnam (Ho Chi Minh City) a return flight costs US$660.

Other Asian countries with limited flights to Japan include India, Nepal and Myanmar (Burma).

Other Regions There are also flights between Japan and South America (via the USA), Africa (via Europe or south Asia) and the Middle East.

Travellers with Special Needs

If you have a special need – a broken leg, a wheelchair, a baby, dietary restrictions, fear of flying – let the airline know early so that it can make arrangements. Also remind the airline when you reconfirm your booking (at least 72 hours prior to departure), and again when you check in at the airport.

SEA
South Korea

South Korea is the closest country to Japan and a popular visa-renewal point. Many long-term visitors to Japan, who are teaching English or who are engaged in some other kind of work, drop over to Korea when their visa is about to expire and then come back to start a fresh stay. For this reason you can expect to have your passport rigorously inspected.

Pusan–Shimonoseki The **Kampu Ferry Service** (in Japan ☎ 0832-24-3000, in Korea ☎ 051-464-2700; W www.kampuferry.co.jp Japanese only) operates the Shimonoseki–Pusan ferry service. There are daily departures at 7pm from Shimonoseki and Pusan, arriving at the other end at 8.30am the next morning. One-way fares range from ¥8500 to ¥18,000. There's a 10% discount on return fares. See the Shimonoseki section of the Western Honshū chapter for more details.

Pusan–Fukuoka An international high-speed hydrofoil service known as the 'Beetle' run by JR Kyūshū (in Japan ☎ 092-281-2315, in Korea ☎ 051-465-6111) connects Fukuoka with Pusan in Korea, taking about three hours (¥13,000, two daily). The Camellia line (in Japan ☎ 092-262-2323, in Korea ☎ 051-466-7799; W www.camellia-line.co.jp Japanese only) also has a regular daily ferry service between Fukuoka and Pusan (¥9000, 14½ hours). See the Fukuoka section of the Kyūshū chapter for more details.

China

The **Japan China International Ferry Company** (in Japan ☎ 06-6536-6541; W www.fune.co.jp/chinjif/index.html Japanese only) connects Shanghai and Osaka/Kōbe. A 2nd-class ticket costs around US$180. A similar service is provided by the **Shanghai Ferry Company** (in Japan ☎ 06-6243-6345, in China ☎ 021-6537-5111; W www.shanghai-ferry.co.jp).

The **China Express Line** (in Japan ☎ 078-321-5791, in China ☎ 022-2420-5777; W www2.celkobe.co.jp) operates a ferry between Kōbe and Tanggu (near Tianjin). Ferries leave from Kōbe every Thursday at noon, arriving in Tanggu the next day. Economy/1st-class tickets cost US$200/US$300.

Orient Ferry Ltd (in Japan ☎ 0832-32-6615, in China ☎ 0532-389-7636; W www.orientferry.co.jp) runs between Shimonoseki and Qingdao, China, with two departures a week. The cheapest tickets cost one-way/return ¥18,000/34,200.

Taiwan

Arimura Sangyō (in Japan ☎ 098-869-1980, in Taiwan ☎ 07-330-9811) operates a weekly ferry service between Okinawa and Taiwan, sometimes via Ishigaki and Miyako in Okinawa-ken. The Taiwan port alternates between Keelung and Kaohsiung. Departure from Okinawa is on Thursday or Friday; departure from Taiwan is usually on Monday. The journey takes about 22 hours. Fares from Okinawa cost from ¥18,000 in second class.

Russia

FKK Air Service (☎ 0766-22-2212; W http://fkk-air.toyama-net.com Japanese only) operates ferries between Fushiki in Toyama-ken and Vladivostok. One-way fares start at ¥25,200.

An even more exotic route is the summertime route between Wakkanai (in Hokkaidō) and Korsakov (on Sahkalin Island) operated by the **East Japan Sea Ferry Company** (in Japan ☎ 0162-23-3780,

in Russia ☎ *4242-42-0917;* Ⓦ *www.kaiferry
.co.jp).* One-way fares start at ¥28,000. The
ferry operates from mid-July to the end of
September.

TRANS-SIBERIAN RAILWAY

A little-used option of approaching or
leaving Japan is the Trans-Siberian Railway.
There are three Trans-Siberian Railway options, one of which is to travel on the
railway to/from Vladivostok and take the
ferry between Vladivostok and Fushiki
in Toyama-ken. The cheaper options are
the Chinese Trans-Mongolia and Russian
Trans-Manchuria routes, which start/finish
in China, from where there are ferry
connections to/from Japan via Tianjin,
Qingdao and Shanghai.

Information on ferry connections between
Japan, Russia and China is included in the
Sea section of this chapter.

More detailed information is also available in a good number of publications –

Bringing Animals to Japan

Japanese regulations on the importation of
live animals are very strict, and are not waived
for guide dogs. Dogs brought from countries
in which rabies has been eradicated need not
be quarantined, provided their owners can
show an exportation certificate *(yūshutsu
shomeisho).* Dogs arriving from countries
in which rabies occurs will be placed into
quarantine for up to six months, unless their
owners can supply an exportation certificate,
veterinary examination certification and written proof of rabies vaccination.

see Lonely Planet's *Trans-Siberian Railway: A Classic Overland Route.* Those
making their way to Japan via China (or
vice versa) should pick up a copy of Lonely
Planet's *China* guide, which has invaluable
information on travel in China as well as
information on Trans-Siberian travel.

Getting Around

Japan is justifiably famous for its extensive, well-organised and efficient transportation network. Schedules are strictly adhered to and late or cancelled services are almost unheard of. All this convenience comes at a price, however, and you'd be well advised to look into money-saving deals whenever possible (see Train Passes & Discount Tickets under Train later in this chapter).

Travel Agencies

Information and tickets can be obtained from travel agencies, of which there are a great number in Japan. Nearly every railway station of any size will have at least one travel agency in the station building to handle all sorts of bookings in addition to train services. JTB (Japan Travel Bureau) is the big daddy of Japanese travel agencies. However, for most train tickets and long-distance bus reservations, you don't need a travel agency – just go to the ticket counters or *midori-no-madoguchi* (green counters) of any major train station.

Discount Ticket Shops Known as *kaku-yasu-kippu-uriba* in Japanese, these stores deal in discounted tickets for trains, buses, domestic plane flights, ferries, and a host of other things like cut-rate stamps and phone cards. You can typically save between 5% and 10% on *shinkansen* tickets. Discount ticket agencies are found around train stations in medium and large cities. The best way to find one is to ask at the *kōban* (police box) outside the station.

Baggage Forwarding

If you have too much luggage to carry comfortably or just can't be bothered, you can do what many Japanese travellers do: send it to your next stop by *takkyūbin* (express shipping companies). Prices are surprisingly reasonable and overnight service is the norm. Perhaps the most convenient service is Yamato Takyūbin, which operates from most convenience stores. Simply pack your luggage and bring it to the nearest convenience store; they'll help with the paperwork and arrange for pick-up. Note that you'll need the full address of your next destination in Japanese, along with the phone number of the place. Alternatively, ask the owner of your accommodation to have them come and pick it up (this is usually possible but might cost extra).

AIR

Air services in Japan are extensive, reliable and safe. In many cases, flying is much faster than even *shinkansen* travel and not that much more expensive. Flying is also an efficient way to travel from the main islands to the many small islands around the coast of Japan.

Domestic Air Services

Japan Air Lines *(JAL;* Ⓦ *www.jal.co.jp/en)* is the major international carrier and also has a domestic network linking the major cities. **All Nippon Airways** *(ANA;* Ⓦ *http:// svc.ana.co.jp/eng/index.html)* is the second largest international carrier and operates a more extensive domestic system. **Japan Air Systems** *(JAS;* Ⓦ *www.jas.co.jp/eng/ index.htm)* only does a couple of overseas routes but flies to many destinations in Japan. **Air Nippon Koku** *(ANK;* Ⓦ *www .air-nippon.co.jp Japanese only)* and **Japan Trans Ocean Air** *(JTA;* Ⓦ *www.jal.co.jp/jta Japanese only)* are smaller domestic carriers. ANK links many smaller towns all over Japan, while JTA is particularly good for connections through Okinawa and the Southwest Islands. In addition to these, **Skymark** *(*Ⓦ *www.skymark.co.jp Japanese only)* is a recent start-up airline that undercuts the prices of the more established airlines.

The Domestic Airfares map shows some of the major connections and one-way fares. Note that return fares are usually around 10% cheaper than buying two one-way tickets. The airlines also have some weird and wonderful discounts if you know what to ask for. The most useful of these are the advance-purchase reductions: both ANA and JAL offer discounts of up to 50% if you purchase your ticket a month or more in advance, with smaller discounts for purchases made one to three weeks in advance. Seniors over 65 also qualify for discounts on most Japanese airlines, but these are sometimes only available if you fly on weekdays.

ANA(w www.ana-sin.com.sg/htm/english /vjf.htm) also offers the Visit Japan Fare for foreign travellers. Provided you reside outside Japan, purchase your tickets outside Japan and carry a valid international ticket on any airline, you can fly up to five times within 60 days on any ANA domestic route for only ¥12,600 per flight (a huge saving on some routes). For more details, see the ANA website.

TRAIN

Japanese rail services are among the best in the world: they are fast, frequent, clean and comfortable. Unfortunately, for long-distance services, they tend to be expensive. The services range from small local lines to the *shinkansen* super-expresses or 'bullet trains' which have become a symbol of modern Japan.

Schedules & Information

The most complete timetables can be found in the *JR Jikokuhyō* (book of timetables; available at all Japanese bookstores; writ-

ten in Japanese). If you can't be bothered to fight your way through that, the Japan National Tourist Organization (JNTO) produces a handy English-language *Railway Timetable* booklet which explains a great deal about the services in Japan and gives timetables for the *shinkansen* services, JR *tokkyū* (limited express services) and major private lines. If your visit to Japan is a short one and you will not be straying far from the major tourist destinations, this booklet may well be all you need.

The TIC offices at Narita airport, Tokyo and Kyoto can also supply information on specific schedules. Major train stations all have information counters, and you can usually get your point across in simplified English.

If you need to know anything about JR, such as schedules, fares, fastest routes, lost baggage, discounts on rail travel, hotels and car rental, call the **JR East-Infoline** (☎ 03-3423-0111; w www.jreast.co.jp/e; *operates 10am-6pm Mon-Fri, closed holidays*). Information is available in English, Korean and Chinese. More information can be found on the website.

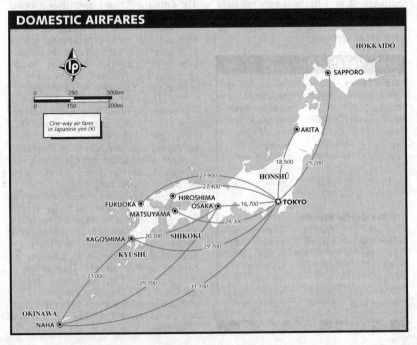

DOMESTIC AIRFARES

Train Stations

Train stations in Japan are usually very well equipped. The main station is often literally the town centre and, in many cases, is part of a large shopping centre with a wide variety of restaurants, bars, fast-food outlets and other facilities.

Meals The Japanese rail system is not renowned for its high-class cuisine, though you may find that the *shinkansen* dining cars turn out pretty good food. Anyway, you certainly won't starve, as apart from the dining cars, there are snacks, drinks, ice creams and meals sold by vendors who prowl the aisles. A good bet is to come prepared with a *bentō* (boxed lunch). At almost every station there is a shop selling *bentō*, typically for ¥1000 or less.

Left Luggage Only major stations have left-luggage facilities, but there are almost always coin-operated storage lockers that cost ¥100 to ¥500 per day, depending on their size. The lockers work until midnight (not for 24 hours) so, after that time, you have to insert more money before your key will work. If your bag is simply too large to fit in the locker, ask someone *'tenimotsu azukai wa doko desu ka'* ('Where is the left-luggage office?').

Train Vocabulary

Train Types

shinkansen	新幹線	bullet train
tokkyū	特急	limited express
shin-kaisoku	新快速	JR special rapid train
kyūkō	急行	express
kaisoku	快速	JR rapid or express
futsū	普通	local
kaku-eki-teisha	各駅停車	local

Other Useful Words

jiyū-seki	自由席	unreserved seat
shitei-seki	指定席	reserved seat
green-sha	グリーン車	first-class car
ōfuku	往復	round trip
katamichi	片道	one way
kin'en-sha	禁煙車	nonsmoking car
kitsuen-sha	喫煙車	smoking car

Japan Railways

Japan Railways (JR) is actually a number of separate private rail systems that provide one linked service. The JR system covers the country from one end to the other and also provides local services around major cities like Tokyo and Osaka. There is more than 20,000km of railway line and about 20,000 services daily. *Shinkansen* lines are totally separate from the regular railways and, in some places, the *shinkansen* stations are a fair distance from the main JR station (as is the case in Osaka). JR also operates buses and ferries, and ticketing can combine more than one form of transport.

For more information on JR, see the earlier Schedules & Information section.

Private Railways

The private train lines usually operate short routes, often no more than 100km in length. Local commuter services are often on private train lines. Unlike JR stations, the private-line stations do not usually form the central focus of a town.

Shinkansen

The fastest and best-known train services in Japan are the *shinkansen* (bullet trains). The *shinkansen* reach speeds of up to 300km/h and some experimental models have gone significantly faster. In addition to being incredibly fast, *shinkansen* are also incredibly safe: in more than 30 years of operation, there has never been a fatality.

The service efficiency starts even before you board the train. Your ticket indicates your carriage and seat number, and platform signs indicate where you should stand for that carriage entrance. The train pulls in precisely to the scheduled minute and, sure enough, the carriage door you want is right beside where you're standing.

On most *shinkansen* routes, there are two or three types of services: faster express services stopping at a limited number of stations and slower local services stopping at all *shinkansen* stations. There is no difference in fare with the exception of the super-express Nozomi service on the Tōkaidō/San-yō *shinkansen* line. There are, however, regular and Green Car (1st class) carriages.

There are a limited number of nonsmoking carriages *(kin'en-sha)*; request one when booking or ask on the platform for the unreserved nonsmoking cars *(kin'en-sha-jiyū-seki)*. Unreserved carriages are available on all but the super-express No-zomi service, but at peak holiday periods they can be very crowded and you may have to stand for the entire trip.

For prices on specific *shinkansen* routes, see the table under Costs.

Other Train Services

In addition to the *shinkansen* routes that run most of the length of Honshū and down into Kyūshū, a network of JR lines, supplemented by a scattering of shorter private lines, cover much of the rest of Japan. Although these services are efficient, they are nowhere near as fast as the *shinkansen*, and typically take about twice as long (see Train Passes & Discount Tickets later in this chapter for more information about non-*shinkansen* trains.)

Classes

All JR trains, including the *shinkansen*, have regular and Green Car carriages. The seating is slightly more spacious in Green Car carriages, but most people will find the regular carriages perfectly acceptable.

The slowest trains stopping at all stations are called *futsū* or *kaku-eki-teisha*. A step up from this is the *kyūkō* (ordinary express), which stops at only a limited number of stations. A variation on the *kyūkō* trains is the *kaisoku* (rapid) service. Finally, the fastest regular (non-*shinkansen*) trains are the *tokkyū* services, which are sometimes known as *shin-kaisoku*.

Women-Only Cars

Several train companies in Japan have recently introduced women-only cars to protect female passengers from *chikan* (men who feel up women on packed trains). These cars are usually available during rush-hour periods on weekdays on busy urban lines. There are signs on the platform indicating where to board these cars, and the cars themselves are usually labelled in both Japanese and English.

Reservations

Tickets for most journeys can be bought from vending machines or ticket counters/reservation offices. For reservations of complicated tickets, larger train stations have

midori-no-madoguchi – look for the counter with the green band across the glass. Major travel agencies in Japan also sell reserved-seat tickets, and you can buy *shinkansen* tickets through JAL offices overseas if you will be flying JAL to Japan.

On *futsū* (local train) services, there are no reserved seats. On the faster *tokkyū* and *shinkansen* services you can choose to travel reserved or unreserved. However, if you travel unreserved, there's always the risk of not getting a seat and having to stand, possibly for the entire trip. This is a particular danger at weekends, peak travel seasons and on holidays. Reserved-seat tickets can be bought any time from a month in advance to the day of departure.

Costs

JR fares are calculated on the basis of *futsū-unchin* (basic fare), *tokkyū-ryōkin* (an express surcharge levied only on express services) and *shinkansen-ryōkin* (a special charge for *shinkansen* services); see the Surcharges entry. The following are some typical fares from Tokyo or Ueno, not including the new Nozomi super express (prices given for *shinkansen* are the total price of the ticket):

destination	basic fare (¥)	shinkansen (¥)
Fukushima	4620	8700
Hakata	13,440	21,720
Hiroshima	11,340	18,050
Kyoto	7980	13,220
Morioka	8190	13,840
Nagoya	6090	10,580
Niigata	5640	10,270
Okayama	10,190	16,360
Osaka	8510	13,750
Sendai	5780	10,590
Shimonoseki	12,810	20,570

Surcharges Various surcharges may be added to the basic fare. These include reserved seat, Green Car, express service and *shinkansen* surcharges. You may also have to pay a surcharge for special trains to resort areas or for a seat in an observation car. The express surcharges (but not the *shinkansen* super-express surcharge) can be paid to the train conductor on board the train.

Further surcharges apply for overnight sleepers, and these vary with the berth type, from ¥5250 for a regular three-tier bunk,

¥6300 to ¥10,500 for various types of two-tier bunks, and up to ¥13,350 to ¥17,180 for a standard or 'royal' compartment. Note that there are no sleepers on the *shinkansen* services as none of these run overnight. Japan Rail Pass users must still pay the sleeper surcharge. Sleeper services mainly operate on trains from Tokyo or Osaka to destinations in Western Honshū and Kyūshū.

The Nozomi super express has higher surcharges than other *shinkansen* services and cannot be used with a Japan Rail Pass. As a guideline, the Nozomi surcharge for Tokyo–Kyoto is ¥6210 as opposed to ¥5240 by other *shinkansen*; for Tokyo–Hakata ¥10,120 as opposed to ¥8280 by other *shinkansen*.

Travel Seasons Some of the fare surcharges are slightly higher (5% to 10%) during peak travel seasons. This applies mainly to reserved seat tickets. Peak season dates are 21 March to 5 April, 28 April to 6 May, 21 July to 31 August, and 25 December to 10 January.

Train Passes & Discount Tickets

If you plan to do any extended travel in Japan, a Japan Rail Pass is almost essential. Not only will it save you lots of money, it will also spare you the hassle of buying tickets each time you want to board a train.

In addition to the Japan Rail Pass, there are various discount tickets and special fares available. The most basic is the return fare discount: if you buy a return ticket for a trip which is more than 600km each way, you qualify for a 10% discount on the return leg. Other special deals are as follows.

Kansai Thru Pass See the Special Ticket Deals section of the Kansai chapter for details on this excellent pass, which allows unlimited travel on all non-JR private train lines and most bus lines in Kansai.

Shūyū-ken & Furii Kippu There are a number of excursion tickets, known as *shūyū-ken* or *furii kippu* (*furii* is Japanese for 'free'). These tickets include the return fare to your destination and give you unlimited JR local travel within the destination area. There are *shūyū-ken* available to travel from Tokyo to Hokkaidō and then

around Hokkaidō for up to seven days. A Kyūshū or Shikoku *shūyū-ken* gets you to and from either island and gives you four or five days of travel around them. You can even go to Kyūshū one way by rail and one way by ferry.

Japan Rail Pass One of Japan's few real travel bargains is the Japan Rail Pass. The pass lets you use any JR service for seven days for ¥28,300, 14 days for ¥45,100 or 21 days for ¥57,700. Green Car passes are ¥37,800, ¥61,200 and ¥79,600, respectively. The pass cannot be used for the new super express Nozomi *shinkansen* service, but is OK for everything else (including other *shinkansen* services). The only surcharge levied on the Japan Rail Pass is for overnight sleepers. Since a reserved seat Tokyo–Kyoto *shinkansen* ticket costs ¥13,220, you only have to travel Tokyo–Kyoto–Tokyo to make a seven-day pass come close to paying off. Note that the pass is valid *only* on JR services; you will still have to pay for private train services.

The pass can only be bought overseas at JAL and ANA offices and major travel agencies. It can only be used by those with a temporary visitor visa (you'll need to show your passport), which means it cannot be used by foreign residents of Japan (those on any visa other than the temporary visitor visa).

The clock starts to tick on the pass as soon as you validate it, which can be done at JR Travel Service Centres located in most major train stations, and at Narita and Kansai airports if you're intending to jump on a JR train immediately. Don't validate it if you're just going into Tokyo or Kyoto and intend to hang around for a few days.

For more details on the pass and overseas purchase locations, visit the JR website's **Japan Rail Pass section** (**w** *www.japanrail pass.net/eng/en01.shtml*).

JR East Pass This is a great deal for those who only want to travel in eastern Japan. The passes are good on all JR lines in eastern Japan (including Tōhoku, Yamagata, Akita, Jōetsu and Nagano *shinkansen*, but not including the Tōkaidō *shinkansen*). This includes the area around Tokyo and everything north of Tokyo to the tip of Honshū, but doesn't include Hokkaidō.

Prices for five-day passes are ¥20,000 for adults over 26, ¥16,000 for youths between 16 and 25, and ¥10,000 for children between six and 11. Ten-day passes are ¥32,000/25,000/16,000 for the same age groups. Four-day 'flexible' passes are also available which allow travel on any four consecutive or nonconsecutive days within any one-month period. These cost ¥20,000/16,000/10,000 for the same age groups. Green Car passes are available for higher prices.

As with the Japan Rail Pass, this can only be purchased outside Japan (in the same locations as the Japan Rail Pass) and can only be used by those with temporary visitor visas (you'll need to show your passport).

For more information on the JR East Pass, visit the website's **JR East Pass section** (**W** *www.jreast.co.jp/eastpass/index.htm*).

JR West San-yō Area Pass

Similar to the JR East Pass, this pass allows unlimited travel on the San-yō *shinkansen* line (including the Nozomi super express) between Osaka and Hakata, as well as local trains running between the same cities. A four-day pass costs ¥20,000 and an eight-day pass costs ¥30,000 (children's passes are half-price). These can be purchased both inside Japan (at major train stations, travel agencies and Kansai airport) and outside Japan (same locations as the Japan Rail Pass) but can only be used by those with a temporary visitor visa. The pass also entitles you to discounts on car rentals at station rent-a-car offices. For more information on this pass, see the website of **JR West** (**W** *www.westjr.co.jp/english /english/index.html*).

JR West Kansai Area Pass

A great deal for those who only want to explore the Kansai area, this pass covers unlimited travel on JR lines between most major Kansai cities, such as Himeji, Kōbe, Osaka, Kyoto and Nara. It also covers JR trains to/from Kansai airport but does not cover any *shinkansen* lines. A one-day pass costs ¥2000 and a four-day pass costs ¥6000 (children's passes are half-price). These can be purchased at the same places as the San-yō area rail pass and also entitle you to discounts on station rent-a-car offices. Like the San-yō Area Pass, this pass can only be used by those with a temporary visitor visa. For more information on this pass, visit the website of **JR West** (**W** *www.westjr.co.jp/ english/english/index.html*).

JR Kyūshū Rail Pass

This pass is valid on all JR lines in Kyūshū with the exception of the *shinkansen* line. It costs ¥15,000 for a five-day pass and ¥20,000 for a seven-day pass. Like the Japan Rail Pass, it must be purchased outside Japan (see the Japan Rail Pass entry earlier for purchase details) and can only be used by those on a temporary visitor visa. The pass can be activated at major train stations in Kyūshū. For more information, visit the website of **JR Kyūshū** (**W** *www.jrkyushu.co.jp/english/ f_railpass1.html*).

Seishun Jūhachi Kippu

If you don't have a Japan Rail Pass, one of the best deals going is a five-day *Seishun Jūhachi Kippu* (literally a 'Youth 18 Ticket'). Despite its name, it can be used by anyone of any age. Basically, for ¥11,500 you get five one-day tickets valid for travel anywhere in Japan on JR lines. The only catches are that you can't travel on *tokkyū* or *shinkansen* trains and each ticket must be used within 24 hours. However, even if you only have to make a return trip, say, between Tokyo and Kyoto, you'll be saving a lot of money.

The tickets are intended to be used during Japanese university holidays. There are three periods of sales and validity: spring – from 20 February to 31 March and valid for use between 1 March and 10 April; summer – from 1 July to 31 August and valid for use between 20 July and 10 September; winter – from 1 December to 10 January and valid for use between 20 December and 20 January. Note that these periods are subject to change. For more information, ask at any JR ticket window or JNTO-operated TIC.

If you don't want to buy the whole book of five tickets, you can sometimes purchase separate tickets at the discount ticket shops around train stations (see Discount Ticket Shops earlier in this chapter).

BUS

Japan has a comprehensive network of long-distance buses. These 'highway buses' are nowhere near as fast as the *shinkansen* but the fares are comparable with those of the *futsū* without any reservation or express surcharges. The trip between Tokyo and Sendai (Northern Honshū), for example, takes about two hours by *shinkansen*, four hours by *tokkyū* and nearly eight hours by bus. Of course, there are also many places in Japan where trains do not run and bus travel is the only public transport option.

Bookings can be made through any travel agency in Japan or at the Green Window in large JR stations. The Japan Rail Pass is valid on some highway buses although, of course, the *shinkansen* would be far preferable! Note, however, that the storage racks on most buses are generally too small for large backpacks, but on most buses you can stow them in the luggage compartment underneath the bus.

Night Services

An option that is becoming increasingly popular among travellers is the network of night buses. They are relatively cheap, spacious (allowing room to stretch out and get some sleep) and they also save on a night's accommodation. They typically leave at around 10pm or 11pm and arrive the following day at around 6am or 7am.

Costs

Some typical long-distance prices out of Tokyo include:

destination	fare (¥)
Aomori	10,190
Hakata	15,000
Hiroshima	12,060
Kyoto	8180
Nagoya	6420
Niigata	5250
Osaka	8610
Sendai	6210

CAR

Driving in Japan is quite feasible, even for the just mildly adventurous. The major roads are signposted in English; traffic rules are generally adhered to and driving is safer than other Asian countries; and gas, while expensive, is not prohibitively so. Indeed, in some areas of the country it can prove much more convenient than other forms of travel and, between a group of people, it can also prove quite economical.

On the Road

Driver's Licence Travellers from most nations are able to drive in Japan with an International Driving Permit backed up by their own regular licence. The international permit is issued by your national automobile association and costs around US$5 in most countries. Make sure it's endorsed for cars and motorcycles if you're licensed for both.

Travellers from Switzerland, France and Germany (and others whose countries are not signatories to the Geneva Convention of 1949 concerning international driver's licences) are not allowed to drive in Japan on a regular international licence. Rather, travellers from these countries must have their own licence backed by an authorised translation of the same licence. These translations can be made by their country's embassy or consulate in Japan or by the Japan Automobile Federation (JAF; see the Maps and Navigation entry for contact details). If you are unsure which category your country falls into, contact the nearest JNTO office (see the Facts for the Visitor chapter for contact details).

Foreign licences and International Driving Permits are only valid in Japan for six months. If you are staying longer, you will have to get a Japanese licence from the local department of motor vehicles. To do this, you will need to provide your own licence, passport photos, Alien Registration Card, the fee, and there's also a simple eyesight test.

Fuel You'll find *gasoreen sutando* (petrol stations) in almost every town in Japan and in service stations along the country's expressways. The cost of petrol ranges from ¥95 to ¥140 per litre.

Maps & Navigation Get yourself a copy of the *Japan Road Atlas* (Shobunsha, ¥2890). It's all in romaji with enough names in kanji to make navigation possible even off the major roads. If you're really intent on making your way through the back blocks, a Japanese map will prove useful even if your knowledge of kanji is nil. The best Japanese road atlases by far are the Super Mapple series (Shobunsha), which are available in bookshops and some convenience stores.

These days, there is a great deal of signposting in romaji so getting around isn't all that difficult. Road route numbers also help; for example, if you know you want to follow Route 9 until you get to Route 36 the frequent roadside numbers make navigation child's play. If you are attempting tricky navigation, use your maps imaginatively – watch out for the railway line, the rivers, the landmarks. They're all useful ways of locating yourself when you can't read the signs. A compass will also come in handy when navigating.

If you're a member of an automobile association in your home country, you're eligible for reciprocal rights at the **Japan Automobile Federation** (JAF; ☎ 03-3436-2811; w *www.jaf.or.jp/e/index_e.htm; Kikaishinkō Kaikan Biru, 3-5-8 Shiba-kōen, Minato-ku, Tokyo 105*). Its office is directly opposite the entrance to Tokyo Tower. JAF publishes a variety of publications, and will make up strip maps for its members.

Road Rules
Driving in Japan is on the left. Apart from being on the wrong side of the road from the continental European or North American perspective, there are no real problems with driving in Japan. There are no unusual rules or interpretations of them and most signposts follow international conventions. JAF has an English-language *Rules of the Road* book for ¥1000. See the previous section for more information about JAF.

Rental
Car rental offices cluster round train stations and the best way to use rental cars in Japan is to take a train for the long-distance part of your trip, then rent a car when you get to the area you want to explore. For example, the northern San-in coast of Western Honshū is a good place to drive – but don't drive there from Tokyo, take the train to Kyoto and rent a car from there.

Japanese car rental companies are set up for this type of operation and offer lots of short-term rates – such as for people who just want a car for half a day. However, they're not much good at one-way rentals; you'll usually have to pay a repositioning charge and if the car has to be brought back from another island, the cost can be very high indeed. Typical one-way charges within the island of Honshū are ¥6000 for 100km and ¥2400 for each additional 50km. It makes a lot of sense to make your

trip a loop one and return the car to the original renting office. Some of the main Japanese car rental companies and their Tokyo phone numbers are:

Dollar Rent-a-Car ☎ 03-3567-2818
Hertz ☎ 0120-489-882
Toyota Rent-a-Lease ☎ 0070-8000-10000

Typical rental rates for a small car is ¥6500 to ¥9000 for the first day and ¥4500 to ¥7000 per day thereafter. Move up a bracket and you're looking at ¥9000 to ¥13,500 for the first day and ¥7000 to ¥9000 thereafter. On top of the rental charge, there's a ¥1000 per day insurance cost.

Many rental places offer unlimited kilometres but you should check before heading out. It's also a good idea to check prices at local rent-a-car places. These places can usually match the rates of the big chains and are a good choice when you just want to rent for three or six hours to get around an island or obscure peninsula.

It's also worth bearing in mind that rental costs go up during peak seasons – 28 April to 6 May, 20 July to 31 August, and 28 December to 5 January. The increase can make quite a difference to costs. A car that costs ¥8800 a day will usually go up to ¥9700 during any of the peak seasons.

Communication can be a major problem when renting a car. Some of the offices will have a rent-a-car phrasebook, with questions you might need to ask in English. Otherwise, just speak as slowly as possible and hope for the best.

Expressways
The expressway system will get you from one end of the country to another but it is not particularly extensive. Also, since all the expressways charge tolls, it is uniformly expensive – about ¥27 per kilometre. Tokyo to Kyoto, for example, will cost about ¥9000 in tolls. The speed limit on expressways is 80km/h but seems to be uniformly ignored. At a steady 100km/h, you will still find as many cars overtaking you as you overtake, some of them going very fast indeed.

There are good rest stops and service centres at regular intervals. A prepaid highway card, available from tollbooths or at the service areas, saves you having to carry so much cash and gives you a 4% to 8%

discount in the larger card denominations. You can also pay tolls with most major credit cards, although some toll-booth operators seem unaware of this. Exits are usually fairly well-signposted in romaji but make sure you know the name of your exit as it may not necessarily be the same as the city you're heading towards.

Parking

In most big cities, free curbside parking spots are almost nonexistent, while in rural areas you'll be able to park your car just about wherever you want to. If you do have the nerve to drive into a big Japanese city, you'll find that you usually have to pay ¥200 per hour for metered street parking, or anywhere from ¥300 to ¥600 per hour for a spot in a multistorey car park. You'll find car parks around most department stores and near some train stations. Fortunately, most hotels have free parking for guests, as do some restaurants and almost all department stores (you'll have to get a stamp inside the store to show that you've actually been shopping there).

MOTORCYCLE
Rental & Purchase

Renting a motorcycle for long-distance touring is not as easy as renting a car, although small scooters are available in many places for local sightseeing.

If you enjoy motorcycles and you're staying long enough to make buying and selling a motorcycle worthwhile, then this can be a great way of getting around the country. A motorcycle provides the advantages of your own transport without the automotive drawback of finding a place to park. Nor do you suffer so badly from the congested traffic.

Although Japan is famed for its large-capacity road burners, most bikes on the road are 400cc or less. This is because a special licence is required to ride a bike larger than 400cc and few Japanese and even fewer foreigners pass the test necessary to get this licence.

The 400cc machines are the most popular large motorcycles in Japan but, for general touring, a 250cc machine is probably the best bet. Apart from being large enough for a compact country like Japan, machines up to 250cc are also exempt from the expensive *shaken* (inspections).

Smaller machines (below 125cc) are banned from expressways and are generally less suitable for long-distance touring but people have ridden from one end of Japan to another on little 50cc 'step-thrus'. An advantage of these bikes is that you can ride them with just a regular driving licence, and you won't need to get a motorcycle licence.

Buying a new machine is no problem, though you will find a better choice of large capacity machines in the big cities. Used motorcycles are often not much cheaper than new ones and, unless you buy from another foreigner, you will face the usual language problems in finding and buying one.

The best place to look for motorcycles in Japan is the Korin-chō motorcycle neighbourhood in Tokyo's Ueno district. There are over 20 motorcycle shops in the area and some employ foreign salespeople who speak both Japanese and English. For used bikes in Kansai check *Kansai Time Out*, *Kansai Flea Market*, or the message board in the Kyoto International Community House.

On the Road

For citizens of most countries, your overseas licence and an International Driving Permit are all you need to ride a motorcycle in Japan (see the Driver's Licence entry for details on which nationalities require different documentation). Crash helmets are compulsory and you should also ensure your riding gear is adequate to cope with the weather, particularly rain. For much of the year the climate is ideal for motorcycle touring, but when it rains it really rains.

Touring equipment – panniers, carrier racks, straps and the like – is readily available from dealers. Remember to pack clothing in plastic bags to ensure it stays dry, even if you don't. An adequate supply of tools and a puncture repair kit can prove invaluable.

Riding in Japan is no more dangerous than anywhere else in the world, which is to say it is not very safe and great care should be taken at all times. Japan has the full range of motorcycle hazards from single-minded taxi drivers to unexpected changes in road surface, heedless car-door openers to runaway dogs.

BICYCLE

Exploring Japan by bicycle is perfectly feasible. The secret of enjoyable touring is to get off the busy main highways and onto the minor roads. This requires careful route planning, good maps and either some ability with kanji or the patience to decipher country road signs, where romaji is much less likely to be used. Favourite touring areas include Kyūshū, Shikoku, the Japan Alps (if you like steep hills!), Noto-hantō and Hokkaidō.

There's no point in fighting your way out of big cities by bicycle. Put your bike on the train or bus and get out to the country before you start pedalling. To take a bicycle on a train you may be required to use a bicycle carrying bag: they're available from good bicycle shops.

See Maps & Navigation earlier in this chapter for information on road maps of Japan. There is also a series of Bridgestone cycling maps *(saikuringu mapu)*. They identify many places in romaji as well as kanji but, as yet, only cover Central Honshū. The cycling maps show where bicycles can be rented, identify special bicycle tracks and biker-friendly accommodation, and even show steep road gradients. For other areas, try the *Touring Mapple* (Shobunsha) series, which is aimed at motorcyclists, but is also very useful for cyclists.

For more information on cycling in Japan, you can check out the excellent **Kancycling website** (**W** www.kancycling.com /index.html).

Purchase & Rental

It is not easy to rent a touring bike for a long trip but, in many towns, you can rent bicycles to explore the town. Look for bicycle-rental outlets near the railway station; typical charges are around ¥200 per hour or ¥1000 per day. Kyoto, for example, is ideally suited to bicycle exploration and there are plenty of cheap rental shops to choose from.

Many youth hostels also have bicycles to rent – there's a symbol identifying them in the *Japan Youth Hostel Handbook*. The so-called cycling terminals found in various locations around the country (see Accommodation in the Facts for the Visitor chapter) also rent bicycles.

If you already have some experience of bicycle touring you will, no doubt, have your own bicycle and should bring this with you. Most airlines these days will accommodate bikes, sometimes as part of your baggage allowance, sometimes free.

Touring cycles are available in Japan but prices tend to be significantly higher than you'd pay back home. And if you're tall, you may not find any suitably sized bikes in stock. One solution for tall riders, or anyone who wants to save money, is to buy a used bike; in Tokyo check the English-language publications and in Kansai check *Kansai Time Out*.

HITCHING

Hitching is never entirely safe in any country in the world, and we don't recommend it. Travellers who decide to hitch should understand that they are taking a small but potentially serious risk. In particular, Japan is a very dangerous place for solitary female hitchhikers; there have been countless cases of solitary female hitchers being attacked, molested and raped. People who do choose to hitch will be safer if they travel in pairs and let someone know where they are planning to go.

Provided you understand the risks and take appropriate precautions, Japan can be an excellent country for hitchhiking. Many hitchhikers have tales of extraordinary kindness from motorists who have picked them up.

The rules for hitchhiking are similar to anywhere else in the world. Dress neatly and look for a good place to hitch – expressway onramps and expressway service areas are probably your best bet.

Truck drivers are particularly good for long-distance travel as they often head out on the expressways at night. If a driver is exiting before your intended destination, try to get dropped off at one of the expressway service areas. The Service Area Parking Area (SAPA) guide maps are excellent for hitchers. They're available free from expressway service areas and show full details of each interchange (IC) and rest stop. These are important orientation points if you have a limited knowledge of Japanese.

For more on hitching in Japan pick up a copy of the excellent *Hitchhiker's Guide to Japan* by Will Ferguson. In addition to lots of general advice, this book details suggested

Cycling in Japan

In 1899 the British adventurer John Foster Frazer, cycling across the country en route from Europe to the USA, declared Japan 'the wheelman's paradise'. Frazer may not have had to contend with the traffic on Route 1 or the bewildering complexities of Tokyo's expressways, but his original judgment remains sound – Japan is still a great country to explore on two wheels.

Unchanged since Foster's day are the topography and the climate, both important considerations for the would-be bicycle tourer. Japan's topographic wild card is its mountains. Even the coastal roads can have their hilly moments.

The Tōkaidō coastline, stretching southwest from Tokyo through Nagoya and past Osaka, is mostly flat, but it is also polluted, congested and unrelievedly boring. Avoid Route 1 at all costs. On the other hand, the Japan Sea coastline – windswept, sometimes hilly but rarely congested – is a cyclist's delight. It provides the cyclist with good roads, abundant wildlife and some of the freshest seafood in Japan. Hokkaidō, Shikoku and Kyūshū offer more of the same on even quieter roads.

That said, my own favourite cycling territory is in the mountains of Central Honshū – hard work but rewarded by spectacular scenery, great hot springs in which to soothe aching bones and, best of all, a glimpse of rural Japan that few city dwellers get a chance to see.

Climatic conditions require some serious consideration, particularly for cyclists planning a lengthy tour of Japan. Winter is something of a mixed bag. November and December are often sunny though cold and can be good months for touring Japan's coastal regions. In January and February, however, snowfalls, rain and cold conditions make much of Japan – particularly the Japan Alps, Northern Honshū and Hokkaidō – unattractive to all but the most masochistic of cyclists. Summer, on the other hand, is swelteringly hot and humid, a good time to stick to the coast or the cooler latitudes of Hokkaidō.

The rainy season is best avoided for obvious reasons. While it generally arrives in May or June and lingers for just a few weeks, it can't always be relied on to end on time, as I discovered on one sodden trip from Niigata to Kyoto. Typhoons blow up with immense ferocity in late summer and can play havoc with a tight itinerary. This leaves spring and autumn, the best seasons to be cycling in Japan: both are blessed with cool weather and minimal rainfall and see the Japanese countryside at its best.

The single biggest frustration for the cyclist in Japan is probably the lack of Romanised street names. This situation is improving gradually, but it can still be maddeningly difficult to find your way out of urban centres onto the road of your choice. (On one memorable occasion, I managed a

---

routes and places to stay on the road. All in all, it's just about invaluable for anyone contemplating a long hitch around Japan.

WALKING

For more information on walking and mountain climbing in Japan, see Hiking & Mountain Climbing in the Facts for the Visitor chapter.

BOAT

Japan is an island nation and there are a great many ferry services both between islands and between ports on the same island. Ferries can be an excellent way of getting from one place to another and seeing parts of Japan you might otherwise miss. Taking a ferry between Osaka (Honshū) and Beppu (Kyūshū), for example, is a good way of

getting to Kyūshū and – if you choose the right departure time – seeing some of the Inland Sea on the way.

The routes vary widely from two-hour services between adjacent islands to 1½-day trips in what are in fact small ocean liners. The cheapest fares on the longer trips are in tatami-mat rooms where you simply unroll your futon on the floor and hope, if the ship is crowded, that your fellow passengers aren't too intent on knocking back the booze all night. In this basic class, fares are usually lower than equivalent land travel, but there are also more expensive private cabins. Bicycles can always be brought along and most ferries also carry cars and motorcycles.

Information on ferry routes, schedules and fares can be found in the comprehen-

Cycling in Japan

90-minute circumnavigation of the Kanazawa ring road that brought me back to where I'd started.) A handy way of avoiding such confusion and the frustration of inner-city traffic is to put your bike on a train. To do this, a carry bag may be required. Specialist carry bags, known in Japanese as *rinko bukuro* or *rinko baggu*, are available in bike shops, though I have made do with a blanket, two garbage bags and some sticky tape without any hassle. Strictly speaking, a ticket is required for your bike on the train (though it is rarely checked). Ask for a *temawarihin kippu* (accompanied-luggage ticket), a bargain at ¥260 and valid for any single journey. Ferries are also an opportunity to rest aching legs, and taking your bike aboard is no problem, though sometimes an extra charge will be required.

The best machine for touring Japan is a lightweight touring road machine or else a suitably equipped hybrid or cross bike. While mountain bikes are all the rage they are hardly required for Japan's well-paved roads. If you do bring a mountain bike, be sure to fit slimmer profile, preferably slick tyres, unless you're planning to spend all your time on mountain trails. Bikes with suspension forks require too much maintenance to consider as viable touring machines.

Perhaps the most important question for the cyclist looking at a holiday in Japan is costs. However you look at it, Japan is not cheap. Try to bring your own bike and accessories – even though Japan produces some of the world's best cycling equipment, prices will be cheaper at home. Camping is a good antidote to Japan's high accommodation costs, and many cyclists sustain themselves on a diet of instant noodles and sandwiches. Bear in mind, however, that after a long rainy day a comfortable inn with home cooking becomes a great temptation and it's easy to stray from a tight budget. Worst of all, if you're really pinching the pennies you'll never get into the bars, restaurants and hot springs where you can meet the Japanese at their most relaxed and welcoming. Even if you're planning to camp out and eat cheaply, it would be wise to budget ¥3600 per day.

Japan is a reasonably safe country to cycle in but, on a cautionary note, accidents happen more frequently than you might imagine. Comprehensive insurance is a must, as is a decent lightweight helmet. Also, despite Japan's reputation as a crime-free country, bicycles do get stolen and, of late, professional gangs of bike thieves have been targeting big cities, especially around train stations. I have lost no less than three expensive bikes over the last eight years. Bring a lock.

For more information on cycling in Japan, check out the Bicycle section earlier in this chapter and the excellent **Kancycling website** (**W** www.kancycling.com/index.html).

John Ashburne

sive *JR Jikokuhyō* and on information sheets from TIC offices. Some TICs also carry the Japan Long Distance Ferry Association's excellent English-language brochure.

Some ferry services and their lowest one-way fares include:

Hokkaidō–Honshū	fare (¥)
Otaru-Maizuru	6700
Otaru-Niigata	5400
Tomakomai-Nagoya	8400
Tomakomai-Ōarai	6400
Tomakomai-Sendai	6600

departing from Tokyo	fare (¥)
Kōchi (Shikoku)	10,600
Nachi-Katsuura (Honshū)	8800
Naha (Okinawa)	20,050
Tokushima (Shikoku)	8610

departing from Osaka/Kōbe	fare (¥)
Beppu (Kyūshū)	7400
Imabari (Shikoku)	4170
Kōchi (Shikoku)	4610
Matsuyama (Shikoku)	5200
Naha (Okinawa)	15,750

departing from Kyūshū	fare (¥)
Hakata-Naha (Okinawa)	13,220
Kagoshima-Naha (Okinawa)	12,070

LOCAL TRANSPORT

All the major cities offer a wide variety of public transport. In many cities you can get day passes for unlimited travel on bus, tram or subway systems. The pass is called an *ichi-nichi-jōsha-ken*. If you're staying for an extended period in one city, commuter passes are available for regular travel.

Train & Subway

Several cities, especially Osaka and Tokyo, have mass transit rail systems comprising a loop line around the city centre and radial lines into the central stations and the subway system. Subway systems operate in Fukuoka, Kōbe, Kyoto, Nagoya, Osaka, Sapporo, Sendai, Tokyo and Yokohama. They are usually the fastest and most convenient way to get around the city.

For subways and local trains you'll most likely have to buy your ticket from a machine. They're pretty easy to understand even if you can't read kanji as there is a diagram explaining the routes; from this you can find what your fare should be. If you can't work the fare out, a solution is to buy a ticket for the lowest fare. When you finish your trip, go to the fare adjustment machine or counter before you reach the exit gate and pay the excess. JR train stations and most subway stations not only have their names posted above the platform in kanji and romaji but also the names of the preceding and following stations.

Bus

Almost every Japanese city has an extensive bus service but it's usually the most difficult public transport system for foreign travellers to use. The destination names are almost always written in kanji and often there are no numbers to identify which bus you want.

Fares are either paid to the driver on entering or as you leave the bus and usually operate on one of two systems. In Tokyo and some other cities, there's a flat fare irrespective of distance. In the other system, you take a ticket as you board which indicates the zone number at your starting point. When you get off, an electric sign at the front of the bus indicates the fare charged at that point for each starting zone number. You simply pay the driver the fare that matches your zone number. There is often a change machine near the front of the bus that can change ¥100 and ¥500 coins and ¥1000 notes.

In many tourist towns there are also *teiki kankō basu* (tour buses), often run from the main railway station. Tours are usually conducted in Japanese but English-language tours are available in popular areas like Kyoto and Tokyo. In places where the attractions are widespread or hard to reach by public transport, tours can be a good bet.

Tram

A number of cities have tram lines – particularly Nagasaki, Kumamoto and Kagoshima in Kyūshū, Kōchi and Matsuyama in Shikoku, and Hakodate in Hokkaidō. These are excellent ways of getting around as they combine many of the advantages of bus travel (particularly the good views) with those of subways (it's easy to work out where you're going). Fares work on similar systems to bus travel and there are also unlimited-travel day tickets available.

Taxi

Taxis are convenient but expensive and are found in even quite small towns; the train station is the best place to look. Drivers are often reluctant to stop and pick you up near a station taxi stand, so either wait at the correct spot for a taxi off the rank or flag one down a couple of streets away. Fares are fairly uniform throughout the country – flagfall (posted on the taxi windows) is ¥600 to ¥660 for the first 2km, after which it's around ¥100 for each 350m (approximately). There's also a time charge if the speed drops below 10km/h. During the day, it's almost impossible to tell if a moving taxi is occupied (just wave at it and it will stop if it's free); at night, vacant taxis are distinguishable by an illuminated light on the roof – an occupied taxi will have its light turned off.

Don't whistle for a taxi, a simple wave should bring one politely to a halt. Don't open the door when it stops, the driver does that with a remote release. The driver will also shut the door when you leave the taxi.

Drivers are normally as polite as anybody else in Japan but, like the majority of Japanese, they are not linguists. If you can't tell the driver where you want to go, it's useful to have the name written down in Japanese. At hotel front desks there will usually be business cards complete with name and location, which are used for just this purpose.

Taxi drivers have just as much trouble finding Japanese addresses as anyone else. Just because you've gone round the block five times does not mean your driver has no idea. Asking directions and stopping at police boxes for help in finding the address is standard practice.

Tipping is not necessary. A 20% surcharge is added after 11pm or for taxis summoned by radio.

Tokyo 東京

☎ 03 • pop 12.2 million

Tokyo, like all great cities, is a conundrum, a riddle of contradictions that springs from tensions between large-scale ugliness and meticulous detail; the frantic rhythms of 20th-century consumer culture and the still, quiet moments that are the legacy of other, older traditions. It is a creative behemoth, inevitably reinventing, re-creating, resolving itself… And it may well be the perfect metaphor for the globe as it spins and wobbles through the 21st century. Naturally, it's a lot of fun.

Tokyo is the nesting place of both Japan Inc and the lineages of the old town of Edo. Reposing by fashionable Ginza and administrative Nihombashi is the Imperial Palace, with its gardens, its closeted Imperial dynasty, and photogenic views. In the heart of Akasaka, surrounded by world-class hotels, trendy boutiques and eateries, is the timeless Hie-jinja shrine. The central areas of Ueno and Asakusa are home to splendid museums and to bustling Sensō-ji, possibly Japan's liveliest Buddhist temple. And just two hours from Tokyo by train are the historic towns of Kamakura and Nikkō, and the scenic regions of Hakone and Mt Fuji.

While Tokyo sports some of the world's biggest and most lavish department stores, the average Tokyo suburb hasn't fallen prey (just yet) to supermarket culture – the streets are lined with tiny specialist shops and restaurants, most of which stay open late into the night. Near soaring office blocks are entertainment quarters – mazes of narrow alleys blazing with neon by night, offering intoxicating escape from the work regimen that is the lot of Tokyo's surging crowds of office workers. And in the shadow of the overhead expressways exist pockets of another Tokyo: an old wooden house, a Japanese inn, an old lady in kimono and *geta* (traditional wooden sandals) slippers sweeping the pavement outside her home with a straw broom.

Tokyo jumps out at you unexpectedly on a crowded street: the woman dressed in kimono buying a burger at McDonald's, the Buddhist monk with an alms bowl poised serenely in the midst of jostling shoppers in Ginza. Look closely – the monk's shockproof watch sports an altimeter.

Highlights

- Wander the streets of Shinjuku, home to Tokyo's busiest train station, rowdiest entertainment district, and some of the best shopping and dining in the country
- Retreat to the calm of Meiji-jingū, one of Japan's finest shrines
- Dip into the old-world hustle and bustle of Asakusa's Sensō-ji, probably the liveliest place of Buddhist worship in all Japan
- Spend a day in Ueno-kōen exploring the museums, including the fine Tokyo National Museum
- Make the morning trip to Tsukiji Fish Market and top it off with a sushi lunch in nearby Ginza
- Party till dawn in the manic entertainment ghetto that is Roppongi

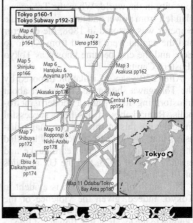

HISTORY

Tokyo is something of a miracle; a city that has literally risen from the ashes (the result of US aerial bombing at the end of WWII) to become one of the world's leading economic centres.

Tokyo used to be known as Edo (literally, 'Gate of the River'), so named for its location at the mouth of the river, Sumidagawa. The city first became significant in 1603, when Tokugawa Ieyasu established his shōgunate (military government) there. From a sleepy backwater town, Edo grew

The Flowers of Edo

Today there is little left of Shitamachi, the old 'downtown', and the only way to get some idea of the circumstances in which the lower classes of old Edo lived is by visiting somewhere like Ueno's Shitamachi History Museum. Edo was a city of wood, and its natural stained-wood frontages and dark-tiled roofs gave the city an attractiveness that is little in evidence in modern Tokyo. Nevertheless, the poor lived in horribly crowded conditions, in flimsy wooden constructions, often with earthen floors. Huge fires regularly swept great swaths through the wooden buildings of the congested city. In a perverse attempt to make the best of misfortune, Edo-dwellers seemed almost to take pride in the fires that periodically purged the city, calling them *Edo-no-hana*, (literally 'flowers of Edo').

The flowers of Edo bloomed with such frequency that it has been estimated that any Shitamachi structure could reckon on a life span of around 20 years, often less, before being destroyed by fire. Preventative measures included building houses that could be completely sealed at the approach of a fire; candles would be left burning inside, starving the houses' interior of oxygen. Private fire brigades operated with standard-bearers who would stake out their territory close to a burning building and exact payment if they managed to save it.

Modern building techniques have eliminated most of Edo's 'flowers', but you can still see the occasional wooden structure that has miraculously survived into the 21st century.

into a city from which the Tokugawa clan governed the whole of Japan. By the late 18th century it had become the most populous city in the world. When the Tokugawa clan fell from power and the authority of the emperor was restored in 1868, the emperor and the capital were moved from Kyoto to Edo, and the city became known as Tokyo (Eastern Capital).

After 250 years of isolation imposed by the Tokugawa shōgunate, Tokyo set about transforming itself into a modern metropolis. Remarkably, it has been successful in achieving this in spite of two major disasters that, in each case, practically levelled the whole city – the great earthquake and ensuing fires of 1923, and the US air raids of 1944 and 1945.

Not much of the old Japan is evident in Tokyo. Indeed, given the violence of the city's history – the periodic conflagrations (known to the locals as the 'flowers of Edo' – see the boxed text), the earthquakes and the destruction brought about through war – it's a wonder that anything is left at all. What you find today is a uniquely Japanese version of a 21st-century city – the bustling heart of the Japanese economic dynamo.

ORIENTATION

Tokyo is a vast conurbation spreading out across the Kantō Plain from Tokyo Bay (Tokyo-wan). The central metropolitan area is made up of 23 *ku* (wards), while outlying areas are divided into 27 separate *shi* (cit-

ies), a *gun* (county) and four island-districts. Nearly everything of interest to visitors lies on or near the JR Yamanote line, the rail loop that circles central Tokyo. Those areas not on the Yamanote line, like Roppongi, Tsukiji and Asakusa, are nonetheless within easy reach, as the whole area is crisscrossed by Tokyo's excellent subway system.

In Edo times, Yamanote referred to 'Uptown': the estates and residences of feudal barons, military aristocracy and other Edo elite, in the hilly regions of the city. Shitamachi, or 'Downtown', was home to the working classes, merchants and artisans. Even today the distinction persists. The areas west of the Imperial Palace (Kōkyo) are the more modernised, housing the commercial and business centres of modern Tokyo; the areas east of the palace, like Asakusa and Ueno, retain more of the character of old Edo.

A trip around the JR Yamanote line makes a good introduction to the city. You might start at Tokyo station, the first point of arrival for many travellers. Near to the station are the Marunouchi and Ōtemachi office districts and the high-class shopping district of Ginza. Continuing north from Tokyo station brings you to Akihabara, the discount electronics centre of Tokyo. Further along is Ueno, home to many of the city's museums. After rounding the top of the loop you descend into Ikebukuro, a bawdy shopping and entertainment district. A few stops further on is Shinjuku, a massive shopping, entertainment and business district considered by many the heart of modern Tokyo. From there, trains continue through to the teen-oriented, fashionable shopping areas of Harajuku, Shibuya and Ebisu. A swing through Shinagawa at the bottom of the loop then brings you back to Tokyo station and completes the loop.

The information in this chapter is presented in the order described above (working anticlockwise around the Yamanote line), with areas not on the Yamanote line covered last.

Maps

We strongly recommend you pick up a copy of the free *Tourist Map of Tokyo* from one of the Tourist Information Centers (TICs – see Tourist Offices later). This excellent map has detailed insets of Tokyo's major neighbourhoods as well as subway and rail maps. For more in-depth exploration of the city, pick up a copy of *Tokyo City Atlas: A Bilingual Atlas* (Kodansha), which includes *banchi* (street address) numbers essential for finding addresses.

Tokyo's train and subway lines are much easier to navigate with the excellent colour-coded map that is available free at subway stations and tourist information counters around town. We've included it in this guide – see the Tokyo Subway map.

Books

There are a number of publications that might supplement the one you have in your hands, particularly if you are planning to become a resident of Tokyo. For a comprehensive guide to the city, pick up Lonely Planet's *Tokyo*.

The Best of Tokyo by Don Morton and Tsunoi Naoko (Tuttle) is a light-hearted look at the city, with recommendations ranging variously from 'best traditional Japanese dolls' to 'best toilet'. *Tokyo for Free* by Susan Pompian (Kodansha) lists more than 400 things that you can do for free in a very expensive city.

Old Tokyo: Walks in the City of the Shogun by Enbutsu Sumiko (Tuttle) details walking tours in Tokyo with fascinating historical and cultural detail. *Little Adventures in Tokyo* (Kodansha) by Rick Kennedy, one of Tokyo's most famous expats, introduces some of his secret finds in and around Tokyo.

Tokyo: A Guide to Recent Architecture by Tajima Noriyuki (Elipsis Könemann) is a great guide to Tokyo's architectural masterpieces and oddities.

INFORMATION

See the Facts for the Visitor chapter for information on foreign embassies and consulates in Tokyo.

Tourist Offices

The Japan National Tourist Organization (JNTO) operates two TICs in the Tokyo area – one on the 1st floor of Terminal 2, Narita airport (☎ 0476-34-6251; open 9am-8pm daily); and one in Yūraku-chō on the 10th floor of the Kōtsu Kaikan Building (Map 1; ☎ 3216-1901; open 9am-5pm Mon-Fri, 9am-noon Sat). The latter has by far the most comprehensive information on travel in Tokyo and Japan, and is an essential port of call. Take exit A8 from Yūraku-chō station.

TIC offices will make accommodation reservations, but only for hotels and ryokan (traditional Japanese inns) that are members of the Welcome Inn group. The Tokyo TIC also offers Teletourist (☎ 3201-2911), a round-the-clock taped information service on current events in town. It can also arrange for tours of the city with volunteer guides.

The Information Bureau of Tokyo operates an information counter (open 9am-6pm Mon-Sat, closed holidays) for foreign travellers; one is on the ground floor of Tokyo station (Map 1) near the central Yaesu exit.

Immigration Offices

The Tokyo Regional Immigration Bureau (☎ 3213-8523) is best reached from Ōtemachi subway station on the Chiyoda line. Take the C2 exit, cross the street at the corner and turn left. Walk past the Japan Development Building; the immigration bureau is the next building on your right.

Money

Banks are open from 9am to 3pm Monday to Friday. Look out for the 'Foreign Exchange' sign outside. Some post offices also offer foreign-exchange services. See the Exchanging Money section in the Facts for the Visitor chapter for more information on changing money.

International ATMs Tokyo has a reasonable number of automated teller machines (ATMs) that accept foreign-issued cards. The best bet for foreign travellers is Citibank, which has 24-hour English-language ATMs, open every day. There are branches in Ōtemachi, Ginza, Akasaka, East and West Shinjuku, Aoyama, Shibuya and Ikebukuro. There are other ATMs that accept foreign-issued cards at Sunny's Card Plaza in the Yaesu Underground Mall beneath Tokyo station; and on the 1st floor of the Yūraku-chō Mullion Building (Map 1).

Credit Cards The main credit-card offices in Tokyo are:

American Express (☎ 0120-020-666, 3220-6100) American Express Tower, 4-30-16 Ogikubo, Suginami-ku; open 24 hours

MasterCard (☎ 5350-8051, 0031 11 3886) 16th floor, Dai Tokyo Kasai Shinjuku Bldg, 3-25-3 Yoyogi, Shibuya-ku

Visa (☎ 5251-0633, 0120-13-3173) 4th floor, Nissho Bldg, 2-7-9 Kita-Aoyama, Minato-ku

Post

The Tokyo central post office is outside Tokyo station (take the Marunouchi exit and then cross the street to the south). Call ☎ 5472-5851 for postal information in English. Poste restante mail will be held at the central post office for 30 days. It should be addressed as follows:

Jane THOMPSON
Poste Restante
Central Post Office
Tokyo, JAPAN

Telephone

Almost all public phones in Tokyo take prepaid phone cards. For domestic directory assistance, call ☎ 104 and ask to be transferred to an English speaker. For details on making international calls from a public phone see the Facts for the Visitor chapter.

Fax

You can send faxes from the front desks of many hotels (some allow nonguests to use their services for a fee), some convenience stores and from Kinko's copy stores (its basic rate to send an international fax is ¥200 plus phone charges).

Email & Internet Access

No longer the Web-access wilderness it was, Tokyo can still be a maddeningly difficult (and pricey) place to get online. **Manga Kissa** the 24-hour comic reading rooms dotted around the major transport hubs usually offer inexpensive Net access, but they are often crowded and smoky. The following are some of the best Net-cafés.

Cafe J Net New New (Map 7; ☎ 5458-5935; ¥300/hr) Shibuya. Open 24 hours.

Gaiax Cafe (Map 5; ☎ 5332-9201; ¥390/30min) Next to the Star Hotel, west Shinjuku. Open 24 hours. A comfortable oddly-painted space with dozens of Macs and PCs.

Hard Internet Cafe T and T (Map 4; ☎ 5950-9983; ¥100/10min) Basement, Liberty Ikebukuro Bldg, Ikebukuro. Open noon to 10pm, closed Sunday and 1st, 3rd and 5th Wednesday of the month.

Manga@Cafe-Gera Gera (Map 5; ☎ 5285-0585; ¥380/1st hr, ¥30/10min thereafter) In front of Shinjuku Komagek. Open 24 hours. This is another late night favourite.

Manga Hiroba (☎ 3497-1751, W www.manga hiroba.com/e/index.html; ¥380/1st hr, ¥150/30min thereafter) Opposite Hub 2, Roppongi. Open 24 hours. Handy for pre-/post-party surfing, but is always crowded.

Sony Style (Map 11; ☎ 5531-2358) 4th floor, Aqua City, Odaiba. Offers the city's hippest free online access. Surf the Net sitting atop ultra-cool dinosaur eggs. OK, they are really chairs, in Sony's vision of our domestic future. You might have to pretend you are going to buy that solar-powered DVD though.

Kinko's, the US-based office-service company, offers 24-hour Internet access at most of its outlets dotted throughout Tokyo. There are handy branches in Ebisu (☎ 5795-1485), Ikebukuro (☎ 5979-5171), Kanda (☎ 3251-7677), Ueno (☎ 5246-9811) and Yaesu (☎ 3278-3911).

Websites

There are thousands of websites about Tokyo. Here are four of the most useful:

Metropolis (W www.metropolis.co.jp) The best all-round site for Tokyo. Lots of events and jobs listings.

Tokyo Journal (W www.tokyo.to) Has interesting articles and interviews from time to time.

Tokyo Meltdown (W www.bento.com/tleisure .html) Young and hip, with especially good record-store listings.

Tokyo Q (**w** http://club.nokia.co.jp/tokyoq/index .html) Great all-round Tokyo site. Plenty of listings of current and upcoming events.

Travel Agencies

In Tokyo there are a number of travel agencies where English is spoken and where discounting on flights and domestic travel is the norm. For an idea of current prices check the *Japan Times* or *Metropolis*.

Four well-established agencies where English is spoken are: **No 1 Travel** in Shinjuku (☎ *3200-8871*), Shibuya (☎ *3770-1381*) and Ikebukuro (☎ *3986-4291*); **STA Travel** which is represented in Ikebukuro (☎ *5391-2922*); **Across Traveller's Bureau** in Shibuya (☎ *5467-0077*), in Shinjuku (☎ *3340-6749*) and in Ikebukuro (☎ *5391-2871*); and **H.I.S** (☎ *3362-3441*) in Takadanobaba.

Bookshops

Tower Books (*Map 7*; ☎ *3496-3661*; *open 10am-11pm daily*) on the 7th floor of the new Tower Records building in Shibuya, has a large selection of English-language books and a fabulous array of magazines and newspapers from around the world. Its magazines are considerably cheaper than elsewhere around town.

One of Japan's better bookshop chains, **Kinokuniya**, has two branches in Shinjuku. There's the old branch (*Map 5*; ☎ *3354-0131*; *open 10am-8pm daily*) on Shinjuku-dōri, and the new branch (*Map 5*; ☎ *5361-3301*; *open 10am-8pm daily*) in the annex of the Takashimaya Times Square complex. The new branch has one of the largest selections of English-language books in Tokyo, on the 6th floor.

Maruzen (*Map 1*; ☎ *3272-7211*; *open 10am-8pm Mon-Sat, 10am-7pm Sun & national holidays*), in Nihombashi near Ginza, has a collection of books almost equal to Kinokuniya's and is always a lot quieter.

Aoyama Book Center (*Map 10*; ☎ *3442-1651*; *open 10am-8pm daily, closed 2nd & 3rd Tues each month*), near Roppongi subway station; and **Yaesu Book Center** (*Map 1*; ☎ *3281-1811*; *open 10am-9pm Mon-Sat, 10am-7pm Sun & national holidays*), next to JR Tokyo station in Nihombashi, both have reasonable selections.

The best used English-language books are in Ebisu at **Good Day Books** (*Map 8*; ☎ *5421-0957*; *open Wed-Mon*). There is

everything from Hesse to Harry Potter, and a good selection of Japan-related art books at, yeehaar, affordable prices.

Tokyo's traditional bookshop area is Jimbō-chō. Mostly catering to Japanese readers, it is still a fascinating place to browse for Edo-period gardening manuals and the like. There's a startling variety of, er, adult literature, too. The annual Jimbō-chō book fair is a bibliophile paradise. It occupies the whole district on 27–28 October.

Libraries

The **National Diet Library** (*Map 9*; ☎ *3581-2331*; *open 9.30am-5pm Mon-Sat*) is a small treasure, with 1.3 million books in Western languages. It is close to Nagata-chō subway station on the Yūraku-chō and Hanzōmon lines.

The **British Council** (*Tokyo colour map*; ☎ *3235-8031*; *open 11am-8pm Mon-Fri*) in Iidabashi, has a comprehensive selection of books and magazines. The **American Center** (☎ *3436-0901*; *open noon-6.30pm Mon-Fri*) in Shiba-kōen, has a similar set-up.

The **Japan Foundation Library** (*Tokyo colour map*; ☎ *5562-3527*; *open 9.30am-5pm Tues-Sat*) is close to Kojimachi station on the Yūraku-chō line. It has some 30,000 English-language publications and is open only to foreigners.

For languages other than English, go to the **Bibliotheque de la Maison Franco-Japonaise** (☎ *5424-1141*; *open 10am-noon & 1pm-6pm Sun-Fri*), close to Ochanomizu station on the JR Chūō line. The **Goethe Institut Tokyo Bibliotek** (☎ *3584-3201*; *open noon-6pm Mon-Thur, noon-8pm Fri*) has around 15,000 volumes. It is close to Aoyama-Itchōme station on the Ginza line.

In Ginza, **Magazine House** (*Map 1*; ☎ *3545-7227*; *open 11am-7pm Mon-Fri*) has a good selection of magazines from all corners of the world.

Newspapers & Magazines

There's plenty of English-language information on Tokyo, starting with the four English-language newspapers (see the Facts for the Visitor chapter for details). The best listings of Tokyo events can be found in Saturday's *Japan Times*.

The *Tokyo Journal* is not the stand-by it once was. Although its Cityscope listings section still makes it worth the purchase price, the magazine is cursed by its hipper-than-thou attitude and annoying graphics style.

These days, the free weekly *Metropolis* is the magazine of choice for most Tokyo residents, although its cultural listings are not as detailed as those in the *Tokyo Journal*. However, for club events and concerts, this is the best magazine.

Cultural Centres

Cultural centres in Tokyo generally act as focal points of the national groups they represent, and usually have good bulletin boards, events, small libraries and language classes.

British Council (Tokyo colour map; ☎ 3235-8031) 1-2 Kagurazaka, Shinjuku-ku (Iidabashi station)

Goethe Institut Tokyo (☎ 3584-3201) 7-5-56 Akasaka, Minato-ku (Akasaka station)

Institute Franco-Japonais du Tokyo (☎ 5261-3933) 15 Ichigaya Funagawarachō, Shinjuku-ku (Iidabashi station)

Conversation Lounges

Mickey House (☎ 3209-9686; *open 5pm-11pm Mon-Sat*) is an 'English bar' that serves ¥350 all-you-can-drink coffee and tea as well as reasonably priced beer and food. Entry is free for English-speaking foreigners. Take the main exit at JR Takadanobaba, go east on Waseda-dōri and look for the Tōzai-line subway station entrance on your left; Mickey House is on the 4th floor of the Yashiro Building.

Useful Organisations & Services

There are innumerable associations for foreign residents and travellers. For the one most suited to your needs and interests, we recommend checking the listings sections of *Metropolis* and *Tokyo Journal*.

There is a lot of information and support available to foreign residents and travellers in Tokyo, including several useful telephone services. For general information try the **Foreign Residents' Advisory Center** (☎ 5320-7744; *open 9.30am-noon & 1pm-4pm Mon-Fri*). **JR English Information** (☎ 3423-0111; *open 10am-6pm Mon-Fri*) offers information on train schedules and fares. **Tokyo English Lifeline** (☎ 5774-0992; *open 9am-4pm & 7pm-11pm daily*) can help with information and counselling.

Laundry

Most hotels, mid-range and up, have laundry services. If you are in a budget ryokan, ask the staff for the nearest *koin randorii* (laundrette). Costs range from ¥150 for a load of washing, and drying costs about ¥100 for 10 minutes.

Kuriningu-yasan (dry-cleaners) are in almost every neighbourhood. The standards are high and some offer rush service. It's about ¥200 for your basic business shirt.

Left Luggage

There are coin lockers in all train and bus stations in Tokyo. Smaller lockers start at ¥300 (you can leave luggage for up to three days). Otherwise, the Akaboshi (Red Cap) luggage service on the Yaesu side of Tokyo station will store small/large bags during the day for ¥300/400 (you must pick up your luggage by the end of the day you leave it). For longer periods, there is an overnight luggage-storage service in Tokyo station that will hold luggage for up to two weeks, with rates starting at ¥500 per bag per day. Ask at the main information counter on the Yaesu side for a map to both of these services.

Medical Services

There are foreign doctors at the **Tokyo Medical and Surgical Clinic** (☎ 3436-3028; *open 9am-5pm Mon-Fri, 9am-1pm Sat, closed holidays*), near Roppongi in Kamiyachō, on the Hibiya subway line. The **International Clinic** (☎ 3583-7831; *open 9am-5pm Mon-Fri, 9am-noon Sat, closed holidays*) in Roppongi also provides services in English.

You can also call the **Tokyo Medical Information Service** (☎ 5285-8181; *operates 9am-5pm Mon-Fri*) for advice about which hospital or clinic can best address your needs. The service operates for nonemergency cases. For emergency or after-hours cases, call the **Tokyo Metropolitan Emergency Translation Service** (☎ 5285-8185; *operates 5pm-10pm Mon-Fri, 9am-10pm Sat, Sun & holidays*).

International Pharmacies The American Pharmacy (Map 1; ☎ 3271-4034; *open 9.30am-7.30pm Mon-Sat, 9.30am-6.30pm Sun & holidays*) is located just around the corner from Tokyo International Forum, near Yūraku-chō station and Hibiya subway station. Another option is the **pharmacy**

(☎ 3442-3181; open 9.30am-7pm daily) at the National Azabu Supermarket, close to Hiro-o subway station.

Emergency

Emergency numbers are: police ☎ 110; and fire and ambulance ☎ 119. You should be able to get your point across in simple English. If you have problems communicating, ring the **Japan Helpline** (☎ 0120-461-997; operates 24hr daily), an emergency number. See Medical Services earlier in this chapter for more information on dealing with a medical emergency.

Dangers & Annoyances

Tokyo can be annoying at times but it is rarely dangerous. If possible, avoid the rail network during peak hours – around 8am to 9.30am and 5pm to 7pm – when the surging crowds would try anyone's patience.

Some travellers may also be disturbed by the overtly sexual nature of some of the signs and sights in Tokyo's red-light districts, like Shinjuku's Kabuki-chō and parts of Ikebukuro.

Earthquakes Check the locations of emergency exits in your hotel and be aware of earthquake safety procedures (see Earthquakes under Dangers & Annoyances in the Facts for the Visitor chapter). If an earthquake occurs, the Japan Broadcasting Corporation (NHK) will broadcast information and instructions in English on all its TV and radio networks. Tune to channel 1 on your TV, or to NHK (639 kHz AM), FEN (810 kHz AM) or InterFM (76.1 FM) on your radio.

CENTRAL TOKYO (MAP 1)
東京中心部

Imperial Palace 皇居

The Imperial Palace, or Kōkyo, is the home of Japan's emperor and the imperial family. The palace itself is closed to the public for all but two days of the year, 2 January and 23 December (the emperor's birthday). Even if you can't enter the palace itself, it is possible to wander around its outskirts and visit the gardens, where you can at least get a view of the palace with the bridge, Nijū-bashi, in the foreground.

The present palace was completed in 1968. It replaced the palace built in 1888, which was destroyed by Allied bombing in WWII. It occupies the site of the castle, Edo-jō, from which the Tokugawa shōgunate ruled all Japan. In its time the castle was the largest in the world, though apart from the massive moat and walls, virtually nothing remains of it today.

It is an easy walk from Tokyo station, or from Hibiya or Nijū-bashi-mae subway stations, to the Nijū-bashi. The walk involves crossing Babasaki Moat and the expansive Imperial Palace Plaza (Kōkyo-mae Hiroba). The vantage point, which is popular with photographers, gives you a picture-postcard view of the palace peeking over its fortifications, behind Nijū-bashi.

Imperial Palace East Garden
皇居東御苑

The Imperial Palace East Garden (Kōkyo Higashi-gyoen; ☎ 3213-2050; admission free; open 9am-4pm Tues-Thur, Sat & Sun, last entry 3pm) is the only quarter of the palace proper that is open to the public. The main entrance is through the Ōte-mon, a 10-minute walk north of Nijū-bashi. This was once the principal gate of Edo-jō; the garden itself lies at what was once the heart of the old castle. You'll be given a numbered plastic token to turn in when you depart. The store inside the garden sells a good map for ¥150.

Kitanomaru-kōen 北の丸公園

This park is quite pleasant, and is a good spot for a leisurely stroll or summer picnic. You can get there from Kudanshita or Takebashi subway stations.

Kitanomaru-kōen contains the **Nihon Budōkan** (☎ 3216-5100), where you may witness a variety of martial arts. South of the Nihon Budōkan is the **Science Museum** (☎ 3822-0111; admission ¥600; open 9am-4.30pm Tues-Sun), which is a decent rainy-day stop for science buffs or those with children in tow. An English booklet is included with the entry fee.

Continuing south from the Science Museum brings you to the **National Museum of Modern Art** (☎ 3214-2561; admission ¥420; open 10am-5pm Tues-Sun). The permanent exhibition here features Japanese art from the Meiji period (1868–1912) onwards. It is worth checking in the *Tokyo Journal* or *Metropolis* to see if any special exhibitions

MAP 1 – CENTRAL TOKYO

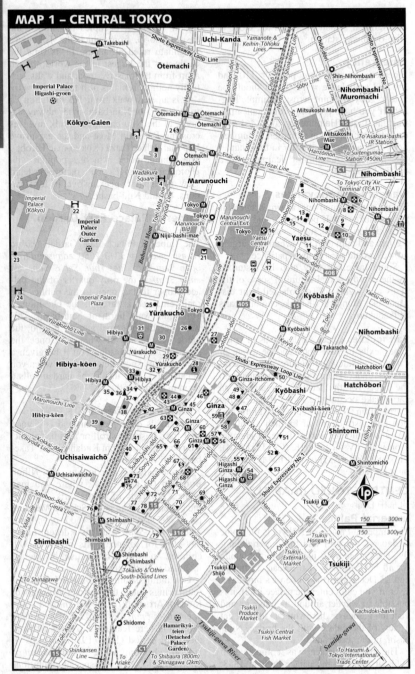

TOKYO

CENTRAL TOKYO – MAP 1

PLACES TO STAY
3 Palace Hotel
パレスホテル
5 Hotel Yaesu-Ryūmeikan
ホテル八重洲龍名館
13 Yaesu Terminal Hotel
八重洲ターミナルホテル
20 Tokyo Station Hotel
東京ステーションホテル
39 Imperial Hotel
帝国ホテル
50 Hotel Seiyo Ginza
ホテル西洋銀座
52 Hotel Ginza Daiei
ホテル銀座ダイエー
69 Renaissance Tokyo Hotel
Ginza Tōbu
ルネッサンス東京ホテル
銀座東武
75 Ginza Nikkō Hotel
銀座日航ホテル
77 Ginza International Hotel
銀座国際ホテル

PLACES TO EAT
9 Mikuniya
美国屋
11 Sushi Tetsu
すし鉄
32 Shin-Hi-No-Moto
新日の基
34 Tonton Honten
豚豚本店
37 Robata
炉端
40 Henry Africa
41 Doutor Coffee
42 Yakitori Alley
やきとりアリー
45 Hina Sushi
ひな寿司
49 Hina Sushi
ひな寿司
51 Chichibu Nishiki
ちちぶにしき
55 Nair's
ナイル
57 Zakuro
ざくろ
58 Restaurant CityMatsuya;
Department Store
松屋百貨店
64 Ginza Palmy Building
銀座パルミビル
65 Ten'ichi
天一
66 New Torigin
ニュー鳥銀

70 Jangara Rāmen
じゃんがらラーメン
71 Sapporo Lion Beer Hall
72 Kyubei
久兵衛
79 Farm Grill

OTHER
1 Ōte-mon
大手門
2 Citibank
4 Wadakura-mon
和田蔵門
6 Tōkyū Department Store
東急百貨店
7 Yamatane Museum of Art
山種美術館
8 Haibara
はいばら
10 Takashimaya Department
Store
高島屋百貨店
12 Maruzen Bookshop
丸善書店
14 Discount Ticket Shop
格安チケット売り場
15 Discount Ticket Shops
格安チケット売り場
16 Daimaru Department
Store
大丸百貨店
17 Airport Limousine
Bus Stop
空港リムジンバス停
18 Yaesu Book Center
八重洲ブックセンター
19 JR Highway Bus Station
ＪＲ高速バスターミナル
21 Central Post Office;
Tokyo Station Plaza
東京ステーションプラザ；
中央郵便局
22 Sakashita-mon
坂下門
23 Nijū-bashi
二重橋
24 Sakurada-mon
桜田門
25 Marunouchi Café
丸の内カフェ
26 Tokyo International
Forum
東京国際フォーラム
27 Sofmap/Muji
ソフマップ/無印
28 Kōtsū Kaikan; TIC
交通会館
29 Bic Camera

30 Kokusai Building; Idemitsu
Art Museum
国際ビル
31 Imperial Theatre
帝国劇場
33 American Pharmacy
アメリカンファーマシー
35 Tokyo Disneyland
Ticket Centre
東京ディズニーラン
ドチケット売り場
36 Godzilla Statue
ゴジラ像
38 Hibiya Chanter; L'Attresco
(Cinema District)
日比谷シャンテ；
ラトレスコ
43 Hankyū & Seibu Depart-
ment Stores; Yūraku-chō
Mullion Building
阪急/西武百貨店
44 Yūraku-chō Mullion
Building
有楽町マリオンビル
46 Printemps Department
Store
プランタン百貨店
47 Itō-ya Stationery Shop
伊東屋
48 Meidiya International
Supermarket
明治屋
53 Magazine House
マガジンハウス
54 Kabuki-za Theatre
歌舞伎座
56 Mitsukoshi Department
Store
三越百貨店
59 Leica Gallery
60 Wakō Department Store
和光百貨店
61 San Ai Building
三愛ビル
62 Sony Building; Maxim's de
Paris; Sabatine di Firenze
63 Hankyū Department Store
阪急百貨店
67 Citibank
68 Matsuzakaya Department
Store
松坂屋百貨店
73 Takumi Souvenirs
たくみ土産物店
74 Hachikan-jinja
八官神社
76 Discount Ticket Shop
格安チケット売り場
78 Hakuhinkan Toy Park
博品館

are being held. Your ticket (hold on to the stub) gives you free admission to the nearby **Craft Museum** (☎ 3211-7781; open 10am-5pm Tues-Sun), which houses a good display of crafts such as ceramics, lacquerware and dolls.

Yasukuni-jinja 靖国神社

If you take the Tayasu-mon exit (just past the Budōkan) of Kitanomaru-kōen, across the road and to your left is Yasukuni-jinja, the Shrine for Establishing Peace in the Empire. Dedicated to the 2.4 million Japanese war-dead since 1853, it is the most controversial shrine in all Japan.

The Japanese constitutional separation of religion and politics and the renunciation of militarism didn't stop a group of class-A war criminals being enshrined here in 1979; it also doesn't stop annual visits by politicians on the anniversary of Japan's defeat in WWII (15 August). The loudest protests are from Japan's Asian neighbours, who suffered most from Japanese aggression. This is not to say you should boycott the shrine; it is well worth a visit. Black vans blasting right-wing propaganda (in Japanese) are often there to remind you where you are, however.

Yūshūkan Museum Next to the Yasukuni-jinja is the Yūshūkan Museum (admission ¥500; open 9am-5pm daily; closed 28-31 Aug & 28-31 Dec), with treasures from Yasukuni-jinja and other items commemorating Japanese war-dead. There are limited English explanations, but an English pamphlet is available. Interesting exhibits include the long torpedo in the large exhibition hall that is actually a *kaiten* (human torpedo), a submarine version of the kamikaze (WWII suicide pilots). There are also displays of military uniforms, samurai armour and paintings of famous battles. Perhaps most interesting of all are the excerpts from books (some in English) arguing that America forced Japan into bombing Pearl Harbor.

Tokyo International Forum
東京国際フォーラム

The forum (☎ 5221-9000; open 8am-11pm daily) in Yūraku-chō, midway between Tokyo station and Ginza, is a remarkable edifice. The prominent glass wing of this convention centre looks like a glass ship plying the urban waters of central Tokyo. In contrast, the west wing is a boxy affair of cantilevered, overhanging spaces and cavernous atria.

Ginza 銀座

Ginza is the shopping area in Tokyo that *everyone* has heard of. Back in the 1870s, Ginza was one of the first areas to modernise, featuring a large number of novel (for Tokyoites of that time) Western-style brick buildings. Ginza was also home to Tokyo's first department stores and other harbingers of the modern world, such as gas lamps.

Today, other shopping districts rival Ginza in opulence, vitality and popularity, but Ginza retains a distinct snob value. It is still the place to go and be seen emptying the contents of a bulging wallet. Even if you are on a tight budget, Ginza is an interesting area in which to browse – the galleries are usually free and there are lots of discount coffee shops.

On Sunday the smaller streets are closed to vehicles, making for a nice stroll. Start your exploration at the Sukiyabashi train crossing, a 10-minute walk from the Kōkyo, directly above Ginza subway station.

Sony Building The Sony Building (☎ 3573-2371; Sukiyabashi train crossing; admission free; open 11am-7pm daily) has fascinating hands-on displays of Sony's many products, including some that have yet to be released. Although there's often a wait, kids love the free video and virtual-reality games on the 6th floor. If nothing else, you can put your feet up and relax for a while in one of the building's two Hi-Vision theatres.

Galleries Ginza is overflowing with galleries, many of them so small that they can be viewed in two or three minutes. Others feature work by unknown artists who have hired the exhibition space themselves. Wander around and visit any of the galleries that seem interesting. They are scattered throughout Ginza but are concentrated in the area south of Harumi-dōri, between Ginza-dōri and Chūō-dōri.

Idemitsu Art Museum (☎ 3213-9402; adult/student ¥800/500; open 10am-5pm Tues-Sun) holds Japanese and Chinese art and is famous for its collection of work by the Zen monk Sengai. It's a five-minute walk from either Hibiya or Yūraku-chō station, on the 9th floor of the Kokusai Building, next door to the Imperial Theatre.

Probably the best of the photographic galleries in the area is **Leica Gallery** (☎ 3567-6706; open 10.30am-5.30pm Tues-Sun) on the 3rd floor of the Matsushima building.

Kabuki-za Theatre Even if you don't plan to attend a kabuki performance, it's worth taking a look at the Kabuki-za Theatre (☎ 5565-6000). See Entertainment later in this chapter for details.

Magazine House Located just around the corner from Kabuki-za is Magazine House (☎ 3381-5058; open 11am-7pm Mon-Fri), which stocks about 1200 magazines from around the world, and although loans cannot be made, you are free to sit down and read anything you please. It also has a coffee shop where you can enjoy a drink while you read.

Hamarikyū-teien 浜離宮庭園

Often referred to in English as the Detached Palace Garden (admission ¥300; open 9am-4.30pm daily), a visit can be combined either with a visit to Ginza or, via the Sumidagawa Cruise, with a visit to Asakusa (see that section in this chapter). The garden has walks, ponds and teahouses.

Tsukiji Fish Market 築地市場

This is where all that seafood comes after it has been fished out of the sea and before it turns up as sushi and sashimi. The day begins very early, with the arrival of fish and its wholesale auctioning. The wholesale market is not open to the general public, which is probably a blessing, given that you'd have to be there before 7am to see the action. You are free to visit the outer market and wander around the wholesalers' and intermediaries' stalls that sell directly to restaurants, retail stores and other buyers. It is a fun place to visit, and you don't have to arrive *that* early: as long as you're there sometime before 10am there'll be something going on. Watch out for your shoes – there's a lot of muck and water on the floor. Be extremely wary of the motorised vegetable-delivery carts that speed around the market, especially around small children.

Hibiya-kōen 日比谷公園

If Ginza has left you yearning for greenery, retrace your steps along Harumi-dōri, back through Sukiyabashi Crossing to Hibiya-kōen. This was Tokyo's first Western-style park, and it makes for a pleasant break, especially if you head for the benches overlooking the pond on the park's eastern side. Also on the park's eastern side, about midway down, is a small restaurant where you can pause for coffee or ice cream.

AKIHABARA 秋葉原

Akihabara is Tokyo's discount electrical and electronics mecca. Nowhere in the world will you find such a range of electrical appliances, and you can easily spend half a day wandering from store to store. Some larger stores (Laox and Sofmap are reliable options) have tax-free sections with export models for sale (don't forget to ask for duty-free).

While prices may be competitive with those you are used to at home, it's unusual to find prices that match those of dealers in Hong Kong or Singapore. You should be able to knock 10% off the marked prices by bargaining, though this is often not the case with the tax-free items in the bigger stores. To find the shops, take the Electric Town exit of Akihabara station. You'll see the sign on the platform if you come in on the JR Yamanote line.

UENO (MAP 2) 上野

Ueno is one of the last places in Tokyo where the old Shitamachi spirit lingers on. Like Asakusa, it is a place where you can catch a glimpse of what life was like before the economic miracle of the 1970s and 80s. The heart of Ueno is crusty old Ameya-yokochō Arcade, a bustling market that feels worlds away from the hyper-trendy shopping meccas of Shibuya and Harajuku. The main reason to visit Ueno, however, is Ueno-kōen, which has the highest concentration of museums and galleries anywhere in Japan. A trip to Ueno, perhaps paired with a jaunt to nearby Asakusa, is the perfect counterpoint to a day spent in ultra-modern Shinjuku.

Ueno-kōen 上野公園

Ueno Hill was the site of a last-ditch defence of the Tokugawa shōgunate by about 2000 Tokugawa loyalists in 1868. They were duly dispatched by the imperial army, and the new

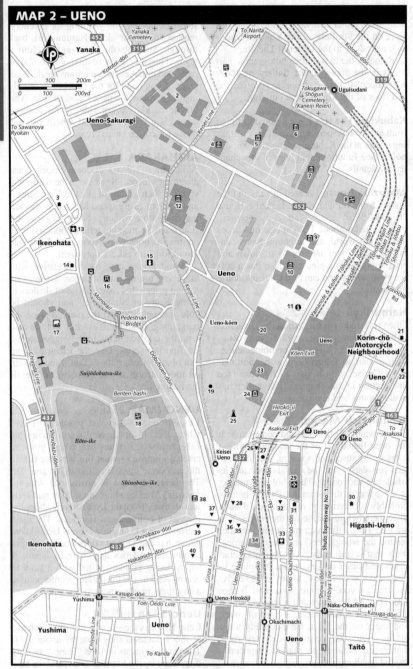

MAP 2 – UENO

PLACES TO STAY		OTHER		13	Police
3	Ryokan Katsutarō 旅館勝太郎	1	Kanei-ji 寛永寺		交番
14	Suigetsu Hotel Ōgaisō 水月ホテル鴎外荘	2	Tokyo University of Fine Arts 東京芸術大学	15	Five-Storeyed Pagoda 五重塔
21	Hotel Green Capital ホテルグリーンキャピタル	4	Gallery of Hōryūji Treasures 法隆寺宝物館	16	Tōshō-gū 東照宮
30	Hotel Sun Targas ホテルサンターガス	5	Hyōkei-kan 表慶館	17	Ueno Zoo 上野動物園
31	Ueno Kinuya Hotel 上野きめやホテル	6	Tokyo National Museum Main Hall 東京国立博物館本館	18	Benzaiten 弁財天
41	Hotel Parkside ホテルパークサイド	7	Gallery of Eastern Antiquities 東洋館	19	Kiyomizu Kannon-dō 清水観音堂
PLACES TO EAT				20	Tokyo Metropolitan Festival Hall 東京文化会館
22	Maguroyāsan まぐろ家さん	8	Rinnō-ji 輪王寺	23	Japan Art Academy 芸術院会館
26	Pronto プロント	9	National Science Museum 国立科学博物館	24	Ueno-no Mori Art Museum 上野の森美術館
28	Ganko Sushi がんこ寿司	10	National Museum of Western Art 国立西洋美術博物館	25	Saigō Takamori Statue 西郷隆盛像
32	Ueno Yabu Soba 上野 藪蕎麦	11	Ueno-kōen Information Centre 上野公園インフォメーションセンター	27	Ameya-yokochō Arcade アメヤ横丁
35	Doutor Coffee			29	Marui Department Store 丸井百貨店
36	Samrat サムラート	12	Tokyo Metropolitan Museum of Art 東京都美術館	33	Warrior Celt
37	McDonald's			34	Ameyoko Centre アメヨコセンタービル
39	Izu-ei 伊豆栄			38	Shitamachi History Museum 下町風俗資料館
40	Musashino 武蔵野				

Meiji government decreed that Ueno Hill would be transformed into Tokyo's first public park. Today, Ueno-kōen may not be the best of Tokyo's parks, but it certainly packs in more attractions than any of the others.

The park is famous as Tokyo's most popular site for *hanami* (blossom viewing) in early to mid-April. Of course, this doesn't mean that Ueno-kōen is the *best* place to see the blossoms (see Shinjuku-gyoen in the Shinjuku section later for an altogether quieter *hanami* spot). In addition to the cherry blossoms, check out the lotuses in the pond, Shinobazu-ike, at the southern end of the park. It's also worth noting that Ueno-kōen is the centre of Tokyo's surprisingly large population of homeless people; their blue tents fill almost every inch of available land in the northern reaches of the park.

Saigō Takamori Statue This slightly unusual statue of a samurai walking his dog, near the southern entrance to the park, is a favourite meeting place. Saigō Takamori started out supporting the Meiji Restoration but ended up ritually disembowelling

himself in defeated opposition to it. The turnabout in his loyalties occurred when the Meiji government withdrew the powers of the military class to which he belonged. See the 'Saigō Takamori' boxed text under Kagoshima in the Kyūshū chapter.

Tokyo National Museum The Tokyo National Museum (☎ 3272-8600; W www.tnm.go.jp; adult/student ¥420/130; open 9.30am-5pm Tues-Sun, 9.30am-8pm Fri Apr-Sept) is the one museum in Tokyo that is worth going out of your way to visit. Not only is it Japan's largest museum, housing some 87,000 items, it also has the world's largest collection of Japanese art. Only a portion of the museum's huge collection is displayed at any one time. Entry is free on the second Saturday of each month.

The museum has four galleries, the most important of which is the **Main Hall** (Hon-kan). It's straight ahead as you enter, and houses a very impressive collection of Japanese art, from sculpture and swords to lacquerware and calligraphy. The **Gallery of Eastern Antiquities** (Tōyō-kan), to the right of the ticket booth, has a collection of art and archaeological finds from all of Asia east of Egypt. The **Hyōkei-kan**, to the left of the ticket booth, has a collection of Japanese archaeological finds. There is a room devoted to artefacts once used by the Ainu, the indigenous people of Hokkaidō.

Finally, and perhaps best of all, there is the **Gallery of Hōryūji Treasures** (Hōryūji Hōmotsu-kan), which houses some of Japan's most important Buddhist artworks, all from Hōryū-ji in Nara.

A nice way to cap off a visit to the museum is with a stroll in the **Tokugawa Shōgun Cemetery**, behind the museum.

Tokyo Metropolitan Museum of Art

The Metropolitan Museum of Art (☎ 3823-6920; w www.tobikan.jp/eng/index.html; admission free, special exhibits ¥900-1000; open 9am-5pm Tues-Sun, closed 3rd Mon each month) has a number of different galleries that run temporary displays (admission fee varies) of contemporary Japanese art. Galleries feature both Western-style art such as oil paintings and Japanese-style art such as sumi-e (ink brush) and ikebana (flower arrangement). Unfortunately, there's a lot of wasted space here and exhibits are not always up to snuff.

National Science Museum

This museum (☎ 3822-0111; admission ¥420; open 9am-4.30pm Tues-Sun) is only visit-worthy for its excellent special exhibitions (usually around ¥500 extra). Look for the life-sized model of the blue whale outside.

National Museum of Western Art

The National Museum of Western Art (☎ 5777-8600; w www.nmwa.go.jp; admission ¥420; open 9.30am-5pm Tues-Thur, Sat & Sun, 9.30am-8pm Fri) has an impressive, though rather indifferently displayed, permanent collection. It frequently hosts special exhibits (you will have to pay extra) on loan from other museums of international repute.

Shitamachi History Museum

This museum (☎ 3823-7451; admission ¥300; open 9.30am-4.30pm Tues-Sun) re-creates life in Edo's Shitamachi, the plebeian downtown quarter of old Tokyo. Exhibits include a merchant's shop, sweet shop, the home and business of a copper-boiler maker, and a tenement house. You are free to handle the displays, making it rather fun.

Ueno Zoo

Established in 1882, Ueno Zoo (☎ 3828-5171; adult/child of high-school age ¥600/200, younger child free; open 9.30am-4.30pm Tues-Sun) was the first of its kind in Japan. It's a good outing if you have children; otherwise, it can be safely dropped from a busy itinerary. The zoo is very popular with Japanese visitors for its pandas (not on view on Friday).

Tōshō-gū

Dating from 1651 this shrine, like its counterpart in Nikkō, is dedicated to Tokugawa Ieyasu, who unified Japan. You'll find more information under History in the Facts about Japan chapter. The shrine (☎ 3822-3455; admission ¥200; open 9am-4.30pm daily winter, 9am-5.30pm daily rest of year) is one of the few extant early-Edo structures, having fortunately survived Tokyo's innumerable disasters.

Ameya-yokochō Arcade アメヤ横丁

Ameya-yokochō was famous as a black-market district after WWII, and is still a lively shopping area where many bargains can be found. Shopkeepers are much less restrained than elsewhere in Tokyo, attracting customers with raucous cries that rattle down the crowded alleyways like the trains overhead. Look for the big romaji (Japanese roman script) sign opposite Ueno station.

AROUND UENO 上野周辺
Kappabashi-dōri かっぱ橋通り

At Tawaramachi (Map 3), just two stops from Ueno subway station on the Ginza line, is Kappabashi-dōri. This is where you go if you're setting up a restaurant. You can get flags that advertise the food in your restaurant, personalised cushions, crockery and, most importantly, all the plastic food you'll ever need. Whether you want a plate of spaghetti bolognaise with an upright fork, a plastic steak and chips, a lurid pizza or a bowl of rāmen (Chinese-style noodles), it's all there. Items aren't particularly cheap, but some of them are very convincing and could make unusual Japanese mementos.

Kappabashi-dōri is a five-minute walk northwest of any of Tawaramachi subway station's exits; look for the giant chef's head atop the Niomi utensil shop.

Rainbow Bridge, Tokyo

Fuji Television Japan Broadcast Center, Tokyo

Tokyo Metropolitan Government Offices

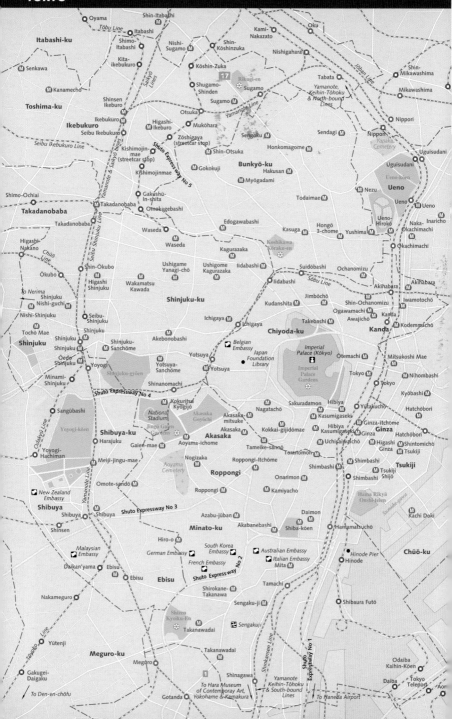

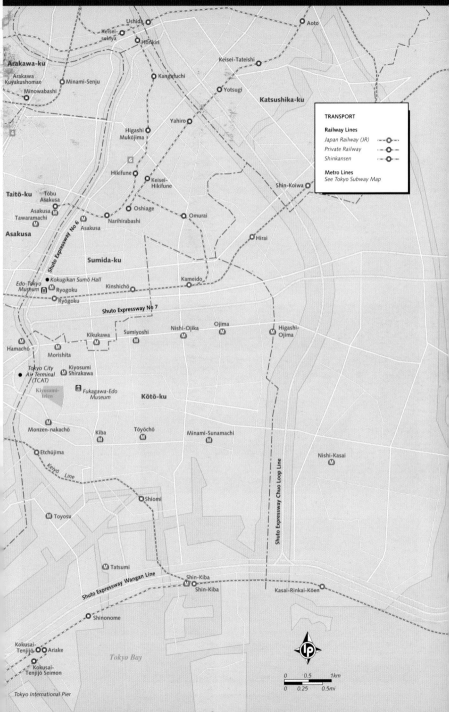

Arakawa-ku

Arakawa
Kuyakushomae
Minami-Senju
Minowabashi

Keisei-
sekiya
Ushida
Horikiri
Aoto

Kangafuchi
Keisei-Tateishi

Yotsugi

Katsushika-ku

Yahiro

Higashi
Mukōjima

Shin-Koiwa

Hikifune
Keisei-
Hikifune

Shin-Koiwa

Taitō-ku
Tōbu
Asakusa
Asakusa
Tawaramachi
Narihirabashi
Asakusa
Oshiage
Omurai

Asakusa

Hirai

Sumida-ku

Kameido

Edo-Tokyo
Museum
Kokugikan Sumō Hall
Ryōgoku
Kinshichō
Ryōgoku

Shuto Expressway No 7

Kikukawa
Sumiyoshi
Nishi-Ojima
Ojima
Higashi-
Ojima

Hamachō

Morishita

Tokyo City
Air Terminal
(TCAT)
Kiyosumi
Shirakawa
Kiyosumi-
teien
Fukagawa-Edo
Museum

Kōtō-ku

Monzen-nakachō
Kiba
Tōyōchō
Minami-Sunamachi

Nishi-Kasai

Etchūjima

Keiyō
Line

Shiomi

Toyosu

Tatsumi
Shin-Kiba
Shin-Kiba
Kasai-Rinkai-Kōen

Shuto Expressway Wangan Line

Shinonome

Kokusai-
Tenjijō
Ariake

Tokyo Bay

Kokusai-
Tenjijō Seimon

Tokyo International Pier

Shuto Expressway Chuo Loop Line

Shuto Expressway No 6

TRANSPORT

Railway Lines
Japan Railway (JR)
Private Railway
Shinkansen

Metro Lines
See Tokyo Subway Map

0   0.5   1km
0   0.25   0.5mi

Takashimaya Times Square, Shinjuku, Tokyo

Freeway flyovers, Tokyo

Tokyo Dome

Tokyo Tower

ASAKUSA (MAP 3) 浅草

Long considered the heart of old Shita-machi, Asakusa is an interesting area to explore on foot. The big attraction is the temple, Sensō-ji, also known as Asakusa Kannon-dō. In Edo times, Asakusa was a halfway stop between the city and its most infamous pleasure district, Yoshiwara. In time, however, Asakusa developed into a pleasure quarter in its own right, eventually becoming the centre for that most loved of Edo entertainments, kabuki. In the very shadow of Sensō-ji a fairground spirit prevailed and a whole range of very secular entertainments were provided, from kabuki theatres to brothels.

When Japan ended its self-imposed isolation with the commencement of the Meiji Restoration, it was in Asakusa that the first cinemas opened, in Asakusa that the first music halls appeared and in Asakusa's Teikoku Gekijo (Imperial Theatre) that Western opera was first performed before Japanese audiences. It was also in Asakusa that another Western cultural import – the striptease – was introduced. A few clubs still operate in the area.

Unfortunately, Asakusa never quite recovered from the bombing at the end of WWII. Sensō-ji was rebuilt, but other areas of Tokyo assumed Asakusa's pleasure-district role. Asakusa may be one of the few areas of Tokyo to have retained something of the spirit of Shitamachi, but the bright lights have shifted elsewhere – notably to Shinjuku.

Sensō-ji 浅草寺

Sensō-ji (☎ 3842-0181) enshrines a golden image of Kannon (the Buddhist Goddess of Mercy) which, according to legend, was miraculously fished out of the nearby Sumida-gawa by two fishermen in AD 628. The image has remained on the spot ever since, through successive rebuildings of the temple. The present temple dates from 1950.

If you approach Sensō-ji from Asakusa subway station, the entrance is via Kaminari-mon (Thunder Gate). The gate's protector gods are Fūjin, the god of wind, on the right; and Raijin, the god of thunder, on the left.

Straight ahead is Nakamise-dōri, the temple precinct's shopping street, where everything from tourist trinkets to genuine Edo-style crafts is sold. There's even a shop selling wigs to be worn with kimono. Try the *sembei* (crackers) that a few shops specialise in – you'll have to queue as they are very popular with Japanese visitors.

Nakamise-dōri leads to the main temple compound. Whether the ancient image of Kannon actually exists is a secret – it's not on public display. Not that this stops a steady stream of worshippers making their way to the top of the stairs to bow and clap. In front of the temple is a large incense cauldron: the smoke is said to bestow health and you will see visitors rubbing it into their bodies through their clothes.

Dembō-in 伝法院

To the left of the temple precinct is Dembō-in (Dembō Garden). Although it is not open to the public, it is possible to obtain a pass by calling in to the main office (☎ 3842-0181) to the left of Sensō-ji's Five-Storeyed Pagoda. The garden is one of Tokyo's best, containing a picturesque pond and a replica of a famous Kyoto teahouse. It's closed on Sunday, holidays and whenever a ceremony is being held in the garden. To avoid disappointment, it's best to call a few days in advance to see if it will be open when you plan to visit.

Sumida-gawa Cruise 隅田川クルーズ

This cruise (every 10 to 15 minutes, from 9.30am to 6pm daily) may not be the most scenic river cruise you've ever experienced, but the *suijō basu* (water bus) is a great way to get to or from Asakusa.

The cruise departs from next to the bridge, Azuma-bashi, in Asakusa and goes to Hamarikyū-teien (see that entry under Ginza, earlier) and Hinode Pier (Tokyo colour map). Probably the best option is to buy a ticket to Hamarikyū-teien (¥620; you'll have to pay an additional ¥300 entry fee for the garden). After looking around the garden it is possible to walk to Ginza in about 10 to 15 minutes. The fare to Hinode Pier is ¥660.

IKEBUKURO (MAP 4) 池袋

Traditionally Shinjuku's poor cousin, bawdy Ikebukuro has been treated to something of a facelift in recent years. Agreed, it shouldn't be high on a busy itinerary, but it's worth noting that its attractions include two of the world's largest department stores (Seibu and Tōbu – the world's largest

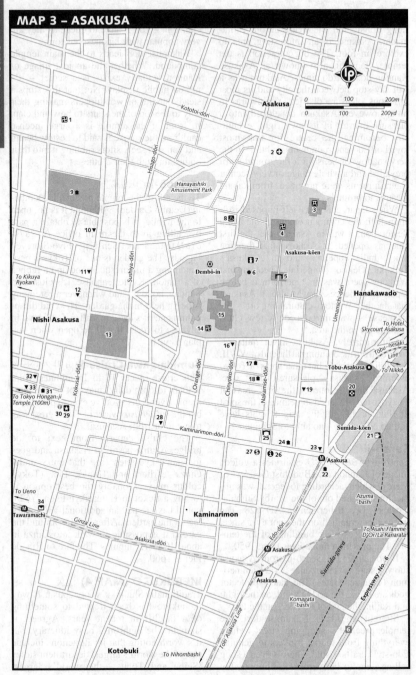

MAP 3 – ASAKUSA

ASAKUSA – MAP 3

PLACES TO STAY		23	Kameya		13	Rox Building
9	Asakusa View Hotel 浅草ビューホテル		かめや			ロックスビル
17	Ryokan Shigetsu 旅館指月	28	Owariya 尾張屋		14	Chingo-dō 鎮護堂
18	Ryokan Mikawaya Bekkan 旅館三河屋別館	32	Vin Chou 萬鳥		15	Dembō-in 伝法院
22	Capsule Hotel Riverside カプセルホテルリバーサイド	33	Sometaro 染太郎		20	Matsuya Department Store 松屋百貨店
24	Asakusa Plaza Hotel 浅草プラザホテル	**OTHER**			21	Sumida-gawa River Cruise
31	Taito Ryokan 台東旅館	1	Banryū-ji 萬隆寺			隅田川水上バス
		2	Sensō-ji Hospital 浅草寺病院		25	Kaminari-mon 雷門
PLACES TO EAT		3	Asakusa-jinja 浅草神社		26	Asakusa Tourist Information Center
10	Akiyoshi 秋吉	4	Sensō-ji 浅草寺			浅草文化観光センター
11	Asakusa Imahan 浅草今半	5	Hōzō-mon 宝蔵門		27	Sumitomo Mitsui Bank 住友三井銀行
12	Raishūken 来集軒	6	Sensō-ji Office 浅草寺事務所		29	Police 交番
16	Daikokuya 大黒屋	7	Five-Storeyed Pagoda 五重塔		30	Public Toilet 公衆便所
19	Tatsumiya 辰巳屋	8	Asakusa Kannon Onsen 浅草観音温泉		34	Post Office 郵便局

is Yokohama Seibu), one of the tallest buildings in Asia (the Sunshine City building), the second-busiest station in Tokyo, the world's largest automobile showroom (Toyota Amlux), and the escalator experience of a lifetime (Tokyo Metropolitan Art Space). Like Shinjuku, Ikebukuro divides into an east side and a west side.

East Side 東池袋

Sunshine City Billed as a 'city in a building', Sunshine City (☎ 3989-3319) is essentially 60 floors of office space and shopping malls, with a few overpriced cultural and entertainment options thrown in. If you have got ¥620 to burn, you can take a lift (operates 10am to 8.30pm) to the lookout on the 60th floor and gaze out on Tokyo's murky skyline. Sunshine City is 300m north of Higashi-Ikebukuro station (take exit 2).

Not in the Sunshine City building itself, but in the Bunka Kaikan of Sunshine City, is the **Ancient Orient Museum** (☎ 3989-3491; admission ¥500, special exhibitions ¥900; open 10am-5pm daily). It is strictly for those with a special interest in ancient odds and ends such as coins and beads.

Also of interest to some might be the **Sunshine Planetarium** (☎ 3989-3475; adult/child ¥1600/800; open noon-5.30pm Mon-

Fri, 11am-6.30pm Sat & Sun), though shows are in Japanese, and **Sunshine International Aquarium** (☎ 3989-3466; adult/child ¥1600/800; open 10am-6pm daily).

Nanjatown (☎ 5950-0765; adult/child ¥300/200; open 10am-10pm daily), also known as nothing less than the Ikebukuro Gyōza Stadium, is a great place to pig out on the famous Chinese dumplings. It's also a spectacle in itself, with 12 shops from across the country competing for the King Gyōza title. We recommend the 'healthy' Kyūshū-based Temujin, which serves its dumplings in a Yuzu citrus, vinegar-soy sauce dip. Don't set foot near the place if you've an aversion to garlic. It's on the 2nd floor of the Sunshine City World Import Mart building.

Department Stores Just why Ikebukuro should have two of the world's largest department stores is a mystery. **Tōbu** (☎ 3981-2211; open 10am-9pm Mon-Sat, 10am-8pm Sun) is the bigger of the two, but **Seibu** (☎ 3981-0111; open 10am-9pm Mon-Sat, 10am-8pm Sun), for many years the world's biggest, still feels bigger and busier. You can easily spend an entire afternoon just wandering around the basement food-floor of Seibu sampling the little tidbits on offer. The 12th floor has an art museum and the

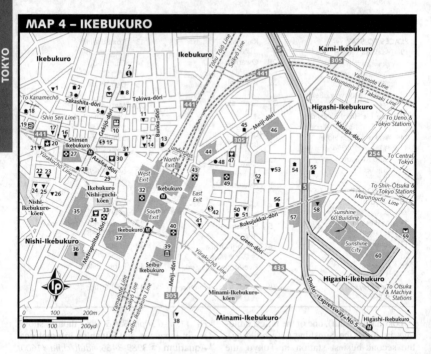

MAP 4 – IKEBUKURO

top floor is restaurant city, with something like 50 restaurants, many of them offering great lunch specials. Tōbu closes on varying days twice monthly.

Art Galleries In the annexe of the Seibu department store is **Seibu Art Gallery**, which has changing art exhibits, usually of fairly high standard. In Tōbu's Metropolitan Plaza is **Tōbu Art Museum**, which also features changing art exhibits. Admission to both galleries varies according to the exhibit.

West Side 西池袋

There's not really a lot to see on the west side, but anyone who hasn't been to Ikebukuro for a couple of years should check out the area between Tokyo Metropolitan Art Space and the southern end of the station. **Metropolitan Plaza** (☎ 5954-1111; restaurants open 11am-10.30pm daily) is packed with classy boutiques, restaurants (8th floor) and a massive HMV (music store, 6th floor – great browsing). Just across the road is the **Spice 2** building (restaurants open 11am-10pm daily), which does a repeat performance of Metropolitan Plaza.

Tokyo Metropolitan Art Space Part of the 'Tokyo Renaissance' plan launched by the Department of Education, this huge cultural bunker was plonked down just where Tokyo needed it most – on Ikebukuro's west side. Designed to host performance art, the building has four halls. Those without a ticket for anything should treat themselves to the soaring escalator ride (it's said to be the world's longest escalator) – it doesn't get much more exciting than this in Ikebukuro!

AROUND IKEBUKURO 池袋周辺
Rikugi-en 六義園

Just three stops from Ikebukuro, near JR Komagome station (Yamanote line), Rikugi-en (Tokyo colour map; ☎ 3941-2222; admission ¥300; open 9am-5pm daily) is one of Tokyo's better gardens. It's a 10-hectare (25-acre) Edo-style kaiyū, or 'many pleasure' garden, built around a tranquil, carp-filled pond. The landscaped views here are said to evoke famous scenes from Chinese and Japanese literature. The garden was established in the late 17th century by Yana-gisawa Yoshiyasu and, after falling

IKEBUKURO – MAP 4

PLACES TO STAY

2	Kimi Ryokan 貴美旅館
8	Ikebukuro Royal Hotel 池袋ロイヤルホテル
13	Hotel Sun City Ikebukuro ホテルサンシティ池袋
18	House Ikebukuro ハウス池袋
36	Hotel Metropolitan ホテルメトロポリタン
45	Hotel Sunroute Ikebukuro ホテルサンルート池袋
54	Hotel Grand City ホテルグランドシティー
55	Ark Hotel アークホテル
56	Hotel Theatre ホテルシアター

PLACES TO EAT

1	Taiwan Hsiao Tiao 台湾小調
4	Sushi Kazu 寿司和
9	Tonerian 舎人庵
11	Doutor Coffee; Tenka Ippin Rāmen ドトールコーヒー； 天下一品ラーメン
12	Matsukaze 松風
14	KFC; Yoshinoya KFC；吉野屋
16	Subway サブウェイ
17	Doutor Coffee ドトールコーヒー
21	Myun ミュン
22	Akiyoshi 秋吉
23	Capricciosa カプリチョーザ

24	Malaychan マレーチャン
25	Chez Kibeau シェ・キーボウ
26	Tonbo とんぼ
38	Mawaru Sushi Hana Kan 回る寿し花館
41	Yamabuki 山吹
51	Komazushi こま寿司
52	Tapa タパ
53	Oriental Kitchen オリエンタルキッチン
58	Nanjatown

OTHER

3	Pharmacy 薬局
5	Pachinko Parlor パチンコパーラー
6	Ikebukuro Post Office 池袋郵便局
7	Kimi Information Center 貴美インフォメーション センター
10	Cinema Rosa シネマロサ
15	Sumitomo Bank 住友銀行
19	Hard Internet Cafe T and T ハードインターネット カフェ T and T
20	Police 交番
27	Marui Department Store 丸井百貨店
28	Kinko's キンコーズ
29	Marui Field Sports Store 丸井フィールド池袋
30	Bobby's Bar ボビーズバー

31	Discount Ticket Shop 格安チケット売り場
32	Tōbu Department Store; Tobu Art Museum 東武百貨店
33	Spice 2 スパイス2
34	The Dubliners ザダブリナーズ
35	Tokyo Metropolitan Art Space 東京芸術会館
37	Metropolitan Plaza; Domani; HMV メトロポリタンプラザ
39	Seibu Irumus-kan イルムス館
40	Seibu Department Store 西武百貨店
42	Fuji Bank みずほ銀行
43	Parco Department Store パルコ
44	Bic Camera (main store) ビックカメラ (本店)
46	Toshima-ku Office 豊島区役所
47	The Black Sheep ザブラックシープ
48	Bic Personal Computer Store ビックカメラパソコン館
49	Mitsukoshi Department Store 三越百貨店
50	Bic Camera ビックカメラ
57	Tōkyū Hands 東急ハンズ
59	Toshima Post Office 豊島郵便局
60	Bunka Kaikan; Ancient Orient Museum 文化会館； 古代オリエント博物館

into disuse, was restored by the founder of the Mitsubishi group, Iwasaki Yataro.

SHINJUKU (MAP 5) 新宿

If you had only a day in Tokyo and wanted to dive headfirst into the modern Japanese phenomenon, Shinjuku would be the place to go. Nearly everything that makes Tokyo interesting rubs elbows here: high-class department stores, discount shopping arcades, flashing neon, government offices, swarming push-and-shove crowds, street-side video screens, stand-up noodle bars, hostess clubs, tucked-away shrines and sleazy strip bars.

Shinjuku is a sprawling business, commercial and entertainment centre that never lets up. Every day approximately two million people pass through the station alone, making it one of the busiest in the world. On the western side of the station is Tokyo's highest concentration of skyscrapers and, presiding over them, Tange Kenzō's Tokyo Metropolitan Government Offices – massive awe-inspiring structures. The eastern side of the station – the more interesting by far – is a warren of department stores, restaurants, boutiques, neon and sleaze.

TOKYO

MAP 5 – SHINJUKU

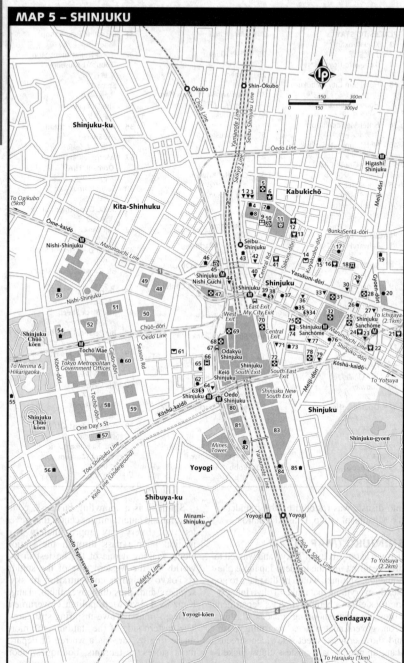

PLACES TO STAY

4 Green Plaza Shinjuku; Green
Plaza Ladies Sauna
グリーンプラザ新宿; グリーン
プラザレディースサウナ
15 Shinjuku-Kuyakusho-Mae
Capsule Hotel
新宿区役所前カプセルホテル
19 Hotel Sun Lite Shinjuku
ホテルサンライト新宿
43 Shinjuku Prince Hotel
新宿プリンスホテル
46 Star Hotel Tokyo
スターホテル東京
53 Hilton Tokyo
ヒルトン東京
54 Century Hyatt Tokyo
センチュリー
ハイアット東京
55 Shinjuku New City Hotel
新宿ニューシティーホテル
56 Park Hyatt Tokyo; New York
Grill; New York Bar
パークハイアット東京;
ニューヨークグリル
57 Shinjuku Washington Hotel
新宿ワシントンホテル
60 Keiō Plaza Inter-Continental
Hotel
京王プラザインター
コンチネンタルホテル
73 Central Hotel
セントラルホテル
82 Hotel Century Southern Tower
ホテルセンチュリー
サザンタワー
85 Shinjuku Park Hotel
新宿パークホテル

PLACES TO EAT

1 Beijing Rāmen
北京
2 Shinjuku Negishi
新宿ねぎし
3 Tainan Taami
台南担仔麺
23 Keika Kumamoto Rāmen
桂花熊本ラーメン
27 Starbucks
スターバックス
29 Canard
カナール
30 Tokyo Dai Hanten; Oriental
Wave
東京大飯店;オリエンタル
ウェーブ
33 Isetan Kaikan; Kushinobō
伊勢丹会館;串の坊
36 El Borracho
エルブラッチョ
40 Ibuki
伊吹
42 Suzuya
すずや

44 Omoide-yokochō
思い出横丁
64 Raobian Gyozakan
老辺餃子館
71 Suehiro
スエヒロ
77 Tsunahachi
つな八
79 Daikokuya
大黒屋

OTHER

5 Hygeai Shopping Centre
ハイジヤショッピングセンター
6 Police
交番
7 Liquid Room; Finlando Sauna
リキッドルーム;
フィンランドサウナ
8 Shinjuku Tōkyū Bunka Kaikan
新宿東急文化センター
9 Shinjuku Joy Cinema
新宿ジョイシネマ
10 Manga@Cafe-Gera Gera
11 Koma Theatre
コマ劇場
12 Loft
ロフト
13 Rock Bar Mother
ロックバーマザー
14 Post Office; Shinjuku Ward
Office
郵便局;新宿区役所
16 Bon's
ボンズ
17 Golden Gai
ゴールデン街
18 Hanazono-jinja
花園神社
20 Isetan Park City
伊勢丹パークシティー
21 Arty Farty
アーティーファーティー
22 Rolling Stone
ローリングストーン
24 Clubhouse
クラブハウス
25 Marui One Department Store
丸井ワールド新宿
26 Minami Sports
ミナミスポーツ
28 Marui Department Store
丸井百貨店
31 Isetan Department Store
伊勢丹百貨店
32 Isetan Department Store
伊勢丹百貨店
34 Citibank
シティーバンク
35 Kinokuniya
紀伊国屋書店
37 Kirin City
キリンシティー
38 Sumitomo Mitsui Bank
住友三井銀行

39 Studio Alta Building
スタジオアルタビル
41 Garam
ガラム
45 Cyber Scholé Internet Café
T-Zone; Gaiax Cafe
サイバースコレ;Tゾーン
47 Odakyū Department Store
小田急百貨店
48 Yasuda Kasai Kaijo Building
安田火災海上ビル
49 Shinjuku Nomura Building
新宿野村ビル
50 Shinjuku Centre Building
新宿センタービル
51 Shinjuku Mitsui Building;
Royal Deli
新宿三井ビル;ロイヤルデリ
52 Shinjuku Sumitomo Building
新宿住友ビル
58 Shinjuku NS Building
新宿NSビル
59 KDD Building
KDDビル
61 Post Office
郵便局
62 Sakuraya Camera
カメラのサクラヤ
63 Citibank
シティバンク
65 Yodobashi Camera
ヨドバシカメラ
66 Highway Bus Station; Haneda
Limousine Bus Stop
高速バスターミナル;
羽田リムジンバス停
67 Narita Limousine Bus Stop
成田リムジンバス停
68 Keiō Department Store
京王百貨店
69 Odakyū Department Store
小田急百貨店
70 My City Department Store
マイシティー百貨店
72 Flags; Gap; Tower Records
フラッグス;ギャップ;
タワーレコード
74 Dubliners; Lion Beer Hall
ダブリナーズ;
ライオンビアホール
75 Mitsukoshi Department Store
三越百貨店
76 Marui City
丸井シティ
78 Mitsukoshi South; IDC
三越南館;IDC
80 JR Shinjuku Building
JR新宿ビル
81 JR East Headquarters
JR西日本本部
83 Takashimaya Times Square
高島屋タイムズスクエアー
84 Kinokuniya
紀伊国屋書店

East Side 東新宿

Shinjuku's east side is an area that is good to wander through and get lost in rather than an area in which to search out particular sights.

Kabuki-chō Tokyo's most notorious red-light district lies east of Seibu Shinjuku station, north of Yasukuni-dōri. This is one of the world's more imaginative red-light areas, with 'soaplands' (massage parlours), love hotels, peep shows, pink cabarets ('pink' is the Japanese equivalent of 'blue' in English), porno-video booths and strip shows that involve audience participation. The streets here are all crackling neon and drunken salarymen. High-pitched female voices wail out invitations to enter their establishments through distorting sound-systems, and Japanese punks earn a few extra yen passing out advertisements for karaoke boxes.

Most of what goes on is very much off limits to foreigners, but it's still an interesting area for a stroll. If you do want to get a peek at the action, try one of the strip bars that deploy foreign touts on the street – count on at least ¥7000 for a show and a drink or two.

Kabuki-chō is not wall-to-wall sex; there are also some very straight entertainment options, including cinemas and some good restaurants.

Hanazono-jinja Nestled in the shadow of Kabuki-chō is this quiet, unassuming shrine. It only takes around 10 minutes to stroll around the grounds, but it's a fine place to sit down and take a break. You hardly know you are in Shinjuku. The shrine is particularly pleasant when it's lit up in the evening. It is 300m north of Shinjuku Sanchome station (take exit B2).

Shinjuku-gyoen This park (☎ 3350-0151; admission ¥200; open 9am-4pm Tues-Sun) is one of Tokyo's best escapes and top cherry blossom-viewing spots and, at 57.6 hectares (144 acres), one of Tokyo's largest parks. It dates back to 1906 and was designed as a European-style park, though a Japanese garden is also included. Other features are a French garden, a hothouse containing tropical plants and, near the hothouse, a pond with giant carp.

West Side 西新宿

Shinjuku's west side is mainly administrative, but the area behind the Keiō department store is home to Tokyo's largest camera stores: Yodobashi Camera and Sakuraya Camera. Yodobashi Camera has practically everything you could possibly want that relates to photography, all at very reasonable prices. It even has a limited selection of second-hand photographic equipment.

Elsewhere, the attractions of Shinjuku's west side are mainly the interiors of buildings and the observation floors of the impressive Tokyo Metropolitan Government Offices.

Metropolitan Government Offices These offices (☎ 5320-7890; admission free; North tower open 9.30am-10pm Tues-Sun, South tower open 9.30am-5.30pm Wed-Mon, 9.30am-7pm Sat & Sun, open later summer, closed 29 Dec-3 Jan) are also known as Tokyo Tochō. These two adjoining buildings are worth a visit for their stunning architecture and for the great views from the **twin observation floors**. On really clear days, you might even spot Mt Fuji to the west.

Despite its critics, most visitors are won over by the buildings' complex symmetry and computer-chip appearance. Particularly impressive is the spacious Citizen's Plaza in front of the No 1 building – more reminiscent of a Roman amphitheatre than anything Japanese.

To reach the No 1 building's observation floors, take one of the two 1st-floor lifts.

Shinjuku NS Building The interior of this building is hollow, featuring a 1600 sq metre atrium illuminated by sunlight, which comes in through the glass roof. Overhead, at 110m, is a 'sky bridge'. The atrium itself features a 29m-tall pendulum clock that is said to be the largest in the world. The 29th and 30th floors have a large number of restaurants, all of which sport excellent views over Tokyo.

Pentax Forum On the 1st floor of the Shinjuku Mitsui Building is Pentax Forum (☎ 3348-2941; admission free; open 10.30am-6.30pm, closed 1 Jan), a must for photography buffs. You can play with the cameras, and there's a good exhibition space.

Cos-play-zoku

When Tokyo's forces of Law and Order donned their riot gear to oust the Takenokozoku – the dancers clad in bright pastel clothes, with 1950s rockabilly haircuts – from Yoyogi-kōen, no-one imagined that the Takenokozoku would be replaced by an even odder, younger crowd.

Enter the Cos-play-zoku, the Costume Play Gang. Mainly teenage girls from the dormitory towns and cities around Tokyo's fringe, the Cos-play-zoku assemble at Harajuku's Jingū-bashi each weekend, bedecked in Gothic make-up, a mixture of SM queen arch-vamp, black taffeta, blue lipstick and cartoon nurse exaggeration.

Cos-play-zoku are united in their fondness for Japanese *visual-kei* (visual type) bands, such as L'Arc En Ciel and Zard, and a sense of pride in their alienation. Many of the girls are *ijime-ko*, kids bullied in school, who find release and expression in their temporary weekend identities.

The end result is Tokyo's most fun circus, as each weekend hordes of excited photographers, bewildered tourists and plain voyeurs gather to catch the show. The girls revel and primp and pose for the cameras until dusk, when they hop back on the trains for the slow return to 'normal' life in the faceless housing blocks of Chiba and Kawasaki.

HARAJUKU & AOYAMA (MAP 6)
原宿・青山

Harajuku and Aoyama are Tokyo in loafers. They're pleasant areas to stroll in and watch locals spend their money in boutiques and bistros. **Takeshita-dōri** swarms with bubble-gum teenagers shopping for illiterate T-shirts and fishnet stockings; **Omote-sandō**, with its alfresco cafés and boutiques, is still the closest Tokyo gets to Paris; the bistro alleys of **Aoyama** sport some of the best international cuisine in town; and **Meiji-jingū** is Tokyo's most splendid shrine.

For unforgettable holiday snaps, check out the Sunday madness at **Jingū-bashi**, right next to Harajuku JR station.

Meiji-jingū 明治神宮

Completed in 1920, the shrine (**W** www .meijijingu.or.jp/english/index.htm; admission free) was built in memory of Emperor Meiji and Empress Shōken, under whose rule Japan ended its long isolation from the outside world. Unfortunately, like much else in Tokyo, the shrine was destroyed in the bombing at the end of WWII. Rebuilding was completed in 1958.

Meiji-jingū might be a reconstruction of the original but, unlike so many of Japan's postwar reconstructions, it is altogether authentic. The shrine itself was built with Japanese cypress, while the cypress for the huge torii (gates) came from Alishan in Taiwan.

Meiji-jingū-neien This garden (admission ¥500; open 9am-4.30pm daily) offers peaceful strolls, being almost deserted on weekdays. It's particularly beautiful in June, when the irises are in bloom.

Meiji-jingū Treasure Museum This museum (admission ¥500; open 9am-4.30pm daily) is an unremarkable collection of items from the lives of the emperor and empress.

Yoyogi-kōen 代々木公園

This is not one of Tokyo's best but, at 53.2 hectares (133 acres), its wooded grounds make for a relaxing walk. It's at its best on a sunny Sunday in spring or autumn.

Ota Memorial Art Museum
太田記念美術館

This museum (☎ 3403-0880; admission ¥500; open 10.30am-5.30pm Tues-Sun), 50m from Meiji Jingumae subway station (take exit 5), has an excellent collection of ukiyo-e (woodblock prints) and offers a good opportunity to see works by Japanese masters of the art, including Hiroshige. There is an extra charge for special exhibits.

Nezu Fine Art Museum
根津美術館

This museum (☎ 3400-2536; **W** www.nezu -muse.or.jp; admission ¥1000; open 9.30am-4pm Tues-Sun) houses a well-known collection of Japanese art including paintings, calligraphy and sculpture. Also on display are Chinese and Korean art exhibits, and teahouses where tea ceremonies are performed. The exhibits are well displayed

MAP 6 – HARAJUKU & AOYAMA

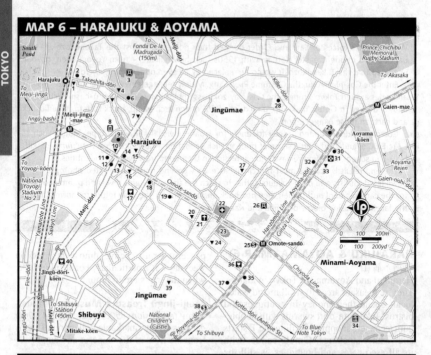

MAP 6 – HARAJUKU & AOYAMA

PLACES TO EAT
1 Doutor Coffee
   ドゥトールコーヒー
4 Shūtarō
   しゅうたろう
5 Rat Gnon Store
7 Son of Dragon
   龍の子
10 Tokyo Apartment Café
13 Lotteria
   ロッテリア
15 Tacos del Amigo
   タコスデルアミーゴ
16 Fujimamas
20 Bamboo Cafe
   バンブーカフェ
24 Hiroba; Organic
   Restaurant Home;
   Crayon House
   広場 ; 自然食レストラン
   HOME ; クレヨンハウス
27 Maisen
   まい泉
33 Tony Roma's;
   Doutor Coffee
   トニーローマーズ ;
   ドゥトールコーヒー
39 Las Chicas
   ラスチカス

OTHER
2 Taurus Vintage Clothing
3 Tōgō jinja
   東郷神社
6 Get Back
   ゲットバック
8 Ota Memorial Art Museum
   大田記念美術館
9 Laforet
   ラフォーレ
11 Chicago Thrift Shop
   シカゴ
12 Condomania
   コンドマニア
14 T'S Harajuku/Gap
17 Oh God; Zest
   オーガット ; ゼスト
18 Kiddyland
   キディーランド
19 Oriental Bazaar
   オリエンタルバザール
21 Tokyo Union Church
   東京ユニオンチャーチ
22 Itō Hospital
   伊東病院
23 Hanae Mori Building; Citibank; Le
   Papillon de Paris; Antique Mall
   森英恵ビル ; シティバンク ;
   ルパピオンドゥパリ ; 骨董街

25 Mizuho Bank
   みずほ銀行
26 Zenkō ji
   善光寺
28 Watari-um Gallery
   ワタリウム美術館
29 Bell Commons
   ベルコモンズ
30 Japan Traditional Craft
   Centre
   日本伝統工芸センター
31 Daimaru Peacock
   Department Store
   大丸ピーコック百貨店
32 Cycland
   サイクランド
34 Nezu Fine Art Museum
   根津美術館
35 Spiral Bldg
   スパイラルビル
36 Mix
   ミックス
37 Kinokuniya International
   Supermarket
   紀ノ国屋
38 Citibank
   シティバンク
40 Crocodile
   クロコダイル

and of high quality. Savour its wonderful, slightly wild ornamental garden.

Galleries

Aoyama is packed with tiny galleries, most of which are free. Up Killer-dōri, in particular, look out for **Watari-um** (☎ 3402-3001; admission ¥1000; open 11am-7pm Tues-Sun), an adventuristic display space with a great art bookshop and probably the best supply of postcards in Tokyo. Exhibits are advertised in the lobby/store area and admission averages ¥700. The futuristic **Spiral Garden** (☎ 3498-1171; open 11am-8pm daily) features changing exhibits, shows, dining and live music.

Kotto-dōri, or 'Antique Street' as it's called in the tourist literature, is a good place to seek out both galleries and souvenirs.

Aoyama Reien 青山霊園

Better known as Aoyama Botchi, this cemetery is perfect for a stroll and provides a nice break from the crowds of Omote-sandō and nearby Roppongi. It's also a good alternative to Ueno-kōen during *hanami* season.

SHIBUYA (MAP 7) 渋谷

Shibuya is a bustling, youth-oriented shopping district where it's easy to get the feeling that everyone over the age of 35 has been sent back to Ueno or Ikebukuro. Like Shinjuku, Shibuya is not exactly rich in sights but it is a good area to stroll around and there's some of the best department-store browsing to be had in all Tokyo. You may want to avoid the area on weekends, when the streets are jammed with fashionable Tokyo kids.

Hachiko Statue ハチ公像

In the 1920s, a professor who lived near Shibuya station kept a small Akita dog, who would come to the station every day to await his master's return. The professor died in 1925, but the dog continued to show up and wait at the station until his own death 11 years later. The poor dog's faithfulness was not lost on the Japanese, and they built a statue to honour his memory.

Tobacco & Salt Museum
たばこと塩の博物館

This small museum (☎ 3476-2041; admission ¥100; open 10am-6pm Tues-Sun, closed 1 Jan & 1st Tues of June) has some fairly interesting exhibits detailing the history of tobacco and the methods of salt production practised in premodern Japan (Japan has no salt mines and until recently harvested salt from the sea). As usual, there's little in the way of English explanations, but a lot of the material is self-explanatory.

Tepco Electric Energy Museum
電力館

Folks with kids in tow and an interest in electric power might want to stop by the Tepco Electric Energy Museum (Denryoku-kan; ☎ 3477-1191; admission free; open 10am-6pm Thur-Tues). It may be seven floors of advertising for Tokyo Electric Power, but the displays are well presented and cover a lot of ground. Anything and everything associated with electricity gets the treatment. It's just north of the Marui One department store, 500m from Shibuya station, exit 7.

Love Hotel Hill

The area around the top of Dōgen-zaka hill is probably the world capital of love hotels. There are love hotels to suit all tastes, from miniature Gothic castles to Middle-Eastern temples (and wait – these are just the buildings – the rooms are even more varied). It's OK to wander in and take a look at the screen with illuminated pictures of the various rooms available.

This area is gradually being invaded by other entertainment options such as alfresco cafés, restaurants, performance halls and so on. **Dr Jeekhan's** is an upmarket video-game parlour. There are two popular nightclubs in the same building (see Shibuya under Bars & Clubs in the Entertainment section, later). Just down the road is the trendy On Air Theatre (east and west branches are on either side of the road).

EBISU & DAIKANYAMA (MAP 8)
恵比寿・代官山

Ebisu and Daikanyama are pleasant alternatives to the crowds and madness of nearby Shibuya and Shinjuku. Daikanyama, in particular, is a great spot for a casual afternoon stroll, with its almost Western ambience and abundant alfresco cafés. However, most people come to Ebisu and Daikanyama at night to sample some of Tokyo's better clubs and bars. If you do come during the

TOKYO

MAP 7 – SHIBUYA

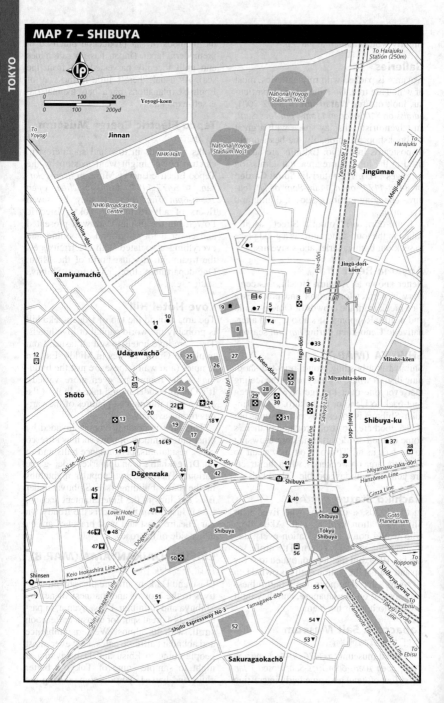

SHIBUYA – MAP 7

PLACES TO STAY
9   Shibuya Tōbu Hotel
    渋谷東武ホテル
37 Shibuya Business Hotel
    渋谷ビジネスホテル
39 Shibuya Tōkyū Inn
    渋谷東急イン

PLACES TO EAT
4   Jūnikagetsu; Hina Sushi
    十二月；雛鮨
5   New York Kitchen
    ニューヨークキッチン
15 Sakana-tei
    酒菜亭
18 Samrat
    サムラート
20 Kushinobō
    串の坊
41 Ubusuna Cafe
43 Tamakyū
    玉久
44 Reikyō
    麗郷
51 Tainan Taami
    台南担仔麺
53 Akiyoshi
    秋吉
54 Kantipur
    カンティプール
55 Fujiya Honten
    富士屋本店

OTHER
1   Eggman
    エッグマン
2   Tepco Electric Energy
    Museum
    電力館
3   Marui One Department
    Store
    丸井ワールド

6   Tobacco & Salt Museum
    たばこと塩の博物館
7   Frontier Shibuya
    フロンティア渋谷
8   Parco Part II
    パルコパート2
10 Cisco Records
    シスコレコード
11 Manhattan Records
    マンハッタンレコード
12 Kanze Nō-gakudō
    観世能楽堂
13 Tōkyū Department Store;
    Bunkamura
    東急百貨店；文化村
14 Bar, Isn't It?
    バーイズントイット
16 Citibank
    シティバンク
17 One-Oh-Nine Building;
    Maruhan Pachinko
    Tower
    109ビル；
    まるはんパチンコタワー
19 Book 1st
    ブックファースト
21 Cafe J Net New New
22 Club Quattro
    クラブクアトロ
23 The Beam; Inti Shibuya
    ザビーム；インティ渋谷
24 Police
    交番
25 Tōkyū Hands
    東急ハンズ
26 Parco Part III
    パルコパート3
27 Parco Part I
    パルコパート1
28 Seibu Seed
    西武SEED

29 Loft Department Store
    ロフト
30 Disney Store; Humax
    Pavilion
    ディズニーストアー；
    ヒューマックス
    パビリオン
31 Seibu Department Store
    西武百貨店
32 Marui Department Store
    丸井百貨店
33 Doi Camera
    カメラのドイ
34 Tower Records; Tower Books
    タワーレコード
35 H.I.S. Travel
    エイチアイエストラベル
36 Marui Young Department
    Store
    丸井ヤング
38 Shibuya Post Office
    渋谷郵便局
40 Hachikō Statue
    ハチ公像
42 109 Building
    109ビル
45 Club Asia
    クラブアジア
46 On Air West
    オンエアーウエスト
47 Dr Jeekhan's; Harlem
    ドクタージーカンズ；
    ハーレム
48 On Air East
    オンエアーイースト
49 Sugar High
    シュガーハイ
50 Shibuya Mark City
52 Cerulean Tower
    セルリアンタワー
56 South Exit Bus Station
    南口バス停

day, most sights worth seeing are in the new Ebisu Garden Place, easily reached from JR Ebisu station by an aerial walkway.

Ebisu Garden Place
恵比寿ガーデンプレイス

This is a complex (☎ 5423-7111) of shops, restaurants and a 39-floor tower, surrounded by an open mall area – perfect for hanging out on warmer days. Garden Place also features the headquarters of Sapporo Breweries, which contains the **Beer Museum Yebisu** (admission free; open 10am-6pm Tues-Sun). There are lots of good exhibits, the best of which is the 'Tasting Lounge', where you can sample Sapporo's various brews (¥200 a glass).

There are lots of outdoor cafés scattered around the complex. If you're hungry, most serve light meals as well. The restaurants on the 38th and 39th floors of **Ebisu Garden Place Tower** offer excellent views.

Tokyo Metropolitan Museum of Photography Japan's first large-scale museum devoted entirely to photography (☎ 3280-0099; permanent/special/all exhibits ¥500/600/1000; open 10am-6pm Tues, Wed, Sat & Sun, 10am-8pm Thur & Fri) is in new premises. The emphasis in this museum is on Japanese photography, but international work is also displayed. From JR Ebisu station take the covered walkway to Ebisu Garden Place.

TOKYO

MAP 8 – EBISU & DAIKANYAMA

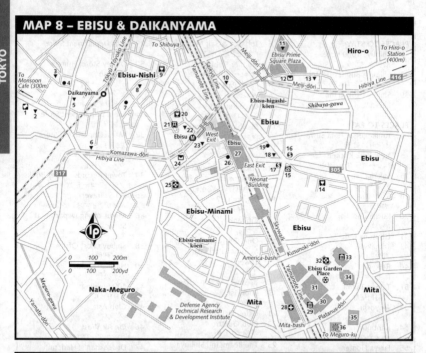

MAP 8 – EBISU & DAIKANYAMA

PLACES TO EAT

2	Caffe Michelangelo カフェミケランジェロ
3	Bombay Bazar ボンベイバザール
5	Café Artifagose カフェアルトファゴス
6	Gazebo Café ガゼボカフェ
8	Café Juliet; KM Fils カフェジュリエット; カーエムフィス
10	Fujii 藤井
11	Shunsenbō 旬泉坊
13	Ippūdō Rāmen 一風堂らーめん
18	Denki Kurage 電気くらげ
22	Nanaki Soba なな樹そば
23	Doutor Coffee ドトールコーヒー

OTHER

1	Danish Embassy デンマーク大使館

4	Kamawanu かまわぬ
7	7-Eleven セブンイレブン
9	Enjoy House エンジョイハウス
12	Post Office 郵便局
14	Lazy Cat
15	Kinko's
16	Mizuho Bank みずほ銀行
17	Sumitomo Mitsui Bank 住友三井銀行
19	Good Day Books グッドデイブックス
20	What the Dickens; Milk ワットザディケンズ;みるく
21	Ebisu-jinja 恵比寿神社
24	Ebisu Eki-mae Post Office 恵比寿駅前郵便局
25	Matsuzakaya Department Store 松坂屋百貨店
26	Shanghai シャンハイ
27	Atre Building

28	Kōseichūō Hospital 厚生中央病院
29	Tokyo Metropolitan Museum of Photography 東京都写真美術館
30	Garden Hall ガーデンホール
31	Ebisu Garden Place Tower ガーデンパレスタワー
32	Mitsukoshi Department Store 三越百貨店
33	Beer Museum Yebisu; Sapporo Breweries HQ 恵比寿麦酒記念館; サッポロビール本社
34	Ebisu Garden Terrace Niban-kan Building 恵比寿ガーデンテラス 弐番館
35	Ebisu Garden Terrace Ichiban-kan Building 恵比寿ガーデンテラス 壱番館
36	Ebisu View Tower 恵比寿ビュータワー

AKASAKA (MAP 9) 浅草

Akasaka is home to Tokyo's heaviest concentration of top-notch hotels and a good selection of mid-range restaurants. Its sights, however, are low-key.

Hie-jinja 日枝神社

The shrine itself (☎ 3581-2471), next to the Capitol Tōkyū Hotel, 250m northwest of Tameike Sanno subway station (exit 5), is not one of Tokyo's major attractions; it's modern, drab and largely cement. The highlight is the walk up to the shrine through a 'tunnel' of orange **torii** (shrine gates), particularly pretty during cherry-blossom season. Unfortunately, Tokyo is now in the process of building a garish new promenade to the shrine and this will add to its decidedly modern feel.

Hotel Sights

Some of Akasaka's luxury hotels are sights in themselves. Hotel New Otani (see Places to Stay, Top End), for example, has preserved part of a **400-year-old garden** that was once the property of a Tokugawa regent. The carp pond is spectacular.

For views over the area (forget the expensive Tokyo Tower), ANA Hotel Tokyo and Akasaka Prince Hotel both offer skyline spectacles from their lofty upper reaches.

Aoyama-dōri 青山通り

Aoyama-dōri runs from Akasaka to Shibuya, taking in the Akasaka Palace grounds (not a major attraction) and Harajuku. Halfway between Akasaka and Aoyama-Itchōme station, on the left-hand side, is the Sōgetsu Kaikan building, headquarters of the **Sōgetsu school of avant-garde flower arrangement**. If you are interested in ikebana, this is a good place to visit. There are displays, a bookshop and coffee shop.

On the 6th floor of the same building is **Sōgetsu Art Museum** (☎ 3408-9112; admission ¥500; open 10am-5pm Mon-Sat), notable for its highly idiosyncratic and eclectic collection of art treasures from across the centuries. Exhibits range from Indian Buddhas to works by Matisse.

ROPPONGI (MAP 10) 六本木

Roppongi is restaurants and nightlife, but mainly nightlife. There's no compelling reason to visit by day, though there are a couple of nearby tourist attractions.

Tokyo Tower 東京タワー

Tokyo's Eiffel Tower-lookalike (☎ 3433-5111; **W** www.tokyotower.co.jp) is more impressive from a distance; up close, the 330m tower is a tourist trap. The **Grand Observation Platform** (admission ¥820; open 9am-10pm daily) is only 150m high; if you want to peer through the smog at Tokyo's uninspiring skyline from 250m, it will cost you a further ¥600 to get to the **Special Observation Platform** (open 9am-8pm daily 16 Mar-15 Nov, 9am-9pm daily Aug, 9am-6pm daily rest of year). The tower also features an overpriced **aquarium** (admission ¥1000; open 10am-9pm daily), a **wax museum** (admission ¥850; open daily), the **Holographic Mystery Zone** (admission ¥400; open daily) and showrooms. A combination ticket costs ¥1900.

Tokyo Tower is a fair trudge from Roppongi; take the Hibiya subway line one stop to Kamiyachō station.

Zōjō-ji 増上寺

Behind Tokyo Tower, Zōjō-ji (☎ 3432-1531) was the family temple of the Tokugawas. It makes a nice stroll if you are in the vicinity.

ODAIBA/TOKYO BAY (MAP 11)
お台場・東京湾

Tokyo is rediscovering the fact that it's a waterfront city, and recent years there's been a spate of development in and around the Tokyo Bay area. Perhaps the most popular Tokyo Bay spot is the Odaiba/Ariake area. Odaiba and Ariake are serviced by the Tokyo Rinkai Shinkōtsū Sen ('Tokyo Waterfront New Transit Line' or 'Yurikamome line'). There's also the extension of the Rinkai Fukutoshin line. See the boxed text 'Odaiba/Tokyo Bay Walking Tour' later for details on some of the area's attractions.

OTHER ATTRACTIONS
Parks & Gardens

If you have been hitting the bitumen and haven't seen a tree for days, there are several parks and gardens to cure what ails you. (Many of these are listed in the relevant area sections earlier in this chapter.) **Koishikawa Kōraku-en** (Tokyo colour map; ☎ 3811-3015; admission ¥300; open 9am-5pm daily) has to be one of the least-visited (by foreigners at least) and best gardens in Tokyo. A stroll-garden with a strong

TOKYO

MAP 9 – AKASAKA

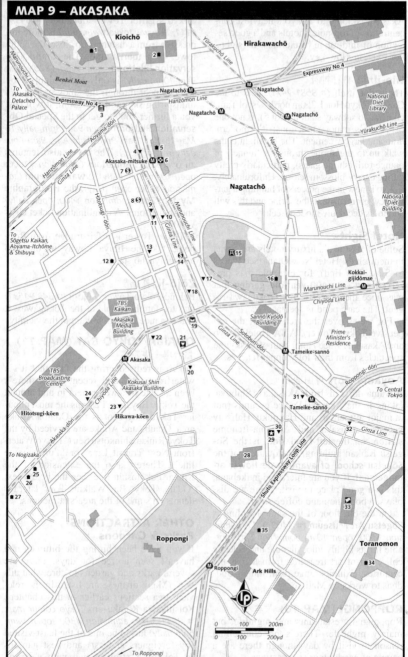

PLACES TO STAY

1 Hotel New Otani; The Bar
   ホテルニューオータニ
2 Akasaka Prince Hotel;
   Top of Akasaka
   赤坂プリンスホテル
5 Akasaka Tōkyū Hotel;
   Kushinobō
   赤坂東急ホテル ;
   串の坊
12 Capsule Hotel
   Fontaine Akasaka
   カプセルホテル
   フォンテーヌ赤阪
16 Capitol Tōkyū Hotel
   キャピタル東急ホテル
25 Capsule Inn Akasaka
   かぷせるイン赤坂
26 Akasaka Yōkō Hotel
   赤坂陽光ホテル
27 Marroad Inn Akasaka
   マロウドイン赤阪
34 Hotel Ōkura
   ホテルオークラ
35 ANA Hotel Tokyo
   全日空ホテル東京

PLACES TO EAT

4 Tsunahachi
   つな八
9 Trattoria Marumo
   トラットリアマルーモ
10 The Taj
   ザタージ
11 Moti Darbar
   モティ
13 Sushi-sei
   寿司清
17 Jangara Rāmen
   じゃんがららあめん
18 Tōfu-ya
   豆腐屋
20 Mugyodon
   ムギョドン
22 Moti Darbar
   モティ
23 Sunaba
   砂場
24 Yakitori Luis
   焼き鳥ルイス
30 Doutor Coffee
   ドトールコーヒー
31 Tony Roma's
   トニーロマーズ

32 Inachū Lacquerware
   いなちゅう漆器

OTHER

3 Suntory Museum of Art
   サントリー美術館
6 Tōkyū Plaza
   東急プラザ
7 International ATM
   キャッシュコーナー
8 Citibank
   シティバンク
14 Sumitomo Mitsui Bank
   住友三井銀行
15 Hie-jinja
   日枝神社
19 Post Office
   郵便局
21 Hobgoblin Tokyo
28 Akasaka Twin Tower
   赤坂ツインタワー
29 Police Station
   交番
33 US Embassy
   アメリカ大使館

Chinese influence, it was established in the mid-17th century. It is next to Kōraku-en Amusement Park (see Amusement Parks later) and Tokyo Dome, near Kōraku-en subway station on the Marunouchi line.

Museums & Galleries

There's an enormous number of museums and galleries in Tokyo. In many cases their exhibits are small and specialised and the admission charges prohibitively expensive for travellers with a limited budget and a tight schedule. For a more complete listing, get hold of the TIC's *Museums & Art Galleries* pamphlet. Better still, look out for *Tokyo Museums – A Complete Guide* by Thomas & Ellen Flannigan, which covers everything from the Tombstone Museum to the Button Museum.

Edo-Tokyo Museum This place (*Tokyo colour map;* ☎ 3626-9974; **W** www.edo-tokyo -museum.or.jp; admission ¥600; open 10am-6pm Tues-Sun) is the best of Tokyo's new museums. Just the building itself, which looks like it has been spirited from the set of *Star Wars*, is a wonder. The Nihom-bashi divides this vast display into re-creations of Edo-period Tokyo and Meiji-period Tokyo. It is close to Ryōgoku station on the JR

Sōbu line, and can be combined with a visit to the Sumō Museum.

Sumō Museum This museum (☎ 3622-0366; admission free; open 10am-4.30pm Mon-Fri), close to the main entrance to Kokugikan Sumō Stadium, is quite a treat, but unfortunately there is nothing in the way of English explanations. See Edo-Tokyo Museum earlier for details on getting there.

Tokyo Metropolitan Teien Museum While this museum (☎ 3443-0201; admission ¥600; open 10am to 6pm daily, closed 2nd & 3rd Wed each month) lacks a permanent display of its own, the building itself was designed by French architect Henri Rapin and it lies in pleasant gardens. Take the east exit of Meguro station (on the Yamanote line), walk straight ahead along Meguro-dōri for around five minutes and look out for the museum on the left. The entry price depends on the exhibition.

The Museum of Emerging Science With the full name of The Museum of Emerging Science and Innovation, and also known as the Miraikan (*Map 11;* ☎ 3570-9150; **W** www.miraikan.jst.go.jp; adult/under 18 ¥500/200; open 10am-5pm Wed-Mon),

MAP 10 – ROPPONGI & NISHI-AZABU

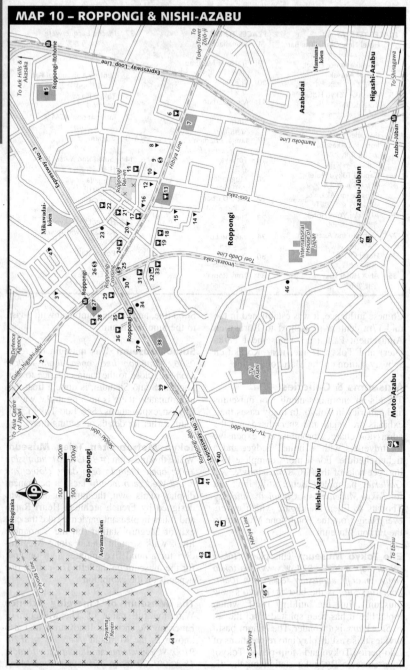

ROPPONGI & NISHI-AZABU – MAP 10

PLACES TO STAY
5 Roppongi Prince Hotel
六本木プリンスホテル
27 Hotel Ibis
ホテルアイビス

PLACES TO EAT
1 Gokoku
五穀
2 Inakaya
田舎屋
3 Havana Café
ハバナカフェ
4 Namban-tei
南蛮亭
8 Humming Bird
ハミングバード
10 Hamburger Inn
ハンバーガーイン・
12 Bikkuri Sushi; Propaganda
びっくり寿司
14 Fukuzushi; Spago
福寿司；スパゴ
15 Hard Rock Café; Tony Roma's
ハードロックカフェ；
トニーロマーズ
16 Bellini's Trattoria
20 Seryna
瀬理奈
30 Almond
アーモンド
39 Bengawan Solo
ベンガワンソロ
40 Maenam
メナム

44 Monsoon Café
モンスーンカフェ
45 Hobson's
ホブソンズ

OTHER
6 Roppongi Pit Inn
六本木ピットイン
7 Axis Bldg; Kisso
アクシスビル；吉左右
9 Sumitomo Mitsui Bank
住友三井銀行
11 Gas Panic Café; Gas Panic
Bar; Club 99 Gaspanic
ガスパニックカフェ；
ガスパニックバー；
クラブ99ガスパニック
13 Paddy Foley's; Roi Building
パディーフォーリーズ；
ロイビル
17 Dusk Till Dawn
18 Cavern Club
カバーンクラブ
19 Pints Sportscafé; Kento's
パインツスポーツバー；
ケントーズ
21 Lexington Queen
レクシントンクイーン
22 Bar, Isn't It?
バーイズントイット
23 Square Building
スクエアービル
24 Motown House 1
モータウンハウス
25 Citibank

26 International ATM
キャッシュコーナー
28 Velfarre
ベルファーレ
29 Geronimo
ジェロニモ
31 Mogambo; Castillo
モガンボ；カスティロ
32 Post Office
郵便局
33 Sweet Basil 139
スイートベイジル139
34 Aoyama Book Center
35 Bauhaus
バウハウス
36 Pylon
37 Meidiya International
Supermarket
明治屋
38 Tōnichi Building
東日ビル
41 BuL-Let's
42 Nishi-Azabu Post Office
西麻布郵便局
43 Yellow
イエロー
46 Swedish Centre; Stockholm
スウェーデンセンター；
ストックホルム
47 Azabu Jūban Onsen;
Koshi-No-Yu Sento
麻布十番温泉；
越の湯銭湯
48 Chinese Embassy
中国大使館

this is undoubtedly Japan's best science museum. Its hands-on exhibits are fun, as well as genuinely educational, whether you're 'driving' a virtual horse around Odaiba, building your own robot, or fathoming how Medaka riverfish could copulate in zero gravity aboard the space shuttle.

To get to the museum, you take the Yurikamome New Transit line to Fune-no-kagakukan, and it's a five-minute walk.

Museum of Maritime Science Also down in the Odaiba/Tokyo Bay area, this large, ship-shaped museum (*Map 11; ☎ 5500-1111; adult/child ¥700/400; open 10am-5pm Mon-Fri, 10am-6pm Sat, Sun & holidays*) is one of Tokyo's better museums. Known as Fune-no-kagakukan, it has four floors of excellent displays dealing with every aspect of ships and shipping, with loads of highly detailed models. The 4m-long version of the largest battleship ever built, the *Yamato*, is stunning in detail and craftsmanship. There are also lots of hands-on exhibits that kids will love.

To get to the museum, you should take the Yurikamome New Transit line from Shimbashi station and get off at the Fune-no-kagakukan stop.

Amusement Parks
Tokyo Disneyland This wonderland (*Tokyo colour map; ☎ 045-683-3777; W www.tokyo disneyresort.co.jp; passport-ticket adult/child 12-17/child 4-11 ¥5500/4800/3700; open 8.30am-10pm daily summer, 10am-6pm daily winter*) is a near-perfect replica of the original in Anaheim, California. Its opening hours vary seasonally – phone ☎ 047-354-0001 to be sure. It's open year-round except for about a dozen days a year (most of them in January). A variety of tickets are available, including an all-inclusive 'passport' that gives you unlimited access to all the rides. As at the original Disneyland, there are often long queues at popular rides (30 minutes to

MAP 11 – ŌDAIBA/TOKYO BAY AREA

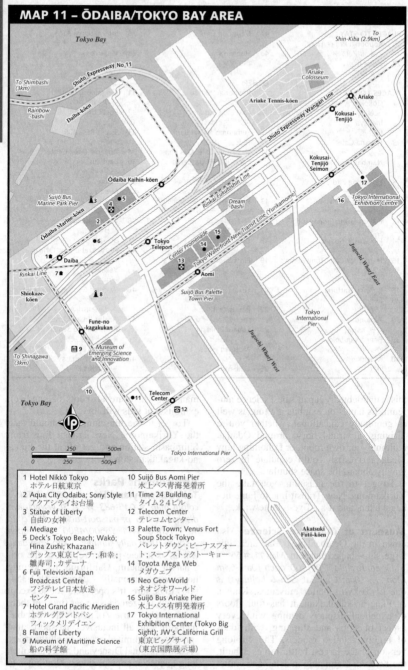

1 Hotel Nikkō Tokyo
  ホテル日航東京
2 Aqua City Odaiba; Sony Style
  アクアシティお台場
3 Statue of Liberty
  自由の女神
4 Mediage
5 Deck's Tokyo Beach; Wakō;
  Hina Zushi; Khazana
  デックス東京ビーチ；和幸；
  雛寿司；カザーナ
6 Fuji Television Japan
  Broadcast Centre
  フジテレビ日本放送
  センター
7 Hotel Grand Pacific Meridien
  ホテルグランドパシ
  フィックメリデイエン
8 Flame of Liberty
9 Museum of Maritime Science
  船の科学館

10 Suijō Bus Aomi Pier
  水上バス青海発着所
11 Time 24 Building
  タイム24ビル
12 Telecom Center
  テレコムセンター
13 Palette Town; Venus Fort
  Soup Stock Tokyo
  パレットタウン；ビーナスフォー
  ト；スープストックトーキョー
14 Toyota Mega Web
  メガウェブ
15 Neo Geo World
  ネオジオワールド
16 Suijō Bus Ariake Pier
  水上バス有明発着所
17 Tokyo International
  Exhibition Center (Tokyo Big
  Sight); JW's California Grill
  東京ビッグサイト
  （東京国際展示場）

one hour is normal). Tokyo Disneyland has a **ticket office** (Map 1; ☎ 3595-1777; open 10am-7pm daily) in Hibiya.

There is now a direct train service to Disneyland: take the Keiyō line from Tokyo station to Maihama station (¥210, 15 minutes).

Kōraku-en Amusement Park Next to Kōraku-en subway station on the Marunouchi subway line, the Kōraku-en Amusement Park (☎ 5800-9999; adult/child ¥1200/600, most rides ¥600, unlimited rides adult/child ¥3300/2600; open 10am-10pm summer, 10am-6pm winter, 10am-8pm rest of year) is of the old rattle-and-shake school, and is popular precisely for that reason. The Ultra Twister roller coaster takes 1st prize for most of the visitors. Geopolis is a new hi-tech addition to the amusement park, with attractions like the Geopanic indoor roller coaster and, our favourite, Zombie Zone.

Baths

A nice hot bath is a great way to relax after a day pounding the pavements of Tokyo. Here are a few of Tokyo's more interesting *sentō* (public baths), *onsen* (mineral hot spring spa) and spas.

Azabu-Jūban Onsen & Koshi-No-Yu Sento (Map 10) You might not expect to find an onsen in the middle of Tokyo, but here it is. The dark, tea-coloured water is scalding hot. Downstairs is a *sentō* (☎ 3404-2610; admission ¥400; open 3pm to 11pm Wednesday to Monday) and upstairs a plusher *onsen* (admission ¥1260; open 11am to 9pm Wednesday to Monday). The water comes from the same source; the only difference is the price and the fact that upstairs there's a room to hang around in after your bath.

Asakusa Kannon Onsen (Map 3; ☎ 3844-4141; admission ¥700; open 6.30am to 6pm Friday to Wednesday) This place calls itself an onsen, but we don't believe it. Nonetheless, this bath, next to Sensō-ji, is worth a try.

Finlando Sauna (Map 5) This is a huge 24-hour complex of baths and steam rooms right in the middle of Shinjuku's Kabuki-chō. This is a good place to escape the madness of the streets outside. Massages (per hour ¥3060) come highly recommended. This complex is men-only.

Green Plaza Ladies Sauna (Map 5; ☎ 3207-4921; admission 6am to 10pm ¥2300, 10pm to 6am ¥3000, for 1½ hours ¥1400) A decent 24-hour bath and spa for women, this place is also in Shinjuku's Kabuki-chō. A 40-minute massage costs ¥3260.

ORGANISED TOURS

One of the most reliable Tokyo-tour operators is **Hato Bus Tours** (☎ 3435-6081). Its Panoramic Tour (¥9800 including lunch) takes in most of Tokyo's major sights. Probably the widest range of Tokyo tours is available from the **JTB's Sunrise Tours office** (☎ 5260-9500). Sunrise offers general sightseeing tours, such as morning tours (¥5000) and afternoon tours (¥5000). Both Hato and Sunrise offer English-speaking guides and/ or taped explanations and headsets.

Night tours of the city are offered by Sunrise Tours and **Gray Line** (☎ 3433-5745). Sunrise's Kabuki Night tour (¥9800) includes a sukiyaki and sake dinner, kabuki at Ginza's Kabuki-za Theatre and a geisha show.

All of these tours pick up guests at various major hotels around town. Sunrise and Gray Line also offer tours to sightseeing spots around Tokyo.

SPECIAL EVENTS

There is a festival of one sort or another every day in Tokyo. Call or visit the TIC for up-to date information. Some of the major celebrations are: Ganjitsu (New Year) when Tokyoites head to Meiji-jingū, Sensō-ji or Yasukuni-jinja; Hanami (Cherry Blossom Viewing) in early to mid-April (chaotic at Ueno-kōen; peaceful at Shinjuku-gyoen); the massive Sanja Matsuri, on the third weekend of May when 100 *mikoshi* (portable shrines) are paraded through Asakusa; the same area's wild Samba Matsuri in late August; and the Bōnen-kai Season in late December. The latter isn't an official festival at all, but the period leading up to New Year, when the Japanese hold their drink-and-be-merry year-end parties.

PLACES TO STAY

In Tokyo you can choose from the whole range of Japanese accommodation, from capsule hotels to ryokan. Budget accommodation in Tokyo is a bit pricier than elsewhere. Hotels are expensive, and to add insult to financial injury, they charge an additional 5% 'metropolitan area' tax. Business hotels are a good compromise solution, with rates in Tokyo from ¥7000 for singles and around ¥10,000 for doubles. Ryokan and *minshuku* (Japanese-style budget B&B) are better still, if you can make a few concessions to Japanese etiquette, with rates from around ¥4500 per person. At youth hostels and so-called *'gaijin* houses' (foreigner houses) you can get single rates down to ¥3500 per person (which is about as low as it gets in Tokyo). There are two caveats however: the youth hostels impose an early evening curfew; and the *gaijin* houses are generally way out in the boondocks and only take long-termers.

Reservations & Information

The Welcome Inn Reservation Center, at Narita airport and at the TIC in Tokyo (Map 1), is a free booking service that will make reservations for you at hotels and ryokan in the Japan Welcome Inn hotel group.

Places to Stay – Budget

If it is imperative that you find inexpensive accommodation, be certain to make a booking before you arrive. Flying into Narita (particularly at night) without accommodation lined up can be nightmarish.

Hostels Tokyo has two standard youth hostels: Tokyo International Youth Hostel in Iidabashi; and Yoyogi Youth Hostel. The usual regulations apply – you have to be out of the building from 10am to 3pm (9am to 5pm at Yoyogi), and you have to be in by 10pm; the latter is a real drawback in a late-night city like Tokyo. There's a three-night limit to your stay and the hostels can often be booked right out during peak holiday periods. You can reserve a room in English at the YHA website (W www.jyh.or.jp).

The **Tokyo International Youth Hostel** (☎ 3235-1107; *dorm beds ¥3500*) doesn't require that you be a member but does ask that you book ahead and provide some identification (a passport will do) when you arrive. To get there, take the west exit (when coming by JR) or the B2b exit (when coming by subway) out of Iidabashi station. It's on the 18th floor of the Central Plaza building, one minute from the station (look for the tall, glass-fronted building). You may be charged an extra fee for air-con in summer and heating in winter, and breakfast/dinner costs ¥400/800. Check-in is 4pm to 9.30pm. The Narita airport TIC (see Tourist Offices in the Information section earlier) has a step-by-step instruction sheet on the cheapest way to get to the hostel from the airport.

Yoyogi Youth Hostel (☎ 3467-9163; *dorm beds members/nonmembers ¥3000/4000*) is the less appealing choice. There are no meals and no cooking facilities. However, all the rooms are singles and are clean. Check-in is from 5pm to 8pm. To get there, take the Odakyū line to Sangūbashi station. Exit the station, turn left and walk 200m, then cross the tracks and turn right. Walk 150m and cross the pedestrian bridge. Continue on in the same direction and enter the National Olympics Memorial Youth Center compound. The guards at the gate have a map to the hostel.

Hotel Skycourt Asakusa (☎ 3875-4411; *6-35-8 Asakusa, Taitō-ku; beds members ¥5000, singles/doubles/twins nonmembers ¥6000/10,500/13,000*), in addition to the others, is a clean, new business-hotel that also functions as a youth hostel. All rooms have baths, TVs and air-con. To get there from Asakusa, walk up Edo-dōri past the Tōbu station (keeping it on your left – see the off-map arrow on Map 3) to the third set of lights. Take the street just to the left of the *kōban* (police box) and walk 100m past the first set of lights.

Ryokan & Guesthouses The best budget choice in Tokyo is **Kimi Ryokan** (*Map 4; ☎ 3971-3766; W www.kimi-ryokan.jp; singles/doubles from ¥4500/6500*) with a good location and clean, inexpensive Japanese-style rooms. Of all the ryokan in Tokyo, the Kimi has the most convivial lounge area. There's a notice board, and the constantly changing ikebana adds cheer to the place. Be sure to book ahead; there's nearly always a waiting list. The Kimi is on the western side of Ikebukuro station.

House Ikebukuro (*Map 4; ☎ 3984-3399; singles/doubles/triples from ¥5000/6000/10,500, 'apartment' rooms for 2/3 people ¥8500/10,500*), also in Ikebukuro, has a variety of rooms, all with shared bathroom and a common kitchen. The best, however, are the apartment-like rooms in the annexe, with en suite, fridge and microwave. Check-in is 3pm.

New Kōyō (☎ 3873-0343; *fax 3873 1358; W www.newkoyo.com; smaller/larger singles with shared bath ¥2500/2700, doubles ¥4800*), a flophouse-turned-guesthouse is the cheapest place to stay in Tokyo. There are small, very basic Western/Japanese-style singles and two doubles. Reserve well

Odaiba/Tokyo Bay Walking Tour

Tokyo Bay (Map 11) makes a nice change from the congestion of central Tokyo. The following day walk takes in a few of the parks, and some of the museums and attractions which have sprung up over recent years. More than a scenic walk, it should be considered a good chance to breathe the sea air and escape the city for a while.

To start, take the Yurikamome line from Shimbashi station near Ginza to Daiba station. The ride itself is interesting, as it crosses **Rainbow Bridge** and affords good views of bay area develop-ments. Upon arrival at Daiba, you have several choices: head to the futuristic Fuji Television Japan Broadcast Center, which offers a studio tour and observation platform; head to Shiokaze-kōen to relax by the sea; or walk over to the Decks Tokyo Beach and Aqua City complex for a bite to eat. Whatever you do, don't miss Tokyo's very own **Statue of Liberty**, studiously turning its back to the Rainbow Bridge.

The **Fuji Television Japan Broadcast Center observatory** (admission ¥500; open 10am-9pm Tues-Sun) is inside the ball-shaped structure on its upper floors. On clear days, it affords good views of the bay and Rainbow Bridge. A ticket to the observatory also gets you into the Fuji Studio Tour, although this is probably of little interest to foreign visitors as it is all in Japanese.

The **Decks Tokyo Beach complex**, **Aqua City** and **Mediage** house dozens of trendy restaurants, shops, the chichi **Sony Style** showroom, and a cinema complex. You could while away a rainy day in here no problem.

Shiokaze-kōen park is a good spot for a waterside picnic on warmer days.

The next stop is either the ship-shaped **Museum of Maritime Science** (Fune-no-kagakukan), or the marvellous, hands-on **Museum of Emerging Science & Innovation** (Miraikan). If you visit the latter add at least an hour – probably two – to your itinerary. See the entry in the Other Attrac-tions section of this chapter for details.

From here you have the option of taking the train or walking to **Palette Town** complete with its humongous Ferris-wheel, Italian Renaissance shopping mall, Venus Fort and state-of-the-art **Toyota Mega Web** showroom. If you walk, en route check out the **Flame of Liberty** statue. You can't miss it – it's like a V2 rocket stuck in a pile of cat-litter.

Once more you can walk or take the train to the next stop: **Tokyo International Exhibition Center** (open daily), better known as 'Tokyo Big Sight'. If you walk (about 20 minutes), follow the 'Center Promenade' walkway. This leads across the flat middle of the island, with the monolithic towers of the bay area rising on all sides. After crossing **Dream Bridge**, Tokyo Big Sight comes into view.

The Big Sight's main hall looks like an Egyptian pyramid which fell to earth upside-down – certainly one of Tokyo's architectural wonders. On the 8th floor of the main hall there is a restaurant and bar, **JW's California Grill** (☎ 5530-1221; open 11.30am-2pm & 5.30pm-9pm Tues-Sun), which serves American-style food at mid-range prices. For a good view of the bay, you can take the lifts or escala-tors to the roof of the hall, which is open to visitors any time a conference is not in session.

From Tokyo Big Sight there are two ways to return to central Tokyo: either take the Yurikamome line from Kokusai Tenjijo Siimon station back to Shimbashi, or walk over to the Rinkai Fukutoshin line (Kokusai Tenjijo station) and go two stops to Shin-Kiba station. There, transfer to the JR Keiyō line, which will take you to Tokyo station in less than 10 minutes.

in advance. It's two stops north of Ueno on the Hibiya line. Take a left out of Minowa station's No 3 exit and walk to the first set of lights. Take a left, walk past three sets of lights and take a right just before the Law-son convenience store; it's on the right in the second block. Check-in is 11am.

Asia Center of Japan (Map 10; ☎ 3402-6111; 8-10-32 Asakusa, Minato-ku; singles/ doubles/twins from ¥7500/9500/12,000), is near Aoyama-Itchōme subway station (Ginza line); it's a popular option. This place attracts many long-term stayers and is often fully booked (call ahead). The station is under the easily recognisable Aoyama Twin Tower building on Aoyama-dōri. Walk past the building towards Akasaka-mitsuke, turn right on Gaien-Higashi-dōri (towards Roppongi),

TOKYO

and the Asia Center is a short walk up the second street on the left. Rooms have pay-TV (rooms with bathrooms are more expensive). Breakfast/lunch/dinner costs ¥580/800/1200. Check-in is 2pm.

Taito Ryokan *(Map 10;* ☎ *3843-2822;* e *jptaito@libertyhouse.gr.jp;* W *www.liberty house.gr.jp, singles/doubles ¥3000/6000)* is great value, with English-speaking managers, and a funky Shitamachi (downtown) location. It can be noisy, and palatial it ain't, but who cares at this price. Take exit 3 from Tawaramachi station (Ginza line), and walk north towards the Asakusa View Hotel, turn left at the police box into Kikusui-dōri, and the ryokan is on the right-hand corner. The website has a map.

Sakura Hotel *(☎ 3261-3939; 2-21-4 Kanda-Jimbōchō, Chiyoda-ku; beds ¥5800, singles/doubles ¥6800/8000)* is a good guesthouse in Jimbōchō, on the Hanzōmon subway line. Beds are in a shared two- or four-person room and there are private singles/doubles. There's a small restaurant/bar on the premises with a small outside terrace. To get there from Jimbōchō station, take the A6 exit and turn right, walk two blocks and turn right at the kōban; the hotel is 200m on the right. Check-in is 1pm.

Ryokan Sansui-sō *(☎ 3441-7475; 2-9-5 Higashi-Gotanda, Shinagawa-ku; twins with bath ¥9000, singles/twins/triples without bath ¥4900/8600/12,000)* is close to JR Gotanda station on the Yamanote line. It's not an ideal location, still, it's only a few stops from Shibuya station, the nearest main station. Take the east exit out of Gotanda station. Turn right, take the first right after the big Tōkyū department store and then the first left. Turn left and then right, walk past the bowling centre and look for the sign on the right directing you down the side-street to the ryokan. Check-in is 2pm.

Ueno may be a bit of a trek from the bright lights, but it's a good sightseeing base, atmospheric, and there are several budget ryokan in the area.

Sawanoya Ryokan *(Map 2;* ☎ *3822-2251; 2-3-11 Yanaka, Taitō-ku; singles with/without bath ¥5000/4700, doubles ¥9400/8800, triples ¥13,500/12,000)* is a good choice within walking distance of Nezu subway station on the Chiyoda line (call for walking directions from the station). If you're coming from Narita airport, it will probably be easier and

just as cheap (if there are more than one of you) to catch a taxi from Ueno station. Check-in is 2pm.

Ryokan Katsutarō *(Map 2;* ☎ *3821-9808; doubles/triples with bath ¥9000/13,200, singles/doubles/triples without bath ¥4500/8400/12,300)* is another good option in the vicinity. Check-in is 3pm.

Sakura Ryokan *(☎ 3876-8118; 2-6-2 Iriya, Taitō-ku; Western-style singles/twins with bath ¥6300/10,600, singles/doubles without bath ¥5300/9600, triples without bath ¥12,600-13,500)* is one stop away from Ueno on the JR Yamanote line (Uguisudani station). It's tricky to find; we suggest calling from the station for directions. A Western breakfast costs ¥500. Check-in is 3pm.

Three stops away from Ueno on the Ginza line is Asakusa, which also has a few reasonably priced ryokan.

Ryokan Shigetsu *(Map 3;* ☎ *3843-2345; Western-style singles/doubles with bath from ¥7300/14,000, Japanese-style singles/doubles ¥9000/15,000)* is a highly recommended clean, comfortable place around the corner from Sensō-ji. There is a good Japanese bath on the top floor, which overlooks Sensō-ji. It has free Net access. Check-in is 3pm.

Ryokan Mikawaya Bekkan *(Map 3;* ☎ *3841-7130; Japanese-style singles/doubles ¥6500/11,000)* is another good option in Asakusa. These are the prices if you reserve through the Welcome Inn Center (see Reservations & Information earlier in this section). Check-in is 3pm.

Kikuya Ryokan *(Map 3;* ☎ *3841-6404/ 4051; 2-18-9 Nishi-Asakusa, Taitō-ku; singles/ doubles/triples ¥4800/8000/11,000)* is in Nishi Asakusa (near Tawaramachi subway station; see off-map arrow on the Asakusa map). It's just off Kappabashi-dōri. This ryokan gets good reports as a quiet and friendly place to stay. Check-in is 2pm.

Capsule Hotels These hotels are generally a male domain (we list two here that accept women), and you find them in large hubs and nightlife districts. Most are open from 5pm to 10am.

Green Plaza Shinjuku *(Map 5;* ☎ *3207- 5411; capsules ¥4200)* is just down the road from the Shinjuku Prince Hotel on Shinjuku's east side. You get your own personal capsule and the price includes admission to the hotel's sauna (see Baths earlier in this chapter). The front desk of this hotel is on the 3rd floor; take the lift from the basement. Check-in is 3pm.

Shinjuku-Kuyakusho-Mae Capsule Hotel (Map 5; ☎ 3232-1110; capsules ¥4200) is right in Shinjuku's sleazy Kabuki-chō. Check-in is 2pm.

Capsule Inn Akasaka (Map 9; ☎ 3588-1811; capsules ¥4000) is in Akasaka, not far from Akasaka station. Check-in is 5pm.

Capsule Hotel Fontaine Akasaka (Map 9; ☎ 3583-6554; capsules men/women Mon-Fri ¥4800/4500, Sat & Sun ¥4500), an upmarket capsule hotel is closer to Akasaka-mitsuke station than Capsule Inn Akasaka. This is one of the few capsule hotels in Tokyo that accepts women. Check-in is 5pm.

Capsule Hotel Riverside (Map 3; ☎ 3844-1155; capsules ¥3300), another capsule hotel that accepts women, is near Asakusa station. Capsules here are a bargain. The entrance is around the back of the building. Check-in is 3pm Monday to Friday and 2pm Saturday and Sunday.

Gaijin Houses These houses are more an option for those planning to stay long-term in Tokyo. Some offer nightly or weekly rates, but many are geared to foreigners working in Tokyo, and charge by the month. If you just want a cheap place to crash and don't mind commuting into town to do your sightseeing, try ringing around the *gaijin* houses when you get to Tokyo.

Long-termers can expect to pay from ¥40,000 to ¥70,000 a month for a tiny private room, with no deposits or key money (a nonrefundable gift to the landlord of one or two months' rent) required.

The best ways to find a *gaijin* house are by word of mouth from other foreigners, looking in *Metropolis*, or going through an agency. Agencies are generally the fastest and easiest way to go, as they have extensive listings and will handle all the arrangements with the landlord. The Tokyo agency with the most listings and best rates is **Fontana** (☎ 3382-0151). Readers have also recommended **Sakura House Management** (☎ 5330-5250; W www.sakura-house.com) in Nishi-Shinjuku.

For more on *gaijin* houses, see the Facts for the Visitor chapter, or W www.gaijin house.com and W www.freesianet.co.jp.

Places to Stay – Mid-Range

Mid-range hotels in Tokyo are mostly business hotels. These cost from ¥7000 for singles and from ¥10,000 for doubles. Since there is little to distinguish one business hotel from another, we recommend choosing one in an area convenient to the sights you'd like to see. Always check what time your hotel locks its doors before heading out at night. Some hotels stay open all night, but many lock up at midnight or 1am.

An adventurous late-night alternative is a love hotel. These can be found in any of Tokyo's entertainment districts – particularly in Shinjuku, Shibuya, Roppongi and Ikebukuro. All-night rooms range in price from ¥6500 to ¥8000, but 'all night' doesn't start until 10pm or 11pm, when the regular hour-by-hour customers have run out of energy.

Central Tokyo (Map 1) This is a convenient but expensive area in which to be based. If you're in Tokyo on business or need to be near Tokyo station for an early morning train, then this is probably your best bet.

Hotel Yaesu-Ryūmeikan (☎ 3271-0971; singles/doubles from ¥8600/15,400), the cheapest deal in the area, has Japanese-style rooms. It's a five-minute walk from Tokyo station. Check-in is 2pm.

Yaesu Terminal Hotel (☎ 3281-3771; singles/doubles or twins ¥10,800/15,800), between Tokyo station and Takashimaya department store, is fairly economical. It has a business-hotel feel and the rooms are quite small, but the prices are good for this area. Check-in is 2pm.

Tokyo Station Hotel (☎ 3231-2511; singles/doubles or twins from ¥10,000/23,000), on the Marunouchi (west) side of the station, is a place you can try if you can't face any more travel upon arriving at Tokyo station. The rooms are pretty basic, but you can't beat the location. Check-in is 2pm.

Hotel Ginza Daiei (☎ 3545-1111; singles/doubles or twins from ¥11,970/14,270), north of Kabuki-za Theatre in Ginza, is a slightly scruffy business hotel. Check-in is 3pm.

Ginza Nikkō Hotel (☎ 3571-4911; singles/doubles/twins from ¥12,000/15,000/16,000), in a prime location right on Sotobori-dōri between Ginza and Shimbashi, is a quality place. Check-in is 1pm.

Ginza International Hotel *(☎ 3574-1121; singles/doubles/twins from ¥13,000/18,000/22,000)* is in a similar class to the Ginza Nikkō and is located nearby. Check-in is from 1pm.

Ueno (Map 2) The ryokan (see Ryokan & Guesthouses earlier) in this area are better value but if they're all full, the business hotels here are generally cheaper than those in other areas around Tokyo.

Hotel Green Capital *(☎ 3842-2411; singles/doubles/twins ¥7500/12,500/15,500)* is a typical business hotel quite close to Ueno station. The rooms are clean and new, and the staff polite. Prices are also competitive. Check-in is 3pm.

Hotel Parkside *(☎ 3836-5711; singles/doubles or twins from ¥9200/16,100, Japanese-style doubles ¥16,600)*, overlooking the park itself, is also a good choice, particularly if you can get a room at the front. The place is pleasant, clean and new. Japanese-style rooms are also available. Check-in is 2pm.

Ueno Kinuya Hotel *(☎ 3836-1911; singles/doubles without bath from ¥7400/11,200)* has decent Japanese-style rooms if the other options are full. Check-in is 1pm.

Hotel Sun Targas *(☎ 3833-8686; singles/doubles/twins from ¥7550/10,000/10,610)*, another business hotel not far from the station, is slightly less appealing than the Ueno Kinuya. Check-in is 4pm.

Suigetsu Hotel Ōgaisō *(☎ 3822-4611; Western-style singles from ¥9300, Japanese-style doubles from ¥16,000)* is on the western side of the park. Those who want a change from the typical Western-style hotel may want to try it. This hotel mostly has Japanese-style tatami (woven floor-mat) rooms, and there are several large Japanese-style baths. Rates include Japanese breakfast. There are also Western-style rooms, with breakfast. Check-in is 3pm.

Asakusa (Map 3) This is an interesting area to stay, if you don't mind sacrificing central location for a funky Shitamachi atmosphere.

Asakusa Plaza Hotel *(☎ 3845-2621; singles/doubles/twins from ¥6900/12,000/16,500)* is a standard-issue business hotel convenient to the sights. Check-in is 4pm.

Hotel Skycourt Asakusa *(☎ 3875-4411)*, another good option, is a business hotel that

doubles as a youth hostel (see the Hostels section earlier).

Ikebukuro (Map 4) There are innumerable business hotels, love hotels and capsule hotels in the Ikebukuro area. Be warned, however, that the capsule hotels in this neighbourhood are not nearly as accustomed to foreign guests as their cousins in Akasaka and Shinjuku.

Hotel Grand City *(☎ 3984-5121; singles/doubles from ¥7300/9000)*, on the east side of Ikebukuro, is a standard business hotel with relatively inexpensive rates. Check-in is 2pm.

Hotel Theatre *(☎ 3988-2251; singles/doubles from ¥8700/14,500)*, also to the east of the station, is centrally located and clean. Check-in is 2pm.

Ikebukuro Royal Hotel *(☎ 5396-0333; singles/twins from ¥8000/12,000)* is another basic business hotel not too far from the station, with a nice shared bathroom. The rooms are nothing special. Check-in is from 3pm.

Hotel Sun City Ikebukuro *(☎ 3986-1101; singles/doubles from ¥7800/12,600)* has basic rooms with a few on-premises drinking and dining options. Check-in is 3pm.

Ark Hotel *(☎ 3590-0111; singles/doubles/twins from ¥8800/14,000/15,000)* has clean, newish rooms and polite staff. Check-in is 3pm.

Hotel Sunroute Ikebukuro *(☎ 3980-1911; singles/doubles/twins from ¥9900/15,000/17,200)*, just along the street from the main Bic Camera store, has pleasant, clean rooms and friendly staff, some of whom speak English. Check-in is 2pm.

Shinjuku (Map 5) This area is a good hunting ground if you're after business hotels accustomed to foreign guests. Moreover, the intense competition in the area helps keep prices down. It's also a pretty convenient area in which to be based.

Hotel Sun Lite Shinjuku *(☎ 3356-0391; singles/doubles/twins ¥8000/11,500/13,500)*, in east Shinjuku, is a good choice. The place is clean and new with small but well-maintained rooms. Check-in is 3pm.

Shinjuku Park Hotel *(☎ 3356-0241; singles/twins from ¥7900/13,800)* is just south of the Takashimaya Times Square complex. While it gets no raves for warm, friendly

TOKYO

service, the rooms are a little larger than at most business hotels and the prices are competitive. Check-in is 3pm.

Central Hotel *(☎ 3354-6611; singles/ doubles or twins from ¥11,000/17,000)*, newly redecorated, is another decent choice in the heart of east Shinjuku. The rooms are pleasant and clean. Check-in is 1pm.

Star Hotel Tokyo *(☎ 3361-1111; singles/ doubles or twins from ¥11,000/17,000)*, in west Shinjuku, is very conveniently located. The rooms and service are average. Check-in is 1pm.

Shinjuku New City Hotel *(☎ 3375-6511; singles/doubles/twins from ¥9000/15,000/ 14,000)*, on the far side of Shinjuku's Chūō-kōen, has rooms slightly larger than usual for a business hotel. Check-in is 3pm.

Shinjuku Washington Hotel *(☎ 3343-3111; W www.wh-rsv.com; singles/doubles/ twins from ¥11,300/17,000/17,500)* offers business-hotel accommodation with lots of restaurants and amenities. Rooms and windows are small, but the views from the upper floors are excellent. Check-in is 2pm.

Shibuya (Map 7) This is an expensive area to base yourself and the pickings are slim. If you're looking for less-expensive business hotels, Ueno, Ikebukuro and even Shinjuku represent much better value for money.

Shibuya Business Hotel *(☎ 3409-9300; singles/doubles/twins from ¥8400/11,600/ 12,300)*, on a backstreet behind Shibuya post office, is the cheapest choice in the area. Rooms are small but sufficient. Check-in is 2pm.

Shibuya Tōbu Hotel *(☎ 3476-0111; singles ¥11,800-13,800, doubles or twins ¥20,000-26,000)* is probably the nicest place to stay in Shibuya. The rooms are clean, the common areas are pleasant, there are loads of in-house restaurants and the staff speak English. Check-in is 2pm.

Shibuya Tōkyū Inn *(☎ 3462-0109; singles/ doubles or twins from ¥12,000/19,000)*, closer to Shibuya station than Shibuya Tōbu Hotel, has similar rooms although it's really not worth paying this much. Check-in is 3pm.

Akasaka & Roppongi These are good areas in which to be based if you want access to central Tokyo and a lively nightlife (it's possible to walk down to Roppongi from Akasaka).

Akasaka Yōkō Hotel *(Map 9; ☎ 3586-4050; singles/doubles from ¥9800/15,500)*, in Akasaka, is a reasonably priced business hotel about midway between Akasaka and Roppongi. Although it's quite simple, the rooms are clean and the staff friendly. Check-in is 3pm.

Marroad Inn Akasaka *(Map 9; ☎ 3585-7611; W www.toto-motors.co.jp; singles/ doubles/twins from ¥9400/10,300/15,000)*, on the same street as Akasaka Yōkō Hotel, 100m closer to Roppongi, is another standard business hotel with similar features. Check-in is 4pm.

Hotel Ibis *(Map 10; ☎ 3403-4411; W www .ibishotel.com; singles/doubles/twins from ¥11,500/14,100/19,000)*, in Roppongi, right near the famous Roppongi crossing, is a clean, modern hotel with a few restaurants and bars in the building. This being Roppongi, you can count on the staff being used to foreign guests. Check-in is 1pm.

Places to Stay – Top End

Although Tokyo is one of the world's most expensive cities, its top-end hotels are no more expensive than similar hotels anywhere else, and you get Japan's legendary high standard of service.

Top-end hotels are found mostly in central Tokyo. Given that all such hotels have very high standards, location should be a prime factor in deciding where you stay. The areas around Ginza and the palace have a certain snob-appeal, but the Akasaka area, which combines a good central location with nearby entertainment options, is an equally good choice. The west side of Shinjuku has a concentration of top-notch hotels, and is a good area in which to see Tokyo at its liveliest.

Among Tokyo's best are: Hotel Seiyo Ginza (which also happens to be the most expensive), Akasaka Prince, Hotel New Otani and Hotel Ōkura. The following prices are for the least-expensive rooms available in each hotel.

Central Tokyo (Map 1) Along with Akasaka, Ginza is home to the thickest concentration of elite hotels anywhere in Tokyo. Prices here reflect the glamorous surroundings and proximity to Tokyo station, great shopping, good restaurants, and the political and financial districts of the city.

Renaissance Tokyo Hotel Ginza Tōbu (☎ 3546-0111; W www.marriott.com; singles/ doubles or twins from ¥17,000/28,000) is a clean, new hotel just south of Kabuki-za Theatre. The restaurants and bars are excellent and its rooms are spacious. Check-in is noon.

Imperial Hotel (☎ 3504-1111; W www. imperialhotel.co.jp; main-building doubles or twins ¥34,000), one of Tokyo's grand old hotels, is within walking distance of the sights of Ginza and Hibiya-kōen. It has all the standard amenities in a very elegant setting, and rooms are large and tastefully appointed. Check-in is noon.

Hotel Seiyo Ginza (☎ 3535-1111; W www .seiyo-ginza.com; rooms ¥40,000-220,000) is the place to try for an experience of over-the-top service in impossibly dignified surroundings. Check-in is 2pm.

Palace Hotel (☎ 3211-5211; W www .palacehotel.co.jp; singles/doubles/twins from ¥23,000/33,000/32,000), directly alongside the Kōkyo, is in the running for the best location in Tokyo. Many rooms here command impressive views over the palace. The service is wonderful and the hotel's restaurants are among the best in Tokyo. Check-in is noon.

Asakusa (Map 3) Just about Asakusa's only luxury hotel is **Asakusa View Hotel** (☎ 3847-1111; singles/doubles/twins from ¥13,000/21,000/31,000). This is a 28-storey building that boasts an assortment of restaurants, a swimming pool, one storey with Japanese-style rooms, and a shopping area. Check-in is 1pm.

Ikebukuro (Map 4) Unless you have a good reason to be based here, there seems little point in paying top-end prices to stay in Ikebukuro.

Hotel Metropolitan (☎ 3980-1111; W www.itbc.co.jp/hotel; singles/doubles or twins from ¥16,500/22,000), on Ikebukuro's west side, is a place you can try if Ikebukuro is where you want to be. This hotel has all the amenities you'd expect, including ample dining and entertainment options, some of which are located on the 27th floor, affording good views over Tokyo and beyond. Check-in is 1pm.

Shinjuku (Map 5) In east Shinjuku, next to Seibu Shinjuku station is **Shin-**juku Prince Hotel (☎ 3205-1111; W www. princehotels.co.jp; singles/doubles/twins from ¥15,000/30,000/28,000), which is a rather drab choice in this price bracket. Check-in is noon.

Keiō Plaza Inter-Continental Hotel (☎ 3344-0111; W www.keioplaza.co.jp; singles/ doubles or twins from ¥18,500/26,000), in west Shinjuku, has 47 floors and provides excellent views of the area and quick access to the station. Check-in is 1pm.

Hilton Tokyo (☎ 3344-5111; W www .hilton.co.jp; singles/doubles or twins from ¥29,000/35,000) offers great service, sports facilities, a convenient location and a variety of good restaurants. Check-in is 2pm.

Century Hyatt Tokyo (☎ 3349-0111; W www.centuryhyatt.co.jp; singles/doubles or twins ¥23,000/32,000), located near Hilton Tokyo, offers a similar level of service and spacious rooms, both Western and Japanese style, and a 28th-floor pool. Check-in is 1pm.

Hotel Century Southern Tower (☎ 5354-0111; W www.southerntower.co.jp; singles/ doubles or twins ¥16,000/22,000), a new place in west Shinjuku, is on the upper floors of the Odakyū Southern Tower building. It has clean and modest rooms with good views. Check-in is 2pm.

Park Hyatt Tokyo (☎ 5322-1234; W www .tokyo.hyatt.com; singles/doubles ¥51,000/ 57,000) on the upper floors of the new 53-floor Shinjuku Park Tower, is an island of luxury in the sky. For a hotel experience unlike any other, check out this breathtaking place. The rooms are new, clean, very stylish, and complemented by some of the most impressive bars and restaurants in Tokyo. Add to this the rooftop pool, the exercise studio overlooking the city, and a great spa-bath and sauna room, and you've got one of the city's best top-end hotels. Even if you don't stay here, at least stop by for a drink in the New York Bar. Check-in is 1pm Monday to Friday and 3pm Saturday and Sunday.

Akasaka & Roppongi Akasaka has a high concentration of luxury hotels because it is a great area in which to be based: there are loads of good restaurants nearby, the political and business centres are within walking distance and Roppongi's nightlife is just down the road.

Akasaka Tōkyū Hotel *(Map 9; ☎ 3580-2311;* W *www.ath-jp.com; singles/doubles/twins from ¥19,000/27,000/28,000)* is right in the heart of Akasaka, just above Akasaka-mitsuke subway station. There are lots of good bars and restaurants scattered throughout the building. Check-in is 1pm.

Capitol Tōkyū Hotel *(Map 9; ☎ 3581-4511;* W *www.capitoltokyu.com; singles/doubles or twins from ¥26,000/38,000)* is an elegant place up on the same hill as Hie-jinja. The hotel is built around a fine Japanese garden, with good restaurants and bars from which to take in the view. In warmer months, you can make use of the outdoor swimming pool. Check-in is noon.

Akasaka Prince Hotel *(Map 9; ☎ 3234-1111;* W *www.princehotels.co.jp/akasaka; Western-style singles/doubles/twins from ¥25,000/37,000/33,000, Japanese-style suites from ¥95,000)*, another skyscraper hotel, is something of a landmark. The rooms provide excellent views and spaciousness, a commodity in short supply in Tokyo. Check-in is noon.

Hotel New Otani *(Map 9; ☎ 3265-1111;* W *www.newotani.co.jp/ja; singles/doubles or twins from ¥26,000/31,000)*, 240m north of Akasaka Mitsuke subway station (exit D), and not far from the Akasaka Prince, is renowned for the Japanese garden around which it is constructed (see Hotel Sights under Akasaka, earlier). The hotel itself is massive, with all the amenities you'd expect from a hotel of this class. Check-in is noon.

Hotel Ōkura *(Map 9; ☎ 3582-0111;* W *www.hotelokura.co.jp; singles/doubles or twins from ¥32,500/40,000)*, near the US embassy, is the home of visiting dignitaries and businesspeople and is at the top of a very exclusive bunch. Check-in is noon.

ANA Hotel Tokyo *(Map 9; ☎ 3505-1111;* W *www.anahotels.com/tokyo/e/index.html; singles/doubles or twins from ¥24,000/32,000)*, midway between Akasaka and Roppongi in the fashionable Ark Hills area, is an excellent choice. This modern 37-storey hotel has all the amenities on offer from fitness clubs to fancy restaurants. Check-in is 1pm.

Roppongi Prince Hotel *(Map 10; ☎ 3587-1111;* W *www.princehotels.co.jp/roppongi; singles/doubles/twins from ¥18,500/23,000/21,500)*, in Roppongi itself, is a good, modern choice. It's built around a huge atrium with an outdoor, heated swimming pool at its

centre. If you run out of things to do inside the hotel, the nightlife of Roppongi is only a 10-minute walk away. Check-in is 1pm.

Near Narita Airport For hotels near Narita airport, see the Narita section of the Around Tokyo chapter.

PLACES TO EAT

No city in Asia can match Tokyo for the sheer variety and quality of its restaurants. As well as refined Japanese cuisine, Tokyo is loaded with great international restaurants – everything from Cambodian to African. One thing to keep in mind is that Japanese food tends to be cheaper than international food. For ¥750 you can get a good bowl of noodles in a *shokudō* (all-round eatery); the same money will buy you a plate of spaghetti in one of Tokyo's many cheap Italian places, but it's sure to be a disappointment. If you fancy international food, be prepared to pay a little extra for the good stuff.

Whatever you choose to eat, you rarely have to look far for a restaurant in Tokyo. Check out the basements and upper floors of the big department stores for *resutoran-gai* (restaurant streets) – these invariably have a good selection of Japanese, Chinese and Italian restaurants with inexpensive lunch-time specials. Train stations are the home of *rāmen* shops, *obentō* (boxed meal) stands and *kareraisu* (curry rice) restaurants. Big commercial districts like the east side of Shinjuku simply brim with restaurants – serving everything from *kaiten-zushi* (revolving, or 'conveyor-belt' sushi) to pizza.

During the day, the best eating areas are the big shopping districts like Shibuya, Shinjuku, Harajuku and Ginza. By night, try Aoyama and Roppongi for some of Tokyo's best international and Japanese food. For something more traditional, try an *izakaya* (Japanese pub/eatery) or Yakitori Alley in central Tokyo, or the down-at-the-heels eating arcade of Omoide-Yokochō in Shinjuku.

If you are going to be in Tokyo for some time, pick up a copy of John Kennerdell's *Tokyo Restaurant Guide* or Rick Kennedy's *Good Tokyo Restaurants*. Alternately, you can check out the **Tokyo Food Page Website** (W www.bento.com /tokyofood.html), or **Tokyo Q's food section** (W http://club .nokia.co.jp/tokyoq), for some up-to-the-minute picks.

TOKYO

Vegetarian

Vegetarian food is less common than you might expect in Tokyo. Luckily, many places that aren't strictly vegetarian, such as Japanese noodle and tōfu (bean curd) shops, serve a good variety of no-meat and no-fish dishes. For more information, pick up the TIC's *Vegetarian & Macrobiotic Restaurants in Tokyo* handout. This lists strictly vegetarian restaurants, wholefood shops, *shōjin-ryōri* (Buddhist-temple fare) restaurants, and Indian restaurants that offer a good selection of vegetarian dishes.

Central Tokyo (Map 1)

Japanese If all you need is a quick bite, you'll find plenty of decent places to eat in the underground mall below Tokyo station. Outside the station, on the Yaesu side, there are some more-interesting choices.

Mikuniya (☎ 3271-3928; meals ¥1800; open 11am-7pm Mon-Sat) is a great place to sample *unagi* (eel) in pleasant surroundings. Its standard *unagi* set is recommended. Mikunya is a member of the Japan Slow Food association.

Sushi Tetsu (☎ 3275-0717; lunch/dinner ¥2500/6000; open 11.30am-2.30pm & 4.30pm-10pm daily), near Mikuniya, is a serious sushi restaurant, and a good alternative to the bad *kaiten-zushi* places nearby.

Tonton Honten (☎ 3508-9454; meals ¥2000; open 1.30pm-10pm daily) is a very friendly, atmospheric *yakitori* (charcoal-broiled chicken and other meats or vegetables, cooked on skewers) joint under the railway tracks in Yūraku-chō's so-called **Yakitori Alley**. It has an English menu. It's in the east–west tunnel beneath the tracks. If Tonton is full, walk out the east side of the tunnel and turn left, where you'll be welcomed by the next-friendliest place

Alternatively head south to Ginza, where restaurants are more plentiful. Although it's expensive in the evening, lunch deals are competitive. A few *resutoran-gai* to check are **Restaurant City** (☎ 3567-1211; open 10am-8pm daily) on the 8th floor of the Matsuya department store; the B2 floor of the **Matsuzakaya department store** (☎ 3572-1111; open 10.30am-7.30pm daily) and the basement floors of the Ginza Palmy Building, where ¥400 buys a decent bowl of *rāmen* at **Naokyū Rāmen** (open 11am-9pm daily).

Jangara Rāmen (☎ 3251-4059; meals ¥1000; open 11am-11pm Mon-Sat; 11am-9.30pm Sun) is the place to head down to for all-the-rage *rāmen*; order *zenbu iri* (all-in) *rāmen* for ¥1000.

Shin-Hi-No-Moto (☎ 3214-8021; meals ¥2500; open 5pm-midnight), another great spot under the tracks, is a lively *izakaya* just around the corner from Yūraku-chō station. The Chinese and Myanmarese staff speak English.

Ginza is also a good place to dip into Japanese beer-hall culture. **Sapporo Lion Beer Hall** (☎ 3571-2590; meals ¥2500; open 11.30am-11pm daily) is the biggest, and a good place to start. The extensive menu includes everything from Japanese snacks to German sausages.

New Torigin (☎ 3571-3334; meals ¥1500; open 4pm-10pm Mon-Fri, 11.30am-9.30pm Sat & Sun), just south of Harumi-dōri, is hidden away down a very narrow back-alley but signposted in English. There's an English menu too, and this authentic, very popular little place does excellent *yakitori*, and the steamed-rice dish known as *kamameshi*.

Robata (☎ 3591-1905; meals ¥2500; open 5pm-11pm daily), back near the railway tracks, is one of Tokyo's most celebrated *izakaya*. A little Japanese is helpful here. It's hard to spot the sign, even if you can read Japanese; it's better just to look for the rustic, weathered facade.

Chichibu Nishiki (☎ 35941-4777; meals ¥2500; open 5pm-10.30pm Mon-Fri), another atmospheric spot in the same price range as Robata, is a traditional *izakaya* with good, cheap food in a very authentic setting. It's tucked away a few blocks behind Kabuki-za.

Hina Sushi (☎ 5531-0017; meals around ¥2500; all-you-can-eat ¥4300; open 11.30am-2pm & 5pm-10.30pm Tues-Fri, 11.30am-10.30pm Sat, 11.30am-9.30pm Sun), the excellent sushi chain, has two branches in Ginza, one of which is located on the 2nd floor of the Nishi Ginza department store. The all-you-can-eat sushi is a steal for this quality.

Of course, Ginza is the place for establishment upmarket dining too. **Ten'ichi** (☎ 3571-1949; lunch/dinner ¥3500/8000; open 11.30am-9.30pm) is *the* place for tempura, assuming you want to splash out.

Jiro Sushi (☎ 3535-7053; meals around ¥30,000; open 11.30am-2pm & 5pm-8.30pm Mon-Sat) is probably the best sushi in Tokyo. It is in the basement of the Tsukamoto building opposite the Sony building. Reservations are essential.

Zakuro (☎ 3535-4421; open 11am-10.30pm daily), another good spot for a splurge on traditional Japanese food, is on the B1 floor of the Ginza Saison Restaurant Plaza, behind Mitsukoshi department store. The speciality here is *shabu-shabu* (thin slices of beef and vegetables cooked in a broth at the table), sets of which start at around ¥5000 at dinner.

Kyubei (☎ 3571-4777/6523; main dishes ¥10,000; open 11.30am-2pm & 5pm-10pm Mon-Sat), in southern Ginza near Shimbashi, is a truly elegant sushi place with prices to match.

International A popular restaurant that is in eastern Ginza towards Tsukiji, **Nair's** (☎ 3541-8246; subway Higashi-Ginza exit 1; lunch/dinner around ¥1500/3000; open 11am-9pm daily) always seems to have a queue at lunch. Japanese showbiz types like to drop by for some incognito Indian.

Farm Grill (☎ 5568-6156; lunch/dinner ¥1500/2300; open 11.30am-11pm daily) is without a doubt the best value in Ginza. It puts out an enormous all-you-can-eat spread of typical Western favourites. The quality of food here is better than at most of Tokyo's all-you-can-eat places, and the desserts and salad bar are excellent. It's under the highway, across the street from the Ginza Dai-Ichi Hotel.

Maxim's de Paris (☎ 3572-3621; subway Ginza exit B9; lunch/dinner with wine ¥6000/20,000; open 11am-3pm & 5.30pm-11pm Mon-Sat), in another price range entirely, is in the Sony Building. The interior and the menu are dead ringers for the original in Paris.

Sabatine di Firenze (☎ 3573-0013; lunch/dinner with wine ¥7000/20,000; open noon-3pm & 5.30pm-11pm daily), in the same building as Maxim's de Paris, serves over-the-top Italian fare for that special night out.

Ueno (Map 2)

Japanese The Ueno area is a happy hunting ground for cheap food. You'll find a good variety of cheap Japanese places in and around Ameyoko acade, where you can also pick up takeaway foods like *yakitori*, rice balls and fruit from vendors.

Ueno Yabu Soba (☎ 3831-4728; meals ¥1800; open 11.30am-11pm Thur-Tues), near the arcade, is a famous *soba* (buckwheat noodles) shop. To really fill up, get the *tenseiro* (noodles topped with shrimp and vegetable tempura) set. The black-on-white sign is in Japanese but the large picture menu makes ordering a snap.

Maguroyāsan (☎ 3844-2732; meals ¥1600; open 11am-3pm & 5pm-11pm Mon-Sat) is an excellent place that is located across from the station. 'Maguro' means tuna, and if it can be made from tuna, it's probably on the menu. Exotic and tasty *maguro gyōza* (tuna-filled dumplings) are unmissable. The lunch sets are great: a large bowl of tuna-topped rice (seafood *donburi*), with salad, or cold *udon* (thick, white noodles). The restaurant is nonsmoking during lunch hours.

Ganko Sushi (☎ 5688-8845; meals ¥1400; open 11.30am-3pm & 4.30pm-11pm daily) is on the 6th floor of the Nagafuji Building. Try it for decent sushi and *teishoku* (set-course meal) deals at lunch and dinner. It has a picture menu and seems fairly accustomed to foreign customers. Try the sushi *mori-awase* (assortment) or the tempura *bentō* for lunch or dinner.

Musashino (☎ 3831-1672; meals around ¥1500; open 11.30am-10pm daily) is a *tonkatsu* (deep-fried breaded pork cutlet, that is served with a special sauce) specialist worth going out of your way for. The *hire katsu* (lean cutlet) *teishoku* is less fatty than the *rōsu katsu*. Both are good.

Izu-ei (☎ 3831-0954; meals from ¥2500; open 11am-9.30pm daily) is an elegant choice for authentic Japanese food. The speciality here is *unagi* and it's tasty. The Izu-ei *unagi bentō* (eel lunch box) includes tempura. There is a limited picture menu.

International Serving up your average Tokyo-Indian fare, and offering a bargain all-you-can-eat lunch is **Samrat** (☎ 5688-3226; meals ¥1000; open 11am-10pm daily).

Asakusa (Map 3)

Japanese The area between Sensō-ji and Kaminarimon-dōri is the best place in Asakusa to seek out Japanese food.

Daikokuya (☎ 3844-1111; open 11.10am-8.30pm daily) near Nakamise arcade, is the place to get tempura, a speciality in Asakusa. It is authentic and the tempura is excellent. Expect to pay about ¥1800 for a meal at lunchtime (try the tempura *donburi*) and at least ¥3000 for dinner.

Owariya (☎ 3845-4500; meals ¥1300; open 11.30am-8.30pm daily), in a similar vein to Daikokuya, serves tempura and a variety of noodle dishes. It's another good place to try the tempura *donburi*.

Tatsumiya (☎ 3842-7373; lunch/dinner ¥850/2500-4000; open 5pm-10pm Tues-Sun) is an old Edo-period restaurant, full of interesting bric-a-brac, that specialises in *nabe ryōri* (stew; literally, 'pot cuisine') during the winter months.

Akiyoshi (☎ 3982-0644; meals ¥3000; open 5pm-11pm daily; subway Asakusa Kaminarimon exit), near the Asakusa View Hotel, is a place to check out for good *yakitori* and a picture menu. In addition to standard *yakitori*, try some *kushi-katsu* (skewers of deep-fried meat, vegetables and seafood) and rice dishes.

Asakusa Imahan (☎ 3842-1800; meals ¥7300; open 11.30am-8.30pm Tues-Sun), just down the street from Akiyoshi, is a great place to try sukiyaki or *shabu-shabu*. The meat is high quality, the preparation excellent and the atmosphere dignified. You're going to have to pay for it, though.

Sometaro (☎ 3844-9502; meals ¥1000; open noon-10pm daily), in Nishi-Asakusa, is good for *okonomiyaki* (meat, seafood and vegetables in a cabbage-and-vegetable batter) in really funky surroundings. You cook it up yourself on a griddle built into your table. Look for the rustic, overgrown facade.

Vin Chou (☎ 3845-4430; meals ¥3000; 5am-11pm Thur-Tues) is, of all things, a French-style *yakitori* joint, offering fois gras with your *tori negi* (chicken and leek). All rather chichi, for this neck of the woods. It's opposite the Taitō Ryokan.

Raishūken (☎ 3844-7409; meals ¥900; open noon-7pm Wed-Mon), a 40-year-old *rāmen* shop in Nishi-Asakusa, is unmissable. The Japanese describe this as *natsukashii no aji*, 'the taste of nostalgia'. Order an *ōmori* – a large bowl of Taiwan-style noodles in a soy-based soup – brilliant!

Kameya (☎ 3831-0912; open 11.30am-9.20pm Wed-Mon), close to Asakusa subway station, is said to be the oldest bar in Japan. There's a beer hall on the ground floor, where you order and pay for beer and food as you enter. Upstairs, Western and Japanese food is served.

International Apart from the standard fast-food offerings, the only decent international choices in Asakusa are just across Azuma-bashi in the **Asahi Beer Flamme D'Or** complex (you can't miss it – it's got the giant 'golden turd' on top).

La Ranarata (☎ 5608-5277; lunch/dinner ¥2500/6000; open 11.30am-2pm & 5pm-9pm Mon-Sat, 11.30am-3pm & 4pm-8pm Sun) has good Milanese cuisine on the 22nd floor of the Asahi Beer building. It has great pizza capricciosa and is an excellent date spot for nonsufferers of vertigo.

Sumida River Brewing Company (☎ 5608-3831; set lunch ¥700; open 11.30am-1.30pm & 5pm-10pm Mon-Fri, 11.30am-10pm Sat & Sun) offers average, but inexpensive, pub food with *ji-biru* (local beer), which start at ¥530 for a small glass.

Ikebukuro (Map 4)

Japanese Ikebukuro is perhaps not the place for a serious Japanese meal but there are plenty of fine places to fill up. At lunchtime, don't forget to check out the restaurant floors in Seibu, Tōbu and Marui department stores.

On the station's eastern side, look for revolving sushi restaurants.

Komazushi (☎ 3590-0581; plates from ¥120; open 11am-10pm daily), a popular place with a friendly atmosphere, is worth recommending. It's near a giant *pachinko* (vertical pinball game) parlour.

Mawaru Sushi Hana Kan (☎ 3988-6124; open 11am-10pm daily), on the same side of the station as Komazushi, is a similar automatic sushi place.

Tonbo (☎ 3983-1686; meals ¥1250; open 11am-3pm & 5pm-9.30pm Mon-Sat), on the west side, serves good *tonkatsu*, fried shrimp and related fare. The *hire katsu teishoku* (set meal with fancier *tonkatsu*) is recommended.

Akiyoshi (☎ 3982-0644; meals ¥3000; open 5pm-11pm daily) is a place to try for a tasty *yakitori* dinner in approachable, laid-back surroundings. There is a large picture menu to help you order. There's

Shibuya district, Tokyo

Ginza district, Tokyo

Passenger ferry on the Sumida-gawa, Tokyo

TOKYO SUBWAY MAP

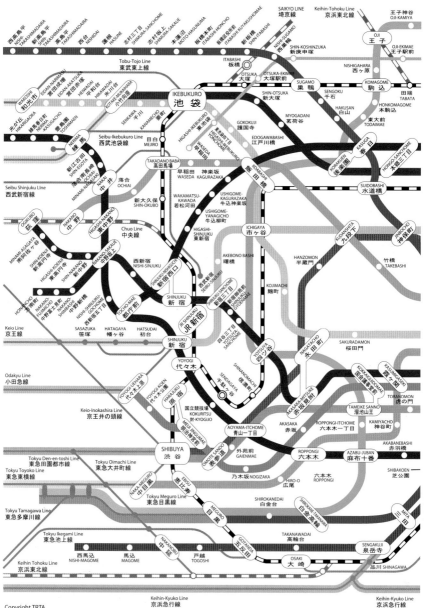

Copyright TRTA

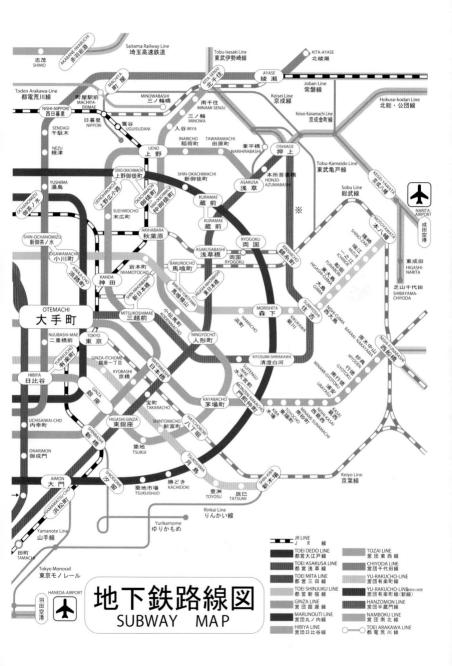

Autumn leaves, Tokyo

Seating outside a noodle shop, Tokyo

Red torii, Hie-jinja, Akasaka, Tokyo

Morning peak hour, Shinjuku station, Tokyo

no English sign, but you can easily spot the long counters and smoky grills from out on the street.

Sushi Kazu (☎ 3980-5225; meals from ¥3000; open 5pm-4am Mon-Sat) is a good, standard-issue sushi bar that is definitely a step up from all those revolving sushi bars in the neighbourhood.

Tonerian (☎ 3985-0254; meals ¥3000; open 5pm-11.15pm daily), one of Ikebukuro's many izakaya, is a busy place with friendly staff. This is the place to learn about good jizake (regional sake) and the master, who speaks English, will be glad to make suggestions. Look for all the empty sake bottles piled up outside.

Matsukaze (☎ 3986-1047; dinner around ¥3500; open 5pm-11.30pm daily), in a similar vein to Tonerian, nearby, is a rustic izakaya that serves interesting twists on all the standard izakaya favourites. Look for the wooden facade.

Tapa (☎ 5954-1180; meals ¥3000; open 4pm-1am Sun-Thur, 4pm-3am Fri & Sat), something between an izakaya and a Spanish tapas bar, is back on the east side, not far from Tōkyū Hands. There's another branch on the 13th floor of Tōbu department store.

Yamabuki (☎ 3971-1287; lunch/dinner ¥980/1100; open 11am-8.45pm daily) is a place to call into for that wonderful Japanese delicacy, unagi; it serves unadon (unagi over rice). There is a picture menu. Look for all the eel in the window.

International There are lots of cheap international places to eat in Ikebukuro. Some of the deals can be found on department-store restaurant floors. In particular, try the 11th–17th floors of Tōbu and the 8th floor of Tōbu's Metropolitan Plaza, where the Italian restaurant **Domani** (☎ 5954-8114; lunch/dinner around ¥1000/2500; open 11am-4.30pm & 5.30pm-9.40pm daily) serves good meals.

Oriental Kitchen (☎ 3982-7721; lunch/dinner ¥100/2000; open 11am-10pm daily), serves a vast all-you-can-eat buffet of just about every major Asian food you'd care to name, although none of it's very special. It's on the 2nd floor of its building; look for the large karaoke-box sign.

Capricciosa (☎ 5396-0773; lunch/dinner ¥2000/3000; open 10am-10pm daily) is the

place to head to for large portions of cheap Italian food.

Malaychan (☎ 5391-7638; lunch sets from ¥700; open 11am-2.30pm & 5pm-11pm daily), located on a corner across from Nishi-Ikebukuro-kōen, is one of Tokyo's few Malaysian restaurants. The food is so-so, but it's easy to order from the big picture menu and the drinks are good. Nasi lemak (rice with assorted dishes) is a filling introduction to Malaysian food at ¥1070.

Myun (☎ 3985-8967; lunch/dinner set ¥1500/3000; open 11am-3pm & 5pm-11pm daily) is a place you can try for reasonable Vietnamese food, which serves a good lunch set and a dinner set with seven items. The only drawback is the music: Japanese pop music. Look for the green sign, streetside.

Taiwan Hsiao Tiao (☎ 3980-7822; lunch sets under ¥1000, dinner around ¥3000; open 11am-2pm & 5pm-2am daily), very near Kimi Ryokan, serves good Taiwanese fare in casual surroundings. Try the steamed gyōza (dumplings), the 'healthy' Chinese sake and the crispy duck dishes. Lunch sets are a bargain.

Chez Kibeau (☎ 3987-6666; dinner with wine ¥5000; open 6pm-midnight Tues-Sun) serves excellent continental cuisine in a pleasant basement that feels far removed from the chaos on the streets above. The owner speaks English and can help with ordering.

Shinjuku (Map 5)

Japanese Shinjuku is a good place to hunt for bargain meals. Some of the cheaper offerings are pretty grim, including some leathery kaiten-zushi, but a little searching turns up some pleasant surprises.

Don't forget to check the offerings on the restaurant floors of east Shinjuku's many department stores. In particular, **Isetan Kaikan** has eight floors of restaurants including a branch of **Kushinobo** (☎ 3356-3865; lunch/dinner ¥860/3500; open 11.30am-9.30pm daily) a kushi-katsu specialist that serves good lunch sets and fancier dinner courses. **Takashimaya Times Square** (☎ 5361-3301; open 10am-9pm daily) also has a restaurant park on its 12th to 14th floors, with 28 restaurants to choose from.

Outside of the department stores you'll also find plenty to choose from. **Tsunahachi** behind Mitsukoshi department store

TOKYO

has excellent tempura at reasonable prices. Its ¥2500 tempura *teishoku* is highly recommended for dinner. Best of all, there's an English menu and the staff seem accustomed to foreign customers.

Suzuya *(Yasukuni-dōri)* has good *tonkatsu*. The *katsu* here are high quality (not greasy) and come in filling sets that include rice and miso soup. We suggest the *hire katsu teishoku* (¥1450). It's on the 2nd floor, with signs at street level on the corner.

Shinjuku Negishi *(☎ 3232-8020; lunch/dinner ¥2000; open 11am-3pm & 5.30pm-10.30pm daily)*, also in Kabuki-chō, serves beef tongue and beef stew. It's tasty stuff, and the set meal it comes with is healthy. This cosy little spot is sandwiched between Beijing Rāmen and Tainan Taami Taiwanese restaurant (see the International section following).

Daikokuya *(☎ 3202-7272; meals from ¥2000; open 5pm-11.30pm Mon-Fri, 3pm-midnight Sat & Sun)* is a good place for hungry, budget-minded travellers, with its all-you-can-eat *yaki-niku* (grilled meat), *shabu-shabu* and sukiyaki courses. There's an all-you-can-drink option too.

Suehiro *(☎ 3356-4656; lunch or dinner ¥1000; open 11pm-3pm & 5pm-10.30pm Mon-Sat, 11am-9.30pm Sun)*, in a similar vein to Daikokuya, specialises in cheap lunch and dinner sets (Japanese versions of Western favourites like steak and burgers).

Ibuki *(☎ 3352-4787; sukiyaki course ¥2500, shabu-shabu ¥3200; open 5pm-11.30pm daily)* is an excellent sukiyaki and *shabu-shabu* restaurant, has an English menu and sign, and gets a lot of foreign visitors. It offers friendly service in a traditional atmosphere.

Keika Kumamoto Rāmen *(☎ 3354-4591; subway Shinjuku-sanchōme exit east; meals ¥800; open 11am-10.45pm daily)* is out towards Shinjuku-sanchōme and the place to try for authentic *rāmen*. The noodles are distinctively chewy and the broth is thick. Try the *chashūmen* (*rāmen* with roast pork). You order and pay as you enter.

For a taste of Occupation-era Tokyo – tiny restaurants packed willy-nilly into a wonderfully atmospheric old alley – try the **Omoide-yokochō** street beside the JR tracks just northwest of Shinjuku station. Here, local workers stop off for *yakitori*, *oden* (fishcakes, tōfu, vegetables and eggs

simmered for hours in a kelp-flavoured broth), noodles and beer before braving the trains back home. It's pointless to make recommendations; most of the places serve the same thing and few have names. What they serve will be piled high on the counters; just point and eat. Expect to pay about ¥3000 per person for a memorable time.

International This is a good place to look for good deals on international food. However, there's a lot of junk mixed in with the bargains in Shinjuku. Beware of all-you-can-eat specials and other such deals – there's a reason why the food is so cheap. In addition to the places listed here, see the Clubhouse entry under Bars & Clubs in the Entertainment section later.

Beijing Rāmen *(☎ 3200-3560; open 11am-9pm daily)* in Kabuki-chō has good Chinese-style *rāmen*. It gets no awards for warm and friendly service, but the noodles are authentic, and so are the Chinese staff. *Rāmen* starts at ¥800 and six *gyōza* go for ¥300.

Tainan Taami *(☎ 3464-7544; dishes ¥300-600; open 11am-2pm & 5pm-2am Mon-Sat)*, offers great Taiwanese cuisine in a rowdy *izakaya* atmosphere. The menu comes complete with photographs of the dishes, which are, as per genre, small.

El Borracho *(☎ 3354-7046; open 5pm-10.30pm daily)* has inexpensive Mexican food in a real hole-in-the-wall atmosphere. Your tacos may not be authentic, but they aren't bad. El Borracho is next to Mos Burger; look for the Aztec motif.

Tokyo Dai Hanten *(☎ 3202-0121; per person around ¥4000; open 11.30am-10.30pm daily)*, on the 3rd floor of the unfortunately named Oriental Wave building, is one of the few possibilities for yum cha or dim sum. For Sunday brunch it serves dim sum à la Hong Kong, bringing it around on trolleys.

Canard *(☎ 3200-0706; lunch/dinner courses from ¥1500/2500; open 11.30am-2pm & 6pm-10.30pm daily)*, tucked into a tiny alley near Hanazono-jinja, serves good French food in cosy surroundings. With wine, the bill adds up.

Raobian Gyozakan *(☎ 3348-5810; courses around ¥3000; open 11.30am-11.30pm daily)* serves authentic thick-skinned Beijing-style *gyōza* and other Chinese fare. The *gyōza* here are so good that you don't need sauce for dipping. However, the portions are small.

New York Grill (☎ 5323-3458; meals ¥6000, Sun brunch ¥3900; open 11.30am-midnight daily), on the 52nd floor of the Park Hyatt Tower, is one place worth going out of your way for among all the fine restaurants in the hotels of west Shinjuku. This is power dining at its best – hearty portions of steak and seafood and a drop-dead view. One bargain worth mentioning is the Sunday brunch. On the way in, you can warm up with a few drinks at the adjoining New York Bar.

Harajuku & Aoyama (Map 6)

Japanese In trendy Harajuku and Aoyama there aren't many Japanese places; international cuisine is the rule here. However, there are a couple of spots worth recommending.

Maisen (☎ 3470-0071; meals around ¥1500; open 11am-11pm daily) is a shrine dedicated to that classic Japanese dish, *tonkatsu*. Its *hire katsu teishoku* is good value and there is a selection of other classic Japanese dishes. **Shūtarō** (☎ 3402-7366; open 11am-10pm daily) is a budget version of Maisen, but it's not quite as good.

International Harajuku and Aoyama have more bistros, cafés and trattorias than most small European cities. The heart of it all is the famous promenade of Tokyo's young and beautiful: Omote-sandō.

Tokyo Apartment Café (☎ 3401-4101; meals from ¥600; open 11am-4am daily) is a popular, inexpensive option opposite Condomania, offering panzerotti, cocktails and, er, Fruits Conscious Frozen.

Rat Ngon Store (☎ 3478-9478; meals from ¥750; open noon-3pm & 6pm-11pm daily) is a friendly, rodentless spot ('rat ngon' means very tasty in Vietnamese), offering reasonably priced, Asian-ish sets. It's near the west end of Takeshita-dōri, behind Pop-land, crammed into a tiny space on the 3rd floor of an apartment building, next to a barber specialising in Afros.

Vegetarians will find more to their liking in the Crayon House building, which houses two organic restaurants. **Hiroba** (☎ 3406-6409; lunch buffet ¥1260; open 11am-10pm daily), the first, does an excellent organic lunch buffet. **Organic Restaur-**

ant Home (☎ 3406-6409; subway Omote-sandō exit B2 & B4; set lunches from ¥1800; open 11am-10pm daily), the second place, is more of a sit-down-and-order spot. Both Japanese- and Western-style dishes are on offer here. There is also a small organic food store.

Fujimamas (☎ 5485-2262; W www.fuji mamas.com; meals from ¥4000; open 11am-10pm daily) is a very pleasant, and hugely popular 'international' restaurant mixing and matching European and Asian ingredients under the auspices of chef/co-owner Mark Vann. Good wines, and especially nice rooms upstairs in what was once a tatami-maker's workshop. It also has a good children's menu and is directly behind the Penny Black store. Reservations are recommended.

Fonda de la Madrugada (☎ 5410-6288; lunch/dinner from ¥3800/6000; open 5.30pm-5am daily) has the best Mexican in Tokyo. Head up past the Turkish embassy to this favourite with expats and the business community. Complete with open courtyards and strolling musicians, everything from the rooftiles to the chefs has been imported from Mexico. It's not cheap, but it's worth the expenditure. Hope you like mariachi though.

Tacos del Amigo (☎ 3405-9996; open 5pm-12.30am Mon-Fri, 5pm-midnight Sat & Sun) is a Mexican restaurant, not far from exit 5 of Meiji Jingumae station, with a pleasant indoor-outdoor atmosphere and it's a good place to combine drinks and dinner. The food is average and the prices a bit steep, but it's fun all the same.

Bamboo Cafe (☎ 3211-0087; light meals ¥1000; open 7am-10pm daily) is yet another outdoor café-style restaurant, where you can have sandwiches made on three different types of bread, and salads to go with them.

Son of Dragon (Ryunoko; ☎ 3402-9419; meals around ¥2500; open 11.30am-3pm & 5pm-9.30pm Mon-Sat) serves pretty good Sichuan cuisine in a smoky basement off Meiji-dōri. Try the *banbanji* (cold chicken and sesame sauce) and any of the noodle dishes.

Tony Roma's (☎ 3479-5214; lunch/dinner ¥1000/3000; open noon-10.30pm daily) on Aoyama-dōri is cholesterol central, *the* place to pig out on American-style ribs and onion rings. There are also passable salads for the nonravenous.

Las Chicas (☎ 3407-6865; lunch/dinner ¥1000/1500; open 11am-11pm daily) will give you a look at expat life in pleasant, expansive surroundings. This is where cool and wannabe-cool expats come to pose and peer. The yuppie-style food is pretty good too – from pizzas to salads to sandwiches – and the wine list is solid. There's also a bar to repair to after dinner.

Shibuya (Map 7)

Japanese Take the briefest of looks around Shibuya, and it will probably occur to you that there must be a lot of restaurants lurking in all those department stores – there are. Try the 7th floor of Parco Part 1 or the 8th floor of the One-Oh-Nine Building.

Jūnikagetsu (means '12 months' for all you language students) is a collection of good restaurants all under one roof. Here, you can choose from *yaki-niku*, *shabu-shabu*, sea-food *teppanyaki* (high-class steak dinner) and, perhaps best of all, sushi served by **Hina Sushi** (☎ 5531-0017; meals from ¥2000; open 11.30am-2pm & 5pm-11.30pm Tues-Fri, 11.30am-10.30pm Sat, 11.30am-9.30pm Sun). Its all-you-can-eat special (¥4300) is good value for this quality.

Tamakyū (☎ 3461-4803; meals from ¥3000; open 4pm-10.30pm Mon-Sat), the creaking little pile of timber that refused to be budged by the 109 Building, is about the only nonshiny thing left in this bit of Shibuya. The adventurous (you will need some Japanese) should show their support by coming here. Inside is a lively little *izakaya*, not one of Tokyo's best, but not bad.

Akiyoshi (☎ 3464-1518; open 5pm-11.30pm daily), a good choice for *yakitori*, is an approachable place with a large picture menu. Dinner here should cost about ¥3000.

Kushinobō (☎ 3496-8978; lunch courses from ¥1000; open noon-2pm & 5pm-10.30pm daily) is the place to sample that great Japanese treat, *kushi-katsu*. It's on the 5th floor of the J&R Building, across from Wendy's. Plan on ¥3000 for dinner.

Sakana-tei (☎ 3780-1313; meals from ¥3500; open 5.30pm-1.30am Mon-Sat) looks more like a concrete modernist bomb shelter than a good value, slightly posh *izakaya* and sake-specialist. But that's what it is, up in Dogenzaka. Handily placed for pre- or

post–Love Hotel Hill nuptials. It is on the 4th floor of the Koike building.

Fujiya Honten (☎ 3461-2128; meals ¥700; open 5pm-9pm daily) is for the bold budget-diner. Venture into this marvellous, legendary old *tachi-nomi* (stand-up-and-drink place) on the southwest side of Shibuya station, and you'll find it filled with post-race punters from the nags at Ōi (Tokyo's famous horse-racing track). Wash down the Oden with beer and sake at rock-bottom prices, and prepare to be engaged in friendly, slurred conversation. Be warned: we've never seen a woman in the place. It's down the small street between Ringer Hut and the spectacles dealer. In the basement, where else?

International There's no shortage of international cuisine here. The best places to look are the small streets around the station and the built-up shopping areas around the giant department stores.

New York Kitchen (☎ 5457-7755; meals from ¥580; open 11am-11pm daily) is one of our favourite stops for lunch. Here you can get proper bagel sandwiches with a variety of fillings. There's also a good deli-bar where you can choose from six or seven different salads etc. There's cheap coffee and espresso as well.

Ubusuna Cafe (☎ 5459-4502; meals ¥800; open 10am-11pm daily) is a good option if you are after a light, inexpensive meal and a coffee, in relaxed surroundings. It is, quite literally, behind the huge liquid-crystal video screen that peers down on Shibuya station, on the 6th floor of the Q-Front building.

Samrat (☎ 3770-7275; meals ¥1000; open 11am-10pm daily) serves the usual Indian curries and curry sets. There's usually a tout outside beckoning people in.

Tainan Taami (☎ 3464-7544; meals ¥3000; open 11am-2pm & 5pm-2am Mon-Sat) is a great choice for good Taiwanese fare in raucous, if slightly smoky, surroundings.

Reikyō (☎ 3461-4220; meals ¥3000; open noon-2pm & 5pm-1am Fri-Wed) offers similar Taiwanese fare and surroundings as Tainan Taami. It's in a triangular red-brick building.

Kantipur (☎ 3770-5358; meals around ¥2800; open 11.30am-3pm & 5pm-11pm daily) is a Nepali restaurant that seems to borrow a lot from India (perhaps *dal bhat* is a limited menu for a restaurant). This place is a little bit back from the street and can be tough to spot.

Ebisu & Daikanyama (Map 8)

Japanese Try the 6th floor of the Atre building, over Ebisu station, for all the standard Japanese favourites. **Fujii** (☎ 5424-6667; open 11am-10pm Mon-Sat), down at street level, is a good place to sample fresh, handmade *udon*. We recommend the tempura udon for ¥1500. There is no English sign, but you'll see food models in the window, just up the street from KFC.

Denki Kurage (☎ 5420-5901; lunch/dinner ¥3000/4000; open 5.30pm-12.30am daily) means 'Electric Jellyfish' but the menu consists of eclectic modern *izakaya* fare in trendy, relaxed surroundings. It's between Good Day books and Kinko's.

Nanaki Soba (☎ 3496-2878; open 11.30am-1.50pm & 5pm-10pm Mon-Sat) is an *izakaya* with standard-issue food, a picture menu and a good selection of sake.

Ippūdō Rāmen (☎ 5420-2225; subway Ebisu exit 1 & 2; meals ¥900; open 11am-4pm daily), on the other side of the station, is nationally famous. It serves Kyūshū-style *rāmen* into which you can grate garlic cloves. You'll queue at peak periods.

Shunsenbō (☎ 5469-9761; subway Ebisu exit 1 & 2; lunch/dinner courses from ¥1000/3800; open 11am-3pm & 5.30pm-11pm daily) specialises in tofu dishes and *shabu-shabu*. Courses are a real bargain considering the quality of the food and the elegant surroundings. Best of all, there's an English menu. It's in the Ebisu Prime Square Plaza complex, on the ground floor.

You'll find Japanese restaurants few and far between in Daikanyama, as the area has its gaze fixed firmly on the West (see the following International section).

International Daikanyama rivals Harajuku and Aoyama as the centre of Tokyo café society and it's a good place to grab a cappuccino and do some people watching. You'll also find plenty of trendy foreign restaurants, some of which are good and some of which are merely fashionable.

Caffe Michelangelo (☎ 3770-9517; meals ¥1000; open 11am-midnight daily) is Tokyo's best impersonation of Paris and it's a good

place to watch the beautiful people on a weekend afternoon. You'll pay for the pleasure, though – coffee starts at ¥600.

Café Artifagose (☎ 5489-1133; meals ¥900; open 11am-8pm daily) is a more reasonable option and has great outdoor seating, good breads and cheeses and a fine selection of drinks. **Gazebo Café**, halfway between Ebisu and Daikanyama is in the same vein as Café Artifagose. The sandwiches are pretty good here but the view leaves something to be desired.

Café Juliet (☎ 3770-5656; meals ¥700; open 11.30am-midnight Tues-Thur, noon-4am Fri & Sat) has a pleasant outdoor eating area, and pasta, sandwiches and similar light fare. The coffee here, though good, is inexplicably expensive. **KM Fils** (☎ 5457-1435; lunch/dinner ¥2500/5000; open noon-2pm & 6pm-10pm Mon & Wed-Fri, 11.30am-2pm & 6pm-9pm Sat & Sun) is a chic place downstairs from Café Juliet where the French fare is decent but overpriced.

Bombay Bazar (☎ 3461-8512; meals around ¥2000; open noon-8pm daily) is an interesting place that, in terms of atmosphere, is the pick of the bunch in Daikanyama. It's a restaurant that *claims* to serve organic food (we doubt it). It makes decent curries and has a varied drink selection. Count on spending around ¥1200 for a drink and a meal.

Monsoon Cafe (☎ 3400-7200; meals around ¥3000; open 11.30am-5am daily) on Kyūyamate-dōri is another good choice and is about 300m past the Danish embassy on the left side of the street. The multilevel affair of outdoor terraces and spacious dining rooms is a great place for a meal and drink on a warm summer evening. The food, though none too special, is an interesting mix of Southeast Asian classics like Vietnamese spring rolls and Malaysian satay.

Akasaka (Map 9)

Japanese Akasaka is packed with excellent Japanese restaurants, though bear in mind that bargains are few and far between. For starters, take a stroll in the streets running off and parallel to Sotoburi-dōri. In this neighbourhood there are branches of expensive restaurant chains such as **Sushi-sei** (☎ 3582-9503; lunch/dinner ¥2000/4000; open 11.30am-2pm & 5pm-11.30pm Mon-Sat), a branch of the famous sushi chain,

TOKYO

where costs of around ¥4000 per person are the norm (although delicious lunch sets are significantly cheaper).

Kushinobo (☎ 3586-7390; dinner courses from ¥2500; open 6pm-9.30pm Mon-Sat) is good for an inexpensive lunch. It's a *kushiage* (skewers of deep-fried meat, seafood and vegetables) and *kushi-katsu* specialist on the 3rd floor of the Akasaka Tōkyū Hotel. **Tsunahachi** (☎ 3588-5110), on the 8th floor of the Belle Vie building, is a good tempura place with similar prices to Kushinobo. **Tōfu-ya** (☎ 3582-1028; lunch/dinner ¥800/4300; open 11.30am-1.30pm & 5pm-11pm Mon-Fri) is the perfect introduction to a largely vegetarian cuisine that many visitors miss out on – some Japanese-language ability will be helpful here.

Sunaba (☎ 3583-7670; meals ¥2000; open 11am-7.30pm Mon-Fri, 11am-7pm Sat) has some of the city's finest buckwheat noodles. They invented *tempura soba*, and serve it in an exquisite, dense, smoky *tsuyu* (dipping sauce) – sublime. It's next to the Kokusai Shin-Akasaka building. There's a sister shop in Nihombashi.

Yakitori Luis (☎ 3506-2306; meals ¥1500; open 5pm-11.15pm Mon-Sat, 5pm-10.30pm Sun), for standard *izakaya* dining close to Akasaka subway station, is a popular *yakitori* haven.

Jangara Rāmen (☎ 3595-2130; meals from ¥580; open 11.45am-2am Tues-Thur, 11.45am-3.30am Sat, 11.45am-1am Fri, Sun & holidays), near the entrance to Hie-jinja, is worth trying for a great bowl of *rāmen*. Live a little and order the *zenbu-iri* all-in *rāmen*.

International Along with nearby Roppongi, Akasaka is one of Tokyo's most cosmopolitan neighbourhoods. While most of the action is in the mid-range bracket, a stroll through the narrow streets just west of Akasaka-mitsuke subway station will turn up a number of good lunch deals.

Moti Darbar (☎ 3582-3620; lunch/dinner ¥800/2000; open 11.30am-11pm daily), part of Tokyo's best Indian chain, is in this neighbourhood. **The Taj** (☎ 3586-6606; lunch buffet ¥1200; open 11.30am-2.30pm & 5pm-10.30pm Mon-Fri, 11am-3pm & 5pm-10pm Sat & Sun), nearby, is a slightly upmarket institution starting to show its age. Nonetheless, the lunch buffet is usually quite

well done; dinners run close to ¥4000 per person.

Trattoria Marumo (☎ 3585-5371; lunch/dinner ¥1500/3000; open 11.30am-midnight daily) is a pizzeria that serves a range of Italian fare for reasonable prices. The atmosphere is pleasant and the food is pretty good. There are loads of food models in the window. There's a more formal Marumo out on Akasaka-dōri.

Mugyodon (☎ 3586-6478; dinner ¥5000; open 5pm-midnight Mon-Sat) is a popular, friendly Korean place open for dinner only. This is your chance to sample the real thing, not the usual Japanese version. It's upstairs from Uskudar Turkish restaurant.

Roppongi (Map 10)

Japanese Roppongi's Japanese restaurants tend to be expensive and very accessible to foreigners. This makes it the perfect area for that long-awaited splurge on a special Japanese meal. That said, there are some cheap spots around if you just fancy a quick bite before hitting the bars.

Bikkuri Sushi (☎ 3403-1489; meals from ¥1000; open 11pm-5am daily) is a long-time favourite for Roppongi revellers and is a late-night *kaiten-zushi* place that's seen it all.

Namban-tei (☎ 3478-5866; meals ¥6000; open 5pm-11pm daily) is something of a Roppongi institution, serving excellent *yakitori* in pleasant surroundings. It won't be cheap but it will be delicious.

Kisso (☎ 3582-4191; main meals around ¥10,000; open 11am-2pm & 5.30pm-10pm Mon-Sat), on the B1 floor of the Axis building, is a good place to sample Japan's gourmet cuisine, *kaiseki ryōri* (beautifully presented multicourse meals). This is without a doubt the most accessible *kaiseki* in all of Tokyo. It's best to order a course and leave everything up to the chef.

Fukuzushi (☎ 3402-4116; meals around ¥10,000; open 11.30am-1.30pm & 5.30pm-10pm Mon-Sat) serves some of the best sushi in town, in an atmosphere that is decidedly more relaxed than at some of the more traditional places in Ginza and Tsukiji. The fish here is fresh, the portions are large and there's even a cocktail bar.

Seryna (☎ 3402-1051; lunch/dinner ¥6000/15,000; open noon-11pm daily) is a long-time expat favourite for entertaining important guests from abroad. There are actually three restaurants under the Seryna roof: Seryna Honten *(shabu-shabu* and *sukiyaki)*, Mon Cher Ton Ton (Kōbe-beef steaks), and Kani Seryna (crab dishes). It's all a bit musty though.

Inakaya *(☎ 3405-9866; meals ¥10000; open 5pm-11pm)*, at the Nogizaka end of Gaien-higashi-dōri in Roppongi, has achieved fame as a top-end *robatayaki* (rustic bar-restaurant serving food grilled over charcoal). It does raucous, bustling, don't-stand-on-ceremony *robatayaki* with gusto. It's possible to spend lots of money here *and* have fun. There is also a branch in Akasaka *(☎ 3586-3054)*.

Gokoku *(☎ 3796-3356; meals ¥6000; open 6pm-midnight Mon-Sat)* is close to the top-end category, but if you're conservative with your drink orders, you can eat for mid-range prices (for Roppongi). The menu changes daily but it is always hearty Edo-style fare.

International It only makes sense that in Roppongi, Tokyo's foreign nightlife playground, there would be a lot of international restaurants. These places range from cheap hamburger joints to expensive imports like Wolfgang Puck's Spago. Whatever it is you fancy, you'll find it here – and the bars and clubs of Roppongi are only a step away.

Havana Café *(☎ 3423-3500; meals ¥1000; open 11.30am-5am Mon-Fri, noon-5am Sat & Sun)* is casual and one of the best places to start a Roppongi evening. In addition to great happy-hour drink specials, it serves reliable stuff like burritos and sandwiches for less than ¥1000. The place opens onto a quiet backstreet, and as you sip that first drink, it's difficult to imagine that Roppongi lurks just round the corner.

Hamburger Inn *(☎ 3405-8980; meals ¥1000; open 11.30am-5am Mon-Sat)* is a Roppongi institution that stays open all night and serves forgettable burgers for around ¥400.

Bellini's Trattoria *(☎ 3470-5650; lunch/ dinner ¥1300/4000; open 11.30am-2am Sun-Thur, 11.30am-3am Fri-Sun)* is worth a try for decent Italian food and excellent streetside people-watching. It has a wide selection of Italian favourites, and lots of drink choices, including cappuccino and espresso.

Bengawan Solo *(☎ 3408-5698; meals ¥1100; open 11.30am-2.30pm & 5pm-9.30pm Mon-Sat)* on Roppongi-dōri is an Indonesian eatery that offers a taste of the south seas. It's been around for ages, and the food never disappoints. The *gado gado* (salad with peanut sauce) lunch is a bargain, and the beef in coconut-cream is delicious. Look for the food models displayed outside.

Maenam *(☎ 3404-4745; meals ¥3500; open 11.30am-4am daily)*, another good Southeast Asian favourite, is a tackily-decorated but competent Thai place down towards Nishi-Azabu.

Monsoon Café *(☎ 3400-7200; meals ¥3500; open 11.30am-5am Mon-Sat)*, next to the Aoyama Reien, serves decent Southeast Asian fare in a semi-outdoor café-style place. This is a good option for tropical drinks and just hanging out. Again, you're looking at around ¥3500 for a good feed with drinks.

Hard Rock Café *(☎ 3408-7018; lunch/ dinner ¥1000/2000; open 11.30am-2am Mon-Thur, 11.30am-4am Fri & Sat, 11.30am-11.30pm Sun & national holidays)* and **Tony Roma's** are in the same building. We figure you know what to expect from the former – loud music, oversized portions of passable American food and plenty of reasonably priced drinks. Tony Roma's is another American joint that serves barbecued spare ribs with all the fixings. At either place, a good dinner is in the ¥3000 range, with Tony Roma's the more expensive of the two.

Spago *(☎ 3423-4025; lunch/dinner ¥3000/ 7000; open 11.30am-2pm & 6pm-10pm daily)* has a Tokyo branch for those who fancy a splurge on somewhat upmarket Western cuisine.

Humming Bird *(☎ 3401-3337; dinner ¥5000; open 11am-3pm & 6pm-2am Mon-Sat, 6pm-10pm Sun)* mixes Vietnamese and French colonial. This is a good value mid-range option, and not a little posh. We recommend the sautéed lobster with mango mint sauce.

Odaiba (Map 11)

Japanese There are several Japanese-style restaurants on this trendy island in the bay. **Hina Sushi** *(☎ 5531-0017; meals ¥4300; open 11.30am-2pm & 5pm-10.30pm daily)*, on Restaurant Row, serves excellent sushi, and offers a good all-you-can-eat lunch. **Wakō** (☎ 3599-6555; meals from ¥1000; open 11am-11pm daily), in the Decks Tokyo Beach complex, is a place to try the *tonkatsu*; standard *teishoku* starts at ¥1000.

International Odaiba is a pleasant place to sample some reasonable international fare, as most of the restaurants have good views of the bay or the beach.

Cafe Coyote (☎ 5531-5007; lunch/dinner from ¥1200/2500; open 5.30pm-2am Tues-Sun) is a Mexican place that serves passable lunches and dinners.

Sam Choy's (☎ 5531-5036; open 5.30pm-11pm, last order 9.30pm, Tues-Fri, 11am-3pm & 5pm-11pm Sat & Sun) nearby, serves whopping portions of decent Hawaiian-Asian seafood for similar prices.

Khazana (☎ 3599-6551; lunch buffet ¥800; open 11am-11pm daily), up on the 5th floor of the Decks Tokyo Beach complex, is an Indian restaurant that serves a good all-you-can-eat buffet lunch. You'll have to come early to get one of the coveted tables out on the deck.

Soup Stock Tokyo (☎ 3599-2333; meals from ¥800; open 11am-11pm daily) is an inexpensive fast-soup restaurant in the Venus Fort shopping complex. Try the garlic soup with *onsen tamago* (hot-spring boiled eggs).

ENTERTAINMENT

Tokyo is very much the centre of the Japanese world, and has the best of everything. On the nightlife front, there are those who maintain that Osaka is more cutting edge, but then Osaka offers nowhere near the diversity of entertainment options available in Tokyo – traditional entertainment such as kabuki, avant-garde theatre, countless cinemas, live houses, pubs and bars. See the special section 'Arts & Architecture' for more information on Japanese theatre.

Kabuki

Kabuki-za Theatre (Map 1; ☎ 5565-6000; admission ¥2400-14,000; times vary), in front of exit 3 of the Higashi Ginza subway station in Ginza, is the simplest way to see kabuki in Tokyo. Performances and times vary from month to month, so you'll need to check with the TIC or with the theatre directly for programme information. Ear-

phone guides providing 'comments and explanations' in English are available for ¥650 plus ¥1000 deposit.

Kabuki performances can be quite a marathon, lasting from 4½ to five hours. If you're not up to it, you can get tickets for the 4th floor from ¥600 to ¥1000 and watch only part of the show (ask for *hitomakumi*) but earphone guides are not available in these seats. Fourth-floor tickets can be bought on the day of the performance. There are generally two performances daily, starting at around 11am and 4pm.

Kokuritsu Gekijō (☎ 3265-7411; admission ¥1500-9200; tickets available 10am-6pm, performance starts 11.30am & 5pm), Japan's national theatre, also has kabuki performances, with ranging seat prices. Again, earphone guides are available. It's near Nagata-chō station on the Yūraku-chō subway line. Check with the TIC or the theatre for performance times.

Nō

Nō (classical Japanese dance-drama) performances are held at various locations around Tokyo. Tickets cost between ¥2100 and ¥15,000, and it's best to get them at the theatre itself. Check with the TIC or the appropriate theatre for times.

Kanze Nō-gakudō (Map 7; ☎ 3469-6421) is about a 15-minute walk west from Shibuya station. **Kokuritsu Nō-gakudō** (☎ 3423-1331; admission ¥2800-5600) – the National Nō Theatre – is located in Sendagaya. Exit Sendagaya station in the direction of Shinjuku on the left and follow the road that hugs the railway tracks; the theatre is on the left.

Bunraku

Kokuritsu Gekijō Theatre (☎ 3265-7411; tickets available 10am-6pm, performance starts 11.30am & 5pm) has performances several times a year, even though Osaka is the home of bunraku (classical puppet t heatre). The theatre is in Hayabusa-chō, near Nagata-chō station on the Yūraku-chō subway line. Check with the TIC or the theatre for information.

Tea Ceremonies

A few hotels in Tokyo hold tea ceremonies that you can see and occasionally participate in for a fee of ¥1000 to ¥1500. **Hotel New**

Otani *(Map 9; ☎ 3265-1111; ceremonies 11am & 1pm Thur-Sat)* has ceremonies on its 7th floor on Thursday, Friday and Saturday at 11am and 1pm. Ring before you go to make sure the day's sitting hasn't been booked out. **Hotel Okura** *(Map 9; ☎ 3582-0111; admission ¥1050; open 10am-4pm Mon-Sat)* and **Imperial Hotel** *(Map 1; ☎ 3504-1111)* also hold daily tea ceremonies.

Bars & Clubs

Bars and clubs change with the weather in Tokyo, which makes the job of coming up with specific recommendations rather difficult. The following is a rundown on bars and clubs popular at the time of writing. For up-to-the-minute information, check the bars and clubs sections of the websites listed in the websites section earlier.

Ueno & Asakusa This is definitely not the place for a night out in Tokyo. However, if you do find yourself up in old Shitamachi at night, try the **Warrior Celt** *(Map 2; ☎ 3841-5400; open 11.30am-10pm Wed-Mon)* pub in Ueno, where drinks are only ¥500 from 5pm to 7pm. It's a friendly place and has a good selection of English and Irish brews. In Asakusa (Map 3), try the beer halls in the **Asahi Flamme D'Or** complex. Otherwise, check the entry for **Kameya** *(Map 3; ☎ 3831-0912; open 11.30am-10pm daily)* under Asakusa in the Places to Eat section earlier.

Ikebukuro (Map 4) There are lots of *izakaya* on both sides of the station (see Japanese in the Ikebukuro entry under Places to Eat). **The Dubliners** *(☎ 5951-3614; open 11am-11pm daily)* is worth a try if you'd prefer something Western-style. It's a faux-Irish pub offering Kilkenny and Guinness draught. **The Black Sheep** *(☎ 3987-2289; open 6.30pm-4.30am Fri & Sat, 6.30pm-12.30am Sun-Thur)* behind Bic Personal Computer Store, is in a similar vein but open much later. The place is often packed on weekend nights when it features live bands.

Bobby's Bar *(☎ 3980-8875; open 11.30am-3am daily)*, on the 3rd floor of the Milano building on the western side of the station, is another late-night option. There's table soccer, darts and good pub grub. Early birds will enjoy the happy hour, 7pm to 9pm Monday to Thursday.

Shinjuku (Map 5) Gaudy Shinjuku is awash with nightspots of every shape and size. Of course, a lot of these fall into the sleazy category and don't cater to foreigners. That said, there's still plenty to do here by night if you have the energy to face the madness of an evening on the streets of Shinjuku.

Clubhouse *(☎ 3359-7785; open 5pm-1am Sun-Thur, 5pm-late Fri & Sat)* is a welcome arrival on the Shinjuku scene. Officially it's a sports bar, but in reality it's just a good, friendly place for a drink, with a selection of imported and domestic brews (including a few of its own custom brews). It also serves a variety of pub food for dinner and a ¥1000 all-you-can-eat international buffet at lunch.

Another popular bar located in the vicinity is **Rock Bar Mother** *(☎ 5285-2936; open 6.30pm-5am daily)*, a tiny basement bar with an extensive CD collection and a friendly crowd.

Rolling Stone *(☎ 3354-7347; admission ¥500, beers ¥600; open 6pm-4am daily)*, out towards Ni-chōme, is a grubby, low-life place that's been around since the dawn of time and still manages to pull in the crowds on Friday and Saturday nights.

Garam *(☎ 3205-8668; admission ¥1000; open 8pm-2am daily)* is a club that feels like a bar. It's a small, friendly place, where the master plays a range of hip-hop, reggae etc.

Liquid Room *(☎ 3200-6831; opening hours depend on the event, so call in advance)* is a mainstay of the Tokyo electronica scene (see the Live Music entry later). It has a small grungy bar and regularly hosts live acts – look out for notices in *Tokyo Journal* and *Metropolis* and in the big CD stores around town.

Golden Gai, lastly, is one of the city's most interesting night zones. Even if you don't feel like a drink, take a night stroll through this warren of tightly packed establishments, just to feel the atmosphere – the whole place seems lost in a boozy, run-down time warp. **Bon's** is one sure-fire spot. There's usually a ¥900 cover, and drinks start at ¥700. Look for it next to the police box.

Harajuku & Aoyama (Map 6) These adjoining areas are a good option when the Roppongi crush is too much to bear.

Oh God (☎ 3406-3206; open 6pm-6am daily) has been going for years; miraculously, it is still going. The format seems a little tired, but if your needs run to pool tables and movie screenings, it's just the ticket.

Mix (☎ 3797-1313; admission with 2 drinks ¥2500; open 10pm-late daily) is a tiny, hole-in-the-wall near the Omotesandō crossing. You can usually count on this club, even when others in the neighbourhood are flat. It's small, smoky, crowded and always friendly. Music ranges from reggae to hip-hop. It's rather hard to find; look for the stairs heading down to the basement.

Las Chicas (☎ 3407-6865; open 6pm-11pm daily) restaurant has a bar and a members' club, both of which are good spots for a drink. It's out towards Shibuya; take exit B2 from Omotesando station.

Lastly, don't forget that Harajuku and Aoyama are all about cafés, and you can spend an evening drinking beer and wine in them just as you might in Paris.

Shibuya (Map 7) Youth-oriented Shibuya is not the best place for a night out in Tokyo, especially if you're elderly travellers (in Shibuya that's anyone over 25).

Bar, Isn't It? (☎ 5784-0362; open 7pm-3am Sun-Thur, 7pm-5am Fri & Sat) is a cavernous place and a cheap choice for those who aren't too picky about where they drink. The deal here is that everything costs ¥500, including the food.

Sugar High (☎ 3780-3022; open 9pm-5am daily), a more atmospheric option, is a stylish but casual club run by two expat Americans. Music runs from lounge to techno and there is a cover of ¥1000 for special events. Its nearby sister operation **Ruby** offers similar fare.

Club Asia (☎ 5458-1996; open 11pm-5am daily) is a massive techno/soul club and worth trying if you want to see what the kids are up to. Events here usually cost ¥2500. It also has a restaurant that serves a variety of Southeast Asian food.

Harlem (☎ 3461-8806; admission ¥2000; open 10pm-5am Tues-Sat) on the 2nd and 3rd floor of Dr Jeekhan's building, is the gathering place of Tokyo's B-boy and B-girl wannabees. The music is soul and hip-hop and the cover includes two drinks.

Ebisu & Daikanyama (Map 8) These two neighbourhoods are excellent choices for a night out in Tokyo, striking the perfect balance between hip and casual. They're especially good if you just can't face the mayhem of Roppongi or Shinjuku.

What the Dickens (☎ 3780-2099; open 5pm-1am Tues & Wed, 5pm-2am Thur-Sat, 3pm-midnight Sun) is a good British pub we like. It has the usual beers on tap, some decent pub-grub and the occasional good live music.

Enjoy House (☎ 5489-1591; open 1pm-2am Mon-Thur, 1pm-4am Fri-Sun, closed Mon & 1st Sun each month), near What the Dickens, is one of Tokyo's better clubs/lounges, where you can kick back and listen to a variety of music, from rock to house, in an opium-den atmosphere. Best of all, there's no cover charge.

Lazy Cat (☎ 3442-8679; open 9pm-5am daily) is a cosy spot run by an expat Liverpudlian, and sometimes has acoustic bands. It's tucked down the small alleyway behind Kinko's.

See International under Ebisu & Daikanyama in the Places to Eat section, earlier, for information on the **Monsoon Café**, a hip place for a drink on the outskirts of Daikanyama.

Akasaka (Map 9) This is an expensive and staid place to drink. The best spots are probably the plush bars in the upper reaches of the area's luxury hotels.

Top of Akasaka (☎ 3234-1121; drinks from ¥1500; open 5pm-2am daily), on the 40th floor of the Akasaka Prince Hotel, is worth a try.

The Bar (☎ 3265-1111; open 5pm-midnight Mon-Fri, noon-midnight Sat & Sun), which is on the 40th floor of the New Otani tower, is a similar spot; otherwise, just walk the 20 minutes to Roppongi and take your pick.

Hobgoblin Tokyo (☎ 3585-3681; W www .hobgoblin-tokyo.com; open 11am-2pm & 5pm-1am Mon-Fri, 5pm-1am Sat) is far better than your average Britpub replica. Run by an Oxfordshire brewery, it has good pub fare and excellent imported microbrews. Try the Black Wych stout. Hobgoblin is in the basement of the building next to the clearly marked Marugen 23 building. It has a branch in Roppongi.

Roppongi (Map 10) This place is not part of Japan – it's a multinational twilight zone where *gaijin* get together with adventurous locals to drink until the first trains at dawn. Because of this, many long-termers avoid it like the plague, leaving it for punters fresh off the plane and gormless riff-raff out trolling for local talent. That said, Roppongi still rocks, and you'll probably want to check it out at least once.

Starting with the bars, right on the famous Roppongi crossing, you'll find **Geronimo** (☎ 3478-7449; *open 6pm-7am daily*), a shot bar that gets packed out with all sorts of off-work expats and a few of their Japanese associates. It has good happy-hour specials from 6pm to 8pm and beer is ¥800 no matter what time you go.

On the southern side of Roppongi-dōri, you'll find two good choices next to one another. **Mogambo** (☎ 3403-4833; *open 6pm-6am daily*) is the sister-club of Geronimo, with a similar crowd and prices. **Castillo** (☎ 3475-1629; *open 3pm-6am Mon-Sat, 2.30pm-midnight Sun*) next door, is a small club/bar that plays disco and soul classics. You can dance or just kick back and relax here, but you can't enter unless you're wearing 'smart casual clothes' (that's what the sign says).

Across the street is another zone thick with drinking places. **Motown House 1** (☎ 5474-4605; **W** www.motownhouse.com; *subway Roppongi exit 3; open 6pm-5am daily*) is on the first street in from the corner,

plays standard rock and roll, and has a long bar and drinks that start at ¥800. **Motown House 2** (☎ 5474-2931; *subway Roppongi exit 3; open 8pm-5am Sun-Thur, 8pm-8am Fri-Sat*) is on the next block.

Dusk Till Dawn (☎ 5771 2258; *subway Roppongi exit 3; open 5pm-late daily*) fills up at happy hour (6pm to 9pm) then keeps on filling up. The name says it all really.

Bar, Isn't It? (☎ 3746-1598; *subway Roppongi exit 3; admission with 1 drink ¥1000; open 6pm-late Thur-Sat*), an offshoot of the successful Osaka bar-chain, is further down the same road, on the 3rd floor of the MT building. The formula here is simple: a big space, so-so bar food and all drinks for ¥500. All together, it works pretty well, and it's a good place to meet people.

Propaganda (☎ 3423-0988; *subway Roppongi exit 3; open 6pm-dawn, happy hour 6pm-9pm & 5.30pm-11pm Mon-Sat*), above Bikkuri Sushi, is an inexpensive shot bar with good happy-hour specials. It's now one of Roppongi's more popular pick-up joints, if that does anything for you.

Gas Panic Bar (☎ 3470-7101; *open 6pm-5am daily*) used to be one big *gaijin* bar. Now it has been split into three bars, and forms one of Roppongi's rowdier cul-de-sacs. Along with the original there's **Club 99 Gas Panic** and **Gas Panic Café**. All three are cheap places to drink, particularly during happy hour. On the down side, these places tend to get packed out with all sorts of yahoos, and fights are not unknown.

Paddy Foley's (☎ 3423-1176; *open 5pm-late daily*) is a decent Irish-style pub, popular with the expat business community. If you want a good pint (about ¥900), convivial surroundings and some space to breathe, join the after-work crowd here.

Velfarre (☎ 3402-8000; *women/men Mon-Fri ¥2000/3000, Sat & Sun ¥3000/4000; open 6pm-midnight Thur-Sun*), on the club front, is Roppongi's disco Hilton. Dance clubs don't get much bigger, flashier or better behaved than this place. The cover includes three drinks. Take exit 4 of Roppongi subway station, and cut down beside the Mizuho bank. Velfarre is in the basement of what looks like a car park.

Lexington Queen (☎ 3401-1661; **W** www .lexingtonqueen.com; *open 8pm-5am daily*) was one of Roppongi's first discos and is still the place that every visiting celebrity ends up in. The cover here is around ¥5000 unless you're a celebrity or model.

Yellow (☎ 3479-0690; admission ¥2000-3500) is a better place to head for electronica and is an interesting, inky space that plays host to some of Tokyo's better club events. It's behind the Hotel Mentels Roppongi, besides a 'coin parking' lot.

BuL-Let's (☎ 3401-4844; admission before/after 11pm free/¥1000), near Yellow, is a mellow basement space that plays worldwide trance and ambient sounds.

Pylon (☎ 3497 1818; W www.club-pylon .com; women/men with 1 drink ¥3000/3500; open 10pm-dawn Sat & sometimes Fri) is a youth-oriented dance club, which plays anything from soul to techno. The cover here includes two drinks. Don't be put off if the entrance looks like you're walking into an underground carpark.

Techno Events Electronica has caught on in Tokyo in a big way. The city attracts some of the world's best DJs and live acts and boasts an impressive line-up of superb local talent. Some of the better events take place in Nishi-Azabu's **Yellow** (Map 10), Shibuya's **Club Asia** (Map 7; see Shibuya under Bars & Clubs earlier) and Shinjuku's **Liquid Room** (Map 5; see the Live Music section). Check *Metropolis* to see what's on while you're in town or stop by Cisco or Tower Records in Shibuya to pick up some flyers.

Gay & Lesbian Venues Tokyo's gay and lesbian enclave is Shinjuku-ni-chōme, the area east of Shinjuku Sanchome station's C8 exit. There are lots of little bars here, but some can be rather daunting to enter. **Arty Farty** (Map 5; ☎ 3356-5388; open 5pm-5am Mon-Sat, 4pm-5am Sun) is an easy place to meet people, with good all-you-can-drink deals. Wednesday is, er, 'Sticky Night'. It's a good place to learn about the area's other possibilities. Only women are admitted on Sunday.

For lesbian offerings and some more gay bars and clubs, check out the *Tokyo Journal's* Cityscope section, which sometimes has a special section called 'Tokyo Out'.

Music

Tokyo is the only city in Asia where you may have the luxury of seeing up-and-coming performers playing in intimate venues. Check the latest issue of *Metropolis* or *Tokyo Journal* or pick up some flyers at Cisco, Manhattan or Tower Records in Shibuya to see who's playing around town. Ticket prices generally range from ¥5000 to ¥8000, depending on the performer and the venue.

Live Music Tokyo's home-grown live-music scene is disappointing given how vibrant the city is in other quarters.

Overseas and local acts perform regularly at **Club Quattro** (Map 7; ☎ 3477-8750) and **On Air West** (Map 7; ☎ 5458 4646) in Shibuya, and at **Liquid Room** (Map 5; ☎ 3200-6811) in Shinjuku. These are places you book tickets for, however, not places you just turn up at in the hope of catching a good live act.

Crocodile (Map 5; ☎ 3499-5205; admission ¥2000), in Harajuku, has live music seven nights a week. There's usually a cover that includes one drink. It's a spacious place with room for dancing if the music allows it.

Loft (Map 5; ☎ 3365-0698) in Shinjuku is a Tokyo institution. Had they been Japanese, the Rolling Stones would have played here long before they cut their first single. It's smoky, loud and lots of fun on a good night.

Milk (Map 8; ☎ 5458-2826) is down in Ebisu, beneath What the Dickens (see Ebisu & Daikanyama under Pubs & Bars earlier), and has live music on Thursday and Friday nights. Check out the kitchen – there's no food but it's a great place to chat and sip on a gin and tonic between sets.

Roppongi (Map 10) is the place for 'oldies-but-goodies'. **Cavern Club** (☎ 3405-5207; admission ¥1300) hosts flawless I-wanna-hold-your-hand covers by four Japanese mop-heads; **Kento's** (☎ 3401-5755; admission ¥1300.) features 1950s standards.

Bauhaus (Map 10; ☎ 3403-0092; admission ¥1800) is where you go to forget the 1950s and forget the Beatles; it's the place for 1970s and 80s rock covers. The cover includes one drink. Bauhaus is on the 6th floor of the Wada building.

Jazz People take their jazz seriously in Tokyo. For listings of performances, you should check the latest issue of *Tokyo Journal* or *Metropolis*.

Blue Note Tokyo (☎ 3407-5781; admission ¥6000-10,000; open 5.30pm-1.30am Mon-Sat), in Aoyama, is Tokyo's big-name jazz venue. The cover charge keeps the riffraff away and aficionados within spitting distance of the greats of jazz. Take exit B3 from Omotesando subway station and walk down Kotto-dōri towards Nishi Azabu; it's is opposite the Idee store.

Sweet Basil 139 (Map 10; ☎ 5474-0139; admission ¥3000-7000; open 6pm-11pm Mon-Sat), a two-minute walk south of Roppongi station (exit 3), is a big, new space that draws similarly big-name acts and is a competitor to the Blue Note. Roppongi Pit Inn (Map 10; ☎ 3585-1063), also in Roppongi, is another spot to check out.

Cinemas

Shibuya and Shinjuku are Tokyo's cinema meccas, but you'll find cinemas near any major train station. Check the Japan Times, Metropolis or the Tokyo Journal to see what's on. Discounted tickets are sold in the basement of the Tokyo Kōtsū Kaikan (Map 1) building in Ginza, Shinjuku's Studio Alta building (Map 5; 5th floor), Harajuku's Laforet building (Map 6; 1st floor) and Shibuya's 109 Building (Map 7; 2nd floor).

SPECTATOR SPORTS
Sumō

Sumō tournaments at Tokyo's Ryōgoku Kokugikan Stadium (☎ 3623-6111) in Ryōgoku take place in January, May and September and last for 15 days. The best seats are all bought up by those with the right connections, but if you don't mind standing, you can get in for around ¥1000. Tickets can be bought up to a month prior to the tournament, or simply turn up on the day (you'll have to arrive very early, say 6am, to be assured of seats during the last days of a tournament). The stadium is adjacent to Ryōgoku station (Sōbu line), on the northern side of the railway tracks. If you can't go in person, NHK televises sumō from 3.30pm daily during each tournament.

Baseball

Although soccer has made some headway in recent years, baseball remains Japan's most popular team sport. There are two professional leagues, the Central and the Pacific.

The baseball season runs from April until the end of October. Check the Japan Times to see who's playing while you're in town. The cheapest unreserved outfield seats start at ¥1500. The two main places to see baseball in Tokyo are the Tokyo Dome a.k.a. Big Egg (☎ 5800-9999), next to Kōraku-en Amusement Park; and Jingū Kyūjo (☎ 3404-8999), close to JR Shitanomachi station.

SHOPPING

Although Tokyo is a notoriously expensive city, the determined shopper can still come up with a few bargains. Naturally, the best one-stop shopping options are the department stores, which stock virtually everything, including souvenirs. Unless a major sale is on, however, department stores are expensive places to shop.

Antiques & Souvenirs

One of the best places to look for antiques and interesting souvenirs is in the basement of the Hanae Mori building, in Harajuku (Map 6), which has more than 30 antique shops. Not far from here, the Oriental Bazaar (Map 6; ☎ 3400-3933; open daily) is an interesting place to rummage through. It has a wide range of good souvenirs – fans, folding screens, pottery etc – some at very affordable prices.

Another great selection of souvenirs can be found in Ueno at the Tokyo National Museum's gift shop (Map 2; ☎ 3822-1111; Ⓦ www.momat.go.jp; open 10am-4.40pm Sat-Thur, 10am-7.30pm Fri summer, 10am-4.30pm daily rest of year, closed Mon and 28 Dec-7 Jan). In addition to art books,

---

Keitai

Japan has been seriously bitten by the Keitai Denwa (Mobile Phone) bug. With over 40 million in use, there's almost one keitai denwa for every three Japanese. When you're riding a busy train in Japan, you may feel like half of those 40 million keitai denwa are in use around you. When they're not talking on their keitai, it seems that young Japanese are busy programming their automatic dial features or downloading wireless email messages. The latest models feature in-built digital video cameras. Hand-held Internet access is de rigeur.

postcards and the like, it has woodblock prints and *komono* (small arts and crafts) and a variety of other Japanese goods at reasonable prices.

Japanese Dolls Next to JR Asakusabashi station, **Edo-dōri** (Map 3) is the place to go if you're interested in Japanese dolls. Both sides of the road have large numbers of shops specialising in traditional as well as contemporary Japanese dolls.

Other Japanese Goods *Washi* (hand-made paper) is one of the cheaper and more interesting souvenir possibilities. One place that stocks a good selection is **Haibara** *(Map 1; ☎ 5379-1111)* in Nihombashi. All the major department stores have a section devoted to *washi*.

Kamawanu *(Map 8; ☎ 3780-0182; open 11am-7pm daily)*, in Daikanyama, is a little shop specialising in *tenugui*, those ubiquitous Japanese hand-towels that you find in *sentō* and *onsen*. It's also got a limited selection of other craft goods.

Photographic Equipment

Check the Shinjuku section for information on the big camera stores there. Ginza's Harumi-dōri is another place for photographic equipment – there are several good second-hand photographic shops where Japanese gear can often be bought at reasonable prices.

Computer Equipment

Akihabara is the place to go for computer equipment, although the vast majority of offerings are aimed at computers with Japanese operating systems. **T-Zone computers** *(☎ 5209-7501; open 11am-8pm Mon-Fri, 10am-8pm Sat, Sun & holidays)* is one store that stocks a small selection of computers with English operating systems, English-language software and related peripherals. It's on the eastern side of Chūō-dōri, 500m northwest of Akihabara.

Clothes

For general off-the-rack wear, Shinjuku (Map 6) and Shibuya (Map 7) are the best areas to shop around and compare prices. The department stores are good places to look. **Seibu**, **Isetan**, **Marui** and **Parco** have a great mix of youth and mature casual-wear

at reasonable (by Tokyo standards) prices. Stores such as **Takashimaya**, **Matsuzakaya** and **Mitsukoshi** (all Map 1) are more conservative. In Shibuya, in particular, try the three Parco stores and **Seed** (Map 7), a Seibu spin-off that brings a host of boutiques together under one roof. **Venus Fort**, down in Odaiba (Map 11), besides being an attraction in itself, specialises in women's fashion.

Areas like Harajuku (Map 6), Aoyama (Map 6) and Nishi-Azabu (Map 10) are the best places for specialised boutiques.

Finally, if you want to see where the Tokyo girls buy those towering high-heel boots, look no further than Shibuya's **Frontier** *(Map 7; ☎ 3464-4579)* shoe shop – last time we checked it had the mother of all high-heel boots on display outside.

Flea Markets

Flea markets sound like promising places to shop for interesting antiques and souvenirs, but bear in mind that this is Tokyo and there are unlikely to be any real bargains. At the very least, take a look at somewhere like the Oriental Bazaar (see the earlier Antiques & Souvenirs section) and make a note of prices before embarking on a flea-market shopping spree. Tokyo's main flea markets are as follows:

Tōgō-jinja (Map 6) JR Harajuku station; open 6am to 3pm on the 1st, 4th and 5th Sunday of each month

Nogi-jinja Nogi-zaka subway station on the Chiyoda line – the shrine is on Gaien-higashi-dōri; open dawn to dusk on the 2nd Sunday of each month

Hanazono-jinja (Map 5) Close to Isetan department store on the eastern side of Shinjuku station; open 5am to 4pm every Sunday

Music

Shibuya (Map 7) is music central; the area northwest of Shibuya station boasts several shops, including branches of the **Recofan** and **Disk Union** chains, which stock rare and second-hand CDs. The best of the lot is the massive Shibuya branch of **Tower Records** – which has the most extensive range in Tokyo. Even if you're not a music lover, the 7th-floor bookshop is worth a look. The big three, Tower Records, **Virgin** and **HMV**, all have several branches in Tokyo.

For LP wax, try the record stores in Shibuya, most notably **Cisco** *(Map 7;*

☎ 3462-0366) for electronica, and **Manhattan** *(Map 7;* ☎ *3477-7737)* for hip-hop (the latter is worth a trip just to glimpse all the B-Boy poseurs).

Kids' Stuff

Japanese are particularly creative when it comes to finding things to keep their kids occupied, and Tokyo has some great toy shops.

Places to take kids to are **Loft** *(Map 7;* ☎ *3462-3807; open 10am-8pm Sun-Wed, 10am-9pm Thur-Sat)* in Shibuya and **Kiddyland** *(Map 6;* ☎ *3409-3431; open 10am-8pm daily, closed 3rd Tues each month)* in Harajuku. The latter has five floors of stuff that your kids would probably be better off not knowing about. **Hakuhinkan Toy Park** *(Map 1;* ☎ *3571-8008;* W *www.hakuhinkan.co.jp; open 11am-8pm daily)* in Ginza is a big toy shop that has a child-oriented theatre and restaurants on its upper floors.

GETTING THERE & AWAY
Air

With the exception of China Airlines, all international airlines use Narita airport rather than the more conveniently located Haneda airport.

Arrival Immigration and customs procedures are usually straightforward, but they can be time consuming for non-Japanese. Note that Japanese customs officials are probably the most scrupulous in Asia; backpackers arriving from anywhere remotely third-worldish (the Philippines, Thailand etc) can expect some questions and perhaps a thorough search.

You can change money in the customs hall after having cleared customs, and in the arrival hall. The rates are the same as those offered in town.

Narita has two terminals, No 1 and No 2. This doesn't complicate things too much as both have train stations that are connected to JR and Keisei lines. The one you arrive at will depend on the airline you are flying with. Both terminals have clear English signposting for train and limousine bus services. The main information counter for foreign travellers is the **TIC** *(*☎ *0476-34-6251)*, on the 1st floor of Terminal 2. There's another information counter, in Terminal 1, that can handle most questions.

Departure Be sure to check which terminal your flight leaves from, and give yourself plenty of time to get out to Narita.

Train

All major JR lines radiate from Tokyo station; northbound trains stop at Ueno station, which, like Tokyo station is conveniently on the JR Yamanote line. Private lines – which are often cheaper and quicker for making day trips out of Tokyo – start from various stations around Tokyo. With the exception of the Tōbu Nikkō line, which starts in Asakusa, all private lines originate somewhere on the Yamanote line.

For fares to major cities from Tokyo, see the table in the Train section of the Getting Around chapter.

Shinkansen There are three *shinkansen* (bullet train) lines that connect Tokyo with the rest of Japan: the Tōkaidō line, which passes through central Honshū, changing its name along the way to the San-yō line before terminating at Hakata in northern Kyūshū; the Tōhoku line, which runs northeast via Utsunomiya and Sendai as far as Morioka, with the Yamagata branch heading from Fukushima to Yamagata and the Akita branch heading from Morioka to Akita; and the Jōetsu line, which runs north to Niigata, with the Nagano branch heading from Takasaki to Nagano-shi.

Of these lines, the one most likely to be used by visitors to Japan is the Tōkaidō line, as it passes through Kyoto and Osaka in the Kansai region. All three *shinkansen* lines start at Tokyo station, though the Tōhoku and Jōetsu lines make a stop at Ueno station.

Other JR Lines The regular Tōkaidō line serves the stations that the Tōkaidō *shinkansen* line zips through without stopping. Trains start at Tokyo station and pass through Shimbashi and Shinagawa stations on the way out of town. There are *kyūkyō* (express) services to Yokohama and to Izu-hantō via Atami, and from there trains continue – very slowly – to Nagoya, Kyoto and Osaka.

Northbound trains start in Ueno. The Takasaki line goes to Kumagaya and, of course, Takasaki, with onward connections from Takasaki to Niigata. The Tōhoku line

TOKYO

follows the Takasaki line as far north as Ōmiya, from where it heads to the far north of Honshū via Sendai and Aomori. Getting to Sendai without paying any express surcharges will involve changes at Utsunomiya and Fukushima. For those intent on saving the expense of a night's accommodation, there are also overnight services.

Private Lines The private lines generally service Tokyo's sprawling suburbia. The Tōkyū Tōyoko line, running between Shibuya station and Yokohama; the Odakyū line, running from Shinjuku to Odawara and the Hakone region; the Tōbu Nikkō line, running from Asakusa to Nikkō; and the Seibu Shinjuku line from Ikebukuro to Kawagoe are the most useful.

Bus

Long-distance buses are generally little or no cheaper than trains, but are sometimes a good alternative for long-distance trips to areas serviced by expressways.

There are a number of express buses running between Tokyo, Kyoto and Osaka. Overnight buses leave at 10pm from the Yaesu side of Tokyo station and arrive at Kyoto and Osaka between 6am and 7am the following day. They cost from ¥8000 to ¥8500 (if you're coming back, you'll save money by buying a return ticket). The buses are a JR service and can be booked at one of the green windows at a JR station.

Buses also run from Tokyo station to Nara, Kōbe, Hiroshima, Fukui, Shimoda, Nagano, Yamagata, Takamatsu, Sendai, Morioka and Aomori. From Shinjuku station there are buses running to the Fuji and Hakone regions, including, for Mt Fuji climbers, direct services to the 5th station (see Climbing Mt Fuji in the Around Tokyo chapter). The Shinjuku long-distance bus station is across from the west exit of Shinjuku station.

Ferry

A ferry journey can be a great, relatively inexpensive way to get from Tokyo to other parts of the country. Prices given here are for 2nd-class travel.

From Tokyo, there are long-distance ferry services to Kōchi (☎ 3578-1127; ¥10,600) and Tokushima in Shikoku and Kitakyūshū (Ocean Ferry; ☎ 3567-0971; ¥8610 and ¥12,600 respectively) in northern Kyūshū;

and to Naha (☎ 5643-6170; ¥22,000) on Okinawa. Long-distance ferry services to Hokkaido are no longer available from Tokyo, however departures from Ibaragi prefecture to Tomakomai in Hokkaidō are (Shousen Mitsui Ferry; ☎ 5501-1855; ¥6400; or Higashi Nihon Ferry; ☎ 3535-0489; ¥6400).

GETTING AROUND

Tokyo has an excellent public transport system. Everything of note is conveniently close to a subway or JR station. Bus services are difficult to use if you don't read kanji (character-script), but the average visitor to Tokyo won't need the buses anyway.

To/From Narita Airport

Narita airport is 66km from central Tokyo, and is used by almost all the international airlines but by only a small number of domestic operators. Travel to or from Tokyo takes from 50 minutes to 1½ hours or more, depending on your mode of transport and destination in town.

Depending on where you're going, it is generally cheaper and faster to travel into Tokyo by train than by limousine bus. However rail users will probably need to change trains somewhere, and this can be confusing on a jetlagged first visit. Limousine buses provide a hassle-free direct route to a number of Tokyo's top hotels (you don't have to be staying at the hotels to use these buses).

Train There are three rail services between Tokyo and both terminals at Narita airport: the private Keisei line (☎ 3621-2242; W www.keisei.co.jp); the JR Narita Express N'EX (W www.jreast.co.jp/e/index.html for information; W www.world.eki-net.com for reservations); and the JR 'Airport Narita' service. The Keisei service arrives at Nippori and Ueno, from either of which you can change to the Yamanote line for access to Ikebukuro, Shinjuku and other destinations. N'EX and the 'Airport Narita' service arrives at Tokyo station (from where you can change to almost any line). N'EX also runs to Shinjuku, Ikebukuro and Yokohama.

The Keisei line has two services: the Keisei Skyliner, which does the trip between Narita and Ueno (¥1920, one hour), and the Keisei tokkyū (limited express; ¥1000, one hour and 11 minutes). Times and fares to and from Nippori are marginally less. Tokkyū services are much more frequent than the Skyliner, and what's another 11 minutes?

The N'EX services are fast, extremely comfortable and include amenities like drink-dispensing machines and telephones. To or from Tokyo station costs ¥2940 and takes 55 minutes; to Shinjuku station it costs ¥3110 and takes 1½ hours; to or from Ikebukuro station costs ¥3110 and takes one hour and 40 minutes; and to or from Yokohama station costs ¥4180 and takes 1½ hours. N'EX services run approximately half-hourly between 7am and 10pm, but Ikebukuro services are very infrequent; in most cases you will be better off heading to Shinjuku and taking the Yamanote line from there. Seats are reserved only, but can be bought immediately before departure if they are available.

'Airport Narita' trains cost ¥1280 and take 1½ hours to or from Tokyo. Trains only run approximately once an hour.

The Keikyū rail line runs between Narita and Haneda airports (¥1560, 1¾ hours), with several direct trains a day.

Limousine Bus Don't be misled by the name; they're just ordinary buses and take 1½ to two hours (depending on the traffic) to travel between Narita airport and a number of major hotels around Tokyo. Check departure times before buying your ticket, as services are not all that frequent. The fare to or from hotels around Asakusa is ¥3000, while to or from Ikebukuro, Akasaka, Ginza, Shiba, Shinagawa, Shinjuku or Haneda airport it is ¥3000. There is also a direct service between the airport and Yokohama (¥3500, two hours).

To/From Haneda Airport
Most domestic flights and China Airlines to/from Taiwan use the convenient Haneda airport.

Transport to or from Haneda airport is a simple matter, as the **Tokyo Monorail** (W www.tokyo-monorail.co.jp) runs from 5.15am to 11.15pm between the airport and Hamamatsu-chō station on the JR Yamanote line with departures every 10 minutes (¥470, 22 minutes).

Taxis from the airport to places around central Tokyo cost around ¥6000. Limousine

buses connect Haneda with TCAT (¥900), Tokyo station (¥900), Ikebukuro and Shinjuku (¥1200) and several other destinations in Tokyo.

There is a direct bus service between Haneda and Narita (¥3000, two hours).

To/From TCAT
Leaving Tokyo, you can get your boarding pass, check your luggage and even clear immigration at **TCAT** (Tokyo City Air Terminal; W www.tcat-hakozaki.co.jp) before taking the bus out to the airport. This service is available to passengers flying on most major airlines; call your airline to check. TCAT is next to Suitengu-mae subway station on the Hanzōmon line, in Nihombashi.

Limousine buses run between Narita and TCAT every 15 minutes (5.45am to 8.50pm, ¥2900). The journey takes about an hour but you may want to leave extra time in case of traffic. There is a frequent shuttle-bus service between TCAT and Tokyo station (¥200), which departs from the Yaesu side of Tokyo station.

Train
Tokyo has a crowded but otherwise awesome rail network. Between the JR and private above-ground and subway lines, you can get to almost anywhere in town quickly and cheaply. But night owls beware: it closes from around midnight until 5am or 6am.

Avoiding Tokyo's rush hour is not often possible, though things tend to quiet down from 10am to 4pm.

JR Lines Undoubtedly, the most useful line in Tokyo is the JR Yamanote line, which does a 35km loop around the city, taking in most of the important areas. You can do the whole circuit in an hour for the ¥130 minimum charge – a great introduction to the city. Another useful above-ground JR route is the Chūō line, which cuts across the centre of town between Shinjuku and Akihabara. Tickets are transferable on all JR lines.

The major JR stations (Tokyo, Shibuya, Shinjuku, Ikebukuro and Ueno) are massive places with thronging crowds and never enough English signposting. Just working out how to buy a ticket can drive a newcomer to the edge of madness. If it's a

TOKYO

JR train you're taking, look for the JR sign (usually green) and the rows of vending machines. If you don't know the fare, put in ¥130 and push the top left-hand button (the one with no price on it). When you get to your destination you can pay the balance at the ticket gate. English signposting points the way to the railway platforms.

If you're going to be doing a lot of travelling on JR lines (even just the Yamanote line) we strongly suggest buying a JR 'Suica' card. These are like train passes that you can insert directly into automated ticket wickets (the correct fare will be deducted automatically). Suica cards come in denominations of ¥1000, ¥3000 and ¥5000 and can be purchased from ticket machines marked with, er, a large watermelon and a penguin, or from ticket windows. Buy one and you'll never go back to waiting in ticket lines and fumbling for change.

For English-language train information, you can call the **JR English Information line** (☎ 3423 0111; open 10am-6pm Mon-Fri).

Subway Lines There are 12 subway lines in Tokyo (13 if you include the Yūraku-chō New Line), of which eight are TRTA lines and four are TOEI lines (**W** www.tokyometro.go.jp). This is not particularly important to remember, as the subway services are essentially the same, have good connections from one to another and can be used with the same subway pass or special transfer tickets. Train lines are colour-coded on the excellent maps that are available free at subway stations and tourist information counters around town.

Ticket prices start at ¥160 for short hops, but if your trip involves a change of train you can be sure it will cost upwards of ¥190. As with the JR system, if you are in doubt at all (there are still subway stations in Tokyo where the only pricing maps are in Japanese), buy a ticket for ¥160 and upgrade if necessary at your destination.

Unless you purchase a special ticket (and this would require Japanese-reading ability), you'll have to buy a separate ticket when you switch from TRTA and TOEI subway lines.

The subway equivalent of the JR Suika card is the SF Metro card. It comes in denominations of ¥1000, ¥3000 and ¥5000 and can be used directly in the automatic ticket gates. Best of all, it's good for travel on both subway systems and saves you time when switching between the two systems.

Discount Tickets & Train Passes There are no massively discounted tickets available for travel around Tokyo. The best deal is the Tokyo Combination Ticket, which allows travel on any subway, tram, TOEI bus or JR train in the metropolitan area until the last train of the day. It costs ¥1580 and is available from subway and JR stations and even post offices.

Bus
Pick up a copy of the free *TOEI Bus Route Guide* from the TIC. When using a bus, it pays to have the name of your destination written in Japanese so that you can either show the driver or match up the kanji with the route map yourself (there's not much in the way of English signposting on buses or at bus stops). It's a flat ¥200 for city destinations.

Car
For those who enjoy a challenge. You'll need an international licence. Three companies that usually have English-speakers on hand are **Dollar Rent-a-Car** (☎ 3567-2818), **Hertz** (☎ 0120-489-882) and **Toyota Rent-a-Lease** (☎ 0070-8000-10000). Typical rates for small cars are ¥8000 or ¥9000 for the first day, and ¥5500 to ¥7000 each day thereafter. On top of this there is a ¥1000-per-day insurance fee. Mileage is usually unlimited.

Taxi
Taxis are so expensive that you should only use them when there is no alternative. Rates start at ¥630, which gives you 2km (1.5km after 11pm), after which the meter starts to clock an additional ¥80 for every 347m; you also click up ¥80 for every two minutes you sit idly gazing at the scenery in a typical Tokyo traffic jam.

Around Tokyo 東京近郊

Tokyo itself may seem like an endless sea of concrete, but there are some surprisingly beautiful oases of green only an hour or so away by train. Apart from the Izu-shotō (also known as the Izu-nana-tō, or Izu Seven Islands) and the islands of Ogasawara-shotō, all the attractions in this chapter can be visited on day trips from Tokyo, although in some cases it would be worth staying away overnight.

The information in this chapter begins with destinations to the north of Tokyo and works anticlockwise to those in the east. The Izu-shotō and Ogasawara-shotō are treated separately at the end of the chapter.

SUGGESTED ITINERARIES

Foremost among the cultural attractions around Tokyo are Nikkō and Kamakura, both of which rate highly among Japan's must-sees. Of these, Nikkō should be given priority, since nowhere else in Japan can compete with it for sheer visual impact. Kamakura, attractive though it is, can be missed *if* you plan a visit to Kyoto, which offers similar attractions on a much grander scale.

Nature lovers will enjoy the hikes in nearby Chichibu-Tama National Park or the ones in the more distant Oze region. And those hankering for a view of Mt Fuji will get an eyeful, providing the weather cooperates, in the lovely Fuji Go-ko (Fuji Five Lakes) region or the popular Hakone area (we suggest the former unless you enjoy a full tourist circus).

If *onsen* (mineral hot springs) are your thing, you can do an *onsen meguri* (hot-spring tour) of the peninsula, Izu-hantō, which also boasts pleasant mountain scenery and a rugged coastline. In the warmer months, you can swim in the Pacific off some of the peninsula's beaches.

Yokohama, south of Tokyo, is a cosmopolitan port city with a fascinating China-town and ebullient nightlife.

Other destinations around Tokyo include Narita, a pleasant temple-town near the New Tokyo International Airport; Kawa-saki, home of Nihon Minka-en, an open-air museum of traditional Japanese houses; and Mito, home to one of Japan's three most famous gardens.

Highlights

- Head into the northern hills to Nikkō, a fabulous complex of overwrought gilded shrines and temples quite unlike anything else in Japan

- Spend a day exploring the Buddhist temples of Kamakura, many of them tucked away in quiet, wooded groves.

- Hike the rugged hills of Chichibu-Tama National Park

- Take an *onsen* (hot spring) tour of Izu-hantō, a lovely peninsula southwest of Tokyo

- Journey to the beautiful Fuji Go-ko region for spectacular views of Mt Fuji; better still, in season, climb the mountain itself

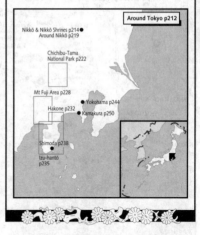

Around Tokyo p212

Nikkō & Nikkō Shrines p214 ● Around Nikkō p219

Chichibu-Tama National Park p222

Mt Fuji Area p228 ● Yokohama p244

Hakone p232 ● Kamakura p250

Shimoda p238

Izu-hantō p235

Lastly, the semitropical Izu-shotō or the more distant Ogasawara-shotō might lure the adventurous traveller with their good beaches and warm climate.

North of Tokyo

North of Tokyo are the prefectures Saitama-ken, Gunma-ken and Tochigi-ken, which include numerous places of interest, such as the Chichibu-Tama National Park, hot springs and the temple- and shrine-centre of Nikkō.

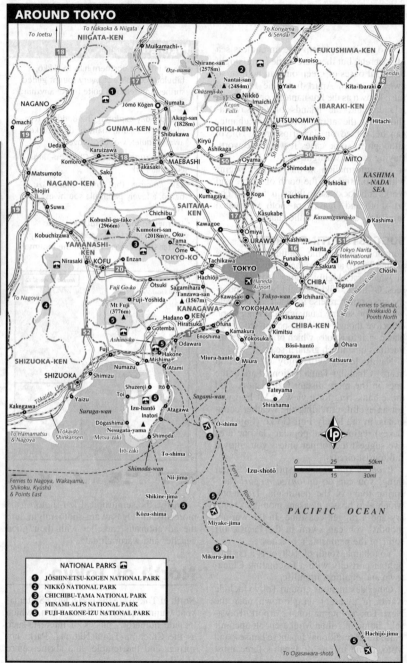

AROUND TOKYO

To Joetsu
To Nakaoka & Niigata
NIIGATA-KEN
Muikamachi
18
17
Oze-numa
Shirane-san
(2578m)
❷
Nantai-san
▲ (2484m)
Chūzenji-ko
Kegon
Falls
Imaichi
Nikkō
To Koriyama
& Sendai
FUKUSHIMA-KEN
Kuroiso
To
Sendai
6
Yaita
Kita-Ibaraki
IBARAKI-KEN
Hitachi

NAGANO
❶
Jōmō Kōgen
Numata
GUNMA-KEN
Akagi-san
(1828m)
Shibukawa
Joetsu Shinkansen
Asama Shinkansen
Omachi
19
Ueda
Karuizawa
Komoro
Saku
18
Takasaki
MAEBASHI
Kiryū
Ashikaga
TOCHIGI-KEN
Oyama
50
UTSUNOMIYA
Mashiko
Shimodate
50
MITO
Ishioka
Tōhoku Shinkansen
Tōhoku Line
KASHIMA-NADA SEA

NAGANO-KEN
Matsumoto
Shiojiri
Suwa
19
Kobuchizawa
YAMANASHI-KEN
Nirasaki
KŌFU
20
Enzan
Kobushi-ga-take
(2966m)
Kumotori-san
(2018m)
Oku-Tama
Ōme
Chichibu
SAITAMA-KEN
Kawagoe
TOKYO-KO
Tachikawa
Hachiōji
Kumagaya
17
Kasukabe
Koga
Tsuchiura
Kasumigaura-ko
6
URAWA
Omiya
Kashiwa
Narita
16
51
Tokyo Narita International Airport
Sakura
Funabashi
Chōshi
Kashima
Kujukuri-hama Coast

❸
To Nagoya
❹
52
Ōtsuki
Sagamihara
Fuji Go-ko
Tanzawa-san
▲ (1567m)
Mt Fuji
(3776m)
❺
▲
Fuji-Yoshida
Gotemba
Hadano
Hiratsuka
Ofuna
Enoshima
KANAGAWA-KEN
TOKYO
Haneda Airport
Kawasaki
YOKOHAMA
Tokyo-wan
Ichihara
Goi
Kisarazu
Kimitsu
Yokosuka
Kamakura
Miura-hantō
Miura
CHIBA
Tōgane
Ferries to Sendai, Hokkaidō & Points North
CHIBA-KEN
Bōsō-hantō
Ōhara

SHIZUOKA-KEN
SHIZUOKA
Shimizu
Ashino-ko
❺
Fuji
Hakone
Mishima
Numazu
Atami
Odawara
Miura-hantō
Kamogawa
Katsuura
Tōkaidō Line
Kakegawa
Yaizu
Suruga-wan
Shuzenji
Itō
❺
Toi
Izu-hantō
Inatori
Atagawa
Sagami-wan
Ō-shima
❺
Tateyama
Shirahama
To Hamamatsu & Nagoya
Tōkaidō Shinkansen
Dōgashima
Nesugata-yama
▲
Metsu-zaki
Shimoda
Irō-zaki
Shimoda-wan
To-shima
Nii-jima
Izu-shotō

0   25   50km
0   15   30mi

Ferries to Nagoya, Wakayama, Shikoku, Kyūshū & Points East

Shikine-jima
❺
Kōzu-shima
❺
Miyake-jima
Ferry Routes
PACIFIC OCEAN

❺
Mikura-jima

NATIONAL PARKS
❶ JŌSHIN-ETSU-KOGEN NATIONAL PARK
❷ NIKKŌ NATIONAL PARK
❸ CHICHIBU-TAMA NATIONAL PARK
❹ MINAMI-ALPS NATIONAL PARK
❺ FUJI-HAKONE-IZU NATIONAL PARK

❺ Hachijō-jima
To Ogasawara-shotō

NIKKŌ 日光
☎ 0288 • pop 17,368

Nikkō is one of Japan's major tourist attractions, due to its splendid shrines and temples – it's worth trying to slot Nikkō into even the most whirlwind tour of Japan. Note, however, that Nikkō can get extremely crowded, so it's best to visit early on a weekday to avoid the hordes (most of the attractions are open from 8am to 5pm, or until 4pm from November to March).

History
Nikkō's history as a sacred site stretches back to the middle of the 8th century, when the Buddhist priest Shōdō (735–817) established a hermitage there. For many years it was a famous training centre for Buddhist monks, before declining into obscurity. That is, until it was chosen as the site for the mausoleum of Tokugawa Ieyasu, the warlord who took control of all Japan and established the shōgunate that ruled for 250 years until the Meiji Restoration ended the feudal era.

Tokugawa Ieyasu was laid to rest among Nikkō's towering cedars in 1617, but it was his grandson Tokugawa Iemitsu who, in 1634, commenced work on the shrine that can be seen today. The original shrine, Tōshō-gū, was completely rebuilt using an army of some 15,000 artisans from all over Japan. The work on the shrine and mausoleum took two years to complete and the results continue to receive mixed reviews.

Tōshō-gū was constructed as a memorial to a warlord who devoted his life to conquering Japan. Tokugawa Ieyasu was a man of considerable determination and was not above sacrificing a few scruples in order to achieve his aims. He is attributed with having had his wife and eldest son executed because, at a certain point, it was politically expedient for him to do so. More than anything else, the grandeur of Nikkō is intended to inspire awe; it is a display of wealth and power by a family that for nearly three centuries was the supreme arbiter of power in Japan.

Information
First stop in Nikkō should be the **Kyōdo Center tourist information office** (☎ 53-3795; open 8.30am-5pm daily) which has a wealth of useful pamphlets and maps. There

is another **tourist information office** (☎ 53-4511) in Tōbu Nikkō station, where you can pick up a town map.

It's a 30-minute walk uphill from the Japan Railways (JR) and Tōbu stations to the shrine area. Bus Nos 1 and 2 go to the Shin-kyō bus stop for ¥190.

Hikers should pick up a copy of *Yumoto-Chūzenji Area Hiking Guide* which has maps and information on local flora and fauna. It costs a pittance (¥150) and is available from some of the pensions in the area, as well as at the information counters in Nikkō.

Tickets Although you can buy separate tickets to Nikkō's attractions, it makes sense to buy a 'combination ticket' for ¥1000, valid for two days. This covers entry to the temple, Rinnō-ji, the shrines, Tōshō-gū and Futarasan-jinja, but not to the Nemuri-Neko (Sleeping Cat) in Tōshō-gū, a sight that will set you back an extra ¥500. Even if you do include a visit to the Nemuri-Neko, buying a combination ticket is still much cheaper than buying each of the tickets separately.

Shin-kyō 神橋
Buddhist monk Shōdō Shōnin, who first established a hermitage in Nikkō in 782, was carried across the river at this point on the backs of two huge serpents, no less. Today's bridge, a reconstruction of the 17th-century original, is currently being refinished.

Rinnō-ji 輪王寺
The original Tendai-sect Rinnō-ji was founded 1200 years ago by Shōdō Shōnin. Sambutsu-dō (Three Buddha Hall) has huge gold-lacquered images, the most impressive of which is of Kannon, the goddess of mercy and compassion. The central image of the *senjū* (1000-armed Kannon) is Amida Nyorai (one of the primal deities in the Mahayana Buddhist cannon), flanked by *batō* (a horse-headed Kannon), whose special domain is the animal kingdom.

Hōmotsu-den (*Treasure Hall; admission ¥300*), also in the temple grounds, has a collection of treasures associated with the temple, but admission is not included in the combination ticket (see Tickets in the earlier information section).

AROUND TOKYO

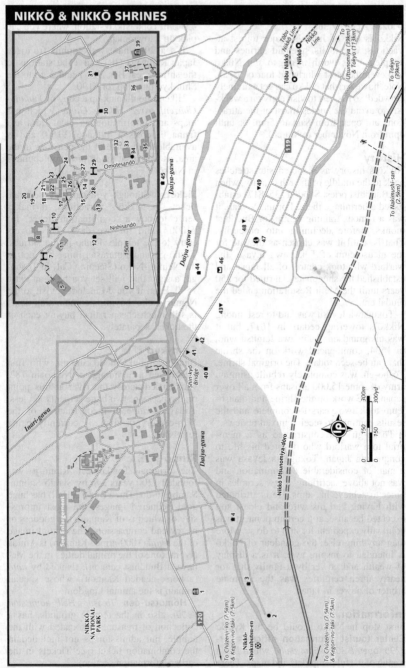

NIKKŌ & NIKKŌ SHRINES

NIKKŌ & NIKKŌ SHRINES

PLACES TO STAY

3 Annex Turtle
   Hotori-An
   アネックスタートル
   ほとり庵
4 Turtle Inn Nikkō
   タートルイン日光
12 Nikkō Pension Green
   Age Inn
   日光ペンション
   グリーンエイジイン
30 Hotel Seikōen
   ホテル清晃苑
31 Nikkō Tōkan-sō
   Ryokan
   日光東観荘
40 Nikkō Kanaya
   Hotel
   日光金谷ホテル
44 Nikkō Daiyagawa
   Youth Hostel
   日光大谷川ユース
   ホステル
45 Nikkō Kōryū Sokushin
   Centre
   日光交流促進センター

PLACES TO EAT

41 Sawamoto
   澤本
42 Hippari Dako
   ひっぱり凧
43 Eddoko
   江戸っ子
48 Hi No Kuruma
   ひの車
49 Yōrō-no-Taki
   養老の滝

OTHER

1 The Nikko Tamozawa
   Goyotei
   日光博物館
2 Ganman-Ga-Fuchi Abyss
   含満ヶ淵
5 Taiyūin-byō
   大献院廟
6 Yasha-mon
   夜叉門
7 Niten-mon
   二天門
8 Futarasan-jinja
   二荒山神社
9 Kara-mon
   唐門
10 Bronze Torii
   銅鳥居
11 Hokke-dō
   法華堂
13 Treasury
   宝物殿
14 Ticket Office
   きっぷ売り場
15 Shinkyūsha
   神厩舎
16 Drum Tower
   鼓楼
17 Honji-dō
   本地堂
18 Tōshō-gū
   東照宮
19 Tomb of Ieyasu
   奥社（徳川家康の墓）
20 Honden
   本殿
21 Honden
   本殿

22 Haiden
   拝殿
23 Sakashita-mon
   坂下門
24 Nemuri-Neko
   眠猫
25 Yōmei-mon
   陽明門
26 Sanjinko
   三神庫
27 Omote-mon
   表門
28 Pagoda (5 storeys)
   五重塔
29 Granite Torii
   一の鳥居
32 Gohhōten-dō
   護法天堂
33 Sambutsu-dō
   三仏堂
34 Ticket Office
   きっぷ売り場
35 Rinnō-ji
   輪王寺
36 Nanshō-in
   南照院
37 Shihonryū-ji
   四本竜寺
38 Hongū
   本宮
39 Kosugi Hōan Museum
   of Art
   小杉放庵
46 Nikkō Post Office
   日光郵便局
47 Kyōdo Center Tourist
   Office
   日光郷土センター

Tōshō-gū 東照宮

A huge stone torii (Shintō shrine entrance gate) marks the entrance to this shrine, while to the left is a five-storey pagoda, originally dating from 1650 but reconstructed in 1818. The pagoda has no foundations and is said to contain a long suspended pole that swings like a pendulum, restoring equilibrium in the event of an earthquake.

The true entrance to the shrine is through the torii at the gate, Omote-mon, protected on either side by Deva kings. Directly through the entrance are the **Sanjinko** (Three Sacred Storehouses). On the upper storey of the last storehouse are imaginative relief carvings of elephants by an artist who famously had never seen the real thing. To the left of the entrance is **Shinkyūsha** (Sacred Stable), a suitably plain building housing a carved white horse. The stable's only

adornment is an allegorical series of **relief carvings** depicting the life cycle of the monkey. They include the famous 'hear no evil, see no evil, speak no evil' threesome who have become emblematic of Nikkō.

Just beyond the stable is a granite font at which, in accordance with Shintō practice, worshippers cleanse themselves by washing their hands and rinsing their mouths. Next to the gate is a **sacred library** containing 7000 Buddhist scrolls and books; it is not open to the public.

Pass through another torii, climb another flight of stairs, and on the left and right are a drum tower and a belfry. To the left of the drum tower is **Honji-dō**. The hall has a huge ceiling-painting of a dragon in flight known as the Roaring Dragon. A monk in attendance will bang two wooden sticks together to demonstrate the strange acoustic properties of the hall; the echo is said to sound like the roar of a dragon – something of a stretch of the imagination.

Next comes **Yōmei-mon**, which, in contrast with the minimalism that is generally considered the essence of Japanese art, is crowded with detail. Animals, mythical and otherwise, jostle for your attention from among the glimmering gold leaf and red lacquerwork. The walls are decorated with intricate patterning, coloured relief carvings and paintings of, among other things, flowers, dancing girls, mythical beasts and Chinese sages. The overall effect is more Chinese than Japanese, and it's a grand spectacle, no matter what the critics say. Worrying that its perfection might arouse envy in the gods, those responsible for its construction had the final supporting pillar on the left-hand side placed upside down as a deliberate error.

Through the Yōmei-mon and to the right is **Nemuri-Neko**. While the sleeping cat is famous throughout Japan for its lifelike appearance, you may feel let down by this tiny wooden feline. **Sakashita-mon** here opens onto a path that climbs up through towering cedars to **Ieyasu's tomb**, a relatively simple affair. If you are using the combination ticket, you will have to pay an extra ¥500 to see the cat and the tomb.

To the left of Yōmei-mon is the **Jin-yōsha**, a storage depot for Nikkō's *mikoshi* (portable shrines) which come into action during the May and October festivals. The **Honden** (Main Hall) and **Haiden** (Hall of Worship) can also be seen in the enclosure.

Futarasan-jinja 二荒山神社

Shōdō Shōnin founded this shrine. It's dedicated to the mountain Nantai, the mountain's consort, Nyotai, and their mountainous progeny Tarō. It's essentially a repeat performance of Tōshō-gū on a smaller scale, but worth a visit all the same.

Taiyūin-byō 大院廟

Taiyūin-byō enshrines Ieyasu's grandson Iemitsu (1604–51) and is very much a smaller version of Tōshō-gū. The smaller size gives it a less extravagant air and it has been suggested that it is more aesthetically worthy than its larger neighbour. Many of the features to be seen in the Tōshō-gū are replicated on a smaller scale: the storehouses,

drum tower and Chinese gate, for example. The shrine also has a wonderful setting in a quiet grove of cryptomeria. Entry is included in the combination ticket (see Tickets under Information earlier).

Kosugi Hōan Museum of Art
小杉放庵美術館

Back toward the river, not far from Nikkō's shrines and temples, is the Kosugi Hōan Museum of Art (☎ 50-1200; admission ¥700; open 9.30am-5pm Tues-Sun). This modern museum holds a collection of landscape paintings by local artist Kosugi Hōan (1920–64). This is a good rainy-day option in Nikkō.

Gamman-Ga-Fuchi Abyss 含満ヶ淵
If the crowds of Nikkō have left you yearning for a little quiet, take the 20-minute walk over to Gamman-Ga-Fuchi Abyss, a collection of statues of Jizō, the patron saint of the souls of departed children, set along a wooded path. One of the statues midway along is known as the Bake-jizō, who mocks travellers foolish enough to try to count all the Jizō (they're said to be uncountable).

The Nikkō Tamozawa Goyōtei
日光田母沢御用邸

The Nikkō Tamozawa Goyōtei (☎ 536767; admission ¥500; open 9am-4.30pm Wed-Mon), where the Emperor spent WWII, has recently been painstakingly restored to its former glory and is well worth a visit.

Special Events
On 16 and 17 April, **Yayoi Matsuri** – a festival procession of portable shrines – is held at Futarasan-jinja.

Tōshō-gū Grand Festival, on 17 and 18 May, is Nikkō's most important annual festival. It features horseback archery (on the first day) and a 1000-strong costumed re-enactment of the delivery of Ieyasu's remains to Nikkō (on the second day).

Tōshō-gū Autumn Festival is held on 17 October and needs only the equestrian archery to be an autumnal repeat of the performance in May.

Places to Stay
Nikkō has lots of good-value lodgings and most places are used to foreign guests.

Thus, it's a good place for a quick night out of Tokyo, and staying the night makes sense if you want to combine a visit to Nikkō with the sights of the lake, Chūzenji-ko and Yumoto Onsen.

Places to Stay – Budget

Nikkō Daiyagawa Youth Hostel (☎ 54-1974; W www.jyh.or.jp; dorm beds ¥2730; breakfast/dinner ¥420/840, closed 25 Dec-1 Jan) is a friendly, comfortable place. It's behind the post office opposite the Shiyakusho-mae bus stop. Check-in is 4pm.

Nikkō Kōryū Sokushin Center (☎ 54-1013; family room with/without bath & toilet ¥5000/4100) is Nikkō's best budget option, with excellent, clean facilities. It is a 10-minute walk from the other hostel on the other side of the river. Check-in is 4pm.

Places to Stay – Mid-Range & Top End

Turtle Inn Nikkō (☎ 53-3168; W http://www .sunfield.ne.jp/~turtle; rooms per person with/without bath ¥5000/4200) is one of the more popular pensions in Nikkō. Breakfast/dinner costs ¥1000/2000 and check-in is 3pm. From the station, take a bus to the Sōgō-kaikan-mae bus stop, backtrack around 50m to the fork in the road and follow the river for around five minutes.

Annex Turtle Hotori-An (☎ 53-3663; rooms ¥5800) is clean and new and further west, over the river but on the same road as Turtle Inn. Japanese- and Western-style rooms are the same price (again there's a seasonal variation). Check-in is 2pm. Breakfast/dinner for ¥1000/2000 are served at its main building, the Turtle Inn.

Nikkō Pension Green Age Inn (☎ 53-3636; rooms per person with/without meals ¥9800/5800) is a pleasant place which looks like a Tudor mansion. The 'with meals' rate includes two meals. Check-in is 3pm.

Nikkō Tōkan-sō Ryokan (☎ 54-0611; rooms per person ¥7000-14,000, minimum 2 people) is clean and spacious and might be a good spot for your ryokan (traditional Japanese inn) experience (if it's not fully booked by bus tours). Rates include two meals and check-in is 3pm.

Hotel Seikōen (☎ 53-5555; rooms per person from ¥13,800) is clean and rates include two meals. Both Western- and Japanese-style rooms are available. Check-in is 2pm.

Nikkō Kanaya Hotel (☎ 54-0001; twins ¥13,000-40,000, doubles ¥15,000-22,000) is not far from the bridge Shin-kyō, and is Nikkō's oldest and classiest hotel. It is good value too. Check-in is 3pm.

Places to Eat

Many travellers staying in Nikkō prefer to eat at their lodgings, but there are also a number of places on the main road between the stations and the shrine area.

Yōrō-no-Taki (☎ 53-4862; dinner ¥2000; open 5pm-11.30pm Wed-Mon) is the only decent izakaya (pub) with cheap beer and a good selection of meals.

Hippari Dako (☎ 53-2933; lunch ¥800; open 11am-7pm daily) is something of a Nikkō institution among foreign travellers, judging from all the testimonials and business cards affixed to the walls. There's an English menu with filling sets of yakitori (chicken on skewers) and rice for ¥800 and yaki-udon (fried noodles) for the same price.

Other options include the following: **Edokko** (☎ 54-0293; lunch ¥1300; open 11am-3pm daily) which does tempura soba (noodle soup with lightly battered seafood and vegetables) for ¥850; **Hi No Kuruma** (☎ 54-2062; meals around ¥2000; open noon-3pm & 5pm-9pm Thur-Tues) an inexpensive okonomiyaki (meat, seafood and vegetables in a cabbage-and-vegetable batter) place; and **Sawamoto** (☎ 54-0163; meals around ¥2000; open 11am-2pm & 5pm-7pm) a good unagi (eel) specialist that serves tasty unagi sets for ¥1700. Sawamoto is closed two or three days a month according to the owner's whim.

There are also enclosed stalls just off Omotesandō selling soba noodles and the like for around ¥800.

Getting There & Away

The best way to visit Nikkō is via the Tōbu-Nikkō line from Asakusa station in Tokyo. The station is in the basement of the Tōbu department store (it's well signposted from the subway). All seats are reserved on tokkyū (limited express) trains (¥2740, one hour 50 minutes) but you can usually get tickets just before setting out. Trains run every 30 minutes or so from 7.30am to 10am; and hourly after 10am. Kaisoku trains (¥1320, two hours, hourly from 6.20am to 4.30pm) require no reservation.

AROUND TOKYO

For trains other than the *tokkyū*, you *may* have to change at Imaichi.

Travelling by JR is costly and time consuming – it's really only of interest to those with a Japan Rail Pass. The quickest way is to take the *shinkansen* (bullet train) from Tokyo to Utsunomiya (¥4510, 50 minutes) and change there for an ordinary train to Nikkō (¥740, 45 minutes).

Nikkō-Kinugawa Free Pass This pass may save you money on a multiday trip around Nikkō. It's valid for two days, costs ¥4940 and is available from Tōbu railways in Asakusa. It includes transport from Asa-kusa to Nikkō (but not the express surcharge) and all bus costs between Nikkō and Chūzenji, Yumoto Onsen, Kinugawa, the plateau of Kirifuri-kōgen, and Ikari-ko as well as cable-car fares around Chūzenji-ko (see Around Nikkō for information on Chūzenji and Yumoto).

AROUND NIKKŌ 日光周辺
☎ 0288

Nikkō is part of the Nikkō National Park, which covers 1402 sq km, sprawling over Fukushima, Tochigi, Gunma and Niigata prefectures. It is a mountainous area, complete with extinct volcanoes, and lakes, waterfalls and marshlands. There are good hiking opportunities in the area and some remote hot-springs resorts.

Yashio-no-yu Onsen
やしおの湯温泉

A 5km bus ride from Nikkō, this modern *onsen (admission ¥500; open 10am-5pm Fri-Wed)* is a good place to relax after a day of traipsing around shrines and temples. It has several different baths, including a *rotemburo* (outdoor spa bath). Take a Chūzenji-bound bus from Nikkō and get off at the Kiyomizu Itchōme stop. The *onsen* is across the river from the bus stop; walk back toward Nikkō, under the Rte 120 bypass and across the bridge.

Chūzenji-ko 中禅寺湖

Ten kilometres west of Nikkō, this lake is chiefly a scenic attraction, and it's probably not worth cutting short your visit to Nikkō in order to see it. If you have plenty of time, however, then the lake and the 97m-high falls, **Kegon-no-taki** are definitely worth

visiting. The waterfall features an elevator (¥530 return) down to a platform where you can observe the full force of the plunging water. Also worth a visit is a third Futarasan-jinja, complementing the *jinja* (shrine) in the Tōshō-gū area and on the mountain Nantai-san.

For good views of the lake and Kegon-no-taki, get off the bus at the Akechi-daira bus stop (the stop before Chūzenji Onsen) and take the Akechi-daira (Akechi Plateau) cable car (¥390/710 one way/return) up to a viewing platform. From this point, it's a pleasant 1.5km walk across the Chanoki-no-daira to a vantage point with great views over the lake, the falls and Nantai-san (2484m). From here you can walk down to the lake and Chūzenji Onsen or take the Chūzenji cable car (¥440/840 one way/return).

As you might expect, Chūzenji-ko has the usual flotilla of cruise boats all clamouring to part you from your yen. The lake, which reaches a depth of 161m, is a fabulous shade of deep blue in good weather, and this, along with the mountainous backdrop, makes for a pleasant cruise. An alternative to a cruise is to hire one of the rowing boats that are available for ¥1000 per hour.

See the Yumoto Onsen entry for information on the Senjōgahara Shizen-kenkyu-rō (Senjōgahara Plain Nature Trail) from Chūzenji-ko to Yumoto.

Places to Stay We recommend staying in Nikkō, which has a greater variety of good-value accommodation. **Chūzenji Pension** (☎ 55-0888; rooms per person from ¥11,000) is worth trying if you prefer to stay in Chūzenji; rates include two meals and check-in is 3pm. To get to the pension from the Nikkō-Chūzenji road (Rte 120), turn left at the lakeside and cross the bridge. The pension is on the left, about 100m down the road.

Getting There & Away There are buses from the Nikkō station area to Chūzenji Onsen (¥1100, 50 minutes).

Yumoto Onsen 湯元温泉

From Chūzenji-ko, you might continue on to the quieter hot-springs resort of Yumoto Onsen by bus (¥840, 30 minutes). Alternatively, you can hike there in three or four hours from the falls, Ryūzu-daki, on the

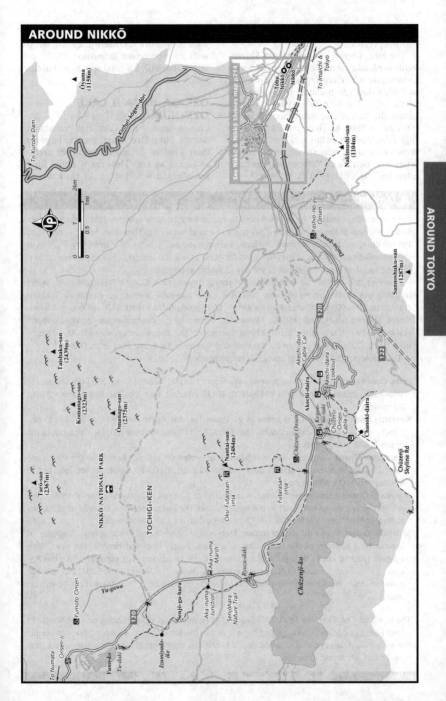

AROUND NIKKŌ

central northern part of Chūzenji-ko (or do this in reverse).

The hike, known as **Senjōgahara Shizen-kenkyu-rō**, takes three hours. From Chūzenji Onsen, take a Yumoto-bound bus and get off at Ryūzu-daki (20 minutes, ¥410), the start of the hike. The hike follows the Yu-gawa across the picturesque marshland of **Senjō-ga-hara**, to **Yuno-ko** (look out for the 75m-high falls, **Yu-daki**, in this area) from where it wends around the western edge of the lake to Yumoto Onsen. From Yumoto, you can catch a bus back to Nikkō (¥1650, 1½ hours).

Before heading back to Nikkō, you might want to stop off at **Onsen-ji**, a small temple with its own *onsen (admission ¥500; open 10am-3pm daily)*; a good spot to rest hiking-weary muscles.

OZE-GA-HARA & LAKE OZE-NUMA 尾瀬沼・尾瀬沼湖

Oze-ga-hara, the 1400m-high marshlands around Lake Oze-numa, are the largest of their kind in Japan, covering an area of around 8 sq km. The area is noted for its birdlife and wildflowers, in particular the

A Day in the Bath

Even the most committed city-lover will need to escape Tokyo at some point, and the perfect antidote to the madness of the metropolis is a day spent at a rural hot spring. These vary from the deluxe to the primitive, but none need break the bank, indeed many public baths offer free entry. Holders of the Japan Railpass can use JR lines to hop as far afield as Niigata, Tochigi or Fukushima prefectures, utilising the *shinkansen* to get out of the city as swiftly as possible.

However, the star in the Kanto area hot-spring firmament is Gunma Prefecture, with water bubbling out of the ground at every turn. It is easily accessible from Ueno station via Takasaki (*shinkansen* ¥4090, 45 minutes; *tokkyū* ¥3190, 80 minutes; *futsū* ¥1890, 110 minutes) and Jomo-Kogen Stations (*shinkansen* ¥5040, 70 minutes) on the Joetsu *shinkansen* line, or via Maebashi (*tokkyū* ¥3190, 100 minutes; *futsū*, ¥1890, two hours) and Shibukawa (*tokkyū* ¥3570, 100 minutes; *futsū* ¥2210, 2¼ hours) on the Takasaki and Ryomo or Agatsuma lines respectively.

The following Gunma springs are highly recommended:

Ikaho Onsen Great public bath with views over Mount Haruna. Take the Jōetsu line from Takasaki to Shibukawa station (*tokkyū/futsū* ¥1410/400, 20/30 minutes), then local bus to the *onsen* (¥550, 20 minutes).

Kusatsu Onsen Quintessential old-time *onsen* town. Take the Agatsuma line from Takasaki to Naganohara Kusatsuguchi station (*tokkyū/futsū* ¥2520/1110, 60/100 minutes), then local bus to the *onsen* (¥670, 30 minutes).

Takaragawa Onsen Complete with river bathing, oft-voted the nation's best. Take the Jōetsu line from Takasaki to Minakami station (*tokkyū/futsū* ¥2360/950, 60/90 minutes), then local bus to the *onsen* (¥1100, 40 minutes).

Minakami Onsen A thriving *onsen* town with a touch of nostalgic naughty-naughty sybaritism, and where you can white-water raft in the summer. Take the Jōetsu line from Takasaki to Minakami station (*tokkyū/futsū* ¥2360/950, 60/90 minutes), then it's a 15-minute walk.

Shiriyaki Onsen Very odd and primitive; literally the 'arse-burning' hot spring, favourite of haemorrhoid sufferers of the Heike clan, where you simply strip and climb in the river. Bring a *bentô* (packed lunch) though, as there's nothing else here), and start out early. Take the Agatsuma line from Takasaki to Naganohara-Kusatsu station (*tokkyū/futsū* ¥2520/1110, 60/100 minutes), then local bus to Hanashiki Onsen (¥800, 30 minutes); from there it's a 10-minute walk.

The beautiful **Chōjūkan inn** (☎ 0273-85-6634) at Hoshi Onsen allows bathing only. Although it's a train ride, bus ride and a hike, getting there is part of the fun. Try to arrive around noon to sample the inn's mountain-vegetable steamed rice. Women can sneak into the (far superior) men's bath here. In fact, it's almost expected.

unfortunately-monickered *mizubashō* (skunk cabbage). Even when the wildflowers aren't in bloom, the hiking is lovely, as much of it is over wooden planks laid across the marshes.

Because Oze is one of the premier hiking destinations around Tokyo, it can be packed on summer weekends. For this reason, we strongly suggest that you go on a weekday during the summer months. Another way to escape the crowds is to ascend the mountain, **Hiuchi-ga-take**, from which there's a great view over the marshes.

During the hiking season (28 May to 10 October) direct overnight buses run from Tokyo and Shinjuku stations to three of the area's trailheads. There is a slight discount for return travel, but basic one-way rates with **Oze Chokutsu Bus** (☎ *03862-0819*) are: ¥4500 to Ōshimizu, ¥5300 to Hatomachi-tōge, and ¥6500 to Numayama-tōge. Make sure you book both ways if you want to use this service.

Otherwise, the best bet for getting into the Oze region is to start from Numata in Gunma-ken. From Ueno station, take a Jōetsu-line *kaisoku* train to Takasaki (1½ hours) and then take a *futsū* (local train) to Numata (45 minutes). The whole journey costs ¥2520. From Numata station there are regular buses to the Ōshimizu trailhead (¥2200, two hours).

CHICHIBU-TAMA NATIONAL PARK 秩父多摩国立公園

While the hikes in Chichibu-Tama National Park cannot compete with those further afield, they do make a pleasant escape from the concrete jungles of Tokyo. The park is divided into the Chichibu and Oku-Tama regions. These two regions are connected by a two-day hiking trail that runs over the top of Kumotori-san (2017m), the highest point in the Tokyo metropolitan area. For those with less time, a trip to the mountaintop shrine complex of Mitake-jinja in the Oku-Tama region, perhaps paired with a hike to the summit of nearby Ōtake-san (1266m), makes a great day trip from the city.

Chichibu Region 秩父周辺
☎ 0494

Before heading on to other destinations, have a look round the small town of Chichibu. There are several interesting old Japanese and Western buildings on the road that leads to **Chichibu-jinja** from Ohanabatake station. The shrine itself is pleasant, although most of the buildings are modern reconstructions.

Southwest of the town, just near the top of Mitsumine-san (1329m), **Mitsumine-jinja** is the starting point for the two-day walk that connects Chichibu with Oku-Tama. The shrine was founded some 2000 years ago and has long been favoured as a mountain retreat by members of the Tendai Buddhist sect. Set in a grove of towering cryptomeria trees, the shrine is worth a visit even if you don't intend to do the hike. Although it's possible to walk up to the shrine in two hours, most people take the Mitsumine-san cable car (¥950/1650 one way/return). The shrine festival on 2 and 3 December is a huge spectacle that attracts 170,000 visitors each year.

To get to the cable car, take the Chichibu Tetsudō line from Ohanabatake station to Mitsumine-guchi station (¥430, 15 minutes) then switch to a Chichibu-ko bound bus and get off at Ōwa (¥300, 15 minutes). The cable-car station is a 15-minute walk uphill across the river from the bus stop.

Nagatoro 長瀞
From mid-March to mid-November boats leave from Oyahana-bashi, 700m from Kami-Nagatoro station, to shoot the **Arakawa River rapids**. The trip costs ¥1550 and lasts 50 minutes. You can also take the **Hodō-san cable car** (one way/return ¥420/720) to the top of Hodō-san (497m), although it isn't as good as the trip up Mitsumine-san (see earlier in this section). The cable car is a 15-minute walk from Nagatoro station.

Places to Stay & Eat Out of town a bit is **Oku-Chichibu Lake View Youth Hostel** (☎ *55-0056*; ⒲ *www.jyh.or.jp; dorm beds ¥3200*). It can be reached on a bus trip from Mitsumine-guchi to the last stop, Chichibu-ko, then it's a 15-minute walk.

New Chichibu (☎ *24-4444; singles/twins ¥4600/7500*) is a business hotel that is a five-minute walk south of Chichibu station. It's the best option in Chichibu itself. Check-in is 3pm to 10pm.

The Chichibu region's speciality is *teuchi soba* (handmade buckwheat noodles). **Soba Fuku** (☎ *23-2572; lunch/dinner ¥1200; open 11.30am-2.30 & 4.30pm-7pm Tues-Sun*) is a good place to try *soba* and is across the

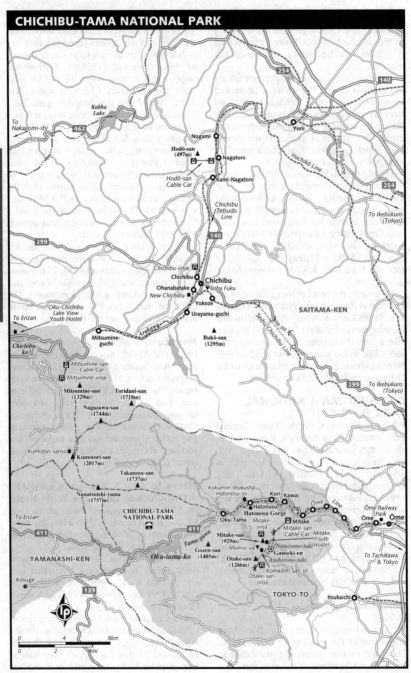

CHICHIBU-TAMA NATIONAL PARK

AROUND TOKYO

Kabba Lake

To Nakagomi-shi

Yorii

Nogami

Hodō-san (497m)

Nagatoro

Hodō-san Cable Car

Kami-Nagatoro

Chichibu Tetsudō Line

To Ikebukuro (Tokyo)

Chichibu-jinja

Chichibu

Chichibu

Ohanabatake

New Chichibu

Soba Fuku

Yokoze

SAITAMA-KEN

Urayama-guchi

Oku-Chichibu Lake View Youth Hostel

To Enzan

Mitsumine-guchi

Arakawa

Bukō-san (1295m)

Chichibu-ko

Seibu Chichibu Line

Mitsumine-san Cable Car

Mitsumine-jinja

Mitsumine-san (1329m)

Toridani-san (1718m)

To Ikebukuro (Tokyo)

Nagazawa-san (1744m)

Kumotori-sanso

Kumotori-san (2017m)

Takanosu-san (1737m)

Nanatsuishi-yama (1757m)

Kokumin-shukusha Hatonosu-so

Kori

Kawai

CHICHIBU-TAMA NATIONAL PARK

To Enzan

Oku-Tama

Hatonosu

Hatonosu Gorge

Mitake-jinja

Mitake

Ōme Line

Ōme Railway Park

Ōme

Tama-gawa

Mitake-san (929m)

Mitake-san Cable Car

Mitake Youth Hostel

YAMANASHI-KEN

Oku-tama-ko

Gozen-san (1405m)

Momiji-ya

Nanyono-taki

Ōtake-san (1266m)

Ganseki-en

Ayahirono-taki

To Tachikawa & Tokyo

Kosuge

Komadori San-so

Ōtake-san-jinja

TOKYO-TO

Itsukaichi

0   4   8km

0   2   mi

street from Seibu Chichibu station; we recommend the *tempura soba*.

Getting There & Away The cheapest and quickest way of getting to the Chichibu area from Tokyo is via the Seibu Ikebukuro line (which becomes the Seibu Chichibu line) from Seibu Ikebukuro station (*futsū* ¥750, 1¾ hours with changes en route; *tokkyū Chichibu 17* ¥1370, 1½ hours direct). Alternatively, JR trains run from Ueno station to Kumagaya station on the Takasaki line (¥1110, one hour and 10 minutes) where you will have to change to the Chichibu Tetsudō line to continue to Chichibu station (¥840, 70 minutes). All things considered, unless you're travelling on a Japan Rail Pass, it's cheaper to set off from Ikebukuro even if you're based in Ueno.

Oku-Tama Region 奥多摩周辺
☎ 0428
Like the Chichibu region, Oku-Tama has some splendid mountain scenery and a few good hiking trails. If you're only coming up for a day trip from Tokyo, this is a better and cheaper choice than the Chichibu region. The highlight of the area is the mountaintop shrine complex of Mitake-jinja and the quaint village surrounding it.

Mitake-san Buses run from Mitake station to the Mitake-san cable-car terminus (¥270, 10 minutes) from where the Mitake-san cable car takes you close to the summit (¥570/1090 one way/return, ¥50 less each way with an Okutama Furii Kippu (Okutama Free Pass). See Getting There & Away later for details. About 20 minutes on foot from the top of the cable car is **Mitake-jinja**, said to date back some 1200 years. The area around the shrine has great views of the surrounding mountains and the Kantō Plain.

If you plan to hike around Mitake-san (926m) pick up the excellent *Okutama Nature Map* from the **Mitake Visitors Center** (☎ 78-8836; open 8am-4pm Tues-Sun) which is 250m beyond the top of the cable car, near the start of the village.

Ōtake-san Hike If you've got the time, the three-hour hike from Mitake-jinja to the summit of Ōtake-san (1266m) and back is highly recommended. Although there's some climbing involved, it's a fairly easy

hike and the views from the summit are excellent – Mt Fuji is visible to the south on clear days. On the way, take the detour down to **Nanoyono-taki**, **Ganseki-en** (a rocky ravine) and **Ayahirono-taki** – all that greenery and silence may come as a shock after a few days cooped up in Tokyo.

Places to Stay & Eat Up on Mitake-san **Mitake Youth Hostel** (☎ 78-8774; W www .jyh.or.jp; dorm beds ¥2750) is very comfortable. It's midway between the top of the cable car and Mitake-jinja. Check-in is 3pm.

Komadori San-sō (☎ 78-8472; rooms per person ¥4500-5000) is further on, just below the shrine. This *minshuku* (Japanese-style B&B) is a friendly place at ease with foreigners. Meals cost extra and check-in is 3pm.

The **Mitake Visitors Center** (☎ 78-9363) has a map to both places (see the earlier Mitake-san section).

Kokumin-shukusha Hatonosu-sō (☎ 85-2340; rooms with 2 meals around ¥7000), down in the valley, is a clean place that's a short walk from Hatonosu station. Exit the station, walk down to and cross the main road, take the road that bears off left just before the tunnel, and you'll see it down on your left. They don't have a room-only option; check-in is 3pm.

We recommend lunch on Mitake-san. **Momiji-ya** (☎ 78-8475; meals from ¥800; open noon-5pm daily) is a *soba* shop on the main walkway to the shrine. The *kamo-nanban* (duck) *soba* is recommended by locals.

Getting There & Away You can get to Oku-Tama by taking the JR Chūō line from Shinjuku station to Tachikawa station (¥450, 26 minutes) and changing there to the JR Ōme line to Oku-Tama station (¥620, one hour and 21 minutes). Unless you've got a Japan Rail Pass, if you visit on weekends or a national holiday, we highly recommend the Holiday Free Pass (¥2040), available at JR ticket windows, which covers return travel between Okutama and Tokyo and unlimited use of JR trains in the Okutama region.

MITO 水戸
☎ 0292 • pop 234,000
The capital of Ibaraki-ken, Mito was once a castle town. Today its only notable attraction

is **Kairaku-en** (admission garden/pavilion free/¥180), one of Japan's three most celebrated landscape gardens (the other two are Kenroku-en in Kanazawa and Kōraku-en in Okayama). The 18-acre gardens date back to 1842 and are popular for their *ume* (plum blossoms) which bloom in late February or early March.

There's an entry charge for the pavilion, **Kobun-tei**, a tasteful reproduction of a Mito clan-lord's villa. To get to the garden take a bus from Mito station to Kairakuen-mae bus

Kumotori-san Track

Kumotori-san (literally, 'Taker of Clouds Mountain'; 2017m), in Chichibu-Tama National Park, straddles the prefectural borders of Yamanashi, Saitama and Tokyo. The hike from the Chichibu region to the Oku-Tama region, over the summit of Kumotori-san, is made easier by the Mitsumine-san cable car (see Chichibu Region in this section) at the Chichibu end, which cuts about 730 vertical metres out of your hike in eight minutes. If you object to having the big climb taken out of your hike, you can always walk up (or do this hike the other way around!).

This hike is a two-day trip, leaving Tokyo on the morning of day one and returning in the evening of day two. There's no real reason to stay in Chichibu or Oku-Tama – one night is spent on the mountain in a mountain hut, camping, or in the emergency hut.

This hike is best from April to December (spring to early winter). The main hut on the track, Kumotori Sansō, is open year round, but if you go in winter, consider weather conditions with common sense.

Day One: Top of Mitsumine Cable Car to Kumotori Sansō; three to five hours

The Mitsumine cable car should have just whipped you up to 1090m. The first 2km of the hike are virtually flat, so you can warm up as you amble through the shrine complex, Mitsumine-jinja. Pass through the complex and head onto the track to start the climb.

The first target is **Kirimo-ga-mine** (1523m) which you should reach in one to 1½ hours from the cable car. Stay on the main ridge and descend briefly before making the long climb to Mae-shiraiwa-san (1776m) where you can rest on some benches. Another short descent and climb brings you to **Shiraiwa-goya**, 1½ hours or so from Kirimo-ga-mine. This hut is open daily from 20 July to 31 August, and on Saturday throughout the rest of the year.

After another 20- to 30-minute climb, you reach Shiraiwa-san (1921m). This is followed by a 30- to 45-minute descent. **Kumotori-Sansō** (☎ 0494-23-3338) is a mountain hut that is open year round. It charges ¥6000/3500 with/without meals, and ¥300 for camp sites nearby. It's a short climb from the low point (about three to five hours from the top of the cable car). If you are adequately prepared and can invest an extra 20 to 30 minutes in climbing, you can stay for free in the **emergency hut** at the summit of Kumotori-san. There are no facilities there: you'll need a sleeping bag and food.

Day Two: Kumotori Sansō to Oku-Tama; five to seven hours

If you stay at the hut or camp, you'll start day two by climbing to the peak. Views of the surrounding mountains from the bald, rocky top are stunning. This is the highest point in Tokyo! Descend from the peak to the south, keep right at all trail junctions, and after 45 minutes you'll come to **Kumotori Oku-tama-goya**, a hut open year round. Camping here is permitted, and there's water available.

The track continues along the ridge to Nanatsuishi-yama (Seven Stone Mountain; 1757m) then carries on along the right side of the main ridge to the **emergency hut** on Takanosu-san (Hawk's Nest Mountain; 1737m). At the intersection thereafter, you can either climb the peak, by going left, or avoid it, by going right. The tracks meet up again on the other side, and descend to a spot just to the north of Mutsuishi-yama (Six Stone Mountain; 1479m). The none-too-steep descent from Kumotori-san should have taken three to 4½ hours to this point.

This is where things steepen. It's a 1½- to two-hour drop to the small village of Oku-Tama, where there is a visitors centre, countless places to eat, and a train to take you back to Tokyo. See Oku-Tama in this chapter for details.

Temple doors, Nikkō, north of Tokyo

Great Buddha, Kamakura, south of Tokyo

Park adjoining Narita-san, Shinshō-ji, Narita

Fuji-Yoshida, with Mt Fuji in the background

Mt Fuji

stop (20 minutes). From Ueno station take the JR Jōban line to Mito (*tokkyū*, one hour and 20 minutes). Ordinary services from Ueno take just under two hours and stop at Kairaku-en station (one stop before Mito).

West of Tokyo

Many of the destinations most popular with Tokyo residents lie to the west of the city, including the scenic Fuji Go-ko region, Mt Fuji itself, the tourist mecca of Hakone and the *onsen* and beach resorts of the Izu-hantō.

MT FUJI AREA 富士山周辺
☎ 0555

Mt Fuji, Japan's most familiar symbol, dominates the region southwest of Tokyo. Although Hakone is probably the most famous spot for Fuji-viewing, those with an aversion to crowds will prefer the scenic Fuji Go-ko region.

Mt Fuji 富士山

Japan's highest mountain stands 3776m high. When it's capped with snow in late autumn, winter and spring, it's a picture-postcard perfect volcanic cone. Fuji-san, as it's known in Japanese (*san* is the Chinese reading of the kanji, or character, for 'mountain'), last blew its top in 1707, covering the streets of Tokyo with volcanic ash. On an exceptionally clear day, you can see Mt Fuji from Tokyo, 100km away, but for much of the year you'd be hard pressed to see it from 100m away. Your best chance of seeing the notoriously shy mountain is in the late autumn, winter and early spring when the air is fairly clear. Even during these times, the mountain may only be visible in the morning before it retreats behind a curtain of haze or clouds.

Information Climbing Mt Fuji, Mt Fuji Climber's Guidebook and Mt Fuji & Fuji Five Lakes brochures are available from the **Tourist Information Center** in Tokyo (*TIC*; ☎ 3201-3331) and provide exhaustive detail on transport to the mountain and how to climb it, complete with climbing schedules worked out to the minute.

During the climbing season, there is climbing information in English (☎ 24-1236; available 9.30am-5.30pm Mon-Fri).

Alternatively, contact the **Kawaguchi-ko Tourist Information Center** (☎ 72-6700; open 8.30am-6pm daily).

Mt Fuji Views You can get a classic view of Mt Fuji from the *shinkansen* as it passes the city of Fuji (sit on the northern side of the train). There are also good views from the Hakone area, Nagao-tōge Pass on the road from Hakone to Gotemba, and the northwest coast of the Izu-hantō. But the best and closest views are from the Fuji Go-ko region where, on a clear day, the hulking presence of the mountain seems to fill the sky.

Climbing Mt Fuji Officially, the climbing season on Mt Fuji is from 1 July to 31 August, and the Japanese, who love to do things 'right', pack in during those busy months. Actually, you can climb Mt Fuji at any time of year, and it may be preferable to do so just outside the official season to avoid the crowds, but keep in mind that transport services may be less frequent and some of the huts may be closed. Of course, any time there's snow on the mountain you'll need the proper equipment and experience to climb Mt Fuji, and a midwinter ascent is strictly for expert mountaineers.

Be warned that there is no free water available on the mountain. Either bring your own or shell out ¥500 for a half-litre bottle.

Although children and grandparents regularly make it to the summit, this is a serious mountain and not to be trifled with. It's high enough for altitude sickness and, as on any mountain, the weather on Mt Fuji can be viciously changeable. On the summit it can go from sunny and warm to wet, windy and cold in remarkably little time. Even if conditions are fine, you can count on it being close to freezing on mornings in season, and much colder out of season. Whatever you do, *don't climb Mt Fuji without clothing appropriate for cold and wet weather*.

The mountain is divided into 10 'stations', from base to summit, but these days most climbers start from one of the four 5th stations, which you can reach by road. From the end of the road, it takes about 4½ hours to climb the mountain and about three hours to descend. Once you're on top, it takes about an hour to make a circuit of the crater. The Mt Fuji Weather Station, on

A Wise Man's Climb

I started out on a hot August night. At 10pm the temperature had been around 27°C (80°F), but by 4am it was below freezing and the wind was whistling past at what felt like hurricane speed. With a surprising number of other *gaijin* (foreigners) and a huge number of Japanese, I reached the top of Mt Fuji.

Climbing Mt Fuji is definitely not heroic: in the two-month 'season', as many as 180,000 people get to the top – 3000-odd every night. Nor is it that much fun – it's a bit of a dusty slog and when you get to the top it's so cold and windy that your main thought is about heading down again. But the climb and the views aren't really what you do it for. To Japanese Fuji-climbers, it's something of a pilgrimage; to *gaijin*, it's another opportunity to grapple with something uniquely Japanese.

Like many other climbers, I made my Fuji climb overnight. At 9.30pm I got off the bus at the Kawaguchi-ko 5th Station, which is where the road ends and you have to start walking. Surprisingly, about half the passengers on my bus were *gaijin*, most of them a group of Americans planning to convert the Japanese to Mormonism! I'd bought a litre of the isotonic drink Pocari Sweat and a packet of biscuits at a 7-Eleven in the town of Kawaguchi-ko, and wearing a shirt and a coat, I was all set. The night was clear, but dark, and I was glad I'd bought some new batteries for my torch before I left Tokyo.

My experience of climbing holy mountains is that you always get to the top too early – you work up a real sweat on the climb and then you freeze waiting for dawn. So I hung around for a while before starting out.

Despite the hordes climbing the mountain, I managed to lose the path occasionally. By the time I reached 2390m I'd already stopped to unzip the lining from my coat. By 11pm I was past 2700m and thinking it was time to slow down if I wanted to avoid arriving too early. By midnight it was getting much cooler, and I zipped the jacket-lining back in place and added more clothes to my ensemble. I was approaching 3000m – virtually halfway – and at this rate I was going to be at the top by 2.30am, in line with the four hours and 35 minutes the tourist-office leaflet said it was supposed to take! In Japan, even mountain climbing is scheduled to the minute.

Although I'd started on my own, some of the faces I met at rest stops were becoming familiar by this point and I'd fallen in with two Canadians and a Frenchman.

Huts are scattered up the mountainside; some stations have a number of huts, and others have none. The proprietors are very jealous of their facilities, and prominent signs, in English and Japanese, announce that even if it is pouring with rain, you can stay outside if you aren't willing to fork over the overnight fee. Fortunately, at 1.30am we were virtually swept into one hut, probably in anticipation of the numerous bowls of *rāmen* (noodles in soup) we would order. We hung out in this comfortable 3400m-high hideaway until after 3am, when we calculated a final hour and a bit of a push would get us to the top just before the 4.30am sunrise.

We made it and, looking back from the top, we saw hordes of climbers heading up towards us. It was no great surprise to find a souvenir shop (there is absolutely no place in Japan where tourists won't find a souvenir shop waiting for them). The sun took an interminable time to rise, but eventually it poked its head through the clouds, after which most climbers headed straight back down. I spent an hour walking around the crater rim, but I wasn't sorry to wave Fuji-san goodbye. The Japanese say you're wise to climb Fuji, but a fool to climb it twice. I've no intention of being a fool.

Tony Wheeler

the southwestern edge of the crater, is on the actual summit of the mountain.

You want to reach the top at dawn – both to see *goraiko* (sunrise) and because early morning is the time when the mountain is least likely to be shrouded in cloud. Sometimes it takes an hour or two to burn the morning mist off, however. To time your ar-

rival for dawn you can either start up in the afternoon, stay overnight in a mountain hut and continue early in the morning, or climb the whole way at night. You do not want to arrive on the top too long before dawn, as it's likely to be very cold and windy, and if you've worked up a sweat during the climb, you'll be very uncomfortable.

Although nearly all climbers start from the 5th stations, it is possible to climb all the way up from a lower level. The low-level trails are now mainly used as short hiking routes around the base of the mountain, but gluttons for punishment can climb all the way on the Yoshida Route from Fuji-Yoshida, or on the Shoji Route from near Shoji-ko. There are alternative sand trails on the Kawaguchi-ko, Subashiri and Gotemba Routes, which you can descend very rapidly by running and *sunabashiri* (sliding), pausing from time to time to get the sand out of your shoes.

5th Stations There are four 5th stations around Mt Fuji and it's quite feasible to climb from one and descend to another. On the northern side of Fuji is the **Kawaguchi-ko 5th Station** (2305m) which is reached from the town of Kawaguchi-ko. This station is particularly popular with climbers starting from Tokyo. The Yoshida Route (which starts much lower down, close to the town of Fuji-Yoshida) is the same as the Kawaguchi-ko Route for much of the way.

The route from the **Subashiri 5th Station** (1980m) meets the Yoshida Route just after the 8th station. The **Gotemba 5th Station** is reached from the town of Gotemba and, at 1440m, is much lower than the other 5th stations. From Gotemba station it takes seven to eight hours to reach the top of Mt Fuji, as opposed to 4½ to five hours on the other routes. The **Fujinomiya (Mishima) 5th Station** (2380m) is convenient for climbers coming from Nagoya, Kyoto, Osaka and western Japan. It meets the Gotemba Route right at the top.

Equipment Make sure you have plenty of clothing suitable for cold and wet weather, including a hat and gloves. Bring drinking water and some snack food. If you're going to climb at night, bring a torch (flashlight) or headlamp, and spare batteries.

Mountain Huts There are 'lodges' dotted up the mountainside, but they're expensive – ¥4000 to ¥4500 for a mattress on the floor squeezed between countless other climbers – and you don't get much opportunity to sleep anyway, as you have to be up well before dawn to start the final slog to the top. The huts also prepare simple meals for their

guests and for passing climbers, and you're welcome to rest inside so long as you order something. If you don't feel like eating, a one-hour rest costs ¥500. Camping on the mountain is not permitted.

Getting There & Away See the Fuji Go-ko section, following, for details on transport to Kawaguchi-ko, the most popular arrival point for Tokyo Fuji-climbers. Travellers intending to head west from the Fuji area towards Nagoya, Osaka and Kyoto can take a bus from Kawaguchi-ko or Gotemba to Mishima station on the *shinkansen* line.

From Kawaguchi-ko, there are bus services up to Kawaguchi-ko 5th Station (¥1700, 55 minutes) from April to mid-November. The schedule varies considerably during that period – call **Fuji Kyūkō bus** (☎ 72-2911) for details. At the height of the climbing season, there are buses until quite late in the evening – ideal for climbers intending to make an overnight ascent.

Taxis operate from the train station to the Kawaguchi-ko 5th station for around ¥8000, plus tolls, which is not much more than the bus fare when divided among four people.

There are also direct buses (¥2600, 180 minutes) from the Shinjuku bus terminal to the Kawaguchi-ko 5th Station. This is by far the fastest and cheapest way of getting from Tokyo to the 5th Station. If you take two trains and a bus, the same trip can cost nearly ¥6000.

From Subashiri, buses to the Subashiri 5th Station cost ¥1220 and take 55 minutes. From Gotemba station they cost ¥1500.

From Gotemba, buses to the Gotemba 5th Station (¥1080, 45 minutes) operate four to six times daily, but only during the climbing season.

The southern route up the mountain is most popular with climbers from western Japan approaching the mountain by *shinkansen*. Bus services run from Shin-Fuji (¥2400) and Mishima train stations (¥2390) to Fujinomiya (Mishima) 5th Station in just over two hours. There are reservation centres in Tokyo (☎ 5376-2222) and in the Fuji area (☎ 72-5111)

Fuji Go-ko 富士五湖

The Fuji Go-ko (Fuji Five Lakes), scattered around the northern side of Mt Fuji, are the

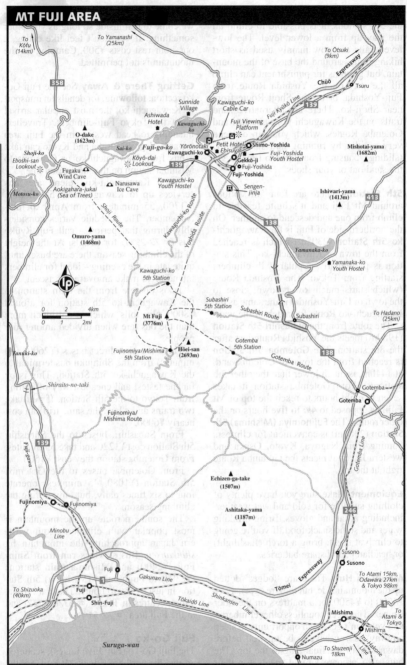

MT FUJI AREA

To Kōfu (14km)

To Yamanashi (25km)

To Ōtsuki (9km)

Expressway

358

Chūō

Tsuru

Fuji Kyūkō Line

139

Sunnide Village

Kawaguchi-ko Cable Car

Ashiwada Hotel

Fuji Viewing Platform

O-dake (1623m)

Kawaguchi-ko

Shoji-ko

Eboshi-san Lookout

Sai-ko

Fuji-go-ko

Yōrōnotaki

Petit Hotel

Shimo-Yoshida

Kawaguchi-ko

Ebisuya

Gekkō-ji

Fuji-Yoshida Youth Hostel

Kōyō-dai Lookout

139

Fuji-Yoshida

Mishotai-yama (1682m)

Motosu-ko

Fugaku Wind Cave

Narusawa Ice Cave

Aokigahara-jukai (Sea of Trees)

Kawaguchi-ko Youth Hostel

Sengen-jinja

Ishiwari-yama (1413m)

413

Omuro-yama (1468m)

Shoji Route

Yoshida Route

Kawaguchi-ko Route

138

Yamanaka-ko

Kawaguchi-ko 5th Station

Yamanaka-ko Youth Hostel

Subashiri 5th Station

Subashiri Route

Mt Fuji (3776m)

Tanuki-ko

Gotemba 5th Station

To Hadano (25km)

Subashiri

138

Shiraito-no-taki

Fujinomiya/Mishima 5th Station

Hōei-san (2693m)

Gotemba Route

Gotemba

Gotemba Line

Fujinomiya/ Mishima Route

Echizen-ga-take (1507m)

139

Fujinomiya

Minobu Line

Ashitaka-yama (1187m)

246

Susono

Susono

To Atami 15km, Odawara 27km & Tokyo 98km

Fuji-gawa

Fuji

Gakunan Line

Shin-Fuji

Tōmei Expressway

To Shizuoka (40km)

Tōkaidō Line

Shinkansen Line

Mishima

Izu-Hakone Line

To Atami & Tokyo

Mishima

Suruga-wan

To Shuzenji 18km

Numazu

0   2   4km
0   1   2mi

perfect reflecting pools for the mountain's majesty. Particularly pleasant during the autumn *kōyō* (maple) season, the lakes make a good overnight trip out of Tokyo. Most folks spend their time in the region doing little more than strolling around and enjoying the views, but those with energy can do some hiking in the mountains above the lakes. Hiking maps are available from the information centres in Kawaguchi-ko and Fuji-Yoshida.

Things to See & Do On the lake of the same name, **Kawaguchi-ko** is the best place from which to explore the Fuji Go-ko area. It's also a popular departure point for climbing Mt Fuji. Start your explorations with a stop at the **Kawaguchi-ko Tourist Information Center** (☎ 72-6700; open 9am-4.30pm daily) which is right outside Kawaguchi-ko station. Around 600m north of the station, on the lower eastern edge of the lake, is the **Kawaguchi-ko cable car** (¥400/700 one way/return) to the **Fuji Viewing Platform** (1104m). You can walk to the cable car from Kawaguchi-ko station; ask at the information centre for a map.

At Fuji-Yoshida, five minutes southeast of Kawaguchi-ko by train, is the atmospheric **Sengen-jinja**, which dates from 1615 (although this area is thought to have been the site of a shrine as early as 788). In the days when climbing Mt Fuji was a pilgrimage and not an annual tourist event, a visit to this shrine was a necessary preliminary to the ascent. The entrance street to the shrine still has some Edo-era pilgrims' inns. From Fuji-Yoshida station you can take a bus to Sengen-jinja-mae (¥150, five minutes) or walk there in about 15 minutes following a map from the **Fuji-Yoshida Tourist Information Center** (☎ 22-7000; open 9am-5.30pm daily), next to Fuji-Yoshida station.

Yamanaka-ko is the largest of the lakes, but it doesn't offer much in the way of attractions – unless you count an enormous swan-shaped hovercraft that does 35-minute circuits of the lake for ¥900.

The area around the smaller **Sai-ko** is less developed than the areas around the larger lakes. There are good views of Mt Fuji from the western end of the lake and from the **Kōyō-dai lookout**, near the main road. Close to the road are the **Narusawa Ice Cave** and the **Fugaku Wind Cave**, both formed by lava flows from a prehistoric eruption of Mt Fuji. There's a bus stop at each of the caves, or you can walk from one to the other in about 20 minutes.

The views of Mt Fuji from further west are not so impressive, but tiny **Shoji-ko** is said to be the prettiest of the Fuji Go-ko. Continue to Eboshi-san, a one- to 1½-hour climb from the road, to a lookout over the **Aokigahara-jukai** (Sea of Trees) to Mt Fuji. The last lake along is **Motosu-ko**, the deepest and least visited of the lakes.

Special Events On 26 and 27 August, the annual **Yoshida no Hi Matsuri** (Fire Festival) is held to mark the end of the climbing season and to offer thanks for the safety of the year's climbers. The first day involves a *mikoshi* (portable shrine) procession and the lighting of bonfires on the town's main street. On the second day, festivals are held at the town's Sengen-jinja.

Places to Stay There are two youth hostels in the Fuji Go-ko area. **Fuji-Yoshida** (☎ 22-0533; ⓦ www.jyh.or.jp; dorm beds ¥2700) is cosy and is around 600m south of Shimo-Yoshida station; exit the station, walk down the main street through three sets of lights, and turn down the alley on the right, before the Lawson convenience store. Check-in is 4pm.

Kawaguchi-ko Youth Hostel (☎ 72-1431; dorm beds ¥2900) is rather regimented and is about 500m southwest of Kawaguchi station; turn left as you come out of the tourist information centre, left again after the 7-Eleven, right after the post office and, finally, left in front of the power station. Check-in is 4pm. There are many hotels, *minshuku* and pensions around the Fuji Go-ko, particularly in Kawaguchi-ko. The **tourist information office** (☎ 72-6700) at Kawaguchi-ko station can make reservations.

Sunnide Village (☎ 76-6004, fax 76-7706; backpacker plan rate ¥4000, rooms per person with bath ¥6000) is the best of the bunch. It commands a magnificent view over Kawaguchi-ko towards Mt Fuji (you can enjoy this view from its outdoor bath). If you go through the Kawaguchi-ko Tourist Information Center you can qualify for its 'backpacker plan' rate. Note that no advance reservations are accepted for this rate; you just have to turn up and hope for the best.

Check-in is 3pm. There's also a free pick-up service from the station (ask the folks at the information centre to call for you).

The Japanese Inn Group is represented in the area by the following two hotels. **Ashiwada Hotel** (*☎ 82-2587; singles/doubles with bath ¥6000/12,000*) is at the western end of Kawaguchi-ko (take the No 6 bus from Kawaguchi-ko to the Nagahama stop, ¥270). Check-in is 2pm.

Petit Hotel Ebisuya (*☎ 72-0165; rooms per person ¥6000*) is just outside Kawaguchi-ko station; check-in is 3pm.

Places to Eat Most people eat where they're staying but there are other options. **Yōrōnotaki** (*☎ 72-0076; lunch/dinner around ¥2000; open 5pm-11pm Mon-Sat*) is opposite the station and worth a try. In Fuji-Yoshida, the 6th floor of the station building is a **restaurant floor**. Otherwise, the **Fuji-Yoshida Tourist Information Center** (*☎ 22-7000*) can make arrangements for you to sample homemade *udon* (thick, white wheat noodles) at private homes for around ¥500.

Getting There & Away Kawaguchi-ko and Fuji-Yoshida are the two main travel centres in the Fuji Go-ko area. Buses (¥1700, 1¾ hours) operate directly to Kawaguchi-ko from the Shinjuku long-distance bus station, outside the western exit of Shinjuku station in Tokyo. There are departures up to 16 times daily at the height of the Fuji climbing season. Some buses continue on to Yamanaka-ko and Motosu-ko. In Tokyo, call **Keiō Kōsoku bus** (*☎ 03-5376-2222*) for reservations and schedule information.

You can also get to the lakes by train, although it takes longer and costs more. JR Chūō-line trains go from Shinjuku to Ōtsuki (*tokkyū* ¥2230, one hour; *futsū* ¥1280, one hour and 50 minutes). At Ōtsuki, cross the platform to the Fuji Kyūkō line, which runs to Kawaguchi-ko (*futsū* only, ¥1110, one hour). The train actually goes to Fuji-Yoshida first (¥990, 50 minutes) then reverses out for the final short distance to Kawaguchi-ko. On Sunday and holidays from March to November there is a direct local train from Shinjuku and Tokyo stations (¥2370 from Shinjuku, ¥2530 from Tokyo, both two hours).

From Fuji-Yoshida and Kawaguchi-ko, buses run north to Kōfu, from where you can continue northwest to Matsumoto.

Getting Around There's a comprehensive bus network in the area, including regular buses from Fuji-Yoshida station that pass by the four smaller lakes and around the mountain to Fujinomiya (¥2150, 1½ hours) on the southwestern side. From Kawaguchi-ko, there are nine to 11 buses daily to Mishima (¥2130, two hours) on the *shinkansen* line.

HAKONE 箱根
☎ 0460 • pop 15,227

Hakone is the Japanese tourist-mecca *par excellence*. If the weather cooperates and Mt Fuji is clearly visible, the Hakone region can make a fun day trip from Tokyo. You can enjoy cable-car rides, visit an open-air museum, poke around smelly volcanic hot springs and cruise Ashino-ko. If it's rainy or cloudy, however, you may simply feel that you're riding a conveyor belt of which the sole purpose is to strip you of your cash.

An interesting loop through the region takes you from Tokyo by train and toy (tiny, local) train to Gōra; then by funicular and cable car up the 1153m-high mountain, Sōun-zan to almost the top, and down to Ashino-ko; by boat around the lake to Moto-Hakone, where you can walk a short stretch of the Edo-era Old Tōkaidō highway; and from there by bus back to Odawara, where you catch the train to Tokyo. (If you're feeling energetic, you can spend 3½ hours walking the old highway back to Hakone-Yumoto, from where you can catch a train back to Tokyo.)

Odawara 小田原

Odawara is famous for its **castle** (*admission ¥400; open 9am-5pm daily, closed 29 Dec-1 Jan*) which is an uninspired reconstruction of the original. It's perhaps only worth visiting during the cherry-blossom season – there are some 1000 *sakura* (cherry) trees planted on the grounds. The castle and surrounding park area is a 10-minute walk southeast of Odawara station. There is very little else of interest in the town, which is principally a transit point for Hakone.

Hakone-Yumoto Onsen
箱根湯元温泉

Yumoto is Hakone's most popular hot-springs resort. It's possible to stop off between Odawara and Gōra, and you might want to spend the day soaking in the baths here if the weather looks dodgy. You might also consider approaching the town on foot from Moto-Hakone via the old Tōkaidō hiking course (see the Moto-Hakone entry later in this section).

Of course, *onsen* are the main attraction of Hakone-Yumoto. **Kappa Tengoku Notemburo** (admission ¥750; open 10am-10pm daily), behind the station, is a popular outdoor bath and worth a dip if the crowds aren't too bad. For something more up-market, try **Ten-zan Notemburo** (admission ¥1000; open 9am-11pm daily) which has a larger selection of indoor and outdoor baths. To get there, take the free shuttle bus from the bridge outside the station.

Hakone Open-Air Art Museum
彫刻の森美術館

The museum (admission ¥1600; open 9am-5pm daily Apr-Nov, 9am-4.30pm daily Dec-Mar) is next to Chōkoku-no-Mori station, one stop before Gōra station. The focus is on Western and Japanese 19th- and 20th-century sculpture. The Hakone Free Pass (see Getting Around later in this section for details) does *not* gain you free admission, though it will earn you a discount.

Gōra 強羅

Gōra is the terminus of the Hakone-Tōzan line and the starting point for the funicular and cable-car trip to Tōgendai on Ashino-ko. The town also has a couple of its own attractions that may be of minor interest to travellers. If you're in this area between 11.30am and 2.30pm, check out **Gyōza Center**, a famous shop with nine kinds of *gyōza* (dumplings). Basic sets with rice and *miso* (soya-bean paste) soup start at ¥900.

Hakone Gōra-kōen Just a short walk beside the funicular tracks up Sōun-zan is the park, Hakone Gōra-kōen (☎ 2-2825; admission ¥900; open 9am-5pm daily, closes slightly later in summer). It has a, er, French rock garden, seasonal flowers, plus alpine and tropical plants.

Hakone Art Museum Further up the hill, 10 minutes from Gōra station, the Hakone Art Museum (admission ¥900; open 9am-4pm Fri-Wed Dec-Mar, 9am-4.30am Fri-Wed Apr-Nov) has a moss garden and a decent collection of ceramics from Japan and China.

Sōun-zan & Ōwakudani
早雲山・大桶谷

From Gōra, continue to near the 1153m-high summit of Sōun-zan by funicular ('cable car' in Japanese; ¥410, 10 minutes). If you don't have a Hakone Free Pass (see Getting Around later in this section), tickets are sold at the booth to the right of the platform exit.

Sōun-zan is the starting point for what the Japanese refer to as a ropeway, a 30-minute, 4km cable-car ride to Tōgendai (¥1330/2340 one way/return). On the way, the gondolas pass through Ōwakudani. Get out here and take a look around the volcanic hot springs – the gondolas pass by every 52 seconds, so you can continue your journey whenever you like. In fine weather Mt Fuji looks fabulous from here.

Ōwakudani is a volcanic cauldron of steam, bubbling mud and mysterious smells. The black boiled eggs on sale here are cooked in the boiling mud. Next to the cable-car stop, there's a building with restaurants and souvenir shops.

Ōwakudani Natural Science Museum (☎ 4-9149; admission ¥400; open 9am-4.30pm daily) has displays relating to the geography and natural history of Hakone.

Ashino-ko 芦ノ湖

Ashino-ko is touted as the primary attraction of the Hakone region; but it's Mt Fuji, with its snow-clad slopes glimmering in reflection on the water, that lends the lake its poetry. And unfortunately the venerable mountain is frequently hidden behind a dirty-grey bank of clouds. If this is the case when you visit, you have the consolation of a ferry trip across the lake; you can always buy a postcard of the view. See Getting Around later in this section for details about transport across the lake.

Komaga-take 駒ヶ岳

The mountain Komaga-take (1357m) is a good place from which to get a view of the lake and Mt Fuji. From Tōgendai, boats run to Hakone-en, from where a cable car (¥620/1050 one way/return) goes to the top. You can leave the mountain by the same route or by a five-minute funicular descent (¥370/630) to Komaga-take-nobori-guchi. Buses run from here to Hakone-machi (¥300), Hakone-Yumoto (¥820) and to Odawara (¥1050).

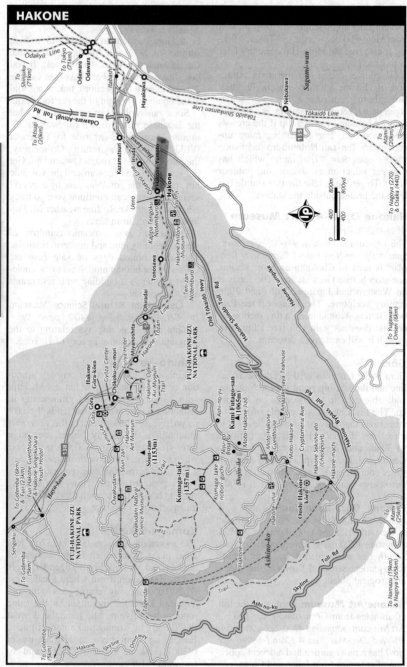

HAKONE

AROUND TOKYO

Rock Carvings Not far from Komaga-take-nobori-guchi is Moto-Hakone Jizō, a group of Buddhas and other figures carved in relief on rocks that lay between Komaga-take and Kami Futago-san (1065m). Although they date from the Kamakura era (1192–1333), most are still fairly well preserved. To get there from the funicular, turn right and follow the road down until you reach a T-junction. Turn left here and then left again; the carvings are around 400m up the road.

Moto-Hakone 元箱根

Moto-Hakone is a pleasant spot with a few places where you can eat or get an over-priced cup of coffee. There are a couple of interesting sights within easy walking distance of the jetty.

Hakone-jinja It is impossible to miss Hakone-jinja (☎ 3-7213; admission ¥300; open 9am-4pm daily) with its red torii rising from the lake. Walk around the lake towards the torii; huge cedars line the path to the shrine, which is in a wooded grove. There is a treasure hall in the grounds.

Cryptomeria Avenue Known as Sugi-namiki, the avenue is a 2km path between Moto-Hakone and Hakone-machi, which is lined with cryptomeria trees that were planted more than 360 years ago. The path runs behind the lakeside road used by buses and other traffic.

Old Tōkaidō Highway Up the hill from the lakeside Moto-Hakone bus stop is the old Tōkaidō highway, the road that once linked the ancient capital, Kyoto, with Edo (now known as Tokyo). It is possible to take a 3½-hour walk along the old road to Hakone-Yumoto station, passing the **Amazake-jaya Teahouse** and **Sōun-ji** along the way.

Hakone-machi 箱根町

Hakone-machi lies further around the lake, beyond Moto-Hakone. The town's main attraction is the **Hakone Sekisho-ato** (Hakone Checkpoint) which was operated by the Tokugawa shōgunate from 1619 to 1869 as a customs post between Edo and the rest of Japan. The present-day checkpoint is a recent reproduction of the original. Further back towards Moto-Hakone is the **Hakone History Museum** (☎ 5-7111; admission ¥200;

open 9am-4.30pm Tues-Sun, closed last Mon each month & New Years Day), which displays a small selection of samurai artefacts.

Special Events

Ashino-ko Kosui Matsuri, held on 31 July at Hakone-jinja near Moto-Hakone, features fireworks displays over Ashino-ko. On 16 August, in the **Hakone Daimonji-yaki Matsuri**, torches are lit on Myojoga-take so that they form the shape of the Chinese character for 'big' or 'great'. The **Hakone Daimyō Gyoretsu parade** on 3 November is a re-enactment by 400 costumed locals of a feudal lord's procession.

Places to Stay

Hakone's local popularity is reflected in the high price of most accommodation in the area. With the exception of two youth hostels and a couple of Welcome Inns, there's little in the way of alternatives.

To get to both **Hakone Sengokuhara Youth Hostel** (☎ 4-8966; w www.jyh.or.jp; dorm beds ¥2900), with check-in 4pm to 6pm, and **Fuji Hakone Guest House** (☎ 4-6577; singles/doubles from ¥5000/10,000), with check-in 3pm – they're in the same place – take a No 4 bus from Odawara station to Senkyōrō-mae bus stop (50 minutes). There's an English sign close by. A natural hot spa is available for bathing.

Moto Hakone Guesthouse (☎ 3-7880; rooms per person ¥5000) is conveniently located in Moto-Hakone. From Odawara station, take a bus from the No 3 stand and get off at the Ashino-ko-en-mae stop (55 minutes). Check-in is 3pm.

Fujiya Hotel (☎ 2-2211; w www.fujiya hotel.co.jp; rooms from ¥20,000) is one of Japan's earliest Western-style hotels and is highly rated on all fronts. There's also a weekday special for foreign travellers of US$120 for double rooms (you can pay the equivalent sum in yen). The hotel is around 250m west of Miyanoshita station on the Hakone-Tōzan line. Check-in is 2pm.

Getting There & Away

There are three ways of getting to the Hakone region from Tokyo: by the Odakyū express bus service, which leaves from the western side of Shinjuku station; by JR from Tokyo station; and by the private Odakyū line from Shinjuku station.

Train JR trains run on the Tōkaidō line between Tokyo station and Odawara (*futsū*, ¥1450, 1½ hours; *tokkyū*, ¥2880, 70 minutes; Kodama *shinkansen* is ¥3130, 35 minutes).

The private Odakyū line (**w** www.odakyu -group.co.jp/english/index.htm) runs into Hakone from Shinjuku station. Quickest and most comfortable is the *Romance Car* to Odawara (¥1720, 1¼ hours) or to Hakone-Yumoto (¥2020, one hour and 25 minutes). There is also a *kyūkō* (regular express) service (¥1150, 1½ hours) to Hakone-Yumoto.

At Odawara, it's possible to change to the narrow gauge, or toy train, Hakone-Tōzan line, which takes you to Gōra (¥650, 50 minutes). Alternatively, if you are already on the Odakyū line, you can continue on to Hakone-Yumoto and change to the Hakone-Tōzan line (¥390 to Gôra, 35 minutes) by walking across the platform.

Bus The Odakyū express bus service has the advantage of running directly into the Hakone region, to Ashino-ko and to Hakone-machi (¥1950, two hours). The disadvantage is that the bus trip is much less interesting than the combination of *Romance Car,* toy train (Hakone-Tōzan line), funicular, cable car and ferry. Buses run from the western exit of Shinjuku station 11 times daily.

Getting Around

Train The Odakyū line offers a Hakone *Furii Pasu* (Free Pass) which costs ¥5500 in Shinjuku or ¥4130 in Odawara (the place to buy it if you are travelling on a Japan Rail Pass) and allows you to use any mode of transport within the Hakone region for four days. The fare between Shinjuku and Hakone-Yumoto is also included in the pass (there's a ¥850 surcharge for the *Romance Car*). This is a good deal for a Hakone circuit, as the pass will save you at least ¥1000 even on a one-day visit to the region.

Bus The Hakone-Tōzan and Izu Hakone bus companies service the Hakone area and between them they manage to link up most of the sights. If you finish up in Hakone-machi, Hakone-Tōzan buses run between here and Odawara for ¥1150. Hakone-en to Odawara costs ¥1270. Buses run from Moto-Hakone to Yumoto for ¥900 every 30 minutes from 10am to 3pm.

Boat Ferry services crisscross Ashino-ko, running between Tōgendai, Hakone-machi and Moto-Hakone every 30 minutes. From Tōgendai, the fare is ¥970 to Moto-Hakone or Hakone-machi; between Moto-Hakone and Hakone-machi it's ¥250. The 'Pirate Ship' has to be seen to be believed – it's tourist kitsch at its worst, but fun all the same.

IZU-HANTŌ 伊豆半島

Eighty kilometres southwest of Tokyo, the peninsula, Izu-hantō, with its abundant *onsen* and rugged coastline, is one of Japan's most popular resort destinations. This means that things can get pretty crowded on the peninsula on weekends and holidays, particularly in summer. Luckily, once you get past the touristy resort of Atami, the crowds usually thin out. And over on the west coast, where transport is by bus only, things are always a lot quieter.

A suggested two- or three-day itinerary for the peninsula involves heading straight down the east coast to Shimoda. After exploring the town, neighbouring Rendai-ji Onsen and perhaps the rugged headlands of the cape, Irō-zaki, catch a bus for the scenic ride across the peninsula to Dōgashima on the west coast. Here, you can bathe in a cliffside *onsen*, swim in the Pacific in warmer months and enjoy stunning views up and down the coast. From Dōgashima, you can catch another bus to the *onsen* village of Shuzen-ji. After sampling the excellent baths there, you can take the Izu-Hakone Tetsudō line to Mishima and from there switch to the JR Tōkaidō line for the trip back to Tokyo.

Atami 熱海

☎ 0557 • pop 42,664

Atami is an overdeveloped hot-springs resort with little to detain foreign travellers. The town's biggest attraction is the over-priced **MOA Art Museum** (*admission ¥1600; open 9.30am-5pm Fri-Wed*). Its collection of Japanese and Chinese art includes a few 'national treasures' and a good number of 'important cultural properties'. Take the bus from stop 4 from outside Atami station to the last stop, MOA bijitsukan (¥160, eight minutes).

Because of Atami's popularity with domestic tourists, rooms are very expensive;

IZU-HANTŌ

To Shimizu (45km) & Shizuoka (59km)
To Tokyo (104km)
Numazu
Mishima
Mishima
To Hakone
Atami
Numazu
Kannami
Atami
Nirayama
Sagami-wan
Ōse-zaki
Mito-hama
Ōhito
Naga-hama
Shuzen-ji
Youth Hostel
Shuzen-ji
Onsen
Shuzen-ji
Shuzen-ji
Itō-hama
Heda
Daruma-yama
(982m)
136
Itō
Itō
Nishi-Izu
Skyline
Kawana
Suruga-wan
Ippeki-ko
Tōi-hama
Tōi
135
Amagi-san
(1406m)
Izu-Kōgen
Ferry to
Ō-shima
(40km)
Amagi Tunnel
Atagawa
Atagawa
136
Dōgashima
Inatori
Sanyo-sō
Youth Hostel
Higashiizu
Matsu-zaki
Matsu-zaki
Kawazu
Ferry to
Ō-shima
414
Rendai-ji
Rendai-ji
Shira-hama
Kanaya Ryokan/Onsen
Shimoda
Hagachi-zaki
Shimoda
Sotoura-kaigan
Gensu
Youth
Hostel
Minamiizu
Kisami
Ō-hama
Ferry to
Nii-jima, Shikine-jima
& Kozu-shima
Irō-zaki
Yumiga-hama

AROUND TOKYO

head down to Itō or Shimoda to find more reasonable lodgings.

Getting There & Away JR trains run from Tokyo station to Atami on the Tōkaidō line (regular train, ¥1890, two hours; Kodama *shinkansen*, ¥3570, 55 minutes; limited express *Odoriko*, ¥4070, one hour and 20 minutes). It's also possible to approach Atami via Shinjuku by taking the Odakyū line to Odawara (¥850, one hour and 10 minutes) and then connecting with the Tōkaidō line to Atami (¥400, 29 minutes).

Itō 伊東
☎ 0557

Itō is another hot-springs resort and is famous as the place where Anjin-san (William

Adams), the hero of James Clavell's book *Shogun*, built a ship for the Tokugawa shōgunate. Itō station has a beachfront **Tourist Information Center** (☎ 37-6105; open 9am-5pm daily), near where bay cruises depart.

Places to Stay For one of the cheapest deals in town, have a look at **Business Hotel Itō** (☎ 36-1515; singles/twins ¥5250/9450). It's a four-storey building about 300m east of the train station, close to the waterfront. Check-in is 4pm.

Getting There & Away Itō is connected to Atami by the JR Itō line (¥320, 25 minutes). The JR limited express *Odoriko* service also runs from Tokyo station to Itō (¥4090, 45 minutes).

AROUND TOKYO

Onsen Mania!

In his quintessential tome *Things Japanese* (1890), humorist and Japan-expert Basil Hall Chamberlain wryly observed 'Cleanliness is one of the few original items of Japanese civilisation'. Chamberlain was impressed by the Japanese mania for *onsen* (mineral hot-spring spas), not least by the pool in rural Gunma-ken where 'the bathers stay in the water for a month on end, with a stone on their lap to prevent them from floating in their sleep'.

A century later, *onsen* addicts may not be weighing themselves down with boulders, but the fascination with hot springs remains as strong as ever, and the activity has developed into a fine art with its own rules of etiquette. Baths are found just about everywhere due to plenty of underground thermal activity – poke a stick in the ground and out comes *o-yu* (literally, 'honourable hot water'). *Onsen* range from pristine mountain retreats to workaday bath houses and kitsch, overdeveloped spa towns.

Getting naked with total strangers is not, for most of us, the cultural norm (California readers, please forgive me), but shy *gaijin* (foreigners) should know that the Japanese perceive bathing as a great social leveller; company presidents rub naked shoulders with truck drivers, priests with publicans – and all revel in the anonymity that nudity allows. Only the *yakuza* (Japanese mafia) stand out with their magnificent *irezumi* (tattoos) or, in Yakuza parlance, *iremono*. They are often happy if you show an interest.

The baths themselves come in as many different shapes and sizes as the customers. Essentially, you will either visit solely for an *o-furo* (literally, 'the honourable bath'); or you will stay at an *onsen ryokan* (traditional hot-spring inn) to enjoy good food, copious amounts of alcohol, karaoke and a soak in the establishment's private baths, either indoors or out. Ryokan will often allow you to have a soak even if you aren't staying there (ask for *ofuro-nomi*). This is an excellent and affordable way to experience some beautiful, traditional baths. Unfortunately, bathing is also big business and rampant commercialism has marred many once-lovely *onsen*.

While famed commercial resorts, such as Dōgo Onsen in Shikoku and Beppu in Kyūshū, provide a good introduction to *onsen*, the effort it takes to seek out less touristed springs is worthwhile. If you find a rare, unvisited bath, the effect is scintillating. A few special *onsen* well worth visiting include Ibusuki and Kurokawa (Kyūshū), Yunomine (Kansai), and Bessho Onsen (central Honshū).

JOHN ASHBURNE

A bather, dressed in a 'modesty' towel, has a good scrub before plunging in to the bath

Onsen Mania!

There are two excellent books devoted to hot springs: *A Guide to Japanese Hot Springs* and *Japan's Hidden Hot Springs*. Both are worth seeking out for anyone looking to *onsen*-hop their way through Japan.

So whether it's being buried up to the neck in a thermally heated sand bath, soaking in a pool in a remote forest or luxuriating in a glitzy resort, the *onsen* experience is one of Japan's greatest treasures. And where else can you safely get naked with a mobster?

Onsen Etiquette

The Japanese hot-spring *o-furo* is blissfully free of the rules and regulations that make life a minefield of potential societal gaffes for the average Japanese citizen. No doubt this liberation from the strictures of polite society is what makes it so popular. The first-time-naked *gaijin* needn't be intimidated – once the basics have been mastered.

Soap is a commodity kept as far from the bath water as possible. Have a rinse in the adjacent shower. If there's no shower, squat on one of the Lilliputian stools provided and ladle hot water over your body, using one of the available buckets, while outside the bath. Then gracefully ease yourself into the water. Incidentally, stealing someone else's bucket or stool while they are soaking is officially frowned upon but, in fact, seems to be an undeclared national pastime.

One should endeavour to slip into the water with the minimum of disturbance, not unlike a cherry blossom petal delicately slipping into a moonlit Kyoto temple pond. Doing a double-pike with a half-somersault into the ornamental stone bath might impress your travelling companions, but not only will it result in cerebral haemorrhaging as you strike cranium to bath-bottom, it will mean instant social death – blood in the bath-water is a strict no-no.

In the event that the water is hot enough to strip the skin off a rhino, it is perfectly acceptable to do a reverse long-jump action, although if you can slowly ease yourself into the superheated water, grimacing is positively encouraged. If you accompany your facial contortions with a long drawn out, anguished 'achee, acheEE, AAAcheeee!' (hot, hooo-ot, HOOoo-ot!), you will be considered a professional.

An essential piece of *onsen* equipment is a 'modesty' towel to delicately cover your most private bits and pieces. Once they are safely underwater, this useful item can be dipped in the water, rinsed out (outside the bath) and placed on your head, a la Northern England male beachgoer, circa 1958. This is rumoured to prevent you from passing out (another minor social infringement). In the more rural, single-sex baths, however, no one bothers with a modesty towel – bathers wibble and wobble around, starkers as the day they were born.

It's that simple. And if you do commit a faux pas, most people are too busy forgetting work and looking forward to a night of karaoke to care. And in the event that you inadvertently fart, just try *kyo tansan wa kitsui desu ne* (Carbonation's strong today, isn't it?).

John Ashburne

Onsen Lingo

dansei-no-yu	男性の湯	male bath
otoko-yu	男湯	male bath
josei-no-yu	女性の湯	female bath
onna-yu	女湯	female bath
konyoku	混浴	mixed bath
kazoku-no-yu	家族の湯	family bath
rotenburo	露天風呂	outdoor bath
kawa-no-yu	川の湯	river bath
dōtsuburo/anaburo	洞窟風呂/穴風呂	cave bath
sunaburo	砂風呂	sand bath

Shimoda 下田
☎ 0558 • pop 27,722

If you only have time for one town on the peninsula, make it Shimoda, the most pleasant of the peninsula's *onsen* towns. Shimoda is famous as the residence of the American Townsend Harris, the first Western diplomat to live in Japan. The Treaty of Kanagawa, which resulted from Commodore Perry's visit (see History in the Facts about Japan chapter) ended Japan's centuries of self-imposed isolation by opening the ports of Shimoda and Hakodate to US ships and establishing a consulate in Shimoda in 1856.

The southern end of town, around **Perry Road**, is perfect for strolling and has a few temples scattered about.

There is a small **information centre** *(open 10am-5pm daily)* near the station, where the staff will help you book accommodation.

Ryōsen-ji & Chōraku-ji Around a 25-minute walk south of Shimoda station is the temple, Ryōsen-ji, famous as the site of another treaty, supplementary to the Treaty of Kanagawa, signed by Commodore Perry and representatives of the Tokugawa shōgunate.

Next to the temple is a small **museum** *(admission ¥500; open 8.30am-5pm, closed 1-3 Aug & 24-26 Dec)* with exhibits relating to the arrival of Westerners in Japan. These include a series of pictures depicting the tragic life of Okichi-san, a courtesan who was forced to give up the man she loved in order to attend to the needs of the barbarian

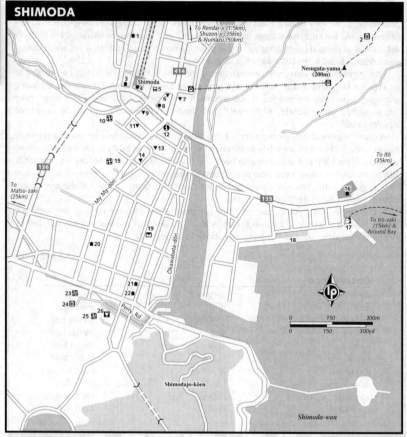

SHIMODA

Harris. When Harris left Japan five years later, Okichi was stigmatised for having had a relationship with a foreigner and was eventually driven to drink and suicide. Downstairs, there's an important collection of erotic Buddhist artwork.

Nearby Ryōsen-ji is Chōraku-ji, another pleasant little temple that's worth a quick look.

Hōfuku-ji Right in the centre of town is Hōfuku-ji, which has a **museum** *(admission ¥300; open 8am-5pm daily)* that memorialises the life of Okichi-san and includes scenes from the various movie adaptations of her life.

Nesugata-yama About 200m east of Shimoda station is the cable-car station to Nesugata-yama (Mt Nesugata; 200m). Cable cars run up every 10 minutes to a park (9am to 5pm) that has a photography museum, a small temple, good views of Shimoda and the bay, Shimoda-wan, and a reasonably priced restaurant. A return cable-car trip, including admission to the park, costs ¥1200.

Beaches There are some good beaches around Shimoda, particularly around Kisami, which is south of town. You can take an Irō-zaki bound bus; ask to be dropped at Ō-hama Iriguchi and walk 10 minutes toward the coast. Further south you can try

the more developed beaches of Yumigahama, which is on the same bus route. Be warned that these places can be packed in late July and August; otherwise, they're relatively quiet.

Bay Cruises Several cruises depart from the Shimoda harbour area. Most popular with Japanese tourists is a 'Black Ship' cruise around the bay (¥920, 20 minutes) which departs every 30 minutes (approximately) from 9.10am to 3.30pm.

Three boats a day (9.40am, 11.20am and 2pm) leave on a course for Irō-zaki. You can leave the boat at Irō-zaki (¥1530, 40 minutes) and travel on by bus northwards up the peninsula, or stay on the boat to return to Shimoda.

Special Events On the third Friday, Saturday and Sunday in May, the **Kuro-fune Matsuri** (Black Ship Festival) is held in Shimoda. It commemorates the first landing of Commodore Perry with parades by the US Navy Marine band and fireworks displays. It's most interesting to see how the Japanese have made a virtue out of this potentially bitter historical event. On 14 and 15 August, the **Shimoda Taiko Matsuri** (Drum Festival) features a spectacular parade of Dashi floats, and some serious Japanese-style drumming. The climax comes on the 15th.

SHIMODA

PLACES TO STAY
1　Kokumin-shukusha New Shimoda
　　国民宿舎ニュー下田
3　Station Hotel Shimoda
　　ステーションホテル下田
16　Hotel Kurofune
　　黒船ホテル
20　Shimoda-ya (Minshuku)
　　下田屋
21　Uraga Hotel
　　ウラガホテル・
22　Ōizu Ryokan
　　大伊豆旅館

PLACES TO EAT
6　McDonald's
7　Izutarō
　　伊豆太郎

9　Matsu Sushi
　　松寿し
11　Musashi
　　むさし
13　Gorosaya
　　ごろさや
14　Isoka-tei
　　磯華亭

OTHER
2　Photography Museum
　　写真記念館
4　Replica of Admiral Perry's Ship, the Susquehanna
　　サスケハナ丸の模型
5　Bus Stop
　　バス停
8　Convenience Store
　　コンビニエンスストアー

10　Tōden-ji
　　稲田寺
12　Tourist Information
　　観光案内所
15　Hōfuku-ji
　　宝福寺
17　Bay Cruises
　　遊覧船
18　Morning Fish Market
　　海の朝市
19　Shimoda Post Office
　　下田郵便局
23　Ryōsen-ji
　　了仙寺
24　Museum
25　Chōraku-ji
　　潮楽寺
26　Ja Jah
　　ジャジャ

Places to Stay The Gensu Youth Hostel (☎ 62-0035; W www.jyh.or.jp; dorm beds ¥2900) is 25 minutes from town on bus No 3; get off at the Yakuba-mae stop (¥630). Check-in is 4pm to 8pm. If you prefer to be in town, you'll have to spend a little more. There are lots of *minshuku* around and the **tourist office** (☎ 22-1531; open 9am-5pm daily) can help with reservations. **Shimoda-ya** (☎ 22-0446; beds with/without meals ¥8500/5500) has beds and offers a rate that includes two meals; check-in is 2.30pm.

Ōizu Ryokan (☎ 22-0123; rooms per person ¥3500) is the city's best bargain, with plain but comfy Japanese-style rooms, all with air-con and TV, and a two-seater hot-spring bath. It is a 10-minute walk south of the station, near Ryōsen-ji. **Kokumin-shukusha New Shimoda** (☎ 23-0222; rooms per person ¥7000) is a drab but friendly place that includes two meals in the rate. Check-in for both is 3pm.

Station Hotel Shimoda (☎ 22-8885; singles/doubles ¥5800/9800), right next to the station, is a business hotel with clean rooms. Check-in is 4pm.

Uraga Hotel (☎ 23-6600; singles/doubles ¥7000/9800) is another good business hotel which has clean new rooms and a 3pm check-in.

Hotel Kurofune (☎ 22-1234; rooms per person with/without meals ¥20,000/10,000) is the posh option; check-in is 3pm.

Places to Eat & Drink Seafood is the speciality in Shimoda and there are lots of good places around to try it. **Isoka-tei** (☎ 23-1200; lunch/dinner from ¥1000/2500; open 11.30am-3pm & 5.30pm-10pm daily) is a friendly place and the best of the bunch. They do hearty seafood sets for lunch and dinner for around ¥1500. There's a picture menu to make ordering easier.

Izutarō (☎ 27-2700; items ¥110-¥450; open 11.15am-2.30pm & 4.30pm-8pm daily) is a standard *kaiten-zushi* (conveyor-belt) spot.

Matsu Sushi (☎ 22-1309; sets from ¥1500; open 11am-8pm Thur-Tues) is another sushi place and is a cut above.

Musashi (☎ 22-0934; ¥800; open 11am-2pm & 5.30pm-7.30pm Wed-Mon) does most Japanese *shokudō* (cafeteria) favourites, including *tempura soba*.

Gorosaya (☎ 23-5638; lunch/dinner ¥1500/3000; open 11.30am-2pm & 5pm-9pm Fri-Wed), more upmarket, does great seafood.

Ja Jah (☎ 27-1611; closed Mon) is a bar and a place to try after dinner to kick back with some good tunes and friendly people. Beers start at ¥600.

Getting There & Away Shimoda is as far as you can go by train on the Izu-hantō. You can take the limited express *Odoriko* from Tokyo station (¥6160, 2¾ hours) or an Izu Kyūkō line train from Itō station (¥1570, one hour). Trains also run from Atami (¥1890, 1½ hours).

Bus platform No 5 in front of the station is for buses going to Dōgashima (¥1360, one hour), while platform No 7 is for those bound for Shuzen-ji (¥2180, two hours).

Rendai-ji & Kanaya Onsen
蓮台寺・金屋温泉

A stop north of Shimoda on the Izu Kyūkō line is Rendai-ji (¥160, five minutes), home to one of the best *onsen* on the peninsula, Kanaya Onsen (admission ¥1000; open 9am-10pm daily). Housed in atmospheric **Kanaya Ryokan** (☎ 22-0325; rooms per person with/without meals ¥15,000/7000), this traditional bath is well worth a side trip from Shimoda. The highlight is the enormous bath on the men's side, inside a weathered wooden hall. Women who want to check out this bath are welcome, but bathing suits are not permitted (towels are). The women's bath is nothing to sneeze at, and both sides have private outdoor baths.

Once you see the lovely ryokan, you may be tempted to stay the night.

From Rendai-ji station, go straight across the river and main road to the T-junction and turn left; the *onsen* is 50m on the right.

Irō-zaki 石廊崎

Irō-zaki, the southernmost point of the peninsula, is noted for its cliffs and lighthouse. It also has a jungle park, a tropical garden and some fairly good beaches. You can get to the cape from Shimoda by boat (see Bay Cruises in the Shimoda section earlier) or by bus (¥930, 45 minutes) from the No 4 bus platform.

Matsu-zaki 松崎
☎ 0558

The attraction of Matsu-zaki is its collection of around 200 **traditional houses** with *namako-kabe* walls – diamond-shaped tiles set in plaster. They're concentrated in the south of town, on the far side of the river.

Places to Stay Several kilometres to the east of town is **Sanyo-sō Youth Hostel** (☎ 42-0408; dorm beds ¥2850). From Shimoda take a bus from the No 5 platform and get off at the Yūsu-hosteru-mae bus stop. Check-in is 4pm to 6.30pm.

Getting There & Away Buses from Shimoda to Dōgashima pass through Matsuzaki. The fare from Shimoda is ¥1170; from Dōgashima ¥490. High-speed ferries also travel from Matsu-zaki to Dōgashima (¥450), Toi (¥1660), Heda (¥2090) and Numazu (¥3400).

Dōgashima 堂ヶ島

From Shimoda, it's a picturesque bus journey to Dōgashima, on the other side of the peninsula. There are no breathtaking views, but the hilly countryside and the narrow road that winds its way past fields and through small rural townships make for an interesting trip.

The main attractions at Dōgashima are the dramatic **rock formations** that line the seashore. The park just across the street from the bus stop has some of the best views. It's also possible to take a boat trip (¥900, 20 minutes) from the nearby jetty to visit the town's famous shoreline **cave**. The cave has a natural window in the roof that allows light to pour in. You can look down into the cave from paths in the aforementioned park.

South of the bus stop, you'll find the stunning **Sawada-kōen Rotemburo onsen** (admission ¥500; open 7am-7pm Wed-Mon Sept-July, 6am-8pm Wed-Mon Aug) perched high on a cliff overlooking the Pacific. Go early in the day if possible; around sunset it's standing room only. Males and females bathe separately.

Getting There & Away Buses to Dōgashima (¥1360, one hour) leave from platform No 5 in front of Shimoda station. From Dōgashima you can catch a bus onward to Shuzen-ji (¥2090, 1½ hours), a journey that affords fantastic views over Suruga-wan north to Mt Fuji. Indeed, when the air is clear and the mountain is blanketed by snow, it's worth the bus fare for

the view alone – you'll swear you're looking at a Hokusai print. The best views are to be had a few kilometres south of Toi.

There are six high-speed ferries between Dōgashima and Numazu (¥3300, 1¼ hours, 10am to 4.45pm), which is connected with Tokyo by the Tōkaidō line.

Shuzen-ji Onsen 修善寺
☎ 0558

Shuzen-ji is one of the peninsula's better *onsen* towns. It's connected to the Tōkaidō line by the Izu-Hakone Tetsudō line, making it, along with Atami, one of the two main entry points to the peninsula. Everything of interest to travellers is in Shuzen-ji Onsen, a bus ride (¥210, 10 minutes) west of Shuzen-ji station.

Things to See & Do In the middle of Shuzen-ji Onsen, you'll find **Shuzen-ji**, an attractive and tranquil temple that dates back to 807. It's said to have been founded by Kōbō Daishi, who established the Shingon sect (see Buddhism under Religion in the Facts about Japan chapter). The present structure dates from 1489.

Of course, the real reason to visit Shuzen-ji is to take a dip in one of its famous *onsen*. Right in the middle of the village you'll find the mineral hot spring **Tokko-no-yu** (admission free; open 24hr) with mixed bathing, on a rocky promontory over the Katsura-gawa. Given the bath's central location and lack of proper walls, it's hardly surprising that naked foreigners become instant tourist attractions.

For a little privacy, head to the wonderful baths at **Kikuya Ryokan** (admission ¥1000) opposite the bus stop. Nonguests are welcome from 11.30am to 2.30pm. This is one of the few places in Japan where the women's baths are better than the men's.

If the baths at Kikuya are out of your price range, try the nameless local *sentō* (public bath) which uses hot-spring water. It's opposite Kikuya, past the bus stop, 50m up a narrow lane on the left. There's no-one on duty here – just put your ¥300 in the box and watch the locals' jaws drop when you enter.

Places to Stay & Eat A 15-minute bus ride from Shuzen-ji station is **Shuzen-ji Youth Hostel** (☎ 72-1222; dorm beds

¥2900). Take a bus from the No 6 platform at Shuzen-ji station to the New Town-guchi stop. It's a five-minute walk from the bus stop. Check-in is 3.30pm to 9.30pm.

Kikuya Ryokan (☎ 72-2000; rooms per person ¥18,000), previously mentioned, is an elegant place, with rates that include two meals; check-in is 3pm.

Sakae-sō (☎ 72-3434; doubles per person ¥6500) is a pleasant minshuku and is a cheaper option. The double occupancy rates include breakfast; check-in is 3pm.

Washoku-dokoro Mizu (☎ 72-0546; lunch/dinner ¥1000/2000; open 11am-2pm & 5pm-8pm Wed-Mon), about 100m east of the bus stop on the main street, is a more elegant choice. Try the tempura-zen set.

Zen-dera (☎ 72-0007; meals around ¥1200; open 10am-4pm Fri-Wed) serves soba which is the local favourite.

Getting There & Away From Tokyo, access to Shuzen-ji is via Mishima on the Tōkaidō line (see the Mishima entry following). Izu-Hakone Tetsudō trains between Mishima and Shuzen-ji (¥500) take around 30 minutes. Buses run between Shuzen-ji and Shimoda (¥2180, two hours) and Shuzen-ji and Dōgashima (¥1970, 1½ hours).

Mishima 三島
☎ 0559

Mishima, on the Tōkaidō line, was once an important post-town on the old Tōkaidō highway. You might pause here before heading into the Izu-hantō or back to Tokyo. The town's main highlight is **Rakuju-en** (admission ¥300; open 9am-5pm Tues-Sun Apr-Oct, 9am-4.30pm Tues-Sun Nov-Mar, 9am-3pm Tues-Sun Dec) a Meiji-era stroll garden three minutes' walk south of the station. Nearby is **Mishima-taisha**, the most important shrine on the Izu-hantō. It's set in pleasantly wooded environs and has a small **treasure hall** (admission ¥500; open 9am-4.30pm daily) with Kamakura-era exhibits on display. The shrine is a five-minute walk from the southeastern gate of Rakuju-en.

Getting There & Away You can take a Tōkaidō-line shinkansen to Mishima from Tokyo (¥3890, one hour and five minutes); futsū trains take twice as long and cost ¥2210.

It's 10 minutes by train from Mishima to Numazu, from where you can continue into the Izu-hantō by boat or by bus (see the Dōgashima section earlier for details).

South of Tokyo

Southwest of Tokyo are the cities of Kawasaki and Yokohama, which have virtually merged with the capital to create one immense urban corridor. Beyond these cities is the fascinating old capital of Kamakura.

KAWASAKI 川崎
☎ 044 • pop 1.28 million

Kawasaki is a sprawling industrial port city, partly built on land reclaimed from Tokyo-wan. Its main attractions are the temple Kawasaki Daishi and Nihon Minka-en, an excellent museum of traditional Japanese houses.

Kawasaki Daishi 川崎大師
Formerly known as Heigen-ji, Kawasaki Daishi (admission free) has a long pedigree (legend has it the temple was founded in 1127) and is Kawasaki's answer to Sensō-ji in Asakusa, Tokyo. Like Sensō-ji, Kawasaki Daishi houses an image that was fished from the water – this time the sea. The image is that of Kōbō Daishi, the founder of the Shingon sect.

The temple is well worth a visit, as there are interesting shops nearby, an impressive five-storey pagoda and very few foreign tourists about.

Nihon Minka-en 日本民家園
Carpenters, architects and those with an interest in old Japan shouldn't miss the Nihon Minka-en (admission ¥500; open 9.30am-4.30pm Tues-Sun), an open-air museum comprised of 24 traditional Japanese buildings brought from all over the country and reassembled on one site. Most are farmhouses, although there is also a Shintō shrine and a kabuki stage.

Special Events
Kawasaki hosts the famous **Jibeta Matsuri**, in which processions of costumed locals parade wooden phalluses to celebrate the vanquishing of a sharp-toothed demon. The demon had taken up residence in a fair

maiden and had already emasculated two bridegrooms before a local blacksmith came up with the ingenious idea of deflowering the maiden with an iron phallus. History doesn't record the said maiden's feelings about this solution, but defeat of the demon gave rise to much celebration and an annual re-enactment of the forging of the metal phallus. Freudians are welcome.

The festival takes place in the late afternoon of the first Sunday in April, and starts with a procession, followed by a re-enactment of the forging, and rounded off with a banquet. The action takes place close to Kawasaki Daishi station.

Try to sneak into the shrine's erotica collection. It's above the souvenir shop, up the back stairs. Naturally.

Getting There & Away
For Kawasaki Daishi, take the JR Tōkaidō line from Tokyo station to Kawasaki station (¥290, 18 minutes). Walk from there to Keikyū Kawasaki station and take a Keikyū Daishi-line train to Kawasaki Daishi station, just three stops away (¥130). From Yokohama it takes just 13 minutes to get to Kawasaki (¥210) on the JR Tōkaidō line. For the Nihon Minka-en, take an Odakyū line train from Shinjuku station to Mukōgaoka-yuen station (¥240, 20 minutes). Then it's a 15-minute walk from the station's southern exit.

YOKOHAMA 横浜
☎ 045 • pop 3.5 million
Japan's second largest city may tread on Tokyo's coat-tails, but this former maritime centre is a vibrant, metropolis in its own right, and makes a pleasant side-trip from the capital. Its nationally renowned Chinatown buzzes with activity, as do the centres of Kannai and Sakuragi-chō, and the new seaside development of Minato Mirai 21. The city really comes into its own at night when the restaurants, clubs and bars that fill the city spring into life. By day, check out the harbour, and the peaceful greenery of Sankei-en.

For a glimpse of the earthy Yokohama that never appears in the tourist literature, take the Keihin-Kyuko train out to Kogane-Cho Station at dusk, where you'll find one of the country's most flourishing red-light districts. It is a veritable United Nations of sleaze, and though decidedly rough, it is rarely dangerous.

Orientation
Most of the sights are quite a way from Yokohama station and it makes more sense to go to Sakuragi-chō or Kannai stations. From Sakuragi-chō station, the Minato Mirai 21 complex is five minutes away by moving walkway. From the Minato Mirai 21 complex, it's possible to walk across Shinko Pier to the park Yamashita-kōen in around 25 minutes. From Yamashita-kōen you can walk on to Chinatown, the Silk Museum, the Foreigners' Cemetery and Harbour View Park.

Information
There is a **Tourist Information Center** (☎ 211-0111; open 9am-6pm daily) directly outside the northern exit of Sakuragi-chō station. The office has English speakers on hand. Be sure to pick up a copy of its free *Yokohama City Guide*, which has detailed maps of Yokohama's most important neighbourhoods.

There's a **Citibank** with a 24-hour international automated teller machine (ATM) outside the western exit of Yokohama station on the 2nd floor of the First Building; look for it on the southwestern side of the Yokohama Bay Sheraton.

Yokohama Station Area
横浜駅周辺
The Yokohama station area is given over unrelentingly to shopping. Its only real attraction is the **Hiraki Ukiyoe Museum** (admission ¥500; open 10.30am-5.30pm daily, sometimes closed Tues) on the 6th floor of the Sogō department store – yes, the largest department store in the world. The museum has a collection of over 8000 wood-block prints, both old and new. Sogō is close to the eastern exit of Yokohama station.

Minato Mirai 21 みなとみらい21
This new development (the '21' stands for '21st century') just north of Sakuragi-chō station is another of those Japanese excursions into the metropolis-of-the-future theme. One of the highlights is the new **Landmark Tower**, which not only is the tallest building in Japan, but also has the world's fastest lift (45km/h). The **Landmark Tower Sky Garden** (admission ¥1000; open 10am-9pm daily Sept-June, 10am-10pm daily July & Aug) observatory is on the 69th floor.

AROUND TOKYO

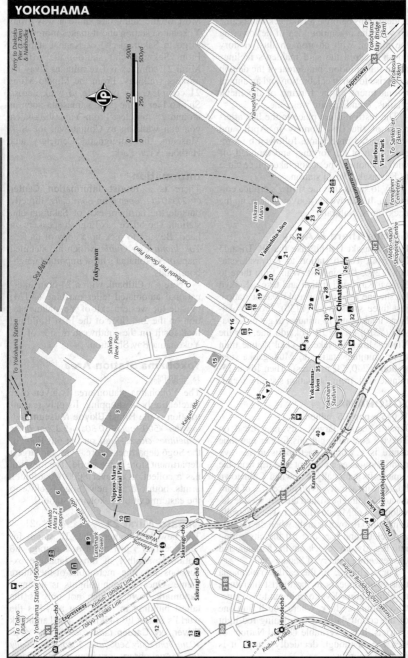

YOKOHAMA

YOKOHAMA

PLACES TO STAY

9 Yokohama Royal Park
Hotel Nikkō; Sirius
横浜ロイヤルパーク
ホテルニッコー
12 Kanagawa Youth Hostel
神奈川ユースホステル
21 Hotel Yokohama
ホテル横浜
22 Hotel New Grand
ホテルニューグランド
23 Star Hotel Yokohama
スターホテル横浜
29 Holiday Inn Yokohama
ホリデイイン横浜
41 Yokohama Isezakichō
Washington Hotel
横浜伊勢佐木町
ワシントンホテル

PLACES TO EAT

16 Suginoki; Scandia
Garden
杉の木；スカンジアガーデン
19 Parkside Gourmet
Plaza
パークサイドグルメプラザ
27 Peking Hanten Honten
北京飯店本店
28 Heichinrō Honten
へい珍楼本店
30 Manchinrō Honten
萬珍楼本店
37 Baikōtei
梅香亭
38 Ali Baba
アリババ

OTHER

1 Gaspanic Yokohama
2 Pacifico Yokohama;
National Convention Hall
of Yokohama;
Yokohama Grand
Intercontinental Hotel
パシフィコ横浜；
国立横浜国際会議場；
横浜グランドインター
コンチネンタルホテル
3 Yokohama World Porters
横浜ワールドポーターズ
みなとみらい）
4 Yokohama Cosmo World
横浜コスモワールド
5 Nippon Maru
コスモクロック
6 Queen's Square Yokohama;
Pan Pacific Hotel Yokohama
クイーンズスクエア横浜；
パンパシフィック
ホテル横浜
7 Yokohama Museum of Art
横浜美術館
8 Mitsubishi Minato Mirai
Industrial Museum
三菱みなとみらい技術館
10 Yokohama Maritime
Museum
横浜マリタイム
ミュージアム
11 Sakuragi-chō Tourist
Information Center
桜木町観光案内所
13 Iseyama-jinja
伊勢山皇大神社

14 Zoo; Nogeyama-kōen
動物園；
野毛山公園
15 Yokohama Customs
House
横浜税関
17 Yokohama Archives of
History
横浜開港資料館
18 Silk Museum
シルク博物館
20 Ken-min Hall
県民ホール
24 Marine Tower
マリンタワー
25 Yokohama Doll
Museum
横浜人形の家
26 Tenchō-mon
天長門
31 Zenrin-mon
善隣門
32 Kantei-byō
関帝廟
33 Windjammer
ウィンドジャマー
34 The Tavern
ザタバーン
35 Kita-mon
北門
36 The Mission to
Seafarers
ミッショントゥシーマン
39 Cape Cod
ケープコッド
40 City Hall
市役所

Across from Landmark Tower you'll find the interesting **Yokohama Maritime Museum** and the **Nippon Maru sailing ship** (admission to both ¥600; open 10am-5.30pm Tues-Sun Jan-Oct, 10am-4.30pm Tues-Sun Nov & Dec, slightly later summer). Beyond the Maritime Museum is **Cosmo World** (open 1pm-9pm Mon-Fri, 11am-10pm Sat & Sun) amusement park, where the price varies according to the ride. The best part of Cosmo World is the **Cosmo Clock Ferris Wheel** (admission ¥700; open 1pm-9pm Mon-Fri, 11am-10pm Sat & Sun), the world's highest at 105m. Near Cosmo World, **Yokohama World Porters** is a huge shopping complex with lots of restaurants on the ground floor.

Northeast of Landmark Tower is **Queen's Square Yokohama**, yet another shopping and dining complex. Check out the street performers doing their thing outside the main entrance. Next along from Queen's Square is the dramatic, sail-shaped **Pacifico Yokohama** complex, housing the National Convention Hall of Yokohama and the Yokohama Grand Intercontinental Hotel.

Behind Landmark Tower, you'll find the **Yokohama Museum of Art** (admission ¥500; open 10am-6pm Fri-Wed) which has a decent collection of modern art. Perhaps more exciting than the art on display is the Tange Kenzō–designed building, particularly the dramatic main hall. Nearby, the **Mitsubishi Minato Mirai Industrial Museum** (adult/child ¥600/200; open 10am-5.30pm Tues-Sun) is one of Japan's better science and technology museums, with a wildly enjoyable helicopter simulator, along with lots of other good hands-on exhibits.

Yamashita-kōen Area
山下公園周辺

This area, east of Kannai station, is traditionally Yokohama's sightseeing district. At the heart of it all is the seafront Yamashita-kōen. Moored alongside the park you'll find the **Hikawa Maru** *(adult/child ¥800/ 400; open 9.30am-7pm daily winter, 9.30am-8pm daily rest of year)*, a retired passenger liner that's a lot of fun for the kids.

Across the street is the **Silk Museum** *(admission ¥300; open 9am-4.30pm Tues-Sun)* which covers all aspects of silk and silk production and has some lovely kimono and obi (sashes) on display. Nearby, the **Yokohama Archives of History** *(admission ¥200; open 9.30am-5pm Tues-Sun)* has a fascinating collection of items related to the history of Yokohama port. Across the street, **Yokohama Customs House** *(admission free; open 10am-4pm Mon-Fri)* has a somewhat less interesting collection of exhibits related to customs and trade.

Back in a southeasterly direction, you'll find **Marine Tower** *(admission ¥700; open 10am-7pm daily winter, 10am-9pm daily rest of year)*, a relic from the early days of Japanese tourism, offering a diminutive (106m) view over the harbour. Other attractions relatively nearby include **Harbour View Park** and the **Foreigners' Cemetery**, the final resting place of 4000 foreign residents and visitors to Yokohama – a look at some of the headstones reveals some fascinating inscriptions.

Chinatown 中華街

Not far from the harbour area is Chinatown (known as 'Chūkagai' in Japanese). This is one of Yokohama's greatest tourist attractions and the tiny streets are often packed with visitors who come to ogle the over-the-top Chinese facades of the neighbourhood's stores and restaurants. Needless to say, food is the main attraction here, but be warned that prices are high. Apart from the food, the only other attractions worthy of exploration are **Kantei-byō**, a Chinese temple in the heart of the district, and the gaily coloured Chinese gates scattered around the area.

Sankei-en 三溪園

Sankei-en *(admission each garden ¥300; open 9am-4.30pm daily, closed 29-31 Dec)* was established in 1906 by a Yokohama silk merchant. The beautifully landscaped gardens feature a 500-year-old three-storey pagoda. There are separate admission charges to the outer and inner gardens. The inner one is a fine example of traditional Japanese garden landscaping. Take the No 8 bus from Yokohama or Sakuragi-chō stations to Honmoku Sankei-en-mae bus stop. Alternatively, take a JR Negishi-line train from Sakuragi-chō to Negishi station and change to a city bus bound for Sakuragi-chō (No 54, 58, 99, 101 or 108). Get off at the Honmoku stop, from which it's an easy five-minute walk to the southern entrance of the park.

Shin-Yokohama Station Area
新横浜駅周辺

Shin-Yokohama Rāmen Hakubutsukan *(☎ 471-0503; admission/meals ¥300/900; open 11am-11pm daily)* is a noodle-nut's paradise. The museum is a kind of *rāmen* theme park that tells the history of the cuisine – and *rāmen* houses – in a replica of a 1958 Shitamachi (downtown district), including eight *rāmen* shops run by masters of the trade from across the country. Currently the most popular eatery is **Sumire**. Avoid this place on public holidays unless you want to wait in line for up to 70 minutes. It's a five-minute walk east from Shin-Yokohama station; turn left after the co-op, and right at the Family Mart convenience store. It is clearly signposted in English and Chinese.

Places to Stay

Kanagawa Youth Hostel *(☎ 241-6503; ⓦ www.jyh.or.jp; dorm beds ¥2600, summer ¥2800)* has friendly new management. You can make reservations in English; check-in is 4pm.

Yokohama Isezakichō Washington Hotel *(☎ 243-7111; singles/doubles/twins from ¥8000/14,200/16,200)* is the cheapest hotel option and is decent; check-in is 2pm.

Star Hotel Yokohama *(☎ 651-3111; singles/doubles ¥9000/15,000)* is the cheapest of a number of hotels along the harbourfront facing Yamashita-kōen. Check-in is 2pm.

Hotel Yokohama *(☎ 662-1321; ⓦ www .theyoko.co.jp; singles/doubles Mon-Thur from ¥16,000/21,000, Fri from ¥18,000/ 24000, Sat & Sun from ¥20,000/27,000)* is an upmarket option.

Hotel New Grand *(☎ 681-1841; singles/ twins Mon-Fri from ¥12,000/20,000, Sat & Sun from ¥20,000/29,000)* has 260 rooms in a prime waterfront location, handy for Yamashita-kōen and Chinatown. Once a favourite of visiting foreign potentates and plenipotentiaries, it is now simply a classy upmarket option with some olde-worlde charm still lingering on despite its 1992 modernisation. Check-in is 2pm.

Holiday Inn Yokohama (☎ 681-3311; **w** www.loonmoongroup.com; twins from ¥20,000) is not far away in Chinatown, but is overpriced.

The city's top hotels can be found in the Minato Mirai 21 area. **Yokohama Royal Park Hotel Nikkō** (☎ 221-1111; **w** www.yrph.com; singles/twins/doubles from ¥29,000/34,000/ 34,000) has the best location, on the upper floors of Landmark Tower. Watch out for their frequent cut-price deals for women travellers. Check-in is 2pm.

Pan Pacific Hotel Yokohama (☎ 682-2222; **w** http://pphy.co.jp; twins from ¥35,000), in the Queen's Square Yokohama complex, is a stylish new place. Check-in is 2pm.

Yokohama Grand Intercontinental Hotel (☎ 223-2222; **w** http://yokohama.japan.inter continental.com/hotel.shtml; singles/doubles from ¥28,000/34,000), in the Pacifico Yoko-hama complex, is another stunningly located hotel; check-in is 2pm.

Places to Eat
In Yokohama, the done thing is to have a bang-up dinner in Chinatown. Plan on spending about ¥5000 per head for a good dinner and perhaps half that for lunch. Most places offer set courses.

Manchinrō Honten (☎ 681-4004; dinner for 2 ¥8000; open 10am-10pm daily) is one of the area's more popular spots for Guang-dong cuisine.

Heichinrō Honten (☎ 681-3001; lunch/ dinner course ¥3000/5000; open 11am-10.15pm daily), an elegant Cantonese spe-cialist, has dim sum sets from ¥2500 and a large picture menu.

Peking Hanten Honten (☎ 681-3535; open 11.30am-2am daily) is a huge place with an English menu and reasonably priced lunch specials.

Back near Yamashita-kōen you'll find the next two places.

Scandia Garden (☎ 201-2262; lunch/ dinner sets from ¥1300/1500; open 11am-midnight daily) is one of Japan's few Danish restaurants.

Suginoki (☎ 212-4143; lunch set/dinner course ¥700/3250; open 11.45am-3pm & 4.30pm-11.15pm Fri-Wed) serves a popular paella. It's worth stopping by just to check out the antique plastic food models in the window – they look like they were set out to tempt Admiral Perry and his crew.

Baikōtei (☎ 681-4870; meals around ¥800; open 11am-9pm Mon-Sat) is a friendly 'retro' spot famed for its Hayashi rice. Look out for the sign which announces Baikō Emmies: English Spoken. It is very near Yokohama-kōen.

Ali Baba (☎ 651-0388; meals around ¥700; open 11.30am-2pm & 5pm-11pm Mon-Sat), nearby, serves good, inexpensive Turk-ish fare. The cross-cultural Doner Don is highly recommended. The Japanese owner speaks English and Turkish.

Entertainment
There is plenty to do in Yokohama in the evening. Many of the city's bars are on the outskirts of Chinatown.

The Tavern (☎ 322-9727; beers from ¥800, pub food ¥1200; open 6pm-1am daily) is a British-style pub with the usual beers on tap and a good selection of pub food. **Wind-jammer** (☎ 662-3966; live music cover ¥500, drinks from ¥900; open 6pm-1.30am daily), a bar-restaurant, is another good spot for a few drinks and the occasional live jazz. It's been jamming for three decades.

The Missions to Seafarers (☎ 662-1871; open 11:30am-11.30pm Mon-Fri, 4pm-11.30pm Sat & Sun) is a far rowdier spot which has cheap beer and billiards. As you might imagine, this place draws an interesting crowd (and you don't have to be a sailor to get in). A similar spot that also attracts a lot of foreigners is **Cape Cod** (☎ 661-0700; beers/cocktails from ¥600/ 950; open 5pm-midnight daily) in the mid-dle of town.

Gaspanic Yokohama (☎ 680-0291; open 6pm-midnight Sun-Wed, 6pm-5am Thur-Sat), a branch of the Roppongi cheap-booze cheap-thrills emporium, peddles it gas and panic in Minato Mirai. Drinks are ¥400 until 9.30pm every day, and on Thursday, all night. The results are not hard to imagine.

Sirius (open 5pm-1am; drinks from ¥1000) bar, on the 70th floor of Landmark Tower, is the antithesis of Gaspanic – an elegant cocktail lounge in the Yokohama Royal Park Hotel Nikkō. The place to go for drinks with a view.

Getting There & Away

Train There are numerous trains from Tokyo – the cheapest being the Tōkyū Tōyoko line from Shibuya station to Sakuragi-chō station (*futsū/kyūkō* ¥290, 44/37 minutes). Trains stop at Yokohama station on the way to Sakuragi-chō station.

The Keihin Tōhoku line goes through Yokohama station (¥450, 40 minutes) to Kannai station (¥380, 47 minutes) from Tokyo and Shinagawa stations. The Tōkaidō line from Tokyo or Shinagawa stations also runs to Yokohama station (¥450, 25 minutes).

To Kamakura, you take the Yokosuka line from Yokohama station (¥330, 25 minutes). The Tōkaidō *shinkansen* stops at Shin-Yokohama station, a fair way to the northwest of town, on its way between Tokyo and the Kansai region. Shin-Yokohama station is connected to Yokohama, Sakuragi-chō and Kannai stations by the Yokohama line and by a less convenient subway line.

Getting Around

To/From the Airport Both trains and buses connect Narita to Yokohama; take the train to be sure of arriving at a particular time. Trains run from Yokohama station. You can choose Narita Express (N'EX) services (¥4180, 1½ hours) or JR Airport Narita services (¥1890, two hours). Limousine buses travel frequently between the Yokohama City Air Terminal (YCAT, in the Sky Building east of Yokohama station, next to Sogō department store) and Narita (¥3500, two hours, depending on traffic).

Bus Although trains are more convenient for getting around town, Yokohama does have an extensive bus network. To travel within the city, you pay a flat fee of ¥210.

Boat The *Sea Bass* ferry connects Yokohama station, the Minato Mirai 21 complex and Yamashita-kōen. Boats run between 10am and 7pm. The full fare from Yokohama station to Yamashita-kōen is ¥600; the trip takes 20 minutes.

KAMAKURA 鎌倉
☎ 0467

The capital of Japan from 1185 to 1333, Kamakura rivals Nikkō as the most culturally rewarding day trip from Tokyo. There are a huge number of Buddhist temples and the occasional shrine dotted around the surrounding countryside, as well as some very pleasant walks. Although Kamakura – like any other major attraction in Japan – gets packed on weekends and in holiday periods, midweek can be very peaceful in the outlying temples.

History

In the 10th century, the power of the emperor in Kyoto was largely ceremonial; real power had for some time rested in the hands of the Fujiwara clan. As the power of the Fujiwara declined, the Taira clan, led by Taira Kiyomori, and the Minamoto clan, led by Minamoto Yoshitomo, began an all-out struggle for supreme power. In 1159 the Taira routed the Minamoto forces.

Although many executions followed, by chance Yoshitomo's third son's life was spared and the boy was sent to spend his days in an Izu-hantō temple. As soon as the boy, Minamoto Yoritomo, was old enough, he began to gather support for a counterattack on his clan's old rivals. In 1180 he set up his base at Kamakura, an area far away from the debilitating influences of Kyoto court life, close to other clans loyal to the Minamoto and, being enclosed by the sea on one side and by densely wooded hills on the others, easy to defend.

With a series of victories over the Taira behind him, Minamoto Yoritomo was appointed shōgun in 1192; he governed Japan from Kamakura. When he died without an heir, however, power passed to the Hōjo, the family of Yoritomo's wife.

The Hōjo clan ruled Japan from Kamakura for more than a century until, in 1333, weakened by the cost of maintaining defences against threats of attack from Kublai Khan in China, the Hōjo clan was defeated by Emperor Go-Daigo. Kyoto once again became capital.

Orientation

Kamakura's main attractions can be seen in a day of walking augmented by the occasional bus ride. Temples are usually well signposted in both English and Japanese. You can either start at Kamakura station and work your way around the area in a circle, or start north of Kamakura at Kita-Kamakura station and visit the temples between there and Kamakura on foot. The itinerary in this section follows the latter route.

Information

The **Kamakura Tourist Information Center** (☎ 22-3350; open 9am-5.30pm daily) is just outside Kamakura station. Maps and brochures are available here and the office should also be able to help you find accommodation.

Engaku-ji 円覚寺

Engaku-ji (☎ 22-0487; admission ¥200; open 8am-5pm daily Apr-Sept, 8am-4pm daily Oct-Mar) is on the left as you exit Kita-Kamakura station. It is one of the five main Rinzai Zen temples in Kamakura. Engaku-ji was founded in 1282, allegedly as a place where Zen monks might pray for soldiers who had lost their lives defending Japan against the second of Kublai Khan's invasion attempts. Today the only real reminder of the temple's former magnificence and antiquity is **San-mon**, a 1780 reconstruction. At the top of the long flight of stairs through the gate is the **Engaku-ji bell**, which was cast in 1301 and is the largest bell in Kamakura. The **Hondō** (Main Hall) inside San-mon is quite a recent reconstruction, dating from the mid-1960s.

Tōkei-ji 東慶寺

Tōkei-ji (admission ¥100; open 8.30am-5pm daily Mar-Oct, 8.30am-4pm daily Nov-Feb), across the railway tracks from Engaku-ji, is notable for its grounds as much as for the temple itself. On weekdays, when visitors are few, it can be a pleasantly relaxing place. Walk up to the cemetery and wander around.

Historically, the temple is famed as having served as a women's refuge. A woman could be officially recognised as divorced after three years as a nun in the temple precincts. Today there are no nuns; the grave of the last abbess can be found in the cemetery.

Jōchi-ji 浄智寺

A couple of minutes further on from Tōkei-ji is Jōchi-ji (admission ¥150; open 9am-4.30pm daily Jan & Feb, 9am-5pm daily Mar-Dec), another temple with pleasant grounds. Founded in 1283, this is considered one of Kamakura's five great Zen temples.

Ennō-ji 円応寺

Across the road from Kenchō-ji is Ennō-ji (admission ¥300; open 9am-3.30pm daily winter, 9am-4pm daily rest of year) which is distinguished primarily by its collection of statues depicting the judges of hell. Presiding over them is Emma, an ancient Hindu deity known in Sanskrit as Yama. The ideas of hell and judgement became important Buddhist concepts with the rise of the Jōdo (Pure Land) school (see Buddhism under Religion in the Facts about Japan chapter).

Tsurugaoka Hachiman-gū 八幡宮

Further down the road, where it turns toward Kamakura station, is Tsurugaoka Hachiman-gū, the main shrine of Kamakura. It was founded by Minamoto Yoriyoshi, of the same Minamoto clan that ruled Japan from Kamakura (see History earlier in this section). There is some debate as to whether Hachiman, the deity to which the shrine is dedicated, has always been regarded as the god of war; the construction of this shrine may simply be a reflection of the fact that Hachiman is also the guardian deity of the Minamoto clan. Whatever the case, this Shintō shrine presents the visitor with an atmosphere drastically different to the repose of the Zen temples clustered around Kita-Kamakura station.

Kamakura National Treasure Museum

At the end of the main avenue, the Kamakura Kokuhō-kan (admission ¥150; open 9am-4.30pm Tues-Sun) is recommended, as it provides your only opportunity to see Kamakura art, most of which is hidden away in the temples.

Daibutsu 大仏

The Kamakura Daibutsu (Great Buddha; admission ¥200; open 7am-6pm daily Mar-Nov, 7am-5pm daily Dec-Feb) was completed in 1252 and is Kamakura's most famous sight. Once housed in a huge hall, the statue today sits in the open, its home having been washed away by a tsunami in 1495. Cast in bronze and weighing close

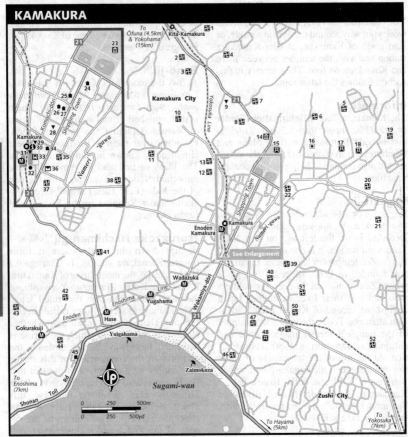

KAMAKURA

to 850 tonnes, the statue is 11.4m tall. Its construction is said to have been inspired by Yoritomo's visit to Nara (where there is another, even bigger, *daibutsu*) after the Minamoto clan's victory over the rival Taira clan. Even though Kamakura's Daibutsu doesn't quite match Nara's in stature, it is commonly agreed that it is artistically superior.

The Buddha itself is the Amida Buddha (*amitābha* in Sanskrit), worshipped by the followers of the Jōdo school as a figure of salvation.

Buses from stop No 2, 7 or 10 in front of Kamakura station run to the Daibutsu-mae stop. Alternatively, take the Enoden Enoshima line to Hase station and walk north for 10 minutes.

Hase-dera 長谷寺

Not far from the Daibutsu-mae bus stop is the temple, Hase-dera (☎ 22-6300; admission ¥300; open 8am-4.30pm daily Oct-Feb, 8am-5.30pm daily Mar-Sept), also known as Hase Kannon-ji. The grounds have a garden and an interesting collection of statues of Jizō, the patron saint of travellers and the souls of departed children. Ranked like a small army of urchins, the statues are clothed, to keep them warm, by women who have lost children by abortion or miscarriage. The main point of interest in the grounds, however, is the Kannon statue.

Kannon (*avalokiteshvara* in Sanskrit), the goddess of mercy, is the Bodhisattva of infinite compassion and, along with Jizō, is one of Japan's most popular Buddhist deities.

KAMAKURA

The 9m-high carved wooden *jūichimen* (11-faced Kannon) here is believed to be very ancient, dating from the 8th century. The 11 faces are actually one primary face and 10 secondary faces, the latter representing the 10 stages of enlightenment. It is commonly believed that the 11 faces allow Kannon, ever vigilant for those in need of her assistance, to cast an eye in every direction.

Other Shrines & Temples

If you're still in the mood for temple tramping, there are plenty more in and around Kamakura, which has somewhere in the vicinity of 70 temples and shrines.

From the Daibutsu it is best to return to Kamakura station by bus and take another bus out to the temples in the eastern part of town. These have the advantage of being even less popular with tourists than the temples in Kita-Kamakura; they may lack the grandeur of some of Kamakura's more famous temples, but they more than make up for this with their charm. There is also a delightfully restful village-like atmosphere in the town's outer fringes.

Zuisen-ji The grounds of this secluded Zen temple (☎ 22-1191; admission ¥100; open 9am-5pm daily) make for a pleasant stroll and include Zen gardens laid out by Kokushi Musō, the temple's founder. It is possible to get there from the Egara Ten-jin shrine on foot in about 10 to 15 minutes; turn right where the bus turns left in front of the shrine, take the next left and keep following the road.

Sugimoto-dera This interesting little temple (☎ 22-3463; admission ¥200; open 8am-4.30pm daily), founded in 734, is reputed to be the oldest in Kamakura. Its ferocious-looking guardian deities and a statue of Kannon are its main draw.

Take a bus from stop No 5 in front of Kamakura station to the Sugimoto Kannon bus stop.

Hōkoku-ji Down the road (away from Kamakura station) from Sugimoto-dera, on the right-hand side, is Hōkoku-ji (☎ 22-0762; admission ¥200; open 9am-4pm daily). This is a Rinzai Zen temple with quiet, landscaped gardens where you can relax under a red parasol with a cup of Japanese tea. This is also one of the more active Zen temples in Kamakura, regularly holding *zazen* classes for beginners. Take bus No 23, 24 or 36 from Kamakura station (¥190, 5 minutes).

Special Events
The **Kamakura Matsuri** is a week of celebrations held from the second Sunday to the third Sunday in April. It includes a wide range of activities, most of which are centred on Tsurugaoka Hachiman-gū.

During the **Bonbori Matsuri**, held from 7 to 9 August, hundreds of lanterns are strung up around Tsurugaoka Hachiman-gū.

The **Hachiman-gū Matsuri** is held from 14 to 16 September. Festivities include a procession of *mikoshi* and, on the last day, a display of horseback archery.

Places to Stay
Kamakura Kagetsuen Youth Hostel (☎ 25-1238; **w** www.jyh.or.jp; dorm beds ¥3150) is right on the beach and has good ocean views. From Kamakura station take an Enoden Enoshima train to Hase station. From there, walk down to the seafront road and walk west for about 10 minutes. The hostel is inside the Kagetsuen Hotel; check-in is 4pm.

Ajisai (☎ 22-3492; rooms per person from ¥6500), back in town, is comfortable and is the cheapest option. Check-in is 3pm to 10pm.

City Pension Shangri La (Shangri La Tsuroka Hotel; ☎ 25-6363; singles/twins ¥6500/13,000) is nearby. Shangri La it ain't – just a handily placed business hotel. Check-in is 3pm to 9pm.

Tsurugaoka Kaikan Hotel (☎ 24-1111; rooms per person from ¥8000) is just a few doors down from Shangri La and is somewhat overpriced; check-in is 2.30pm.

Hotel Kamakura Mori (☎ 22-5868; twins per 1/2 people ¥13,500/18,000) is a similar hotel and is clean and new. Rates do not include meals; check-in is 3pm.

Komachi-sō (☎ 23-2151; singles/twins ¥5000/9000) is a *minshuku* that receives positive reports from readers, not least because it offers that Kamakura rarity *sudomari* (accommodation only) and a good breakfast at ¥1000. Check-in is 4pm.

Places to Eat
Komachi-Ichiba (☎ 24-7921; lunch/dinner around ¥1200/2500; open 11.30am-2.30pm & 4pm-10.30pm daily) is the city's best lunch and dinner deal, with great local fresh seafood set courses and local sake. It is on the 2nd floor of the station building, above the TIC. Its sister operation, a tempura shop next door, shares the same kitchen and same hours, and is also good value.

Kawagoeya (☎ 24-2580; meals around ¥1200; open 11am-8pm Fri-Wed) is a good *soba* restaurant specialising in Kyoto-style buckwheat noodles. It's to the left of Kamakura station's East exit, in the basement below McDonald's.

There are plenty of other choices on the Komachi-dōri shopping street or the main road to Tsurugaoka Hachiman-gū, both of which run northeast from the station.

Chaya Kado, (☎ 23-1673; meals around ¥1600; open 10am-5pm daily) up in Kita-Kamakura, is this *soba* shop which does sets like tempura and *oden gozen*; various morsels simmered in a rich broth.

Getting There & Away
Yokosuka line trains run to Kamakura from Tokyo (¥890, 56 minutes), Shimbashi and Shinagawa stations. It's also possible to catch a train from Yokohama (¥330, 27 minutes) on the Yokosuka line. If you're planning to get off at Kita-Kamakura station, it's the stop after Ōfuna.

It's possible to continue on to Enoshima from Kamakura, either via the Enoden Enoshima line from Kamakura station (¥250, 25 minutes) or by bus from stop No 9 in front of Kamakura station (¥300, 35 minutes).

JR Kamakura-Enoshima Free Pass This pass is valid for two days, covers the trip to and from Tokyo, and allows unlimited use of JR trains around Kamakura, the Shōnan monorail between Ōfuna and Enoshima, and the Enoden Enoshima line between Fujisawa and Enoshima. From Tokyo station the pass costs ¥1970; from Yokohama station ¥1130.

Getting Around

You can walk to most temples from Kamakura or Kita-Kamakura stations. Sites in the west, like the Daibutsu, can be reached via the Enoden Enoshima line from Kamakura station. Alternatively, you can take buses from Kamakura station. Bus trips around the area cost either ¥170 or ¥190. Another good option is to rent a bicycle; there's a rental shop just outside the eastern exit of Kamakura station that charges ¥500/1500 per hour/day.

ENOSHIMA 江ノ島

Seven kilometres west of Kamakura, the tiny island of Enoshima is a good side-trip from Kamakura if you've got some time left after seeing all those temples. The island, dubbed in a startling leap of hyperbolic faith 'The Miami Beach of the East', is connected to the mainland by a 600m causeway. After crossing the causeway on foot, you have the choice of hiking to Enoshima-jinja or taking the 'outdoor escalator' (¥300). The shrine houses a *hadaka-benzaiten* – a nude statue of the Indian goddess of beauty *(admission to enter the hall housing the statue ¥150)*.

Getting There & Away

Frequent buses and trains run between Kamakura and Enoshima (see Getting There & Away under Kamakura). To return to Tokyo, you can retrace your steps to Kamakura or take the Odakyū line back to Shinjuku from Katase Enoshima station *(kyūkō/tokkyū ¥610/1220, two hours)*. To get to the station from the island, walk back across the causeway, turn left over the river and look for the faux-Chinese station building.

East of Tokyo

Much of Chiba-ken, to the east and southeast of Tokyo, is suburbia. There are few compelling reasons to visit the area. However, a large majority of visitors to Japan will arrive or depart from Narita airport and, if you have a few hours to kill at the airport, there are some points of interest in the town of Narita.

NARITA 成田
☎ 0476 • pop 97,421
Narita is a pleasant temple town that makes a perfect trip for those stuck on a long layover at Tokyo Narita International Airport. It's also ideal for your first or last night in Japan.

Information

Pick up a copy of the map pamphlet *Narita* at the **Narita Tourist Information Center** *(☎ 24-3198; open 8.30am-5.15pm daily)* just outside the eastern exit of JR Narita station. You might also stop by the **Narita Tourist Pavilion** *(☎ 24-3232; Omotesandō; open 10am-5pm Tues-Sun)* to see its exhibits on Narita's history.

Things to See & Do

The town is centred on the impressive **Narita-san Shinshō-ji** and its attractive grounds, **Narita-san-kōen**. While the temple was founded some 1000 years ago, the main hall is a 1968 reconstruction. The temple itself remains an important centre of the Shingon sect of Buddhism and attracts as many as 10 million visitors a year. Entrance is allowed until 3.30pm.

In Narita-san-kōen, you'll find the **Narita-san Calligraphy Museum** *(admission ¥500; open 9am-4pm Tues-Sun)* which has a good collection of *shodō* (calligraphy) for real aficionados. The **Reikōkan Historical Material Museum** *(☎ 22-0234; admission ¥300; open 9am-4pm Tues-Sun)*, under the temple's upper pagoda, and its nearby annex house a collection of artefacts from 18th-century Japanese life and various temple treasures – again, probably of interest only to real aficionados. Even if you skip both of these attractions, be sure to stroll along the ponds at the eastern edge of the park. The town's Omotesandō street is also an interesting walk.

Boso no Mura *(☎ 95-3333; admission free; open 9am-4.30pm)* is a replica of a traditional Japanese village, and an excellent place to kill several hours, with free paper-making, wood-working and even blacksmithing. You can also dress up in samurai armour or kabuki costume. It is a five minute walk from JR Ajiki station.

AROUND TOKYO

Special Events

The main festivals in Narita-san Shinshō-ji are **Setsubun** (last day of winter in the Japanese lunar calendar), which is on 3 or 4 February, and **Hatsumōde** (First Shrine Visit) which is on 1 January. Things get very hectic at the temple on both these occasions, and a high level of crowd-tolerance is a must.

Places to Stay

Narita is a pleasant place to stay and a good choice for those with early flights. **Ohgiya Ryokan** (☎ 22-1161; rooms per person with/without bath ¥9100/6300) is a member of the Japanese Inn Group and is a Japanese-style inn. It's a 10-minute walk from JR Narita or Keisei Narita stations. Check-in is 3pm.

Kirinoya Ryokan (☎ 22-0724; singles/doubles ¥5000/9000), near Narita-san-kōen, is another good choice. The owners are friendly and maintain the place as a 'ryokan museum' – it's filled with all sorts of interesting historical bric-a-brac. Meals are also served. Both places are on the *Narita* map pamphlet given out at the tourist information office. Check-in is 1pm to 11pm.

Being so close to the airport, Narita has a representative selection of upmarket hotels including, **ANA Hotel Narita** (☎ 33-1311; W www.anahotels.com/narita; singles/doubles from ¥14,000/21,000), **Holiday Inn Tōbu Narita** (☎ 32-1234; W www.sixcontinents hotels.com/h/d/HI/hd/narja; singles/doubles from ¥9500/15,000) and **Hotel Narita Tokyū** (☎ 33-0109; W www.panpac.com/japan/nar ita/hotels/hotel.html; singles/twins/doubles from ¥9000/15,000/15,000). If you don't mind paying a little more, the ANA is the pick of the bunch (check-in 1pm; check-in for the other two is 2pm).

All three hotels operate regular shuttle buses to and from the airport; ask at the hotel reservation counter in the arrivals hall for the correct boarding stand. Coming from Tokyo, it's best to go to the airport and then take the shuttle bus to your hotel.

Places to Eat

Omotesandō is packed with good places to eat. **Kikuya** (☎ 22-0236; lunch/dinner from ¥1000/1500; open 10am-8.30pm daily) is the best and serves lunch sets of typical Japanese fare. Look for the English sign reading 'Chrysanthemum Housu' (sic) across from the Tourist Pavilion.

The Barge Inn (☎ 23-2546; meals from ¥950; open 4pm-2am daily, lunch specials 11am-2pm Sat & Sun only) is a good choice if you hanker for some English-pub fare or a pint or two. English is spoken.

Getting There & Away

From Tokyo Narita international airport you can take either the Keisei line (*futsū* or *kyūkō* but not the Skyliner, ¥250, five minutes) or JR (*futsū* or *kyūkō* – the N'EX usually doesn't stop – ¥190/230 from Terminal 2/1, five minutes). From Tokyo, the easiest way to get to Narita is via the Keisei line from Ueno (*kyūkō*, ¥810, 85 minutes) or the JR Airport Narita from Tokyo station (¥1110, 80 minutes). For information on using these services, see the Getting Around section in the Tokyo chapter.

Izu-shotō 伊豆七島

The semitropical Izu-shotō, known in English as Izu Seven Islands, are peaks of a submerged volcanic chain that projects far down into the Pacific from the Izu-hantō. Until the beginning of the 20th century, the island chain was a place of exile; now it's a popular holiday destination for Tokyo residents. Activities on the islands include swimming, snorkelling, diving, fishing, dolphin watching, bicycling, hiking and relaxing in outdoor *onsen*.

Although it's relatively expensive to reach the islands, free camp sites are available on most of them and you can take your food over on the ferry. To escape the crowds, avoid holiday periods and head for the more remote islands, such as the fascinating Hachijō-jima, hands-down the pick of the bunch.

Getting There & Away

Ferries to the islands leave from Tokyo's Takeshiba Pier (10 minutes from Hama-matsu-chō station). Most ferries from Tokyo depart at 10pm and arrive at the islands early the next morning. Some of the islands are also serviced by ferries from Atami and Itō. Call **Tōkai Kisen ferry service** (☎ 5472-9009) for departure times and reservations (in Japanese). The islands, Ō-shima, Mi-yake-jima and Hachijō-jima, have airports and can be reached by plane from Tokyo's Haneda airport.

Getting Around
Island-hopping is possible but requires some serious planning, as services vary seasonally and departures can be quite infrequent. If you do intend to island-hop, consult with the **Tokyo TIC** (☎ *3201-3331; open 9am-5pm Mon-Fri, 9am-12pm Sat*) to choose the best route and schedule. If you have money to burn, you can also travel from island to island by helicopter. Rates average ¥10,000 per flight and there is usually one flight per day to and from each island. Call **Tokyo Island Shuttle** (☎ *2-5222*) for details.

Ō-SHIMA 大島
☎ 04992
Due to its proximity to the mainland, Ō-shima is the most popular island in the group. It's also the largest, at 91 sq km. Be warned that Ō-shima is overrun with young Tokyoites on weekends and holidays. Unless you really love crowds, avoid the island during these times, or head to the more southerly islands.

Information
Pick up the TIC's informative *Oshima Island* pamphlet or call the **Izu Seven Islands Tourist Federation** (☎ *3436-6955*) in Tokyo for more information before setting out. Once on the island, stop by the helpful **Ōshima Tourist Association** (☎ *2-2177*). It's right at the pier, visible as soon as you get off the ferry. While you're there, pick up some half-price *onsen* tickets.

Things to See & Do
The main attraction of Ō-shima is the active volcano **Mihara-yama**, which last erupted in November 1986 forcing the evacuation of island residents to Tokyo. Buses run to the summit from Motomachi port (¥680, 25 minutes).

Onsen are the island's other main attraction. **Hama-no-yu** (*admission ¥400; open 1pm-7pm daily*), 10 minutes' walk north of the port, has good ocean views but gets packed out on weekends. It's mixed bathing but swimsuits are permitted. A quieter place is **Ōshima Onsen Hotel** (*admission ¥800; open 1pm-9pm daily*), an outdoor *onsen* with a good view of Mihara-yama. Take a bus from Motomachi port and get off at Mihara-yama *onsen* stop.

Places to Stay & Eat
Umi-no-furusato-mura (☎ *4-1137; camping with/without own tent ¥2000/4000, plus per person ¥200/300*) camping ground is the cheapest place to stay, with pre-pitched tents for six people. It's on the opposite side of the island and not serviced by any bus – try hitching. **Izu Oshima Kokumin-shukusha** (☎ *2-1285; rooms per person ¥8000*), not far from the pier, is an institutional place where rates include two meals; check-in is 4pm. **Tachibana-sō** (☎ *2-2075; rooms per person with/without 2 meals ¥6300/4200*) is a typical old *minshuku* and is a more interesting choice. It's conveniently located on the main road, five minutes' walk straight in from the pier. Check-in is 11am.

Kāchan (☎ *2-1127; meals from ¥1000; open 11am-3pm & 5pm-9pm Wed-Mon*) is a cosy *izakaya* on the seaside road less than five minutes north of the pier. They are particularly proud of their Iso udon – a rice bowl topped with a variety of sashimi and Bekkō-zushi, literally 'Tortoise-shell sushi'. Look for the wooden front decorated with glass net-floats.

Getting There & Away
There are three flights a day from Tokyo (Haneda) to Ō-shima with Air Nippon Koku (ANK; ¥10,500, 40 minutes).

Ferry services run daily to Ō-shima from Tokyo (2nd class, ¥3810, 7½ hours). From Atami there are two express ferries daily (2nd class, ¥4500, one hour). There's also a daily ferry from Itō (2nd class, ¥3500, 1½ hours).

TO-SHIMA 利島
☎ 04992
To-shima, 27km southwest of Ō-shima, is the smallest island in the Izu-shotō, with a circumference of only 8km. The island is mountainous, although its volcano is now dormant, and there are no swimming beaches. Much of the island is used for the cultivation of camellias, which makes it a picturesque place to visit between December and February, when the flowers are in bloom.

Places to Stay
The island has six *minshuku* with prices of ¥6000 to ¥6800 with two meals. For information contact the **Izu Seven Islands Tourist Federation** (☎ *03-3436-6955; open 9am-10pm daily*).

Getting There & Away

There's a daily ferry from Tokyo to To-shima (2nd class, ¥4240, 9½ hours).

NII-JIMA 新島
☎ 04992

Nii-jima has an area of 23 sq km and its beaches have made it so popular that there are now over 200 *minshuku* on the island. Even with this abundance of accommodation, it's a good idea to ring the **Niijima Tourist Association** (☎ 5-0048) for help with reservations if you're visiting during a holiday period.

There's a daily ferry from Tokyo to Nii-jima (2nd class, ¥5120, 10 hours).

SHIKINE-JIMA 式根島
☎ 04992

Six kilometres south of Nii-jima is tiny Shikine-jima, with an area of only 3.8 sq km. The island has swimming beaches, *onsen* and plenty of accommodation.

Ferries to Shikine-jima depart Tokyo once daily (2nd class, ¥5120, 10 hours). Six ferries a week leave from Shimoda on the Izu-hantō (2nd class, ¥3600, 3½ hours).

MIYAKE-JIMA 三宅島
☎ 04994

Miyake-jima is 180km south of Tokyo. It is the third-largest island in the Izu group, with a circumference of 36km. The island's volcano **Osu-yama** is said to erupt every 20 years and last did so in 1983, destroying one of the island's main tourist attractions, the pond Shinmyō-ike. Miyake-jima's attractions include some good beaches as well as three *onsen*, the best of which is **Furusato-no-yu** (*admission ¥500; open 11am-7.30pm Thur-Tues*). It's in the Ago area; walk from Ago bus stop towards the ocean for about 10 minutes. The best place to see the island's birds is Tairō-ike on the south coast. As with the other islands in the chain, Miyake-jima gets packed on weekends.

Places to Stay

For information (in Japanese) on reasonably priced *minshuku*, contact the **Miyake-jima Tourist Association** (☎ 6-1144). Many of the *minshuku* have very thin walls, so you really must emphasise that you want a quiet, private place. There are free camping grounds at Sagiga-hama, Okubo-hama and Miike-hama; you'll need your own equipment, however. All have toilets, cooking facilities and cold showers. Book through the tourist association.

Getting There & Away

Daily ferries depart Tokyo at 10.30pm (2nd class, ¥5730, 6½ hours). There are also daily boats to and from Hachijō-jima (2nd class, ¥1860, 4½ hours). From Tokyo (Haneda) there are two flights a day with Air Nippon (¥11,050, 50 minutes) – you can call ☎ 0120-029-222 toll free.

Getting Around

Chō-ei buses make clockwise and anti-clockwise circuits (¥860) of the island several times a day. Bicycle rentals are available for ¥1000/1500 a half/full day, or ¥400 per hour. Motorcycle rentals are also available, from ¥2000 for three hours.

HACHIJŌ-JIMA 八丈島
☎ 04996

Hachijō-jima (68 sq km) is 290km south of Tokyo. It is the southernmost and second-largest island in the Izu-shotō. Its distance from Tokyo keeps it relatively free of the crowds that descend on the more northerly islands of the Izu group. It also attracts an interesting mix of surfers, stoners, ecologists and refugees from the big-city rat race.

Information

Before leaving Tokyo, pick up the TIC's informative *Hachijo-jima & Aogashima Islands* pamphlet. The **Hachijō-jima Tourist Organisation** (☎ 2-1377) can answer questions in Japanese. After arrival, you can get information at the **Tourist Information Office** (☎ 2-1121) in the town hall, in the centre of the island on the main road.

Things to See & Do

The address is Tokyo prefecture, but the vibe is Okinawa. Hiking, climbing, watersports and seeking out glow-in-the-dark mushrooms are all favourite activities.

The island is dominated by two dormant volcanoes, **Hachijō-Fuji** and **Mihara-yama**, whose slopes are covered with lush semi-tropical vegetation.

Hachijō-jima's highlights include good beaches, a botanical garden, and two historical sights, **Tametomo-jinja** and **Sofuku-ji**.

There are also some great *onsen* in which to soak after a day of sightseeing.

Urami-ga-taki Onsen *(admission free; open 10am-9pm daily)* is not to be missed. It's tucked into a thick forest overlooking a waterfall. It has mixed bathing. Take a Sueyoshi-bound bus from the port (you may have to change at Kashitate Onsen Mae) to Nakata-Shōten Mae and walk for 20 minutes towards the ocean. Another good choice is **Sueyoshi Onsen Miharashi-no-yu** *(admission ¥500; open 10.30am-9.30pm Wed-Mon)* with separate bathing for men and women, which has a great view over the Pacific – try going at sunset. Take the same bus that goes to Urami-ga-taki Onsen and get off at Sueyoshi.

History buffs will be interested in the **Tama-ishi-gaki walls** that the exiled population on the island built to prevent landslides and to protect themselves from typhoons. The walls are made from the uncannily round volcanic rocks that the exiles carried by hand up from the shoreline. These can be seen in the Ōsato-chiku area on the southwest coast of the island.

Project WAVE (☎ 2-5407; e wave@isis .ocn.ne.jp) offers a variety of eco-tourism options, including hiking, bird watching, sea kayaking and scuba-diving. Its owner, Iwasaki-san, speaks English.

Places to Stay

Ashitaba-sō (☎ 7-0434; *rooms per person ¥6500*) is a good *minshuku* that includes two meals in the rates. The owner is a friendly, chatty fellow who serves heaped portions of locally caught seafood. Reservations 24 hours in advance (in Japanese) are required; check-in at 11am.

Hachijō-jima Kokusai Kankō Hotel (☎ 2-0671; *rooms per person ¥7000*) is a newish place with comfortable rooms. In summer it becomes a bonkfest for holidaying university students from around the Kansai region. Expect dodgy chat-up lines, Hawaiian shirts and an excess of blonde hair-dye. Actually it's fun if you're in the mood, and there's a great communal bath.

Sokodo Camp-jō (☎ 2-1121) camping area is next to the Sokodo port and is free. Toilets, cold showers and cooking facilities are available. You must reserve (in Japanese only) a spot at the ward office.

Places to eat are a little thin on the ground here. Generally, however, your lodging will provide meals. If you intend to camp it's best to bring food with you.

Getting There & Away

In the summer season, ferries depart Tokyo daily at 10.30pm and travel via Miyake-jima (2nd class, ¥7180, 11 hours). Departures are less frequent outside the summer (June to August) season. Alternatively, there is a more frequent air service between Haneda airport and the island with Air Nippon (¥13,400 if booked a day in advance, five flights a day, one hour). Air Nippon's toll-free information line is ☎ 0120-029-222.

Getting Around

You can negotiate most of the island by bicycle and there are rental places along the main street. The airport has a scooter rental place that offers good deals. Otherwise, the Chō-ei bus covers the island's most important destinations.

Ogasawara-shotō
小笠原諸島

Although technically part of the prefecture Tokyo-to, these islands are far to the south of the Izu-shotō. They have a climate similar to that of the Nansei-shotō (Southwest Islands, often referred to as Okinawa) and, like these islands, remained occupied by US forces until 1968, long after the occupation of the mainland islands had ended.

The main group of islands includes **Chichi-jima** (Father Island), **Haha-jima** (Mother Island) and **Ani-jima**, on which you will find a number of *minshuku* and where **scuba diving** is popular. Further south are the Kazan-shotō (Volcano Islands) which include **Iwo-jima**, one of the most famous battle sites of WWII. The island is still off limits to visitors because of the live ammunition there.

Boats to Chichi-jima leave approximately once a week from Tokyo (2nd class, ¥22,570, 25 to 30 hours). For more information, call **Ogasawara Kaiun** (☎ 3451-5171). Boats between Chichi-jima and Haha-jima leave daily (2nd class, ¥3780, two hours).

Central Honshū 本州中部

Central Japan, 'Chūbu' in Japanese, stretches between Tokyo and Kyoto, the Pacific and the Sea of Japan. It features rugged seascapes in the north, the spectacular mountain ranges and highlands of the Japan Alps in the centre, and the urban, densely populated Pacific coast to the south. Local colour is as diverse as the landscapes: refined arts and excellent craftsmanship, cosy thatched-roof architecture, significant castles and spiritual centres, sea fishing, cormorant fishing and historic heritage.

This chapter covers the prefectures at the heart of the region: Aichi-ken, Gifu-ken, Nagano-ken, Toyama-ken, Ishikawa-ken and Fukui-ken.

For a lightning trip, visit at least Takayama and Kanazawa. With a couple more days, add Matsumoto, the Unesco World Heritage sites of the Shōkawa Valley, the old Nakasendō post road up the Kiso Valley or the peninsula Noto-hantō. Nature lovers and sports enthusiasts will want to explore the hot springs and hiking trails of Chūbu-Sangaku (Japan Alps) National Park.

Nagoya is the transport hub of southern Chūbu. The mountainous inland area is served by the JR Takayama and Chūō lines, which run roughly parallel from north to south with hubs in Takayama and Matsumoto, respectively. Other useful rail connections are provided by the JR Nagano *shinkansen* (bullet trains), which link Tokyo with Nagano. In the northern area, the JR Hokuriku line follows the coast along the Sea of Japan, linking Fukui, Kanazawa and Toyama.

Bus is the main form of transport in the mountainous midsection, but schedules can be inconvenient or, between November and May, stop entirely (except for ski resorts). If you can get a couple of people together, renting a car may be the most affordable, time-efficient and pleasant option; new expressways make getting around remarkably quick, and some of the views are awesome.

Highlights

- Visit Takayama, a small, beautiful city known for its traditional architecture and skilled woodworkers
- See Shōkawa Valley, a remote agricultural region where traditional customs and farmhouses remain largely intact
- Explore the National Treasure castles at Matsumoto and Inuyama
- Relax at Bessho Onsen, an ancient mineral hot spring and rural temple retreat, easily accessible from Tokyo
- Walk the Nakasendo, an old post road with beautifully preserved Edo-period villages
- Follow the superb mountain scenery and hiking trails of Chūbu-Sangaku National Park
- Enjoy the cultural and artistic treasures of Kanazawa
- Discover the lovely coastline and fine seafood of peninsula Noto-hantō

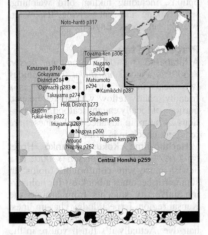

Nagoya 名古屋

☎ 052 • pop 2,184,000

Nagoya, Japan's fourth-largest city, isn't a traditional tourist destination, but it has a number of worthwhile sights. In spirit, this major industrial centre, the capital of Aichi-ken, feels like a scaled-down, far more relaxed version of Tokyo. English-language signs make it easy to get around, and there are some interesting restaurants, shops and nightspots, particularly in the Sakae entertainment district.

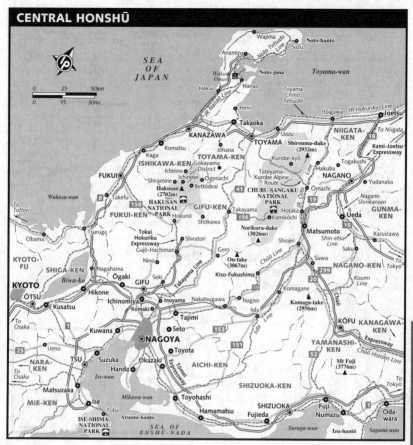

CENTRAL HONSHŪ

Nagoya is also a convenient hub for day trips. See the Around Nagoya section later in this chapter, and Ise-jingū in the Kansai chapter.

HISTORY

Nagoya rose to power as a castle town during the feudal age. Three of Japan's great historical heroes, Oda Nobunaga, Toyotomi Hideyoshi and Tokugawa Ieyasu, were born here or nearby; Tokugawa Ieyasu built the castle, Nagoya-jō, for one of his sons from 1610 to 1614. Not much of the past remains, however. During WWII, the city was flattened by US aerial bombing, which also claimed most of Nagoya-jō.

Nagoyans are famed for their thrift, counterbalanced by lavish displays of wealth (including outrageous weddings), and their love of *pachinko* (Japanese pinball).

ORIENTATION

Nagoya was completely rebuilt after WWII, on a grid with wide avenues. On the western edge of the city centre, Nagoya station, known locally as Meieki, is a city in itself with shops, restaurants, hotels and observation decks in two gleaming 50-plus-storey towers, the city's most useful landmark. Several train lines converge here: *shinkansen* platforms are on the west side of the station, while on the east side you'll find the private Meitetsu and Kintetsu lines as well as the subway and bus stations.

From the east exit, Sakura-dōri runs towards the TV tower, in the centre of the

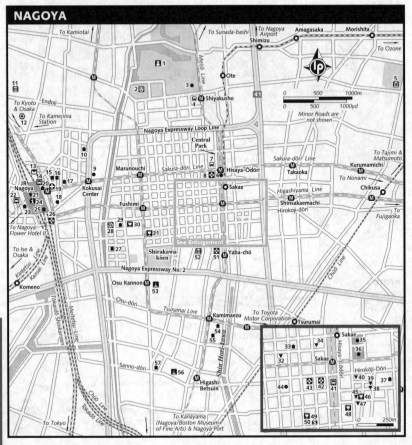

park-like Hisaya-ōdōri. South of the TV tower is the Sakae entertainment district. The castle, Nagoya-jō, is just north of the city centre. Nagoya's major sights can be knocked off in a day or two.

INFORMATION
Tourist Offices

Nagoya has a **tourist information office** (☎ 541-4301; open 9am-7pm daily) in the central concourse of Nagoya station, with smaller **offices** at the north exit of Kanayama station (☎ 323-0161; open 9am-7pm daily), south of the city centre, and in the Oasis 21 building in Sakae (☎ 963-5252; open 10am-8pm daily). All have English-language maps of the city, information on sights and accommodation, and at least one English speaker behind the counter. Information is available on the Web at ⓦ www.ncvb.or.jp.

Nagoya International Centre (☎ 581-0100; open 9am-8.30pm Tues-Sat, 8am-5pm Sun & holidays) is a 10-minute walk east of the Nagoya station along Sakura-dōri, on the 3rd floor of the Kokusai Center building. Staff here speak English (and many other languages) and have a wealth of information on both Nagoya and regional destinations. There are also extensive lists of restaurants, bars and accommodation, though staff are not allowed to make recommendations. Staff can also help arrange home visits with Japanese families, and you'll find a library, TV newscasts from overseas and a bulletin board for postings.

NAGOYA

PLACES TO STAY
10 Kimiya Ryokan
きみや旅館
15 Royal Park Inn Nagoya
ロイヤルパークイン名古屋
16 Hotel Sun Plaza
17 Fitness Hotel 330 Nagoya
フィットネスホテル
330名古屋
20 Hotel Associa Nagoya
Terminal
ホテルアソシア名古屋
ターミナル
23 Nagoya Flower Hotel 1
名古屋フラワーホテル
25 Nagoya Marriott
Associa Hotel; Takashimaya
Department Store
名古屋マリオットアソシア
ホテル；高島屋
サンプラザホテル
27 Aichi-ken Seinen-kaikan
Youth Hostel
愛知県青年会館
29 Hilton Nagoya
ヒルトン名古屋
33 Nishiki Washington Hotel
Plaza
錦ワシントンホテルプラザ
37 Nagoya Tōkyū Hotel
名古屋東急ホテル
54 Ryokan Meiryū
旅館名龍
55 Yamazen Ryokan
山善旅館
57 Ryokan Marutame
旅館丸為

PLACES TO EAT
21 Sumiyoshi; Doeriya
すみよし；どえりや
32 Ebisuya
えびすや
34 Torigin Honten
鳥銀本店
38 Bali Hai
バリハイ
39 Tōen
桃園

40 Nova Urbana
ノバウルバナ
45 Ka-ren
花蓮
47 Yagiya China
やぎやチャイナ

OTHER
1 Nagoya-jō
名古屋城
2 Nagoya Noh Theatre
名古屋能劇場
3 Aichi Prefectural
Gymnasium
愛知県立体育館
4 Bus to Tokugawa
Museum
5 Tokugawa Art Museum
徳川美術館
6 Nagoya TV Tower
テレビ塔
7 Airport Bus Stop
空港バス亭
8 Tokyu Hands
Department Store
東急ハンズ
9 Kokusai Centre –
Nagoya International
Centre
国際センタービル
11 Toyota Commemorative
Museum of Industry and
Technology
12 Noritake Garden
ノリタケの森
13 Eki-mae Post Office
駅前文室郵便局
14 City Bus Station;
Matsuzakaya Department
Store
市バスターミナル；
松坂屋デパート
18 Toyota Building
トヨタビル
19 Dai-Nagoya Building;
Tachino Clinic
大名古屋ビル
22 Airport Bus Stop
空港バス

24 Tourist Information
観光案内所
26 Meitetsu & Kintetsu
Department Stores; Meitetsu
Shin-Nagoya Station;
Meitetsu Grand Hotel
名鉄デパート；近鉄デパート；
名鉄グランドホテル
28 Chikōraku
知好楽
30 Elephants Nest
エレファントネスト
31 Shooters
シューターズ
35 Oasis 21; Tourist Information;
Bus Terminal
オアシス21；観光案内所、
バスターミナル
36 Aichi Arts Center
愛知芸術文化センター
41 Sakae Bus Station
栄バスターミナル
42 Mitsukoshi Department Store
三越デパート
43 Maruei Department Store;
Skyle Building; Media Wave
丸栄；スカイルビル；
メディアウエーブ
44 iD
46 Lush – Underground; Club
Atlantic
48 Red Rock Bar & Grill
49 Citibank ATM
50 Club Wall; Metro Club
51 Matsuzakaya Department
Store
松坂屋デパート
52 Nadya Park; International
Design Centre Nagoya; Loft
Department Store;
Kinokuniya Books
ナデイアパーク；
国際デザインセンター；
ロフト；紀伊国屋
53 Osu Kannon Temple
54 Higashi Betsuin
東別院

Money & Post

There's a small **post office** with an **ATM** inside Nagoya station, and a seriously large one, **Eki-Mae Post Office**, north of the station's east exit.

Citibank has 24-hour Cirrus ATM access at its branch in the Sugi building, three minutes' walk southwest from exit 7 of Sakae station. There is also a **Citibank ATM** on the 1st floor of the arrival lobby at Nagoya airport.

Email & Internet Access

Above Nagoya station, on the 12th floor of the north tower, **Cafe Quatre** (☎ 562-1517; ¥300/30min) has Internet access with the purchase of a drink. The Internet café **Chikōraku** (☎ 204-0237; ¥480/1st hr), near the Aichi-ken Seinen-kaiken Youth Hostel, serves free soft drinks. In Sakae are **Kinko's** (☎ 231-9211; ¥100/1st 10min, ¥1100/1st hr) and, on the 9th floor of the Skyle Building, **Media Wave** (☎ 264-6550; ¥600/30min).

Publications

The Best of Nagoya is a handy brochure with most tourist information you'll need. Useful English-language maps include the *Goodwill Guide*, *Live Map Nagoya*, the advertising-sponsored *Info Guide* and a public transport map. English-language listings publications include *Japanzine*, *Avenues* and *Nagoya Calendar*.

Emergency

Nagoya International Centre (☎ 581-0100) can provide all the emergency advice you need (see Information earlier in this section). The **Kyukyuiryō Jōhō Sentā** *(Emergency Medical Information Centre;* ☎ 263-1133) can advise (in Japanese only) where to receive weekend and holiday

emergency treatment. The **Tachino Clinic** (☎ 541-9130) has staff who speak English, French, German and Spanish. It's in the Dai-Nagoya building, opposite the east exit of Nagoya station.

THINGS TO SEE & DO

Nagoya-jō 名古屋城

Tokugawa Ieyasu built Nagoya-jō (☎ 231-1700; admission ¥500; open 9am-4.30pm daily) on the site of an older castle for his ninth son in 1610–1614. Although it was destroyed in WWII and replaced in 1959 with a ferroconcrete replica, it is nonetheless worth a visit for the impressive museum inside, featuring armour, treasures, and histories of the Oda, Toyotomi and Tokugawa families. An elevator will save

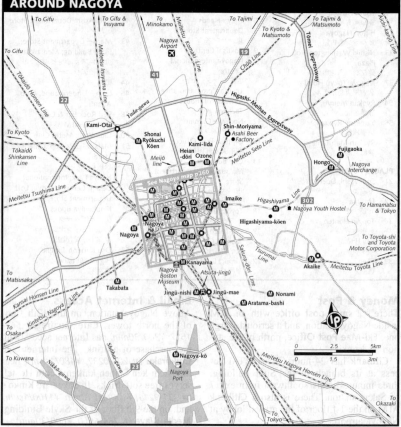

you from climbing stairs. Note the 3m-long replicas of the famous *shachi-hoko,* gilded dolphin-like sea creatures at either end of the roof (and in every souvenir shop).

Within the castle grounds, the garden, **Ninomaru-en,** has a teahouse in an attractive setting. The elegant **Nagoya Noh Theatre** (☎ *231-0088; admission free; open 9am-5pm daily*) features a small museum on nō, just southwest of the castle grounds.

The castle is a five-minute walk from Shiyakusho station on the Meijō subway line.

Atsuta-jingū 熱田神宮

One of the most sacred Shintō shrines, the 3rd-century Atsuta-jingū (☎ *671-4151; admission free; open 24hr*) is said to house the *kusanagi-no-tsurugi* (sacred sword – literally, the 'grass-cutting sword'), one of the *sanshu no jingi,* three regalia that were, according to legend, handed down to the imperial family by the goddess Amaterasu Ōmikami (the other two are the curved jewels at the imperial palace in Tokyo and the sacred mirror housed at Ise Jingū). You won't be able to view the regalia, but don't feel left out; no-one but the emperor and a few selected Shintō priests ever gets to see them.

There is a small **museum** (☎ *671-0852; admission ¥300; open 9am-4.30pm daily, closed last Wed each month & the following day*), housing Tokugawa-era swords, masks and paintings, including some important cultural properties.

The shrine is about five minutes' walk from exit 2 of Jingū-nishi station on the Meijō subway line. Or, take the Meitetsu Nagoya Honsen line to Jingū-mae and then walk west for five minutes.

Tokugawa Art Museum
徳川美術館

This important collection (☎ *935-6262; admission ¥1200; open 10am-5pm Tues-Sun*) includes furnishings, armour, calligraphy, painted scrolls, lacquerware and ceramics that previously belonged to the Tokugawa family. A priceless 12th-century scroll depicting *The Tale of Genji* is locked away except for a short stint in late November; the rest of the year, visitors must remain content with a video.

The museum is three minutes' walk from the Shindeki bus stop, east of Nagoya-jō.

Take a bus from Shiyakusho subway station (near Nagoya-jō) or from stop No 4 at the Meitetsu bus centre.

Noritake Garden ノリタケの森

On the grounds of one of Japan's best-known porcelain makers (*established 1876;* ☎ *561-7290; admission ¥500; open 10am-6pm Tues-Sun*), a new **craft centre** (*open 10am-5pm Tues-Sun*) offers a peek at the production process, a porcelain museum, and a chance to glaze your own dish or cup (¥1500). Signage is in English throughout the grounds. Naturally, there are ample shopping opportunities – the 'Box' outlet store offers 40% discounts on discontinued items – though no overseas shipping as of this writing. Admission to the grounds and shops is free. It's a 15-minute walk north of Nagoya station, or a few minutes by bus.

Nadya Park ナデヤパーク

A futuristic, skyscraper museum/shopping complex in Sakae, Nadya Park houses the **International Design Centre Nagoya** (☎ *265-2106; admission ¥300; open 11am-8pm Wed-Mon*) on the 4th floor, a secular shrine to the deities of conceptualisation, form and function, and a fascinating place to spend an hour or more. Exhibits (adventurously presented, with most signage in English) trace the history of design from Art Deco to the present.

Also in Nadya Park is the Loft department store, which shopping buffs will find equally fascinating. Kinokuniya bookstore is on the 6th floor of Loft, with a decent English-language selection.

Nadya Park is five minutes' walk northwest of Yaba-chō station on the Meijō line, or eight minutes' walk southwest of Sakae station on the Higashiyama and Meijō lines.

Nagoya/Boston Museum of Fine Arts 名古屋ボストン美術館

This excellent museum (☎ *684-0101; admission special & long-term exhibitions ¥1200, long-term exhibitions only ¥400; open 10am-5pm Tues-Thur, Sat & Sun, 10am-9pm Fri*) is a collaborative effort between Japanese backers and the Museum of Fine Arts, Boston. Rotating exhibits showcase both Japanese and non-Japanese masterpieces, with good English signage.

The museum is to the right of the south exit of Kanayama station.

Nagoya Port Area 名古屋港

Redeveloped to attract tourists, the cargo port now boasts several mildly interesting attractions. The hi-tech **Port of Nagoya Public Aquarium** (☎ 654-7080; admission ¥2000; open 9.30am-8pm Tues-Sun late July-Aug, to 5pm Dec-Mar, to 5.30pm rest of year) is one of Japan's largest. The **Port Tower** (☎ 652-1111; admission ¥300; museum open 9.30am-5pm Tues-Sun) offers good views of the harbour, the **Maritime Museum** and the **Fuji Antarctic Exploration Ship**. All of them can be visited with a combination ticket for ¥2400, which must be purchased before 1pm. Attractions are signposted in English. Take the Meijō subway line to Nagoya-kō station.

Factory Tours

The commercially curious can consider free forays into famous factories.

Toyota Motor Corporation is an hour east of Nagoya, and two-hour tours of its main plant in **Toyota City** can be made by reservation (☎ 0565-28-2121; tours 11am weekdays). To get there, take the Tsurumai subway line (it becomes the Meitetsu Toyota Line) to Toyota-shi, transfer to a bus (stop No 4, bound for Higashi-Okazaki or Toyota-kinen-byōin) and get off at Toyota-honsha-mae. If you can't make it out to the factory, you might visit the **Toyota Commemorative Museum of Industry and Technology** (☎ 551-6115; admission ¥500; open 9.30am-5pm Tues-Sun), north of Noritake Garden.

Lager lovers might tour the Nagoya factory of **Asahi Beer** (reservations ☎ 792-8966). Japanese-language tours are held weekdays (1¼ hours) from 9.30am to 3pm; you can sample the wares (free!) for up to 20 minutes. Catch one of four free shuttle buses per day from the Meitetsu bus centre (stop No 6) or take the JR Chūō line to Shin-Moriyama station and walk 15 minutes east.

SPECIAL EVENTS

The festival **Atsuta Matsuri**, held in early June at Atsuta-jingū, features displays of martial arts, sumō matches and fireworks. Street vendors peddle their wares by the light of thousands of lanterns.

On the first Saturday and Sunday of June, the **Tennō Matsuri** takes place in Deki-machi. Large karakuri (mechanical puppets) are paraded on floats in the precincts of the shrine, Susano-o-jinja.

The Nagoya Basho **sumō tournament** takes place at the **Aichi Prefectural Gymnasium** (☎ 962-9300) from the first to the third Sunday of July. Non-reserved seats (from ¥2800) are available from the box office on the day of the bout from 8.30am. Arrive early in the afternoon and you can walk unchallenged to the very front of the arena to watch the lower-ranked wrestlers up close. It's also a great photo opportunity. The gymnasium is in the grounds of Nagoya-jō.

The **Minato Matsuri**, held around 20 July at Nagoya port, features a street parade with more than 1500 dancers, as well as a water-logging contest that dates back to the Edo period (1600–1867).

Nagoya Matsuri, held in mid-October in Hisaya-ōdōri-kōen (aka Central Park, north of the TV Tower), is the big event of the year. It includes costume parades, processions of floats with karakuri puppets, folk dancing, music and a parade of decorated cars.

In late October to late November, the **Kiku-no-hana Taikai** (Chrysanthemum Exhibition) sets the grounds of Nagoya-jō awash in colour; a separate ningyō (doll) exhibit incorporates the flowers into scenes from Japanese history and legend.

The Ōsu Kannon temple hosts a colourful **antique market** on the 18th and 28th of each month.

And Nagoya is gearing up for the **World Expo 2005**, to be held in Aichi-ken. The theme of the expo (Ⓦ www.pref.aichi.jp /index-e.html) is sustainable development.

PLACES TO STAY

Accommodation in Nagoya is clustered largely around Nagoya station and Sakae. Nagoya's excellent subway system means that basing yourself in either area is no impediment to reaching the other.

PLACES TO STAY – BUDGET
Hostels

Centrally located **Aichi-ken Seinen-kaikan Youth Hostel** (☎ 221-6001, fax 204-3508; dorm beds ¥2850) is usually the first budget place to be booked out. Private single rooms and Japanese-style family rooms are also available for an extra charge. The hostel is a 20-minute walk southeast of Nagoya station. Alternatively, you can take bus No 20 from the stop in front of the Toyota building and get off at the Nayabashi stop.

From there, it's three minutes south on foot. Check-in is between 3pm and 8pm.

Nagoya Youth Hostel (☎ 781-9845, fax 781-9023; dorm beds ¥2200) is out of the city centre, east of town near the park, Higashiyama-kōen. It has free washer and dryer. From Nagoya station, take the Higashiyama subway line to Higashiyama-kōen station. From exit 2, turn left and follow the main road, Higashiyama-dōri, to the next main intersection, where you'll see signs for the hostel. Check-in is until 9pm.

PLACES TO STAY – MID-RANGE
Ryokan

The simple, family-style **Kimiya Ryokan** (☎ 551-0498, fax 565-0465; e hott@hotmail .com; rooms per person ¥4500) is north of the Nagoya International Centre building. Request a garden-view room.

Near Kamimaezu subway station on the Meijō line are two well-run places: **Ryokan Meiryū** (☎ 331-8686, fax 331-6119; w www.japan-net.ne.jp/~meiryu; singles/doubles ¥5000/ 8000) has English-speaking staff, air-con and TV in each room, as well as a coin laundry and a nice communal bath. **Yamazen Ryokan** (☎ 321-1792, fax 321-3076; rooms per person with/without breakfast ¥5700/ 5000) has a kindly, welcoming atmosphere and a 40-plus-year history, although staff don't speak much English.

Ryokan Marutame (☎ 321-7130, fax 321-3626; w www.jin.ne.jp/marutame; singles/ doubles ¥5000/9500) is an up-to-date place three blocks west of Higashi Betsuin subway station on the Meijō line (exit 4).

About 30 minutes' subway ride from Nagoya station, **Petit Ryokan Ichifuji** (☎ 914-2867, fax 981-6836; w www.jin.ne.jp/ichifuji; singles/doubles from ¥4800/8400) is run by a friendly couple and offers clean, comfortable Japanese-style rooms and a communal hinoki-iburo (cypress wood bath). Take the Meijō subway line to Heiandōri station, turn right out of exit 2 and walk south for three minutes. The ryokan is signposted in English.

Hotels

Most of the business hotels in the Nagoya station area are fairly pricey; the cheapest are around the less-used west exit.

Nagoya Flower Hotel Part II (☎ 451-2200; rooms per person ¥5700) is the least expensive, about six minutes' walk from the station.

Nagoya Flower Hotel I (☎ 451-2222, fax 451-3462; singles/doubles from ¥6000/ 9800) is just outside the station's west exit. Upper-storey rooms are in better condition, but cost more.

Hotel Sun Plaza (☎ 563-0691, fax 563-0698; singles/twins from ¥6400/12,300), a few minutes' walk east of the station, is business-hotel standard.

Fitness Hotel 330 Nagoya (☎ 562-0330, fax 562-0331; w www.misawa-resort.co.jp; singles/twins/doubles from ¥7500/11,000/ 12,000), further east of Hotel Sun Plaza, is somewhat more contemporary.

Nishiki Washington Hotel Plaza (☎ 962-7111, fax 962-7122; singles/doubles from ¥5455/11,256), in Sakae, is a simple but reasonably priced business hotel, and is one of the better deals.

Places to Stay – Top End

Hotel Associa Nagoya Terminal (☎ 561-3751, fax 581-3236, toll-free 0120-489-174; w www.associa.com/nth; singles/doubles from ¥9900/15,000) has a range of rooms, including Japanese style; discounts are available for Japan Rail Pass holders.

Meitetsu Grand Hotel (☎ 582-2211, fax 582-2230; w www.meitetsu-gh.co.jp; singles/doubles/twins from ¥9,500/15,000/ 16,500), towering above the Meitetsu/Melsa department store and station complex, is rather dapper. Twin rooms are decent sized, although the cheapest singles have no windows.

Royal Park Inn (☎ 581-4411, fax 581-4427; w www.royalpark-nagoya.com; singles/ twins ¥9500/17,000), northeast of the station, is recently renovated.

Nagoya Tōkyū Hotel (☎ 251-2411, fax 251-2422; w www.nagoyatokyu.com; singles/ twins/doubles ¥15,000/25,000/23,000) is top-of-the-line in Sakae – large and classy.

Nagoya Marriott Associa Hotel (☎ 584-1111, fax 584-1112; w www.associa.com /english/nma; singles/doubles from ¥17,000/ 24,000) has spacious rooms and deluxe, well, everything. It's literally Nagoya's uppermost lodging, in the south tower above Nagoya station.

Hilton Nagoya (☎ 212-1111, toll-free 0120-489-852, fax 212-1225; e mail@nagoya .hilton.co.jp; singles/doubles from ¥21,000/ 27,000) is another posh choice; rooms blend Japanese and Western touches.

PLACES TO EAT

Nagoya's most famous regional dish is *kishimen* (flat, handmade noodles, served either cold or in hot broth). The other culinary star is *kōchin* (free-range chicken). While there are, naturally, restaurants throughout the city the greatest concentration is in Sakae.

Ebisuya (☎ 961-3412; dishes ¥650-1700) is the city's best-known *kishimen* restaurant.

Torigin (☎ 973-3000; dishes ¥380-1800; open dinner) is a *kōchin* restaurant that's nearly as famous. Chicken is served in many forms, including *kushiyaki* (skewered), *kara-age* (deep-fried chicken pieces), *zōsui* (mild rice hot-pot) and sashimi (what you think it is). Some may find the individual dishes a little dainty for the price, but *teishoku* (set menus) are available from ¥2900.

Ka-ren (☎ 262-4550; dishes ¥380-1080) is a good bet for Shanghainese food, while **Tōen** (☎ 264-7188; dishes ¥300-3000) has sassy Cantonese dishes, most under ¥1000.

Yagiya China (☎ 241-7022; dishes ¥300-850; open dinner) has a tropical-meets-tatami look, Sino-Japanese dishes and an English menu. **Bali Hai** (☎ 241-8801; dishes ¥480-1200) is a slick and stylish Pan-Asian place.

Nova Urbana (☎ 263-0354; dishes ¥300-1800) celebrates Japan's Brazilian ties with an all-you-can-eat dinner buffet (men ¥2580, women ¥1980), including *churrasco* grills. After dinner, it doubles as a samba club.

And along Hisaya-ōdōri-kōen and around Nadya Park are a number of Western eateries, trattoria and coffee houses, from cosy to trendy.

Even if you're just passing through Nagoya station, don't feel left out. There are some nice **bentō stands**, and locals say that the humble stand-up noodle counter **Sumiyoshi** (dishes ¥340-600, pay before entering at vending machines outside the door), on the southbound *shinkansen* platform, is the best 'secret' spot for *kishimen*; the identical northbound version apparently pales in comparison. **Doeriya** (☎ 583-6300), on track 3, has grills, vegies, noodles etc for just ¥100 each, though some dishes count as two (eg, *donburi*=rice+topping); it's popular with salarymen and budget travellers.

ENTERTAINMENT

Nagoya's nightlife might not match Tokyo's or Osaka's, but what it lacks in scale it makes up for in ebullience. Among the more popular spots is **Lush** (☎ 242-1388). The dance club **iD** (☎ 251-0382) is five floors, each with different music and a young-ish Japanese crowd. **Plastic Factory** (w www.mangafrog.com) is in an actual former plastic factory, five minutes' walk from exit 2 of the Imaike subway station, east of the city centre.

Shooters (☎ 202-7077) is a sports bar with both Japanese and foreign staff, and drink specials most nights. Food includes burgers, pasta and Tex-Mex. It's near exit 5 of Fushimi subway station. **Elephant's Nest** (☎ 232-4360), near the Hilton, is a comfy British place with darts, and in Sakae **Red Rock Bar & Grill** (☎ 262-7893) has an open feel and an Australian owner.

Metro Club (☎ 090-3950-7983) is a monthly gay and lesbian dance party. It meets on the second Saturday of the month at **Club Wall** (☎ 251-5609). **Plastic Factory** also occasionally hosts gay events. Unfortunately, Nagoya's full-time gay bars are known for being foreigner-unfriendly.

Nagoya also offers live jazz, rock and classical music, including some well-known Japanese and international artists. Check English-language listings magazines for dates and times.

SHOPPING

Nagoya and the surrounding area are known for arts and crafts, including *arimatsunarumi shibori* (elegant tie-dying), cloisonne (enamelling on silver and copper), ceramics and Seki blades (swords, knives, scissors etc).

The major shopping centres are in Sakae and around Nagoya station. For souvenir items (such as handmade paper, pottery and tie-dyed fabric) you can browse in the giant department stores, such as **Matsuzakaya**, **Maruei** and **Mitsukoshi** in Sakae, or **Takashimaya** or **Meitetsu/Melsa**, near Nagoya station.

For more shopping possibilities see also Noritake Garden under Things to See & Do earlier in this chapter.

GETTING THERE & AWAY
Air

Nagoya airport (☎ 0568-29-0765) is linked by air with most of Japan's major cities. If you're coming from Tokyo, however, the *shinkansen* is much quicker (two hours); the bus from the airport to Nagoya's city centre alone takes some 30 minutes.

A number of international carriers use Nagoya airport to destinations around the Pacific Rim.

A new airport, **Central Japan International Airport (Centrair)**, is being built on a man-made island in Ise-wan (Ise Bay), south of the city, and should open by March 2005, in time for the World Expo.

Train

Nagoya is a major *shinkansen* stop. Fares cost will cost you from Tokyo (Hikari, ¥10,070, two hours), Osaka (¥5670, one hour), Kyoto (¥4930, 44 minutes) and Hiroshima (¥12,920, three hours).

Ise-shima National Park is connected with Nagoya on the private Kintetsu line, which runs via Ise-shi station and Toba to Kashikojima. *Tokkyū* (limited express trains) run to Ise (¥2690, 80 minutes). JR offers connecting service to Ise. The Kintetsu line also has indirect services to Nara (*tokkyū*, ¥3750, 2½ hours).

To the Japan Alps, you can take the JR Chūō line to Nagano (Shinano *tokkyū* ¥6620, three hours) via Matsumoto (¥5360, two hours). A separate train serves Takayama (Hida *tokkyū*, ¥5870, 2½ hours).

Gifu connects with Nagoya station on the JR Tōkaidō line (¥450, 18 minutes), as well as the Meitetsu Nagoya line (¥540, 25 minutes).

Direct trains serve Inuyama from Nagoya via the Meitetsu Inuyama line (*kyūkō* [ordinary express train] ¥540, 30 minutes). JR travellers can connect via Gifu to Unuma, and walk across the river from Inuyama.

Bus

JR and Meitetsu highway buses (☎ 563-0489) operate services between Nagoya and Kanazawa (¥4060, four hours, 10 daily), Kyoto (¥2500, 2¾ hours, 19 daily), Osaka (¥2900, 3¼ hours, six daily), and Tokyo (¥5100, six hours, 13 daily). They also run overnight buses to Hiroshima (¥8400, nine hours), Kōchi (¥9070, 9¾ hours), Fukuoka (¥10,500, 11 hours) and Nagasaki (¥12,230, 12 hours).

Boat

The **Taiheiyo ferry** (☎ 203-0227) runs between Nagoya and Tomakomai (Hokkaidō,

¥10,500,40 hours) via Sendai (¥7800, 21 hours) every second evening. Take the Meijō subway south to its terminus at Nagoya-kō station and head for Nagoya-futō pier.

GETTING AROUND
To/From the Airport

Express buses run between Nagoya airport and Meitetsu bus station, on the 3rd floor (¥870, 30 minutes, every seven minutes), just southeast of JR Nagoya station. Less frequent buses serve the Marriott Associa Hotel, the west exit of Nagoya station and the northwest exit of Hisaya-ōdōri subway station in Sakae (¥730, 25 minutes). Taxis take around 30 minutes and cost about ¥5000.

Subway

Nagoya has an excellent subway system with four lines, all clearly signposted in English and Japanese. The most useful lines for visitors are the Meijō (purple), Higashiyama (yellow) and Sakura-dōri (red) lines. The last two run via Nagoya station. Fares cost ¥200 to ¥320. If you plan to do a lot of travel by bus and subway, you can save money with a one-day pass (¥850), available at subway stations. The one-day 'Ikomai Pass' (¥1300) includes all transport plus free or discounted admission to selected attractions.

Bus

There is an extensive city bus system (¥200 per ride), although the subway is easier for those with limited grasp of Japanese. The city bus centre is on the 2nd floor of Matsuzakaya department store, just northeast of Nagoya station; some buses operate from the Meitetsu bus station.

Around Nagoya
名古屋近辺

The main destinations in this area, consisting of outlying Aichi-ken and southern Gifu-ken, are Inuyama, Gifu (easy day trips from Nagoya) and Gujō-Hachiman (an hour bus ride north from Gifu). Inuyama has a noteworthy castle and some worthwhile side trips, both Inuyama and Gifu are famed for *ukai* (cormorant fishing), and Gujō-Hachiman is an attractive town surrounded by mountains and crisscrossed by

CENTRAL HONSHŪ

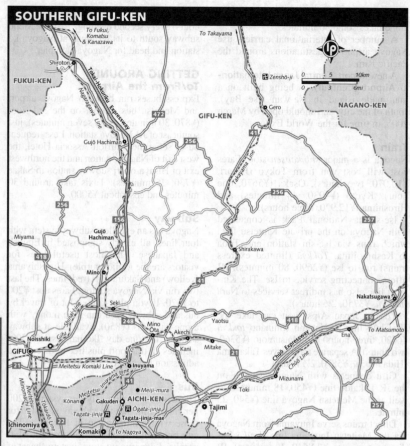

SOUTHERN GIFU-KEN

rivers. Ceramic art enthusiasts will want to visit Tajimi, famed for Mino pottery, east of Nagoya.

TAJIMI 多治見
☎ 0572 • pop 94,000

The Mino district has an almost 1800-year history as a centre for pottery, and Tajimi, at Mino's heart, calls itself Japan's ceramics capital. Mino-yaki (Mino ware) gained fame, particularly during the Momoyama period, for distinctive traits, including the milky *yuzu-hada* (citron skin) glaze of the Shino style and the irregular shapes of the Oribe style.

The **tourist office** (☎ 24-6460; open 9.30am-4pm Thur-Tues), above the police box to the right from the station's south

exit, can provide the latest information and a simple Japanese map of the town.

In the hills east of town, the **Gifu-ken Tōji Shiryōkan** (*Prefectural Ceramic Museum*; ☎ 23-1191; admission ¥300; open 9.30am-4.30pm Tues-Sun) is in an understated modern building. There's little English signage, but you can ask for an English leaflet or just let the works (both ancient and *very* contemporary) speak for themselves. Next door, **Tōji no Sato** (☎ 25-2233; prices from ¥1000; open 9.30am-4.30pm Tues-Sun, reservation required) is a workshop where you can create your own ceramic masterpiece (eg, cup or dish), which staff will later fire and/or glaze and then ship for you. Depending on the technique you choose, firing can take up to five days! Both locations are five minutes' walk from Higashimachi bus stop (¥250 from Tajimi station, six buses most days). A taxi from Tajimi station costs about ¥1350.

A new **Ceramic Park** (☎ 28-3200) was set to open as we went to press, featuring works from around the world in the **Tōgei Bijutsu-kan** (Contemporary Ceramic Art Museum), as well as conference facilities and a tearoom.

Local producers gather to display their creations, and bargains are to be found, at the twice-annual **Tajimi Chawan Matsuri** (Teacup Festival) during mid-April and mid-October. The rest of the year, the Mino-yaki Danchi (Mino-ware Village) has many dealers; it's reachable by bus from north of Tajimi station (¥300, 10 minutes, several daily).

Tajimi is easily reached from Nagoya on the JR Chūō line (*kaisoku* [rapid train] ¥650, 25 minutes).

INUYAMA 犬山
☎ 0568 • pop 69,000

The highlights of Inuyama are its castle, the garden Uraku-en and national treasure teahouse Jō-an, and activities such as *ukai*. The castle's riverside setting is quite attractive – it inspired a turn-of-the-last-century Japanese geologist to christen the area the 'Japan Rhine' – and the city has been beautifying its streetscapes, particularly south of the castle. Other attractions in the area include the architecture of Meiji-mura Museum, boat trips down the Kiso-gawa, and some rather racy shrines.

Orientation & Information
The castle and *ukai* area are within easy walking distance of Inuyama-yūen station on the Meitetsu Komaki line. However, the **tourist office** (☎ 61-1800; open 9am-5pm daily) is in Inuyama station, one stop south, where the Meitetsu Komaki line meets up with the Meitetsu Inuyama line; it has useful English-language pamphlets and maps, and can book accommodation. Web information is available at **w** www.city.inu yama.aichi.jp/inuyama/e_index.html.

Inuyama-jō 犬山城
Japan's oldest castle (☎ 61-1711; admission ¥400; open 9am-5pm daily), this National Treasure is said to have originated with

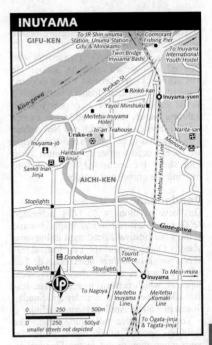

a fort in 1440; the current *donjon* (main keep) dates from 1537 and has withstood war, earthquake and restoration to remain an excellent example of Momoyama-period architecture. Stone walls reach 5m high, and inside are narrow, steep staircases and military displays. From the top storey, there's a fine view of mountains and plains.

It is also the nation's only privately owned castle, having been in (and out, and in) the hands of the Naruse family since 1617.

The castle is a 15-minute walk west of Inuyama-yūen station. Just south are the shrines Haritsuna Jinja and Sanko-Inari Jinja, the latter with interesting statues of *komainu* (protective dogs).

Uraku-en & Jo-an Teahouse
有楽園・茶室如安

The strolling garden Uraku-en (☎ 61-4608; admission ¥1000; open 9am-5pm daily Mar-Nov, 9am-4pm daily Dec-Feb) is 300m east of Inuyama-jō, in a corner of the grounds of the Meitetsu Inuyama Hotel. Its National Treasure Jo-an Teahouse is rated as one of the finest in Japan. It was constructed in 1618 in Kyoto by Oda Urakusai, a younger

CENTRAL HONSHŪ

brother of Oda Nobunaga, and it spent time in Tokyo and Kanagawa prefecture before being moved here in 1972.

Urakusai was a renowned tea master who founded his own tea ceremony school. He was also a closet Christian whose adopted name (the Portuguese 'Joan') was bestowed on the teahouse. Visitors may peek into the teahouse but are not allowed inside, except for four days each in March and November.

In what has to be Japan's most annoying use of enforced footwear, you must swap your shoes for open-toed sandals before entering the gravel-path garden.

Dondenkan どんでん館

This new pavilion (☎ 65-1728; admission ¥200; open 9am-5pm daily) displays some of the yatai (festival floats) used in Inuyama Matsuri. Dating back to 1650, the festival features a parade of 13 three-tiered floats decked out with lanterns and karakuri (mechanical puppets), which perform to music. The festival takes place on the Saturday and Sunday closest to 7 and 8 April, at Haritsuna Jinja.

You may notice tall, thin garage-like buildings around town; these house the yatai when they're not in the Dondenkan or parades.

Cormorant Fishing

Ukai takes place close to Inuyama-yuen station, by Twin-Bridge Inuyama-bashi. Book your ticket in Inuyama in the morning or reserve at the **dock office** (☎ 61-0057; July & Aug ¥2800, June & Sept ¥1980), near the cormorant fishing pier.

Sailings are generally at 7.30pm nightly except after heavy rainfall or on the night of a full moon.

Kiso-gawa Rapids Trip

Flat-bottomed wooden boats shoot the rapids on a 13km section of the Kiso-gawa. The ride takes an hour and costs ¥3400/1700 for adults/children; it entails little risk, except of a soaking. Contact **Nihon Rhein Kankō** (☎ 0574-28-2727). There is a free shuttle bus from Inuyama-yūen station.

Places to Stay & Eat

Inuyama International Youth Hostel (☎ 61-1111, fax 61-2770; tatami rooms per person from ¥2900, singles ¥3700, Western-style twins ¥6400) is Inuyama's cheapest option.

There are comfortable rooms with your own sink and toilet; advance booking is recommended. It's about a 25-minute walk northeast of Inuyama-yūen station.

Minshuku Yayoi (☎/fax 61-0751; rooms per person with 2 meals from ¥6000), across from Inuyama-yūen station, is friendly and simple, with comfy tatami rooms and shared facilities. It prides itself on its home cooking.

Rinkō-kan (☎ 61-0977, toll free 0120-61-0977, fax 61-2505; e rinkokan@triton.ocn.ne.jp; rooms per person with/without 2 meals ¥10,000/5400), overlooking the river, is a cheery hot-spring hotel with Japanese rooms, popular with the cormorant fishing crowd. It is known for its rotemburo (open-air baths), Jacuzzi and local cuisine.

Getting There & Away

Inuyama is connected with Nagoya (¥540, 30 minutes) and Shin-Gifu station in Gifu city (¥440, 35 minutes) via the Meitetsu Inuyama line. Alternatively, from JR Unuma station on the JR Takayama line, a short walk across the river, there are frequent trains to JR Gifu station (¥320, 30 minutes).

AROUND INUYAMA 犬山近辺
Meiji-mura Museum 明治村

Few Meiji period buildings have survived war, earthquake or rabid development, but this open-air museum (☎ 67-0314; admission ¥1600; open 9.30am-5pm daily Mar-Oct, 9.30am-4pm daily Nov-Feb, closed Mon Dec-Feb) has brought together more than 65 of them from all over Japan – public offices, private homes, banks, and some trains and buses. Among them is the entryway designed by Frank Lloyd Wright for Tokyo's Imperial Hotel – that building has since been replaced by a more generic version. The clash of Western and Japanese architectural styles provides a sense of that period's cultural schizophrenia. Allow at least half a day to enjoy the place at an easy pace.

A bus to Meiji-mura (¥410, 20 minutes) departs every 30 minutes from Inuyama station.

Ōgata-jinja 大縣神社

This 2000-year-old shrine (☎ 67-1017) is dedicated to the female Shintō deity Izanami, and draws women devotees seeking marriage or fertility. The precincts of the shrine contain rocks and other items resembling female genitals.

The popular **Hime-no-Miya Grand Festival** takes place here on the Sunday before 15 March (or 15 March if it's a Sunday). Locals pray for good harvests and prosperity by parading through the streets bearing a portable shrine with replicas of female genitals.

Ōgata-jinja is a 30-minute walk southeast of Gakuden station on the Meitetsu Komaki line.

Tagata-jinja 田県神社

Izanagi, the male counterpart of Izanami, is commemorated at this shrine (☎ 76-2906). The main hall of the shrine has a side building containing a collection of phalluses, left as offerings by grateful worshippers.

The **Tagata Hōnen Sai Festival** takes place on 15 March at the Tagata-jinja when the highly photogenic, 2m-long, 60kg 'sacred object' is paraded, amid much mirth, around the neighbourhood. Arrive well before the procession starts at 2pm.

Tagata-jinja is five minutes' walk west of Tagata-jinja-mae station, one stop south of Gakuden station on the Meitetsu Komaki line.

YAOTSU 八百津

☎ 0574 • pop 13,950

This little town has become a pilgrimage site as the birthplace of Sugihara Chiune, Japan's consul in Lithuania during early WWII. Sugihara saved some 6000 Jews from Nazi extinction by issuing transit visas against Japanese government orders; the 'Sugihara survivors' escaped to Kobe and Japanese-controlled Shanghai and, later, to other countries. The story is the subject of the 1997 Academy Award–winning short film *Visas and Virtue*.

On Yaotsu's Jindō-no-oka (Hill of Humanity) is a **museum** (admission ¥300; open 9.30am-5pm Tues-Sun) with photos of this inspiring story. Further information can be found at **w** www.town.yaotsu.gifu.jp, or contact the **city office** (☎ 43-2111, ext 252, English speaker available).

Yaotsu is easiest reached by car, but from Nagoya you can take the Meitetsu Hiromi line to Akechi (¥900, one hour), then transfer to the Yao bus (¥400, 25 minutes) to Yaotsu; it's a short taxi ride to the museum. The city office may be able to

help with logistics if you phone at least a day in advance.

GIFU 岐阜

☎ 058 • pop 410,000

Gifu was hit by a colossal earthquake in 1891 and given a thorough drubbing in WWII, so the city centre is not much to look at. That said, visitors come for *ukai* and handicrafts, as well as a reasonably colourful district in the sidestreets north of the station and a postwar reconstruction of Gifu-jō atop the nearby mountain Kinka-zan.

Orientation & Information

JR Gifu station and Meitetsu Shin-Gifu station are separated by several minutes' walk in the southern part of the city centre.

The **tourist information office** (☎ 262-4415; open 9am-7pm daily Mar-Dec, to 6pm Jan-Feb) on the 2nd floor of the JR station provides English-language city maps and accommodation lists.

NTT Multimedia Gallery (☎ 0120-102-950; Kinkabashi-dōri; open 10am-6.30pm daily), a few minutes' walk north from JR Gifu station, has free Internet access, but it's limited to 10 minutes.

Cormorant Fishing

The *ukai* season in Gifu (where Charlie Chaplin fished) lasts from 11 May to 15 October. Boats depart every evening, except after heavy rainfall or on the night of a full moon.

Tickets are sold at hotels or, after 6pm, at the **booking office** (☎ 262-0104 for advance reservations) just below the bridge, Nagarabashi. Tickets cost ¥3300/2900 for adults/children, and reservations are advised. Food and drink are not provided on the boats, so bring your own for the two-hour boat ride. Cheaper boats cost ¥3000/2600 per adult/child, but you can't take food aboard.

Fishing takes place around Nagarabashi, which can be reached by the No 11 bus from JR Gifu station. You can also get a good view of the action by walking along the river east of the bridge.

Gifu-kōen 岐阜公園

This park has a **history museum** (☎ 265-0010; admission ¥300; open 9am-5pm Tues-Sun) and a cable car (☎ 262-6784; ¥1050 return; available 9am to 5pm daily mid-October to mid-March, to 10.30pm late July to August, to 6pm other times) up to the summit of Kinka-zan. From here you can check out **Gifu-jō** (☎ 263-4853; admission ¥200; closes 30min before ropeway), a small but picturesque modern reconstruction of the original castle.

Shōhō-ji 正法寺

The main attraction of this orange-and-white temple (☎ 264-2760; admission ¥150; open 9am-5pm daily) is the papier-mache daibutsu (Great Buddha), which is nearly 14m tall and was created from about a tonne of paper sutras. Completed in 1832, the daibutsu took 38 years to make. The temple is a short walk southwest of Gifu-kōen.

Places to Stay

Gifu has plenty of accommodation, and the tourist information office at the station can provide a list and a helpful map. Most lodgings are north of the station.

Weekly Shō (☎ 272-9730, toll free 0120-626-540, fax 262-6542; singles/twins from ¥3000/5000) is bargain-priced. It has basic Western-style rooms and, despite its name, nightly rates; you can clean your room yourself with a vacuum provided, or pay extra to have it serviced.

Yamaguchiya Honkan (☎ 262-4650; rooms per person ¥4000) is a cosy ryokan and gets many repeat customers; it's in the middle of the shopping district.

Grand Palais Hotel (☎ 65-4111, fax 263-5233; w www.grandpalais.co.jp; singles/twins from ¥6200/11,000) feels like it stepped out of the 1970s. It's among a number of business hotels near the station.

Gifu Grand Hotel (☎ 233-1111, fax 233-1122; w www.gifugrandhotel.co.jp; rooms per person from ¥12,000) is one of the swankiest choices. It's about 15 minutes by car from the train stations.

Shopping

Gifu is famous for kasa (oiled paper parasols) and chōchin (paper lanterns), which are stocked in all the souvenir shops. The tourist information office has a map to speciality stores.

Sakaida Eikichi Honten (☎ 271-6958; open 9am-5pm Mon-Fri) both makes and sells kasa (umbrellas). It often shuts down at lunch time. It's a 12-minute walk southeast of JR Gifu station.

Ozeki Shōten (☎ 263-0111; open 9am-5pm Mon-Sat) is a chōchin factory and shop. Visitors are not permitted into the workshop, but a display explains the processes of frame building, pasting and painting. Phone ahead as there are sometimes random closures. Take the No 11 bus to the Daigaku-byōin-mae stop, and from there it's a short walk east down the main road.

Getting There & Away

The JR Tōkaidō line will get you here from Nagoya (¥450, 18 minutes). Meitetsu line trains from Shin-Gifu serve Inuyama (¥440, 35 minutes) and Shin-Nagoya station (¥540, 25 minutes).

SEKI 関
☎ 0575 • pop 76,000

Seki, not to be confused with Seki-ga-hara, is renowned as an ancient swordsmithing centre. It still produces a few katana (Japanese swords); however, there isn't a lot of growth in the sword market so the emphasis of production has been switched to more mundane razor blades, knives, scissors etc.

Swordsmithing demonstrations take place on 2 January, the first Sunday of March, April, June and November, and the second weekend in October. For the latest information, contact the **Seki Tourism Association** (☎ 23-6753). There are several minshuku and ryokan around Seki; some visitors combine a stay with dinner on a boat while watching ukai (11 May to 15 October).

The **Seki Festival** is held on the third weekend in April; a parade of elaborate floats winds through the town.

From Gifu, trains run on the Meitetsu Minomachi line to Seki in 50 minutes, departing from a separate platform. There are also buses from Gifu to Seki that take about 40 minutes.

GUJŌ HACHIMAN 郡上八幡
☎ 0575 • pop 16,800

This comfortable town is nestled in the mountains at the confluence of the Yoshida-gawa, the Nagara-gawa and some smaller rivers. The **tourist office** (☎ 67-0002; open 8.30am-5pm daily) is by the bridge Shin-bashi in the centre of town, about five minutes' walk from the Jōka-machi Plaza bus terminal.

Gujō Hachiman's main claim to fame is the **Gujō Odori Matsuri**, Japan's third-largest dance festival. Following a tradition dating to the 1590s, townsfolk let down their hair with frenzied folk dancing on 31 nights between early July and early September. Visitor participation is encouraged, and during the four main days of the festival (13–16 August) the dancing goes all night.

On the site of the tiny hilltop castle, **Gujō Hachiman-jō** (☎ 65-5839; admission ¥300; open 8am-6pm daily June-Aug, 9am-5pm daily Sept-May), had been a humble fortress dating back to about 1600; the current, grander building dates from only 1933. It contains weapons, armour and the like, and offers nice views. From the bus terminal it's about a 20-minute walk.

The famous spring, **Sōgi-sui**, near the centre of town, is something of a pilgrimage site, named for a Momoyama-era poet. People who rank such things place Sōgi-sui at the top of the list for clarity.

Gujō Tōsenji Youth Hostel (☎ 67-0290, fax 67-0291; beds per person ¥3200, closed early to mid-Aug) is an attractively refurnished facility in a temple, though there are only Japanese-style loos and no bath on the premises (there's a *sentō* nearby).

Satō Minshuku (☎ 65-2316; rooms per person with 2 meals from ¥7000), practically across from the bus terminal, is a welcoming, old-style place furnished with some antiques.

Bizenya Ryokan (☎ 65-2068, fax 67-0007; rooms per person with 2 meals ¥10,000) is patrician and well-staffed, with large rooms without private facilities, and a nice garden. It's between the bus terminal and the tourist office.

The most convenient access to Gujō Hachiman is via bus from Gifu (¥1480, one hour). The town centre is easily walkable, but the tourist office rents bicycles (¥300/1500 per hour/day).

Hida District
飛騨地域

Gifu-ken's major attractions are in this ancient, mountainous region. Hida is known for *gassho-zukuri* (hands-in-prayer) architecture and a strong craft tradition, as well as beef and *soba* (buckwheat noodles). This section also includes the Unesco World Heritage

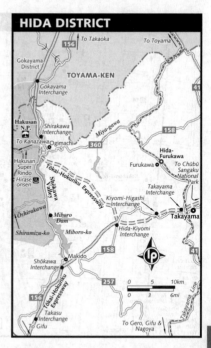

sites of Shirakawa-gō and nearby Gokayama, though the latter is not part of Hida.

TAKAYAMA 高山
☎ 0577 • pop 67,600

With its traditional inns, shops and sake breweries, Takayama is a rarity – a city (admittedly a small one) that has managed to retain its traditional charm. It should be a high priority on any visit to central Honshū. Give yourself two days to enjoy the place; it's easily tackled on foot or bicycle.

Takayama was established in the late 16th century, as the castle town of the Kanamori family, although in 1692 it was placed under direct control of the *bakufu* (shōgunate) in Edo. The present layout dates from the Kanamori period, and sights include more than a dozen museums, galleries and exhibitions covering lacquer and lion masks, folkcraft and architecture.

Takayama remains the region's administrative and transport hub, and it makes a good base for trips around Hida and Chūbu-Sangaku National Park.

The Takayama Festival (April and October; see Special Events later) is rated as one

CENTRAL HONSHŪ

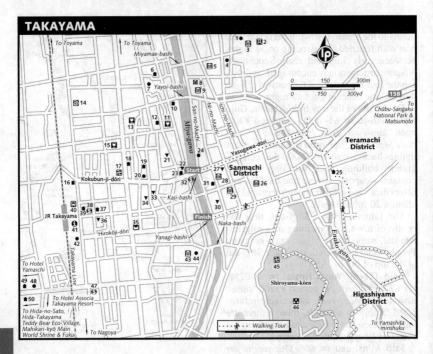

TAKAYAMA

of Japan's three great festivals and attracts over half a million spectators. If you plan to visit Takayama during the festival, book your accommodation well in advance, or visit as a day trip in from a nearby town.

Orientation

All the main sights, except Hida-no-Sato (Hida Folk Village), are in the centre of town, a short walk east from the station. Streets are arranged in a grid pattern. From the station, Kokubun-ji-dōri, the main street, heads east, across the river Miya-gawa (about 10 minutes' walk), where it becomes Yasugawa-dōri. South of Yasugawa-dōri is the historic Sanmachi district of immaculately preserved old homes.

Hida no Sato is a 10-minute bus ride west of the station.

Information

The **tourist information office** (☎ 32-5328; open 8.30am-5pm daily Nov-Mar, 8.30am-6.30pm daily Apr-Oct), directly in front of JR Takayama station, has English-speaking staff, as well as English-language maps and information on sights and accommoda-

tion. It can also provide English-language pamphlets on Takayama's festivals, as well as English-language bus schedules for services between Takayama and Chūbu-Sangaku National Park and the Shōkawa Valley. On the Web, visit ⓦ www.hida.jp/e-taka.htm.

To arrange a home visit, home stay or volunteer interpreter for non-Japanese languages (including sign language), contact the city's **International Affairs Office** (☎ 32-3333, ext 2407) one month in advance.

Postal ATMs are at the main post office on Hirokōji-dōri, a few blocks east of the station. **Ōgaki Kyōritsu Bank** also has foreign card ATMs southeast of the station and near the Miya-gawa Morning Market. **Jōroku Bank**, one block east of the station, can change cash or travellers' cheques.

Internet access (occasionally slow) is available free of charge at **Takayama Municipal Office** (open 9am-5pm Mon-Fri), seven minutes' walk north of the station.

Takayama-jinya 高山陣屋

Originally built in 1615 as the administrative centre for the Kanamori clan,

CENTRAL HONSHŪ

TAKAYAMA

PLACES TO STAY
6 Murasaki Ryokan
むらさき旅館
10 Sumiyoshi Ryokan
旅館寿美吉
12 Takayama City Hotel
Four Seasons
高山シティホテルフ
オーシーズン
16 New Alps Hotel
ニューアルプスホテル
18 Minshuku Kuwatani-ya
民宿桑谷屋
19 Rickshaw Inn
力車イン
23 Hotel Alpha One
ホテルアルファワン
25 Hida Takayama
Tenshō-ji
Youth Hostel
飛騨高山天照寺
ユースホステル
31 Ryokan Gōto
旅館河渡
37 Best Western Hotel
ベストウェスタンホテル
39 Country Hotel Takayama
カントリーホテル高山
49 Sōsuke
惣助
50 Takayama Green Hotel
高山グリーンホテル

PLACES TO EAT
21 Tom's Bellgins Bell
トムの店ベルギンズベル
22 Rengaya
レンガ屋

27 Ebisu
恵比寿本店
30 Noguchiya Tofu Restaurant
豆腐料理のぐちや
33 Suzuya
寿々や
34 Bandai Kadomise
萬代角店
36 Yamamotoya
やまもとや生そば

OTHER
1 Takayama Yatai Kaikan
(Festival Floats Exhibition
Hall)
高山屋台会館
2 Sakurayama Hachiman-gū
桜山八幡宮
3 Nikko-kan
日光館
4 Shishi Kaikan (Lion Mask
Exhibition Hall)
獅子会館
5 Inrō Bijutsukan
(Inro & Netsuke Museum)
印籠美術館
7 Shunkei Kaikan
(Lacquerware Exhibition Hall)
春慶会館
8 Yoshijima-ke
吉島家住宅
9 Kusakabe Mingeikan
日下部民芸館
11 Tonio Pub
13 Red Hill Pub
14 Takayama Municipal Office
高山市役所
15 Bagus

17 Hida Kokubun-ji
飛騨国分寺
20 Hara Cycle
ハラサイクル
24 Miya-gawa Morning Market
宮川朝市
26 Takayama Museum of Local
History
高山市郷土館
28 Fujii Folkcraft Art Gallery
藤井美術民芸館
29 Hirata Folk Art Museum
平田記念館
32 Ōgaki Kyōritsu Bank
大垣共立銀行
35 Main Post Office
高山郵便局
38 Jōroku Bank
十六銀行
40 Takayama Bus Station
高山バスターミナル
41 Tourist Information Office
観光案内所
42 Eki Rent-a-Car System
駅レンタカー
43 Takayama-jinya
高山陣屋
44 Jinya-mae Morning Market
陣屋前朝市
45 Shōren-ji
照蓮寺
46 Takayama-jō Ruins
高山城跡
47 Ōgaki Kyōritsu Bank
大垣共立銀行
48 Nippon Rent-a-Car
ニッポンレンタカー

Takayama-jinya *(Historical Government House;* ☎ *32-0643; admission ¥420; open 8.45am-5pm daily Mar-Oct, 8.45am-4.30pm daily Nov-Feb)* is now the only remaining prefectural office of the Tokugawa shōgunate; the main gate was once reserved for high officials. The present main building dates from 1816, and it was used as a local government office until 1969.

As well as government offices, a rice granary and a garden, there's a torture chamber with explanatory detail. Guided tours in English take place every 45 minutes.

Sanmachi 三町
The centre of the old town, this district of three main streets (Ichi-no-Machi, Ni-no-Machi and San-no-Machi) is lined with traditional shops, restaurants, museums

and private homes. Sake breweries are easily recognised by the round baskets of cedar fronds hanging above the entrances, though most of the year they just sell their wares (see Special Events later).

Fujii Folkcraft Art Gallery This gallery *(☎ 35-3778; admission ¥700; open 9am-5pm daily)* displays folkcraft and ceramics from Japan (particularly from the Muromachi and Edo periods), China and Korea. It's in an old merchant's house.

Hirata Folk Art Museum This museum *(Hirata Kinen-kan;* ☎ *33-1354; admission ¥300; open 9am-5pm daily)* is a merchant's house dating from the turn of the century, displaying items from everyday rural Japanese life.

Takayama Museum of Local History

This museum (☎ 32-1205; admission ¥300; open 8.30am-5pm daily Mar-Nov, 9am-4.30pm daily Dec-Feb, closed Mon Nov-Mar) is devoted to the crafts and traditions of the region. Pride of place is allotted to images carved by Enkū, a woodcarving priest who wandered this region in the 17th century.

Merchant Houses
吉島家日下部民芸館

North of Sanmachi are two excellent examples of Edo period merchants homes, with the living quarters in one section and the warehouse in another. Design buffs will revel at **Yoshijima-ke** (Yoshijima house; ☎ 32-0038; admission ¥500; open 9am-5pm daily Mar-Nov, 9am-4.30pm Wed-Sun Dec-Feb), well covered in architectural publications. Its lack of ornamentation allows you to focus on the lovely, spare lines, soaring roof and skylight. Down the block, the folk-art collection **Kusakabe Mingeikan** (Kusakabe Folk Art Museum; ☎ 32-0072; admission ¥500; open 8.30am-5pm daily Mar-Nov, 8.30am-4.30pm daily Dec-Feb) is fitted out as it would have been if you had walked in to talk business in the late 1890s.

Shunkei Kaikan 春慶会館

Unlike many other Japanese lacquer styles, Takayama's Shunkei lacquerware is designed to show off the wood grain; this exhibition hall (☎ 32-3373; admission ¥300; open 8am-5.30pm daily Apr-Oct, 9am-5pm daily Nov-Mar) features more than 1000 Shunkei pieces, with an exhibit showing production techniques.

Inrō Bijutsukan 印籠美術館

Traditional kimono do not have pockets, so fashionable Japanese used to carry inrō (medicine boxes) on strings held in place by netsuke (toggles). Both are elaborately designed and carved creations in wood, bone, stone and ivory, and are among Japan's most celebrated works of art. This museum (☎ 32-8500; admission ¥500; open 9am-5pm Wed-Mon Apr-Nov) displays some 300 rare and historic examples.

Takayama Yatai Kaikan
高山屋台会館

The Festival Floats Exhibition Hall (☎ 32-5100; admission ¥820; open 8.30am-5pm daily Mar-Nov, 9am-4.30pm daily Dec-Feb) features a rotating selection of four of the 23 multi-tiered yatai (floats) used in the Takayama Festival. These spectacular creations, some dating from the 17th century, are prized for their flamboyant carvings, metalwork and lacquerwork. A famous feature of some floats is karakuri, marionettes that perform amazing tricks and acrobatics courtesy of eight accomplished puppeteers using 36 strings. A video gives a sense of the festival.

Although the hall can be crowded, it tries to respect the festival's religious significance.

Your ticket also admits you to the **Sakurayama Nikkō-kan** next door, with amazingly detailed models of the famous shrines at Nikkō; you can also visit the shrine **Sakurayama Hachiman-gū**, where the festival is based.

You may pass some unusual slender garages around town with three-storey doors; these house the yatai that are not in the museum.

Shishi Kaikan 獅子会館

Just south of the Yatai Kaikan is the Lion Mask Exhibition Hall (☎ 32-0881; admission ¥600; open 8.30am-5.30pm late Apr-late Oct, 9am-5pm late Oct-late Apr). It has a display of over 800 lion masks and musical instruments connected with the lion dances that are commonly performed at festivals in central and northern Japan. Admission includes twice-hourly demonstrations of karakuri – a good opportunity for a close-up view of these marvellous puppets in action.

Hida Kokubun-ji 飛騨国分寺

The original temple (☎ 32-1295; admission ¥300; open 9am-4pm daily) was built in the 8th century; the oldest of the present buildings dates from the 16th century. The temple's treasure hall houses some Important Cultural Properties, and the gingko tree in the courtyard is impressively gnarled and in remarkably good shape, considering it's believed to be 1200 years old.

Teramachi & Shiroyama-kōen
寺町・城山公園

These hilly districts in the east side of town are linked by a walking trail, particularly enjoyable in the early morning or late afternoon. Teramachi has over a dozen temples (one houses the youth hostel) and shrines that you can wander around before taking in the lush greenery of the park. Various trails lead through the park and up the mountainside to the ruins of the castle, **Takayama-jō**. As you descend, you can take a look at the temple, **Shōren-ji**, which was transferred to this site from the Shōkawa Valley when a dam was built there in 1960.

The walk takes a leisurely two hours, and from the temple it's a 10-minute walk back to the centre of town.

Hida-no-Sato 飛騨の里

This large open-air museum (☎ *34-4711; admission ¥700; open 8.30am-5pm daily)* is highly recommended for dozens of traditional houses, dismantled at their original sites throughout the region and rebuilt here. During clear weather, there are good views across the town to the peaks of the Japan Alps. Allow at least three hours to explore the whole place on foot.

Hido-no-Sato is in two sections. The western section features 12 old houses and a complex of five traditional buildings with artisans demonstrating folk arts and crafts. Many are in Hida's distinctive *gasshō-zukuri* style (see the boxed text 'Hida's Gasshō-Zukuri' below). Displays are well presented and offer an excellent chance to see what rural life was like in previous centuries.

The eastern section of the village, which is a pleasant walk away, is centred around the Omoide Taikenkan, where you can try making candles, *senbei* (rice crackers) etc. Other buildings include the Go-kura Storehouse (used for storage of rice as payment of taxes) and the Museum of Mountain Life.

Hida-no-Sato is a 30-minute walk from Takayama station, but the route through urban sprawl is not enjoyable. Either hire a bicycle in town, or take the Hida-no-Sato bus (¥250, 10 minutes) from Stop 2 at the bus station. A discount ticket 'Hida-no-Sato setto ken' is available, combining the return fare and admission to the park for ¥900. Be sure to check return times for the bus.

Hida-Takayama Teddy Bear Eco-Village

飛騨高山テディベアエコビレッジ

Within a late-19th-century *gasshō* house (☎ *37-2525; adult/child ¥600/400; open 10am-6pm daily mid-Mar–late Nov, 10am-5pm daily late Nov–mid-Mar)*, and in other buildings, some 800 furry friends convey an environmentalist message. Travellers with children seem to enjoy this quirky museum, and Japanese high-school girls find it *kawaii* (cute).

Hida's Gasshō-Zukuri

Winter in the Hida region can be fierce, and inhabitants faced snow and cold long before the advent of propane heaters and 4WD vehicles. One of the most visible symbols of that adaptability is *gasshō-zukuri* architecture, seen in the steeply slanted straw-roofed homes that still dot the landscape around the region.

The sharply angled roofs were designed to prevent heavy snow accumulation, a serious concern in a region where nearly all mountain roads close from December to April. The name *gasshō* comes from the Japanese word for 'praying', because the shape of the roofs was thought to resemble two hands clasped in prayer. *Gasshō* buildings often featured pillars crafted from stout cedar trees to lend extra support. The attic areas were ideal for silk cultivation.

Larger *gasshō* buildings were inhabited by wealthy families, up to 30 people under one roof. Peasant families lived in huts of the size that are now used as tool sheds.

The *gasshō-zukuri* building has become an endangered species, with most examples having been gathered together and preserved in folk villages, including Hida-no-Sato in Takayama, and in the Shōkawa Valley. This sometimes means that two homes that are now neighbours were once separated by several days or weeks of travel on foot or sled. But local authorities have worked hard to recreate their natural surroundings, making it possible to imagine what life in the Hida hills might have looked like hundreds of years ago.

Mahikari-kyō Main World Shrine
真光教

Dominating Takayama's western skyline is the golden roof of the Main World Shrine (☎ 34-7008; admission free; open 8.30am-4.30pm daily, closed for monthly religious holidays) of the new religion Mahikari-kyō, which is said to combine Buddhism and Shintō. Opinion is divided on whether its believers are harmless loop-the-loops or anti-Semitic doomsday cultists. A guided tour might allow you to decide for yourself (call in advance for an English-speaking guide; an English pamphlet is available).

Morning Markets

Asa-ichi (morning markets) take place every morning from 7am to 11am, starting an hour earlier from April to October. The Jinya-mae Market is in front of Takayama-jinya; the Miya-gawa Market is larger, along the east bank of the Miya-gawa, between Kaji-bashi and Yayoi-bashi. The markets provide a pleasant way to start the day, with a stroll past gnarled farmers at their vegetable stands and stalls selling crafts, pickles, souvenirs and that all-important steaming cuppa joe.

Special Events

Takayama's famed festival is in two parts: Sannō Matsuri takes place on 14 and 15 April; a dozen yatai, decorated with carvings, dolls, colourful curtains and blinds, are paraded through the town. In the evening the floats are decked out with lanterns, and the procession is accompanied by sacred music. Hachiman Matsuri, on 9 and 10 October, is a slightly smaller version starting at Sakurayama Hachiman-gū.

If you plan to visit Takayama during either of these times, you must book accommodation months in advance and expect to pay a 20% premium. Or you could stay elsewhere in the region and commute to Takayama.

Most of the sake breweries in Sanmachi, many dating back to the Edo period, only sell their wares most of the year, but in January and February several of them arrange tours and tastings.

Places to Stay

The tourist information office (☎ 32-5328; open 8.30am-5pm daily Nov-Mar, 8.30am-6.30pm daily Apr-Oct) assists with reservations.

Places to Stay – Budget

Hostel The Hida Takayama Tenshō-ji Youth Hostel (☎ 32-6345, fax 32-6392; dorm beds ¥2800) is in an attractive temple in Teramachi, although some guests gripe about its lights-out and wake-up schedule. The hostel is a 25-minute walk across town from the train station, or board the bus for Shin-Hotaka, get off at the Betsuin-mae stop and walk east about five minutes.

Minshuku About 10 minutes by bus south of town is Hotel Yamaichi (☎ 34-6200, fax 34-6201; W www.kbnet.jp.org/11pm/kamaya /hyoshi.html; Japanese/Western rooms per person from ¥3800/4800). The building is old, but the owners are friendly; the couple of Western rooms have private facilities. If the owners can't pick you up, they'll pay half the taxi fare.

Places to Stay – Mid-Range

Ryokan Near Shunkei Kaikan, Murasaki Ryokan (☎ 32-1724, fax 33-7512; rooms per person with/without 2 meals from ¥7500/ 4000) features Japanese-style rooms and a dazzling wall of flowers along the front of the building, the product of decades of work.

Minshuku The good-value Rickshaw Inn (☎ 32-2890, fax 32-2469; W www.rickshawinn .com; Japanese-style rooms per person ¥4900, singles/twins with bath ¥6000/11,000, without bath ¥4200/8400) is a very pleasant place to stay. It's a modern minshuku with Southeast Asian touches, both Japanese and Western-style rooms and a small kitchen. The owners speak English, are very friendly and dispense excellent English-language information.

Minshuku Kuwataniya (☎ 32-5021, fax 36-3835; W http://kuwataniya.com; rooms per person with 2 meals from ¥7000), close to the train station, is Takayama's longest-running minshuku (since the 1920s), with both Japanese and Western-style rooms, hot-spring bath and free bicycle use. Dinner always features Hida's famed beef.

Sosuke (☎ 32-0818, fax 33-5570; W www .irori-sosuke.com; rooms per person with 2 meals from ¥7500), west of the train station, across from Takayama Green Hotel, has friendly, English-speaking staff. The handsomely renovated building retains a traditional style, including an *irori* (hearth), though it is on a busy road.

Yamashita (☎ 33-0686, fax 32-8513; *rooms per person with 2 meals ¥8500*) is a farmhouse-style *minshuku* in Enakochō, about 10 minutes by car south of the city centre; pick-up from the train station is available. Dinner is served around the *irori*. It's a good option if you don't mind staying in the outskirts of town.

Hotels The **New Alps Hotel** (☎ 32-2888, fax 33-6687; *rooms per person from ¥4200*) is just a minute's walk from the train station. Rooms are nothing special, though it's cheap and convenient.

Hotel Alpha One (☎ 32-2211, fax 32-7720; *singles/twins/doubles ¥5313/13,629/ 12,474*) is well located near the Miya-gawa and has pleasant enough business hotel-style rooms. Look for the Greek character 'alpha' and the numeral '1' on the sign outside.

Country Hotel Takayama (☎ 35-3900, fax 35-3910; *singles/twins from ¥5900/7800*) is directly across from the station. It's new and has slightly larger, up-to-date rooms, though off echo-ey tiled hallways.

Takayama City Hotel Four Seasons (☎ 36-0088, fax 36-0080; *singles/twins from ¥6900/13,000*) has nicer-than-average business hotel rooms and a communal *onsen* (mineral hot-spring bath).

Best Western Hotel (☎ 37-2000, fax 37-2005; *singles/twins from ¥7500/16,000*), one minute from the station, was recently built and has comfortable rooms. It costs a bit more, but it makes up for it in polish.

Places to Stay – Top End

Ryokan Most of Takayama's ryokan cost between ¥8000 and ¥15,000 per person (with two meals); in some cases you may need to speak some Japanese before the proprietors will take you. Most rooms in places listed here don't have private facilities.

Sumiyoshi Ryokan (☎ 32-0228, fax 33-8916; *rooms per person with 2 meals ¥8000-13,000*) is a delightfully traditional place in an old merchant's house; some rooms have river views.

Ryokan Gōto (☎/fax 33-0870; *rooms per person with breakfast from ¥9000*) is another traditional inn in the heart of Sanmachi; you know you're somewhere special when you have to crouch to enter the front door.

Hotels The *onsen* hotel **Takayama Green Hotel** (☎ 33-5500, fax 32-4434; **w** *www .takayama-gh.com; rooms per person with 2 meals from ¥15,000*) has Japanese, Western and combination rooms, in a tower southwest of the station.

Hotel Associa Takayama Resort (☎ 36-0001, fax 36-0188; **w** *www.associa.com/tky; rooms per person from ¥13,500*) is luxurious. It has both indoor and outdoor hot-spring baths and a tennis court, and all rooms boast views of the Japan Alps. It's several kilometres south of town, but a free shuttle bus serves the train station hourly.

Places to Eat

Takayama's culinary treats include *soba*, *hoba-miso* (sweet miso paste cooked on a *hoba* [magnolia] leaf) and *sansai* (mountain vegetables). Popular street foods include *mitarashi-dango* (skewers of grilled rice balls seasoned with soya sauce), *shio-sembei* (salty rice crackers) and skewers of grilled Hida beef (among the finest grades of meat in Japan, though relatively new on the scene).

Most restaurants, especially in the historic Sanmachi district, close by between 7pm and 9pm. After that, your best bets are near the train station. In that area, **Yamamotoya** (☎ 33-7777; *dishes ¥500-900, sets from ¥1100*) serves *soba*, *tempura* and *katsudon* (fried pork cutlet over rice).

Suzuya (☎ 32-2484; *sets ¥1200-3000; open 11am-7.30pm Wed-Mon*), in the centre of town, is a rustic, longstanding favourite serving the local specialities. **Bandai Kadomise** (☎ 33-5166; *sets ¥1400-3000*) has a similar feel for lunch and dinner. Both have English menus.

Ebisu (☎ 32-0209; *mains ¥750-1480*) is a historic (110 year-old) little *soba* restaurant in Sanmachi. There is no English menu.

Noguchiya Tofu Restaurant (☎ 33-7563; *sets ¥750-2100; open lunch daily*) features tasty varieties of hot and cold tofu dishes, and a picture menu.

Rengaya (☎ 36-1339; *dishes ¥350-800; open dinner*), near Hotel Alpha One, is a Western-style *izakaya* (Japanese-style pub) seemingly staffed by off-duty schoolgirls. It has some good *ji-bīru* (local beer) and an English menu.

Tom's Bellgins Bell (☎ 33-6507; *mains ¥550-2500*) is for if you feel like a complete change. It's a couple of blocks northwest of

Kaji-bashi. Its amiable Swiss owner fulfils all those cravings for fondue and rosti. Look for the sign reading 'I found my heart in Takayama'.

Entertainment

Pubs & Bars An excellent selection of domestic and imported brews can be found at **Red Hill Pub** (☎ 33-8139; open 7pm-midnight Tues-Sun). It's a pretty popular spot with locals and tends to get crowded after 11pm. **Tonio Pub** is an English-style place closer to the river, with Guinness on tap and reasonable prices (for Japanese bars).

Bagus (☎ 36-4341; open 7pm-2am Mon-Sat) is a friendly, youthful reggae bar between the train station and Takayama Municipal Office.

Shopping

Takayama is renowned for crafts. *Ichii ittobori* (woodcarvings) are fashioned from yew and can be seen as intricate components of the *yatai* floats or for sale as figurines. Woodworking expertise also extends to furniture (see the boxed text 'Hida's Takumi Woodworkers' on the next page).

Shunkei lacquerware was introduced from Kyoto several centuries ago and is used to produce boxes, trays and flower containers. The city-run exhibition hall, **Shunkei Kaikan**, has adjacent shops with outstanding lacquerware and porcelain, and, occasionally, good deals.

Local pottery styles range from the rustic Yamada-yaki to the decorative Shibukusa-yaki.

Around town, good places to find handicrafts are Sanmachi, the morning markets, and the section of Kokubun-ji-dōri between the Miya-gawa and the train station. Probably the most common souvenirs are *sarubobo* (monkey babies), dolls of red cloth dressed in blue fabric, with pointy limbs and featureless faces. These are said to date from the time when locals had to make toys out of materials on hand.

Getting There & Away

Bus The bus station is on your left outside the train station. Many roads in this region close in the winter, so bus schedules vary seasonally and don't run at all in winter on some routes. For exact dates, check with the tourist offices.

Keiō Highway Buses (☎ 32-1688) connect Takayama and Shinjuku (¥6500, 5½ hours, several daily, reservations required).

For getting around in Chūbu-Sangaku National Park, see the boxed text later in this chapter.

Train Takayama is connected with Nagoya on the JR Takayama line (Hida *tokkyū*, ¥5870, 2¼ hours, 10 daily). Some of these continue to Toyama (¥3280, 1½ hours).

Express trains run from Osaka (¥8070, five hours) and Kyoto (¥7440, 4½ hours), although it's usually faster to take the *shinkansen* and change in Nagoya.

Car At the train station you'll find **Eki Rent-a-Car System** (☎ 33-3522), and there's a branch of **Nippon Rent-a-Car** (☎ 34-5121), southwest of the train station, near Sosuke *minshuku*.

Getting Around

Most sights in Takayama can be covered easily on foot. You can amble from the train station across to Teramachi in 25 minutes.

Bus The only place you'll really need to take the bus is to Hida-no-Sato (¥220, 10 minutes, half-hourly).

Cycling Takayama is a good place to explore by bicycle. Some lodgings rent or loan cycles, or try **Hara Cycle** (☎ 32-1657; Kokubunji-dōri; bike rental ¥300/1300 per hour/day).

FURUKAWA 古川

☎ 0577 • pop 18,000

Furukawa is home of the Hadaka Matsuri (Naked Festival). Now that we have your attention, you should also know that this town, only 15 minutes from Takayama, makes a nice day trip the rest of the year too, thanks to a couple of worthwhile museums and some lovely streetscapes.

Orientation & Information

Furukawa's train and bus stations adjoin each other east of the town centre, and the sights are within 10 minutes' walk. There's an **information office** (☎ 73-3180; open 8.30am-5.30pm daily) at the bus station, which offers an English pamphlet and

Hida's Takumi Woodworkers

Some 1300 years ago there lived a carpenter named Takumi, said to be so skilled that word of his work spread as far as the capital, Heian-kyō (now Kyoto).

At that time, the Japanese regions had to pay taxes in rice, which posed a problem for Hida, with little farmland but many forested mountains. So in the year 718, in lieu of taxes, Hida was permitted to send Takumi – and a cadre of carpenters and carvers – to construct the legendary shrines and temples of Kyoto and Nara.

Today, 'Takumi' has become a general term for woodworkers of great skill and precision. Takumi work appears in homes, furniture, and statues and *karakuri* puppets for Hida's famed *yatai*, festival floats that are storeys tall.

Takumi's name has been adopted by woodworking shops throughout Hida, and you can learn more about Takumi-style woodworking at the Takumi-kan in Furukawa.

Japanese maps, but if you don't speak Japanese you'll be better off getting information in Takayama; staff in either city can book accommodation in Furukawa.

Things to See

If you're not in town for the festival, the **Matsuri Kaikan** (Festival Museum; ☎ 73-3511; admission ¥800; open 9am-5pm daily Apr-Nov, 9am-4.30pm daily Dec-Mar) shows it in all its glory. You can don 3-D glasses to watch a video of the festivities, see some of the *yatai* that are paraded through the streets, try manipulating *karakuri* like those used on the *yatai*, and watch craftsmen demonstrating *kirie* (paper cut-outs) or *ittobori* (wood carving).

Across the square, **Takumi-kan** (Takumi Craft Museum; ☎ 73-3321; admission ¥200; open 9am-5pm daily Mar-Nov, 9am-4.30pm daily Dec-Feb) is a must for woodworkers, craftspeople and design fans. There's a hands-on room where you can try assembling blocks of wood cut into different joint patterns – not as easy as it sounds.

The museums are one gateway to the historic district, **Setakawa to Shirakabe-dozo**, handsome riverside streets filled with white- and darkwool-walled shops, storehouses and private homes. Among them is **Mishima-ya** (☎ 73-4109), a shop that has made candles for over two centuries; traditional shapes are concave or tapered with the wide end at the top.

Special Events

The **Furukawa Matsuri**, as the Hadaka Matsuri is formally known, takes place every 19 and 20 April. The highlight is the Okoshi Daiko, when squads of boisterous young men dressed in loincloths parade through town at midnight, competing to place small drums atop a stage bearing a giant drum. OK, it's not *naked*-naked, but we didn't make up the name.

During the **Kitsune-bi Matsuri** (Fox Fire Festival), on 16 October, locals make up as foxes, parade through the town by lanternlight and enact a wedding at the shrine, Okura Inari-jinja. The ceremony, deemed to bring good fortune, climaxes with a bonfire at the shrine.

Places to Stay & Eat

Hida Furukawa Youth Hostel (☎/fax 75-2979; e hidafyh@d2.dion.ne.jp; beds with/without 2 meals ¥4600/3100; open 11 Apr-29 Mar) is friendly and attractive, with 22 beds. It's surrounded by farmland about 6km from the town centre, or 1.2km west of Hida-Hosoe station (two stops north of Hida-Furukawa). The park, Shinrin-kōen, is across the street. Rooms are both Japanese and Western style.

Ryokan Tanbo-no-Yu (☎ 73-2014, fax 73-6454; rooms per person with 2 meals ¥7000), in the town centre, has spacious Japanese rooms without private facilities, plus a bath with red-brown waters said to be good for cuts, bruises and rheumatism. Visitors can bathe for ¥500. No English is spoken.

Kitchen Kyabingu (☎ 73-4706; dishes ¥350-2400; open Tues-Sun) is a busy, cosy lunch spot in the historic district, serving delicious Hida-gyu (Hida beef). Most people seem to order the beef curry with rice (¥800) or the *teishoku* starring sizzling steak on a hot iron plate (¥2400).

Getting There & Around

There are some 20 daily connections each way between Takayama and Furukawa. Hida-Furukawa train station is three stops north of Takayama (*futsū* [ordinary train], ¥230, 15 minutes), or you can bus it (¥360, 30 minutes). Central Furukawa is an easy stroll, or there's bike rental at the station.

SHŌKAWA VALLEY REGION
庄川

This remote, dramatically mountainous district between Takayama and Kanazawa is best known for farmhouses in the thatched-roof, A-frame style called *gasshō-zukuri* ('hands-in-prayer'; see the boxed text 'Hida's Gasshō-Zukuri' earlier). They're rustic and lovely, particularly in clear weather or in the snow, and they hold a special place in the Japanese heart. The valley's main centres are Shirakawa-gō to the south and Gokayama about 30 minutes' drive to the north (technically not in Hida but in Toyama-ken). Route 156 connects the two.

In the 12th century, the region's remoteness and inaccessibility are said to have attracted stragglers from the Taira clan, virtually wiped out by the Genji clan in a brutal battle in 1185. During feudal times Shirakawa-gō, like the rest of Hida, was under direct control of the shōgun, while Gokayama was a centre for the production of gunpowder for the Kaga region.

Fast-forward to the 1960s: when construction of the gigantic Miboro Dam was about to submerge some local villages, many *gasshō* houses were moved to their current sites for safekeeping. Although much of what you'll find has been specially preserved for, and supported by, tourism, it still presents a view of rural life found in few other parts of Japan.

Most of Shirakawa-gō's sights are in the community of Ogimachi. In Gokayama, the community of Ainokura has the greatest concentration, although other sights are spread throughout hamlets over several kilometres along route 156. If your time is limited, visit Ogimachi or Ainokura (both Unesco World Heritage sites, along with the Gokayama settlement of Suganuma).

One of the draws of the region is the opportunity to spend the night in a *gasshō-zukuri* house that's been turned into an inn. Advance reservations are highly recom-mended, and the Shirakawa-gō tourist office can help with local bookings (in Japanese). Takayama's tourist office can help if you don't speak Japanese. Don't expect rooms with private facilities, but some inns have *irori* for guests to eat around.

Bus services to and around the region are infrequent and vary seasonally, so it's important to check schedules. For maximum flexibility (and perhaps even a cost saving), you may prefer to rent a car. Either way, traffic can be severe on weekends and throughout the peak tourist times of May, August and October. Expect snow, and lots of it, between late December and late March.

Shirakawa-gō 白川郷
☎ 05769

The region's central settlement, **Ogimachi**, has over 110 *gasshō-zukuri* buildings and is the most convenient place to orient yourself for tourist information and transport.

Information Ogimachi's main **tourist office** (☎ 6-1013; w www.shirakawa-go.org; open 9am-5pm daily) is next to Gasshō-zukuri Minka-en. The office has a Japanese map of Shirakawa-gō, including a detailed map of Ogimachi. No English is spoken.

To reach the office, walk west from the main road, pass the shrine Akiba-jinja, and cross Deai-bashi, the suspension footbridge over the river.

Shiroyama Tenbōdai To get your bearings, this lookout on the site of the former castle offers a famous, sprawling view of the flatlands below. It's a 15-minute walk via the road behind the east side of town, or you can climb the path (five minutes) from near the intersection of routes 156 and 360.

Gasshō-zukuri Minka-en This folklore park (☎ 6-1231; admission ¥500; open 8am-5.30pm Fri-Wed Aug, 8.40am-5pm Fri-Wed Apr-Nov, 9am-4pm Fri-Wed Dec-Mar) is a well-presented group of over a dozen *gasshō-zukuri* buildings, collected from the surrounding region and reconstructed in this open-air museum amid seasonal flowers. Several of the houses are used for demonstrating regional crafts, such as woodwork, straw handicrafts and ceramics – many items are for sale.

OGIMACHI

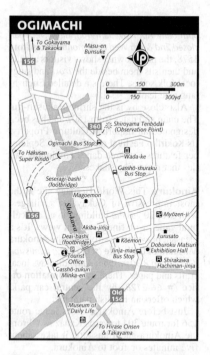

To Gokayama & Takaoka

Masu-en Bunsuke

156

0   150   300m
0   150   300yd

Shiroyama Tenbōdai (Observation Point)

360

Ogimachi Bus Stop

To Hakusan Super Rindō

Wada-ke

Gasshō-shuraku Bus Stop

Seseragi-bashi (footbridge)

Magoemon

Shōkawa

Myōzen-ji

156

Akiba-jinja

Deai-bashi (footbridge)

Kōemon

Furusato

Tourist Office

Jinja-mae Bus Stop

Doburoku Matsuri Exhibition Hall

Gasshō-zukuri Minka-en

Shirakawa Hachiman-jinja

Museum of Daily Life

Old 156

To Hirase Onsen & Takayama

You can wander away from the houses for a pleasant stroll through the trees further up the mountain. Feel free to take a picnic, but Shirakawa-gō has a rule that you must carry your trash out of town.

Wada-ke The largest *gasshō* house (☎ 6-1058; admission ¥300; open 9am-5pm daily, closed occasionally) in Shirakawa-gō once belonged to a wealthy silk-trading family and dates back to the mid-Edo period. Appropriately, you'll find silk-harvesting equipment upstairs, as well as a valuable lacquerware collection.

Myōzen-ji This temple in the centre of Ogimachi has a museum (☎ 6-1009; admission ¥300; open 8.30am-5pm daily Apr-Nov, 9am-4pm daily Dec-Mar) displaying the traditional paraphernalia of daily rural life.

Doburoku Matsuri Exhibition Hall Shirakawa-gō's big festival is held in mid-October at the shrine Shirakawa Hachiman-jinja, and features coordinated dancing groups of locals, including the lion dance and much *niwaka* (improvised buffoonery).

But the real star is *doboroku*, and very potent unrefined sake. Perhaps the most illustrative part of this exhibition hall (☎ 6-1655; admission ¥300; open 9am-4pm daily Apr-Nov) is the video of the festival (in Japanese).

Onsen In Hirase Onsen, about 13km south of Ogimachi on route 156, the **Kyōdō Yokujō** (public bath, ☎ 5-2412; admission ¥330; open 10am-10pm Fri-Wed Apr-Nov, 12pm-9pm Fri-Wed Feb & Mar) is ageing but a good place to soak up the local atmosphere; its waters are said to be beneficial for the skin and fertility. About another 15km up the Ōshirakawa river (via a mountain road full of blind curves), **Ōshirakawa Rotemburo** (☎ 090-2770-2893; admission ¥200; open 8.30am-5pm daily July-Oct, to 6pm July & Aug) is much admired for its views of an emerald-green pool.

Places to Stay & Eat Some Japanese is helpful in making reservations at one of Ogimachi's many *gasshō-zukuri* inns. In the town centre are **Kōemon** (☎ 6-1446, fax 6-1748; rooms per person ¥7700), handsomely updated with darkwood panelling, and **Furusato** (☎ 6-1033; rooms per person ¥8000), a much-photographed place near Myōzen-ji, run by a kindly older lady. **Magoemon** (☎ 6-1169, fax 6-1851; rooms per person ¥8500) has slightly larger rooms, some with river views. All prices include two meals but not the nightly surcharge for heating (¥300) during cold weather.

The town centre has a number of casual restaurants (look for *soba* or *hoba miso*), mostly open at noon only. **Masu-en Bunsuke** (☎ 6-1268; dishes ¥300-500; teishoku from ¥1500), uphill from the town centre, specialises in trout cuisine, in an attractive setting with its own trout ponds.

Gokayama District 五箇山
☎ 0763

Gokayama is so isolated that road links and electricity didn't arrive until 1925.

Communities with varying numbers of *gasshō-zukuri* buildings are scattered over many kilometres along route 156. The following briefly describes the communities and sights you'll come across as you travel north from Shirakawa-gō or the Gokayama exit from the Tōkai-Hokuriku Expressway; if your time is limited, head straight for Ainokura.

CENTRAL HONSHŪ

Nishi-Akao In this settlement, about 300m north of the Kami-Taira Michi-no-Eki (information/tourist plaza), the 17th-century house **Iwase-ke** (☎ 67-3338; admission ¥300; open 8am-5pm daily) was once the local centre for the production of gunpowder. Out the back, a garden slopes up a hill, and a pond was built to catch snow as it slid off the roof. The nearby temple **Gyōtoku-ji** (☎ 67-3302; admission ¥200; open 9am-5pm daily) has a museum featuring works by masters of the *mingei* (folk-art) movement, including Kawai Kanjirō, Bernard Leach and the eccentric genius potter-painter, Munakata Shikō.

Suganuma This World Heritage site, 2km beyond Nishi-Akao and down a steep hill, features an attractive group of *gasshō-zukuri* houses worth a stroll. The **Minzoku-kan** (Folklore Museum; ☎ 67-3652; admission ¥300; open 9am-4pm May-Nov) consists of two houses with items from traditional life and exhibits on traditional gunpowder production.

About 1km further up route 156, **Kurōba Onsen** (☎ 67-3741; admission ¥600; open 11am-9pm Wed-Mon Apr-Oct, 11am-8pm Nov-Mar) is a complex with baths overlooking the river.

Kaminashi About 4km beyond Suganuma is Kaminashi. The house museum **Murakami-ke** (☎ 66-2711; admission ¥300; open 8.30am-5pm daily Apr-Nov, 9am-4pm daily Dec-Mar, closed 2nd & 4th Wed each month) dates from 1578; the proud owner shows visitors around and then sits them beside the *irori* and sings local folk songs. There's a detailed English-language leaflet.

Also close by is the shrine **Hakusan-gū**. The main hall dates from 1502 and has been designated an Important Cultural Property. Its **Kokiriko Festival** on 25 and 26 September features a unique dance employing rattles that move like snakes.

Ainokura This World Heritage site is the most impressive of Gokayama's villages, with over 20 *gasshō* buildings in an agricultural valley with fine mountain views. It's a pleasant place just to stroll, and the **Ainokura Museum of Daily Life** (☎ 66-2732; admission ¥200; open 8.30am-5pm daily) displays local crafts and paper. There's an **information office** (☎ 66-2123) by the central car park, which offers an English pamphlet.

Just before Ainokura, buses leave route 156 for route 304 towards Kanazawa. From the Ainokura-guchi bus stop it takes about five minutes on foot to Ainokura.

Continue up route 156 for several kilometres until **Gokayama Washi-no-Sato** (Gokayama Japanese Paper Village; ☎ 66-2223; admission ¥200; open 8.30-5pm daily), where you will find exhibits of *washi* (Japanese handmade paper) art and a chance to make your own (reservation required).

Places to Stay Ainokura is a great place for a *gasshō-zukuri* farmhouse stay, as you'll have the place to yourself after the tour buses leave. Try the welcoming **Yomoshiro** (☎ 66-2377, fax 66-2387), **Goyomon** (☎ 66-2154, fax 66-2227), with excellent views from the 2nd storey, or **Chōyomon** (☎ 66-2755, fax 66-2765), with its atmospheric, darkwood sliding doors. All cost around ¥7500 per person, including two meals. Ainokura also has a **camping ground** (☎ 66-2123; per person ¥500; open mid-Apr–late Oct, unless there's snow).

Kokuminshukusha Gokayama-sō (☎ 66-2316, fax 66-2717; rooms per person with 2 meals ¥7500), in Kaminashi, doesn't have the charm of its *gasshō-zukuri* neighbours, but some rooms on the 3rd floor have nice valley vistas.

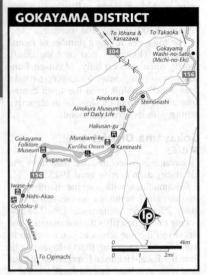

GOKAYAMA DISTRICT

To Jōhana & Kanazawa | To Takaoka

Gokayama Washi-no-Sato (Michi-no-Eki)

304

156

Ainokura — Shimonashi

Ainokura Museum of Daily Life

Hakusan-gu

Gokayama Folklore Museum

Murakami-ke

Kurōba Onsen — Kaminashi

Suganuma

156

Iwase-ke

Nishi-Akao

Gyōtoku-ji

Shōkawa

To Ogimachi

0 | 2 | 4km

0 | 1 | 2mi

Nakaya (*☎ 67-3252, fax 67-2765; rooms per person with 2 meals ¥6800*) is a friendly little *minshuku* in Nishi-Akao.

Getting There & Away

Bus Schedules change annually, but here's the latest as we went to press. Between April and October, five buses a day operated by **Nōhi Bus Company** (*☎ 0577-32-1688*) link Shirakawa-gō with Takayama (¥2400, 1¾ hours). Of these, two continue via Gokayama to Kanazawa (¥1800, 1⅓ hours).

Between Ogimachi and Gokayama, **Kaetsuno Bus** (*☎ 0766-22-4888*) operates four buses a day stopping at all the major sights and continuing to Takaoka on the JR Hokuriku Line (1⅔ hours). If you wish to get off somewhere other than an official stop (eg, at Kuroba Onsen), let the driver know.

Car From Takayama (the most popular starting point), the trip takes about two hours, but by the time you read this, new interchanges should have opened up on the Tōkai-Hokuriku Expressway, dramatically trimming travel times from Kanazawa, Toyama and, eventually, Nagoya. Interchanges are at Gokayama and Shōkawa. From Hakusan, the scenic toll road Hakusan Super-Rindō ends near Ogimachi (cars ¥3150). During colder months, be sure to check first on road conditions with regional tourist offices.

People do hitch, although one should take the usual precautions.

GERO 下呂
☎ 0576 • pop 15,178

Hida's southern gateway, Gero is favoured by Japanese tourists for its numerous *onsen*, even if its name in Japanese is an unfortunate homonym for 'vomit'. The town's sprawl of concrete buildings dampens its appeal, but the waters, reputedly beneficial for rheumatism, athletic injuries and complexion, are excellent.

Gero is fairly compact; you can walk nearly anywhere from the train station within 20 minutes. Day-use bathing prices hover around ¥1000 per visit, but the ¥1200 'Yumeguri Tegata' is a wooden plaque on a rope (and a nice souvenir) that allows one-time access to three among a selection of *onsen*. It's available at the **tourist information office** (*☎ 25-4711; open 8.30am-5.30pm daily*), outside the train station, where you can also make lodging reservations and pick up an English-language map.

Gero boasts its own hot-spring temple – **Onsen-ji** – overlooking the town, while on the edge of the centre is **Gero Onsen Gasshō Village** (*☎ 25-2239; admission ¥800; open 8.15am-5pm daily*), the most polished of its ilk with 10 buildings from the Shirakawa-gō area; there's a museum of *komainu*, stone dog sculptures often seen in pairs guarding Shintō shrines and said to have roots back to the Egyptian sphinx. One train station (3.2km) away, **Jōmon Kōen** (*Jōmon Park; ☎ 25-4174; admission free; open 9am-5pm Tues-Sun*) offers clues to this ancient era via stone and earthenware.

The **Gero Onsen Matsuri** (Hot Spring Festival), from 1 to 3 August, is a lively one. On 1 August, men clad in *fundoshi* (loincloths) and toting fireworks perform a dance to Ryūjin, the Dragon God. The following day sees a parade of women dressed as geisha, and the local Gero Odori folk dance.

Places to Stay

Most lodgings are across the river from the train station, and even the simplest have *onsen*-fed baths.

Katsuragawa Minshuku (*☎ 25-2615; singles/twins ¥4000/7000*), facing the river, about 12 minutes' walk from the station, might interest budget travellers, though it's small and no meals are served.

Miyanoya Minshuku (*☎ 25-2399, fax 25-3367; rooms per person with 2 meals from ¥6500*), a few minutes further on Onsen-gai (Onsen St), is ageing but has a friendly but simple atmosphere and a games room.

Ogawaya (*☎ 25-3121, fax 25-3268; e yado@gero-ogawaya.net; rooms per person with 2 meals ¥18,000*) is a large, elegant Japanese-style resort; its many baths include a *rotemburo* and a 25m indoor pool. Most rooms face the river.

Getting There & Away

Tokkyū trains serve Gero from Gifu (¥3280, 67 minutes), Nagoya (¥4300, 1½ hours) and Takayama (¥1990, 40 minutes). If you're heading to the Kiso Valley (see the Nagano-ken section later in this chapter), two buses a day to Nakatsugawa (¥1700, 50 minutes) will save you hours, yen and hardship over the train.

Chūbu-Sangaku National Park
中部山岳国立公園

Also called Japan Alps National Park, Chūbu-Sangaku provides some of Japan's most spectacular mountain scenery. Highlights include hiking the valleys and peaks of Kamikōchi, skiing at Norikura, and Shirahone Onsen, a gem of a hot-spring resort. The northern part of the park extends to the Tateyama-Kurobe Alpine Route, covered later in this chapter.

ORIENTATION & INFORMATION
The park straddles the border between Gifu-ken and Nagano-ken, with the Gifu-ken (western) side also known as Oku-Hida Onsen, while the Nagano-ken (eastern) side is Azumi-mura. Several maps and pamphlets are published by the Japan National Tourist Organization (JNTO) and local tourist authorities in English (particularly the one put out by Azumi-mura), with more detailed hiking maps in Japanese.

GETTING THERE & AROUND
The main gateway cities are Takayama to the west and Matsumoto to the east. Service from Takayama is by bus, while most travellers from Matsumoto catch the private Matsumoto Dentetsu train to Shin-Shimajima station (¥680, 30 minutes) to transfer to buses. Within the park, the main transit hubs are Hirayu Onsen and Kamikōchi.

Sample Bus Routes: Chubu-Sangaku National Park

Within the park, bus fares and schedules change seasonally and annually, so we're not even going to attempt to provide details. However, the following are fares and travel times on common bus routes in and around the area as we went to press. Discounted return fares are listed, where available. Depending on your intended route, the Free Coupon (¥6400), valid for three days, may be the most economical option. You can find current fare and schedule information at tourist offices in Matsumoto and Takayama, or at Ⓦ www.alpico.co.jp/access/route_k/honsen/info_e.html or Ⓦ www.alpico.co.jp/access/express/kamikochi_takayama/info_e.html.

from	to	fare (¥; one way or one way/return)	duration (mins; one way)
Takayama	Hirayu Onsen	1530	55
	Kamikōchi	2000	80
Matsumoto	Shin-Shimajima	680 (train)	30
		750 (bus)	
	Kamikōchi	2500/4600	100
	Shin-Hotaka	2800/5000	120
Shin-Shimajima	Naka-no-yu	1650	50
	Kamikōchi	2050/3500	70
	Shirahone Onsen	1400/2300	75
	Norikura Tatami-daira	3150	105
Kamikōchi	Naka-no-yu	680	20
	Hirayu Onsen	1050/1800	30
	Shirahone Onsen	1500	40
Hirayu Onsen	Naka-no-yu	540	10
	Shin-Hotaka	870	35
	Norikura Tatami-daira	1050	45

Bus schedules are known to change annually, and at the time of writing, the schedules shortchanged visits to some areas and *long*changed others. Before setting out, it is essential that you check the schedules. Note that some individual communities within the park cover a lot of ground, so if you're arriving by bus make sure to ask which stop to get off. You may also consider the three-day 'Free Coupon' (¥6400) for unlimited transport within the park and connections to Matsumoto and Takayama. See the boxed text 'Sample Bus Routes: Chūbu-Sangaku National Park' on the previous page for fares and travel times.

Renting a car may save money, time and nerves. However, some popular routes, particularly the Norikura Skyline Road (linking Hirayu Onsen and Norikura) and the road between Nakanoyu and Kamikōchi, are open only to buses and taxis.

KAMIKŌCHI 上高地
☎ 0263

The park's biggest draw, Kamikōchi has some of the most spectacular scenery in Japan and a variety of hiking trails from which to see it. In the late 19th century, foreigners 'discovered' this mountainous region and coined the term 'Japan Alps'. A British missionary Reverend Walter Weston toiled from peak to peak and sparked Japanese interest in mountaineering as a sport. He is now honoured with his own annual festival (first Sunday in June, the official opening of the hiking season), and Kamikōchi has become a base for strollers, hikers and climbers.

Kamikōchi is closed from mid-November to late April, and in peak times (late July to late August, and during the foliage season in October), it is busier than Shinjuku station. Between June and mid-July is the rainy season, which makes outdoor pursuits depressingly soggy.

It's perfectly feasible to visit Kamikōchi as a day trip, but you'll miss out on the pleasures of staying in the mountains and taking early morning or late evening walks before the crowds appear.

Orientation
Private cars are prohibited between Nakanoyu and Kamikōchi; access is only by bus or taxi, and then only as far as the

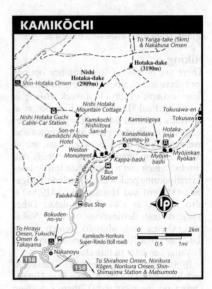

Kamikōchi bus station. A short distance on foot from the bus station, the Azusa-gawa is spanned by Kappa-bashi (named for a water sprite of Japanese legend), from where a variety of trails snake into the mountains.

Information
There is an **information office** (☎ 95-2405; open 9am-5pm daily late Apr–mid-Nov) at the bus station. It has leaflets and maps but is geared mostly to booking accommodation. Non-Japanese speakers may want to book through the tourist information office in Takayama, which has English-speaking staff.

Day Walks
The river valley has lots of basically level, short-distance walks. A three-hour round trip starts east of Kappa-bashi along the right-hand side of the river past Myōjin-bashi (45 minutes) to Tokusawa (45 minutes) before returning. By Myōjin-bashi is the idyllic pond **Myōjin-ike**, which marks the innermost shrine of the **Hotaka-jinja**. There's also a trail on the other side of the river, but it's partly a service road.

West of Kappa-bashi, you can amble along the right-hand side of the river to **Weston Monument** (15 minutes) or keep to the left-hand side of the river and walk to the pond **Taishō-ike** (20 minutes). There's

CENTRAL HONSHŪ

also a pleasant, clearly signposted 3km hike uphill, from the Taishō-ike bus stop.

Hiking

There are dozens of long-distance options for hikers and climbers, varying in duration from a couple of days to a week. *Hiking in Japan* by Paul Hunt, Mason Florence et al provides practical advice. Large Japanese-language maps of the area show routes and average hiking times between huts, major peaks and landmarks. Favourite trails and climbs (which can mean human traffic jams on trails during peak seasons) include Yariga-take (3180m) and Hotaka-dake (3190m) – also known as Oku-Hotaka-dake. Other more distant destinations include Naka-busa Onsen and Murodō, which is on the Tateyama-Kurobe Alpine Route (see Toyama-ken later in this chapter).

If you want to hike between Kamikōchi and Shin-Hotaka Onsen (see Shin-Hotaka Onsen on the next page), there's a steep trail that crosses the ridge below Nishi Hotaka-dake (2909m) at Nishi Hotaka San-sō (Nishi Hotaka Mountain Cottage) and continues to Nishi Hotaka-guchi, the top station of the cable car for Shin-Hotaka Onsen. The hike takes nearly four hours (because of a steep ascent). Softies might prefer to save an hour of sweat and do the hike in the opposite direction.

Those heading off on long hikes or climbs should be properly prepared. Even in summer, temperatures can plummet, or the whole area can be covered in sleeting rain or blinding fog. On the other hand, in clear weather it's possible to see all the way to Mt Fuji.

Onsen

Kamikōchi Onsen Hotel (☎ 95-2311; *admission ¥600)* and **Son-ei Kamikōchi Alpine Hotel** (☎ 95-2231; *admission ¥500)* open their baths to the public. The latter is an artificially heated *reisen* (cold mineral spring).

The area's best-kept secret is at Na-kanoyu, just before the bus-only tunnel branches up to Kamikōchi proper. Go in the small store next to the Nakanoyu bus stop, pay ¥500, get the key and cross the road bridge where you'll find a door set in the mountainside. Open this and inside is **Bokuden-no-yu**, a tiny gem of a hot-spring

cave bath, dripping with minerals. It is yours privately until you return the key.

Places to Stay & Eat

Accommodation in Kamikōchi is pricey, and advance reservations are essential.

Kamikōchi Konashidaira Kyampu-jō (☎ 95-2321; *camp sites per person from ¥700, bungalows ¥6000),* about 15 minutes' walk from the bus station, has camp sites, rental tents from ¥2000 and a few bungalows.

Among the hotels, all rates quoted here include two meals, and some lodgings shut down their electricity generators in the middle of the night (emergency lighting stays on).

Kamikōchi Nishiitoya San-sō (☎ 95-2206, fax 95-2208; **w** *www.nishiitoya.com; bunk beds ¥7500, rooms per person ¥13,000)* is Kamikōchi's cheapest; its history goes back to the early 20th century.

Myōjinkan Ryokan (☎ 95-2036; **w** *www .myojinkan.co.jp/index3.html; dorm beds ¥8000, rooms per person from ¥10,000)* is up along the river, near Myōjin-ike and backed by the peak Myōjin-dake.

Son-ei Kamikōchi Alpine Hotel (☎ 95-2231, fax 95-2520; *dorm beds ¥8500, private rooms per person from ¥13,000)* has some dorm-style 'hikers' beds', private Japanese rooms with private toilet, and a glass en-closed bath.

Tokusawa-en (☎ 95-2508; *camping per person ¥500, Japanese dorms per person ¥9000, private rooms per person from ¥13,000)* is a marvellously secluded place, about 3km northeast of Kappa-bashi; rooms do not have private facilities.

Dotted along the trails and around the mountains are dozens of spartan *yama-goya* (mountain huts), which provide two meals and a bed from around ¥7000 per person; some also serve simple lunches. The bus station and some stops along the trails have vending machines and some food stands (the bus station has a cafeteria).

HIRAYU ONSEN 平湯温泉
☎ 0578

This hot-spring resort is a busy hub for bus transport on the Gifu-ken side of the park. It has a cluster of *onsen* lodgings and an excel-lent modern hot-spring complex, and even the bus terminal has a **rotemburo** (*admission ¥600; open 8am-5pm daily).* The **information** office (☎ 9-3030; open 9am-5pm daily), opposite the bus station, has leaflets and maps and can book accommodation.

The hot-spring complex **Hirayu-no-mori** (☎ 9-3338; admission ¥500; open 10am-9pm daily), uphill from the bus station, boasts one indoor and six outdoor baths. It's great either for a quick dip between buses, or as part of a day excursion from Takayama.

Although Hirayu is not remote and relaxing in the way other Chūbu-Sangaku villages are, there are some nice inns within a few minutes' walk of the bus station.

Ryosō Tsuyukusa (☎ 9-2620, fax 9-3581; rooms per person with 2 meals ¥7000) is a friendly place with a cosy wooden *rotemburo* with mountain views.

Eitarō (☎ 9-2540, fax 9-3526; rooms per person with 2 meals ¥10,000) is a bit fancier, also with a *rotemburo*.

Hirayu-kan (☎ 9-3111, fax 9-3113; rooms per person with 2 meals from ¥13,000) is top of the line, with both Japanese- and Western-style rooms, a splendid garden, and indoor and outdoor baths.

Hirayu Camping Ground (☎ 9-2610, fax 9-2130; camp sites per person ¥600, parking ¥1500) is about 700m from the bus station.

For drivers, the 4km-plus Abō tunnel from Hirayu Onsen eastward into the park costs ¥600 each way.

FUKUCHI ONSEN 福地温泉
☎ 0578

This relatively untouristed hot spring, a short ride north of Hirayu Onsen, has rural charm, a morning market and two outstanding baths.

Yumoto Chōza (☎ 9-2146, fax 9-2010; rooms per person with 2 meals from ¥18,000) is one of central Honshū's finest *onsen* ryokan, with excellent mountain cuisine served at *irori*, elegant traditional architecture, and five indoor and two outdoor pools. Reservations are essential.

Mukashibanashi-no-sato (☎ 9-2793; bath ¥500; open 8am-5pm daily) is a restaurant-cum-hot-spring in a traditional farmhouse. Its small indoor and outdoor baths are excellent, and are free on the 26th of each month. Out the front, there's an *asa-ichi* (morning market; open 6am-10pm Apr-late Nov).

By bus, get off at Fukuchi-onsen-ue bus stop for Mukashibanashi-no-sato or Fukuchi-onsen-shita for Yumoto Chōza.

SHIN-HOTAKA ONSEN
新穂高温泉
☎ 0578

This hot-spring resort, north of Fukuchi Onsen, is home to the Shin-Hotaka cable car, reportedly the longest of its kind in Asia, whisking you up close to the peak of Nishi Hotaka-dake (2909m) for a superb mountain panorama. The **cable car** (☎ 9-2252; one way/return ¥1500/2800; open 8.30am-5.30pm daily late July-late Aug, 8.30am-3.45pm daily late Aug-late July) is near the Shin-Hotaka Onsen bus station.

If you are fit, properly equipped and have ample time, there are a variety of hiking options from Nishi Hotaka-guchi (the top cable-car station). In a little under three hours you can hike over to **Kamikōchi**.

Also near the bus station is a rather spartan **public onsen** (admission free). During summer it gets crowded with tourists, but in the off season your only company is likely to be a few weary shift workers from the electric plant across the river.

Places to Stay
This far up into the mountains, most options charge ¥12,000 to ¥16,000 per night. Accommodation is clustered around the Shin-Hotaka Onsen-guchi and Shin-Hotaka Onsen bus stops (a few kilometres apart).

Shin-Hotaka Campground (☎ 9-2513; camp sites ¥600; open July & Aug) is up near the Shin-Hotaka Onsen bus stop.

Yamanoyado (☎ 9-2733, 9-3215; rooms per person with 2 meals ¥8000), near Shin-Hotaka Onsen-guchi, is a functional *minshuku* and one of the cheapest.

Mahoroba (☎ 9-2382, 9-3077; rooms per person with 2 meals ¥8000) is a friendly place with a very nice *rotemburo* (mostly *konyoku* [mixed bathing] except for women-only hours). It's near Naka-o Onsen bus stop, two stops past Shin-Hotaka Onsen-guchi. Upon request (in Japanese), someone will pick you up at the bus stop. Otherwise you'll have to walk uphill for about 1km.

NORIKURA-KŌGEN & NORIKURA ONSEN
乗鞍高原・乗鞍温泉
☎ 0263

Norikura-kōgen, the alpine plateau below the mountain Norikura-dake (3026m) is blissfully free of Kamikōchi crowds and offers cycling, hiking and skiing. It is famous for the Norikura Skyline Road (closed from November to May; closed to private vehicles all year), a scenic route that leads to the Norikura Tatami-daira bus stop at the foot of the mountain. From there, a trail leads to the peak in about 40 minutes. You might glimpse a *raichō* (ptarmigan), the prefectural symbol, or if you're really fortunate, the magnificent *inuwashi* (dog eagle).

Norikura Onsen is a collection of hot-spring accommodation on the plateau. You'll find the **tourist office** (☎ 93-2147; open 9am-5pm daily Mar-Oct, 9am-4.30pm daily Nov-Feb) at Kankō Centre. Its main bus stops are Kankō Centre, Suzuran and Ski-jō-mae, near the bulk of the accommodation.

Norikura Onsen is surrounded by well-marked **trails**, one of the best being the 40-minute woodland walk from the Suzuran bus stop to the beautiful waterfall, **Zengoro-no-taki**.

Places to Stay

Norikura Tatami-daira is not an ideal place to stay, but there are several dozen lodgings in Norikura Onsen.

Norikura Kōgen Onsen Youth Hostel (☎ 93-2748, fax 93-2162; Japanese dorm rooms per person ¥3200) is the cheapest option, with wooden *onsen* and great local information. It's at the end of the road, a 10-minute trek from the Ski-jō-mae bus stop.

Also near this bus stop are **Ryokan Mitake-sō** (☎ 93-2016; rooms per person with 2 meals ¥8000-10,000), an unassuming place with a *rotemburo*, and the cosy, Western-style **Pension Chimney** (☎ 93-2902; rooms per person with 2 meals ¥7500).

SHIRAHONE ONSEN 白骨温泉
☎ 0263

Intimate and dramatic, this hot-spring resort straddles a deep gorge and features some traditional inns with open-air baths. It could easily be visited as part of a trip to Kamikōchi or Norikura (an 8km hike away).

It is said that bathing here for three days ensures three years without a cold, and the milky-blue hydrogen sulphide waters have a wonderful silky feel. The riverside **kōshū rotemburo** (public outdoor bath; admission ¥500; open 9.30am-5pm daily) is in the village centre. Diagonally opposite, the **tourist information office** (☎ 93-3251;

open 9am-5pm daily) maintains a list of inns that have opened their baths to the public that day (admission from ¥600). **Awanoyu** (☎ 92-2101), furthest up the hill, allows *konyoku* (mixed bathing).

Budget travellers may wish to dip and move on; nightly rates start at ¥9000 with two meals, and advance reservations are highly recommended. **Tsuruya Ryokan** (☎ 93-2331, fax 93-2029; rooms per person with 2 meals ¥10,000) has both contemporary and traditional touches, great indoor and outdoor baths, and fine views of the gorge.

Nagano-ken 長野県

Nagano-ken is one of the most enjoyable regions to visit in Japan, not only for the beauty of its mountainous terrain (it claims to be 'the Roof of Japan'), but also for the traditional architecture and culture in many parts of the prefecture. Agriculture is still a major source of income here (in season, local apples are the size of grapefruits), but the lack of pollution has also attracted growing numbers of companies from the electronics and precision manufacturing industries in search of a dust-free environment.

Apart from the sections of the prefecture in Chūbu-Sangaku National Park, there are several quasi-national parks that attract large numbers of campers, hikers, mountaineers and hot-spring aficionados. Skiers can choose from dozens of resorts; the ski season lasts from late December to late March.

KISO VALLEY REGION 木曽
☎ 0264

Thickly forested and Alpine, southwest Nagano-ken is traversed by the twisting, craggy former post road, the Nakasendō. Like the more famous Tokaidō, the Nakasendō connected Edo (present-day Tokyo) with Kyoto, enriching the towns along the way. Today, several small towns feature carefully preserved architecture of those days, making this a highly recommended visit.

It was not always so. Kiso *hinoki* (Japanese cypress) was so highly prized that it was used in the construction of the Edo and Nagoya castles; it is still used for the reconstruction of Ise Jingū, Shintō's holiest shrine, every 20 years. To protect this asset, the region was placed under control of the

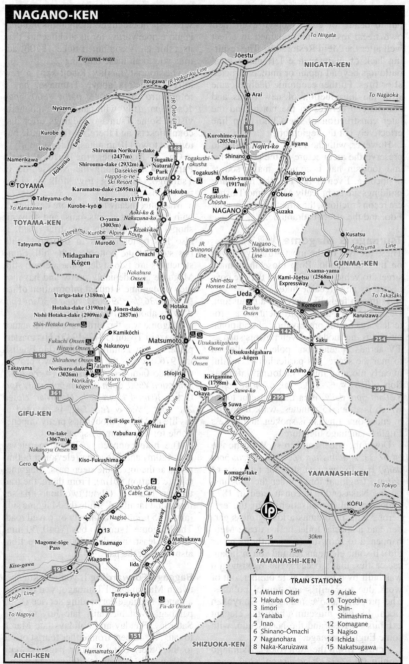

NAGANO-KEN

TRAIN STATIONS

1	Minami Otari	9	Ariake
2	Hakuba Oike	10	Toyoshina
3	Iimori	11	Shin-Shimashima
4	Yanaba		
5	Inao	12	Komagane
6	Shinano-Ōmachi	13	Nagiso
7	Naganohara	14	Ichida
8	Naka-Karuizawa	15	Nakatsugawa

CENTRAL HONSHŪ

Tokugawa shōgunate, and locals could be put to death for cutting down even their own trees; restrictions remained in effect well after the Meiji Restoration. The resulting lack of maintenance left many local buildings beyond repair or unreconstructed after fires. Further economic decline came with the introduction of new roads and commercial centres to the north, and the later construction of the Chūō train line effectively cut the region off.

However, with the 1960s came a move to preserve the architecture of the post towns, and tourism has become a major source of income. Even if most of the remaining buildings are technically Meiji- and Taishō-era reconstructions, the streetscapes are pure Edo, and the effect is dramatic.

Tsumago & Magome 妻籠・馬籠

These are two of the most attractive towns on the Nakasendō. Both close their main streets to vehicular traffic, and they're connected by an agreeable hike.

Tsumago feels like an open-air museum. Designated by the government as a protected area for the preservation of traditional buildings, no modern developments such as TV aerials or telephone poles are allowed to mar the scene; it's particularly beautiful in early morning mist. The **tourist information office** (☎ 57-3123; fax 57-4036; open 8.30am-5pm daily) is in the centre of town, which is about 15 minutes' walk from end to end. Some English is spoken, and there's English-language literature.

Down the street and across, **Waki-honjin** (☎ 57-3322; admission ¥600; open 9am-5pm daily) is a former rest stop for retainers of daimyō (regional lords under the shōguns) on the Nakasendō. Reconstructed in 1877 under special dispensation from the emperor Meiji, it contains a lovely moss garden and a special toilet built in case Meiji happened to show up (apparently he never did). If some elements remind you of Japanese castles, that's because the Waki-honjin was built by a former castle builder, out of work due to Meiji's anti-feudal policies. The property also contains the **Shiryōkan** (local history museum) housing elegant exhibits on Kiso and the Nakasendō, with some English signage.

Across from the Shiryōkan, **Tsumago Honjin** (☎ 57-3322; admission ¥300; open 9am-5pm daily) is where the daimyō themselves spent the night, though this building is more noteworthy for its architecture than its exhibits. A combined ticket (¥700) admits you to all these buildings.

The tourist facility **Kisoji-kan**, a few hilly kilometres above Tsumago, has a **rotemburo** (☎ 58-2046; baths ¥800; open 10am-8pm daily) with panoramic mountain vistas. Some Tsumago lodgings offer discount tickets, and there's a free shuttle bus to/from town (10 minutes, at least hourly).

On 23 November, the **Fuzoku Emaki Parade** is held along the Nakasen-dō in Tsumago, featuring townsfolk in Edo-period costume.

Magome, meanwhile, is more developed, with houses, restaurants, inns (and souvenir shops) lining a steep pedestrian road. It also has better access to transport, with bus stops at the bottom of the hill. Some structures are Edo style, some are not; still, Magome is undeniably pretty and has nice views. Magome's **tourist information office** (☎ 59-2336; fax 59-2653; open 8.30am-5pm daily) is about halfway up the road.

Magome was the birthplace of the author Shimazaki Tōson (1872–1943). His masterpiece, Ie (The Family), published in English in 1976, records the decline of two provincial Kiso families. A **museum** (☎ 59-2047; admission ¥500; open 8.30am-5pm daily Apr-Oct, 8.30am-4.15pm daily Nov-Mar; closed 2nd Tues, Wed & Thur Dec) is devoted to his life and times, though it's pretty impenetrable for non-Japanese-speakers.

The **hike** connecting Tsumago (elevation 420m) and Magome (elevation 600m) peaks at the top of the steep pass, Magome-tōge (elevation 801m). From there, the trail to/from Tsumago (about two hours) passes forest and farmland, while the Magome side (about 45 minutes) is largely on paved road. The Magome-Tsumago bus (¥640, 30 minutes, at least four daily in each direction) also stops at the pass.

Baggage Forwarding If you're hiking between Magome and Tsumago, you can use a handy baggage-forwarding service (¥500 per bag; available daily late July to Aug, Saturday, Sunday and holidays late March to late November) from either tourist office to the other. Deposit your bags between 8.30am and 11.30am for delivery by 1pm.

Places to Stay It's worth a stay in these towns, particularly Tsumago, to have them to yourself once the day-trippers clear out. Both tourist information offices can help book accommodation at numerous ryokan (from around ¥9000 per person) and *minshuku* (from around ¥7000); prices include two meals.

Minshuku Daikichi *(☎ 57-2595, fax 57-2203; rooms per person ¥7500, singles ¥8000)*, in Tsumago, feels very traditional – although it was actually constructed in the 1970s – and every room has a view. It's at the edge of town (take the right-hand fork uphill from the centre).

Matsushiro-ya *(☎ 57-3022, fax 57-3386; rooms per person ¥10,000; closed Wed)* is one of Tsumago's standout lodgings, in the centre, on the village's most picturesque street. Parts of the inn date back to 1804.

Fujioto *(☎ 57-3009, fax 57-2239; rooms per person ¥10,000)* is also excellent, and much photographed. You will find it near Tsumago's Waki-Honjin and features large rooms, a graceful garden and some English-speaking staff.

Magome-Jaya *(☎ 59-2038, fax 59-2648; rooms per person with/without 2 meals from ¥6200/3200)* is a comfy, well-kept place in the centre of Magome. If you don't plan on dining in, bring your own food; restaurants and food shops close by suppertime.

A popular street food in both towns is *gohei-mochi*, skewered rice dumplings that are coated with sesame-walnut sauce.

Getting There & Away Nakatsugawa and Nagiso stations on the JR Chūō line provide access to Magome and Tsumago respectively, though both are still at some distance. Nakatsugawa is connected with Nagoya (Shinano *tokkyū*, ¥2740, 47 minutes) and Matsumoto (Shinano *tokkyū*, ¥3980, 70 minutes). A few *tokkyū* a day stop in Nagiso; otherwise it's about 20 minutes from Nakatsugawa by occasional *futsū* (¥320).

Highway buses operate between Magome and Nagoya's Meitetsu Bus Centre (¥1810, 1½ hours), as well as Tokyo's Shinjuku station (¥4500, 4½ hours). If you're heading to/from the Hida district, two daily buses each way between Nakatsugawa and Gero (¥1700, 50 minutes) will save loads of money, time and grief.

Buses leave hourly from outside Nakatsugawa station for Magome (¥540, 30 minutes). There's also infrequent bus service between Magome and Tsumago (¥640, 30 minutes).

From Tsumago, you can catch the bus to Nagiso station (¥270, 10 minutes), or if you're still in the mood to hike, walk there in one hour. To/from Kisoji-kan, the shuttle bus serves Nagiso station.

Narai 奈良井
☎ 0264

Narai was the wealthiest of the 11 post towns in the Kiso Valley. Today it is the route's least-touristed, most relaxing and, arguably, best-preserved town, with a high proportion of Edo-period buildings. Its single main street extends for about 1km to your left as you exit the train station.

Although, unlike Magome and Tsumago, Narai allows cars down its main street, this adds to its authenticity as a working rural community, not simply a living museum.

Things to See At intervals along the street are five old wells used by thirsty Edo period travellers. The **sake brewery** is easily recognised by its basket of fronds hanging from the roof above the entrance. Side streets on the right-hand side lead to tranquil temples.

Many of the houses lining the main street functioned as inns during the heyday of the Nakasendō; now they're museums, shops or private homes, though some still operate as ryokan.

Nakamura-tei *(☎ 34-2655; admission ¥200; open 9am-5pm daily Apr-Oct, 9am-4pm Tues-Sun Nov-Mar)* was once a shop selling lacquer combs and is now a museum with excellent architectural details and an English-language pamphlet explaining local architecture. At the end of town, the **Narakawa Folklore Museum** *(☎ 34-2654; admission ¥200; open 9am-5pm daily Apr-Oct, 9am-4pm Tues-Sun Nov-Mar)* is 1970s concrete, but has nice presentations of lacquer, lanterns and procession poles.

Narai grew prosperous thanks to **Torii-tōge**, the steep pass to the south; travellers caught their breath in Narai before or after negotiating the pass. If *you* want to walk it, Torii-toge is about one hour from town, and another hour to the station at Yabuhara.

CENTRAL HONSHŪ

Places to Stay & Eat In an updated, 170-year-old wooden structure, **Iseya** (☎ 34-3051, fax 34-3156; rooms per person with 2 meals ¥7500) is a marvellous *minshuku*. Ask for a room in the original front building.

Echigoya Shokudo (☎ 34-3048; meals ¥600-1900) serves *soba* in a comfy setting, while **Tsuchiya** (☎ 34-3102; cakes ¥400) is a coffee shop in an old house with handsome woodwork.

Shopping Hand-crafted lacquerware, particularly lunch-boxes, is produced and sold at **Hananoya** (☎ 34-3071). This lacquerware is usually called *bento-bako* but here called *men-pa* when made from local *hinoki* (Japanese cypress). Narai's other famous product is *hyaku-sō-gan* (100-herb balls), tiny pills taken 20 at a time that are meant to be good for digestion.

Getting There & Away Narai is reachable by *futsū* from Matsumoto (¥570, 45 minutes). Express trains do not stop at Narai.

MATSUMOTO 松本
☎ 0263 • pop 200,000

From the moment you step off the train and hear the piped-in voice singing 'Ma-*tsumo-toooh*', you sense you're somewhere different. Matsumoto has a superb castle, some pretty streets, and an atmosphere that's both laid-back and surprisingly cosmopolitan.

The city has been around since at least the 8th century. Formerly known as Fukashi, it was the castle town of the Ogasawara clan during the 14th and 15th centuries, and it continued to prosper through the Edo period. Today, Matsumoto's street aesthetic combines the black-and-white of its castle with *namako* (lattice-patterned) *kura* storehouses and 21st-century Japanese architecture; plus, views of the Japan Alps are never much further than around the corner. Parts of the city centre were recently given a contemporary makeover, and the area by the Metoba-gawa and the Nakamachi district boasts smart galleries, comfortable cafés and reasonably priced, high-quality accommodation.

Asama Onsen and Utsukushi-ga-hara are day trips, while Hotaka can be either a day trip or the start of a hiking route. Matsumoto is also a regional transit hub, including trips to Chūbu-Sangaku National Park.

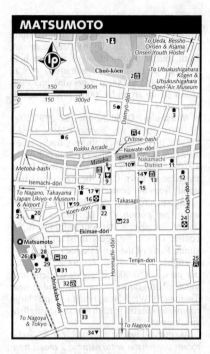

Orientation & Information

For a castle town, Matsumoto is relatively easy to get around. Although small streets radiate somewhat confusingly from the train station, soon you're on a grid. Any place on our Matsumoto map is within 15 minutes' walk of the train station.

The **tourist information office** (☎ 32-2814; open 9.30am-6pm daily Apr-Oct, 9.30am-5.30pm daily Nov-Mar) is at street level outside Matsumoto station's eastern exit. English-speaking staff have English-language pamphlets and maps, and can book accommodation in town.

The main **post office** is located on Honmachi-dōri. The café **People's** (☎ 37-5011; ¥200/hr; open 6pm-1am daily) has Internet access.

Matsumoto-jō 松本城

Even if you only spend a couple of hours in Matsumoto, make sure you visit this castle (☎ 32-2902; admission ¥520; open 8.30am-6pm daily late July-Aug; 8.30am-5pm daily rest of year), one of four castles declared National Treasures (the others are Hikone, Himeji and Inuyama).

MATSUMOTO

PLACES TO STAY
3 Hotel Kagetsu
   ホテル花月
6 Nishiya
   にしや旅館
11 Marumo
   まるも旅館
12 Nunoya
   ぬのや旅館
18 Roynet Hotel
   ロイネットホテル
20 Hotel Iidaya
   ホテル飯田屋
21 Hotel New
   Station
   ホテルニュー
   ステーション
22 Ichiyama
   いちやま
29 Ace Inn
   エースイン
31 Matsumoto
   Tōkyū Inn
   松本東急イン
33 Hotel Buena
   Vista
   ホテルブエナビスタ

PLACES TO EAT
8 Caviar
   キャヴィアール
10 Delhi
   デリー
14 Kissa-kan
   喫茶館
15 Nomugi
   野麦
17 Kura
   蔵
19 Robata Shōya
   炉ばた庄屋
34 Tamita Gumtree
   タミタガムトリー

OTHER
1 Matsumoto-jō
   松本城
2 Matsumoto City Museum/
   Japan Folklore Museum
   松本市立博物館
4 Yohashira Jinja
5 Seikando
7 Matsumoto Timepiece
   Museum
   松本市時計博物館

9 Coat
   コート
13 Naka-machi
   Chic-Kan
   中町蔵シック館
16 Parco Department Store
   パルコ
23 Main Post Office
   中央郵便局
24 Berami (Belle Amie)
   ベラミ
25 Fukashi-jinja
   深志神社
26 Tourist Information
   Office
   観光案内所
27 Eki Rent-a-Car
28 Nippon Rent-a-Car
   日本レンタカー
30 Matsumoto Bus Station;
   Espa Building; Marui
   Restaurant
   松本バスターミナル;
   エスパ；
   まるゐ
32 People's
   ピープルズ

The three-turreted *donjon* was built circa 1595, in contrasting black and white, which has led to the nickname Karasu-jō (Crow Castle). Steep steps lead up six storeys, with impressive views from each level. Lower floors house displays of guns, bombs and gadgets with which to storm castles, and a delightful *tsukimi yagura* (moon-viewing pavilion), a dainty retreat for those moments of peace. The basics are explained via English signs, and you may be able to catch a free tour with an English-speaking volunteer guide.

The castle grounds (and your admission ticket) also include the **Matsumoto City Museum/Japan Folklore Museum** (☎ 32-0133), with small exhibits on local history and a collection of Tanabata dolls (see Shopping later).

Nakamachi 中町
This former merchant district is a really excellent place to take a stroll, as most of its storehouses have been transformed into galleries, craft shops and cafés. **Nakamachi Chic-Kan** (☎ 36-3053; *open 9am-10pm daily*) showcases locally produced arts and crafts and there's a relaxing coffee house next door.

Matsumoto Timepiece Museum
松本時計博物館
Honda Chikazō (1896–1985), inventor of the rolling-ball clock, bequeathed his collection of 320 rare and antique clocks and watches to the city. This new museum (☎ 36-0969; *admission ¥520; open 9am-5pm Tues-Sun*) displays about one-third of them at any one time; with any luck, you'll see some marvellous Edo-period wooden clocks. Thanks to meticulous maintenance, they all seem to be running on time.

Japan Ukiyo-e Museum
日本浮世絵美術館
This museum (☎ 47-4440; *admission ¥1000; open 10am-5pm Tues-Sun*) is a must for ukiyo-e (woodblock print) lovers. Several generations of the Sakai family have collected over 100,000 prints, paintings, screens and old books – the largest private collection in the world. English labelling is minimal, but an explanatory leaflet in English is provided.

The museum is about 3km from Matsumoto station or 15 minutes' walk from Ōniwa station on the Matsumoto Dentetsu line (¥170, seven minutes) or about ¥2000 by taxi.

CENTRAL HONSHŪ

Asama Onsen 浅間温泉

This hot-spring resort northeast of town isn't rustic, but its history is said to reach back to the 10th century and include writers and poets. The waters are also said to be good for gastrointestinal and skin troubles, and women's disorders. Among dozens of baths and inns (and the youth hostel), **Hot Plaza Asama** (*☎ 46-6278; admission ¥840; open 10am-8pm Wed-Mon*) has many pools in a traditional building. Buses from Matsumoto station take about 20 minutes.

Utsukushi-ga-hara-kōgen
美ヶ原高原

From April to mid-November, this alpine plateau is a popular excursion from Matsumoto. There are pleasant walks and the opportunity to see cows in pasture (a constant source of Japanese fascination).

Utsukushi-ga-hara Bijutsukan (*Utsukushi-ga-hara Open-Air Museum; ☎ 0268-86-2331; admission ¥1000; open 9am-5pm daily late Apr-late Nov*) is in the same vein (with the same owner) as the Hakone Open-Air Museum, a large sculpture garden (some 450 pieces) with fine views of the surrounding mountains.

Most Japanese visitors reach the museum by car. Buses (¥1300, 80 minutes) run several times daily in midsummer with spotty-to-nonexistent service the rest of the season; check before you go. Taxis to the museum start at a cool ¥10,700 (yes, one way). See Getting There & Away later in this section for car-rental information.

Special Events

On 23 and 24 July, the **Tenjin Matsuri** at Fukashi-jinja features elaborately decorated *dashi*, and a fireworks display. The second day is liveliest.

During August, the atmospheric **Takigi Nō Matsuri** features nō (classical Japanese dance-drama) by torchlight, performed outdoors on a stage in the park below the castle.

Phallic merriment is to be had at the **Dōsojin Matsuri**, held in honour of *dōsojin* (roadside guardians), on the fourth Saturday in September at Utsukushigahara Onsen.

Around the beginning of October, the **Yohashira Jinja Matsuri** (aka Shintōsai) features displays of fireworks and large dolls, while around the same time, Asama Onsen celebrates the **Asama Hi-Matsuri**, a spec-

tacular fire festival with torch-lit parades that are accompanied by drumming.

Around 3 November, the **Oshiro Matsuri** (Castle Festival) is held – a cultural jamboree including costume parades, puppet displays and flower shows.

Places to Stay – Budget

Although hardly fancy, **Asama Onsen Youth Hostel** (*☎ 46-1335; beds ¥3200; open 4 Jan-27 Dec*) offers quick access to nearby *onsen* and significant discounts to Hot Plaza Asama. Doors close at 9pm.

From Matsumoto bus station, take bus No 6 to Shita-Asama (¥300) or bus No 7 to Dai-Ichi Kōkō-mae (¥240). Either bus takes 20 minutes, and the hostel is then five minutes' on foot.

In a quiet neighbourhood between the station and the castle, the ryokan **Nishiya** (*☎/fax 33-4332; rooms per person ¥3600*) is showing its age, but remains popular.

Places to Stay – Mid-Range

Ryokan In Nakamachi, **Nunoya** (*☎/fax 32-0545; rooms per person ¥5000*) is in a traditional wooden building with good-quality tatami rooms. You can get breakfast for an additional ¥500.

Marumo (*☎ 32-0115, fax 35-2251; rooms per person with breakfast ¥6000*), around the corner, by Metoba-gawa, is delightful, with its own bamboo garden and coffee shop. Although rooms are not huge, it's quite popular, so book ahead.

Enjyoh Bekkan (*☎ 33-7233, fax 36-2084; singles/doubles from ¥5300/9800*) is outside town, at Utsukushi-ga-hara Onsen. It has pleasant, large rooms, a nice garden, and indoor hot-spring baths available day and night. From Matsumoto, take the bus to Utsukushi-ga-hara Onsen (¥330, 20 minutes); it's 300m to the ryokan.

Hotels In the station area, this category consists mostly of cramped, charmless business hotels.

Ace Inn (*☎ 35-1188, fax 35-1102; w http://ace.alpico.co.jp; singles/twins ¥6700/9700*) is new and about the nicest option near the station. Rooms are tiny, but rates include a simple breakfast and free Internet access in the lobby.

Matsumoto Hotel Kagetsu (*☎ 32-0114, fax 33-4775; w www.mcci.or.jp/www/kagetsu;*

rooms per person from ¥6500) is a neat alternative across town, with nice-sized Japanese- or Western-style rooms with full facilities, plus generous communal baths. Rooms in the newer building cost a little more but are smarter. Look for Internet specials.

Roynet Hotel (☎ 37-5000, fax 37-5505; w www.roynet.co.jp; singles/doubles ¥6953/ 9524), in the town centre, is new and has relatively large rooms at business-hotel prices. Roynet/Royal Hotels kai-in (members) get these rates. To become a kai-in, fill out a form and pay a one-time ¥500 charge when you check in.

Places to Stay – Top End

Matsumoto Tōkyū Inn (☎ 36-0109, fax 36-0883; singles/twins from ¥8300/14,000) is not particularly exciting, but it's polished, efficient and close to the train station.

Ichiyama (☎ 32-0122, fax 32-2968; singles/doubles with breakfast Apr-Nov ¥10,000/16,000, Dec-Mar ¥9000/15,000) is a central, up-to-date, well-kept place with kindly staff and a dozen generous Western- and Japanese-style rooms.

Hotel Buena Vista (☎ 37-0111; singles/ twins from ¥13,090/17,000) has spacious public areas and pleasant (if not huge) rooms with nice amenities and CNN.

Places to Eat & Drink

Matsumoto is renowned for shinshū-soba, eaten either hot (kake-soba; in broth) or cold (zaru-soba; with wasabi and soya-based sauce). Other regional specialities include basashi (raw horsemeat), hachinoko (bee larvae), and inago (crickets). Tamer are oyaki, little wheat buns filled with various vegetables.

Nomugi (☎ 36-3753; soba ¥1000; closed Tues & sometimes Wed), in Nakamachi, is one of central Japan's finest soba shops. Its owner used to run a French restaurant in Tokyo before returning to his home town. There's one dish: zaru-soba in a hand-crafted wicker basket; in colder seasons there's also hot kake-soba (¥1200).

Robata Shōya (☎ 37-1000; dishes ¥250-980) is a fun corner place with a large selection of grills, seasonal specials and a (sort of) English menu.

Marui (☎ 36-2337; dishes ¥300-600, sets ¥800-1800) is for tofu lovers. It's served den-gaku (topped with miso), with kara-age (fried morsels of chicken) and dozens of other ways. It's one of several restaurants on the 7th floor of the Espa (bus terminal) building.

Kura (☎ 33-6444; dishes from ¥300, teishoku ¥900-2000), located near Nakamachi, serves Japanese dishes (sushi, tempura etc) for lunch and dinner in a stylish former warehouse like its namesake. There's an English menu.

For curry in a kura, **Delhi** (☎ 35-2408; dishes ¥600-800), in Nakamachi, is well regarded for its food and old-fashioned atmosphere. It's one of many little cafés and markets around Nakamachi (south of the river) and Nawate-dōri (north of the river).

Caviar (☎ 38-0007; 2nd floor, Atrium bldg; mains ¥700-1200), nearby, is an intimate, contemporary salon de vin with nice pasta sets (from ¥1500).

Tamita Gumtree (☎ 33-8828; dishes ¥280-900; open nightly Mon-Sat), on the south side of the city centre, is a laid-back café/bar serving homestyle cooking (both Japanese and Western). It's popular with gaijin (foreigners), and there's an Australian owner.

Coat (☎ 34-7133) is an uber-sophisticated bar where the bartender, Hayashi-san, is one of Matsumoto's newest celebrities. His 'otomenadeshiko' cocktail won first prize at the 2001 Japan Bartenders Association competition; the first one will set you back ¥1800 (after that, ¥1000).

Shopping

Matsumoto is synonymous with temari (balls embroidered in geometric patterns) and doll-making. You can find both at **Berami** (Belle Amie; ☎ 33-1314; closed Wed) on Ōhashi-dōri. Dolls styles include Tanabata (flat wood or cardboard cut-outs dressed in paper) and Oshie-bina (dressed in fine cloth). Takasago street, one block south of Nakamachi, also has several doll shops.

Collectors of old books will be agog at the selection (and seeming disorganisation) at **Seikandō** (☎ 32-2333), near the castle. And Nawate-dōri north of the river is a colourful place for souvenirs and cafés.

Getting There & Away

For information about reaching Chūbu-Sangaku National Park, see its section earlier in this chapter.

CENTRAL HONSHŪ

Air Matsumoto airport has flights to Fukuoka, Osaka and Sapporo.

Train Matsumoto is connected with Tokyo's Shinjuku station (*Super Azusa, Azusa,* ¥6510, 2¾ hours, hourly), Nagoya (Shinano *tokkyū,* ¥5670, two hours) and Nagano (Shinano *tokkyū,* ¥2570, 50 minutes; *futsū,* ¥1110, 70 minutes). On the JR Ōito Line, trains serve Hotaka (¥320, 30 minutes) and Hakuba (Azusa *tokkyū,* ¥2570, 55 minutes; *futsū,* ¥1110, 1½ hours).

Bus The company **Alpico/Matsumoto Dentetsu** (☎ 35-7400) runs buses between Matsumoto and Shinjuku in Tokyo (¥3400, 3½ hours, 14 daily), Osaka (¥5710, 5½ hours, two daily) and Nagoya (¥3460, 3½ hours, four daily). All departures are from Matsumoto bus station, in the basement of the Espa building across from the train station (reservations advised).

Car Renting a car often turns out to be the best way to do sidetrips. **Nippon Rent-A-Car** (☎ 33-1324) has the best deals (from about ¥5000 a day), just outside the train station. **Eki Rent-A-Car** (☎ 32-4690) is a few doors down.

Getting Around

The castle and the city centre are easily covered on foot. The 'town sneaker' bus loops through the centre for ¥100 (9am to 6pm).

To/From the Airport An airport shuttle bus connects Matsumoto airport with the city centre (¥540, 25 minutes). Buses are timed to flights. A taxi costs around ¥4500.

HOTAKA 穂高
☎ 0263 • pop 32,880

Not to be confused with Shin-Hotaka in Chūbu-Sangaku National Park, Hotaka is home to Japan's largest wasabi (Japanese horseradish) farm. It is an easy day trip from Matsumoto or a popular starting point for mountain hikes.

The **tourist office** (☎ 82-9363; *open 9am-5pm daily Jun-Oct, 9am-4pm daily Nov-May*) and **bicycle rental** (the recommended way to get around; ¥300 per hour) are outside the Hotaka station exit. Both have basic maps which, while in Japanese, are sufficient for navigation.

Dai-ō Wasabi-Nōjo 大王わさび農場

A visit to the Dai-ō Wasabi Farm (☎ 82-2118; *admission free; open 8.30am-5.30pm daily July & Aug, shorter hours rest of year*) is *de rigeur* for wasabi lovers, and even wasabi haters may have fun. An English map guides you among wasabi plants (wasabi is grown in flooded fields), restaurants, shops and workspaces, all set amid rolling hills. There are lots of free sampling opportunities; wasabi finds its way into everything from wine to rice crackers, ice cream to chocolate. 'Wasabi juice' (¥400) is a kind of milk shake.

The farm is about 15 minutes' bike ride from Hotaka station. There are also some calmer municipal wasabi fields.

Rokuzan Bijutsukan 碌山美術館

About 10 minutes' walk from the station, the Rokuzan Art Museum (☎ 82-2094; *admission ¥700; open 9am-5.10pm daily Apr-Oct, to 4.10pm Nov-Mar, closed Mon Nov-Apr*) showcases the work of Meiji-era sculptor Rokuzan Ogiwara (whom the Japanese have labelled the 'Rodin of the Orient') and his Japanese contemporaries. Strolling through the four buildings and garden, you may be struck by how much cross-cultural flow there was between East and West.

Nakabusa Onsen 中房温泉

Seasonal buses from Hotaka station serve these remote hot springs (*admission ¥1610/50min; open daily mid-July–mid-Aug, weekends late May-early Nov*). A taxi costs ¥7000. From here, there are several trails for extended mountain hikes, and *onsen* accommodation (see Places to Stay).

Jōnen-dake 常念岳

From Hotaka station, it takes about 30 minutes by taxi to reach Ichi-no-sawa, trailhead for experienced hikers to climb Jōnen-dake (2857m) – the ascent takes about 5½ hours. There are many options for mountain hikes extending over several days in the region, but you must be properly prepared. Hiking maps and information are available at regional tourist offices, although the more detailed maps are in Japanese.

Places to Stay

Most people visit Hotaka as a day trip from Matsumoto, but some accommodation is available.

Azumino Pastoral Youth Hostel (☎ 83-6170; beds ¥3100; open 8 Feb-16 Jan) is 4km west of Hotaka station (a one-hour walk).

Nestled up near Nakabusa Onsen are two inns where you can soak up the nourishing minerals of the local hot springs.

Nakabusa Onsen Ryokan (☎ 090-8771-4000; rooms per person with 2 meals from ¥8000) can accommodate up to 250 people (usually in shared rooms) and has several bathing pools. Ariake-so Kokuminshukusha (☎ 090-2321-9991; rooms per person with 2 meals from ¥9500) is a smaller affair.

Getting There & Away
Hotaka is about 30 minutes (¥320) from Matsumoto on the JR Ōito line.

HAKUBA & AROUND 白馬
☎ 0261
Skiing in winter, and hiking and mountaineering in summer, attract large numbers of visitors to this quite pleasant town surrounded by mountain majesties in northern Chūbu-Sangaku National Park. Hiking trails tend to be less clogged during September and October, but even in mid-summer you should be prepared for hiking over snow-covered terrain on the highest peaks.

Shirouma-dake 白馬岳
The ascent of this mountain (2932m) is a popular hike, but you should be properly prepared. Mountain huts provide meals and basic accommodation, about one hour out and at the summit.

Buses leave Hakuba station for the trailhead at Sarukura (¥980, 30 minutes, late May to September). From here, you can hike west to the peak in about six hours. A more leisurely option is a return trip via the same trail as far as Daisekkei (Great Snowy Gorge), about 1¾ hours away.

The trail southwest of Sarukura leads uphill for three hours to Yari Onsen, and its open-air hot spring with breathtaking mountain views. There's also a mountain hut if you feel compelled to stay.

Tsugaike Natural Park 栂池自然園
This park (Tsugaike Shizen-en; admission ¥300) lies north of Shirouma Norikura-dake in an alpine marshland. A three-hour hiking trail covers most of the park, which is renowned for its alpine flora.

During summer there are one to two buses an hour (¥540, 30 minutes) to Tsugaike-kōgen; from there you'll find a gondola and ropeway into the park. From the park to Shirouma, allow seven hours' hike.

Happō-o-ne Ski Resort
八方尾根スキーリゾート
This is a busy ski resort in the winter and a popular hiking area in the summer. From Hakuba station, a five-minute bus ride takes you to Happō; from here it's a 10-minute walk to the gondola (open 8am to 5pm) base station. From the top station of the cable car you can use two more chairlifts (open 8am to 4.30pm), and then hike along a trail for an hour or so to the pond Happō-ike on a ridge below Karamatsu-dake. From here you can follow a trail for an hour up to Maru-yama, continue for 1½ hours to the Karamatsu-dake San-sō (mountain hut) and then climb to the peak of Karamatsu-dake (2695m) in about 30 minutes. The return fare is ¥2260 if purchased at the Hakuba tourist office, ¥2600 otherwise.

Nishina San-ko 仁科三湖
While travelling south from Hakuba, Nishina San-ko (Nishina Three Lakes) provide some short walks. Nakazuna-ko and Aoki-ko are close to Yanaba station, and Kizaki-ko is next to Inao station.

Places to Stay & Eat
There are over 800 lodgings around Hakuba.

Hakuba Shukuhaku Joho Centre (☎ 72-6900, fax 72-6922; e 6900@hakuba1.com) helps arrange rooms starting at about ¥7000 per person with two meals. Staff speak English.

Lodge Hakuba (☎ 72-3095, fax 72-3774; rooms per person from ¥6500), near the cable car base lodge at Happō-o-ne, is a hiker/skier place.

Wade Ryokan (☎ 72-2435, fax 72-2363; rooms per person with 2 meals ¥7500), nearby, is a kokumin-shukusha (people's lodge). Travellers enjoy this place.

Hajimeno Ippo (☎ 75-3527; dorm beds with 2 meals Apr-Nov ¥3800, Dec-May ¥4800) is a Toho network minshuku 12 minutes' on foot from Iimori station (one stop south of Hakuba). It's sometimes closed in June and November.

Gravity Worx (☎ 72-5434; *dishes ¥580-940; open noon-10pm Wed-Mon off season, daily rest of year*), one minute's walk from Hakuba station, is a friendly snowboard shop/café serving homemade pizza, pasta and cakes. It's a popular hangout for *gaijin* (English is spoken).

Getting There & Away

Hakuba is connected with Matsumoto by the JR Ōito line (*tokkyū*, ¥2770, one hour; *futsū*, ¥1110, 1¾ hours). Continuing north, you can change trains at Minami Otari to meet the JR Hokuriku Honsen line at Itoigawa, with connections towards Niigata, Toyama and Kanazawa. From Nagano, buses leave from in front of Nagano station (¥1400, one hour).

NAGANO 長野
☎ 026 • pop 360,000

Nagano, the prefectural capital, has been around since the Kamakura period, when it was a temple town centred around its temple, Zenkōji. The temple is still Nagano's main attraction, drawing more than four million visitors every year.

After a brief flirtation with international fame hosting the 1998 Winter Olympics, Nagano has reverted to its friendly small-town self, though just a bit more worldly. Nagano is also an important transport hub and, not surprisingly, the mountains surrounding the city offer superb recreational opportunities.

Orientation & Information

As a temple city, Nagano is on a grid with Zenkōji occupying a place of prominence, overlooking the city centre from the north. Chūō-dōri leads south from the temple, doing a quick dogleg before hitting JR Nagano station, 1.8km away; it is said that street-planners considered Zenkōji so holy that it should not be approached directly. Bus stops and the private Nagano Dentetsu train line are just outside the JR station's Zenkōji exit.

In JR Nagano station, Nagano city **Tourist Information Center** (☎ 226-5626; *open 9.30am-6pm daily*) has good English-language colour maps and guides to both Nagano and the surrounding areas. Staff can also book accommodation in the city centre.

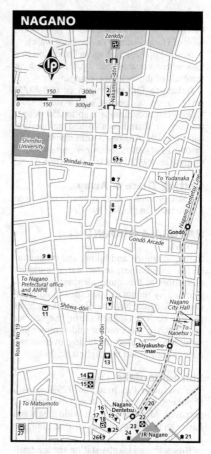

The **International Relations Section** of Nagano City Hall (☎ 224-5121; *open 8.30am-5.15pm Mon-Fri*) has both English and Chinese speakers available. In the Kenchō (prefectural office), **Anpie** (*Association of Nagano Prefecture for Promoting International Exchange*; ☎ 235-7186; *open 8.30am-5.15pm Mon-Fri*) can also help English-speaking visitors and it has an international lounge.

There's a **post office** and an international **ATM** in the West Plaza Nagano building opposite the station's Zenkōji exit, below the huge TV screen. **Heiandō bookstore** upstairs has a selection of English-language books.

Media Space (☎ 224-2227; *¥200/30min, ¥950/day*) has Internet access. It's above

NAGANO

PLACES TO STAY
3 Zenkō-ji Kyōju-in Youth Hostel
善光寺教授院
ユースホステル
5 Gohonjin Fujiya
御本陣藤屋
7 Shimizuya Ryokan
旅館清水屋
9 Hotel Saihokukan
ホテル犀北間
12 Nagano Washington Hotel
長野ワシントンホテル
21 Hotel Sunroute Nagano Higashi-guchi
ホテルサンルート長野東口
24 Hotel Metropolitan Nagano
ホテルメトロポリタン長野
25 Hotel Ikemon
ホテル池紋

PLACES TO EAT
2 Marusei
丸清
8 Ōtaya
太田屋
10 Taj Mahal
タージマハール
16 Chō Bali Bali
チョーバリバリ
17 La Tavola nel Bosco
ボスコ
19 Kinryū Hanten
金龍飯店
20 Motojiya
元庄屋
23 Oyaki Kōbō
お焼き工房

OTHER
1 Sanmon
三門
4 Niō-mon
仁王門
6 Eighty-Two Bank
八十二銀行

11 Central Post Office
中央郵便局
13 Groovy
グルービー
14 Liberty
リバーテイー
15 Again/Comme Ca Department Store
18 Media Space; Mister Donut
メデイアスペース；ミスタードーナツ
22 Midori Department Store
みどりデパート
26 West Plaza Nagano Bldg.; ATM; Post Office; Heiandō Bookstore
ウエストプラザ長野；郵便局；平安堂
27 Bus Terminal
バスターミナル

Mister Donut, a minute's walk from the train station.

Zenkōji 善光寺

This temple (☎ 186-026-234-3591; admission ¥500; open 4.30am-4.30pm daily summer, 6am-4pm daily winter, sliding hours rest of year) is believed to have been founded in the 7th century, and is the home of the Ikkō-Sanzon, allegedly the first Buddhist image to arrive in Japan (in 552, from Korea). The image has quite a history; it's been the subject of disputes, lost, recovered and, finally, installed again. Don't expect to see it, however; it is said that 37 generations of emperors have not seen the image, though visitors may view a copy every seven years (see Special Events later).

Zenkōji's immense popularity stems partly from its liberal welcoming of believers from all Buddhist sects, including women; its chief officiants are both a priest and a priestess. Despite its name, Zenkōji has nothing to do with Zen. There are some 200 other Zenkōji temples throughout Japan.

The original site was south of the current temple, off what's now the busy shopping street Nakamise-dōri; however, in that location it was destroyed some 11 times by fires originating in neighbouring homes

and businesses – and rebuilt each time with donations from believers throughout Japan. Finally, the Tokugawa shōgunate decreed that the temple be moved to its present, safer location. The current building dates from 1707 and is a National Treasure.

Visitors ascend to the temple via Nakamise-dōri and the impressive gates Niōmon and Sanmon. In the Hondō (main hall), the Ikkō-Sanzon image is in an ark left of the central altar, behind a dragon-embroidered curtain. To the right of the altar, visitors may descend a staircase to a pitch-black tunnel that symbolises death and rebirth and provides the closest access to the hidden image; taller visitors: watch your head! As you navigate the twisting tunnel, dangle your arm along the right-hand wall until you feel something heavy, moveable and metallic – said to be the key to salvation.

It's worth getting to the temple shortly after it opens to witness the morning service and the *ojuzu chodai*, in which the priest or priestess touches the Buddhist holy beads to the heads of all who line up and kneel. Check with the tourist information centre or the Zenkōji office for the times of the service.

Any bus from bus stop No 1 in front of Nagano station will get you to Zenkōji (¥100).

CENTRAL HONSHŪ

Zenkōji Legends

Few Japanese temples have the fascination of Zenkōji, thanks in part to the legends related to it. Among them:

- **Ikkō-Sanzon** This image, containing three statues of the Amida Buddha, was brought to Japan from Korea in the 6th century and remains the temple's raison-d'etre. It's wrapped like a mummy and kept in an ark behind the main altar, and it's generally said that nobody has seen it for 1000 years. However, in 1702, in response to rumours that the ark was empty, the shōgunate ordered a priest to confirm its existence and take measurements – that priest remains the last confirmed person to view it.

- **Following an Ox to Zenkōji** Long ago, an impious old woman was washing her kimono when an ox appeared, caught a piece of the cloth on his horn and ran away with it. The woman was as stingy as she was impious, and she gave chase for hours. Finally, the ox led her to Zenkōji, and she fell asleep under its eaves. The ox came to her in a dream, revealed himself to be the image of the Amida Buddha and disappeared. The woman saw this as a miracle and became a pious believer. Today, people in Kantō say, 'I followed an ox to Zenkōji' to mean that something good happened unexpectedly.

- **The Doves of Sanmon** Zenkōji's pigeon population is renowned, making the rattan *hatto-guruma* (wheeled pigeon) a favourite Nagano souvenir. Natives claim the birds forecast bad weather by roosting on the Sanmon gate, but many visitors also claim to see five white doves in the plaque above the central portal. They're talking about the short strokes on the three characters that make up 'Zenkōji'. In the upper character (善, 'zen') they're the two uppermost strokes; in the middle character (光, 'kō') they're the strokes on either side of the top; and in the 'ji' (寺) it's the short stroke on the bottom left.

- **Binzuru** A follower of Buddha, Binzuru trained in healing. He was due to become a *bosatsu* (Bodhisattva, or enlightened one) and go to the land of the immortals, but the Buddha instructed him to remain on earth and continue to do good works. At most temples with images of Binzuru, he's outside the main hall, but at Zenkōji you'll find his statue just inside. His body is worn from all the visitors who have touched it to help heal ailments of the corresponding parts of their own bodies; you can see the lines where the face was once replaced.

Special Events

Gokaichō Matsuri is held at Zenkōji once every seven years from early April to mid-May, when five million pilgrims come to view a copy of Zenkōji's sacred image of the Buddha – the only time it can be seen. Unfortunately, the next festival isn't until 2010.

Courses

Travellers interested in Japanese cultural pursuits, such as martial arts, traditional music and even Zen, can check with any of the information centres to arrange one-day study courses. Staff will make arrangements or referrals to English speaking help.

Places to Stay

Shukubō (temple lodgings) are available at Zenkōji's subtemples. Contact the tourist of-

fice or Zenkōji (☎ 186-026-234-3591); if it's the latter be sure to dial all the digits to permit caller ID, without which staff might not pick up the phone. Rooms with two meals generally cost ¥7000 to ¥10,000 per person.

Places to Stay – Budget

Zenkō-ji Kyōju-in Youth Hostel (☎ 232-2768, fax 232-2767; beds ¥3000) is in a handsome, 100-plus year-old sub-temple of Zenkōji. Be sure to reserve. No meals are served.

Places to Stay – Mid-Range

Ryokan Downhill from Zenkōji, **Shimizuya Ryokan** (☎ 232-2672, fax 234-5911; rooms per person with 2 meals from ¥8000) is a very agreeable place with traditional touches.

Hotels There are a number of business hotels around the train station.

Hotel Ikemon (☎ 227-2122, fax 227-6600; singles/doubles/twins ¥5670/7560/9450) is nothing special, though it's cheap and has a can't-beat-it location across from the station's Zenkōji exit.

Hotel Sunroute Nagano-Higashiguchi (☎ 264-7700, fax 264-6611; singles/twins/doubles from ¥7700/13,700/14,700), outside the other station exit, is the newest and nicest business hotel.

Nagano Washington Hotel (☎ 228-5111; singles/twins from ¥6000/13,700) is your best bet in the town centre, with business-standard rooms and a few restaurants.

Places to Stay – Top End
Gohonjin Fujiya (☎ 232-1241, fax 232-1243; e fuziya@avis.ne.jp; Chūō-dōri; rooms per person with 2 meals from ¥9000) is Nagano's most famous and venerable hotel, in business for 17 generations. The current building (circa 1923) is rather Western-looking but functions as a traditional Japanese inn.

Hotel Metropolitan Nagano (☎ 291-7000, fax 291-7007; singles/doubles/twins from ¥8000/17,000/16,000), by the train station, is upscale and up-to-date. Japan Rail Pass holders get a 20% discount.

Saihokukan (☎ 235-3333, fax 235-3365; singles/twins from ¥6500/15,000) is a modern, Western hotel with an uppercrust feel. It's the local hotel of choice of the Imperial family.

Places to Eat & Drink
Nagano is famed for *soba*, and many restaurants around Zenkōji serve it.

Marusei (☎ 232-5776; dishes ¥600-1300; open 11am-4pm Thur-Tues), on Nakamise-dōri, serves *soba* and the famous *tonkatsu* (pork cutlets); the Marusei *bentō* (¥1300) lets you try both.

Ōtaya (☎ 232-6348; soba or teishoku ¥600-1840), down the hill, specialises in home-made *soba*.

The best variety of restaurants is in the station area.

Motojiya (☎ 226-3322; dishes ¥450-900), an *izakaya*, serves grills, sashimi and small dishes, plus *shabu-shabu* and sukiyaki from ¥1800.

Kinryū Hanten (☎ 228-2111; mains ¥710-1030) is the city's best loved Chinese place, with *teishoku*, dumplings and an English menu.

Cho Bali Bali (☎ 229-5226; mains ¥500-600) is funky and has dishes from across Asia, some nicely spicy.

La Tavola nel Bosco (☎ 264-6270; mains ¥800-1400) is a trattoria popular with local foreigners (though you may want to take along a Japanese speaker).

Oyaki Kōbō (☎ 223-4537; oyaki around ¥125 each) is good for quick bites; try its *oyaki*.

There are several restaurants on the 5th floor of **Midori department store**, to the right as you exit the train station. Most *teishoku* costs ¥800 to ¥1200.

Taj Mahal (☎ 234-1343; mains ¥600-1200), closer to the town centre, is a popular Indian place serving course menus from ¥1480, and lunch specials.

Groovy (☎ 227-0480; w http://nagano .cool.ne.jp/jazzgroovy) is a live house that's popular with local jazz lovers. It's between Taj Mahal and the train station.

Liberty (☎ 224-2870) is a *gaijin* pub down the alley behind Again/Comme Ça department store.

Getting There & Away
Nagano *shinkansen* trains run twice hourly from Tokyo station (Asama, ¥7970, 1¾ hours). The JR Shinonoi line connects Nagano with Matsumoto (*tokkyū*, ¥2770, one hour) and Nagoya (*tokkyū*, Y6930, three hours).

TOGAKUSHI 戸隠
☎ 026 • pop 5200
This mountainous, forested region northwest of Nagano is a popular destination for hikers – particularly during late spring and autumn – and skiers in winter. Togakushi's elevation makes it unsuitable for rice-growing, but it has been famed for *soba* for centuries.

Three sub-shrines (Hōkōsha, Chūsha and Okusha), each separated by several kilometres, make up the Togakushi Shrine. One bus line serves all three, but the greatest concentration of sights and accommodation is in the community of Chūsha, near the Chūsha-Miyamae bus stop. Here you'll find the historic, wooded Chūsha shrine; one tree here is said to be 800 years old. Nearby hiking trails lead throughout the area; it takes about 45 minutes to Okusha, partly via a tree-lined path. In winter, Okusha is inaccessible except by hearty snowshoers.

In Chūsha, **Togakushi Kōgen Yokokura Ryokan Youth Hostel** (☎ 254-2030; *dorm beds with/without 2 meals ¥4750/2950*) is in an early Meiji-era building (Japanese toilets only), near the entrance to a ski area. Ryokan-quality private rooms are available from ¥7000 per person, with two meals. Prices at other ryokan start at around ¥8000 per person. To savour local *soba*, try **Uzuraya** (☎ 254-2219; *dishes ¥800-1700*), also in Chūsha.

Buses via the scenic **Togakushi Birdline Highway** depart from Nagano approximately once an hour between 6.55am and 6.45pm and arrive at Chūsha Miyamae bus stop in about an hour (¥1160) – do not get off at Chūsha bus stop, which is basically a bus transit point. To Okusha the fare is ¥1360. If you plan to take many buses, look into the Togakushi Kōgen Free Kippu pass (¥2500), valid on area buses for three days.

OBUSE 小布施
☎ 026 • pop 12,000

This little town northeast of Nagano occupies a big place in Japanese art history. The famed ukiyo-e (woodblock print) artist Hokusai (1760–1849) worked here during his last years, making it a pilgrimage site for his legions of fans. The museum **Hokusai-kan** (☎ 247-5206; *admission ¥500; open 9am-5pm daily*) displays some 30 of his prints at any one time.

Nearby, Hokusai's patron, Takai Kōzan, is commemorated in the **Takai Kōzan Kinenkan** (☎ 249-4049; *admission ¥200; open 9am-5pm daily*). This businessman was also an accomplished artist, albeit of more classical forms than Hokusai's.

Obuse also has 10 other **museums**, covering topics including bonsai and Japanese lamps.

To reach Obuse, take the Nagano Dentetsu line from Nagano (*tokkyū*, ¥750, 22 minutes; *futsū*, ¥650, 30 minutes). The coffee shop at the train station has some maps and pamphlets. The Hokusai and Takai museums are 10 minutes on foot from the train station.

Obuse also boasts the nearest *rotemburo* to Nagano, **Anakannon-no-yu** (☎ 247-2525; *admission ¥500; open 10am-10pm daily May-Sept, 10am-9pm daily Oct-Apr*); bring a towel. It's about 30 minutes' walk from the train station, or occasional buses are available.

YUDANAKA 湯田中
☎ 0269 • pop 18,000

This region of hot springs and winter Olympic sites is perhaps best known for **Jigokudani Onsen** (Hell Valley Hot Springs) and the monkeys who soak in its waters. There are also hiking and winter sports activities.

Jigokudani Yaen-kōen (*Wild Monkey Park*; ☎ 33-4379; *admission ¥500; open 8.30am-5pm daily Apr-Oct, 9am-4pm daily Nov-Mar*) allows you to commune with the bathing monkeys.

Kōraku-kan (☎ 33-4376; *rooms per person with 2 meals from ¥10,545*), across the river, is where monkeys get to commune with bathing humans. Accommodation at this *onsen* ryokan here is pretty basic (although the mountain vegetable tempura has received good reviews), but the pleasant indoor and concrete riverside outdoor *onsen* are available 24 hours for guests. For day visitors (8am to 10am and noon to 3pm) entry costs ¥400. From Yudanaka station, take the bus for Kanbayashi Onsen Guchi and get off at Kanbayashi Onsen (¥220, 15 minutes, several daily), one stop before the end. From here walk uphill along the road about 400m (a sign at the trailhead reads 'Monkey Park') and follow the trail for a tree-lined 1.6km to the ryokan and Yaen-kōen.

Uotoshi Ryokan (☎ 33-1215, fax 33-0074; ⓦ www.avis.ne.jp/~miyasaka; *rooms per person with/without two meals from ¥7300/3800*), which is located in town, is not fancy but commendably hospitable. The English-speaking owner may demonstrate *kyūdō* (Japanese archery) on request. You can arrange to be picked up at Yudanaka station, or walk from there to the ryokan (seven minutes).

Yuyado Sekiya (☎ 33-2268, fax 33-5885; *rooms per person with 2 meals from ¥12,000*) is a posh place by Kanbayashi Onsen bus stop. It's in a woodsy setting with lovely indoor and outdoor baths.

From Nagano, take the Nagano Dentetsu line to the terminal at Yudanaka (*tokkyū*, ¥1230, hourly). Note that some trains do not go all the way to Yudanaka.

BESSHO ONSEN 別所鴛泉
☎ 0268 • pop 1600

If you're visiting just one central Honshū hot-spring town, Bessho is a good choice; it's almost as convenient from Tokyo as from Nagano, and it retains much old-world charm. Bessho's excellent waters, reputed to cure diabetes and constipation while beautifying your complexion, bring in tourists aplenty, but overall it feels undeveloped.

Bessho is mentioned in *The Pillow Book* by the Heian era poetess Sei Shōnagon and flourished as an administrative centre during the Kamakura period (1185–1333). It is still referred to as 'Little Kamakura' for dramatic temples constructed at that time. The national treasure **Anraku-ji** (☎ 38-2062; admission ¥100; open sunrise-sunset), renowned for its octagonal pagoda, is 10 minutes on foot from Bessho Onsen station, while **Chūzen-ji** (☎ 38-4538; admission ¥100; open 9am-4pm daily) and **Zenzan-ji** (☎ 38-2855; admission ¥100; open 9am-5pm daily) are both a very enjoyable 5km hike away.

There are three **public baths** (admission ¥150; open 6am-10pm daily), all located centrally. Ō-yu has a small *rotemburo*, Ishi-yu is famed for its stone bath, and Daishi-yu, most frequented by the locals, is known for being relatively cool.

Bessho Onsen Ryokan Association (☎ 38-2020, fax 38-8887) can help with hotel bookings. **Ueda Mahoroba Youth Hostel** (☎ 38-5229, fax 38-1714; dorm beds with/ without 2 meals ¥4500/2900) is comfortable and secluded, eight minutes' walk from the train station (no *onsen*).

Ryokan Katsura-sō (☎ 38-2047, fax 38-3929; e katsuraso@po7.ueda.ne.jp; rooms per person with 2 meals ¥10,000) is friendly and serves really excellent *sansai* cuisine. The rooms on upper floors have valley views.

Ryokan Hanaya (☎ 38-3131, fax 38-7923; rooms per person with 2 meals from ¥17,000) is splendidly traditional and very elegant. It's often booked out.

To reach Bessho Onsen, take the JR Nagano *shinkansen* to Ueda (from Tokyo, ¥6490, 1½ hours; from Nagano, ¥1410, 13 minutes) then change to the private Ueda Kōtsū line to Bessho Onsen (¥570, 27 minutes, about hourly).

KARUIZAWA 軽井沢
☎ 0267 • pop 17,290

Karuizawa is Japan's Aspen, a mountain resort where the nation's wealthy, famous and powerful go to see and be seen.

Nary a trace remains of Karuizawa's days as a post town on the Nakasendō, but during the Meiji era it became a favourite getaway for Western missionaries. Japanese politicians and cultural figures soon followed, and today the town centre is full of fashionable folk eating in fashionable cafés and shopping for fashionable clothes in fashionable outlet stores. It even has its own Ginza district, to mirror the one in Tokyo, and at peak times it can seem almost as crowded.

Outside the city centre, you can see the natural scenery that attracted the first visitors. A popular warm-weather hike runs some 10km from the bus stop at Mine-no-chaya (¥860, 30 minutes) via the waterfall Shiraito-no-taki to the **former Hotel Mikasa** (1906; ☎ 45-8695; admission ¥400), one of the first buildings by Japanese architects to mix styles both Western (eg, glass windows) with Japanese (they slide). From here it's another 4km to the train station by foot or bus (¥270, eight minutes). The main ski resorts are past Mine-no-chaya in Gunma-ken; there's also one by the Karuizawa Prince Hotel, but some find it overpriced.

Closer in, it's worth a stroll through the wooded lanes encircling the city centre to see how Japan's other 2% lives. Vacation homes and corporate and academic guesthouses sit on plots of land that would fit a Tokyo apartment complex; some architecturally adventurous examples are in the vicinity of the pond **Kumoba-ike**.

There are well over 100 lodgings in Karuizawa. *Minshuku* cost from ¥6500 and pensions from ¥8000 per night.

Wings Club (☎ 42-4110, fax 42-8173; rooms per person with breakfast from ¥7000) is an attractive, New England style B&B, seven minutes' walk from the station.

Sunshine Hotel (☎ 42-5259, fax 42-6632; singles/doubles from ¥6600/10,000), about one minute's walk from the station, is less homey and has larger-than-average business-style rooms; rates can rise significantly in the high season.

Karuizawa is easily reached on the Nagano *shinkansen* from Tokyo (¥5550, 1½ hours) or Nagano (¥3380, 30 minutes).

CENTRAL HONSHŪ

Toyama-ken 富山県

TOYAMA 富山
☎ 076 • pop 321,000

Toyama is a heavily industrialised city with few tourist attractions, but you may well be passing through en route to the northern Japan Alps or the Japan Sea coast.

If you have time, **Chokei-ji** (☎ 441-5451; admission free; open 24hr) is known for 500 statues of *rakan* (Buddha's disciples), and the **Toyama Folkcraft Village** (☎ 433-8270; admission ¥630; open 9am-4.30pm Tues-Sun) consists of museums displaying local crafts.

Information

The **information office** (☎ 432-9751; open 8.30am-8pm daily), outside Toyama station's south exit, has useful maps and pamphlets on the Tateyama-Kurobe Alpine Route, Unazuki Onsen and Gokayama (see Shōkawa Valley in the Hida District section), and staff speak English. JNTO issues a leaflet entitled *Tateyama, Kurobe & Toyama*, which has details on transport links and accommodation.

Places to Stay & Eat

There are many lodgings within a few minutes' walk from the train station's south exit.

Relax Inn (☎ 444-1010; fax 444-2288; W www.relax-inn.co.jp; singles/doubles from ¥800/8800) is a new business hotel, and is cheap and professional.

Toyama Excel Hotel Tōkyū (☎ 441-0109, fax 441-0179; W www.tokyuhotels.co.jp; singles/twins from ¥8300/13,500) has large rooms, in a tower above the C in C shopping centre.

Toyama station delicacies include *oshi-zushi* (fish that's been pressed down onto rice, from ¥130) from *bentō* merchants, and irresistible cinnamon cream puffs from **Maple House** (☎ 441-1193) for ¥120 each.

Yakuto (☎ 425-1871, courses from ¥2000) serves *yakuzen-ryōri*, a local speciality made with medicinal herbs; it's by the Nishi-cho tram stop, 10 minutes' ride from the station.

Getting There & Away

Air Daily flights operate between Toyama and major Japanese cities. There are less frequent flights to Seoul and Vladivostok.

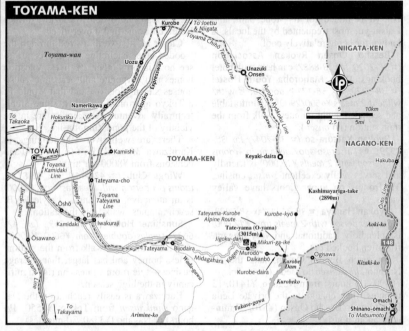

TOYAMA-KEN

Train The JR Takayama line links Toyama with Takayama (*tokkyū* ¥3080, 1½ hours; *futsū* ¥1620, 2¼ hours). The Toyama Chiho Testudo (aka Chitetsu) line links Toyama with Tateyama, the starting (or finishing) point for those travelling the Tateyama-Kurobe Alpine Route. Chitetsu also links Toyama with Unazuki Onsen, the starting point for a trip up Kurobe-kyō.

The JR Hokuriku line runs west to Kanazawa (*tokkyū* ¥2410, 35 minutes; *futsū* ¥950, one hour), Kyoto (Rai-chō *tokkyū* ¥7560, three hours) and Osaka (¥8290, 3½ hours). The same line runs northeast via Naoetsu (¥3980, 1¼ hours) to the ferry terminal for Sado-ga-shima and Niigata (¥7130, three hours), and Aomori at the very tip of Northern Honshū.

TATEYAMA-KUROBE ALPINE ROUTE 立山 黒部アルペンルート

JNTO publishes a leaflet entitled *Tateyama, Kurobe & Toyama* with details on this route, which extends between Toyama and Shinano-ōmachi. The route is divided into nine sections using various modes of transport. The best place to take a break, if only to escape the Mickey Mouse commentaries and enjoy the tremendous scenery, is Murodō. Transport buffs will want to do the lot, but some visitors find that a trip from Toyama as far as Murodō is sufficient, therefore skipping the expense of the rest. Transport costs for the 90km trip from Toyama to Shinano-ōmachi (between Hotaka and Hakuba; see the Nagano-ken section earlier) add up to ¥10,320 for adults.

Peak season is between August and late October, and transport and accommodation reservations are strongly advised for travel in these months. Better yet, avoid this period.

The route is closed from late November to late April. For the precise dates, which vary each year, check with a tourist office.

The Route

This route will take you from Toyama to Shinano-ōmachi, but travel is possible in either direction. From Toyama station, take the chug-a-lug Toyama Tateyama line (¥1170, 50 minutes) through rural scenery to Tateyama (at an altitude of 475m). If you are making an early start or a late finish on the route, there are plenty of ryokan in Tateyama.

From Tateyama, take the cable car (¥700, seven minutes) to **Bijodaira** and then the bus (¥1660, 50 minutes) via the spectacular alpine plateau of Midagahara Kōgen to **Murodō** (altitude 2450m). You can break the trip at Midagahara and do the 15-minute walk to see **Tateyama caldera** – the largest non-active crater in Japan. The upper part of the plateau is often covered with deep snow until late into the summer – the road is kept clear by piling up the snow to form a virtual tunnel.

At Murodō, the natural beauty of the surroundings has been somewhat spoilt by a monstrous bus station to service the annual flood of visitors. From here, there are various options for short hikes. To the north, just 10 minutes away on foot, is the pond, **Mikuri-ga-ike**. Twenty minutes further on again is **Jigokudani Onsen** (Hell Valley Hot Springs): no bathing here, unless you don't mind boiling bath water. To the east, you can hike for about two hours – including a very steep final section – to the peak of **O-yama** (3003m) for an astounding panorama. For the keen long-distance hiker who has several days or even a week to spare, there are fine routes south to Kamikōchi or north to Keyaki-daira in the Kurobe-kyō.

Continuing on the route from Murodō, there's a bus ride (¥2100, 10 minutes) to Daikanbō, via a tunnel dug through Tateyama. By our calculations this is roughly 3½ times the per-minute cost of a Tokyo to Kyoto *shinkansen*.

At **Daikanbō** you can pause to admire the view before taking the cable car (¥1260, seven minutes) to Kurobe-daira, where another cable car whisks you down (¥840, five minutes) to Kurobeko beside the vast **Kurobe Dam**.

There's a 15-minute walk from Kurobeko to the dam, where you can descend to the water for a cruise, or climb up to a lookout point, before taking the trolley bus to **Ogisawa** (¥1260, 16 minutes). From here, a bus ride (¥1330, 40 minutes) takes you down to Shinano-ōmachi station – at an altitude of 712m. From here there are frequent trains to Matsumoto (one hour), from where you can connect with trains for Tokyo, Nagoya and Nagano.

There's no denying that it's a unique way to travel, but not everyone will agree it's worth the cost.

CENTRAL HONSHŪ

KUROBE-KYŌ & UNAZUKI ONSEN 黒部峡・宇奈月温泉
☎ 0765

From Unazuki Onsen, the Kurobe Kyōkoku mountain train (aka *torokko*) provides a superbly scenic Alpine run through Kurobe-kyō, Japan's deepest gorge. The train operates from late April through November. Train buffs especially love this service, with open carriages used on most runs (surcharge for enclosed carriages). A museum across from the *torokko* station details the mountain train's raison-d'etre, the Kurobe dam (technological marvel or environmental desecration? You decide). From the other end, Keyaki-daira, you can hike to an observation point for a panorama of the northern Japan Alps. Keyaki-daira is also linked with Hakuba and Murodō by trails suitable for well-prepared, seasoned hikers with several days to spare.

Places to Stay
There's no shortage of large luxury hotels in Unazuki Onsen, starting from about ¥15,000 during *torokko* season and ¥10,000 other times; however, some lovely corporate guest houses welcome non-employees at more reasonable rates. The **Unazuki Ryokan Association** (☎ 62-1021, fax 62-1025, *in Japanese only*) can help with lodgings.

Etsuzan-so (☎ 62-1016, fax 62-1017; *rooms per person with 2 meals from ¥7700*) is NTT-owned, and has large rooms and indoor *onsen* overlooking the gorge.

Kurobe-so (☎ 62-1149, fax 62-1856; *rooms per person with 2 meals from ¥9130*) is a larger affair close to the train stations and has a rooftop bath with wide views.

If you take the *torokko* to Kuronagi station (¥480, 25 minutes) and hike about 20 minutes through the woods, you'll reach **Kuronagi Onsen Ryokan** (☎/fax 62-1820; *rooms per person with 2 meals from ¥9000*). This informal place looks like it may have been built for dam workers, but has a riverside *kon-yoku* (mixed bathing) *rotemburo* as well as a separate women' bath. Be mindful of the *torokko* schedules – if you miss the train, you won't make it here.

Getting There & Away
Take the Toyama Chihō Tetsudō line (next to JR Toyama station) to Unazuki Onsen (¥1790, 1½ hours, hourly). If you're arriving on the JR Hokuriku line from the north, change to the Toyama Chihō Tetsudō line at Uozu (¥900, 40 minutes).

From Unazuki Onsen station, it's a five-minute walk to the Kurobe Kyōkoku Tetsudō (*torokko*). The fare from Unazuki Onsen to the terminus at Keyaki-daira is ¥1440 (80 minutes).

Ishikawa-ken 石川県

This prefecture, made up of the former Kaga and Noto fiefs, offers visitors a nice blend of cultural and historical sights and natural beauty. Kanazawa, the Kaga capital and power base of the feudal Maeda clan, boasts several excellent museums, traditional architecture and one of Japan's most famous gardens. To the north, the peninsula, Noto-hantō, has beautiful seascapes, rolling hills and quiet fishing villages. Hakusan National Park, near the southern tip of the prefecture, offers some great hiking, though it can be tough to reach even during peak season.

KANAZAWA 金沢
☎ 076 • pop 458,000

During the 15th century, Kanazawa came under the control of an autonomous Buddhist government, which was ousted in 1583 by Maeda Toshiie, head of the powerful Maeda clan.

Then the fun started.

Three centuries of bountiful rice production made the Kaga region Japan's wealthiest; it was known as Kaga-Hyaku-Man-Goku for the one million *koku* (about five million bushels) of rice produced annually. Wealth allowed the Maedas to patronise cultural and artistic pursuits (see the boxed text 'Get Lacquered, Go to Pot, Dye and Be Gilded' later in this section), and today Kanazawa remains one of Japan's key cultural centres.

During WWII, the absence of military targets spared Kanazawa from destruction, thus preserving several historical and cultural sites – the former samurai and geisha districts boast some of Japan's loveliest streetscapes – plus the big-ticket Kenroku-en. That said, Kanazawa is also a modern city, the capital of Ishikawa-ken, with more than its fair share of functional urban architecture.

The main sights can be hurriedly seen in a day or so, and side trips to Noto-hantō and Eihei-ji in Fukui-ken are highly recommended.

Orientation

Kanazawa is a sprawling city with a labyrinthine layout befitting its castle-town past, but bus service makes it easy to get from the train station to the main sightseeing districts, which can then be covered on foot.

The Katamachi district is the commercial and business hub. A useful orientation point in Katamachi is the Kohrinbo 109 department store; from here it's a short walk east to Kenroku-en and its surrounding attractions. The samurai houses in the Nagamachi district are a short walk west from Kohrinbo 109. Northeast of Katamachi, across the Asano-gawa, is the picturesque Higashi geisha district; the hills of Higashi-yama to its east are popular for walks and city views. Just south of Katamachi, across the Sai-gawa, is the Teramachi temple district.

Information

Inside Kanazawa station, the **tourist information office** *(☎ 232-6200; open 9am-7pm daily)* provides the excellent bilingual map *Kanazawa Japan* (with details on sights, crafts and local specialities) and can help with hotel bookings. Some staff speak English.

An essential visit for anyone planning an extended stay in Kanazawa is the **Ishikawa Foundation for International Exchange** *(☎ 262-5931; open 9am-6pm Mon-Sat, 9am-5pm Sun)*. It has reams of information, foreign periodicals and satellite TV news, as well as free Internet access in its library. It's on the 3rd floor of the Rifare building, a few minutes' walk southeast of the train station.

The most convenient **post office** is in Katamachi, close to Kohrinbo 109 department store. There's also a branch inside Kanazawa station.

Bookshops Some English-language titles are carried by both **Meitetsu Book Centre** *(☎ 260-2555)*, in the Rifare building, and **Kikuya Bookstore** *(☎ 220-5055)*, beneath Kohrinbo 109.

Things to See & Do

This list is arranged in geographical order so that it can be used as a walking tour. To hit just the highlights with a good balance of history, culture and local colour, try Kenroku-en, the Ishikawa Prefectural Museum for Traditional Products & Crafts, the Honda Museum, the Nagamachi and Higashi Geisha districts, the Ōhi Pottery Museum and Ōmichō Market.

Nagamachi District Once inhabited by samurai, this attractive, well-preserved district framed by two canals features winding streets lined with tile-roofed mud walls. **Nomura Samurai House** *(☎ 221-3553; admission ¥500; open 8.30am-5.30pm daily Apr-Sept, to 4.30pm Oct-Mar)*, though partly transplanted from outside Kanazawa, is worth a visit for its decorative garden.

In another former samurai house is **Saihitsu-an** *(Yūzen Silk Centre; ☎ 264-2811; admission ¥500; open 9am-noon & 1pm-4.30pm Fri-Wed)*, where you can watch the process of *Kaga yūzen* kimono-dyeing (see the boxed text 'Get Lacquered, Go to Pot, Dye and Be Gilded' later in this chapter).

Towards the Sai-gawa, **Shinise Kinenkan** *(☎ 220-2524; admission free; open 9am-5pm daily)* offers a peek at a former pharmacy and, upstairs, a moderate assortment of local traditional products. If the flowering tree made entirely of candy gives you a sweet tooth, slake it at **Murakami** *(☎ 223-2800)*, a handsome *wagashi* (Japanese candy) shop next to the Nomura samurai house.

Kenroku-en Kanazawa's star attraction, Kenroku-en *(☎ 234-3800; admission ¥300; open 7am-6pm daily Mar-15 Oct, 8am-4.30pm 16 Oct-Feb)* is ranked by Japanese as one of their nation's three top gardens – the other two are Kairaku-en in Mito and Kōraku-en in Okayama.

The name (*kenroku* means 'combined six'), referring to a renowned garden from Sung Dynasty China that required six attributes for perfection: seclusion, spaciousness, artificiality, antiquity, abundant water and broad views (on clear days to the Sea of Japan). Originally, Kenroku-en formed the outer garden of Kanazawa-jō, but from the 17th century onwards it was enlarged until it reached completion in the early

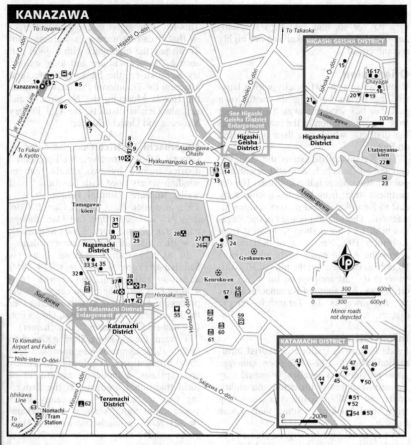

KANAZAWA

19th century; the garden was opened to the public in 1871. In winter, the branches of Kenroku-en's trees are famously suspended with rope via a post at each tree's centre, forming elegant conical shapes that protect the trees from breaking under Kanazawa's heavy snows. In spring, irises turn Kenroku-en's waterways into rivers of purple.

Kenroku-en is certainly attractive, but enormous crowds can diminish the intimacy and enjoyment of the garden. Visit at opening time and you'll have the place to yourself. An hour later, tour buses begin to descend.

Ishikawa-mon Across the moat from Kenroku-en, this elegant gate with lead tiles

(useful if ammunition ran short) is all that's left of Kanazawa-jō, which burnt down so many times that the locals obviously got sick of rebuilding it.

Seison-kaku Villa A Maeda lord built this stylish retirement villa (☎ 221-0580; admission ¥600; open 8.30am-4.30pm Thur-Tues), on the southeastern edge of Kenroku-en, for his mother in 1863. It's worth a visit for the elegant chambers and furnishings. A detailed English-language pamphlet is provided.

Ishikawa Prefectural Museum for Traditional Products & Crafts Behind Seison-kaku, this museum (☎ 262-2020; admission ¥250; open 9am-5pm daily; closed

KANAZAWA

PLACES TO STAY
5 Kanazawa Station Hotel
金沢ステーションホテル
6 Garden Hotel Kanazawa
ガーデンホテル金沢
13 Matsumoto
まつ本
16 Minshuku Yōgetsu
民宿陽月
22 Kanazawa Youth Hostel
金沢ユースホステル
30 New Grand Hotel
金沢ニューグランドホテル
32 Yamadaya
山田家
37 Kanazawa Excel Hotel
金沢エクセルホテル
47 Murataya Ryokan
村田屋旅館
51 Kanazawa Washington Hotel
金沢ワシントンホテル
53 Matsui Youth Hostel
松井ユースホステル

PLACES TO EAT
20 Jiyūken
自由軒
33 Murakami Sweet Shop
お菓子の村上
41 Janome-sushi
蛇の目寿司
43 Legian; Polé Polé Bar
レギアン、ポレポレ
44 Tamazushi
玉寿司
46 Shiruberu
汁べる
50 Kopkunka
コックンカ
52 Pilsen
ぴるぜん

OTHER
1 JR Rent-a-Cycle
ＪＲレンタサイクル
2 Tourist Information Office
観光案内所

3 Post Office
郵便局
4 Hokutetsu Kankō Bus
Company
北鉄観光バスターミナル
7 Ishikawa Foundation for
International Exchange;
Rifare Building; Meitetsu
Book Centre
国際交流センター；
リファーレ；
めいてつブックセンタ
8 Hokuriku Bank
北陸銀行
9 Musashi-ga-tsuji Bus Stop
10 Meitetsu Marukoshi
Sky Plaza Department Store
名鉄丸越スカイプラザ
11 Ōmichō Market
近江町市場
12 Ishikawa Bank
石川銀行
14 大樋美術館
15 Sakuda Gold Leaf
Company
作田金箔
17 Shima Geisha House
志摩
18 Kaikarō
懐花楼
19 Higashi-yu Public Bath
東湯
21 Coin Laundry
コインランドリー
23 Yūsu-Hosteru-Mae Bus Stop
24 Kenroku-en-shita Bus Stop
兼六園下バス停
25 Kankō Bussankan (Ishikawa
Local Products Shop)
石川観光物産館
26 Bus Stop
27 Ishikawa-mon
石川門
28 Kanazawa-jō Ruins
金沢城跡
29 Oyama-jinja
尾山神社

31 Post Office
郵便局
34 Nomura Samurai
House
野村家跡
35 Saihitsu-an (Yūzen Silk
Centre)
彩筆庵
36 Shinise Kinenkan
老舗記念館
38 Daiwa Department Store
ダイワ
39 Atrio Shopping Plaza
40 Kohrinbo 109 Department
Store; Kikuya Bookstore
香林坊１０９；喜久屋書店
42 Post Office
郵便局
45 Katamachi Intersection
片町交差点
48 100 Yen Shop
１００円ショップ
49 100 Yen Shop
54 I no Ichiban
いの一番
55 International lounge
56 Ishikawa Prefectural Art
Museum
石川県立美術館
57 Seison-kaku Villa
成巽閣
58 Ishikawa Prefectural
Museum for Traditional
Products & Crafts
石川県立伝統産業工芸館
59 Ishikawa Prefectural Nō
Theatre
石川県立能楽堂
60 Honda Museum
本多 品館
61 Nakamura Memorial
Museum
中村記念美術館
62 Myōryū-ji (Ninja-dera)
妙竜寺（忍者寺）
63 Kutani Kosen Gama Kiln
久谷光仙窯

every 3rd Thur Apr-Nov, every Thur Dec-Mar) is not flashy but offers fine displays of over 20 regional crafts. Be sure to pick up the free English-language headphone guide. If you come across a must-buy, the museum has an English-language map to shops on nearby Hirosaka street (see Shopping later in this chapter).

Ishikawa Prefectural Art Museum This museum (☎ 231-7580; admission ¥350; open 9.30am-5pm daily) specialises in antique exhibits of traditional arts, with special emphasis on colourful Kutani-yaki porcelain, Japanese painting, and *Kaga yūzen* (silk-dyed) fabrics and costumes. Admission costs more for special exhibitions.

Nakamura Memorial Museum This museum (☎ 221-0751; admission ¥300; open 9.30am-5pm daily) is reached via a narrow flight of steps below the Ishikawa Prefectural Art Museum. Rotating exhibits usually include *chanoyu* utensils, calligraphy and traditional crafts from the collection of a wealthy sake brewer Nakamura Eishun.

CENTRAL HONSHŪ

Get Lacquered, Go to Pot, Dye and Be Gilded

Much as the Medici family was the patron of some of the great artists of the Italian Renaissance, during the Edo Period, Kanazawa's ruling Maeda family fuelled the growth of important crafts. Many of these crafts are still practised today, including:

Kanazawa & Wajima Lacquerware

This luminous black lacquerware starts with hard, durable wood, such as *zelkova* or Japanese chestnut, finely carved with any defects removed or filled. Many layers of undercoating and middle coating are applied, each rubbed down with *washi* (Japanese paper) before the next application. Before the final topcoat, decoration is applied through *maki-e* (painting) or gilding. With the last coat of lacquer, artists must take great care that dust does not settle on the final product.

Ōhi Pottery

A central aesthetic to tea ceremony is *wabi-sabi*: introspective, humble and understated, yet profound and prepared with great thought. Ōhi pottery seems its ceramic equivalent, with deliberately simple, almost primitive designs, rough surfaces, irregular shapes and monochromatic glazes, typically in black or amber. Little surprise, then, that Ōhi ware has long been used by tea practitioners; the same family, with the professional name Chōzaemon, have been keepers of the Ōhi tradition since the early Edo period.

Kutani Porcelain

Known for elegant shapes and bold hues of red, blue, yellow, purple and green, Kutani ware could hardly be more different from Ōhi pottery. Kutani ware is said to date back to the early Edo period,

---

Honda Museum Members of the Honda family were chief retainers to the Maeda clan, and this museum (☎ 261-0500; admission ¥500; open 9am-5pm daily, closed Thur Nov-Feb) exhibits the family collection of armour, household utensils and works of art. The bulletproof coat and the family vase are particularly interesting, and there's a detailed catalogue in English.

Gyokusen-en For more intimacy and fewer crowds than Kenroku-en, this Edo-period garden (☎ 221-0181; admission ¥500; open 9am-4pm daily Mar-early Dec) rises up a steep slope. You can take tea here for an additional ¥500.

Ōhi Pottery Museum This museum (☎ 221-2397; admission ¥700; open 9am-5pm daily) was established by the Chōzaemon family, now in its 10th generation. The first Chōzaemon developed this brooding style in nearby Ōhi village, using special slow-fired amber glaze, specifically for use in *chanoyu*.

Higashi Geisha District North of the Ōhi Pottery Museum and across Asano-gawa, this enclave of narrow streets was established early in the 19th century as a centre for geisha to entertain wealthy patrons. **Higashi Chayagai** (east tea house street) is romantically preserved with the slatted, wooden facades of geisha houses.

One famous, traditional former geisha house is **Shima** (☎ 252-5675; admission ¥400; open 9am-6pm daily); note the case of elaborate combs and *shamisen* picks. Across the street, **Kaikarō** (☎ 253-0591; admission ¥700; open 9am-5pm daily) is an early-19th-century geisha house strikingly refinished with contemporary fittings and art; the red lacquered staircase near the entryway is a bold introduction.

The **Sakuda Gold Leaf Company** (☎ 251-6777; admission free; open 9am-6pm daily) is a good place to observe the *kinpaku* (gold leaf) process and pick up gilded souvenirs (including pottery, lacquerware and, er, golf balls). You'll be offered a free cup of tea containing flecks of gold leaf, meant to be good for rheumatism. Even the walls of the loos are lined with gold and platinum.

On most nights you can visit the local *sentō* (public bath), **Higashi-yu** (admis-

Get Lacquered, Go to Pot, Dye and Be Gilded

and it shares design characteristics with Chinese porcelain and Japanese Imari ware. Typical motifs include birds, flowers, trees and landscapes.

Kaga Yūzen Silk Dyeing

This kimono dyeing technique is characterised by sharp colours (red, ochre, green, indigo and purple) and realistic depictions of nature, such as flower petals that have begun to brown around the edges.

It's highly specialised, labour-intensive work. A pattern is drawn on the fabric with grey-blue ink from spiderwort flowers, and the lines are traced over with rice paste using a cone like a fine pastry tube; this keeps the dyes from running as they are painted onto the silk. The colours are filled in and coated with more rice paste, and then the entire sheet of silk is dyed with the kimono's background colour.

Only then is the fabric rinsed clean (traditionally in a river) and steamed to fix the colours. White lines between the elements, where the initial spiderwort ink has washed away, are a characteristic of *Kaga yūzen*. To dye one kimono takes about three months.

Gold Leaf

It starts with a lump of pure gold the size of a ¥10 coin, which is rolled to the size of a tatami mat, as little as .0001mm thick. The gold leaf is cut into squares of 10.9cm – the size used for mounting on walls, murals or paintings – or then cut for gilding on lacquerware or pottery. Tiny particles find their way into tea, sweets and hand lotion. Kanazawa makes over 98% of Japan's gold leaf.

---

sion ¥350), and there's a **coin laundry** by Asano-gawa.

Teramachi District Beside Sai-gawa, southwest of the city centre, this old neighbourhood was established as a first line of defence and still contains dozens of temples and narrow backstreets – a good place for a peaceful stroll. The temple **Myōryū-ji** (☎ 241-0888; *admission ¥700; open 9am-4.30pm daily Mar-Nov, 9am-4pm daily Dec-Feb; reservations required*), better known as **Ninja-dera**, is a five-minutes walk from the river. Completed in 1643, it was designed as a hideout in case of attack, and contains hidden stairways, escape routes, secret chambers, concealed tunnels and trick doors. The popular name refers to the temple's connection with ninjutsu (the art of stealth) and the ninja (practitioners of ninjutsu). Admission is by tour only (in Japanese).

The nearby **Kutani Kosen Gama Kiln** (☎ 241-0902; *admission free; open 9am-4.30pm daily*) is a must for lovers of pottery. The kiln is in an area of the city that was known as the Nishi Geisha District, a precinct that had similar functions to its counterpart in the eastern part of the city.

Ōmichō Market A warren of several hundred shops, many of which specialise in seafood, this market is a great place to break from sightseeing and watch daily life. It's between Katamachi district and Kanazawa station; the most convenient bus stop is Musashi-ga-tsuji.

Courses

Japanese-language classes are offered through the **Ishikawa Foundation for International Exchange** (☎ 262-5931). The **Ishikawa International Lounge** (☎ 221-9901) offers calligraphy and other Japanese arts, crafts, games and cultural pursuits.

Special Events

Kagatobi Dezomeshiki Early January. Scantily clad firemen brave the cold, imbibe sake and demonstrate ancient firefighting skills on ladders.

Asano-gawa Enyūkai Second weekend of April. Performances of traditional Japanese dance and music are held on the banks of Asano-gawa.

Hyakumangoku Matsuri Second Saturday in June. This is the main annual festival in Kanazawa, commemorating the first time the region's rice production hit 1,000,000 *koku* (around 150,000 tonnes), under the leadership of the first Lord Maeda. The highlight is a huge parade of townsfolk dressed in costumes from the 16th century. Other events include *takigi nō* (torch-lit performances of nō drama), *tōrō nagashi* (lanterns floated down the river at dusk) and a special *chanoyu* at Kenroku-en.

Places to Stay
The **tourist information office** (☎ 232-6200; *open 9am-7pm daily*) can help with accommodation reservations; the main concentration of lodgings is in Katamachi and the Kanazawa station area, while Nagamachi and Higashiyama retain a more traditional atmosphere.

Places to Stay – Budget
Hostels Tucked away in Katamachi, **Matsui Youth Hostel** (☎ 221-0275; *beds ¥3100*) is small and relaxed, but closes at 10pm.

Kanazawa Youth Hostel (☎ 252-3414, fax 252-8590; e *kanazawa@jyh.gr.jp; dorm beds ¥2900; closed early–mid-Feb*) commands a superb position in the hills to the east of the city. Rooms are Japanese and Western, and some private rooms are available (extra charge). Unfortunately, bus services are infrequent. From the station, take bus No 90 for Utatsuyama-kōen and get off after about 25 minutes at the Yūsu-Hosteru-mae bus stop.

Places to Stay – Mid-Range
Ryokan Friendly **Yamadaya** (☎/fax 261-0065; *rooms per person with no meals/breakfast/2 meals ¥4000/4500/6000*) is in a former samurai house in Nagamachi. There's free Internet access for guests.

Murataya Ryokan (☎ 263-0455, fax 263-0456; e *murataya@spacelan.ne.jp; rooms per person ¥4500*) is well-kept and friendly. It's in the centre of Katamachi's restaurants and nightlife, and maintains an English-language map of local establishments.

Minshuku A stay at historic, humble **Yōgetsu** (☎ 252-0497; *rooms per person with/without breakfast ¥5000/4500*), a former geisha house next door to Shima, allows you to have the Higashi geisha district practically to yourself at night.

Hotels Although it's the cheapest near the station, **Kanazawa Station Hotel** (☎ 223-2600; *singles/doubles/twins from ¥5600/9000/10,000*) is showing its age (with basic business hotel rooms).

Garden Hotel Kanazawa (☎ 263-3333, fax 263-7761; e *info@gardenhotel-kanazawa.co.jp; singles/doubles/twins from ¥6930/10,000/13,200*), nearby, has some renovated rooms.

Kanazawa Washington Hotel (☎ 224-0111, fax 224-2800; *singles/doubles/twins from ¥7505/16,170/18,480*) is in the heart of Katamachi's nightlife. It's well located but rooms are cramped.

New Grand Hotel (☎ 233-1311, fax 233-1591; *singles/doubles or twins from ¥8500/16,000*) offers good value, with nice-sized, smart rooms in two buildings near Katamachi.

Places to Stay – Top End
Kanazawa Excel Hotel (☎ 231-2411, fax 263-0154; w *www.tokyu-kanazawa.com; singles/twins from ¥12,500/19,500*) is recently renovated and the city's most upmarket hotel. It's adjacent to the Kohrinbō 109 department store.

Matsumoto (☎ 221-0302, fax 221-0303; *rooms per person with breakfast ¥15,000*) is a swanky ryokan with huge rooms with private bath. Its restaurant is also excellent; dinner costs an extra ¥10,000. It's on the little street west of Ishikawa Bank.

Places to Eat
Kanazawa's Kaga ryōri (Kaga cuisine) is characterised by seafood; even the most humble *bentō* (box lunches) at the train station nearly all feature some type of fish. *Oshi-zushi*, which is a thin layer of fish pressed atop vinegared rice and cut into pieces, is said by some to be the precursor to modern sushi. Another favourite is *jibuni*, which is duck or chicken coated with flour and boiled with shiitake mushrooms and green vegetables.

Janome-sushi (☎ 231-0093; *sets from ¥2000*), near Kohrinbō 109, is well regarded for sushi and Kaga cuisine.

For delicious and relatively cheap sushi, try one of the tiny restaurants that line the walkways of **Ōmichō Market**. Not many have English menus, but you should be able to make yourself understood. A lot of places here also serve seafood *donburi* (seafood served atop a deep bowl of rice). *Teishoku* (daily specials) cost ¥800 to ¥1200. Restaurants here close around 7pm to 8pm.

Tamazushi (☎ 221-2644; sets ¥1000-3000), down near Sai-gawa in Katamachi, has a most hard-earned reputation as one of Kanazawa's best sushi restaurants. Sushi *teishoku* are displayed in the front window.

Shiruberu (☎ 224-0077; dishes ¥450-700), at Katamachi intersection, is a contemporary *izakaya* with a hip crowd; it gets crowded on weekends.

Try the following restaurants for international cuisine:

Legian (☎ 262-6510; most dishes ¥600-1000) is a popular, authentic Indonesian spot by the river; look for lunch specials.

Kopkunka (☎ 222-0002; dishes ¥800-1300) serves Thai food. It's one block southeast of Katamachi crossing – look for the yellow sign.

Pilsen (☎ 221-0688; dishes ¥600-1800), on the next block, is named for the birthplace of beer, but is more interesting for its German–Japanese menu; where else can you get a sausage plate *and* warm tofu-mushroom salad at the same meal?

If you're in the mood to browse, there are several handsome **restaurants** northwest of Tamazushi.

Jiyūken (☎ 252-1996; most mains ¥650-2850), in the Higashi geisha district, has been serving *yō-shoku* (Japanese takes on Western cuisine: beef stew, grilled chicken, omelettes etc) since 1909. The *teishoku* is a steal at ¥880.

Entertainment

Nō theatre is alive and well is Kanazawa, and performances are held once a week during summer at **Ishikawa Prefectural Nō Theatre** (☎ 264-2598).

Most of Kanazawa's bars and clubs are holes-in-the-wall, jam-packed into high rises in Katamachi. Some are straightforward bars; others are barely disguised girlie clubs.

In the same building (and sharing the same owners) as Legian restaurant, **Polé Polé** (☎ 260-1138) draws an interesting mix of *gaijin* and locals. It's very grungy and dark, the floor is littered with peanut shells, and the music (reggae) is loud. **I no Ichiban** (☎ 261-0001), an *izakaya* that also serves just drinks, is so cool that it's almost unrecognisable from the street; look for the wood-panel screen and tiny stand of bamboo.

Shopping

For a quick view or purchase of Kanazawa crafts, you can visit **Kankō Bussankan** (*Ishikawa Local Products Shop*; ☎ 222-7788). The **Hirosaka** district, between Kohrinbō and Kenroku-en, has some nice shops on its south side; most locals recommend that you shop for local crafts in department stores. At the other end of the spectrum, the **100 Yen Shop** has an amazing assortment, from housewares to toys, in the middle of the trendy **Tatemachi** pedestrian street in Katamachi.

Getting There & Away

Air Komatsu airport has air connections with Tokyo, Sendai, Fukuoka and Sapporo. There's also an international connection with Seoul.

Bus There are regular expressway bus services from the Hokutetsu bus station in front of Kanazawa station's east exit, to Tokyo (Ikebukuro, ¥7840, 7½ hours), Yokohama (¥8250, 7½ hours), Kyoto (¥4060, four hours) and Nagoya (¥4060, four hours). See the following Noto Hantō section for bus services there. Some buses also stop at Kenroku-en-shita bus stop.

Train Kanazawa is linked to southwestern destinations by the JR Hokuriku line: Fukui (*tokkyū*, ¥2950, 50 minutes), Kyoto (*tokkyū*, ¥6710, 2¼ hours) and Osaka (*tokkyū*, ¥7440, 2¾ hours). The same line runs northeast to Toyama (*tokkyū*, ¥2610, 35 minutes) and further north up the coast. To travel to Takayama (*tokkyū*, ¥5840, 2¼ hours), you need to change at Toyama. The quickest way to travel between Tokyo and Kanazawa is via the Jōetsu *shinkansen* at Echigo-Yuzawa (¥12,710, 3¾ hours). For more information on Echigo-Yuzawa see the Northern Honshū chapter.

The JR Nanao line connects Kanazawa with Wakura Onsen on Noto-hantō (*tokkyū*, ¥2220, one hour).

Getting Around

To/From the Airport Buses connect Komatsu airport with Kanazawa station (¥1100, 40 minutes, timed to airplane departures and arrivals). Buses leave from the Hokutetsu bus station and also stop at Kohrinbo 109 department store.

Bus The bus network is extensive, and any bus from station stop 6, 7 or 8 will take you to the city centre (fares from ¥200, day pass ¥900). The Hokutetsu Kankō bus company also operates the 'Kanazawa Loop Bus', circling all the major tourist attractions in 45 minutes. Buses leave approximately every 15 minutes from 8.30am to 6pm (day pass ¥500).

Bicycle Rental is available at **JR Rent-a-Cycle** (☎ 261-1721; ¥400/2hr, ¥1200/day), left of the station's west exit.

NOTO-HANTŌ 能登半島

For an enjoyable combination of rugged seascapes, traditional rural life and a light diet of cultural sights, this peninsula atop Ishikawa-ken is highly recommended.

Although day trips from Kanazawa are offered, they don't do the peninsula justice; buzzing through the sights leaves little time to savour the pace of rural life as the locals do. Unless you're under your own power, a speedy trip may not be an option anyway: train service was recently scaled back and bus service is infrequent. With your own car, the new Noto Toll Rd offers a quick, not-too-outrageously expensive compromise.

Orientation & Information

Noto juts out from Honshū like a boomerang, with few sights dotting its flat west coast, while the town of Wajima is the hub of the rugged north, known as Oku-Noto.

Kanazawa **tourist information office** (☎ 076-232-6200) can handle most queries regarding Noto-hantō. The office stocks the *Easy Living Map* of Ishikawa-ken, including the peninsula. JNTO's leaflet *Noto Peninsula* also has concise information.

On the peninsula, the best tourist office is at Wajima, on the north coast. Telephone information about Noto can be obtained through the **Noto tourist office** in the city of Nanao (☎ 0767-53-7767 in Japanese).

Special Events

Noto-hantō has dozens of festivals throughout the year. On 31 July, the small community of Kōda on Noto-jima (off the peninsula's east coast) hosts a spectacular **fire festival**.

Gojinjō Daikō Nabune Matsuri, held in Wajima between 31 July and 1 August, features wild drumming performed by drummers wearing demon masks and seaweed headgear. The **Wajima Taisai** (late August) features the towering, illuminated *kiriko* festival floats for which the region is famous.

Accommodation

The peninsula has plenty of accommodation, though reservations are advised during the peak months of July and August. A night or two in a Japanese inn will also net you healthy portions of delicious sashimi, grilled fish and shellfish.

There are camping grounds tucked away in a few pockets of the peninsula, although most are difficult to reach using public transport. Call ahead to reserve sites, especially in summer.

Shopping

Particularly in Oku-Noto, you won't have to look far before you see shops groaning with the main regional craft – lacquerware. A large proportion of Wajima's townsfolk are engaged in producing *Wajima-nuri*, lacquerware renowned for its durability and rich colours.

Getting There & Around

Air By the time you read this, a new airport should have opened in the centre of Oku-Noto, with flights to Tokyo-Haneda.

Train It was once possible to take the train all the way to Wajima, but train service to Wajima has been suspended. The private Noto Tetsudō line runs from Wakura Onsen, via Anamizu as far as Takojima in northeastern Noto. See 'Bus' following for connections from Wakura Onsen to Wajima. If you're heading to the west Noto coast, you'll do better to get off the train at Hakui, Noto's western bus hub. Whatever your plan, check departure and arrival times to avoid long waits.

Bus Hokutetsu Kankō bus company's Oku-noto express buses run between Kanazawa and Wajima (¥2200, two hours), with a few continuing to Sosogi. There are five buses a day between Wakura Onsen and Wajima (¥1200, one hour).

Given the quite infrequent service, many visitors opt for the daily **tour buses**

NOTO-HANTŌ

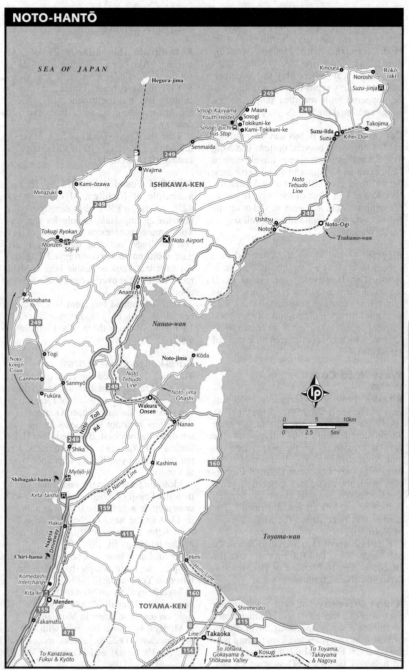

SEA OF JAPAN

Hegura-jima

Kinoura
Noroshi
Rokō-
zaki
Suzu-jinja

249

Sosogi Kajiyama
Youth Hostel
Sosogi-guchi
Bus Stop
Maura
Sosogi
Tokikuni-ke
Kami-Tokikuni-ke

249

Takojima

Suzu-Iida
Suzu
Kihei-Don

Senmaida

Wajima

Kami-ōzawa

ISHIKAWA-KEN

Minazuki

249

Noto
Tetsudo
Line

Ushitsu
Notoro

Noto-Ogi

Tokugi Ryokan
Monzen
Sōji-ji

Noto Airport

Anamizu

Tsukumo-wan

Sekinohana

249

Nanao-wan

Togi

Noto-
Kongō
Coast

Ganmon

Sanmyō

249

Noto-jima

Kōda

Noto
Tetsudo
Line

Fukūra

Noto-jima
Ōhashi

Wakura
Onsen

Nanao

Shika

Kashima

160

Myōjō-ji

JR Nanao Line

Shibagaki-hama

Keta-taisha

159

Haku

Nagisa Driveway

415

Toyama-wan

Chiri-hama

Himi

Komedashi
Interchange

Kita-ke

Himi Line

Menden

159

160

Takamatsu

471

Shinminato

415

TOYAMA-KEN

8

JR Hokuriku Line

Takaoka

8

156

To Kanazawa,
Fukui & Kyōto

To Jōhana,
Gokayama &
Shōkawa Valley

Kosugi

To Toyama,
Takayama
& Nagoya

0   5   10km
0   2.5   5mi

CENTRAL HONSHŪ

(☎ 076-234-0123) from Kanazawa, with one way/return fares from ¥3500 to ¥7200. Depending on the itinerary, the ticket price includes transport, lunch, Japanese-speaking guide and admission fees. Some tours operate all year, others May to November, and the guide's rapid-fire commentary can be peppered with recorded jungle noises, songs and breaking waves.

Car Given the lack of bus service, renting a car has become a popular option. The Noto Toll Rd makes it possible to travel between Kanazawa and Wajima in about two hours; the toll road goes only as far as Anamizu – take Route 1 the rest of the way. If you're planning to include a visit to sights on the west coast, you should allow a full day to reach Wajima.

Bicycle A stay along the coasts should appeal to cyclists as the coastal terrain is mostly flat. However, some inland roads are quite steep and have blind curves; this is also true along the Noto-kongō coast. The tourist information offices have a very good map (in Japanese) called *Noto Hantō Rōdo Mappu*, which covers the area on a scale of 1:160,000.

West Noto Coast
☎ 0767

Kita-ke From this sprawling, 300-plus year-old house (☎ 28-2546; *admission ¥700; open 8am-5pm daily*), the Kita family once administered over 100 villages at the pivotal crossroads of the Kaga, Echizen and Noto districts. The house and some furnishings are Important Cultural Properties; inside the house and adjacent museum are displays of weapons, ceramics, farming tools, fine and folk art, and documents. The garden was once called the Moss Temple of Noto.

Kita-ke is about 1km from the Komedashi exit on the Noto Toll Rd; by train, take the JR Nanao line to Menden or Hōdatsu stations; it's about 20 minutes' walk.

Nagisa Driveway The 8km beach linking the towns of Chiri-hama and Hakui at times resembles a sandy speedway, with droves of buses, motorcycles and cars roaring past the breakers. **Hakui** is both the western transit hub and Japan's UFO-viewing capital,

with flying-saucer-shaped snacks on sale everywhere to prove it.

Keta-taisha This shrine (☎ 22-0602; *admission ¥100; open 8.30am-4.30pm daily*), set in a wooded grove with sea views, is said to have been founded in the 1st century BC, but the architectural style of the present building dates from the 17th century.

Take the Togi-bound bus from Hakui to Ichinomiya bus stop (10 minutes, approximately 10 buses daily).

Myōjō-ji Founded in 1294 by Nichijō, a disciple of Nichiren, Myōjō-ji (☎ 27-1226; *admission ¥500; open 8am-5pm daily*) remains an important temple for the sect. The temple complex is composed of several buildings, including the strikingly elegant **Gojū-no-tō** (Five-Storeyed Pagoda). An excellent book available here explains more than you'd ever dreamed of knowing about the religion.

The Togi-bound bus from Hakui station can drop you at Takidani-guchi (¥390, 18 minutes); from there, it's 15 minutes' walk.

Noto-kongō Coast ☎ 0768
This rocky, cliff-lined shoreline extends for about 16km between Fukūra and Sekino-hana, and includes a variety of rock formations such as the gate-shaped Ganmon. The ride offers pleasant sea views as the road winds along the coast. Buses go from Hakui station to Fukūra (¥1110, 70 minutes, four per day); often you'll have to change buses at Sanmyō.

Monzen, further up the coast, is home to majestic **Sōji-ji** (☎ 42-0005; *admission ¥400; open 8am-5pm daily*), the temple established in 1321 as the head of the Sōtō school of Zen. After a fire severely damaged most of the buildings in 1898, the temple was restored, but it now functions as a branch temple; the main temple has been transferred to Yokohama.

Tokugi Ryokan (☎ 42-0010; *rooms per person with 2 meals ¥7000*) is simple and right on the main street in Monzen.

Monzen is also a bus hub with service to Kanazawa (¥2200, 2½ hours), Hakui (¥1510, 1½ hours) and Wajima (¥740, 35 minutes).

Wajima 輪島
☎ 0768 • pop 27,300

This fishing port, the largest town in Oku-Noto, is a historic centre for the production of lacquerware and has become a significant, if understated, centre for tourism. The town centre is nicely refurbished, and the morning market is fun.

The **tourist information office** (☎ 22-1503; open 7am-10pm daily) at Wajima station provides English leaflets and maps, and the staff can book accommodation (from 9am to 6pm, in person only). Note that although trains no longer run to the station, it is still a bus hub.

Wajima Shikki Shiryōkan/Shikki Kaikan
The lacquerware hall and museum is in the centre of town next to the Shin-bashi. The 2nd-floor museum (☎ 22-2155; admission ¥200; open 8.30am-5pm daily) displays lacquerware production techniques and some impressive old pieces, including bowls that were being swilled out of when Hideyoshi was struggling to unify Japan 500 years ago. There's a **shop** (admission free) downstairs where you can purchase contemporary works. None are cheap, but they are undeniably beautiful.

Wajima Urushi Art Museum
In the southwest corner of the town centre, this stately contemporary museum (☎ 22-9788; admission ¥600; open 9am-5pm daily, closed when changing exhibits) has a large, rotating collection of lacquerware in galleries on two floors; works are both Japanese and foreign, ancient and contemporary. It's about 15 minutes' walk west of the train station.

Kiriko Kaikan
A selection of the impressive, illuminated lacquered floats used in the Wajima Taisai and other regional festivals is on display in this hall (☎ 22-7100; admission ¥500; open 8am-6pm daily mid-July–Aug, 8am-5pm daily rest of year). Some of the floats are up to 15m tall. From the train station, it is 20 minutes on foot or you can take the bus to Tsukada bus stop (six minutes).

Hegura-jima
For a nice day trip, take the ferry to Hegura-jima, which boasts a lighthouse, several shrines and no traffic. Bird watchers flock to the island in spring and autumn. If you want to extend your island isolation by staying overnight, there are plenty of *minshuku*.

Weather permitting, there are two daily ferries (☎ 22-4381) each way from late July to late August (¥1900 each way), with one each way daily the rest of the year.

Places to Stay & Eat
Wajima has dozens of *minshuku*, where meals include copious and delicious seafood; the **tourist information office** (☎ 22-1503) can book accommodation from 9am to 6pm (in person only).

Asunaro (☎/fax 22-0652; rooms per person ¥6800), about 15 minutes' on foot from the station, is hardly fancy but kindly and home style, with an *onsen* and an *irori*.

Fukasan (☎ 22-9933, fax 22-9934; rooms per person with 2 meals ¥7000), by the harbour, is a contemporary *minshuku* with rustic elegance, an *onsen* and waves crashing outside your window.

Sodegahama Campground (☎ 22-2211, fax 22-9920; camp sites ¥600; open late July & Aug; office open 4pm-9am daily) is about 10 minutes by bus west of town. Take a Monzen-bound bus to Sodegahama or hike for 20 minutes.

If you're not eating at your inn, there are some lovely restaurants by the harbour, though some close by early evening.

Madara-kan (☎ 22-3453; sets ¥800-3000) serves local specialities, including *zosui* (rice hot-pot), *yaki-zakana* (grilled fish) and seasonal seafood; there are pictures in the window. **Yabu Honten** (☎ 22-2266; dishes ¥450-1300) is a tidy noodle shop on the main pedestrian street.

Shopping
The **asa-ichi** (morning market; open 8am-noon, closed 10th & 25th each month) is highly entertaining, though undeniably touristed. Fishwives ply their wares, everything from raw abalone to load-of-baloney, with plenty of sass and humour that cuts across the language barrier. To find the market, walk north along the river from the Wajima Shikki Shiryōkan and turn right just before Iroha-bashi. The **yu-ichi** (evening market; open 3.30pm-dusk) is lower-key, across the river on the grounds of Sumiyoshi-jinja.

Getting There & Away
See 'Getting There & Away' earlier in this section for

CENTRAL HONSHŪ

information on reaching Wajima. From Wajima, buses bound for Ushitsu stop in Sosogi (¥740, 40 minutes). Buses to Monzen (¥740, 35 minutes) leave every one to two hours.

Sosogi & Northeast Soto Coast
曽々木
☎ 0768
Heading east from Wajima you'll pass the famous, slivered *dandan-batake* (rice terraces) at Senmaida before arriving in the village of Sosogi. After the Taira were defeated in 1185, one of the few survivors, Taira Tokitada, was exiled to this region. The Tokikuni family, which claims descent from Tokitada, eventually divided into two parts and established separate family residences here.

The first residence, **Tokikuni-ke** (*Tokikuni Residence;* ☎ 32-0075; admission ¥500; open 8.30am-4.30pm daily Apr-Nov, 9am-4.30pm daily Dec-Mar), built in 1590 in the style of the Kamakura period, is a designated National Important Cultural Property and has a *meishō tei-en* (famous garden).

A few minutes' walk away, **Kami Tokikuni-ke** (*Upper Tokikuni Residence;* ☎ 32-0171; admission ¥420; open 8.30am-6pm daily Apr-Sep, 8.30am-5pm daily Oct-Mar), with its impressive thatched roof and elegant interior, was constructed early in the 19th century. Entry to either home includes an English leaflet. From Wajima station, the bus ride takes about 40 minutes.

If you visit the Sosogi coast in winter, look for *nami-no-hana* (flowers of the waves), masses of foam that form when waves gnash the rocky shore.

The road northeast from Sosogi village passes the remote cape Rokō-zaki and rounds the tip of the peninsula to less dramatic scenery on the eastern coast. At the cape, you can amble up to **Noroshi lighthouse**; a nearby signpost marks the distances to faraway cities. A coastal **hiking trail** runs west along the cape. The scenery is nice, and during the week when the tourist buses run less frequently, the town of Noroshi reverts to its true role as a sleepy fishing village.

Places to Stay Sosogi village is an agreeable choice for an overnight; there are many options.

Sosogi Kajiyama Youth Hostel (☎ 32-1145; rooms per person ¥2900) is seven minutes on foot from the Sosogi-guchi bus stop, practically across from the rock formation *mado-iwa* (window rock). The hostel is a convenient base for walking along the nearby coastal hiking trail.

Yokoiwaya (☎ 32-0603, fax 32-0663; rooms per person from ¥7000) is about six minutes' walk from the bus stop, with comfortable rooms and outstanding seafood dinners – in most Japanese cities the dinner alone would easily cost this price.

Garō Minshuku Terai (*Terai's Art Gallery Minshuku;* ☎ 86-2038; rooms per person with 2 meals ¥6500), in Noroshi, is one of the more unusual places to stay; artwork adorns the walls and shelves.

Rokō-zaki Lighthouse Pension (☎/fax 86-2030; rooms per person with 2 meals ¥8800) feels rather youthful and has both Japanese and Western-style rooms with sink and toilet (some with private bath).

HAKUSAN NATIONAL PARK 白山
☎ 0761
Travellers with a thirst for exercise (and time on their hands) may want to venture into this national park, in the southeast corner of Ishikawa-ken and spilling over into neighbouring Fukui, Toyama and Gifu prefectures. The park has several peaks above 2500m; the tallest is Hakusan (2702m), a sacred mountain that, along with Mt Fuji, has been worshipped since ancient times. In summer, hiking and scrambling uphill to catch mountain sunrises are the main activities, while in winter, skiing and *onsen* bathing take over.

For information, you can phone the **Hakusan Tourism Association** (☎ 93-1001), which also handles reservations for the Murodō Centre (see Places to Stay following), or the **Shiramine Town Hall** (☎ 98-2011). Japanese skills are helpful at both places.

The alpine section of the park is crisscrossed with trails, offering hikes of up to 25km. For hikers who are well equipped and in no hurry, there is a 26km trek to Ogimachi in Shōkawa Valley. However, camping is prohibited in the park except at designated camping grounds, meaning you'll have to either hike very fast or break the rules.

Nagoya-jō, central Honshū

Matsumoto-jō, Matsumoto, central Honshū

Paper lanterns, Fukashi-jinja, Matsumoto

Traditional stone lanterns, Sengen-jinja, Mt Fuji

Kenroku-en, Kanazawa, central Honshū

Sake barrels from Nagoya

Those looking to hike on and around the peaks are required to stay overnight at either Murodō Centre or Nanryū Sansō Mountain Lodge (see Places to Stay following). Getting to either of these requires a hike of 3½ to five hours. That doesn't stop the park from swarming with visitors, however.

The surrounding area of the park is dotted with little villages offering *onsen*, *minshuku* and ryokan accommodation and camping grounds.

Places to Stay

Murodō Centre *(☎ 93-1001; dorm rooms per person with 2 meals ¥7700; open 1 May-15 Oct)* and **Nanryū Sansō Mountain Lodge** *(☎ 98-2022; camping per person ¥300; dorm rooms per person with 2 meals ¥7300; open July-Sept)* are your two choices in the alpine area of the park. Both are rather cramped; when the lodges are full, each person gets about one tatami mat's worth of sleeping space. Murodō can hold up to 750 people in its four lodges, while Nanryū is smaller (holding 150 people) but has private cabins for up to five people for ¥12,000 (meals available for extra). There is also a **camping ground** *(tent rental ¥2200)* at Nanryū, which is the only place in the alpine area where camping is permitted. During the July to August peak season, reservations must be made at least one week in advance for both Murodō and Nanryū.

The closest access point is Bettōde-ai. From here it's 6km to Murodō (about 4½ hours' walk) and 5km to Nanryū (3½ hours). You can also access the lodges from trailheads at Ichirino and Chūgū Onsen, but these involve hikes of around 20km.

Ichirino, Chūgū Onsen, Shiramine and Ichinose all have **minshuku** and **ryokan**. Per person rates with two meals start at ¥7000.

There are several camping grounds in the area. **Ichinose Yaeijō** *(☎ 98-2121; camping per person ¥300)* has 20 camp sites near Ichinose, which is in turn close to the trailhead at Bettōde-ai. **Midori no Mura Campground** *(☎ 98-2716, camping per person ¥400, bungalows ¥6000)*, near Shiramine, has tents and bungalows for rent. There is also a **camping ground** near Chūgū Onsen. Most of the camping grounds are only open from June to October, with the exception of the one at Nanryū Sansō Mountain Lodge, which operates year-round.

Getting There & Away

This is not easily done, even during the peak summer period. The main mode of transport is the Hokuriku Tetsudō (aka Hokutetsu) Kankō bus from Kanazawa station to Bettōde-ai. From late June to mid-October, up to three buses operate daily (¥2000, two hours).

Hokutetsu also has daily departures for Ichirino and Chūgū Onsen. Check with the Kanazawa **tourist information office** *(☎ 232-6200; open 9am-7pm daily)* or the Hokutetsu bus station by Kanazawa station for the latest schedule.

If you're driving from the Shōkawa Valley, you can take the spectacular toll road, Hakusan Super-Rindō (cars ¥3150).

Fukui-ken 福井県

FUKUI 福井
☎ 0776 • pop 252,000

Fukui, the prefectural capital, was given quite a drubbing in 1945 during the Allied bombing, and what was left largely succumbed to a massive earthquake in 1948. It was totally rebuilt and is now a major textile centre. There's no real reason to linger here, but Fukui makes a useful sightseeing base. Between 19 and 21 May, Fukui celebrates the **Mikuni Matsuri** with a parade of giant warrior dolls.

Fukui City Sightseer Information *(☎ 20- 5348; open 8.30am-5pm daily)* is inside Fukui station, and can provide pamphlets in English (no English spoken). Northwest of the station are the central business district and the walls of what was once Fukui castle. On the other side of the castle grounds, **Fukui International Activities Plaza** *(☎ 28-8800; open 9am-6pm Tues-Sun, to 8pm Thur)* has lots of English-language information and free Internet access.

Fujin Seinen-kan Youth Hostel *(☎/fax 22-5625; Japanese-style dorms per person ¥3200)*, around 500m northwest of the station near Chūō-kōen, is rather drab.

Hotel Riverge Akebono *(☎ 22-1000, toll-free ☎ 0120-291-489, fax 22-8023; singles/doubles ¥6200/11,000)*, on the bank of the Asuwa-gawa, 10 minutes' walk from

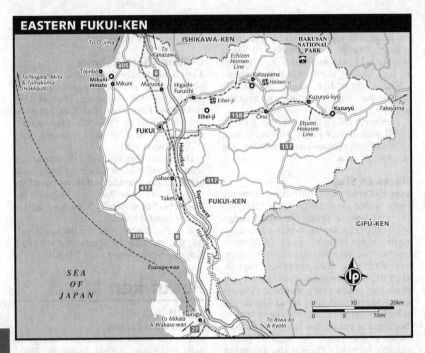

EASTERN FUKUI-KEN

CENTRAL HONSHŪ

the station, has nice rooms with private facilities and common baths on the top floor 'observation deck' (bathers observe the city; not the other way around). 'Businessman support' specials often include breakfast for the same price. From the main street perpendicular to the station, turn left after Tsuchiya furniture store.

A delicious regional speciality is *oroshi soba* (*soba* noodles topped with grated daikon and shaved bonito flakes).

Ori-Ori-ya (☎ 27-4004, skewers ¥100-300), close to Hotel Rivierge Akebono, is an ingenious *izakaya* where you select your own ingredients and grill them yourself at the table.

Fukui is connected by the JR Hokuriku line with Kanazawa (¥2430, 50 minutes) and Tsuruga (¥2100, 40 minutes); there's also convenient access to Nagoya (¥5040, 2½ hours), Kyoto (¥ 4300, 1½ hours) and Osaka (¥5340, two hours).

EIHEI-JI 永平寺
☎ 0776

Founded in 1244 by Dōgen, Eihei-ji is now one of the two head temples of the Sōtō sect of Zen Buddhism and is ranked among the most influential centres of Zen in the world. It is a palpably spiritual place – amid mountains, mosses and ancient cedars. At most times some 150 priests and disciples are in residence, and serious students of Zen should consider a retreat here.

The **temple** (☎ 63-3102; admission ¥400; open 5am-5pm daily) is geared to huge numbers of visitors who come either as sightseers or for the rigorous Zen training. Among the approximately 70 buildings, the standard circuit concentrates on seven major ones: *tosu* (toilet), San-mon (main gate), *yokushitsu* (bath), *daikuin* (kitchen), Butsuden (Buddha Hall), Hattō (Dharma Hall) and Sō-dō (Priests' Hall). You walk among the buildings on wooden walkways in your stockinged feet. A new **Shōbōkaku** exhibits many Eihei-ji treasures.

The temple is frequently closed for periods varying from a week to 10 days. Before you visit, be sure to check ahead with the temple, a nearby tourist office or **Japan Travel-Phone** (☎ toll free 0088-22-4800).

You can attend the temple's three-day, two-night *sanzensha* (religious trainee programme), which follows the monks' training schedule, complete with 3am prayers, cleaning, *zazen* (sitting meditation) and ritual meals in which not a grain of rice may be left behind. It costs ¥9000, and reservations must be made at least a fortnight in advance. Call ☎ 63-3640 or fax 63-3631 for bookings. Japanese ability is not necessary, but it helps to be able to sit in the half-lotus position. Everyone who has completed this course agrees it is a remarkable experience. A single night's stay, *sanrōsha*, is also possible for ¥8000 (with two meals; reserve at least one month in advance). If you'd like to eat a special vegan lunch (¥3000) you must confirm this before your arrival.

Places to Stay
There's a somewhat offputting tourist village beneath the temple.

Eihei-ji Monzen Yamaguchi-sō *(☎/fax 63-3122; beds ¥2900)*, on the tourist village's edge, is a secluded youth hostel; it has Japanese-style toilets only. It's five minutes on foot from Eihei-ji.

Green Lodge *(☎/fax 63-3126; rooms per person with 2 meals ¥7300)*, close to Eihei-ji, is a two-storey inn which offers basic accommodation.

Getting There & Away
From Fukui, take the Keifuku bus (¥720, one hour) from stop No 5, a couple blocks from Fukui station. As we went to press, the bus company was experimenting with nonstop buses (35 minutes).

TŌJINBŌ 東尋坊
On the coast about 25km northwest of Fukui are the towering rock columns and cliffs at Tōjinbō, a too-popular tourist destination that's also a place of legend: one says that Tōjinbō was an evil Buddhist priest who was cast off the cliff by angry villagers in 1182. It is said that the sea surged for 49 days thereafter, a demonstration of the priest's fury from beyond his watery grave.

Visitors can take a boat trip (¥1010, 30 minutes) to view the **rock formations** or travel further up the coast to **O-jima**, a small island with a shrine that is joined to the mainland by a bridge.

At least three buses serve Tōjinbō daily (¥1110, one hour) from bus stop No 7 near Fukui station.

TSURUGA 敦賀
Tsuruga, south of Fukui and north of Biwa-ko, is a thriving port and major train junction. The **Shin Nihonkai ferry company** *(☎ 0770-23-2222; ⓦ www.snf.co.jp)* operates 11 sailings a week to Tomakomai (Hokkaidō; from ¥6700 2nd class, 19 hours nonstop); of these, four stop en route at Niigata (¥4100, 9½ hours) and Akita (¥5600, 18¾ hours). Buses timed to ferry departures serve Tsuruga-kō port from Tsuruga station (¥340, 20 minutes).

MIKATA-GO-KO 三方五湖
Unfortunately, bus services around the coast from Obama to the Mikata-go-ko (Mikata Five Lakes) have disappeared, and unless you have a vehicle or hitch, you'll have to take the inland route on the train.

Sightseeing boats (¥1210, 40 minutes, depart hourly from 10am to 3pm) go out on the impressive lakes from Lake Center, a 10-minute ¥270 bus ride from JR Mihama station.

The new **Mikata Jōmon Museum** *(☎ 0770-45-2270; admission ¥500; open 9am-5pm daily; closed 1st Mon each month)* is on the south shore of Mikata-ko. You'll find artifacts from the Jōmon period discovered throughout the region, including ceramics, canoes and, surprisingly, lacquerware; there's a good English-language headphone guide. The building itself is shaped like a *kofūn* (ancient burial mound).

North of the lakes is the **Mihama-sō Youth Hostel** *(☎ 0770-32-0301; rooms ¥2900; meals available)*, and there is **camping** near the beach at Mihama.

OBAMA 小浜
Obama is a port town with the ruins of the castle, **Obama-jō**, and a number of interesting old temples. There is a **tourist information office** *(☎ 0770-52-2082; open 9am-5pm daily)* opposite the station, but staff don't speak English.

Tour buses operate from JR Obama station on half-day (¥3200) and day tours (¥4900) around the city's temples, and also popular are **boat trips** (¥2000, hourly) around the picturesque **Sotomo coastline**, with its inlets, arches and caves, just north of Obama. The tourist information office can arrange 10% off the price of the boat trips. It also rents bicycles (¥300/2hr, ¥1000/day).

For accommodation, try **Business Hotel Rengatei** (*☎ 0770-52-1004; singles ¥6000*), two minutes' walk from the station.

TAKAHAMA 高浜

The **beaches** on the Sea of Japan coast around Takahama, at the western extreme of Fukui-ken, are extremely popular in summer. Shirahama and Wada beaches, in particular are packed with sun-worshippers. Wakasa-Takahama station is on the JR

Obama line, while one stop east is Wakasa-Wada station. Wada is very well organised, with rental boats, beach volleyball, eateries on the beachfront and a really great range of accommodation.

Try **Hirata Ryokan** (*☎ 0770-72-0261*), though rates will depend on when you turn up. There is a good beachfront **camping area**, and about 1km east of the station is a big new *onsen* complex called **Onsen Yupple**.

Kansai 関西周辺

52 Kansai Region

KANSAI REGION

For fans of traditional Japanese culture, Kansai is an unmissable destination. Nowhere else in the country can you find so much of historical interest in such a compact area. And, since plenty of international carriers now fly into Kansai international airport, it is perfectly possible to make Kansai your first port of call in Japan.

Kansai's major drawcards are Kyoto and Nara. Kyoto, with its myriad temples and gardens, was the imperial capital between 794 and 1868, and is still considered by most Japanese to be the cultural heart of Japan. Nara predates Kyoto as an imperial capital and also has an impressive array of temples, burial mounds and relics. Both cities should feature prominently in even the busiest travel itinerary.

Osaka, like Tokyo, is a great place to sample Japanese city life in all its busy, mind-boggling intensity, while Kōbe is one of Japan's most cosmopolitan and attractive cities. Himeji, west of Kōbe, has the best of Japan's many feudal castles.

The main attractions of the prefecture Mie-ken, are Ise-jingū, Japan's most sacred Shintō shrine, and the seascapes around the peninsula, Shima-hantō. Wakayama-ken offers *onsen* (hot-spring spas), a rugged coast and the temple complex of Kōya-san, Japan's most important Buddhist centre.

Finally, the northern coast of Kansai, known as the San-in Coast, has some fabulous scenery, a number of good beaches and the lovely Tango-hantō (Tango Peninsula).

SUGGESTED ITINERARIES

Kyoto should be given the highest priority by any visitor to Japan. Not only does the city have an almost endless list of things to see and do, it also has cheap lodgings, great food, wonderful shops and pleasant hikes in its surrounding hills.

If you only have a week or less in Kansai, base yourself in Kyoto and take day trips to Nara and Osaka and perhaps an overnight trip to the mountaintop temple complex of Kōya-san. If you're keen on Japanese castles, you might also take a day trip out to Himeji to see the castle, Himeji-jō, visiting Kōbe on the way there or back if you have the time.

Highlights

- Visit Kyoto, Japan's cultural capital, with more than 2000 temples and shrines
- Sample the bustling nightlife of Osaka, Japan's most down-to-earth city
- Uncover the roots of Japanese culture in Nara, the country's ancient capital
- Soak in open-air hot springs in mountainous Wakayama-ken
- Spend a quiet night in atmospheric temple lodgings atop sacred Kōya-san
- Explore the fabulous coastline and rolling hills of the Tango-hantō (Tango Peninsula) in northern Kyoto-fu

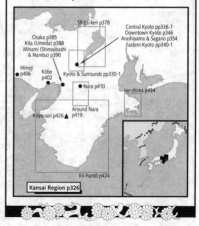

Shiga-ken p378

Central Kyoto pp336-7
Downtown Kyoto p346
Arashiyama & Sagano p354
Eastern Kyoto pp340-1

Osaka p385
Kita (Umeda) p388
Minami (Shinsaibashi & Namba) p390

Himeji p406

Kōbe p402

Kyoto & Surrounds pp330-1

Nara p410

Ise-shima p434

Around Nara p419

Kōya-san p426

Kii-hantō p424

Kansai Region p326

If you have two weeks, you can travel to some of Kansai's more distant sights. In addition to the Kyoto-based itinerary listed earlier, you could head down to Mie-ken's Ise-jingū, and perhaps hit some of the attractions in southern Nara.

In three weeks you can include destinations that are even more remote, such as the *onsen* in Wakayama-ken's Hongū region and the seaside spa town of Shirahama.

SPECIAL TICKET DEALS

The **Kansai Thru Pass** is an excellent way to get around Kansai on the cheap. This pass, available at the travel counter in the arrivals hall of Kansai international airport and at the main bus information centre in front of

KANSAI

KANSAI REGION

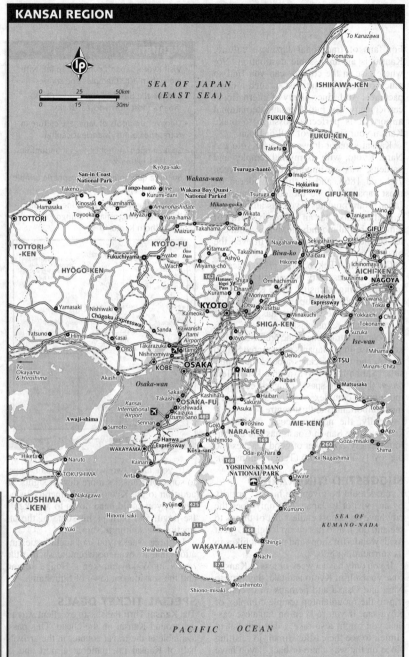

SEA OF JAPAN
(EAST SEA)

To Kanazawa

Komatsu

ISHIKAWA-KEN

FUKUI

FUKUI-KEN

Takefu

Kyōga-saki

San-in Coast
National Park

Wakasa-wan

Tango-hantō

Tsuruga-hantō

Imajō

Hokuriku
Expressway

GIFU-KEN

Takeno

Kinosaki

Kumihama

Ine
Kurumi-dani

Wakasa Bay Quasi -
National Parked

Tsuruga

Mino

Hamasaka

Toyooka

Miyazu

Amanohashidate

Mikata-go-ko

Mikata

Tanigumi

GIFU

TOTTORI

Yura-hama

Maizuru

Takahama

Obama

TOTTORI
-KEN

HYŌGO-KEN

Fukuchiyama

KYOTO-FU

Ayabe

Ōno
Dam

Kitamura

Takashima

Nagahama

Sekigahara

Ogaki

Bisai

Wachi

Miyama-chō

Ashyū

Biwa-ko

Maibara

Ichinomiya

AICHI-KEN

Yamasaki

Nishiwaki

Chūgoku Expressway

Sanda

Hanase
tōgei
Pass

Shiga

Ōhara

Ōmihachiman

Meishin
Expressway

Tsushima

NAGOYA

Kurama

Moriyama

Kuwana

Tokai

Tatsuno

Himeji

Kasai

Ono

Kawanishi
Itami
Airport

Kameoka

KYOTO

Ōtsu

Kusatsu

Minakuchi

Yokkaichi

Chita

To
Okayama
& Hiroshima

Takarazuka

Nishinomiya

Itami

Uji

Jōyō

SHIGA-KEN

Ueno

Suzuka

Tokoname

KŌBE

OSAKA

Nara

TSU

Ise-wan

Mihama

Akashi

Osaka-wan

Nabari

Minami-Chita

Sakai

Kashihara

Haibari

Matsusaka

Kansai
International
Airport

Takaishi

OSAKA-FU

Kishiwada

Kaizuka

Asuka

Sakurai

Ise

Toba

Sennan

Izumi-Sano

Gojō

Yoshino

NARA-KEN

MIE-KEN

Goza-misaki

Hanwa
Expressway

Hashimoto

Kōya-san

Ōdai-ga-hara

Owase

Kii-Nagashima

Shima

WAKAYAMA

Kainan

YOSHINO-KUMANO
NATIONAL PARK

Hiketa

Naruto

Arita

TOKUSHIMA

Ryūjin

Kumano

SEA OF
KUMANO-NADA

TOKUSHIMA
-KEN

Nakagawa

Hinomi-saki

Tanabe

Hongū

Awaji-shima

Sumoto

Yūki

Shirahama

WAKAYAMA-KEN

Shingū

Nachi

Kushimoto

Shiono-misaki

PACIFIC OCEAN

KANSAI

Kyoto station, allows unlimited travel on all bus and train lines in Kansai except the Japan Railways (JR) line (the pass covers travel on the Nankai line, which serves Kansai international airport). It also qualifies you for discounts at several attractions around Kansai.

When you buy the pass, be sure to pick up the handy companion English guide map, which shows all the bus and train lines available.

Two-day passes cost ¥3800 and three-day passes cost ¥5000. It's possible to purchase multiple passes for longer explorations of Kansai. Like the Japan Rail Pass, however, these passes are only available to travellers on temporary visitor visas (you'll have to show your passport).

Kyoto 京都

☎ 075 pop • 1.4 million

If there are two cities in Japan that *have* to be included in anyone's Japan itinerary, they are Tokyo and Kyoto. Some of what you'll see in Tokyo, you'll also find in Kyoto: lots of concrete and neon. But Kyoto, more than any other city in the country, offers what a great many Westerners long for in Japan: raked pebble gardens, the sensuous contours of a temple roof, the tripping step of a latter-day geisha in pursuit of a taxi.

Despite this, first impressions are likely to be something of an anticlimax. If you take the time to seek it out, however, you will be impressed by how much there is to see: more than 2000 temples and shrines, a trio of palaces and dozens of gardens and museums. Months, or even years, could be spent exploring Kyoto and turning up still more surprises.

HISTORY

The Kyoto basin was first settled in the 7th century, and by 794 it had become Heian-kyō, the capital of Japan. Like Nara, a previous capital, the city was laid out in a grid pattern modelled on the Chinese Tang dynasty capital, Chang'an (contemporary Xi'an). Although the city was to serve as home to the Japanese imperial family from 794 to 1868 (when the Meiji Restoration took the imperial family to the new capital, Tokyo), the city was not always the focus of Japanese political power. During the Kamakura period (1185–1333), Kamakura served as the national capital, and during the Edo period (1600–1867), the Tokugawa shōgunate ruled Japan from Edo (now Tokyo).

The problem was that from the 9th century, the imperial family was increasingly isolated from the mechanics of political power, and the country was ruled primarily by military families, or shōgunates. While Kyoto still remained capital in name and was the cultural focus of the nation, imperial power was, for the most part, symbolic and the business of running state affairs was often carried out elsewhere.

Just as imperial fortunes have waxed and waned, the fortunes of the city itself have fluctuated dramatically. During the Ōnin War (1466–67), which marked the close of the Muromachi period, the Kyoto Gosho (Imperial Palace) and most of the city was destroyed. Much of what can be seen in Kyoto today dates from the Edo period (1600–1867). Although political power resided in Edo, Kyoto was rebuilt and flourished as a cultural, religious and economic centre. Fortunately Kyoto was spared the aerial bombing that razed other Japanese urban centres in the closing months of WWII.

Today, even though it has seen rapid industrialisation, Kyoto remains an important cultural and educational centre. It has some 20% of Japan's National Treasures and 15% of Japan's Important Cultural Properties. Perhaps more impressive, Kyoto is home to a total of 17 Unesco World Heritage sites (see the boxed text 'Unesco World Heritage Sites'). In addition, there are 24 museums and 37 universities and colleges scattered

Unesco World Heritage Sites

Thirteen of Kyoto's Buddhist temples, three Shintō shrines and one castle are designated World Heritage sites. Each of the 17 sites has buildings or gardens of immeasurable historical value and all are open for public viewing.

Castle Nijō-jō

Shrines Kamigamo-jinja, Shimogamo-jinja, Ujigami-jinja

Temples Byōdō-in, Daigo-ji, Enryaku-ji, Ginkaku-ji, Kinkaku-ji, Kiyomizu-dera, Kōzan-ji, Ninna-ji, Nishi Hongan-ji, Ryōan-ji, Saihō-ji, Tenryū-ji, Tō-ji

KANSAI

throughout the city. Even though the city centre looks remarkably like the centre of a dozen other large Japanese cities, a little exploration will turn up countless reminders of Kyoto's long history.

SUGGESTED ITINERARY

Kyoto is worth considering as a base for travel in Japan, especially as it is within easy reach of Osaka Itami and Kansai international airports. And Kyoto is by far the best choice as a base for travel in Kansai because it has a wealth of accommodation and is close to Nara, Osaka, Kōbe, Mie-ken and Wakayama-ken.

It is difficult to suggest a minimum itinerary for Kyoto – you should certainly consider it a city you must see while you are in Japan and allocate as much time as possible. The absolute minimum amount of time you should spend in Kyoto is two days, during which you could just about scratch the surface by visiting the Higashiyama area in eastern Kyoto. Five days would give you time to include Arashiyama, northwestern Kyoto and central Kyoto. Ten days would allow you to cover these areas and also northern, southern and southeastern Kyoto, while leaving a day or so for places farther afield or for in-depth exploration of museums, shops and culture.

Kyoto is also an excellent place to indulge specific cultural interests, whether they be in the arts, Buddhism or crafts. The best place to find information on these subjects is the Tourist Information Center (TIC – see Information opposite).

A final word of advice is that it's easy to overdose on temples in Kyoto. If you don't find temples to your liking, there are plenty of other options. Instead, go for a hike in the mountains (see the various hikes covered in boxed text in this chapter), browse in the shops around Shijō-dōri (see Shopping later in this chapter), do some people-watching on Kiyamachi-dōri or, best of all, find a good restaurant and sample some of the finest food in all of Japan (see Places to Eat later in this chapter).

WHEN TO GO

Without a doubt, the best times to visit Kyoto are the climatically stable seasons of spring (March to May) and autumn (late September to November).

The highlight of spring is the cherry blossom season, which usually arrives in Kyoto in early April. Bear in mind, though, that the blossoms are notoriously fickle, blooming any time from late March to mid-April.

Autumn is an equally good time to travel, with pleasant temperatures and soothing autumn colours. The shrines and temples of Kyoto look stunning against a backdrop of blazing leaves, which usually peak between late October and mid-November.

Japanese people are well aware that Kyoto is most beautiful at these times and the main attractions can be packed with local tourists. Likewise, accommodation can be hard to find; if you do come at these times, be sure to book well in advance.

Travelling in either winter or summer is a mixed bag. Mid-winter (December to February) weather can be quite cold (but not prohibitively so), while the extremely sticky summer months (June to August) can turn even the briefest excursion out of the air-conditioning into a soup bath.

June is the month of Japan's brief rainy season, which varies in intensity from year to year; some years there's no rainy season, other years it rains virtually every day.

ORIENTATION

Kyoto is a fairly easy city to find your way around. Kyoto station (which serves Japan and Kintetsu Railways) is in the south, and from there Karasuma-dōri runs north past Higashi Hongan-ji to the commercial centre of town. The commercial and nightlife centres are between Shijō-dōri and Sanjō-dōri (to the south and north, respectively) and between Kawaramachi-dōri and Karasuma-dōri (to the east and west, respectively).

Although some of Kyoto's major sights are in the city centre, most of Kyoto's best sightseeing is on the outskirts of the city, in the eastern and western parts of town. These areas are most conveniently reached by bus or bicycle. Outside the city itself, the mountain villages of Ōhara, Kurama and Takao make wonderful day trips and are easily accessible by public transport.

Kyoto has retained a grid system based on the classical Chinese concept. This system of numbered streets running east to west and avenues running north to south makes it relatively easy to move around with the help of a map from the TIC.

Efficient bus services crisscross the city. There's a simplified bus map on the reverse of the TIC Kyoto map. The quickest way to move between the north and south of the city is to take the subway.

Maps

Available at the TIC, the *Tourist Map of Kyoto-Nara* fulfils most map needs and includes a simplified map of the subway and bus systems. You might also want to pick up a copy of the Japanese city bus map at any major bus stop; even if you don't read Japanese, the detailed route maps are useful. The TIC also has a leaflet called *Walking Tour Courses in Kyoto* which has detailed walking maps for major sightseeing areas in and around Kyoto (Higashiyama, Arashiyama, Northwestern Kyoto and Ōhara).

INFORMATION
Tourist Offices

The best source of information on Kyoto, the Kansai region and Japan in general is the Japan National Tourist Organization's (JNTC) TIC *(Map 1;* ☎ *371-5649; open 9am-5pm Mon-Fri, 9am-noon Sat, closed holidays)*. It's a one-minute walk north of Kyoto station, just past Kyoto Tower on the west side of Karasuma-dōri.

The **Welcome Inn Reservation Centre**, in the TIC, can make reservations for you at member ryokan (traditional inns) and hotels (for more on this see the later Places to Stay section). Volunteer guides can also be arranged through the TIC with one day's notice.

While you're at the TIC, be sure to check its upcoming-events board to see what's on while you're in town.

The **Kyoto City Tourist Information Center** *(*☎ *343-6656; open 8.30am-7pm daily)* is inside the new Kyoto station building, on the 2nd floor just across from Café du Monde. Though it's geared towards Japanese visitors, English-speaking staff are usually on hand and can be of assistance when the TIC is closed.

Money

Most of the major banks are near the Shijō-Karasuma intersection, two stops north of Kyoto station on the Karasuma line subway. International transactions (like wire transfers) can be made at **Tokyo Mitsubishi Bank** (Map 3), which is one block southwest of this intersection. Other international transactions can be made at **Citibank** (Map 3), just west of this intersection. Finally, you can change travellers cheques at most post offices around town, including the **Kyoto Central Post Office** (Map 1) next to Kyoto station.

International ATMs There's an **international ATM** *(Map 1; available 10am-9pm daily)* on the B1 floor of the Kyoto Tower Hotel, very close to the TIC and Kyoto station. In the middle of town, you'll find another **international ATM** *(Map 1; available 7am-11pm daily)* in the Zest underground mall, 200m west of the Kawaramachi-Oike intersection, near exit 7. Also in the middle of town, the **All Card Plaza** *(Map 3; open 9am-8pm, closed 1-3 January)* in the Teramachi shopping arcade just north of Shijō-dōri provides card services for most major international banks and credit cards. **Citibank** (listed earlier under Money) has a 24-hour ATM that accepts most foreign-issued cards. Lastly, note that all the post offices in Kyoto have ATMs that accept most international bank cards. These ATMs are open the same hours as the post office in question (usually 9am to 5pm Monday to Friday, sometimes Saturday morning from 9am to noon).

Post

The **Kyoto Central Post Office** *(Map 1; open 9am-7pm Mon-Fri, 9am-5pm Sat, 9am-12.30pm Sun & holidays)* is conveniently located next to Kyoto station (take the Karasuma exit, as the post office is on the northwestern side of the station). There's an after-hours service counter on the southern side of the post office, which is open 24 hours a day, 365 days a year.

Telephone

There are pay phones all over town. However, international pay phones are becoming increasingly hard to find. Your best bet is the lobby of any major hotel.

Email & Internet Access

One of the cheapest Internet places in town is the **Kyoto Prefectural International Centre** *(Map 1;* ☎ *342-5000; ¥250/30min; open 10am-6pm, closed 2nd & 4th Tues each month)*, on the 9th floor of the Kyoto station building.

KYOTO & SURROUNDS

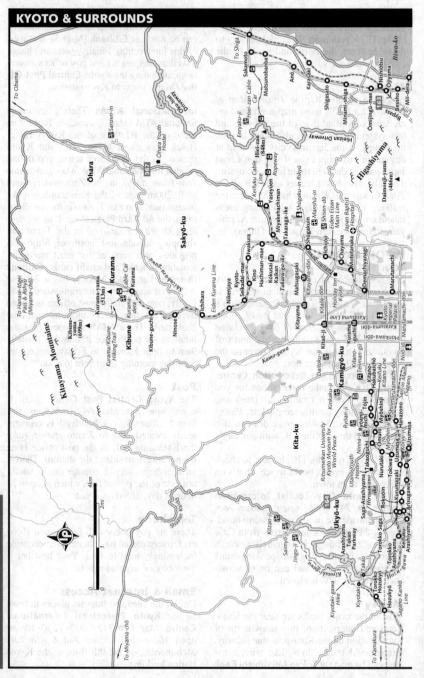

To Obama

To Shiga

Biwa-ko

Sakamoto

Matsunobanba

Ano

Karasaki

Minami-shiga

Shigasato

Omijingu-mae

Nishihotsu

Bessho

Ojiyama

Mii-dera

Bypass

Hiei-zan Cable Car

Hieizan Driveway

Enryaku-ji

Hiei-zan (848m)

Keifuku Cable
Line

Higashiyama

Daimonji-yama
(466m)

Keifuku Cable Ropeway
Line

Ohara

Ohara Youth
Hostel

Yase-yuen

Miyakehachiman

Shugakuin

Shigaku-in Rikyū

Marishō-dō

Shisen-dō

Eiden Eizan
Main Line

Japan Baptist
Hospital

Ichijōji

Sakyō-ku

Kurama

Kurama-yama
(513m)

Cable Car

Kurama-
dera

Iwakura

Takaraga-ike

Chayama

Mototanaka

Demachiyanagi

Marutamachi

Kyoto-
Seikadai-mae

Kino
Hachiman-mae

Kokusai
Kaikan

Matsugasaki

Kitayama-dōri

Kitaōji-dōri

Holiday Inn
Kyoto

Kitayama

Nikenjaya

Eiden Kurama Line

Ichihara

Ninose

Kibune-guchi

Kibune

Kibune-
yama
(699m)

Kurama/Kibune
Hiking Trail

Kurama-
guchi

Kita-ku

Kitayama Mountains

To Hanase-tōgei
Pass & Ashyū
(Miyama-chō)

Kitaōji

Daitoku-ji

Kitano
Hakubaichō

Kitano-
Tenmangū

Teimani- in

Kinkaku-ji

Kamigyō-ku

Shin-Mann

Nijō-jō

Shimabara-chō

Karasuma-dōri

Honkawa-dōri

Marutamachi-dōri

Kyoto
Imperial
Palace

Kamo-gawa

Kita-ku

Ritsumeikan University
Kyoto Museum for
World Peace

Ryōan-ji

Myōshinji

Tōjin

Ninna-ji

Ryōanji
Uchi

Omuro

Narutaki

Uzumasa

Hanazono

Kyoto-
gosho

Ukyō-ku

Utano Youth
Hostel

Tokiwa

Kurumazaki

Katsugawa

Uzumasa

Saga-Arashiyama

Rokuōin

Torokko Saga

Saga

Keifuku-
Arashiyama

Arashiyama

Matsuo

Hirosawa

Takaosguchi

Saimyō-ji

Arashiyama
Takao
Parkway

Jingo-ji

Takao

Torokko
Arashiyama

Torokko
Hozukyō

Kiyotaki-gawa
Hike

Kyōtaki

Toi Line

Hozu-gawa

Sagano Line

Torokko
Hozukyō

Kozan-ji

Kiyotaki

Sagano Kankō
Line

To Kamakura

To Miyama-chō

0   4km

0   2mi

KANSAI

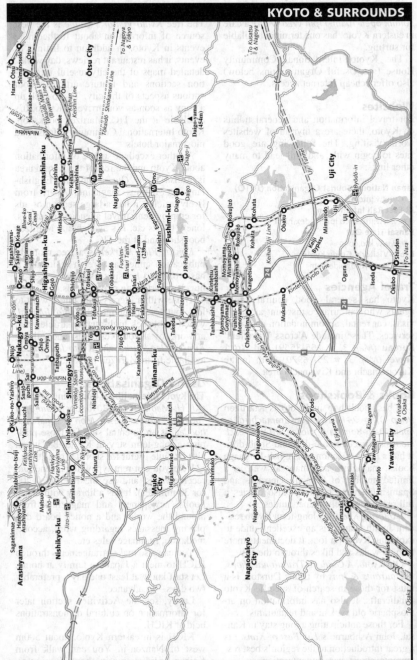

KANSAI

Buttercups *(Map 2; ☎ 751-9537; ¥250/ 30min; open 10am-11pm Wed-Mon)*, a café in eastern Kyoto, has one terminal available for surfing.

The Kyoto International Community House (see Useful Organisations below) also offers cheap Internet access.

Websites

For travel information and general tidbits on Kyoto, there are a myriad of websites worth visiting. The following are good sites to begin with, and will lead to many other links:

Japan National Tourist Organization (JNTO)
  Ⓦ www.jnto.go.jp
JR East Rail Information
  Ⓦ www.jreast.co.jp/e/index.html
Kansai Time Out
  Ⓦ www.kto.co.jp
Kyoto Visitor's Guide Kyoto
  Ⓦ www.kyotoguide.com

Travel Agencies

Kyoto has several good central travel agents who can arrange discount air fares, visas, car rental, accommodation and other services. These include **A'cross Travellers' Bureau** *(Map 3; ☎ 255-3559)* and **No 1 Travel** *(Map 3; ☎ 251-6970)*, both in the Kawaramachi and Kiyamachi area.

Books & Bookshops

The best bookshop in Kyoto is **Maruzen** *(Map 3; ☎ 241-2161; Kawaramachi-dōri; open 10am-8pm daily, closed 3rd Wed each month)*, between Sanjō-dōri and Shijō-dōri. It has a large selection of English-language books, magazines and maps as well as a limited number of French-, German- and Spanish-language books. It also carries a full range of Lonely Planet guides.

Exploring Kyoto, by long-term Kyoto resident Judith Clancy, is an excellent guide to exploring Kyoto on foot. It documents more than 25 walks and hikes through the city.

Old Kyoto: A Guide to Traditional Shops, Restaurants & Inns by Diane Durston, is a must for those in search of specific Kyoto handicrafts. It also has information on atmospheric old ryokan and restaurants.

For those anticipating a long stay in Kansai, John Ashburne's *The Best of Kansai* is a great introduction to the region's best restaurants, shops, bars and attractions.

Newspapers & Magazines

The free *Kyoto Visitor's Guide* is the best source of information about forthcoming events in Kyoto. In addition to listings of events, it has restaurant reviews, day walks, detailed maps of the city, useful information sections and feature articles about various aspects of the city. Try to pick up a copy as soon as you arrive in Kyoto. It's available at the TIC, Maruzen bookshop, Kyoto International Community House and most major hotels.

Another excellent source of information about Kyoto and the rest of the Kansai area is *Kansai Time Out*, a monthly English-language listings magazine. Apart from lively articles, it has a large section of ads for employment, travel agencies, meetings, lonely hearts etc. It's available at Maruzen bookshop and at the TIC.

Kansai Flea Market is a free monthly publication aimed at foreign residents. It has work and housing listings, as well as hugely entertaining personal ads.

Those with a literary bent might want to look out for the nonprofit *Kyoto Journal*, which publishes high-quality articles and artwork by Kyoto residents and others. *Kansai Flea Market* and *Kyoto Journal* are available from Maruzen bookshop.

Useful Organisations

The **Kyoto International Community House** *(KICH; Map 2; ☎ 752-3010; open 9am-9pm Tues-Sun, closed Tues if Mon is a national holiday)* is an essential stop for those planning a long-term stay in Kyoto, but it can also be quite useful for short-term visitors.

Here you can rent typewriters, send and receive faxes, and use the Internet (¥200 for 30 minutes). It has a library with maps, books, newspapers and magazines from around the world, and a notice board displaying messages regarding work, accommodation, rummage sales etc.

You can also make arrangements through KICH to meet a Japanese family at home. Let staff know at least one day – preferably two days – in advance.

Lastly, see the Activities section later for information on cultural demonstrations held at KICH.

KICH is in eastern Kyoto, about 500m west of Nanzen-ji. You can walk from Keihan Sanjō station in about 30 minutes.

Alternatively, take the Tōzai line subway from central Kyoto and get off at Keage station, from which it's a five-minute walk downhill.

Medical Services

Kyoto Holiday Emergency Clinic (☎ 811-5072) is actually spread over three different hospitals according to the type of complaint. If you require urgent attention, contact the clinic and they will direct you to the appropriate hospital.

For non-urgent medical attention, try the **Japan Baptist Hospital** (*Kyoto & Surrounds map;* ☎ *781-5191; open 8.30am-11am & 1pm-3.45pm Mon-Fri*), which usually has some English-speaking doctors on its staff; you can visit without an appointment. It's in northeastern Kyoto; to get there take bus No 3 from the intersection of Shijō and Kawaramachi streets (30 minutes), and get off at the Baptist Byōin-mae stop. It's a short walk up the hill.

The TIC has listings of additional hospitals, clinics and dentists with English-speaking doctors and can help you find one to meet your needs.

KYOTO STATION AREA 京都駅周辺

Although most of Kyoto's attractions are further north, there are a few attractions within walking distance of the station. And now that it's been redone, the station itself is something of an attraction.

Kyoto Station 京都駅

Kyoto's new station building is a striking steel and glass structure – a futuristic cathedral for the transportation age. Unveiled in September 1997, the building met with some decidedly mixed reviews. Some critics assailed it as out of keeping with the traditional architecture of Kyoto; others loved its wide-open spaces and dramatic lines.

Whatever the critics' views, you'll be impressed by the huge atrium that soars over the main concourse. Take some time to explore the many levels of the station, all the way up to the 15th-floor observation level. If you don't suffer from fear of heights, try riding the escalator from the 7th floor on the eastern side of the building up to the 11th-floor aerial skywalk high over the main concourse.

In the station building you'll find several **food courts** (see the Places to Eat section),

the **Kyoto Prefectural International Centre**, a **Joypolis game centre**, a performance space and **Isetan department store**.

Nishi Hongan-ji 西本願寺

In 1591, Toyotomi Hideyoshi built this temple (*Map 1; admission free; open 5.30am-5pm daily, slightly longer hours spring & summer*), known as Hongan-ji, as the new headquarters for the Jōdo Shin-shū (True Pure Land) school of Buddhism, which had accumulated immense power. Later, Tokugawa Ieyasu saw this power as a threat and sought to weaken it by encouraging a breakaway faction of this school to found Higashi Hongan-ji (*higashi* means 'east') in 1602. The original Hongan-ji then became known as Nishi Hongan-ji (*nishi* means 'west'). It now functions as the headquarters of the Hongan-ji branch of the Jōdo Shin-shū school, with over 10,000 temples and 12 million followers worldwide.

The temple contains five buildings, featuring some of the finest examples of architecture and artistic achievement from the Azuchi-Momoyama period (1568–1600). Unfortunately, the Goe-dō (Main Hall) is presently being restored and will be 'under wraps' until 2010. Nonetheless, it's worth a visit to see the Daisho-in Hall, which has sumptuous paintings, carvings and metal ornamentation. A small garden and two nō (classical Japanese dance-drama) stages are connected with the hall. The dazzling Karamon has intricate ornamental carvings. Both the Daisho-in Hall and the Kara-mon were transported here from Fushimi-jō.

If you'd like a guided tour of the temple (in Japanese only), reservations (preferably several days in advance) can be made either at the **temple office** (☎ 371-5181) or through the TIC. The temple is a 12-minute walk northwest of Kyoto station.

Higashi Hongan-ji 東本願寺

When Tokugawa Ieyasu engineered the rift in the Jōdo Shin-shū school of Buddhism, he founded this temple (*Map 1; admission free; open 5.50am-5.20pm daily, slightly longer hours spring & summer*) as competition for Nishi Hongan-ji. Rebuilt in 1895 after a fire, it's certainly monumental in its proportions, but it's less impressive artistically than its counterpart. A curious item on display is a length of rope made from hair donated by female believers, which was used to haul the timber for the reconstruction. The temple, which is a five-minute walk north of Kyoto station, is now the headquarters of the Ōtani branch of the Jōdo Shin-shū school of Buddhism.

Tō-ji 東寺

This temple *(Kyoto & Surrounds map; admission to grounds free, admission to Kondō & Treasure Hall ¥500; open 9am-4.30pm daily)* was established in 794 by imperial decree to protect the city. In 818, the emperor handed the temple over to Kūkai, the founder of the Shingon school of Buddhism. Many of the buildings were destroyed by fire or fighting during the 15th century; most of those that remain date from the 17th century.

The Kōdō (Lecture Hall) contains 21 images representing a Mikkyō (Esoteric Buddhism) mandala. The Kondō (Main Hall) contains statues depicting the Yakushi (Healing Buddha) trinity. In the southern part of the garden stands the five-storey pagoda, which burnt down five times, was rebuilt in 1643 and is now the highest pagoda in Japan, standing 57m high.

The **Kōbō-san market/fair** is held here on the 21st of each month. The fairs held in December and January are particularly lively.

Tō-ji is a 15-minute walk southwest of Kyoto station.

Umekōji Steam Locomotive Museum 梅小路蒸気機関車館

A hit with steam-train buffs and kids, this museum *(Kyoto & Surrounds map; adult/child ¥400/100; open 9.30am-5pm Tues-Sun)* features 18 vintage steam locomotives (dating from 1914 to 1948) and related displays. It's in the former Nijō station building, which was recently relocated here and carefully reconstructed. For an extra ¥200 (¥100 for children), you can take a 10-minute ride on one of the fabulous old trains (departures at 11am, 1.30pm and 3.30pm). From Kyoto station, take bus No 33, 205 or 208 to the Umekō-ji Kōen-mae stop (make sure you take a west-bound bus).

CENTRAL KYOTO 京都中央

Central Kyoto looks much like any other Japanese city, but there are a few major sights in the area, such as Kyoto Gosho, Nijō-jō and several museums.

Kyoto Gosho 京都御所

The original imperial palace (Map 1) was built in 794 and was replaced numerous times after destruction by fire. The present building, on a different site and smaller than the original, was constructed in 1855. Enthronement of a new emperor and other state ceremonies are still held there.

The Gosho does not rate highly in comparison with other attractions in Kyoto and you must apply for permission to visit (see the following section). However, you shouldn't miss the park surrounding the Gosho (see the Kyoto Imperial Palace Park entry opposite).

To get there, take the Karasuma line subway to Imadegawa or a bus to the Karasuma-Imadegawa stop and walk southeast.

Reservation & Admission Permission to visit the Gosho is granted by the Kunaichō, the **Imperial Household Agency** *(☎ 211-1215; open 8.45am-noon & 1pm-4pm Mon-Fri, closed national holidays),* which is inside the walled park surrounding the palace, a short walk from Imadegawa station on the Karasuma line. You have to fill out an application form and show your passport. Children can visit if accompanied by adults over 20 years of age (but are forbidden entry to the other three imperial properties of Katsura Rikyu, Sentō Gosho and Shūgaku-in Rikyu). Permission to tour the palace is usually granted the same day (try to arrive at the office at least 30 minutes before the start of the tour you'd like to join). Guided tours, sometimes in English, are given at 10am and 2pm from Monday to Friday. The tour lasts about 50 minutes.

The Imperial Household Agency is also the place to make advance reservations to see the Sentō Gosho, Katsura Rikyu and Shūgaku-in Rikyu. Application forms are also available from JNTO offices outside the country and JNTO-run TICs inside Japan.

Sentō Gosho 仙洞御所

This palace (Map 1) is a few hundred metres southeast of the main Kyoto Gosho. Visitors must obtain advance permission from the Imperial Household Agency and be over 20 years old (see the preceding section for details). Tours (in Japanese) start at 11am and 1.30pm. The gardens, which were laid out in 1630 by Kobori Enshū, are the main attraction.

Kyoto Imperial Palace Park
京都御苑

The Kyoto Gosho is surrounded by the spacious Kyoto Imperial Palace Park *(Map 1; admission free; open dawn-dusk daily)*, which is planted with a huge variety of flowering trees and open fields. It's perfect for picnics, strolls and just about any sport you can think of. Take some time to visit the pond at the park's southern end, which contains gorgeous carp. The park is most beautiful in the plum- and cherry-blossom seasons (March and April respectively). It is between Teramachi-dōri and Karasuma-dōri (to the east and west) and Imadegawa-dōri and Marutamachi-dōri (to the north and south).

Nijō-jō 二条城

This castle (Map 1) was built in 1603 as the official Kyoto residence of the first Tokugawa shōgun, Ieyasu. The ostentatious style of construction was intended as a demonstration of Ieyasu's prestige and to signal the demise of the emperor's power. As a safeguard against treachery, Ieyasu had the interior fitted with 'nightingale' floors (floors that sing and squeak at every move, making it difficult for intruders to move about quietly) and concealed chambers where bodyguards could keep watch.

After passing through the grand Kara-mon gate, you enter **Ninomaru Palace** *(admission palace & garden ¥600; open 8.45am-4pm daily, closed 26 Dec-4 Jan)*, which is divided into five buildings with numerous chambers. The Ohiroma Yon-no-Ma (Fourth Chamber) has spectacular screen paintings. Don't miss the excellent **Ninomaru Palace Garden**, which was designed by the tea master and landscape architect Kobori Enshū.

The neighbouring **Honmaru Palace** dates from the middle of the 19th century and is only open for special viewing in the autumn.

While you're in the neighbourhood, you might want to take a look at the garden, **Shinsen-en**, just south of the castle (it's outside the walls and therefore free). This forlorn garden, with its small shrines and pond, is all that remains of the original imperial palace, abandoned in 1227.

To reach the castle, take bus No 9 from Kyoto station to the Nijō-jō-mae stop. Alternatively, take the Tōzai line subway to the Nijō-jō-mae station.

Nijō Jinya 二条陣屋

A few minutes' walk south of Nijō-jō Nijō Jinya *(Map 1; admission ¥1000)* is one of Kyoto's hidden gems. Seldom seen by short-term visitors, it was built as a merchant's home in the mid-1600s and served as an inn for provincial feudal lords visiting the capital. What appears to be an average Edo-period mansion, however, is no ordinary dwelling.

The house contains fire-resistant earthen walls and a warren of 24 rooms that were ingeniously designed to protect the *daimyō* (domain lords) against possible surprise attacks. Here you'll find hidden staircases, secret passageways and a whole array of counter-espionage devices. The ceiling skylight of the main room is fitted with a trap door through which samurai could pounce on intruders, and sliding doors feature alternating panels of translucent paper to expose the shadows of eavesdroppers.

One-hour tours are conducted several times a day in Japanese and advance reservations must be made (ring ☎ 841-0972, Japanese only). Those who don't speak Japanese are asked to bring a Japanese-speaking guide.

Museum of Kyoto 京都文化博物館

Housed in and behind the former Bank of Japan, a classic brick Meiji-period building, this museum *(Map 3; ☎ 222-0888; admission ¥500, extra for special exhibits; open 10am-7.30pm daily, closed 3rd Wed each month)* is worth visiting if a special exhibit is on. The regular exhibits consist of models of ancient Kyoto, audiovisual presentations and a small gallery dedicated to Kyoto's film industry. On the 1st floor, the Roji Tempō is a reconstructed Edo-period merchant area showing 10 types of exterior lattice work (this section can be entered for free; some of the shops sell souvenirs and serve local dishes). The museum has English-speaking volunteer tour guides. The entrance is on Takakura-dōri, just north of Sanjō-dōri. The museum is a three-minute walk southeast of the Karasuma-Oike stop on the Karasuma and Tōzai subway lines.

Pontochō 先斗町

Pontochō-dōri (Map 3), a traditional nightlife district, is a narrow alley running between Sanjō-dōri and Shijō-dōri just west of Kamo-gawa. It's best visited in the evening,

KANSAI

MAP 1 – CENTRAL KYOTO

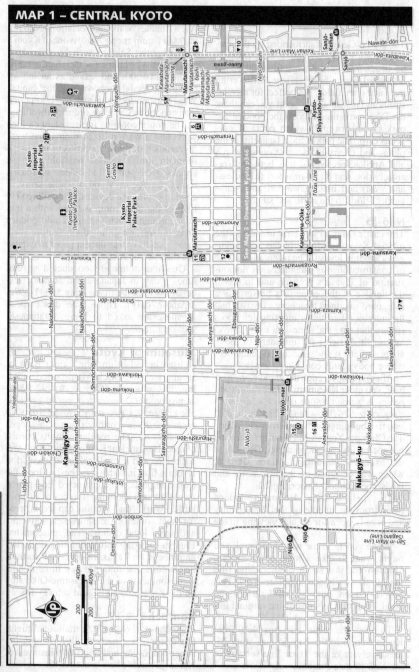

KANSAI

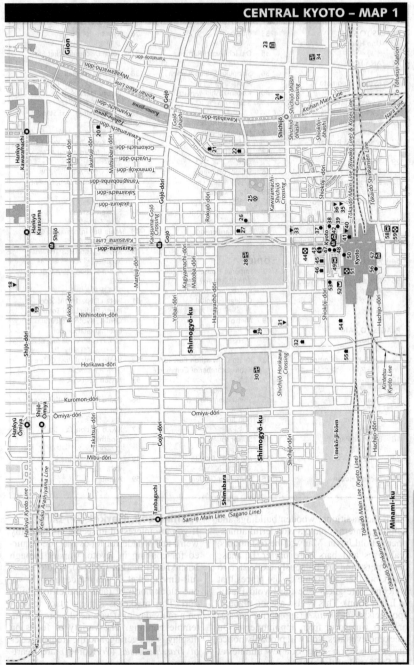

CENTRAL KYOTO – MAP 1

MAP 1 – CENTRAL KYOTO

PLACES TO STAY

7	Uno House 宇野ハウス
14	ANA Hotel 全日空ホテル
20	Ryokan Hinomoto 旅館ひのもと
21	Riverside Takase リバーサイド高瀬
22	Yuhara Ryokan ゆはら旅館
27	Matsubaya Ryokan 松葉屋旅館
29	Tour Club 旅倶楽部
32	Budget Inn Kyoto バジェットイン京都
41	Hotel Granvia Kyoto ホテルグランビア京都
45	Hotel New Hokke Kyoto ホテルニュー法華京都
46	Kyoto New Hankyū Hotel 京都新阪急ホテル
54	APA Hotel APAホテル
55	Rihga Royal Hotel Kyoto ; Kitchō リーガロイヤルホテル都 ; 吉兆

PLACES TO EAT

5	Shuhari シュハリ
8	Earth Kitchen Company アースキッチンカンパニー
10	Mikō-an 彌光庵
13	Obanzai おばんざい
17	Mukade-ya 百足屋
18	Bistro de Paris パリの食堂
24	Amazon アマゾン
31	Second House セカンドハウス
33	Iimura いいむら
35	Dai Ichi Asahi Rāmen 第一旭ラーメン
36	Shinpuku Saikan Ramen 新福菜館ラーメン
40	Kaiten-zushi Iwamaru 回転寿司岩丸

TEMPLES & SHRINES

2	Nashinoki-jinja 梨木神社
3	Rozan-ji 廬山寺
6	Shimogoryō-jinja 下御霊神社
28	Nishi Hongan-ji 西本願寺
30	Higashi Hongan-ji 東本願寺
34	Sanjūsangen-dō 三十三間堂

OTHER

1	Imperial Household Agency 宮内庁京都事務所
4	Kyoto Prefectural Medical College Hospital 京都府立医科大学付属病院
9	Metro メトロ
11	Meix メイックス
12	Kyoto Convention Bureau/ Kyoto Chamber of Commerce 京都コンベンションビューロ ー／京都商工会議所
15	Shinsen-en Garden 神泉苑
16	Nijō Jinya 二条陣屋
19	Shikunshi 四君子
23	Museum of Kyoto 京都文化博物館
25	Shōsei-en Garden 渉成園
26	Kyōsen-dō 京扇堂
37	Tōkai Discount Ticket Store トーカイ格安きっぷ売場
38	Renaissance Hall ルネッサンスホール
39	Paruru Plaza Kyoto ぱるるプラザ京都
42	Kyoto Station Taxi Stand (North) 京都駅前タクシーのりば（北）
43	TIC; Kyoto Tower; Kyoto Tower Hotel; International ATM 旅行案内所；京都タワー；京都 タワーホテル；国際ATM
44	Platz Kintetsu Department Store プラッツ近鉄百貨店
47	Sunken Garden サンクガーデン
48	Main Bus Information Center 総合バス案内所
49	Kyoto Station Bus Terminal 京都駅前バスターミナル
50	Kyoto Station Main Entrance/ Exit 京都駅烏丸中央口
51	Isetan Department Store; Kyoto Prefectural Tourism Center; Kyoto Prefectural International Center 伊勢丹百貨店；京都府観光セン ター；京都府国際センター
52	Kyoto Central Post Office 京都中央郵便局
53	Nissan Rent-A-Car 日産レンタカー
56	Kyoto Station South Entrance/ Exit 京都駅八条口
57	Kyoto Station Taxi Stand (South) 京都駅前タクシーのりば（南）
58	Airport Limousine Bus Stop 京都駅八条口アバンティ前バス亭
59	Avanti アバンティ

when the traditional wooden buildings and hanging lanterns create a wonderful atmosphere of old Japan. Many of the restaurants, teahouses and bars here prefer Japanese customers (and are hideously expensive to boot), but there are some casual places that welcome foreigners (see the Kyoto Places to Eat section). This is also a good place to spot geisha and *maiko* (apprentice geisha) on their way to or from appointments. On weekend evenings, you will probably notice one or two if you stand for a few minutes at the Shijō end of the alley.

Nishiki-kōji Market 錦小路市場

If you are interested in seeing all the really weird and wonderful foods that are required for cooking in Kyoto, wander through Nishiki-kōji market (Map 3), Kyoto's best full-time market. It's in the centre of town, one block north of (and parallel to) Shijō-dōri. This market is a great place to visit on a rainy day or if you need a break from temple hopping. The variety of foods on display is staggering, and the frequent cries of *Irasshiamase!* (Welcome!) are heartwarming.

KANSAI

EASTERN KYOTO 京都東部

The eastern part of Kyoto, notably the Higashiyama (Eastern Mountains) district, merits top priority for its fine temples, peaceful walks and traditional night entertainment in Gion.

Allocate at least a full day to cover the sights in the southern section, and another full day for the northern section. The JNTO leaflet, *Walking Tour Courses in Kyoto* covers the whole of eastern Kyoto (pick up a copy at the TIC).

Sanjūsangen-dō 三十三間堂

The original Sanjūsangen-dō *(Map 1; admission ¥600; open 8am-5pm daily 1 Apr-15 Nov, 9am-4pm daily 16 Nov-31 Mar)* was built in 1164 at the request of the retired emperor Go-shirakawa. The temple burnt to the ground in 1249 but a faithful copy was constructed in 1266.

The temple's name refers to the 33 *sanjūsan* (bays) between the pillars of this long, narrow building that houses 1001 statues of the 1000-armed Kannon (the Buddhist goddess of mercy). The largest Kannon is flanked on either side by 500 smaller Kannon images, neatly lined up in rows.

There are an awful lot of arms, but if you're picky and think the 1000-armed statues don't have the required number of limbs, then you should remember to calculate according to the nifty Buddhist mathematical formula that holds that 40 arms are the equivalent of 1000 arms, because each saves 25 worlds. Visitors also seem keen to spot resemblances between friends or family members and any of the hundreds of images.

At the back of the hall are 28 guardian statues in a great variety of expressive poses. The gallery on the western side of the hall is famous for the annual **Tōshi-ya Matsuri**, held on 15 January, during which archers shoot arrows the length of the hall. The ceremony dates back to the Edo period, when an annual contest was held to see how many arrows could be shot from the southern end to the northern end in 24 hours. The all-time record was set in 1686, when an archer successfully landed over 8000 arrows at the northern end.

The temple is a 1.5km east of Kyoto station; alternatively, take bus No 206 or 208 and get off at the Sanjūsangen-dō-mae stop.

It's also very close to Keihan Shichijō station. From the station, walk north on Karasuma-dōri, then turn right onto Shichijō-dōri and walk east; the temple is on the right.

Kyoto National Museum 京都国立博物館

The Kyoto National Museum *(Map 1; admission ¥420, extra for special exhibitions; open 9am-4pm Tues-Sun)* is housed in two buildings opposite Sanjūsangen-dō. There are excellent displays of fine arts, historical artefacts and handicrafts. The fine arts collection is especially highly regarded, containing some 230 items that have been classified as National Treasures or Important Cultural Properties.

Kawai Kanjirō Memorial Hall 河井寛次郎博物館

This museum *(Map 2; admission ¥900; open 10am-4.30pm Tues-Sun, closed 10-20 Aug & 24 Dec-7 Jan)* was once the home and workshop of one of Japan's most famous potters, Kawai Kanjirō. The house is built in rural style and contains examples of his work, his collection of folk art and ceramics, and his kiln.

The hall is a 10-minute walk north of the Kyoto National Museum. Alternatively, take bus No 206 or 207 from Kyoto station and get off at the Umamachi stop.

Kiyomizu-dera 清水寺

This temple *(Map 2; admission to main hall ¥300, other areas free; open 6am-6pm daily)*, was first built in 798, but the present buildings are reconstructions dating from 1633. As an affiliate of the Hossō school of Buddhism, which originated in Nara, it has successfully survived the many intrigues of local Kyoto schools of Buddhism through the centuries and is now one of the most famous landmarks of the city. This, unfortunately, makes it a prime target for busloads of Japanese tourists, particularly during cherry-blossom season. Some travellers are also put off by the rather mercantile air of the temple – endless stalls sell good-luck charms, fortunes and all manner of souvenirs.

The main hall has a huge veranda that is supported by hundreds of pillars and juts out over the hillside. Just below this hall is the waterfall, **Otawa-no-taki**, where

MAP 2 – EASTERN KYOTO

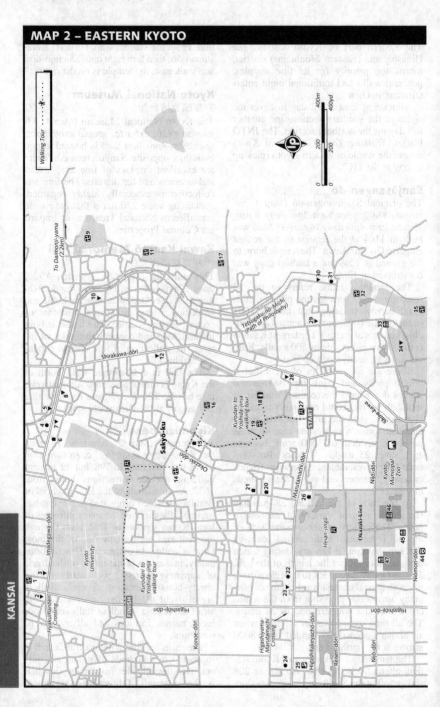

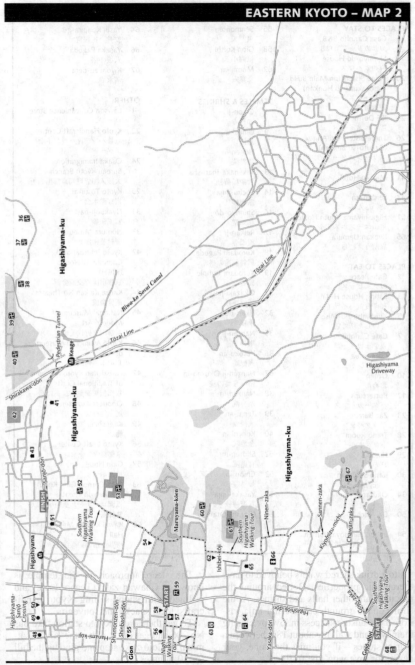

EASTERN KYOTO – MAP 2

KANSAI

MAP 2 – EASTERN KYOTO

PLACES TO STAY

6 Casa Carinho B&B
カサカリーニョB&B
15 Shinnyo-dō House
真如堂ハウス
20 Three Sisters Inn Main Building (Rakutō-sō Honkan)
スリーシスターズイン洛東荘本館
21 ISE Dorm
アイエスイードーム
26 Three Sisters Inn Annex (Rakutō-sō Bekkan)
スリーシスターズイン洛東荘別館
41 Miyako Hotel
都ホテル
43 Seishin-an
せいしん庵
51 Higashiyama Youth Hostel
東山ユースホステル
65 Ryokan Uemura
旅館うえむら

PLACES TO EAT

2 Café Peace
カフェピース
3 Eating House Hi-Lite
和洋食堂ハイライト
5 Kuishinbō-no-Mise
くいしん坊の店
7 Café Carinho
カフェカリーニョ
8 Gargantua
ガルガンチュア
10 Omen
おめん
12 Buttercups
バターカップス
23 Zac Baran
ザックバラン
28 Tranq Room
トランクルーム
29 Hinode
日の出
30 Kanō Shōju-an
叶匠寿庵
34 Okutan
奥丹
50 Dai-kitchi
大吉
54 Imobō Hiranoya Honten
いもぼう平野屋本店

55 Senmonten
泉門天
58 Gion Koishi
祇園小石
62 Momiji-an
紅葉庵

TEMPLES & SHRINES

1 Chion-ji
知恩寺
9 Ginkaku-ji
銀閣寺
11 Hōnen-in
法然院
13 Takenaka-Inari-sha
竹中稲荷社
14 Sōchu-jinja
宗忠神社
16 Shinnyo-dō
真如堂
17 Reikan-ji
霊鑑寺
18 Kurodani Pagoda
黒谷五重の搭
19 Kurodani Temple
黒谷
27 Okazaki-jinja
岡崎神社
32 Eikan-dō
永観堂
35 Nanzen-ji
南禅寺
36 Kōtoku-an
高徳庵
37 Nanzen-ji Oku-no-in
南禅寺奥の院
38 Nanzen-in
南禅院
39 Tenju-an
天授庵
40 Konchi-in
金地院
52 Shōren-in
青蓮院
53 Chion-in
知恩院
59 Yasaka-jinja
八坂神社
60 Higashi-Ōtani
東大谷
61 Kōdai-ji
高台寺

64 Yasui Konpira-gū
安井金比羅宮
66 Yasaka Pagoda
八坂の搭
67 Kiyomizu-dera
清水寺

OTHER

4 Lawson Convenience Store
ローソン
22 Kyoto Handicraft Centre
京都ハンディクラフトセンター
24 Osaka Immigration Bureau Kyoto Branch
大阪入国管理局京都出張所
25 Kyoto Tōsuikai
京都踏水会
31 Nyakuōji-bashi
若王子橋
33 Nomura Museum
野村美術館
42 Kyoto International Community House (KICH)
京都市国際交流会館
44 Kanze Kaikan Nō Theatre
観世会館
45 National Museum of Modern Art
京都国立近代美術館
46 Kyoto Municipal Museum of Art
京都市美術館
47 Fureai-Kan Kyoto Museum of Traditional Crafts
京都伝統産業ふれあい館
48 Onouechikuzaiten
尾上竹材店
49 Kagoshin
籠新
56 Kyoto Craft Center
京都クラフトセンター
57 Gion Hotel
祇園ホテル
63 Gion Corner; Gion Kōbu Kaburen-Jō Theatre
祇園コーナー；祇園甲部歌舞練場
68 Kawai Kanjirō Memorial Hall
河井寛次郎記念館

KANSAI

visitors drink sacred waters believed to have therapeutic properties. Dotted around the precincts are other halls and shrines. At the shrine on the grounds called Jishu-jinja, visitors try to ensure success in love by closing their eyes and walking about 18m between a pair of stones – if you miss the stone, your desire for love won't be fulfilled!

The steep approach to the temple is known as Chawan-zaka (Teapot Lane) and is lined with shops selling Kyoto handicrafts, local snacks and souvenirs.

To get there from Kyoto station take bus No 206 and get off at either the Kiyōmizu-michi or Gojō-zaka stop and plod up the hill for 10 minutes.

Southern Higashiyama Walking Tour (Map 2)

Time Half a day to a full day
Distance About 5km
Major Sights Kiyomizu-dera, Kōdai-ji, Yasaka-jinja

One of the most enjoyable strolls around the back streets and temples of Kyoto follows a winding route between Kiyomizu-dera and Maruyama-kōen (see the Eastern Kyoto map in this chapter or, for more details, the TIC's *Walking Tour Courses in Kyoto*).

The walk begins near the Gojō-zaka slope. Start your walk after a look at the pottery shops on the slope near the northwestern corner of the intersection of Gojō-dōri and Higashiōji-dōri. Cross Higashiōji and head east (uphill) until you reach the first fork in the road; bear right and continue up to **Kiyomizu-dera**. When you reach the top, the temple entrance will be on your left. Take a short detour uphill to the right for an amazing view of the neighbouring cemetery before heading towards the temple.

After touring Kiyomizu-dera, exit down **Kiyomizu-michi**, a steep approach road to the temple. After walking about 200m, you'll see a small street on your right down a flight of steps. This is **Sannen-zaka**, lined with old wooden houses and traditional shops and restaurants. There are also pleasant teahouses with gardens. It's a good place to relax over a bowl of steaming noodles.

Halfway down Sannen-zaka, the road bears sharp left. Follow it a short distance, then turn right and walk down a flight of steps into **Ninen-zaka**, a street lined with historic houses, shops and tea-houses. At the end of Ninen-zaka, zigzag left then right and continue north for five minutes to reach the entrance of **Kōdai-ji**, on the right up a long flight of stairs. Just before this entrance you can detour into **Ishibei-kōji** on your left – perhaps the most beautiful street in Kyoto, though it's actually a cobbled alley which is lined on both sides with elegant, traditional Japanese inns and restaurants.

Exit Kōdai-ji the way you came and walk to the 'T' in the road; turn right here and zigzag right and left into **Maruyama-kōen** (Map 2), a pleasant spot to take a rest. From the park, head west into the grounds of **Yasaka-jinja**. From here you can exit west to Shijō-dōri, or head back through the park and north towards **Chion-in** and **Shōren-in**. From either temple it's about a 10-minute walk back to the bright lights of Shijō-dōri.

Kōdai-ji 高台寺

Kōdai-ji *(admission ¥600; open 9am-4.30pm daily)* was founded in 1605 by Kita-no-Mandokoro in memory of her late husband, Toyotomi Hideyoshi. The extensive grounds include gardens designed by the famed landscape architect Kobori Enshū, and teahouses designed by the renowned master of the tea ceremony Sen-no-Rikyū.

The temple is a 10-minute walk north of Kiyomizu-dera (see the preceding section). Check at the TIC for the scheduling of summer and fall night-time illuminations of the temple (when the gardens are lit by multicoloured spotlights).

Maruyama-kōen 円山公園

This park is a great place to escape the bustle of the city centre and amble around gardens, ponds, souvenir shops and restaurants. Peaceful paths meander through the trees and carp glide through the waters of a small pond in the centre of the park.

For two weeks in early April, when the park's many cherry trees come into bloom, the calm atmosphere of the park is shattered by hordes of revellers enjoying *hanami* (blossom viewing). The centrepiece is a massive *shidarezakura*, a weeping cherry tree – truly one of the most beautiful sights in Kyoto, particularly when lit from below at night. For those who don't mind crowds, this is a good place to observe the Japanese at their most uninhibited. It is best to arrive early and claim a good spot high on the eastern side of the park, from which point you can safely peer down on the mayhem below.

The park is a five-minute walk east of the Shijō-Higashiōji intersection. To get there from Kyoto station, take bus No 206 and get off at the Gion stop.

Yasaka-jinja 八坂神社

This colourful shrine (Map 2) is just down the hill from Maruyama-kōen. It's considered the guardian shrine of neighbouring Gion and is

KANSAI

sometimes endearingly referred to as 'Gion-san'. This shrine is particularly popular as a spot for *hatsu-mōde* (the first shrine visit of the new year). If you don't mind a stampede, come here around midnight on New Year's Eve or over the next few days. Surviving the crush is proof that you're blessed by the gods! Yasaka-jinja also sponsors Kyoto's biggest festival, Gion Matsuri (see Special Events later in this chapter).

Gion 祇園周辺

Gion is a famous entertainment and geisha district on the eastern bank of Kamo-gawa. Modern architecture, congested traffic and contemporary nightlife establishments rob the area of some of its historical beauty, but there are still some lovely places left for a stroll. Gion falls roughly between Sanjō-dōri and Gojō-dōri (north and south, respectively) and Higashiyama-dōri and Kawabata-dōri (east and west, respectively).

Hanami-kōji is a street running north to south that bisects Shijō-dōri. The southern section is lined with 17th-century trad-itional restaurants and teahouses, many of which are exclusive establishments for geisha entertainment. If you wander around here in the late afternoon or early evening, you can often glimpse geisha or *maiko* on their way to or from appointments.

If you walk north from Shijō-dōri along Hanami-kōji, the fourth intersection you will come to is **Shinmonzen-dōri**. Wander in either direction along this street, which is packed with old houses, art galleries and shops specialising in antiques. Don't expect flea-market prices.

For more historic buildings in a waterside setting, wander down **Shirakawa Minami-dōri**, which is parallel with, and a block south of, the western section of Shinmonzen-dōri. This is one of Kyoto's most beautiful streets, especially in the evening.

Chion-in 知恩院

Chion-in *(Map 2; admission to main hall ¥400, other areas free; open 9am-4.30pm daily Mar-Nov, to 4pm daily Dec-Feb)* was built in 1234 on the site where a famous

---

The Living Art of the Geisha

Behind the closed doors of the exclusive teahouses and restaurants that dot the back streets of Kyoto, women of exquisite grace and refinement entertain gentlemen of considerable means. Patrons may pay more than $3000 to spend an evening in the company of two or three geisha – kimono-clad women versed in an range of visual and performing arts, including playing the three-stringed *shamisen*, singing old teahouse ballads and dancing.

An evening in a Gion teahouse begins with an exquisite *kaiseki* dinner. While their customers eat, the geisha or *maiko* (apprentice geisha) enter the room and introduce themselves in Kyoto dialect.

A *shamisen* performance, followed by a traditional fan dance, is often given, and all the while the geisha and *maiko* pour drinks, light cigarettes and engage in charming banter.

It is virtually impossible to enter a Gion teahouse and witness a geisha performance without the introduction of an established patron. With the exception of public performances at annual festivals or dance presentations, they perform only for select customers. While geisha are not prostitutes, those who decide to open their own teahouses once they retire at 50 or so may receive financial backing from well-to-do clients.

Knowledgeable sources estimate that there are perhaps 80 *maiko* and just over 100 geisha in Kyoto. Although their numbers are ever-decreasing, geisha (*geiko* in the Kyoto dialect) and *maiko* can still be seen in some parts of Kyoto, especially after dusk in the back streets between the Kamo-gawa and Yasaka-jinja and along the narrow Pontochō alley. Geisha and *maiko* can also be found in other parts of the country, most notably Tokyo. However, it is thought that there are less than 1000 geisha and *maiko* remaining in all Japan.

The best way to get a feel for the world of *geiko* and *maiko* is the take a walking lecture with **Peter MacIntosh** (☎ 090-5169-1654; **W** www.kyotosightsandnights.com). Morning and evening tours (¥4000 and ¥3000, respectively) take in the major Kyoto geisha district and chances of spotting geisha are high. Peter can also arrange an evening with a geisha for those interested.

Kurodani to Yoshida-jinja Walk (Map 2)

Time Two to three hours
Distance About 4km
Major Sights Kurodani temple, Shinnyo-dō temple, Yoshida-jinja

This fine walk (see the Eastern Kyoto map) is a good way to escape the crowds that flock to the northern Higashiyama area's better-known sights. You might try doing it in the late afternoon or evening, but time it so that you don't get stuck here after dark, as the cemeteries around here can be distinctly spooky once the sun goes down.

The walk starts a few metres west of Okazaki-jinja (look for a narrow alley on the west side of the shrine). Walk up the alley, climb the steps and continue straight on for 75m to the base of the Kurodani cemetery. Climb to the pagoda at the top of the steps for a good view over Kyoto.

Return to the bottom of the steps, cross the stone bridge, turn right and walk up the steps to the main precinct of **Kurodani temple**. If you look south from the wide-open plaza in front of the main hall of the temple, you will see the impressive San-mon, or main gate, of the temple.

Facing the main hall, turn left and then quickly right and walk out of the grounds of Kurodani, passing a statue of the seated Buddha. Further along, you pass another cemetery on the right, and several subtemples. Continue straight ahead for about 200m, go through a wooden gate and continue on for another 100m to the entrance to **Shinnyo-dō** on your right. After exploring this temple, retrace your steps and walk west to a stone torii at the base of a hill. Climb the steps here to **Muretada-jinja**. Next, walk straight ahead through another stone torii and ascend through a procession of orange torii to **Takenaka-Inari-sha**, a small shrine near the top of Yoshida-yama.

From here, take the steps that lead west over the crest of the hill. Descend through a small park down to the left. Take the first trail down the hill on the right, bearing west (downhill). A few zigzags down the fall line bring you to the back of **Yoshida-jinja**. After exploring the shrine, you can descend its main stone steps to the west and walk out to Higashioji-dōri, where you can catch buses to all parts of Kyoto.

priest by the name of Hōnen had taught and eventually fasted to death. Today it is still the headquarters of the Jōdo school of Buddhism, which was founded by Hōnen, and a hive of activity. For visitors with a taste for the grand, this temple is sure to satisfy.

The oldest of the present buildings date back to the 17th century. The two-storey San-mon, a Buddhist temple gate at the main entrance, is the largest temple gate in Japan and prepares you for the massive scale of the temple. The immense main hall contains an image of Hōnen. It's connected to another hall, the Dai Hōjō, by a 'nightingale' floor. The massive scale of the buildings reflects the popularity of the Jōdo school, which holds that earnest faith in the Buddha is all you need to achieve salvation.

After visiting the main hall, with its gold altar, you can walk around the back of the same building to see the temple's gardens. On the way, you pass a darkened hall with a small statue of Amida Buddha on display, glowing in the darkness. It makes a nice contrast to the splendour of the main hall.

The giant bell, cast in 1633 and weighing 74 tonnes, is the largest in Japan. The combined muscle-power of 17 monks is needed to make the bell ring for the famous ceremony that heralds the new year.

The temple is close to the northeastern corner of Maruyama-kōen. From Kyoto station take bus No 206 and get off at the Chion-in-mae stop or walk up (east) from the Keihan Sanjō or Shijō station.

Shōren-in 青蓮院

Shōren-in *(Map 2; admission ¥400; open 9am-4.30pm daily)* is hard to miss, with the giant camphor trees growing just outside its walls. This temple was originally the residence of the chief abbot of the Tendai school of Buddhism. The present building dates from 1895, but the main hall has sliding screens with paintings from the 16th and 17th centuries. Often overlooked by the crowds that descend on other Higashiyama temples, this is a pleasant place to sit and think while gazing out over the beautiful gardens.

KANSAI

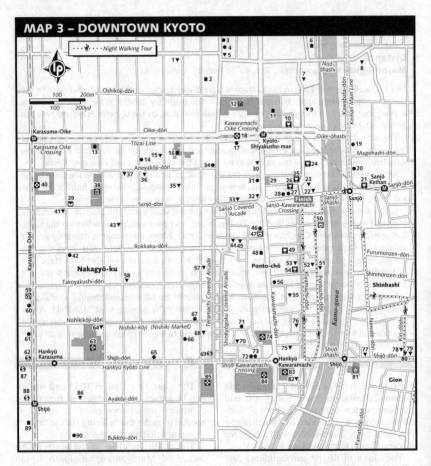

MAP 3 – DOWNTOWN KYOTO

The temple is a five-minute walk north of Chion-in (see the Chion-in section for transport details).

National Museum of Modern Art
国立近代美術館

This museum (*Map 2; admission ¥420, more for special exhibits; open 9.30am-5pm Tues-Sun*) is renowned for its collection of contemporary Japanese ceramics and paintings. Exhibits are changed on a regular basis (check with the TIC or *Kansai Time Out* for details).

Fureai-Kan Kyoto Museum of Traditional Crafts 伝統産業会館

While you're in the Heian-jingū area (see the Heian-jingū section following), you could check out some of its interesting displays of traditional Kyoto crafts. Exhibits include woodblock prints, lacquerware, bamboo goods and gold-leaf work.

Heian-jingū 平安神宮

Heian-jingū (*Map 2; admission to shrine free, garden ¥600; open 8.30am-5.30pm daily 15 Mar-31 Aug, to 4.30pm daily other times*) was built in 1895 to commemorate the 1100th anniversary of the founding of Kyoto. The buildings are colourful replicas, reduced to two-thirds of the size of the Kyoto Gosho of the Heian period.

The spacious garden, with its large pond and Chinese-inspired bridge, is also meant to represent the kind of garden that was popular in the Heian period. About 500m

DOWNTOWN KYOTO – MAP 3

PLACES TO STAY
2 Hiiragiya Ryokan Annex
柊屋旅館別館
6 Hotel Fujita Kyoto
ホテルフジタ京都
11 Kyoto Hotel
京都ホテル
13 Hotel Gimmond
ホテルギンモンド
16 Hiiragiya Ryokan
柊屋旅館
48 Sun Hotel Kyoto
サンホテル京都
89 Karasuma Kyoto Hotel
からすま京都ホテル

PLACES TO EAT
1 Shin-shin-tei
新進亭
5 Le Bouchon
ルブシュン
7 Ganko Nijō-en
がんこ二条苑
8 Chabana
ちゃばな
9 Merry Island Cafe
メリーアイランド
15 Yoshikawa
吉川
22 Ganko Zushi
がんこ寿司
23 Morita-ya
モリタ屋
30 Kerala
ケララ
32 Musashi Sushi
むさし寿司
33 Tagoto Honten
田毎本店
35 Misoka-an Kawamichi-ya
晦庵河道屋
36 Café Kocsi
カフェコチ
37 Kōsendō-sumi
光泉洞寿み
41 Biotei
びお亭
43 Inoda Coffee
イノダコーヒー
44 Uontana
魚棚
45 Kane-yo
かねよ
51 Uzuki
うずき
52 Zu Zu
厨厨
53 Hati Hati
八チ八チ
55 Zappa
ザッパ
57 Device Café
ディバイスカフェ
58 Tōsai
豆菜

64 Daniel's
ダニエルズ
68 Yak & Yeti
ヤック＆イェティ
70 Tomi-zushi
とみ寿司
75 Shirukō
志る幸
76 The 844 Store Café
八四四
77 Yagura
やぐ羅
78 Gonbei
権兵衛
79 Kagizen Yoshifusa
鍵善良房
80 Ōharameya
大原女屋
82 Takasebune
高瀬船
86 Uosue
うをすえ

OTHER
3 Ippō-dō
一保堂
4 Kakimoto Washi
紙司柿本
10 Horiuchi Color
堀内カラー
12 Kyoto City Hall
京都市役所
14 Zest Underground Shopping
Mall; Kinokuniya
ゼスト御池；紀伊国屋
17 ANA Office
全日空
18 The Hill of Tara
ザヒルオヴタラ
19 Kitazawa Bicycle Shop
キタザワサイクル
20 Rental Cycle Yasumoto
バイクプール安本
21 Pig & Whistle
ピッグ＆ホイッスル
24 Teddy's; Ace Café
テディーズ；エースカフェ
25 Katsuryoku-ya
活力屋
26 Backgammon
バックギャモン
27 H.I.S. Travel Agency
エイチアイエス旅行会社
28 Meiji-ya
明治屋
29 Asahi Kaikan; Asahi
Cinema; Kōjitsu
朝日会館；朝日シネマ；
コージツ
31 Medic
メディック
34 Kyōkyu-dō
鳩居堂
38 Museum of Kyoto
京都文化博物館

39 Nakagyō Post Office
中京郵便局
40 Shinpukan
新風館
42 A'cross Travellers' Bureau
アクロストラベラーズビュ
ーロー
46 Book 1st
ブックファスト
47 Sukara-za Theatre
スカラ座
49 Sama Sama
サマサマ
50 Pontochō Kaburen-jō
Theatre
先斗町歌舞練場
54 Ing ; Dua Orang
イング ；ヅアオラン
56 Maruzen
丸善
59 Kinko's
キンコーズ
60 Japan Foundation Kyoto
Office
国際交流基金京都支部
61 Nippō Rent-a-Car
日邦レンタカー
62 UFJ Bank
UFJ銀行
63 Daimaru Department
Store
大丸百貨店
65 Tanakaya
田中彌
66 Kodak Imagica
コダックイマジカ
67 Aritsugi
有次
69 All Card Plaza
オールカードプラザ
71 No 1 Travel
ナンバーワントラベル
72 Discount Ticket Shop
格安きっぷ売り場
73 Erizen
ゑり善
74 OPA
オーパ
81 Minami-za Theatre
南座
83 Hankyū Department Store
阪急百貨店
84 Takashimaya Department
Store
高島屋百貨店
85 Fujii Daimaru Department
Store
藤井大丸百貨店
87 Citibank
シティバンク
88 Tokyo Mitsubishi Bank
東京三菱銀行
90 Morita Washi
森田和紙

KANSAI

in front of the shrine there is a massive steel torii (Shintō shrine entrance gate). Although it appears to be entirely separate from the shrine, this is actually considered the main entrance to the shrine itself.

Two major events are held here: **Jidai Matsuri** (Festival of the Ages), on 22 October, and **Takigi Nō**, from 1 to 2 June. Jidai Matsuri is described later in the Special Events section, while details for Takigi Nō are under Traditional Dance Theatre & Music in the Entertainment section.

Take bus No 5 from Kyoto station or Keihan Sanjō station and get off at the Kyoto Kaikan Bijutsu-kan-mae stop and walk north, or walk up from Keihan Sanjō station (15 minutes).

Nanzen-ji 南禅寺

This is one of the most pleasant temples in all Kyoto, with its expansive grounds and numerous subtemples *(Map 2; admission to most areas free, admission to inner buildings & garden ¥500, to San-mon ¥300; open 8.40am-4.30pm daily)*. It began as a retirement villa for Emperor Kameyama but was dedicated as a Zen temple on his death in 1291. Civil war in the 15th century destroyed most of the temple; the present buildings date from the 17th century. It operates now as headquarters for the Rinzai school of Zen.

At its entrance stands the massive San-mon. Steps lead up to the 2nd storey, which has a fine view over the city. Beyond the gate is the Hōjō, a hall with impressive screens painted with a vivid depiction of tigers.

Within the precincts of the same building, the **Leaping Tiger Garden** is a classic Zen garden well worth a look. While you're in the Hōjō, you can enjoy a cup of tea while sitting on tatami (tightly woven matting) and gazing at a small waterfall (¥400, ask at the reception desk of the Hōjō).

Perhaps the best part of Nanzen-ji is overlooked by most visitors: **Oku-no-in**, a small shrine/temple hidden in a forested hollow behind the main precinct. To get there, walk up to the red brick aqueduct in front of the subtemple of Nanzen-in. Follow the road that runs parallel to the aqueduct up into the hills, past several brightly coloured torii until you reach a waterfall in a beautiful mountain glen. Here, pilgrims pray while standing under the waterfall, sometimes in the dead of winter. Hiking trails

lead off in all directions from this point; by heading due north, you'll eventually arrive at the top of Daimon-ji-yama (two hours), and by going east you'll eventually get to Yamashina (also about two hours).

Most of the grounds can be explored free of charge. From JR Kyoto or Keihan Sanjō station, take bus No 5 and get off at the Nanzen-ji Eikan-dō-michi stop. You can also take the Tōzai line subway from the city centre to Keage and walk for five minutes downhill.

Dotted around the grounds of Nanzen-ji are several subtemples that are often skipped by the crowds and consequently easier to enjoy.

Nanzen-in This subtemple *(Map 2; admission ¥350; open 8.40am-4.30pm daily)* is on your right if you are facing the Hōjō – follow the path under the aqueduct. It has an attractive garden designed around a heart-shaped pond. This garden is best in the morning or around noon, when sunlight shines directly into the pond, illuminating the colourful carp.

Tenju-an This temple *(Map 2; admission ¥300; open 8.40am-4.30pm daily)* stands at the side of the San-mon, a four-minute walk west of Nanzen-in. Constructed in 1337, the temple has a splendid garden and a great collection of carp in its pond.

Konchi-in When leaving Tenju-an, turn left and continue for 100m – Konchi-in *(Map 2; admission ¥400; open 8.30am-5pm daily Mar-Nov, to 4.30pm daily Dec-Feb)* is down a small side street on the left. The stylish gardens fashioned by the master landscape designer Kobori Enshū are the main attraction.

Nomura Museum 野村美術館

The Nomura Museum *(Map 2; admission ¥700; open 10am-4.30pm Tues-Sun)* is a 10-minute walk north of Nanzen-ji. Exhibits include scrolls, paintings, tea-ceremony implements and ceramics that were bequeathed by the wealthy business magnate Tokushiki Nomura.

Eikan-dō 永観堂

Eikan-dō *(Map 2; admission ¥600; open 9am-4pm daily)*, also known as Zenrin-ji, is made interesting by its varied architecture, gardens and works of art. It was founded in 855 by the priest Shinshō, but the name was changed to Eikan-dō in the 11th century to honour the philanthropic priest Eikan.

The best way to appreciate this temple is to follow the arrows and wander slowly along the covered walkways connecting the halls and gardens.

In the Amida-dō Hall, at the southern end of the complex, is the statue of Mikaeri Amida (Buddha Glancing Backwards).

From the Amida-dō Hall, head north to the end of the covered walkway. Change into the sandals provided, then climb the steep steps up the mountainside to the Taho-tō (Taho Pagoda), where there's a fine view across the city.

Tetsugaku-no-Michi (Path of Philosophy) 哲学の道

The Tetsugaku-no-Michi has long been a favourite with contemplative strollers who follow the traffic-free route beside a canal lined with cherry trees that are spectacular when in bloom. It only takes 30 minutes to complete the walk, which starts just north of Eikan-dō and ends at Ginkaku-ji. During the day, be prepared for crowds of tourists; a night stroll will definitely be quieter.

A map of the walk is part of the *Walking Tour Courses in Kyoto* leaflet, available at the TIC.

Hōnen-in 法然院

This fine temple *(Map 2; admission to grounds free; open 7am-4pm daily)* was established in 1680 to honour Hōnen, the charismatic founder of the Jōdo school. This is a lovely, secluded temple with carefully raked gardens set back in the woods. Be sure to visit in early April for the cherry blossoms and early November for the maple leaves, when the main hall is opened for a special viewing.

The temple is a 12-minute walk from Ginkaku-ji (see the following section), on a side street just east of Tetsugaku-no-Michi. Look for the sign, then cross the bridge over the canal and follow the road uphill through the bamboo groves.

Ginkaku-ji 銀閣寺

Ginkaku-ji *(Map 2; admission ¥500; open 8.30am-5pm daily 15 Mar-30 Nov, 9am-4.30pm daily other times)* is definitely worth a visit, but be warned that bus loads of visitors often jam the narrow pathways.

In 1482, Shōgun Ashikaga Yoshimasa constructed a villa here as a genteel retreat from the turmoil of civil war. The villa's name translates as 'Silver Pavilion', but the shōgun's ambition to cover the building with silver was never realised. After Yoshimasa's death, the villa was converted into a temple.

You approach the main gate between tall hedges, before turning sharply into the extensive grounds. Walkways lead through the

---

Daimonji-yama Climb

Time Two hours
Distance 5km
Major Sights Ginkaku-ji, Daimonji Yaki site

Located directly behind Ginkaku-ji, Daimonji-yama is the main site of the Daimonji Yaki fire festival. From almost anywhere in town the Chinese character for *dai* (great) is visible in the middle of a bare patch on the face of this mountain. On 16 August, this character is set ablaze to guide the spirits of the dead on their journey home. The view of Kyoto from the top is unparalleled.

Take bus No 5 to the Ginkaku-ji michi stop and walk up to Ginkaku-ji. Here, you have the option of visiting the temple or starting the hike immediately. To find the trailhead, turn left in front of the temple and head north for about 50m towards a stone torii (shrine gate). Just before the torii, turn right up the hill.

The trail – a broad avenue through the trees – proper starts just after a small car park on the right. A few minutes of walking brings you to a red banner hanging over the trail (warning of forest fires). Soon after this you must cross a bridge to the right then continue up a smaller, switchback trail. When the trail reaches a saddle not far from the top, go to the left. You climb a long flight of steps before coming out at the top of the bald patch. The sunset from here is great, but bring a torch.

gardens, which include meticulously raked cones of white sand (probably symbolic of a mountain and a lake), tall pines and a pond in front of the temple. A path also leads up the mountainside through the trees.

From JR Kyoto or Keihan Sanjō station, take bus No 5 and get off at the Ginkaku-ji-michi stop. From Demachiyanagi station or Shijō station, take bus No 203 to the same stop.

NORTHWESTERN KYOTO
京都北西部

The northwestern part of Kyoto is predominantly residential, but there are several superb temples with tranquil gardens in secluded precincts. For Zen fans, a visit to Daitoku-ji and Ryōan-ji is recommended. Kinkaku-ji is another major attraction. JNTO's *Walking Tour Courses in Kyoto* leaflet also covers this area, but most of the walk is along unremarkable city streets.

Those who have the time and inclination to escape the tourist trail might also consider a visit to the Takao District.

Daitoku-ji 大徳寺

The precincts of this temple (Kyoto & Surrounds map), which belongs to the Rinzai school of Zen, contain an extensive complex of 24 subtemples, of which two are mentioned in following sections; eight are open to the public. If you want to examine Zen culture intensively, this is the place to visit.

Daitoku-ji itself is on the eastern side of the grounds. It was founded in 1319, burnt down in the next century and rebuilt in the 16th century. The San-mon contains an image of the famous tea master, Sen-no-Rikyū, on the 2nd storey.

According to some historical sources, Toyotomi Hideyoshi was so enraged when he discovered he had been demeaning himself by walking *under* Rikyū that he forced the master to commit seppuku (ritual suicide) in 1591.

Two subtemples particularly worth a visit are **Daisen-in**, for its two famous (if small) gardens, and **Kōtō-in** for its lovely maples in autumn.

Admission charges to the various subtemples vary but are usually around ¥400. Those temples that accept visitors are usually open from 9am to 4.30pm daily. The temple bus stop is Daitoku-ji-mae and

convenient buses from Kyoto station are Nos 205 and 206. Daitoku-ji is also a short walk west of Kitaō-ji subway station on the Karasuma line.

Kinkaku-ji 金閣寺

Kinkaku-ji, the famed Golden Temple, is one of Japan's best-known sights *(Kyoto & Surrounds map; admission ¥400; open 9am-5pm daily)*. The original building was constructed in 1397 as a retirement villa for Shōgun Ashikaga Yoshimitsu. His son converted it into a temple. In 1950, a young monk consummated his obsession with the temple by burning it to the ground. The monk's story was fictionalised in Mishima Yukio's *The Golden Pavilion*.

In 1955, a full reconstruction was completed that exactly followed the original design, but the gold-foil covering was extended to the lower floors.

To get to the temple from Kyoto station, take bus No 205 and get off at the Kinkaku-ji-michi stop. From Keihan Sanjō, take bus No 59 and get off at the Kinkaku-ji-mae stop.

Ritsumeikan University Kyoto Museum for World Peace
立命館国際平和ミュージアム

While you're in northwestern Kyoto, you might want to drop by this excellent little museum *(Kyoto & Surrounds map; admission ¥300; open 9.30am-4.30pm Tues-Sun, closed day after national holidays & 20 July-31 August)*, which has exhibits covering Japan's actions leading up to WWII, the events of WWII and the conventional and atomic bombing of Japan by Allied forces at the end of the war. It's an educational, if sobering, way to spend an hour or two in Kyoto. It's a 15-minute walk east of Ryōan-ji.

Ryōan-ji 龍安寺

This temple *(Kyoto & Surrounds map; admission ¥500; open 8am-5pm daily Apr-Nov, 8.30am-4.30pm daily Dec-Mar)* belongs to the Rinzai school of Zen and was founded in 1450. The main attraction is the garden arranged in the *kare-sansui* (dry-landscape) style. An austere collection of 15 rocks, apparently adrift in a sea of sand, is enclosed by an earthen wall. The designer, who remains unknown, provided no explanation.

The viewing platform for the garden can be packed solid but the other parts of the temple grounds are also interesting and less of a target for the crowds. Among these, Kyoyo-chi pond is perhaps the most beautiful, particularly in autumn. Probably the best advice for Ryōan-ji is to come as early in the day as possible.

From Keihan Sanjō station, take bus No 59 to the Ryōan-ji-mae stop.

Ninna-ji 仁和寺

Ninna-ji (Kyoto & Surrounds map; open 9am-4.30pm daily) was built in 842 and is the head temple of the Omura branch of the Shingon school of Buddhism. The present temple buildings, including a five-storey pagoda, are from the 17th century. The extensive grounds are full of cherry trees that bloom in early April.

Admission to most of the grounds is free, but separate admission fees are charged for some of the temple's buildings, many of which are closed most of the year. To get there, take bus No 59 from Keihan Sanjō station and get off at the Omuro Ninna-ji stop. From Kyoto station take bus No 26.

Myōshin-ji 妙心寺

Myōshin-ji (Kyoto & Surrounds map; admission ¥400; open 9.10am-noon & 1pm-3.40pm daily), a vast temple complex dating back to the 14th century, belongs to the Rinzai school of Zen. There are over 40 temples, but only four are open to the public.

From the northern gate, follow the broad stone avenue flanked by rows of temples to the southern part of the complex.

The real highlight here is the wonderful garden of Taizō-in (admission ¥400; open 9am-5pm daily), a temple in the southwestern corner of the grounds.

The northern gate of Myōshin-ji is an easy 10-minute walk south of Ninna-ji; or take bus No 10 from Keihan Sanjō station to the Myōshin-ji Kita-mon-mae stop.

Kitano-Tenman-gū 北野天満宮

This shrine (Kyoto & Surrounds map; admission free; open 5.30am-dusk daily) is of moderate interest. However, if you're in town on the 25th of any month, be sure to catch the Tenjin-san market/fair held here. This is one of Kyoto's two biggest markets and is a great place to pick up some interesting souvenirs. The markets held in December and January are particularly colourful.

From Kyoto station, take bus No 50 and get off at the Kitano-Tenmangū-mae stop. From Keihan Sanjō station, take bus No 10 to the same stop.

Kōryū-ji 広隆寺

Kōryū-ji (Kyoto & Surrounds map; admission ¥600; open 9am-5pm daily Mar-Nov, to 4.30pm daily Dec-Feb), one of the oldest temples in Japan, was founded in 622 to honour Prince Shōtoku, who was an enthusiastic promoter of Buddhism.

The Hattō (Lecture Hall), to the right of the main gate, houses a magnificent trio of 9th-century statues: Buddha flanked by manifestations of Kannon.

The Reihōkan (Treasure House) contains numerous fine Buddhist statues, including the Naki Miroku (Crying Miroku) and the world-renowned Miroku Bosatsu, which is extraordinarily expressive. A national upset occurred in 1960 when an enraptured (at least that's what he said) student clasped the statue and snapped off its little finger.

Take bus No 11 from Keihan Sanjō station, get off at the Ukyō-ku Sogo-chosha-mae stop and walk north. The temple is also close to Uzumasa station on the Keifuku Arashiyama line.

Takao District 高雄周辺

This is a secluded district tucked far away in the northwestern part of Kyoto. It is famed for autumn foliage and the temples of Jingo-ji, Saimyō-ji and Kōzan-ji.

Jingo-ji (admission ¥400; open 9am-4pm daily) is the best of the three temples in the Takao District. This mountain temple sits at the top of a long flight of stairs that stretch up from Kiyotaki-gawa to the temple's main gate. The Kondō (Gold Hall) is the most impressive of the temple's structures; it's roughly in the middle of the grounds, at the top of another flight of stairs.

After visiting the Kondō, head in the opposite direction along a wooded path to an open area overlooking the valley. Don't be surprised if you see people tossing small disks over the railing into the chasm below. These are kawarakenage – light clay disks that people throw to rid themselves of their bad karma. Be careful: it's addictive, and at ¥100 for two, it can become expensive. You

KANSAI

Kiyotaki-gawa Hike (Kyoto & Surrounds map)

Time About two hours
Distance 5km
Major Sights Jingo-ji, Kiyotaki-gawa and Hozu-gawa

This is one of the better hikes in the Kyoto area, especially in autumn when the maples set the hillsides ablaze with colour. Start from **Jingo-ji** (see the Jingo-ji section of this chapter for transport details). The trail begins at the bottom of the steps leading up to the temple and follows Kiyotaki-gawa south (downstream).

After about one hour of riverside walking, you come to the small hamlet of **Kiyotaki**, with its quaint riverside inns and restaurants. Just before the town there's a trail junction that can be confusing: the trail leaves the riverside for a while and comes to a junction on a hillside. At this spot, head uphill back towards the river, not further into the woods. After passing through the town, cross a bridge and continue downstream. The trail hugs the river and passes some excellent crystal-clear swimming holes – great on a hot summer day.

After another 30 minutes or so you come to a road. Turn right, walk through the tunnel and continue along this road for another 30 minutes to reach Hozukyō station. The riverside below the bridge here is a popular summer picnic and swimming spot – bring a bathing suit and picnic basket and join the fun (but be warned that currents can be treacherous – parents take note). From Hozukyō station you can catch a train back to Kyoto (¥230, 20 minutes).

---

can buy the disks at a nearby stall. The trick is to flick the disks very gently, convex side up, like a Frisbee. When you get it right, they sail all the way down the valley, taking all that bad karma away with them.

The other two temples are within easy walking distance of Jingo-ji; **Saimyō-ji** (admission free; open 9am-5pm daily) is the better of the two. It's about five minutes' walk north of the base of the steps that lead up to Jingo-ji (follow the river upstream). To get to **Kōzan-ji** (admission ¥600; open 8.30am-5pm daily) you must walk back up to the main road and follow it north for about 10 minutes.

There are two options for bus services to Takao: an hourly JR bus from Kyoto station which takes about an hour to reach the Takao stop station (get off at the Yamashiro-Takao stop); and Kyoto city bus No 8 from Shijō-Karasuma (get off at the Takao stop). To get to Jingo-ji from these bus stops, walk down to the river then look for the steps on the other side.

Hozu-gawa Trip 保津川下り

The Hozu-gawa river trip (☎ 0771-22 5846; per person ¥3900) is a great way to enjoy the beauty of Kyoto's western mountains without any strain on the legs. The river winds through steep, forested mountain canyons before it arrives at its destination,

Arashiyama. Between 10 March and 30 November, there are seven trips (from 9am to 3.30pm) a day. During the winter, the number of trips is reduced to four a day and the boats are heated. There are no boat trips from 29 December to 4 January.

The ride lasts two hours and covers 16km between Kameoka and Arashiyama through occasional sections of white water – a scenic jaunt with minimal danger. The boats depart from a dock that is eight minutes on foot from Kameoka station. Kameoka is accessible by rail from Kyoto station or Nijō station on the JR San-in (Sagano) main line. The Kyoto TIC provides a leaflet in English and a photocopied timetable sheet for rail connections. The train fare from Kyoto to Kameoka is ¥400 one way by regular train (don't spend the extra for the express as it makes little difference in time).

ARASHIYAMA & SAGANO
嵐山・嵯峨野

Arashiyama and Sagano are two districts well worth a visit in this area if you feel like strolling in pleasant natural surroundings and visiting temples tucked into bamboo groves. The JNTO leaflet *Walking Tour Courses in Kyoto* has a good map of the area, and you should make an effort to pick up a copy before heading out. Note

Yasaka-jinja, Kyoto, Kansai

Nijō-jō, Kyoto, Kansai

Replica of a 16th-century castle, southern Kyoto, Kansai

Kinkaku-ji, Kyoto, Kansai

Stepped path through bamboo forest near Adashino Nembutsu-ji, Sagano, Kyoto, Kansai

Sloping stone walls of Nijō-jō, Kyoto, Kansai

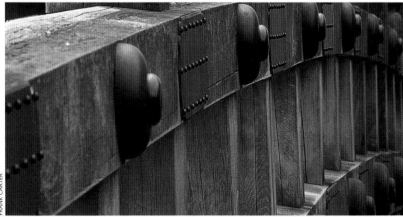

Detail of historic bridge, Nijō-jō, Kyoto, Kansai

that Arashiyama is wildly popular with Japanese tourists and can be packed, particularly in the cherry-blossom and maple-leaf seasons.

Bus No 28 links Kyoto station with Arashiyama. Bus No 11 connects Keihan Sanjō station with Arashiyama. The most convenient rail connection is the ride from Shijō-Ōmiya station on the Keifuku-Arashiyama line to Arashiyama station. You can also take the JR San-in line from Kyoto station or Nijō station and get off at Saga Arashiyama station (be careful to take only the local train, as the express does not stop in Arashiyama).

Togetsu-kyō 渡月橋

The bridge, Togetsu-kyō, is the main landmark in Arashiyama, a couple of minutes on foot from the station. Upon arrival here, you may wonder why the Japanese make such a fuss about this place; it's not very beautiful, particularly with all the tacky shops and vending machines nearby. The best advice is to head north immediately to the quieter regions of Sagano.

The area around the bridge, however, is a good spot to watch *ukai* (cormorant fishing) on summer evenings. If you want to get close to the action, you can pay ¥1700 to join a passenger boat. The TIC can provide a leaflet and further details.

Kameyama-kōen 亀山公園

Just upstream from Togetsu-kyō, behind Tenryū-ji, this park is a nice place to escape the crowds of Arashiyama. It's laced with trails, the best of which leads to a lookout over Katsura-gawa and up into the Arashiyama mountains. Keep an eye out for the monkeys; and keep children well away from the occasionally nasty critters.

Tenryū-ji 天竜寺

Tenryū-ji *(admission ¥500; open 8.30am-5.30pm daily Apr-Oct, to 5pm daily Nov-Mar)* is one of the major temples of the Rinzai school of Zen. It was built in 1339 on the former site of Emperor Go-Daigo's villa after a priest had dreamt of a dragon rising from the nearby river. The dream was interpreted as a sign that the emperor's spirit

---

Arashiyama-Sagano Walking Tour

Time Half a day
Distance About 3km
Major Sights Temples, shrines, gardens, bamboo forests

There is a detailed map for the walk described here in the *Walking Tour Courses in Kyoto* leaflet, available at the Kyoto TIC. This walk begins at **Tenryū-ji**, which is famous for its Zen garden (if you'd like to skip the temple and save on the entry fee, you can bypass it by walking 200m north of the temple on the main road and taking a left).

Otherwise, after checking out the temple, exit via the north gate, take a right and walk down the hill for a few metres to see humble **Nonomiya-jinja**. From the shrine, head back up the hill, passing through a wonderful grove of bamboo. At the top of the hill, you will see the entrance to **Ōkōchi-sansō**, a wonderful stop, provided it's not swarming with crowds.

Continuing north from Ōkōchi-sansō, you'll cross two sets of train tracks and descend past **Okura-ike**, a small pond. On the left you'll soon see a set of stone steps which lead up to the pleasant grounds of **Jōjakkō-ji**. A few minutes further brings you to a charming poet's hut. Continuing northwest from here you'll reach **Nison-in**, in an attractive setting on the wooded hillside.

Return to the main road from Nison-in and follow it gradually northwest for a few minutes. This will bring you to the narrow alley that leads up to **Giō-ji** and **Takiguchi-dera**, two wonderfully atmospheric little hillside temples. Returning to the main road, follow it up to **Adashino Nembutsu-ji**. It's worth entering this temple to admire its stone Buddhas. From here it is a short climb past a few of Sagano's remaining thatched-roof houses to the huge orange **Atago Torii**.

From here, tired legs can catch a Kyoto bus (No 72) from the Toriimoto bus stop back to Arashiyama (it continues to Kyoto station).

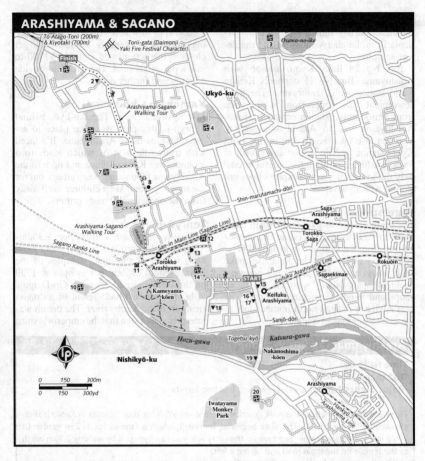

ARASHIYAMA & SAGANO

was uneasy and the temple was constructed as appeasement – hence the name *tenryū* (heavenly dragon). The present buildings date from 1900, but the main attraction is the 14th-century Zen garden.

Ōkōchi sansō 大河内山荘

This villa *(admission ¥900; open 9am-5pm daily)* is the home of Ōkōchi Denjiro, an actor in samurai films. The gardens allow fine views over the city and are open to visitors. The admission fee is hefty but includes tea and a cake. The villa is a 10-minute walk through bamboo groves north of Tenryū-ji.

Temples North of Ōkōchi Sansō

If you continue north of Ōkōchi Sansō, the narrow road soon passes stone steps on your left which lead up to the pleasant grounds of **Jōjakkō-ji**. If you walk north for another 10 minutes, you will come to **Nison-in**, which is in an attractive setting up the wooded hillside.

If you have time for a detour, there are several small temples west of Nison-in that you might like to visit. **Adashino Nembutsu-ji** *(admission ¥500; open 9am-4.30pm daily)* is a rather unusual temple where the abandoned bones of paupers and destitutes without next of kin were gathered. Thousands of stone images are crammed into the temple grounds, and these abandoned souls are remembered each year with candles here in the **Sentō Kuyō ceremony** held on the evenings of 23 and 24 August.

KANSAI

ARASHIYAMA & SAGANO

1	Adashino Nembutsu-ji 化野念仏寺	8	Rakushisha 落柿舎	14	Tenryū-ji 天竜寺
2	Bokuseki 木石	9	Jōjakkō-ji 常寂光寺	15	Gyātei ぎゃあてい
3	Daikaku-ji 大覚寺	10	Daihikaku Senkō-ji 大悲閣千光寺	16	Seizansō-dō 西山艸堂
4	Seiryō-ji 清涼寺	11	Ōkōchi-sansō Villa 大河内山荘	17	Kushi-tei 串亭
5	Giō-ji 祇王寺	12	Nonomiya-jinja 野宮神社	18	Yodōfu Sagano 湯豆腐嵯峨野
6	Takiguchi-dera 滝口寺	13	Tenryū-ji North Gate 天竜寺北門	19	Togetsu-tei 渡月亭
7	Nison-in 二尊院			20	Hōrin-ji 法輪寺

Daikaku-ji 大覚寺

Daikaku-ji *(admission ¥500; open 9am-4.30pm daily)* is a 25-minute walk northeast of Nison-in. It was built in the 9th century as a palace for Emperor Saga, who converted it into a temple. The present buildings date from the 16th century but are still palatial in style, with some impressive paintings. The large pond, Osawa-no-ike, was once used by the emperor for boating.

Close to the temple entrance, there are separate terminals for Kyoto city buses (bus No 28 connects with Kyoto station) and Kyoto buses (No 71 connects with Kyoto station and No 61 with Keihan Sanjō station).

SOUTHWESTERN KYOTO
京都南西部

Katsura Rikyū 桂離宮

Katsura Rikyū *(Katsura Detached Palace; Kyoto & Surrounds map; admission free)* is considered to be one of the finest examples of Japanese architecture. It was built in 1624 for the emperor's brother, Prince Toshihito. Every conceivable detail of the villa, the teahouses, the large pond with islets and the surrounding garden has been given meticulous attention.

Tours, in Japanese, start at 10am, 11am, 2pm and 3pm and last about 40 minutes. You should be there 20 minutes beforehand. An explanatory video is shown in the waiting room and a leaflet is provided in English. You *must* make reservations in advance through the Imperial Household Agency (see Kyoto Gosho earlier in this chapter). Visitors must be over 20 years of age.

To get to the villa from Kyoto station, take bus No 33 and get off at the Katsura Rikyū-mae stop, which is a five-minute walk from the villa. The easiest access from the city centre is to take a Hankyū line train from Hankyū Kawaramachi station to Hankyū Katsura station, which is a 15-minute walk from the villa. Don't take an express *(tokkyū)* train as they don't stop in Katsura.

Saihō-ji 西芳寺 (苔寺)

The main attraction at this temple (Kyoto & Surrounds map) is the heart-shaped garden, designed in 1339 by Musō Kokushi. The garden is famous for its luxuriant mossy growth, hence the temple's other name, Koke-dera (Moss Temple). Visiting the temple is recommended only if you have the time and patience to follow the reservation rules. If you don't, visit nearby Jizo-in (see that section following) to get a sense of the atmosphere of Saihō-ji without the expense or fuss.

Take bus No 28 from Kyoto station to the Matsuo-taisha-mae stop and walk 15 minutes southwest. From Keihan Sanjō station, take Kyoto bus No 63 to Koke-dera, the last stop, and walk for two minutes.

Reservations To visit Saihō-ji, you must make a reservation. Send a postcard at least one week before the date you wish to visit and include details of your name, number of visitors, address in Japan, occupation, age (you must be over 18) and desired date (choice of alternative dates preferred). The address is Saihō-ji, 56 Kamigaya-chō, Matsuo, Nishikyō-ku, Kyoto-shi 615-8286. Enclose a stamped self-addressed postcard for a reply to your Japanese address. You might find it convenient to buy an *ōfuku-hagaki* (send and return postcard set) at a Japanese post office.

KANSAI

You should arrive at the time and on the date indicated by the temple office. After paying your ¥3000 'donation', you must spend up to 90 minutes copying or chanting sutras (collection of dialogues and discourses) or doing Zen meditation before finally being guided around the garden for 90 minutes.

Jizo-in 地蔵院

This delightful little temple *(Kyoto & Surrounds map; admission ¥400; open 9am-5pm daily)* could be called the 'poor man's Saihō-ji'. It's only a few minutes' walk south of Saihō-ji, in the same atmospheric bamboo groves. While the temple does not boast any spectacular buildings or treasures, it has a nice moss garden and is almost completely ignored by tourists, making it a great place to sit and think. For directions, see the earlier Saihō-ji section.

SOUTH & SOUTHEASTERN KYOTO 京都南部・南東部

The district to the south of Kyoto is mostly devoted to industry, but Tōfuku-ji and Fushimi-Inari Taisha (Fushimi-Inari Shrine) are worth a visit.

To the southeast, Daigo-ji offers scope for a gentle hike to complement the architectural splendours. The city of Uji isn't exactly part of Kyoto, but it's easy to reach on a day trip or as a convenient stop when travelling between Kyoto and Nara.

Tōfuku-ji 東福寺

Founded in 1236 by the priest Enni, Tōfuku-ji *(Kyoto & Surrounds map; admission to main hall ¥400, to subtemples ¥300, grounds free; open 9am-4pm daily)* now belongs to the Rinzai sect of Zen Buddhism. Since this temple was intended to compare with Tōdai-ji and Kōfuku-ji in Nara, it was given a name combining characters from the names of each of these temples.

Despite the destruction of many of the buildings by fire, this is still considered one of the five main Zen temples in Kyoto. The huge San-mon is the oldest Zen main gate in Japan. The *tosu* (lavatory) and *yokushitsu* (bathroom) date from the 14th century. The present temple complex includes 24 subtemples; at one time there were 53.

The **Hōjō** was reconstructed in 1890. The gardens, laid out in 1938, are worth a visit. As you approach the northern gardens, you cross a stream over Tsūten-kyō (Bridge to Heaven), which is a pleasant leafy spot – the foliage is renowned for its autumn colour. The northern garden has stones and moss neatly arranged in a chequerboard pattern.

The nearby **Reiun-in** subtemple receives few visitors to its attractive garden.

Tōfuku-ji is a 20-minute walk southeast of Kyoto station. You can also take a local train on the JR Nara line and get off at Tōfukuji station, from which it's a 10-minute walk southeast.

Fushimi-Inari Taisha 伏見稲荷大社

This intriguing shrine (Kyoto & Surrounds map) was dedicated to the gods of rice and sake by the Hata family in the 8th century. As the role of agriculture diminished, deities were enrolled to ensure prosperity in business. Nowadays, the shrine is one of Japan's most popular, and is the head shrine for some 30,000 Inari shrines scattered the length and breadth of Japan.

The entire complex, consisting of five shrines, sprawls across the wooded slopes of Inari-yama. A pathway wanders 4km up the mountain and is lined with hundreds of red torii. There are also dozens of stone foxes. The fox is considered the messenger of Inari, the god of cereal grains. The Japanese traditionally see the fox as a sacred, somewhat mysterious figure capable of 'possessing' humans – the favoured point of entry is under the fingernails. The key often seen in the fox's mouth is for the rice granary.

The walk around the upper precincts of the shrine is a pleasant day hike. It also makes for a very eerie stroll in the late afternoon and early evening, when the various graveyards and miniature shrines along the path take on a mysterious air.

To get to the shrine from Kyoto station, take a JR Nara line train to Inari station. From Keihan Sanjō station take the Keihan line to Fushimi-Inari station. There is no admission charge for the shrine. The shrine is just east of both of these stations.

Daigo-ji 醍醐寺

Daigo-ji (Kyoto & Surrounds map) was founded in 874 by the priest Shobo, who gave it the name of Daigo. This refers to the five periods of Buddha's teaching, which were often compared to the five forms of milk prepared in India, the highest form of which is called *daigo* (ultimate essence of milk).

The temple was expanded into a vast complex of buildings on two levels – Shimo Daigo (Lower Daigo) and Kami Daigo (Upper Daigo). During the 15th century, the buildings on the lower level were destroyed, with the sole exception of the five-storey pagoda. Built in 951, this pagoda still stands and is lovingly pointed out as the oldest of its kind in Japan and the oldest existing building in Kyoto.

In the late 16th century, Hideyoshi took a fancy to Daigo-ji and ordered extensive rebuilding. It is now one of the main temples of the Shingon school of Buddhism. To explore Daigo-ji thoroughly and leisurely, mixing hiking with temple viewing, you will need at least half a day.

Entry to the grounds is free except during the spring *hanami* and fall foliage seasons, when it's ¥600.

To get to Daigo-ji, take the Tōzai line subway from central Kyoto to the last stop, Daigo, and walk east (towards the mountains) for about 10 minutes. Make sure that the train you board is bound for Daigo, as some head to Hama-Ōtsu instead.

Sampō-in This was founded as a subtemple of Daigo-ji in 1115, but received a total revamp under Hideyoshi's orders in 1598. It is now a fine example of the amazing opulence of that period *(admission ¥500; open 9am-5pm daily)*. The Kanō paintings and the garden are special features.

Hōju-in Treasure House This museum *(admission ¥700; open 9am-5pm daily)*, close to Sampō-in, is only open to the public for a limited time during the year. Despite the massive admission fee, it really should not be missed if you happen to be there at the right time. The display of sculptures, scrolls, screens, miniature shrines and calligraphy is superb.

Climb to Kami Daigo From Sampō-in in Shimo Daigo (Lower Daigo), walk up the large avenue of cherry trees, through the Niō-mon and past the pagoda. From there you can continue for a pleasant climb through Kami Daigo (Upper Daigo), browsing through temples and shrines on the way. Allow yourself 50 minutes to reach the top.

Uji 宇治

Uji is a small city to the south of Kyoto. Its main claims to fame are Byōdō-in, tea cultivation and *ukai*. The stone bridge at Uji – the oldest of its kind in Japan – has been the scene of many bitter clashes in previous centuries.

Between 17 June and 31 August, *ukai* trips are organised in the evening around 7pm on the Uji-gawa. Prices start at ¥1800 a person. The TIC has a leaflet with up-to-date information about how to book.

Uji can be reached by rail in about 40 minutes from Kyoto on the Keihan Uji line or JR Nara line.

When arriving in Uji by Keihan train, leave the station, cross the river via the first bridge on the right, you'll find the tourist information office on the left, next to a *kōban* (police box). When coming by JR, the temple and the information office are about 10 minutes' walk east (towards the river) of Uji station.

Byōdō-in This temple *(admission ¥600; open 8.30am-5pm daily Mar-Nov, 9am-4pm daily Dec-Feb)* was converted from a Fujiwara villa into a Buddhist temple in 1052. The Hōō-dō (Phoenix Hall), more properly known as the Amida-dō, was built in 1053 and is the only original remaining building. The phoenix was a popular mythical bird in China and was revered by the Japanese as a protector of Buddha. The architecture of the building resembles the shape of the bird, and there are two bronze phoenixes perched opposite each other on the roof. The building was originally intended to represent Amida's heavenly palace in the Pure Land. This building is one of the few extant examples of Heian-period architecture, and its graceful lines make one wish that far more of its type had survived Kyoto's past.

Inside the hall is the famous statue of Amida and 52 Bosatsu (Bodhisattvas) dating from the 11th century and attributed to the priest-sculptor Jōchō.

The temple, complete with its reflection in a pond, is one of Japan's top attractions and draws huge crowds. For a preview without the masses, take a look at the ¥10 coin.

NORTHERN KYOTO 京都北部

The area north of Kyoto is perfect for an exploration of its rural valleys and lovely mountainous areas. The twin valleys of Kurama and Kibune are perhaps the most pleasant day trip in the Kyoto area, giving one the feeling of being deep in the country without the necessity of long travel. Ōhara also makes another pleasant day trip, perhaps combined with an excursion to Hiei-zan and Enryaku-ji or Shūgaku-in Rikyū.

Shūgaku-in Rikyū 修学院利休

This imperial villa (Kyoto & Surrounds map), or detached palace, was begun in the 1650s by the abdicated emperor Go-Mizunoo, and work was continued after his death in 1680 by his daughter Akenomiya.

Designed as an imperial retreat, the villa grounds are divided into three large garden areas on a hillside: lower, middle and upper. The gardens' reputation rests on their ponds, pathways and impressive use of 'borrowed scenery' in the form of the surrounding hills; the view from the Rinun-tei Teahouse in the upper garden is particularly impressive.

Tours, in Japanese, start at 9am, 10am, 11am, 1.30pm and 3pm (50 minutes). Admission is free, but you must make advance reservations through the Imperial Household Agency (see Kyoto Gosho earlier in this chapter for details).

From Kyoto station, take bus No 5 and get off at the Shūgaku-in Rikyū-michi stop. The trip takes about an hour. From the bus stop it's a 15-minute walk to the villa. You can also take the Eiden Eizan line from Demachiyanagi station to the Shūgaku-in stop and walk east about 25 minutes towards the mountains.

Shisen-dō & Manshū-in
詩仙堂・曼殊院

Both these temples (Kyoto & Surrounds map) are in the vicinity of Shūgaku-in Rikyū. Due to their somewhat inconvenient location, they are less popular with tourists than the main Higashiyama temples further south.

Shisen-dō (admission ¥500; open 9am-5pm daily) was built in 1641 by Jōzan, a scholar of Chinese classics and a landscape architect, who wanted a place to retire to at the end of his life. The garden is a fine place to relax, with only the rhythmic 'thwack' of a bamboo sōzu (animal scarer) to interrupt your snooze.

The temple is a five-minute walk from the Ichijōji-sagarimatsu-mae bus stop on the No 5 route.

Manshū-in (admission ¥500; open 9am-4.30pm daily) was originally founded by Saichō on Hiei-zan, but was relocated here at the beginning of the Edo period. The architecture, works of art and garden are impressive.

The temple is about 30 minutes' walk north of Shisen-dō.

Hiei-zan & Enryaku-ji
比叡山・延暦寺

A visit to 848m-high Hiei-zan and the vast Enryaku-ji complex (Kyoto & Surrounds map; admission ¥550; open 8.30am-4.30pm daily, earlier in winter) is a good way to spend half a day hiking, poking around temples and enjoying the atmosphere of a key site in Japanese history.

Enryaku-ji was founded in 788 by Saichō, also known as Dengyō-daishi, the priest who established the Tendai school. From the 8th century the temple grew in power; at its height it possessed some 3000 buildings and an army of thousands of sōhei, or warrior monks. In 1571, Oda Nobunaga saw the temple's power as a threat to his aims to unify the nation and he destroyed most of the buildings, along with the monks inside. This school did not receive imperial recognition until 1823. Today only three pagodas and 120 minor temples remain.

The complex is divided into three sections – Tōtō, Saitō and Yokawa. The Tōtō (eastern pagoda section) contains the Kompon Chū-dō (primary central hall), which is the most important building in the complex. The flames on the three Dharma (the law, in Sanskrit) lamps in front of the altar have been kept lit for over 1200 years. The Daikō-dō (great lecture hall) displays life-size wooden statues of the founders of various Buddhist schools. This part of the temple is heavily geared to group access, with large expanses of asphalt for parking.

The Saitō (western pagoda section) contains the Shaka-dō, which dates from 1595 and houses a rare Buddha sculpture of the Shaka Nyorai (Historical Buddha). The Saitō, with its stone paths winding through forests of tall trees, temples shrouded in mist and the sound of distant gongs, is the most atmospheric part of the temple. Hold onto your ticket from the Tōtō section, as you may need to show it here.

The **Yokawa** is of minimal interest and a 4km bus ride away from the Saitō area. The Chū-dō (central hall) here was originally built in 848. It was destroyed by fire several times and has undergone repeated reconstruction (the most recent in 1971). If you plan to visit this area as well as Tōtō and Saitō, allow a full day for in-depth exploration.

Getting There & Away You can reach Hiei-zan and Enryaku-ji by either train or bus. The most interesting way is the train/cable-car/ropeway route described below. If you're in a hurry or would like to save money, the best way is a direct bus from Sanjō Keihan or Kyoto stations.

By train, take the Keihan line north to the last stop, Demachiyanagi, and change to the Yase-yūen/Hiei-bound Eizan Dentetsu Eizan-line train (be careful not to board the Kurama-bound train which sometimes leaves from the same platform). At the last stop, Yase-yūen (¥260), board the cable car (¥530, nine minutes) and then the ropeway (¥310, three minutes) to the peak, from which you can walk down to the temples.

By bus, take Kyoto bus (not Kyoto city bus) No 17 or 18, which run from Kyoto station to the Yase-yūen stop (¥390, about 50 minutes). From there it's a short walk to the cable car station.

Alternately, if you want to save money (by avoiding the cable car and ropeway), there are direct Kyoto buses from Kyoto and Keihan Sanjō stations to Enryaku-ji, which take about 70 and 50 minutes respectively (both cost ¥800).

Ōhara 大原

Ōhara, a quiet farming town about 10km north of Kyoto, provides a glimpse of old rural Japan along with a picturesque temple, Sanzen-in. It's most popular in autumn, when the maple leaves change colour and the mountain views are spectacular. From late October to mid-November avoid this area on weekends, as it will be packed.

From Kyoto station, Kyoto bus Nos 17 and 18 run to Ōhara (¥580, one hour). From Keihan Sanjō, take Kyoto bus No 16 or 17 (¥470, 45 minutes). Be careful to board a tan Kyoto bus, not a green Kyoto city bus

of the same number. Allow half a day for a visit, possibly twinned with an excursion to Hiei-zan and the Enryaku-ji. JNTO includes a basic walking map for the area in its leaflet *Walking Tour Courses in Kyoto*.

Sanzen-in Founded in 784 by the priest Saicho, Sanzen-in *(admission ¥600; open 8.30am-4.30pm daily Mar-Nov, to 4pm daily Dec-Feb)* belongs to the Tendai sect of Buddhism. Saicho, considered one of the great patriarchs of Buddhism in Japan, also founded Enraku-ji on nearby Hiei-zan. The temple's Yusei-en is one of the most photographed gardens in Japan, and rightly so. Take some time to sit on the steps of the Shin-den Hall and admire its beauty.

After seeing Yusei-en, head off to the Ojo-gokuraku Hall (Temple of Rebirth in Paradise) to see the impressive Amitabha trinity, a large Amida image flanked by attendants Kannon and Seishi, gods of mercy and wisdom, respectively. After this, walk up to the hydrangea garden at the back of the temple, where, in late spring and summer, you can walk among hectares of blooming hydrangeas.

If you feel like a short hike after leaving the temple, head up the hill around the right side of the temple to the **Soundless Waterfall** (you'll note that it sounds pretty much like any other waterfall). The sound of this waterfall is said to have inspired Shomyo Buddhist chanting.

To get to Sanzen-in, follow the signs from Ōhara's main bus stop up the hill past a long arcade of souvenir stalls. The entrance is on your left as you crest the hill.

Kurama & Kibune 鞍馬・貴船

Only 30 minutes north of Kyoto on the Eiden Eizan main line, Kurama and Kibune are a pair of tranquil valleys long favoured by Kyoto-ites as places to escape the crowds and stresses of the city below. Kurama's main attractions are its mountain temple and its *onsen* (hot spring bath). Kibune, over the ridge, is a cluster of ryokan overlooking a mountain stream, which is best enjoyed in the summer, when the ryokan serve dinner on platforms built over the rushing waters of Kibune-gawa, providing welcome relief from the summer heat.

The two valleys lend themselves to being explored together. In the winter, one can

KANSAI

start from Kibune, walk for an hour or so over the ridge, visit Kurama-dera and then soak in the *onsen* before heading back to Kyoto. In the summer, the reverse is best; start from Kurama, walk up to the temple, then down the other side to Kibune to enjoy a meal suspended above the cool river.

If you happen to be in Kyoto on the night of 22 October, be sure not to miss the **Kurama-no-hi Matsuri** (Kurama Fire Festival), one of the most exciting festivals in the Kyoto area (see Special Events later in this chapter for details).

To get to Kurama and Kibune, take the Eiden Eizan line from Kyoto's Demachi-yanagi station. For Kibune, get off at the second-to-last stop, Kibune Guchi, take a right out of the station and walk about 20 minutes up the hill. For Kurama, go to the last stop, Kurama, and walk straight out of the station. Both destinations are ¥410 and take about 30 minutes to reach.

Kurama-dera This temple (admission ¥200; open 9am-4.30pm daily) was established in 770 by the monk Gantei from Nara's Tōshōdai-ji. After seeing a vision of the deity Bishamon-ten, guardian of the northern quarter of the Buddhist heaven, he established Kurama-dera in its present location, just below the peak of Kurama-yama. Originally belonging to the Tendai sect, Kurama has been independent since 1949, describing its own brand of Buddhism as Kurama Kyō.

The entrance to the temple is just up the hill from the Eiden Eizan main line's Kurama station. A tram goes to the top for ¥100; alternatively, hike up by following the main path past the tram station. The trail is worth taking if it's not too hot, as it winds through a forest of towering old-growth cryptomeria trees. At the top, there is a courtyard dominated by the Honden (Main Hall). Behind the Honden, a trail leads off to the mountain's peak.

At the top, those who want to continue to Kibune can take the trail down the other side. It's a 45-minute hike from the Honden of Kurama-dera to the valley floor of Kibune. On the way down there are two pleasant mountain shrines.

Kurama Onsen One of the few *onsen* within easy reach of Kyoto, Kurama Onsen

(open 10am-9pm daily) is a great place to relax after a hike. The outdoor bath, with a fine view of Kurama-yama, costs ¥1100. The inside bath costs ¥2300, but even with the use of sauna and locker thrown in, it's difficult to imagine why one would opt for the indoor bath. For both baths, buy a ticket from the machine outside the door of the main building (instructions are in Japanese and English).

To get to Kurama Onsen, walk straight out of Kurama station, turn left up the main road and follow it for about 10 minutes. You'll see the baths down on your right. There's also a free shuttle bus that runs between the station and the *onsen*, leaving approximately every 30 minutes.

Kibune The main attractions here are the dining platforms above the river, which are open from 1 June to the end of September. In addition to these, all the ryokan in the valley are open year round and serve as romantic escapes for travellers willing to pay mid-level ryokan prices. **Kibune-jinja**, halfway up the valley, is worth a quick look, particularly if you can ignore the unfortunate plastic horse statue at its entrance. Admission is free.

From Kibune you can hike over the mountain to Kurama-dera, along a trail that starts halfway up the village on the eastern side (or vice versa – see Kurama-dera earlier).

BATHS

After a day spent marching from temple to temple, nothing feels better than a good hot bath. Kyoto is full of *sentō* (public baths), ranging from small neighbourhood baths with one or two tubs to massive complexes offering saunas, mineral baths and even electric baths. The following bath is worth a visit and could even double as an evening's entertainment. If you don't feel like making the trek to Funaoka Onsen, there's probably a *sentō* within a few minutes' walk of where you're staying (just ask the proprietor of your lodgings or at any *kōban*).

Funaoka Onsen 船岡温泉

This old bath on Kuramaguchi-dōri is the best in all Kyoto (Kyoto & Surrounds map; admission ¥350; open 3pm-1am Wed-Mon). It boasts an outdoor bath, a sauna, a

The Japanese Bath

The *o-furo* (Japanese bath) is a ritual that has to be learnt at an early stage and, like so many other things in Japan, is initially confusing but quickly becomes second nature. The all-important rule for using a Japanese bath is that you wash outside the bath and use the bath itself purely for soaking. Getting into a bath unwashed or, equally dreadful, without rinsing all the soap off your body, would be a major error.

People bathe in the evening, before dinner; a pre-breakfast bath is thought of as distinctly strange. In a ryokan there's no possibility of missing bath time: you will be told clearly when to bathe lest you not be washed in time for dinner. In a ryokan or in a *sentō* (public bath), the bathing facilities will either be communal (but sex segregated) or there will be smaller family bathing facilities for families and couples.

Take off your *yukata* (light cotton kimono) or clothes in the ante-room to the bath and place them in the baskets provided. The bathroom has taps, plastic bowls (wooden ones in very traditional places) and stools along the wall. Draw a stool up to a set of taps and fill the bowl from the taps or use the bowl to scoop some water out of the bath itself. Sit on the stool and soap yourself. Rinse thoroughly so there's no soap or shampoo left on you, then climb into the bath. Soak as long as you can stand the heat, then leave the bath, rinse yourself off again, dry off and get dressed.

cypress-wood tub, an electric bath, a herbal bath and a few more for good measure. Be sure to check out the *ranma* (carved wooden panels) in the changing room. Carved during Japan's invasion of Manchuria, they offer insight into the prevailing mindset of that era (frankly, we're surprised that they haven't been taken down).

To find it, head west about 400m on Kuramaguchi-dōri from the Kuramaguchi/Horiikawa intersection. It's on the left not far past Lawson convenience store. Look for the large rocks out the front.

ACTIVITIES

Kyoto International Community House (KICH) Cultural Demonstrations

KICH (☎ *752-3512; per class ¥500, per 3-month semester ¥3000)* offers an intriguing variety of introductory courses in Japanese culture, which are open to all for observation (free) and participation.

They also offer Japanese-language and calligraphy classes. Ask at KICH for details of classes, some of which may not be listed here.

The basic demonstration schedule is as follows, but confirm times and reserve a place:

The Way of Tea (tea ceremony) 2pm to 4pm Tuesday
The Koto (a Japanese string instrument) 2pm to 4pm Wednesday

See KICH under Useful Organisations earlier in this chapter for more details.

ORGANISED TOURS

JTB Sunrise Tours *(☎ 341-1413; W www.jtb.co.jp/sunrisetour/kyoto)* offers morning, afternoon and all-day bus tours year-round with English-speaking guides. Morning and afternoon tours cost ¥5300, while all-day tours with a buffet lunch included are ¥11,200. Pick-ups are available at all of Kyoto's larger hotels.

One of the greatest ways to acclimatise to Kyoto is to spend a few hours with the popular **Johnnie Hillwalker** *(☎ 622-6803; W http://web.kyoto-inet.or.jp/people/h-s-love; adult/child ¥2000/¥1000; Mon, Wed & Fri Mar-Nov).* Hirooka Hajime (his Japanese name) leads an intimate, four-hour English-language tour, starting from the northern side of Kyoto station.

The course covers some lesser-visited sights in central and eastern Kyoto. Reservations aren't necessary; just show up at the Sunken Garden (it's not really a garden, so don't be confused) in front of Kyoto station between 10am and 10.15am on the days the tour is given. The price includes all fees, and payment is in cash only.

See also the **Kyoto Cycling Tour Project** entry under Bicycle Rentals in the later Getting Around section. These folks conduct some great tours of the city on bicycles – a really excellent way to see Kyoto!

SPECIAL EVENTS

There are hundreds of festivals in Kyoto throughout the year. Listings can be found on the TIC's forthcoming-events board or in *Kyoto Visitor's Guide, Kansai Time Out* or the weekend editions of the English-language newspapers available in Japan. The following are some of the major or most spectacular festivals. These attract hordes of spectators from out of town, so book accommodation well in advance.

February

Setsubun Matsuri at Yoshida-jinja (3 or 4 February; check with the TIC) This festival is held on the day of *setsubun*, which marks the last day of winter in the Japanese lunar calendar. In this festival, people climb up to Yoshida-jinja in the northern Higashiyama area to watch a huge bonfire. It's one of Kyoto's more dramatic festivals. The action starts at dusk.

May

Aoi Matsuri (Hollyhock Festival; 15 May) This festival dates back to the 6th century and commemorates the successful prayers of the people for the gods to stop calamitous weather. Today, the procession involves imperial messengers in ox carts and a retinue of 600 people dressed in traditional costume; hollyhock leaves are carried or used as decoration. The procession leaves at around 10am from the Kyosho Gosho and heads for Shimogamo-jinja, where ceremonies take place. It sets out from here again at 2pm and arrives at Kamigamo-jinja at 3.30pm.

July

Gion Matsuri (17 July) Perhaps the most renowned of all Japanese festivals, this one reaches a climax on the 17th with a parade of over 30 floats depicting ancient themes and decked out in incredible finery. On the three evenings preceding the main day, people gather on Shijō-dōri, many dressed in beautiful *yukata* (light summer kimono), to look at the floats and carouse from one street stall to the next.

August

Daimon-ji Gozan Okuribi (16 August) This festival, commonly known as Daimon-ji Yaki, is performed to bid farewell to the souls of ancestors. Enormous fires are lit on five mountains in the form of Chinese characters or other shapes. The fires are lit at 8pm and it is best to watch from the banks of Kamo-gawa or pay for a rooftop view from a hotel. Better yet, head up to Hirosawano-ike (Kyoto & Surrounds map) in northwestern Kyoto, rent a rowing boat and watch *torii-gata* (the character for 'gate') burn over the pond. Here, in addition to the burning figure, people float hundreds of lanterns with burning candles inside them on the surface of the pond – the effect is magical.

October

Kurama-no-hi Matsuri (Kurama Fire Festival; 22 October) In perhaps Kyoto's most dramatic festival, huge flaming torches are carried through the streets by men in loincloths. The festival climaxes around 10pm at Yuki-jinja in the village of Kurama, which is 30 minutes by train from Kyoto station on the Eiden Eizan Line. The train leaves from Demachiyanagi station.

Jidai Matsuri (Festival of the Ages; 22 October) This festival is of recent origin, only dating back to 1895. More than 2000 people, dressed in costumes ranging from the 8th century to the 19th century, parade from Kyoto Gosho to Heian-jingū.

PLACES TO STAY

Kyoto has the widest range of foreigner-friendly accommodation in all Japan, with a variety of options in every budget range. Choices range from the country's finest and most expensive ryokan to youth hostels and funky old guesthouses.

Keep in mind that the most convenient areas in which to be based, in terms of easy access to shopping, dining and most of the major attractions, are eastern and central Kyoto.

The **Kyoto TIC** (☎ 371-5649) offers advice and accommodation lists, and can help with reservations at its **Welcome Inn Reservation counter** (*open 9am-noon & 1pm-4.30pm Mon-Fri*). There's another Welcome Inn Reservation counter in the international arrivals lobby of Kansai airport (☎ 0724-56-6025; *open 9am-8.30pm daily*).

Transport info is from Kyoto station unless otherwise noted.

See the Osaka Places to Stay section for details on hotels near Itami and Kansai airports.

PLACES TO STAY – BUDGET
Central Kyoto

The best budget guesthouse in town is the excellent **Tour Club** (*Map 1;* ☎ 353-6968; ⓦ www.kyotojp.com; *dorm beds ¥2300, twins/triples ¥6900/8900*). Run by a charming and informative young couple, this clean new guesthouse is already a favourite of many foreign visitors. Facilities include Internet access, bicycle rentals, laundry, money exchange and free tea and coffee. It's a 15-minute walk from Kyoto station; turn north from Shichijō-dōri at the Second House coffee shop (looks like a bank) and keep an eye out for the Japanese flag.

Budget Inn *(Map 1; ☎ 344-1510; w www .budgetinnjp.com; dorm beds ¥2300, triples/ quads ¥8900/10,900)*, under the same management as the Tour Club, is another great choice. There are four dorm rooms and four private tatami-mat rooms with private bath, and the facilities and service are similar to those at the Tour Club. It's a seven-minute walk from Kyoto station; from the station, walk west on Shiokōji-dōri and turn north at the Esso station and look for the English-language sign out front.

Uno House *(Map 1; ☎ 231-7763; dorm beds from ¥1650, private rooms ¥2250-5200)* is a long-time fixture of the Kyoto guesthouse scene and has a convenient central location and casual atmosphere. Sure, it's a little noisy and run down, but you can't beat the price. Take the Karasuma line subway from Kyoto station, get off at the Marutamachi stop (seven minutes) and walk east for 10 minutes.

Eastern Kyoto

Shinnyo-dō House *(Map 2; e divyam@ mac .com; B&B per person ¥4000)* is a charming B&B with an excellent location for sightseeing in the Ginkaku-ji/Yoshida-yama area. The one guest room, which sleeps up to three people, looks out over a small Japanese garden. The house is a late-Edo-period samurai house located just outside the main gate of Shinnyo-dō, a temple famed for its maple leaves and cherry blossoms. There is a private entrance and no curfew. Reservation is via email only.

Casa Carinho B&B *(Map 2; w www .gotokandk.com; B&B per person ¥4000)* is another great B&B. Located close to Ginkaku-ji, this cosy guesthouse has two Japanese-style rooms, and is run by a charming couple with a wealth of inside information on Kyoto. Reservation is via email only.

Higashiyama Youth Hostel *(Map 2; ☎ 761-8135; beds with 2 meals ¥4800)* is close to the sights of Higashiyama. It's very regimented, but if you're the kind of person who likes being in bed by 9.30pm, this might suit. To get there, take bus No 5

from Kyoto station (stand A1, 30 minutes) to the Higashiyama-Sanjō stop.

ISE Dorm *(Map 2; ☎ 771-0566; rooms per person ¥2800, per month from ¥45,000)* provides basic short- and long-term accommodation. Facilities on offer include phone, fridge, air-con, shower and washing machine. On the negative side, the place can be noisy. Take bus No 206 from Kyoto station (stand D2, 30 minutes) to the Kumano-jinja-mae stop.

Northwestern Kyoto

The friendly and well-run **Utano Youth Hostel** *(Kyoto & Surrounds map; ☎ 462-2288; dorm beds Dec-Mar, July & Aug ¥2800, rest of year ¥2650)* is the best youth hostel in Kyoto. Bear in mind, though, that while it's conveniently located for touring sights in northwest Kyoto, it's something of a hike to those in other areas of the city. From Keihan Sanjō station, take bus No 10 or 59 (stands 3 and 2, respectively, 40 minutes) to the Yuusu-hosteru-mae stop. The hostel is a one-minute walk up the hill from the stop.

PLACES TO STAY – MID-RANGE

Kyoto is a good place in which to sample the ryokan experience, and there are dozens of inexpensive ryokan in the city that specialise in serving foreign guests. Keep in mind, though, that staying in a ryokan can be like staying at someone's home; if you want real freedom you should consider staying in a business hotel instead.

Central Kyoto & Kyoto Station Area

Ryokan There are several foreigner-friendly ryokan in central Kyoto, all of which are members of the Japanese Inn Group. At all these places, there are common baths, and breakfast is available for an additional fee.

Ryokan Hinomoto *(Kyoto & Surrounds map; ☎ 351-4563; singles ¥4000-4500, doubles ¥8000-8500)* is most convenient to the city's nightlife action and has a nice wooden bathtub. Take bus No 17 or 205 from Kyoto station (stand A2, 15 minutes) and get off at the Kawaramachi-matsubara stop.

Matsubaya Ryokan *(Map 1; ☎ 351-4268; singles/doubles from ¥4700/9400, triples ¥13,200)* is a welcoming place 10-minutes' walk north of Kyoto station.

Riverside Takase *(Map 1; ☎ 351-7925; singles/doubles from ¥3500/7000, triples ¥9400)* has five decent rooms. It's a 15-minute walk from Kyoto station or take bus No 17 or 205 from Kyoto station (stand A2, 10 minutes) and get off when you arrive at the Kawaramachi-Shōmen stop.

Yuhara Ryokan *(Map 1; ☎ 371-9583; singles/doubles ¥4000/8000)* has a family atmosphere and a riverside location popular with foreigners. Follow the directions for the Riverside Takase, mentioned previously. This place comes recommended by readers.

Hotels The new business hotel **APA Hotel** *(Map 1; ☎ 365-4111, fax 365-8720; singles/ twins from ¥7500/15,000)* has competitive rates. It's only five minutes on foot from Kyoto station, making it a good choice for those with early morning departures.

Hotel New Hokke Kyoto *(Map 1; ☎ 361-1251; singles/doubles/twins from ¥7200/ 11,000/13,000)* is directly opposite the northern side of Kyoto station. It sometimes offers special rates on double and twin rooms – ask when reserving or checking in.

Karasuma Kyoto Hotel *(Map 3; ☎ 371-0111; singles/twins/doubles from ¥8800/ 16,000/20,000)* is a good midtown choice, with clean, fairly new rooms. It's a five-minute walk from Shijō station on the Karasuma line subway.

Sun Hotel Kyoto *(Map 3; ☎ 241-3351; singles/doubles/twins ¥7000/12,200/12,200)* is our favourite business hotel in Kyoto with small but clean rooms. It's right in the heart of Kyoto's nightlife district. From Kyoto station take bus No 5 (stand A1, 20 minutes) to the Kawaramachi-Sanjō stop and backtrack for 100m.

Hotel Gimmond *(Map 3; ☎ 221-4111; singles/doubles/twins from ¥8300/14,000/ 14,500)*, centrally located and clean, is justifiably popular with foreign visitors. It's very close to Oike station on the Karasuma line subway.

Eastern Kyoto

Ryokan A good choice is **Three Sisters Inn Main Building** *(Map 2; Rakutō-so Honkan; ☎ 761-6336; singles/doubles/triples from ¥8900/13,000/19,500)*, with comfortable rooms. It is well situated in Okazaki for exploration of the Higashiyama area. Take bus No 5 from Kyoto station (stand A1, 30

minutes), get off at Dōbutsuen-mae stop and walk for five minutes.

Three Sisters Inn Annex *(Map 2; Rakutō-so Bekkan; ☎ 761-6333; singles/doubles with bath ¥10,810/18,170, without bath ¥5635/ 11,270, triples with bath ¥23,805)*, in the same neighbourhood, is run by another one of the three eponymous sisters, and is an excellent choice. The features are basically the same as at the main building, but it's somewhat more intimate and the garden walkway adds to the atmosphere. Directions are the same as for the main building.

Ryokan Uemura *(Map 2; ☎/fax 561-0377; rooms per person ¥9000)* is a beautiful little ryokan at ease with foreign guests. It's on a quaint cobblestone alley, just down the hill from Kōdai-ji. Rates include breakfast, and there is a 10pm curfew. Book well in advance, as there are only three rooms. Note that the manager prefers bookings by fax and asks that cancellations also be made by fax (with so few rooms, it can be costly when bookings are broken without notice). Take bus No 206 from Kyoto station (stand D2, 15 minutes) and get off at Yasui bus stop, then walk in the direction of Kōdai-ji.

Seishin-an *(Map 2; ☎ 761-3400; singles/ doubles from ¥15,000/17,000)* is an attractive ryokan near the Kyoto International Community House. It's got a pretty, semi-enclosed garden and spacious rooms. Check-in is from 3.30pm and there is a 10.30pm curfew. To get there, take the Tōzai line subway, get off at Keage station and walk back down Sanjō-dōri.

Northern Kyoto

Hotels Up in the north end of town, near Takano, is **Holiday Inn Kyoto** *(Kyoto & Surrounds map; ☎ 721-3131; singles/doubles/ twins from ¥8000/12,000/12,000)*. It has good facilities but is a bit of a hike to the major attractions.

PLACES TO STAY – TOP END
Central Kyoto

Detailed directions are not provided for places in this price range, as you will probably be travelling to them from the station by taxi (refer to maps for locations).

Ryokan Impossibly elegant **Hiiragiya Ryokan** *(Map 3; ☎ 221-1136; rooms per person ¥25,000-80,000)* is favoured by celebrities from around the world. Room rates include two meals. **Hiiragiya Ryokan Annex** *(Map 3; ☎ 231-0151; rooms per person from ¥12,000)*, close by, also offers top-notch ryokan service (with two meals) and surroundings, but at slightly more affordable rates.

Hotels In the middle of town, **Hotel Fujita Kyoto** *(Map 3; ☎ 222-1511; singles/doubles/ twins from ¥13,000/23,000/16,000)* has good rooms. It is convenient to the nightlife areas and many sightseeing spots

ANA Hotel *(Map 1; ☎ 231-1155; singles/ doubles/twins from ¥13,000/19,000/19,000)* is a good choice in terms of on-site facilities (pool, restaurants, shopping). It's just opposite Nijō-jō.

Kyoto New Hankyū Hotel *(Map 1; ☎ 343-5300; singles/doubles/twins from ¥12,000/22,000/22,000)*, across the street from Kyoto station, has clean but rather drab rooms.

Hotel Granvia Kyoto *(Map 1; ☎ 344-8888; singles/doubles/twins from ¥14,000/ 18,000/20,000)*, built into the station building right over Kyoto station, is gleaming and new and takes the prize in terms of convenient location. It has an extensive variety of restaurants and bars on its premises, and spacious and modern rooms.

Kyoto Hotel *(Map 3; ☎ 211-5111; singles/ doubles/twins from ¥16,000/31,000/25,000)* is an enormous new place right in the centre of town at the Oike-Kawaramachi intersection and commands an impressive view of the Higashiyama mountains. Rooms here are spacious and well maintained.

Rihga Royal Hotel Kyoto *(Map 1; ☎ 341-2311; singles ¥13,000-20,000, doubles ¥21,000-30,000, twins ¥18,000-30,000)* is a large hotel with a swimming pool and several good restaurants on the premises. It's a 10-minute walk from Kyoto station.

Eastern Kyoto

Hotels Perched on the Higashiyama mountains, **Westin Miyako Hotel** *(Map 2; ☎ 771-7111; Western-style singles/doubles/twins from ¥23,000/23,000/23,000, Japanese-style rooms from ¥35,000)* is a graceful hotel and a choice for visiting foreign dignitaries. The hotel surroundings stretch over 6.4 hectares of wooded hillside and landscaped gardens. Prices are higher on weekends.

PLACES TO EAT

Kyoto is famed for *kyō-ryōri*, a local variation on *kaiseki* cuisine. A *kyō-ryōri* course might cost ¥6000 a person, a full spread ¥15,000, and then there are exclusive establishments where you can shell out ¥50,000 (if you are deemed fit to make a reservation). For lesser mortals with punier budgets, some restaurants do a *kyō-ryōri/kaiseki bentō* (boxed lunch) at lunch time for around ¥2500.

Luckily, there's a lot more to the Kyoto restaurant scene than elite restaurants serving rarefied food. Kyoto has great restaurants in every price bracket and it's one of the best places in Japan to make a thorough exploration of Japanese cuisine. And if you get tired of Japanese food, there are heaps of great foreign restaurants about town.

The places listed in this section are generally open daily, unless otherwise noted.

Kyoto Station

The new Kyoto station building is chock-a-block with restaurants. For a quick cuppa while waiting for a train try **Café du Monde** on the second floor overlooking the central atrium. Or you just might want to snag a few pieces of sushi off the conveyor belt at **Kaiten-zushi Iwamura**, on the ground floor at the east end of the station building.

For more substantial meals there are several food courts scattered about. On the 10th floor on the west side of the station building, the **Cootocco** food court has a variety of fast food restaurants, including **Bibimba Tai-ō**, which serves nice *bibimba* (a Korean rice and vegetable dish) for ¥600.

Proper sit-down meals can be found in the two food courts on the 11th floor on the west side of the building: **The Cube** food court and Isetan department store's **Eat Paradise** food court (the latter is better for Japanese food).

In addition to these, you'll find several other good choices near the station including: **Dai Ichi Asahi Rāmen** *(Map 1; ☎ 351-6321; rāmen from ¥600; open 5.30am-2am Fri-Wed)*, an unprepossessing noodle joint that brings to mind the film *Tampopo*; and **Shinpuku Saikan Rāmen** *(Map 1; ☎ 371-7648; rāmen from ¥600; open 7.30am-11pm Thur-Tues)*, another classic *rāmen* joint famous for its chicken-flavoured broth. These two places are next to each other – Shinpuku is further north.

Iimura *(Map 1; ☎ 351-8023; set lunch ¥650-1000; open 11.30pm-2pm Wed-Sun)*, about 10 minutes' walk north of the station, is a classic little restaurant that's popular with locals who come for its ever-changing set Japanese lunch. Just say *kyō no ranchi* (today's lunch) and you should be fine. It's in a traditional Japanese house, set back a bit from the street.

Second House *(Map 1; ☎ 342-2555; coffee from ¥400; open 10am-11pm daily)* is a good spot for a cuppa or light lunch when you're near Nishi Hongan-ji. It's in an old bank building.

Lastly, if you're departing by train from Kyoto station and want to pick up some nibblies for the ride, head downstairs to the B1 floor of **Porta underground shopping arcade**. Here, you can purchase excellent sushi *bentō* at **Kyōtaru** and good bread and pastries at **Shinshindō**. Both are near the north *(kita)* entrance/exit of the Karasuma line subway.

Central Kyoto

The thickest concentration of Japanese and international restaurants in Kyoto can be found in the streets between Shijō and Oike (south to north) and Karasuma and Kawabata (west to east). Also, across the river in Gion you'll find hundreds more restaurants, though these tend to be a little more forbidding, as they cater mainly to salarymen on expense accounts.

Japanese A great place to try a range of healthy and well-prepared Japanese dishes is **Tōsai** *(Map 3; ☎ 213-2900; open 5pm-10pm daily, closed 1st Sun each month)*. There are plenty of choices here for vegetarians (the name of the place means 'Bean/Vegetable'). It's just east of a corner, next to a tiny parking lot – look for the traditional Japanese exterior.

Kōsendō-sumi *(Map 3; ☎ 241-7377; lunch from ¥870; open 11.30am-3pm Mon-Sat, closed holidays)* is a good pick for a pleasant lunch while in the city centre. It's in an old Japanese house and serves a daily set lunch of simple Japanese fare. It's near the Museum of Kyoto.

Tagoto Honten *(Map 3; ☎ 221-3030; noodle dishes from ¥700; open 11am-9pm daily)* is one of Kyoto's oldest and most revered *soba* restaurants. It makes a good

break for those who have overdosed on *rāmen*. It's in the Sanjō covered arcade. There is an English menu.

Gonbei *(Map 3; ☎ 791-4534; noodle dishes from ¥580; open 11.30am-10pm Fri-Wed)* is a quaint little Gion noodle house with an English menu.

Yagura *(Map 3; ☎ 561-1035; open 11am-9.30pm Fri-Wed)* is a classic little noodle house where the house speciality, *nishin soba* (*soba* noodles with fish), goes for ¥1000. We love the funky wooden interior of this place. It's between a *rāmen* joint and a Japanese gift shop – look for the bowls of noodles in the window.

Kane-yo *(Map 3; ☎ 221-0669; unagi over rice from ¥850; open 11.30am-8.30pm)* is a good place to try *unagi* (eel). You can sit downstairs with a nice view of the waterfall or upstairs on the tatami. The *kane-yo donburi* set (¥850) is great value; it's served until 3pm. Look for the barrels of live eels outside and the wooden facade.

Musashi Sushi *(Map 3; ☎ 222-0364; all plates ¥100; open 11am-9.30pm daily)* is the place to go to try *kaiten-zushi* (conveyorbelt sushi). Sure, it's not the best sushi in the world, but it's cheap, easy and fun. Look for the mini-sushi conveyor belt in the window. It's just outside the entrance to the Sanjō covered arcade.

Biotei *(Map 3; ☎ 255-0086; lunch ¥800; open 11.30am-2pm & 5pm-8.30pm Tues-Sat, closed holidays)*, diagonally across from the Nakagyō post office, is a favourite of Kyoto vegetarians. Best for lunch, it serves a daily set of Japanese vegetarian food (the occasional bit of meat is offered as an option, but you'll be asked your preference).

Uosue *(Map 3; ☎ 351-1437; open 11am-2pm & 5pm-10pm Mon-Sat, closed holidays)* is one of the best value Japanese places in town. For lunch, try the wonderful *nijū bentō* for ¥1000. At dinner, their *omakase ryōri cōsu* is a great way to sample *kaiseki* cuisine without breaking the bank: it's only ¥3800. It's next to a tiny shrine – keep an eye out for the sake barrels out front.

Uontana *(Map 3; ☎ 221-2579; dinner from ¥3000; open noon-3pm & 5pm-10pm Thur-Tues)* is a slick upscale *izakaya* (Japanese pub-style venue) where you can try a range of sake and elegantly presented Japanese fare. There is an English menu.

The **844 Store Café** (Map 3; ☎ 241-2120; dishes from ¥700; open 5pm-12pm Wed-Mon) is another favourite of Kyoto vegetarians. It's an offbeat little café which serves things like vegie *gyōza* (Chinese dumplings) and assorted rice and tōfu dishes. It's a colourful place down a tiny alley.

Takasebune (Map 3; ☎ 351-4032; lunch/dinner from ¥1000/5000; open 11am-3pm & 4.30pm-9.30pm Tues-Sun) is a decent tempura and sashimi specialist located in a classic old Japanese house behind Hankyū department store. There's a simple English menu.

Zu Zu (Map 3; ☎ 231-0736; dinner from ¥3000; open 6pm-1.30am daily) is a fun little Ponto-chō *izakaya*. There is no English menu so your best bet is to ask the waiter for a recommendation or point at what other diners are eating. The fare is sort of nouveau-Japanese – things like shrimp and tōfu or chicken and plum sauce. Look for the white stucco exterior and black bars on the windows.

Tomi-zushi (Map 3; ☎ 231-3628; dinner ¥3000; open 5pm-midnight Fri-Wed) is one of our favourites for good sushi in lively surroundings. Here, you rub elbows with your neighbour, sit at a long marble counter and watch as some of the fastest sushi chefs in the land do their thing. Go early or wait in line. It's near the Shijō-Kawaramachi crossing. Look for the lantern and the black and white signs.

Ganko Zushi (Map 3; ☎ 255-1128; lunch/dinner ¥1000/3000; open 11.30am-11pm daily), near Sanjō-Ōhashi bridge, is a good place for sushi or just about anything else. Look for the large display of plastic food models in the window.

Ganko Nijō-en (Map 3; ☎ 223-3456; lunch/dinner from ¥2800/2500; open 11.30am-9.30pm daily) is an upscale branch of Ganko Zushi that serves sushi and *kaiseki* sets. There's a picture menu and you can also stroll in the stunning garden before or after your meal. You will find it near the Nijō-Kiyamachi crossing.

Shirukō (Map 3; ☎ 221-3250; lunch or dinner from ¥2600; open 11.30am-8.30pm Thur-Tues) is a good spot to try Kyoto *obanzai-ryōri* (home-style cooking). The restaurant features more than 10 varieties of miso soup, and the *rikyū bentō* (¥2600) is a bona fide work of art. It's down a pedestrian

street near Shijō-Kawaramachi crossing. Look for the *noren* (Japanese curtains) and the rustic façade.

Misoka-an Kawamichi-ya (Map 3; ☎ 221-2525; dishes ¥550-3800; open 11am-8pm Fri-Wed) is the place to head for a taste of some of Kyoto's best *soba* noodles in traditional surroundings. They've been hand-making noodles here for 300 years. Try a simple bowl of *nishin* (topped with fish) *soba*, or the more elaborate *nabe* dishes (cooked in a special cast-iron pot). Look for the *noren* and the traditional Japanese exterior.

Uzuki (Map 3; ☎ 221-2358; dinner from ¥5000; open 5pm-12pm Thur-Tues) is an elegant Ponto-chō *kaiseki* restaurant with a great platform for riverside dining in the summer. It's best to have a Japanese speaker call and reserve for you here.

Morita-ya (Map 3; ☎ 231-5118; meals from ¥3800; open noon-11pm daily) is Kyoto's most famous beef restaurant. It serves excellent sukiyaki and *shabu-shabu* in traditional tatami rooms, some overlooking the Kamo-gawa. It's on Kiyamachi-dōri, down a narrow alley paved with stones.

Mukade-ya (Map 1; ☎ 256-7039; meals from ¥3000; open 11am-2pm & 5pm-9pm Thur-Tues) is an atmospheric restaurant located in an exquisite *machiya* (traditional Japanese townhouse) west of Karasuma-dōri. For lunch try the *bentō*: two rounds (five small dishes each) of delectable *obanzai* fare (¥3000). *Kaiseki* courses start at ¥5000.

Yoshikawa (Map 3; ☎ 221-5544; lunch ¥2000-4000, dinner ¥6000-12,000; open 11am-2pm & 5pm-8.30pm Mon-Sat) is the place to go for delectable tempura. It offers table seating, but it's much more interesting to sit and eat around the small counter and observe the chefs at work. It's near Oike-dōri.

North of Oike-dōri are some more interesting choices.

Shin-shin-tei (Map 3; ☎ 221-6202; rāmen from ¥570; open 10.30am-5pm Mon-Sat, closed holidays) is famous for its *shiro miso rāmen* (white miso rāmen). The place may not look like much, but the rāmen here is excellent. Look for the yellow and black sign.

Obanzai (Map 1; ☎ 223-6623; lunch/dinner ¥840/2100; open 11am-2pm & 5pm-9pm, closed Wed night) is a little out of the way, but good value. Obanzai serves a good buffet-style lunch/dinner of mostly organic food. It's northwest of the Karasuma-Oike crossing, set back from the street a bit.

Earth Kitchen Company *(Map 1; ☎ 771-1897; lunch ¥700; open 10.30am-6.30pm Mon-Fri, 10.30am-3.30pm Sat, closed holidays)*, located on Marutamachi-dōri near the Kamo-gawa, is a tiny spot that seats just two people but does a bustling business serving tasty takeaway lunch *bentō*. If you fancy a picnic lunch for your temple-hopping, this is the place.

Chabana *(Map 3; ☎ 751-8691; okonomiyaki from ¥600; open 5pm-4am daily)* is a classic *okonomiyaki* (assorted fillings cooked in batter on a grill) joint, good for a late-night snack. If you don't have a favourite just ask for the mixed *okonomiyaki* (¥750). It's on Nijō-dōri. Look for the rotating light outside.

Mikō-an *(Map 1; ☎ 751-5045; lunch/ dinner ¥800/1000; open 11am-11pm Mon-Sat, to 10pm Sun, 2pm-8pm holidays)* is a great choice for a vegetarian lunch or dinner. Just ask for the *setto* (set meal). It's on Kawabata-dōri north of Nijō-dōri. Look for the white front and the small sign with the name written in English on street level.

Most *kaiseki ryōri* places are rather forbidding if you don't speak Japanese. One exception to this is **Kitchō** *(Map 1; ☎ 371-7580; lunch/dinner from ¥3500/8000; open daily)*, a *kaiseki* restaurant located on the B1 floor of the Rhiga Royal Hotel Kyoto not far from Kyoto station. The hotel location means that they're used to foreign customers and there's an English menu to ease the pain of ordering.

Sweet, Tea & Coffee Shops The following places are all in Gion, just east of the Kamo-gawa.

Ōharameya *(Map 3; ☎ 561-1905; sweet set ¥2500; open 11am-7.30pm daily)* is the place to get a thorough education in Japanese sweets. To do so, ask for the full course *amato kaiseki* (sweet set). It's got food models in a glass case out the front.

Kagizen Yoshifusa *(Map 3; ☎ 525-0011; tea from ¥400; open 9am-5.30pm Thur-Tues)* is one of Kyoto's oldest and best known *okashi-ya* (sweet shops). It sells a variety of traditional sweets and has a cosy tearoom upstairs where you can sample cold *kuzukiri* (transparent arrowroot noodles),

served with a *kuro-mitsu* (sweet black sugar) dipping sauce. It's in a traditional *machiya* up a flight of stone steps.

Inoda Coffee *(Map 3; ☎ 221-0507; coffee from ¥440; open 7am-6pm daily)* is a Kyoto coffee institution with branches throughout the city centre. Though slightly overrated for the price, the old-Japan atmosphere at its main shop on Sakaimachi-dōri, south of Sanjō-dōri, is worth a try. It's in a converted *machiya*.

Amazon *(Map 1; ☎ 561-8875; coffee from ¥300; open 7.30am-6pm Thur-Tues)* is a typical Japanese coffee shop that turns out some surprising tasty sandwiches. It's good for a bite or a cuppa while heading to/from Sanjūsangen-dō.

International We go to **Kerala** *(Map 3; ☎ 251-0141; lunch/dinner from ¥850/3500; open 11.30am-2pm & 5pm-9pm daily)* for reliable Indian lunch sets. We find that the dinners, however, are a little overpriced. It's on the 2nd floor; look for the display of food in the glass case on street level.

Bistro de Paris *(Map 1; ☎ 256-1825; lunch/ dinner from ¥850/2500; open 11.30am-1.30pm & 5.30pm-9.30pm Tues-Sun)* is our choice for tasty French cuisine – nothing too fancy, just good. It's near the Shijō-Karasuma crossing.

Daniel's *(Map 3; ☎ 212-3268; lunch/ dinner from ¥750/1800; open 11.30am-3pm & 5.30pm-10pm daily)*, behind Daimaru department store, is a cramped Italian restaurant that does good work with pasta and fish dishes. It's on the second floor.

Merry Island Café *(Map 3; ☎ 213-0214; lunch ¥800; open 11.30am-11pm Tues-Sun)*, behind the Kyoto Hotel, is a good place for coffee or a light lunch. In warm weather the front doors are opened and the place takes on the air of a sidewalk café.

Hati Hati *(Map 3; ☎ 255-1555; dishes from ¥600; open 6pm-2am Wed-Mon)* is our pick for the best Indonesian restaurant in Kyoto. Run by an Indonesian expat, the food is authentic and the atmosphere is cool. It's sometimes closed for private functions. It's downstairs in the Kankō building – look for the white, brick building and the green entry to the stairs.

Shuhari *(Map 1; ☎ 222-6815; lunch from ¥850; open 11.30am-3pm & 5pm-10pm Mon-Fri, 11.30am-10pm Sat & Sun, bar*

Entrance of Kōtoku-an subtemple, Nanzen-ji, Kyoto, Kansai

Tombstone and wooden prayer tablets

Rope with *omikuji* (fortunes) tied around it

Daitoku-ji entrance, Kyoto, Kansai

Akashi Kaikyō Suspension Bridge linking Honshū with Awaji-shima

Kyoto Tower reflected in the glass walls of Kyoto station, Kansai

View over Kyoto to the mountains of Arashiyama, Kyoto, Kansai

open 10pm-2am Sat) is a great example of a new type of Kyoto restaurant: modern cuisine served in a *machiya*. In this case, the cuisine is French, and the emphasis is on tasty fish dishes. There's an English sign.

Le Bouchon *(Map 3; ☎ 211-5220; open 11.30am-2.30pm & 5.30pm-9.30pm Fri-Wed)* is a reliable little French place where there is usually a cheap lunch set on offer (around ¥900). À la carte dinners will run closer to ¥2500. We imagine that the French menu will be a relief after fighting your way through all those Japanese menus.

Yak & Yeti *(Map 3; ☎ 213-7919; lunch sets from ¥650; open 11.30am-4.30pm & 5pm-9.30pm Tues-Sun)* is a little Nepalese place that serves reliably good curry sets for lunch and tasty à la carte dinners. One visit and you'll see why many Kyoto-ites make this a regular pit stop.

Café Kocsi *(Map 3; ☎ 212-7411; open noon-10.30pm Fri-Wed)* is a homey little café which serves good coffee, tea, cakes and sandwiches. It's on the 2nd floor of a white building on a corner; look for the blackboard sign on street level.

Device Café *(Map 3; ☎ 213-7733; open 11am-9pm daily)* is a mod new spot with an English menu featuring a wide variety of Asian and European dishes. Lunch here should cost about ¥1000. It's upstairs in a model steel-girder building.

Zappa *(Map 3; ☎ 255-4437; dishes from ¥700; open 6pm-midnight Mon-Sat)* is a cosy little place that serves up savoury Southeast Asian fare. Prices are reasonable and the music is groovy (but no Frank Zappa?!). It's down a narrow alley between Kiyamachi-dōri and Kawaramachi-dōri; turn south at the wooden torii.

Eastern Kyoto

Japanese Filling noodle and rice dishes are served at **Hinode** *(Map 2; ☎ 751-9251; noodle dishes from ¥400; open 11am-6pm Mon-Sat)*, a pleasant little shop with an English menu. Plain *udon* (thick, white noodles) here is only ¥400, but we recommend you spring for the *nabeyaki udon* (pot-baked udon in broth) for ¥800. This is a good spot for lunch when temple-hopping near Ginkaku-ji or Nanzen-ji.

Omen *(Map 2; ☎ 771-8994; noodles ¥1000; open 11am-10pm Fri-Wed)* is a noodle shop that is named after the thick, white noodles served in a hot broth with a selection of seven fresh vegetables. Just say *omen* and you'll be given your choice of hot or cold noodles, a bowl of soup to dip them in and a plate of vegetables (you put these into the soup along with some sesame seeds). It's a great bowl of noodles but that's not the end of the story: everything in the frequently changing menu is delicious. Best of all, there's a menu in English. It's about five minutes' walk from Ginkaku-ji in a traditional Japanese house with a lantern outside.

Okutan *(Map 2; ☎ 771-8709; set meals ¥3000; open 11am-6pm Fri-Wed)*, just outside the grounds of Nanzen-ji, is a fine restaurant located inside the garden of Chōshō-in. Try a course of *yudōfu* (tōfu cooked in a pot) together with vegetable side dishes.

Senmonten *(Map 2; ☎ 531-2733; 10 dumplings ¥460; open 6pm-2am Mon-Sat)* serves only one thing: crisp fried *gyōza* – they're the best in town. Look for the metal and glass front door.

Imobō Hiranoya Honten *(Map 2; ☎ 561-1603; set meals ¥2400; open 10.30am-8pm daily)*, tucked inside the north gate of Maruyama-kōen, is a traditional restaurant that specialises in *imobō*, a dish consisting of a local type of sweet potato and dried fish. All meals are served in restful, private tatami rooms. There is an English menu.

The neighbourhood around Kyoto University is crammed with good cheap restaurants, many of them along Imadegawa-dōri.

Eating House Hi-Lite *(Map 2; ☎ 721-1997; set meals from ¥500; open 11am-11.30pm Mon-Fri, 11am-10.30pm Sat, closed holidays & 2nd Sat each month)* is where Kyoto University students go for cheap, filling meals. Try the *cheezu chicken katsu teishoku* (fried chicken with cheese set meal) for ¥540; it's a little greasy but how can you complain at these prices? The name is written in English on the sign.

Kuishinbō-no-Mise *(Map 2; ☎ 712-0656; set meals from ¥500; open 11.30pm-2pm & 6pm-11pm Thur-Tues)* is similar to Hi-Lite. The daily lunch/dinner specials are a great value (at dinner ask for the *sabisu-teishoku* – daily set meal). Look for the photos of dishes displayed on the front of the restaurant.

Lastly, **Dai-kitchi** *(Map 2; ☎ 771-3126; dinner about ¥3000; open 5pm-1am Thur-Tues)* is a good *yakitori* (skewered meats

KANSAI

or vegetables) joint with a friendly owner. It's on Sanjō-dōri; look for the red lanterns outside.

International   Located near Ginkaku-ji, **Café Carinho** *(Map 2; ☎ 752-3636; coffee from ¥280, lunch from ¥880; open 11am-7.30pm Tues-Thur & Sun, 11am-11pm Fri & Sat)* is a cosy little café. It serves good, strong Brazilian coffee, tasty cakes and some excellent sandwiches. The friendly owner speaks English.

Buttercups *(Map 2; ☎ 751-9537; coffee from ¥300, meals from ¥580; open noon-10pm Wed-Mon)* is a favourite of the local expat community and a great place for lunch, dinner or a cup of coffee. There is an international menu and this is one of the only places in town where you can get a proper salad.

Zac Baran *(Map 2; ☎ 751-9748; dishes from ¥500; open 5pm-5am daily)*, near the Kyoto Handicraft Centre, is a good spot for a light meal or a drink. It serves a variety of spaghetti dishes, as well as a good lunch special. Look for the picture of the Freak Brothers near the downstairs entrance. If you fancy dessert when you're done, step upstairs to the **Second House Cake Works**.

Tranq Room *(Map 2; ☎ 762-4888)* is a hip new spot in the northern Higashiyama area. Stop in for a cup of coffee or sample some of the tasty pan-Asian fare. There's a picture menu and the owner speaks English. While you're there, check out the upstairs gallery.

Café Peace *(Map 2; ☎ 707-6856; lunch from ¥780; open 11.30am-11pm daily)* is a pleasant spot for a cuppa or a light meal. It's on the 3rd floor but there's a small sign on street level.

Gargantua *(Map 2; ☎ 751-5335; lunch/dinner from ¥1500/3500; open noon-2pm & 5.30pm-10.30pm Wed-Mon)* is an intimate French spot on Imadegawa-dōri that does some creative takes on standard French dishes. Look for the white front.

Sweet & Tea Shops   We go to **Gion Koishi** *(Map 2; ☎ 531-0301; tea from ¥400; open 10.30am-6.30pm daily)* when we want to cool down on a hot summer day in Gion. The speciality here is *uji kintoki* (¥700), a mountain of shaved ice flavoured with green tea, sweetened milk and sweet beans (it tastes a lot better than it sounds, trust

us). This is only available in the summer months. Look for the models of the sweets and tea out front.

Momiji-an *(Map 2; ☎ 551-0420; tea & sweet beans ¥600; open 9am-5pm Fri-Wed)*, located in a rustic old Kyoto house overlooking Maruyama-kōen, is a great spot for a rest while touring the Higashiyama area. Ask for the *usucha* (thin green tea).

Kanō Shōju-an *(Map 2; ☎ 751-1077; open 10am-4.30pm Thur-Tues)* is a delightful tea house off the Tetsugaku-no-Michi where you can enjoy Japanese tea and a sweet (¥1050, ask for *tenzen*).

Arashiyama & Sagano

Yudōfu Sagano *(☎ 871-6946; open 11am-7pm daily)* is a good place to try that classic Arashiyama dish: *yudōfu*. Lunch and dinner courses go for ¥3800 (simply ask for the *yudōfu cosu*). Look for the wagon wheels outside.

Kushi-tei *(☎ 861-0098; lunch or dinner from ¥2500-3000; open noon-9.30pm Thur-Tues)* is a good spot to try *kushi katsu* (skewers of deep-fried goodies). For lunch, ask for the *ohiru osusume kōsu* (¥2500, lunch special). There's a small English sign.

Gyātei *(☎ 862-2411; lunch ¥1800; open 11am-2.30pm & 5pm-9.50pm Tues-Sun)*, just beside the station, offers an all-you-can-eat lunch buffet of Japanese fare (over 30 dishes). It's not the pinnacle of Japanese cuisine, but if volume is what you're after, this is the place. Look for the ochre building.

Seizansō-dō *(☎ 861-1609; courses from ¥3000; open 11.30am-5pm Thur-Tues)* specialises in *yudōfu*. Ask for the *yudōfu teishoku*, which is good value at ¥3000. The seven-course meal includes a pot of fresh *yudōfu* and an array of tōfu-based dishes displaying the creative possibilities of bean curd. The entrance is just to the left of the entrance to Tenryū-ji.

Togetsu-tei *(☎ 871-1310; lunch from ¥3000; open 11am-7pm daily)*, on the south side of Togetsu-kyō Bridge, has great riverside views and tatami-mat seating. Try the *tōfu ryōri hana setto* (tōfu full course, ¥3500). It's on the island just across the bridge from central Arashiyama.

Bokuseki *(lunch from ¥1800; open 10am-5pm Thur-Tues)*, on the road up to Adashino Nembutsu-ji, serves three different lunch sets featuring tōfu and fish. You can also get coffee, tea and sweets here. There's a small English sign.

Kurama

Yōshūji (☎ 741-2848; meals from ¥1000; open 10am-5.30pm Wed-Mon) serves superb *shōjin ryōri* (temple food) in a delightful old Japanese farmhouse with an *irori* (open hearth). The house special, a sumptuous selection of vegetarian dishes served in red lacquered bowls, is called *kurama-yama shōjin zen* (¥2500). Or if you just feel like a quick bite, try the *uzu-soba* (*soba* with mountain vegetables, ¥1000 – you dump all the vegies in the dipping broth). It's just below the main gate to Kurama-dera.

Kibune

Visitors to Kibune from June to September should not miss the chance to cool down by dining at one of the picturesque restaurants beside the Kibune-gawa. Known as *kawadoko-ryōri*, meals are served on platforms suspended over the river as cool water flows just underneath. Most of the restaurants offer some kind of lunch special for around ¥3000. For a full *kaiseki* spread (¥5000-10,000), have a Japanese person call to reserve in advance. In the cold months you can dine indoors overlooking the river.

Tochigiku (☎ 741-5555; meals from ¥3500; open 11am-7pm daily) is one of the better places in Kibune and offers sukiyaki and *kaiseki* sets. It's a 10-minute walk downstream from the centre of the village; the name Tochigiku is written in small Roman letters on the sign that faces downriver.

Ōhara

Seryō-jaya (☎ 744-2301; lunch sets from ¥1000; open 9am-4.30pm daily), just by the gate to Sanzen-in, serves wholesome *sansai ryōri* (mountain vegetable cooking), fresh river fish and *soba* noodles topped with grated yam.

Uji

Kawabun (☎ 0774-21-2556; donburi from ¥750; open 11am-6pm daily) is a simple *shokudō* (dining hall) close to Byōdō-in where you can sample Uji sweets, Uji tea and simple meals. You might consider the *cha soba* (tea *soba* noodles, ¥700). It's the last restaurant in the row before the park area; look for the black-and-white sign.

Self-Catering

If you want a break from eating out, there are plenty of options for self-catering in Kyoto. To do all your food shopping under one roof, try one of Kyoto's many *shōtengai* (market streets). The best of these is **Demachiyanagi Shōtengai**, a humble shopping street in the northern part of town. **Nishiki Market**, in the centre of town, is a much more upscale version that caters primarily to Kyoto restaurateurs.

ENTERTAINMENT

Most of Kyoto's cultural entertainment is of an occasional nature, and you'll need to check with the TIC or a magazine like *Kansai Time Out* to find out whether anything interesting coincides with your visit. Regular cultural events are generally geared at the tourist market and tend to be expensive and, naturally, somewhat touristy.

In addition to cultural entertainment, Kyoto has a great variety of bars, clubs and discos, all of which are good places to meet Japanese folks.

Traditional Dance, Theatre & Music

Gion Corner (Map 2; ☎ 561-1119; admission ¥2800; shows every evening at 7.40pm & 8.40pm 1 Mar-29 Nov; closed 16 Aug) presents shows which are a sort of crash course in Japanese traditional arts. You get a chance to see snippets of the tea ceremony, Koto music, flower arrangement, *gagaku* (court music), *kyōgen* (ancient comic plays), *Kyōmai* (Kyoto-style dance) and bunraku (puppet plays). However, these are rather touristy affairs and may not satisfy those in search of more authentic experiences. On top of this, 50 minutes of entertainment for ¥2800 is a little steep by anyone's standards.

Geisha Dances

Annually in autumn and spring, geisha and their *maiko* apprentices from Kyoto's five schools dress elaborately to perform traditional dances in praise of the seasons. The cheapest tickets cost about ¥1650 (unreserved on tatami mats), better seats cost ¥3000 to ¥3800, and spending an extra ¥500 includes participation in a quick tea ceremony. The dances are similar from place to place and are repeated several

KANSAI

times a day. Dates and times vary, so check with the TIC.

Gion Odori (☎ 561-0160) Gion Kaikan Theatre, near Yasaka-jinja; 1 to 10 November
Kamogawa Odori (☎ 221-2025) Pontochō Kaburen-jō Theatre, Pontochō; 1 to 24 May
Kitano Odori (☎ 461-0148) Kamishichiken Kaburen-jō Theatre, east of Kitano-Tenman-gū; 15 to 25 April
Kyō Odori (☎ 561-1151) Miyagawa-chō Kaburen-jō Theatre, east of the Kamo-gawa between Shijō-dōri and Gojō-dōri; from the first to the third Sunday in April
Miyako Odori (☎ 561-1115) Gion Kōbu Kaburen-jō Theatre, near Gion Corner; throughout April

Kabuki

Minami-za *(Map 3; ☎ 561-0160)*, in Gion, is the oldest kabuki theatre in Japan. The major event of the year is the Kao-mise Festival (1–26 December), which features Japan's finest kabuki actors. Other performances take place on an irregular basis. Those interested should check with the TIC. The most likely months for performances are May, June and September.

Nō

For performances of nō, the main theatre is the **Kanze Kaikan Nō Theatre** *(Map 2; ☎ 771-6114)*. Takigi-Nō is a picturesque form of nō performed in the light of blazing fires. In Kyoto, this takes place in the evenings of 1 and 2 June at Heian-jingū – tickets cost ¥2000 if you pay in advance (ask at the TIC for the location of ticket agencies) or you can pay ¥3300 at the entrance gate.

Musical Performances

Musical performances featuring the koto, *shamisen* and *shakuhachi* are held in Kyoto on an irregular basis. Performances of *bugaku* (court music and dance) are often held at Kyoto shrines during festival periods. Occasionally contemporary *butō* dance is also performed in Kyoto. Check with the TIC to see if any performances are scheduled to be held while you are in town.

Bars

All the places in this section are generally open daily from evening until late.

The Hill of Tara (Map 3), near the Oike-Kawaramachi intersection, is one of our favourite places for a drink in Kyoto. It's a convivial Irish-style pub with Guinness on tap and occasional live Irish music. They also serve a variety of Irish pub food.

Pig & Whistle (Map 3), a British-style pub with darts, pint glasses and, of course, fish and chips, is one of Kyoto's most popular *gaijin* bars. It's a good place to meet Japanese folks and local expats.

Sama Sama (Map 3), another place we highly recommend, is a great little bar/restaurant built with an interior that looks like a cave (but brighter than that image suggests). The Indonesian-born owner turns out great Indonesian food and is happy to chat in English, Japanese or Bahasa Indonesia. Drinks here might be a touch more expensive than at some other spots around town, but it's worth it for the great atmosphere.

Zappa *(Map 3; ☎ 255-4437; open 6pm-midnight Mon-Sat)* can't be beaten if you're looking for a more intimate venue. It's a cosy, little place that once played host to David Bowie (he's said to have discovered the place by chance and decided to drop in for a drink). They serve savoury Southeast-Asian fare and a few Japanese tidbits for good measure. It's down a narrow alley; turn south at the wooden torii.

Ing (Map 3) is another one of our favourite spots. This little joint is the place for cheap bar snacks and drinks, good music and friendly company. It's on the 2nd floor of the Royal building; you'll know you're getting close when you see all the hostesses out trawling for customers on the streets nearby.

Dua Orang (Map 3) is a cool bar with an Indonesian theme (it also serves good Indonesian food). The interior is pleasantly bohemian and you might easily forget you're in Kyoto while drinking here. It's on the 5th floor of the Royal building (same building as Ing – see the previous entry).

Teddy's (Map 3) is part club and part bar. It really gets going late in the evening when the tables are cleared away and the dancing starts (usually to dancehall reggae). On weekend nights there's a cover charge of ¥500. It's on the 7th floor of the Empire building.

Katsuryoku-ya *(Map 3; ☎ 213-2572)* is an interesting pan-Asian themed *izakaya* – an underground grotto with lots of cool nooks and a bar in the back. It's a good place to combine a few drinks and some tasty nibbles (there's a picture menu). It's downstairs on the corner next to a canal.

Ace Café (Map 3; 10th floor, Empire Bldg) is a hip café/bar where you can enjoy a light lunch during the day, or a few drinks in the evening, all while enjoying a first-class view over eastern Kyoto and the Higashiyama mountains.

Backgammon (Map 3), on a little alley north of Sanjō-dōri, is a Kyoto late-night institution. Small, dark and loud, it's a place for serious drinking. Check out the crow's nest drinking area at the top of the ladder – if you don't want to climb down for the next round, staff will send it up to you in a special drinks lift.

Lastly, if you happen to be in Kyoto in the summer, many hotels and department stores operate rooftop beer gardens with all-you-can-eat-and-drink deals and good views of the city. Check the *Kyoto Visitor's Guide* for details.

Clubs

Metro (Map 1) is one of the most popular clubs in town. It's part disco, part live house and even hosts the occasional art exhibition. Every night is a different theme; check the *Kansai Time Out* for forthcoming events. On weekends there's usually an admission charge of between ¥1500 and ¥2000 (with one drink), while Wednesday and Thursday are usually free. It's inside the exit 2 of the Keihan Marutamachi station.

SHOPPING

The heart of Kyoto's shopping district is around the intersection of Shijō-dōri and Kawaramachi-dōri. The blocks running north and west of here are packed with all sorts of stores selling both traditional and modern goods. Kyoto's largest department stores (Hankyū, Takashimaya, Daimaru and Fujii Daimaru) are grouped together in this area.

The TIC has shopping maps and can help you track down specialist shops. *Old Kyoto: A Guide to Traditional Shops, Restaurants & Inns* by Diane Durston is useful for finding unusual traditional items sold (and often produced) by elegant shops with vintage character.

Japanese Arts & Crafts

Not far from Shijo-Karasuma, the **Morita Washi** (Map 3; ☎ 341-1419; open 9.30am–5.30pm daily) sells a fabulous variety of handmade *washi* (Japanese paper) for reasonable prices.

North of city hall, Teramachi-dōri, between Oike-dōri and Marutamachi-dōri, there are a number of classic old Kyoto shops and it is pleasant for strolling around and window-shopping. Two shops worth a look are: **Ippō-dō** (Map 3; ☎ 211-3421; open 9am–7pm Mon-Sat), an old-fashioned teashop selling all sorts of Japanese tea; and **Kakimoto Washi** (Map 3; ☎ 211-3481; open 9am–6pm Mon-Sat), another shop dealing in exquisite *washi*.

In eastern Kyoto, the paved streets of Ninnen-zaka and Sannen-zaka (close to Kiyomizu-dera) are renowned for their crafts and antiques. You'll also find a lot of pottery shops on Gojō-dōri, between Kawabata-dōri and Higashiōji-dōri.

If you want to do all your shopping under one roof, the following places offer a wide selection of Kyoto handicrafts. The **Kyoto Handicraft Centre** (Map 2; ☎ 761-5080; open 9.30am–6pm daily), just north of the Heian-jingū, is a huge cooperative that sells, demonstrates and exhibits crafts (wood-block prints and *yukata* are a good buy here). It's the best spot in town for buying Japanese souvenirs and is highly recommended. **Kyoto Craft Centre** (Map 2; ☎ 561-9660; open 10am–6pm Thur-Tues), near Maruyama-kōen, also exhibits and sells a wide range of handicraft and souvenirs.

Food & Kitchen Utensils

Nishiki-kōji (Map 3), in the centre of town, is Kyoto's most fascinating food market. See the entry in the Central Kyoto section for details on this market. If you do choose to visit, be sure to stop into the knife shop **Aritsugu** (☎ 221-1091; open 9am–5.30pm daily) near the eastern end of the market. Here, you can find some of the best kitchen knives available in the world, as well as a variety of other kitchenware.

For an even more impressive display of foodstuffs, check out the basements of any of the big department stores on Shijō-dōri (perhaps Daimaru has the largest selection). It's difficult to believe the variety of food on display, as well as some of the prices (check out the ¥10,000 melons or the Kōbe beef, for example).

KANSAI

Antiques

The place to look for antiques in Kyoto is Shinmonzen-dōri, in Gion. The street is lined with great, old shops, many of them specialising in one thing or another (furniture, pottery, scrolls, prints etc). You can easily spend an afternoon strolling from shop to shop here, but be warned: if something strikes your fancy you're going to have to break out the credit card – prices here are steep!

Markets

If you're in town when one of the following markets is on, by all means go! Markets are the best places to find antiques and bric-a-brac at reasonable prices and are the only places in Japan where you can actually bargain for a better price.

On the 21st of each month, **Kōbō-san Market** is held at Tō-ji to commemorate the death of Kōbō Daishi (Kūkai), who in 823 was appointed abbot of the temple.

Another major market, **Tenjin-san Market**, is held on the 25th of each month at Kitano Tenman-gū, marking the day of the birth (and, coincidentally, the death) of the Heian-era statesman Sugawara Michizane (845–903).

If you aren't in Kyoto on the 21st, there's also a regular antiques fair at Tō-ji on the first Sunday of each month.

GETTING THERE & AWAY
Air

Kyoto is served by Osaka Itami airport, which handles mostly domestic traffic, and the new Kansai international airport (KIX), which handles most international flights. There are frequent flights between Tokyo and Itami (¥16,700, 70 minutes) but unless you're very lucky with airport connections you'll probably find it as quick and more convenient to take the *shinkansen* (bullet trains). There are ample connections to/from both airports, though the trip to/from Kansai international airport can be both expensive and time consuming.

Train
Shinkansen (Tokyo, Osaka, Nagoya & Hakata) Kyoto is on the Tōkaidō–San-yō Hikari *shinkansen* line (to/from Tokyo ¥13,220, two hours 50 minutes; to/from Nagoya ¥5440, 44 minutes; to/from Osaka

¥1380, 15 minutes; to/from Hakata ¥15,210, three hours 40 minutes). Other stops on this line include Hiroshima, Okayama, Kōbe and Yokohama.

Osaka The fastest train other than the *shinkansen* (see the preceding section) between Kyoto station and Osaka is the JR *shinkaisoku* (special rapid train), which takes 29 minutes (¥540). In Osaka, the train stops at both Shin-Osaka and Osaka stations.

There is also the cheaper private Hankyū line, which runs between Hankyū Kawaramachi, Karasuma and Ōmiya stations in Kyoto and Hankyū Umeda station in Osaka (*tokkyū* [limited express] Umeda–Kawaramachi, ¥390, 40 minutes).

Alternatively, you can take the Keihan main line between Demachiyanagi, Sanjō, Shijō or Shichijō stations in Kyoto and Keihan Yodoyabashi station in Osaka (*tokkyū* to/from Sanjō ¥400, 45 minutes). Yodoyabashi is on the Midō-suji subway line.

Nara Unless you have a Japan Rail Pass, the best option is the Kintetsu line (sometimes written in English as the Kinki Nippon railway) linking Kyoto (Kintetsu Kyoto station, on the south side of the main Kyoto station building) and Nara (Kintetsu Nara station). There are direct limited-express trains (¥1110, 33 minutes) and ordinary express trains (¥610, 45 minutes), which may require a change at Saidai-ji.

The JR Nara line connects Kyoto station with JR Nara station (*shinkaisoku* ¥690, 46 minutes) but departures are often few and far between.

Tokyo The *shinkansen* line has the fastest and most frequent rail links (see the earlier *Shinkansen* section). The journey can also be undertaken by a series of regular JR express trains, but keep in mind that it takes around eight hours and involves at least two (often three or four) changes along the way. The fare is ¥7980. Get the staff at the ticket counter to write down the exact details of each transfer for you when you buy your ticket.

Bus
The overnight bus (JR Dream Kyoto Go) runs between Tokyo station (Yaesu-guchi long-distance bus stop) and Kyoto station

(the long-distance bus stop is adjacent to the city bus terminal).

The trip takes about eight hours and there are usually two departures nightly in either direction, at 10pm and 11pm. The fare is ¥8180/14,480 one way/return. You should be able to grab some sleep in the reclining seats. There is a similar service to/from Shin-juku station's Shin-minami-guchi in Tokyo.

Other JR bus possibilities include (fares are given as one way/return) Kanazawa (¥4060/7310), Tottori (¥3870/6970), Hiro-shima (¥6620/11,720), Nagasaki (¥11,310/20,380) and Kumamoto (¥10,800/19,440).

Hitching

Although we never recommend it, for long-distance hitching, head for the Kyoto-Minami Interchange of the Meishin Expressway, about 4km south of Kyoto station. Take the No 19 bus from Kyoto station and get off when you reach the Meishin Expressway signs. From here you can hitch east towards Tokyo or west to southern Japan.

GETTING AROUND
To/From the Airport

Osaka Itami Airport There are frequent limousine buses between Osaka Itami air-port and Kyoto station (the Kyoto station airport bus stop is opposite the southern side of the station, in front of Avanti de-partment store). Buses also run between the airport and various hotels around town, but on a less regular basis (check with your hotel). The journey should take around 55 minutes and the cost is ¥1370. Be sure to allow extra time in case of traffic.

At Itami, the stand for these buses is out-side the arrivals hall; buy your tickets from the machines and ask one of the attendants which stand is for Kyoto.

MK Taxi (☎ 702-5489) also offers lim-ousine van service to/from the airport for ¥2000 (call at least two days in advance to reserve) or ask at the information counter in the arrivals hall on arrival in Osaka.

Kansai International Airport (KIX)

The fastest, most convenient way to travel between KIX and Kyoto is on the special Haruka airport express, which makes the trip in about 75 minutes. Most seats are reserved (¥3490) but there are usually two cars on each train with unreserved seats (¥2980). Open seats are almost always available, so you don't have to purchase tickets in advance. First and last departures from Kyoto to KIX are 5.45am and 8.16pm; first and last departures from KIX to Kyoto are 6.29am and 10.18pm.

If you have time to spare, you can save some money by taking the *kanku kaisoku* (Kansai airport express) between the air-port and Osaka station and taking a regular *shinkaisoku* to/from Kyoto. The total jour-ney by this method takes about 90 minutes with good connections and costs ¥1800, making it the cheapest option.

It's also possible to go by limousine bus between Kyoto and KIX (¥2300, about two hours). In Kyoto, the bus departs from the same spot as the Itami-bound bus (see the previous Osaka Itami Airport section).

A final option is the **MK Taxi Sky Gate Shuttle limousine van service** (☎ 702-5489), which will pick you up anywhere in Kyoto city and deliver you to KIX for ¥3000. Call at least two days in advance to reserve. The advantage of this method is that you are delivered from door to door and you don't have to lug your baggage through the train station. MK has a counter in the arrivals hall of KIX, and if there's room they'll put you on the next van to Kyoto. A similar service is offered by **Yasaka Taxi** (☎ 803-4800).

Bus

Kyoto has an intricate bus network that is an efficient way to get around at moder-ate cost. Many of the bus routes used by foreign visitors have announcements in English. The core timetable for buses is between 7am and 9pm, though a few run earlier or later.

The bus terminal at Kyoto station is on the northern side of the station and has three main departure bays (departure points are indicated by the letter of the bay and number of the bus stand within that bay).

The TIC's *Kyoto Transportation Guide* is a good map of the city's main bus lines, with a detailed explanation of the routes and a Japanese/English communication guide on the reverse side.

Bus stops throughout the city usually dis-play a map of bus stops in the vicinity on the top section. On the bottom section there's a timetable for the buses serving that stop.

KANSAI

Unfortunately, most of this information is written in Japanese, and those who don't read the language will simply have to ask locals waiting at the stop for help.

Entry to the bus is usually through the back door and exit is via the front door. Inner city buses charge a flat fare (¥220), which you drop into the clear plastic receptacle on top of the machine next to the driver. The machine gives change for ¥100 and ¥500 coins or ¥1000 notes, or you can ask the driver.

On buses serving the outer areas, you take a *seiri-ken* (numbered ticket) when entering. When you leave, an electronic board above the driver displays the fare corresponding to your ticket number.

To save time and money, you can buy a *kaisū-ken* (book of five tickets) for ¥1000. There's also a one-day card (*shi-basu senyō ichinichi jōshaken kaado*) valid for unlimited travel on city buses and subways that costs ¥500. A similar pass (*Kyoto kankō ichinichi jōsha-ken kaado*) that allows unlimited use of the bus *and* subway costs ¥1200. A two-day bus/subway pass (*futsuka jōshā-ken*) costs ¥2000. *Kaisū-ken* can be purchased directly from bus drivers. The other passes and cards can be purchased at major bus terminals and at the main bus information centre.

The main bus information centre is located in front of Kyoto station. Here, you can pick up bus maps, purchase bus tickets and passes (on all lines, including highway buses), and get additional information. Nearby, there's an English/Japanese bus information computer terminal; just enter your intended destination and it will tell you the correct bus and bus stop.

When heading for locations outside the city centre, be careful which bus you board. Kyoto city buses are green, Kyoto buses are tan and Keihan buses are red and white.

Subway

The quickest way to travel between the north and the south of the city is to take the Karasuma line subway, which operates from 5.30am to 11.30pm. The minimum fare is ¥200.

There's also the new Tōzai line subway, which runs east–west across the city, from Daigo station in the east to Nijō station in the west, stopping at Sanjō-Keihan en route.

Taxi

Kyoto taxi fares start at ¥630 for the first 2km. The exception is **MK Taxis** (☎ 702-5489), which start at ¥580.

MK Taxis also provide tours of the city with English-speaking drivers. For a group of up to four people, prices start at ¥12,620 for a three-hour tour. Another company offering a similar service is **Kyōren Taxi Service** (☎ 672-5111).

Cycling

Kyoto is a great city to explore on a bicycle; with the exception of outlying areas it's mostly flat and there is a new bike path running the length of the Kamo-gawa.

Unfortunately, Kyoto must rank near the top in having the world's worst public facilities for bike parking and the city regularly impounds bikes parked outside of regulation bike-parking areas. If your bike does disappear, check for a poster in the vicinity (in both Japanese and English) indicating the time of seizure and the inconvenient place you'll have to go to pay a ¥2000 fine and retrieve your bike.

Bicycle Rentals About 15 minutes' walk northwest of Kyoto station is **Tour Club** (☎ 353-6968), which rents mountain bikes and shopping bikes for ¥630 per day. For more on Tour Club, see the earlier Places to Stay section.

Another good spot to rent a bike is **Kyoto Cycling Tour Project** (KCTP; ☎ 354-3636; Ⓦ www.kctp.net/en/index.html). These folks rent mountain bikes (from ¥1500 per day) which are perfect for getting around the city. Bicycles can be delivered upon request (¥500) or you can pick them up at one of their three locations around town (see their website for details and maps). KCTP also conducts a variety of bicycle tours of Kyoto – an excellent way to see the city (check the website for details). Finally, KCTP produces a useful map of recommended cycling routes in Kyoto; pick one up from them when you pick up your bike.

Near Sanjō station on the Keihan line, **Kitazawa Bicycle Shop** (☎ 771-2272; open 8am-5pm daily) rents out bicycles for ¥200 per hour and ¥1000 per day. It's a 200m walk north of the station next to the river on the east side.

Nearby on Kawabata-dōri, north of Sanjō-dōri, **Rental Cycle Yasumoto** (☎ 751-0595; open 9am-5pm daily) offers a similar deal.

Most rental outfits require you to leave ID such as a passport or driver's licence.

Shiga-ken 滋賀県

Just across the Higashiyama mountains from Kyoto is Shiga-ken, a small prefecture dominated by Biwa-ko, Japan's largest lake. The prefecture has a variety of attractions that are easily visited as day trips from Kyoto. Ôtsu and Hikone are the major sightseeing centres. Hiei-zan and Enryaku-ji are covered under Northern Kyoto this chapter.

JNTO publishes a leaflet entitled *Lake Biwa, Ôtsu & Hikone*, which has useful maps and concise information. It's available at any JNTO-operated TIC, including the Kyoto TIC.

ŌTSU 大津
☎ 077 • pop 286,000

Ôtsu has developed from a 7th-century imperial residence (the city was capital of Japan for just five years) into a lake port and major post station on the Tōkaidō highway between eastern and western Japan. It is now the capital of Shiga-ken.

The **information office** (☎ 522-3830; open 8.45am-5.25pm daily) is at JR Ōtsu station. Some English is spoken here, and it has an excellent free map of the area entitled the *Biwako Ôtsu* Guide Map.

Mii-dera 三井寺

Mii-dera (admission ¥500; open 8am-5pm daily), formally known as Onjō-ji, is a short walk northwest from Keihan Hama-Ōtsu station. The temple, founded in the late 7th century, is the head branch of the Jimon branch of the Tendai school of Buddhism. It started its days as a branch of Enryaku-ji on Hiei-zan, but later the two fell into conflict, and Mii-dera was repeatedly razed by Enryaku-ji's warrior monks.

Special Events

The **Ōtsu Matsuri** takes place on 7 and 8 October at Tenson-jinja, close to JR Ōtsu station. Ornate floats are displayed on the first day and paraded around the town on the second day. If you're in town on 8 August, be sure to catch the **Ōtsu Dai Hanabi Taikai** (Ōtsu Grand Fireworks Festival), which starts at dusk. The best spots to watch are along the waterfront near Keihan Hama-Ōtsu station. Be warned that trains to and from Kyoto are packed for hours before and after the event.

Getting There & Away

From Kyoto you can either take the JR Tōkaidō line from JR Kyoto station to Keihan Hama-Ôtsu station (¥190, 10 minutes), or travel on the Kyoto Tōzai subway line from Sanjō Keihan station to Hama-Ôtsu station (¥390, 25 minutes).

SAKAMOTO 坂本

Sakamoto station is the main station for access from Shiga-ken to Enryaku-ji.

Hiyoshi-taisha 日吉大社

If you fancy a detour on your visit to Hiei-zan, Hiyoshi-taisha (Hie-taisha; admission ¥300; open 9am-4.30pm daily) is a 15-minute walk from Sakamoto station. Dedicated to the deity of Hiei-zan, the shrine is closely connected with Enryaku-ji.

Getting There & Away

Sakamoto is best reached by taking the Kyoto Tōzai line subway from Sanjō-Keihan station in Kyoto to Keihan Hama-Ôtsu station; change there to a Keihan-line Sakamoto-bound *futsū*. The total fare is ¥590, and with good connections the trip takes about 40 minutes. You can also take the JR line to the Hiei-zan Sakamoto station – be careful to take the Kosei (West Lake) line (¥320, 20 minutes).

HIRA-SAN 比良山

Hira-san is the high mountain range that rises to the west of Biwa-ko. It is a great hiking destination and there are many excellent hiking courses crisscrossing the peaks. It is best accessed by the JR Kosei line, which leaves from Kyoto station (but be careful to board a Kosei-line train, as most trains on that track head to the other side of the lake).

A good base for hiking in the area is the **Maiko Hut** (☎ 077-596-8190; w www.trekstation.co.jp/index5.html; dorm beds

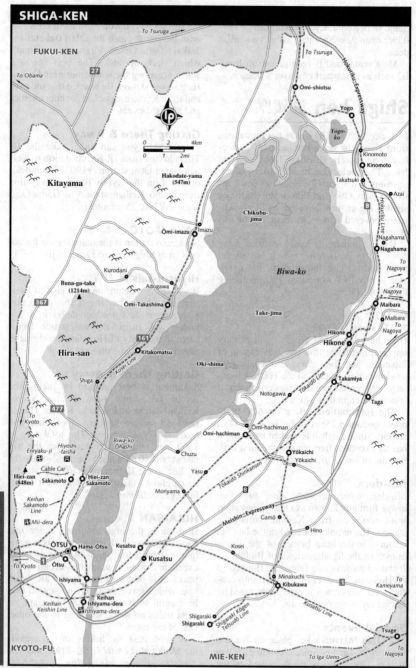

SHIGA-KEN

FUKUI-KEN

To Obama

To Tsuruga

27

To Tsuruga

To Tsuruga

Hokuriku-Expressway

Ōmi-shiotsu

Yogo

Yogo-ko

Kinomoto

Kinomoto

Takatsuki

Azai

8

0   2   4km
0   2mi

Hakodate-yama
(547m)

Kitayama

Ōmi-imazu   Imazu

Chikubu-
jima

Nagahama

Nagahama

To
Nagoya

Hokuriku Line

Buna-ga-take
(1214m)

Kurodani

Adogawa

Biwa-ko

To
Nagoya

367

Ōmi-Takashima

Take-jima

Maibara

Maibara
To
Nagoya

Hira-san

Kosei Line

Kitakomatsu

Hikone

Hikone

161

Shiga

Oki-shima

Notogawa

Tōkaidō Line

Takamiya

Taga

477

To
Kyoto

Biwa-ko
Ōhashi

Ōmi-hachiman   Ōmi-hachiman

Yōkaichi

Yōkaichi

Enryaku-ji

Hiyoshi
-taisha

Chuzu

Yasu

Tōkaidō Shinkansen

Cable Car

Hiei-zan
(848m)

Sakamoto

Hiei-zan
Sakamoto

Moriyama

Gamō

Meishin-Expressway

Keihan
Sakamoto
Line

Hino

8

Mii-dera

Kusatsu   Kusatsu

Kosei

To Kyoto

ŌTSU

Hama-Ōtsu

Minakuchi

To
Kameyama

Ōtsu

Kibukawa

1

KANSAI

Ishiyama

Keihan
Keishin Line

Keihan
Ishiyama-dera

Kusatsu Line

Ishiyama-dera

Shigaraki   Shigaraki Kōgen
Tetsudō Line

Shigaraki

To Iga-Ueno

To
Nagoya

Tsuge

KYOTO-FU

MIE-KEN

¥3500, private rooms per person from ¥4000). The folks here will happily pick you up at Ōmi-maiko station (about 30 minutes from Kyoto) on the Kosei line if you call ahead to make arrangements. They can also arrange guided walks in the Hira-san range in English.

Several good hikes in the Hira-san range are described in Lonely Planet's *Hiking in Japan*, including the superb Yatsubuchi-no-taki hike, which we reckon is the best one-day hike near Kyoto.

ISHIYAMA-DERA 石山寺

This temple *(admission ¥500; open 8am-4.30pm daily)*, founded in the 8th century, now belongs to the Shingon sect. The room next to the Hondō (Main Hall) is famed as the place where Lady Murasaki wrote *The Tale of the Genji*.

The temple is a 10-minute walk south from Keihan Ishiyama-dera station. Take the Kyoto Tōzai line subway from Sanjō-Keihan station in Kyoto to Keihan Hama-Ōtsu and change there to a Keihan-line Ishiyama-dera-bound *futsū* (¥520, minutes). Alternatively, take the JR Tōkaidō line from JR Kyoto station to JR Ishiyama-dera station. *Kaisoku* (rapid) and *futsū* trains run this route (¥230, 10 minutes). Switch at JR Ishiyama-dera station to the Keihan line for the short journey to Keihan Ishiyama-dera station (¥160, three minutes).

HIKONE 彦根
☎ 0749 • pop 106,000

Hikone is the second-largest city in the prefecture and of special interest to visitors for its lovely castle, which dominates the town.

Orientation & Information

There is a good **tourist information office** (☎ 22-2954), on your left as you leave the station, with helpful maps and literature. The *Street Map & Guide to Hikone* has a map on one side and a suggested one-day bicycle tour of Hikone's sights on the back.

The castle is straight up the street from the station – about a 10-minute walk away.

Hikone-jō 彦根城

This castle *(admission ¥500; open 8.30am-5pm daily)* was completed in 1622 by the Ii family, who ruled as *daimyō* (feudal lords) over Hikone. It is rightly considered one of the finest remaining castles in Japan. Much of it is original, and you can get a great view across the lake from the upper storeys. The castle is surrounded by more than 1000 cherry trees, making it a popular spot for spring-time *hanami* activities.

After visiting the castle, don't miss nearby **Genkyū-en** *(admission included in castle ticket; open 8.30am-5pm daily)*, a lovely Chinese-influenced garden that was completed in 1677. Ask someone at the castle to point you in the right direction. There's a teahouse in the garden where ¥500 gets you a cup of *matcha* (powdered green tea) and a sweet to enjoy as you gaze over the scenery.

Special Events

The **Hikone-jō Matsuri** takes place at the castle during the first three days in November. At this time children dress up in the costume of feudal lords and parade around the area.

Perhaps more interesting, however, is the **Birdman Contest**, held on the last Friday and Saturday of August at Matsubara Beach in Hikone. Here you will find that contestants launch themselves over Lake Biwa in all manner of flimsy human-powered flying machines. It's really a whole lot of fun to watch.

Places to Eat

If you're hungry after visiting the castle, try **Suihama** restaurant, which is on the left 1½ blocks down the street from the station as you walk to the castle. There's a small picture menu and the *higawari okazu teishoku* (daily lunch special) costs ¥650.

Getting There & Away

Hikone is less than an hour travelling time (*shinkaisoku*, ¥1110) from Kyoto on the JR Tōkaidō line. If you take the *shinkansen*, it is best to ride from Kyoto to Maibara (25 minutes) and then backtrack from there on the JR Tōkaidō line to Hikone (¥180, five minutes). Maibara is a major rail junction, the meeting place of the JR Tōkaidō, Hokuriku and Tōkaidō *shinkansen* lines. By *shinkaisoku*, Maibara is 52 minutes from Kyoto on the JR Tōkaidō line (¥1110).

NAGAHAMA 長浜
☎ 0749 • pop 61,063

Nagahama is interesting for its old *machiya* and *kura* (storehouses), which can be found in the streets east of the station. Some of the old buildings have been converted into atmospheric shops and are worth popping into as you explore the area. The speciality of the area is glass, and Nagahama's artisans produce a variety of high-quality and interesting work – souvenir hunters take note! Several of the buildings have also been converted into restaurants.

There is a **tourist information office** (☎ 63-7055; open 10am-5pm daily) just outside the station, where you can pick up a detailed Japanese-language map of the area.

If you're in the area from 14 to 16 April, check out the **Nagahama Hikiyama Matsuri**, in which costumed children perform Hikiyama *kyōgen* (comic drama) on top of a dozen festival floats decked out with elaborate ornamentation.

Places to Stay & Eat
Kokumin-shukusha Hōkō-sō (☎ 62-0144; rooms per person ¥8000) is five minutes' walk west of the station in Hōkōen Park (*kokumin-shukusha* are people's lodges – cheap accommodation).

There are two classic old *shokudō* in town on the right side of Ekimae-dōri, about a block east of the station. **Tora-ya** (open Fri-Wed) is the best place for cheap eats in town, with such things as *kitsune donburi* (rice with pieces of fried tōfu) for only ¥350 (look for the dilapidated old house on the corner). **Nakajima Shokudō** is a step up in price and comfort (look for the wooden front and the food models). Both of these places are time machines back to a forgotten Japan and are well worth stopping for.

For something more upscale, along with a tasty brew to wash it down with, try the **Nagahama Roman Beer** hall, a microbrewery and restaurant about 10 minutes' walk from the station (ask the folks at the tourist information office to point it out on a map).

Getting There & Away
Nagahama is a 10-minute ride north of Maibara on the JR Hokuriku line (*shinkaisoku*, ¥190, 10 minutes). See the Hikone Getting There & Away section for transport details to Maibara.

Northern Kansai & the San-in Coast
関西北部・山陰海岸

The spectacular coastline east from Tottori all the way to the Tango-hantō (peninsula) in Kyoto-fu is known as the **San-in Kaigan Kokuritsu Kōen** – the San-in Coast National Park. There are sandy beaches, rugged headlands, rocky islets and a cruisy atmosphere.

There are train lines the length of the area, but they spend a fair bit of time inland and in tunnels. The best way to see the coastline is on wheels, whether it be a rental car, a motorbike, a bicycle or by thumb. If you stick to the trains, make the effort to get off every now and then.

ORGANISATION
The text in this section moves from west to east, starting at the Tottori-ken/Hyōgo-ken border. It is a continuation of the route along the San-in Coast described in the Western Honshū chapter. If you're heading east to west, read this section backwards. See San-In Coast National Park in the Western Honshū chapter for more details on this area.

MOROYOSE 諸寄
If you want to check out life in a small Sea of Japan fishing village, Moroyose, in Hyōgo-ken near the border with Tottori-ken, provides a great chance. There is the convenient Moroyose station on the JR San-in line, a sandy beach, an *asa-ichi* (morning fish market) at 9am Sunday to Friday at the port, and the **Youth Hostel Moroyose-sō** (☎ 0796-82-3614; beds ¥2700; meals available), just a short stroll from it all.

Just over the hill to the east is **Hamasaka**, which has cruises (from ¥1000), an *onsen* and a beach backed by a huge stand of pine trees among which you can camp.

TAKENO 竹野
Takeno is a gem of a fishing village/summer resort that is full of accommodation and eateries. It is extremely popular in summer. There is an **information office** (☎ 0796-47-1080; open 8.30am-5pm daily) on the main beachfront, a couple of kilometres north of Takeno station on the JR San-in line. There is good summer swimming, and **Bentenhama**

camping area is a short walk away among pine trees that are bent at awkward angles by the winter winds. **Kitamaekan** *(open daily)* is an *onsen* complex where the baths are on the second floor with a great view of the beach and sea. **Hamaya Ryokan** *(☎ 0796-47-0028; rooms per person with 2 meals ¥10,000)* is right on the beachfront next to the information office, but if it's full there are plenty of other options.

KINOSAKI 城崎
☎ 0796

Inland off the coast, on the Maruyama-gawa, is the lovely little *onsen* town of Ki-nosaki, which makes a pleasant overnight excursion from Kyoto, Osaka or Kōbe. It is a laid-back place to roam around and soak in hot springs.

Kinosaki's biggest attraction are its **onsen** *(admission ¥500; open daily)*, of which there are six open to the public. Guests staying in town stroll the canal from bath to bath wearing *yukata* and *geta* (wooden sandals). Most of the *ryokan* and hotels in town have their own *uchi-yu* (private baths), but also provide their guests with free tickets to the ones outside *(soto-yu)*. A seventh public bath-house, **Sato-no-yū** *(admission ¥800)*, has recently opened in a massive building next to the station. Outside its entrance is an *ashi-no-yū*, a 'foot-bath' where you can soak your feet for free.

The town also has a ropeway up to the **Onsen-ji**, the temple built to commemorate the founding of the *onsen* in 738. The tem-ple is halfway up, but if you go to the top, there are some fine views out to the coast.

Savoury crab from the Sea of Japan is a speciality in Kinosaki during the winter months.

On 14 and 15 October the **Danjiri Matsuri** sees teams of *mikoshi* (portable shrine) bear-ers clashing for pole position to get to the local shrine.

Information

Opposite the station is an **information office** *(☎ 32-4141; open 9am-6pm daily)* where the staff are extremely enthusiastic. They can provide an English brochure/map, suggest accommodation and make book-ings. A smattering of English is spoken. The same office has rental bicycles avail-able for ¥400 for two hours or ¥800 a day.

If you're just passing through, you could leave your bags in a coin locker, pick up a bicycle, go for a ride, have a bath or just soak your feet, and then carry on.

Places to Stay

If you don't mind paying a bit of money, Kinosaki is a great place to experience a night in a traditional Japanese inn. **Nishimura Honkan Ryokan** *(☎ 32-2211; rooms per person from ¥28,000)* is a classic and the ultimate of inns here.

Far more affordable, and still of a high standard, is **Tsuruya** *(☎ 32-2924; rooms per person with breakfast ¥7000)* where Mr Ta-mura, who speaks English, will attend to your needs. Tsuruya is near the base of the rope-way, a ten-minute walk from the station.

Other options are **Tsutaya** *(☎ 32-2511)* along the canal, as well as **Mikuniya** *(☎ 32-2414)*, in front of the JR Kinosaki station. Both have per person rates with two meals starting at ¥15,000.

Getting There & Away

Kinosaki is on the JR San-in line, 10 minutes north of Toyooka, 2½ hours from Osaka, and three hours from Kyoto. There are various train options, so it would pay to check at an information office.

CONTINUING EAST INTO KYOTO-FU

If you're using the JR San-in line, unfortu-nately it disappears inland and there isn't another JR line on the coast until the JR Obama line at Nishi-Maizuru, some 60km to the east. There's some great stuff coming up though, including Amanohashidate, and for-tunately the Kita-Kinki Tango Miyazu-sen, a private line, picks up the link. If you're on a JR pass, this section will cost you extra. From Kinosaki, take the JR San-in line into Toyooka, a largish town that serves as a train junction, change to the Kita-Kinki Tango Miyazu-sen, and carry on east.

If you're heading westwards along the coast and want to visit Amanohashidate, you'll have to change to the Kita-Kinki Tango Miyazu-sen at Nishi-Maizuru.

KUMIHAMA 久美浜

The second station out from Toyooka is Kumihama, which is in Kyoto-fu. The large seawater bay named **Kumihama-wan** is connected out to the Sea of Japan through a narrow gap at its northern end that has a bridge across it. There are free bicycles for use (¥1000 deposit) at the station, where there is an **information office** (☎ 0772-82-1781; open 9am-5.30pm daily). It's 16km for the full loop around the bay and a great bike ride if the weather is halfway decent. There's a good swimming beach out on the Sea of Japan coast. If you want to stay out there, try the **Hamanoji Ryokan** (☎ 0772-83-1096; rooms per person with/without meals ¥12,000/6000).

TANGO-HANTŌ 丹後半島

At the eastern end of the San-in Coast National Park is the Tango-hantō, which juts north into the Sea of Japan. The train line cuts across its base to Amanohashidate, so if you want to check out the peninsula, you'll have to take to the road. A bus runs around the peninsula, passing a number of small scenic fishing ports. At the end of the peninsula, a large car park and restaurant mark the start of the 40-minute round-trip walk to the **Kyōga-saki Lighthouse**.

The village of **Ine**, on a perfect little bay on the eastern side of the Tango-hantō, is particularly interesting. There are *funaya* houses that are built right out over the water, under which boats are drawn in, as if in a carport. The best way to check it out is by boat, and **Ine-wan Meguri** tour boats putter around the bay (¥650, 30 minutes) from March to December. Buses (¥1100) reach Ine in half an hour from Amanohashidate.

Places to Stay

One of the best ways to see the Tango-hantō is with **Two to Tango** (e divyam@mac.com; w www.gotokandk.com/tango.html; lodging & 3-day all-inclusive tour per person ¥100,000). This is an exclusive tour of the Tango Peninsula offered by a French expat who's lived in Kyoto-fu for 20 years. You stay in a secluded farmhouse in Kurumi-dani (in the heart of the Tango-hantō) and make trips over scenic roads to excellent *onsen*, restaurants and lovely beaches. Everything is taken care of, including the driving. The tour gives you an intimate look at a side of Japan rarely glimpsed by foreign travellers and it's perfect for a gentle entry into the country or to wind down after a hectic trip.

There are several fine *minshuku* (B&B-style accommodation) in the town of Ine including **Yoza-sō** (☎ 0772-32-0278; rooms per person with 2 meals ¥8000).

WAKASA-WAN 若狭湾

The area east of Tango-hantō is known as the **Wakasa-wan Kokutei Kōen** (Wakasa Bay Quasi-National Park), and includes parts of northern Kyoto-fu and western Fukui-ken. It is fairly easily accessed from the cities of Kansai and has beaches that are very popular in summer.

Amanohashidate 天橋立

☎ 0772

Amanohashidate (Bridge to Heaven) is rated as one of Japan's 'three great views', along with Miyajima (near Hiroshima) and the islands of Matsushima-wan (near Sendai). The 'bridge' is really a long, narrow tree-covered (8000 pine trees!) sand-spit, 3.5km in length. Just a couple of narrow channels prevent it from cutting off the top of the bay, Miyazu-wan, as a separate lake. The sand-spit itself is very pleasant, and someone with a good deal of foresight has done a great job keeping the construction and concrete boys away. There is good swimming, as well as beach showers, toilet facilities and covered rest areas the length of the spit.

The town of Amanohashidate consists of two separate parts, one at each end of the spit. At the southern end there are a number of hotels, ryokan, restaurants, a popular temple and JR Amanohashidate station. There's an **information counter** (☎ 22-8030; open 10am-6pm daily) stocking an English brochure at the train station.

At the other end, a funicular railway (¥640 return) and a chair lift run up the hillside to the Kasamatsu-kōen vantage point from where the view is said to be one of the best three in the land. From here, incidentally, you're supposed to view the sand-spit by turning your back to it, bending over and observing it framed between your legs! (It supposedly makes the Amanohashidate look like it is 'floating'.) There is a bus from the top of the lift along to Naria-ji, number 28 on the 33 Temples of Kannon pilgrimage. Proving that mountain temples are not short of cash, Naria-ji has recently opened a gaudy five-storey 33m pagoda. If you don't want to fork out for the lift up to Kasamatsu-kōen, you can walk up in about 20 minutes. The walkway is to the left of the lift station.

A bridge and swing bridge cross the two channels at the southern end of the sand spit, and cycling along the length of the spit is a popular activity.

Places to Stay At the northern end of Ichinomiya is **Amanohashidate Youth Hostel** (☎ 27-0121; beds with/without 2 meals ¥4000/2700), a modern-thinking YH that even has beer on tap in its dining room. To get there take a bus from JR Amanohashidate station and get off at the Jinjamae bus stop (20 minutes), from where it's a 1km walk (with signs from the bus stop). If you've got plenty of time, allow an hour to walk along the spit to get there.

There are a number of ryokan and hotels near the station at the southern end of the 'bridge', though they're generally fairly expensive. Best deals are **Maruyasu Minshuku** (☎ 22-2310; rooms per person with/without meals ¥7200/4900) and **Young Inn Amanohashidate** (☎ 22-0650; singles/twins ¥5500/9000). **Toriki Ryokan** (☎ 22-0010; rooms ¥12,000) includes two meals. **Shoero Ryokan** is similarly priced and also includes meals.

Getting There & Away The Kita-kinki Tango Tetsudō line runs between JR stations at Toyooka to the west and Nishi-Maizuru to the east. Amanohashidate station is on this line, 1¼ hours from Toyooka (futsū ¥1160) and 40 minutes from Nishi-Maizuru (futsū ¥620). There are several direct trains from Kyoto daily, but JR pass holders will have to fork out for the Kita-kinki Tango Tetsudō part of the route.

Getting Around You can cross the 'bridge to heaven' on foot, bicycle or on a motorcycle of less than 125cc capacity. Bicycles can be hired at a number of places for ¥400 for two hours or ¥1600 a day. Tour boats (¥520) also operate across Miyazu-wan.

YURA-HAMA 由良浜
Further around the coast to the east is Yura-hama, served by Tango-yura station on the Kita-Kinki Tango Miyazu-sen. There is a nice beach here, and at its eastern end the Yura-gawa flows out into the bay. The river valley has strong steady winds, and the area

around the mouth of the river is one of Japan's most popular windsurfing spots. If you're keen to have a go at windsurfing, try renting from **Marina Fiji** (☎ 0772-26-0243) on the beachfront. It also rents small yachts and jet-skis. **Yamada-sō** (☎ 0772-26-0047; rooms per person from ¥4000) is on the beachfront a bit further west.

MAIZURU 舞鶴
There's nothing overly appealing about the two ports of Nishi-Maizuru and Higashi-Maizuru, but they play important parts in the area's transportation networks. If you've come from the west on the Kita-Kinki Tango Tetsudo trains as described in the text, **Nishi-Maizuru** is the end of the line and where the JR Obama line comes out to meet the coast. If you're on your way to Amanohashidate, this is where you'll have to change to the private line.

There are regular ferry services to Otaru in Hokkaidō from **Higashi-Maizuru** (and also from Tsuruga at the eastern end of the Wakasa-wan – see Fukui-ken in the Central Honshū chapter). This is a cheap and interesting way of getting to Hokkaidō. The cheapest tickets are ¥7000 for the 30-hour journey. Call **Shin-Nihonkai Ferry** (☎ 06-6345-2921) for details.

CONTINUING EAST INTO FUKUI-KEN
The lovely coastal scenery of Wakasa-wan continues east along the coast into Fukui-ken. For details on this part of the coast, see Fukui-ken in the Central Honshū chapter.

Osaka 大阪

☎ 06 • pop 2.48 million
Osaka is the working heart of Kansai. Famous for its down-to-earth citizens and hearty cuisine, Osaka combines a few historical and cultural attractions with all the delights of a modern Japanese city. Indeed, Osaka is surpassed only by Tokyo as a showcase of the Japanese urban phenomenon.

This isn't to say that Osaka is an attractive city; almost bombed flat in WWII, it appears an endless expanse of concrete boxes punctuated by pachinko parlours and elevated highways. But the city somehow manages to rise above this and exert a peculiar charm.

KANSAI

By night, the city really comes into its own; this is when all those drab streets and alleys come alive with flashing neon, beckoning residents and travellers alike with promises of tasty food and good times.

Osaka's highlights include Osaka-jō and its surrounding park, Osaka Aquarium with its enormous whale shark, the *Blade Runner* nightscapes of the Dōtombori area and the wonderful Open Air Museum of Old Japanese Farmhouses. But Osaka has more to offer than its specific sights; like Tokyo, Osaka is a city to be experienced in its totality, and casual strolls are likely to be just as rewarding as structured sightseeing tours.

HISTORY

Osaka has been a major port and mercantile centre from the beginning of Japan's recorded history. It was also briefly the first capital of Japan (before the establishment of a permanent capital at Nara). During its early days, Osaka was Japan's centre for trade with Korea and China, a role which it shares today with Kōbe and Yokohama.

In the late 16th century, Osaka rose to prominence when Toyotomi Hideyoshi, having unified all of Japan, chose Osaka as the site for his castle. Merchants set up around the castle and the city grew into a busy economic centre. This development was further encouraged by the Tokugawa shōgunate, which adopted a hands-off approach to the city, allowing merchants to prosper unhindered by government interference.

In the modern period, Tokyo has usurped Osaka's position as economic centre of Japan, and most of the companies formerly headquartered in Osaka have moved east. Nonetheless, Osaka remains an economic powerhouse and the prefecture has recorded a GDP bigger than the individual GDPs of all but eight countries in the world in the past several years. However, the city has been hard hit by Japan's ongoing recession and many businesses have closed, particularly those that used to cater to businessmen out entertaining clients.

ORIENTATION

Osaka is usually divided into two areas: Kita and Minami. Kita (Japanese for 'north') is the city's main business and administrative centre and contains two of its biggest train stations, JR Osaka and Hankyū Umeda.

Minami (Japanese for 'south') is the city's entertainment district and contains the bustling shopping and nightlife zones of Namba and Shinsaibashi. It's also home to two major train stations, JR Namba and Nankai Namba stations.

The dividing line between Kita and Minami is formed by two rivers, the Dōjimagawa and the Tosabori-gawa, between which you'll find Nakano-shima, a peaceful green island that is home to the Museum of Oriental Ceramics. About 1km southeast of Nakano-shima you'll find Osaka-jō and its surrounding park, Osaka-jō-kōen.

To the south of the Minami area you'll find another group of sights clustered around Tennō-ji station. These include Shitennō-ji, Tennō-ji-kōen, Den-Den Town (the electronics neighbourhood) and the retro entertainment district of Shin-Sekai.

The bay area, to the west of the city centre, is home to another set of attractions including the excellent Osaka Aquarium and Universal Studios Japan theme park.

Keep in mind that, while JR Osaka station is centrally located in the Kita area, if you're coming from Tokyo by *shinkansen* you will arrive at Shin-Osaka station, which is three stops (about five minutes) north of Osaka station on the Midō-suji subway line.

Maps

At the visitors' information offices (see the following section) you can pick up a free copy of the excellent *Osaka City Map*, which has a subway/train map and detailed insets of the city's most important areas.

INFORMATION
Tourist Offices

The Osaka Tourist Association operates **visitors information offices** in Shin-Osaka (☎ 6305-3311), Osaka (☎ 6345-2189; Kita), Namba (☎ 6643-2125; Minami) and Tennō-ji (☎ 6774-3077) stations, the main office being the one in Osaka station. All are open from 8am to 8pm daily and close from 31 December to 3 January. Many travellers have problems finding the tourist office in Osaka station. To get there from JR trains, go out the Midō-suji ticket gate/exit, turn right, walk about 50m and look for it on your left, tucked into a corner. From the subway, go out exit No 9, turn left, walk past a café and look for it on your left.

KANSAI

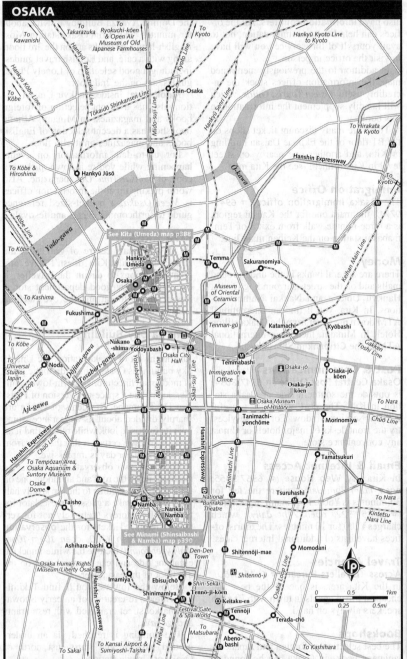

OSAKA

To Kawanishi

To Takarazuka

To Ryokuchi-kōen & Open Air Museum of Old Japanese Farmhouses

To Kyoto

Hankyū Kyoto Line to Kyoto

Hankyū Takarazuka Line

Kyoto Line

Hankyū Kōbe Line

To Kōbe

Tōkaidō Shinkansen Line

Shin-Osaka

Hankyū Senri Line

To Kōbe & Hiroshima

Hankyū Jūsō

To Hirakata & Kyoto

Yodo-gawa

To Kyoto

Hanshin Expressway

Kōbe Line

To Kōbe

See Kita (Umeda) map p388

Hankyū Umeda

Temma

Sakuranomiya

Keihan Main Line

To Kashima

Osaka

Museum of Oriental Ceramics

Fukushima

Tenman-gū

Katamachi

Kyōbashi

Gakken Toshi Line

To Kōbe

Nakano-shima

Yodoyabashi

Osaka City Hall

Tēmmabashi

Osaka-jō

Osaka-jō-kōen

To Universal Studios Japan

Noda

Yotsubashi Line

Midō-suji Line

Sakai-suji Line

Immigration Office

Osaka Museum of History

To Nara

Osaka Loop Line

Dōjima-gawa

Tosaburi-gawa

Aji-gawa

Tanimachi-yonchōme

Tanimachi Line

Morinomiya

Chūō Line

Hanshin Expressway

Chūō Line

To Tempōzan Area, Osaka Aquarium & Suntory Museum

Osaka Dome

National Bunraku Theatre

Tsuruhashi

Tamatsukuri

To Nara

Hanshin Expressway

See Minami (Shinsaibashi & Namba) map p390

Namba

Nankai Namba

Kintetsu Nara Line

Taisho

Den-Den Town

Shitennōji-mae

Momodani

Ashihara-bashi

Osaka Human Rights Museum/Liberty Osaka

Imamiya

Shin-Sekai

Shitennō-ji

Nankai Line

Ebisu-chō

Tennō-ji-kōen

Keitaku-en

Shinimamiya

Festival Gate & Spa World

Tennō-ji

Terada-chō

To Kansai Airport & Sumiyoshi-Taisha

To Sakai

Abeno-bashi

To Matsubara

To Kashihara

0   0.5   1km

0   0.25   0.5mi

KANSAI

Osaka and Kansai international airports also have **information counters**. All the offices can help book accommodation, but to avail yourself of this service you will have to visit the office in person.

In addition to the previously mentioned map, the information offices stock the incredibly useful *Osaka Tourist Guide*, which will handily supplement the information in this book.

There are many discount ticket shops on the B1 floor of the Ekimae Daisan building in Kita, and another one nearby on street level in Kita-Shinchi (see the Kita map).

Immigration Office

The **Osaka immigration office** (☎ 6941-0771), the main one for the Kansai region, is a three-minute walk from exit 3 of Temmabashi station on the Keihan main line.

Money

There are several banks in the underground malls and on the streets surrounding Osaka, Hankyū Umeda and Nankai Namba stations. In Kita, you'll find an international ATM down the street from the Osaka Hilton Hotel. In Minami, there's an international ATM at the **Citibank** in Shinsaibashi.

Post & Communications

Osaka Central Post Office (☎ 6347-8034) is outside the southern side of Osaka station in Kita. The post office has a useful 24-hour service window. For fax services, try the front desks of major hotels or almost any convenience store.

Email & Internet Access

In Kita, try **Web House** (☎ 6367-9555; *open 11am-8pm daily*) where the fee for 30 minutes is ¥600. In Minami, try **Kinko's** (☎ 6245-1922; *open 24hr daily*), which charges ¥200 for 10 minutes. The tourist offices have lists of additional Internet cafés.

Travel Agencies

A'cross Travellers Bureau (☎ 6345-0150), in the Kita area, is one of the best and cheapest travel agents in town with English speakers always on hand.

Bookshops

The best selection of foreign and Japanese-language books in Osaka can be found at the huge new **Junkudō** bookstore, inside the Dōjima Avanza Building in Kita, about ten minutes' walk from Osaka station. Most English-language books are on the 3rd floor, along with a café, and English travel guides, including a good selection of Lonely Planet guides, are on the 2nd floor.

Kinokuniya, inside Hankyū Umeda station, also has a decent selection of foreign books and magazines. In Minami, **Athens** bookshop has a decent selection of English books and magazines on its 4th floor.

For up-to-date information on events happening while you're in town, pick up a copy of *Kansai Time Out* magazine. Also worth picking up at the information offices is *Meet Osaka*, a pocket-sized reference guide to forthcoming events and festivals.

KITA AREA キタ

By day, Osaka's centre of gravity is the Kita area. While Kita doesn't have any great attractions to detain the traveller, it does have a few good department stores, lots of places to eat and the eye-catching Umeda Sky building.

Umeda Sky Building

梅田スカイビル

Just northwest of Osaka station, the Umeda Sky building is Osaka's most dramatic piece of modern architecture. The twin-tower complex looks like a space-age version of Paris' Arc De Triomphe. Residents of Osaka are sharply divided about its appearance: some love its futuristic look while others find it an eyesore. What is certain is that the view from the top on a clear day is impressive.

There are two observation galleries: an outdoor one on the roof and an indoor one on the floor below. Getting to the top is only half the fun as you take a glassed-in escalator for the final five storeys (definitely not for vertigo sufferers). Tickets for the **observation decks** (*admission ¥700; open 10am-10pm daily year-round*) include the white-knuckled escalator ride and can be purchased on the 3rd floor of the east tower.

Below the towers, you'll find **Takimi-koji Alley**, a re-creation of an early Showa-era market street crammed with restaurants and *izakaya*.

The building is reached via an underground passage that starts just north of Osaka or Umeda stations.

CENTRAL OSAKA
Osaka-jō 大阪城
Osaka-jō *(Osaka Castle; admission ¥500; open 9am-5pm daily)* was built as a display of power by Toyotomi Hideyoshi after he achieved his goal of unifying Japan. One hundred thousand workers toiled for three years to construct an 'impregnable' granite castle, finishing the job in 1583. However, it was destroyed just 32 years later, in 1615, by the armies of Tokugawa Ieyasu.

Within 10 years the castle had been rebuilt by the Tokugawa forces, but it was to suffer a further calamity when another generation of Tokugawas razed it rather than let it fall to the forces of the Meiji Restoration in 1868.

The present structure is a 1931 concrete reconstruction of the original, which was refurbished at great cost in 1997 (serious fans of Japanese castles should head west to see the castle at Himeji). The interior of the castle houses an excellent collection of displays relating to the castle, Toyotomi Hideyoshi and the city of Osaka. On the 8th floor, there is an observation deck which offers excellent views of Osaka and surrounding areas.

The castle and park are at their best in the spring cherry-blossom and fall-foliage seasons.

The Ōte-mon gate, which serves as the main entrance to the park, is a 10-minute walk northeast of Tanimachi-yonchōme station (sometimes written Tanimachi 4-chome) on the Chūō and Tanimachi subway lines. You can also take the Osaka Loop line, get off at Osaka-jō-kōen station and enter through the back of the castle.

Osaka Museum of History
大阪歴史博物館
Just southwest of Osaka-jō, the new Osaka Museum of History *(Osaka Reki-shi Hakubutsukan; admission ¥600; open 9.30am-5pm Mon, Wed, Thur, Sat & Sun, 9.30am-8pm Fri)* is housed in a fantastic new building adjoining the Osaka NHK Broadcast Center. The display floors of the museum occupy the 7th–10th floors of the new sail-shaped building.

The displays are broken into four sections by floor; you start at the top and work your way down, passing in time from the past to the present. The displays are very well done and there are plenty of English explanations; taped tours are available.

The museum is a two-minute walk northeast of Tanimachi-yonchōme station.

Nakano-shima 中之島
Sandwiched between Dōjima-gawa and Tosabori-gawa, this island is a pleasant oasis of trees and riverside walkways in the midst of Osaka's unrelenting grey. It's also home to **Osaka City Hall**, the Museum of Oriental Ceramics (see following) and **Nakano-shima-kōen**. The latter, on the eastern end of the island, is a good place for an afternoon stroll or picnic lunch.

Museum of Oriental Ceramics
東洋陶磁美術館
With more than 2700 pieces in its permanent collection, this museum *(admission ¥500; open 9.30am-5pm Tues-Sun)* has one of the finest collections of Chinese and Korean ceramics in the world. At any one time, about 300 of the pieces from the permanent collection are on display, and there are often special exhibits (which cost extra).

To get to the museum, go to Yodoya-bashi station on either the Midō-suji line or the Keihan line (different stations). Walk north to the river and cross to Nakano-shima. Turn right, pass the city hall on your left, bear left with the road, and look for the squat brown brick building.

MINAMI AREA ミナミ
A few stops south of Osaka station on the Midō-suji subway line (get off at either Shinsaibashi or Namba stations), the Minami area is the place to spend the evening in Osaka. Its highlights include the Dōtombori Arcade, the National Bunraku Theatre, Dōgusuji-ya Arcade and Amerika-Mura.

Dōtombori 道頓堀
Dōtombori is Osaka's liveliest nightlife area. It's centred around **Dōtombori-gawa** and **Dōtombori Arcade**, a strip of restaurants and theatres where a peculiar type of Darwinism is the rule for both people and shops: survival of the flashiest. In the evening, head to **Ebisu-bashi** bridge to sample the glittering nightscape, which brings to mind a scene from the science-fiction movie *Blade Runner*.

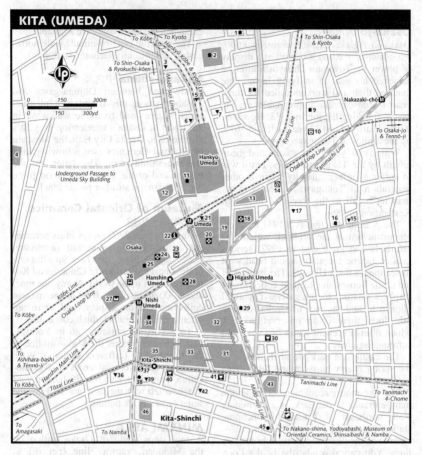

KITA (UMEDA)

Only a short walk south of Dōtombori Arcade, you'll find **Hōzen-ji**, a tiny temple hidden down a narrow alley. The temple is built around a moss-covered **Fudō-myōō statue**. This statue is a favourite of people employed in *mizu shobai* (the water trade) who pause before work to throw some water on the moss-covered statue. Nearby, you'll find **Hōzen-ji Yokochō**, a tiny alley filled with traditional restaurants and bars.

Next to Hōzen-ji, the small **Kamigata Ukiyo-e Museum** (*admission ¥500; open 11am-8pm Tues-Sun*) houses a small collection of ukiyo-e prints in the Nishiki-e style. While the collection is poorly displayed and dimly lit, it does offer a chance to see some original ukiyo-e prints. Oddly, the 3rd floor of the museum is devoted to displays on rice

and rice growing, making this museum a rival of Tokyo's Tobacco and Salt Museum in terms of bizarre museum collections. The odd pairing celebrates the fact that profits from Osaka's rice trade were used to support the work of Osaka's ukiyo-e artists.

To the south of Dōtombori, in the direction of Nankai Namba station, you'll find a maze of colourful arcades with more restaurants, *pachinko* parlours, strip clubs, cinemas and who knows what else. To the north of Dōtombori, between Midō-suji and Sakai-suji, the narrow streets are crowded with hostess bars, discos and pubs.

Dōgusuji-ya Arcade 道具筋屋
If you desperately need a *tako-yaki* (octopus ball) fryer, a red lantern to hang

KITA (UMEDA)

PLACES TO STAY

1 Hotel Sunroute Umeda
ホテルサンルート梅田
2 Hotel Hankyū International
ホテル阪急インターナシ
ョナル
8 Osaka Tōkyū Hotel
大阪東急ホテル
9 Hotel Green Plaza Osaka
ホテルグリーンプラザ大阪
11 Hotel New Hankyū
新阪急ホテル
16 New Japan Sauna & Capsule
Hotel
ニュージャパンサウナ＆カプ
セルホテル
25 Granvia Hotel Osaka
グランヴィアホテル大阪
29 Umeda OS Hotel
梅田ＯＳホテル
34 Osaka Hilton Hotel; Windows
on the World
大阪ヒルトンホテル；ウイン
ドーズオンザワルド

PLACES TO EAT

3 Kantan
カンタン
5 Kappa Yokochō Arcade;
Pina Khana; Gataro
かっぱ横丁；ピーナカナ；
がたろ
6 Isaribi
漁火
7 Hatago
旅篭
15 Herradura
ヘラドラ

17 Café Org
カフェオーグ
21 Shin-Umeda Shokudō-Gai;
Kiji ; Maru
新梅田食道街；きじ；丸
36 Shabu-zen; Blue Note
Osaka
しゃぶ禅；ブルーノート大阪
39 Court Lodge
コートロッジ
42 Genki Sushi
元気寿司

OTHER

4 Umeda Sky Building
梅田スカイビル
10 Osaka Nōgaku Hall
大阪能楽会館
12 Yodobashi Umeda Building
ヨドバシ梅田
13 Hankyū Hep Five Complex;
Ferris Wheel
阪急ヘップファイブ；大観
覧車
14 Web House
ウェブハウス
18 Hankyū Navio Store
阪急ナビオ
19 Hankyū Grand Building
阪急グランドビル
20 Hankyū Department Store
阪急百貨店
22 Osaka Visitors Information
Umeda Office
大阪観光案内所（梅田案
内所）
23 City Bus Terminal
市バスターミナル

24 Daimaru Department
Store
大丸百貨店
26 JR Highway Bus Terminal
JR高速バスターミナル
27 Osaka Central Post Office
大阪中央郵便局
28 Hanshin Department Store
阪神百貨店
30 Pig & Whistle
ピッグアンドホイッスル
31 Ekimae Daisan Building ;
Aruna
駅前第三ビル；アルナ
32 Ekimae Daiyon Building
駅前第四ビル
33 Ekimae Daini Building
駅前第二ビル
35 Ekimae Daiichi Building
駅前第一ビル
37 International ATM
国際ATM
38 A'cross Travellers Bureau
アクロストラベラーズビュ
ーロー
40 Karma
カルマ
41 Canopy
キャノピー
43 Dōwa Kasai Building
同和火災ビル
44 American Consulate
アメリカ領事館
45 Discount Ticket Shop
格安チケット売り場
46 Dōjima Avanza Building ;
Junkudō Bookstore
堂島アバンザ；ジュンク堂

outside your shop or plastic food-models to lure the customers in, this shopping arcade is the place to go. You'll also find endless knives, pots, pans and just about anything else that's even remotely related to the preparation and consumption of food.

National Bunraku Theatre
国立文楽劇場

Although bunraku, or puppet theatre, did not originate in Osaka, the art form was popularised here. The most famous bunraku playwright, Chikametsu Monzaemon (1653–1724), wrote plays set in Osaka concerning the classes that traditionally had no place in Japanese art: merchants and the denizens of the pleasure quarters. Not surprisingly, bunraku found an appreciative audience among these people, and a theatre was established to put on the plays of Chikametsu

in Dōtombori. Today's theatre is an attempt to revive the fortunes of bunraku.

Performances are only held at certain times of the year: check with the tourist information offices. Tickets normally start at around ¥2300; programme guides in English and earphones are available.

Amerika-Mura アメリカ村

Amerika-Mura (which means 'America Village') is a compact enclave of trendy shops and restaurants, with a few discreet love hotels thrown in for good measure. The best reason to come is to check out the hordes of colourful Japanese teens living out the myth of *Amerika*.

In the middle of it all is Amerika-Mura Triangle Park, an all-concrete park with benches where you can sit and watch the parade of fashion victims. Amerika-Mura

KANSAI

MINAMI (SHINSAIBASHI & NAMBA)

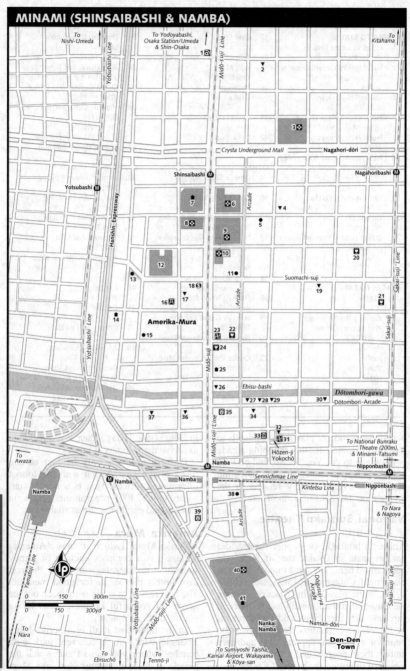

To Nishi-Umeda

To Yodoyabashi, Osaka Station/Umeda & Shin-Osaka

To Kitahama

Yotsubashi Line

Midō-suji Line

Crysta Underground Mall

Nagahori-dōri

Shinsaibashi

Nagahoribashi

Yotsubashi

Hanshin Expressway

Arcade

Yotsubashi Line

Sakai-suji Line

Amerika-Mura

Suomachi-suji

Midō-suji

Sakai-suji

Midō-suji Line

Ebisu-bashi

Dōtombori-gawa

Dōtombori-Arcade

Hōzen-ji Yokochō

To National Bunraku Theatre (200m), & Minami-Tatsumi

Namba

Sennichmae Line

Nipponbashi

Namba

Namba

Kintetsu Line

Nipponbashi

To Awaza

To Nara & Nagoya

Arcade

Yamatōji Line

0   150   300m
0   150   300yd

To Nara

Nankai Namba

Dōgusuji-ya Arcade

Nansan-dōri

Den-Den Town

Sakai-suji Line

To Ebisuchō

To Tennō-ji

To Sumiyoshi Taisha, Kansai Airport, Wakayama & Kōya-san

KANSAI

MINAMI (SHINSAIBASHI & NAMBA)

is one or two blocks west of Midō-suji, bounded on the north by Suomachi-suji and the south by Dōtombori-gawa.

TENNŌ-JI & AROUND 天王寺公園
Shitennō-ji 四天王寺
Shitennō-ji (admission free; open 8.30am-4.30pm daily), founded in 593, has the distinction of being one of the oldest Buddhist temples in Japan, although none of the present buildings are originals; most are the usual concrete reproductions, with the exception of the big stone torii. The torii dates back to 1294, making it the oldest of its kind in Japan. Apart from the torii, there is little of real historical significance, and the absence of greenery in the raked-gravel grounds makes for a rather desolate atmosphere. The adjoining **museum** (admission ¥200) is of limited interest.

The temple is most easily reached from Shitennōji-mae station on the Tanimachi subway line. Take the southern exit, cross to the left side of the road and take the small road that goes off at an angle away from the

subway station. The entrance to the temple is on the left.

Tennō-ji-kōen 天王寺公園
A visit to this park can easily be combined with a visit to Shitennō-ji and Shin-Sekai (see the following section).

The park has a botanical garden, a zoo and a circular garden known as Keitaku-en (admission ¥150; open 9.30am-5pm Tues-Sun). However, the best reason to visit the park is for the Sunday karaoke songfests held on the road that runs through the middle of the park. Here, enterprising members of Tennō-ji's sizable homeless population rig up generators and karaoke machines and charge passers by ¥50 or ¥100 to belt out classic enka (folk ballads) numbers.

The park is above Tennō-ji station, which is on the Midō-suji subway line and the Osaka Loop line.

Shin-Sekai 新世界
For something completely different, take a walk through this retro entertainment

KANSAI

district just west of Tennō-ji-kōen. At the heart of it all you'll find crusty old Tsūten-kaku tower, a 103m-high structure that dates back to 1912 (the present tower was rebuilt in 1969). When the tower first went up it symbolised everything new and exciting about this once-happening neighbourhood (*shin-sekai* is Japanese for 'New World').

Now, Shin-Sekai is a world that time forgot. You'll find ancient *pachinko* parlours, run-down theatres, dirt-cheap restaurants and all manner of raffish and suspicious characters.

Festival Gate フェスティバルゲート

South of Shin-Sekai and west of Tennō-ji-kōen you'll find the new entertainment complex of Festival Gate (*admission free; open 10am-10pm daily*), which is really an amusement park surrounded by a huge shopping/dining complex. The rides are in the open atrium of the complex and the roller coaster snakes its way over and around the walls of the places, offering tantalizing glimpses of the city and the nearby Spa World bathing complex. It's a good spot to bring the kids, but you'll really have to shell out the yen to enjoy yourself here.

Spa World スパワールド

Next door to Festival Gate is the super-spa known as Spa World (*admission 3hr/all day Mon-Fri ¥2400/2700, Sat, Sun & holidays ¥2700/3000; open 10am-9am the following day*). Billed as the world's largest spa, it consists of two floors of baths, one Asian themed and one European themed, and a rooftop waterworld with pools and waterslides, along with restaurants and relaxation areas.

The Asian and European bath floors are sex segregated; one month the ladies get the Asian bath floor and the men the European bath floor, and then it switches to the opposite, so you'll have to visit twice to sample all the baths (they're fairly similar, so you're not missing much if you don't). We particularly like the *rotemburo* (outdoor bath) on the roof, where you can show off your tan to folks whizzing by on the Festival Gate roller coaster (and from which you can see Tsūten-kaku tower rising like a retro space ship to the north). Be sure to bring a bathing suit if you want to visit the waterworld (or you can rent one for ¥300).

OTHER ATTRACTIONS

Tempōzan Area 天保山エリア

Trudging through the streets of Kita or Minami, you could easily be forgiven for forgetting that Osaka is actually a port city. A good remedy for this is a trip down to Tempōzan, the best of Osaka's burgeoning seaside developments. On an island amid the busy container ports of Osaka Bay, Tempōzan has several attractions to lure the travellers, especially those with children in tow.

Before hitting the main attractions, you might want to get some perspective on it all by taking a whirl on the **Giant Ferris Wheel** (*Daikanransha; admission ¥700; open 10am-10pm daily*). Said to be the largest ferris wheel in the world, the 112m-high wheel offers unbeatable views of Osaka, Osaka Bay and Kōbe. Give it a whirl at night to enjoy the vast carpet of lights formed by the Osaka/Kōbe conurbation.

Next to the ferris wheel, you'll find **Tempōzan Marketplace**, a shopping and dining arcade that includes the **Naniwa Kuishinbō Yokochō**, a faux-Edo-period food court where you can sample all of Osaka's culinary specialities.

Osaka Aquarium Although it's fairly expensive, Osaka Aquarium (*adult/child ¥2000/900; open 10am-8pm daily*) is well worth a visit. It's centred around the world's largest aquarium tank, which is home to the aquarium's star attraction, a whale shark, which shares its quarters with an astonishing variety of lesser sharks, rays, tuna and other fish.

A walkway winds its way around the main tank and past displays of life found on eight different ocean levels. The giant spider crabs in the Japan Ocean Deeps section look like alien invaders from another planet. Presentations have both Japanese and English captions and an environmentally friendly slant to them.

Take the Chūō subway line to the Osaka-kō, from which it's about a five-minute walk to the aquarium. Get there for opening time if you want to beat the crowds – on weekends and holidays long queues are the norm.

Suntory Museum On the southern side of Osaka Aquarium is the Suntory Museum complex (*admission ¥1000; open 10.30am-7.30pm daily*), which holds an IMAX 3-D theatre and an art gallery with a collection of modern art posters and glass artwork. The building itself, designed by Andō Tadao, is at least as impressive as any of the displays. The **IMAX theatre** (admission ¥1000; open 11am-8pm Tues-Sun) usually has screenings on the hour; check the *Meet Osaka* guide to see what's showing.

Osaka Human Rights Museum/ Liberty Osaka
大阪人権博物館／リバティ大阪

This museum (admission ¥250; open 10am-5pm Tues-Sun), which goes by two names, is dedicated to the suffering of Japan's Burakumin people and other oppressed groups, including Koreans, the handicapped, the Ainu and women. The most fascinating exhibits deal with the Burakumin, outcasts in Japan's four-tiered caste system that was officially outlawed in 1879 under the Emancipation Edict issued by the Meiji government.

An English-language leaflet is available, and you can borrow a tape recorder and English tape for free. Take the JR Osaka Loop line to Ashihara-bashi station, exit via the southern exit, walk south down the main street for five minutes and the museum is on the right of the pedestrian crossing.

Open Air Museum of Old Japanese Farmhouses
日本民家集落博物館

In Ryokuchi-kōen this fine open-air museum (admission ¥500; open 10am-5pm daily Apr-Oct, 10am-4pm daily Nov-Mar) features 11 traditional Japanese country houses and other structures brought here from all over Japan. All have been painstakingly reconstructed and filled with period-era tools and other displays. Most impressive is the giant *gasshō-zukuri* (thatch-roofed) farmhouse from Gifu-ken.

The park-like setting, with plenty of trees and bamboo, gives the whole museum a pleasantly rustic air – and the whole place comes alive with fiery red maple leaves during the November foliage season. For anyone even remotely interested in traditional Japanese architecture, we highly recommend this excellent attraction. An English-language pamphlet is available.

To get there, take the Midō-suji subway line to Ryokuchi-kōen and walk northwest into the park.

Sumiyoshi Taisha 住吉大社

This shrine (admission free; open dawn-dusk daily) is dedicated to Shintō deities associated with the sea and sea travel, in commemoration of a safe passage to Korea by a 3rd-century empress.

Having survived the bombing in WWII, Sumiyoshi Taisha actually has a couple of buildings that date back to 1810. The shrine was founded in the early 3rd century and the buildings that can be seen today are faithful replicas of the originals. They offer a rare opportunity to see a Shintō shrine that predates the influence of Chinese Buddhist architectural styles.

The main buildings are roofed with a kind of thatch rather than the tiles used on most later shrines. Other interesting features are a collection of more than 700 stone lanterns donated by seafarers and business people, a stone stage for performances of *bugaku* and court dancing and the attractive Taiko-bashi, an arched bridge set in a park.

It's next to both Sumiyoshi-taisha station on the Nankai main line and Sumiyoshi-tori-mae station on the Hankai line (the tram line that leaves from Tennō-ji station).

Universal Studios
ユニバーサルスタジオジャパン

Universal Studios Japan (☎ 4790-7000; adult/child ¥5500/3700; open 9am-7pm daily) is Osaka's answer to Tokyo Disneyland. Closely based on its two sister parks in the United States, the park features a wide variety of rides, shows, restaurants and other attractions.

To get there, take the JR Loop Line to Nishi-kujō station, switch to one of the distinctively painted Universal Studio shuttle trains and get off at Universal City station. From Osaka station the trip costs ¥170 and takes about 20 minutes. There are also some direct trains from Osaka station (ask at the tourist office for times; the price is the same).

SPECIAL EVENTS
The major festivals held in Osaka include the following:

January
Toka Ebisu (9 to 11 January) Huge crowds of more than a million people flock to the Imamiya Ebisu Shrine to receive bamboo branches

hung with auspicious tokens. The shrine is near Imamiya Ebisu station on the Nankai line.

Doya Doya (14 January) Billed as a 'huge naked festival', this event involves a competition between young men, clad in little more than headbands and loincloths, to obtain the 'amulet of the cow god'. This talisman is said to bring a good harvest to farmers. The festival takes place from 2pm at Shitennō-ji.

April
Shōryō-e (22 April) Shitennō-ji holds afternoon performances of *bugaku*. Performances are usually held from 1pm to 5pm.

June
Otaue Shinji (14 June) Women and girls dressed in traditional costume commemorate the establishment of the imperial rice fields. The festival is held at Sumiyoshi Taisha.

July
Tenjin Matsuri (25 July) This is one of Japan's three biggest festivals. Try to make the second day, when processions of *mikoshi* and people in traditional attire start at Temman-gū and end up in O-kawa (in boats). As night falls, the festival is marked with a huge fireworks display.

September
Kishiwada Danjiri Matsuri (14 to 15 September) Osaka's wildest festival, a kind of running of the bulls except with *danjiri* (festival floats), many weighing over 3000kg. The *danjiri* are hauled through the streets by hundreds of people using ropes, and in all the excitement there have been a couple of deaths – take care and stand back. Most of the action takes place on the second day. The best place to see it is west of Kishiwada station on the Nankai Honsen line (from Nankai station).

PLACES TO STAY
There are plenty of places to stay in and around the two centres of Kita and Minami. It's possible to base yourself in Kyoto when exploring Osaka, and you'll find more budget accommodation in the old capital, which is about a ½ hour away by train. If you plan to sample some of Osaka's nightlife, it's probably best to stay in Osaka – unless you're one of those rare folks who actually enjoys riding the first train at dawn with a hangover.

PLACES TO STAY – BUDGET
Osaka Shiritsu Nagai Youth Hostel (☎ 6699-5631; *dorm beds from ¥2500, rooms per person ¥3000, family room per person*

¥3500) is the nearest youth hostel to the centre of Osaka. Bed price varies, depending upon the season. There are also private rooms and a family room for up to four people. Take the Midō-suji subway line south from the centre of town to Nagai station, go out exit No 1 and walk for 10 minutes towards the stadium. The hostel is at the back of the stadium. Or (for Japan Rail Pass holders), take the JR Hanwa line to Tsuruoaka station and walk southeast for five minutes.

Osaka-fu Hattori Ryokuchi Youth Hostel (☎ 6862-0600; *dorm beds ¥2500*) is about 15 minutes from Kita or 30 minutes from Minami and no membership is necessary. Take the Midō-suji line to Ryokuchi-kōen station, take the western exit, enter the park and follow the path past a fountain and around to the right alongside the pond.

New Japan Sauna and Capsule Hotel (☎ 6312-0610; *capsules ¥2600, sauna ¥800*) is located in one of Kita's busiest entertainment districts; this is the place to stay if you miss the last train. It's also the place to give the capsule hotel experience a try.

PLACES TO STAY – MID-RANGE
Kita Area
There are a few business hotels scattered around Hankyū Umeda and Osaka stations.

Hotel Sunroute Umeda (☎ 6373-1111; *singles/doubles/twins from ¥8400/13,000/ 15,000*) is perhaps the best value and is a reasonable business hotel just north of Hankyū Umeda.

Hotel Green Plaza Osaka (☎ 6374-1515; *singles/doubles/twins from ¥6800/14,000/ 9800*) is not far from the Osaka Nōgaku Hall, and is drab but economical.

Umeda OS Hotel (☎ 6312-1271; *singles/ doubles/twins from ¥8300/14,800/11,800*) is a step up and is clean, modern and about five minutes south of Osaka station.

Minami Area
Considering the wealth of dining and entertainment options in the area, the Minami area is probably the best place in Osaka to be based.

Asahi Plaza Hotel Amenity Shinsaibashi (☎ 6212-5111; *singles/twins from ¥7800/14,500*) is right in the heart of the nightlife action and has decent rooms.

Holiday Inn Nankai Osaka (☎ 6213 8281, fax 6213 8640; *singles/doubles/twins* from ¥12,000/20,000/19,000), located just a short walk from the Dōtombori area, is the most reasonably priced hotel (as opposed to business hotel) in Minami.

Itami Airport
Hotel Crevette (☎ 6843-7201; singles/ doubles/twins from ¥6500/15,000/12,000) is the best deal near Itami. Prices are discounted if you make reservations at the main tourist information counter at the airport. The folks at the information counter can also arrange for the hotel's shuttle bus to pick you up. They also have a regular shuttle bus to the airport for departures.

PLACES TO STAY – TOP END
Kita Area
This area is brimming with top-end accommodation.

Osaka Tōkyū Hotel (☎ 6373-2411; singles/doubles/twins from ¥10,000/16,000/ 18,000), northeast of Hankyū Umeda station, has the cheapest rooms in this bracket.

Hotel New Hankyū (☎ 6372-5101; singles/doubles/twins from ¥12,500/25,000/ 19,500), next to Hankyū Umeda station, is a reasonable choice with decent rooms.

Granvia Hotel Osaka (☎ 6344-1235, fax 6344 1130; singles/doubles/twins from ¥13,500/29,000/25,000) can't be beaten for convenience: it's located directly over Osaka station. Rooms and facilities are of a high standard.

Osaka Hilton Hotel (☎ 6347-7111; singles/doubles/twins ¥27,000/33,000/ 33,000), just outside Osaka station, is one of the city's more luxurious hotels.

Hotel Hankyū International (☎ 6377-2100; singles/doubles/twins from ¥27,000/ 40,000/42,000), north of Hankyū Umeda station, is the most luxurious hotel in town.

Minami Area
While most of Osaka's luxury hotels are in Kita, you'll find a few top-end choices in Minami as well.

Hotel Nikkō Osaka (☎ 6244-1111; singles/doubles/twins from ¥18,500/ 28,500/28,500), in Shinsaibashi, is a good choice, with excellent facilities and a convenient location.

Nankai South Tower Hotel (☎ 6646-1111; singles/doubles/twins from ¥18,000/ 27,000/30,000) is the most impressive

hotel in the area and is directly above Nankai Namba station. Rooms are clean and well appointed. The views from the rooms are great and the facilities are excellent.

Kansai International Airport
Hotel Nikkō Kansai Airport (☎ 0724-55-1111; singles/doubles/twins from ¥19,000/ 26,000/28,000) is expensive but is the only hotel at the airport, with clean new rooms. You should definitely ask for a discount or promotional rate outside peak travel times.

PLACES TO EAT
What Osaka offers is a chance to enjoy what ordinary Japanese enjoy – good food and drink in a rowdy atmosphere. The Osakans call it *kuidaore*, which means 'eat until you drop'. Osaka presents ample opportunities to do just that, with thousands of restaurants lining its cramped streets.

Kita
Japanese A great place for a cheap lunch or dinner while in Kita is the **Shin-Umeda Shokudō-Gai** which is located across the street from the Umeda Visitors Information Office under the JR tracks. There are heaps of good restaurants here that vie for the lunch/ dinner custom with cheap set meals, many of which are displayed outside, making ordering easier. Two that we really like are **Kiji**, a good *okonomiyaki* place (try the mixed *okonomiyaki* for around ¥800), and an *oden* and fish specialist called **Maru** (☎ 6361-4552), where the lunchtime sashimi set meal costs about ¥800. Check the Kita map for the kanji and look for it on the sign (there's usually a girl outside beckoning customers).

Another good food court in Kita is the **Kappa Yokochō Arcade**, just north of Hankyū Umeda station. Here, you'll find **Gataro** (☎ 6373-1484; dinner around ¥3000), a cosy little spot that does creative twists on standard *izakaya* themes. Look for the glass front on the left as you head north in the arcade.

Outside of the food arcades, there are many other good choices.

Hatago (☎ 6373-3400; all items ¥300), in a restored farmhouse, is a great spot to sample *robotayaki* (fireside) cooking. It's fun watching the chefs whirl the food around on paddles as they labour over the grill. Look for the low doorway and the wooden façade. They also do cheap lunch sets (usually displayed outside).

Isaribi (☎ 6373-2969; dinner from ¥2300), another *robotayaki* place, is down a flight of stairs outside Hankyū Umeda station. It's a second choice after Hatago.

Shabu-zen (☎ 6343-0250; dinner sets from ¥3300), on the 10th floor of the AX building, is the place to go for delicious *shabu-shabu* sets in a pleasant setting.

If you find yourself in need of a bite while in the Kita-Shinchi area, try **Genki Sushi**, an automatic sushi place where you can have an all-you-can eat sushi binge for ¥900 to ¥1300 (at these prices, you shouldn't be surprised that it's not the best sushi around).

International There are several cafés and bakeries in Osaka station itself. Otherwise, you might try the offerings in the nearby Osaka Hilton, which has a wide variety of restaurants on its two basement floors. You could also try some of the following spots.

Court Lodge (curry sets from ¥800) is a tiny hole-in-the-wall spot which serves filling sets of Sri Lankan food. Look for the beer signs in the window.

Pina Khana (☎ 6375-5828; lunch/dinner from ¥850/3000), a crowded spot in the Kappa Yokochō Arcade, is our favourite Indian restaurant in Kita. Another good Indian restaurant is the small **Aruna** (☎ 6345-5211; lunch/dinner from ¥800/2000) on the B1 floor of the Ekimae Daisan Building.

Café Org (☎ 6312-0529; drinks/meals from ¥250/700) is an open-plan, casual café where you can grab a light meal or a quick pick-me-up while exploring Kita. Decent sandwiches start at ¥300 here.

Herradura (☎ 6361-1011; dinner ¥2500) is an intimate spot for Mexican food, including taco platters and frozen margaritas.

For a tasty *mukokuseki* (international or no-national cuisine) in a pleasant Japanese setting, try **Kantan** (☎ 6373-3223; dishes from ¥1000; open dinner only). There are two tasty *omakase* courses (tasting courses) which cost ¥3000 and ¥5000.

Minami

Japanese Dōtombori is crammed with restaurants, most of which are bad. They cater to the hoards of Japanese tourists who descend on the area. If you must eat here, the best of

a bad lot are the following four places: **Kani Dōraku** (lunch/dinner from ¥1600/3000), a crab specialist; **Ganko Sushi** (set meals from ¥1000), a sushi specialist; **Zuboraya** (fugu sashimi ¥1800, full dinners from ¥3000), a *fugu* (Japanese puffer fish) specialist; and **Chibō** (okonomiyaki from ¥750), a good place to try one of Osaka's most popular dishes: *okonomiyaki*. Chibō's *modan yaki* (a kind of *okonomiyaki*) is a good bet at ¥950.

Otherwise, we recommend eating at one of the many restaurants off the main Dōtombori strip.

One of our favourite Minami eateries is **Dai-sushi** (☎ 6212-6567; open 5pm-5am daily). This place is the most elegant automatic sushi place we've ever seen – it's all smooth lines, polished metal and cool tunes. There's a picture menu and all the automatic sushi favourites are available, each with a twist to set it apart from the usual conveyor-belt fare. You pay more for the pleasure – plan on at least ¥3000 for a decent feed.

Shabu-zen (☎ 6213-2953; shabu-shabu from ¥3000), on the 6th floor of the Gurukas building beside the Dōtombori-gawa, is an approachable place to sample *shabu-shabu* and sukiyaki.

Gin Sen (☎ 6213-7234; all-you-can-eat kushi-katsu lunch/dinner ¥1980/2980) serves delicious *kushi katsu*, a greasy but tasty treat. It's on the 2nd floor of the Gurukas building.

Nishiya (☎ 6241-9221; noodle dishes from ¥800) is an Osaka landmark that serves udon noodles and a variety of hearty *nabe* (iron pot) dishes for reasonable prices. Look for the semi-rustic facade and the food models.

Tempura Maki (☎ 6211-8284; courses from ¥3900), in the atmospheric Hōzen-ji Yokochō, is a good place to splash out on a tempura feast.

International Dōtombori's most popular Thai place is **Kuntep** (☎ 4708-0088; lunch buffet/dinner ¥980/2000). It serves fairly authentic versions of the standard favourites like green curry and fried noodles. Look for the small sign – it's on the B1 floor.

Santana (☎ 6211-5181; lunch/dinner sets from ¥1000/2000) is our favourite Indian place in Minami, with lots of vegie choices and delicious samosas.

La Bamba (☎ 6213-9612; dinner from ¥2000) is Minami's most popular Mexican restaurant and serves some mean guacamole and tasty fajitas.

Namaste (☎ 6241-6515; lunch/dinner from ¥750/2000), up in the Shinsaibashi area, is a friendly Indian restaurant that serves filling set meals at reasonable prices.

Uncle Steven's (☎ 6211-7574) is worth a stop if you find yourself in Amerika-Mura and fancy some spicy food, music and beer. It's more of a restaurant than bar, but you can definitely do some drinking here.

ENTERTAINMENT
Traditional Japanese Entertainment

The National Bunraku Theatre (☎ 6212-2531), described earlier, is Osaka's main bunraku (Japanese puppet) theatre.

Osaka Nōgaku Hall (☎ 6373-1726), a five-minute walk east of Osaka station, holds nō shows about twice a month, most of which cost ¥4000.

Unfortunately, neither place has regularly scheduled shows. The best thing is to check with the tourist information offices about current shows, check the listings in the *Meet Osaka* guide or look in *Kansai Time Out*.

Bars & Clubs

Osaka is a hard working city, but when quitting time rolls around, Osakans know how to party. Take a stroll through Minami on a Friday night and you'd be excused for thinking that there is one bar for every resident of the city. Whatever your taste, you're sure to find something to your liking among this vast array of bars and clubs.

For up-to-date listings of forthcoming club events, check *Kansai Time Out*. To supplement the bars and club listings in the section, pick up a copy of *Kansai Scene*.

The places listed in this section are generally open daily from evening until late.

Kita Area Although Minami is Osaka's real nightlife district, there are plenty of bars, clubs and *izakaya* in the neighbourhoods to the south and east of Osaka station (but be warned that most of the places in Kita-Shinchi cater only to Japanese salarymen on expense accounts).

Karma (☎ 6344-6181) is a very long-standing club that is popular with Japanese

and foreigners alike. On weekends they usually host techno events with cover charges averaging ¥2500.

Canopy is a café-style bar that pulls in a crowd of local expats for after-work snacks and drinks. The happy hour special here is a good and popular deal.

Pig & Whistle (☎ 6361-3198), part of Kansai's biggest British-style pub chain, is the place to go for pints of Guinness and fish and chips.

Windows on the World (☎ 6347-7111) is an unbeatable spot for drinks with a view – it's on the 35th floor of the Osaka Hilton. Be warned that there's a ¥2500 per person table charge and drinks average ¥1000.

Minami This is the place for a wild night out in Osaka. You simply won't believe the number of bars, clubs and restaurants they've packed into the narrow streets and alleys of Dōtombori, Shinsaibashi, Namba and Amerika-Mura. Go on a weekend night and you'll be part of a colourful human parade of Osaka characters – this is one of Japan's best spots for people-watching.

American Beauty (☎ 6489-2299) is a cosy little downstairs bar where the music runs to rock and roll and the crowd includes both foreigners and Japanese. Bonus points for guessing the origin of the name (hint: it's the name of one of their best albums).

Murphy's (☎ 6282-0677) is one of the oldest Irish-style pubs in Japan. This is a good place to rub shoulders with local expats and Japanese. It's on the 6th floor of the Reed Plaza Shinsaibashi building (look for the 'retro futuristic' building).

Pig & Whistle (☎ 6213-6911) is like its sister branches in Kita and Kyoto: a good place to go for a pint and a plate of fish and chips.

Rakan (☎ 6213-4000) lures foreigners and Japanese alike with special theme nights and good drinks. It doesn't usually get going until late.

Arc en Ciel (☎ 6646-1119) is where we go when we want something a little swanky. It's on the 36th floor of the Nankai South Tower Hotel. The view is fantastic and the prices are too: there's a ¥1500 per person table charge and drinks average ¥1200.

Tin's Hall (☎ 6773-5955) is the best bar down south in the Tennō-ji area. It's a casual spot with good burgers and a great happy hour special: beers are only ¥300 from 6pm to 9pm. To get there, leave Tennō-ji station by the north exit, go right and walk along the main road, turn right one block beyond the Tōei Hotel and look for it on the right.

Live Music

If you are interested in live blues and jazz, check *Kansai Time Out* to see who's scheduled to play at the **Blue Note Osaka** (☎ 6342-7722) which is a short walk from the Osaka Hilton. It draws some fairly big-name acts; the price of tickets to shows averages ¥7000.

SHOPPING

Osaka has almost as many shops as it has restaurants. Look for department stores in the area around JR Osaka and Umeda stations. Most of the major department stores are represented here.

Osaka's speciality is electronics, and **Den Den Town** is Osaka's version of Tokyo's Akihabara. Taking its name from the Japanese word for electricity, *denki*, Den Den Town is an area of shops almost exclusively devoted to electronic goods. To avoid sales tax, check if the store has a 'Tax Free' sign outside and bring your passport. Most stores are closed on Wednesday. Take the Sakaisuji subway line to Ebisu-cho station and exit at No 1 or No 2 exit. Alternatively, it's a 15-minute walk south of Nankai Namba station.

For anything related to cooking and eating, head to the **Dōgusiji-ya Arcade** in Minami (see earlier in this chapter). Also in Minami, you'll find **Naniwa Camera**, which has the lowest prices on cameras, equipment and film in town. For used camera equipment, try the many shops on the ground floors of the Ekimae Dai-San buildings (there are four of them) south of Osaka station.

GETTING THERE & AWAY
Air

Osaka is served by two airports: the old Itami airport, which now handles only domestic traffic, and the new Kansai international airport (KIX), which handles all international and some domestic flights.

Train

Shinkansen Osaka is on the Tōkaidō/San-... ...ansen line that runs between Tokyo

and Hakata in Kyūshū (Hikari *shinkansen* to/from Tokyo ¥13,750, three hours; Hikari *shinkansen* to Hakata ¥14,590, 2¾ hours). Other cities on this line include Hiro-shima, Kyoto, Kōbe and Okayama.

Kyoto The fastest way to travel by train between Kyoto and Osaka, other than *shinkansen*, is to catch the JR *shinkaisoku* (¥540, 29 minutes).

Another choice is the cheaper private Hankyū line that runs between Hankyū Umeda station in Osaka and Hankyū Ka-waramachi, Karasuma and Ōmiya stations in Kyoto (*tokkyū* to Kawaramachi ¥390, 42 minutes).

Alternatively, you can take the Keihan main line between Sanjō, Shijō or Shichijō stations in Kyoto and Keihan Yodoyabashi station in Osaka (*tokkyū* to Sanjō ¥400, 48 minutes). Yodoyabashi is on the Midō-suji subway line.

Nara The JR Kansai line links Osaka (Namba and Tennō-ji stations) and Nara (JR Nara station) via Hōryū-ji (*kaisoku* ¥540, 35 minutes).

The private Kintetsu Nara line also connects Osaka (Kintetsu Namba station) with Nara (Kintetsu Nara station). *Kyūkō* and *futsū* services take about 35 minutes and cost ¥540. *Tokkyū* trains do the journey in five minutes less time but at almost double the cost, making them a poor option.

Kōbe The fastest way between Kōbe and Osaka is the JR *shinkaisoku* that runs between Osaka station and Kōbe's Sannomiya and Kōbe stations (¥390, 21 minutes).

There is also the private Hankyū line, which takes a little more time but is cheaper. It runs from Osaka's Hankyū Umeda station to Kōbe's Sannomiya station (*tokkyū* ¥310, 27 minutes).

Bus

There is a long-distance highway bus service between Osaka and cities all across Honshū, Shikoku and some cities in Kyushū. Destinations include Tokyo (¥8610, eight hours), Nagasaki (¥11,000, 10 hours) and Kago-shima (¥12,000, 12 hours). Buses usually depart from either Osaka, Hankyū Umeda or Namba stations; check with the tourist information offices for more details.

Boat

Ferries to Shanghai in China depart Osaka twice a month (2nd class ¥20,000). The ferries leave from the Osaka Nankō international ferry terminal, which can be reached by taking the New Tram service from Suminoe-kōen station to Nankoguchi station. You can ring the **Nitchū Kokusai ferry company** (☎ 6536-6541, in Japanese) for details, but Osaka tourist information offices are a better source of information on schedules and bookings.

Ferries also depart from Nankō ferry terminal and Kanome-futō and Benten-futō piers for various destinations around Honshū, Kyūshū and Shikoku. Kyūshū destinations include Beppu (¥7030) and Miyazaki (¥8380). Other possibilities in Kyūshū are Shinmoji in the north of the island near Shimonoseki and Shibushi in the south of the island. Possibilities in Shikoku are Kōchi (¥4610), Matsuyama (¥5000), Takamatsu (¥6100, hydrofoil) and Tokushima (¥4620, hydrofoil). Note that prices listed here are for a 2nd-class ticket, which, on overnight ferries, usually means a place on a tatami floor in a large, open room.

For detailed information about sailing schedules and bookings contact the tourist information offices.

GETTING AROUND
To/From the Airport

Itami Airport There are frequent limousine buses running between the airport and various parts of Osaka. Buses run to/from Shin-Osaka station every 15 minutes from about 6.30am to 7.30pm (¥490, 25 minutes). Buses run at about the same frequency to/from Osaka and Namba stations (¥620, 30 minutes). At Itami, buy your tickets from the machine outside the arrivals hall.

There are also direct airport buses to/from Kyoto (¥1370) and Kōbe (¥1020).

Kansai International Airport There are a variety of routes between KIX and Osaka. Limousine buses travel to/from Shin-Osaka, Osaka Umeda, Kyobashi, Tenmabashi, Osaka City Air Terminal (OCAT) Namba, Uehonmachi, Tennō-ji and Nanko (Cosmo Square) stations. The fare is ¥1300 for most routes and the journeys take an average of 50 minutes, depending on traffic

conditions. OCAT, in JR Namba station, allows passengers on Japanese and some other airlines to check in and deposit baggage before boarding trains to the airport. Check with your airline for details.

The fastest way by train to/from the airport is the private Nankai express Rapit, which departs from Nankai Namba station on the Midō-suji subway line (¥1400, 30 minutes). The JR Haruka limited airport express operates between the airport and Tennō-ji station (¥2270, 31 minutes) and Shin-Osaka (¥2980, 48 minutes).

Regular JR express trains called *kanku kaisoku* also operate between the airport and Osaka station (¥1160, 66 minutes), Kyōbashi station (¥1160, 70 minutes), Tennō-ji station (¥1030, 50 minutes) and JR Namba station (¥1030, 61 minutes).

Train & Subway

Osaka has a good subway network and, like Tokyo, a JR loop line (known in Japanese as the JR *kanjō-sen*) that circles the city area. In fact, there should be no need to use any other form of transport while you are in Osaka unless you stay out late and miss the last train.

There are seven subway lines, but the one that most short-term visitors are likely to find most useful is the Midō-suji line, which runs north to south stopping at Shin-Osaka, Umeda (next to Osaka station), Shinsaibashi, Namba and Tennō-ji stations. Most rides cost between ¥200 and ¥300.

If you're going to be using the rail system a lot on any day, it might be worth considering a 'one-day free ticket'. For ¥850 (¥650 on Fridays and the 20th of every month) you get unlimited travel on any subway, the New Tram line and all city buses (but not the JR line). Note, however, that you would really have to be moving around a lot to save any money with this ticket. These tickets can be purchased from some of the ticket machines in most subway stations; push the button for 'one-day free ticket' then press the illuminated button reading '¥850'.

Bus

Osaka does have a bus system, but it is nowhere near as easy to use as the rail network. Japanese-language bus maps are available from the tourist offices.

KANSAI

Kōbe 神戸

☎ 078 • pop 1.42 million

Perched on a hillside overlooking Osaka-wan, Kōbe is one of Japan's most attractive cities. It's also one of the country's most famous, largely as a result of the tragic earthquake of 17 January 1995, which levelled whole neighbourhoods and killed more than 6000 people. Fortunately, the city has risen, Phoenix-like, from the ashes and is now more vibrant than ever.

One of Kōbe's best features is its relatively small size – most of the sights can be reached on foot from the main train stations. Of course, it must be noted that none of these sights are attractions you really must see: Kōbe is likely to appeal more to residents than to travellers. However, it does have some good restaurants, cafés and bars and is a good place for a night out in Kansai if you just can't face the mayhem of Osaka.

ORIENTATION

Kōbe's two main entry points are San-nomiya and Shin-Kōbe stations. Shin-Kōbe station, in the northeast of town, is where the *shinkansen* stops. A subway (¥200, one minute) runs from here to the busier Sannomiya station, which has frequent rail connections with Osaka and Kyoto. It's possible to walk between the two stations in around 15 minutes. Sannomiya station marks the city centre, although a spate of development in Kōbe Harbor Land is starting to swing the city's centre of gravity to the southwest. Before starting your exploration of Kōbe, pick up a copy of the *Kōbe Town Map* at one of the two information offices (see Information following).

INFORMATION

The city's main **tourist information office** (☎ 322-0220; open 9am-7pm daily) is outside Sannomiya station. There's a smaller **information counter** on the 2nd floor of Shin-Kōbe station. Both information centres carry the useful *Kōbe Town Map* and the *Kōbe Guide Map*, both free.

There's an international ATM in the Sannomiya Sentah Gai shopping arcade. Behind Kōbe city hall there's a **Citibank** with machines that also accept a variety of cards.

There's are several **discount ticket shops** ..ankyū Sannomiya station.

Bookshops

There's a branch of **Maruzen** near Nan-kinmachi (Chinatown). For second-hand books, try **Wantage Books** (☎ 232-4517; open 9.30am-5.30pm Mon-Fri), up near Shin-Kōbe station. It has a great selection and low prices, and all proceeds go to charity. In the same building is the office of *Kansai Time Out*, Kansai's best 'what's on' magazine.

KITANO 北野

Twenty minutes' walk north of Sannomiya is the pleasant hillside neighbourhood of Kitano, where local tourists come to enjoy the feeling of foreign travel without leaving Japanese soil. A European/American atmosphere is created by the winding streets and *ijinkan* (literally 'foreigners' houses') that housed some of Kōbe's early Western residents. Admission to some is free, to others ¥300 to ¥700, and most are open from 9am to 5pm daily. Although these brick and weatherboard dwellings may not hold the same fascination for Western travellers that they hold for local tourists, the area itself is pleasant to stroll around and is dotted with good cafés and restaurants.

SHIN-KŌBE CABLE CAR & NUNOBIKI HABU-KŌEN
新神戸ロープウェイ・布引ハーブ園

The Shin-Kōbe cable car ('ropeway' in Japanese; one way/return ¥550/1000; operates 9.30am to 5pm daily winter, to 8pm autumn and spring, to 9pm summer) leaves from behind the OPA shopping centre near Shin-Kōbe station and ascends to a mountain ridge 400m above the city. The views from the top over Kōbe and the bay are particularly pretty after sunset. There's a complex of gardens, restaurants and shops below the top station known as the Nunobiki Habu-kōen (*Nunobiki Herb Garden; admission ¥200*). Note that you can easily walk down to the bottom station from the Herb Garden in about 30 minutes.

KŌBE CITY MUSEUM
神戸市立博物館

Kōbe City Museum (*Kōbe Shiritsu Hakubut-sukan; admission ¥200, extra for special exhibits; open 10am-4.30pm Tues-Sun*) has a collection of so-called Namban (literally 'southern barbarian') art and occasional special exhibits. Namban art is a school

Abandoned fishing boat, Miyazu-wan, Kansai

Okuno-in, Kōya-san, Kansai

Funaya (boat houses), Ine, northern Kyoto-fu, Kansai

Osaka-jō and the city, Kansai

Summit sign, Miune, Tokushima-ken, Shikoku

of painting that developed under the influence of early Jesuit missionaries in Japan, many of whom taught Western painting techniques to Japanese students.

NANKINMACHI (CHINATOWN)
南京町

Nankinmachi, Kōbe's Chinatown, is not on a par with Chinatowns elsewhere in the world, but it is a good place for a stroll. It's particularly attractive in the evening, when the lights of the area illuminate the gaudily painted facades of the shops. Unfortunately most of the restaurants in the area are overpriced and somewhat disappointing (we list a good exception in the Places to Eat section). The best idea is to grab a takeaway snack here and eat elsewhere.

KŌBE HARBOR LAND & MERIKEN PARK
神戸ハーバーランド・メリケンパーク

Five minutes' walk southeast of Kōbe station, Kōbe Harbor Land is awash with new mega-mall shopping and dining developments. This may not appeal to foreign travellers the way it does to the local youth, but it's still a nice place for a stroll in the afternoon. For a good view of the area, take the free glass lift to the 18th floor of the **Ecoll Marine building**.

A five-minute walk to the east of Harbor Land you'll find Meriken Park, on a spit of reclaimed land jutting out into the bay. The main attraction here is the **Kōbe Maritime Museum** (*Kōbe Kaiyō Hakubutsukan; admission ¥500; open 10am-5pm Tues-Sun*). The museum has a small collection of ship models and displays, with some English explanations.

Just east of the Maritime Museum, the **Port of Kōbe Earthquake Memorial Park** (*open 24hr daily*) preserves part of a concrete pier that was destroyed in the 1995 earthquake. The extent of the damage should give you a good idea just how strong the earthquake was.

ROKKO ISLAND 六甲アイランド

An artificial island, the main attraction here is the **Kōbe Fashion Museum** (*Kōbe Fashion Bijutsukan; admission ¥500; open 11am-5.30pm Sat-Tues & Thur, 11am-7.30pm Fri*). The museum's collection of mostly foreign fashion is not quite up to the dramatic building in which it's housed but it's worth a look if you're interested in fashion. To reach the museum, take the Rokko Liner monorail (¥240) from JR Sumiyoshi (four stops east of Sannomiya) and get off at the Island Centre stop.

SPECIAL EVENTS

Luminarie, Kōbe's biggest yearly event, is held every evening from around 12 to 25 December to celebrate the city's miraculous recovery from the 1995 earthquake (check with the Kōbe Tourist Information Office to be sure of the dates as they change slightly every year). The streets southwest of Kōbe City Hall are decorated with countless illuminated metal archways, which when viewed from within look like the interior of some otherworldly cathedral.

PLACES TO STAY – MID-RANGE

Green Hill Hotel Urban (☎ 222-1221; *singles/doubles or twins from ¥6500/13,000*) is a good value place and also has a convenient location not far from Shin-Kōbe station.

Green Hill Hotel Kōbe (☎ 222-0909; *singles/twins from ¥7500/10,000*) has rooms that are slightly better than at the Hotel Urban, making it another good business hotel choice.

Hotel Tor Road (☎ 391-6691; *singles/ doubles or twins from ¥7500/15,000*), on the hill leading up to Kitano, is a pleasant little hotel with fairly large rooms.

Kōbe Washington Hotel Plaza (☎ 331-6111; *singles/doubles or twins from ¥7014/ 15,152*), close to Sannomiya station, has small but clean rooms.

PLACES TO STAY – TOP END

Shin-Kōbe Oriental Hotel (☎ 291-1121; *singles/doubles or twins from ¥13,000/ 23,000*), towering above Shin-Kōbe station, claims the best views of any hotel in town.

Hotel Ōkura Kōbe (☎ 333-0111; *singles/ doubles/twins from ¥16,000/19,000/20,000*), on the waterfront behind Meriken Park, is the most elegant hotel in town and has fine rooms.

PLACES TO EAT

The restaurants in this section are open during usual business hours (11am to 2pm, 5pm to 10pm) unless otherwise noted.

KANSAI

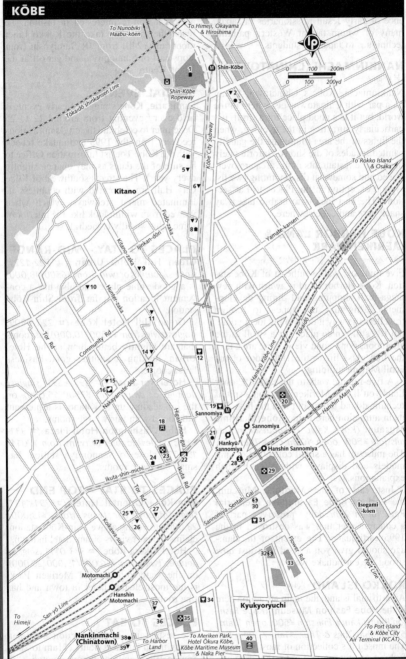

KŌBE

To Nunobiki
Haabu-kōen

To Himeji, Okayama
& Hiroshima

Shin-Kōbe

1

Shin-Kōbe
Ropeway

▼ 2
● 3

Tōkaidō Shinkansen Line

Kitano

Kōbe City Subway

4 ▲
5 ▼
6 ▼

To Rokko Island
& Osaka

▼ 7
8 ▲

Yamate-kansen

Ijinkan-dōri

Kitano-zaka

▼ 9

▼ 10

Hunter-zaka

Tor Rd

Community Rd

▼ 11

Nakayamate-dōri

14 ▼
13

Hankyū Kōbe Line

12

Fudō-zaka

▼ 15
16

19 ▼
Sannomiya

20

Tōkaidō Line

Hanshin Main Line

18

21

Sannomiya

Higashimon-gai

17 ▲

24 23
22

Ikuta Rd

Hankyū
Sannomiya

Hanshin Sannomiya

28

29

Ikuta-shin-michi

Isogami
-kōen

25 ▼
26

27

Sannomiya-Sentah Gai

30

31

Koikawa-suji

Flower Rd

Port Line

32

33

Motomachi

San-yō Line

Hanshin
Motomachi

To Himeji

37

36

34

Kyukyoryuchi

35

Nankinmachi
(Chinatown)

38 ●
39 ▼

To Harbor
Land

To Meriken Park,
Hotel Ōkura Kōbe,
Kōbe Maritime Museum
& Naka Pier

40

To Port Island
& Kōbe City
Air Terminal (KCAT)

0   100   200m
0   100   200yd

KANSAI

KŌBE

PLACES TO STAY		14	Gaylord	20	Daiei Department Store
1	Shin-Kōbe Oriental Hotel;		ゲイロード		ダイエー百貨店
	Shin-Kōbe Oriental City;	15	Kōkaen	21	Discount Ticket Shop
	OPA Shopping Centre		鴻華園		格安切符売り場
	新神戸オリエンタルホテル ;	25	Modernark Pharm	22	Higashimon-gai Gate
	新神戸オリエンタルシティ ;		モダンアークファーム		(South)
	オーパ	26	Tutto Benne; Patisserie Tooth		東門街街 （南）
4	Green Hill Hotel Kōbe		Tooth	23	Tōkyū Hands Department
	グリーンヒルホテル神戸		トゥートベーネ；トゥース		Store
8	Green Hill Hotel Urban		トゥース		東急ハンズ
	グリーンヒルホテルアーバン	27	Aja Kaja	28	Tourist Information Office
17	Hotel Tor Road		アジャカジャ		観光案内所
	ホテルトアロード	37	Kintoki	29	Sogō Department Store
24	Kōbe Washington Hotel		金時		そごう百貨店
	Plaza	39	Motomachi Gyōza-en	30	International ATM
	神戸ワシントンホテルプラザ		元町ぎょうざ苑		国際ATM
				31	Polo Dog
PLACES TO EAT		OTHER			ポロドッグ
2	Yoshinoya	3	Wantage Books; Kansai	32	Citibank
	吉野屋		Time Out Office		シティバンク
5	Nailey's		ワンテージ書店；関西タイム	33	Kōbe City Hall
	ネイリーズ		アウト事務所		神戸市役所
6	Native	12	Oto-ya	34	Dubliners
	ネイテイブ		音屋		ダブリナーズ
7	Mikami	13	Higashimon-gai Gate (North)	35	Daimaru Department Store
	みかみ		東門街街 （北）		大丸百貨店
9	Upwards	16	South Korea Consulate	36	Maruzen Books
	アプワーズ		韓国領事館		丸善書店
10	Tada	18	Ikuta-jinja	38	Nankinmachi Square
	多田		生田神社		南京町広場
11	Court Lodge	19	Ryan's Irish Pub	40	Kōbe City Museum
	コートロッジ		ライアンズ		神戸市立博物館

Japanese

Although Kōbe is more famous for its international cuisine, there are plenty of good Japanese restaurants to be found.

Yoshinoya (☎ 265-6269; *gyū-don* from ¥400), close to Shin-Kōbe station, is a fast food *gyū-don* (beef over rice) specialist that is good for a quick, light meal (to order a regular-sized bowl of beef over rice just say *gyū-don nami*).

Native (☎ 242-7677; *lunch/dinner around* ¥1000/3000) is a small, modern café/restaurant that serves light and healthy Japanese fare.

Tada (☎ 222-1715; *lunch/dinner from* ¥600) is a casual *okonomiyaki* place in Kitano with counter seating. It also serves *teppanyaki* (grilled meat) beef from ¥1100 for a set.

Mikami (☎ 242-2500; *lunch/dinner from* ¥400; open Mon-Sat) is a friendly spot for good-value lunch and dinner sets of standard Japanese fare. Noodle dishes are available from ¥400 and *teishoku* (set meals) from ¥600. There is also an English menu.

Kintoki (☎ 331-1037; *lunch/dinner from* ¥500) is a good place to go for a taste of what Japan was like before it got rich. It's an atmospheric old *shokudō* that serves the cheapest food in the city. You can order standard noodle and rice dishes from the menu (plain *soba* noodles are ¥250 and a small rice is ¥160) or choose from a variety of dishes laid out on the counter.

Sazanka (☎ 333-3528; *dinner from* ¥7,000) is a good *teppanyaki* restaurant on the first floor of Hotel Ōkura Kōbe. This is the place to sample that most precious of meats: Kōbe beef.

International

Kōbe has loads of international restaurants, including good Indian, Chinese and Italian restaurants. There are also lots of trendy café-style spots in Kōbe, including a clutch of restaurants just north of Motomachi station in the fashionable Tor Road area.

Aja Kaja (☎ 393-2775; *curry sets* ¥950) is a dimly lit Indian restaurant that is a favourite of the locals.

KANSAI

Gaylord (☎ 251-4359; lunch/dinner from ¥900/3000) is a large Indian eatery where you have to pay a little more to enjoy excellent set meals and delicious curries.

Court Lodge (☎ 222-5504; lunch/dinner from ¥1000/2000), right in the heart of Kitano, is a Sri Lankan place that serves tasty set meals and delicious Ceylon tea.

Patisserie Tooth Tooth (☎ 334-1350; lunch/dinner from ¥1000/2500), near Motomachi station, is a fashionable European-style café-restaurant that serves light meals.

Tutto Benne (☎ 230-3350; tea ¥400, lunch ¥900) is a trendy little spot for a variety of café drinks and mouth-watering pastries.

Modernark Pharm (☎ 391-3060; lunch/dinner from ¥900/1500) is an interesting little restaurant that serves tasty sets of Japanese and Western dishes, including burritos and rice dishes.

Nailey's (☎ 231-2008; coffee from ¥400, lunch/dinner from ¥900/1200) is a hip little café that serves espresso, light lunches and dinners. This is also a good spot for an evening drink.

Upwards (☎ 230-8551; lunch/dinner from ¥900/2000) is a fashionable eatery in Kitano that serves light Italian fare in an airy, open space. It's another good spot for a drink in the evening.

Motomachi Gyōza-en (☎ 331-4096; 6 dumplings ¥340) is the best spot in Nankin-machi for Chinese dumplings (that's about all this place serves). Try its wonderful fried dumplings (yaki gyōza) at lunch or dinner. At dinner they also make steamed gyōza (sui gyōza). Use the vinegar, soy sauce and miso on the table to make a dipping sauce. The red sign is in Japanese only, so you may have to ask someone to point out the store.

Lastly, **Kōkaen** (☎ 231-7079; lunch/dinner from ¥1000/2000) is a favourite of local cognoscenti for authentic Chinese and Vietnamese food.

ENTERTAINMENT

Kōbe has a large foreign community and a number of bars that see mixed Japanese and foreign crowds. For Japanese-style drinking establishments, try the izakaya in the neighbourhood between the JR tracks and Ikuta-jinja. Also bear in mind that a lot of Kōbe's nightlife is centred around the city's many cafés, most of which transform into bars come evening (see Places to Eat earlier).

Ryan's Irish Pub (☎ 391-6902) is an Irish-owned pub with Guinness on tap, traditional Irish pub fare, occasional live music, and a good crowd of regulars.

Dubliners (☎ 334-3614) is another decent Irish-style pub that is part of the Sapporo Lion House beer hall chain. It also serves lunch and dinner during the day.

Polo Dog (☎ 331-3944), a short walk from Sannomiya station, is a small casual bar at home with foreign customers.

Oto-ya (☎ 321-4880) is a live house (small indie music venue) that attracts some good local bands. Check Kansai Time Out to see what's happening while you're in town.

GETTING THERE & AWAY
Train
JR Sannomiya station is on the JR Tōkaidō line as well as the private Hankyū and Hanshin lines (both of which run to/from Osaka). The fastest way between Kōbe and Kyoto or Osaka is the JR shinkaisoku (to/from Kyoto ¥1050, 54 minutes; to/from Osaka station ¥390, 21 minutes).

The Hankyū line is the more convenient of the two private lines (limited express to/from Osaka's Hankyū Umeda station ¥310, 27 minutes; tokkyū to/from Kyoto – change at Osaka's Jūsō station – ¥600, one hour).

Shin-Kōbe station is on the Tōkaidō/San-yō shinkansen line (Hikari shinkansen to/from Fukuoka ¥14,270, two hours 43 minutes; Hikari shinkansen to/from Tokyo ¥14,270, three hours nine minutes).

Boat
There are regular ferries between Kōbe and Shikoku (Imabari and Matsuyama) and Kyūshū (Ōita). Most ferries depart from Rokko Island and are operated by **Diamond Ferry Company** (☎ 857-9525, in Japanese). The cheapest fares are as follows: Imabari ¥4300, Matsuyama ¥5200 and Ōita ¥7400.

Osaka-Shanghai ferries also stop in Kōbe. For more information, see the Osaka Boat section.

GETTING AROUND
To/From the Airport
Itami Osaka Airport It's possible to take a bus directly to/from Osaka's Itami airport (¥1020, 40 minutes). In Kōbe, the buses stop on the southwestern side of Sannomiya station.

Kansai International Airport

There are a number of routes between Kōbe and KIX. By train, the fastest way is the JR *shinkaisoku* to/from Osaka station, and the JR *kanku kaisoku* between Osaka station and the airport (total cost ¥1660, total time 90 minutes with good connections). There is also a direct limousine bus to/from the airport (¥1800, 70 minutes). The Kōbe airport bus stop is on the southwestern side of Sannomiya station.

Public Transport

Kōbe is small enough to travel around on foot. JR, Hankyū and Hanshin railway lines run east to west across Kōbe, providing access to most of Kōbe's more distant sights. A subway line also connects Shin-Kōbe station with Sannomiya station (¥200, one minute). There is also a city loop bus service which makes a grand circle tour of most of the city's sightseeing spots (¥250 per ride, ¥650 for an all-day pass). The bus stops at both Sannomiya and Shin-Kōbe stations; look for the retro-style green buses.

Himeji 姫路

☎ 0792 • pop 479,000

If you see no other castles in Japan you should at least make an effort to visit Himeji-jō, unanimously acclaimed as the most splendid Japanese castle still standing. It's also known as Shirasagi, the 'White Egret', a title that derives from the castle's stately white form. The surrounding town itself is pretty drab, but the nearby Hyōgo Prefectural Museum of History and Kōko-en are worth a visit.

Himeji can easily be visited as a day trip from Kyoto, Osaka or Kōbe. On the way to Himeji, take a look out the train window at the new Akashi Kaikyō Suspension Bridge. Its 3910m span links the island of Honshū with Awaji-shima, making it the longest suspension bridge in the world. It comes into view on the southern side of the train about 10km west of Kōbe.

ORIENTATION & INFORMATION

There's a **tourist information counter** (☎ 85-3792) at the station; it's on the ground floor to the right as you come off the escalator. Between 10am and 3pm, English-speaking staff are on duty and can help with hotel/ryokan reservations etc. The castle is a 15-minute walk straight up the main road from the north exit of the station. If you don't feel like walking, free rental cycles are available; inquire at the information counter.

HIMEJI-JŌ 姫路城

Himeji-jō *(admission ¥600; open 9am-4pm daily Sept-May, 9am-5pm daily June-Aug, closed 29-31 Dec)* is the most magnificent of the handful of Japanese castles that survive in their original (nonconcrete) form. Although there have been fortifications in Himeji since 1333, today's castle was built in 1580 by Toyotomi Hideyoshi and enlarged some 30 years later by Ikeda Terumasa. Ikeda was awarded the castle by Tokugawa Ieyasu when the latter's forces defeated the Toyotomi armies. In the following centuries the castle was home to 48 successive lords.

The castle has a five-storey main donjon (heavily fortified central tower) and three smaller donjons, and the entire structure is surrounded by moats and defensive walls punctuated with rectangular, circular and triangular openings for firing guns and shooting arrows. The walls of the donjon also feature *ishiotoshi* – openings that allowed defenders to pour boiling water or oil onto anyone who made it past the defensive slits and was thinking of scaling the walls. All things considered, visitors are recommended to pay the admission charge and enter the castle by legitimate means.

It takes around 1½ hours to follow the arrow-marked route around the castle. English-speaking guides are sometimes available and can really add a lot to your tour of the castle. Unfortunately appointments aren't accepted and it's hit or miss whether any will be available on the day of your visit – ask at the ticket office of the castle and hope for the best. The guide service is free.

KŌKO-EN 好古園

Just across the moat on the western side of Himeji-jō, you'll find Kōko-en *(admission ¥300; open 9am-6pm daily June-Aug, 9am-5pm daily Sept-May)*, a reconstruction of the former samurai quarters of the castle. There are nine separate Edo-style gardens, two ponds, a stream, a tea arbor (¥500 for *matcha* and a Japanese sweet) and the restaurant **Kassui-ken**, where you can enjoy lunch while gazing over the gardens. While the garden doesn't have the subtle beauty of some of Japan's older gardens, it is well done and especially lovely in the autumn foliage season.

HYŌGO PREFECTURAL MUSEUM OF HISTORY

兵庫県立博物館

This museum *(Hyōgo Kenritsu Rekishi Hakubutsukan; admission ¥200; open 10am-5pm Tues-Sun, closed the day after national holidays)* has good displays on Himeji-jō and other castles around Japan. In addition to the displays on castles, the museum covers the main periods of Japanese history with some English explanations. At 11am, 2pm and 3.30pm you can even try on a suit of samurai armour or a kimono (ask at the front desk).

The museum is a five-minute walk north of the castle.

ENGYŌ-JI 円教寺

Around 8km northeast of Himeji station, this mountaintop temple complex *(admission ¥300; open 8.30am-5pm daily)* is well worth a visit if you've got time after visiting the castle. The temple and surrounding area is most beautiful in the April cherry-blossom season or November *momiji* (maple-leaf) season. Eight of the temple buildings and seven Buddha images have been designated Important Cultural Properties. Take your time to explore the temple grounds, which continue quite a way up the mountain (Shosha-zan) from the cable-car stop.

To get there, take bus No 6 or 8 from Himeji station (¥260, 25 minutes). Get off at Shosha, and board the cable car (one way/return ¥500/900).

SPECIAL EVENTS

The **Nada-no-Kenka Matsuri**, held on 14 and 15 October, involves a conflict between three *mikoshi* that are battered against each other until one smashes. Try to go on the second day, when the festival reaches its peak (around noon). The festival is held five minutes' walk from Shirahamanomiya station (10 minutes from Himeji station on the Sanyō-Dentetsu line); follow the crowds.

PLACES TO STAY

Himeji is best visited as a day trip from other parts of Kansai. If you'd like to stay, however, there are plenty of choices.

HIMEJI

HIMEJI

PLACES TO STAY		OTHER		12	Seiden Electronics Shop
11	Himeji Washington Hotel Plaza 姫路ワシントンホテルプラザ	1	Hyōgo Prefectural Museum of History 兵庫県立歴史博物館		セイデンデンキ
21	Hotel Sun Garden Himeji ホテルサンガーデン姫路	2	Himeji-jinja 姫路神社	14	Discount Ticket Shop 格安切符売り場
22	Hotel Himeji Plaza ホテル姫路プラザ	3	Himeji City Museum of Art 姫路市立美術館	15	San-yō Department Store; San-yō Himeji 山陽百貨店；山陽姫路駅
		4	Castle Ticket Office 姫路城切符売り場	16	City Bus Terminal 市バスターミナル
PLACES TO EAT		5	Gokoku-jinja 護国神社	17	Shinki Bus Terminal 神姫バスターミナル
7	Morijū 森重	6	Himeji Post Office 姫路郵便局	18	Himeji North Exit 北口
9	Bistro Angelot ビストロアンジェロ	8	Yamatoyashiki Department Store ヤマトヤシキ百貨店	19	Himeji South Exit 南口
10	Fukutei ふく亭			20	City South Bus Terminal 市バス南ターミナル
13	Sekishin 赤心				

Himeji Washington Hotel Plaza (☎ 25-0111; singles/doubles from ¥6750/13,508) is the best mid-range choice in town. It's within easy walking distance of the castle and lots of restaurants.

Hotel Himeji Plaza (☎ 81-9000; singles/doubles from ¥5900/12,300), on the other side of the station, is similar in quality but is a bit of a hike to the castle and restaurants.

Hotel Sun Garden Himeji (☎ 22-2231; singles/doubles ¥8800/17,000) is a stone's throw from the station. It has clean and fairly spacious rooms and is the best choice for those who want something nicer than a business hotel.

PLACES TO EAT

The **food court** in the underground mall at JR Himeji station has all the usual Western and Japanese dishes. It's just to the right as you exit the north ticket gate of the station.

Sekishin (☎ 22-3842; tonkatsu ¥550, rice ¥200) is a tiny hole-in-the-wall joint that serves tasty tonkatsu (pork cutlets). You might also try its special tonjiru (miso soup with bits of fatty pork). Look for the white curtains with red kanji.

Fukutei (☎ 23-0981; lunch/dinner ¥1400/5000; open Fri-Wed) is a good spot for a nice lunch of simple kaiseki fare. From 11am to 2pm, try its mini-kaiseki course (¥1400). Look for the glass door and menu in the window.

Bistro Angelot (☎ 26-1113; lunch from ¥1000; open Wed-Mon) is a casual French/Italian place that serves reasonable lunch courses. Look for the green awning.

Morijū (☎ 23-2517; meals from ¥2500; open Tues-Sun) is another good spot for an elegant dinner of things like unagi mamushi (eel over rice, ¥2800) and kaki nabe (oyster cooked in a stew pot, ¥2500 per person). Some Japanese ability would be helpful here. Look for the black-and-white sign; it's next to a two-car parking lot.

GETTING THERE & AWAY

The best way to Himeji from Kyoto, Osaka or Kōbe is a shinkaisoku on the JR Tōkaidō line (to/from Kyoto, ¥2210, 1½ hours; to/from Osaka, ¥1450, one hour; to/from Kōbe, ¥950, 40 minutes). From Okayama, to the west, a tokkyū JR train on the San-yō line takes 1½ hours and costs ¥1450. You can also reach Himeji from these cities via the Tōkaidō/San-yō shinkansen line, and this is a good option for Japan Rail Pass holders.

Nara 奈良

☎ 0742 • pop 363,000

Japan's first real capital, Nara, is the number-two tourist attraction in Kansai after Kyoto. Like Kyoto, Nara is uninspiring at first glance, but careful inspection will reveal the rich history and hidden beauty of the city. Indeed, with eight Unesco World Heritage sites, Nara is second only to Kyoto as a repository of Japan's cultural legacy. Whatever you do, try to go to Nara on a fine day, as visiting the sites requires a lot of walking, and it's no fun at all in bad weather.

KANSAI

Unesco World Heritage Sites

In 1998, eight sites in Nara met the criteria to be designated World Heritage sites by the United Nations. They are the Buddhist temples of Tōdai-ji, Kōfuku-ji, Gango-ji, Yakushi-ji and Tōshōdai-ji; the shrine, Kasuga Taisha; Kasuga-yama Primeval Forest; and the remains of Heijō-kyō Palace.

Each of these sites is considered to be of immeasurable historical value. All are open for public viewing. Five are covered in detail in the text; of the remaining three, Kasuga-yama Primeval Forest is directly behind Kasuage Taisha, Gango-ji is in Naramachi, and the Heijō-kyō Palace Ruins are 10 minutes' walk east of Saidai-ji station on the Kintetsu line.

SUGGESTED ITINERARY

Nara is so small that it's quite possible to pack the most worthwhile sights into one full day. It's preferable to spend at least two days here, but this will depend on how much time you have for the Kansai region. Those with time to spare should allow a day for Nara-kōen and another day for the sights in western and southwestern Nara. If you only have one day in Nara, spend it walking around Nara-kōen; you would only exhaust yourself if you tried to fit in some of the more distant sights as well.

HISTORY

Nara is at the northern end of the Yamato plain, where members of the Yamato clan rose to power as the original emperors of Japan. The remains of these early emperors are contained in *kofun* (burial mounds), some of which date back to the 3rd century AD.

Until the 7th century, however, Japan had no permanent capital, as native Shintō taboos concerning death stipulated that the capital be moved with the passing of each emperor. This practice died out under the influence of Buddhism and with the Taika reforms of 646, when the entire country came under imperial control.

At this time it was decreed that a permanent capital be built. Two locations were tried before a permanent capital was finally established at Nara (which was then known as Heijōkyō) in 710. Permanent status,

however, lasted a mere 75 years. When a priest by the name of Dōkyō managed to seduce an empress and nearly usurp the throne, it was decided to move the court to a new location, out of reach of Nara's increasingly powerful clergy. This led to the new capital being established at Kyoto, where it remained until 1868.

Although brief, the Nara period was extraordinarily vigorous in its absorption of influences from China, a process that laid the foundations of Japanese culture and civilisation. The adoption of Buddhism as a national religion made a lasting impact on government, arts, literature and architecture. With the exception of an assault on the area by the Taira clan in the 12th century, Nara was subsequently spared the periodic bouts of destruction wreaked upon Kyoto, and a number of magnificent buildings have survived.

ORIENTATION

Nara retains the grid pattern of streets laid out in Chinese style during the 8th century. The two main train stations, JR Nara station and Kintetsu Nara station, are roughly in the middle of the city, and Nara-kōen, which contains most of the important sights, is on the eastern side, against the bare flank of Wakakusa-yama. Most of the other sights are southwest of the city and are best reached by buses that leave from both train stations (or by train in the case of Hōryū-ji). It's easy to cover the city centre and the major attractions in nearby Nara-kōen on foot, though some may prefer to rent a bicycle (see the Getting Around section).

Maps

Nara tourist information offices have two very useful maps: the *Strolling Around Nara* map, which is best for sightseeing within the city limits, and the *Japan, Nara Prefecture* map, which is best for outlying areas. In addition, their hand-out titled *Nara* has a basic map and useful transport information.

INFORMATION

If you're heading to Nara from Kyoto, the **TIC** in Kyoto has good information on the city. In Nara, the best source of information is the **Nara City Tourist Center** (☎ 22-3900; open 9am-9pm daily). It's a short walk from JR Nara or Kintetsu Nara station.

The tourist centre can put you in touch with volunteer guides who speak English and other foreign languages, but you must book at least one day in advance. Two of these services are the **YMCA Goodwill Guides** (*☎ 45-5920*) and **Nara Student Guides** (*☎ 26-4753*). These services are a pleasant way to meet the Japanese – the guides are often students keen to practise their foreign languages. Remember that the guides are volunteers, so you should offer to cover their day's expenses; however, most temple and museum admission fees are waived for registered guides, so you needn't worry about those.

There are three more tourist information offices in Nara that stock maps and have staff who can answer basic questions in English: the **JR Nara station office** (*☎ 22-9821*), the **Kintetsu Nara station office** (*☎ 24-4858*) and the **Sarusawa information office** (*☎ 26-1991*). All three are open from 9am to 5pm daily. The JR Nara station office may be able to help with ryokan and *minshuku* reservations.

There is an ATM that accepts international cards on the ground floor of the building opposite Kintetsu Nara station. In the same building you can purchase tickets for highway buses (to Tokyo etc), airport buses (to Kansai airport) and tour buses (around Nara and surrounding areas).

Outside the NTT office on Sanjō-dōri there is a bank of international phones. For internet, try the Hotel Asyl's **Suien tea lounge** (*☎ 22-2577; 2hr Internet free with purchase of ¥500 drink; open 8am-10.30pm daily*).

The Nara City Tourist Center office also has comprehensive listings of places to stay, information on bus tours, hiking maps and the like.

NARA-KŌEN AREA 奈良公園
The park was created from wasteland in 1880 and covers a large area at the foot of Wakakusa-yama. The JNTO's leaflet entitled *Walking Tour Courses in Nara* includes a map for this area. We also include a walking tour of the area in this section (see the Nara-kōen Walking Tour boxed text). This walking tour is probably the best way to get the most out of a day in Nara and is highly recommended.

The park is home to about 1200 deer, which in pre-Buddhist times were considered messengers of the gods and today

enjoy the status of National Treasures. They roam the park and surrounding areas in search of hand-outs from tourists, often descending on petrified children who have the misfortune to be carrying food. You can buy *shika-sembei* (deer biscuits) from vendors for ¥150 to feed to the deer.

Kōfuku-ji 興福寺
This temple was transferred here from Kyoto in 710 as the main temple for the Fujiwara family. Although the original temple complex had 175 buildings, fires and destruction as a result of power struggles have left only a dozen still standing. There are two pagodas – a three-storey one and a five-storey one – dating from 1143 and 1426 respectively. The taller of the two pagodas is the second tallest in Japan, outclassed by the one at Kyoto's Tō-ji by only a few centimetres.

The **Kōfuku-ji National Treasure Hall** (*Kokuhō-kan; admission ¥500; open 9am-4.30pm daily*) contains a variety of statues and art objects salvaged from previous structures. A descriptive leaflet in English is provided.

Nara National Museum
奈良国立博物館
The Nara National Museum (*Nara Koku-ritsu Hakubutsukan; admission ¥420, special exhibitions ¥830; open 9am-4.30pm daily*) is devoted to Buddhist art and is divided into two wings. The western gallery has a fine collection of *butsu-zō* (statues of the Buddha), while the new eastern gallery displays sculptures, paintings and calligraphy.

A special exhibition featuring the treasures of the Shōsō-in Hall, which holds the treasures of Tōdai-ji, are displayed here in May, as well as from 21 October to 8 November (call the Nara City Tourist Center to check, as these dates vary slightly each year). The exhibits include priceless items from the cultures along the Silk Road. If you are in Nara during these periods and are a fan of Japanese antiquities, you should make a point of visiting the museum, but be prepared for crowds – these exhibits get packed!

Isui-en & Neiraku Art Museum
依水園・寧楽美術館
This garden, dating from the Meiji era, is beautifully laid out and features abundant greenery and a pond filled with ornamental

KANSAI

NARA

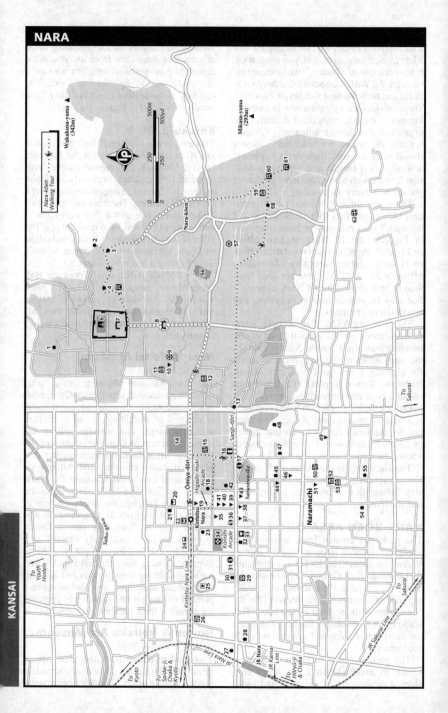

Wakakusa-yama
(342m)

Mikasa-yama
(293m)

Nara-kōen
Walking Tour

Nara-kōen

500m
500yd
0   250   500m
0   250   500yd

To
Youth
Hostels

To
Kyoto

To
Saidai-ji,
Osaka &
Kyoto

Saho-gawa

Kintetsu Nara Line

JR Nara Line

JR Nara

JR Kansai
Line

To
Hōryū-ji
& Osaka

Omiya-dōri

Kintetsu
Nara

Higashi-muki
Arcade

Konishi
Arcade

Sanjō-dōri

Sarusawa-ike

Naramachi

JR Sakurai Line

To
Sakurai

To
Sakurai

NARA

PLACES TO STAY

21	Green Hotel Ashibi グリーンホテルあしび
27	Nara Kokusai Hotel 奈良国際ホテル
28	Super Hotel スーパーホテル
30	Hotel Fujita Nara ホテルフジタ奈良
32	Ryokan Hakuhō 旅館白鳳
45	Ryokan Matsumae 旅館松前
47	Hotel Sunroute Nara ホテルサンルート奈良
48	Nara Hotel 奈良ホテル
54	Ryokan Seikan-sō 旅館静観荘

PLACES TO EAT & DRINK

10	Sanshū 三秀
19	Tsukihi-tei 月日亭
33	Rumours ルーマーズ
35	Hira-no-le 平の家
37	Kyōshō-An 京匠庵
38	Miyono 三好野
39	Beni-e べに江
40	Okaro おかろ
41	Za Don ザ どん
43	Drink Drank ドリンクドラク
44	Hirasō 平宗
46	Tempura Asuka 天ぷら飛鳥
49	Kosode 小袖
51	Harishin はり新

OTHER

1	Shōsō-in Treasure Repository 正倉院
2	Nigatsu-dō Hall 二月堂
3	Sangatsu-dō Hall 三月堂
4	Shōrō Belfry 鐘楼
5	Tamukeyama-jinja 手向山神社
6	Tōdai-ji Daibutsu-den 東大寺大仏殿
7	Tōdai-ji Chū-mon 東大寺中門
8	Tōdai-ji Nandai-mon 東大寺南大門
9	Isui-en 依水園
11	Neiraku Art Museum 寧楽美術館
12	Nara National Museum 奈良国立博物館
13	Ichi-no-Torii 一の鳥居
14	Nara Prefectural Office 奈良県庁
15	Kōfuku-ji National Treasure Hall 興福寺国宝館
16	Kōfuku-ji Five-Storey Pagoda 興福寺五重塔
17	Sarusawa Tourist Information Office 猿沢観光案内所
18	Kōfuku-ji Hokuen-dō Hall 興福寺北円堂
20	Post Office 郵便局
22	Tour Bus Tickets; Highway Bus Tickets; Airport Bus Tickets; International ATM 観光バス切符売り場；高速バ ス切符売り場；エアポートリ ムジン；バス切符売り場； 国際ATM

23	Kintetsu Sunflower Rent-a-Cycle 近鉄サンフラワー レンタサイクル
24	Local Bus Stop 市バス停
25	Emperor Kaika's Tomb 開化天皇陵
26	Hotel Asyl Nara; Suien Tea Lounge ホテルアジール奈良； 水煙
29	International Phones 国際電話
31	Nara City Tourist Centre 奈良市観光センター
34	Vivre Department Store ビブレ
36	SMBC Bank SMBC銀行
42	Kōfuku-ji Nanen-dō Hall 興福寺南円堂
50	Gangō-ji 元興寺
52	Naramachi Monogatari-kan 奈良町物語館
53	Naramachi Shiryō-kan Museum 奈良町資料館
55	Naramachi Koushi-no-le ならまち格子の家
56	Nara Prefectural Public Hall 奈良県民ホール
57	Kasuga Taisha-en 春日大社庭園
58	Ni-no-Torii 二の鳥居
59	Kasuga Taisha Hōmotsu-den 春日大社宝物殿
60	Kasuga-taisha 春日大社
61	Wakamiya-jinja 若宮神社
62	Shin-Yakushi-ji 新薬師寺

carp (admission museum & garden ¥600; open 9.30am-4pm Wed-Mon). It's without a doubt the best garden in the city and well worth a visit. For ¥450 you can enjoy a cup of tea on tatami mats overlooking the garden or have lunch in nearby Sanshū restaurant, which also shares the view.

The adjoining art museum (Neiraku Bijutsukan), which displays Chinese and Korean ceramics and bronzes, is something of an anticlimax after the garden.

TŌDAI-JI 東大寺

This temple, with its vast Daibutsu-den Hall and enormous bronze Buddha image, is Nara's star attraction. For this reason, it is often packed with groups of school children being herded around by microphone-wielding tour guides. Nonetheless, it is an awe-inspiring sight and should be high on any sightseeing itinerary.

On your way to the temple you'll pass through **Nandai-mon**, an enormous gate

Nara-kōen Walking Tour

Time Half a day
Distance About 5km
Major Sights Tōdai-ji, Kōfuku-ji, Kasuga-taisha

This walk meanders through the pleasantly wooded hills of Nara-kōen, taking in some of Nara's most important sights along the way. Start from the No 2 exit of Kintetsu Nara station. Walk straight up Ōmiya-dōri, passing **Kōfuku-ji** on your right (you can visit it now, or leave it until the return leg). After Kōfuku-ji, you have the option of taking a left to visit Isui-en, one of Nara's finest gardens. Otherwise, continue straight on, passing the **Nara National Museum** on your right. At the next traffic light, take a left, passing an arcade of souvenir stalls, some of which sell *shika-sembei* (deer crackers), to the delight of the hoards of deer in the park. At this point, you'll see the massive **Nandai-mon**, the main gate of **Tōdai-ji**. Stop in the gate to admire the **Niō guardians** and then continue to the temple.

After visiting Tōdai-ji, take the path that leads uphill from the southeast corner of the temple (just in front of the torii for Tamukeyama-jinja). The path curves around and climbs to the **Shōrō Belfry**, then climbs to an open plaza in front of **Sangatsu-dō** and **Nigatsu-dō** halls. The view from the veranda of Nigatsu-dō is one of the best in Nara, taking in the graceful curves of the Daibutsu-den and most of the Nara plain.

Exit the plaza and head south, passing between a log cabin-like structure and gaudy Tamukeyama-jinja. Follow the broad path through the woods, descend two staircases and follow the signs reading 'Kasuga Shrine'. You'll come to a road that leads uphill to the left; follow it along, passing under the bare slopes of Wakakusa-yama. At Musashino Ryokan (look for the small English sign), walk straight down the steps, cross a bridge, jog left, and at the T-junction, take a left up to **Kasuga-taisha** (you'll have to work around the side of it to find the main entrance).

After visiting the shrine, leave via the main entrance and bear left up the path to **Wakamiya-jinja**, passing several small shrines on the way. After visiting the shrine, retrace your steps towards Kasuga-taisha, and take a left down the steps which lead back towards the centre of town. You'll pass first through **Ni-no-Torii** and then continue down the broad wooded arcade to **Ichi-no-Torii**. Cross the street and you'll soon see the pagoda of Kōfuku-ji. Walk through the Kōfuku-ji grounds, passing between the **Nanen-dō** and **Hokuen-dō** halls, and take the narrow lane that leads down to Higashi-muki Arcade. A quick right here will bring you back to where you started.

containing two fierce looking **Niō guardians**. These recently restored wooden images, carved in the 13th century by the sculptor Unkei, are some of the finest wooden statues in all of Japan, if not the world. They are truly dramatic works of art and seem ready to spring to life at any moment.

Daibutsu-den Hall 大仏殿

Tōdai-ji's Daibutsu-den *(Hall of the Great Buddha; admission ¥500; open 8am-4.30pm daily Nov-Feb, 8am-5pm daily Mar, 7.30am-5.30pm daily Apr-Sept, 7.30am-5pm daily Oct)* is the largest wooden building in the world. Unbelievably the present structure, rebuilt in 1709, is a mere two-thirds of the size of the original! The Daibutsu (Great Buddha) contained within is one of the largest bronze figures in the world and was

originally cast in 746. The present statue, recast in the Edo period, stands just over 16m high and consists of 437 tonnes of bronze and 130kg of gold.

The Daibutsu is an image of the Dainichi Buddha, the cosmic Buddha believed to precede all worlds and their respective historical Buddhas. Historians believe that Emperor Shōmu ordered the building of the Buddha as a charm against smallpox, which had ravaged Japan in preceding years. Over the centuries the statue took quite a beating from earthquakes and fires, losing its head a couple of times in the process (note the slight difference in colour between the head and the body).

As you circle the statue towards the back, you'll see a wooden column with a hole through its base. Popular belief maintains that those who can squeeze through the hole, which is exactly the same size as one of the Great Buddha's nostrils, are ensured of enlightenment. It's great fun to watch the kids wiggle through nimbly and the adults get wedged in like champagne corks – you wonder how often they have to call the fire department to extricate trapped visitors. A hint for determined adults: it's a lot easier to go through with both arms held above your head.

Shōsō-in Treasure Repository
正倉院

The Shōsō-in Treasure Repository is a short walk north of Daibutsu-den. The building was used to house fabulous imperial treasures and its wooden construction allowed precise regulation of humidity through natural expansion and contraction. The treasures have been removed and are shown twice a year, in spring and autumn, at the Nara National Museum (see the entry earlier in this section). The Shōsō-in building is open to the public at the same time.

Nigatsu-dō & Sangatsu-dō
二月堂・三月堂

These two halls are an easy walk east of the Daibutsu-den; follow the path that winds uphill starting from the southeast corner of the Daibutsu-den.

Nigatsu-dō *(admission free)* is famed for its *Omizutori Matsuri* (see Special Events later in this chapter for details) and a splendid view across Nara, which makes the climb up the hill worthwhile – particularly at dusk. Opening hours here are the same as those of the Daibutsu-den.

A short walk south of Nigatsu-dō is Sangatsu-dō *(admission ¥400)*, which is the oldest building in the Tōdai-ji complex. This hall contains a small collection of fine statues from the Nara period. It's open the same hours as the Daibutsu-den.

Kasuga Taisha 春日大社

This shrine *(admission ¥500; open 9am-4pm daily)* was founded in the 8th century by the Fujiwara family and completely rebuilt every 20 years according to Shintō tradition, until the end of the 19th century. It lies at the foot of the hill in a pleasant, wooded setting with herds of sacred deer awaiting hand-outs.

The approaches to the shrine are lined with hundreds of lanterns, and there are many hundreds more in the shrine itself. The **lantern festivals** held twice a year at the shrine are a major attraction. For details about these and other festivals held at the nearby Wakamiya-jinja, see the later section on Nara Special Events.

The **Hōmotsu-den** *(Treasure Hall; admission ¥420; open 9am-4pm daily)* is just north of the entrance torii for the shrine. The hall displays Shintō ceremonial regalia and equipment used in *bugaku*, nō and *gagaku* performances.

Shin-Yakushi-ji 新薬師寺

This temple *(admission ¥500; open 9am-5pm daily)*, a pleasant 15-minute walk from Kasuga Taisha, was founded by Empress Kōmyō in 747 in thanks for her husband's recovery from an eye disease. Most of the buildings were destroyed or have been reconstructed, but the present main hall dates from the 8th century. The hall contains sculptures of Yakushi Nyorai (Healing Buddha) and a set of 12 divine generals.

NARAMACHI ならまち

South of Sanjō-dōri and Sarusawa-ike pond you will find Naramachi, with many well-preserved *machiya* and *kura* (traditional storehouses). It's a nice place for a stroll before or after hitting the big sights of Nara-kōen, and there are several good restaurants in the area to entice hungry travellers (see Places to Eat & Drink later in this chapter).

Highlights of Naramachi include the **Naramachi Shiryō-kan Museum** *(☎ 26-5187; admission free; open 10am-4pm Tues & Wed, Fri-Sun)*, which has a decent collection of bric-a-brac from the area, including a display of old Japanese coins and bills.

Naramachi Koushi-no-Ie *(☎ 23-4820; admission free; open 9am-5pm Tues-Sun)* is a traditional Japanese house which, unfortunately, has been a little too thoroughly restored.

While you're in the neighbourhood, check out the **Naramachi Monogatari-kan** *(☎ 26-3476; open 10am-4.30pm daily)*, an interesting little gallery that holds some worthwhile exhibitions.

Lastly Naramachi is also home to **Gangō-ji** *(admission ¥400; open 9am-5pm daily)*, a small temple that is one of Nara's

KANSAI

Unesco World Heritage sites. Despite it's World Heritage listing, it's not particularly interesting and probably only merits a quick glance from outside.

TEMPLES SOUTHWEST OF NARA

The most important temples southwest of Nara are Hōryū-ji, Yakushi-ji and Tōshōdai-ji. These three can be visited in one afternoon. The best way to do this is to head straight to Hōryū-ji (the most distant from the centre of Nara) and then continue by bus No 52, 97 or 98 (¥560, 40 minutes) up to Yakushi-ji and Tōshōdai-ji, which are a 10-minute walk apart (for more on getting to/from these temples, see the respective entries).

Hōryū-ji 法隆寺

This temple (admission ¥1000; open 8am-4pm daily 22 Feb-3 Nov, 8am-3.25pm daily 4 Nov-21 Feb) was founded in 607 by Prince Shōtoku, considered by many to be the patron saint of Japanese Buddhism. Legend has it that Shōtoku, moments after birth, stood up and started praying. A statue in the treasure museum depicts this auspicious event. Hōryū-ji is renowned not only as the oldest temple in Japan but also as a repository for some of the country's rarest treasures. Several of the temple's wooden buildings have survived earthquakes and fires to become the oldest of their kind in the world. The temple is divided into two parts, **Sai-in** (West Temple) and **Tō-in** (East Temple).

The entrance ticket allows admission to Sai-in, Tō-in and the Great Treasure Hall. A detailed map is provided and a guidebook is available in English and several other languages. The JNTO leaflet called *Walking Tour Courses in Nara* includes a basic map for the area around Hōryū-ji.

The main approach to the temple proceeds from the south along a tree-lined avenue and continues through Nandai-mon and Chū-mon before entering the Sai-in precinct. As you enter this precinct, you'll see the **Kondō** (Main Hall) on your right and a pagoda on your left.

The Kondō houses several treasures, including the triad of the **Buddha Sākyamuni**, with two attendant Bodhisattvas. Though it is one of Japan's great Buddhist treasures, it is dimly lit and barely visible (you may want to bring a flashlight). Likewise the pagoda contains clay images depicting scenes from the life of Buddha that are barely visible without a flashlight.

On the eastern side of Sai-in are the two concrete buildings of the **Daihōzō-den** (Great Treasure Hall), containing numerous treasures from Hōryū-ji's long history. Renowned Buddhist artefacts in this hall include the Kudara Kannon and two miniature shrines: the Tamamushi Shrine and the Shrine of Lady Tachibana.

The **Tamamushi Shrine** is named for the insect *tamamushi*, or jewel beetle, the wings of which were used to decorate it. The colour in the original has faded, but an example of fresh *tamamushi* wings is on display and one can only imagine how the shrine must have looked when it was entirely covered with shimmering blue-green wings.

Getting There & Away To get to Hōryū-ji, take the JR Kansai line from JR Nara station to Hōryū-ji station (¥210, 10 minutes). From there, a bus shuttles the short distance between the station and Hōryū-ji (No 72, ¥170, eight minutes), or you can walk it in 20 minutes. Alternatively, take bus No 52, 60, 97 or 98 from either JR Nara station or Kintetsu Nara station and get off at the Hōryū-ji mae stop (¥760, 40 minutes by No 60 bus, 60 minutes by others).

Yakushi-ji 薬師寺

Yakushi-ji (admission ¥500; open 8.30am-5pm daily) was established by Emperor Temmu in 680. With the exception of the **East Pagoda**, the present buildings either date from the 13th century or are very recent reconstructions.

The main hall was rebuilt in 1976 and houses several images, including the famous **Yakushi Triad** (the Buddha Yakushi flanked by the Bodhisattvas of the sun and moon), dating from the 8th century. Originally gold, a fire in the 16th century turned the images an appealingly mellow black.

The East Pagoda is a unique structure because it appears to have six storeys, but three of them are *mokoshi* (lean-to additions), which give a pleasing balance to its appearance. It is the only structure to have survived the ravages of time, and dates from 730.

Behind the East Pagoda is **Tōin-dō** (East Hall), which houses the famous Shō-Kannon image, built in the 7th century and showing obvious influences of Indian sculptural styles.

Getting There & Away To get to Yakushi-ji, take bus No 52, 63, 70, 97 or 98 from either JR Nara station or Kintetsu Nara station and get off at the Yakushi-ji Higashiguchi stop (¥240, 20 minutes).

Tōshōdai-ji 唐招提寺

This temple (*admission ¥600; open 8.30am-4.30pm daily*) was established in 759 by the Chinese priest Ganjin (Jian Zhen), who had been recruited by Emperor Shōmu to reform Buddhism in Japan. Ganjin didn't have much luck with his travel arrangements from China to Japan: five attempts were thwarted by shipwreck, storms and bureaucracy. Despite being blinded by eye disease, he finally made it on the sixth attempt and spread his teachings to Japan. The lacquer sculpture in the Miei-dō Hall is a moving tribute to Ganjin: blind and rock steady. It is shown only once a year, on 6 June – the anniversary of Ganjin's death.

If you're not lucky enough to be in Nara on that day, it's still well worth visiting this temple to see the fantastic trinity of Buddhas in the **Kon-dō** hall of the temple. The centrepiece is a seated image of Rushana Buddha, which is flanked by two standing Buddha images, Yakushi-nyorai and Senjū-Kannon.

Tōshōdai-ji is a 10-minute walk north of Yakushi-ji's northern gate; see that section for transport details from Nara.

ORGANISED TOURS

Nara Kōtsū (☎ 22-5263) runs daily bus tours on a variety of routes, two of which include Nara city sights only and two of which include more distant sights like Hōryū-ji and the burial mounds around Asuka (see Around Nara later in this chapter). An explanation tape in English is available for all but the Asuka route. Prices for the all-day trips average ¥7000 for adults (which includes all temple fees and tape-recorder rental). Lunch at a Japanese restaurant on the route is optional (reserve when buying your ticket). Nara Kōtsū has offices in JR Nara station and across the street from Kintetsu Nara station.

SPECIAL EVENTS

Nara has plenty of festivals throughout the year. The following is a brief list of the more interesting ones. Because the dates for some of these festivals vary, it's best to check with the Nara or Kyoto tourist information offices.

January
Yamayaki (Grass Burning Festival) Early January (the day before Seijin-no-hi). This festival commemorates a feud many centuries ago between the monks of Tōdai-ji and Kōfuku-ji: Wakakusa-yama is set alight at 6pm, with an accompanying display of fireworks. Arrive earlier to bag a good viewing position in Nara-kōen.

February
Mantōrō (Lantern Festival) Early February. Held at Kasuga Taisha at 6pm, this is a festival renowned for its illumination, with 3000 stone and bronze lanterns; a *bugaku* dance also takes place in the Apple Garden on the last day. Also held around 14 August in O-bon.

March
Omizutori (Water-Drawing Ceremony) 1 to 14 March. The monks of Tōdai-ji enter a special period of initiation during these days. On the evening of 12 March, they parade huge flaming torches around the balcony of Nigatsu-dō (in the temple grounds) and rain down embers on the spectators to purify them. The water-drawing ceremony is performed after midnight.

May
Takigi Nō 11 to 12 May. Open-air performances of nō held after dark by the light of blazing torches at Kōfuku-ji and Kasuga Taisha.

October
Shika-no-Tsunokiri (Deer Antler Cutting) Sundays & national holidays in October. Those pesky deer in Nara-kōen are pursued in a type of elegant rodeo into the Roku-en (deer enclosure) close to Kasuga Taisha. They are then wrestled to the ground and their antlers sawn off. Tourist brochures hint that this is to avoid personal harm, though it's not clear whether they are referring to the deer fighting each other or the deer mugging the tourists.

PLACES TO STAY

Although Nara is favoured as a day trip from Kyoto, accommodation can still be packed out for festivals and holidays and at weekends, so make reservations in advance if you plan to visit at these times. The Nara City Tourist Center has extensive lists of hotels, *minshuku*, pensions and ryokan. The JR Nara station tourist office may be able to help with *minshuku* and ryokan reservations.

Youth Hostels

Nara-ken Seishōnen Kaikan Youth Hostel (*☎/fax 22 5540; dorm beds or private rooms per person ¥2650-3350*) is a nondescript, concrete place with friendly staff. From JR Nara station or Kintetsu Nara station, take bus No 12, 13, 131 or 140 and get off at the Ikuei-gakuen bus stop, from where it's a five-minute walk.

Nara Youth Hostel (*☎ 22-1334, fax 22-1335; dorm beds ¥3000*) is a nicer hostel than the above. From either JR or Kintetsu Nara station, take bus No 108, 109, 111, 113 or 115 and get off at the Shieikyūjō-mae bus stop, from where it's a one-minute walk.

Ryokan

Ryokan Seikan-sō (*☎/fax 22-2670; per person without bath from ¥4000*), a friendly place with wooden architecture and a pleasant garden, is probably the best-value ryokan in Nara.

Ryokan Matsumae (*☎ 22-3686; per person without bath from ¥5000*) lacks the atmosphere of the Seikan-sō but has a very convenient location.

Ryokan Hakuhō (*☎ 26-7891, fax 26 7893; per person without bath from ¥5000*), in the centre of town five minutes walk from JR Nara station, is starting to show its age and has less atmosphere than the Seikan-sō.

Hotels

The cheapest hotel in town is the **Super Hotel** (*☎ 20-9000; singles/doubles from ¥4800/6800*), a no-frills place across from JR Nara station. It only opens for check in after 3pm.

Close to Kintetsu Nara station, **Green Hotel Ashibi** (*☎ 26-7815, fax 24-2465; singles/doubles/twins from ¥6400/11,000/12,000*) is a small business hotel with some of the cheapest rooms in this range.

Hotel Fujita Nara (*☎ 23-8111, fax 22-0255; singles/doubles/twins from ¥6500/10,000/12,000*) is a clean, new hotel with a convenient location. During off-peak times, you might get a reduced rate if you reserve through the Kintetsu Nara tourist information office.

Hotel Sunroute Nara (*☎ 22-5151, fax 27-3759; singles/doubles/twins from ¥8800/

17,000/16,500*) is a basic business hotel near the southwest corner of Nara-kōen.

Nara Kokusai Hotel (*☎ 26-6001, fax 23-1552; singles/doubles/twins from ¥5000/8500/12,000*), right outside JR Nara station, has decent rooms and a great location for those with early-morning train departures.

Built near the turn of the century, **Nara Hotel** (*☎ 26-3300, fax 23-5252; singles/doubles/twins from ¥14,000/23,000/22,000*) still ranks as one of the city's premier hotels. Rooms in the old wing have much more character than those in the new wing.

PLACES TO EAT & DRINK

Nara is full of good restaurants, most of which are in the vicinity of Kintetsu Nara station or in Naramachi.

Kyōshō-An (*☎ 27-7715; green tea from ¥400*) is a simple little Japanese tea shop where you can sample green tea and traditional Japanese sweets. It's on the second floor – look for the pictures on the sign outside. We recommend this spot for a cool drink or sweet on a hot day.

Drink Drank (*☎ 27-6206; smoothies ¥400, lunch sets ¥850; open Thur-Tues*) is a new shop that serves a variety of fresh fruit drinks and light lunches including sandwiches and soup.

Harishin (*☎ 22-2669; open Tues-Sun*) is an elegant *kaiseki* place for a special lunch or dinner in Nara. Offerings include the *kamisumira bentō* for ¥2500 or the mini *kaiseki* course for ¥3500.

Kosode (*☎ 27-2582; green tea with Japanese sweet ¥400*) is a charming little tea room-cum-gallery in Naramachi that we highly recommend for a break when strolling the area. In addition to the pottery on display, it offers a kimono-fitting service (¥5000 for men and women).

Za Don (*☎ 27-5314; donburi from ¥400*), in the Higashi-muki arcade, serves the eponymous *donburi* (rice bowl with various toppings) for absurdly low prices. It's healthy Japanese fast food and there's a picture menu to make ordering easier.

Okaro (*☎ 24-3686; okonomiyaki from ¥680*) is a homey spot in the Higashi-muki arcade for simple *okonomiyaki* – look for the food models in the window.

Hira-no-Ie (*☎ 26-3918; okonomiyaki from ¥680*) is another good spot for some *okonomiyaki* and similar dishes.

Tsukihi-tei (☎ 23-5470; *lunch/dinner from ¥1000/1500*), on the second floor at the north end of the Higashi-muki arcade, serves simple *kaiseki* sets at reasonable prices. The *tenshin bentō*, a good bet at ¥1500, includes sashimi, rice, vegetables and other tidbits.

Beni-e (☎ 22-9493) is one of our favourites in Nara. It serves good tempura sets for ¥1500/2000/2500 (*hana*, *tsuki* and *yuki* sets respectively). It's located a little back from Higashi-muki arcade, behind a shoe store.

Miyono (☎ 22-5239; *lunch/dinner from ¥650)* does good-value sets of typical Japanese fare. Stop by and check the daily lunch specials on display outside.

Hirasō (☎ 22-0866; *lunch/dinner from ¥2100/4000)*, in Naramachi, does set meals including local specialities like *kaki-no-ha sushi* (persimmon leaf sushi).

Tempura Asuka (☎ 26-4308; *lunch/dinner from ¥1500/3500)* serves attractive tempura and sashimi sets in a relatively casual atmosphere. At lunchtime try its nicely presented *yumei-dono bentō* for ¥1500.

Located beside Isui-en, one of Nara's finest gardens, **Sanshūtei** (☎ 22-2173; *lunch from ¥1200; open 11.30am-2pm Wed-Mon)* is one of the city's most interesting places to eat. Guests sit on tatami mats and enjoy the food while gazing out over the garden. Unfortunately, the main dish is enough to challenge even the most adventurous of eaters: *tororo*, a gooey dish made from grated yam, barley and rice. There are only two choices: *mugimeshitororo* (*tororo* without eel, ¥1200) or *unatoro gozen* (*tororo* with eel, ¥2400).

Lastly, **Rumours** (☎ 26-4327), an English-style pub, is a decent spot for a few evening drinks and a good spot to meet local residents and other travellers.

GETTING THERE & AWAY
Train
Kyoto Unless you have a Japan Rail Pass, the best option is the Kintetsu line, which runs between Kintetsu Kyoto station (in Kyoto station) and Kintetsu Nara station. There are direct *tokkyū* trains (¥1110, 33 minutes) and *kyūkō* trains (¥610, around 45 minutes) that may require a change at Saidai-ji.

The JR Nara line connects JR Kyoto station with JR Nara station (*kaisoku*, ¥690, 46

minutes) but departures are sometimes few and far between.

Osaka The Kintetsu Nara line connects Osaka (Kintetsu Namba station) with Nara (Kintetsu Nara station). *Kaisoku* and *futsū* services take about 35 minutes and cost ¥540. *Tokkyū* services do the journey in five minutes less but cost almost double, making them a poor option.

The JR Kansai line links Osaka (Namba and Tennō-ji stations) and Nara (JR Nara station). A *kaisoku* costs ¥540 and takes 46 minutes between Namba and JR Nara station. A *kaisoku* costs ¥450 and takes 31 minutes between Tennō-ji and JR Nara station.

Bus
There is an overnight bus service between Tokyo's Shinjuku (highway bus terminal) and Nara (¥8400/15,120 one way/return). The bus leaves Nara at 10.30pm and reaches Tokyo the next day at 6.15am. The bus from Tokyo leaves at 11.15pm and arrives in Nara the next day at 6.50am. In Nara, call ☎ 22-5110 or check with the Nara City Tourist Center for more details. In Tokyo, call ☎ 03-3928-6011.

GETTING AROUND
To/From the Airport
Nara is served by Kansai international airport. There is a limousine bus service between Nara and the airport with departures roughly every hour in both directions (¥1800, 1½ hours). At Kansai international airport ask at the information counter, and in Nara visit the ticket office in the building across from Kintetsu Nara station. Reservations are a good idea and can be made on ☎ 22-5110.

For domestic flights, there are limousine buses to/from Osaka's Itami airport (¥1440, 80 minutes).

Bus
Most of the area around Nara-kōen is covered by two circular bus routes. Bus No 1 runs anticlockwise and bus No 2 runs clockwise. There's a ¥180 flat fare. You can easily see the main sights in the park on foot and use the bus as an option if you are pushed for time or get tired of walking.

The most useful buses for western and southwestern Nara (Tōshōdai-ji, Yakushi-ji and Hōryū-ji) are Nos 52, 97 and 98, which

KANSAI

link all three destinations with the Kintetsu and JR stations. Buses run about every 30 minutes between 8am and 5pm, but are much less frequent outside these times.

Taxi

Taxis are plentiful but expensive. A taxi ride from JR Nara station to either of the youth hostels costs about ¥1000.

Cycling

Nara is a convenient size for getting around on a bicycle. **Kintetsu Sunflower Rent-a-Cycle** (☎ 24-3528) is close to the Nara City Tourist Center. Weekday rates are ¥300 per hour and ¥900 per day on weekdays and ¥350 and ¥1000 on weekends. It's just off Konishi Arcade, down a small street, the entrance to which is opposite a supermarket.

Around Nara
奈良周辺

Southern Nara-ken was the birthplace of imperial rule and is rich in historical sites that are easily accessible as day trips from Osaka, Kyoto or Nara, provided that you make an early start. Of particular historical interest are the *kofun* that mark the graves of Japan's first emperors; these are concentrated around Asuka and Sakurai (see the 'Kofun Burial Mounds' boxed text in this chapter). There are also several isolated temples where you can escape the crowds that plague Nara's city centre. Further afield, the mountaintop town of Yoshino is one of Japan's cherry-blossom meccas.

Easily reached by rail, Yamato-Yagi and Sakurai serve as useful transport hubs for the region. Keep in mind that the Kintetsu line is far more convenient than JR for most of the destinations in this section.

If you're starting from Nara, you may want to pick up a copy of the detailed *Japan: Nara Prefecture* map at any of the tourist information offices in Nara city before starting out.

AROUND YAMATO-YAGI
大和八木周辺

Easily reached on the Kintetsu line from Osaka, Kyoto or Nara, Yamato-Yagi is the most convenient transport hub for sights in southern Nara-ken. From Kyoto take the Kintetsu Nara/Kashihara line direct (*kyūkō*, ¥860, one hour). From Nara take the Kintetsu Nara line to Saidaiji and change to the Kintetsu Kashihara line (*kyūkō*, ¥430, 30 minutes). From Osaka's Uehonmachi station, take the Kintetsu Osaka line direct (*kyūkō*, ¥540, 35 minutes).

Imai-chō   今井町

Southwest of Yamato-Yagi is Imai-chō, a neighbourhood with several classic *machiya* preserved virtually intact from the Edo period. It's a pleasant place to walk around and seven of the buildings are open to the public (*admission ¥170; open 10am-noon & 1pm-5pm daily*). The most interesting of these is the huge **Imanishike Jyūtaku** (Imanishi House), which was completed in 1650. The **Imai Machinami Koryū Sentaa** (☎ 0744-24-8710; open 9am-5pm Tues-Sun), on the neighbourhood's southeast corner, has Japanese-language maps of the area.

To get to Imai-chō, take a train one stop south from Yamato-Yagi to Yagi-nishiguchi (¥150, one minute). The neighbourhood is a 10-minute walk southwest of the station; take the western exit out of the station, go right across the bridge over the canal and walk under the JR tracks.

Kashihara   橿原

Three stops south of Yamato-Yagi, on the Kintetsu Kashihara line, is Kashihara-jingū-mae station (¥200 from Yamato-Yagi, five minutes). There are a couple of interesting sights within easy walking distance of this station.

Kashihara-jingū This shrine, at the foot of Unebi-yama, dates back to 1889, when many of the buildings were moved here from Kyoto Gosho. The shrine buildings are built in the same style as those of Ise-jingū's Grand Shrine (Japan's most sacred shrine) and are a good example of classical Shintō architecture. The shrine is dedicated to Japan's mythical first emperor, Jimmu, and an annual festival is held here on 11 February, the legendary date of Jimmu's enthronement. The vast, park-like grounds are pleasant to stroll around. The shrine is five minutes' walk from Kashihara-jingū-mae station; take the central exit out of the station and follow the main street in the direction of the mountain.

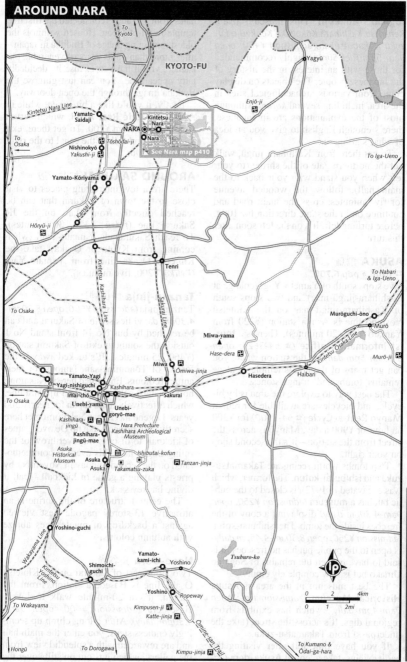

AROUND NARA

To Kyoto

KYOTO-FU

To Kyoto

Kintetsu Nara Line

Yamato-Saidaji

NARA

Kintetsu Nara

Nara

See Nara map p410

Enjō-ji

Yagyū

To Iga-Ueno

Nishinokyō
Yakushi-ji

Tōshōdai-ji

To Osaka

Yamato-Kōriyama

To Osaka

Hōryū-ji

Kansai Line

Tenri

Kintetsu Kashihara Line

Sakurai Line

Murōguchi-ōno

Murō

To Nabari
& Iga-Ueno

Miwa-yama

Hase-dera

Miwa

Ōmiwa-jinja

Hasedera

Haibari

Kintetsu Osaka Line

Murō-ji

Yamato-Yagi

Yagi-nishiguchi

Imai-chō

Kashihara

Sakurai

Sakurai

To Osaka

Unebi-yama

Unebi-
goryō-mae

Kashihara-
jingū

Nara Prefecture
Kashihara Archeological
Museum

Kashihara-
jingū-mae

Asuka
Historical
Museum

Ishibutai-kofun

Asuka

Asuka

Takamatsu-zuka

Tanzan-jinja

Wakayama Line

Yoshino-guchi

Shimoichi-
guchi

Kintetsu
Yoshino
Line

Yamato-
kami-ichi

Yoshino

Tsuburo-ko

To Wakayama

Yoshino

Ropeway

Kimpusen-ji

Katte-jinja

Hongū

To Dorogawa

Ōmine-san Trail

Kimpu-jinja

To Kumano &
Ōdai-ga-hara

0   2   4km
0   1   2mi

KANSAI

Nara Prefecture Kashihara Archaeological Museum This museum *(Nara Ken-ritsu Kashihara Kōkogaku Kenkyūjo Fuzoku Hakubutsukan; admission ¥400; open 9am-5pm Tues-Sun)* is highly recommended for those with an interest in the history of the Japanese people. The objects on display come from various archaeological sites in the area, including several *kofun*. Although most of the explanations are in Japanese, there's enough English to give you an idea of what's going on.

To get there from Kashihara-jingū, walk out the northern gate of the shrine (to your left when you stand with your back to the main hall), follow the wooded avenue for five minutes, cross the main road and continue on in the same direction for 100m before turning left. It's on the left soon after this turn.

ASUKA 飛鳥
☎ 0744 • pop 6,700

Five stops south of Yamato-Yagi (change at Kashihara-jingū-mae) and two stops south of Kashihara-jingū-mae on the Kintetsu Yoshino line is Asuka station (¥220 from Yamato-Yagi, 20 minutes). There's a **tourist information office** *(☎ 54-3624; open 8.30am-5pm daily)* at the station where you can get maps of the area's temples, palace remains, tombs and strange stones.

The best way to explore the area is by bicycle, and bicycles are available for rent at **Manyō Rent-a-Cycle** *(☎ 54-3500)* for ¥300 an hour or ¥900 a day. Manyō is across the street from the station – it's the second shop on your right.

Two tombs worth seeing are **Takamatsu-zuka** and **Ishibutai-kofun**. The former, which was excavated in 1972), is closed to the public but has a **museum** *(admission ¥250; open 9am-4.30pm daily)* displaying a copy of the frescoes inside the tomb. The Ishibutai-kofun *(admission ¥250; open 8.30am-4.45pm daily)* is open to the public but has no frescoes. It is said to have housed the remains of Soga no Umako but is now completely empty.

The best museum in the area is **Asuka Historical Museum** *(admission free; open 9am-4pm daily)*, which has exhibits from regional digs. It's across the street (take the underpass) from Takamatsu-zuka.

If you have time left after visiting the earlier sights, take a look at **Asuka-dera** *(ad-* *mission ¥300; open 9am-5pm daily)*, which dates from 596 and is considered the first true temple in all of Japan. Housed within is the oldest remaining image of Buddha in Japan – after more than 1300 years of venerable existence, you'll have to excuse its decidedly tatty appearance. You can just glimpse the Buddha image through the open doorway.

Lastly, if you'd like a bite to eat while in Asuka, try **Café Rest Asibi**, which serves simple meals from ¥700. To get there, exit the station, and follow the canal to the right for about 150m.

AROUND SAKURAI 桜井周辺
There are a few interesting places to visit close to the town of Sakurai that can be reached directly from Nara on the JR Sakurai line *(futsū, ¥320, 30 minutes)*. To reach Sakurai via Yamato-Yagi (when coming from Kyoto or Osaka), take the Kintetsu Osaka line from Yamato-Yagi *(kyūkō, ¥200, five minutes)*.

Tanzan-jinja 談山神社
Tanzan-jinja *(admission ¥500; open 8.30am-4.30pm daily)* lies south of Sakurai and can be reached by bus No 14 from stand No 1 outside the southern exit of Sakurai station (¥460, 25 minutes). It's tucked away in the forests of Tōnomine-san, famous for their autumn colours. Enshrined here is Nakatomi no Kamatari, patriarch of the Fujiwara line, which effectively ruled Japan for nearly 500 years. Legend has it that Nakatomi met here secretly with prince Naka no Ōe over games of kickball to discuss the overthrow of the ruling Soga clan. This event is commemorated on the second Sunday in November by priests playing a game of kickball – call it divine hackey sack.

The central structure of the shrine is an attractive 13-storey pagoda best viewed against a backdrop of maple trees ablaze with autumn colours.

Hase-dera 長谷寺
Two stops east of Sakurai on the Kintetsu Osaka line is Hasedera station. From the station, it's a 20-minute walk to lovely Hase-dera *(admission ¥500; open 9am-4.30pm daily)*. After a long climb up seemingly endless steps, you enter the main hall and are rewarded with a splendid view from the gallery, which juts out on stilts over the

Kofun Burial Mounds

The origins of the Japanese imperial line and the Japanese people in general are shrouded in mystery. Much of what we do know comes from large, earthen burial mounds scattered around the islands of Honshū, Kyūshū and Shikoku. These burial mounds, called *kofun*, served as tombs for members of Japan's early nobility, primarily members of the imperial household. The practice of building these mounds started quite suddenly in the 3rd century and died out gradually, finally ending in the 7th century. It was during this period that the forerunners of the present imperial family, the Yamato clan, were consolidating their power as rulers over Japan's warring factions.

The practice of *kofun* burial started in the region known today as Kinai, which encompasses Kyoto, Osaka and Nara. Early burial mounds were built on hilltops overlooking fertile land, usually in a round or keyhole shape. Along with the imperial corpse, a variety of both military and ceremonial objects were buried, many of which were Chinese in origin, testifying to the extent to which early Japanese civilisation was influenced by continental culture. This influence was the result of frequent contact between Japan and Korean and Chinese cultures present on the Korean peninsula.

In the 4th century the practice of *kofun* burial spread along the inland sea to western Honshū, Shikoku and Kyūshū, and finally to regions in the east near present-day Tokyo. Mounds of this period contain, along with the body, vast amounts of funerary objects, most of them continental in origin and military in nature. One mound, the **Ōjin mausoleum** in Ariyama, was found to contain about 3000 swords buried in a separate treasure mound. The richness of these tombs gives some indication of the absolute power held by these early emperors over the labour and resources of their societies.

Some of the largest mounds were built in the 5th century, including the tomb believed to house the remains of Emperor Nintoku, in southern Osaka. This keyhole-shaped mound is 28m high, 486m in length and covers an area of 32 hectares. The volume of material in this mound is said to be greater than that of the Great Pyramid of Cheops. The use of moats to surround and protect the central chamber also appeared during this period.

Under the influence of Buddhism, which favoured cremation over burial, the practice of *kofun* burial gradually died out and disappeared by the end of the 7th century.

Some of the best-preserved mounds are in Nara-ken, concentrated around the village of Asuka. Most interesting is the stone Ishibutai-kofun, said to house the remains of Soga no Umako, a 7th-century noble. Its exposed stone burial chamber looks over the Nara plain and speaks of a time in Japanese history when the emperor held power over his subjects not unlike the power wielded by some of history's other great tomb builders, the Pharaohs of ancient Egypt.

---

mountainside. Inside the top hall, the huge Kannon image is well worth a look. The best times to visit this temple are in the spring, when the way is lined with blooming peonies, and in autumn, when the temple's maple trees turn a vivid red. From the station, walk down through the archway, cross the river and turn right onto the main street that leads to the temple.

Murō-ji 室生寺

This temple *(admission ¥500; open 8am-5pm daily)* was founded in the 9th century and has strong connections with Esoteric Buddhism (the Shingon sect). Women were never excluded from Murō-ji as they were from other Shingon temples, and it is for this reason that it came to be known as 'the Woman's Koya'.

Unfortunately the temple's lovely five-storey pagoda, which dates from the 8th or 9th century, was severely damaged in a typhoon in the summer of 1999. In the process of being repaired, it lost some of its rustic charm. Nonetheless Murō-ji is a secluded place in thick forest and is well worth a visit.

Murōguchi-ōno station on the Kintetsu Osaka line is two stops east of Hasedera station. It's a 15-minute bus ride from Murōguchi-ōno station to Murō-ji on bus No 43, 44, 45 or 46 (¥400).

YOSHINO 吉野
☎ 07463 • pop 11,216

Yoshino is Japan's top cherry-blossom destination, and for a few weeks in early to mid-April, the blossoms of thousands of cherry

KANSAI

trees form a floral carpet gradually ascending the mountainsides. It's definitely a sight worth seeing, but the narrow streets of the village become jammed tight with thousands of visitors at this time, and you'll have to be content with a day trip unless you've booked accommodation long in advance. Once the *sakura* (cherry-blossom) petals fall, the crowds depart and Yoshino reverts back to a sleepy village with a handful of shrines and a couple of temples to entertain day-trippers.

History

In early times the remote, mountainous regions around Yoshino were considered the mysterious abode of the *kami* (Shintō gods) and later became a centre for Shugendō, a Buddhist school that incorporated ancient Shamanistic rites, Shintō beliefs and ascetic Buddhist traditions. The school has its origin in the banding together of Buddhist hermits who practised their faith deep in the mountains, though the legendary En-no-Gyōja, to whom powers of exorcism and magic are ascribed, is frequently referred to as the founder of the school.

Yoshino came to historical prominence in the years following Emperor Go-Daigo's efforts to wrest imperial rule from the Kamakura shōgunate. In 1333, Emperor Go-Daigo successfully toppled the Kamakura shōgunate with the help of disgruntled generals. The return to imperial rule, known as the Kemmu Restoration, only lasted three years, however. Go-Daigo failed to reward his supporters adequately and was ousted in a revolt by one of his generals, Ashikaga Takauji, who set up a rival empire.

Go-Daigo beat a hasty retreat to the remote safety of Yoshino, where he set up a competing court. This period of rivalry between the two courts (known as Nanbokuchō – the Northern and Southern Courts period) continued for about 60 years, ending only when Ashikaga made a promise (which was not kept) that the imperial lines would alternate.

Information

The village's main **tourist information office** is about 400m up the main street from the top cable-car station, on your right just after Kimpusen-ji. The staff don't speak much English but are quite helpful and have a specially prepared English-Japanese phrase-book to help foreign travellers. They can help with *minshuku* bookings if necessary.

Things to See

As you walk up the main street, you pass through two torii before coming to the stone steps leading to the Ni-ō-mon of **Kimpusen-ji** *(admission ¥400; open 8am-4.30pm daily)*. Check out the fearsome **Kongo Rikishi** (guardian figure statues) in the gate and then continue on to the massive **Zaō-dō Hall** of the temple. Said to be the second-largest wooden building in Japan, the hall is most interesting for its unfinished wooden columns. For many centuries Kimpusen-ji has been one of the major centres for Shugendō, and pilgrims have often stopped here to pray for good fortune on the journey to Ōmine-san.

About 500m further up the street, where the road forks, is **Katte-jinja**. Take the left fork and then the next right up the hill. You soon pass **Zenkō-in** on your left and **Chikurin-in** on your right (see Places to Stay & Eat). A few minutes' walk further on there is another fork, where you'll find some steps leading up to a wooden torii. Take the left fork and the next right up the hill for the 3km hike to **Kimpu-jinja**, a small shrine in a pleasantly wooded mountain setting. If you don't fancy this somewhat strenuous uphill hike, there are plenty of smaller shrines on the streets and alleys off Yoshino's main street.

Places to Stay & Eat

Yoshino-yama Kizō-in *(☎ 2-3014; beds ¥4800)* is a temple that doubles as the local youth hostel and is the cheapest option in town. It's a pleasant place to stay, and several of the hostel's rooms look out across the valley. See the earlier Things to See section for directions to the temple.

Chikurin-in *(☎ 2-8081; rooms per person from ¥15,000)* is not far past Kizō-in, on the opposite side of the street, and is an exquisite temple that now operates primarily as a ryokan. Both present and previous emperors have stayed here, and a look at the view afforded by some of the rooms explains why. Rates include two meals. Reservations are essential for the cherry-blossom season, a good idea at all other times. Even if you don't plan to stay at the temple, you should at least visit its splendid **garden** *(admission*

¥300), said to have been designed by the famous tea master Sen no Rikyū.

The speciality of Yoshino is *kaki-no-ha sushi* (mackerel sushi wrapped in persimmon leaves). Almost every store and restaurant in town sells it and you can buy two pieces to take away for ¥250. For proper meals try **Yatsuko**, opposite the tourist information office. It has the usual *shokudō* favourites. **Hatsu-on** restaurant, closer to the top cable-car station, is in an atmospheric old wooden building, and serves tempura *donburi* for ¥1300.

Finally, if you'd just like a cup of Japanese tea to pick you up, try the atmospheric **Hōkon-an** teahouse, where you can sip your tea while enjoying a lovely view over the valley. The *matcha* (powdered green tea; ¥600) comes with a Japanese sweet. Look for the rustic wooden façade on the left, just past the post office as you walk away from the cable-car.

Getting There & Away

The village of Yoshino is on a shoulder of Yoshino-yama, at the bottom of which is Yoshino station. From Yoshino station, you can take the cable car to the village (¥350/600 one way/return) or walk up in 15 minutes on the path that leaves from beside the cable-car station.

To get to Yoshino station from Kyoto or Nara, take the Kintetsu Nara/Kashihara line (it changes name halfway) to Kashihara-jingū-mae (*kyūkō* from Kyoto, ¥860, 70 minutes; *kyūkō* from Nara, ¥480, 40 minutes) and change to the Kintetsu Yoshino line (*kyūkō*, ¥460, 52 minutes).

You can take a direct train on the Kintetsu Minami-Osaka/Yoshino lines from Osaka (Abenobashi station, close to Tennō-ji station) to Yoshino (*kyūkō*, ¥950, 1½ hours).

The closest JR station to Yoshino is Yoshino-guchi, where you can transfer to trains to/from Nara, Osaka and Wakayama.

Kii-hantō 紀伊半島

The remote and mountainous Kii-hantō (Kii Peninsula) is a far cry from central Kansai's bustling urban sprawl. Most of the peninsula's attractions are found in Wakayama-ken, including the mountaintop temple complex of Kōya-san, one of Japan's most important Buddhist centres. Other Wakayama-ken attractions include the *onsen* clustered around the village of Hongū, the beachside hot spring resort of Shirahama, and the rugged coastline of Shiono-misaki and Kii-Ōshima.

The JR Kii main line (Kinokuni line) runs around the coast of the Kii-hantō, linking Shin-Osaka and Nagoya stations (some trains originate/terminate at Kyoto station). Special Kuroshio and Nankii *tokkyū* trains can get you around the peninsula fairly quickly, but once you step off these express trains, you're at the mercy of slow local trains and buses, so plan accordingly. We present the information in this section anticlockwise, working from Wakayama-shi around the horn to Mie-ken, but it's perfectly possible to do this the other way round (perhaps starting in Ise).

JNTO publishes a leaflet called *Shirahama and Wakayama Prefecture* that provides concise details about sights and transport in the area.

WAKAYAMA 和歌山

☎ 0734 • pop 387,000

Wakayama, the prefectural capital, is a pleasant little city useful as a transport hub for travellers heading to other parts of the prefecture. The city's main attraction is **Wakayama-jō** *(admission grounds free, castle's keep ¥350; open 9am-4.30pm daily)*, a 20-minute walk from JR Wakayama station. The original castle was built in 1585 by Toyotomi Hideyoshi and destroyed by bombing in WWII. The present structure is a concrete post-war reconstruction; it's picturesque from afar and unprepossessing up close. However, the gardens surrounding the castle are well worth a stroll if you're in the area.

Places to Stay & Eat

The most relaxing place to stay in Wakayama is the Shinwaka Ura area, a pleasant collection of *minshuku* and ryokan on a point southwest of the city. **Kokumin-shukusha Shinwaka Ura Lodge** *(☎ 44-9000; rooms per person with/without 2 meals ¥6500/4500)* is the most reasonable place. Take bus No 24 from the No 2 stop in front of JR Wakayama station to the last stop, Shinwaka Ura (¥380, 40 minutes). Continue on in the same direction along the

KANSAI

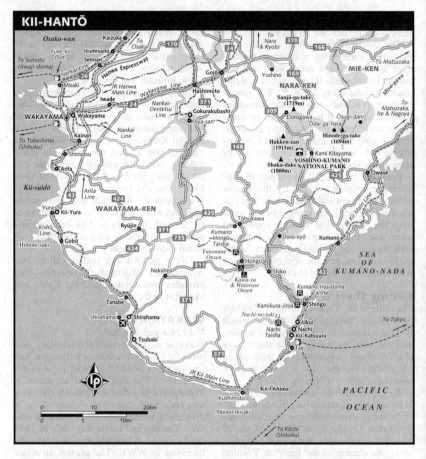

KII-HANTŌ

main road, go through the tunnel and look for it on your left.

Otherwise, **Hotel Granvia Wakayama** (☎ 25-3333; singles/doubles from ¥8800/15,500) is right outside the station and offers new, clean rooms.

For a bite to eat, head to the restaurant arcade on the basement floor beneath JR Wakayama station. Among the choices here, you'll find **Mendori-tei**, which serves excellent *kushi-age* (deep-fried seafood on skewers) and *kushi-katsu* dishes (try their *kushi-age teishoku* for ¥750). Look for the red curtains. Otherwise, two blocks south and one block west of JR Wakayama station, you'll find **Ide** (open 1pm-1am Fri-Wed), where you can sample the local speciality, *shoyū rāmen* (soy sauce *rāmen*) for ¥500.

But call it *chuka soba* (Chinese noodles) or you'll get funny looks from the staff!

Getting There & Away

Wakayama is serviced by JR *tokkyū* trains from Shin-Osaka and Kyoto, but unless you've got a Japan Rail Pass it's cheaper to take a local train on the JR Hanwa line from Osaka's Tennō-ji station (*futsū*, ¥830, one hour). From Osaka's Namba station you can also take the private Nankai line to Wakayama-shi station (*kyūkō*, ¥1400, one hour), which is linked to JR Wakayama station by the JR Kisei main line (*futsū*, ¥180, six minutes).

Wakayama is a convenient starting point for the trip to Kōya-san (see the following Kōya-san section for transport details).

KANSAI

From Wakayama-kō port, there's a ferry service to Tokushima on **Shikoku** (☎ *31-4431*); a 2nd-class ticket is ¥1730. From Fuke-kō port, just north of Wakayama, **Awaji-shima** (☎ *0724-69-3821*) ferries go to Sumoto; the trip takes 30 minutes and a 2nd-class ticket is ¥1980. Ask at the tourist office in JR Wakayama station for details on getting to the respective piers.

KŌYA-SAN 高野山
☎ 0736 • pop 7000

Kōya-san is a raised tableland in northern Wakayama-ken covered with thick forests and surrounded by eight peaks. The major attraction on this tableland is the monastic complex, also known as Kōya-san, which is the headquarters of the Shingon school of Esoteric Buddhism. Though not quite the Shangri-la it's occasionally described as, it is one of the most rewarding places to visit in Kansai, not just for the natural setting of the area but also as an opportunity to stay in temples and get a glimpse of long-held traditions of Japanese religious life.

More than a million visitors come here annually so you should be prepared for congestion during peak holiday periods and festivals. Summer is a popular time to visit and escape from the lowland heat. You can miss large crowds by getting up really early for a stroll around the area before returning to take part in the morning religious service usually held around 6am. Late-night strolls are peaceful and quiet, and spring and autumn foliage are especially attractive. Some hardy visitors even enjoy wandering round Kōya-san in the snow.

Although you could visit Kōya-san as a day trip from Nara, Kyoto or Osaka, it's much better to reduce the travel stress and stay overnight in one of the town's excellent *shukubō* (temple lodgings). Be sure to bring some warm clothes when you go, as up on the mountain it tends to be around 5° colder than down on the plains.

Whenever you go, you'll find that getting there is half the fun – the train winds through a series of tight valleys with mountains soaring on all sides, and the final vertiginous cable car leg is not for the faint of heart.

History

The founder of the Shingon school of Esoteric Buddhism, Kūkai (known after his death as Kōbō Daishi), established a religious community here in 816. Kōbō Daishi travelled as a young priest to China and returned after two years to found the school. He is one of Japan's most famous religious figures and is revered as a Bodhisattva, scholar, inventor of the Japanese kana syllabary and as a calligrapher. He is believed to be simply resting in his tomb, not dead but meditating, awaiting the arrival of Miroku (Maitreya, the future Buddha).

Over the centuries, the temple complex grew in size and attracted many followers of the Jōdo (Pure Land) school of Buddhism. During the 11th century, it became popular with both nobles and commoners to leave hair or ashes from deceased relatives close to Kōbō Daishi's tomb, handy for his reawakening. This practice continues to be very popular today and accounts for the thousands of tombs around Okuno-in.

In the 16th century, Oda Nobunaga asserted his power by slaughtering large numbers of monks at Kōya-san. The community subsequently suffered confiscation of lands and narrowly escaped invasion by Toyotomi Hideyoshi. At one stage, Kōya-san numbered about 1500 monasteries and many thousands of monks. The members of the community were divided into *gakuryō* (clergy), *gyōnin* (lay priests) and *hijiri* (followers of Pure Land Buddhism).

In the 17th century, the Tokugawa shōgunate smashed the economic power of the lay priests, who managed considerable estates in the region. Their temples were destroyed, their leaders banished and the followers of Pure Land Buddhism were bluntly pressed into the Shingon school. During the Edo period, the government favoured the practice of Shintō and confiscated the lands that supported Kōya-san's monastic community. Women were barred from entry to Kōya-san until 1872.

Kōya-san is now a thriving centre for Japanese Buddhism, with more than 110 temples remaining and a population of 7000. It is the headquarters of the Shingon school, which numbers 10 million members and presides over nearly 4000 temples all over Japan.

Orientation & Information

There's a small **information office** at the top cable-car station. However, the main office of the **Kōya-san Tourist Association**

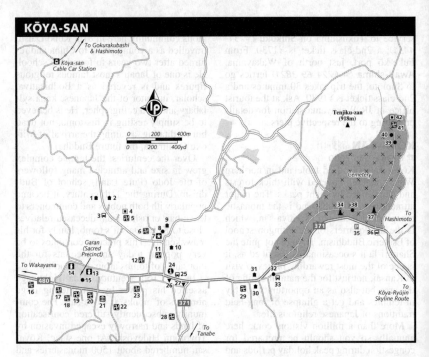

KŌYA-SAN

To Gokurakubashi & Hashimoto

Kōya-san Cable Car Station

To Wakayama

To Tanabe

To Hashimoto

To Kōya-Ryūjin Skyline Route

Tenjiku-zan (918m)

Cemetery

Garan (Sacred Precinct)

0 200 400m
0 200 400yd

(☎ 56-2616, fax 56-2889; open 8.30am-5.30pm daily June-Aug, 8.30am-4.30pm daily Sept-May) is in the centre of town in front of the Senjūin-bashi-mae bus stop. Staff speak some English, and brochures and maps are available. For a better map of the area, pick up a copy of the Japanese map from the bus office outside the top cable-car station.

The precincts of Kōya-san are divided into the Garan (Sacred Precinct) in the west and Okuno-in, with its vast cemetery, in the east.

Note that there is a joint ticket (*shodōkyōtsu-naihaiken*; ¥1500) that covers entry to Kongōbu-ji, the Kondō, Daitō, Treasure Museum and the **Tokugawa Mausoleum** (*Tokugawa-ke Reidai; admission without joint ticket ¥200*). It can be purchased at the information office.

Okuno-in 奥の院

Any Buddhist worth their salt in Japan has had their remains, or just a lock or two of hair, interred at this temple to ensure pole position when the future Buddha and Kūkai return to the world.

The best way to approach Okuno-in is to walk or take the bus east to Ichi-no-hashi-mae bus stop. From here you cross the bridge, Ichi-no-hashi, and enter the cemetery grounds along a winding, cobbled path lined by tall cypress trees and thousands of tombs. As the trees close in and the mist swirls, the atmosphere can be quite ghostly, especially as night falls. Among the interesting graves and monuments to look out for are the **North Borneo War Victim Memorial**, which commemorates Japanese, Malay and Australian soldiers killed in North Borneo in WWII (look for the flags), and the **White Ant Memorial**, built by a pesticide company to expiate its guilt for the murder of legions of the little critters.

The **Tōrō-dō** (Lantern Hall), the main building of the complex, is at the northernmost end of the graveyard. It houses hundreds of lamps, including two believed to have been burning for more than 900 years. Behind the hall you can see the closed doors of the Gobyō, Kūkai mausoleum.

On the way to the Lantern Hall is Mimyo-no-hashi bridge. Worshippers ladle water from the river and pour it over the

KŌYA-SAN

	PLACES TO STAY & EAT	8	Kōya Town Office 高野町役場	28	Kongōsanmai-in 金剛三昧院
1	Haryō-in 巴陵院	11	Ichijō-in 一乗院	29	Karukaya-dō 苅萱堂
2	Rengejō-in 蓮華定院	12	Kongōbu-ji 金剛峯寺	32	Ichi-no-hashi 一の橋
9	Kōya Youth Hostel 高野ユースホステル	13	Dai-tō 大塔	33	Ichi-no-hashi-mae Bus Stop 一の橋前バス停
10	Muryōkō-in 無量光院	14	Sai-tō 西塔	34	North Borneo War Victim Memorial
20	Henjōson-in 遍照尊院	15	Kondō (Main Hall) 金堂		北ボルネオ没者墓所
26	Nankai-shokudō 南海食堂	16	Sainan-in 西南院	35	Naka-no-hashi Parking
27	Hanabishi Honten 花菱本店	17	Hōon-in 報恩院		中の橋駐車場
30	Eikō-in 恵光院	18	Hōki-in 宝亀院	36	Okuno-in-mae Bus Stop
31	Shojōshin-in 清浄心院	19	Yōchi-in 桜池院		奥の院前バス停
		21	Treasure Museum	37	White Ant Memorial 白蟻墓
	OTHER		霊宝館	38	Naka-no-hashi
3	Isshi-guchi-mae Bus Stop 一心口バス停	22	Jōju-in 成就院		中の橋
4	Tokugawa Mausoleum 徳川家霊台	23	Tentoku-in 天徳院	39	Mimyo-no-hashi 御廟橋
5	Nan-in 南院	24	Kōya-san Tourist Association Office	40	Miroku-ishiū みろく石
6	Fukuchi-in 福智院		高野山観光協会	41	Okuno-in ; Tōrō-dō 奥の院、灯ろう堂
7	Kōya Police Station 高野警察署	25	Senjūin-bashi-mae Bus Stop 千手院橋前バス停	42	Kūkai Mausoleum 空海の墓

nearby Jizō statues as an offering for the dead. The inscribed wooden plaques in the river are in memory of aborted babies and those who died by drowning.

Between the bridge and the Tōrō-dō is a small wooden building the size of a large phone booth which contains the **Miroku-ishi**. Pilgrims reach through the holes in the wall to try to lift a large, smooth boulder onto a shelf. The interesting thing is that the stone is supposed to weigh more or less according to the weight of sin of the pilgrim. We can only report that the thing is damn heavy!

Buses return to the centre of town from the terminus just across from the concrete shopping complex.

Kongōbu-ji 金剛峯寺

This is the headquarters of the Shingon school and the residence of Kōya-san's abbot. The present structure dates from the 19th century and is definitely worth a visit (admission ¥500; open 8.30am-4.30pm daily).

The main hall's Ohiro-ma room has ornate screens painted by Kanō Tanyu in the 16th century. The Yanagi-no-ma (Willow Room) has equally pretty screen paintings of willows but the rather grisly distinction of being the place where Toyotomi Hidetsugu committed *seppuku* (ritual suicide by disembowelment).

The rock garden is interesting for the sheer number of rocks used in its composition, giving the effect of a throng of petrified worshippers eagerly listening to a monk's sermon.

Admission includes tea and rice cakes served beside the stone garden.

Garan 壇上伽藍

This is a temple complex of several halls and pagodas (admission to each building ¥200; open 8.30am-4.30pm daily). The most important buildings are the Dai-tō (Great Pagoda) and Kondō (Main Hall). The Dai-tō, rebuilt in 1934 after a fire, is said to be the centre of the lotus flower mandala formed by the eight mountains around Kōya-san. The nearby Sai-tō (Western Pagoda) was most recently rebuilt in 1834 and is more subdued. It's well worth going into the Dai-tō to see the

KANSAI

Dainichi-nyōrai (Cosmic Buddha) and his four attendant Buddhas.

Treasure Museum 霊宝館

The Treasure Museum *(Reihōkan; admission ¥600; open 8.30am-4.30pm daily)* has a compact display of Buddhist works of art, all collected in Kōya-san. There are some very fine statues, painted scrolls and mandalas.

Special Events

The **Aoba Matsuri** is a festival held on 15 June to celebrate the birth of Kōbō Daishi. Various traditional ceremonies are performed at the temples around town.

A more interesting festival is the **Rōsoku Matsuri** (Candle Festival), which is held on 13 August. In remembrance of dead relatives, thousands of mourners light candles along the approaches to Okuno-in.

Places to Stay

There are more than 50 temples in Kōya-san offering *shukubō*. It is well worth staying the night at a temple here, especially to sample *shōjin-ryōri* (vegetarian food – no meat, fish, onions or garlic). Because *shukubō* is intended for religious pilgrims, in the morning you'll be asked to participate in *o-inori* (Buddhist prayer services) or *o-tsutome* (work). While participation is not mandatory, taking part in these practices would enable you to appreciate the daily workings of a Japanese temple.

Kōya-san's temples have recently formed a group to fix prices and now almost all lodgings start at ¥9000 a person including two meals. **Haryō-in** *(☎ 56-2702; rooms per person ¥6500)* is one exception to this and functions as a *kokumin-shukusha* and has rates that include two meals.

During the high season and holidays you should make advance reservations by fax through the Kōya-san Tourist Association or directly with the temples. If you arrive in Kōya-san after hours or you want to do things yourself, the following *shukubō* have English-speaking staff and are at the lower to middle end of the price spectrum.

Eikō-in *(☎ 56-2514; rooms per person with 2 meals ¥10,000)* is one of the nicer temples in town. It's run by a friendly bunch of young monks and the rooms look onto beautiful gardens. Rates here are an exception to the ¥9000 set price at most other

temples. This is also one of the two temples in town (the other is Kongōbu-ji) where you can study *zazen* (sitting Zen meditation). Call ahead to make arrangements.

Henjōson-in *(☎ 56-2434)* is another good choice. Here you get a pleasant room with a garden view, tatami furnishings, an excellent vegetarian dinner served in your room and the use of terrific wooden bathtubs. There's even a temple bar!

Other good choices include elegant **Rengejō-in** *(☎ 56-2233)*, friendly **Shojōshin-in** *(☎ 56-2006)* and down-to-earth **Muryōkō-in** *(☎ 56-2233)*.

Kōya Youth Hostel *(☎ 56-3889; beds ¥3200)* is a friendly and comfortable choice if the prices at the temples are out of your range. It's closed for parts of December and January. Call ahead for reservations.

Places to Eat

The culinary speciality of Kōya-san is *shōjin ryōri*, which you can sample at your temple lodgings. Two tasty tōfu specialities are *goma-tōfu* (sesame tōfu) and *kōya-tōfu* (local tōfu). If you're just in town for the day, you can try *shōjin ryōri* at any of the temples that offer *shukubō*. Ask at the Kōya-san Tourist Association office and staff will call ahead to make reservations. Prices are fixed at ¥2500, ¥3500 and ¥5000, depending on how many courses you have.

There are various coffee shops dotted around town where you can have breakfast; a convenient one is at the main crossroads close to the tourist office. **Nankai-shokudō** is worth a try at lunch. All the standard lunch items are represented by plastic food models in the window. *Katsu-don* (pork cutlet over rice) is ¥800 and noodle dishes start at ¥520. It's diagonally across from the main tourist office.

For something nicer, try **Hanabishi Honten** *(☎ 56-2236)* which serves well-prepared sets of standard Japanese dishes for around ¥2000. Look for the food models in the window (which will also help ordering, if necessary).

Getting There & Away

All rail connections to and from Kōya-san run via Gokurakubashi, which is at the base of the mountain. A cable car runs frequently from the base to the top of the mountain (five minutes, price included in most train tickets). From the cable-car station, you must take a bus into the centre of town, as walking is prohibited on the connecting road.

From Osaka (Namba station) you can travel directly by *kyūkō* on the Nankai–Dentetsu line to Gokurakubashi station (¥1230 including cable-car ticket, 1½ hours). For the slightly faster *tokkyū* service with reserved seats you pay a supplement of ¥760.

From Wakayama you can go by rail on the JR Wakayama line to Hashimoto (¥820, one hour) and then continue on the Nankai-Dentetsu line to Gokurakubashi station (¥810 including cable-car ticket, 45 minutes).

From Kyoto it's probably best to go via Namba in Osaka (see earlier in this section). From Nara, you can take the JR line to Hashimoto, changing at Sakurai and Takadate en route.

Getting Around

Buses run on three routes from the top cable-car station via the centre of town to Ichi-no-hashi and Okuno-in. The fare to the tourist office in the centre of town at Senjūin-bashi is ¥280. The fare to the final stop, Okuno-in, is ¥450. An all-day bus pass (*ichi-nichi furee kippu*; ¥800) is available from the bus office outside the top cable-car station, but once you get into the centre of town you can reach most destinations quite easily on foot (including Okuno-in, which takes about 30 minutes).

If you don't feel like walking, bicycles can be rented for ¥400 an hour or ¥1200 for the day at the **Kōya-san Tourist Association Office**.

SHIRAHAMA 白浜
☎ 0739 • pop 20,000

Shirahama, on the southwest coast of Kii-hantô, is Kansai's leading beach/*onsen* resort and has all the trappings of a major Japanese tourist attraction – huge resort hotels, aquariums, amusement parks, the lot. However, because the Japanese like to do things according to the rules – and the rules say the only time you can swim in the ocean is from late July to the end of August – the place is almost deserted outside the season and you'll have the place to yourself.

There are several good *onsen* in town (two of which are free), there is a fantastic white-sand beach, and the rugged sea coast

south of the town is stunning. This is a great place to visit in, say, June or September, and we've swum in the sea here as late as mid-October (just keep in mind that jellyfish can be found in the ocean here in late July and August).

There's a **tourist information office** (☎ 42-2240; open 9.15am-5pm daily) in the station, where you can pick up a map to the main sights and accommodation. Since the station is a fair distance from the main sights, you'll need to take a bus (¥330, 20 minutes to the beach, ¥980 for an all-day pass) or rent a bicycle if you arrive by rail. The JR office at the station rents bicycles (regular/mountain bikes ¥1000/2000 per day, discount for JR ticket holders – save your ticket).

Shirara-hama Beach 白良浜
Shirara-hama, the town's main beach, is famous for its white sand. If it reminds you of Australia don't be surprised – the town had to import sand from down under after the original stuff washed away. This place is packed during July and August. In the off-peak season, it can actually be quite pleasant. The beach is hard to miss, as it dominates the western side of town. **Shirasuna-yu** (*open 10am-7pm Tues-Sun*) is a free open-air *onsen* off the boardwalk in the middle of the beach. You can soak here and then dash into the ocean to cool off – not a bad way to spend an afternoon.

Onsen
In addition to its great beach, Shirahama has some of Japan's oldest developed *onsen* (they're even mentioned in the Nihon Shoki, one of Japan's earliest literary texts).

The free **Sakino-yu Onsen** (*open 8am-6.30pm Thur-Tues June-Aug, 8am-5pm Thur-Tues Sept-May*) is sensational. It is built on a rocky point with great views of the Pacific Ocean (and you can climb down the rocks to cool off if the waves aren't too big). Come early in the day to beat the crowds. It's 1km south of the main beach; walk along the seafront road and look for the point below the big Hotel Seymor. The baths are segregated by sex.

Other baths include **Shirara-yu** (*admission ¥300; open 7am-10.30pm Wed-Mon, noon-10.30pm Tues*), a pleasant bath right on the north end of Shirara-hama, and

Murono-yu *(admission ¥300; open 7am-10.30pm Fri-Wed, noon-10.30pm Thur)*, a simple *onsen* not far from Sakino-yu, in front of Shirahama post office.

Senjō-jiki, Sandan-heki & Isogi-kōen
千畳敷・三段壁・いそぎ公園
Just around the point south of the Sakino-yu *onsen* are two of Shirahama's natural wonders: Senjō-jiki and Sandan-heki. Senjō-jiki (Thousand Tatami Mat Point) is a wildly eroded point with stratified layers that actually resemble the thousand tatami mats it is named for.

More impressive is the 50m cliff face of Sandan-heki (Three-Step Cliff), which drops away vertiginously into the sea (there are signs in Japanese warning off suicidal jumpers). While you can pay ¥1200 to take a lift down to a cave at the base of the cliff, it's better simply to clamber along the rocks to the north of the cliff – it's stunning, particularly when the big rollers are pounding in from the Pacific.

If you'd like to enjoy more rugged coastal scenery, walk south along the coast another 1km from Sandan-heki to Isogi-kōen, where the crowds are likely to be thinner and the scenery just as impressive.

These attractions can be reached on foot or bicycle from the main beach in around 30 minutes, or you can take a bus from the station (¥430, 25 minutes to Senjō-jiki, from which you can walk to the others).

Places to Stay & Eat
Ohgigahama Youth Hostel *(☎ 22-3433; beds ¥2300)* is friendly, comfortable and the cheapest option if you don't mind staying outside the town of Shirahama. The hostel is 10 minutes on foot from Kii-Tanabe station, which is three stops north of Shirahama station on the JR Kisei line. Meals are not served.

In Shirahama itself, there are several *kokumin-shukusha* and *minshuku*. **Katsuya** *(☎ 42-3814; rooms per person with/without 2 meals ¥8000/5000 20 July-31 August, ¥7000/4000 rest of year)* is the best of these and is central, being only two minutes' walk from the main beach. It's built around a small Japanese garden and has its own natural hot-spring bath. **Kokumin-shukusha Hotel Shirahama** *(☎ 42-3039)*

is a good bet if Katsuya is full, and offers similar rates. The tourist information office at the station has maps to both places.

There are many restaurants in the streets around these accommodation. **Kiraku** serves standard *teishoku* for around ¥800. **Ginchiro** *(☎ 42-2514; open 11am-2pm & 4pm-9pm Thur-Tues; set meals ¥1800)* is more upmarket, serving tempura and *unagi* set meals (there's a picture menu). The tourist information office at the station can provide a map to both places. Alternatively, ask directions at your accommodation venue.

If you're on a tight budget, you can save money by self-catering; there are plenty of convenience stores in town and **Sakae Supermarket** is five minutes' walk from the main beach.

Getting There & Away
Shirahama is on the JR Kii main line. There is a *tokkyū* train from Shin-Osaka station (¥5250, 2¼ hours). The same line also connects Shirahama to other cities on Kii-hantō such as Kushimoto, Nachi, Shingū and Wakayama City.

KUSHIMOTO, CAPE SHIONO-MISAKI & KII-ŌSHIMA
串本・潮岬・紀伊大島
☎ 0735
The southern tip of Kii-hantō has some stunning coastal scenery. Shiono-misaki, connected to the mainland by a narrow isthmus, has some fine rocky vistas, but the real action is over on Kii-Ōshima, a rocky island accessible by a newly completed bridge.

The main attraction on Kii-Ōshima is the coastal cliffs at the eastern end of the island, which can be viewed from the park around **Kashino-zaki Lighthouse**. Just before the park, you'll find the **Turko-kinenkan Museum** *(☎ 65-0628; admission ¥250; open 9am-5pm daily)*, which commemorates the sinking of the Turkish ship *Ertugrul* in 1890. Backtracking about 1km towards the bridge, there are small English signs to the **Japan-US Memorial Museum** *(☎ 65-0099; admission ¥250; open 9am-5pm Tues-Sun)*, which commemorates the visit of the United States' ship *Lady Washington* in 1791, a full 62 years before Commodore Perry's much more famous landing in Yokohama in 1853. There is a lookout just beyond the museum from which you can see the magnificent

Umi-kongō formations along the eastern point of the island.

If you're without your own transport, the best way to explore Kii-Ōshima is by renting a cycle at Kushimoto station (¥600/1000 per four hours/day, discount for JR ticket holders), but be warned that there are a few good hills en route and these bikes are not performance vehicles. Otherwise, there are buses from the station, but take note of schedules as departures are few and far between.

Kushimoto itself is renowned for the Hashi-kui-iwa, a line of pillar-like rocks that have been imaginatively compared to a line of hooded monks heading towards Kii-Ōshima. To see the rocks, take a Shingū-bound bus from Kushimoto station, and get off five minutes later at the Hashi-kui-iwa stop (¥130).

Misaki Lodge Youth Hostel (☎ 62-1474; beds per person ¥4550, rooms per person ¥7000) is the best place to stay in the area. It's in a good position, on the southern side of the cape overlooking the Pacific. It's also a minshuku, offering large rooms and including two meals in the rates. Take a Shiono-misaki–bound bus from Kushimoto station (20 minutes) and get off at the last stop, Sugu-mae.

Kushimoto is one hour from Shirahama by JR tokkyū, and three hours (¥6080) from Shin-Osaka. Futsū services are significantly cheaper but take almost twice as long.

NACHI & KII-KATSUURA
那智・紀伊勝浦

The Nachi and Kii-Katsuura area has several sights grouped around the sacred **Nachi-no-taki**, Japan's highest waterfall (133m). **Nachi Taisha**, near the waterfall, was built in homage to the waterfall's kami. Although it is one of the three great shrines of Kii-hantō, it is gaudy and a long climb from the waterfall car park. If you do decide to visit this shrine, you can take a trail from there to two hidden waterfalls above the main falls: these are seldom visited by tourists and are worth seeing. You can also pay ¥200 at the base of the falls to hike up to a lookout that affords a better view of the falls.

The **Nachi-no-Hi Matsuri** (Fire Festival) takes place at the falls on 14 July. During this lively event mikoshi are brought down from the mountain and met by groups bearing flaming torches.

Buses from Nachi station to the waterfall take 20 minutes and cost ¥470. From Kii-Katsuura station buses take about 30 minutes and cost ¥600.

Getting There & Away
Kii-Katsuura can be reached by JR Kii main line trains from Shin-Osaka station (tokkyū, ¥6500, four hours) and from Nagoya station (tokkyū, ¥7310, 3½ hours). Futsū are significantly cheaper but take almost twice as long.

SHINGŪ 新宮
☎ 0735 • pop 33,000

This town is nothing exceptional to look at but functions as a useful transport hub for access to the three major Shintō shrines of the area, known as the **Kumano San-zan** (Kumano Hayatama Taisha, Kumano Hongū Taisha and Nachi Taisha). There's a helpful **information office** (☎ 22-2840) at the station.

If you're killing time between trains or buses, you could visit the colourful **Kumano Hayatama Taisha**, a 15-minute walk northwest of Shingū station. The shrine's **Boat Race Festival** takes place on 16 October. Another shrine worth looking at is **Kamikura-jinja**, which is famous for its **Otō Matsuri** (6 February), during which more than 1000 people carrying torches ascend the slope to the shrine. The shrine is a 15-minute walk west of the station.

Hase Ryokan (☎ 22-2185; rooms per person with/without 2 meals & shared bath ¥6000/4000) is a two-minute walk north of the station and slightly more upmarket than the hostel. Call from the station and someone will collect you or ask at the information office for a map. If you'd prefer a hotel, **Shingū Station Hotel** (☎ 21-2200; singles/doubles from ¥5500/9000) is a short walk south of the station and has reasonable rooms.

There are several places to eat around the station. **Marusan**, an atmospheric little shokudō a minute's walk from the station – go past the kōban (police box) but don't cross the tracks – has good set meals for around ¥1000 and food models in the window to help you order. If you're up for something a little more special, get the folks at the information office to draw you a map to **Ajino-sankin** (☎ 22-2373; open lunch & dinner daily), which offers excellent sets of locally caught sashimi for around ¥1500. It's about a 20-minute walk from the station.

Getting There & Away

The JR Kii main line connects Shingū with Nagoya station (*tokkyū*, ¥6990, three hours) and Shin-Osaka station (*tokkyū*, ¥6810, four hours).

There are buses between Shingū and Hongū, about half of which make a loop of the three surrounding *onsen* (Watarase, Yunomine and Kawa-yu). See the following Hongū section for details.

HONGŪ 本宮

Hongū itself isn't particularly interesting but it makes a good starting point for the *onsen* villages nearby. Hongū is also home to **Kumano Hongū Taisha**, one of the three famous shrines of the Kumano Sanzan. The shrine is close to the Ōmiya Taisha-mae bus stop (the buses listed in this section stop here).

Nara Kōtsū and JR buses leave for Hongū from Gojō in the north (¥3250, four hours), Kii-Tanabe in the west (¥2000, two hours) and Shingū in the southeast (¥1500, 1½ hours). Shingū is the most convenient of these three access points (departures are most frequent from there). Most Hongū buses also stop at Kawa-yu, Watarase and Yunomin *onsen* (in that order), but be sure to ask before boarding. Keep in mind that departures are few in any direction, so jot down the times and plan accordingly.

YUNOMINE, WATARASE & KAWA-YU ONSEN

☎ 07354

These three *onsen* are among the best in all of Kansai. Because each has its own distinct character, it's worth doing a circuit of all three. There are several ryokan and *minshuku* in the area, but if you are on a tight budget, it's possible to camp on the riverbanks above and below Kumano Hongū Taisha. See the Hongū section earlier for transport details.

Yunomine Onsen 湯峰温泉

The town of Yunomine is nestled around a narrow river in a wooded valley. Most of the town's *onsen* are contained inside ryokan or *minshuku* but charming little **Tsubo-yu Onsen** (*admission ¥260; open 6am-9.30pm Thur-Tues, 8am-9.30pm Wed*) is open to all. It's right in the middle of town, inside a tiny wooden shack built on an island in the river. Buy a ticket at the *sentō* next to Tōkō-ji, the town's main temple. The *sentō* itself is open the same hours as the *onsen* and entry is ¥300; of the two baths at the *sentō*, we suggest the *kusuri-yu* (medicine water), which is 100% pure hot spring water.

While you're at Yunomine, try your hand at cooking some *onsen tamago* – eggs boiled in the hot water of an *onsen*. There is a pool of hot-spring water just downstream from Tsubo-yu for cooking. The shop across from the temple sells bags of five eggs for ¥200. Put them in the water before you enter the bath and they should be cooked by the time you get out.

Yunomine has plenty of *minshuku* and ryokan for you to choose from. **Yunotanisō** (☎ 42-1620; rooms per person with/without 2 meals ¥7500/5000) is at the upper end of the village and has pleasant tatami rooms. There's also an excellent *rotemburo* on the premises. **Yoshino-ya** (☎ 42-0101; **w** www.mountaintrad.co.jp/yoshinoya in Japanese; singles/doubles with 2 meals from ¥7800/15,600) is a slightly more upscale place with a lovely *rotemburo*. It's near Tsubo-yu.

Kawa-yu Onsen 川湯温泉

Kawa-yu Onsen is a natural wonder, where geothermally-heated water percolates up through the gravel banks of the river that dissects the town. You can make your own private bath here by digging out some of the stones and letting the hole fill with hot water; you can then spend the rest of the day jumping back and forth between the bath and the cool waters of the river. Admission is free and the best spots along the river are in front of Fujiya ryokan. We suggest bringing a bathing suit unless you fancy putting on a 'naked *gaijin*' show for the whole town. In the winter, from 1 December to 28 February, bulldozers are used to turn the river into a giant 1000-person *rotemburo*.

If you don't fancy splashing about in the river, try the **Kawa-yu Koshū Yokujō** (*admission ¥200; open 8am-9pm daily, closed 1st & 3rd Wed each month*), a public bath that uses natural hot-spring water. It's near the town's footbridge.

Places to Stay The cheapest place in Kawa-yu is **Kajika-sō** (☎ 42-0518; hostel/minshuku beds per person ¥5070/8000), a combination youth hostel/minshuku.

Hotels in Kawa-yu, as in other Japanese onsen towns, tend to be expensive. **Pension Ashita-no-Mori** (☎ 42-1525; rooms per person ¥10,650) is a pleasant wooden building. **Fujiya** (☎ 42-0007; rooms per person from ¥15,000), next door, is a more upmarket ryokan with tasteful rooms. Rates at both include two meals.

Watarase Onsen 渡瀬温泉

This onsen (admission ¥700; open 6am-9.30pm daily) is built around a bend in the river directly between Yunomine Onsen and Kawa-yu Onsen. It's not as interesting as its neighbours, but it does boast the largest rotemburo in Kansai.

DORO-KYŌ 瀞峡

Doro-kyō Kankō-sen (☎ 0735-22-6220, Japanese only) runs glass-roofed boats which leave from Shiko for a dramatic two-hour trip (¥3340) on the Kitayama-gawa through Doro-kyō, one of Japan's finest gorges. Boats generally operate from 9.30am to 2.10pm (slightly longer in summer). Buses connect Shiko with Shingū station (42 minutes). There are special bus/boat tickets available from Shingū for ¥5200 (ask at the ticket office by the station).

Ise-Shima 伊勢志摩

The Ise-Shima region, on Mie-ken's Shima-hantō, is most famous for Ise-jingū, Japan's most sacred Shintō shrine. It also encompasses the tourist mecca of Toba and some pleasant coastal scenery around Kashikojima and Goza. Ise-Shima is easily reached from Nagoya, Kyoto or Osaka and makes a good two-day trip.

JNTO publishes Ise-Shima, a leaflet providing basic mapping and concise travel information for the area.

ISE 伊勢
☎ 0596 • pop 99,000

Although the town of Ise is rather drab, it's worth making the trip here to visit the spectacular Ise-jingū. This is arguably Japan's most impressive shrine; its only rival to this claim is Nikkō's Tōshō-gū, which is as gaudy as Ise-jingū is austere.

If you have some time to kill in town after visiting the shrines, take a stroll down atmospheric **Kawasaki Kaiwai**, a street lined with traditional Japanese houses. It's a little tricky to find; the best way is to head to Hoshide-kan (see Places to Stay), take a right and walk towards the canal. Kawasaki-kaiwai is the street just before the canal.

Ise-jingū 伊勢神宮

Dating back to the 3rd century, Ise-jingū is the most venerated Shintō shrine in Japan (admission free; open sunrise-sunset daily). Shintō tradition has dictated for centuries that the shrine buildings (about 200 of them) be replaced every 20 years with exact imitations built on adjacent sites according to ancient techniques – no nails, only wooden dowels and interlocking joints. Upon completion of the new buildings, the god of the shrine is ritually transferred to its new home in the Sengū No Gi ceremony, first witnessed by Western eyes in 1953. The wood from the old shrine is then used to reconstruct the torii at the shrine's entrance or is sent to shrines around Japan for use in rebuilding their structures. The present buildings were rebuilt in 1993 (for the 61st time) at a cost exceeding ¥5 billion.

The reason for this expensive periodic rebuilding is not clear. The official version holds that rebuilding the shrine every 20 years keeps alive traditional carpentry techniques. Perhaps the real reason goes back to pre-Buddhist Japanese taboos concerning death. Before the establishment of a permanent capital at Nara it was thought that the emperor's residence was defiled by death. This meant that the entire capital had to be razed and rebuilt with the passing of each emperor. This thinking may have carried over to the dwellings of Shintō gods resulting in the periodic reconstruction of the shrines, which continues to this day.

Visitors to the shrine are often shocked to discover that the main shrine buildings are almost completely hidden from view. Only members of the imperial family and certain shrine priests are allowed to enter the sacred inner sanctum. This is unfortunate, as the buildings are stunning examples of pre-Buddhist Japanese architecture. Don't despair, though, as determined neck craning

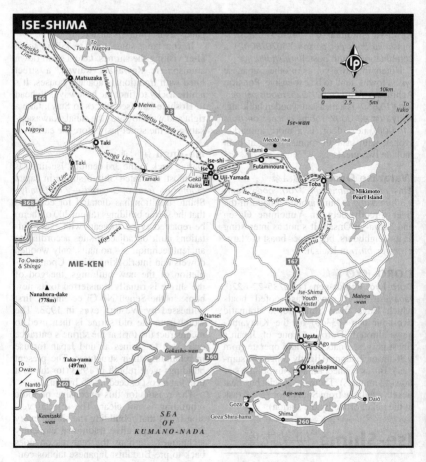

ISE-SHIMA

over fences allows a decent view of the upper parts of the buildings. You can also get a good idea of the shrine's architecture by looking at any of the lesser shrines nearby which are exact replicas built on a smaller scale.

There are two parts to the shrine, **Gekū** (Outer Shrine) and **Naikū** (Inner Shrine). The former is an easy 12-minute walk from Ise-shi station; the latter is accessible by bus from the station or from outside Gekū (see below for details). If you only have time to visit one of the shrines, Naikū is by far the more impressive of the two.

Smoking is prohibited throughout the grounds of both shrines and photography is forbidden around the main halls of both shrines.

Gekū The Outer Shrine dates from the 5th century and enshrines the god of food, clothing and housing, Toyouke-no-Ōkami. Daily offerings of rice are made by shrine priests to the goddess, who is charged with providing food to Amaterasu-Ōmikami, the goddess enshrined in the Naikū.

A stall at the entrance to the shrine provides a leaflet in English with a map. The main hall is approached along an avenue of tall trees and surrounded by closely fitted wooden fences that hide most of the buildings from sight. You can get a decent idea of the shape of the main building by craning your neck over the fences, or by looking at some of the smaller shrine buildings around the compound, which are smaller copies of the main hall.

To the left of the main hall is an empty plot of land on which will be built the main hall when the shrine is next rebuilt in 2013.

From Ise-shi station or Uji-Yamada station it's a 12-minute walk down the main street to the shrine entrance.

Naikū The Inner Shrine is thought to date from the 3rd century and enshrines the sun goddess, Amaterasu-Ōmikami, who is considered the ancestral goddess of the imperial family and the guardian deity of the Japanese nation. Naikū is held in even higher reverence than Gekū because it houses the sacred mirror of the emperor, one of the three imperial regalia (the other two are the sacred beads and the sacred sword).

Since being enshrined here in the 3rd century, this mirror has not been seen by human eyes. Members of the imperial family technically have the right to see it, but apparently none of them have ever tried to exercise this right. It stands on a wooden pedestal wrapped in a brocade bag. As each bag wears thin, the bag with the mirror inside is simply placed inside another bag. This ensures that the mirror is never sullied by the gaze of a human and has resulted in what one writer has suggested must be the world's best collection of Japanese brocade weaving.

A stall just before the entrance to the shrine provides the same English leaflet given out at Gekū. Next to this stall is the Uji-bashi, which leads over the crystal-clear Isuzu-gawa into the shrine. One path leads to the right and passes Mitarashi, a place for pilgrims to purify themselves in the river before entering the shrine. This isn't easy, as the river is teeming with gargantuan carp awaiting hand-outs.

The path continues along an avenue lined with towering cryptomeria trees to the main hall. Photos are only allowed from the foot of the stone steps. Here too, you can only catch a glimpse of the structure, as four rows of wooden fences obstruct the view. If you're tempted to jump the fence when nobody's around, think again – they're watching you on closed-circuit TV cameras not so cleverly disguised as trees!

A better view of the shrine can be had by walking along its front (western) side towards the separate Aramatsurinomiya shrine. Here, you can see a large section of the shrine, and on sunny days the cypress wood of the shrine gleams almost as brightly as the gold tips of its roof beams.

To get to Naiku, take bus No 51 or 55 from bus stop No 11 outside Ise-shi station or the stop on the main road in front of Gekū (¥410, 15 minutes). Get off at Naikū-mae stop. From Naikū there are buses back to Ise-shi station via Gekū (¥410, 15 minutes from bus stop No 2). Alternatively, a taxi from Ise-shi station to Naiku costs ¥630.

Special Events

Since Ise-jingu is Japan's most sacred shrine, it's not surprising that it's also a favourite destination for *hatsu-mōde*. Most of the action takes place in the first three days of the year, when millions of worshippers pack the area and accommodation is booked out for months in advance.

The **Kagurai-sai Matsuri**, celebrated on 5 and 6 April, is a good chance to see performances of *kagura* (sacred dance), *bugaku*, nō and Shintō music.

Places to Stay

There are plenty of places to stay in Ise itself, but you'll also find lots of *minshuku* and ryokan in Futami, Kashikojima or Goza. Be aware that prices for all ryokan and *minshuku* go up on weekends and holidays.

Hoshide-kan (☎ 28-2377; e hoshidekan@ cool.ne.jp; per person with/without 2 meals ¥6500/4800), in Ise itself, is a quaint wooden ryokan with some nice traditional touches. Take the road that heads north from between Ise-shi and Uji-Yamada stations (to find this, exit Ise-shi station and walk east); it's on the right about 700m after crossing the tracks.

On the same road but closer to Ise-shi station, **Ise City Hotel** (☎ 28-2111; w www .greens.co.jp/hotel_e/17.html; singles/doubles ¥6200/13,000) is a good business hotel with small but adequate rooms.

Ise-Shima Youth Hostel (☎ 05995-5-0226; beds ¥4400) is a safer choice and is an excellent place built on a hill overlooking an attractive bay. It's close to Anagawa station on the Kintetsu line (only *futsū* trains stop). Walk east out of the station along the waterfront road; it's uphill on the right.

KANSAI

Places to Eat

There are lots of places to eat around Ise-shi station. If you walk straight out of the station and take your second right (at a mini clock tower), you'll find a couple of cheap *shokudō*.

For more upscale fare, head to the atmospheric Kawasaki-Kawai street. Here, you'll find **Ajikko** (*☎ 25-9696; open noon-2pm & 6pm-11pm Fri-Wed)*, a pleasant little *robotayaki* restaurant where you'll probably need a Japanese speaker in your group to handle the ordering. If you just fancy a cup of coffee, don't miss **Kawasaki-kan** (*☎ 29-5200; open 9am-4pm Tues-Sun)*, a coffee shop inside an old Japanese *kura*. It's also in Kawasaki Kaiwai.

Near Naikū, try the shopping arcade just outside the shrine compound. **Nikōdōshiten** is a good place to try some of the local specialities in a rough, roadhouse atmosphere. A light lunch of Ise-udon is ¥400. *Ōasari* (large steamed clams) or *sazai* (another type of shellfish) are also tasty and cost ¥400. The restaurant is about 100m north of the entrance to the arcade. **Akafuku Honten** is about 200m further on – follow your nose to get there. Here *akafuku mochi*, a kind of Japanese sweet, is served with tea for ¥340. Look for the large, steaming cauldrons and the queue out the front.

Getting There & Away

Ise is well endowed with direct rail connections for Nagoya, Osaka and Kyoto. For those without a Japan Rail Pass, the Kintetsu line is by far the most convenient way to go. Note that there are two stations in Ise – Ise-shi station and Uji-Yamada station – which are only a few hundred metres apart; most trains stop at both.

From Nagoya, the *tokkyū* service on the Kintetsu line takes one hour and 20 minutes to reach Ise-shi station (¥2690) and another 30 minutes to reach its terminus at Kashiko-jima (¥3480). A JR *kaisoku* from Nagoya takes up to two hours (¥2250).

From Osaka (Uehonmachi or Namba stations), the Kintetsu limited express takes about two hours to Ise-shi station and costs ¥3030. The same train continues on to Kashikojima (¥3810, 30 minutes).

From Kyoto, the Kintetsu *tokkyū* takes two hours and 10 minutes to Ise-shi station (¥3520) and continues for another 30 minutes to its terminus in Kashikojima (¥4320).

If you're only going from Ise-shi to Kashikojima, take a Kintetsu *futsū* (¥670, 55 minutes). JR doesn't serve Kashikojima.

If you're taking JR from Kyoto or Osaka to Ise-shi you'll have to change up to four times and pay ¥2210 from Kyoto and ¥3260 from Osaka. Inquire at the station office for transfer details.

FUTAMI 二見

The big attractions here are Futami Okitama-jinja and the Meoto-iwa (Wedded Rocks). These two rocks are considered to be male and female and have been joined in matrimony by *shimenawa* (sacred ropes), which are renewed each year in a special festival on 5 January. The rocks are a 20-minute walk from the station. The shrine is on the shore opposite the rocks. Futami can be reached from Ise by JR (*futsū* ¥200, 10 minutes). Get off at Futaminoura station.

TOBA 鳥羽

Unless you have a strong interest in pearls or enjoy a real tourist circus, you can safely give this place a miss. The JR line runs from Ise-shi station via Futami to Toba and then on to Kashikojima. **Ise-wan Ferry Corporation** (*☎ 0559-25-2880)* has ferry connections from Toba-ko port to Irako on Atsumi-hantō in Aichi-ken (¥1050, 55 minutes). Boats leave from Ise-wan ferry terminal, two minutes' walk south of Mikimoto Pearl Island. Toba can be reached from Ise in 20 minutes by both the Kintetsu line (*kyūkō*, ¥320) or the JR line (*futsū* ¥230).

Mikimoto Pearl Island
ミキモト真珠島

Although this is the classic Japanese tourist trap, it does have lots of good exhibits about cultured pearls and their production. And, miracle of miracles, there are even plenty of English explanations.

The establishment is a monument to Kokichi Michimoto, who devoted his life to producing cultured pearls: after irritating a lot of oysters with a variety of objects, he finally succeeded in 1893.

The demonstration halls show all the oyster tricks from growing and seeding to selecting, drilling and threading the finished product.

There is an **observation room** (*admission ¥1500; open 8.30am-5pm daily June-Aug, 9am-4.30pm daily Sep-May*) from which you can watch a boat put into view and drop off the *ama* (women divers) in their white outfits. There are several thousand *ama* still operating in these coastal areas – but despite valiant efforts by regional tourist organisations to make you think they're after pearls, they are actually after shellfish or seaweed. There is a taped commentary in English that tells you all about the divers and their watery ways. Just ask if you'd like the attendant to put in a tape in another language.

Toba Aquarium 鳥羽水族館

This rather expensive aquarium (*admission ¥2400; open 8.30am-5pm daily 21 Mar-30 Nov, 9am-5pm daily 1 Dec-20 Mar*) has some interesting fish and marine mammal displays and some good shows. It would make a good destination for those with children or if the rain puts a damper on outdoor activities.

AGO-WAN, KASHIKOJIMA & GOZA 英虞湾・賢島・御座

Ago-wan is a pleasant stretch of coastline, with sheltered inlets and small islands. Kashikojima, an island in the bay, is the terminus of the Kintetsu line, only 40 minutes from Ise-shi to Kashikojima (¥670, about one hour), and a good base for exploration of Ago-wan. The island itself is probably of little interest to foreign travellers as it is dominated by large resort hotels.

Those in search of peace and quiet might want to take a ferry to Goza on the other side of the bay (¥600, 25 minutes). The ferry terminal is right outside Kashikojima station (buy your tickets from the **Kinki Kankōsen** office near the terminal). The ride is a good way to see the sights in the bay. There are also sightseeing boats that do a loop around the bay for ¥1500.

Goza is a sleepy fishing community where the main attractions are the fish market and Goza Shira-hama, a long white-sand beach on the southern side of town. There are small signs in English from the ferry pier to the beach; just follow the main road over the hill and across the peninsula. The beach is mobbed in late July and early August but is quite nice at other times. After the beginning of August, there may be some *kurage* (jellyfish) in the water, so ask the locals about conditions.

If you'd like to stay in Goza, there are tons of *minshuku*, some of which close down outside of summer. **Shiojisō** (☎ 0599-88-3232; *rooms per person from ¥7500*), just off the beach (look for the sign reading 'Marine Lodge Shiojisō' in English), is one of the better *minshuku*. Rates include two meals.

SOUTH OF KASHIKOJIMA 賢島以南

If you want to continue down Kii-hantō but avoid the tortuous coastal road, backtrack to Ise and then take a train on the JR Kisei main line. This line crosses from Mie-ken into Wakayama-ken and continues down to Shingū on its way round Kii-hantō, finally ending up in Osaka's Tennō-ji station.

Western Honshū 本州西部

Western Honshū is also known as Chūgoku or, literally, the 'Middle Lands'; 'Chūgoku' is written in Japanese using the same characters that the Chinese use for 'China'. Over time, much of the artistic and cultural influences from China and Korea that were to shape Japanese society, entered through this region.

Chūgoku is split down the middle by rugged mountains that have produced two distinct coastlines. To the south of the mountains and facing the Inland Sea (Seto-Nai-Kai) is the San-yō, while to the north and facing the Sea of Japan is the San-in. While San-yō literally means 'on the sunny side of the mountains', San-in means 'in the shade of the mountains', and this very effectively describes how western Honshū developed over time. Basking in the sunshine and with easy access to the seats of power in Kyoto, the San-yō developed into the prosperous industrial region it is today. The San-in, however – relatively inaccessible and with inhospitable winters – lagged behind, but as a consequence, has retained much of its natural beauty, including rocky coastlines, sandy beaches and significantly fewer people.

As a visitor, which way you go depends on how much time you have and what you want to see and do.

Most visitors to the region choose the southern route through the San-yō region, heavily industrialised and densely populated – and if you've already done the Tokyo–Osaka route by train, this will leave you feeling that Japan is one continuous urban sprawl. There are, however, a number of interesting cities, including Kurashiki and Hiroshima. The island-dotted waters of the Inland Sea, sandwiched between Honshū and Shikoku, are also reached from ports on the San-yō coast. If you don't have much time, this is the way to go as the Tokyo–Kyoto–Osaka–Hakata *shinkansen* (bullet train) rail route runs along the San-yō coast.

A great alternative for those with time on their hands, however, is the San-in coast. By Japanese standards, the north coast is comparatively uncrowded and rural. The coastline is stunning and there are all sorts of interesting little places to drop into. Despite the lower population density in

Highlights

- Visit the sombre, affecting Hiroshima Peace Museum, then walk out into the city's vibrant, party-filled streets
- Clamber up the crumbling volcano of Daisen from the ancient temple, Daisen-ji
- Examine the intriguing sealife at Karato Ichiba, Shimonoseki's early-morning fish markets
- Seek out the hidden-away rural 'health spa', Tawarayama Onsen, and its curious phallic temple dedicated to the Goddess of Mercy
- Wander around Izumo Taisha, where the Shintō gods go on holiday, and then taste the local wines at Shimane Winery
- Potter through the well-preserved warehouses and wonderful museums along the canal in Kurashiki
- Relax on the beach while staying at Okayama-ken's International Villa, on Shiraishi-jima in the Inland Sea

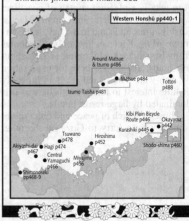

the north, travel along the San-in coast is likely to be slower, as the train services are less frequent and not as fast as those in the south. If you take the attitude that half the fun of travel is getting there, then the San-in coast will provide some great experiences.

Another alternative for those with private transport is the Chūgoku Expressway, which runs the full length of western Honshū, more or less equidistant from the north and south coasts. Attractions along this route are limited and it's basically just a way to breeze through Chūgoku.

SUGGESTED ITINERARIES

If you've got the time and the inclination, and are feeling adventurous, head along the San-in coast and have a look at a part of Japan few foreigners see.

If on a tight schedule, use the *shinkansen* along the San-yō and be sure to at least drop into Hiroshima.

If you can't make up your mind which way to go, try a bit of both. There are a number of train lines crossing the mountains between the two coastlines, and it shouldn't be hard to find someone to help figure out the train timetables.

CHAPTER ORGANISATION

The first part of this chapter is organised for those taking the San-yō route west from Kansai through to Kyūshū. It covers Okayama-ken, Hiroshima-ken, the Inland Sea (east to west) and Yamaguchi-ken. The second part (from p471) covers the San-in coast starting at the western end and coming back towards Kansai. Northern Yamaguchi-ken, Shimane-ken and Tottori-ken are covered. If you're going the other way, read the sections back-to-front.

Okayama-ken 岡山県

The prefecture of Okayama-ken includes the cities of Okayama and Kurashiki, along with other interesting towns and visitor attractions. The Seto-ōhashi forms the main road and rail link from Honshū to Shikoku. Some of Okayama's islands are included in the Inland Sea section of this chapter.

Bizen 備前

☎ 0869 • pop 30,000

East of Okayama city on the JR Akō line is the 700-year-old pottery region of Bizen, renowned for its unglazed Bizen-yaki pottery. Much prized by tea-ceremony connoisseurs, Bizen ceramics are earthy, dramatic and, more often than not, rather expensive. At Imbe station, the drop-off point to explore the area, there is a **tourist information counter** (☎ 64-1100; open 9am-6pm Wed-Mon), which has a useful

English-language pamphlet on the history of Bizen-yaki.

On the 2nd floor of the station is the **Bizen Ceramic Crafts Museum** (admission free; open 9.30am-5.30pm Wed-Mon) and on the north side of the station are the **Okayama Prefectural Bizen Ceramics Art Museum** (admission ¥500; open 9.30am-4.30pm Tues-Sun) and the **Bizen Ceramics Center** (☎ 64-2453; admission free; open 10am-4.30pm Tues-Sun), all of which display the pottery of the area. Of all the galleries in Bizen's main street, **Kibi-dō** (☎ 64-4467; open 10am-6pm daily) is the oldest and most interesting.

There are several kilns in the area that offer a chance to try your hand at making Bizen-yaki (around ¥3000; reservations necessary). Try **Bishū Gama** (☎ 64-1160), where some English is spoken. In about two hours you can sculpt a masterpiece, but you'll need to arrange to have your creation shipped to you after it's been fired. **Bizen-yaki Traditional Pottery Centre** (☎ 64-1001), on the 3rd floor of Imbe station, holds workshops (¥3000) on weekends and holidays from April to November.

If you have come from Himeji or points east, you'll need to change to the JR Akō line at Aioi and get off at Imbe station, after possibly making a train change at Banshū-Akō. You can carry on along the JR Akō line to get to Okayama.

OKAYAMA 岡山

☎ 086 • pop 630,000

Okayama is a bustling, modern city and the prefectural capital. It is so close to Kurashiki that it's very easy to stay in one town and day trip to the other. There are a number of places to visit, including one of Japan's 'big three' gardens.

Orientation & Information

The town's main street, Momotarō-dōri, leads directly from the station to near the castle, Okayama-jō, and the garden, Kōraku-en. Tramlines run down the middle of the street.

JR Okayama station has a **tourist information counter** (☎ 222-2912; open 9am-6pm daily). The staff are helpful and can provide excellent English advice about Okayama and Kurashiki. **Okayama International Exchange Centre** (☎ 256-2000;

WESTERN HONSHŪ

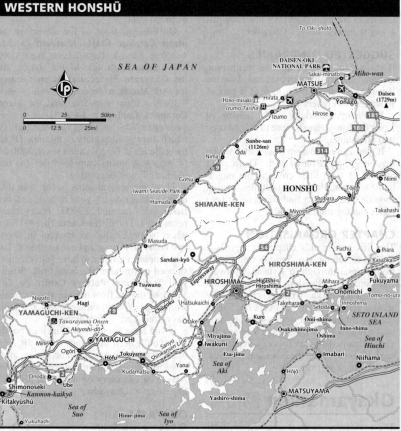

open 9am-5pm Tues-Sun), a short walk west of the station, is also a good information source. There is Internet access (¥300 for 30 minutes) and brochures on all towns in the prefecture and on the International Villas (see the Around Okayama section later).

The **Kinokuniya** and **Maruzen** bookshops both have English-language sections that are pretty reasonable.

Post The Okayama main post office faces Okayama station, on the east side.

Email & Internet Access The **Okayama Prefectural Office** *(Kenchō)* and **Okayama City Office** *(Shiyakusho)* both have free Internet access from 9am to 4pm Monday to Friday.

Kōraku-en 後楽園

Kōraku-en *(admission ¥350; open 7.30am-6pm daily spring & summer, 8am-5pm daily autumn & winter)* means 'the garden for taking pleasure later', taken from the Chinese proverb that 'the lord must bear sorrow before the people and take pleasure after them'. The Japanese penchant for rating and numbering things is apparent at Kōraku-en, said to be one of the three finest gardens in Japan. The other two are the Kairaku-en in Mito (see the Around Tokyo chapter) and Kenroku-en in Kanazawa (see the Central Honshū chapter).

Constructed between 1687 and 1700, Kōraku-en is a garden for strolling in. Part of its attraction in crowded Japan is its expanse of flat lawn, but there are also

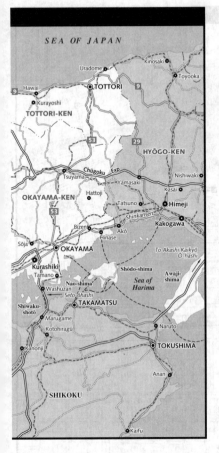

and only the small *tsukima-yagura* (moon-viewing turret) survived. The castle was rebuilt in 1966, a modern reinforced concrete construction like most post-war reconstructions. Nevertheless, there is an interesting display inside, much of it labelled in English. The information office provides an English brochure on the castle.

Museums

There are a number of museums and galleries in the 'Okayama Culture Zone'. Close to the castle's back entrance, near the corner of the moat, the **Hayashibara Museum of Art** (*admission ¥300; open 9am-4.30pm daily*) houses a private collection of Japanese and Chinese artefacts. Beside the main entrance to Kōraku-en is the worthwhile **Okayama Prefectural Museum** (*admission ¥200; open 9am-5pm Tues-Sun*), with displays about local history. Just north of Kōraku-en is the **Yumeji Art Museum** (*admission ¥700; open 9am-5pm Tues-Sun*), displaying work by famed artist Yumeji Takehisa.

Just north of the end of Momotarō-dōri, where the tram line turns south, is the excellent **Okayama Orient Museum** (*admission ¥300; open 9am-5pm Tues-Sun*). Behind this museum is the **Okayama Prefectural Museum of Art** (*admission ¥300; open 9am-4.30pm Tues-Sun*).

Other Attractions

The canal-like **Nishi-gawa**, not far east of the station, is flanked by gardens and sculptures and makes for a pleasant short stroll.

Southeast of central Okayama is **Tōko-en** (*admission ¥400; open 9am-5pm daily*), which is easy to overlook in a town with one of the 'big three' gardens. The garden circles a large pond and actually predates Kōraku-en by 70 years. Beyond Tōko-en is the temple, **Sōgen-ji** (*open 6am-6pm daily*), which also has a noted Zen garden.

Special Events

The **Saidai-ji Eyō** (Naked Festival) takes place from midnight on the third Saturday in February at the temple Kannon-in, in the Saidai-ji area. A large crowd of near-naked men fight for two sacred *shingi* (wooden sticks), while seasonally freezing water is poured over them. For such a masochistic purification ritual everyone seems to have a good time.

attractive ponds, a hill in the centre, a curious, tiny tea plantation and rice paddy, and a neatly placed piece of 'borrowed scenery' in the shape of Okayama-jō. Look for the nō stage, the pretty little Ryuten Building where poetry composing contests were once held, and the nearby Yatsu-hashi zigzag bridge.

From the station take the Higashi-yama tram to the Shiro-shita stop (¥100).

Okayama-jō 岡山城

Known to locals as U-jō (*admission ¥300; open 9am-5pm daily*), the 'Crow Castle' was built in 1597; it's said that its very striking black colour was a *daimyō*'s (domain lord's) jest at Himeji's pristine 'White Egret Castle'. Like many other great castles in Japan, U-jō was destroyed in WWII,

OKAYAMA

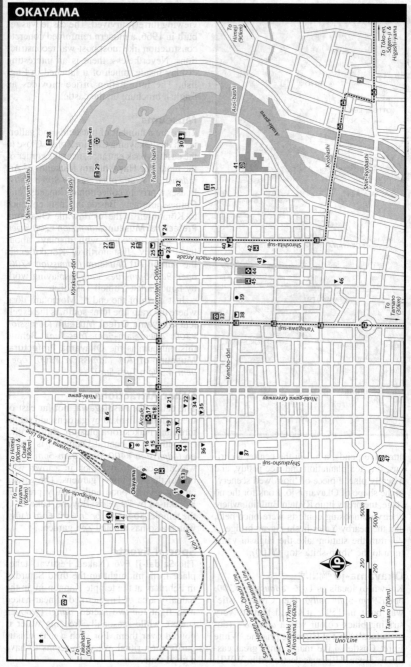

OKAYAMA

Places to Stay – Budget
Okayama Seinen-kaikan Youth Hostel
(☎ 252-0651; beds ¥2800; meals available)
is a 10-minute walk west of the train station. Nearer the station are **Matsunoki Ryokan** (☎ 253-411; per person with/without meals ¥8000/5000) and **Okayama Green Hotel** (☎ 225-7211; singles from ¥4500).

Places to Stay – Mid-Range & Top End
Okayama Castle Hotel (☎ 234-5678; singles/doubles ¥5500/11,000) is southeast of the station. **Washington Hotel Plaza** (☎ 231-9111; singles ¥7600) is found further down Momotarō-dōri and is decent value.

Okayama has no centrally located traditional accommodation. **Saiwai-sō** (☎ 254-0020; singles from ¥7090), near the station's west exit, is at least a business hotel with tatami (woven floor covering) rooms. Rates include two meals.

Granvia Hotel (☎ 233-3131; rooms from ¥9500) is next to the station and rather plush. **Hotel New Okayama** (☎ 223-8211; singles/

twins from ¥9000/14,000) is conveniently placed and has comfortable rooms.

Places to Eat & Drink
The small street parallel to, and immediately south of, Momotarō-dōri has a varied collection of places to eat. **Murasaki** is a popular robatayaki (yakitori-ya with a deliberately rustic, friendly, homey atmosphere) with a fully illustrated menu. **Pizza & Salad St Moritz** is nearby on the 2nd floor of the Communication Building.

Curiously, Okayama is brimming with Italian restaurants. There are two branches of **Pizza Patio** in town, one close to the station and one by Ote-machi arcade. Both have an excellent selection of pizzas and pasta dishes for ¥700. **Jolly Fox**, just north of the Chisan Hotel, is popular, woodsy and serves pastas, pizza and praiseworthy salads.

Zen is a good-value 'Beer and Herb' restaurant with an English-language menu. **Eikokuryō-Honkoku**, near Zen, is a trendy, graffiti-daubed izakaya (Japanese version of a pub).

Momotarō, the Peach Boy

Okayama-ken and neighbouring Kagawa-ken on the island of Shikoku are linked with the legend of Momotarō, the tiny 'Peach Boy' who emerged from the stone of a peach and, backed up by a monkey, a pheasant and a dog, defeated a three-eyed, three-toed, people-eating demon. There are statues of Momotarō at JR Okayama station and the main road of Okayama is named after him. Megi-shima, off Takamatsu in Shikoku, is said to be the site of the clash with the demon.

Momotarō may actually have been a Yamato prince who was deified as Kibitsuhiko. His shrine, the Kibitsu-jinja, is visited on the Kibi Plain bicycle ride (see the boxed text 'Kibi Plain Bicycle Route' later).

Bukkake-tei, in the Omote-machi arcade, is a renowned noodle shop. **Sushi Land – Marine Polis**, is a revolving sushi restaurant in the arcade behind the New Okayama Hotel.

Hunters and **Desperado** are both popular bars with the local foreign community.

Getting There & Away

Okayama airport is 20km northwest of the station. There are domestic flights to Japan's major cities and some international ones. A bus runs to/from the airport (¥680, 40 minutes).

Okayama is connected by the Sanyō Hikari *shinkansen* to Hakata (Fukuoka; ¥12,060, two hours) to the west, and to Osaka (¥5860, 45 minutes), Kyoto and Tokyo. The JR Hakubi line runs between Okayama and Yonago (¥4620, two hours) in Tottori-ken on the San-in coast.

When travelling west to Kurashiki, it's quicker to transfer from the *shinkansen* at Okayama than at Shin-Kurashiki. You also change trains at Okayama if you're heading to Shikoku across the Seto-ōhashi.

Getting Around

Getting around Okayama is a breeze since the Higashi-yama tram route will take you to all the main attractions. Trams charge a standard ¥140 to anywhere in town.

JR Rent-a-cycle offers bike hire for ¥350/600 per half-/full day; it's at the southeast end of the station building. Next door is the office of **Eki Rent-a-Car** (☎ 224-1037).

AROUND OKAYAMA

In a brave attempt to attract foreign visitors to the less frequently visited areas of the region, the Okayama Prefectural Government has established six **International Villas** scattered around the prefecture. These places are highly recommended. Rates are ¥2500 a night for members and ¥3000 for nonmembers, but since membership costs only ¥500, it's a good idea to sign up. The accommodation is of a very high quality, and the villas are well equipped, with cooking facilities, instructions in English on where to shop locally or where to find local restaurants and bicycles for visitors' use. The villas provide an ideal opportunity to get away and see a side to Japan that not many foreigners see.

The villa at **Fukiya**, in the mountains in the west of the prefecture, is modelled after the traditional *shoyu gura* (soya sauce storehouse) that once stood on the site. Fukiya is an old copper mining town.

The **Koshihata villa**, in the north of Okayama prefecture, is a renovated *kayabuki* (thatched-roof farmhouse) in a peaceful mountain valley surrounded by forest and rice paddies.

In central Okayama, the **Takebe villa** is on the side of the Asahi River. The modern buildings were designed by a local architect; nearby is Yahata Onsen, with a variety of hot baths.

Hattoji, high up on a plateau in the east of the prefecture, is home to the **Hattoji villa**, in a thatched-roof farmhouse. The building has a traditional clay *genkan* (foyer area where shoes are removed or replaced when entering or leaving a building) and features a sunken *irori* hearth in the floor, used for cooking and heating.

The **Ushimado villa**, on the Inland Sea coast east of Okayama city, is a modern glass-enclosed structure perched high above the old village. The views are stunning and there are a variety of activities in the area.

On **Shiraishi-jima** in the Inland Sea, south of Kasaoka in the west of the prefecture, is a modern villa with great views and easy access to the island's main beach and hiking trails. See the boxed text 'Taking it Easy in the Inland Sea' later in this chapter.

For reservations or more information, contact the **Okayama International Villa Group** (☎ 086-256-2535; **W** www.harenet .ne.jp/villa) at the Okayama International Exchange Centre. Members of the staff here speak English and they have English-language brochures for each villa.

KURASHIKI 倉敷
☎ 086 • pop 450,000

Kurashiki's claim to fame is a small quarter of picturesque buildings around a stretch of moat. There are a number of old black-tiled warehouses that have been converted into an eclectic collection of museums. Bridges arch over, willows dip into the water, carp cruise the canal and the whole effect is quite delightful – it's hardly surprising that the town is a favourite with tourists, or that *kurashiki* means 'warehouse village'.

In the feudal era, the warehouses were used to store rice brought by boat from the surrounding rich farmlands. As this phase of Kurashiki's history faded, the town's importance as a textile centre increased and the Kurabō Textile Company expanded. Ōhara Keisaburō, the owner of the company,

gathered together a significant collection of European art and, in the 1920s, opened the Ōhara Museum. It was the first of a series of museums that have become the town's principal attraction and is still its finest.

Beware that many of Kurashiki's prime attractions, and most of the eateries, close on Monday.

Orientation & Information

It's about 1km from the station to the old Bikan area and, if you walk, the typical urban Japanese scenery makes you wonder whether you are in the right town. But when you turn into the canal area, everything changes; Ivy Square is just beyond the canal. A number of shops along the main street, Kurashiki Chūō-dōri, sell Bizen-yaki.

The staff at the station's **information counter** (☎ 426-8681; *open 9am-6pm daily summer, 9am-5pm daily winter*) have very good English-language brochures and will make accommodation bookings. There is also a helpful tourist information office called the **Kurashikikan** (*open 9am-6pm daily summer, 9am-5pm daily winter*) near the bend in the canal. If you're in Kurashiki

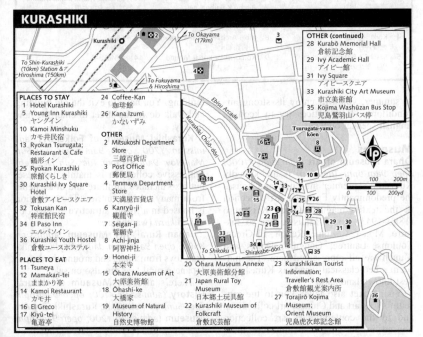

KURASHIKI

To Okayama (17km)
Kurashiki
To Shin-Kurashiki (10km) Station & Hiroshima (150km)
To Fukuyama & Hiroshima
Ebisu Arcade
Kurashiki Chūō-dōri
Tsurugata-yama kōen
To Shikoku
Shirakabe-dōri
Kurashiki-gawa

PLACES TO STAY	24	Coffee-Kan 珈琲館
1	Hotel Kurashiki	26 Kana Izumi かないずみ
5	Young Inn Kurashiki ヤングイン	
10	Kamoi Minshuku カモ井民宿	**OTHER**
13	Ryokan Tsurugata; Restaurant & Cafe 鶴形イン	2 Mitsukoshi Department Store 三越百貨店
25	Ryokan Kurashiki 旅館くらしき	3 Post Office 郵便局
30	Kurashiki Ivy Square Hotel 倉敷アイビースクエア	4 Tenmaya Department Store 天満屋百貨店
32	Tokusan Kan 特産館民宿	6 Kanryū-ji 観龍寺
34	El Paso Inn エルパソイン	7 Seigan-ji 誓願寺
36	Kurashiki Youth Hostel 倉敷ユースホステル	8 Achi-jinja 阿智神社
		9 Honei-ji 本栄寺
PLACES TO EAT	15	Ōhara Museum of Art 大原美術館
11	Tsuneya	18 Ōhashi-ke 大橋家
12	Mamakari-tei ままかり亭	19 Museum of Natural History 自然史博物館
14	Kamoi Restaurant カモ井	
16	El Greco	
17	Kiyū-tei 亀遊亭	

| **OTHER (continued)** |
28	Kurabō Memorial Hall 倉紡記念館
29	Ivy Academic Hall アイビー館
31	Ivy Square アイビースクエア
33	Kurashiki City Art Museum 市立美術館
35	Kojima Washūzan Bus Stop 児島鷲羽山バス停

20	Ōhara Museum Annexe 大原美術館分館	23	Kurashikikan Tourist Information; Traveller's Rest Area 倉敷館観光案内所
21	Japan Rural Toy Museum 日本郷土玩具館	27	Torajirō Kojima Museum; Orient Museum 児島虎次郎記念館
22	Kurashiki Museum of Folkcraft 倉敷民芸館		

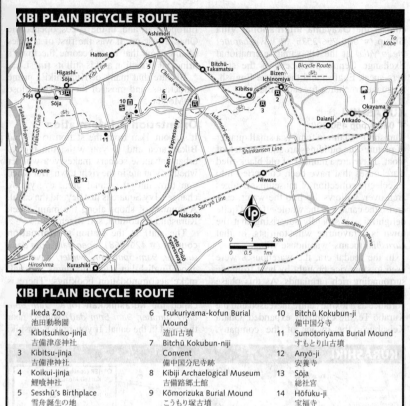

KIBI PLAIN BICYCLE ROUTE

1 Ikeda Zoo 池田動物園	6 Tsukuriyama-kofun Burial Mound 造山古墳	10 Bitchū Kokubun-ji 備中国分寺
2 Kibitsuhiko-jinja 吉備津彦神社	7 Bitchū Kokubun-niji Convent 備中国分尼寺跡	11 Sumotoriyama Burial Mound すもとり山古墳
3 Kibitsu-jinja 吉備津神社	8 Kibiji Archaelogical Museum 吉備路郷土館	12 Anyō-ji 安養寺
4 Koikui-jinja 鯉喰神社	9 Kōmorizuka Burial Mound こうもり塚古墳	13 Sōja 総社宮
5 Sesshū's Birthplace 雪舟誕生の地		14 Hōfuku-ji 宝福寺

in summer, you will enjoy its strong air-conditioner. Both offices try to keep an English-speaker on hand.

Museums

Ōhara Museum of Art *(admission ¥1000; open 9am-5pm Tues-Sun)* is undoubtedly Kurashiki's premier museum, and houses the predominantly European art collection of the textile magnate Ōhara Keisaburō (1880–1943). Rodin, Matisse, Picasso, Pissarro, Monet, Cézanne, Renoir, El Greco, Toulouse–Lautrec, Gauguin, Degas and Munch are all represented here. The museum's neo-classical facade is Kurashiki's best-known landmark.

Your ticket also takes you to the museum's folk art and Chinese art collections, and to the contemporary art collection housed in an annexe behind the main

building. You have to exit the old building and walk down the street to enter the new gallery.

Kurashiki Museum of Folkcrafts *(admission ¥700; open 9am-5pm Tues-Sun Mar-Nov, 9am-4.15pm Tues-Sun Dec-Feb)* impressive collection is mainly Japanese, but also includes furniture and other items from many other countries. The collection is housed in a rustic, attractive complex of linked *kura* (warehouses).

Japan Rural Toy Museum *(admission ¥500; open 9am-5pm daily)* displays folk-craft toys from Japan and around the world. Japanese rural toys are also on sale.

There's also the **Museum of Natural History** *(admission ¥100; open 9am-5pm Tues-Sun)*, as well as the **Kurashiki City Art Museum** *(admission ¥200; open 9am-5pm Tues-Sun)*. The recently restored **Ōhashi-ke**

Kibi Plain Bicycle Route

To access this excellent cycling course, take a local JR Kibi line train from Okayama for three stops to Bizen Ichinomiya, ride the 15km route to Sōja, drop off your bike and take a JR Hakubi line train back through Kurashiki to Okayama. Most of the course is on a cycling road that cars are not allowed to use. Bicycles cost ¥200 per hour or ¥1000 for the day.

Uedo Rental Bicycles (☎ 0862 84-2311; open 9am-6pm daily) is just outside JR Bizen Ichinomiya station. Pick up your bike and free Japanese-language route map here. You'll want to use this map in conjunction with the one here as it is a larger scale. Turn right, then right again to cross the railway line and in just 300m you reach **Kibitsuhiko-jinja**, the shrine which fronts a large pond. From here you soon pick up the bicycle path following a canal through the fields until it rejoins the road just before the temple, Fudenkai-ji. Just 200m further is the **Kibitsu-jinja**, where a wide flight of steps leads up to its attractive hilltop setting. The shrine, built in 1425, is unusual in having both the oratory and main sanctum topped by a single roof. The legendary Peach Boy, Momotarō, is connected with the shrine.

Pedalling on, you pass **Koikui-jinja**, which is also connected with the legendary figure Kibitsuhiko, and reach the huge 5th-century **Tsukuriyama-kofun Burial Mound**, rising like a rounded hill from the surrounding plain. You really need to be in a hot-air balloon or a helicopter to appreciate that it's really a 350m-long keyhole-shaped mound, not a natural hill. Just north of here is the **birthplace** of famous artist Sesshū (1420–1506). He was once a novice monk at **Hōfuku-ji**, which is 3km northwest of JR Sōja station.

Finally, there are the foundation stones of the **Bitchū Kokubun-niji Convent**, the nearby **Kibiji Archaeological Museum** (closed Mon), the excavated **Kōmorizuka Burial Mound** and Bitchū Kokubunji, with its picturesque five-storey pagoda. From here it's a few more kilometres into Sōja.

There are countless drink-vending machines along the way, and occasionally the bicycle path passes close enough to a main road to divert for food. On arrival at Sōja station, return your bicycle to **Araki Rental Bicycles** (☎ 0866 92-0233; open 9am-6pm daily). If this ride appeals to you, you can easily plot others on the network of tracks that cover the area.

(Ōhashi House; admission ¥300; open 9am-5pm Tues-Sun) is a reasonable example of a late 18th-century merchant's house. It's a shame, however, that the spacious tatami rooms aren't furnished.

Ivy Square アイビースクエア
The Kurabō textile factories have moved to more modern premises and the fine Meiji-era factory buildings (dating from 1889 and remodelled in 1974) now house a hotel, restaurants, shops and yet more museums. Ivy Square, with its ivy-covered walls and open-air café, is the centre of the complex.

The **Torajirō Kojima Museum** (admission ¥350; open 9am-5pm Tues-Sun) displays work by the local artist who helped Ōhara establish his European collection, along with some fine pieces from the Middle East in the associated **Orient Museum**.

Shrines & Temples
Achi-jinja tops Tsurugata-yama-kōen; the park overlooks the old area of town. The temples Honei-ji, Kanryū-ji and Seigan-ji are also found in the park.

Places to Stay
Kurashiki is a great town if you're keen to stay in a traditional Japanese inn, with an ample selection of *minshuku* (Japanese equivalent of a B&B) and ryokan. The information offices will help with advice and bookings.

Places to Stay – Budget
Kurashiki Youth Hostel (☎ 422-7355; beds ¥2800) is south of the canal area. It's a long climb to its hilltop location, but the view is great, the staff are very friendly and meals are available. **Kurashiki Young Inn** (☎ 425-3411; singles/twins ¥4000/7000) is quite a bargain. There are slightly more expensive rooms with bathrooms.

Places to Stay – Mid Range
There are several good-value *minshuku* conveniently close to the canal. **Tokusan Kan**

(☎ 425-3056; per person with meals ¥7000) is found near Ivy Square. **Kamoi Minshuku** (☎ 422-4898; per person with meals ¥7000) is easy to find at the bottom of the steps to the Achi-jinja. The Kamoi also has a popular restaurant by the canal.

The best place to look for hotels is around the popular canal area, or near the train station. The **Kurashiki Ivy Square Hotel** (☎ 422-0011; singles with/without bath ¥11,000/700, doubles or twins with bath ¥27,000, without bath ¥11,500-12,800) is part of the Ivy Square complex. **Hotel Kurashiki** (☎ 426-6111; singles/twins from ¥8500/16,000), in the station building, is JR-operated.

Places to Stay – Top End

Ryokan Tsurugata (☎ 424-1635; per person ¥15,000-35,000) is canal-side and dates from 1744. The ryokan's restaurant serves nonguests, mainly at lunchtime, and there is also a café. **Ryokan Kurashiki** (☎ 422-0730; per person ¥20,000), also by the canal, is old, elegant and expensive.

El Paso Inn (☎ 421-8282; doubles/twins from ¥9900/11,000) is a stylish hotel, again close to the canal.

Places to Eat

Don't leave eating out too late. Many of the restaurants you may notice at lunchtime will be closed by early evening. The day-trippers will have disappeared by then and many of the visitors staying in Kurashiki will be eating in their ryokan or minshuku. The following restaurants are in the Bikan area near the canal.

Kamoi Restaurant, located beside the canal, is run by the same people as the popular Kamoi Minshuku. **Mamakari-tei**, not far from the Ryokan Kurashiki, is a cosy, traditional spot named and famed for the local sardine-like fish it dishes out daily (served both raw and cooked). If you're not a sardine lover, try the tōfu manjū (fried tofu patties). **Tsuneya** is a welcoming place frequented more by locals than tourists. It specialises in sumibiyaki (charcoal-grilled dishes). **Kiyū-tei** is a steakhouse in an old traditional Japanese house at the northern end of the canal.

Kana Izumi is just back from the canal and is a pleasant, modern restaurant with plastic meals displayed in the window and a fully illustrated menu. There's a snack bar in Ivy Square and several restaurants in and near the square.

El Greco, by the canal near the Ōhara Museum (you can't miss its ivy-clad walls), is a fashionable place for coffee and cakes. It has an English-language menu. **Coffee-Kan** is another great spot for coffee – and coffee only. It's the cavernous tavern just beside the Ryokan Kurashiki.

There are also a number of places to eat along Kurashiki Chūō-dōri.

Getting There & Away

Kurashiki, only 17km from Okayama, is not on the shinkansen line, despite there being a Shin-Kurashiki station. Travelling westwards, it's usually faster to disembark at Okayama and take a San-yō line futsū (local train) to Kurashiki. If you're eastbound, get off at Shin-Kurashiki station, two stops on the San-yō line from Kurashiki.

Getting Around

It's only a 15-minute walk from the station to the canal area, where almost everything is within a few minutes' stroll. There are rental bicycles (¥350 for four hours, ¥650 per day) at the JR station.

TAKAHASHI 高梁
☎ 0866

Built along the banks of the Takahashi-gawa, this pleasant, small town, midway between Kurashiki and the central Chūgoku Expressway, gets few Western visitors even though it has a temple with a very beautiful Zen garden and is overlooked by an atmospheric old castle.

Orientation & Information

Bitchū-Takahashi is Takahashi's train station. The **tourist information counter** (☎ 22-6789; open 8am-6pm Mon-Sat) in the bus terminal beside the train station has some information in English as well as maps in Japanese. The temple, Raikyū-ji, is about 1km to the north of the station, on the east side of the tracks, though to get there you'll need to walk north on the west side and then cross over. Bitchū-Matsuyama-jō is about 5km north of the station, up a steep hillside. If you are not up to walking or cycling up there, a taxi should cost about ¥1500. There are bicycles for hire at the station.

Raikyū-ji 頼久時

The classic Zen garden (admission ¥300; open 9am-5pm daily) in this small temple is the work of the master designer Kobori Enshū and dates from 1604. It contains all the traditional elements of this style of garden, including stones in the form of turtle and crane islands, and a series of topiary hedges to represent waves on the sea. It even incorporates the mountain Atago-san in the background, as 'borrowed scenery'.

Bitchū-Matsuyama-jō 備中松山城

High above Takahashi stands Japan's highest castle (admission ¥300; open 9am-4pm daily) at 430m, a relic of an earlier period when fortresses were designed to be hidden and inaccessible, unlike later, much larger constructions designed to protect the surrounding lands. The road winds up the hill to a car park, from where it's a steep climb to the castle itself. On a dark and overcast day you can almost feel the inspiration for a film like Akira Kurosawa's Throne of Blood.

The castle was originally established in 1240 and in the following centuries was enlarged until it finally covered the whole mountaintop. It fell into disrepair after the Meiji Restoration, but the townspeople took over its maintenance from 1929. It was finally completely restored in the 1950s and has recently undergone further repairs and additions.

Other Attractions

Takahashi has some picturesque old samurai streets with traditional walls and gates, mainly in the area around Raikyū-ji. Around 500m to the north of Raikyū-ji is the Takahashi Bukeyashiki-kan (admission ¥300; open 9am-5pm daily), a well-preserved samurai residence dating from the 1830s. If you walk up to Raikyū-ji, you'll pass the Local History Museum (Kyōdō shiryō-kan; admission ¥300; open 9am-5pm daily), which is a fine wooden Meiji structure dating from 1904. It has displays of items associated with the area's mercantile and agricultural past.

Places to Stay & Eat

Takahashi Youth Hostel (☎ 22-3149; beds ¥2700) is located about 1km north of the station, just south of Raikyū-ji. Takahashi-shi Cycling Terminal (☎ 22-0135; ¥5000 including meals) is a 20-minute bus trip from the JR station. You can rent bicycles from the terminal (¥500 for four hours), but think twice before setting out to ride up to the castle! Midori Ryokan (☎ 22-2537; per person with/without meals ¥8000/4200) is a very attractive place and is just west of the station.

Most of the eating options are around the station.

Getting There & Away

Although Takahashi is not on any of the regular tourist routes through western Honshū, it would not take a great effort to to include it in an itinerary. The town is about 50km north of Okayama or 60km from Fukuyama. It's on the JR Hakubi line from Okayama (¥820, 50 minutes) so a stop could be made when travelling between Okayama on the San-yō coast and Yonago (near Matsue) on the San-in coast.

Hiroshima-ken
広島県

In addition to Hiroshima city's atomic bomb–related attractions, the prefecture has a number of other places of interest including nearby Miyajima, with the famed Itsukushima-jinja, the quaint fishing village of Tomo-no-ura and the natural setting of the Sandan-kyō gorge in the north of the prefecture.

SOUTHERN HIROSHIMA-KEN
広島県南部
Fukuyama 福山

Fukuyama is a modern industrial town of little interest to the tourist, but its convenient location on the Osaka-Hakata shinkansen route makes it a good jumping-off point for the pretty fishing port of Tomo-no-Ura; or for Onomichi, which in turn is a jumping-off point for the Inland Sea.

If you do have a few hours to spend in Fukuyama, you can visit the art gallery and museum, and the reconstructed castle. There's an information office (☎ 0849-22-2869; open 8.30am-5pm daily) in the station with helpful staff and English maps. If you are going on to Tomo-no-ura, pick up an English-language brochure/map at the information office before you go. There are plenty of hotels around Fukuyama Station should you need to stay.

Tomo-no-ura 鞆の浦

The delightful fishing port of Tomo-no-ura, with its numerous interesting temples and shrines, is just half an hour by bus south of Fukuyama. In feudal days, due to its central location on the Inland Sea, the port played an important role as host to fishing boats that would wait in the harbour to determine the next shift in the tides and winds before heading back out to sea.

Get your English-language map/brochure at the JR Fukuyama station information desk before you go, detailing Tomo-no-ura's sights; an extremely enjoyable few hours can be had on foot or by bicycle exploring the village. Rental bicycles are available (¥100 for two hours; ¥500 deposit) from next to the ferry building. To get your bearings, climb up to the ruins of the castle, Taigashima-jō.

Uonosato (admission free; open 9am-5pm Tues-Sun) is a snack-food factory that processes most of the locally-caught fish. You can watch the workers making prawn *sembei* crackers and even have a go at it yourself.

Ferries run on a regular basis to nearby Sensui-jima from the harbour area (¥240 return, five minutes), and there are some quiet walking trails and a camping area on the island.

Kokuminshukusha Sensui-jima (☎ 0849-70-5050; per person with meals ¥7300), on the island, is your best bet in the area for reasonably priced accommodation. Back on the mainland, **Tomo Seaside Hotel** (☎ 0849-83-5111; per person ¥12,000-35,000) is near the bus terminal, with prices depending on how extravagantly you want to be fed.

If you set aside a day to travel from Kurashiki to Hiroshima you can spend a pleasant morning exploring Tomo-no-ura, get back to Fukuyama for lunch, and visit Onomichi in the afternoon before heading to Hiroshima. It's only 14km from Fukuyama to Tomo-no-Ura; frequent buses run from bus stop No 11 outside JR Fukuyama station (¥530, 40 minutes).

Onomichi 尾道

Onomichi is an undistinguished-looking industrial town at first glance, hemmed in against the sea by a backdrop of hills. Yet along the base of this backdrop is a fascinating temple walk that is well signposted in English. An English-language map that details the route is available at the **information office** (☎ 0848-20-0005; open 9am-6pm daily) in the new building to the right as you leave the station. The walk itself is pleasant, although you'd have to be obsessed to want to visit all 25 temples and shrines. Rental bicycles are available for ¥500 per day – ask at the information office.

A lot of the nicer accommodation in Onomichi is very expensive, though there are a few business hotels that have reasonable rates, including **Onomichi Dai-Ichi Hotel** (☎ 0848-23-4567; singles ¥5500) and **Hotel Alpha 1 Onomichi** (☎ 0848-25-5600; singles from ¥5000). **Nishiyama Bekkan** (☎ 0848-37-3145; per person with meals ¥24,000) is top-notch and set in exquisite grounds.

Onomichi is at the Honshū end of the island-hopping Shimanami-kaidō bridge system to Shikoku. As such it is a gateway to Inno-shima, Ikuchi-jima and Ōmi-shima (see the Inland Sea section later).

The information office can supply its curiously named 'Setouchi Shimanami University Campus Map', an English-language brochure/map of the islands and the bridge links to Imabari on Shikoku; it details Shimanami's '100 Places of Scenic Beauty'. The islands can be reached by bus or ferry from Onomichi.

The Shin-Onomichi *shinkansen* station is 3km north of the JR San-yō line station. Buses connect the two stations, but it's easier to reach Onomichi on the JR San-yō line and change to the *shinkansen* line either at Fukuyama (to the east) or Mihara (to the west).

Mihara 三原

Mihara is on the San-yō *shinkansen* line and on the JR San-yō line. It is a convenient ferry departure or arrival point for Setoda on Ikuchi-jima, for other islands of the Inland Sea and for Shikoku. The harbour is directly south of the station. There is a **tourist information office** (☎ 0848-67-5877; open 8am-7pm Mon-Fri, 10am-6pm Sat & Sun) in the modern JR station, which can provide useful English-language brochures and maps of the area.

NORTHERN HIROSHIMA-KEN
広島県北部
Sandan-kyō 三段峡

The gorge, Sandan-kyō, about 60km northwest of Hiroshima, is an area that you could get lost in for a few days. A mostly paved trail follows the Shiki-gawa through an 11km gorge, providing visitors to Hiroshima with accessible, beautiful Japanese nature. The hike is very popular in autumn when the leaves change colour. Pick up a copy of Lonely Planet's *Hiking in Japan* for details.

Buses run from the Hiroshima bus centre to Sandan-kyō station (¥1400, two hours), at the southern end of the gorge. Trains also go to JR Sandan-kyō station (¥1100, two hours), which is the terminus of the JR Kabe line.

HIROSHIMA 広島
☎ 082 • pop 1,100,000

A busy, prosperous and attractive city, Hiroshima will forever be remembered for that terrible instant on 6 August 1945 when it became the world's first atomic-bomb target. Hiroshima's Peace Memorial Park is a constant reminder of that tragic day and attracts visitors from all over the world. Yet Hiroshima is far from a depressing place; on the contrary, its citizens have recovered from nuclear holocaust to build a thriving and internationally minded community.

The city's history dates back to 1589, when the feudal lord Mōri Terumoto named the city and established a castle.

Orientation & Information

Hiroshima (meaning 'broad island') is built on a series of sandy islands on the delta of the Ōta-gawa. JR Hiroshima station is east of the city centre and, although there are a number of hotels around the station, the central area, with its very lively entertainment district, is much more interesting.

Peace Memorial Park and most of the atomic bomb reminders are at the northern end of an island immediately west of the city centre.

Hiroshima's main east–west avenue is Heiwa-Ōdōri (Peace Boulevard), but the busiest road (with the main tram lines from the station) is Aioi-dōri, which runs parallel to Heiwa-Ō-dōri. Just south of Aioi-dōri, and again parallel to it, is the busy Hon-dōri shopping arcade. You should be able to find a bank easily.

Tourist Offices There are two information offices (☎ 261-1877; open 9am-5.30pm daily) in JR Hiroshima station (one at the north exit, the other at the south), where the English-speaking staff can make accommodation bookings. For the benefit of those arriving by sea, Hiroshima's port, Ujina, also has an information counter, but it's next to useless.

The most comprehensive information about the city and the island of Miyajima can be found at **Hiroshima Rest House** (☎ 247-6738; open 9.30am-6pm daily Apr-Sept, 8.30am-5pm daily Oct-Mar) in the Peace Park, next to Motoyasu-bashi; pick up a **Seto Inland Sea Welcome Card**, which can get you discounts on all sorts of things in Hiroshima, Yamaguchi and Ehime prefectures.

Finally, the **International Conference Centre Hiroshima** (☎ 247-9715; open 9am-7pm daily May-Nov, 10am-6pm daily Dec-Apr) also in the Peace Memorial Park, has English-language information, newspapers and satellite TV. Pick up the free bilingual map, *Welcome to Hiroshima* and check out W www.tourism.city.hiroshima.jp.

Post The **main post office** (open 9am-7pm Mon-Fri, 9am-5pm Sat, 9am-12.30pm Sun) is near the Shiyakusho-mae tram stop. **Higashi post office** (open 9am-7pm Mon-Fri, 9am-noon Sat), near the south exit of the station, is more convenient. **Naka post office** is next to the Sogō department store and is also handily located.

Email & Internet Access There are a number of Internet cafés in Hiroshima. **I Love You** runs operations on the 6th floor of the building (yellow sign down the side) immediately to the east of JR Hiroshima, and near the Peace Memorial Park end of the Hondori Arcade. **Pas.Time** is in the other end of the arcade.

Bookshops With a lot of second-hand English-language book bargains, **Book Nook** (☎ 244-8145; open 10am-9pm Mon-Fri, 10am-6pm Sat) has a handy notice board and friendly advice. It's near the Hiroshima Kokusai Hotel.

English-language books can also be found at **Kinokuniya bookshop** on the 6th floor of the Sogō department store.

WESTERN HONSHŪ

HIROSHIMA

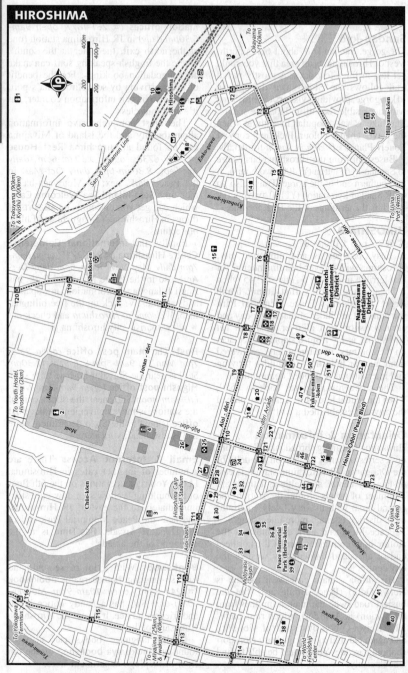

To Tokuyama (90km)
& Kyūshū (200km)

San-yō Shinkansen Line

JR Hiroshima

To Okayama (160km)

Enkō-gawa

Kyōbashi-gawa

To Ujina
Port (4km)

Shukkei-en

Hijiyama-kōen

Jonan-dōri

Moat

Moat

To Youth Hostel,
Hiroshima (2km)

Chūō-kōen

Aioi-bashi

Ryjo-dōri

Hiroshima Carp
Baseball Stadium

Aioi-dōri

Hon-dōri Arcade

Shintenchi
Entertainment
District

Nagarekawa
Entertainment
District

Ebisu-dōri

Chūō-dōri

Fukuro-machi-kōen

Heiwa-Ōdori (Peace Blvd)

To Ujina (4km)
Port (4km)

Motoyasu-gawa

To Yokogawa
terminus X, T16

To Miyajima (25km)
& Iwakuni (40km)

Tenma-gawa

Peace Memorial
Park (Heiwa-kōen)

Motoyasu-
bashi

To World
Friendship
Center

Ōta-gawa

HIROSHIMA

PLACES TO STAY
6 Hiroshima Ekimae Green Hotel
　広島駅前グリーンホテル
7 Hotel Sun Palace
　ホテルサンパレス
8 Hotel Yamato
　ホテルやまと
14 Mikawa Ryokan
　三河旅館
20 Hiroshima Kokusai Hotel
　広島国際ホテル
32 Hiroshima Green Hotel
　広島グリーンホテル
38 Minshuku Ikedaya
　民宿池田屋
40 Aster Plaza International Youth House
45 ANA Hotel Hiroshima
　広島全日空ホテル
51 Sera Bekkan
　世羅別館
52 Hiroshima Tōkyū Inn
　広島東急イン

PLACES TO EAT & DRINK
16 Harry's Bar
22 Andersen's
23 Sam's 13 Cafe
26 Pacela Building; Tandoor
41 Otis
44 Kemby's
47 Pizza Mario Expresso
49 Michan
　みっちゃん
50 Okonomi-mura
　お好み村
53 Mac
54 Jacara

OTHER
1 Pagoda of Peace
　平和塔
2 Hiroshima-jō
　広島城
3 Science & Culture Museum for Children
　こども文化科学館
4 Hiroshima Museum of Art
　広島美術館
5 Hiroshima Prefectural Art Museum
　県立美術館
9 Higashi Post Office
　東郵便局
10 Tourist Information
　観光案内所
11 Tourist Information
　観光案内所
12 I Love You Internet
13 Nippon Rent-a-Car
15 World Peace Memorial Cathedral
　世界平和記念堂
17 Mitsukoshi Department Store
　三越百貨店
18 Tenmaya Department Store
　天満屋百貨店
19 Fukuya Department Store
　福屋百貨店
21 Book Nook
24 I Love You Internet
25 Sogō Department Store; Sogō Bus Terminal; Kinokuniya Bookshop
　そごう百貨店；
　そごうバスターミナル；
　紀伊国屋書店
27 Naka Post Office
　中郵便局
28 KDD (International Telephone)
29 ANA
　全日空
30 A-Bomb Dome
　原爆ドーム
31 Atomic Bomb Hypocentre
　爆心地
33 Korean A-Bomb Memorial
　韓国人原爆犠牲者慰霊碑
34 Children's Peace Memorial
　原爆の子の像
35 Hiroshima Rest House
　広島市レストハウス
36 Cenotaph; Flame of Peace
　原爆慰霊碑；平和の灯
37 Laundrette
　コインランドリー
39 International Conference Centre Hiroshima
42 Peace Memorial Museum
　平和記念資料館
43 Peace Memorial Hall
　平和記念館
46 Former Bank of Japan Building
　旧日本銀行
48 Parco
55 Hiroshima City Museum of Contemporary Art
　広島現代美術館
56 Hiroshima City Manga Library
　広島まんが図書館

TRAM STOPS
T1 Hiroshima-ekimae
　広島駅前
T2 Enkōbashi
　猿こう橋
T3 Matoba-chō
　的場町
T4 Danbara ōhata-chō
　段原大畑町
T5 Inarimachi
　稲荷町
T6 Kanayama-chō
　銀山町
T7 Ebisu-chō
　胡町
T8 Hatchōbori
　八丁堀
T9 Tatemachi
　立町
T10 Kamiya-chō
　紙屋町
T11 A-Bomb Dome (Genbaku Dōmu)
　原爆ドーム前
T12 Honkawa-chō
　本川町
T13 Tōkaichimachi
　十日市町
T14 Dobashi
　土橋
T15 Teramachi
　寺町
T16 Betsuin-mae
　別院前
T17 Jogakuin-mae
　女学院前
T18 Shukkeien-mae
　縮景院前
T19 Katei Saibansho-mae
　家庭裁判所前
T20 Hakushima Line Terminus
　白島
T21 Hon-dōri
　本通
T22 Fukuro-machi
　袋町
T23 Chūden-mae
　中電前

The A-Bomb Dome 原爆ドーム

The symbol of the destruction visited upon Hiroshima is the A-Bomb Dome (Gembaku Dōmu), across the river from Peace Memorial Park. Declared a **Unesco World Heritage** site in December 1996, the building was the Industrial Promotion Hall until the bomb exploded almost directly above it. Its propped-up ruins, floodlit at night, have been left as an eternal reminder of the tragedy.

Peace Memorial Park
平和記念公園

Cross over into Peace Park (Heiwa-kōen), dotted with memorials including the **cenotaph** that contains the names of all the known victims of the bomb. The cenotaph frames the **Flame of Peace**, which will only be extinguished once the last nuclear weapon on earth has been destroyed, and the A-Bomb Dome across the river.

Just north of the road crossing through the park is, for many, the most poignant memorial in the park – the **Children's Peace Memorial**, inspired by leukaemia victim Sadako. When Sadako developed leukaemia at 10 years of age she decided to fold 1000 paper cranes, the symbol of longevity and happiness in Japan, and was convinced that if she could achieve that target she would recover. She died before reaching her goal, but her classmates folded the rest. The story inspired a nationwide bout of paper-crane folding, which continues to this day. Strings of paper cranes from all over Japan are kept on display around the memorial.

Nearby is the recently relocated **Korean A-bomb Memorial**. Great numbers of Koreans were shipped from their homeland to work as slave labourers in Japanese factories during WWII, and more than one in 10 of those killed by the atomic bomb was a Korean.

Peace Memorial Museum
平和記念資料館

The A-bomb museum *(admission ¥50; open 9am-6pm daily May-Nov, 9am-5pm daily Dec-Apr)*, as the Peace Memorial Museum is commonly known, expresses a simple message driven home with sledgehammer force. The exhibits tell the story of the bomb and the destruction it wrought on Hiroshima and its people. It is a must for all visitors.

Hiroshima-jō 広島城

Hiroshima-jō *(admission ¥320; open 9am-4.30pm daily Oct-Mar, 9am-5.30pm daily Apr-Sept)*, also known as 'Carp Castle', was originally constructed in 1589; however, much of it was dismantled following the Meiji Restoration, leaving only the donjon, main gates and turrets. The remainder was totally destroyed by the bomb and rebuilt in modern ferro-concrete in 1958.

Shukkei-en 縮景園

Modelled after Xi Hu (West Lake) in Hangzhou, China, Shukkei-en *(admission ¥250; open 9am-6pm daily Apr-Sept, 9am-5pm daily Oct-Mar)* dates from 1620 but was badly damaged by the bomb. The garden's name literally means 'shrunk' or 'contracted view', and it attempts to re-create grand vistas in miniature. It may not be one of Japan's celebrated classic gardens, but it makes for a pleasant stroll.

Next to the garden is the splendid **Hiroshima Prefectural Art Museum** *(admission ¥500; open 9am-5pm Tues-Sun)*, featuring Salvador Dali's 'Dream of Venus' and the staggering artwork of Hirayama Ikuo, who was in the city during the bombing. A ticket for entry to garden and museum is ¥600 (enter the garden through the museum).

Other Attractions

Hijiyama-kōen, directly south of JR Hiroshima station, is noted for its cherry blossoms in spring, and hosts two worthy attractions: **Hiroshima City Museum of Contemporary Art** *(permanent exhibition admission ¥320; open 10am-5pm Tues-Sun)* has excellent displays by Japanese and foreign modern artists, while the **Hiroshima City Manga Library** *(admission free; open 10am-5pm Tues-Sun)* is a small comic museum.

Hiroshima Museum of Art *(admission ¥1000; open 9am-5pm daily)* and the **Science & Culture Museum for Children** *(admission free, planetarium ¥440)* are both in Chūō-kōen (Central Park), just southwest of the castle.

There are a variety of lunch and dinner cruises that run from Hiroshima to Miyajima and back, while on Monday and Friday from March to September, day cruises operate through the Inland Sea. Ask at one of the information offices for details.

A love of baseball is not a prerequisite for having a great time at a **Hiroshima Carp** game. It's just as much fun watching the rowdy, organised enthusiasm of the crowd, especially when the Tokyo Giants come to town. Ask at the information office if there are any home games while you are in Hiroshima. The **stadium** is just north of the Peace Park and outfield tickets start at ¥1500.

Miyajima (see the Miyajima information section later) can be easily visited as a day trip from Hiroshima. The tram company has a special '1 Day Passport' that includes a return tram trip to Miyajima-guchi, return ferry to Miyajima, and unlimited daily tram transport for just ¥840. You can buy the ticket at various big hotels, various tram stops, and at the Peace Park Rest House information office.

Special Events

On the 6 August, the anniversary of the atomic bombing, a memorial service is held in the Peace Memorial Park and thousands of paper lanterns for the souls of the dead are floated down the Ōta-gawa from in front of the A-bomb Dome.

Places to Stay – Budget

Hiroshima Youth Hostel (☎ 221-5343; beds ¥2440; meals available) is inconveniently located about 2km north of the city centre. A much better option is to stick near the centre of town.

Minshuku Ikedaya (☎ 231-3329; rooms per person ¥4200) is convenient and set up to cater to foreigners. It's on the western side of Peace Memorial Park in a quiet area, an easy walk via the park from the town centre. **Mikawa Ryokan** (☎ 261-2719; singles/doubles ¥3500/6000) is a short stroll from JR Hiroshima station. Both of these places have Japanese-style rooms.

World Friendship Center (☎ 503-3191; per person with breakfast ¥3500) is run by an antinuclear nonprofit organisation. The information offices can supply a brochure and instructions on how to get there.

Aster Plaza International Youth House (☎ 247-8700; per person ¥3620) is a municipal cultural centre a block south of the Peace Park. It's supposed to be for students, but puts up foreign tourists in its sizable Western-style rooms. You'll need to show your passport.

Places to Stay – Mid-Range

Near the station are **Hotel Yamato** (☎ 263-6222; singles/doubles ¥6000/12,000), overlooking the Enkō-gawa; **Hotel Sun Palace** (☎ 264-6111; singles/doubles ¥6000/10,000) right next door; and **Hiroshima Ekimae Green Hotel** (☎ 264-3939; singles/doubles ¥6300/10,000).

In central Hiroshima, **Hiroshima Kokusai Hotel** (☎ 248-2323; singles/doubles ¥7000/12,500) is in a very convenient loca-

tion. **Hiroshima Green Hotel** (☎ 248-3939; singles/doubles ¥6200/9200), down-at-heel, is redeemed by its proximity to the riverside and the Peace Memorial Park.

Places to Stay – Top End

Sera Bekkan (☎ 248-2251; rooms with 2 meals from ¥12,000) is a centrally located traditional Japanese ryokan near Fukurō-machi-kōen.

ANA Hotel Hiroshima (☎ 241-1111; singles/twins or doubles from ¥11,000/20,000) is a luxurious hotel in central Hiroshima. **Hiroshima Tōkyū Inn** (☎ 244-0109; singles/doubles ¥8700/16,000) is at the northwest corner of Heiwa-Ōdōri and Chūō-dōri.

Places to Eat & Drink

Hiroshima is noted for its seafood (particularly oysters), as well as hiroshima-yaki, a local version of okonomiyaki (egg-based savoury pancakes) made with soba (thin buckwheat noodles) and fried egg. **Okonomi-mura** (open 11am-2am daily) is an amazing grouping of some 30 minirestaurants on the 2nd, 3rd and 4th floors of the Shintenchi Plaza Building behind the Parco department store. All specialise in hiroshima-yaki (most under ¥1000) and the boisterous atmosphere alone is worth the visit. A few have English menus and display photos of meals. **Michan** on Chūō-dōri is another popular spot to taste hiroshima-yaki.

The **Pacela building**, next to Sogo Department Store, has all sorts of eateries, with the entire 7th to 10th floors set aside for restaurants. Most have plastic replicas to help you choose. **Tandoor**, on the 7th floor, is a popular Indian restaurant with good lunchtime specials.

The popular Mario Italian restaurants serve pasta and pizza and are a great bet for an inexpensive lunch or dinner. **Pizza Mario Expresso** is a local favourite across from Fukurō-machi-kōen. **Andersen's**, is a popular restaurant complex, with an excellent bakery section – it's good for an economical breakfast and for watching the world pass by from the tables in the front window. **Otis** has Tex-Mex food near the Aster Plaza south of the Peace Park.

Hiroshima has an estimated 4000 bars. Shintenchi and Nagarekawa are the entertainment districts.

Mac, much loved by resident *gaijin*, has an astoundingly wide selection of CDs and LPs, while **Sam's 13 Cafe** is reputed to have the widest range of beers in the city.

Jacara is a popular dance club, while **Kemby's** is an American-style beer-and-burger place, popular despite being off the party track in Ōtemachi.

Harry's Bar is a bit more upmarket.

Getting There & Away

Hiroshima's main airport is 40km east of the city with bus connections to/from Hiroshima station (¥1300). There are flights to/from all Japan's major cities, and some international flights. Hiroshima Nishi airport is 4km southwest of the city centre on the coast. It handles more regional services and there are buses to/from the city centre (¥240).

Hiroshima is an important stop on the Tokyo–Osaka–Hakata *shinkansen* route. Hiroshima to Hakata (Fukuoka) takes 1¼ hours and costs ¥8700; to Osaka it's 1½ hours (¥9950); and to Tokyo five hours (¥18,050).

The JR San-yō line passes through Hiroshima onwards to Shimonoseki, hugging the coastline much of the way. The ordinary local services move along fairly quickly and are the best way to visit the nearby attractions of Miyajima and Iwakuni. Long-distance buses connect Hiroshima with all the major cities.

Hiroshima is an important port with ferry connections to other cities. The Hiroshima to Matsuyama ferry (¥2500, 2¾ hours, 10 daily) and hydrofoil (¥5800, 1¼ hours, 10 daily) services are a popular way of getting to or from Shikoku. Ferries also operate to Imabari on Shikoku.

Getting Around

Hiroshima has an extensive, easy-to-use and rather fun streetcar service that will get you pretty well anywhere you want to go for a flat fare of ¥150 (¥100 on the short No 9 route). There is even a tram that runs all the way to Miyajima port (¥270). If you have to change trams to get to your destination, you should ask for a *norikae-ken* ticket. Pay when you get off.

Rental bicycles are available at **Nippon Rent-a-car** (☎ 264-0919) near the station, but it doesn't have many bikes.

MIYAJIMA 宮島
☎ 0829 • pop 22,000

Correctly known as Itsuku-shima, Miyajima is easily reached from Hiroshima. The famous 'floating' torii (Shintō shrine gate) of the shrine Itsukushima-jinja is one of the most photographed tourist attractions in Japan – it's classified as one of Japan's 'three best views' (the other two are the sandspit at Amanohashidate on the northern coast of Kyoto prefecture, and the islands of Matsushima near Sendai, northern Honshū). Apart from the shrine, the island has some other interesting temples, some good walks and even some remarkably tame deer that wander the streets – watch for signs warning of the dangers of fraternising with horned species.

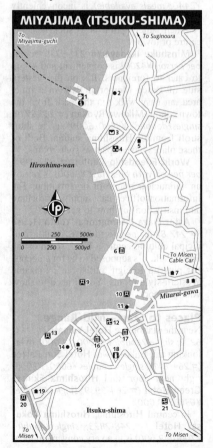

MIYAJIMA (ITSUKU-SHIMA)

To Miyajima-guchi

To Suginoura

Hiroshima-wan

0   250   500m
0   250   500yd

To Misen Cable Car

Mitarai-gawa

Itsuku-shima

To Misen

To Misen

Orientation & Information

There's an **information counter** (☎ 44-2011; open 9am-6pm daily) in the ferry terminal. The staff are enthusiastic and can give you a map and brochure in English. Turn right as you emerge from the building and follow the waterfront to get to the shrine and the centre of the island's small town. The shopping street, packed with souvenir outlets and restaurants, is a block back from the waterfront.

Itsukushima-jinja 厳島神社

The shrine (admission ¥300; open 6.30am-sunset daily), which gives the island its real name, dates from the 6th century (in its present form from 1168). Its pier-like construction is a result of the island's holy status: commoners were not allowed to set foot on the island and had to approach the shrine by boat, entering through the **floating torii** out in the bay. Much of the time, however, the shrine and torii are surrounded not by water but by mud. The view of the torii, which is immortalised in thousands of travel brochures, requires a high tide.

On one side of the floating shrine is a **floating nō stage** built by a Mōri lord. The orange torii, dating from 1875 in its present form, is often floodlit at night.

The **Treasure House** (admission ¥300; open 8.30am-5pm daily) has a collection of painted sutra scrolls dating from the 12th century that is only rarely on display and the exhibits are not of great interest except, perhaps, to the scholarly.

Temples & Historical Buildings

Topping the hill immediately north of Itsukushima-jinja is **Senjō-kaku** (Pavilion of 1000 Mats; admission ¥100; open 9am-4pm daily), built in 1587 by Toyotomi Hideyoshi. This huge and atmospheric hall is constructed with equally massive timber pillars and beams, and the ceiling is hung with paintings. It looks out to a colourful five-storey pagoda dating from 1407. Senjō-kaku should have been painted to match but was left unfinished when Toyotomi died.

Miyajima has numerous other temples, including **Daigan-ji** just south of the shrine, which is dedicated to the god of music and dates from 1201. The colourful and glossy **Daishō-in**, just behind the town, can be visited on the way down Misen (see the Misen section following). This is a temple with everything: statues, gates, pools, carp, you name it. The rituals performed at the main Itsukushima-jinja are also administered by Daigan-ji. South of Itsukushima-jinja is the picturesque pagoda, **Tahō-tō**.

Miyajima History & Folklore Museum 歴史民俗資料館

Set in a fine garden, this museum (admission ¥300; open 8.30am-5pm Tues-Sun) combines a 19th-century merchant's home with exhibits on trade in the Edo period, as well as displays connected with the island. There's an excellent English-language brochure.

Misen 弥山

The ascent of Misen (530m) is the island's finest walk, although the uphill part of the

MIYAJIMA (ITSUKU-SHIMA)

PLACES TO STAY		2	Hall of Industrial Traditions (Handicraft Display) 伝統産業会館	13	Kiyomori-jinja 清盛神社
5	Guest House Kikugawa 菊がわ			14	Aquarium 水族館
7	Miyajima Grand Hotel Arimoto 宮島グランドホテル 有もと	3	Post Office 郵便局	16	Miyajima History & Folklore Museum 歴史民俗資料館
8	Iwasō Ryokan 岩惣	4	Castle Ruins 城跡	17	Treasure House 宝物館
15	Mizuhasō 水羽荘	6	Senjō-kaku 千畳閣	18	Tahō-tō Pagoda 多宝塔
19	Miyajima Mori-no-yado 宮島森の宿	9	Floating Torii 大鳥居		
		10	Itsukushima-jinja 厳島神社	20	Ōmoto-jinja 大元神社
OTHER		11	Nō Stage 能舞台	21	Daishō-in 大聖院
1	Ferry Terminal; Information 宮島港；観光案内所	12	Daigan-ji 大願寺		

round trip can be avoided by taking the two-stage ropeway or cable car (¥900/1500 one way/return). The cable car leaves you about a 20-minute walk from the top. Around the cable-car station there are monkeys as well as deer. On the way up look for the **giant pot** said to have been used by the Buddhist saint Kōbō-daishi (AD 774–835), and kept simmering ever since! It's in the smaller building beside the main temple hall, also said to have been used by the founder of the Shingon sect.

There are superb views from the summit and a variety of routes leading back down. The descent takes a good hour and walking paths also lead to other elevated points on the island, or just follow the gentle stroll through **Momiji-dani** (Maple Valley), which leads to the cable-car station.

A four-hour hike of Misen is detailed in Lonely Planet's *Hiking in Japan*.

Other Attractions

Miyajima also has an **aquarium** featuring 'panda dolphins', a popular beach, a seaside park and, across from the ferry landing, a display of **local crafts** in the Hall of Industrial Traditions.

Special Events

Festivals on the island include **fire-walking** rites by the island's monks on 15 April and 15 November, and the **Kangensai Boat Festival** in summer (held on different dates every year).

Places to Stay

There is little inexpensive accommodation on Miyajima. **Miyajima-guchi Youth Hostel** (☎ 56-1444; beds ¥2730; meals available) is a nearby option, on the mainland near the ferry terminal and JR Miyajima-guchi station.

If you can afford to stay on the island, it's well worth it – you will be able to enjoy the island in the evening, minus the day-tripping hordes. Cheapest options are **Mizuhaso** (☎ 44-0173; per person ¥6000) across the road from the aquarium, and **Guest House Kikugawa** (☎ 44-0039; per person ¥6000, with 2 meals ¥10,000), a moderately priced place just back from the ferry landing. **Miyajima Mori no yado** (☎ 44-0430; per person with 2 meals ¥8700) is southwest of the shrine.

At large, pleasant **Iwasō Ryokan** (☎ 44-2233) and **Miyajima Grand Hotel Arimoto** (☎ 44-2411) you'll pay at least ¥15,000 per person with meals. There are a number of expensive hotels and ryokan along the waterfront. The information office is happy to help with accommodation bookings.

Although there are many restaurants and cafés on Miyajima, most cater to day-trippers and close early.

Getting There & Away

The mainland ferry terminal for Miyajima is near Miyajima-guchi station on the JR San-yō line between Hiroshima and Iwakuni. Miyajima trams from Hiroshima terminate at the Hiroden-Miyajima stop by the ferry terminal. The tram (¥270, 70 minutes) takes longer than the *futsū* (¥400, 25 minutes), but runs more frequently and can be boarded in central Hiroshima.

From the terminal, ferries shuttle across to Miyajima (¥170, 10 minutes). One of the ferries is operated by JR, so JR pass-holders should make sure they use this one. High-speed ferries (¥1460, 20 minutes, eight times daily) operate direct to Miyajima from Hiroshima's Ujina Port.

Miyajima can be easily visited as a day trip from Hiroshima (see the Hiroshima section earlier). The tram company has a special '1 Day Passport' that includes a return tram trip to Miyajima-guchi, return ferry to Miyajima and unlimited tram transport for the day for just ¥840. You can buy the ticket at various big hotels, various tram stops, and at the Peace Park Rest House information office.

Getting Around

Bicycles can be rented from the JR office in the ferry building, but walking around is quite easy. A free bus operates from in front of the Iwasō Ryokan to the Misen cable-car station.

The Inland Sea
瀬戸内海

The Inland Sea (Seto-Nai-Kai) is bounded by the major islands of Honshū, Kyūshū and Shikoku, with four narrow channels connecting it with the ocean. To the west the Kanmon-kaikyō separate Honshū from Kyūshū and lead to the Sea of Japan; to the south, leading to the Pacific, the Hoya-kaikyō separate Kyūshū from Shikoku; at the other end of Shikoku, the Naruto-kaikyō and Kitan-kaikyō straits flow each side of Awaji-shima.

The most interesting area of the Inland Sea is the island-crowded stretch from Takamatsu (Shikoku) and Okayama west to Hiroshima. There are said to be more than 3000 islands (depending on what you define as an 'island'), and there seems to be just as many different ferry services linking them.

There are a number of ways of seeing the Inland Sea. One is to simply travel through it on the numerous ferries criss-crossing or even running its full length. Alternatively, visit individual islands for a first-hand experience at your own pace of a part of Japan which, though rapidly changing, is still way slower than the fast-moving metropolitan centres.

It is even possible to visit some islands by bus. There are now three separate bridge systems linking Honshū with Shikoku, with the western-most, known as the Setonai Shimanami Kaidō, crossing 10 bridges and nine islands. Needless to say, increasing accessibility is doing a lot to change lifestyles in the Inland Sea.

Information

Brochures, maps and general tourist information are readily available, but Donald Richie's *The Inland Sea*, originally published in 1971 and now available in paperback, makes an excellent introduction to the region. Although much of the Inland Sea's slow-moving and easy-going atmosphere has disappeared since his book was published (and indeed he emphasised its rapidly changing nature even at that time), it still provides some fascinating insights.

Getting Around

Besides the regular ferry services between Honshū, Shikoku and the various islands, **SKK** *(Seto Naikai-kisen;* ☎ *082-253-1212)* offers day cruises on the Inland Sea from Hiroshima. These are seasonal, on certain days of the week, and are declining in number.

The Japan Travel Bureau (JTB) and other tour operators also have seasonal overnight cruises running in the Inland Sea. Check with local tourist offices for details on times and current prices.

It is possible to take a ferry through the Inland Sea from Kansai to Kyūshū. Unless you check the timings carefully though, you may end up going through the Inland Sea at night, and by just travelling through, you won't get a chance to taste the lifestyle on any of the islands. **Kansai-kisen** *(*☎ *06-6572-5181;* Ⓦ *www.kanki.co.jp Japanese only)* has daily Osaka–Beppu ferries, while **Diamond Ferry** *(*☎ *078 857-9525)* runs between Kōbe and Oita on Kyūshū.

Chapter Organisation

This section on the Inland Sea starts with its largest island, Awaji-shima, in the east. It then works its way westwards. Islands that are close to and associated with particular places on Honshu or Shikoku are included in those sections. For instance, Miyajima is included in the Hiroshima section and Megi-jima in the Kagawa section of the Shikoku chapter.

AWAJI-SHIMA 淡路島
☎ 0799

Awaji-shima, the Inland Sea's largest island, forms the region's eastern boundary and connects with Honshū via the **Akashi Kaikyō-ōhashi** – at 3.91km, the longest suspension bridge in the world. Life on the island has changed considerably since the bridge opened, and Awaji-shima is now part of a road link from Kansai to Shikoku. At the southern end of the island, the **Naruto-ōhashi** spans the Naruto-kaikyō (Naruto Channel) across the well known **Naruto Whirlpools** to connect Shikoku with Awaji-shima (see the Tokushima section of the Shikoku chapter).

The northern part of the island will be long remembered as the epicentre of the massive January 1995 earthquake which claimed over 6000 lives, mostly in and around the Kōbe area. The island also provided most of the material used to build the island on which Kansai's international airport sits in Osaka Bay.

The island is relatively flat and has some good beaches. It was the original home of *ningyō jōruri* puppet theatre, which preceded the development of bunraku theatre. Short performances are given several times daily in the small puppet theatre in Fukura, at the southern end of the island. Near the Kōshien ferry terminal, at **Onokoro Ai-rando-kōen** (admission ¥1200; open 9.30am-5.30pm Wed-Sun), a bizarre grouping of miniature replica world-sightseeing attractions (constructed 1/25 their original size) include the Taj Mahal, the Parthenon, Pisa's leaning tower and other international favourites.

Of the island's beaches, Ōhama, about halfway down the east coast is sandy and attracts crowds in summer, while Goshiki, about halfway down the west coast, is better for swimming and known for its spectacular sunsets.

SHŌDO-SHIMA 小豆島
☎ 0879 • pop 40,000
Famed for its vast olive groves and as the location for the Japanese film classic *Twenty-Four Eyes*, Shōdo-shima translates literally as 'island of small beans'. A very mountainous island, it offers a number of interesting places to visit and makes an enjoyable escape from big-city Japan. The second-largest island in the Inland Sea, Shōdo-shima even has a miniature version

of neighbouring Shikoku's 88 Temple Circuit. Administratively, Shōdo-shima is part of Shikoku's Kagawa-ken.

Orientation & Information
Tonoshō, at the western end of the island, is the usual arrival point from Takamatsu, Uno or Okayama and makes a good base from which to explore the island, although there are another six ports with ferry connections to here and there. At Tonoshō you'll find an **information office** (☎ 62-5300; open 8.30-5.15pm daily) just inside the ferry building, with a very good English-language brochure on everything the island has to offer.

Coastal Area
Moving around the island anticlockwise, the island's olive-growing activities are commemorated at **Olive Park** (admission free; open 8.30am-5pm daily) on the south coast, where there are fake Grecian ruins and olive chocolate for sale. **Shōdo-shima Folk Museum** (admission ¥310; open 9am-5pm Tues-Sun) is right there, as is the brand new **Sun Olive Onsen** (admission ¥700),

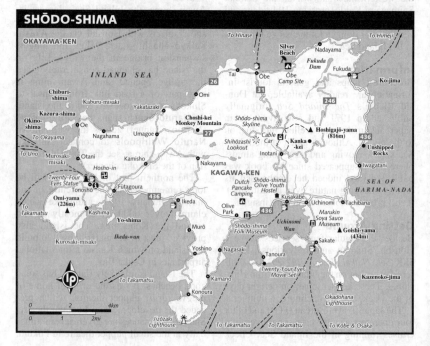

SHŌDO-SHIMA

featuring stunning views from a variety of baths, a restaurant and a training room. Shōdo-shima is serious about olives – it even has Milos in Greece as a sister island.

Between Kusakabe and Sakate, cool off with a soya sauce–flavoured ice cream at the **Marukin Soya Sauce Historical** museum.

Just north of Sakate is the turn-off to the small village of **Tanoura**, the site of the village school in the novel *Twenty-Four Eyes* and the later film of the same name. The real school and its movie set version are both open for inspection *(combined ticket ¥750; open 9am-5pm daily)*. A statue of the film's teacher and her pupils, known as the 'Group Statue of Peace', stands outside the Tonoshō ferry terminal.

South of Fukuda, on the eastern side of the island, huge rocks cut for Osaka-jō now lie jumbled down a cliff-side at **Iwagatani**. The unused rocks are classified as *zanseki* (rocks left over) or *zannen ishi* (rocks that were sorry not to be in time for shipment) and each bears the seal of the general responsible for their quarrying and dispatch. The northeastern corner of the island is still one big quarry to this day. More unshipped castle rocks can be seen on the northern coast at **Omi**, along with the site of a shipyard used by Toyotomi Hideyoshi.

There are a number of swimming beaches around the island.

Central Mountains

The **Kanka-kei cable car** (one way/return ¥700/1250) is the main attraction in the central mountains, making a spectacular trip up through the Kanka-kei gorge. An alternative for keen walkers is a 3½-hour return trip climbing up the Omote 12 views track and down the Ura 8 views trail. From the top of the cable car, you can hike to the island's high point, Hoshigajō-yama (816m), in an hour.

As you descend on the road from the top towards Tonoshō, you pass **Choshi-kei Valley & Monkey Park** *(admission ¥370; open 8.10am-4.50pm daily)* where monkeys from around the world are kept in cages. Wild monkeys come for a daily feed – they are used to people and will come right up to you.

Between Tonoshō and Otani is the temple, **Hosho-in**, famed for its huge juniper tree that is said to have been planted by Emperor Ojin 1500 years ago. The circumference of the trunk is 17m.

Shōdo-shima Pilgrimage

Shōdo-shima's 88 sacred places are known to Buddhist pilgrims as a miniature version of the Shikoku pilgrimage (see the boxed text '88 Sacred Temples of Shikoku' in the Shikoku chapter). The pilgrimage covers 150km and takes about a week to complete on foot. Many of the sacred places are in secluded mountain settings that keen hikers will enjoy getting to. If you're keen you can call the **Shōdo-shima Pilgrim Association** *(☎ 62-0227 in Japanese only)*.

Special Events

The village, Shikoku-mura, at Yashima, just outside Takamatsu on Shikoku, has a village kabuki theatre that was originally from Shōdo-shima. **Farmers' kabuki performances** are still held on the island on 3 May at Tonoshō and on Sports Day (around 10 October) in other centres.

Places to Stay & Eat

Shōdo-shima Olive Youth Hostel *(☎ 82-6161; beds ¥3100; meals available)* is on the south coast. **Uchinomi-chō Cycling Terminal** *(☎ 82-1099; per person with/without meals ¥2835/5250)*, in Sakate at the ferry terminal, rents bikes (¥500 for four hours, ¥50 each extra hour).

Tonoshō has a variety of hotels, ryokan and *minshuku*, particularly along the road running straight back from the waterfront. **Maruse Minshuku** *(☎ 62-2385; rooms with/without 2 meals ¥6000/4500)* is neat and tidy and is next to the post office.

If you want something more upmarket, **Resort Hotel Olivean** *(☎ 65-2311; from ¥13,000)* has it all.

There are a number of camping grounds around the island, including **Dutch Pancake Camping** *(☎ 82-4616)*, up behind the Sun Olive Onsen. It's run by a Dutchman and his Japanese wife who are planning, but have yet to build, a pancake café on site.

Getting There & Away

There is a variety of ferry services from Honshū and Shikoku to various ports on the island. Popular jumping-off points include Uno on Honshū (trains go to Uno from Okayama) and Takamatsu on Shikoku. There are high-speed ferries (¥1000, 35 minutes) and regular ferries (¥500, around an hour) from Takamatsu to Tonoshō.

Getting Around

There are plenty of bus services around the island and a host of bus tours (¥3000 to ¥5000) that seem to set off with every ferry arrival at Tonoshō. Alternatively, you can rent a car, a scooter, a mountain bike or a bicycle from agencies near the Tonoshō ferry terminal. Ask exactly where at the information office. With adequate time, touring by bicycle presents a great way to see the island.

NAO-SHIMA 直島

Nao-shima is an island that is well worth a look, if not an overnight stay. The island features the **Benesse Island Nao-shima Cultural Village** (W www.naoshima-is.co .jp/english), which features some stunning art and architecture in a project that was originally started by the Fukutake Shoten publishing company to display its collection of contemporary art. Fukutake Shoten became the Benesse Corporation (hence the name) and managed to get award-winning architect Andō Tadao to design its **Nao-Shima Contemporary Art Museum** (admission ¥1000; open 8am-5pm daily). It seems a little strange to come to Nao-shima to see

them, but there are works here by Andy Warhol, David Hockney and Jasper Johns among others.

Stranger still is the opportunity to stay in an encampment of Mongolian pao (circular tents) at the **Nao-shima International Campground** (☎ 087-892-2030; per person ¥4500) which is part of the complex. There's also Benesse House and its annex for upmarket accommodation – check out rates on the village website and preview each room and its particular commissioned piece of art. The museum also restores and preserves old houses on the island, with a contemporary artist turning a house into a work of art that is then exhibited permanently. Three such houses have been completed for viewing.

Although much closer to Honshū, Nao-shima is officially part of Shikoku's Kagawa-ken. It can be reached from Takamatsu in Kagawa by ferry (¥510, one hour), or from Uno in Okayama-ken (¥280, 20 minutes). Uno is at the end of the JR Uno line from Okayama. Travelling via Nao-shima is a good way to get from Honshū to Shikoku, or vice versa.

INNO-SHIMA 因島

Inno-shima and the islands Ikuchi-jima and Ōmi-shima are now linked with Honshū and Shikoku as three of the nine islands crossed as part of the Setonai Shimanami Kaidō

Taking it Easy in the Inland Sea

If you want to experience the Inland Sea on some smaller islands, unconnected to the mainland by bridges, consider Shiraishi-jima and Manabe-jima (administratively, the islands are part of Kasaoka City). The starting point is Kasaoka, about 40 minutes west of Okayama on the JR San-yō line and it is only a five-minute stroll from Kasaoka station down to the rickety ferry terminal.

From there, take a ferry to Shiraishi-jima (¥500, 35 minutes or ¥900, 20 minutes; nine daily) where the Okayama International Villa Group has one of its villas. The modern building is in an idyllic location with great views and access to the beach, rocky coastline and hiking trails. Costs are ¥3000 per person per night for nonmembers. You can get more information and make bookings by contacting the organisation directly (see the Around Okayama section earlier).

Next up is the ferry to Manabe-jima (¥450, 35 minutes) where **Santora Youth Hostel** (☎ 0865-68-3515; W www.oka.urban.ne.jp/home/suntora; beds ¥2900; meals available) is beachside and set to take care of your every need. Residents call their island hana-no-shima (flower island) – due to its mild, frost-free climate, a large variety of flowers are cultivated.

When you've had enough of island life, head back to Kasaoka or carry on to Tadotsu in Kagawa-ken on Shikoku by ferry. At the time of research, the only connections to Tadotsu were on Tuesdays, Thursdays and Saturdays. The ferry company is **Sanyō Kisen** (☎ 0865-69-7080), and should you be in need of accommodation in Kasaoka, **Kasaoka-ya Youth Hostel** (☎ 0865-63-4188; beds ¥2900; meals available) is an eight-minute walk from JR Kasaoka station.

system. Famed for its flowers and abundance of fruit, Inno-shima is connected by bridge to Mukai-shima and on to Onomichi. The island has a moderately interesting **pirate castle** (admission ¥310; open 9am-5pm daily) and, atop Shirataki-yama, there are 500 rakan statues, the disciples of Buddha. On the first Saturday and Sunday in September, there's the lively **Suigun Furusato Matsuri** with boat races and jindaiko drumming.

IKUCHI-JIMA 生口島
☎ 08452
Ikuchi-jima is known for its citrus groves and beaches, including the man-made Sunset Beach on its west coast that may not rival Hawaii's Sunset Beach for waves, but definitely defeats it in terms of summer swimmers.

Setoda, the main town on the island, is noted for the temple, **Kōsan-ji** (combined ticket ¥1000; open 9am-4pm daily), a wonderful exercise in kitsch. Local steel-tube magnate Kanemoto Kōzō devoted a large slab of his considerable fortune – starting in 1935 – to re-creating numerous important temples and shrines, all in this one spot and all in grateful homage to his mother. If you haven't got time to visit the originals, this is an interesting substitute.

The admission ticket for Kōsan-ji includes the **1000 Buddhas Cave**, the **art museum** and the **treasure house**. It costs another ¥300 to visit Kōzō's mother's quarters. The extraordinary 1000 Buddhas Cave includes an introductory 'hell', as well as winding tunnels and spiral stairs lined with 1000 Buddhas.

To get to the temple, turn right as you leave the boat landing then left up the shop-lined 600m-long street. **Setoda History & Folklore Museum** (admission free; open 10am-4pm Wed-Mon) is at the start of this street. Halfway up the same street you can turn left towards a temple on the hillside; around the back of this temple and much further up the hill is **Kōjō-ji**, dating from 1403, with a three-storey pagoda and fine views over the island. You can also get there by turning left from the pier (towards the bridge) and heading straight up the hill.

Places to Stay
Setoda Shimanami Youth Hostel (☎ 7-3137; beds ¥2500; meals available) is one of the island's two youth hostels. **Setoda Youth**

Hostel (☎ 7-0224; beds ¥2700; meals available), a short walk from the dock, is easily spotted as it has a huge rainbow painted on one side. It offers similar prices.

Getting There & Away
You can get to Ikuchi-jima by ferries from Mihara or Onomichi on Honshū. Mihara has the widest range of services, some continuing on to Ōmi-shima and Imabari on Shikoku. It pays to shop around at the harbour area. Fares range from ¥300 to ¥1400, depending on the speed and luxury of the ferry. No matter how you want to travel, you shouldn't have to wait more than an hour. It seems a bit of a shame to do so, but yes, you can get to Setoda by bus from Onomichi.

ŌMI-SHIMA 大三島
This hilly island boasts the mountain god's treasure house, **Ōyamatsumi-jinja** (admission including Kaiji Museum ¥1000; open 8.30am-5pm daily), which commanded much respect from the Inland Sea's pirates between the 12th and 16th centuries. In fact, the pirates were more like a local navy than real pirates but, until Toyotomi Hideyoshi brought them to heel, they wielded real power in these parts. Along the way, reputedly Japan's largest collection of armour was built up in the shrine's treasure house. Around 80% of the armour and helmets designated as National Treasures are held here, but despite the importance of the collection, it's probably of more interest to those with a specific interest in Japanese military accoutrements than to the average visitor.

In an adjacent building known as the **Kaiji Museum** there is a boat used by Emperor Hirohito in his marine science investigations, together with a natural-history exhibit. The shrine's history is actually one of the most ancient in Japan, ranking with the shrines at Ise and Izumo.

Miyaura port is a 15-minute walk from the shrine.

Getting There & Away
You can get to Ōmi-shima by ferry service from Onomichi, Mihara or Setoda on the neighbouring island of Ikuchi-jima; and also from Takehara, further west on the Honshū coast. There is a highway bus that

links Ōmi-shima with Onomichi; the bus station is on the eastern side of the island below the Tatara Ōhashi, the bridge that links Ōmi-shima with Ikuchi-jima.

Yamaguchi-ken

山口県

Yamaguchi, at the western end of Honshū, straddles both the southern San-yō coast and the northern San-in coast. The great bridge Kintai-kyō at Iwakuni is a southern highlight, while Shimonoseki acts as the gateway to Kyūshū and Korea. The northern stretch includes the historically important town of Hagi and, in the central mountains, the vast cave at Akiyoshi-dai. Pick up a **Seto Inland Sea Welcome Card** at one of the information offices for discounts on all sorts of things in Yamaguchi, Hiroshima, and Ehime prefectures.

IWAKUNI 岩国

☎ 0827 • pop 110,000

The five-arched bridge, Kintai-kyō, is Iwakuni's major attraction, although the town also has a US military base (an 'unattraction' perhaps?) and a number of points of interest in the Kikko-kōen area, near the bridge.

Orientation & Information

Iwakuni has three widely separated areas, which at first can be somewhat confusing for visitors. To the far west of the town centre is the Shin-Iwakuni *shinkansen* station, which is totally separate from the rest of town. Its **tourist information office** (☎ 46-0656; open 10.30am-4.30pm daily) is very helpful. In the central area is the old part of town with the bridge, the samurai quarter and the castle. There is a **Tourist Information Center** (open 8.30am-5.30pm daily) located near the bridge. To the east, in the modern part of town, the JR Iwakuni station has a helpful **Tourist Information Center** (☎ 21-6050; open 9am-5pm Tues-Sun), as well as hotels, restaurants, bars and other conveniences.

At the bridge, the cable car can be seen climbing the mountains on the far side. The castle overlooks the town from the right of the cable car.

Kintai-kyō 錦帯橋

Kintai-kyō (Brocade Sash Bridge) was built in 1673 and washed away by a flood in 1950. It was authentically rebuilt in 1953, albeit with some cunningly concealed steel reinforcements. The bridge is immediately recognisable by its five steep arches. In the feudal era only samurai could use the bridge, which connected their side of the river with the rest of the town; commoners had to cross the river by boat. Today visitors pay a ¥220 toll to walk across and back. The ticket office at the entrance to the bridge also sells an all-inclusive *setto-ken* ticket (¥840) that covers the bridge (normally ¥220 on its own), the return cable-car trip (normally ¥540), and entry to Iwakuni-jō (normally ¥260), a saving of ¥180 for all three. The bridge and castle are floodlit nightly.

Samurai Quarter

Some traces remain of the old samurai quarter on the far side of the bridge. Beside the bottom of the cable car, is the **Iwakuni Historical Museum** (admission ¥500; open 9am-5pm Fri-Wed), with its extensive collection of samurai armour and equipment. It's said to be one of the best collections in Japan, but is unlikely to impress those already suffering from artefact overload.

The old samurai quarter is now part of **Kikko-kōen** and includes picturesque moats and remnants of feudal buildings.

Iwakuni-jō 岩国城

The original castle was built on the mountain between 1603 and 1608, but seven years later the *daimyō* was forced to dismantle it and move down to the riverside. The castle was rebuilt in 1960 during Japan's great castle-reconstruction movement; but modern Japanese castles were built for tourism, not warfare, so it now stands photogenically high on the hillside, a short distance in front of its initial hidden location. The well beside the path indicates where it was originally built.

You can get to the castle by cable car (one way/return ¥320/540), or by the road (for walking only) from beside the youth hostel. See the Kintai-kyō section earlier for details of all-inclusive tickets.

Other Attractions

Iwakuni is famed for its albino snakes, said to embody the spirit of the goddess of good

Ema (votive plaques), Miyajima

Statues of Buddha's disciples, Daigan-ji, Miyajima, western Honshū

A-Bomb Dome, Hiroshima, western Honshū

Statue of a mother with children cowering from the Hiroshima blast

Seto-ōhashi, leading from Honshū to Shikoku

The 'Floating Torii', Itsukushima-jinja, Miyajima, western Honshū

fortune, Benzaiten; visitors come to pray here for good luck in business. The **Imazu White Snake Viewing Facility** on the far side of the bridge (admission free; open 9am-5pm daily) has four of these strange-looking creatures.

Ukai (cormorant fishing) takes place at Kintai-kyō every night from June to August, except when rain makes the water muddy or on full-moon nights. For ¥3500 you can watch this colourful and exciting method of fishing using birds.

Places to Stay
Central Iwakuni is not an overly enticing place to spend the night, though there are a number of business hotels near the JR station. There's virtually nothing around Shin-Iwakuni station.

Iwakuni Youth Hostel (☎ 43-1092; beds ¥2700; meals available) is close to most of the attractions on the samurai-quarter side of the Kintai-kyō bridge.

There are a number of traditional ryokan located near Kintai-kyō, including **Hangetsu-an** (☎ 41-0021; per person with 2 meals ¥9000). **Shiratame Ryokan** (☎ 41-0074; per person with 2 meals ¥18,000), nearby, is a little more luxurious. Both ryokan offer local specialities, such as *ayu* (sweetfish) and the unusual nine-hole *renkon* (lotus-root). Ask the information office to make a booking.

Getting There & Away
Iwakuni is only 44km from Hiroshima. Shin-Iwakuni station is on the *shinkansen* line, while JR Iwakuni station is on the JR San-yō line. Kintai-kyō is about 5km from either. Buses shuttle back and forth between JR Iwakuni station and the bridge (¥240), and between Shin-Iwakuni station and the bridge (¥280).

YAMAGUCHI 山口
☎ 083 • pop 140,000
During the Sengoku-jidai, or Warring States period (1467–1573), Yamaguchi prospered as an alternative capital to chaotic Kyoto. In 1550 the Jesuit missionary Francis Xavier paused for two months in Yamaguchi on his way to the imperial capital, but quickly returned to the safety of this provincial centre when he was unable even to find the emperor in Kyoto! In the following cen-

turies, Yamaguchi took turns with Hagi as the provincial capital and, like Hagi, Yamaguchi played an important part in the Meiji Restoration. Today it's a pleasantly peaceful town with a number of interesting attractions.

Orientation & Information
Ekimae-dōri is the main shopping street, running straight up from the station and crossing the main shopping arcade before it reaches Route 9. There's a very helpful **information office** (☎ 933-0090; open 9am-6pm daily) on the 2nd floor of the train station, with English-language brochures. If you're desperate to get on a computer, ask here and they'll either let you on theirs or tell you where the latest Internet café is. (At the time of writing, the only one had just closed.)

Xavier Memorial Chapel
ザビエル記念聖堂
The chapel overlooks the town centre from a hilltop in Kameyama-kōen. Built in 1952 to commemorate the 400th anniversary of Francis Xavier's visit to the city, it burned down under mysterious circumstances in 1991 and was rebuilt in 1998.

Art Gallery & Museums
At the foot of the hill stands the **Yamaguchi Prefectural Art Museum** (admission ¥190; open 9am-4.30pm Tues-Sun), where frequent special exhibitions are held. Just north is the **Yamaguchi Prefectural Museum** (admission ¥130; open 9am-4.30pm Tues-Sun). **Yamaguchi History Museum** (admission ¥100; open 9am-5pm Tues-Sun) is just off Route 9.

Kōzan-kōen & Rurikō-ji
香山公園・瑠璃光寺
Further north again from the town centre is Kōzan-kōen, where the five-storey pagoda of Rurikō-ji, dating from 1404, is picturesquely sited beside a small lake. A small **museum** (admission ¥300; open 9am-5pm daily) has photos and details of all 40 Japanese five-storey pagodas, plus a map indicating where they're located. It's illuminated at night. Rurikō-ji, with which the pagoda is associated, is also in the park and was moved here from a small village.

The park's teahouse was also moved here, where the Yamaguchi *daimyō* held

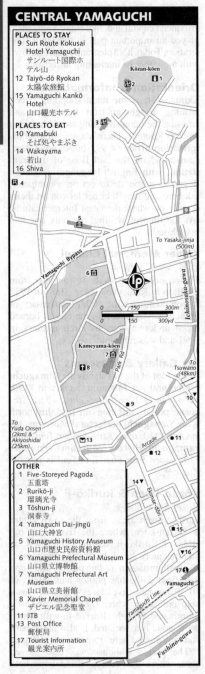

CENTRAL YAMAGUCHI

PLACES TO STAY
9   Sun Route Kokusai
    Hotel Yamaguchi
    サンルート国際ホ
    テル山
12 Taiyō-dō Ryokan
    太陽堂旅館
15 Yamaguchi Kankō
    Hotel
    山口観光ホテル

PLACES TO EAT
10 Yamabuki
    そば処やまぶき
14 Wakayama
    若山
16 Shiva

OTHER
1   Five-Storeyed Pagoda
    五重塔
2   Rurikō-ji
    瑠璃光寺
3   Tōshun-ji
    洞春寺
4   Yamaguchi Dai-jingū
    山口大神宮
5   Yamaguchi History Museum
    山口市歴史民俗資料館
6   Yamaguchi Prefectural Museum
    山口県立博物館
7   Yamaguchi Prefectural Art
    Museum
    山口県立美術館
8   Xavier Memorial Chapel
    ザビエル記念聖堂
11 JTB
13 Post Office
    郵便局
17 Tourist Information
    観光案内所

secret talks in the house under the pretext of holding a tea ceremony. The park is also the site of the temple, **Tōshun-ji**, and the graves of the Mōri lords.

Jōei-ji 常栄寺

Jōei-ji, 3km northeast of the JR station, was originally built as a house and is notable for its beautiful Zen **garden** *(admission ¥300; open 8am-5pm daily)* designed by the painter Sesshū. Visitors bring *bentō* (boxed lunches) and sit on the veranda to eat while admiring the garden.

Other Attractions

Just west of the city is the hot-spring resort of **Yuda Onsen**; it's rather developed and concrete-clad. You can use the baths at **Ryokan Kamefuku** *(admission ¥750)*, **Kokuminshukusha Koteru** *(admission ¥350)* and, for a taste of luxury, at the traditional ryokan **Umenoya** *(admission ¥800)*. The town also has two *ashi no yu* (foot baths), where you can sit and bathe your feet for free. Buses run regularly from Yamaguchi station (10 minutes).

North of Route 9, the river **Ichinosaka-kawa** has a particularly pretty stretch lined with cherry trees. Naturally, they're at their best during the spring blossoming time, but they're also lovely on summer evenings when large fireflies flit through the trees.

During the **Gion Matsuri** festival, held 20–27 July, the Sagi-mai (Egret Dance) is held at Yasaka-jinja. On 6–7 August, during the Chōchin Tanabata Matsuri, 10,000 decorated lanterns illuminate the city.

Ogōri, only 10km southwest of Yamaguchi, is of no particular interest except as a place to change trains. It is at the junction of the San-yō Osaka-Hakata *shinkansen* line and the JR Yamaguchi line, which passes through Yamaguchi and continues on to Tsuwano and Masuda on the San-in coast.

Places to Stay

The information office is happy to make accommodation bookings.

Yamaguchi Youth Hostel *(☎ 928-0057; beds ¥2600; meals available)* is about 4km from Miyano station (two stops east of Yamaguchi). The information office in Yamaguchi station can tell you how to get there by bus from outside the station. You can rent bicycles at the hostel and a bicycle tour map is available.

Sun Route Kokusai Hotel Yamaguchi (☎ 923-3610; singles/twins ¥6000/7900) is one of the usual assortment of modern business hotels. **Yamaguchi Kankō Hotel** (☎ 922-0356; per person ¥6000-7000) and **Taiyō-dō Ryokan** (☎ 922-0897; per person ¥6000-7000) both have two meals included in their rates.

Yuda Onsen, 10 minutes from the station by bus, has a number of traditional ryokan, including the expensive but historically interesting **Matsudaya Hotel** (☎ 922-0125; per person ¥22,000-39,000). An extremely good deal in Yuda Onsen is **Saekiya Ryokan** (☎ 922-0838; per person with breakfast ¥5000) just back off the main street, with large traditional rooms.

Places to Eat

The arcade off Ekimae-dōri has lots of restaurants, coffee bars and fast-food places. **Yamabuki**, a few streets northeast from the arcade and Ekimae-dōri, is a pleasant old *soba* shop where you can eat well for ¥500.

There are a number of good places along Ekimae-dōri. **Shiva** is an excellent Indian eatery, with lunch specials and a fully illustrated menu. **Wakayama** has reasonably priced, excellent seafood.

Getting There & Away

The Yamaguchi *futsū* service connects the city with Ogōri (¥230, 15 minutes), which is on the main Tokaidō *shinkansen* line. JR and Bōchō Kōtsu buses run between Yamaguchi and Hagi (¥1680, 70 minutes), and between Yamaguchi and Akiyoshi-dai (¥1130, one hour).

Getting Around

Bicycles can be rented from the train station, a good idea since the town's attractions are somewhat scattered (it's 8km just to Jōei-ji and back) and the traffic is reasonable. The first two hours cost ¥310, or it's ¥820 daily.

AKIYOSHI-DAI 秋吉台
☎ 0837

The rolling Akiyoshi-dai tablelands are about halfway between Yamaguchi and Hagi on the northern San-in coast. The green fields are dotted with curious rock spires, and

beneath this picturesque plateau are hundreds of limestone caverns, the largest of which, **Akiyoshi-dō** (admission ¥1200; open 8.30am-4.30pm daily) is open to the public.

Akiyoshi-dō is of interest principally for its size (the stalagmites and stalactites are not particularly noteworthy). In all, the cave extends about 10km, with a river flowing through it and a pathway running through for about 1km. At the midpoint of the cave trail you can take a lift up to the surface, where there is a lookout over the surrounding country. There are entrances to the cave at both ends of the pathway as well as at the lift. Buses run between the two ends if you do not want to retrace your steps.

The cave and tablelands are both pretty interesting, but get less so if shared with busloads of visitors. If you're feeling claustrophobic in the cave, go for a wander out on the plentiful hiking trails on Japan's largest karst plateau.

Places to Stay

Akiyoshi-dai Youth Hostel (☎ 62-0341; beds ¥2600; meals available) is large and somewhat institutional.

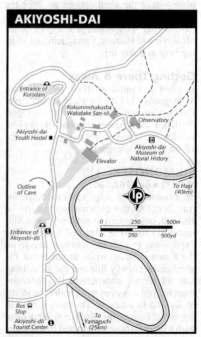

AKIYOSHI-DAI

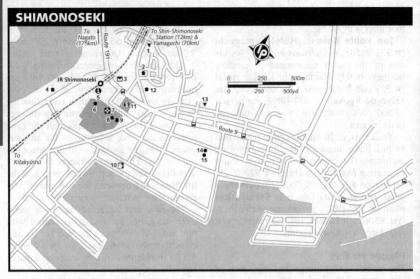

SHIMONOSEKI

There is a variety of accommodation around the cave area. **Kokuminshukusha Wakatake Sansō** (☎ 62-0126; rooms with/without meals ¥6400/4500) is a good value place – take the meal options as, once the day-trippers have left, open restaurants are hard to find. You would probably be better off staying in Hagi or Yamaguchi and visiting here as a day trip.

Getting There & Away

It takes a around an hour by bus from Yamaguchi (¥1130) or Hagi to the cave. Buses also run to the cave from Ogōri (¥1070, 1¼ hours) and Shimonoseki (¥1730, two hours). If you've got a JR pass, take the JR bus from Yamaguchi.

SHIMONOSEKI 下関
☎ 0832 • pop 260,000

Shimonoseki is an important crossroads for travellers. At the extreme western tip of Honshū, only a narrow strait separates Shimonoseki from the island of Kyūshū. The expressway crosses the Kanmon-kaikyō on the Kanmon-bashi; while another road, the *shinkansen* railway line and the JR railway line all tunnel underneath. If you really want to, you can even walk under the straits to Kyūshū in a tunnel! The town is also an important connecting point to South Korea, with a daily ferry service to and from Pusan.

Shimonoseki has a number of points of interest and some excellent, if potentially deadly, cuisine.

Information

There's a **tourist information office** (☎ 32-8383; open 9am-7pm daily) in JR Shimonoseki station and another (☎ 56-3422; open 9am-7pm daily) in the Shin-Shimonoseki *shinkansen* station, two stops north of the JR station on the JR Sanyō line. Beside JR Shimonoseki station is the large Sea Mall Shimonoseki shopping centre, and just east is the new Kaikyō Yume Tower (which looks like a midget skyscraper topped by a futuristic billiard ball). A ¥600 ticket to the tower gets you to the **observatory** (open 9.30am-9.30pm daily) on the 30th floor, where you can take in an impressive 360° view of the surrounding scenery.

Located on the 4th floor of the International Trade Building (which is next to the tower) is the **International Exchange Room 'Global Salon'** (open 10am-8pm Tues-Sun), where there is a small library and also Internet access (¥300 per 30 minutes). Shimonoseki was the venue for the 2002 International Whaling Convention – an interesting choice considering the city's history as a whaling port – and meetings took place in the conference rooms on the top floors.

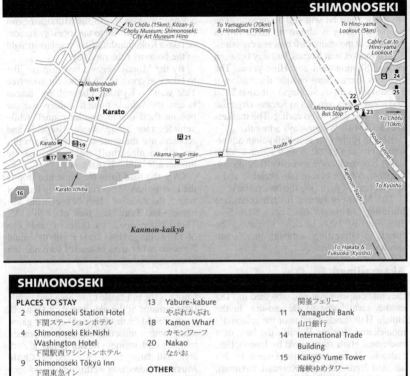

SHIMONOSEKI

To Chōfu (15km); Kōzan-ji;
Chofu Museum; Shimonoseki;
City Art Museum Hino

To Yamaguchi (70km)
& Hiroshima (190km)

To Hino-yama
Lookout (5km)

Cable Car to
Hino-yama
Lookout

Nishinohashi
Bus Stop

20▼

Karato

Mimosusōgawa
Bus Stop

To Chōfu
(10km)

Karato

19

17   18

Karato Ichiba

Akama-jingū-mae

Route 9

Kanmon-bashi

To Kyūshū

16

Kanmon-kaikyō

To Hakata &
Fukuoka (Kyūshū)

Road Tunnel

Kanmon-kaikyō

SHIMONOSEKI

PLACES TO STAY		
2	Shimonoseki Station Hotel 下関ステーションホテル	
4	Shimonoseki Eki-Nishi Washington Hotel 下関駅西ワシントンホテル	
9	Shimonoseki Tōkyū Inn 下関東急イン	
12	Hotel 38 Shimonoseki; Internet café ホテル38 下関	
17	Shimonoseki Grand Hotel 下関グランドホテル	
24	Kaikyō View Shimonoseki 海峡ビューしものせき	
25	Hinoyama Youth Hostel 下関火の山ユースホステル	

PLACES TO EAT		
1	Yasumori Yakinikuya やすもり焼肉や	

13	Yabure-kabure やぶれかぶれ	
18	Kamon Wharf カモンワーフ	
20	Nakao なかお	

OTHER		
3	Post Office 郵便局	
5	Tourist Information 観光案内所	
6	Daimaru Department Store 大丸	
7	Sea Mall Shimonoseki Shopping Centre シーモール下関	
8	Daiei Department Store	
10	Ferry Terminal; Kampu Ferry Service フェリーターミナル；	

	関釜フェリー	
11	Yamaguchi Bank 山口銀行	
14	International Trade Building	
15	Kaikyō Yume Tower 海峡ゆめタワー	
16	Kaikyōkan Aquarium 海峡館水族館	
19	Former British Consulate (Museum) 旧英国領事館	
21	Akama-jingū 赤間神宮	
22	Walking tunnel to Kyūshū	
23	Dan-no-ura Memorial 壇ノ浦記念	

There is also an Internet café (¥500 per 30 minutes) located on the 1st floor of the Hotel 38 Shimoseki, about a two-minute walk from the station.

Money If you are arriving from Korea, note that there is no money exchange in the ferry terminal. The information office in the station can give you a list of places where you can change money, and of international ATM services.

Karato Ichiba 唐戸市場

A highlight for any trip to Shimonoseki is an early rise and a visit to the Karato Ichiba fish markets, although it's not recommended for squeamish types. The interesting stuff is on show from 4am to 8am, so if you like to sleep in, forget it. The markets actually kick off at 2am for those in the industry, but the public is welcome from 4am, the earlier you get there the better. It's a great opportunity to try sashimi for breakfast (in the restaurant on the 2nd floor), and the fish doesn't get any fresher – a fair bit will still be moving. The people-watching is almost as much fun as goggling at the many different sea creatures.

The market is at Karato, halfway between central Shimonoseki and Hino-yama. The first bus leaves from outside the station at 5.55am (6.14am on Sundays) – it costs ¥190 and takes seven minutes to Karato. Organise a taxi if you want to go earlier. The markets are closed two Wednesdays a month.

Also in Karato, the new **Kaikyokan aquarium** *(admission ¥1800; open 9.30am-5.30pm daily)* has stacks of impressive fish, shows, displays, a huge blue-whale skeleton and a special tank of *fugu* (see the boxed text).

The Meiji-era former **British consulate building** *(admission free; open 9am-5pm Tues-Sun)* of 1906 is close at hand. The facade is interesting, although there's not much of interest inside.

Akama-jingū 赤間神宮
Bright vermilion, this shrine is dedicated to the child emperor Antoku, who died in 1185 in the naval battle of Dan-no-ura. In the Hōichi Hall stands a statue of the splendidly monickered 'Earless Hōichi', the hero of a traditional ghost story retold by Japanophile, Lafcadio Hearn (otherwise known by his adopted Japanese name, Koizumi Yakumo). The shrine is between Karato and Hino-yama. Get off the bus (¥230, 10 minutes) at the Akama-jingū-mae bus stop.

Hino-yama 火の山
About 5km northeast of JR Shimonoseki station there are superb views over the Kanmon-kaikyō from the top of 268m-high Hino-yama. Walk, drive or travel by ropeway

(one way/return ¥200/400) to the top. Take a Ropeway-mae bus to the Mimosusōgawa bus stop and walk up to the ropeway station, or take a Kokuminshukusha-mae bus straight to the bottom of the ropeway.

By the Mimosusōgawa bus stop are lifts to take you down to the tunnel for your free 1km walk to Kyūshū. The walkers' tunnel is also the vehicle tunnel: walkers use the bottom third of the circular tunnel, while vehicles race along above. Bicycles and scooters use the same section as the walkers. It's a nice stroll around the seaside promenade on the Kyūshū-side.

Over the road from the same bus stop is the Dan-no-ura Memorial, marking the spot where the decisive clash between the Minamoto and Taira clans took place in 1185. This is where one of the ladies of the House of Taira plunged into the sea with the infant Emperor in her arms instead of surrendering to the enemy.

Chōfu 長府
Chōfu is the old castle town area and, while little remains of the old coastal castle itself, there are old earth walls and samurai gates, along with a museum and some important temples and shrines. **Kōzan-ji** has a Zen-style hall dating from 1327, and the **Chōfu Museum** *(admission ¥200; open 9am-5pm Tues-Sun)* is also in the temple grounds.

Shimonoseki City Art Museum Hino *(admission ¥200; open 9.30am-4.30pm Tues-Sun)*, also in Chōfu, features contemporary Japanese artists.

Places to Stay – Budget
Near the station, the **Hotel 38 Shimonoseki** *(☎ 23-1138)* has it all. There's an Internet

---

Fugu

Fugu are known in English as 'globefish' or 'blowfish', and you won't have to go to the Karato Ichiba to see your first in Shimonoseki. The city revels in its reputation as the *fugu* capital of Japan, and paintings and sculptures of the fish are everywhere.

Eating raw *fugu* is considered somewhat adventurous since the fish's liver and other organs contain tetrodotoxin, a poison that makes cyanide look like chicken feed. Chefs in *fugu* restaurants need to train for three years just to get a licence so they can prepare the fish. Despite the precautions, every now and then people die – Kabuki actor Bandō Mitsugoro, considered a national treasure, keeled over after a *fugu* party in 1975, which really put the fish on the front pages.

Fugu used to be a winter dish, eaten mainly between October and March, but it is now available year-round, thanks to *fugu* farms off Kyūshū.

café (¥500 per 30 minutes) on the 1st floor, a capsule hotel on the 5th floor (men only, ¥2500, 6pm to 10am), a coin laundry and rooms starting at ¥4500 per person. Close by is **Shimonoseki Station Hotel** (☎ 32-3511; singles/doubles from ¥5500/8800).

Hinoyama Youth Hostel (☎ 22-3753; beds ¥2500; meals available) is at the base of Hino-yama, near the lower ropeway station. You can take a Hino-yama bus from the station. Also at Hino-yama is **Kaikyō View Shimonseki** (☎ 23-0117; rooms ¥6000), a kokuminshukusha (people's lodge).

Places to Stay – Mid-Range & Top End

Beside the station is the **Shimonoseki Tōkyū Inn** (☎ 33-0109), with rooms starting at ¥8000. **Shimonoseki Eki-Nishi Washington Hotel** (☎ 31-5000; singles/twins ¥7000/14,000) is on the west side of the station.

If you want to be around the action of the fish markets, **Shimonoseki Grand Hotel** (☎ 31-5000; singles/twins ¥8000/14,000) is in Karato.

Places to Eat

There are no shortages of places to eat around the station. Head down to the combined Daimaru and Daiei department store basements, as well as the Sea Mall Market in the huge Sea Mall complex, and check out the goodies and eateries.

The best spot for a raw-fish breakfast is the 2nd floor of the Karato Ichiba market. There are stalls in the markets at lunchtime too, serving sushi and delicious deep-fried *fugu* for ¥500 a plate. Next door is the **Kamon Wharf** complex with more than 40 shops, the majority of them eateries.

For *fugu* try **Yabure-Kabure**, not far from the station, or **Nakao** in Karato, but plan to spend at least ¥5000 per person for dinner. Nakao's set lunches are good value.

Meat eaters should head for **Yasumori Yakinikuya**, a *yakiniku* (meat and vegetable grill) restaurant a short walk north of the station.

Getting There & Away

Shinkansen trains stop at Shin-Shimonoseki station, two stops from JR Shimonoseki station. There are frequent trains and buses between the two.

From Shimonoseki, the bridge and tunnels connect roads and rail lines in Honshū with Kyūshū. Eastbound road users can take Route 191 along the northern San-in coast, Route 2 along the southern San-yō coast or the Chūgoku Expressway through Central Honshū.

Ferries run regularly from early morning to late at night from the Karato area of Shimonoseki to Moji-ko in Kyūshū (¥270). From Shin-moji in Kita-kyūshū there are ferries to Kōbe, Osaka and Tokyo in Honshū and to Matsuyama in Shikoku.

Ferries to Korea and China

The **Kampu Ferry Service** (☎ 24-3000) operates the Shimonoseki–Pusan ferry from the Shimonoseki International Ferry Terminal (Shimonoseki-kō Kokusai Taminaru), a short walk from the station. Head up to the 2nd floor (open 10.30am-5.30pm daily) of the enormous, desolate terminal building for bookings. There are daily departures at 7pm from Shimonoseki, arriving in Pusan at 8.30am the following morning. Boarding time is between 6pm and 6.20pm and one-way fares start at ¥6800 for students (¥8500 for an open tatami area), continuing upwards for cabins; there's a 10% discount on return fares. Return ferries from Pusan run to the same time schedule, departing Pusan at 7pm and arriving in Shimonoseki at 8.30am.

If you need a visa for South Korea, arrange it before coming to Shimonoseki. This route is used by many long-term Western residents in Japan, so expect to have your passport rigorously inspected on returning into Japan.

Orient Ferry Ltd (☎ 32-6615) runs between Shimonoseki and Qingdao, China, with a set schedule of departures – generally twice a week. Call for exact dates and times; cheapest tickets cost ¥18,000/34,200 one way/return.

The San-in Coast to Tottori

The rest of this Western Honshū chapter deals with travel along the San-in coast from Shimonoseki in the west to Tottori in the east. The section of the coast from Tottori eastwards to Wakasa-wan is included in the Kansai chapter.

WESTERN HONSHŪ

SHIMONOSEKI TO HAGI

There are three different routes between Shimonoseki and Hagi. One goes around the coast, which is served by the JR San-in line, and features some great coastal scenery, some small fishing villages and interesting countryside at this western extremity of Honshū. **Ōmi-shima**, with its scenic, rocky coast, is immediately north of **Nagato** and connected to the mainland by a bridge. The island is part of the Kita Nagato Coastal Park, which extends eastwards beyond Hagi. **Ōmi-shima Kanko-kisen** (☎ 0837-26-0834) runs 1½-hour cruises (¥2200) around the island.

An alternative is to travel via the Aki-yoshi cave and tablelands area (see the Akiyoshi-dai section earlier).

The third option is to take the JR Mine line from Asa, east of Shimonoseki, to Nagato, then change to the JR San-in line to Hagi.

Tawarayama Onsen 俵山温
☎ 0837

This is a gem of an *onsen*, a fascinating backwater (literally) given over to *toji*, or 'curative bathing'. It's well off the beaten track, and very serious about its purpose – there are no karaoke bars, no *pachinko* (vertical pinball game) halls, no neon, no restaurants; bathers come here for their health, staying for weeks at a time in the 40-odd ryokan, but bathing mainly in the two public baths, **Machi-no-yu** and **Kawa-no-yu**. The latter, overlooking the river, is the most pleasant. There is an endless supply of little old people wandering down the narrow main street in their *yukata*. For a place to stay, try **Izumiya** (☎ 29-0231; per person with 2 meals ¥8000), which has a huge garden.

About 2km west of the *onsen* village is the remarkable temple, **Mara Kannon**. 'Kannon' is the Buddhist deity of compassion, while 'mara' is the most graphic word imaginable for the male procreative organ, somewhere off the vulgar scale beyond 'knob end'. Put the two together and you have this astonishing little temple asking for compassion for knob ends that aren't working properly. It looks more like a garden shed than a place of worship, and it's festooned with phallic statuary. Worshippers bring little statues of erect penises and write their wishes on the side of them – to produce a healthy child, to stop bed wetting, to undergo a desired 'size change', and so on – leaving them before Kannon.

The old guy in the souvenir shop in Tawarayama Onsen, who sells the little statues for ¥850 (should you want one), swears that he personally knows of a case where a couple who had given up all hope of having a baby rapidly produced one after visiting the temple. He also sells marvellous little ashtrays in the shape of the female sexual organ.

There are so many little phallic statues at the temple that a separate little building out the back contains the overflow. On 1 May, it's the scene of a highly photographic fertility rite, the **Mara Kannon Matsuri**. Call the ryokan and check the date – sometimes it's on the 3rd.

Take the JR Mine line from Asa to the south, or Nagato to the north, to Nagato-Yumoto. Buses run from there up to Tawarayama Onsen (¥520, 20 minutes). There's also a direct bus from Shimonoseki (¥1610, two hours).

HAGI 萩
☎ 0838 • pop 50,000

Hagi has an interesting combination of temples and shrines, a fascinating old samurai quarter, some picturesque castle ruins and fine coastal views. The town also has important historical connections with the events of the Meiji Restoration. It is ironic that Hagi's claim to fame is its role in propelling Japan directly from the feudal to the modern era, while its attractions are principally its feudal past. Hagi is also noted for its fine ceramics.

History

Hagi in Honshū and Kagoshima in Kyūshū were the two centres of unrest that played the major part in the events leading up to the Meiji Restoration. Japan's long period of isolation from the outside world under the Tokugawa rule had, by about the mid-19th century, created tensions approaching breaking point. The rigid stratification of society had resulted in an oppressed peasantry, while the progressive elements of the nobility realised Japan had slipped far behind the rapidly industrialising European nations and the USA. The arrival of Commodore Perry brought matters to a humiliating head as the 'barbarians' simply dictated their terms to the helpless Japanese.

Japan could not stand up against the West if it did not adopt Western technology, and this essential modernisation could not take place under the feudal shōgunate. Restoring the emperor to power, even if only as a figurehead, was the route the progressive samurai chose and Shōin Yoshida of Hagi was one of the leaders in this movement. On the surface, he was also a complete failure. In 1854, in order to study first hand the ways of the West, he attempted to leave Japan on Perry's ship, only to be handed over to the authorities and imprisoned in Edo (Tokyo).

When he returned to Hagi he hatched a plot to kill a shōgunate official, but talked about it so much that word leaked out to his enemies. He was arrested again and, in 1859 at the age of 29, he was executed. Fortunately, while Shōin was a failure when it came to action, he was a complete success when it came to inspiration and in 1865 his followers led a militia of peasants and samurai that overturned the Chōshū government of Hagi. The Western powers supported the new blood in Hagi and Kagoshima, and when the shōgunate army moved against the new government in Hagi, it was defeated. That the downfall of the shōgunate had come at the hands of an army not just of samurai, but of peasants as well, was further proof of the changes taking place.

In late 1867, the forces of Kagoshima and Hagi routed the shōgunate, the emperor was restored to nominal power and in early 1868, the capital was shifted from Kyoto to Tokyo, as Edo soon became known. To this day, Hagi remains an important site for visitors interested in the history of modern Japan, with Shōin Yoshida 'living on' at the Shōin-jinja.

Orientation & Information

Hagi consists of three parts. Western and central Hagi are effectively an island created by the rivers, the Hashimoto-gawa and Matsumoto-gawa; while eastern Hagi (with the major JR station, Higashi-Hagi) lies on the eastern bank of the Matsumoto-gawa.

The main road through central Hagi starts from JR Hagi station and runs north, past the bus station in the centre of town. There's a wide variety of shops along Tamachi arcade, close to the bus station. West of this central area is the old samurai quarter of Jōkamachi, with its picturesque streets and interesting old buildings. More interesting old buildings can be found in Horiuchi to the northwest and Teramachi to the northeast of Jōkamachi.

Hagi's **tourist information office** (☎ 25-3145; open 9am-5pm daily) is just beside Higashi-Hagi station. Pick up the concise but informative English-language *Hagi Sightseeing Guide* (¥200).

Hagi Pottery & Kilns

Connoisseurs of Japanese pottery rank *hagi-yaki*, the pottery of Hagi, second only to Kyoto's *raku-yaki*. As in other pottery centres in Japan, the craft came from Korea when Korean potters were brought back after Toyotomi Hideyoshi's unsuccessful invasion in the late 1500s. There are a number of shops and kilns where you can see the pottery being made, and also browse through the finished products. *Hagi-yaki* is noted for its fine glazes and delicate pastel colours. The small notch in the base of each piece is also a reminder of the pottery's long history. In the feudal era only samurai were permitted to use the pottery, but by cutting a tiny notch in some pieces, the potters 'spoilt' their work so it could then be used by common folk.

The **Hagi-jō Kiln** in Horiuchi has particularly fine pieces. The western end of Hagi has several interesting pottery kilns near the park, Shizuki-kōen. *Hagi-yaki* pottery can also be inspected at the **Hagi-yaki Museum** (*Hagi-yaki Togei Kaikan*) near the park; there is a big souvenir area downstairs.

Swede **Bertil Persson** (☎ 25-2693), who has lived in Hagi for over 30 years, has his own kiln and is happy to meet anyone seriously interested in ceramics.

During the first week of May, the Hagi-yaki Matsuri takes place at the city gymnasium, with works on sale from 51 local kilns.

If the idea of making your own piece of *hagi-yaki* appeals, there are six operations in town offering the opportunity. There are lots of options, and the information office has a handout on where, when and how much.

HAGI

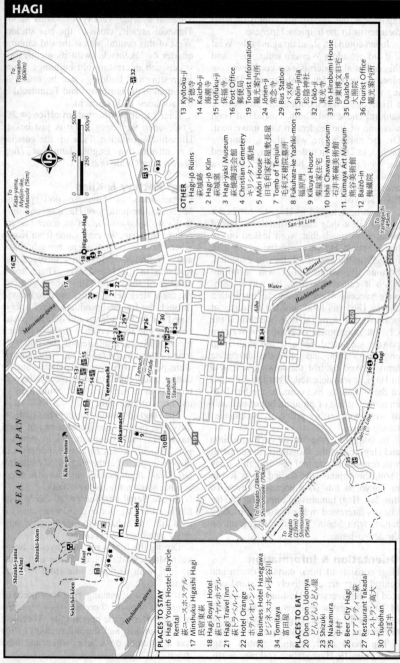

SEA OF JAPAN

To Kasa-yama,
Myōjin-ike,
& Masuda (5km)

San-in Line

To Tsuwano
(60km)

To Yamaguchi
(45km)

To Nagato (28km)
& Shimonoseki (70km)

To Nagato
(23km) &
Shimonoseki
(95km)

Matsumoto-gawa

Hashimoto-gawa

Channel

Water

Aiba

San-in Line

Shizuki-yama
(143m)

Shizuki-kōen

Sekichō-kōen

Kiku-ga-hama

Horiuchi

Jōkamachi

Teramachi

Tamachi Arcade

Baseball Stadium

Moat

PLACES TO STAY
6 Hagi Youth Hostel; Bicycle
   Rental
   萩ユースホステル
17 Minshuku Higashi Hagi
   民宿東萩
18 Hagi Royal Hotel
   萩ロイヤルホテル
21 Hagi Travel Inn
   萩トラベルイン
22 Hotel Orange
   ホテルオレンジ
28 Business Hotel Hasegawa
   ビジネスホテル長谷川
34 Tomitaya
   富田屋

PLACES TO EAT
20 Don Don Udonya
   どんどんうどん屋
23 Shizuki
   指月
25 Nakamura
   中村
26 Beer City Hagi
   ビアシティ萩
27 Restaurant Takadai
   レストラン高大
30 Tsubohan
   つぼ半

13 Kyōtoku-ji
   享徳寺
14 Kaichō-ji
   海潮寺
15 Hofuku-ji
   保福寺
16 Post Office
   郵便局
19 Tourist Information
   観光案内所
24 Jōnen-ji
   常念寺
29 Bus Station
   バス停
31 Shōin-jinja
   松陰神社
32 Tōko-ji
   東光寺
33 Itō Hirobumi House
   伊東博文旧宅
35 Kumaya Art Museum
   熊谷美術館
36 Tourist Office
   観光案内所

OTHER
1 Hagi-jō Ruins
   萩城跡
2 Hagi-jō Kiln
   萩城窯
3 Hagi-yaki Museum
   萩焼陶芸会館
4 Christian Cemetery
   キリシタン墓地
5 Mōri House
   旧毛利家屋敷長屋
7 Tomb of Tenjun
   毛利天樹院墓所
8 Fukuhara-ke Yashiki-mon
   福原門
9 Kikuya House
   菊屋家住宅
10 Ishii Chawan Museum
   石井茶碗美術館
11 Kumaya Art Museum
   熊谷美術館
12 Baizō-in
   梅蔵院

Hagi-jō Ruins & Shizuki-kōen
萩城跡・指月公園

There's not much of the old Hagi-jō to see, apart from the typically imposing outer walls and its surrounding moat. The castle *(admission with Mōri House ¥210; open 8am-4.30pm daily winter, 8am-6.30pm daily rest of year)* was built in 1604. It was dismantled in 1874 during the Meiji Restoration – since Hagi played a leading part in the end of the feudal era and the downfall of the shōgunate, it was appropriate that the town also led the way in the removal of feudal symbols.

Now the grounds are a pleasant park with the **Shizukiyama-jinja**, **Hanano-e Teahouse** (Hanano-e Satei) and other buildings. From the castle ruins you can climb the hillside to the peak of Shizuki-yama (143m).

Sekichō-kōen 石彫公園

About a five-minute walk to the west of Shizuki-kōen is the new park Sekichō-kōen (Sculpture Park), with its collection of sculptural works from around the world. Admission is free.

Mōri House 旧毛利家萩屋敷長屋

South of the park is Mōri House *(admission with Hagi-jō ¥210; open daily)*, a terrace house where samurai soldiers were once barracked. There's an interesting Christian cemetery to the south of the samurai house.

Jōkamachi, Horiuchi & Teramachi Areas
城下町・堀内・寺町

Between the modern town centre and the moat that separates western Hagi from central Hagi is the old samurai residential area, with many streets lined with whitewashed walls. This area is fascinating to wander around and there are a number of interesting houses and temples, particularly in the area known as Jōkamachi. Teramachi is noted particularly for its many fine old temples.

Kikuya House The Kikuya family were merchants rather than samurai, but their wealth and special connections allowed them to build a house well above their station. The house *(admission ¥500; open 9am-5pm daily)* dates from 1604 and has a fine gate, attractive gardens and numerous examples of construction details and materials that would normally have been forbidden to the merchant class.

Kumaya Art Museum This museum *(admission ¥700; open 9am-5pm Tues-Sun)* in Jōkamachi has a small collection, including tea bowls, screens and other items displayed in a series of small warehouses dating from 1768. The Kumaya family handled the trading and commercial operations of Hagi's ruling Mōri family.

Other Buildings The Horiuchi and Teramachi areas are dotted with temples and shrines. **Fukuhara-ke Yashiki-mon**, is one of the finest of the samurai gates in Horiuchi. Nearby is the **Tomb of Tenjuin**, dedicated to Mōri Terumoto, the founder of the Mōri dynasty. There are numerous old temples in the Teramachi area including the two-storey **Kaicho-ji**; **Hōfuku-ji**, with its Jizō statues (the Buddha for travellers and the souls of departed children); **Jonen-ji**, with its gate carvings; and **Baizo-in**. Large **Kyotoku-ji** has a fine garden.

Tōkō-ji 東光寺

East of the river stands this pretty temple *(admission ¥200; open 8.30am-5pm daily)*, with the tombs of five Mōri lords. The odd-numbered lords (apart from No 1) were buried here; the even-numbered ones were buried at the temple, Daishō-in. The stone walkways on the hillside behind the temple are flanked by almost 500 stone lanterns erected by the lords' servants.

Shōin-jinja 松陰神社

This Meiji-era shrine is dedicated to Shōin Yoshida. His life is illustrated in the nearby **Shōin Yoshida Rekishikan** *(Shōin Yoshida History Hall; admission ¥650; open 9am-5pm daily)*. South of the shrine, **Itō Hirobumi House** is the early home of the four-term prime minister who was a follower of Shōin Yoshida, and who later drafted the Meiji Constitution. Shōin Yoshida's tomb is near Toko-ji.

Daishō-in 大照院

South of the centre, near JR Hagi station, this funerary temple *(admission ¥200; open 8am-5pm daily)* was the resting place for the first two Mōri generations and after that, all even-numbered generations of the Mōri lords. Like the better known and more visited Tōkō-ji, it has pathways lined by stone lanterns erected by the Mōri lords' faithful retainers. The original Mōri lord's grave is accompanied by the graves of seven of his principal retainers, all of whom committed *seppuku* (ritual suicide) after their lord died. An eighth grave is that of a retainer to one of the retainers who also joined in the festivities. The shōgunate quickly banned similar excessive displays of samurai loyalty.

Myōjin-ike & Kasa-yama
明神池・笠山

About 5km east of the town is the 112m dormant volcano of Kasa-yama. It's hardly a whopper, but there are some great things to do here. The pond at the mountain's base, Myōjin-ike, is actually connected to the sea and shelters a variety of saltwater fish.

Further up the mountain is **Hagi Glass Associates** (☎ 26-2555), where quartz basalt from the volcano is used to make extremely tough glassware. There is a showroom and a shop, and visitors can make their own piece of glassware. Next door is Hagi's own beer factory, where you can check out how the beer is made and taste the brew.

The road continues to the top of Kasa-yama, from where there are fine views along the coast, and an intriguingly tiny 30m deep crater. Kasa-yama is close enough to make a good bicycle ride from Hagi.

Places to Stay
The information office will help with accommodation bookings.

Hagi Youth Hostel (☎ 22-0733; beds ¥2800; closed mid-Jan–mid-Feb) is south of the castle at the western end of the town; Tamae is the nearest JR train station. **Minshuku Higashi Hagi** (☎ 22-7884; singles/twins ¥4000/7000), near Higashi Hagi station, is a friendly, family-run place where English is spoken. **Hotel Orange** (☎ 25-5880; singles/twins ¥5000/9000) is just across the river from Higashi-Hagi station; the receptionist speaks English.

In the mid-range, **Hagi Travel Inn** (☎ 25-2640; singles ¥6000) is near Higashi-Hagi station. **Business Hotel Hasegawa** (☎ 22-0450; singles ¥6000) is across from the bus station.

Hagi Royal Hotel (☎ 25-9595; per person ¥10,000), right by Higashi-Hagi station, and **Tomitaya** (☎ 22-0025; per person ¥10,000), near Hagi station, are more upmarket. Rates for both include two meals.

Places to Eat
Hagi prides itself on *uni* (sea urchin) and **Tsubohan**, near the bus station, is the most economical place to sample this gourmet delicacy – try *unikama setto* (*uni* on rice). **Nakamura** is also good for seafood.

There are a couple of places worth looking out for, both in the east of town. **Shizuki**, in a Tudor-fronted building, has French cuisine and although a lot of it is pretty expensive, there are some good set lunches and dinners. **Restaurant Takadai** is well known for its Hagi cuisine and has a pricey but excellent special lunch.

Don Don Udonya has excellent *udon* noodles and set meals for a reasonable price.

Beer City Hagi has plenty of beer and some quality food.

Getting There & Away
The JR San-in line runs along the north coast through Tottori, Matsue, Masuda and Hagi to Shimonoseki.

JR buses connect Hagi with Ogōri (via Akiyoshi-dai), which is south of Hagi on the Tokyo–Osaka–Hakata *shinkansen* line. There are buses from Yamaguchi, and buses also go to Tsuwano (¥2080, two hours) to the east in Shimane-ken.

Hagi is served by Iwami airport, an hour to the northeast near Masuda in Shimane-ken. There are daily flights to/from Tokyo and Osaka, with a bus connecting Hagi with all flights.

Getting Around
Hagi is a good place to explore by bicycle and there are plenty of rental places, including one at the youth hostel and several around the castle and JR Higashi-Hagi station.

There is also a new bus system, designed for visitors, that takes in Hagi's main attractions. The information office has a pamphlet showing the exact routes and timetable. One trip costs ¥100, and a one-/two-day pass is ¥500/700.

From Hagi, the JR San-in line and Route 191, the main road, pretty much hug each other and the coastline up to the prefectural border with Shimane-ken. If you're going to Tsuwano, there is a direct bus from Hagi, but if you've got a JR Pass, you'll want to go by train up the coast to Masuda, then change to the JR Yamaguchi line for Tsuwano.

Shimane-ken 島根県

Along the northern San-in coastline on the Sea of Japan, Shimane-ken is well worth making the effort to get to. Cities are few and far between, and the pace of life is decidedly slower than on the Sanyō coast. Highlights include Tsuwano, one of Japan's many 'little Kyotos'; the great shrine at Izumo; and Matsue, where the writer and Japanophile Lafcadio Hearn lived and produced some of his best-known works.

TSUWANO 津和野
☎ 0856
In the far western reaches of Shimane-ken, about 40km east of Hagi, is Tsuwano, a pleasant and relaxing mountain town with some fine castle ruins, interesting old buildings and a wonderful collection of carp swimming in the roadside water channels – the 65,000 or so of these colourful fish outnumber the local population tenfold! The town is noted as a place to get to by the superb old steam-train service from Ogōri and as a place to explore by bicycle, of which there are quite a phenomenal number for rent.

Orientation & Information
Tsuwano is a long, narrow town wedged into a deep north–south valley. The Tsuwano-kawa, JR Yamaguchi line and main road all run down the middle of the valley. The staff at the **tourist information office** (☎ 72-1771; open 9am-5pm daily), by the train station, are very helpful and have excellent English information on hand. Try to pick up the bilingual booklet *Yū ni shin sai Tsuwano* (¥200), which translates as 'make yourself at home' in the local dialect.

Tsuwano-jō 津和野城
The ruins of Tsuwano-jō seem to brood over the valley, with the broken stone walls draping along the ridge. The castle was originally constructed in 1295 and remained in use until the Meiji Restoration. A decrepit

old single-seater chairlift takes you up and down the hillside for ¥450, from where there's a further 15-minute walk to the castle ruins. At the top is a splendid view over the town and surrounding mountains. If you've got the energy and time, it's possible to follow a trail on foot all the way up from Taikodani-Inari-jinja.

Taikodani-Inari-jinja
太鼓谷稲成神社
Just above the castle chairlift station, this brightly painted shrine is one of the largest Inari shrines in Japan. You can walk up to it from the main road through a 'tunnel' created by more than 1100 red torii. Festivals are held here on 15 May and 15 November every year.

The Sagi Mai Matsuri (Heron Dance Festival), which includes a procession of dancers dressed as herons, is performed on 20 and 27 July at Yasaka-jinja, near the start of the torii tunnel.

Tonomachi District 殿町
Only the walls and some fine old gates remain from the former samurai quarter of Tonomachi. 'Ditches' (the word used in the local tourist brochure) is too plain a word to apply to the water channels that run alongside the picturesque Tonomachi road: the crystal-clear water in the channels is home to tens of thousands of large and healthy carp. It's said that these fish were bred to provide a potential source of food should the town ever be besieged. (The feared attack never came and the fish have thrived.)

The **Catholic church** is a reminder that Nagasaki Christians were once exiled here, while just north of the river is the **Yōrō-kan**, a school for young samurai in the late Edo period. The building now houses the **Minzoku Museum** (admission ¥200; open 8.30am-5pm daily), an interesting little folk art museum, with all sorts of farming and cooking equipment.

Nearby the post office, the **Katsushika Hok-usai Museum** (admission ¥500; open 9.30am-5pm daily) features a collection by the master Edo-period paint er Hokusai and his disciples.

Chapel of St Mary マリア聖堂
The tiny Maria-Seido Chapel dates from 1951, when a German priest built it as a

memorial to the exiled Catholics who died in the final period of Christian persecution, before the anti-Christian laws were repealed in 1872.

Other Attractions

The beautiful former residences of Nishi Amane, who played an important part in the Meiji Restoration government, and Mori Ōgai, a highly regarded novelist, are in the south of the town. At the rear of the latter is the **Mori Ōgai Memorial Museum** (admission ¥500; open 9am-5pm Tues-Sun), a striking modern building that houses many of the writer's personal effects. Entry to the grounds of the residence only (which is far more interesting than the museum) is ¥100. **Itahashi Antique Doll Museum** (admission ¥800; open 9.30am-5.30pm Fri-Wed) houses an astounding collection of fine European antique dolls, though the entry fee keeps most without such a penchant away. Perhaps more interesting (and still with a bit of European flavour) is the **Morijuku Museum** (admission ¥500; open 9am-5pm daily), an old farmhouse with a room of Goya etchings and paintings by local artists. Make sure you see the pinhole camera feature on the 2nd floor (the proprietor will gladly show you).

Tsuwano Dento Kōugeisha (admission ¥320; open 8.30-5pm daily) has paper-making displays.

Tsuwano Documentary Photography Gallery (admission ¥200; open 9am-4.45pm daily) has a small but excellent collection dedicated to contemporary photojournalism. The standing collection features work by Tsuwano-born Kuwabara Shisei, mostly shot in Vietnam, South Korea and Minamata. It's in the same building as the information office, next to the station.

There are a number of sake breweries in town, some of which you can stop in for tastings. Try **Hashimoto**, where Toba-san, one of the resident staff, can answer your questions in English while you sample the local brew.

South of the town is the shrine, **Washibara Hachiman-gū**, about 4km from the station, where archery contests on horseback are held on 2 April.

If you feel like a long soak in a bath, head down to the new onsen complex south of town – it costs ¥500.

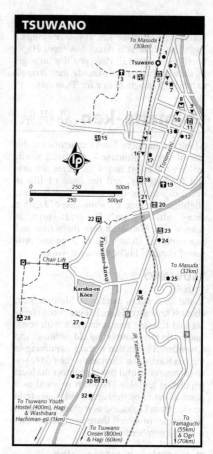

Places to Stay

The information counter next to the train station will help with bookings for the town's many minshuku and ryokan.

Tsuwano Youth Hostel (☎ 72-0373; beds ¥2900; breakfast ¥600) is 2km south of the station, beside a small temple.

Wakasagi-no-yado Minshuku (☎ 72-1146; per person with 2 meals ¥7000) is a pleasant, friendly and frequently recommended place; staff will even pick you up at the station. **Hoshi Ryokan** (☎ 72-0136; per person with 2 meals ¥6000) is centrally located.

Kokuminshukusha Aono-sansō (☎ 72-0436; per person with 2 meals ¥6800) is a government-run place away from the centre and across the river.

TSUWANO

PLACES TO STAY
7 Hoshi Ryokan
    星旅館
13 Meigetsu Ryokan
    明月
17 Tsuwano Kankō Hotel
    津和野観光ホテル
25 Kokuminshukusha
    Aonesansō
    国民宿舎青根山荘
26 Wakasagi-no-Yado Minshuku
    民宿わかさぎの宿

PLACES TO EAT
6 Shō-kyoto
    小京都
9 Furusato
    ふるさと
10 Roku-roku
    六六
14 Waraji-ya
    わらじ屋
16 Tsurube
    つるべうどん屋

21 Azemichi
    あぜみち

OTHER
1 Eki Rent-a-Cycle
    駅貸し自転車
2 Kamai Shōten
3 Chapel of St Mary
    マリア聖堂
4 Kōmyō-ji
    光明寺
5 Tsuwano Photography Gallery;
    Tourist Information Centre
    観光案内所; 産業資料館
8 Post Office
    郵便局
11 Katsushika Hokusai Museum
    葛飾北斎美術館
12 Hashimoto Sake Brewery
    橋本酒店
15 Yōmei-ji
    永明寺
18 Bus Station
    バスターミナル

19 Catholic Church
    津和野カトリック教会
20 Yōrōkan; Minzoku Museum
    養老館
22 Taikodani-Inari-jinja
    太鼓谷稲成神社
23 Museum Morijuku
    杜塾美術館
24 Kusakari Jitensha
    くさかり自転車
27 Dentō Kōgeisha
    津和野伝統工芸舎
28 Tsuwano-jō Ruins
    津和野城跡
29 Nishi Amane House
    西周旧宅
30 Itahashi Antique Doll
    Museum
    板橋アンティック.
    ドール美術館
31 Mori Ōgai House;
    Memorial Museum
    森鴎外記念館
32 Tachibana Cycle

At the top end of the scale, **Meigetsu Ryokan** (☎ 72-0685; per person ¥10,000-20,000) is a traditional and more-expensive ryokan. This is a place where, by request, you may get to try Tsuwano's famine food: carp! **Tsuwano Kankō Hotel** (☎ 72-0333; per person with 2 meals ¥12,000) is right in the centre of town.

Places to Eat

Most visitors to Tsuwano eat in their *minshuku* or ryokan, so dining possibilities are limited. **Furusato**, in Gion-chō across from the post office, is a good lunch spot and serves the local speciality *uzume-meshi*: rice served in a soup with tofu, mushrooms and mountain vegetables.

Shō-kyoto is in front of the station and has cheap, curries, *katsudon* (pork cutlet served over rice) and coffee. **Roku-roku** is an *izakaya* that's a short walk southwest of the post office; in the evening it's the best bet, as it's inexpensive, friendly, and a good place for meeting partying locals. The *kabuto-ebi shio-yaki*, a kind of grilled and salted minilobster (¥500), is highly recommended. **Waraji-ya**, rustic and traditional, serves noodles and has an *irori* (open fireplace). Just down the road, **Tsurube** specialises in *udon* noodles. **Azemichi** boasts *chōgekikara rāmen*, spicy hot Chinese noodles.

Getting There & Away

The JR Yamaguchi line runs from Ogōri on the south coast through Yamaguchi to Tsuwano and on to Masuda on the north coast. Tsuwano is connected with Ogōri (1¼ hours) and Masuda (40 minutes). A bus runs between Tsuwano and Hagi (¥2080, two hours).

During the late April to early May Golden Week holiday, from 20 July to 31 August, as well as sometimes on Sundays and national holidays, a popular steam locomotive service operates between Ogōri and Tsuwano. The SL Yamaguchi-gō is a restored 1937 locomotive pulling antique carriages that travels from Ogōri to Tsuwano in the morning, then waits for three hours before making the return journey. The train trip costs ¥1650 and takes two hours each way. Ask for up-to-date details and book well ahead of your intended dates at JR and tourist information offices.

Getting Around

Tsuwano is packed with bicycle rental places and rates start at ¥400 for two hours, or ¥800 for a day.

MASUDA 益田

This is a modern industrial town with two temples, **Mampuku-ji** and **Iko-ji**. Both have notable gardens said to have been designed by the famed painter Sesshū. The temples are about 10 minutes by bus from the JR station.

Masuda is the junction for the JR Yamaguchi line – which runs between Ogōri, Yamaguchi, Tsuwano and Masuda – and the JR San-in line, which runs from Shimonoseki, through Hagi and Masuda and up the coast. *Futsū* trains run from Masuda to Tsuwano (¥570, 40 minutes), Higashi-Hagi (¥1110, 80 minutes) and Izumo (¥3750, three hours).

Iwami Seaside Park 石見海浜公園

About 5km northeast of Hamada is Iwami Seaside Park (☎ 0855 28-2231), great for camping, swimming and playing on a white, sandy beach. This place is really set up for fun. There are plenty of options, including auto-camping (camping beside your car), free tent sites, and cabins that sleep six people for ¥5760, four for ¥3760 and three for ¥3190. Facilities include floodlit tennis courts, a sports ground, coin laundry, coin showers and even frisbee golf. Plus you can rent just about everything you need on the spot. It's an ideal place for a reasonably priced family holiday. The Park is open year round and reservations are advised.

Just up the road is the enormous new **Aquas Shimane Aquarium** (☎ 0855 28-3900; adult/students ¥1500/500; open 9am-5pm Wed-Mon), which is like a theme park full of fish. It's great stuff for the family, with a 'touching pool' (where kids can touch the fish), white dolphins, sharks, seals, and even Shimane-ken's official fish, the *ago* (flying fish).

Nima 仁摩

Nima is home to the **Nima Sand Museum** (admission ¥700; open 9am-5pm daily, closed 1st Wed each month), which houses the world's biggest sand timer – this monster is turned over at midnight on the 31 December each year, and has exactly the right number of grains of sand to last through to the same time the next year. The 5m-long timer is suspended high in one of the museum's glass pyramids and contains about one tonne of sand.

Also in Nima is the very pleasant **Youth Hostel Jofuku-ji** (☎ 0854 88-2233; beds ¥2600; meals available) and if you haven't

had the chance to stay at a Buddhist temple, this is a great place to start. The priest and his wife are very friendly, there is a splendid view out over the coast and the 20-minute walk from Nima station through the paddy fields and up to the temple is quite enjoyable. Take your shoes in overnight or they might be burgled by the local badger.

Sanbe-san 三瓶山

About 20km inland from Ōda is Sanbe-san, which reaches 1126m and has four separate peaks known as the Father, the Mother, the Child and the Grandchild. It takes about an hour to climb from **Sanbe Onsen**, where there is a dip in the *onsen* awaiting your return. It is also a popular ski centre in winter. Buses run between Ōda and Sanbe Onsen (¥830, 40 minutes).

IZUMO 出雲

☎ 0853 • pop 85,000

Only 33km west of Matsue, Izumo has one major attraction – the great Izumo Taisha shrine. It is also home to the Shimane Winery, which is bound to be a major attraction for some!

Orientation & Information

Izumo Taisha is several kilometres northwest of central Izumo. The shrine area, basically one main street running straight up to the shrine, has a train station and a range of accommodation and restaurants. There's a friendly **tourist information office** (☎ 53-2298; open 9am-5.30pm daily) in the train station, with English-language information. Izumo Taisha can easily be visited as a day trip from Matsue.

Izumo Taisha 出雲大社

This is the oldest Shintō shrine in Japan and is second in importance only to the shrines of Ise. Although it is only a shadow of its former self – the buildings once towered to a colossal 48m, whereas today they are a more modest 24m – this is still an enormously significant structure, both architecturally and spiritually.

A shrine has existed on the site for the last 1500 years. The current main shrine was last rebuilt in 1744, its 25th reincarnation, whereas the surrounding buildings date back to 1874. All are constructed in the *Taisha-zukuri* style, considered Japan's old-

IZUMO TAISHA

```
0        200      400m
0        200      400yd
Approximate Scale
```

To Hino-misaki
(10km)

To
Shimane
Winery
(2km),
Hirata
& Matsue
(38km)

To
Matsue
Onsen
(38km)

To
Izumo
(6km) &
Matsue
(38km)

Ichibata Izumo
Taisha

Hori-kawa

431

161

161

1 Shōkokan (Treasure Hall)
   彰古館
2 Honden (Main Hall)
   本殿
3 Haiden (Hall of Worship)
   拝殿
4 Shinko-den (Treasure House)
   神祐殿
5 Ichibata Bus Terminal
   一畑バス停
6 Inabaya Ryokan
   いなばや旅館
7 Business Hotel Taisha
   ビジネスホテル大社
8 Yashiroya
   やしろや
9 Takenoya Ryokan
   竹野屋旅館
10 Fujiwara Ryokan
   藤原旅館
11 Post Office
   郵便局
12 Ebisuya Youth Hostel
   えびすやユースホステル
13 Tourist Information
   観光案内所

est form of shrine architecture. The wooded grounds are pleasant to wander through and the shrine itself enjoys the 'borrowed scenery' of Yakumo Hill as a backdrop.

The shrine is dedicated to Okuninushi, the *kami* (Shintō spirit god) of marriage, among other things. Hence, visitors to the shrine summon the deity by clapping four times rather than the normal two – twice for themselves and twice for their partner or partners to be.

The **Haiden** (Hall of Worship) is the first building inside the entrance torii; huge *shimenawa* (twisted straw ropes) hang over the entry. The main building is the largest shrine in Japan but the **Honden** (Main Hall) cannot be entered. The shrine compound is flanked by *jūku-sha*, long shelters where

Japan's eight million Shintō spirit gods stay when they turn up for their annual shindig.

On the southeastern side of the compound is the **Shinko-den** (*Treasure House; admission ¥150; open 8.30am-4.30pm daily*), with a collection of shrine paraphernalia. Behind the main shrine building in the northwestern corner is the former **Shōkōkan** (Treasure Hall), which boasts a large collection of images of Okuninushi in the form of Daikoku, a cheerful chubby character standing on two or three rice bales with a sack over his shoulder and a mallet in his hand. Usually you will see his equally happy son Ebisu standing beside him with a fish tucked under his arm.

Hino-misaki 日御碕

It's less than 10km from Izumo Taisha to the cape, Hino-misaki, where you'll find a picturesque lighthouse, some fine views and an ancient shrine. On the way, you'll pass the pleasant **Inasa-no-hama**, a good swimming beach just 2km from Ichibata Izumo Taisha station. Buses run regularly from the station to the cape, via the beach (¥840, 35 minutes). **Hinomisaki-jinja** is near the cape bus terminus. From the car park, coastal paths lead north and south offering fine views, particularly from the top of the **lighthouse** (*admission ¥150; open 9am-4.30pm daily*).

Special Events

The lunar calendar month corresponding to October is known throughout Japan as Kan-nazuki (Month without Gods). In Izumo, however, it is known as Kan-arizuki (Month with Gods), for this is the month when all the Shintō gods congregate for an annual get-together at Izumo Taisha.

In accordance with the ancient calendar, the **Kamiari-sai** ('the gods are here!') **festival** takes place from 11 to 17 October.

Places to Stay & Eat

There's no pressing reason to stay overnight in Izumo Taisha since it's easy to day trip there from Matsue or to simply pause there while travelling along the coast. If you do want to stop, there are a host of places along the main street of Izumo Taisha, which runs down from the shrine to the train station.

Ebisuya Youth Hostel (*☎ 53-2157; beds ¥2900; meals available*) is just off the main

Shimane Winery

There aren't many wineries in the world where they put out huge punchbowls of their product along with ladles and plastic cups and invite you to do as much 'tasting' as you like. But at the Shimane Winery (☎ 0853 53-5577) it's basically 'no holds barred', although it would be a shame to go over-board at the punchbowls and possibly ruin it for the next foreigner who comes along.

Besides tasting, you can view the winery in action, buy a few bottles, enjoy a meal in the barbecue restaurant or sober up in the coffee shop. The winery is 2km east of Izumo Taisha on Route 431. You can't miss this massive Spanish-looking complex, with its white walls and orange-tiled roof.

---

street, near the station. Also on the budget side is **Business Hotel Taisha** (☎ 53-2194; per person from ¥5500), near the entrance to the shrine.

There are a host of ryokan in Izumo, including **Inabaya Ryokan** (☎ 53-3180; per person ¥10,000-28,000), the classy **Takenoya Ryokan** (☎ 53-3131; per person ¥12,000-35,000) and **Fujiwara Ryokan** (☎ 53-2009; per person ¥12,000). All rates include two meals.

Izumo's *soba* gets high praise, particularly the dish known as *warigo*, where a broth is poured over the noodle. There are a number of noodle shops along the main street, though most close early once the day-trippers have gone. **Yashiroya** is a local favourite, off to the right of the shrine entrance.

Getting There & Away
The private Ichihata line starts from Matsue Shinjiko-onsen station in Matsue and runs on the northern side of Shinji-ko to Izumo Taisha station (¥790, 55 minutes). The JR line runs from JR Matsue station to JR Izumo station (¥740, one hour), where you transfer to an Ichihata line train to Izumo Taisha. The first option is easier and more frequent, with more than 20 services a day. If you're coming from the west, change at JR Izumo station.

The one-day L&R 'Free Kippu' ticket (¥1500) allows unlimited travel on Ichihata trains and Shinji-ko Lakeside buses.

Izumo has an airport with flights to/from all Japan's major cities.

MATSUE 松江
☎ 0852 • pop 150,000
Matsue straddles the Ōhashi-gawa river, which connects Shinji-ko to Nakanoumi-ko and then the sea. There's a compact area

in the north with almost all of Matsue's interesting sites: an original castle, a fine samurai residence, the former home of writer Lafcadio Hearn and a delightful teahouse and garden.

Information
There is a new **tourist information office** (☎ 21-4034; open 9am-6pm daily) in front of the JR station with a surprising amount of English information, and extremely helpful English-speaking staff. The office will help with finding and reserving accommodation, and can arrange a free English-language tour – the **Matsue Goodwill Guide** – if you call a few days in advance.

There is also information, a small library and free Internet access at the **Shimane International Centre** (☎ 31-5056; open 9am-7pm Mon-Fri, 9am-5pm Sat) on the 2nd floor of the Kunibiki Messe building, about a 10-minute walk from the station. The information office is much better for accom-modation-type questions though.

Email & Internet Access Free Internet access is available at the International Centre, **NTT** (open 9am-4pm Mon-Fri), and at Terazuya Ryokan (see Places to Stay).

Matsue-jō 松江城
The castle (admission ¥550; open 8.30am-6.30pm daily summer, 8.30am-5pm daily rest of year) in Matsue is not huge or im-posing but it is original, dating from 1611. Modern Japan has so many rebuilt castles, externally authentic-looking but internally totally modern, that it can almost be a shock to step inside one where the con-struction is wood, not concrete. With a 'Universal Pass' (¥920), which combines entry to the castle, Buke Yashiki Samurai Residence and the Koizumi Yakumo (Laf-

cadio Hearn) Memorial Museum, you can save 20%.

The regional **Matsue Cultural Museum** (admission free; open 8.30am-5pm daily) is within the castle precincts. The road alongside the moat on the northeastern side of the castle is known as Shiomi Nawate and was, at one time, a narrow lane through the old samurai quarter. The high tile-topped walls still remain from that era and there are a number of places of interest.

There is a fun **boat tour** (admission ¥1200; open 9am-5pm winter, to 6pm summer), which circumnavigates the castle moat and then zips you around some of the city's canals.

Koizumi Yakumo (Lafcadio Hearn) Residence 小泉八雲旧宅

Hearn was a British writer (although he was born in Greece in 1850, he was educated in France and the UK and lived in the USA from 1869) who came to Japan in 1890 and remained there for the rest of his life. Hearn's adopted Japanese name was Koizumi Yakumo and his first book on Japan, *Glimpses of Unfamiliar Japan*, is a classic, providing an insight into the country at that time. The Japanese have a great interest in the outsider's view of their country so Hearn's pretty little house is an important attraction, despite the fact that he only lived in Matsue for just over a year. While you're admiring the garden you can read his essay *In a Japanese Garden*, which describes how it looked a century ago. Hearn's former residence (admission ¥250; open 9am-4.30pm daily) is at the northern end of Shiomi Nawate.

Exotic Dishes from the Lake

Matsue's *kyodo ryōri*, or regional cuisine, includes 'seven exotic dishes from Shinji-ko'. They are:

suzuki or *hōsho yaki*	steam-baked and paper-wrapped bass
shirauo	whitebait tempura or sashimi
amasagi	sweet tempura or teriyaki
shijimi	tiny shellfish in miso shiro
moroge ebi	steamed shrimp
koi	baked carp
unagi	broiled freshwater eel

Koizumi Yakumo (Lafcadio Hearn) Memorial Museum 小泉八雲記念館

Nextdoor to Hearn's home is this Memorial Museum (admission ¥300; open 8.30am-6.30pm daily summer, 8.30am-5pm daily rest of year), with displays about Hearn's life, writing and Matsue residence. There are a stack of Japanese newspapers on which Hearn had written simple words and phrases to teach English to his son. There is an English-language brochure and map showing points of interest around the town mentioned in his writings.

Tanabe Art Museum 田部美術館

The Tanabe Art Museum (admission ¥500; open 9am-5pm Tues-Sun) principally has on display family items from the many generations of the region's Tanabe clan, particularly tea bowls and other tea ceremony paraphernalia.

Buke Yashiki Samurai Residence 武家屋敷

The Buke Yashiki (admission ¥300; open 8.30am-6.30pm daily summer, 8.30am-5pm daily rest of year) is a well-preserved, middle Edo-period samurai residence from 1730. There's a useful English-language leaflet that describes the various rooms and their uses in this large, spartan residence. (This was not the home of a wealthy samurai.)

Meimei-an Teahouse 明々庵

A little further south is the turn-off to the delightful Meimei-an teahouse (admission ¥300; open 9am-5pm daily), with its well-kept gardens and fine views to Matsue-jō. The teahouse was built in 1779 and was moved to its present site in 1966. Look for the steep steps up from the road to the thatched-roof building.

Shimane Prefectural Art Museum 島根県立博物館

This impressive, futuristic-looking museum (admission ¥300; open 10am-6.30pm Tues-Sun) displays work by Monet, Rodin and current Japanese artists. It's in a fabulous location overlooking the lake, and on a sunny day it's fun to wander around the outdoor sculptures. It's a 15-minute walk west of the station.

WESTERN HONSHŪ

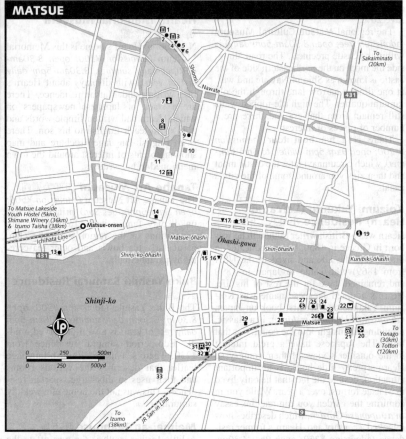

MATSUE

Other Attractions

Matsue has its own *onsen* area, just north of the lake near Matsue-onsen station on the Ichihata line. There are a number of hotels and ryokan in the area, as well as O-yu-kake Jizō, a popular 'hell', or *jigoku* – very hot springs that are definitely not for bathing.

The fine sunset views over lake **Shinji-ko** are best appreciated from the Matsue-ōhashi bridge. The **Matsue Folk Art Centre** (Matsue Meisan Sentaa), in the *onsen* area by the lake, displays regional crafts, as does the **Matsue Prefectural Product & Craft Centre** just southeast of the castle in the town centre.

Places to Stay – Budget

The best budget option is **Terazuya** (☎ 21-3480; rooms with/without 2 meals ¥7000/

4000), a clean, friendly, family-run ryokan that is located near the Matsue Tenmangū shrine. There is some English spoken here and free Internet access. If you ask nicely, the father will sing traditional songs for you, the mother will perform the tea ceremony and the son will show you his calligraphy expertise. (The singing is quite enthralling.)

Business Ishida Hotel (☎ 21-5931; rooms ¥4000) is one of the standard business hotels around the station. **Young Inn Matsue** (☎ 22-2000; per person ¥3300) is a small, bargain priced hotel.

Matsue Lakeside Youth Hostel (☎ 36-8620; beds ¥2800; meals available) is about 5km from the centre of town and inconvenient to get to.

MATSUE

PLACES TO STAY	OTHER	
14 New Urban Hotel ニューアーバンホテル	1 Koizumi Yakumo (Lafcadio Hearn) Memorial Museum 小泉八雲記念館	12 Shimane Prefectural Art Museum 島根県立博物館
15 Young Inn Matsue ヤングイン松江		13 Matsue Folk Art Centre
18 Matsue Washington Hotel 松江ワシントンホテル	2 Koizumi Yakumo (Lafcadio Hearn) Residence 小泉八雲旧宅	19 Kunibiki Messe Building くにびきメッセ
24 Matsue Tōkyū Inn 松江東急イン	3 Tanabe Art Museum 田部美術館	20 SATY サティ
28 Green Hotel Matsue グリーンホテル松江	5 Buke Yashiki Samurai Residence	21 NTT
29 Business Ishida Hotel ビジネス石田ホテル	武家屋敷	22 Post Office 郵便局
32 Terazuya 旅館寺津屋	7 Matsue-jō 松江城	23 Ichihata Department Store 一畑百貨店
	8 Matsue Cultural Museum 松江郷土館	25 Nippon Rent-a-car
PLACES TO EAT		26 Tourist Information 観光案内所
4 Yakumo-an 八雲庵	9 Moat Boat Tours 乗船場	27 Shimane Gōdō Bank 島根合同銀行
6 Yakumo-an Bekkan 八雲庵別館	10 Matsue Prefectural Product & Craft Centre 物産観光館	31 Matsue Tenmangū 松江天満宮
16 Filaments		33 Shimane Prefectural Art Museum 島根県立美術館
17 Kawa-kyō かわきょう	11 Prefecture Hall 県庁	
30 Bus Stop Café		

Places to Stay – Mid-Range & Top End

Matsue Tōkyū Inn (☎ 27-0109; singles/ twins ¥7500/12,300) is just across the road from the station. **Green Hotel Matsue** (☎ 27-3000; singles/twins ¥6200/10,600) is in front of the station.

Matsue Washington Hotel (☎ 22-4111; singles/twins ¥7400/13,000) is across the river from the JR station, but still convenient to the town centre.

New Urban Hotel (☎ 23-0003; singles ¥6000) and its neighbouring annex, towards Matsue Onsen station, is an interesting option. The top floor of the complex boasts a huge hot-spring bath.

Places to Eat

Yakumo-an is a good spot to pause for lunch if you're wandering Shiomi Nawate. It is next to the samurai house, and is a delightfully genteel noodle house with a pond full of very healthy-looking carp. The local speciality, warigo-style noodles, costs ¥600. **Yakumo-an Bekkan** is a pleasant teahouse annex, just on the other side of Buke Yashiki, with a tea-and-sweets set for ¥550.

Kawa-kyō, near the Washington Hotel north of the river, offers the seven local 'exotic dishes from the lake' (see the earlier boxed text) on an English-language menu with prices ranging from ¥250 for shijimi to ¥1500 for hōsho yaki.

Bus Stop Cafe, opposite the Terazuya Ryokan, offers pasta and a livelier crowd, and for a few drinks at night head to **Filaments**, where owner Sam has thousands of CDs.

The tourist office at the station can also recommend restaurants, of which there are a lot around the station.

Getting There & Away

Matsue is on the JR San-in line, which runs along the San-in coast. You can head down to Okayama on the south coast via Yonago on the JR Hakubi line. It's ¥480 to Yonago (35 minutes); then ¥4620 to Okayama (two hours).

Matsue is serviced by both Izumo and Yonago airports, with daily flights to all the major cities.

Highway buses also operate to/from all Japan's major cities.

Getting Around

Matsue has an efficient new Lake Line Bus, which runs a set route around the city's major attractions, departing every 24 minutes from 8.40am to 6.26pm. Get a map of the route from the information office at the station, where the buses depart from. There are about 30 stops and the full route takes 70 minutes. The system is set up for visitors: one ride costs ¥100, but a day ticket is only ¥500 and brings discounts on many of the attractions.

If you're planning to visit Izumo Taisha, make sure you invest in the one-day L&R 'Free Kippu' ticket (¥1500), which allows unlimited travel on Ichihata trains and Shinji-ko lakeside buses.

Matsue is a good place to explore by bicycle: these can be hired opposite Matsue station at Nippon Rent-a-car for ¥500 for two hours or ¥1100 per day.

AROUND MATSUE & IZUMO
Shinji-ko 宍道湖
Sunset over the Yomega-shima islet in Shinji-ko is a photographer's favourite and the lake also provides the region's seven favourite local delicacies. At the western end of the lake, the garden in Gakuen-ji in Hirata is noted for its autumn colours.

At the southwestern corner of the lake, the town of Shinji has one of the finest ryokan in Japan, **Yakumo Honjin** (☎ 66-0136; *rooms per person ¥15,000*). Parts of the inn are 250 years old; if you stay here ask for the old wing or you'll end up in the modern air-conditioned one. Casual visitors can have a look around for ¥300.

Shimane-hantō 島根半島
North of Matsue, the coastline of the peninsula, Shimane-hantō, has some spectacular scenery, particularly around Kaga; you can enter the **Kaga-no-Kukedo** cave by boat.

Fūdoki-no-Oka & Shrines
風土記の丘
About 5km south of Matsue, around the village of Yakumo-mura, there are interesting shrines and important archaeological finds. The Fūdoki-no-Oka hill is a 1st-century AD archaeological site, its finds displayed in the **Fūdoki-no-Oka Archaeological Museum** (*admission ¥300; open 9am-5pm Tues-Sun*). Take the Yakumo bus (¥300, 20 minutes, every 30 minutes) bound from Terminal 4 at Matsue station and get off at Fūdoki-no-Oka Iriguchi.

Nearby is **Okadayama Kofun**, an ancient burial mound. *Haniwa* pottery figures were found here, similar to those of Miyazaki on Kyūshū.

West of Fūdoki-no-Oka is the ancient shrine, **Kamosu-jinja**, dedicated to Izanami, the mother of the Japanese archipelago. The shrine's Honden (Main Hall) dates from 1346.

A little further west is **Yaegaki-jinja**, dedicated to the gods of marriage and commemorating a princess's rescue from an

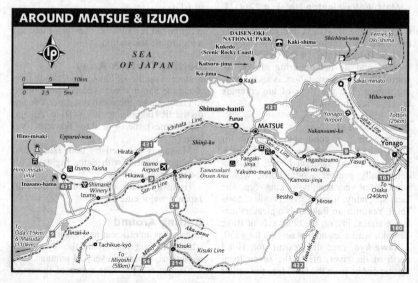

AROUND MATSUE & IZUMO

eight-headed serpent. The events are illustrated in fine 12th-century **wall paintings**. Just for good measure, there are a number of phallic statues around, including one strategically placed in a hole in a tree trunk that apparently represents a vagina!

Adachi Art Museum 足立美術館
East of Matsue in Yasugi is the Adachi Art Museum (admission ¥2200; open 9am-5pm daily). It is set in exquisite extensive gardens (all 43,000 square metres of 'em), and features wonderful artworks by the likes of painter Yokoyama Taikan, mingei (folk craft) potter Kawai Kanjiro and, best of all, firebrand ceramicist Kitaoji Rosanjin. It is worth getting out here early in the day just to slowly lap up the art. A beautifully illustrated English-language pamphlet is available.

OKI-SHOTŌ 隠岐諸島
Directly north of Matsue are the islands of the Oki-shotō, with spectacular scenery and steep cliffs. They are strictly for those who want to get away from it all. At one time, the islands were used to exile political prisoners and daimyō (and, on one occasion, an emperor) who came out on the losing side of political squabbles.

The islands consist of the larger Dōgo island and the three smaller Dōzen islands, plus associated smaller islands. The 7km-long cliffs of the Oki Kuniga coast of **Nishi-no-shima**, at times falling 250m sheer into the sea, are particularly noteworthy. **Kokubun-ji** on Dōgo dates from the 8th century. **Bullfights** are an attraction on Dōgo during the summer months – not man-versus-bull, but bull-versus-bull.

If you're keen to go, allow at least a couple of days, and pop into the information office at Matsue station to sort out a few things before you head off. There's a simple English-language brochure and map of the islands that is called Oki National Park, as well as a Japanese-only website ⓦ www.e-oki.net.

The islands have numerous minshuku and other forms of accommodation, as well as plenty of places to camp.

There are ferry services to the Oki-shotō from Shichirui or Sakai-minato. For Dōgo-shima, from Matsue bus terminal take the 7.55am bus to Shichirui (¥990, one hour) then the 9.20am ferry (¥2530, 2½ hours). Flights operate to Dōgo island from Izumo and Osaka.

Tottori-ken 鳥取県

If you like spectacular coastal scenery, sand dunes, onsen hot springs and volcanoes, then Tottori-ken is a great place to visit, especially in summer.

Yonago 米子
Yonago is a sizable city and important railway junction – here, the JR San-in line, which runs along the Sea of Japan coast, is met by the JR Hakubi line coming up from Okayama on the Sanyō side of the mountains.

There is an **information office** (☎ 0859 22-6317; open 9am-6pm daily) in JR Yonago station, and things to do include a visit to the **Yonago Water Bird Park** (admission ¥210; open 9am-5.30pm Wed-Mon), which boasts over 50 kinds of birds, including the 'whistling swan'.

Kaike Onsen is on the coast, north of the station, and is the largest onsen area in the San-in region, with endless hot water, plenty of accommodation, a sandy swimming beach and pine trees.

Yonago's airport has daily flights to/from Japan's major cities.

Daisen 大山
Although it's not one of Japan's highest mountains, at 1729m Daisen looks very impressive because it rises straight from sea level – its summit is only about 10km from the coast.

The popular climb up the volcano is a five-to-six hour return trip from the ancient **Daisen-ji**. There are fine views over the coast and, in perfect conditions, all the way to the Oki-shotō. Pick up a copy of Lonely Planet's Hiking in Japan for detailed information on hiking Daisen.

Buses run to the temple from Yonago (¥800, 50 minutes). **Daisen Youth Hostel** (☎ 0859 52-2501; beds ¥2750; meals available) is a short walk from Daisen-ji.

The mountain snags the northwest monsoon winds in the winter, bringing deep snow and tons of enjoyment for skiers at what is western Japan's top ski area.

Along the Coast to Tottori

Tottori is known for its nashi pears, and those with a penchant for them may wish to visit the **Tottori Nijisseiki Pear Museum** (*admission ¥500; open 9am-5pm daily*) in Kurayoshi.

Just north of Kurayoshi is **Lake Tōgo**, which has **Hawai Onsen** on its western side and **Tōgo Onsen** on its eastern side. There is a ton of accommodation around, including **Koho-ji Youth Hostel** (*☎ 0858 35-2054; beds ¥2850; onsen ¥100; meals available*), which is attached to a Buddhist temple on the western side.

North of the lake is the **Lake Tōgo Hawai Seaside Park**, which has camping and a swimming beach. The likeness of the town's name to the popular Pacific islands is not lost on the people of Hawaii, but though there's a nice beach, it's not Waimea Bay. It does have a sister-city in Hawaii though.

Travelling eastwards, there is a succession of impressive swimming beaches split by rocky headlands all the way to Tottori city, notably Ishiwaki, Ide-ga-hama, Aoya, Hamamura Onsen and the extremely popular Hakuto. It's packed with surfers on weekends in summer. If you're on the train, you'll miss a lot of it as the line runs a fair way inland. You may wish to get out and hitch instead.

TOTTORI 鳥取

☎ 0857 • pop 150,000

Tottori is a large, busy town some distance back from the coast. The main coast road passes through Tottori's northern fringe in a blizzard of car dealers, *pachinko* parlours and fast-food outlets. The town's main attraction is its famous sand dunes. There's a helpful **tourist information booth** (*☎ 22-3318; open 9.30am-6.30pm daily*) inside the station, with English-language pamphlets and maps.

Tottori-sakyū (The Dunes)

鳥取砂丘

Used as the film location for Teshigahara Hiroshi's classic 1964 film *Woman in the Dunes*, the Tottori sand dunes are on the coast about 5km from the city. There's a viewing point on a hillside overlooking the dunes, along with a huge car park and the usual assortment of tourist amenities. The dunes stretch for over 10km along the coast and, at some points, can be about 2km wide. The

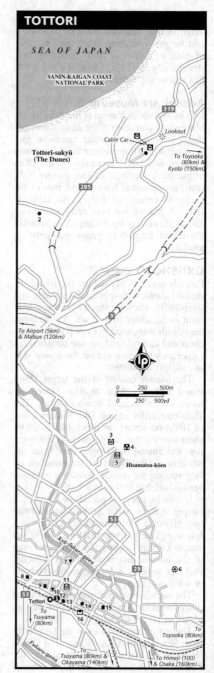

TOTTORI

PLACES TO STAY
8 Tottori Green Hotel Morris
   鳥取ホテルグリーンモリス
9 Hotel Taihei
   ホテル太平
13 Tottori Washington Hotel
   鳥取ワシントンホテル
15 Matsuya-sō
   まつや荘

PLACES TO EAT
7 Flags
10 Daizen
   大善

OTHERS
1 Tottori Sand Dunes Centre
   砂丘センター
2 Tottori Cycling Terminal
   サイクリングターミナル
3 Tottori Prefectural Museum
   鳥取県立博物館
4 Tottori-jō Ruins
   鳥取城跡
5 Jinpū-kaku Villa & Museum
   仁風閣

6 Kannon-in
   観音院
11 Folkcraft Museum
   民芸美術館
12 Tourist Information Booth
   観光案内所
14 Ekimae Ichiba
   駅前市場
16 Post Office
   郵便局

section where the dunes are highest is popular with parapenters who fly off on the incoming sea breezes. You can even get a 'Lawrence of Arabia' photo with a camel while wearing Arab headgear if you choose. It's quite easy to get away from it all out on the sand, which has tracks all over the place.

Use the city's Loop Bus (see Getting Around later) to get out to Tottori-sakyū. The bus stop for the dunes is *Sakyū-Sentā* (Dunes Centre).

About 1km southwest of the lookout it's possible to rent bicycles at the **Tottori Cycling Terminal** (¥300 for four hours). Get off the bus at Kodomo-no-kuni iriguchi (Children's World entrance). You can even stay at the **Cycling Terminal** (☎ 29-0800; per person ¥2730), but it's a bit isolated. There's a camping area next door.

Other Attractions

Tottori's other attractions are mainly concentrated in a compact little group about 1.5km northeast of the station.

Only the foundations remain of **Tottori-jō**; the castle overlooked the town from the hillside. Below the castle walls is the European-style **Jinpū-kaku Villa** (admission ¥150; open 9am-5pm Tues-Sun) dating from 1906 and now used as a museum. Across from this building is the modern **Tottori Prefectural Museum** (admission ¥180; open 9am-5pm Tues-Sun).

Tottori also has an interesting little **Folkcraft Museum** (admission ¥500; open 10am-5pm Thur-Tues) near the JR station, with items from Japan, Korea, China and even Europe. East of the station is the 17th-century garden **Kannon-in** (admission ¥600; open 9am-5pm daily).

Ekimae Ichiba (open 4am-6pm) is a fascinating fish market near the station. The city also has a number of *onsen* in hotels and ryokan available for public bathing. The information office has a map of the city.

Places to Stay & Eat

Matsuya-sō (☎ 22-4891; per person with/without meals ¥6000/3500) is the cheapest lodging, about a 10-minute walk from the station. It's pleasant and comfortable.

Tottori Green Hotel Morris (☎ 22-2331; singles ¥5000) is one of the cheaper places around; the sign in English outside says 'Hotel Morris'. **Hotel Taihei** (☎ 29-1111; singles/twins ¥5300/9500) and the **Tottori Washington Hotel** (☎ 27-8111; singles/twins ¥6700/13,500) are near the station.

There are plenty of places to eat around the station. For quantity and quality at a reasonable price, try the *teishoku* (set menu meals) at the raucous **Daizen**, on the right as you enter the arcade. The *irrashai*s (welcome) and *arigato gozaimashita*s (thank you very much) are deafening in this eatery. **Flags**, a few streets north from the station on the left, is a good little pizzeria with its own coffee shop next door.

A bit more upmarket and traditionally Japanese are **Takumi Kappo** and **Jujuan**.

Getting There & Away

The coastal JR San-in line runs through Tottori from Matsue (¥2210, 2¼ hours) and on to Toyo'ōka (*futsū*, ¥1450, two hours) and Kyoto. The JR Inbi line connects with Tsuyama and on to Okayama (¥4880, two hours) on the San-yō coast.

Tottori airport is just west of town, with flights to/from Tokyo.

Can You Eat Natto?

Sooner or later, should you spend any length of time eating with Japanese acquaintances, you'll see your hitherto gracious hosts – amid much winking and elbow nudging – suddenly perform a culinary Jekyll and Hyde, in the game of 'Let's Gross Out the Gaijin'.

The rules, unstated but recognised intuitively by all, are simple: produce the weirdest food you can, and present it to the foreign guest in a situation so laced with *giri* (social obligation) that they are forced to eat it. Watch as they turn the same colour as freshly salted squid intestines. Suggested weapons in this game of gastronomic sabotage are *natto* (fermented soy beans, best topped off with a raw quail's egg); *inago* (locusts), good and crunchy; and *uni* (sea urchin), orangey-yellow with the consistency and shape of wet brains.

If that fails to work, bring out the heavy guns. *Odori-dako* – octopus chopped up but very much alive, wriggling and adhering itself to the roof of one's mouth – should do the trick, but if all else fails there's one infallible weapon: *shira-ko* (raw cod sperm).

However, *gaijin* visitors are not without their own culinary arsenal. If you want to be on equal terms, stuff your backpack with liquorice bootlaces, steak & kidney pie, Vegemite, or, horror of horrors, rice pudding. If you can get your hosts into a French restaurant, order snails and see who consumes them!

Getting Around

Tottori has a new and efficient Loop Bus for visitors, but at the time of research, it only ran from 18 July to 31 August on Saturday, Sunday and public holidays. You can get a map and timetable from the information office.

The bus connects all of the major attractions, including the sand dunes, and costs ¥200 per ride or ¥600 for a day pass. If you are in Torttori outside these dates, a bus runs every 30 minutes from 8.45am from in front of the station to the dunes.

Rental bicycles are available near the station. For more deatils ask at the information office.

SAN-IN COAST NATIONAL PARK
山陰海岸国立公園

The spectacular coastline east from the Tottori dunes all the way to the peninsula, Tango-hantō, in Kyoto-fu is known as the San-in Kaigan Kokuritsu Kōen – the San-in Coast National Park. There are sandy beaches, rugged headlands, rocky islets and a cruisy atmosphere.

There are train lines the length of the area, but they spend a fair bit of time inland and in tunnels. The best way to see the coastline is on wheels, whether it be a rental car, a motorbike, a bicycle or by thumb. If you stick to the trains, make the effort to get off every now and then.

Uradome Kaigan 浦富海岸

First up of interest is Uradome Kaigan. Cruises (☎ 0857 73-1212; 40 minutes; ¥1200; available March to November) leave Ōtani-sanbashi, which is about 35 minutes east of Tottori by bus from JR Tottori station. The same bus travels via the dunes, so it's possible to visit the dunes and do the cruise as a day trip from Tottori. Boat is the only way to see the craggy cliffs and islets, with pines clinging precariously to their sides.

Uradome and **Makidani**, two very popular beaches, are a few kilometres east. The closest station is Iwami on the JR San-in line, 2km from the coast, where there is an **information office** (☎ 0857 72-3481; open 9am-6pm Tues-Sun); you can rent bicycles or arrange accommodation here. **Seaside Uradome** (☎ 0857 73-1555; per person with/without meals ¥10,000/6000) is located on the sandy beachfront. There is camping at Makidani beach.

Higashi-hama 東浜

The next train station heading eastwards is Higashi-hama and if you're riding the train, this is one to hop off at. It's all of 100m from the station to a long, sandy beach where you can take a stroll or a dip and contemplate the fact that Japan is not all urban sprawl after all.

The Tottori-ken/Hyōgo-ken border is on the next headland.

Northern Honshū 本州の北部

As we turn the corners of the narrow road to the deep north, we may soar with exhilaration, or we may fall flat on our faces...

Bashō, 1644–94

The northern part of Honshū, known in Japanese as Tōhoku, comprises the prefectures of Fukushima-ken, Miyagi-ken, Iwate-ken, Aomori-ken, Akita-ken and Yamagata-ken. This chapter begins with Fukushima-ken, then moves north along the eastern side of Tōhoku, continues round the northern tip, and finally travels down the western side covering Niigata-ken and the island, Sado-ga-shima.

The region used to be known as Michinoku meaning, 'the end of the road' and, even today, its six prefectures are among the least developed for tourism in Japan. However, if you do venture north, you will find the region has its fair share of hidden gems, especially for those seeking traditional rural life and unspoilt natural scenery.

The few major cities make for a good place to get organised before heading off into the back country, with hikes along spectacular rocky coastlines, and volcanic regions where hot springs are tucked away in the mountains. Several excellent ski resorts benefit from the long and severe winters and heavy snowfalls. Tōhoku is also studded with cultural sights – temples, samurai villas, traditional farmhouses and vibrant festivals.

The region was originally inhabited by a people known in previous centuries as the Ezo. The Ezo are believed to have been related to the Ainu, who now live in Hokkaidō. Although the Ezo were conquered and pushed back during the Kamakura period, it wasn't until the 17th century that the area came under complete government control.

During the Meiji era, the region suffered from years of neglect. This trend was only reversed after WWII, with a drive for development based heavily on industrial growth. Despite this, the region still relies heavily on agriculture and many Japanese consider it a place in the back of beyond. Tōhoku people remain popular targets for Japanese comedians.

Highlights

- Wallow in the glorious tranquillity of the island of Kinkasan
- Soak away your stress with a dip in the Zaō Onsen Dai-rotemburo outdoor hot springs
- Get a taste for city life northern style with a big night out in Morioka
- Watch the sun go down over delightful Tazawa-ko, then head for a herbal bath
- Try your hand at being a pilgrim hiking the sacred trio of Dewa Sanzan mountains
- Consult the *itako* at an Osore-zan spiritual festival, or just sample the spooky ambience of Japan's most remote peak

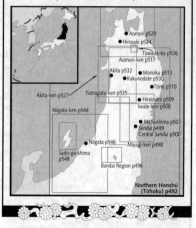

Aomori p520
Hirosaki p524
Towada-ko p526
Aomori-ken p517
Akita p532
Morioka p513
Kakunodate p530
Tōno p510
Akita-ken p527
Yamagata-ken p535
Hiraizumi p509
Iwate-ken p508
Niigata-ken p544
Matsushima p503
Sendai p499
Central Sendai p500
Niigata p546
Miyagi-ken p498
Sado-ga-shima p548
Bandai Region p496
Northern Honshū (Tōhoku) p492

SUGGESTED ITINERARIES

In addition to straight coastal or central routes, the following are interesting, yet practical, east–west tours.

Bashō fans can easily follow in their haiku-scribbling hero's footsteps with a two-week itinerary, taking in Yamadera, Tsuroka, Dewa Sanzan, Hirosaki, Hiraizumi, Matsushima and Naruko Onsen.

One week is enough to take in some of the colourful northern festivals, including the Akita Kantō Matsuri, Hirosaki's Neputa Matsuri and Aomori's Nebute Matsuri, or to enjoy a week of soaking at the holy trinity of northern *onsen*: Zaō, Naruko and Aoni.

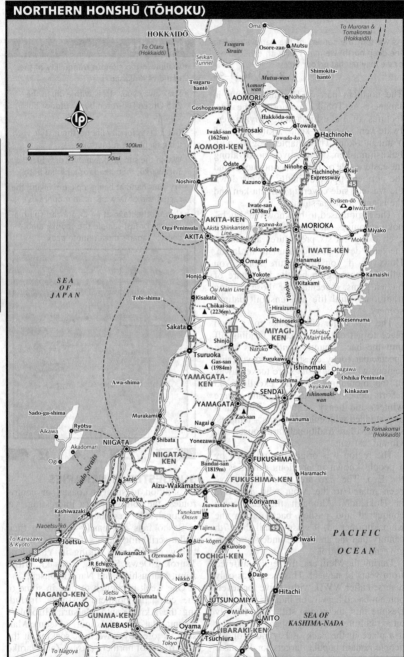

NORTHERN HONSHŪ (TŌHOKU)

NORTHERN HONSHŪ

HOKKAIDŌ

To Otaru
(Hokkaidō)

To Muroran &
Tomakomai
(Hokkaidō)

Ōma

Tsugaru
Straits

Osore-zan ▲ Mutsu

Seikan
Tunnel

Shimokita-
hantō

Mutsu-wan

Tsugaru-
hantō

Aomori-
wan

AOMORI

Noheji

Goshogawara

Hakkōda-san

Towada

Hachinohe

Iwaki-san
(1625m) ▲ Hirosaki

Towada-ko

AOMORI-KEN

Ōdate

Ninohe

Hachinohe
Expressway

Kuji

Noshiro

7

Kazuno

Tōhoku

45

Ryūsen-dō

Iwaizumi

Iwate-san
(2038m) ▲

Tōhoku
Hosen Line

MORIOKA

Miyako

Oga

Tazawa-ko

IWATE-KEN

Moichi

Oga Peninsula

Akita Shinkansen
Line

AKITA

Kakunodate

Expressway

Hanamaki

Ōmagari

Tōno

Kamaishi

Honjō

Yokote

Tōhoku

Kitakami

Ōu Main Line

Tobi-shima

Kisakata

Hiraizumi

Chōkai-san
(2236m) ▲

Ichinoseki

Kesennuma

SEA
OF
JAPAN

Sakata

7

MIYAGI-
KEN

Tōhoku
Main Line

Shinjō

Naruko

Tsuruoka

Gas-san
(1984m) ▲

Furukawa

Ishinomaki

Onagawa

YAMAGATA-
KEN

Awa-shima

Matsushima

Oshika Peninsula

Ayukawa

SENDAI

Ishinomaki-
wan

Kinkazan

YAMAGATA

Zaō-san ▲

Sado-ga-shima

Ryōtsu

Murakami

Nagai

Iwanuma

Aikawa

Akadomari

Shibata

Yonezawa

To Tomakomai
(Hokkaidō)

NIIGATA

NIIGATA-
KEN

Bandai-san
(1819m) ▲

FUKUSHIMA

Ogi

49

Haramachi

Sanjō

Aizu-Wakamatsu

FUKUSHIMA-KEN

Nagaoka

Inawashiro-ko

Kōriyama

Kashiwazaki

Yunokami
Onsen

Naoetsu-kō

Tajima

49

Iwaki

To Kanazawa
& Kyōto

Jōetsu

Muikamachi

Aizu-kōgen

Kuroiso

PACIFIC

8

Itoigawa

JR Echigo
Yūzawa

Ozenuma-ko

TOCHIGI-KEN

Daigo

OCEAN

18

Jōetsu
Line

Nikkō

Hitachi

NAGANO-KEN

Numata

Mashiko

SEA OF
KASHIMA-NADA

NAGANO

GUNMA-KEN

UTSUNOMIYA

MITO

MAEBASHI

Oyama

IBARAKI-KEN

To Nagoya

To
Tokyo

Tsuchiura

0   50   100km
0   25   50mi

Both itineraries are best in summer, but book accommodation well in advance if you're planning to travel during festival times.

INFORMATION

As Tōhoku is less travelled by foreigners, and sources of tourist information about it are less common outside major cities, your queries may be answered more easily by phoning the **Japan Travel-Phone** (within Japan toll-free ☎ 0088-22-4800).

Exploring Tōhoku by Jan Brown is a detailed guide to the region with comprehensive background information and useful indexes with place names in kanji (Chinese script used for writing Japanese). The Tōhoku Tourism Promotion Council publishes *Japan Tōhoku*, a glossy brochure that includes an English map and details of sights, festivals and transport.

For some literary refreshment en route, dip into any of the many translations of *Oku-no-Hosomichi (The Narrow Road to the Deep North)*, which contains classic haiku penned by Bashō, perhaps the most famous Japanese poet, on his travels through central and southern Tōhoku in 1689. If you'd like to bring yourself up to date, read *The Narrow Road to the Deep North: Journey into Lost Japan* by Lesley Downer, which is an account of a walk that retraced Bashō's celebrated trip.

GETTING AROUND

Transport in the region focuses on three major railway lines. Two of these run north–south down the east and west coasts, the third snakes down between them in the centre, closely following the Japan Railways (JR) Tōhoku *shinkansen* (bullet train) line, which links Tokyo with Morioka in about 2½ hours.

Transport connections in the region have been accelerated with the opening of the 1997 Akita *shinkansen* line from Morioka to Akita, the 1999 extension of the Yamagata *shinkansen* north to Shinjō and the extension to the Tōhoku *shinkansen* as far as Hachinohe, which opened in December 2002.

Exploration of the more remote parts of Tōhoku are generally possible with local train and bus connections but car hire is often preferable. Roads and connections can be severely affected by winter weather.

Fukushima-ken
福島県

AIZU-WAKAMATSU 会津若松
☎ 0242 • pop 120,000

This rather drab place has few attractions to offer the traveller outside being a stopoff en route to Mount Bandai.

At the **tourist information office** (☎ 32-0688; open 8.45am-5.15pm daily), inside Aizu-Wakamatsu station, staff speak English and offer useful English-language maps and brochures, as does the **tourist information annexe** at the castle, Tsuruga-jō.

The Japan National Tourist Organisation (JNTO) leaflet *Aizu-Wakamatsu and Bandai* has details of sights and accommodation.

The **post office** (with ATM service) is located along Chūō-dōri, the main drag.

Iimori-yama 飯盛山

This mountain is home to the graves of 19 teenage members of the Byakkotai (White Tigers Band), who retreated from imperial forces and committed ritual suicide in 1868. The standard account of this tragedy maintains that the boys killed themselves after they looked down from the hilltop and thought they saw the town and its castle in flames. In reality, only the town was alight and it would be weeks until the town was finally defeated by food shortages. The event has received attention not only from Japanese nationalists but also from overseas fascist organisations.

Apart from the **Byakkotai Kinenkan** (*Byakkotai Memorial Hall; admission ¥400*), there's also **Sazae-dō** (*admission ¥300; open 8.15am-sunset daily Apr-Oct, 9.30am-4.30pm daily Nov-Mar*), an 18th-century hexagonal hall where 33 Kannon (Buddhist goddess of mercy) represent the famous pilgrimage of Kansai.

The hill is a steep climb on foot; alternatively, use the hillside escalator (¥250).

From stop No 5 outside Aizu-Wakamatsu train station, buses run to Iimori-yama (¥220, 15 minutes) before continuing to Tsuruga-jō via Aizu Bukeyashiki.

Tsuruga-jō 鶴ヶ城

Tsuruga-jō is nicknamed Crane Castle, and the present building is a 20th-century reconstruction containing an historical **museum** *(admission ¥400; open 8.30am-4.30pm daily)*. On the castle grounds, **Rinkaku** *(admission ¥200, combined castle ticket ¥500; open 8.30am-4pm daily)* is a 400-year-old teahouse that was rescued from the castle's destruction by a local family and returned here in 1990.

Buses leaving from stop No 5 outside Aizu-Wakamatsu train station run to the Tsuruga-jō-kitaguchi stop (¥210, 15 minutes).

Oyaku-en 御薬園

Oyaku-en *(admission ¥310; open 8.30am-5pm daily)* is a garden complex with a large central carp pond and a section devoted to the cultivation of medicinal herbs, as encouraged by former Aizu lords.

Buses from stop No 4 outside Aizu-Wakamatsu train station bound for Higashi-yama Onsen stop at the Oyaku-en Iriguchi stop (¥240, 10 minutes) before continuing to Aizu Bukeyashiki.

Aizu Bukeyashiki 会津武家屋敷

Visitors to this large-scale reconstruction of an opulent samurai villa from the Edo period *(admission ¥850; open 8.30am-5pm daily Apr-Oct, 9am-4.30pm daily Nov-Mar)* are given a useful English guide map. Buses from stop No 4 outside Aizu-Wakamatsu train station bound for Higashiyama Onsen stop at the Bukeyashiki-mae stop (¥290, 15 minutes).

Special Events

The highlight of the **Aizu Aki Matsuri** (Aizu Fall Festival), 22 to 24 September, is a morning parade on the 23rd with armoured warriors.

Places to Stay & Eat

The **tourist information office** offers an English-language map detailing the unspectacular accommodation options.

Aizuno Youth Hostel *(☎ 55-1020; dorm/private rooms ¥2000/4000)* is comfortable but a 20-minute walk from Aizu-Takada station along the Tadami line from Aizu-Wakamatsu (¥230, 20 minutes); seven trains run daily but only one in the afternoon.

Minshuku Takaku *(☎ 26-6299; rooms with 2 meals from ¥6000)* is a traditional but comfortable place five minutes east of Aizu Bukeyashiki and its accompanying bus stop.

Green Hotel Aizu *(☎ 24-5181; singles/doubles/triples ¥5600/9500/15,600)* is the best business-hotel option with Western-style rooms and a restaurant. It's located five minutes southeast of the station.

Aside from chain restaurants, Aizu is not blessed with eateries. Nanokamachi-dōri, a 20-minute walk south of the train station where it crosses Chūō-dōri, is the best hunting ground. **Takino** *(open 11am-9pm daily)* is a traditional restaurant serving *wappa-meishi* (salmon and vegetables served over rice in a steamer) from about ¥1500, while **Matsuta-ya** *(open 10am-5pm Thur-Tues)* serves *dengaku*, snacks grilled over charcoal on skewers for about ¥200 each.

Getting There & Away

From Tokyo, take the JR Tōhoku *shinkansen* to Kōriyama (¥7970, 1¼ hours), then change to a *kaisoku* (a rapid service stopping at limited stations) train on the JR Banetsu-sai line for Aizu-Wakamatsu (¥1110, 1¼ hours). There are two daily *kaisoku* train between Aizu-Wakamatsu and Niigata (¥2210, 2½ hours); express buses to Niigata run four times daily (¥2000, 1¾ hours).

Heading to Nikkō (¥3390, 3½ hours) or Asakusa (¥4540, five hours), take a combination of private train lines from JR Aizu-Wakamatsu station via Yunokami Onsen and Aizu-Kōgen station, eventually transferring to a train bound for Asakusa via Shimo-imaichi (where you can connect with trains to Tōbu-Nikkō station); trains run hourly.

Getting Around

From Aizu-Wakamatsu station, two bus lines conveniently circle the main sights – one running clockwise, another anticlockwise. A one-day pass (¥920) is available from the **bus information office** which is outside the station.

ŌUCHIJUKU 大内宿

An important post town on the Aizu Nishi-kaidō route, as well as a battle site during the Boshin Civil War, Ōuchijuku was forgotten after the construction of a new highway further east. Now designated as a special preservation area for historic buildings, the town's main street is lined with an impressive number of traditional inns, farmhouses, restaurants and shops, all earning their livelihood from travellers much as they did during the Edo era. The **Ōuchijuku Machinami Tenjikan** (*Ōuchijuku Cultural Museum; admission ¥250; open 9am-4.30pm daily*) is a reconstruction of an inn that was originally used by travelling feudal lords.

After meandering through town, turn off at the torii (Shintō shrine entrance gate) and follow a dirt road out into the fields to the shrine, **Takakura-jinja**, dedicated to Prince Mochihito Takakura, the second son of Emperor Goshirakawa, who allegedly fled here after being defeated by the Heike clan. On 2 July, **Hange Matsuri** commemorates his flight with a feudal procession through town.

Ōuchijuku is an easy day trip from Aizu-Wakamatsu, otherwise a *minshuku* for the night costs about ¥6500 per person, including two meals.

From JR Aizu-Wakamatsu station, take the private Aizu Tetsudō line to Yunokami Onsen (¥1000, 40 minutes), for connections to Tokyo (Asakusa) or Nikkō (see Aizu-Wakamatsu Getting There & Away). There is no bus service to Ōuchijuku from Yunokami Onsen – either walk, hitch the 6km or take a taxi (¥1700). The route is signposted from Yunokami-onsen station; ask station staff for the English-language sketch map before setting out.

KITAKATA 喜多方
☎ 0241 • pop 40,000

Kitakata has two claims to fame: 2600 coloured *kura* (mud-walled storehouses), which now function as living quarters, sake breweries and workshops, and 120 *rāmen* (Chinese egg noodles in soup) shops.

Staff at the tiny **tourist information kiosk** (☎ 24-2633), to the left of Kitakata station's exit, speak no English – they merely hand out copies of a small English-language map.

Bicycle rental is available outside the station (¥1500 per day), while a horse-drawn carriage circles town from April to October (¥1300, 90 minutes); Japanese commentary only.

Among the scant sites, the **Yamatogawa Sake Brewing Museum** (*open 9am-4.30pm daily*) and Anshoji shrine are both free to visit and a 15-minute walk north of Kitakata station.

Places to Stay & Eat

Sasaya Ryokan (☎ 22-0008; *rooms per person with 2 meals from ¥6500*) is a traditional place, 1km north of the station.

Kitakata's best-known *rāmen* shop is the 70-year-old **Genraiken** (*open 10am-7.30pm Wed-Mon*), which is packed at lunchtime for ¥800 sets; look out for the red facade and dragon sign outside.

Getting There & Away

Kitakata is an easy half-day trip from Aizu-Wakamatsu, accessible by train along the JR Banetsu-saisen line (¥320, 15 minutes).

INAWASHIRO-KO 猪苗代湖
☎ 0242 • pop 18,000

Although the fourth-largest lake in Japan, Inawashiro-ko town is merely a stopoff en route to the scenic Bandai-san area.

The **tourist information office** (☎ 62-2048; *open 8.30am-5pm daily*), to the left outside JR Inawashiro station, has scant maps; no English is spoken.

The JR Banetsu-saisen line connects Aizu-Wakamatsu with Inawashiro (*kaisoku* ¥480, 35 minutes). Hourly buses also run between Aizu-Wakamatsu station and Inawashiro station (¥1140, 45 minutes); frequent buses to Bandai-kōgen (¥870, 30 minutes) leave from opposite the station.

BANDAI-SAN & BANDAI-KŌGEN
磐梯山・磐梯高原
☎ 0241 • pop 4000

Bandai-san erupted on 15 July 1888 destroying dozens of villages and their inhabitants. The aftershock completely rearranged the landscape, creating the plateau, Bandai-kōgen, and damming local rivers, which then formed numerous lakes and ponds.

Now a national park, the area offers spectacular scenery with ample scope for hiking and skiing in winter. The most popular – and often crowded – walk follows a 3.7km nature trail around **Goshiki-numa** (Five-Coloured Lakes); trailheads are located at Goshiki-numa Iriguchi and the Bandai-kōgen bus stop, the main transport hubs on the edge of Hibara-ko. Bandai-san (1819m) itself can be climbed in a day with an early start; the most popular route starts from the Bandai-kōgen bus stop and climbs up through the skiing ground to the summit.

NORTHERN HONSHŪ

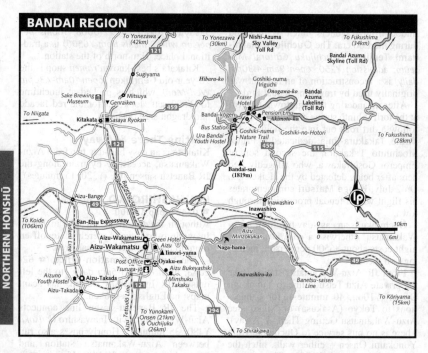

BANDAI REGION

There is a new **visitors centre** (open 9am-5pm Wed-Mon) near the Goshiki-numa Iriguchi trailhead.

Places to Stay & Eat

The best option is the faded but friendly **Ura Bandai Youth Hostel** (☎ 32-2811; e urabandai-YH@nifty.com; beds members/nonmembers ¥2990/3520, with 2 meals ¥4460/4990). It is open from late April to late November, has an 11pm curfew, and laundry and bicycle hire (¥1000 per day). Next to one of the Goshiki-numa trailheads, it is a seven-minute track walk from the Goshiki-numa Iriguchi bus stop and signposted right from the car park. The adjoining camp site has ¥1000 tents and ¥5000 cabins.

Walking north across the street from the bus stop, several *minshuku* cater to hikers and skiers. Taking the first left, **Pension Emu** (☎ 32-2228; rooms per person with 2 meals from ¥8000) is a friendly place with some English spoken. Further north, **Goshiki-no-Hotori** (☎ 32-2356; rooms per person with 2 meals from ¥7000) has an English sign hanging outside and provides free transport to skiing grounds in winter.

Fraser Hotel (☎ 32-3470; rooms per person with 2 meals weekday/weekend from ¥14,000/12,000), the upmarket option, is northeast of the Goshiki-numa Iriguchi bus stop along the highway and next to a convenience store.

Next to same the bus stop, a simple but satisfying restaurant offers ¥800 *rāmen* while, across the intersection opposite the bus stop, Ishikawa Kōbō is a small coffee shop that hires bikes for ¥1000 per day.

Getting There & Away

Frequent buses depart stop No 3 outside Inawashiro station and pass by the Goshiki-numa Iriguchi stop (¥750, 25 minutes) heading onto the Bandai-kōgen bus stop (¥870, 30 minutes).

From Aizu-Wakamatsu to Fukushima via the Bandai-Kōgen bus stop, the Skyline sightseeing bus (¥8000, eight hours) runs once daily along scenic toll roads from late April to early November. The bus makes a 30-minute stop at the Jōdodaira lookout, where you can climb to the top of Azuma-kofuji (1707m) in 10 minutes. Across the road, Issaikyō-yama (1949m) belches steam

Hachiman-gū Matsuri, Morioka, northern Honshū

Tōno Matsuri parade, northern Honshū

Masked dancer, Tōno Matsuri parade

Young musicians, Hachiman-gū Matsuri, Morioka

Azumakofuji, Fukushima-ken, northern Honshū

Bandai-san summit, Fukushima-ken, northern Honshū

in dramatic contrast to its passive neighbour; a steep 45-minute climb is rewarded with sweeping views from the top.

Miyagi-ken 宮城県

SENDAI 仙台
☎ 022 • pop 1,008,000

Sendai – Tōhoku's largest and most cosmopolitan city – can feel rather parochial after Tokyo. But, if you're heading north, it's an ideal base to arrange tickets, exchange your rail pass, sort out post, check email and see some bright lights before heading to nearby rural *onsen* (mineral hot spring spa) or along the Oku-Matsushima coast.

The dominant figure in Sendai's history is Date Masamune (1567–1636), who earned the nickname Dokuganryū (One-Eyed Dragon) after he caught smallpox as a child and went blind in his right eye. Date adopted Sendai as his base and, in a combination of military might and administrative skill, became one of the most powerful feudal lords in Japan. An accomplished artist and scholar, Date also raised Sendai to the status of cultural centre of the Tōhoku region.

Unfortunately, there's not much evidence of high culture these days. During WWII, Sendai was demolished by Allied bombing, and the city was later rebuilt with wide streets and boulevards laid out in a grid pattern. From the station, the broad sweep of Aoba-dōri, lined with many of the major department stores, banks and hotels, leads west to Aoba-yama. The main shopping areas are the series of arcades along Chūō-dōri and Ichibanchō-dōri, which intersect just east of Kokubunchō-dōri, the main drag of the largest entertainment district in Tōhoku.

Information

Inside the station's west exit, the **tourist information office** (☎ 222-4069; open 8.30am-8pm daily) is highly efficient but can get really crowded. English-speaking staff provide English-language maps and pamphlets, and can advise on travel to Matsushima and other regional attractions. It's also worth knowing that the nearby **Travel Service Centre** is – apart from Misawa in Aomori-ken – the furthest place north to exchange your JR East rail pass (see Train Passes in the Getting Around section); it's open every day of the year. Miyagi **Goodwill Guides** (☎ 275-3796) are available for free sightseeing tours of Sendai.

Near the Sendai City Museum, the **Sendai International Centre** (☎ 265-2471; W www.sira.or.jp/english; open 9am-8pm daily) is a fantastic resource for visitors and foreign residents. There is an information desk with English-speaking staff, as well as an international newspaper library, bulletin board, CNN broadcasts, free Internet and a Visa ATM. The centre also operates the invaluable **Sendai English Hotline** (☎ 224-1919; 9am-8pm daily). To get there from Sendai station, take the Loople bus (see the Sendai Getting Around section), or a city bus from stop No 9 at the west bus pool to Loople bus stop No 5 marked Hakubutsukan/Kokusai Centre-mae.

There's a **post office** on level one of JR Sendai station, while the **central post office**,

---

NJR Sendai Station Quick Reference Guide

Navigating your way around JR Sendai station can seem daunting at first, but make it your friend and it will serve you well.

Level three – *Shinkansen* tracks, JR ticket office and small lockers.

Level two – JR lines, the tourist information office (see above) and **Travel Service Centre** (open 10am-7pm Mon-Fri, 10am-6pm Sat & Sun) to exchange rail passes, are both located at the west exit.

From the main exit, overhead walkways lead to shops and to the west bus pool. The bus ticket office is next to stop No 15.3 for the Loople sightseeing bus (stop 15.3), city buses and airport limousines (stop 15.2).

Level one – At the west exit, there's a **post office** (open 9am-6pm Mon-Fri), which offers cash advances and has an international ATM, several bakery cafés (Delina is particularly good) and a Body College relaxation station (15-minute back rub ¥1500, 20-minute foot rub ¥2400).

At the east exit, you can leave larger luggage (from 6am to 11pm ¥410, overnight ¥650) at the parcel storage office.

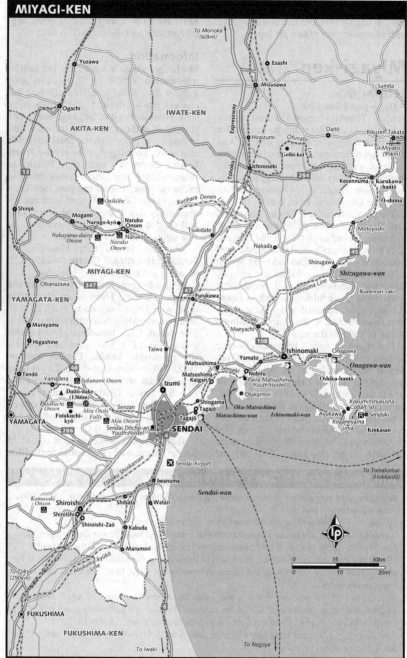

MIYAGI-KEN

To Morioka (60km)

Yuzawa

Esashi

Sumita

Ogachi

Mizusawa

IWATE-KEN

AKITA-KEN

Hiraizumi

Daitō

Rikuzen-Takata

Ōfunato Line

Geibi-kei

To Miyako (95km)

Ichinoseki

Kesennuma

Karukawa-hantō

Shinjō

Onikōbe

Kurihara Denen Line

Tōhoku Shinkansen

Ō-shima

Mogami

Naruko-kyō

Naruko Onsen

Nakayama-daira Onsen

Naruko Onsen

Tsukidate

Nakada

Shizugawa

Motoyoshi

Shizugawa-wan

Obanazawa

MIYAGI-KEN

Furukawa

Kesennuma Line

Kamiwari-zaki

YAMAGATA-KEN

Murayama

Ishinomaki Line

Maeyachi

Higashine

Taiwa

Yamato

Ishinomaki

Onagawa

Tendō

Yamadera

Sakunami Onsen

Izumi

Matsushima

Senseki Line

Nobiru

Paira Matsushima Youth Hostel

Oshika-hantō

Onagawa-wan

Daitō-dake (1366m)

Futakuchi Onsen

Akiu Ōtaki Falls

Matsushima-Kaigan

Otakamori

Oku-Matsushima

Kokuminshukusha Cobalt-sō

Futakuchi-kyō

Akiu Onsen

Shiogama

Matsushima-wan

Ishinomaki-wan

Ayūkawa

Koganeyama-jinja

YAMAGATA

Sendai Dōchū-an Youth Hostel

Senzan Line

Tagajō

Kinkasan

SENDAI

Senjōjiki

Tōhoku Shinkansen

Sendai Airport

To Tomakomai (Hokkaidō)

Kamasaki Onsen

Iwanuma

Sendai-wan

Shiroishi

Shibata

Watari

Shiroishi

Shiroishi-Zaō

Kakuda

Jōban Line

To Tokyo (290km)

Marumori

Abukuma-kyūkō Line

FUKUSHIMA

FUKUSHIMA-KEN

To Iwaki

To Nagoya

0   15   30km

0   10   20mi

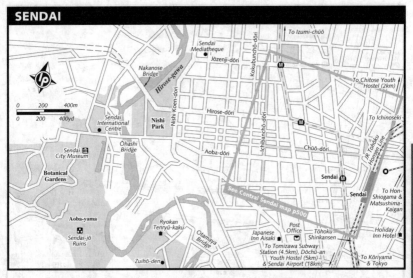

SENDAI

NORTHERN HONSHŪ

100m south of the Sendai Kokusai Hotel, is open 24 hours for post. Both offer ATM service and cash advances on foreign-issued credit cards (8am to 11pm Monday to Friday, 9am to 9pm Saturday, 9am to 7pm Sunday).

Free Internet access is available in the **Netto U Plaza** *(open 10am-8pm daily)*, on the 5th floor of the AER building, which is connected to the station's west exit by pedestrian walkway. Hitachi's **HIT Plaza** *(open 10am-7pm Mon-Fri, 10am-6pm Sat & Sun)* charges ¥300 per hour of Internet use.

On the 1st floor of the AER building, the huge **Maruzen** bookshop has a comprehensive range of English-language magazines and books.

For medical emergencies, **Sendai City Hospital Critical Care Centre** *(☎ 263-9900; 3-1 Shimizu Kōji, Wakabayashi-ku)* is open 24 hours.

Zuihō-den 瑞鳳殿

Zuihō-den *(admission ¥550; open 9am-4.30pm daily Apr-Oct, 9am-4pm daily Nov-Mar)*, the mausoleum of Date Masamune, was originally built in 1637 but later destroyed by WWII bombing. The present building is an exact replica of the original, faithful to the ornate and sumptuous style of the Momoyama period.

From Sendai station, take the Loople bus to stop No 4 (15 minutes).

Sendai City Museum 仙台市博物館

A scale model of Sendai-jō and exhibitions of samurai armour are the main attractions at this museum *(admission ¥400; open 9am-4.15pm Tues-Sun)*.

From Sendai station, take the Loople bus to stop No 5 (20 minutes).

Sendai-jō Ruins 仙台城跡

Sendai-jō was built on Aoba-yama in 1602 by Date Masamune. It was nicknamed Aoba-jō (Green Leaves Castle) for a nearby spring that flowed even during times of drought. The castle's partial destruction during the Meiji era was completed by WWII bombing. The castle ruins – a restored *sumiyagura* (turret) and that's about it – are presided over by a statue of Date on horseback. At the **Aoba Castle Exhibition Hall** *(admission ¥700; open 9am-5pm daily Apr-Oct, 9am-4pm daily Nov-Mar)*, a computer-generated film depicts the castle's former glory; English-language headsets are available.

From Sendai station, take the Loople bus to stop No 6 (25 minutes).

Sendai Mediatheque せんだいメディアテーク

Opened in 2001, this multimedia library and digital arts space *(w www.smt.city.sendai.jp /en; open 9am-8pm daily, library open 10am-8pm Tues-Sun)* is the city's new cultural

NORTHERN HONSHŪ

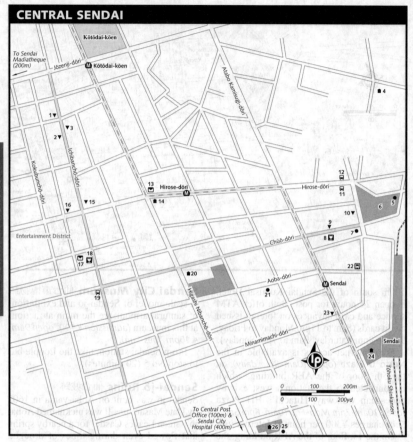

CENTRAL SENDAI

hub with workshops, exhibitions and free Internet access.

From Sendai station, take the Loople bus to stop No 9 (50 minutes).

Special Events

The **Tanabata Matsuri** (Star Festival), held from 6 to 8 August, is the big tourist event in Sendai. According to Chinese legend, a princess and a peasant shepherd were in love but forbidden to meet. The only time of year when the star-crossed lovers could sneak a tryst was when the stars Vega and Altair met in the Milky Way on 7 July. Sendai seems to have stretched the dates a bit, but celebrates in grand style by decorating the main streets and holding afternoon parades along Jōzenji-dōri. Several million

visitors ensure that accommodation is booked solid at this time.

Other major festivals include the lively **Jōzenji Street Jazz Festival**; 500 buskers from across Japan performing during the second weekend in September. From 12 to 31 December, the **Pageant of Starlight** illuminates Aoba-dōri and Jōzenji-dōri with festive lights and, if you're in Sendai on the evening of 14 January, Ōsaki Hachiman-gū shrine plays host to **Donto-sai**, whereby men brave subzero weather conditions to hop around almost naked in a show of collective madness.

Places to Stay – Budget

The best budget option is the **Dōchū-an Youth Hostel** (☎ 247-0511; beds members/ nonmembers ¥2950/3350), which is set

CENTRAL SENDAI

PLACES TO STAY		
4	Roynet Hotel	
	ロイネットホテル仙台	
14	Takenaka Ryokan	
	竹中旅館	
20	Tokyo Dai-Ichi Hotel	
	Sendai	
	東京第一ホテル仙台	
24	Metropolitan Hotel	
	Sendai	
26	Sendai Kokusai Hotel	
	仙台国際ホテル	

PLACES TO EAT		
1	Hoshiyama Kōhī-ten	
	ホシヤマ珈琲店	
2	Chibou	
	千房	
3	Heiroku Sushi	
	回転寿司	

9	Umai Sushikan	
	うまい鮨歓	
10	Sari	
	佐利	
15	Asian Kitchen	
16	Tonton Rāmen;	
	Soba-no-Kanda;	
	Don-tei	
	とんとんラーメン;	
	そばの神田;	
	どん亭	
23	Asian Kitchen 2	

OTHER		
5	Maruzen Bookstore (1/F)	
	AER Building	
	丸善仙台アエル店	
6	AER Building; Netto U	
	Plaza (5/F)	
	アエル	

7	Tokyo Ticket	
	東京チケット	
8	Vilevan	
11	Bus Stop No 40	
	バス乗り場40番	
12	Bus Stop No 41	
	バス乗り場41番	
13	Post Office	
	郵便局	
17	Post Office	
	郵便局	
18	Bar Isn't It?	
19	Loople Bus Stop No 2	
21	HIT Plaza	
22	Loople Bus & Limousine	
	Bus Stops	
25	Sky Symphony Building	
	View Plaza	
	仙台スカイシンフォニ	
	ービルビュープラザ	

NORTHERN HONSHŪ

in an old farmhouse and has a deservedly strong reputation for hospitality. The genial owner offers bike hire, cheap laundry, vegetarian-friendly home cooking and has a fantastic old cedar bath to soak in. The only problem is that the hostel is located 5km south of Sendai at the end of the subway line in Tomizawa (¥290, 12 minutes), then a further 15-minute walk (ask in the station for a sketch map). Alternatively, you can walk to the hostel in 20 minutes from JR Nagamachi station (¥240, 10 minutes).

Closer to the city, **Chitose Youth Hostel** (☎ 222-6329; beds members/nonmembers ¥3000/4000) is a 20-minute walk from Sendai station's west exit. Take any bus going via Miyamachi from stop No 17 at the west bus pool, and get off at Miyamachi-ni-chōme; the hostel is tucked down a small side street three blocks east of the bus stop.

Places to Stay – Mid-Range
Ryokan Sendai can be a hard place to find a cheap room – advance reservations are recommended. **Takenaka Ryokan** (☎ 225-6771; rooms per person ¥4200), next to Hirose-dōri subway station, is a popular place, while **Japanese Inn Aisaki** (☎ 264-0700; singles/twins from ¥4700/8400) is a rather faded place near the post office with Western-style rooms.

Ryokan Tenryū-kaku (☎ 222-9957; rooms per person with 2 meals ¥6500), in a peaceful setting near the entrance to Zuihō-den, is a reliable option but rather far from the action.

Hotels You can sometimes find good deals on the city's numerous business hotels in low season. A smart new option is **Roynet Hotel** (☎ 722-0055; singles/doubles ¥6953/ 8191), 10 minutes north of the station, which has a coin laundry and a 24-hour Royal Host restaurant. If it's full, **Tokyo Dai-Ichi Hotel Sendai** (☎ 262-1355; singles/twins from ¥5800/12,000) is central.

Places to Stay – Top End
If you value comfort, **Sendai Kokusai Hotel** (☎ 268-1112; singles/doubles ¥11,500/ 18,000) is a classy place next to the Sky Symphony building, while the **Metropolitan Hotel Sendai** (☎ 268-2525; singles/twins ¥10,000/18,000) offers JR Pass holders a 10% discount. The smartest of all is the new **Holiday Inn Sendai** (☎ 256-5111; singles/ doubles/triples ¥9500/16,500/20,500), a 10-minute walk from the station's east exit.

Places to Eat
The shopping arcades along Chūō-dōri and Ichibanchō-dōri are the best hunting ground for cheap eats. Try **Sari**, off the eastern end of Chūō-dōri, for Sendai's speciality dish, gyūtan (grilled beef tongue), for ¥700. Near the junction of Ichibanchō-dōri and Hirose-dōri, **Soba-no-Kanda** has ¥400 noodle dishes while **Don-tei** upstairs has decent ¥680 ten-don (tempura over rice), and **Ton-ton Rāmen** next door serves huge bowls of noodles from ¥900. All these places are open 11.30am to 2pm and 5pm to 10pm daily.

For something a little smarter, the two branches of **Asian Kitchen** (open 11am-10pm daily) serve *izakaya*-style Asian fusion cuisine from ¥780 per dish.

Two popular *kaiten sushi* (sushi train or conveyor-belt sushi) restaurants are **Umai Sushikan** (open 11am-9pm daily) and **Heiroku Sushi** (open 11am-9pm daily), with sushi from ¥66 and ¥100 per plate respectively. Opposite the latter, **Chibou** (open 11.30am-2pm & 5pm-11pm daily) is a 3rd floor fun DIY *okonomiyaki* (savoury pancake with meat, vegetables and seafood mixed into the batter) eatery; meals for two cost from ¥1200.

Finally, **Hoshiyama Kōhii-ten** serves the most refined and expensive coffee in Sendai at ¥1000 per cup.

Entertainment

The main hotspot, **Bar Isn't It?**, in the Ichibanchō-dōri arcade, prices all drinks at ¥500 and hosts regular promotional and club nights till very, very late.

For a laid-back jazz vibe, **Vilevan** (open 11am-midnight) has live performances on some weekends and a decent – though not cheap – menu with good vegetarian options.

Getting There & Away

Discount train and flight tickets are available at Tokyo Ticket in the Chōu-dōri arcade.

Air From Sendai airport, 18km south of the city centre, there are international flights to Seoul (¥63,940, 2¾ hours), Beijing (¥111,400, six hours), Dailan (¥94,100, 3¼ hours), Guam (¥75,700, 3¾ hours), Hong Kong (¥111,500, five hours), Shanghai (¥87,500, 3¼ hours) and Honolulu (¥159,220, 7¼ hours).

Domestic destinations include Kansai (¥23,400, 1½ hours), Sapporo (¥24,000, 1¼ hours), Nagoya (¥21,600, 1¼ hours), Okayama (¥27,000, 1½ hours), Hakodate (¥23,000, one hour), Hiroshima (¥31,500, 1½ hours) and Fukuoka (¥33,300, two hours). From Tokyo, the *shinkansen* is so fast that it's not worth flying.

Train From Sendai, the JR Tōhoku *shinkansen* line runs south to Tokyo (¥10,080, two hours), and north to Morioka (¥5780, 50 minutes) for transfers to the Akita *shinkansen* line. Sendai is connected by the JR Senzan line to Yamagata (*kaisoku* ¥1110, one hour) and by the JR Senseki line to Matsushima-kaigan (*kaisoku* ¥400, 25 minutes).

Bus Sendai has a huge – and initially confusing – network of bus services with numerous stops scattered around JR Sendai station. Ask the tourist information office for a bilingual leaflet listing relevant bus numbers, destinations and their appropriate bus stops.

From stop No 42 outside the station's east exit, there are five buses daily to Shinjuku (¥6210, 5½ hours) and Niigata (¥4500, four hours).

From stop No 41, north of the station, buses daily run to Tokyo (¥6210, 7½ hours) at 11am, 10.40pm and 12.10am. From stop No 40 across the street, night buses to Kyoto and Osaka depart at 7.30pm (¥12,230, 12½ hours) as well as day buses to Morioka (¥2850, 2¾ hours), Akita (¥4000, 3¾ hours) and Aomori (¥5700, five hours). Discounted return tickets are available for most routes from Tokyo Ticket.

Boat Sendai-kō is a major port with ferries once daily to Tomakomai on Hokkaidō (¥7600, 14¾ hours); ferries depart at noon every second day for Nagoya (¥4900, 21 hours). To get to Sendai-kō, take a *futsū* (local) train on the JR Senseki line to Tagajō station (¥230); it's then a 10-minute taxi ride. There are also five direct buses from stop No 34 at Sendai station, but only until 6pm (¥490, 40 minutes).

Getting Around

Airport limousines from stop 15.2 at the station's west bus pool depart frequently for the airport between 6.45am and 6.15pm (single/return ¥910/1640, 40 minutes).

The tourist Loople bus leaves from the west bus pool's stop No 15.3 every 30 minutes from 9am to 4pm, making a useful sightseeing loop around the city (¥250 per ride) in a clockwise direction. A one-day pass costs ¥600 and comes with an English-language booklet detailing the bus route and sightseeing discounts for pass holders. Passes can be purchased from the bus ticket office by stop No 15.3.

Sendai's single subway line runs from Izumi-Chūō in the north to Tomizawa in the south but doesn't cover any tourist attractions; single tickets range from ¥200 to ¥290.

AROUND SENDAI 仙台周辺

Tōhoku Shinkansen Repair Depot (*Tōhoku Shinkansen Nosharyōkichi*; ☎ 022-356-5223) is a major inspection facility for Japan's famed *shinkansen*. Over a thousand technicians work day and night on assembly, testing, repairs and development. Free (but short) bus tours of the 53-hectare depot are scheduled at 10am, and 1pm and 3pm on weekdays (Japanese commentary only). Advance bookings are necessary, especially for the festivities of the annual *Shinkansen Matsuri* at the end of August.

The depot is a 10-minute walk from JR Rifu station, 15 minutes by train from Sendai (¥230) with a change at Iwakiri station.

AKIU ONSEN 秋保鴛泉

☎ 022 • pop 4800

This *onsen* is a good base for side trips into the mountains to see **Akiu Ōtaki**, a 55m-high waterfall, and the gorge, **Futakuchi-kyō**, with its *banji-iwa* (rock columns). There are hiking trails along the river valley and a trail from Futakuchi Onsen to the summit of **Daitō-dake** (1366m) that takes about three hours. Hiking maps are available at the **tourist information office** (☎ 398-2323; open 9am-6pm daily) in Akiu Onsen.

There are numerous hotels, *minshuku*, and camping grounds scattered throughout the area. **Banjisan-sō** (☎ 399-2775; rooms per person with 2 meals from ¥8400) is at Futakuchi Onsen, fairly close to trailheads for Daitō-dake and Futakuchi-kyō.

Getting There & Away

Buses leave frequently from stop No 8 at the west bus pool for Akiu Onsen (¥780, 50 minutes), but only a few continue to Akiu Ōtaki (¥1070, 90 minutes).

MATSUSHIMA 松島

☎ 022 • pop 17,500

Matsushima and the islands in the bay Matsushima-wan constitute one of the *Nihon Sankei* (Three Great Sights) of Japan – the other two are the floating torii of Miya-jima island and the sandspit at Amanohashidate. Bashō was reportedly so entranced by the surroundings in the 17th century that his flow of words was reduced to simply, '*Matsushima, ah! Matsushima!*

Matsushima!' Not really his most inspired work.

It's a picturesque place but also very heavily touristed – head further east for impressive seascapes where you can find better accommodation *and* escape the coach parties.

Confusingly, Matsushima station is on the Tōhoku main line but Matsushima-Kaigan station, on the JR Senseki line, is actually closer to the main sights; there's no connecting bus between them.

The **tourist information office** (☎ 354-2263; open 10am-5pm daily) outside Matsushima-Kaigan station provides maps; luggage storage is available next door (¥200 per day). **Goodwill Guides** (☎ 258-1295) are available with three day's notice.

MATSUSHIMA

1 Sakuragawa Ryokan
  桜川旅館
2 Zuigan-ji
  瑞巌寺
3 Donjiki Chaya
  どんじき茶屋
4 Kanran-tei; Matsushima Hakubutsukan
  観らん亭; 松島博物館
5 Tourist Information Office
  松島観光案内所
6 Cruise Boats
  松島観覧船
7 Godai-dō
  五大堂
8 Matsushima Kankō Hotel (Ryokan Matsushima-jō)
  松島観光ホテル
9 Matsushima Century Hotel
  松島センチュリーホテル

Matsushima

To Nobiru (11km) & Ishinomaki (16km)

Tōhoku Main Line

Senseki Line

Fukuura Bridge

Matsushima-Kaigan

Matsushima-wan

Fukuura-jima

O-shima

0 150 300m
0 150 300yd

To Sendai (23km)

Zuigan-ji 瑞巌寺
One of Tōhoku's finest Zen temples, Zuigan-ji (admission ¥700; open 8am-5pm daily Apr-Sept, 8am-3.30pm daily Oct-Mar) was founded in 828. The present buildings were constructed in 1606 by Date Masamune to serve as a family temple. Look out for the painted screens and interior carvings of the main hall and the Seiryū-den (Treasure Hall) displaying works of art associated with the Date family. The temple is approached along an avenue lined with tall cedars with weathered Buddhas and altars to the sides.

Godai-dō 五大堂
The interior of this small wooden temple is only open once every 33 years. If you miss the next viewing in 2006, make do with the 12 animals of the Chinese zodiac carved in the eaves and the view out to sea.

Kanran-tei 観らん亭
This pavilion was presented to the Date family by Toyotomi Hideyoshi in the late 16th century and served as a genteel venue for tea ceremonies and moon viewing (the names means 'a place to view ripples on the water'). The garden includes the **Matsushima Hakubutsukan** (admission ¥200; open 8.30am-5pm daily Apr-Oct, 8.30am-4.30pm daily Nov-Mar), a small museum housing a collection of relics from the Date family.

Fukuura-jima 福浦島
This island is connected to the mainland by a 252m-long red wooden bridge (admission ¥200; open daily 8am-5pm Mar-June, 8am-6pm July & Aug), and makes for a leisurely half-hour walk around the botanical gardens. The bridge gate remains open on the return side after hours for stragglers.

Special Events
Seafood lovers will appreciate the **Matsu-shima Kaki Matsuri** (Matsushima Oyster Festival), which is held on the first weekend in February. On 15 August, Tōrō Nagashi Hanabi Taikai honours the souls of the departed with the O-Bon (Festival of the Dead) ritual of floating lighted lanterns out to sea (see the Facts for the Visitor chapter).

Places to Stay
Given the tourist-trap rates, Matsushima is better suited to day-trippers.

Sakuragawa Ryokan (☎ 354-2513; rooms per person with 2 meals from ¥9000) is rather overpriced but does the job; it's two minutes from Takagimachi station, one stop past Matsushima-kaigan.

Closer to the sights, you can find good deals at the **Matsushima Century Hotel** (☎ 354-4111; singles/twins ¥6500/13,400) if you take a room with a view of the car park rather than the sea; the interior is smart with a pool and sauna.

Matsushima Kankō Hotel (☎ 354-2121; rooms per person with breakfast ¥6300-10,300) is a ryokan that looks like a castle, hence its other name, Ryokan Matsushima-jō.

Cheaper options can be found along the coast in Nobiru (see the Oku-Matsushima section below).

Places to Eat
Restaurants line the main drag but, again, tourist rates apply. **Donjiki Chaya** (open 9am-5pm daily), a charming teahouse 50m southwest of the entrance to Zuigan-ji, serves delicious tricoloured *dango* (dumplings) for ¥450 and iced *matcha* (powdered green tea) for ¥350 as well as noodles; a handwritten English menu hangs out front.

Getting There & Away
The most convenient route to Matsushima Kaigan is from Sendai via the JR Senseki line (*kaisoku* ¥400, 30 minutes). Alternatively, boat trips (¥1420, 50 minutes) to Matsushima along the celebrated coastline depart Shiogama Pier every 30 minutes between 9am and 4pm from April to November, and hourly the rest of the year. Get off two stops before Matsushima Kaigan at Hon-Shiogama (¥320, 20 minutes). The harbour is 10 minutes on foot from Hon-Shiogama station – turn right as you exit.

Beware: the ear-shattering Japanese commentary is enough to make you jump overboard. Equally irritating are the punters feeding seagulls on loop cruises from Matsushima through the pine-covered islets (¥1400, 45-minutes), which run between 8.30am and 4.30pm.

OKU-MATSUSHIMA 奥松島
☎ 0225 • pop 11,700
On the eastern curve of Matsushima-wan, Oku-Matsushima is less tourited and offers several trails for exploration by bicycle

or on foot. Although not the cleanest, the swimming beaches are popular with day-trippers from Sendai.

To reach Oku-Matsushima from Matsu-shima-kaigan, take the JR Senseki line six stations east (two stops by *kaisoku*) to Nobiru (¥230). Inside Nobiru station, the **tourist information office** (☎ 88-2611; *open 8.30am-5.30pm daily*) has a few bicycles for rent, otherwise you really need a car. From the station you can cycle the 5km to Otakamori, where a 20-minute climb up the hill is rewarded with a fine panorama of the bay.

Places to Stay

Paira Matsushima Youth Hostel (☎ 88-2220; *beds members/nonmembers ¥3500/4100, breakfast/dinner ¥600/1000*) is smart but can get very busy. Bicycle rental is available for ¥800 per day and the hostel can provide directions for the hiking trails. To get to the hostel from Nobiru station, walk across the bridge and towards the ocean for about 15 minutes until you reach an intersection with a blue youth hostel sign pointing down the road to the right. From there it's about 800m. Staff at the tourist information office can give you a map to the hostel.

The roads running along the beach are packed with *minshuku*; **Minshuku Bōyō-sō** (☎ 88-2159; *rooms per person with 2 seafood meals from ¥6500*), near the intersection with the youth hostel sign, is a reliable place.

Oshika-hantō
牡鹿半島

AYUKAWA 鮎川
☎ 0225 • pop 5500

Along the peninsula, this once major whaling centre is now a dreary fishing port with a small tourist information office (☎ 45-3456; *open 8am-5pm daily*) and bus terminal, which serves solely as a jumping off point for exploring Kinkasan island – try not to miss the boat. If you do, **Minami-sō** (☎ 45-2501; *rooms per person with 2 meals from ¥6000*), behind the bus station, is friendly.

Getting There & Away

The main gateway to this beautiful, secluded peninsula is JR Ishinomaki station, outside which the **tourist information office** (☎ 93-6448; *open 8.30am-5pm daily*) has combined rail, bus and ferry timetables. From Sendai, the JR Senseki line runs to Ishinomaki (*kaisoku* ¥950, one hour) via Matsushima-kaigan and Nobiru. Ishinomaki can also be reached via the JR Ishinomaki line from Ichinoseki on the Tōhoku main line.

From bus stop No 2 outside Ishinomaki station, seven buses to Ayukawa run daily between 7am and 6pm (¥1460, 90 minutes). It's a delightfully scenic trip.

Ferries leave from Ayukawa pier – opposite the bus station – for Kinkasan (¥900, 30 minutes).

KINKASAN 金華山
☎ 0225 • pop 32 people, 240 monkeys and 600 deer

Kinkasan (Golden Mountain) is considered one of the three holiest places in Tōhoku, and women were banned until the late 19th century. Today, an overnight stay is one of the highlights of a Tōhoku excursion and ideal for both sexes seeking tranquillity from frenetic Japanese daily life. The island features a pyramid-shaped mountain (445m), an impressive shrine, a handful of houses around the boat dock, mostly untended trails and the odd snake. There is no tourist information, no Internet and no convenience store on the island – so come prepared.

Most visitors seem to be day-trippers, which means the island is delightfully deserted in the early morning and late afternoon.

On the first and second Sunday in October, there's a deer-horn cutting ceremony to stop the deer from injuring each other during mating season. On the last weekend in July, the **Ryūjin Matsuri** (Dragon Festival) features giant dragon floats supported by up to 50 dancers.

Turning left from the boat dock, it's a steep 20-minute walk uphill to **Koganeyama-jinja**, which was built in 794 by Emperor Shōmu as thanks for finding gold here to finish the Great Buddha at Nara's Tōdai-ji. Below the shrine are grassy expanses where cheeky deer cadge titbits from visitors – guard your packed lunch closely.

Walking up from the shrine to the mountain summit (allow one hour) is a steep 1.5km hike with no path per se, although a handrail marks a rudimentary guide in parts. At the 1km mark, a small shrine indicates the remaining and increasingly steep path ahead. From the shrine at the summit there are magnificent views out to sea and across to the peninsula.

From there, it's a 50-minute hike downhill to **Senjōjiki** (1000 Tatami Mats Rock), a large formation of white rock on the eastern shore of the island and a further hour to the lighthouse propping up the southeast corner. From there, it takes roughly 90 minutes to follow the dirt trail along the shore and cross back over the summit to the dock area. Note: locals advise it is no longer possible to hike around the northern side of the island due to landfall, only the southern side is considered safe.

There's a very basic sketch map of the island outside the ticket window at the Kinkasan ferry pier. It has neither contour lines nor scale and its only use is to demonstrate the kanji for various places on the island (this may be useful when you come across one of the weather-beaten trail markers).

Hiking around the island is a great way to find solitude as some areas are deserted, but be prepared to find some trails almost fully overgrown. Stock up on supplies and find out what time it gets dark before setting out. If you get lost, head south and downhill towards the sea. The dirt trail that once circled the entire island (24km) along the shore is no longer safe at the northern edge.

Places to Stay & Eat

Koganeyama-jinja (☎ 45-2264; e kinkasan@ cocoa.ocn.ne.jp; rooms per person ¥9000), on the shrine grounds, offers basic temple lodgings with two meals and, if you get up before 6am, a chance to attend morning prayers. Advance reservations by phone or email are mandatory.

Minshuku Shiokaze (☎ daytime 45-2666, evening ☎ 45-2244; rooms per person ¥6000) is the archetypal friendly, family-run minshuku, 500m south along the headland from the pier. Expect simple but airy rooms, great food and panoramic views out to sea. The owners can also advise on the safest hiking routes. You must book well in advance, though, as they actually live in Ayukawa and only come out to Kinkasan if they have customers.

There's only a greasy rāmen shop near the pier so either eat at your lodgings or bring a lot of supplies from the mainland.

Getting There & Away

From April to early November ferries depart Ayukawa for Kinkasan almost hourly between 8.30am and 3.40pm (¥900 one way, 30 minutes); the last return ferry is at 4pm. Service is greatly reduced the rest of the year. There are three daily high-speed catamarans between Kinkasan and Onagawa, the eastern gateway to the peninsula, from April to early November (¥1600 one way, 30 minutes). The last departure from Onagawa is at 1.20pm. Some of the boats have open-air fantail decks, which make for a pleasant ride.

From mid-May to October there is a daily boat at 12.50pm going from Kinkasan to Shiogama-kō.

Ferry reservations (☎ 53-3121) are required at peak times.

ONAGAWA 女川

This fishing town is another access point for Kinkasan. Onagawa is also the terminus for the JR Ishinomaki line, 30 minutes from JR Ishinomaki station (¥320), where you can either catch a train southwest towards Sendai or west towards Furukawa on the Tōhoku shinkansen line (a change of train may be necessary, en route, at Kogota).

From Onagawa station, walk straight to the waterfront, turn right and walk about 200m to the pier. The ferry ticket office is down a side street opposite the pier, little more than a hole in the wall on the right-hand side and two doors down from a convenience store where you should stock up for the trip.

NARUKO ONSEN 鳴子鴬泉
☎ 0229 • pop 9000

A hot-spring spa resort in the northwestern corner of Miyagi-ken with good hiking and bathing options, Naruko is famous for its distinctive style of lacquerware and its kokeshi (wooden dolls with brightly painted floral designs).

The entrance to **Naruko-kyō** can be reached in 20 minutes on foot from Naruko station. Alternatively, buses (¥200, seven minutes) run from 8.50am to 4pm. From the entrance, a pleasant 4km trail leads along the river valley to Nakayama-daira. If you turn right just after the bridge, but before reaching the gorge, you'll find the old **Shitomae checkpoint** and the start of a quiet 5km country path along the route Bashō once walked. The last bus back to the station leaves at 4.29pm.

The helpful **tourist information office** (☎ 83-3441; open 8.30am-6pm daily) inside JR Naruko Onsen station (tucked away behind a tourist video viewing theatre) has useful English language maps and brochures; they also book accommodation. The must-see is the town's fabulously atmospheric wooden bath house *onsen* **Taki-no-yu** (admission ¥150; open 7.30am-10pm daily), which has hardly changed in 150 years.

Places to Stay & Eat
Overnighting poses a dilemma as the better ryokan and hotels in the station area are ludicrously overpriced, while cheaper options are shabby.

Walking northwest from the station, the first budget option you'll pass is **Ryokan Sumei-sō** (☎ 83-2114; rooms for up to 2 people with 2 meals ¥6000, each additional person ¥1000), which has basic but clean rooms. It's five minutes down the main street on the left before the railway tracks. Next along, **Ryokan Okasakiso** (☎ 83-4050; rooms per person ¥3800) is the cheapest and shabbiest deal in town.

Across the train tracks and 10-minutes from the station, **Ryokan Takishima** (☎ 83-3054; rooms for 1-2 people with 2 meals ¥6550-13,300) has rather a 'One Flew Over the Cuckoos Nest' feel but does the job.

Getting There & Away
From JR Sendai station, take the JR Tōhoku *shinkansen* to Furakawa (¥1820, 15 minutes) then transfer to the JR Rikuu-tōsen line for Naruko Onsen (¥850, 40 minutes). Naruko Onsen has infrequent connections to Shinjō (¥950, one hour) for transfers to the Yamagata *shinkansen* line or local trains west to Sakata (¥950, one hour) and Tsuroka (¥1100, 1¼ hours).

Iwate-ken 岩手県

HIRAIZUMI 平泉
☎ 0191 • pop 9000
From 1089 to 1189, three generations of the Fujiwara family created a political and cultural centre in Hiraizumi that allegedly

approached the grandeur and sophistication of Kyoto. This short century of fame and prosperity was brought to an end when Minamoto Yoritomo ordered the annihilation of the Fujiwara clan and the destruction of Hiraizumi.

Today, only a couple of the original temple buildings remain and Hiraizumi is now a rather drab and sleepy town with little sign of life after 6pm.

Information
Turning right outside Hiraizumi station, the **tourist information office** (☎ 46-2110; open 8.30am-5pm daily Apr-Oct, 8.30am-4.30pm daily Nov-Mar) is only useful for some English-language pamphlets. Luggage storage (¥200) is available until 6pm in the souvenir shop to the left of the station exit.

The JNTO leaflet *Sendai, Matsushima and Hiraizumi* has useful information.

The post office is behind Ryokan Komatsushiro, 400m west of the station heading towards Mōtsū-ji; Iwate bank also has foreign exchange. Free Internet access is available at the public library (open 8.30am-5pm Tues-Sun), 1500m west of the station.

Some of the sights in outlying areas are best reached by bus from Ichinoseki station. Inside Ichinoseki station, **tourist information office** (☎ 23-2350; open 9am-5.30pm daily) staff speak no English and have scant resources. For a snack between connections, **Chokurian**, 150m north of the station to the right of the car park, does a decent ¥1100 tempura udon lunch.

Chūson-ji 中尊寺
This temple (open 8am-5pm daily Apr-Mar, 8.30am-4.30pm daily Nov-Mar) was originally established in 850 by the priest Ennin, who established most of Tōhoku's other famous temples. However, it was the first lord of the Fujiwara clan who decided in the early 12th century to expand the site into a complex with more than 40 temples. A massive fire in 1337 destroyed most of the complex. The steep approach to the temple follows a long, tree-lined avenue past the Hon-dō (Main Hall) to an enclosed area with the splendid Konjiki-dō (Golden Hall).

The ¥800 entrance fee is also valid for admission to Kyōzō, Sankōzō and Konjiki-dō.

NORTHERN HONSHŪ

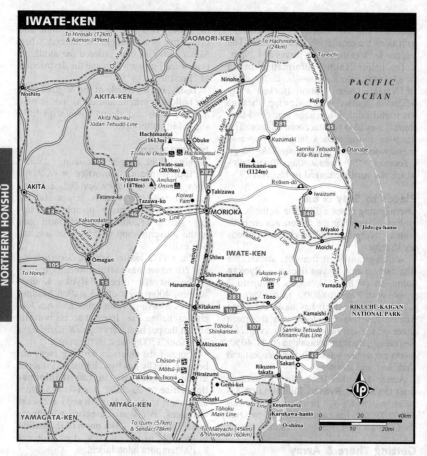

IWATE-KEN

Sankōzō The temple treasury contains the coffins and funeral finery of the Fujiwara clan: scrolls, swords and images transferred from halls and temples that no longer exist.

Konjiki-dō A national treasure, built in 1124, Konjiki-dō *(open 8am-4.30pm daily Apr-Oct, 8.30am-4pm daily Nov-Mar)* is packed with gold ornamentation, black lacquerwork and inlaid mother-of-pearl. The centrepiece of the hall is a statue of Amida with attendants. Beneath the three side altars are the mummified remains of three generations of the Fujiwara family.

Kyōzō Built in 1108, this sutra treasury is the oldest structure in the temple complex. The original collection of more than 5000

sutras was damaged by fire and the remains have been transferred to the Sankōzō.

Mōtsū-ji 毛越寺
This temple *(admission ¥500; open 8.30am-5pm daily Apr-Oct, 8.30am-4.30pm daily Nov-Mar)*, 800m west of the station, once rivalled Chūson-ji. All that remains now is the attractive Jōdo-en (Paradise Garden). The temple and gardens attract large numbers of visitors for the **Ayame Matsuri** (Iris Festival), held from late June to mid-July. Entry is free to guests of the youth hostel on temple grounds.

Takadachi Gikei-dō 高館義経堂
This small memorial *(admission ¥200; open 8.30am-5pm daily Apr-Oct, 8.30am-*

4.30pm daily Nov-Mar) honours Minamoto Yoshitsune, who grew up with and trained under the Fujiwara clan but left Hiraizumi to fight by his brother Yoritomo's side until the brothers had a serious falling out.

Having been betrayed, Yoshitsune was attacked at Takadachi and, seeing no escape, he set his castle on fire, killed his family and then himself to avoid the shame of capture. According to local legend, it was actually Yoshitsune's loyal retainer, the giant Benkei, who sacrificed himself while Yoshitsune fled from Japan to become – wait for it – Ghengis Khan.

Following the train tracks 20 minutes north of the station, the memorial is located 700m from the entrance of Chūson-ji.

Takkoku-no-Iwaya Bishamon-dō
達谷窟

Five kilometres southwest of Mōtsū-ji, this cave temple *(admission ¥300; open 8.30am-6pm daily Apr-Oct, 8.30am-5pm daily Nov-Mar)* is dedicated to Bishamon, the Buddhist guardian deity of warriors. The present structure is a replica of the temple built here in 801 by a famous general after a victorious battle against the Ezo, the original inhabitants of northern Honshū.

You can cycle to the cave along a paved path from Mōtsū-ji in about 25 minutes.

Geibi-kei 巖美渓

Flat-bottomed boats with singing boatmen (¥1500, 90 minutes) depart hourly (8.30am to 4.30pm daily April to October, 9am to 3pm November to March) to ferry passengers through this huge natural gorge. Take the bus from stop No 7 outside Ichinoseki station (¥620, 40 minutes, hourly) or take the train from Ichinoseki to Geibikei station on the JR Ōfunato line *(kaisoku* ¥480, 25 minutes).

Special Events

The **Haru-no-Fujiwaru Matsuri** (Spring Fujiwara Festival) from 1 to 5 May features a costumed procession, performances of nō (classical Japanese dance-drama) at Chūson-ji and traditional *ennen-no-mai* (longevity dances) at Mōtsū-ji, as well as an enormous rice cake–carrying competition in memory of the giant Benkei. A similar **Aki-no-Fujiwaru Matsuri** (Autumn Fujiwara Festival) takes place from 1 to 3 November.

HIRAIZUMI

1 Kyōzō 経蔵	7 Mōtsū-ji 毛越寺
2 Konjiki-dō 金色堂	8 Mōsū-ji Youth Hostel 毛越寺ユースホステル
3 Sankōzō 讃衡蔵	9 Ryokan Komatsushiro 旅館こまつし１゛ろ
4 Chūson-ji 中尊寺	10 Post Office 郵便局
5 Takadachi Gikei-dō 高館義経堂	11 Tourist Information; Bike Hire 旅行案内所
6 Minshuku Yoshitsune-sō 民宿義経荘	12 Hiraizumi Bank 13 Public Library

NORTHERN HONSHŪ

Places to Stay & Eat

Mōtsū-ji Youth Hostel *(☎ 46-2331; dorm/ private room ¥2800/4000)* is part of the temple and a peaceful, if a bit mouldy, place to stay. Breakfast/dinner costs ¥600/ 800; there's a 9pm curfew and free *zazen* meditation sessions in summer.

Minshuku Yoshitsune-sō *(☎ 46-4355; rooms per person with 2 meals ¥6300)* is the best option for a quiet place to stay; it's only 400m from the entrance of Chūson-ji.

Ryokan Komatsushiro *(☎ 46-3323; rooms per person with 2 meals ¥8000)* is a stuffy but clean place 500m west of the station.

Getting There & Away

From Sendai, the JR Tōhoku *shinkansen* runs to Ichinoseki (¥1620, 35 minutes), where you can either take a bus via Hirai-zumi station to Chūson-ji (¥350, 22 minutes) or a local train on the JR Tōhoku main line (*futsū* ¥140, eight minutes).

Ichinoseki is connected to Morioka by the JR Tōhoku *shinkansen* (¥5400, 40 minutes) and the JR Tōhoku main line (*futsū* ¥1620, 90 minutes).

Getting Around
Frequent buses from Ichinoseki run to Hiraizumi station (see earlier) and onto Chūson-ji (¥140, 10 minutes). Bicycle rental is available for ¥1000 per day outside Hiraizumi station (9am to 4pm, closed November to March).

TŌNO 遠野
☎ 0198 • pop 20,000
Tōno excited attention at the beginning of the 20th century when a collection of regional folk tales were compiled by Yanagida Kunio and published under the title *Tōno Monogatari*. The English translation by Robert Morse, *Legends of Tōno*, is available at the Tōno Municipal Museum. The tales cover a racy collection of topics from supernatural beings to the strange ways of the rustic folk in traditional Japan.

One legend relates the history of Oshira-sama, a fertility goddess who was once just a local girl. Against her father's wishes,

she married her horse. The outraged father hung the horse from a mulberry tree and beheaded it, after which the unhappy bride took her own life; they were both whisked away to paradise. Oshira-sama dolls are still important ceremonial objects for *itako* mediums (see Shimokita-hantō later in this chapter).

Today there's little excitement about Tōno. A rather lacklustre place, the town itself is wholly unremarkable while the more rewarding surrounding countryside is fairly inaccessible without your own transport.

Information
The small and rather unhelpful **tourist information office** (*☎ 62-1333; open 8am-6pm daily*) is to the right as you exit JR Tōno station. They don't speak a word of English but can provide an English-language brochure entitled *Come and See Traditional Japan in Tōno*, which includes a useful scaled map of the three main cycling routes. Bicycle rental is available from the station concourse at ¥1000 per day and also at the youth hostel; it's a convenient alternative to the infrequent bus services.

Tōno's main post office is a 10-minute walk southeast of the train station. Free Internet access is available at the **city library** (*open 9am-5pm Tues-Sun*), downstairs from the Tōno Municipal Museum.

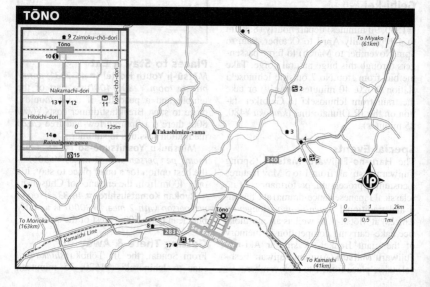

TŌNO

Tōno Municipal Museum
遠野市立博物館

On the upper floors of the city library, this museum (admission ¥300; open 9am-4.30pm daily Apr-Oct, 9am-4.30pm Tues-Sun Nov-Mar; closed last day each month) has exhibits of folklore and audiovisual presentations of the legends of Tōno.

Tōno Mukashibanashi-mura
遠野昔話村

Tōno Mukashibanashi-mura (admission ¥310; open 9am-4.30pm daily Apr-Nov, 9am-4.30pm Tues-Sun Dec-Mar; closed last day each month) is a folktale village with a restored ryokan where Yanagida Kunio (1875–1962; famous for documenting and preserving much of Tōno's folklore and customs) once stayed and an exhibition hall for folk art. A combined ticket for the Tōno Municipal Museum costs ¥500.

Fukusen-ji 福泉寺

This temple (admission ¥300; open 8am-5pm daily Apr-Oct, 9am-4pm daily Nov-Dec, 9am-4pm Sun Jan-Mar) lies 8.5km northeast of Tōno station. Founded in 1912, its major claim to fame is the wooden Fukusen-ji Kannon statue (17m high), which is supposedly the tallest of its type in Japan. If you're not cycling, take a bus bound for Sakanoshita and get off at Fukusen-ji (¥370, eight per day).

Tōno Furusato-mura
遠野ふるさと村

About 3.5km beyond Fukusen-ji, this is the largest folk village in Tōno, comprised of several different farmhouses, a water wheel and a folkcraft gallery (admission ¥200; open 9am-5pm daily). Guides are on hand to explain (in Japanese only) the relevant history and farming culture. If you are not cycling, buses run once or twice an hour from Tōno station (¥490, 25 minutes).

Jōken-ji 常堅寺

Jōken-ji is a peaceful temple 2.5km south of Fukusen-ji with a famous deity image Obinzuru-sama, which some believe will cure their illness if they rub the part on its body that corresponds to the part where their own body ailment is.

Behind the temple are a stream and a small pool, Kappa-buchi. Kappa are considered to be mischievous, mythical creatures but legend has it that the kappa in this pool once put out a fire in the temple. The lion statue was erected as a gesture of thanks to honour the kappa. See Japanese Gods & Mythical Creatures in the Facts about Japan chapter for more details about kappa.

Also in this vicinity is Denshōen (admission ¥310; open 9am-4.30pm daily, closed last day each month), a small folk village.

From Tōno station, you can take a direct bus to Denshōen-mae (¥300, 15 minutes), or more frequent buses bound for Sakanoshita to the Nitagai stop (¥290, 12 minutes), which is 10 minutes on foot from Denshōen.

Gohyaku Rakan 五百羅漢

On a wooded hillside above the Unedori-sama shrine, about 2.5km southwest of Tōno station, are the Gohyaku Rakan (500 Disciples of Buddha). These rock carvings were fashioned by a priest to console the spirits of those who died in a famine in 1754.

NORTHERN HONSHŪ

TŌNO			
PLACES TO STAY		**OTHER**	10 Tourist Information Office
3	Tōno Youth Hostel 遠野ユースホステル	1 Tōno Furusato-mura 遠野ふるさと村	旅行案内所
8	Minshuku Magariya 民宿曲り屋	2 Fukusen-ji 福泉寺	11 Post Office 郵便局
9	Minshuku Tōno 民宿とおの	4 Denshōen 伝承園	14 Tōno Mukashibanashi-mura 遠野昔話村
		5 Jōken-ji 常堅寺	15 Tōno Municipal Library & Museum 遠野市立図書館/博物館
PLACES TO EAT		6 Kappa-buchi カッパ淵	16 Unedori-sama 卯子酉様
12	Ume-no-ya Restaurant うめのや	7 Chiba Family Magariya 千葉家の曲り屋	17 Gohyaku Rakan 五百羅漢
13	Taigetsu Coffee Shop 待月		

NORTHERN HONSHŪ

Chiba Family Magariya
千葉家の曲り屋

Nine kilometres west of Tōno station, this traditional L-shaped farmhouse *(admission ¥350; open 8.30am-5pm daily)* has been restored to give an impression of the traditional lifestyle of a wealthy farming family of the 18th century. Unless you want to fork out several thousand yen for the taxi ride, you'll have to cycle here.

Special Events
The Tōno Matsuri takes place on 14 September with *yabusame* (horseback archery), traditional dances and costume parades.

Places to Stay & Eat
There is a scattering of *minshuku* around the station; **Minshuku Tōno** *(☎ 620-4396; with 2 meals ¥6000)* is the best of an unremarkable bunch and just behind the station.

Better accommodation is a real hike from the city. **Tōno Youth Hostel** *(☎ 62-8736; beds members/nonmembers ¥3150/3850)* provides a good base for cycling or walking around the area; bicycle rental is available for ¥500 per day. The owner is friendly and speaks some English. There is no curfew, but reception closes at 9pm. From Tōno station, take a bus bound for Sakanoshita to the Nitagai stop *(¥290, 12 minutes)*. From there, it's a 10-minute walk to the hostel.

Minshuku Magariya *(☎ 62-4564; rooms per person with 2 meals from ¥10,500)*, 3km southwest of the station, is an atmospheric place where you stay inside a traditional farmhouse. No English is spoken. From the station, take a bus to the *basu-sentā* (bus centre) then walk for 30 minutes on foot to the *minshuku*. Better still, take a taxi.

Taigetsu *(open 11.30am-2pm & 5pm-9pm daily)*, marked with a coffee and snack sign, has reasonable snacks from ¥500; **Ume-no-ya** *(open 11.30am-2pm & 5pm-9pm daily)*, opposite, has similar deals. They are located 350m south of the train station.

Getting There & Away
On the JR Kamaishi line, local trains connect Tōno with Shin-Hanamaki on the Tōhoku *shinkansen* line *(¥740, one hour)* and Hanamaki on the Tōhoku main line *(¥820, 70 minutes)*.

There are two afternoon buses from Morioka at 2.15pm and 3.30pm to Kamai-shi that stop at Tōno's Topia department store *(¥1890, two hours)*. In the reverse direction, buses to Morioka pass by at 7am and 10am.

MORIOKA 枢岡
☎ 019 • pop 288,000

Morioka is the capital of Iwate-ken, which dates back to the early Edo period when it was the castle town of the Nambu clan. Today, this surprisingly compact city has a vibrant foreign community (powered by an exchange programme with Victoria in Canada; more from **w** www.victoria-morioka.com), a decent nightlife scene and one of the nicest coffee shops in northern Japan. It's also a good staging point to make use of city facilities before venturing off the *shinkansen* line into the wilds of the far north.

Orientation & Information
The city centre is east of the station, on the other side of the Kitakami-gawa. Ōdōri, which heads over the Kaiun bridge up to the park Iwate-kōen, is the main shopping street.

The highly efficient **Kita Tōhoku information centre** *(☎ 625-2090; open 9am-5.30pm daily)* is on the 2nd floor of Morioka station at the north exit, next to the *shinkansen* ticket gate. Staff speak excellent English and have a good supply of brochures about the city and region as a whole. There's a useful **post office** kiosk opposite (without ATM) open daily from 9.15am to 8.15pm.

There's a second **tourist information office** *(☎ 604-3305; open 9am-8pm, closed 2nd Tues each month)* across town on the 2nd floor of Odette Plaza. Free Internet access is available as are tourist brochures, phonecards and stamps; English is spoken.

The **Iwate International Plaza** *(☎ 654-8900; open 10am-9pm Mon-Fri, 10am-5pm Sat, Sun & holidays)*, 15 minutes southeast of the station, is an excellent resource for visitors and long-term residents, with helpful English-speaking staff, a foreign newspaper library, local what's on information and free Internet. The latter requires registration and, sometimes, queuing.

The **central post office** is downtown, but there's a useful branch with ATM facilities five minutes east of the station. **Iwate Bank** along Ōdōri also changes money.

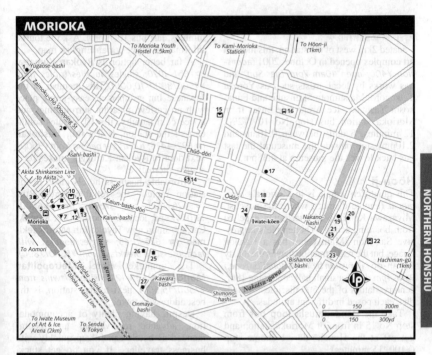

MORIOKA

MORIOKA

PLACES TO STAY
3 Hotel Metropolitan Morioka
ホテルメトロポリタン盛岡
4 Capsule Hotel; Gen Plaza
カプセルホテルゲンプラザ
9 Toyoko Inn Moriokaekimae
東横イン盛岡駅前
13 Hotel Ruiz
ホテルルイズ
25 Taishōkan
大正館
26 Ryokan Kumagai
熊ヶ井旅館

PLACES TO EAT
7 Azumaya
東家
8 Pyon Pyon Sha
ぴょんぴょん舎

11 Cappuccino Shiki
カプチノ詩季
12 Koiwai Regley
小岩井リグレ
18 Sara Sara
24 Ana Kura
穴蔵

OTHER
1 Ono Sensai-sho
小野染彩所
2 Kōgensha Craft Shop
光原社
5 JR Bus Station;
Dendenmushi Bus Stop
6 24-hour Lawson
Convenience Store
10 Post Office
郵便局

14 Iwate Bank
岩手銀行
15 Main Post Office
中央郵便局
16 Honchō-dōri 1-chōme
Stop
17 Morioka Court of Justice;
Rock-splitting Cherry Tree
19 Gozaku
ござ九
20 Workshop Kamasada
21 Iwate Bank (Ex-Head
Office)
岩手銀行（旧本店）
22 Morioka Bus Centre
盛岡バスセンター
23 Odette Plaza
27 Iwate International Plaza
岩手県立国際交流プラザ

The JNTO brochure *Morioka and Riku-chu Kaigan National Park* is worth taking the time to read.

Iwate-kōen 岩手公園

Iwate-kōen, 20 minutes east of the station, is where Morioka-jō once stood. Now ruined,

only the moss-covered stone foundation walls remain as a testament to Edo-period life. The grounds contain Sakurayama-jinja and a totem pole presented by Morioka's sister city in British Columbia, a collaborative effort of a Native North American chief and a local woodcarver.

Iwate Museum of Art
岩手県立美術館

Located 2km west of the station, this modern art complex opened in October 2001 *(admission ¥400; open 10am-7pm Tues-Sun)* and has works by local artists such as Yorozu Tetsugoro, Matsumoto Shunsuke and Funakoshi Yasutake. Ice Arena line buses from Morioka station bus stop No 10 *(¥290, 12 minutes, 5 daily between 9.10am and 2.10pm)* stop outside the museum; the last bus back leaves the museum at 4.38pm.

Hōon-ji 報恩寺

This quiet Zen temple is in Morioka's *teramachi* (temple district), where the novelist, Miyazawa Kenji, lived after being expelled from boarding school. The temple's impressive San-mon (Main Gate) has a Kannon image, but the real attraction here is the musty **Rakan-dō** *(admission by ¥300 donation; open 9am-4pm daily)*, a small hall containing 18th-century statues of the 500 disciples of Buddha, each posed in different attitudes.

Take the **Dendenmushi loop bus** from stop No 15 in front of Morioka station and get off at the Honchō-dōri 1-chōme stop *(¥100, 15 minutes)*.

Special Events

The **Chagu-Chagu Umakko Matsuri**, on the second Saturday of June, features a parade of brightly decorated horses and children in traditional dress. Starting outside town, the procession passes near Iwate-kō in the afternoon (the best views are from Nakanohashi). Iwate was historically famous for breeding horses and the festival allegedly originated when farmers took their horses to shrines to rest them after harvest and pray for their health. The name 'chagu-chagu' is said to describe the sound of the horses' bells.

During the **Hachiman-gū Matsuri** from 14 to 16 September, portable shrines and colourful floats are paraded to the rhythm of *taiko* (drums); there are displays of *yabusame* (horseback archery) on the 15th.

Places to Stay

Inconveniently located in Takamatsu and rather run down, **Morioka Youth Hostel** *(☎ 662-3175; dorm beds ¥2900)* is the cheapest option. From stop No 11 at Morioka station, buses depart frequently for Matsuzono bus terminal – get off at the

Takamatsu-no-ike-guchi stop *(¥210, 20 minutes, last bus 10.40pm)*. Ask the tourist information office for an English map.

A far better option is **Ryokan Kumagai** *(☎ 651-3020; singles/doubles/triples from ¥4500/8000/10,000)*. This member of the Japanese Inn group is an easy-going place with no curfew, pleasant surroundings and a free coin laundry; it's 10 minutes southeast of the station. If it's full, **Taishōkan** *(☎ 622-4436; rooms per person from ¥3500)*, next door to Ryokan Kumagai, makes for a simple alternative.

Affordable business hotels close to the station include the reliable **Hotel Ruiz** *(☎ 625-2611; singles/twins from ¥6500/13,000)* and, located opposite Orix Rent-A-Car, the smart new **Toyoko Inn Moriokaekimae** *(☎ 625-1045; singles/doubles with Japanese-style breakfast from ¥5300/7800)*.

The upmarket **Hotel Metropolitan Morioka** *(☎ 625-1211; singles/twins from ¥7500/15,500)*, next to the station, is the best address in town.

Despite having plenty of accommodation, advance reservations are recommended as hotels can fill up quickly with business travellers. If you do get stuck, there's a clean and convenient **capsule hotel** *(capsule ¥2800, bath ¥1000 extra)* on the 3rd floor of the Gen Plaza. Sadly, this minimalist delight accepts men only.

Places to Eat

The local speciality dish is *Wanko soba*, an all-you-can-eat noodles feast whereby you aren't allowed to stop until you manage to put the lid back on your bowl before the staff can fill it up again. This memorable experience costs around ¥3000 from **Azumaya** *(open 11am-8pm Wed-Sun)* on the 2nd floor of the Miurabiru building.

Morioka's other speciality is *reimen*, soba noodles served with Korean *kim chi* (spicy pickles). **Pyon Pyon Sha** *(1st floor, Jaren Jaren Bldg; open 11am-11pm daily)* has great ¥1500 cold soba *reimen* and hot *onmen reimen* sets. Wash it down with a local Ginga Kogen beer *(¥500)*.

Koiwai Regley *(open 7am-9.30pm Mon-Sat, 9am-8pm Sun)* bakery/restaurant, 100m west of the station, is a safe bet for good-value ¥800 Western-style set menus and uses ingredients from the renowned Koiwai farm outside the city. Opposite,

Cappuccino Shiki *(open 7.30am-9pm Tues-Fri, 9am-8pm Sat & Sun)* is an atmospheric old coffee shop that does good ¥600 toasted sandwiches, affordable breakfast sets and a decent cappuccino.

On the 2nd floor of the East 21 building opposite the park, **Sara Sara** is a smart, chilled-out place for drinks and dinner. Not the cheapest with meals around ¥3500 but, hey, it's worth splashing out for.

Also worth seeking out for a treat, **Ana Kura**, located in the basement of the Sai-ensougoubiru building under the restaurant Rasen, is a friendly *izakaya* with great sashimi. Better still, there's a free banana for every customer as you leave – hence it's known to local ex-pats as the Banana Bar.

The enormous **Fasen** food plaza in the basement of Morioka station is a good spot for a snack before your train.

Shopping

The Morioka region is famous for its *nanbu tetsubin* (cast ironware). One of the best places to browse is at **Workshop Kamasada**, which sells affordable gift items alongside tea kettles that cost as much as a small car. It's located across the Nakatsu-gawa near Gozaku, a traditional merchant's area of *kura* warehouses, coffee shops, and craft studios. To get there, take the Dendenmushi bus from Morioka station to Morioka bus centre. From there it's a three-minute walk to the old Iwate Bank building at the southwestern corner of the street leading to Gozaku.

The attractive Zaimoku-chō district, five minutes from the station, is home to quality craft shops for lacquerware and fabrics, including **Kōgensha** *(open 10am-6pm daily, closed 15th each month)*, a craft and coffee shop located in a garden overlooking the river. For hand-woven and dyed fabrics, check out the impressive selection at **Ono Sensai Sho** – the emperor himself allegedly came by to do some window shopping.

Getting There & Away

On the JR Tōhoku *shinkansen* line, the fastest trains from Tokyo (Ueno) reach Morioka in a mere 2½ hours (¥13,840). From Morioka, the Akita *shinkansen* line runs west to Akita (¥3990, 90 minutes) via Tazawa-ko and Kakunodate, which can also be reached by infrequent local trains on the JR Tazawa-ko line. From Morioka you can continue north to Aomori on the JR Tōhoku mainline *(tokkyū* ¥5460, 2¼ hours).

The bus terminal at Morioka station is well organised and has abundant English signs and a directory matching buses to their relevant stops, as well as journey times and fares. Popular destinations include Iwate-san, Miyako, Ryūsen-dō, Towada-ko and Tazawa-ko. See the relevant sections for more details.

The easiest access to the Hachimantai area, northwest of Morioka, is also by bus. Buses run from stop No 4 at Morioka station to Hachimantai Chōjō (¥1890, two hours, four daily).

Long-distance buses leave the station for Aomori (¥3160, three hours), Hirosaki (¥2930, 2½ hours) and Sendai (¥2850, 2¾ hours). There is one night bus to Tokyo leaving at 10.40pm (¥7850, 7½ hours) and one to Yokohama (¥8950, eight hours) leaving at 10.10pm.

Getting Around

Morioka is navigable easily on foot. Most local buses depart from the station, although there are also some departures from the Morioka bus centre close to Iwate-kōen. The Dendenmushi tourist bus makes a convenient loop around town, departing in a clockwise direction from stop No 15 in front of Morioka station (anti-clockwise from No 16) between 9am and 6pm. It costs ¥100 per ride, or ¥300 for a one-day pass.

IWATE-SAN 岩手山

The volcanic peak of Iwate-san (2038m) is a dominating landmark northwest of Morioka, and a popular destination for hikers. Four walking trails are open between July and October but periodically close due to volcanic activity. Check with tourist information in Morioka for the latest conditions. If you want to stay near Iwate-san, **Amihari Onsen**, at the start of one of the main trails to the summit, has numerous *minshuku*. Railway enthusiasts prefer the **Steam Locomotive Hotel** *(☎ 692-4316; rooms per person from ¥4000)*, on the Koiwai farm, where you sleep in old train compartments. From early May to early November, buses from Morioka bound for Amihari Onsen (¥1140, one hour) pass by Koiwai farm (¥720, 35 minutes). Before Amihari, there's a bus stop at Omisaka for the trailhead.

MIYAKO 宮古
☎ 0193 • pop 550,000

Miyako is a drab little town in the centre of the far more rewarding Rikuchū-kaigan National Park, a 180km stretch of interesting rock formations and seascapes along the eastern coastline of Tōhoku, from Kesennuma in the south to Kuji in the north.

The small **tourist information office** (☎ 62-4060; open 9am-6pm daily), to the right of the train station's exit, dishes out copies of *The Mystic Seaside*, an English-language brochure with details of sights.

Jōdo-ga-hama 浄土ヶ浜

Jōdo-ga-hama, an attractive beach with white sand is the area's main draw.

From stop No 3 outside Miyako station, frequent buses bound for the beach (¥210, 20 minutes) stop in front of a concrete souvenir centre, from where a path leads down to the excursion boat dock. Apart from tame cruises to a few rock formations, there are also departures every hour or two between 8.30am and 3.35pm for **Tarō**, a charming fishing village further north up the coast (¥1420, 40 minutes, late-April to October). Afterwards you can return to Miyako by bus or by train on the private Sanriku-Tetsudō line.

To escape the crowds, follow the walking trails through pine forests on the steep slopes above, from where there are good views across the beach. One trail leads along the coast for a two-hour hike to the visitors centre at the cape, Ane-ga-misaki, from where you can catch a bus back to Miyako station (¥360, 30 minutes, last bus 7.49pm).

Places to Stay & Eat

Suehiro-kan Youth Hostel (☎ 62-1555; *beds members/nonmembers ¥2850/3000*) has decent shared Japanese-style rooms and offers breakfast (¥600) and dinner (¥1000). Reception closes at 9pm, but there is no curfew. Walk north from Miyako station and turn right at the intersection with the main street; heading west, the hostel is 20m further down on the right-hand side.

Yamadaya Ryokan (☎ 62-3155; *rooms per person with 2 meals ¥8000*) is an upmarket but rather frosty place comprising two buildings opposite each other two blocks down the street immediately to the right as you exit the station.

On the way you'll pass **Uomoto** *(open 11am-2pm & 5pm-10pm Mon-Sat)*, a traditional seafood restaurant with indoor fish pools and a picture menu; try the tempura *teishoku* (set meal) for ¥1400.

Janome Sushi *(open 10am-9pm Thur-Tues)*, 50m north of the station on the left, has excellent set menus from ¥1350 and delicious fresh sushi (¥1000).

Getting There & Away

The JR Yamada line links Morioka with Miyako (*kaisoku* ¥1890, two hours) then continues south down the coast to Kamaishi (¥1110, 75 minutes) and inland to Tōno (¥1800, 2½ hours).

The private Sanriku-Tetsudō Kita-Rias line runs north from Miyako past Tarō (¥440) along the coastline to Kuji (¥1800, 90 minutes). From Kuji, you can connect with JR trains to Hachinohe (¥1280, two hours).

From stop No 6 in front of Miyako station there are frequent buses to Morioka (¥1970, 2¼ hours) and two buses daily to Tokyo at 6am and 9pm (¥9170, 9½ hours).

RYŪSEN-DŌ 龍泉洞

Close to Iwaizumi (northwest of Miyako), Ryūsen-dō *(admission ¥1000; open daily 8.30am-6pm May-Oct, 8.30am-5pm daily Nov-Apr)* is one of Japan's three largest stalactite caves. It contains a huge underground lake, said to be one of the clearest in the world. Admission also includes entry to the adjacent Ryūsen Shin-dō, a cave in which stone tools and earthenware were found.

From Morioka there are direct buses to Ryūsen-dō (¥2590, 2½ hours, four to six per day). From Miyako, the most convenient route is to take a train on the private Sanriku-Tetsudō Kita-Rias line to Omoto (¥750, 30 minutes), where you can change to a bus to the cave (¥600, 35 minutes).

Aomori-ken 青森県

As the least explored area of Tōhoku, parts of Aomori-ken are rather inaccessible and have poor transport links. Ideal to get away from it all, it is one place where a car is useful and a good place to practise your hitchhiking (see Hitching in the Getting Around section). The mooted extension of the *shinkansen* to Aomori remains unsubstantiated.

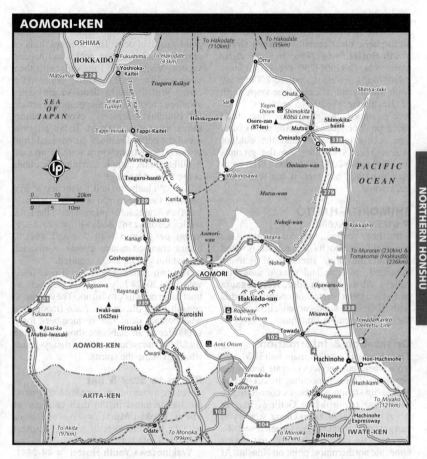

AOMORI-KEN

As a special incentive for foreign tourists, however, Aomori-ken has introduced the free Aomori Welcome Card, which entitles travellers to numerous generous discounts, including 50% off some intra-regional transport. The card is issued on the spot (upon production of passport) at tourist information centres in Mutsu (Shimokita-hantō), Hachinohe, Aomori, Hirosaki and Towada-ko, and remains valid for one year.

HACHINOHE 八戸
☎ 0178 • pop 240,000

Hachinohe recently replaced Morioka as the new terminus for Tōhoku *shinkansen* trains from Tokyo (¥14,840, three hours, 15 trains daily) and, as such, is set to see major redevelopment in forthcoming years as the transport hub for the north. New limited express connections to Aomori, Hirosaki and Hakodate were to be introduced, plus one new *shinkansen* route daily between Sendai and Hachinohe, at the time of writing.

Hachinohe-kō, 15 minutes by taxi from Hon-Hachinohe station on the JR Hachinohe line, and two stops east of Hachinohe station (¥180), is a hub for travellers to Hokkaidō by ferry; Tomakomai (¥3970, nine hours, three per day), Muroran (¥3970, eight hours, once daily).

Local trains ultimately for Aomori (*tokkyū*, ¥1620, 1½ hours) run via Noheji (¥950, 45 mins) for connections on the JR Ominato line to Shimokita station (¥1100, 45 minutes) on the Shimokita-hantō.

New accommodation is springing up around the Hachinohe terminus but the most atmospheric place remains **Kawayo Green Youth Hostel** (☎ 56-2756; beds members/nonmembers ¥3250/4250, breakfast/dinner ¥630/1050), a well-signposted 800m walk from Mukaiyama station, three stops north of Hachinohe (¥320, 15 minutes). This well-equipped hostel offers great food using produce from the farm; guests have free access to Internet and the outdoor onsen. There's camping on the grounds for ¥800 plus ¥2000 car parking. The complex is so big, however, it can feel rather impersonal.

SHIMOKITA-HANTŌ 下北半島
☎ 0175 • pop 90,000

Sometimes called Masakari-hantō (axe peninsula) due to its shape, this isolated peninsula has long stretches of sparsely inhabited coastline and remote mountain valleys. At its western edge, **Hotokegaura** is a spectacular stretch of coastline dotted with 100m-tall wind-carved cliffs, which are said to resemble Buddhas.

Orientation & Information
The Shimokita-hantō's main hub is Mutsu, from where bus services operate across the peninsula. Train connections are centred on Shimokita station with buses connecting to Mutsu bus terminal (see Getting There & Away). North of Mutsu is Ōhata, where you can get buses to the Yagen Onsen resort. To the east is the cape, Shiriya-zaki, to the west Ōma, the northernmost point on Honshū. At the bottom tip of the peninsula is Wakino-sawa, popular with nature lovers.

The tiny **tourist information office** (☎ 22-0909; open 9am-6pm daily May-Oct, 9am-6pm Wed-Mon Nov-Apr) inside Masakari Plaza has few resources and staff speak little English; better information is available in Aomori.

Stock up with supplies before heading to the peninsula – facilities are limited.

Osore-zan 恐山
A barren volcanic mountain Osore-zan (admission ¥500; open 6am-6pm daily May-Oct) is considered one of Japan's most sacred places. It's certainly an eerily atmospheric place and popular with pilgrims seeking to commune with the dead, especially parents who have lost their children. Several statues of the stone child guardian deity Jizō overlook hills of craggy, sulphur-strewn rocks and hissing vapour. Visitors help lost souls with their underworld penance by adding stones to the cairns. With the murky **Usuri-ko** and ravens swarming about, it's an appropriate setting for Buddhist purgatory; even the name, Osore, means fear or dread. Today, pilgrims dread the hefty donations encouraged from visitors, funds from which were being used to build a hotel complex on temple grounds at the time of writing.

You can bathe on hell's doorstep at free onsen to the side as you approach the main hall (sex-segregated options are on the left), while **Osore-zan Bodai-ji** (☎ 22-3825; rooms per person with 2 meals ¥5000) offers cramped tatami rooms – advance reservations in Japanese required.

The two annual Osore-zan Taisai festivals (held 20–24 July and 9–11 October) attract huge crowds of visitors. They come to consult blind old crones, itako (mediums), who contact dead family members for a ¥3000 fee in an elaborate show of reciting Buddhist sutras and rattling rosary beads while invoking the spirits.

Places to Stay & Eat
There are numerous places clustered around the bus terminal in the drab confines of Mutsu; **Ryokan Murai** (☎ 22-4755; rooms with 2 meals from ¥6500), next to Masakari Plaza, is a safe bet.

Wakinosawa Youth Hostel (☎ 44-2341; w www.wakinosawa.com; beds members/nonmembers ¥2850/3850), perched on a hillside 15 minutes west of the ferry pier, has a basic but rustic feel and the helpful owners drive guests to a local onsen (¥200) before dinner. Suspension of ferry services from Aomori, however, make it rather isolated – best for photographers and nature fans joining the owner's excursions to observe 'snow monkeys' (Japanese macaque).

Yagen Onsen offers upmarket accommodation; try **Hotel New Yagen** (☎ 34-3311; rooms with 2 meals ¥15,000-25,000) that offers a 10% discount for Aomori Card holders.

The 2nd-floor restaurant in **Masaraki Plaza** (open 10am-6pm daily) offers reasonable ¥1000 set menus.

Getting There & Away

On the JR Ōminato line, there are two to four direct *kaisoku* trains daily from Aomori via Noheji to the terminus at Ōminato – get off one stop before at Shimokita station (¥1890, 1¾ hours) for buses to Mutsu. The Shimokita-Kōtsū line to Ohata closed in March 2001; bus connections now run from the Mutsu bus terminal to Ohata (¥440, 40 minutes).

From Shimokita station, frequent buses run to the Mutsu bus terminal (¥230, 10 minutes). Three direct buses run daily between Mutsu bus terminal and Aomori (¥2520, 2½ hours); others run via Noheji (¥1450, 90 minutes) onto Aomori (¥1260, one hour).

From Ōma, there are two daily ferries (four in summer) to Hakodate on Hokkaidō (¥1170, 1¾ hours). From Kanita, two ferries run daily (three in summer) to Wakinosawa (¥1120, one hour).

Getting Around

Buses to destinations across the peninsula run from the Mutsu bus terminal.

Between May and October, regular buses run from Wakinosawa to Mutsu (¥1790, 90 minutes), from where four buses leave for Osore-zan between 9am and 3.30pm (¥750, 30 minutes); the last bus back leaves Osore-zan at 4.50pm and Aomori Card holders are discounted 50%.

Nine buses daily ply the northern shore of the peninsula, passing Ōhata, Shimofuro Onsen and Ōma before terminating at Sai (¥2260, two hours). Buses for Yagen Onsen start from Ōhata (¥540, 30 minutes).

Six JR buses run daily between Ominato station (not the Mutsu bus terminal) and Wakinosawa (¥1790, 1¼ hours); JR rail pass holders travel free.

Between April and October, round-trip sightseeing boats for Hotokegaura depart Wakinosawa at 10.45am and 2.45pm (¥3800, two hours), returning from Sai (¥2170, two hours); services are often suspended in poor weather.

AOMORI 青森
☎ 017 • pop 300,000

Aomori is the prefectural capital and an important centre for shipping and fishing. It was bombed heavily during WWII and has since been completely rebuilt. The city remains somewhat behind Japan's economic mainstream with a fishing town air, yet has enough city attractions to keep visitors occupied.

Aomori is also a useful transport hub for ferries to Hokkaidō or visits to Shimokita-hantō, Towada-ko and the scenic region around Hakkōda-san.

Information

Aomori is easily covered on foot but bike hire *(available 9am-5pm Jun-Nov)* is available for ¥100 per day opposite the city **tourist information office** *(☎ 723-4670; open 8.30am-5.30pm daily)*, which is on the left as you exit the station's central exit. There's only one English-speaking staff member, but good English-language pamphlets and the excellent *City of Aomori map*.

On the ground floor of the distinctive pyramid-shaped ASPAM building, the prefectural **tourist information counter** *(☎ 734-2500; open 9am-6pm daily)* is only useful for picking up brochures. Avoid paying ¥400 for ASPAM's top floor **Viewing Plaza** – just ride the glass lifts for great views across Aomori-wan.

Aomori's **main post office** is east of the city centre, but there's a smaller **branch post office** within easy reach of the station, all with ATM service.

Free Internet access is available on the 4th floor of the **AUGA** building *(open 10am-9pm daily)* with terminals both in the DoCoMo shop and behind the children's playground.

Things to See & Do

The **Nebuta-no-sato Museum** *(admission ¥630; open 9am-5.30pm daily Apr-Nov, 9am-8pm daily June–mid-Sept)* has a flavour of Aomori's legendary Nebuta Matsuri. Buses to the museum, 9km south of town, leave fairly frequently from stop No 9 outside the train station for the Nebuta-no-sato iriguchi stop (¥450, 30 minutes); free for rail pass holders.

An impressive sight is **Shōwa Daibutsu** *(admission ¥400; open 8am-5.30pm daily Apr-Oct, 9am-4.30pm daily Nov-Mar)*, Japan's largest outdoor Buddha at a height of 21m and weighing 220 tonnes. The breezy temple grounds are full of spinning pinwheels left by parents for their dead children. Buses from Aomori station are timed so that you have about an hour to look around before catching the next bus back (¥540, 45 minutes).

The **Munakata Shikō Memorial Museum** (admission ¥300; open 9.30am-4.30pm Tues-Sun Apr-Oct, 9.30am-4pm Tues-Sun Nov-Mar) houses a collection of wood-block prints, paintings and calligraphy by Munakata Shikō, an Aomori native who won international fame. The building itself is azekura-style, with walls of geometric wooden planks fitted together without upright supports. Buses bound for Nakatsutui leave from stop No 2 outside the train station for the Munakata Shikō Kinenkan-dōri stop (¥190, 15 minutes).

The **Aomori Cultural Museum** (admission ¥310) has selected folk crafts but far more rewarding displays can be found at **Keikokan** (Museum of Historical Folkcraft; admission free; open 9am-4pm Fri-Wed). The museum explores the region's natural history and tells the story of the Ainu people (see Population

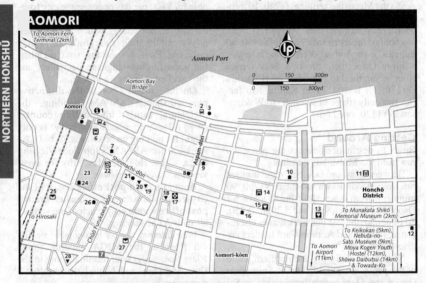

AOMORI

PLACES TO STAY

7   Aomori Grand Hotel
    青森グランドホテル
9   Hotel JAL City Aomori
    ホテルJALシティ青森
10 Takko Ryokan
    田子藍館
12 Hyper Hotel
    ハイパーホテル青森、ハイパ
    ーホテル青森II
16 Aomori Plaza Hotel
    青森プラザホテル
24 Capsule Hotel
26 Daini Ryokan
    大二旅館

PLACES TO EAT

18 Strauss
    シュトラウス
19 Kakigen
    柿源

20 Spage-tei Aomori
    スパゲティー青森
23 Fish & Fresh Food Market
    市場団地
28 Kotobukiya
    ことぶきや

OTHER

1   Tourist Information Office
    松島観光案内所
2   Bus Stand
    バス乗り場
3   ASPAM Building (Aomori
    Prefectural Centre for
    Industry and Tourism)
    アスパム青森観光物産館
4   JR Highway Bus Stop
    JRハイウエイ バス乗り場
5   Bicycle Hire
6   Aomori City Buses
    青森駅前市営バス停

8   HoHo Massage
    好好マッサージ
11 Aomori Cultural Museum
    青森郷土館
13 Rick's Bar
    リックズバー
14 Shrine
    善知鳥神社
15 Crazy Horse Bar
    クレージーホースバー
17 Vivre Department Store
    ヴィヴレ
21 24-hour Lawson
    Convenience Store
22 AUGA Building;
    Internet 4/F
    アウガビル（インターネット
    アクセス）
25 Branch Post Office
27 Main Post Office
    郵便局

& People in the Facts about Japan chapter). Buses from stops No 4 or 5 outside the station run to the Kami-tamagawa stop (¥290, 25 minutes); free for JR rail pass holders.

Finally, take the weight off your feet at **HoHo massage** *(open 10am-8pm daily; foot massage ¥2000/40min)*. They're a friendly bunch and offer great reflexology foot massage.

Special Events

The **Nebuta Matsuri**, held from 2 to 7 August, is renowned throughout Japan for its parades of colossal illuminated floats accompanied by thousands of rowdy, chanting dancers. The parades start at sunset and last for hours, except on the final day when the action starts around noon. Further details can be found at w www.nebuta.or.jp /english/index_e.htm.

Places to Stay

A popular place to break the journey between Tokyo and Hokkaidō, Aomori can be a ludicrously difficult place to find cheap accommodation – even off-peak. Book well ahead, especially if you're coming for the Nebuta Matsuri.

Places to Stay – Budget

Aomori's best budget option is the **Moya Kogen Youth Hostel** *(☎ 764-2888; beds members/nonmembers ¥3300/4200, breakfast/dinner ¥500/1000)*, a modern if a little austere hostel inconveniently located 12km from the station. The English-speaking owner loves Ireland and, if you're lucky, will have a new case of Guinness in the fridge. If you're unlucky, he'll play you his favourite Enya CD at dinner. Buses from stop No 9 outside the train station stop outside the hostel (¥590, 40 minutes); free for rail pass holders. The last bus leaves at 8.20pm.

In the town centre, **Takko Ryokan** *(☎ 722-4825; rooms per person with 2 meals from ¥6500)* is a smarter option.

If you're stuck, two last resorts are the basic **Daini Ryokan** *(rooms per person from ¥3000)*, and a **capsule hotel** *(¥3000)*, located between the station police box and the market; the latter is for men only.

Places to Stay – Mid-Range

Aomori Grand Hotel *(☎ 723-1011; singles/doubles from ¥6000/12,000)*, just east of the station, has rooms with sea views, and staff will exchange money after the banks close at 3pm. The equally suitable **Aomori Plaza Hotel** *(☎ 775-4311; singles/twins ¥5500/10,000)* is a bit further from the station.

Aomori also has two members of the **Hyper Hotel** chain, one conveniently located in the Honchō nightlife district *(☎ 773-3000; singles/twins with breakfast ¥4800/5800)* and with coin laundry.

Six minutes east of the station near ASPAM, **Hotel JAL City** *(☎ 732-2580; singles/doubles ¥8200/11,000)* is the smartest option in town with international standard facilities.

Places to Eat & Drink

Shinmachi-dōri, the main shopping street running east from the station, has the best

---

Nebuta or Neputa?

Even Japanese people muddle up Aomori's Nebuta and Hirosaki's Neputa festivals – not only do they sound confusingly alike, but both take place at the beginning of August.

Historical accounts of the origins of both festivals do not always agree, but Hirosaki's Neputa Matsuri is generally said to signify ceremonial preparation for battle. The fan-shaped Neputa floats are rotated during festival parades so that the heroic *kagami-e* painting on the front and the tearjerker *miokuri-e* ('seeing-off picture') on the back can both be viewed.

Aomori's Nebuta Matsuri, on the other hand, celebrates the triumphant return from battle. The most dramatic account of this festival's origins is the tale of Sakanoue Tamuramaro, an 8th-century general who was sent by the imperial palace to quash a rebellion by the native Ezo tribe. The crafty Tamuramaro is said to have used giant lanterns, along with drums and flutes, to lure the unsuspecting Ezo from their redoubts, after which they were swiftly subdued.

Others theorise that Nebuta began as a way to ward off the stupor that comes with late summer heat. Aomori's more boisterous of the two parades makes for a wake-up call.

pickings, notably **Kakigen** *(open 11am-2.30pm & 5pm-9pm daily)* for its speciality Aomori scallops. Ask for mouth-watering *hotate batā yaki teishoku* (scallops grilled with butter) for ¥1300. In the basement next door, **Spage-tei Aomori** *(open 11am-8.30pm Tues-Sun)* has ¥1000 pasta dishes and an English menu.

The Hotel JAL City's in-house restaurant has a great value soup, buffet, dessert and coffee set lunch daily from 11am to 2.30pm for ¥1500; stock up for the day and show your Aomori Card (see earlier) for a 10% discount.

If you feel like bargaining, there are good deals on set lunches in the **fish and fresh food market**, just south of the station.

Kotobukiya *(☎ 722-7134; open 6pm-midnight daily)*, a 15-minute walk south of Aomori station, offers nightly dinner shows featuring traditional *tsugaru-jamisen* music from ¥6000; reservations required.

The relaxed café **Strauss** *(1st-floor café open noon-6.30pm daily, ground-floor cake shop open 10am-6.30pm daily)* has a 1920's feel and has excellent ¥400 coffee; it's located behind the Vivre department store.

Honchō is the nightlife area and home to two bars popular with local English teachers. **Crazy Horse** is a Grateful Dead–style bar with ¥500 drinks, which stays open until the last person falls down. Heading east from the station, take the first right on Aspam-dōri; it's two blocks further east on the right. Further east, **Rick's Bar** has decent ¥800 cocktails and a pool table.

Getting There & Away

Air There are frequent flights from Aomori airport to Tokyo (¥2300, 1¼ hours), Nagoya (¥24,800, 1½ hours), Osaka (¥27,900, 1½ hours), Sapporo (¥16,200, 40 minutes), and Fukuoka (¥36,000, 2 hours), and an international connection to Seoul (¥51,200, 3 hours). Airport buses are timed to flights and depart from in front of the ASPAM building and Aomori station (¥560, 40 minutes).

Train The JR Tsugaru Kaikyō line runs from Aomori via the Seikan Tunnel to Hakodate on Hokkaidō (*tokkyū* ¥4830, two hours). *Kaisoku* trains do the trip in 2½ hours, and on some of these services (¥3150) you take the Seikan Tunnel tour

(see boxed text 'Seikan Tunnel Tour' in the Hokkaidō chapter).

The JR Tōhoku main line runs south from Aomori to Morioka (*tokkyū* ¥5460, 2¼ hours), from where you can zip back to Tokyo in 2½ hours on the *shinkansen*. The Ōu main line runs via Hirosaki to Akita (¥1680, 2½ hours) where you can pick up the Akita *shinkansen*.

Bus Between April and mid-November, JR runs five to eight buses daily from stop No 8 outside the train station to Towada-ko (¥3000, three hours); the last bus leaves at 2.30pm. The bus reaches stops at the Hakkōda ropeway (¥1070, 50 minutes), then runs via the glorious Sukayu Onsen (¥1300, one hour) (see Hakkōda-san later in this chapter) onto the Oirase Valley and the lake.

JR also operates six buses daily to both Morioka (¥3160, three hours) and Sendai (¥5700, five hours), and one night bus to Tokyo (¥10,190, 10 hours); buses depart from the Highway Bus stop (No 10) outside the station-side tourist information office.

To visit Osore-zan (Shimokita-hantō), direct buses leave the ASPAM building at 12pm, 2pm and 5.20pm for Mutsu via Noheji (¥2520, 2¾ hours).

It's worth knowing that rail pass holders travel free on JR buses, while Aomori Card holders qualify for a 50% discount on all fares. Reservations (from the JR counter inside the station tourist information office) are recommended.

Boat Passenger ferries to Hakodate leave year round (¥850, 3¾ hours), while one ferry leaves for Muroran (Hokkaidō) daily at 14.45pm. Coming back, an overnighter leaves Muroran at 11.25pm (¥3460, 6¾ hours each way).

The ferry terminal, on the western side of the city, is a 10-minute taxi ride from Aomori station (¥1000).

HAKKŌDA-SAN 八甲田山
☎ 017

Just south of Aomori, Hakkōda-san is a scenic region of peaks popular as a day trip with hikers, *onsen* enthusiasts and skiers.

The Hakkōda ropeway (cable car) whisks you up Tamoyachi-dake to the 1324m summit (¥1150 one way, ¥1800 return; open daily 9am to 4.20pm). From there you can follow a network of hiking trails. One particularly pleasant route scales the three peaks of Akakura-dake (1548m), Ido-dake (1550m) and Ōdake (1584m), and then winds its way down to Sukayu Onsen, which is about 10 minutes by bus beyond the cable car station, in the direction of Towada-ko. This 8km hike can be done in a leisurely four hours.

Sukayu Onsen Ryokan (☎ 738-6400; *rooms per person with/without 2 meals from ¥15,000/8000*) is right at the end of the trail and popular with hikers. Budget-conscious travellers can soak in the ryokan's 1000-person cedar bath (*open 9am-5pm*) for just ¥500 and use the camping ground 10 minutes southeast.

JR buses from stop No 8 outside Aomori station pass by the Hakkōda Ropeway-eki stop (¥1070, 50 minutes). In winter, buses terminate at the next stop, Sukayu Onsen (¥1300, one hour); JR rail pass holders travel free, Aomori Card holders are discounted 50%.

HIROSAKI 弘前
☎ 0172 • pop 176,000

Founded in the 17th century, this castle town was once one of the leading cultural centres of Tōhoku. Today it's a drab place and one not particularly welcoming towards foreigners. Given its poor accommodation options, better push on to the livelier Aomori.

Information

The **tourist information office** (☎ 32-0524; *open 8.45am-6pm daily Apr-Oct, 8.45am-5pm daily Nov-Mar*) is to the right as you exit Hirosaki station. Staff speak no English and can only really offer the *Hirosaki City* brochure with a basic map. They do help book accommodation upon payment of ¥2000 (deductible from the room charge).

Equally unspectacular, the **Hirosaki Sightseeing Information Centre** (☎ 37-5501; *open 9am-6pm daily Apr-Oct, 9am-5pm daily Nov-Mar, later during festivals*), inside the Kankōkan (Tourism Building) on the south side of Hirosaki-kōen, has basic information. Internet access is available but, frustratingly, email is blocked. To check mail, head to the **Renaisse Avenue mall** (*open 10am-9pm daily*), where Internet access costs ¥100 per hour in what looks like a store room.

The main **post office**, a 20-minute walk northwest of the station, has a 24-hour postal service, and ATM service that is available until 7pm weekdays, 5pm weekends.

Tsugaruhan Neputa-mura
津軽藩ねぷた村

This museum (*admission ¥500; open 9am-5pm daily Apr-Nov, 9am-4pm daily Dec-Mar*) has a fine display of Neputa floats that are paraded during the Neputa Matsuri. Just south, the **Genbē craft shop** has fine examples of Tsugaru lacquerware, nicknamed *baka-nurii* (fool's lacquer) for its more than 40 layers of multicoloured designs.

Hirosaki-jō 弘前城

Construction of the castle was completed in 1611, but it was burnt down in 1627 after being struck by lightning. One of the castle's corner towers was rebuilt in 1810 and now houses a small **museum** (*admission ¥300; open 9am-5pm daily Apr-Nov*) of samurai artefacts. The castle grounds attract crowds for *hanami* (cherry blossom viewing) during late April and early May. **Fujita Kinen Tei-en** (*admission ¥300; open 9am-5pm Tues-Sun Apr-Nov*) is a well-manicured garden outside the southwest corner of the park.

Zenrin-gai 禅林街

This temple district is a peaceful place for a stroll, following the central avenue – flanked by temples on either side – to **Chōshō-ji**. After passing through the impressive temple gate, continue past a large 14th-century bell to the main hall, which dates from the 17th century. Turning left, a path through the trees leads to a row of mausoleums built for the early rulers of the Tsugaru clan, which dominated the region around Hirosaki during the Edo period.

To get here take a bus from stop No 6 outside Hirosaki station to the Daigaku-byōin stop (¥170, 15 minutes); from here it's a further 10-minute walk southwest. Otherwise you could do the 30-minute walk or take a taxi (¥1000).

Special Events

From 1 to 7 August, Hirosaki celebrates its **Neputa Matsuri**, a festival famous throughout Japan for its illuminated floats parading every evening to the accompaniment

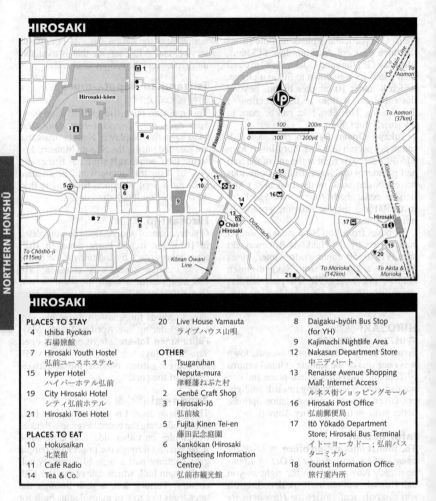

HIROSAKI

PLACES TO STAY
- 4 Ishiba Ryokan
     石場旅館
- 7 Hirosaki Youth Hostel
     弘前ユースホステル
- 15 Hyper Hotel
     ハイパーホテル弘前
- 19 City Hirosaki Hotel
     シティ弘前ホテル
- 21 Hirosaki Tōei Hotel

PLACES TO EAT
- 10 Hokusaikan
     北菜館
- 11 Café Radio
- 14 Tea & Co.

- 20 Live House Yamauta
     ライブハウス山唄

OTHER
- 1 Tsugaruhan
- 2 Neputa-mura
     津軽藩ねぷた村
- 3 Hirosaki-Jō
     弘前城
- 5 Fujita Kinen Tei-en
     藤田記念庭園
- 6 Kankōkan (Hirosaki
     Sightseeing Information
     Centre)
     弘前市観光館

- 8 Daigaku-byōin Bus Stop
     (for YH)
- 9 Kajimachi Nightlife Area
- 12 Nakasan Department Store
     中三デパート
- 13 Renaisse Avenue Shopping
     Mall; Internet Access
     ルネス街ショッピングモール
- 16 Hirosaki Post Office
     弘前郵便局
- 17 Itō Yōkadō Department
     Store; Hirosaki Bus Terminal
     イトーヨーカドー；弘前バス
     ターミナル
- 18 Tourist Information Office
     旅行案内所

of flutes and drums. Like its more rowdy counterpart held in Aomori, this festival attracts thousands of visitors – book accommodation well in advance if you plan to attend.

Places to Stay

The cheapest option is **Hirosaki Youth Hostel** (☎ 33-7066; beds members/nonmembers ¥2950/4000, breakfast ¥630), which is pretty shabby and poorly signposted. Take a bus from stop No 6 outside Hirosaki station to the Daigaku-byōin stop (¥170, 15 minutes); the hostel is located 250m further west down an alleyway.

Many of Hirosaki's ryokan do not accept foreign guests; the upmarket **Ishiba Ryokan** (☎ 32-9118; rooms per person with 2 meals from ¥8000) is one that does and offers Aomori Card holders a 10% discount. It's a 20-minute walk from the station near the Mototera-machi bus stop.

The tourist office encourages foreigners to stay at business hotels. **Hirosaki Tōei Hotel** (☎ 33-8111; singles/doubles from ¥6000/9600) is one of the better options with a coin laundry and downstairs café for decent ¥800 breakfasts. If it's full, **Hyper Hotel** (☎ 31-5000; singles/twins ¥4800/6800) is typically adequate chain fare.

City Hirosaki Hotel (☎ 37-0109; singles/ twins ¥8800/15,000) is the smartest and closest place to the station; Aomori Card holders are discounted 10%.

Places to Eat & Drink
Hokusaikan has three floors of eateries, ranging from a poor imitation Irish pub (open 11am to 11pm) to an *izakaya* (open noon to 1am) on the top floor. **Tea & Co.** *(open 10am-8pm daily)*, just across the river, is a charming little café serving ¥480 *caffè latte* and lovely ¥350 cakes.

Otherwise, the 7th floor of the **Nakasan department store** has several restaurants with point-and-eat displays. Next door, **Cafe Radio** *(open 11.30am-10pm Wed-Mon)* has ¥800 pizza and pasta sets.

Live House Yamauta (☎ 36-1835; open *5pm-11pm daily, closed alternate Mon)* makes for a different (but not cheap) night out. Run by a family who serve local dishes, the hosts give twice-nightly performances of folk music on *tsugaru-jamisen*, a traditional instrument. Expect to pay around ¥3000 per person.

Kajimachi is the town's diminutive entertainment district but many bars refuse foreign customers (for more information on interacting with locals see Society & Conduct in the Facts about Japan chapter).

Getting There & Away
Hirosaki station is on the JR Ōu main line that runs north to Aomori (*futsū* ¥650, 50 minutes) and south to Akita (*tokkyū* ¥3870, two hours).

Most local buses stop at the train station as well as the Hirosaki bus terminal adjacent to Itō Yōkadō department store. The latter only services connections to Sendai (¥5090, 4½ hours, three per day) and Iwaki-san (¥1780, 80 minutes, six to eight per day) with a change at Dake Onsen.

AONI ONSEN 青荷鴛泉
Aoni Onsen (☎ 0172 54-8588; rooms per person with 2 meals from ¥8500) is a seriously atmospheric but seriously isolated rustic group of ryokan in a time warp, where oil lamps replace electricity and bathing is elevated to a fine art. Advance reservations are mandatory; the adjoining camping ground charges ¥1000 even if you bring your own tent. You can just use the baths for ¥500.

Aoni Onsen is most accessible by car. By public transport, take the private Kounan tetsudō line from Hirosaki to Kuroishi (¥420, 35 minutes, four daily); Kounan buses connect with arriving passengers for Niji-no-ko (¥660, 10 minutes) from where four shuttle buses run to Aoni daily (free, 30 minutes). This journey helps filter out the true *onsen* buffs.

IWAKI-SAN 岩木山
Soaring above Hirosaki is the sacred volcano of Iwaki-san (1625m), which is a popular peak for both pilgrims and hikers.

From early April to late October, there are up to eight buses daily from the Hirosaki bus terminal to Dake Onsen (¥900, 50 minutes), where you transfer to a shuttle bus to Hachigōme (¥880, 30 minutes), at the foot of the ski lift. Open from mid-April to mid-October, the lift (¥410/750 one way/ return, 45 minutes) to the summit (Eighth Station) provides the easiest access, but it is also possible to hike to the top in about four hours starting from **Iwaki-jinja**.

In Hyakuzawa Onsen, **Kokuminshuku-sha Iwaki-sō** (☎ 0172 83-2215; rooms per person with 2 meals weekdays/weekends & holidays ¥6500/7500) is a safe bet. From Hirosaki bus terminal stop No 3, take a bus bound for Iwaki-sō and get off at the last stop (¥660, one hour).

TOWADA-KO 十和田湖
☎ 0176 • pop 6000
This 327m deep crater lake has some impressive scenery and opportunities for hiking and skiing. Sadly, it's also a major tourist trap so best enjoyed as a day trip – especially as accommodation quickly books out even in low season.

Nenokuchi, a small tourist outpost on the eastern shore of the lake, marks the entrance to the 14km **Oirase Valley Nature Trail**, a three-hour hike around the lake best hiked early morning or late afternoon to avoid the coach parties. The path ends at Yakeyama, from where frequent buses return to Nenokuchi (¥660, 30 minutes) and Yasumiya (¥1100, one hour).

The lake's tourist hub, **Yasumiya**, offers numerous boat tours of the lake, the best of which is the one-hour cruise between Yasumiya and Nenokuchi (¥1320 one way). Boats leave roughly hourly between 8am

TOWADA-KO

and 4pm from April to early November. You can hire mountain bikes at the dock for ¥1500 per day from April to November.

The unremarkable hole-in-the-wall **Tourist Information Center** (☎ 75-2506; open 8am-5pm daily), just north of the JR bus station, only has Japanese-language hiking maps but does help arrange accommodation. **Goodwill Guides** (☎ 53-4430) are available for the area but a hefty two-week notice period is required.

Places to Stay & Eat
There are three camping grounds around the edge of the lake. **Towada-ko Oide Campground** (☎ 75-2366; camp sites ¥300; open Apr-Oct), about 4km west of Yasumiya, is the cheapest and most basic option. JR buses from Yasumiya to Towada-Minami pass by the Oide Kyampu-jo-mae stop (¥220).

Rooms at the **Hakubutsukan Youth Hostel** (☎ 75-2002; dorm beds ¥3200) are squeezed into the old wing of the Towada-ko Grand Hotel but are not available when the hotel is booked out.

Oirase Youth Hostel (☎ 74-2031; beds ¥2800), near the Yakeyama bus stop, is a relaxed place with no curfew but quite a trek from Yasumiya. Buses running between Towada-ko and Aomori pass by the Yakeyama bus stop (¥1100, one hour), from

where it's 200m up a small hill past the Oirase Grand Hotel car park to the hostel.

Minshuku line the track leading out of Yasumiya away from the lake. A few minutes northwest of the bus station, **Koku Minshukusha** (rooms per person ¥4350) has decent rooms.

Five minutes north of the bus station, **Shinsyuya**, a gloriously chaotic eatery on the 2nd floor above a souvenir shop, has set meals from ¥1300.

Getting There & Away
There are two bus centres in Yasumiya, one for JR buses and one for other services. Both are a couple of minutes on foot from the pier.

From April to November, JR buses run to Aomori (¥3000, three hours) – see Aomori Getting There & Away earlier – and there's a 50% discount for Aomori Card holders. There are three buses daily between April and early November to Morioka (¥2420, 2¼ hours). From late April to September, there is one bus at 8.45am to Hachimantai Chōjō, the main point of access for the Hachimantai region (¥2300, 2¼ hours).

The nearest train station is at Towada-Minami, on the JR Hanawa line with connections to Morioka (*kaisoku*, ¥1800, 1¾ hours). Up to four connecting buses run daily between 8am and 4.40pm (¥330, one hour).

Akita-ken 秋田県

HACHIMANTAI 八幡平
This mountain plateau area is popular with hikers, skiers and *onsen* enthusiasts.

Transport connections revolve around Hachimantai Chōjō, the main access point for the summit, which offers gentle walks. Longer hikes are possible over a couple of days from nearby **Tōshichi Onsen**, a 2km walk downhill from the Hachimantai Chōjō car park.

West of the summit, the Aspite Line Hwy, open late April to November, winds past several hot springs resorts before joining Route 341, which leads either south to Tazawa-ko or north towards Towada-ko.

There is a small visitors centre next to the car park at Hachimantai Chōjō where you can purchase regional contour maps (Japanese only) and consult bilingual

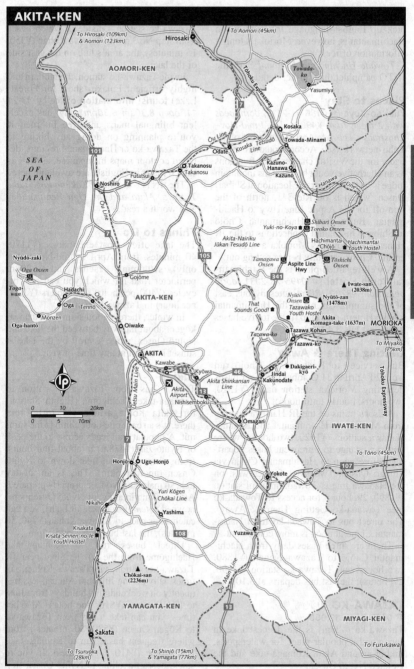

AKITA-KEN

To Hirosaki (109km) & Aomori (123km)

To Aomori (45km)

HIROSAKI

AOMORI-KEN

Towada-ko

Yasumiya

Gonō Line

Tōhoku Expressway

Kosaka

Ōu Line

Kosaka Tetsudō Line

Towada-Minami

Odate

Kazuno-Hanawa

Takanosu

Takanosu

Kazuno

SEA OF JAPAN

Noshiro

Fūtatsui

Hanawa Line

Ōu Line

Akita-Nairiku Jūkan Tesudō Line

Yuki-no-Koya

Shibari Onsen

Toroko Onsen

Hachimantai Chōjō

Hachimantai Youth Hostel

Nyūdō-zaki

Oga Onsen

Gojōme

Tamagawa Onsen

Aspite Line Hwy

Tōshichi Onsen

Iwate-san (2038m)

Toga-wan

Hadachi

AKITA-KEN

That Sounds Good!

Nyūtō Onsen

Tazawako Youth Hostel

Nyūtō-zan (1478m)

Oga

Tennō

Oga-hantō

Monzen

Oiwake

Ōga Line

Akita Komaga-take (1637m)

MORIOKA

Tazawa-ko

Tazawa Kohan

To Miyako (75km)

Tazawa-ko

AKITA

Kawabe

Kyōwa

Dakigaeri-kyō

Jindai

Kakunodate

Akita Airport

Akita Shinkansen Line

Nishisemboku

Uetsu Main Line

Omagari

IWATE-KEN

Tōhoku Expressway

Honjō

Ugo-Honjō

To Tōno (45km)

Yokote

Nikaho

Yuri Kōgen Chōkai Line

Yashima

Kisakata

Kisata Seinen-no-Ie Youth Hostel

Yuzawa

Chōkai-san (2236m)

Ōu Main Line

YAMAGATA-KEN

MIYAGI-KEN

Sakata

To Tsuruoka (28km)

To Shinjō (15km) & Yamagata (77km)

To Furukawa

0   10   20km

0   5   10mi

hiking sketch maps. The best place to pick up English-language information on Hachimantai is, however, Morioka's tourist information office.

Towada-Hachimantai National Park, the JNTO pamphlet, has further details.

Places to Stay

Yuki-no-Koya (☎ *0186-31-2118; dorm beds with 2 meals from ¥4900; closed mid-Nov–Christmas & Feb-late Apr)* is a member of the Toho network (see Accommodation in the Facts for the Visitor chapter) and functions as an alternative youth hostel. This mountain lodge is in a quiet riverside location at Shibari Onsen, which is on Rte 341, north of the turn-off for the Aspite Line Hwy to Hachimantai. Buses from Hachimantai Chōjō to Shibari Onsen, and connections to the JR Hanawa line towards Morioka are, at best, erratic. Check carefully before setting out.

A well-regarded place is the **Hachimantai Youth Hostel** (☎ *0195-78-2031; dorm beds from ¥3200)*, 20 minutes by bus east of the summit. Get off at the Hachimantai Kankō Hoteru-mae stop (three to five buses daily, last bus 3.40pm).

Getting There & Away

Bus services to Hachimantai Chōjō run from 20 April to 31 October with four buses departing Morioka station daily (¥1320, two hours, hourly until noon).

Kaisoku trains on the JR Hanawa line run from Morioka to Hachimantai and Kazuno-Hanawa stations (¥1620, two hours), where you can change to infrequent buses departing before noon to Hachimantai Chōjō via Shibari Onsen. Two stops further west on the Hanawa line is Towada-minami station (¥1890, 2½ hours) for access to Towada-ko (see Towada-ko Getting There & Away). The direct bus to Towada-ko from Hachimantai Chōjō at noon is more convenient.

There are three buses daily from Hachimantai Chōjō to Tazawa Kohan (¥1880, two hours) and Tazawa-ko station (¥1990, 2¼ hours); the last bus departs at 3.10pm.

TAZAWA-KO 田沢湖
☎ 0187 • pop 13,000

Tazawa-ko (423m) is the deepest lake in Japan and a popular place for watersports, hiking around Akita Komaga-take and the isolated Nyūtō Onsen.

The main access to the area is via JR Tazawa-ko station, outside of which buses from stop No 3 run to Tazawa Kohan (¥350, 15 minutes), the area's hub on the east side of the lake.

Inside Tazawa-ko station, the modern and highly efficient Folake (short for Forest-Lake) **tourist information office** (☎ *43-21 11; open 8.30am-6.30pm daily)* has excellent bilingual maps and free Internet. If you're planning on doing any hiking in the Tazawa-ko or Hachimantai regions, detailed contour maps in Japanese, as well as sketch maps in English, are available here.

The JNTO brochure *Kakunodate, Lake Tazawa, Akita and the Oga Peninsula* is also worth a read.

Things to Do

The lake offers boat excursions (¥1170, 40 minutes, from April to mid-November only), swimming beaches and a 20km perimeter road for which you can rent bicycles (¥400 per hour) or scooters (¥1200 per hour) in Tazawa Kohan.

In winter, there's good skiing at Tazawa-kōgen, about halfway between the lake and Nyūtō Onsen, while a stroll by the lake at sunset is a treat at any time of year.

Hiking

Take a bus from Tazawa-ko station to Komaga-take Hachigōme (Eighth Station) for **Akita Komaga-take** (1637m). From there, it's an easy one-hour climb to the summit. A popular trail leads across to the peak of Nyūtō-zan (1478m) in about four hours, from where you can hike down to Nyūtō Onsen (another 5km). This is an all-day trek, so make sure you are properly prepared. After soaking in a few of Nyūtō Onsen's renowned *rotemburo* (open-air bath), you can catch a bus back to Tazawa Kohan (¥740, 50 minutes); the last bus leaves at 5.55pm.

Direct buses run to Komaga-take Hachigōme from the bus terminal near JR Tazawa-ko station, via Tazawa Kohan, six times daily during July and August, less frequently on weekends and holidays from June to late October (¥810, one hour). At other times, you can take a bus from Tazawa-ko to Kōgen Onsen (¥580, 30 minutes), from where frequent buses run to Komaga-take Hachigōme (¥410, 30 minutes). If you're stuck, buses travelling to Nyūtō Onsen stop at Komaga-take Tozan-guchi (¥460, 40 minutes), 7km from Komaga-take Hachigōme.

Places to Stay – Budget

Tazawa-ko Youth Hostel (☎ 43-1281; dorm beds ¥2900, breakfast/dinner ¥800/1000) is a ramshackle place that has seen better days. Bike rental is available for ¥300 per day, the cheapest rate in town. It's 10 minutes from Tozawa Kohan bus station; coming from Tazawa-ko station, get off at the Kōen-iriguchi stop across from the road the hostel's front door.

Places to Stay – Mid-Range & Top End

It's worth splashing out for the charming **That Sounds Good!** (☎ 43-0127; e san zoku@hana.or.jp; rooms per person with 2 meals from ¥8500), where the excellent atmosphere justifies the above average rates. The owners, the Sasaki family, are big jazz fans and often host impromptu jazz nights; they also help organise outdoor activities. It's a pleasant 30-minute stroll north of Tazawa Kohan bus terminal, otherwise call ahead for a pick-up; advance reservations are mandatory during peak seasons.

The Nyūtō Onsen area is home to seven rustic ryokan but some will only let foreigners use the onsen, not stay overnight. Foreigners are welcome at **Tsuru-no-yu Onsen Ryokan** (☎ 46-2139; rooms per person ¥8500, bath ¥400; open 8am-5pm Tues-Sun, closed Nov-Mar), and **Tae-no-yu Onsen Ryokan** (☎ 46-2740; rooms per person ¥10,000-13,000, bath ¥1000; open 9am-3pm daily). Both rates include two meals.

If you just fancy a dip in a rotemburo, stay at the **Nyūtō camping ground** (sites ¥1100 plus ¥400 per person) and head for **Magoroku Onsen Ryokan** (☎ 46-2224; bath ¥400; open 7am-6pm daily) or **Ganiba Onsen Ryokan** (☎ 46-2021; bath ¥500; open 8am-6pm daily), which has a mixed-sex rotemburo for the more adventurous.

Before setting out, check with the **tourist information office** at Tazawa-ko station; they also provide a sketch map of the area detailing appropriate bus stops and directions.

Regular buses run from Tazawa Kohen to Nyūtō Onsen (¥850, 40 minutes); the last bus back leaves at 6.40pm.

Places to Eat

Heart Herb (open 10am-9pm daily) offers relaxing herbal baths (¥400) all year round, and has a good café for ¥880 lunch sets (closed Dec-Mar).

ORAE (open 11am-9pm daily) has set menus from ¥820 and serves up local microbrews from ¥480 a glass – try the caramel beer. There's a relaxed outdoor deck. Both are a 15-minute walk north of the Tazawa Kohan bus terminal, where there's also a cluster of snack bars.

Getting There & Away

On the Akita shinkansen line, Tazawa-ko is within easy reach of Morioka (¥1470, 30 minutes), Kakunodate (¥1050, 15 minutes) and Akita (¥2770, one hour). Local trains run infrequently along the JR Tazawa-ko line to Morioka (¥740, 60 minutes) and Kakunodate (¥320, 20 minutes).

If you're heading west, it's easiest to take the bus from Tazawa Kohan via Tazawa-ko station to Kakunodate (¥850, 45 minutes, seven per day); departures before 4.10pm continue to Akita (¥1680, 2¼ hours). From December to March, services to and from Tazawa Kohan, but not Tazawa-ko station, are suspended.

Between 20 April and 31 October, three buses daily leave Tazawa-ko station for Hachimantai Chōjō (¥1990, 2¼ hours); the last bus leaves at 12.40pm.

KAKUNODATE 角館

☎ 0187 • pop 15,000

This small town, with its samurai district dating from 1620, puffs itself up as Tōhoku's answer to Kyoto but, frankly, Kyoto has nothing to worry about. There's little reason to overnight here as the main sights are covered easily in a day trip from Tazawa-ko, Morioka or Akita, which have far better facilities for travellers.

The **tourist information office** (☎ 54-2700; open 9am-6pm daily Apr-Oct, 9am-5pm daily Nov-Mar), in a small building that looks like a traditional storehouse, outside the JR Kakunodate station, helps with reservations and has an English-language map.

Outside the station, bicycle rental is available for ¥300 per hour, or you can hire a Japanese-speaking rickshaw driver in summer only to explain the local sights (¥3,000 for two people).

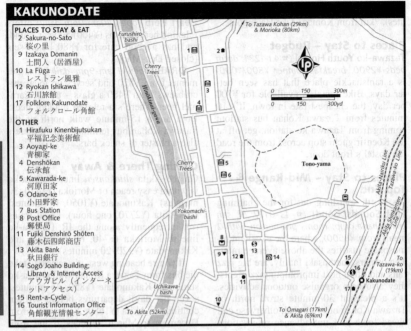

KAKUNODATE

PLACES TO STAY & EAT
2 Sakura-no-Sato
   桜の里
9 Izakaya Domanin
   土間人（居酒屋）
10 La Fūga
   レストラン風雅
12 Ryokan Ishikawa
   石川旅館
17 Folklore Kakunodate
   フォルクロール角館

OTHER
1 Hirafuku Kinenbijutsukan
   平福記念美術館
3 Aoyagi-ke
   青柳家
4 Denshōkan
   伝承館
5 Kawarada-ke
   河原田家
6 Odano-ke
   小田野家
7 Bus Station
8 Post Office
   郵便局
11 Fujiki Denshirō Shōten
   藤木伝四郎商店
13 Akita Bank
   秋田銀行
14 Sogō Joaho Building;
   Library & Internet Access
   アウガビル（インターネ
   ットアクセス）
15 Rent-a-Cycle
16 Tourist Information Office
   角館観光情報センター

Free **Internet access** is available at the library *(open 9am-7pm Tues-Sun)* in the Sogō Joaho building. Cash service is available at the **post office** and **Akita bank**.

Samurai Residences

The interiors of **Kawarada-ke** and **Odano-ke** can be viewed for free, while **Bukeyashiki Shiryōkan** *(admission ¥300; open 8.30am-5pm daily)* is a cramped museum exhibiting samurai equipment.

Further north, **Aoyagi-ke** *(admission ¥500; open 9am-5pm daily Apr-Nov, 9am-4pm daily Dec-Mar)* is actually a conglomeration of mini-museums with folk art and Aoyagi family heirlooms.

Denshōkan 伝承館

This museum *(admission single/combined ¥300/510; open 9am-4.30pm daily Apr-Nov, 9am-4pm daily Dec-Mar)* houses various exhibits and has demonstrations of *kabazaiku* (cherry-bark craft). The discount combined ticket allows entry to the nearby **Hirafuku Kinenbijutsukan** *(open 9am-4.30pm daily Apr-Nov)*, which displays Japanese and Western modern art.

Special Events

In the samurai district, the **cherry trees** beside the river (originally brought from Kyoto) attract crowds of visitors in late April.

From 7 to 9 September, Kakunodate celebrates the **Hikiyama Matsuri** in which participants haul around enormous seventonne *yama* (wooden carts).

Places to Stay & Eat

Kakunodate has poor options for overnighting. **Sakura-no-Sato** *(☎ 55-5652; rooms with/without 2 meals ¥6500/4500)* is the cheapest option, but it's unremarkable and a 2km hike from the station. Closer to town, **Ryokan Ishikawa** *(☎ 54-2030; room with 2 meals from ¥9000)* is the best of a bad bunch.

Folklore Kakunodate *(☎ 53-2070; twins/ 4-person rooms off-season ¥12,000/20,000, high season ¥14,000/23,000)* is a Western-style hotel next to Kakunodate station; prices decrease for multiple-day stays.

The one place definitely worth seeking out in town is **La Fuga** *(☎ 54-2784; open 11am-2pm & 5pm-8.30pm Tues-Sun)*, which not only does excellent ¥800 set lunches and ¥1200 pizzas, but the friendly owners, the Miuras, provide a lifeline to stranded foreigners and local English teachers.

Domanin (open 11am-midnight daily) is a funky izakaya-style eatery with meals around ¥2000 and ¥500 beers.

Shopping

Kakunodate is renowned for kabazaiku, household or decorative items covered in cherry bark, a craft first taken up by poor samurai. It's worth spending more on the genuine article made entirely from wood, rather than the cheaper version with a tin inner core. High-quality kabazaiku can be found at **Fujiki Denshirō Shōten** (open 10am-3pm daily, closed winter), which has its own workshop nearby.

Getting There & Away

The Akita shinkansen line connects Kakunodate with Tazawa-ko (¥1050, 13 minutes), Morioka (¥2260, 50 minutes) and Akita (¥2430, 45 minutes). Infrequent local trains run on the JR Tazawa-ko line from Kakunodate east to Tazawa-ko (¥320, 20 minutes) and Morioka (¥1110, one hour). Infrequent connections west to Akita require a change of trains at Ōmagari.

Buses run from Kakunodate to Tazawa Kohan (¥850, 45 minutes) and Tazawa-ko station (¥490, 35 minutes), as well as to Akita (¥1330, 90 minutes). From December to March, these buses do not stop at Tazawa Kohan.

Kakunodate bus station is 10 minutes north of the train station.

AKITA 秋田
☎ 018 • pop 319,000

Akita, the prefectural capital, is a large commercial city with a lively nightlife area. However, foreign students causing problems in Akita have recently provoked something of a backlash against gaijin. It's worth remembering that not many foreigners make it this far north so some awareness of cultural issues would be advised (see Society & Conduct in the Facts about Japan chapter).

Information

The **tourist information office** (☎ 832-7941; open 9.30am-5pm daily), opposite the shinkansen tracks on the 2nd floor of

Akita's ultra-modern station, offers maps and advice but staff speak no English. The prefectural **tourist information office** (☎ 836-7835; open 9am-7pm Thur-Tues) is located inside the distinctive Atorion building, which also houses an observatory and a **NTT Internet station** (admission free; open 10am-4.30pm Thur-Tues).

On the 2nd floor of the Castle Hotel plaza, **Digital Lounge** (open 9am-midnight daily) has Internet access for ¥300 per hour.

The post office, including ATM service for foreign-issued cards, is located five minutes west of the train station's west exit, in the backstreets near the market.

Things to See

Senshū-kōen, once the site of Kubota-jō and now home to the castle ruins, is 10 minutes west of the station. At the park's northern end, **Osumi-yagura**, a reconstruction of one of the eight turrets of Kubota-jō, was under renovation at the time of writing. Near **Hachiman Akita-jinja**, the **Omonogashira-obansho** guardhouse is the only remaining original castle building, while the tiny **Satake Historical Museum** (admission ¥100; open 9am-4.30pm daily) borders the southeast corner.

The **Masakichi Hirano Art Museum** (admission ¥610; open 10am-5pm Tues-Sun May-Sept, 10am-4.30pm Tues-Sun Oct-Apr) is noted for its enormous canvas painting Events of Akita, which measures 3.65m by 20.5m and depicts traditional Akita life throughout the seasons.

The **Kanto Festival Centre** (Neburi Nagashi-kan; admission ¥100; open 9.30am-4.30pm daily, 9am-9pm during festivals), 10 minutes west of the park across the river, has comprehensive exhibitions of the prefecture's major festivals.

Five minutes south, past Daiei department store, the **Akarengakan Museum** (admission ¥200; open 9.30am-4.30pm daily), in a Meiji-era Renaissance-style red brick building, has wood-block prints of traditional Akita life by self-taught folk artist Katsuhira Tokushi. A combined ticket with the Kantō Festival Centre is available at either place for ¥250.

Special Events

From 4 to 7 August, Akita celebrates the **Kantō Matsuri** (Pole Lantern Festival), one of the most famous festivals in Tōhoku. Starting in the evening along Kantō Ōdori, more than 160 men balance giant poles, weighing 60kg and hung with illuminated lanterns, on their heads, chins, hips and shoulders to the beat of *taiko* drumming

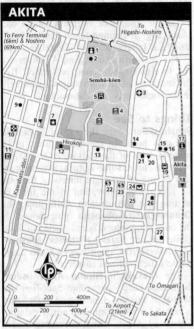

groups. During the day, exhibitions of music and pole-balancing are held in Senshū-kōen. See 🅦 www.kantou.gr.jp.

Places to Stay

The best option in town is **Ryokan Kohama** (☎ 832-5739; *singles/doubles from ¥5500/ 10,000, breakfast/dinner ¥1000/2000*), a member of the Japanese Inn group run by a friendly kimono-clad mama-san and her chatty parrot, is 10 minutes on foot south of Akita station. If it's full, **Ryokan Chikuba-sō** (☎ 832-6446; *rooms per person with 2 meals ¥7000*), slightly closer to the station, makes for a plan B.

The cheapest business hotel rooms are found at **Hotel Hawaii Eki-mae** (☎ 833-1111; *singles/twins with bath ¥6000/9000, without bath ¥4100/5500*), a short walk from the station. Don't expect any hula skirts. Directly opposite, **Akita View Hotel** (☎ 832-1111; *singles/twins from ¥8800/ 16,000*) is smart with a gym, pool and sauna but, like the Hawaii, is geared towards Japanese businessmen.

For a splurge, **Akita Castle Hotel** (☎ 834-1117; *singles/doubles ¥9000/13,000*) is the best address in town.

Places to Eat

Local specialities include two types of hot-pot – *kiritanpo* (chicken with rice cakes) and *shottsuru* (local fish *hatahata* with green onions and tofu). You can sample

---

AKITA

PLACES TO STAY & EAT

8	Gado Gado
12	Akita Castle Hotel; Akita Castle Plaza; (2/F) Digital Lounge 秋田キャッスルホテル; キャッスルズアーケード; (2F) デジタルラウンジ
14	Hotel Hawaii Eki-mae ホテルハワイ駅前
18	Topico Plaza; Suginoya (3/F) トピコプラザショッピングモール3F 杉野屋
20	Merry Xmas Café
21	Akita View Hotel 秋田ビューホテル
26	Ryokan Chikuba-sō 旅館竹馬荘
27	Ryokan Kohama 小浜旅館

OTHER

1	Osumi-yagura 御隅櫓
2	Omonogashira-obansho
3	Municipal Emergency Hospital 私立夜間休日応急診療所
4	Satake Historical Museum 佐竹史料館
5	Hachiman Akita-jinja 八幡秋田神社
6	Masakichi Hirano Art Museum; Prefectural Art Museum
7	Police
9	Kantō Festival Centre ねぶり流し館
10	New City Plaza; Daiei Department Store ニューシティプラザ; ダイエー

11	Akarengakan Museum 赤れんが郷土館
13	Atorion Building; Prefectural Tourist Information Centre (2/ F); NTT Internet Centre (5/F) アトリオンビル（5F）NTT インターネットセンター
15	24-hour Lawson Convenience Store
16	Akita Ticket
17	Tourist Information Office 松島観光案内所
19	Bus Station バスのりば
22	Iwate Bank 岩手銀行
23	Akita Bank 秋田銀行
24	Post Office 郵便局
25	Market

these and ¥1480 set meals at **Suginoya** *(open 10am-9pm daily)* on the 3rd floor restaurant arcade of Akita station's Topico plaza.

Opposite Akita Ticket, 150m west of the station, **Cafe Merry Xmas** *(open 7am-8pm Mon-Fri, 9am-8pm Sat & Sun)*, despite the name, does a surprisingly good ¥480 *caffè latte* and a ¥650 sandwich set lunch.

Gado Gado, just across Saiwai bridge, is a smart basement Asian food market with ¥1000 set lunches and ¥1400 dinners.

For the more adventurous, the **market** *(open 6am-5pm Mon-Sat)* is a good place to negotiate a cheap snack.

Kawabata-dōri is the main nightlife area, a 15-minute walk west of the station. Note: some bars do not welcome foreigners.

Getting There & Away

There are flights from Akita's airport south of town to Nagoya, Osaka, Sapporo and Tokyo. Buses run from outside JR Akita station (¥890, 40 minutes).

The JR Akita *shinkansen* line runs via Tazawa-ko and Kakunodate to Morioka (¥3990, 90 minutes), cutting total travel time between Akita and Tokyo to four hours (¥16,300). Painfully infrequent local trains chug along the Ōu line to Ōmagari where you change to the JR Tazawa-ko line for Kakunodate (¥1280, 90 minutes) and Tazawa-ko (¥1620, two hours). The JR Uetsu line connects Akita with Niigata via Sakata and Tsuruoka *(tokkyū* ¥6510, 3¾ hours).

Ten buses run daily from Akita station to Kakunodate (¥1330, 90 minutes) and eight daily to Tazawa-ko (¥1680, two hours). Direct night buses to Tokyo (Shinjuku) run from the Nagasakiya bus terminal via Akita station at 9pm and 10pm (¥9450 one way, 9½ hours).

On Tuesday, Wednesday, Friday and Sunday, Shin Nihonkai morning ferries connect Akita with Niigata (¥2270, 6½ hours) and Tsuruga (¥5620, 19½ hours). On Tuesday, Thursday, Saturday and Sunday, ferries run to Tomakomai on Hokkaidō (¥3830, 11½ hours).

One bus daily at 7.25am runs to Akita's port, 8km northwest of the station (¥390, 30 minutes).

Discounted air and rail tickets are available at Akita Ticket near the station.

KISAKATA 象潟
☎ 0184 • pop 13,300

Kisakata, a small but lively Japan Sea coast town, is dominated by **Chōkai-san** (2236m), Tōhoku's second highest peak, which is known as 'Dewa Fuji' and is an object of veneration by the same *yamabushi* (mountain priests) who worship at Dewa Sanzan in Yamagata-ken.

The hole-in-the-wall **tourist information office** *(☎ 43-2174; open 8.30am-5.15pm daily)*, inside the station waiting room, has photocopied contour maps for hiking Chōkai-san and information on local sights, such as **Kanman-ji** (visited by Bashō) just north of the town centre.

The most convenient access to Chōkai-san is via bus from Kisakata station to Hokodate (5th Station; ¥980, 40 minutes), from where the summit is a four-and-a-half hour climb. Buses run on weekends and holidays from July to September; two buses leave Kisakata station daily at 5.50am and 7.45am from mid-July to mid-August; the last bus back from Hokodate leaves at 4.20pm.

Places to Stay & Eat

Kisakata Seinen-no-Ie Youth Hostel *(☎ 43-3154; dorm beds ¥2500)* is more a place to crash than stay, but it's cheap with no curfew. From Kisakata station, it's a 10-minute walk southwest to the main intersection where a blue-and-white hostel points the way.

Next door is a **camping ground** *(camp sites ¥600, plus ¥400 per person; open July-Sept)* while, nearby, **Minshuku Rofusō** *(☎ 43-2228; rooms per person with 2 meals ¥6000)* is a simple but effective place to overnight.

Masaen *(open 11.30am-2.30pm & 5.30pm-9pm daily)* is a great little eatery with generous ¥800 set menus and free coffee located 300m west of the station. It's worth changing trains at Kisakata just for a decent meal here.

Getting There & Away

Local trains on the scenic JR Uetsu main line connect Kisakata with Sakata (¥650, 40 minutes) for connections to Tsuruoka (¥1120, 30 minutes). Local trains head north on the same line to Akita (¥1110, 1¼ hours).

Yamagata-ken
山形県

SAKATA 酒田
☎ 0234 • pop 100,000

Sakata is an utterly bland and ugly concrete place – make it a day trip to Tobi-shima island or the excellent Ken Domon Museum of Photography rather than overnight.

City maps and bicycle rental are free at the small and rather unhelpful **tourist information office** (☎ 24-2454; open 9am-5.30pm daily Apr-Oct, 9am-5pm daily Nov-Mar) inside JR Sakata station. Luggage storage at the station costs ¥410 per item.

The **post office** is 150m from the station opposite the Tokyo Inn; there's no public Internet access in Sakata.

The **Homma Art Museum** (admission ¥700; open 9am-5pm daily Mar-Oct, 9am-4.30pm Tues-Sun Nov-Feb) is five minutes northwest of the station.

The town's only major attraction, the **Ken Domon Memorial Museum** (admission ¥420; open 9am-4.30pm daily Apr-Nov, 9am-4.30pm Tues-Sun Dec-Mar), is several kilometres from the station across Mogamigawa. Domon Ken believed that photography should touch on social issues, and his photographs often provide sensitive insight into the underside of Japanese life in the postwar years. He is also renowned for his photos of Buddhist images in Nara and Kyoto. If you're not cycling, take the Run Run loop bus from Sakata station to the Domon Ken Kinenkan-mae stop (¥100, 20 minutes).

Special Events
On 15 and 17 February, farmers perform kabuki at Hie-jinja in Kuromori, 50 minutes by bus from Sakata. If you plan to attend, you must make reservations several months in advance.

Places to Stay
Sakata has few decent options to overnight. If you must stay overnight, **Kameya Ryokan** (☎ 22-0585; rooms per person with 2 meals from ¥5800) is a traditional place 10 minutes from the station by Yagumo-jinja.

Hotel Alpha One Sakata (☎ 22-6111; singles/doubles from ¥5350/11,200) has typical chain hotel rooms but is, at least, next to the station for a quick getaway.

Getting There & Away
From Sakata station, buses to Shōnai airport (¥790, 30 minutes) are timed to coincide with check-in for flights to Tokyo, Kansai and Sapporo.

The JR Uetsu main line runs north from Sakata to Kisakata (futsū, ¥650, 40 minutes) and Akita (¥1890, 1¾ hours). The same line runs south to Tsuruoka (¥1110, 30 minutes) and Niigata (tokkyū, ¥4620, two hours). There are infrequent but scenic connections via Shinjō (¥950, one hour) onto Narugo Onsen (¥950, one hour).

There are up to seven buses daily from Sakata to Sendai (¥2750, three hours, last bus 4.20pm) via the Tsuruoka bus terminal (¥820, 50 minutes). There is one night bus to Tokyo (Shibuya, Ikebukuro) departing Sakata at 9.30pm (¥7870, nine hours).

TOBI-SHIMA 飛島
☎ 0234

A mere speck of an island (2½ sq km), Tobi-shima's main attractions are rugged cliffs, sea caves, scuba diving and, reportedly, excellent fishing. You can also organise boat trips out to smaller islands.

Rates at the island's ryokan vary seasonally from ¥7000 to ¥10,000 per person, with two meals; minshuku cost around ¥7000 with two meals. **Sawaguchi Ryokan** (☎ 95-2246; beds ¥2200-2400), the island's youth hostel, is seven minutes on foot from the ferry pier; bicycle rental is available.

Ferries run at least once (often twice) daily from Sakata-kō to the island (¥2040, 90 minutes). Advance reservations (☎ 22-3911) are recommended in summer. To get to Sakata-kō, take the Run Run bus to ferry terminal stop (¥100).

MOGAMI-KYŌ 最上峡
Boat tours are operated through this gorge on a section of the Mogami-gawa between Sakata and Shinjō. It's harmless fun complete with a boatman singing a selection of local folk tunes.

From Sakata, trains on the JR Rikuusaisen line run to Furukuchi station (¥740, 55 minutes); you may have to change trains en route at Amarume. From Furukuchi station, it's eight minutes on foot to the boat dock. Boats depart up to nine times daily from 9am to 4.30pm during the main season from April to November (¥1970). The boat trip takes an

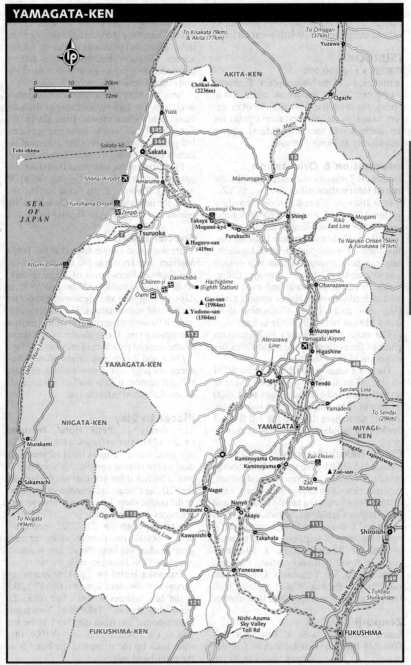

YAMAGATA-KEN

0   10   20km
0   6   12mi

To Kisakata (9km)
& Akita (77km)

To Omagari
(37km)

AKITA-KEN

Yuzawa

Chōkai-san
(2236m)

Ogachi

Yuza

Ou Main Line

Tobi-shima

Sakata-kō

Sakata

Shōnai Airport

Amarume

Mamurogawa

Kusanagi Onsen

Shinjō

Riku
East Line

Mogami

Yunohama Onsen

Zenpō-ji

Takaya

Mogami-kyō

Furukuchi

SEA
OF
JAPAN

Tsuruoka

Haguro-san
(419m)

Atsumi Onsen

Chūren-ji

Dainichibō

Ōami

Hachigōme
(Eighth Station)

Gas-san
(1984m)

Yudono-san
(1504m)

Obanazawa

To Naruko Onsen (5km)
& Furukawa (41km)

Murayama

Yamagata Airport

Higashine

Aterazawa
Line

YAMAGATA-KEN

Sagae

Tendō

Yamadera

Senzan Line

To Sendai
(29km)

NIIGATA-KEN

YAMAGATA

MIYAGI-
KEN

Zaō Onsen

Zaō-san

Zaō
Bōdaira

Yamagata Expressway

Murakami

Kaminoyama Onsen

Kaminoyama

Nagai

Yamagata Shinkansen

Sakamachi

To Niigata
(49km)

Oguni

Yoneska Line

Imaizumi

Nanyō

Akayu

Shiroishi

Kawanishi

Takahata

Yonesaka Line

Tōhoku Shinkansen

Yonezawa

Tōhoku Expressway

FUKUSHIMA-KEN

Nishi-Azuma
Sky Valley
Toll Rd

FUKUSHIMA

Tōhoku Shinkansen

NORTHERN HONSHŪ

hour to reach **Kusanagi Onsen** where passengers are met by shuttle buses heading to Takaya station on the JR Rikuu-saisen line.

TSURUOKA 鶴岡
☎ 0235 • pop 100,000

In the middle of the Shōnai plain, Tsuruoka was formerly an important castle town. Today, the town itself has little to offer except to act as the primary access point for the nearby trio of sacred mountains, known collectively as Dewa Sanzan.

Information & Orientation
Exiting JR Tsuruoka station to the right, the **tourist information office** (*☎/fax 25-7678; open 9.30am-12.30pm & 1.30pm-5pm daily winter, 9.30am-12.30pm & 1.30pm-5.30pm daily rest of year*) are helpful despite speaking little English, and can help book accommodation. If you speak a little Japanese, they can help arrange classes in *e-rōsoku* (candle-painting), tea ceremony, calligraphy, flower arrangement and even *zazen* (seated meditation) at places around town. They also have a lot of information about Dewa Sanzan but, sadly, little in English.

The main shopping area is 20 minutes south of the station but the station area has all you need for a short visit.

There's a small post office with an ATM service 300m south of the station. Next to several point-and-eat restaurants with ¥800 set menus, free Internet access is available from 10am to 8pm daily on the 3rd floor of the Marica Building opposite the station.

Chidō Hakubutsukan 致道博物館
Founded in 1950 by the former Lord Shōnai in order to develop and preserve local culture, this museum (*admission ¥700; open 9am-4.30pm Tues-Sun*) has a family residence and two Meiji-era buildings, a traditional storehouse and *kabuto-zukuri* ('samurai helmet'–style thatched roof farmhouse). The museum is west of Tsuruoka-kōen, a 10-minute bus ride from Tsuruoka station. Frequent buses bound for Yunohama Onsen from stop No 1 at the station pass by the Chidō Hakubutsukan-mae stop (¥200, 10 minutes).

Zenpō-ji 善法寺
Seven kilometres west of Tsuruoka, this Sōtō Zen Buddhist temple, with its five-tier pagoda and large gateway, dates from the 10th century when it was dedicated to the Dragon King, guardian of the seas. Check out the imposing wooden fish hanging from the ceilings and paintings depicting fishing scenes, the latter donated by local fishing companies hoping to gain favour from the gods of the seas.

Near the temple is a more contemporary attraction, the famous *jinmen-gyo* (human-faced fish). When viewed from above, the fish actually do look to have human faces, but picking them out from the dozens of ordinary carp sharing the pond can be tricky.

From the station, take a bus bound for Yunohama Onsen to the Zenpō-ji stop (¥580, 30 minutes). If you're in the mood for surf and sand, the beach at **Yunohama Onsen** is a 10-minute bus ride away, or 4km on foot.

Special Events
Tsuruoka's best-known festival is the **Tenjin Matsuri**, also known as the Bakemono Matsuri (Masked Faces Festival). People used to stroll around in masks and costume for three days, serving sake and keeping an eye out for friends and acquaintances. The object was to make it through all three days without anyone recognising you. The festival is now reduced to one masked parade held only on 25 May.

On 1 and 2 February, night nō performances are held near Tsuruoka in Kurokawa village; reserve tickets well in advance via Tsuruoka tourist information.

Places to Stay
The family-run **Petit Hotel Tsuruoka** (*☎ 25-1011; singles/twins ¥6000/11,400*) is a good-value business hotel located right next to the station complex. It's starting to look a bit faded but you can use the laundry for ¥100 and meals are sometimes available in the coffee shop downstairs – reservations are necessary for meals.

Nara Ryokan (*☎ 22-1202; rooms per person ¥4600*), five minutes along the main street leading out from the station, is a modern place with Japanese-style rooms.

Tsuruoka Hotel (*☎ 22-1135; rooms per person with/without 2 meals ¥8500/5500*) is the best address in town but rather far from the station. Take the Yunohama Onsen-bound bus from stop No 1 at the station to the Hitoichi-dōri stop (¥100), then walk back up the street and the hotel is on the right-hand side.

Getting There & Away

Flights from Shōnai airport link Tsuruoka with Tokyo Haneda, Kansai and Sapporo. Bus departures from Tsuruoka station coincide with flights (¥740, 30 minutes).

From Tsuruoka station, the JR Uetsu main line runs north to Sakata (*tokkyū* ¥480, 30 minutes) for connections to Kisakata, and to Akita (*tokkyū* ¥35830, 90 minutes); it takes a scenic route south to Niigata (*tokkyū* ¥3890, two hours) across a backdrop of crashing waves.

Taking the train to Yamagata usually requires three changes, one at the very least. Despite the extension of the Yamagata *shinkansen* line to Shinjō, it's still more convenient to take the bus.

A series of scenic local trains along the JR Rikuu-sai and Rikuu-tō lines connect Tsuruoka to Naruko Onsen (Miyagi-ken) (¥1890, two hours 20 minutes) via a change at Shinjō. Between trains, there's an excellent free Internet area in Shinjō station's tourist information office.

Buses, run by the **Shōnai Kōtsū Bus Company**, run from the town's bus terminal (by the Dai-ichi Hotel) via the station. There are up to seven highway buses a day from Tsuruoka to Sendai (¥2550, 2½ hours) – these buses that do not pass the station. Night buses to Tokyo (Ikebukuro, Shibuya) depart from in front of the Tokyo Dai-ichi Hotel in Tsuruoka (¥7540, eight hours).

Regular buses between Tsuruoka and Yamagata (¥2150, 1¾ hours) run via the Yudono-san Hotel (¥1330, 50 minutes), which provides access to Yudono-san. Services are often cut back during the winter months due to snowdrifts. Between July and early November, there are also up to four direct buses between Tsuruoka and Yudono-san that stop by the hotel on the way up to the Sennin-zawa trailhead (¥1480, 80 minutes). For details on buses to Haguro-san and Gas-san, see the Dewa Sanzan Getting There & Away section later.

DEWA SANZAN 出羽三山
☎ 0235

Dewa Sanzan is the collective title for three sacred peaks – Haguro-san, Gas-san and Yudono-san – that have been worshipped for centuries by *yamabushi* (pilgrims) and followers of the Shugendō sect (see Religion in the Facts about Japan chapter.)

During the pilgrimage season, you can see white-clad pilgrims (equipped with wooden staff, sandals and straw hat) stomping along mountain trails or sitting under icy waterfalls as part of arduous ascetic exercises intended to train both body and spirit.

Theoretically, if you hiked at a military pace and timed the buses perfectly, you might be able to cover all three peaks in one day. However, this would leave you no time to enjoy the scenery, and chances of missing a key bus connection are good. If you want to tackle all three mountains it's best to devote at least two days; book accommodation and stock up on maps at the tourist office in Tsuruoka before setting off.

Haguro-san 羽黒山

Haguro-san (414m) has easiest access, ensuring a steady flow of tourists. At the base of the mountain is Haguro village, consisting of *shukubō* (pilgrims' lodgings) and the **Ideha Bunka Kinenkan** (admission ¥400; open 8.30am-5pm Wed-Mon), a small history museum featuring films of *yamabushi* rites and festivals.

The orthodox approach to the shrine on the summit requires pilgrims to climb 2446 steps but buses also run to the top. However, the climb is well worth the trouble and can be done in a leisurely 50 minutes – take your time and enjoy the views.

From Haguro centre bus station, walk straight ahead through the torii gate and continue across a bridge into beautiful cryptomeria woods with trees forming a canopy overhead. En route, you pass **Gojū-no-tō**, a weather-beaten five-storey pagoda dating from the 14th century. Then comes a very long slog up the hundreds of stone steps arranged in steep sections. Pause halfway at the **teahouse** (open 8.30am-5pm Apr-Nov) for refreshment and breathtaking views. If you detour to the right just past the teahouse, you will come upon the temple ruins of **Betsu-in**, visited by Bashō during his pilgrimage here.

The scene at the top is a slight anticlimax. There are several shrines, often crowded with visitors except during early mornings or late afternoons, and an uninspiring history museum. From the top you can either walk or catch a bus back down to the bottom. In summer there are two buses in the morning that go on to Gas-san (see Getting There & Away).

Gas-san 月山

Accessible from June to September, Gas-san (1984m), the highest of the three sacred peaks, attracts pilgrims to **Gassan-jinja** *(admission with ritual purification ¥500; open 6am-5pm daily)*, a shrine on the peak itself. The peak is usually accessed from the trail-head at Hachigōme (Eighth Station). The trail passes through an alpine plateau to the Kyūgōme (Ninth Station) in 1¾ hours and then grinds uphill for 70 minutes.

The steep descent down the other side to Yudono-san-jinja takes another 2½ hours (keep choosing the right fork). After about 45 minutes of this descent, you also have the choice of taking the trail to Ubazawa, the main ski resort on Gas-san, which has its own cable car. If you continue to Yudono-san, you'll eventually have to descend rusty ladders chained to the cliffside and carefully pick your way down through a slippery stream bed at the end of the trail.

Yudono-san 湯殿山

Accessible from June to October, the Sennin-zawa trailhead for Yudono-san (1504m) is approached via a 3km toll road from the Yudono-san Hotel. From there it's a 10-minute hike further up the mountain to **Yudonosan-jinja** *(admission ¥500; open 6am-5pm daily Apr-Nov)*. This sacred shrine has the strictest rituals of the three with pilgrims required to perform a bare-foot purification ritual under cascading water.

Dainichibō & Chūren-ji
大日坊・注連寺

Off Rte 112 between Yudono-san and Tsuruoka, these two ordinary country temples house the exotic mummies of former priests who have become 'Buddhas in their own bodies'. Outlawed since the 19th century, the ascetic practice of self-mummification involved coming as close to death as possible through starvation before being buried alive while meditating. The mummy at Dainichibō, *(admission ¥500; open 8am-5pm)*, dressed in bright orange robes and quite ghoulish, is the more accessible of the two. However, beware of the hard sell:

Be prepared to sit cross-legged on tatami through about one hour of sales speech entirely in Japanese held by a rotund priest (obviously not sharing the ascetic practices of his predecessor)

about the history of the temple mixed up with hints at the bargain prices of different items on sale at the temple, for example telephone cards.

Alexander Engelhardt

The Chūren-ji *(admission ¥500; open 8am-5pm daily)* mummy is allegedly a reformed murderer who became a powerful Buddhist priest, and is more atmospheric.

Both temples are five minutes on foot from the Ōami bus stop, which is approximately halfway between Tsuruoka (¥950) and Yudono-san (¥910). Buses are spaced about two hours apart, which is enough time to look around.

Special Events

The Dewa Sanzan-jinja, on the peak of Haguro-san, is the site of several major festivals. During the **Hassaku Matsuri** (24 to 31 August), *yamabushi* perform ancient fire rites to pray for a bountiful harvest. During the Shōrei-sai festival on New Year's Eve, they perform similar rituals in competition with each other after completing 100-day-long austerities.

If just being an observer isn't enough, you can join a *yamabushi* training camp. On selected weekends in July and September, the **Ideha Bunka Kinenkan** (☎ 62-4727) run three-/eight-day courses for ¥20,000/40,000 that include fasting, mountain sprints and 4.30am wake-up calls. **Dewa Sanzan-jinja** (☎ 62-2355) runs even more intensive 'real' *yamabushi* courses, as well as five-day training programs for women during early September (¥40,000). Such Buddhist boot camps are not for the faint-hearted.

Places to Stay & Eat

There are more than 30 *shukubō* (temple lodgings) in the Tōge district of Haguro village charging around ¥7000 to ¥8000 per person, including two meals. Beware: many only welcome repeat guests and exclude foreigners.

One temple lodging open to all is **Seikan** (☎ 62-2357; rooms per person ¥7000), at the top of Hagar-san, with airy rooms and spectacular views; rates include two of the temple's gourmet vegetarian meals. Advance reservations are mandatory. Also friendly is **Sanrōjō** (☎ 54-6131; rooms with 2 meals from ¥7000) beside the Sennin-zawa bus terminal. You may be expected to join in prayers.

Both also serve vegetarian lunches to non-guests from ¥1500 – reservations required.

Yudono-san Hotel (☎ 54-6231; rooms per person from ¥8500) is basic and rates, which include a vegetarian dinner, are not great value but it's a convenient place to start or finish the Yudono-san to Gas-san hike.

Getting There & Away
Buses to Haguro centre bus station depart Tsuruoka roughly hourly (¥680, 35 minutes), continuing to Haguro-sanchō (Haguro summit) less frequently between 8.30am and 4.30pm (¥990, 55 minutes).

From early July to late August, and then on weekends and holidays until late September, there are two buses from Haguro-sanchō at 10am and 11.10am allowing pilgrims to travel towards the peak of Gas-san, as far as Hachigōme (¥1240, 50 minutes). Two buses at 6am and 7am also run from Tsuruoka direct to Gas-san Hachigōme (¥1650, 90 minutes) during these times.

Buses from Tsuroka pass by the Yudono-san Hotel en route to Yamagata (¥1750, 1¼ hours, last bus 4pm) as they do to Tsuruoka via Ōami (¥1330, 50 minutes, last bus 4.30pm).

Between June and early November, there are up to four more buses from the Sennin-zawa trailhead at Yudono-san to Tsuruoka (¥1480, 80 minutes), which also pass by the hotel and Ōami.

YAMAGATA 山形
☎ 023 • pop 250,000
Yamagata is the prefectural capital, a thriving industrial city and a major student town. For the traveller, the city makes for a useful base for day trips to Yamadera, Tendō and Takahata, as well as the skiing and hiking region around Zaō Onsen.

Orientation & Information
From the station, Ekimae-dōri runs east past several hotels before intersecting Nanokamachi-dōri, the main shopping and eating drag, and home to the **central post office**, which has ATM service.

On the 2nd floor of Yamagata station, the **tourist information office** (☎ 631-7865; open 10am-6pm Mon-Fri, 10am-5pm Sat & Sun) is located opposite the *shinkansen*

tracks. The helpful prefectural **tourism information office** (☎ 630-2371; open 9.30am-8pm daily) is on the 1st floor of the Kajo Central Building, which is joined to the station complex by walkways. There's a branch post office on the same floor.

On the 2nd floor of Kajo Central, **NTT PAL** has free Internet access from 10am to 6pm Saturday to Wednesday only.

Hirashimizu Pottery District
平清水陶器地域
Located along the Hazukashii-kawa (Shy River), these recently revived kilns turn out beautiful spotted-glaze pieces, nicknamed *nashi-seiji* (peach skin), all displayed for sale in attached workshops. The renowned **Shichiemon-gama** (☎ 642-7777; open 9am-3pm daily) offers instruction in pottery making. To get there, buses bound for Nishi-Zaō or Geikō-dai run hourly or half-hourly from stop No 5 outside Yamagata station to the Hirashimizu stop (¥200, 15 minutes).

Special Events
In early August, the **Hanagasa Matsuri** features large crowds of dancers wearing *hanagasa* (flower-laden straw hats) and singing folk songs. The lyrics are said to be derived from the impromptu, often salacious tunes once improvised by construction workers to keep time to the rhythm of their labour.

Places to Stay & Eat
Yamagata Youth Hostel (☎ 688-3201; rooms per person with 2 meals ¥4400) is small and often booked out. It's located a five-minute walk from the Kurosawa Onsen bus stop, 25 minutes by bus from Yamagata station bound for Takamatsu-Hayama Onsen.

Yamashiroya Ryokan (☎ 622-3007; rooms per person ¥4400) is a simple but friendly place 150m north of the station's east exit. It's located next to a fruit shop. En route you'll pass **Ekimaramen!**, which does decent ¥800 *rāmen*.

Confusingly, there are several Green Hotels in Yamagata. The best value and closest to the station is **Green Hotel Kasumi-cho** (☎ 622-2636; Western-style rooms with private bath from ¥5600), five minutes east of the station. It's marked with an English sign; reception is on the 2nd floor.

Yamagata International Documentary Film Festival

The innovative Yamagata International Documentary Film Festival (YIDFF) was established in 1989 to mark the 100th anniversary of the municipalisation of Yamagata. The biennial festival was the first of its kind in Asia, and served to put this little-known city, considered to be somewhat *inaka* (outback) to southern Japanese, on the map.

Yamagata takes on an exciting, international flavour during the festival week in October with films from over 70 countries screened. The International Competition and Asia Program constitute the bulk of the festival, and additional categories include retrospectives, symposiums and a Japan panorama. Prizes are awarded to outstanding works.

All screenings contain both English and Japanese subtitles and most festival publications are bilingual; simultaneous interpreting (via headphones) is available at some symposiums.

The next festivals take place in 2003 and 2005.

For more information contact the **YIDFF Organising Committee Office** (☎ 023-624-8368, fax 023-624-9618; ℮ yidff.info@city.yamagata.yamagata.jp) or check **W** www.city.yamagata.yamagata.jp/yidff.

Jennifer Swanton

Pizzeria Buono, turning right at the COCO21 building on the road leading to Night Dew (see Entertainment), does good pizza and pasta sets from ¥2000. Opposite COCO21, the Onuma department store's 7th floor has several point-and-eat places.

Skylark *(open 7am-2am daily)*, inside the station's east exit, does good ¥600 breakfast sets until 10am; there are free refills on drinks.

Entertainment

Home from home for local foreign residents is **Night Dew**, run by the affable Sato-san who is a mine of local information. There's no cover charge and all beers are ¥500; Internet is free after 8pm and the bar closes when the last person falls over. It's located three blocks east of Nanokamachi-dōri; look for a small English sign on your left.

On the same road, **Youyake Koyake** is a buzzy *izakaya* popular with students and open late.

Getting There & Away

There are flights from Yamagata airport to Kansai (¥24,300, 1¼ hours), Nagoya (¥24,000, one hour), Sapporo (¥22,100, 1¼ hours) and Tokyo (¥15,000, one hour). Buses to the airport run from Yamagata station (¥710, 45 minutes, four daily).

The JR Senzan line connects Yamagata with Yamadera and Sendai (*kaisoku* ¥1110, one hour). The JR Ōu main line runs south to Yonezawa (*futsū* ¥820, 45 minutes)

and north to Ōma-gari for connections to Tazawa-ko and Akita (*kaisoku* ¥3570, four hours).

The JR Yamagata and Tōhoku *shinkansen* lines connect Yamagata with Yonezawa (¥1860, 35 minutes), Fukushima (¥2910, 1¼ hours) and Tokyo (¥10,060, three hours).

Travellers to Tsuruoka are advised to take the bus via the Yudono-san Hotel (¥2150, 1¾ hours).

Buses start from the Yama-kō bus station inside the Daiei department store's basement on Ekimae-dōri; most stop at Yamagata station before leaving town. There are frequent buses from Yamagata to Zaō Onsen (¥840, 40 minutes) and five buses daily to Yamadera (¥580, 40 minutes).

Frequent highway buses run to Sendai (¥1000, one hour), two buses run daily to Niigata (¥3500, 3¾ hours). A night bus to Tokyo (Asakusa, Ueno) departs at 9.30pm (¥6420, six hours).

TENDŌ 天童

☎ 023 • pop 63,000

Producing over 90% of Japan's chess pieces annually, Tendō makes an interesting half-day excursion from Yamagata. Begun by poor samurai during the Edo period, the making of chess pieces here has become an exquisite art. The **Tendō Shōgi Museum** *(admission ¥300; open 9am-6pm Thur-Tues)* is part of JR Tendō station and displays chess sets from Japan and abroad.

You can see chess pieces being made at the **Eishundō** museum, a 15-minute walk straight out from the station, just past the Tendō Park Hotel. Across the street, the **Hiroshige Art Museum** (*admission ¥600; open 8.30am-6pm Wed-Mon Apr-Oct, 9am-5pm Wed-Mon Nov-Mar*) displays wood-block prints by famous Edo-period master Hiroshige

The **Tourist Information Center** (☎ 653-1680; *open 9am-5.30pm daily*), on the 2nd floor of JR Tendō station, has details of local attractions, including the eccentric **Tendō Mingeikan** (*admission ¥700; open 8am-6pm daily*) a folkcraft museum housed in a *gasshō-zukuri* farmhouse.

On the last weekend in April, Tendō-kōen hosts the theatrical *Ningen Shōgi* – outdoor chess matches using real people as pieces. The tradition is credited to Toyotomi Hideyoshi who once played a similar match with his son in Kyoto. More details on becoming a human 'piece' are available at W www.ikechang.com/chess/piece-e.htm.

Tendō is six stops north of Yamagata by local train (¥230) or 50 minutes by bus from Yamagata station (¥440).

ZAŌ-SAN 蔵王山
☎ 023 • pop 18,000

The Zaō Quasi-National Park region is highly popular with skiers from December to April and hikers in summer. The main ski resorts are around **Zaō Onsen** and **Zaō Bōdaira**. In winter, free shuttles connect the extensive networks of ropeways and lifts; one-day passes start at ¥4600 (discounted night skiing ¥2000).

In summer you can make your way up to **Okama**, a volcanic crater lake atop Zaō-san, considered by many to be the area's premier sight. The most convenient access is via Katta Chūsha-jo car park, where the **Zaō Sky Cable** takes you to within spitting distance of the Okama overlook (¥700 one way, ¥1200 return, open from 8.30am to 5pm daily).

There are numerous trails around the area, including a one-hour walk over to Jizōsanchō-eki, from where you can hike or catch the **Zaō Ropeway** double chair lifts down through *Juhyō-kōgen* (Ice Monster Plateau) to Zaō Onsen (¥700 one way, ¥1200 return; open from 8.30am to 5pm daily). The 'monsters', best viewed from late February to early March, are really

just frozen conifers covered in snow by Siberian winds.

After a long day of hiking or skiing, you can soak at **Zaō Onsen Dai-rotemburo** (*admission ¥450; open 6am-sunset daily*) where each outdoor hot-spring pool can hold up to 200 people. Bring a towel – they cost ¥300 here.

Near Zaō bus terminal, the **tourist information office** (☎ 694-9328; *open 9am-5.30pm daily*) has maps and can advise on transport and accommodation.

There's plenty of accommodation in the area but advance reservations are essential if visiting during peak seasons or on weekends; all rates include two meals.

At Zaō Onsen, **Pension Boku-no-Uchi** (☎ 694-9542; *rooms per person with 2 meals from ¥6700*), located next to a Lawson convenience store, is a friendly family-run place with possibly *the* hottest *onsen* bath in Japan. Closer to the bus station, **Lodge Chitoseya** (☎ 694-9145; *rooms per person with 2 meals from ¥7000*) is a comfortable place.

At Zaō Bōdaira, decent options are **Pension Alm** (☎ 679-2256; *rooms per person ¥7800*) and **Pension Ishii** (☎ 679-2772; *rooms per person ¥8000*); both rates include two meals.

Buses from stop No 1 outside Yamagata station depart frequently for Zaō Onsen (¥840, 40 minutes). To cope with demand during the winter – there are more than a million visitors to the region – there is a regular bus service direct from Tokyo. Between late April and early November, there are two buses daily at 9.20am and 12.50pm connecting Yamagata station via Zaō Onsen with Katta Chūsha-jo (¥1630, 90 minutes); buses in the reverse direction leave from Katta at 12.30pm and 3.30pm.

YAMADERA 山寺
☎ 023 • pop 1600

Yamadera's main attraction is **Risshaku-ji** (*open 8.30am-4.30pm daily*), a temple which was founded here in 860 with sacred flames brought from Enryaku-ji near Kyoto. It's often besieged with tourists so visit in the early morning or late afternoon if you're hoping for some meditative moments. The temple is actually a cluster of buildings and shrines perched on wooded slopes. From **Hihōkan**, the temple treasury, you pay a ¥300 entry fee to start the steep climb up hundreds of steps through the trees to the *Oku-no-in* (Inner Sanctuary) where trails lead off on either side to small shrines and lookout points.

There is a small **tourist information office** (☎ 695-2816; open 9am-5pm daily) near the bridge before reaching Risshaku-ji aka Yamadera. The staff can provide English-language pamphlets but no English is spoken.

Five minutes from the station, **Bashō Kinenkan** (admission ¥400; open 9am-4.30pm Tues-Sun) is a very quiet museum exhibiting scrolls and calligraphy related to the poet's famous northern journey as well as documentary videos of the places he visited.

Pension Yamadera (☎ 695-2134; rooms per person with 2 meals from ¥8500) is a clean place right by the station.

The JR Senzan line links Yamadera with Yamagata station (*kaisoku*, ¥230, 10 minutes) and Sendai (¥820, 50 minutes). There are also infrequent buses from Yamagata station to Yamadera (¥580, 40 minutes).

TAKAHATA 高畠
☎ 0238 • pop 27,000

Takahata is a pleasant rural place to while away an afternoon along the **Mahoroba Cycling Road** passing ancient burial mounds, an historical park and the eye-catching three-storey pagoda of **Atsuku Hachiman-jinja**. You can negotiate the 6km path in a three-hour round trip and afterwards reward yourself with a dip in the **Mahoroba Onsen** (admission ¥200; open 7am-9.40pm daily) actually *inside* the train station.

The station itself was built to resemble a fairy castle in honour of local children's author Hamada Hirosuke. A small but friendly **tourist information desk** (☎ 57-3844; open 9am-5pm daily) rents bicycles (¥500 for three hours) and provides maps of the cycling route that include background on local sights, including the **Takahata Winery**.

Fukuyoshi, 10 minutes south of the station opposite the winery, is a good spot for a ¥600 *rāmen* lunch.

Takahata is on the JR Ōu main line, south of Yamagata (*futsū* ¥650, 40 minutes) and closer to Yonezawa (¥190, 10 minutes).

YONEZAWA 米沢
☎ 0238 • pop 940,000

During the 17th century, the Uesugi clan built their castle in this town that later developed into a major centre for silk weaving. Today it's a quiet place but worth a brief stopover – if only to sample some famous Yonezawa beef.

You can pick up maps and information at the helpful **tourist information office** (☎ 24-2965; open 8am-6pm daily) inside the station. Rental bicycles (¥525 for two hours) are available outside and are a good alternative to the infrequent buses that ply the main street between the station and the sights.

Internet access (¥480/hr with a soft drink) is available at the 9's Square complex, 500m east of the station's east exit.

At the south entrance of **Matsugasaki-kōen, Yonezawa City Museum** (admission ¥400; open 9am-5pm Tues-Sun) is a small museum with artefacts of the Uesugi clan. **Uesugi-jinja**, built on the castle ruins in 1923, is inside the park grounds with a nearby treasury, **Keishō-den**, which displays armour and works of art belonging to several generations of the Uesugi family. Just south of the shrine is **Uesugi Kinenkan** (admission free; open 9am-5pm Thur-Tues), a Meiji-era residence with more relics from the Uesugi family.

To get to the park, take a bus from stop No 2 from outside the station bound for Shirabu Onsen to the Uesugi-jinja-mae stop (¥190, 10 minutes).

The clan mausoleum **Uesugi-ke Gobyōsho** (admission ¥200; open 9am-5pm daily), 1km west of the park, has several generations of the Uesugi clan entombed in gloomy individual mausoleums.

Special Events
The **Uesugi Matsuri** starts off with folk singing on 29 April and mock ceremonial preparation for battle in Matsugasaki-kōen on the evening of 2 May. The real action takes place on 3 May with a re-enactment of the battle of Kawanakajima featuring over 2000 participants.

Places to Stay & Eat
The best spot in town is **Hotel Otowaya** (☎ 22-0124; singles/doubles from ¥5000/6000), an atmospheric, 100-year-old castle-like building three minutes from the station. It was the only inn in town not to be destroyed by the Japanese military or US occupying authorities at the end of World War II. Former prime ministers, famous kabuki

actors and pop stars have all stayed. Rooms listed above are in the modern addition.

Hotel Eastplaza Yonezawa (☎ 24-0026; *singles/doubles from ¥4800/5600*) is a smart new business hotel 250m east of the station's east (rear) exit.

Marbled Yonezawa beef is renowned but expect to pay at least ¥3000 for a nice bite of steak at the likes of **Gourmet Kozo Mankichi** (*open 11.30am-2pm & 5pm-10pm Tues-Sun*). **Marubun**, however, does an excellent *yakiniku teishoku* (grilled beef set) for ¥1100. It's on the right-hand side of the street leading out from the station and is *not* the one with a cow sign outside, it's actually tucked away in a recess a few doors down.

Getting There & Away

The JR Ou main line runs north from Yonezawa to Yamagata (¥820, 50 minutes) and east to Fukushima (¥740, 45 minutes). The JR Yonesaka and Uetsu main lines link Yonezawa with Niigata (*kaisoku*, ¥2520, four hours, five times daily) via a change at Sakamachi. There's one daily direct train at 6.20pm (three hours).

Niigata-ken 新潟県

NIIGATA 新潟

☎ 025 • pop 520,000

Niigata, the lively prefectural capital, is an important industrial centre, a major transport hub and the gateway to Sado-ga-shima.

Orientation & Information

Higashi Ōdori is the main thoroughfare leading north from the station. Across the Bandai bridge, Furumachi is the downtown shopping area and home to the vibrant Honcho market area. A major new exhibition and business area is currently under construction near the port. The centre is easily covered on foot otherwise a flat rate ¥180 fare operates on city buses.

To the left of Niigata station's Bandai exit (leave luggage in the station office for ¥420 per item) is the **Tourist Information Center** (☎ 241-7914; *open 8.30am-5.15pm daily*). The English-speaking staff provide excellent maps and brochures for both Niigata and Sado-ga-shima; they also book same-day accommodation. The

Niigata International Friendship Centre (☎ 225-2777/2727; *open 10am-6pm Thur-Tues*), three blocks west of Bandai bridge on the 3rd floor of Miyoshi Mansion, has CNN broadcasts, a small library and helpful staff. Their monthly *Niigata English Journal* lists local events and free Japanese culture classes.

The JNTO leaflet *Niigata and Sado Island* also has useful information.

The **central post office**, five minutes northeast of the station, has poste restante and ATM cash service until 11pm weekdays, 7pm weekends. The SMBC bank off Masaya-koji also accepts foreign credit cards.

Free Internet access is available at **Banana** (*open 11am-7.50pm Mon-Fri, 10am-7.50pm Sat, 11am-7pm Sun*), inside the station's Bandai exit. Registration is required. **Internet Cafe Aqua** (*¥300/30min*) has Net access and printing on the 3rd floor of the Stork Building in Furumachi.

Things to See

The **Northern Culture Museum** (*admission ¥700; open 8.30am-5pm daily Mar-Nov, 9am-4.30pm daily Dec-Feb*) is located 10km southeast of Niigata in an attractive garden complex. Amongst traditional earthen warehouses and individual tea arbours, Sanraku-tei is a diminutive teahouse dating from 1890 where everything, even the flooring and furniture, are triangular. Buses leave roughly hourly between 10am and 4.40pm from stop No 7 at the Bandai bus centre (not the railway station) for the Somi stop outside the museum (¥500, 45 minutes).

Next to the **Prefectural Government Memorial Hall** (*admission free; open 9am-4.30pm Tues-Sun*), **Hakusan-jinja** is dedicated to the local god of marriage. The grounds contain a fine lotus pond and the historic teahouse **Enkikan** (*admission free, tea ¥300; open 9am-5pm Tues-Sun*). Take the buses from stop No 8 at the station to Shiyakusho-mae (¥180, 15 minutes).

Just north of the station, the **Tsurui Museum of Art** (*admission ¥500; open 10am-5pm Mon-Sat*) exhibits Japanese arts and local crafts.

The city's newest attraction is **Ryutopia** (*open 9am-10pm daily, closed 2nd & 4th Mon each month*), a major performing arts

NORTHERN HONSHŪ

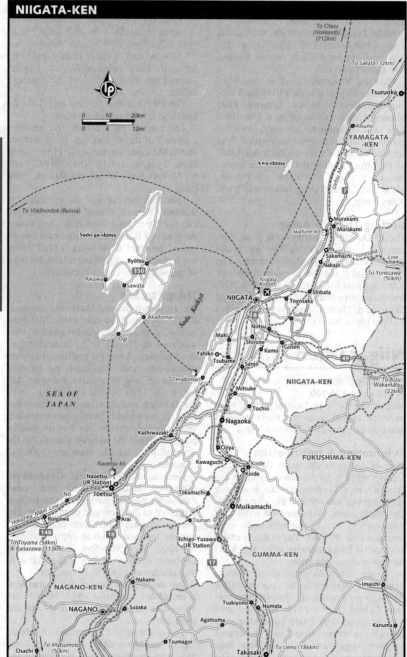

NIIGATA-KEN

To Otaru (Hokkaidō) (712km)

To Sakata (32km)

Tsuruoka

0   10   20km
0   6   12mi

Atsumi

YAMAGATA -KEN

Awa-shima

To Vladivostok (Russia)

Sado-ga-shima

Uetsu Main Line

Ryōtsu

Murakami

Iwafune-ko   Murakami

Aikawa   Sawata

Sakamachi   Yonesaka   Line

Akadomari

Sado Kaikyō

Nakajō   To Yonezawa (50km)

Niigata Airport

Ogi

NIIGATA   Toyosaka   Shibata

Suibara

Maki   Niitsu

SEA OF JAPAN

Yahiko   Shirone   Kamo

Tsubame   Sanjō   Gosen   49

Teradomari

Mitsuke   NIIGATA-KEN   To Aizu-Wakamatsu (22km)

Tochio

Nagaoka

Kashiwazaki

Ojiya   FUKUSHIMA-KEN

Naoetsu-ko   Kawaguchi   Koide

Naoetsu (JR Station)   Kōide

Nō   Jōetsu   Tōkamachi

Hokuriku Main Line   Muikamachi

Itoigawa   Arai   Tsunan

To Toyama (54km) & Kanazawa (113km)   148   18   Echigo-Yuzawa (JR Station)   GUMMA-KEN

17

Nakano

NAGANO-KEN

Imaichi

NAGANO   Suzaka   Tsukiyono   Numata

Agatsuma   Kanuma

Osachi   To Matsumoto (50km)   Tsumagoi

To Ueno (186km)   Takasaki

centre with a 1900-seat concert hall and a 900-seat theatre. For a free view across the cityscape, head for the 6th floor observation deck.

Special Events
During the **Niigata Matsuri** from 7 to 9 August, the streets are filled with afternoon parades of colourful floats and shrines. At night, thousands of folk dancers parade across the Bandai Bridge. A bumper fireworks display on the final day lights up the passage of decorated boats carrying the shrine of the local god of the sea across the Shinano-gawa.

Places to Stay
The area between the station and post office is the prime hunting ground for Niigata's business hotels, which dominate a fiercely competitive accommodation market – bargain hard for deals around ¥5000.

Opposite the post office, **Dormy Inn** (☎ 247-7755; singles/doubles ¥4800/9600) is modern and clean with its own laundry. Don't bother paying ¥6600 for a private bathroom, the public bath and sauna is perfectly good. Further down the road, **Super Hotel** (☎ 247-9000; rooms for 2 people from ¥4800) has the best deal in town with a decent free breakfast included and use of your own Wee Willie Winkie sleeping gown.

Niigata Keihin Hotel (☎ 249-1177; singles/doubles from ¥5800/10,600) has classy rooms while its 1st-floor café has an all-you-can-eat breakfast buffet for ¥780 on offer. **Hotel Sunroute** (☎ 246 6161; singles/doubles from ¥7700/13,200) is a cut above.

The cluster of **Single Inns** near the station are now looking rather faded but, if you're stuck, they still have singles from ¥4380.

If you desperately want Japanese-style lodgings, **Ryokan Ueda** (☎ 225-1111; rooms from ¥6500) is a clean Welcome Inn group member located just across Bandai bridge.

Places to Eat & Drink
The area north of the station has good budget options with **Menkomachi** serving *rāmen* and *gyōza*; up the street, **Enka of Moon** is an upmarket *izakaya* with plenty of seafood on the menu. Next door, **Pizza**

Piatto does ¥500 pizza or ¥550 toasted sandwich set lunches.

The **Patio** mall in the station also has rich pickings. Try **Bakery Saint Etolie** for a snack before catching your train.

Rivage (open 11.30am-2.30pm & 5pm-10pm daily), on the 3rd floor of Ryutopia, does an excellent value set lunch (¥1200) and has great views.

Expats favour the **Immigrant's Cafe** (☎ 242-2722; ⓦ www.immigrantscafe.com), although more for the atmosphere than the food. English-speaking staff serve Asian and Mexican mains around ¥1000, there's a happy hour (from 5.30pm to 7.30pm Sunday to Thursday) with ¥500 drinks and lunch sets start from ¥680 – get there before noon and eat for ¥500.

Irish pub **The Black Pig** (open 6.30pm-midnight daily) is another popular haunt located one block west of the Meidi-ya Grocery Store, which carries imported brands from overseas.

Getting There & Away
Northeast of the city, Niigata airport has international flights to Seoul (¥48,200, 2¼ hours), Shanghai (¥79,800, three hours), Harbin (¥80,400, 2½ hours), Xian (¥112,300, 6¼ hours) and Guam (¥75,100, 3¾ hours), and domestic flights to Osaka (¥22,100, one hour), Nagoya (¥21,500, 55 minutes), Hiroshima (¥33,000, 1¾ hours), Fukuoka (¥35,000, 1½ hours), Okinawa (¥43,000, 2¾ hours) and Sapporo (¥25,000, 1¼ hours). **Kyokushin Air** (☎ 273-0312) light aeroplanes link Niigata with Ryōtsu on Sado-ga-shima (¥7350, 25 minutes). Buses run from stop No 11 outside Niigata station to the airport every half hour from 7am to 8.40pm (¥350, 25 minutes).

The JR Jōetsu *shinkansen* line runs from Niigata to Echigo-Yuzawa (¥4730, 40 minutes) and on to Tokyo (Ueno; ¥10,070, two hours); change at Takisaki for the Nagano *shinkansen*. On the JR Uetsu line, there are *tokkyū* trains north from Niigata to Tsuruoka (¥3890, two hours) and Akita (¥6510, 3½ hours).

Long distance buses use the covered Bandai bus centre across the river. Buses link Niigata with Sendai (¥4500, four hours), Yamagata (¥3500, 3¾ hours), Aizu-Wakamatsu (¥2000, 1¾ hours), Kanazawa (¥4580, five hours) and Nagano (¥3060,

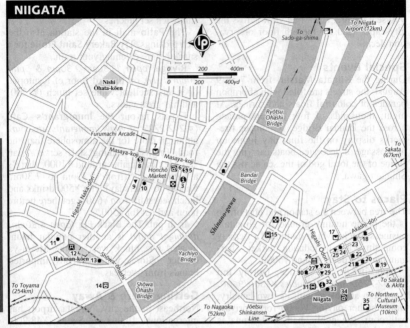

NIIGATA

3½ hours). There are also night buses to Tokyo (Ikebukuro) (¥5250, five hours) and Kyoto/Osaka (¥9450, 9½ hours). Most buses also pass by Niigata station on their way out of town.

Shin-Nihonkai (☎ 273-2171) ferries from Niigata to Otaru (Hokkaidō) are excellent value (¥5420, 18 hours, daily except Monday). Buses leave stop No 3 at Niigata station for Rinko-nichōme. For Niigata-kō port, get off at Suehiro-bashi (¥180, 20 minutes).

From the **Sado Kisen** terminal, there are frequent ferries and hydrofoils to Ryōtsu on Sado-ga-shima (see Sado-ga-shima Getting There & Away later). Buses to the terminal (¥180, 15 minutes) leave from stop No 6 at the station 45 minutes before sailing.

To/From Russia Every Monday and Friday **Dalavia Far East Airways** (☎ 257-9291) flies from Niigata to Khabarovsk (Russia) for connections with the Trans-Siberian Railway. **Vladivostok Airlines** (☎ 279-5105) has flights every Thursday and Sunday to Vladivostok. Discounted round-trip tickets are available from **Kinki**

Nihon Touristo (☎ 241-4891) on Higashi Ōdori. Ferries to Russia no longer connect from Niigata; they now run from Fushiki in Toyama prefecture to Zalvino (five hours from Vladivostok).

You can start the long paper chase for a Russian visa at **Niigata's Russian Consulate-General** (☎ 244-6015; **W** www.visatorus sia.com/russianvisa.nsf/index.html).

SADO-GA-SHIMA 佐渡島
☎ 0259 • pop 80,000

In medieval times, this was an island of exile for intellectuals who had fallen out of favour with the government. Among those banished here were Emperor Juntoku, nō drama master Ze-Ami and Nichiren, the founder of one of Japan's most influential Buddhist sects. When gold was discovered near Aikawa in 1601, there was a sudden influx of gold-diggers – often vagrants shipped from the mainland as prisoners and made to work like slaves.

Today Japan's sixth largest island relies on its booming tourist trade. To escape the coach parties and uncover the unhurried pace of life and natural scenery for which

NIIGATA

PLACES TO STAY

2	Ryokan Ueda 植田旅館
18	Super Hotel スーパーホテル新潟
19	Single Inn Niigata 3 シングルイン新潟3
20	Hotel Sunroute ホテルサンルート新潟
21	Single Inn Niigata 1 シングルイン新潟1
22	Single Inn Niigata 2 シングルイン新潟2
23	Dormy Inn ドーミーイン新潟
30	Niigata Keihin Hotel 新潟京浜ホテル

PLACES TO EAT & DRINK

9	The Black Pig
25	Immigrant's Café イミグランツカフェ
27	Enka of Moon 月のえんか
28	Pizza Piatto ピザピアット
29	Menkomachi 麺小町

OTHER

1	Sado Kisen Ferry Terminal 佐渡汽船 フェリーターミナル
3	Niigata International Friendship Centre 新潟国際友好会館
4	Itō Yōkadō Supermarket イトーヨーカドー
5	Mizoho Bank みずほ銀行
6	Internet Café Aqua インターネットカフェアクア
7	Naka Post Office 中郵便局
8	Sumitomo Mitsui Bank 住友銀行
10	Meidi-ya Grocery Store 明治屋
11	Town Hall 市役所
12	Hakusan-jinja; Enkikan 白山神社；燕喜館
13	Prefectural Government Memorial Hall 新潟県政記念館
14	Ryutopia Building; Rivage Restaurant (3/F) りゅうとぴあ
15	Bandai Bus Centre 万代バスセンター
16	Daiei Department Store ダイエー
17	Central Post Office 中央郵便局
24	24-hour Lawson Convenience Store
26	Tsurui Museum of Art 敦井美術館
31	Bus Terminal バスターミナル
32	Tourist Information Centre; Local Bus Information Office 観光案内センター
33	JR Station Bandai Exit
34	Banana Internet インターネット
35	Russian Consulate 新潟ロシア領事館

NORTHERN HONSHŪ

the island is traditionally famous, you need to get right off the beaten track. This may well require your own transport and a minimum of two days. The best season to visit is between late April and mid-October – during winter, the weather can be foul, much of the accommodation closed and transport is slashed to a bare minimum.

Before heading to Sado, stock up on supplies – there's little at the ferry terminal or on the boat to tempt tastebuds.

Budget travellers beware: a weekend in Sado can potentially burn a serious hole in your wallet.

Information

The island's main **Tourist Information Center** (☎ 23-3300; open 8.30am-5pm daily, 8.30am-7pm daily June-Aug, closed Sat afternoon & Sun Nov-Apr) in Ryōtsu is squeezed in between coffee and souvenir shops. Cross the street from the ferry terminal and head west. Staff speak some English and provide maps, timetables and pamphlets covering the entire island.

There are also centres in Aikawa (☎ 74-3773), Ogi (☎ 86-3233) and Mano (☎ 55-3589) open from 9am to 5.30pm daily April to October (but staff don't speak English) and small post offices with ATM facilities

(open until 7pm weekdays and weekend mornings) in all the island's main towns.

Ryōtsu 両津

Sado's main hub is the best place to pick up information before heading onto more interesting parts of the island. The central area is a 10-minute walk north of the ferry terminal. From bus stop No 2 outside the terminal, buses run to **Sado Nōgaku-no-sato** (☎ 23 5000; open 8.30am-5pm daily), a hi-tech museum of nō drama (¥800 one way, including entry fee).

Sawata 佐和田

The town of Sawata, 15km southwest of Ryōtsu, is on the main road between Ryōtsu and Aikawa. If you get off the bus 1km east of town at Kaminagaki (¥150), you can walk for about 30 minutes into the hills to **Myōshō-ji**, a temple belonging to the Nichiren sect.

Near the bus terminal in Sawata, the **Silver Village Sado** holds three traditional puppet performances daily in the afternoon from April to November (¥350). There's also a good ¥900 lunch buffet (¥1000 weekends and holidays).

Along the Kawaharada-honmachi shopping street, **Cafe Mundo** (☎ 57-3383; open 10am-5pm Tues-Sun) is a friendly bilingual

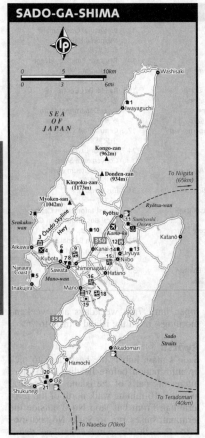

SADO-GA-SHIMA

PLACES TO STAY & EAT

1 Sotokaifu Youth Hostel
外海府ユースホステル

2 Sado Belle Mer Youth Hostel
ユースホステル

5 Minshuku Nanaura-so
民宿七浦荘

6 Sado Hakusan Youth Hostel
佐渡白山ユースホステル

7 Silver Village Sado
シルバービレッジ佐渡

8 Ryokan Urashima
旅館浦島

10 Minshuku Tokaen
民宿桃華園

11 Sado Seaside Hotel
佐渡シーサイドホテル

13 Minshuku Kunimisō
民宿くにみ荘

14 Green Village Youth Hostel
グリーン Village ユースホステル

20 Ryosō Sakaya
民宿さかや

21 Ogi Sakuma-sō Youth Hostel
小木佐久間荘ユースホステル

OTHER

3 Aikawa Kyodo Hakubutsukan
相川Kyodo博物館

4 Sado Kinzan Gold Mine
佐渡金山

9 Myōshō-ji
妙照寺

12 Sado Nogaku-no-sato
佐渡能楽の里

15 Konpon-ji
根本寺

16 Myosen-ji
妙宣寺

17 Sado Rekishi Denshokan; Mano-gū
佐渡歴史伝承館；真野宮

18 Kokubun-ji
国分寺

19 Mano Go-ryo
真野御陵

coffee shop while **Trek Sado** (☎ 57-2430), who organise group hiking trips, run their business from Twin QP toy shop (sparse English spoken).

From stop No 1 outside the ferry terminal, frequent buses run from Ryōtsu to Sawata (¥600, 45 minutes) and onto Aikawa (¥390, 20 minutes) on the Hon-sen Line.

Aikawa 相川

From a tiny hamlet, Aikawa developed almost overnight into a boom town when gold was discovered nearby in 1601. Private mining continued until the end of the Edo period and the town once numbered 100,000 inhabitants. Today the population has dwindled to a few thousand and tourism is the main business.

From Aikawa bus terminal, it's a 40-minute walk up a steep mountain (buses run occasionally in high season) to **Sado Kinzan Gold Mine** (admission ¥600; open 8am-5pm daily Apr-Oct, 8.30am-4.30pm daily Nov-Mar). Visitors descend into the chilly depths, where mechanical puppets dramatise the tough existence of former miners. A further 300m up the mountain is Dōyū-no-Wareto, the original opencast mine where you can still see the remains of the workings.

You can return on foot down the mountain road to Aikawa in about half an hour. On the way you'll pass several temples and **Aikawa Kyōdo Hakubutsukan** (☎ 74-4313;

admission ¥300; open 8.30am-5pm daily Mar-Nov; 8.30am-5pm Mon-Fri, 8.30am-noon Sat Dec-Feb), a folk museum with more exhibits from the old mine.

Aikawa bus terminal, a major transport hub for bus services on the island, has regular buses to Ryōtsu (¥780, one hour), and connections to Ogi (¥810, 90 minutes) and Sawata (¥260, 40 minutes).

Senkaku-wan 尖閣湾

A 20-minute bus ride north of Aikawa (¥280) on the Kaifu Line, this bay features striking rock formations, which can be viewed on 30-minute boat excursions that depart four times daily from April to October in a glass-bottom vessel (¥850).

The scenery along the coast road further north is more interesting; take a local bus from Aikawa to Iwayaguchi (¥1010, 70 minutes). There's a **youth hostel** at Iwayaguchi (see Places to Stay later).

Mano 真野

Mano was the provincial capital and cultural centre of the island from early times until the 14th century. Buses between Ryōtsu and Mano on the No 2 Minami-sen line stop in front of **Konpon-ji** *(admission ¥300; open 8am-5.30pm daily)*, a temple standing on the location where Nichiren was first brought when exiled.

There are several other temples in the vicinity of Mano, many of which lie along a peaceful 7km nature trail that begins just west of Konpon-ji near the Danpū-jo bus stop. It's a short walk from there to **Myōsen-ji** *(admission free; open 8am-5pm daily)* temple with its distinctive five-storey pagoda. The temple was founded by Endo Tamemori, a samurai who became Nichiren's first disciple on Sado-ga-shima.

The trail then passes through rice fields and up old wooden steps set into the hill-side to **Kokubun-ji**, Sado-ga-shima's oldest temple, now sadly neglected but still atmospheric. Another 3km brings you past great lookout points to **Mano Go-ryō**, tomb of Emperor Juntoku. From there, it's a short walk down to **Sado Rekishi Denshōkan** *(admission ¥700; open 8am-5.30pm daily)*, where robots animate dioramas of Sado's history and festivals. Next door is **Mano-gū**, a small shrine dedicated to Emperor Juntoku. It's a 15-minute walk back to the main road.

Mano's **tourist information office** rents bicycles (¥1100 per day) and has sketch maps of the hiking trail (see Information).

Buses connect Mano with Ryōtsu (¥630, 40 minutes) and Sawata (¥260, 15 minutes) on the Minami-sen Line, and Ogi (¥830, 50 minutes) on the Ogi Line.

Akadomari 赤泊

This port provides an alternative ferry connection to Teradomari (Niigata-ken). Local buses link Akadomari with Ogi (¥570, 25 minutes) and Sawata (¥830, 60 minutes).

Ogi 叙り

Ogi is a drowsy port on the island's southern tip kept in business by a ferry connection to Naoetsu. The big tourist attraction here is a ride in a *taraibune* (tub boat) rowed by women in traditional fisherwomen's costumes; a 10-minute spin costs ¥450 and runs 8am to 5pm in summer.

Buses run hourly between Ogi and Sawata via Mano (¥910, 65 minutes), direct buses between Ogi and Ryōtsu (one hour 40 minutes) run only during certain festivals.

Special Events

There seem to be festivals happening almost every week during summer. The island is famed for its *okesa* (folk dances), *onidaiko* (demon drum dances) and *tsuburosashi* (a phallic dance with two goddesses). The big four are:

Aikawa Kinzan Matsuri (25–27 July) Fireworks, *okesa* and float parades
Ryotsu Tanabata Matsuri (6–8 August) *Onidaiko* and Sado's biggest firework display
Sawata Shishi-ga-jo Matsuri (10–11 August) Beach volleyball and fireworks
Ogi Minato Matsuri (28–30 August) Lion dances, folk songs, tub-boat races and fireworks

Places to Stay

The island is well furnished with guesthouses, youth hostels and even camping but you must book accommodation well in advance in the hectic summer months – ask the tourist information offices for help if necessary.

Places to Stay – Budget

Most youth hostels have only around 20 beds, so it's important to book in advance.

Festive Sado

One of Sado's biggest draws for foreign visitors is the Earth Celebration, a three-day music, dance and arts festival usually held during the third week in August. The focal point of the festival is performances by the world-famous Kodo Drummers, who live in a small village north of Ogi, but tour eight months out of the year. The group was formed in the early 1980s to help revive interest in the art of *taiko* (drumming) and all members are required to adhere to strict physical and mental as well as spiritual training regimens.

The main concerts during the Earth Celebration feature original compositions by Kodo group members, often incorporating Buddhist ceremonial flutes and cymbals. Other festival performances range from African dance to Irish folk music. International guest performers and Japanese artists offer workshops throughout the festival, though the latter usually require participants to have basic Japanese-language ability. There's a competitive sign-up lottery for the workshops and you'll have to submit an application by June to even be considered.

Evening performances usually cost around ¥4000, and there are various package deals available; everyone seems to feel it's worth the fairly high ticket prices. Details for each year's festival and workshop availability are provided by the organisers, **Kodo** (☎ 0259 86-3630; **W** *www.kodo.or.jp*). You will need to buy tickets (available from Japan Railways [JR] East reservation centres, Ticket Pia and Lawson convenience stores) and arrange accommodation seriously in advance.

The following rates are low season per person prices based on member prices and dorm beds; add ¥1000 for nonmembers and ¥1200 for two meals.

Green Village Youth Hostel (☎ 22-2719; *beds ¥2900*) is a cheerful spot west of Ryōtsu. From Ryōtsu, take a bus bound for Sawata on the Minami-sen bus line and get off at the Uryūya stop (¥350, 10 minutes). Be careful not to take buses bound for Aikawa via Sawata because they follow a different route. Bike rental is available (¥1000 per day).

Sado Belle Mer Youth Hostel (☎ 75-2011; *beds ¥3200*) is in the tourist area of Senkaku-wan. From Aikawa, take the Kaifu Line to the Minami-Himezu stop (¥310, 20 minutes); from there it's a five-minute walk in the direction of the shore.

Sado Hakusan Youth Hostel (☎ 52-4422; *beds ¥2700*) is inland in a farming area. Take the Hon-sen Line from Ryōtsu bound for Aikawa to Kubota (about 2km west of Sawata). From there, it's a 25-minute walk up the side street opposite the bus stop. Phone ahead for a pick-up.

Sotokaifu Youth Hostel (☎ 78-2911; *beds ¥2300*) is in a tiny fishing hamlet in the middle of nowhere. From late April to early August one bus leaves Ryōtsu daily at 9.10am and runs along the Soto-kaifu Line round the northern tip of the island to deposit you at the Iwayaguchi bus stop – in front of the hostel door (¥1180, 90 minutes). There are eight buses daily to Iwayaguchi from Aikawa on the Kaifu line (¥1010, 70 minutes).

Ogi Sakuma-sō Youth Hostel (☎ 86-2565; *beds ¥2700; open Mar-Nov*) is a 20-minute walk from Ogi, in the island's far south. Guests can use nearby *onsen*.

Places to Stay – Mid-Range

Minshuku The prices for *minshuku* average ¥7000 with two meals but prices rise during summer and festivals and you should bargain hard in low season.

Nanaura-sō (☎ 76-2735) has several rooms with balconies overlooking the ocean and the owners speak some English. From Aikawa, take the Nanaura-kaigan Line to the Nagatemisaki-iriguchi stop (¥330) or, better still, call ahead for a pick-up. It can also be reached from Sawata, which is the southern terminus for the Nanaura-kaigan-sen line. Note that the Hon-sen line, which also links Sawata with Aikawa, follows a different road that won't get you to the *minshuku*.

Kunimisō (☎ 22-2316) is one of Sado's most popular *minshuku* due to its collection of *bunya* puppets, which the owner demonstrates to guests. It is 15 minutes by bus from Ryōtsu to the Uryūya bus stop (same as the Green Village Youth Hostel), then a long walk; phone ahead for a pick-up.

Tokaen (☎ 63-2221) does decent vegetarian food and offers guests a spin in its *shio-gama buro* rock salt sauna. Take the Hon-sen Line to the Shinbo stop (¥400).

Ryosō Sakaya (☎ 86-2535) is conveniently located a few minutes' walk east of the Ogi ferry terminal – ideal for taking the ferry to or from Naoetsu. Rooms are basic but clean.

Ryokan Sado's upscale accommodation comes with a criminally high price tag. Welcome Inn group member **Sado Seaside Hotel** (☎ 27-7211; *rooms per person with/ without meals from ¥7500/5500*), at Sumiyoshi Onsen about 2km from Ryōtsu, is the one exception in the area. It's a bit faded but cheery enough with free Internet, an *onsen* bath and a very obliging free shuttle service to and from the port. Try for a room with an ocean view.

Urashima (☎ 57-3751; *twins with 2 meals peak/off-peak from ¥12,000/8000*) has a smart space-capsule design overlooking the beach and is noted for its food – the owner is a chef known for his Japanese fusion cuisine.

Getting There & Away
Kyokushin Air (☎ 23-5005) flights link Ryōtsu with Niigata (¥7350 one way, ¥11,020 return, 25 minutes, three to four flights daily). Buses between the airport and Ryōtsu bus terminal are timed to flights (¥240, 15 minutes).

Sado Kisen passenger ferries and hydrofoils run between Niigata and Ryōtsu. There are up to six regular ferries per day (¥2060 one way, two hours 20 minutes). As many as 10 jet foils daily zip across in merely an hour, but service is greatly reduced between December and February (¥5960 one way, ¥10,730 return). Before embarking, you need both a ticket from the vending machines and to fill in a white passenger ID form.

From Naoetsu-kō, southwest of Niigata, there are ferry and hydrofoil services to Ogi, in the southwest part of Sado-ga-shima. Between April and late November, there are four or more regular ferry departures daily (2½ hours) and two hydrofoils (one hour). During the rest of the year the hydrofoil service is suspended and regular ferries run only twice daily. Fares are the same as for the Niigata-Ryōtsu service. From JR Naoetsu

station, it's a 10-minute bus ride (¥160) and then a 15-minute walk to the port.

From Akadomari, on the southern edge of Sado-ga-shima, there are ferries to Teradomari, a short distance southwest of Niigata (¥1410, two hours, up to three daily, suspended mid-January to mid-February). However, Teradomari port is only convenient if you have your own transport.

Getting Around
Local buses are fine on the main routes – between Ryōtsu and Aikawa, for example. However, services to other parts of the island are often restricted to two or three a day and, in winter, services are sharply restricted.

If you plan to make extended use of local buses, a vital piece of paper is the *All You Need Sado Island Timetable*, the island's bus timetable in English, available from the ferry terminals and tourist information offices, as is the ¥2000 unlimited ride bus pass, a good value option valid for two consecutive days at weekends only (sightseeing buses excluded). Buses operate a 'hop-on hop-off' system: get on at the back, take a ticket and pay as you alight according to the price board above the driver.

The *teiki kankō* (sightseeing buses) have neat but hectic packaged itineraries with prices from ¥4000 to ¥8000. One useful itinerary is the Panorama Course which follows the spectacular Ōsado Skyline Hwy from Ryōtsu to Aikawa – there is no local transport alternative for this route (¥3040, 2½ hours).

To explore less touristed areas, car hire is desirable. There are numerous car hire firms close to the Ryōtsu terminal; rates start from ¥7000 per day to ¥9000 for 24 hours.

Otherwise, cycling is an enjoyable way to potter around off the beaten track. Bicycle rental is available in Ryōtsu, Aikawa and Ogi from **Naka O Cycle** (☎ 27-2907; *¥500/day*). Failing that, Sado is pretty hitchhiker friendly.

ECHIGO-YUZAWA ONSEN
越後湯沢鴛泉
☎ 025 • pop 9000
Echigo-Yuzawa Onsen was the setting for Nobel Prize-winning writer Kawabata Yasunari's *Snow Country*, a novel about decadent *onsen* geisha. A few items in his

NORTHERN HONSHŪ

memory are on display at the **Yukiguni-kan** (History & Folk Museum; admission ¥300; open 9am-4.30pm daily), 500m north of the station. Today, the town is primarily a skiing and snowboarding retreat for weekending Tokyo residents. The ski season runs December to May; check **w** www.skijapanguide.com for the latest conditions. There are opportunities for hiking in summer around **Yuzawa Kōgen**, an alpine plateau accessed via ropeway (¥1200 return) from the town.

There are, confusingly, two exits from the station. The east exit is the main one with the **tourist information office** (☎ 785-5505; open 9am-5pm daily) located to its left outside the station. To the right of the west exit, an **accommodation office** books rooms at the numerous *minshuku*, hotels and ski lodges in town. You pay them a ¥2000 deposit and they issue you with a receipt to take your guesthouse.

The station's northwest corner has bag and ski lockers; if you can't wait to visit a local *onsen*, **Ponsyukan** (admission ¥800)

is an in-station *onsen* next to Yuzawa plaza within the station concourse.

Overlooking the town and its own skiing grounds, **NASPA New Ōtani Resort** (☎ 780-6111, toll-free 0120-227021; **w** www.naspa.co.jp/english; rooms weekdays/weekends from ¥16,000/19,000) has luxurious Western-style rooms for up to three people – good value if you share. Free shuttles run between the station and the resort and, in winter, to many major ski areas.

Asahikan (☎ 787-3205; rooms per person from ¥7000) is a friendly *minshuku* located at the base of the Yuzawa Park ski area. Closer to the station, **Tatumoto** (☎ 784-2371; rooms per person from ¥7000) is 250m from the east exit, while **Migata** (☎ 784-2518; rooms per person from ¥7000) is five minutes southwest of the west exit. All are Japanese-style and rates include two meals. In peak ski season, prices start from ¥8500.

Echigo-Yuzawa station is on the JR Jōetsu *shinkansen* line between Niigata (¥4740, 45 minutes) and Tokyo (Ueno) (¥5980, 1¼ hours).

Hokkaidō 北海道

Many Japanese consider Hokkaidō, the northernmost and second largest of Japan's islands, to be their nation's Canada or Great American West. Hokkaidō is known for wildlife and mountains, greenery and agriculture, snowy winters, temperate summers and a heritage including indigenous people. The island comprises one-fifth of Japan's land area but contains only 5% of the nation's population (about 5,721,000), so by Japanese standards it feels positively vast, and the spirit of the Dōsanko (as Hokkaidō's residents are known) is both frontier-like and unmistakably Japanese.

While Hokkaidō's southern cities have sites of historical and cultural interest, the island's real treasures lie in its wilderness regions, with superb hiking, camping, skiing, relaxing in hot springs and observing nature. However, during peak travel times it can seem as if the rest of the country has come along with you.

Hokkaidō has four major regions, nicknamed Dō-nan (southern), Dō-ō (central), Dō-hoku (northern) and Dō-tō (eastern).

SUGGESTED ITINERARIES

You should allow a week just to skim the surface of Hokkaidō's offerings. Travel times between destinations can be surprisingly long, and it is essential that you check operating dates for transport services, as they vary seasonally.

If you are short of time, stick to the southern and central regions: Sapporo (the main population centre), Hakodate, Tōya-ko, Niseko and Biei are all within fairly easy reach of connections with Honshū.

Hokkaidō's stellar national parks include Shikotsu-Tōya National Park, southwest of Sapporo; Daisetsuzan National Park, occupying much of the central region; Akan National Park to its east; and Shiretoko National Park at Hokkaidō's eastern reaches.

Public transport provides relatively easy access to Shikotsu-Tōya and Daisetsuzan national parks, but you might consider a car for Shiretoko and Akan national parks – car rental is available in larger cities.

If time is not a concern, you can't get much further away from it all than Wakkanai and the scenic islands of Rebun-tō and Rishiri-

Highlights

- Glimpse the towering ice sculptures at Sapporo's Yuki Matsuri (Snow Festival)
- Encounter the culture of the indigenous Ainu people
- Walk through the aftermath of volcanic eruptions near Tōya-ko
- Catch a ferry to Rishiri-tō and Rebun-tō, islands with spectacular hiking and seascapes
- Explore the dramatic mountain scenery and remote hot springs of Daisetsuzan National Park
- Discover the peninsula, Shiretoko-hantō, one of Japan's most pristine wilderness areas
- Take in Akan National Park's crystal-clear lakes

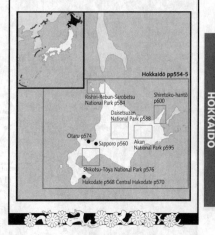

Hokkaidō pp554-5

Rishiri-Rebun-Sarobetsu National Park p584

Shiretoko-hantō p600

Daisetsuzan National Park p588

Otaru p574

Sapporo p560

Akan National Park p595

Shikotsu-Tōya National Park p576

Hakodate p568 Central Hakodate p570

tō, the nation's northernmost region, or the windswept southern cape, Erimo-Misaki.

HISTORY

Until the Edo period, Hokkaidō, or Ezo as the Japanese called it, was largely left to its indigenous inhabitants – notably the Ainu, who referred to it as Ainu Moshiri, Ainu meaning 'human' and Moshiri meaning 'island' or 'world'.

The Muromachi period marked the first appearance of settlers from Honshū. In the

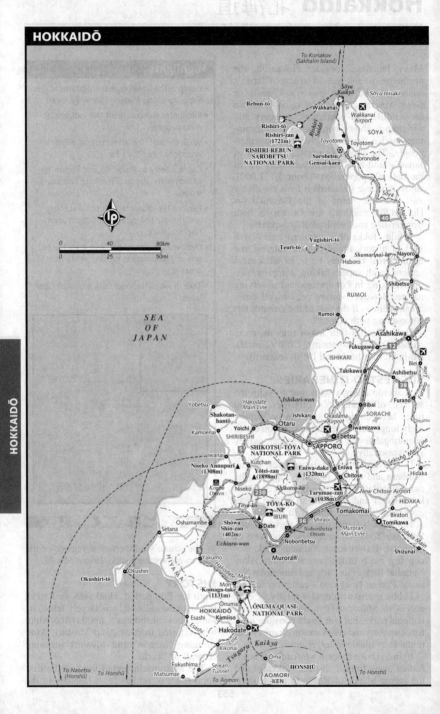

HOKKAIDŌ

To Korsakov
(Sakhalin Island)

Sōya
Kaikyō
Sōya-misaki

Rebun-tō
Wakkanai
Wakkanai
Airport

SŌYA

Rishiri-tō
Rishiri-zan
(1721m)

Rishiri-
Sudo
Toyotomi
Toyotomi

RISHIRI-REBUN-
SAROBETSU
NATIONAL PARK

Sarobetsu
Gensai-kaen
Horonobe

Sōya

40

Sōya
Main
Line

Yagishiri-tō

Teuri-tō

Shumarinai-ko
Nayoro

Haboro

Shibetsu

RUMOI

0   40   80km
0   25   50mi

SEA
OF
JAPAN

Rumoi

Asahikawa

Fukagawa
12

Biei

ISHIKARI

Takikawa

Ashibetsu
38

Furano

Furano
Line

Hakodate
Main Line

Ishikari-wan

Bibai

SORACHI

Yobetsu

Shakotan-
hantō

Iwamizawa

Yoichi
Ishikari
Okadama
Airport

Kamoenai
SHIRIBESHI

Ebetsu
Otaru
SAPPORO

Sekisho Main Line

SHIKOTSU-TŌYA
NATIONAL PARK

-Iwanai
Kutchan
Eniwa-dake
(1320m)
Eniwa

Niseko Annupuri
(1308m)
Yōtei-zan
(1898m)
Chitose

Hidaka

Kanro
Onsen
Niseko
230
Shikotsu-ko

New Chitose Airport

HIDAKA

TŌYA-KO
NP
IBURI
Tarumae-zan
(1038m)

Tomakomai

Oshamambe
Shōwa
Shin-zan
(402m)
Tōya-ko
Shiraoi

Biratori
Tomikawa

Setana
Date
Noboribetsu
Onsen

Muroran
Main Line

Hidaka Main

Uchiura-wan
Noboribetsu

Shizunai

HIYAMA
Yakumo
5

Murorán

Okushiri-tō
Okushiri

Hakodate Main
Line

Mori
Komaga-take
(1131m)
Ōnuma

HOKKAIDŌ
Kamiiso
ŌNUMA QUASI-
NATIONAL PARK

Esashi

Esashi
Line
Hakodate

Fukushima
Kikonai
Ōma

To Naoetsu
(Honshū)
To Honshū
Matsumae
Seikan
Tunnel
To Aomori

Tsugaru
Kaikyō

HONSHŪ

AOMORI
-KEN
To Honshū

HOKKAIDŌ

JAPAN'S 'NORTHERN TERRITORIES'

SEA OF OKHOTSK

PACIFIC OCEAN

Etorofu-tō

Kunashiri-tō

Shikotan-tō

JAPAN

Habomaisho Islands

Nemuro

HOKKAIDŌ

RUSSIA

Nosappu-misaki

0   100km

SEA OF OKHOTSK

Mombetsu

Saroma-ko

Shiretoko-misaki

SHIRETOKO NATIONAL PARK

Rausu-dake (1660m)

Iwaobetsu

Utoro

Rausu

Nemuro Kaikyō

To Etorofu-tō

Kunashiri-tō

ABASHIRI

Engaru

Abashiri

Shari

87

335

RUSSIA

Sekihoku Main Line

Kamikawa

Sōunkyō

Rubeshibe

Kitami

Memanbetsu Airport

Bihoro

Nokke Kaikyō

Habomai Islands

Kuro-dake (1984m)

Asahi-dake (2290m)

39

Kussharo-ko

AKAN NATIONAL PARK

Mashū-ko

Shibetsu

DAISETSUZAN NATIONAL PARK

Furusato-Ginga Line

O-Akan-dake (1371m)

Naka-Shibetsu

Nemuro-wan

Tokachi-dake (2077m)

Nukabira-ko

Akan-ko

Akan Kohan

Teshikaga

NEMURO

Nemuro

Shikaribetsu-ko

Mé-Akan-dake (1499m)

Senmō Main Line

Shibecha

Ashoro

KUSHIRO

Shimizu

Nemuro Main Line

Obihiro

Ikeda

Shiranuka

Kushiro Airport

44

Kushiro

Akkeshi

38

KUSHIRO SHITSUGEN NATIONAL PARK

TOKACHI

Hirō

Line

Samani

PACIFIC OCEAN

Erimo-Misaki

HOKKAIDŌ

Ainu Renaissance

Although Ainu culture was once pronounced dead, the past few decades have seen people of Ainu descent assert their ethnicity both politically and culturally.

In 1899 the Hokkaidō Former Natives Protection Act formalized decades of Meiji-era discrimination against the Ainu, denying them land ownership and giving the governor of Hokkaidō sole discretion over the management of communal Ainu funds. Thus, the Ainu became dependent on the welfare of the Japanese state. Although this law had been amended over the years, many Ainu people objected to it down to its title, which used the word *kyūdo-jin* ('dirt' or 'earth' people) to describe them. It was once the standard among people of Ainu descent to hide their ethnicity out of fear of discrimination in housing, schools and employment; out of an estimated 100,000 Ainu, only 25,000 acknowledged it publicly.

But in the 1980s various Ainu groups called for the law's repeal, and in 1998 the Japanese government replaced the law with one that allocated government funds for Ainu research and the promotion of Ainu language and culture, as well as better education about Ainu traditions in public schools. The Ainu have begun to step more into the open, and travellers to Hokkaidō now have a better chance than ever of enjoying authentic Ainu festivals, cultural performances and exhibitions of traditional arts.

Most large Hokkaidō cities have some sort of Ainu museum, but the best are in the small central Hokkaidō towns of Shiraoi and Biratori.

Shiraoi's **Poroto Kotan** (☎ 0144-82-3914; admission ¥683; open 8am-5pm daily Apr-Oct, 8.30am-4.30pm daily Nov-Mar) is a lakeside village of reconstructed traditional Ainu buildings, anchored by the **Ainu Museum** (Ainu Minzoku Hakubutsukan). Museum exhibits are labelled in both Japanese and English, and in the village you may catch demonstrations of Ainu crafts and cultural performances. The museum maintains an educational website at W www.ainu-museum.or.jp/english/english.html. The only drawback: access to Poroto Kotan is via a gauntlet of tourist shops.

In the village of Nibutani, in the northern part of Biratori, **Nibutani Ainu Culture Museum** (☎ 01457-2-2892; admission ¥400; open 9am-5pm daily mid-Apr–mid-Nov, 9am-5pm Tues-Sun mid-Nov–mid-Apr, closed 16 Dec-15 Jan) has arguably better collections more attractively displayed, although most exhibits are in Japanese only. Visitors could easily spend half a day watching documentary videos about Ainu folkcrafts, traditional dances, epic songs and traditional ceremonies. Other highlights include a loom for weaving traditional tree-bark cloth and some enormous canoes hewn from entire tree trunks.

Across Nibutani's main street, amid some traditional huts, the **Kayano Shigeru Ainu Memorial Museum** (☎ 01457-2-3215; admission ¥400; open 9am-5pm daily Apr-Nov, other times by appointment) houses the private collection of Kayano Shigeru, the first person of Ainu descent to be elected to the Japanese Diet. Upstairs, the museum focuses on indigenous peoples worldwide. Signage is in Japanese only. Kayano was also the author of important books about the Ainu, including *Our Land Was a Forest: an Ainu Memoir*. Another book *Race, Resistance and the Ainu of Japan*, by Richard Siddle, is a contemporary history of the Ainu struggle for self-determination. A combined ticket for both Nibutani museums costs ¥700.

Shiraoi can be reached via several bus or train connections daily from Sapporo or Noboribetsu. Unfortunately, access to Nibutani is a trial without one's own transport – check with the museums or tourist offices for updated transit links.

Elsewhere around the island, you may catch performances of Ainu song and dance. Akan Kohan, in Akan National Park, has a theatre with daily shows, and there are occasional musical performances at Marukipune restaurant near Kawayu Onsen. Obihiro-based Kamuy-to Upopo, a group of traditional dancers, sometimes tours; officially designated as an Important Intangible Living National Treasure, the troupe is led by elder Ainu women who chant the Ainu epics from memory.

Other useful sources of information include the **Foundation for the Research and Promotion of Ainu Culture** (☎ 011-271-4171; W www.frpac.or.jp) in Sapporo, the **Ainu Culture Centre** (☎ 03-3245-9831) in Tokyo and the **Ainu Association of Hokkaidō** (☎ 011-221-0462) in Sapporo.

16th century, the Matsumae clan established a foothold on the southwestern tip of the island, negotiating a trading monopoly with the Ainu, who in turn received a share of the taxes paid on commercial shipping.

At the time of the Meiji Restoration (1868), the island's population was 120,000, but the Meiji era saw a major shift in Japan's approach to its northernmost territory. The Kaitakushi (Colonial Office) was established to encourage vigorous expansion and immigration from Honshū, and the new name Hokkaidō (literally 'North Sea Road') was adopted. By 1900 the population had reached over one million. Meanwhile, various Ainu customs were banned, such as women's tattoos and men's earrings, and the Ainu were forced into de facto second-class citizenship.

The comparison of Hokkaidō to North America has some historical roots: Japan looked eastward to develop Hokkaidō, and that influence is plain even today. Sapporo's grid-like layout was planned by a US architect and mimicked in other Hokkaidō cities; US agricultural experts introduced farm-style architecture that has endured as a characteristic of Hokkaidō's landscape; and many lodge owners will proudly tell you that their log cabins are Canadian in style and materials.

Sapporo's hosting of the 1972 Winter Olympics brought world attention to the region. Restrictions on the Ainu were gradually lifted through the 20th century, culminating in a landmark 1998 law that helped further Ainu culture.

Today, Hokkaidō's sparsely populated landmass and extensive coastline have helped to make it Japan's largest food producer, and the island supports forestry and pulp and paper industries. Tourism is also a major source of income, particularly for remote communities, as Hokkaidō has become a top destination for Japanese tourists to ski or to beat the heat of Honshū's summers.

CLIMATE

While Hokkaidō does not have a rainy season, the beginning of summer can be wet and miserable. From May to October the island attracts hikers and campers, with the biggest crowds from June through August. Transport services are more frequent and extensive in the high season, although accommodation can book out. It's possible to avoid the crowds by timing your trip to take advantage of the last of the autumn weather from October to early November.

After November, winter sets in, and the next five months are characterised by heavy snowfall and subzero temperatures. During this period, the majority of tourists are skiers, though some visitors come specifically to see the Sapporo Yuki Matsuri (Sapporo Snow Festival) in February.

Whatever time of year, don't underestimate the weather – take clothing that will keep you warm and dry.

INFORMATION

English-language information can be scarce in Hokkaidō's more remote regions, so it's a good idea to stop in Sapporo to pick up information, organise transport and make bookings before hitting the trail. Sapporo's excellent tourist information offices have English-language maps and pamphlets for just about every area on the island, as well as comprehensive bilingual booklets (¥400 each) covering camping, trekking/*onsen* (mineral hot-spring baths), skiing and youth hostels.

You can always use the English-language **Japan Travel-Phone** (☎ 0088-22-4800 toll free) if you're having trouble communicating (see Tourist Offices in the Facts for the Visitor chapter). Comprehensive *jikokuhyō* (timetables) for train, bus and air routes are available in Japanese at most bookshops, and most lodgings know the regional timetables.

Money

Thanks to Japan's postal savings system, getting cash from foreign ATM cards is simple, even in remotest Hokkaidō. Some post offices, as well as banks, handle foreign exchange, though mostly in the bigger cities.

Email & Internet Access

The idea of Internet cafés is slowly catching on, though only in the larger cities. If you ask politely, you *may* be able to log on at tourist information offices or lodgings.

ACCOMMODATION

If you plan to visit Hokkaidō during peak seasons (generally June through August and, in Sapporo, during the Snow Festival), it's extremely wise to book accommodation well in advance. Hordes of holiday-makers put such a squeeze on accommodation at all levels that even a big city like Sapporo can be booked out.

Hokkaidō has Japan's largest concentration of youth hostels; many are in superb surroundings, and offer excellent food, advice on outdoor pursuits and a surprisingly laid-back atmosphere. As a rule, reception closes at around 8pm or 9pm and curfew is at 10pm or 11pm. Toho network inns offer a flexible and reasonably priced alternative to youth hostels.

There are also innumerable 'rider houses', which provide spartan shared accommodation from around ¥1000 a night. If you can read some Japanese, pick up a *Touring Mapple Hokkaidō*, available at most bookshops. It indicates all the rider houses and also suggests cheap places to eat along the way.

In big cities and resort areas, you'll find a good range of business hotels, *minshuku*, and some lovely upmarket lodgings. Some of these have separate rates for peak and off-peak periods, while others have Byzantine pricing schemes that seem to change weekly. Where appropriate, this chapter lists both peak and off-peak rates.

FOOD

Hokkaidō is famous throughout Japan for its fresh foods. In summer, stands all over the island hawk locally harvested corn *(tōkibi)*, milk *(gyūnyū)* and other dairy products, potatoes *(jaga-imo)* and melon *(meron)*. Seafood is the speciality in ports and islands, particularly squid *(ika)*, crab *(kani)*, salmon roe *(ikura)* and sea urchin *(uni)*.

Hokkaidō is also loved for its *rāmen*, Chinese-style egg noodles in soup. Choose your broth – miso (fermented soya-bean paste), *shōyu* (soya sauce) or *shio* (salt) – and toppings, including locally popular butter and corn.

To wash it all down, Sapporo introduced Japan to domestically brewed beer with the nation's first brewery (still standing). Furano and Ikeda are known for their wines, though we'll leave the assessment of the quality up to you.

GETTING THERE & AWAY

While Sapporo is the hub of Hokkaidō's air traffic, smaller cities also have flights to Tokyo, Osaka and other Honshū destinations. You can save up to 30% by purchasing tickets during sales or buying them from discount ticket outlets in major cities.

Two of the fastest rail connections to Hakodate and Sapporo from Tokyo are the Hokutosei Express, which is a direct sleeper, and a combination of the *shinkansen* (bullet train) to Morioka followed by a *tokkyū*

Seikan Tunnel Tour

According to feng shui, the Chinese art of geomancy, Japan is shaped like a mighty dragon, with Hokkaidō as its head, Honshū as the body and the southern islands forming the tail. So practitioners of the art were not surprised at the large number of accidents and fatalities during the 17-year construction of the Seikan Tunnel (the world's longest, 53.85km), linking Hokkaidō with Honshū. The tunnel, they say, cuts like a knife across the 'neck' of the dragon at the straits of Tsugaru Kaikyō.

If that doesn't deter you, you can tour the tunnel, beginning at either the Yoshioka-kaitei (Hokkaidō) or Tappi-kaitei (Honshū) stations, both more than 100m below sea level. You'll wind through a maze of service corridors and passageways – staff use bicycles and even cars to make their rounds. Longer tours include some of the tunnel's unique features, such as a 600m-long cable-car link to the shore of Honshū and a narrow passageway between the railway tracks that gives visitors a worm's eye view of trains roaring past.

You must reserve your tunnel tour at least one day in advance from travel agencies or Japan Railways (JR) reservation centres in either Aomori (Honshū) or Hakodate (Hokkaidō). Only a few trains a day in either direction allow actual through-train/tour combinations. If you already have your train fare or a rail pass, the standard Yoshioka-kaitei or Tappi-kaitei station tour (in Japanese only) costs ¥840 extra; tours last from one to 2½ hours, depending on train schedules. For ¥2040, you can take the tour that continues from Tappi-kaitei station via the cable car formerly used by construction workers up to the Seikan Tunnel Museum on dry land. Return-trip tours from Aomori (¥4320) and Hakodate (¥4040) include the museum.

(limited express) via Aomori. Cassiopeia luxury express sleepers follow the same route, but the cheapest twin rooms with TV and attached bath cost a whopping ¥30,570 a person – that is if you can even get a ticket for this popular service.

The cheapest way to visit Hokkaidō is by long-distance ferry from Honshū – if you travel overnight, you save the cost of a night's accommodation. Important ports include Muroran, Otaru and nondescript Tomakomai. Most boats are quite comfortable (some even have saunas or gyms). All ferry prices quoted in this chapter are for the cheapest 2nd-class open sleeping-mat areas. However, these can be jam-packed during peak season, when it may be worth the extra ¥2000 or so for a shared 2nd-class berth. **Cruise System** (☎ 03-5276-4231) in Tokyo offers Toho Ferry Packs entitling you to discounts on 2nd-class ferry tickets in combination with a stay at a Toho network inn.

Ferry to/from Russia

From early May to mid-September ferries run regularly between Wakkanai in Hokkaidō and Korsakov on Russia's Sakhalin Island.

Most Japanese tourists who make this trip go with a tour group. Making the journey alone is possible but requires time and patience. To get a Russian visa you need to have an invitation letter from a hotel or tourist organisation in Sakhalin and must apply at a Russian consulate (there's one in Sapporo) at *least* one week in advance. More details can be found at the website W www.embassy-avenue.jp.

In Sapporo, **Japan Eurasia Association** (☎ 011-707-0933) can assist with arrangements for Japan residents. For information about tours, try **Falcon Japan** (☎ 011-207-3370).

GETTING AROUND

When planning a route around Hokkaidō, it's essential to remember the time and expense required by the sheer size of the place.

A network of internal flights radiating from Sapporo makes it possible for those in a hurry to travel the long distances quickly, though at a price.

Hokkaidō's rail network has only a few major lines with fast and frequent services, while the remainder have mainly slow or in-

frequent trains. JR Hokkaidō offers discounted return tickets on many routes that may reduce the expense somewhat. S-kippu (S-tickets) are valid on unreserved seats for four to six days from the time you start your outbound trip and offers savings of 20% to 40% of the cost of two one-way tickets. The R-kippu offers similar discounts for reserved seats.

Apart from a few clustered blackout days during peak periods, JR offers the seven-day Hokkaidō Free Kippu (¥23,750), entitling you to travel on almost all JR trains and buses on the island. The Hokkaidō Pair Kippu (¥43,220) does the same for two people travelling together. The Hokkaidō Rail Pass – available only to foreigners – starts at ¥14,000 for three days.

Hokkaidō's bus network is far more extensive than its train network. Inter-city buses are usually almost as quick as the trains, tend to run more often and cost less. However, to more remote regions, buses tend to run infrequently or only during the peak season, and fares are often expensive.

Hokkaidō is one of the few places in Japan where renting a car makes sense; roads are uncrowded, vistas are vast, and you can reach remote areas at your own pace. Major cities have car-rental agencies. Rates start at around ¥6100 for 24 hours, including insurance; Internet rates can be lower, or ask about special plans. There are usually also surface roads near expressways if cash is tight.

Bicycle and motorcycle travel are also popular in Hokkaidō; many of the roads around the coast have low gradients and stunning scenery. Residents and even passing tourists seem happy to offer rides to hitchhikers, but some single travellers (especially women) have reported being harassed. If you ask around, it's sometimes possible to arrange a ride with other guests at youth hostels – managers usually seem to know who's going where.

Sapporo 札幌

☎ 011 • pop 1.83 million

Lively, prosperous Sapporo is Hokkaidō's administrative hub and main population centre. Its breezy, cosmopolitan atmosphere, with tree-lined boulevards and long central park, offers a peek at modern Japan without the pressing crowds that prevail in

SAPPORO

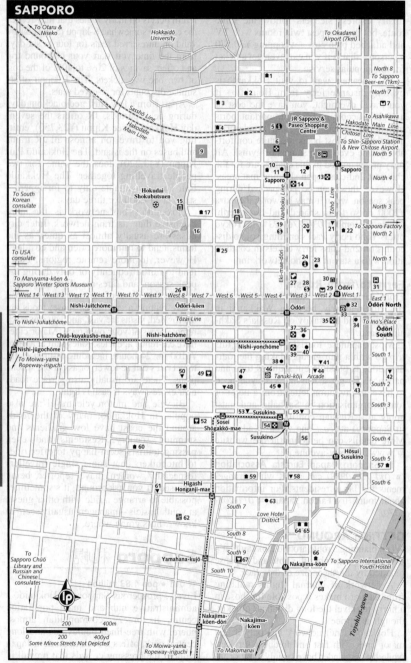

To Otaru &
Niseko

Hokkaidō
University

To Okadama
Airport (7km)

North 8

To Sapporo
Beer-en (1km)

North 7

🏠 1

🏠 2

🏠 3

Sasshō Line

Hakodate
Main Line

JR Sapporo &
Paseo Shopping
Centre

5 🏠 1

6

9

🏠 8

North 5

Hakodate Main Line

Chitose Line

To Asahikawa

To Shin-Sapporo Station
& New Chitose Airport

Sapporo

North 4

North 3

North 2

North 1

To South
Korean consulate

Hokudai
Shokubutsuen

10

11 🏠

🏠 17

15 🏛

18 🏛

16

🏠 25

12

13 🏠

Sapporo

🏠 14

19
🏠

20
▼

21

🏠 22

To Sapporo Factory

24
🏠

23
●

To USA
consulate

To Maruyama-kōen &
Sapporo Winter Sports Museum

West 14 West 13 West 12 West 11 West 10 West 9 West 8 West 7 West 6 West 5 West 4

26 🏠

Nishi-Juitchōme

Ōdōri-kōen

Eki-mae-dōri

Wanboku Line

Tōhō Line

27
●

28
🏠

30 🏛

29 🏠

Ōdōri
West 1

East 1

🏠 31

Ōdōri
North

Ōdōri

🏠 32

33

West 3 West 2

Ōdōri

34

To Ino's Place

Tōzai Line

35 🏠

Ōdōri
South

To Nishi-Juhatchōme

Chūō-kuyakusho-mae

Nishi-hatchōme

37 ●
🏠 36

Nishi-jūgochōme

To Moiwa-yama
Ropeway-iriguchi

Nishi-yonchōme

38 ●

39 ●

40 ●

41
▼

South 1

South 2

50
▼

49 🏠

47
●

46 ●

44
▼

42
▼

51 ●

▼ 48

45 ●

Tanuki-kōji Arcade

43
▼

South 3

53 ▼

Susukino

55 ▼

🏠 52

Sōsei
Shōgakkō-mae

54 🏠

Susukino

56

South 4

🏠 60

Susukino

Hōsui
Susukino

57

South 5

🏠 59

▼ 58

South 6

61
🏠

Higashi
Honganji-mae

🏠 62

63
●

Love Hotel
District

64 65

South 7

South 8

Yamahana-kujō

67

South 9

66

Nakajima-kōen

To Sapporo International
Youth Hostel

To
Sapporo Chūō
Library and
Russian and
Chinese
consulates

South 10

68
▼

Nakajima-
kōen-dōri

Nakajima-
kōen

Toyohira-gawa

0   200   400m
0   200   400yd
Some Minor Streets Not Depicted

To Moiwa-yama
Ropeway-iriguchi

To Makomanai

SAPPORO

PLACES TO STAY
1 Tōyoko Inn Sapporo
   Hokudai-mae
   東横イン札幌北大前
2 Yūgiri Ryokan
   夕霧旅館
3 Izumiya Bekkan
   泉屋別館
4 Sapporo House
   Youth Hostel
   札幌ハウスユースホステル
9 Keiō Plaza Hotel Sapporo
   京王プラザホテル札幌
10 Sapporo Washington Hotel 1
   札幌第1ワシントンホテル
17 Nakamuraya Ryokan
   中村屋旅館
22 Hotel New Ōtani Sapporo
   ホテルニューオータニ札幌
25 Hotel Sapporo Garden Palace
   ホテル札幌ガーデンパレス
26 Hotel Center Park
   ホテルサンターパーク
57 Tōyoko Inn Sapporo
   Susukino Minami
   東横イン札幌すすきの南
59 Safro Spa
   サフロサウナ
60 Sapporo Inn NADA
   札幌インNADA
64 Hotel Sunlight
   ホテルサンライト
65 Sapporo Marks Inn
   札幌マークスイン
66 Art Hotels Sapporo
   アートホテルス札幌

PLACES TO EAT
20 Uoya Itchō
   うおや一丁
21 Tokei-dai Rāmen
   時計台ラーメン
41 Danchū
   暖中
42 Ni-jō Ichiba Market
   二条市場
43 Delhi Restaurant
   デリ
44 Uoya Itchō
   うおや一丁
48 Cafe & Deli Sū'a; Sa Pa
   カフェとデリスーア；
   サパ

50 Warung Hutan
53 Ebi-kani Gassen
   えびかに合戦
55 Ebi-kani Gassen
   えびかに合戦
56 Rāmen Yokochō Alley
   ラーメン横丁
58 Tokei-dai Rāmen
   時計台ラーメン
61 Gojōgen Rāmen
   五丈原ラーメン
68 Kirin Beer-En
   キリンビール園

ENTERTAINMENT
49 Gaijin Bar
   ＧＡＩＪＩＮ バー
51 Garage
52 Precious Hall
   プレシャスホール
63 King Xmhu
   キングシェムー
67 Mugishū-tei
   麦酒亭

OTHER
5 Sapporo International
   Information Corner
6 Daimaru
7 Sapporo Central
   Post Office
   札幌中央郵便局
8 Sapporo Eki-mae Bus Terminal;
   Bic Camera; Esta
   札幌駅前バスターミナル；
   ビックカメラ；エスタ
11 Cathay Pacific
12 Seibu Loft
   西武ロフト
13 Tōkyū Department
   Store
   東急デパート
14 Seibu Department Store
   西武デパート
15 Hokkaidō University
   Ainu Museum
   北方民族資料館
16 Kaderu 2.7 Community
   Centre; Ainu
   Association of
   Hokkaidō
   かでる2.7；
   北海道アイヌ協会

18 Old Hokkaidō Government
   Building, Archives of
   Hokkaidō
   旧道庁
19 Citibank
23 Tokei-dai (Clock Tower)
   時計台
24 Sapporo International
   Plaza information
   札幌国際プラザ
27 Australian Consulate
   オーストラリア領事館
28 Tokyo-Mitsubishi Bank
   東京三菱銀行
29 Ōdōri Post Office
   大通り郵便局
30 Sapporo City Hall
   札幌市役所
31 Chūō Bus Terminal
   中央バスターミナル
32 TV Tower
   テレビ塔
33 NTT Aurora Bell;
   Aurora Town Shopping
   Centre NTT
   オーロラベル；
   オーロラタウン
34 Kinokuniya Books
   紀伊国屋書店
35 Marui Imai Department Store
   丸井今井デパート
36 Maruzen Books
   丸善
37 Mitsukoshi Department Store
   三越デパート
38 Tower Records
   タワーレコード
39 Parco Department Store
   パルコデパート
40 Virgin Megastore CD
   & Video
   バージンメガストアー
45 New Day Books
   ニューデイブックス
46 Hot Station
   漫画喫茶ホットステーション
47 Royal Gift Ticket Shop
   ロイヤルギフト
   チケットショップ
54 Robinson's Department Store
   ロビンソン札幌
62 Higashi Hongan-ji
   東本願寺

HOKKAIDŌ

cities like Tokyo and Osaka. Even if that doesn't appeal, Sapporo is a useful stopover to pick up information before heading out into the hinterlands.

ORIENTATION

Sapporo is one of the only major cities in Japan where it's almost possible to find places in the city centre by their addresses. Blocks are numbered according to the points of the compass (north, east, south, west), with the centre point near the TV Tower. For example, Sapporo's landmark Tokei-dai (Clock Tower) is in the block of North 1, West 2 (in Japanese 'Kita Ichi-jo, Nishi Ni-cho-me'). Street names reflect this numbering pattern, with the exception of Ōdōri along Ōdōri-kōen, which divides north and south. This section uses a shorthand for addresses in central Sapporo (eg, for the Tokei-dai, 'N1W2').

Northwest of Sapporo station is the Hokkaidō University area, with its student hangouts. South of the station, Eki-mae-dōri (West 3-4) makes a beeline through the city's administrative, commercial and entertainment areas, crossing Ōdōri on the way. South of Ōdōri, the Chūō shopping district features many department stores and restaurants, the covered Tanuki-kōji shopping arcade and the underground shopping plazas Aurora Town and Pole Town. Between South 4 and South 9 is Susukino, the largest entertainment district north of Tokyo. From Sapporo station to Ōdōri, it's a leisurely 15-minute walk.

INFORMATION
Tourist Offices
Sapporo has several tourist offices with helpful English-speaking staff. The **Sapporo International Information Corner** (☎ 213-5062; open 9am-5pm daily summer, closed 2nd & 4th Wed each month rest of year) is located inside the western concourse JR reservation centre at Sapporo station. The **Sapporo International Plaza** i counter (☎ 211-3678; N1W3; open 9am-5.30pm daily) is on the 1st floor of the MN building, just opposite the clock tower.

Both are full of information about Sapporo – at the very least pick up the excellent *Sapporo Sightseeing Guide* brochure and a map – and the rest of Hokkaidō. For city information and event listings, check out the free bilingual magazine *Xene* and the pamphlet *What's On in Sapporo*. You may also organise youth hostel membership at the International Plaza location. Although the staff at these counters cannot book accommodation, they can make recommendations according to your budget. There is another **information counter** (☎ 232-7712; open 10am-6pm Mon-Fri) in the Ōdōri subway station, near exit 14. Here you *can* book lodgings, but there is not as great a selection of information.

Those planning a long-term stay in Sapporo should visit the 3rd-floor **help desk** (open 9am-5.30pm Mon-Sat) upstairs from the International Plaza; there are notice boards and a selection of foreign newspapers and magazines here.

Web information is available at **w** www .city.sapporo.jp, or email **e** plazai@poplar .ocn.ne.jp.

Money
In addition to **postal ATMs**, you'll find an **ATM corner** in the Paseo shopping centre adjacent to the eastern concourse of Sapporo station, and **Citibank** (☎ 221-7610; N2W4) has 24-hour ATMs.

Email & Internet Access
NTT offers 15 minutes of free Internet access at its showroom **NTT Aurora Bell** (☎ 212-4261; Ōdōri W1; open 10am-8pm daily), near the TV Tower entrance to the Aurora Town underground shopping centre, though locals gripe that it does not allow access to all ISPs. In the basement of the Paseo shopping centre at Sapporo station is **Bon de Bon** (☎ 213-5726; ¥200/30min; open 10am-8.30pm daily), a pleasant café with Internet terminals. Rates at the *manga kissa* (comic book café) **Hot Station** (☎ 223-5422; S2W4, 5th floor; from ¥500/hr), off Tanuki-kōji, include unlimited soft drinks.

Bookshops & Library
In the Chūō shopping district, **Kinokuniya** (☎ 231-2131; Ōdōri W1) has a small selection of foreign books on its 2nd floor, and **Maruzen** (☎ 241-7250; S1W3) has a larger selection in its basement. Head to **Tower Records** (☎ 241-3851; S2W4) in the Pivot (in Japanese: Pībō) building for a dizzying array of English-language music and entertainment books. Inexpensive used books can be found at **New Day** (☎ 223-6819; S3W4) on the 5th floor of the Arche building on Tanuki-kōji.

The **Sapporo Chūō Library** (☎ 512-7320; S22W13; open 9.15am-7pm Wed-Fri, 9.15am-5.15pm Sat & Sun, noon-7pm Tues) has over 2500 English-language titles and copies of English-language newspapers. Take the tram to the Chūō-Toshokan-mae stop.

Consulates
Sapporo has a few consulates:

Australia (☎ 242-4381) 5th floor, North 1, West 3-2, Chuo-ku, N1W3
China (☎ 563-5563) S13W23
Russia (☎ 561-3171) S14W12
South Korea (☎ 621-0288) N3W21
USA (☎ 641-1115) N1W28

THINGS TO SEE & DO
Historic Buildings

Perhaps no building exemplifies Sapporo's 19th-century heritage better than the **Tokei-dai** (*clock tower, 1878;* ☎ *231-0838; N1W2; admission ¥200; open 9am-5pm Tues-Sun*). Though hardly imposing, this two-storey American-style wood structure is *the* city symbol. Inside is a museum of local history. The building was renovated in 1998, but the clock itself did not need repair; thanks to meticulous maintenance, the Boston-made masterwork has allegedly never missed tolling the hour.

Several blocks away, the distinctive neo-baroque **Old Hokkaidō Government Building** (also called Akarenga, meaning 'red bricks') houses the **Archives of Hokkaidō** (☎ *231-4111; N3W6; admission free; open 9am-5pm daily*), with historical documents, photographs and other items relating to the Kaitakushi, Hokkaidō's colonial office during the early Meiji period. There's little English signage, so nonspeakers of Japanese may find the beautifully restored building more interesting than the exhibits.

TV Tower テレビ塔

If the Tokei-dai is Sapporo's 19th century icon, this Eiffel Tower-shaped affair at the east end of Ōdōri-kōen is its 20th century counterpart. It offers good city views from its 90m-high **viewing platform** (☎ *241-1131; Ōdōri W1; admission ¥700; open 9am-9pm daily late Apr-late Oct, 9am-10pm daily July-Aug, 9.30am-9pm daily rest of year*) and lots of tourist shops down below. You can get a view that's almost as good, free of charge, from the *shiyakusho* (city hall) **observation deck** (*N1W2; open 10am-4pm Mon-Fri, closed winter & during inclement weather*) just northwest of the TV tower; it's on the 19th floor.

Hokudai Shokubutsuen 植物園

This botanical garden and museum complex (☎ *251-8010; N3W8; admission ¥400; open 9am-4pm Tues-Sun late April-Sept, 9am-3pm Tues-Sun Oct-early Nov*), run by Hokkaidō University, has some 4000 varieties of Hokkaidō flora on 14 hectares, and it's a relaxing spot for an afternoon nap. The garden's **museum**, of local fauna, claims to be Japan's oldest (1882). Between early November and April, only the **greenhouse**

(*admission ¥110; open 10am-3pm Mon-Sat*) is open to visitors.

Near the main gate is a small **Ainu Museum**, with Ainu tools, clothing, household utensils and ceremonial objects. For more Ainu information, head diagonally across the street to the Kaderu 2.7 community centre, where the **Ainu Association of Hokkaidō** (☎ *221-0462; 7th floor, N2W7; open 9am-5pm Mon-Sat*) has its offices and a modest display room. Both collections have some English signage.

Sapporo Beer-En サッポロビール園

Sapporo is both a city *and* a beloved brand name. The Sapporo Beer Garden and Museum (☎ *731-4368; N7E9; admission free; daily tours depart 8.40am-4.40pm June-Aug, 9am-3.40pm Sept-May*) is Japan's first brewery (1876, still in operation) and the nation's only beer museum. Factory/museum tours take 40 minutes; before setting off, ask for the (heavily accented) English-language audiotape. Although the tour is – let's be frank – a giant advertisement, that's offset by the option to spend 20 minutes tanking up on free beer and snacks when it finishes.

The sprawling 'Biergarten', occupying the rest of the property, includes dining halls in the original brewery building (it feels positively Teutonic inside) plus outdoor seating in summer. See Places to Eat later in this section.

You can take bus 88 from the city centre, or walk about 10 minutes from the Higashi-Kuyakusho-mae subway station on the Tōhō line (from exit 3, turn left, walk straight, then turn left again when the road signs indicate Naebo; the Beer-En is about 200m ahead on the right). Note that Sapporo is also home to 'Sapporo Factory', an elaborate shopping mall in another (former) brewery.

Sapporo Winter Sports Museum
札幌ウィンタースポーツミュージアム

At the foot of the awe-inspiring ski-jump (134m) used in Sapporo's Olympics, this new museum (☎ *631-2000; admission ¥600; open 9am-6pm May-Oct, 9.30am-5pm Nov-Apr, closed last Tues each month*) dares you not to break a sweat as you try computer-simulated challenges in hockey, cross-country skiing, speed-skating and ski-jumping. A well-done English-language audio guide takes you

HOKKAIDŌ

through a history of winter sporting and the Sapporo Olympics. You can also ride the chairlift (☎ 641-1972) to the top of the *real* jump, or hike it. The chairlift costs ¥250/500 one way/return and operating hours vary. From the bus terminal at Maruyama-kōen subway station (Tōzai line), take bus Nishi 14 and get off at Ōkurayama-Kyōgijo. From there it's a 10-minute walk.

Moiwa-yama Ropeway
藻岩山ロープウェイ

When the weather is clear, the panoramic views from the summit of Moiwa-yama (531m) are breathtaking, especially at night. A ropeway (cable car; ☎ 561-8177) and chairlift whisk you to the top in eight minutes. Passage costs ¥1300 for a return trip. Operating hours vary throughout the year: 9.30am to 9pm mid-April to October; 9.30am to 10pm July and Aug; 9.30am to 5pm 1 to 9 November; 10am to 7pm from 20 December through March; and closed 10 November to 19 December and early April. The ropeway is an eight-minute walk uphill from the Moiwa-yama Ropeway-iriguchi tram stop. Discount coupons (less ¥200) are available on the tram. Be sure the driver stamps yours.

Hokkaidō Kaitaku-no-Mura
北海道開拓の村

Covering some 54 hectares in the suburbs, Hokkaidō Kaitaku-no-Mura (*Historical Village of Hokkaidō;* ☎ 898-2692; *admission ¥610, discounts Dec-Mar; open 9.30am-4pm Tues-Sun*) exhibits over 50 buildings from the 'pioneer' period of Japanese expansion into Hokkaidō. Most are quaint wooden originals rebuilt here in four main areas: town, farm, fishing and mountain village. Horse-drawn trolleys and, in winter, sleighs ply the main street. Direct buses to Kaitaku-no-Mura depart from Sapporo station between 9am and 10.30am (¥230, one hour). Buses in the opposite direction leave the village between 1.15pm and 5.50pm. You could also take the Tōzai subway line to Shin-Sapporo station, changing there to a bus bound for Kaitaku-no-Mura (¥200, 15 minutes).

SPECIAL EVENTS

The **Sapporo Yuki Matsuri** (Sapporo Snow Festival), held in early February and centred on Ōdōri-kōen, is Hokkaidō's major annual event. Thousands of visitors arrive to see dozens of large, and in some cases amazingly elaborate, ice and snow sculptures. Book accommodation well in advance, or take a course in igloo construction.

Though the **Yosakoi Sōran Festival** started only in 1992, it has emerged as one of Sapporo's leading festivals. In early June, the city centre is filled with hundreds of colourfully costumed synchronised dance groups, including the barely walking (children), the barely walking (grandmas) and some high-styling folks in between, all performing to traditional and modern music.

The **Hokkaidō-jingū Matsuri** (Hokkaidō Shrine Festival) takes place in Maruyama-kōen from 14 to 16 June. It features portable shrines and costume processions and performances of nō (classical Japanese dance-drama) and *kagura* (sacred music and dances).

The **Sapporo Summer Festival** (approximately 21 July to 20 August) kicks off with 2½ weeks of beer gardens in Ōdōri-kōen. It features the **Pacific Music Festival**, which was started by legendary conductor Leonard Bernstein.

PLACES TO STAY

A stay around Sapporo station or Ōdōri offers convenient access to transport and sights; however, if you're targeting Sapporo's nightlife you'll be better off staying down in the Susukino district. Book well ahead during peak times.

PLACES TO STAY – BUDGET

Sapporo House Youth Hostel (☎ 726-4235, fax 726-4236; e yh-sappo@crocus.ocn.ne.jp; N6W6; beds ¥2670) is easily reached – just 10 minutes' walk from Sapporo station. Although it has both Japanese- and Western-style rooms, it loses points for being somewhat dingy and adjoining the noisy train tracks.

Sapporo International Youth Hostel (☎ 825-3120; w www.youthhostel.or.jp/kokusai; dorm beds ¥3200, private rooms per person 3800) is spotless and new, and gives some hotels a run for their money. It's one subway stop south of Susukino – exit No 2 from Gakuen-Mae station on the Tōhō line.

Ino's Place (☎ 832-1828, fax 814-9277; w www.inos-place.com; dorm beds from

¥3400) is a new backpackers' hostel, with private rooms and friendly, English-speaking staff. We've received enthusiastic feedback about this place. Take the Tōzai subway line to Shiroishi station (four stops from Ōdōri); it's about a seven-minute walk.

Sapporo Inn NADA (☎ 551-5882, fax 551-0303; e nada@sapporo.email.ne.jp; S5W9; beds peak/off-peak from ¥3700/3500, plus ¥500 per person for private room) is a cosy, five-room, Toho-network establishment. It's perennially popular, on a quiet block near Susukino's bustling entertainment area. From Susukino subway station, walk west along the tram tracks and continue west to S4W9, head south and turn right after four short blocks.

Yugiri Ryokan (☎/fax 716-5482; e mail@ yugiri.co.jp; N7W5; rooms per person ¥3900) has a home-like character. It's near Hokkaidō University, five minutes' walk northwest of Sapporo station. Management don't speak English, but they do try very hard to please.

Izumiya Bekkan (☎/fax 736-2501; e chouba@mb.infosnow.ne.jp; N7W6; rooms per person ¥4000) is a nearby ryokan that's friendly and a tad more institutional and professional.

Safro Spa (☎ 531-2233, fax 531-9981; beds from ¥3500), in Susukino, offers a unique stay in capsule-hotel berths (separate floors for women and men). It also offers use of its luxurious natural hot-spring baths, sauna and enormous swimming pool.

PLACES TO STAY – MID-RANGE

Toyoko Inn Sapporo Hokudai-mae (☎ 717-1045, fax 717-1046; w www.toyoko -inn.co.jp; N8W4; singles/doubles peak from ¥6300/8800, off-peak ¥4300/6800) is a business hotel by the university. It's quite modern and convenient, if a little bit cramped.

Nakamuraya Ryokan (☎ 241-2111, fax 241-2118, e nakamuraya@nakamuraya.ry okan.co.jp; N3W7; rooms per person peak ¥7000-8000, off-peak ¥6000-7000), just east of the botanical garden, is welcoming despite its office-building facade. Japanese-style rooms have private bath, and there are also large communal baths.

Hotel Center Park (☎ 231-5651, fax 231-5693; e cepark@rose.ocn.ne.jp; Ōdōri Nishi 8-chome; singles/doubles/twins peak ¥8000/ 12,000/15,000, off-peak ¥6500/10,000/

12,000) is quirky and friendly, and well equipped for sports enthusiasts. It has less-expensive rooms without private facilities, and any guest can use the large common baths.

Sapporo Washington Hotel 1 (☎ 251-3211; singles/twins peak from ¥8800/17,200, off-peak ¥7000/12,400) is a reliable business hotel across from Sapporo station. Singles without windows cost ¥4500.

Tōyoko Inn Sapporo Susukino Minami (☎ 551-1045, fax 561-2045; w www.toyoko -inn.co.jp; S6E2; singles/doubles peak ¥6800/ 8800, off-peak ¥4800/6800), located in Su-sukino, has up-to-date business hotel–style furnishings.

The following two simpler business hotels sit along a pleasant canal in central Susukino.

Sapporo Marks Inn (☎ 512-5001, toll-free 0120-27-2400, fax 512-3999; e marks003@ seagreen.ocn.ne.jp; S8W3; singles/doubles peak ¥7200/8500, off-peak ¥5600/7500) allows 15% off with a ¥1000 one-year membership card, valid at all Marks Inns nationwide (you can purchase it there).

Hotel Sunlight (☎ 562-3111, fax 512-6727; S8W3; singles/twins peak from ¥7000/ 12,000, off-peak ¥6000/11,000) has both Western- and Japanese-style rooms.

If all else fails, try the love-hotel area south of King Xmhu disco in Susukino (see Entertainment later in this section). With names like Hotel LAX and Hotel Apple, most places are easily recognised. Neon signs hanging out the front state the rates: an all-night 'stay' (as opposed to a two-hour 'rest') costs from ¥3500 for basic rooms up to ¥10,000 for very wacky theme accommodation.

PLACES TO STAY – TOP END

Hotel Sapporo Garden Palace (☎ 261-5311, fax 251-2938; N1W6; singles/doubles peak from ¥8500/15,000, off-peak ¥6700/12,400) is contemporary, lovely and sleek, north of Ōdōri.

Art Hotels (☎ 511-0101, fax 562-0145; e info-sapporo@arthotels.co.jp; S9W2; singles/twins peak from ¥12,500/19,000, off-peak ¥9000/14,000), in Susukino, is a towering and new place. Rates may seem steep, but they include smartly decorated rooms, breakfast, use of the natural spa and impressive views from upper floors.

Keio Plaza (☎ 271-0111, fax 271-1488; Ⓦ www.keioplaza-sapporo.co.jp; N5W7; singles/twins peak from ¥13,000/25,000, off-peak ¥10,000/19,000) offers the space for which Hokkaidō is famous, with huge lobby and rooms, plus pool and fitness facilities.

Hotel New Ōtani Sapporo (☎ 222-1111, fax 222-5521; N2W1; singles/doubles ¥14,000/25,000) has opulent rooms, is central and has occasional seasonal specials.

PLACES TO EAT
Japanese
Some of Sapporo's leading eateries seem to offer you *all* of Hokkaidō's bounty in one sitting, with all-you-can-eat (and sometimes drink) sets.

Sapporo Beer En (☎ 731-4368; N7E9; courses ¥2000-4000) serves 'Genghis Khan' barbeque – you grill mounds of lamb and vegetables at your table. See also the earlier Things to See & Do section.

Kirin Beer En (☎ 533-3000; S10W1; courses ¥2000-5500), not to be outdone, has a similar setup in its 'Spacecraft' hall. In both places you have 100 minutes to grill up and fill up; your choice of meat and side dishes determines the price.

Both of these beer gardens have à la carte options (most dishes cost ¥400 to ¥1200), though not necessarily in the same rooms.

Ebi-kani Gassen (☎ 210-0411, S4W5 • ☎ 231-3043, S4W2; all-you-can-eat ¥2000-5000) is among Sapporo's many crab places. Its two locations are busy, informal and fun, high above Susukino; it also has a regular menu (dishes from about ¥300).

For *rāmen*, **Rāmen Yokochō** (Rāmen Alley) in Susukino is crammed with 16 shops (and Japanese visitors), while locals say the queue is worth the effort at **Gojōgen** (☎ 561-3656; S7W8; *rāmen* from ¥700). In two locations, **Tokei-dai Rāmen** (☎ 242-0272; N2W2 • ☎ 531-1401; S6W3; *rāmen* from ¥650) also serves jumbo *gyoza* (pork dumplings) that live up to their name (¥500 per plate).

Uoya Itcho (☎ 232-0343; N2W3 • ☎ 232-3773; S3W5; most dishes ¥300-780) is a lively *izakaya* and has picture menus starring Hokkaidō-grown ingredients. Locations are north of the Clock Tower, beneath Hotel Hokke Club, and one block north of Tanuki-kōji.

Ni-jō Ichiba (open 7am-6pm) is for self-caterers. It's a sprawling market around 10 minutes on foot south of Ōdōri subway station. It specialises in fish and seafood, but you can find produce too.

International
Danchū (☎ 200-3581; S2W2; mains ¥800-1200) serves steamed dumplings and larger Chinese plates in a contemporary rustic setting.

Delhi Restaurant (☎ 231-8461; S3W1; mains ¥700-900) offers authentic Indian fare near the east end of Tanuki-kōkoji.

Warung Hutan (☎ 281-0216; S2W8; dishes ¥300-980), outside the arcade's west end, is airy and tropical, with tasty Indonesian and Southeast Asian fare. **Sa Pa** (☎ 231-5333; S3W6; mains ¥500-900) specialises in delicious Vietnamese stall food. Both of these places are open only for dinner.

At lunch you can try the Vietnamese deli **Sư'a** (☎ 231-5333; S3W6) beneath Sa Pa.

And as you'd expect, fast-food and coffee options abound throughout the city centre.

ENTERTAINMENT
Susukino is wall-to-wall bars, karaoke parlours and kinky soaplands, most of which are prohibitively expensive and probably of little interest to *gaijin* (foreigners). That said, local tourist offices maintain extensive lists of places that expats and visitors have enjoyed, and, as with any city, it's best to ask around to find out what's hot

Gaijin Bar (☎ 272-1033; S2W7) is a good starting point. It's in the M's Space building, a rabbit warren of tiny bars and cafés north of Tanuki-kōji. It's friendly and busy with local expats. **Mugishutei** (☎ 512-4774; S9W5) is an institution, run by a American resident of Sapporo – look for the sign reading 'Beer Inn', downstairs in the Ouda building.

King Xmhu (say 'King Moo'; ☎ 531-1388; S7W4; cover free-¥5000) is one dance club that has to be mentioned. It's worth a look even if you don't venture into the fabulous interior: King Xmhu himself, massively carved in stone, presides wearily bemused over Susukino's neon playground.

Garage (☎ 252-0878; S3W8) offers a more underground Japanese scene. It's a funky café/record store/clothing store on a block of such places; club music plays constantly. It's open during the day.

Precious Hall (☎ 513-2111; S4W7; cover charge varies), in the basement of the Dai 9 Green building, is where the crowd migrates after 10pm.

GETTING THERE & AWAY

Discount tickets for flights, trains and long-distance buses are available at **Royal Gift ticket shop** (☎ 219-6066; S2W5; open 10am-7.30pm Mon-Fri, 10am-5pm Sat) in Tanuki-kōji.

Air

Flights connect Sapporo with major cities throughout Japan. Standard fares from Tokyo are around ¥25,000, but off-peak fares can be as low as ¥15,000. **Air Do** (☎ 200-7333; N5W6) is known for low fares. Special fares to Ōsaka start as low as ¥11,000. Always ask about special and advance-purchase fares.

Several international airlines have offices in Sapporo: **All Nippon Airways** (☎ 0120-029-333 toll-free; N4W4); **Japan Airlines** (☎ 0120-255-931 toll-free; N2W4); **Continental Micronesia** (☎ 221-4091; N1W3); **Korean Air** (☎ 210-3311; N4W5); and **KLM-Royal Dutch Airlines** (☎ 232-0775; N2W4).

Sapporo's main airport is New Chitose Airport (Shin-Chitose Kūkō), about 40km south of the city. There's a smaller airport at Okadama, about 10km north of the city.

Train

Two of the fastest rail connections from Tokyo are the Hokutosei Express, a direct sleeper to Sapporo (¥23,520, or ¥9450 with a JR Pass, 16 hours, three a day), and a combination of the *shinkansen* to Morioka followed by a *tokkyū* via Aomori (¥21,670, 10 hours). There is also sleeper service to Osaka (¥27,130, or ¥10,960 with a JR Pass, 22½ hours).

Between Sapporo and Hakodate, *tokkyū* trains take 3½ hours (¥8080). S-kippu (¥14,160) are also available on this route.

Trains run west to Otaru (*kaisoku* [rapid train] ¥620, 30 minutes). There's frequent service northeast to Asahikawa (*tokkyū* ¥3690, 1½ hours; *kaisoku* ¥2420, 2½ hours; S-kippu cost ¥4940). To Wakkanai, there's a sleeper service (¥15,960) that leaves Sapporo at 11pm and arrives via Asahikawa in Wakkanai at 6am, and few daytime *tokkyū* trains (¥9660, six hours). S-kippu cost ¥14,000 to Wakkanai.

Bus

Sapporo is linked with the rest of Hokkaidō by a long-distance bus network. The main bus terminal (Sapporo Eki-mae) is southeast of Sapporo station, beneath the Bic Camera/Esta shopping centre. Just across the river, some buses also leave from the Chūō bus station (southeast of Sapporo station), and Ōdori bus centre southeast of the TV Tower.

Buses depart from Sapporo Eki-mae bus terminal several times a day for destinations, including Wakkanai (¥5750, six hours), Asahikawa (¥2000, two hours), Muroran (¥2000, 2¼ hours), Noboribetsu Onsen (¥1900, 2½ hours), Tōya-ko Onsen (¥2700, 2¾ hours) and Furano (¥2100, 2½ hours).

From the Chūō bus station there are a few departures a day to Obihiro (¥3670, four hours) and Abashiri (¥6210, six hours). Buses to Hakodate depart from both the Chūō bus station and Ōdori bus centre (¥4680, five hours). Discounted return tickets are available for most routes.

GETTING AROUND
To/From the Airports

New Chitose Airport is accessible from Sapporo by *kaisoku* train (¥1040, 36 minutes) or bus (¥820, 70 minutes). The airport has its own train station, car-rental counters, and convenient bus services to various Hokkaidō destinations, including Shikotsu-ko, Tōya-ko Onsen, Noboribetsu Onsen and Niseko.

For Okadama airport, buses leave every 20 minutes or so from in front of the ANA ticket offices, opposite Sapporo station (¥310, 30 minutes).

Subway

Sapporo's three subway lines are the most efficient way to get around. Fares start at ¥200, and one-day passes cost ¥800; there are also ¥1000 day passes that include Sapporo's buses and trams as well.

Bus & Tram

Sapporo station is the main terminus for local buses. From late April to early November, tourist buses loop through major sights and attractions from 9am to 5.30pm; a one-day pass costs ¥750, single trips ¥200 to ¥230.

There is a single tram line that heads west from Ōdori, turns south and then loops back to Susukino. It's convenient for Moiwa-yama, and the fare is a flat ¥170.

HOKKAIDŌ

Dō-nan (Southern Hokkaidō) 道南

HAKODATE 函館

☎ 0138 • pop 291,700

Laid-back Hakodate is a convenient gàteway to Hokkaidō and a key seafood trading centre. It was one of the first ports opened under the Kanagawa Treaty of 1854, following which a small foreign community took root; that legacy can still be seen in the city's Motomachi district.

Hakodate is fairly spread out. The station area is more functional than beautiful, but it is a good, central place for hotels. The western area, a quick tram or bus ride away, houses Motomachi and the bulk of the historical sights on the way up the mountain, Hakodate-yama. There are some nice shops and restaurants in the harbour area between the station and Motomachi. Several kilometres east of the station are the remains of the fort, Goryō-kaku.

Hakodate Tourist Information Center (☎ 23-5440; open 9am-7pm daily Apr-Oct, 9am-5pm daily Nov-Mar) is to the right as you exit the station. It has English-language maps and information, including the useful *Hakodate Guide Map* and *Romantic Hakodate*. There is also an information desk in the park Motomachi-kōen. Web information can be found at **w** www.city.hakodate .hokkaido.jp

Motomachi District 元町

This district, on Hakodate-yama's lower reaches, has several 19th-century Western-style buildings and is a pleasant place to stroll.

Motomachi's most recognised building is the **Russian Orthodox Church** (aka Greek Orthodox Church; ☎ 23-7387; admission ¥200; open 10am-5pm Mon-Fri, 10am-4pm Sat, 1pm-4pm Sun, closed 26 Dec-Feb), an attractive reconstruction dating from 1916; you have to take your shoes off to enter.

Other sights worth checking out are the **Hakodate City Museum of Northern Peoples** (☎ 22-4128), with displays of traditional tools and ceremonial objects used by the Ainu and other indigenous peoples (Japanese signage only), and the **Old Public**

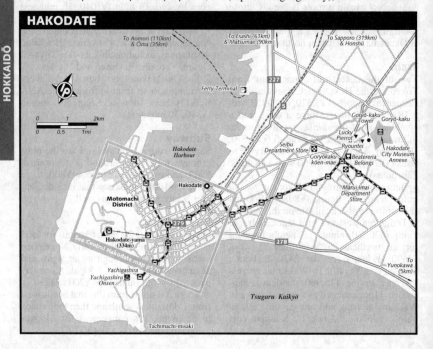

HAKODATE

Hall of Hakodate Ward (☎ 22-1001) which also offers nice views from atop Motomachi Park. Homesick Brits might stop for tea at the **Old British Consulate** (☎ 27-8159; *tea set ¥1000*). Admission for these sights costs ¥300 (discounted combination tickets available). They're open 9am to 7pm from April to October and 9am to 5pm from November to March.

West of Motomachi are several impressive **Buddhist temples**. Further on, the **Foreigners' Cemetery** provides unique insights into local history; some graves combine Japanese and imported elements.

To reach Motomachi, take tram No 5 from Hakodate station to the Suehiro-chō stop, then walk uphill for about 10 minutes.

Hakodate-yama 函館山

On a clear night, picture-postcard views of Hakodate can be enjoyed from the summit of this mountain (334m). A ropeway (cable car; ☎ 23-3105) whisks you to the top in a few minutes. One way/return costs ¥640/1160, and operating hours are from 10am to 10pm (until 9pm from November to late April).

From Hakodate station, take tram No 2 or 5 to the Jūjigai stop (¥200). The ropeway station is then a seven-minute walk uphill. From late April to mid-November you can also take a bus directly from the station to the summit (¥360, 30 minutes).

If you feel fit, a trail winds up the mountain, though it's closed from late October to late April.

Goryō-kaku 五稜郭

Japan's first Western-style fort was built here in 1864 in the shape of a five-pointed star (*goryō-kaku* translates as 'five-sided fort'), designed to trap attackers in deadly crossfire. Five years later, forces loyal to the Tokugawa shōgunate, who had declared their own independent republic recognised by France and Britain only a year earlier, held out here for just seven days before surrendering to the troops of the Meiji Restoration. Today you can view Goryō-kaku's imposing outer walls (which you can ascend), landscaped grounds and the **Hakodate City Museum Annexe** (☎ 51-2548; *admission ¥100; open 9am-4.30pm daily Apr-Oct, 9am-4pm daily Nov-Mar*), which displays weaponry and the inevitable blood-stained uniforms.

Close to the park's entrance is the boxy, 60m **Goryō-kaku Tower** (☎ 51-4785; *admission ¥630; open 8am-7pm daily late Apr-late Oct, 9am-6pm daily late Oct-late Apr*), which provides a bird's-eye view of the ruins and city. For a bottom-up perspective, you can rent a rowboat for the 2km circuit around the moat.

To reach the fort, take tram No 2 or 5 to the Goryōkaku-kōen-mae stop (¥220, 15 minutes). From there, it's a 10-minute walk.

Other Attractions

Early birds might enjoy the **Asa-Ichi** (*morning market; open 5am-noon daily*) near Hakodate station, specialising in seafood and produce. Many restaurants here serve *donburi* (rice bowls) topped with squid, crab or salmon roe. Most of the commerce is over by 8am, after which it gets busy with tourists.

If you fancy catching your own squid, the cruiser **Comfortable Octopus** (☎ 26-8410; *admission ¥6000*) offers two-hour expeditions (cooking fees extra).

The enormous mineral hot spring spa at **Yachigashira Onsen** (☎ 22-8371; *admission ¥370; open 6am-9.30pm, closed 2nd & 4th Fri each month*) is not a major attraction, but it offers a good opportunity to take a look at Japanese *onsen* culture. To get there, take tram No 2 from Hakodate station to Yachigashira, the final stop (¥220). East of the town centre, the Yunokawa district has many high-end hot-springs resorts; some allow day-use.

Special Events

On the third weekend in May, the festival **Hakodate Goryōkaku Matsuri** features a parade of townsfolk dressed in the uniforms of the soldiers who took part in the Meiji Restoration battle of 1868.

During the **Hakodate Minato Matsuri** (Hakodate Port Festival), held in early August, groups of seafood-fortified locals (reputedly 10,000 of them!) move like waves doing the energetic 'squid dance'.

Places to Stay

In summer, Hakodate can be swamped with tourists en route to other parts of Hokkaidō, and accommodation can be scarce. If you have trouble booking, call into the tourist information centre. Staff will know which lodgings, if any, have vacancies.

HOKKAIDŌ

Places to Stay – Budget

The **Hakodate Youth Guesthouse** (☎ 26-7892, fax 26-0989; e hakodate-ygh@biglobe.ne.jp; dorm beds Oct-June ¥3800, July-Sept ¥4500) is a quick walk from Hōrai-chō tram stop. Beds are in two- or three-person dorms. It keeps an irregular winter schedule, so phone ahead.

Niceday Inn (☎ 22-5919; dorm beds ¥3000), on a sidestreet near the morning market, has received enthusiastic reviews from readers. Its bunk-bed rooms are rather cramped, but the friendly management speaks English.

Minshuku Kumachi (☎ 22-3437, 27-1580, fax 50-4643; rooms per person ¥3800), down the block, is in a kindly older house with basic Japanese-style rooms.

Places to Stay – Mid-Range

The spanking-new business hotel **Tōyoko Inn Daimon** (☎ 24-1045, fax 24-1046; w www.toyoko-inn.com; singles/twins peak ¥6800/8800, off-peak ¥4800/6800) is a few blocks southeast of the station and offers complementary Internet access in the lobby.

Auberge Kokian (☎ 26-5753, fax 22-2710; e kokian@hakodate.or.jp; rooms per person ¥6000-8000), dating from 1897, has typical Hakodate architecture: Japanese facade downstairs, Western upstairs. Rooms are atmospheric, small-ish and Western style. Add ¥5000 per person for two meals.

Places to Stay – Top End

When members of the Imperial household visit Hakodate, they stay at the harbourside **Hakodate Kokusai Hotel** (☎ 23-5151, fax 23-0239; e kokusaihotel@hakodate.ne.jp; singles/twins from ¥10,000/20,000). Rooms in the annexe are newer, though pricier.

Hakodate Harborview Hotel (☎ 22-0111, fax 23-0154; singles/doubles peak ¥11,000/18,000, off-peak ¥9000/13,000) is an up-to-date high-rise adjacent to the station.

Places to Eat

Hakodate's breakfast of champions is seafood donburi at the **Asa-Ichi** (morning market) – particularly topped with ikura (salmon roe).

You can also breakfast or lunch across the street at **Kamome Rāmen** (☎ 22-1727; rāmen ¥550-1100), topping your noodles with roast pork, crab, shrimp, squid or sea urchin.

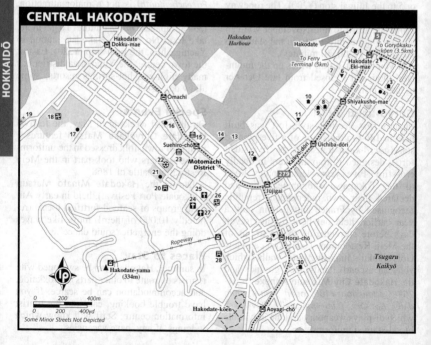

CENTRAL HAKODATE

The Don (☎ 22-7736; *dishes ¥450-690*), down the street from the station, offers more conventional *donburi* toppings (eg, chicken and egg, tempura).

Jolly Jellyfish (☎ 23-1932; *mains ¥580-1800*) bar and restaurant, at the foot of Hakodate-yama, has reasonably priced seafood, pizza and Thai dishes. It's open late and is popular with local expats.

Hakodate Beer (☎ 23-8000; *dishes ¥350-2500*), next to the Hakodate Kokusai Hotel, is an enormous place with pizza, grills and occasional live music. You can sample all four varieties of microbrew produced here for ¥1200.

Heading west along the harbour, the Nishi-hatoba district has trendy **eateries** in converted Western-style buildings.

Ryountei (☎ 54-3221; *set menus ¥800-2000*), adjacent to Goryō-kaku Tower, has lovely, fresh seafood, counter or *zashiki* (tatami) seating, and a picture menu.

Lucky Pierrot (☎ 55-4424; *dishes ¥150-720*), diagonally across the street, is a branch of the wildly popular, only-in-Hakodate fast-food chain, with burgers, curries, spaghetti and some Chinese-inspired choices.

Entertainment

Beateria Belongs (☎ 31-4108) is a stand-up bar with foreign and Japanese clientele. For a sophisticated atmosphere and night-time harbour views, try the 9th-floor **Gagyu** lounge in the Hakodate Kokusai Hotel annexe (☎ 23-5151, fax 23-0239; e *kokusaiho tel@hakodate.ne.jp*).

Getting There & Away

All Nippon Airlines and Japan Airlines connect Hakodate airport with Nagoya, Kansai, Sendai, Niigata, Hiroshima, Fukuoka and Tokyo. All Nippon Kōkū has flights from Hakodate to Sapporo's Okadama airport (from ¥9000 off-peak, 45 minutes).

Trains link Hakodate and Aomori via the Seikan Tunnel (*tokkyū* ¥5340, two hours). Cheaper *kaisoku* trains make the trip in about 2½ hours (¥3460). Some of these trains also give you the option of taking the Seikan Tunnel Tour (see the boxed text 'Seikan Tunnel Tour' earlier in this chapter).

Hokutosei Express sleeper trains serve Tokyo's Ueno station (¥21,000, 12 hours); there's also a sleeper service to Osaka (¥23,100, 17 hours). Either trip costs ¥9450 with a JR Pass. A combination of *tokkyū* and *shinkansen* (from Morioka) takes about seven hours to Tokyo (¥17,640).

JR's Hakodate main line runs north from Hakodate to Sapporo (*tokkyū* ¥8080, 3½ hours) via New Chitose Airport; S-kippu costs ¥14,160.

HOKKAIDŌ

CENTRAL HAKODATE

PLACES TO STAY
1   Hakodate Harborview Hotel
    函館ハーバービュー
    ホテル
3   Tōyoko Inn Daimon
    東横イン大門
8   Minshuku Kumachi
    民宿くまち
9   Niceday Inn
    ナイスディイン
10 Hakodate Kokusai Hotel
    函館国際ホテル
12 Auberge Kokian
    ペンション古稀庵
30 Hakodate Youth Guesthouse
    函館ユースゲストハウス

PLACES TO EAT
2   The Don
    ザー丼
6   Kamome Rāmen
    かもめラーメン
7   Asa-Ichi (Morning Market)
    朝市

11 Hakodate Beer
    函館ビール
13 Nishi Hatoba District
    西はとば
29 Jolly Jellyfish
    ジョリー・ジェリフィッシュ

OTHER
4   NTT
5   Hakodate Municipal
    Office
    函館市役所
14 Comfortable Octopus Dock
    カンファタブル・オクトパス
    のりば
15 Hakodate City Museum of
    Northern Peoples
    函館市北方民族資料館
16 Chinese Memorial Hall
    中華会館
17 Old Russian Consulate
    旧ロシア領事館
18 Kōryō-ji
    高龍寺

19 Foreigners Cemetery
    外人墓地
20 Funadama-jinja
    船魂神社
21 Old Public Hall of Hakodate
    Ward
    旧函館区公会堂
22 Motomachi-kōen; Old
    Prefectural Office; Tourist
    Information
    元町公園；観光案内所
23 Old British Consulate
    旧イギリス領事館
24 Russian Orthodox Church
    ハリストス正教会
25 Roman Catholic Church
    カトリック教会
26 Higashi Hongan-ji
    東本願寺
27 Hakodate Episcopal Church
    of Japan
    聖ヨハネ教会
28 Gokoku-jinja
    護国神社

Buses depart from in front of Hakodate station for Sapporo's Chūō bus station and Ōdōri bus centre (¥4680, five hours, five a day). There are also two night buses leaving around midnight for the same fare. Buses for Esashi leave six times a day (¥1830, 2¼ hours).

Ferries depart year round for Aomori (¥1850, 3¾ hours, up to nine a day) and Ōma on the peninsula, Shimokita-hantō (from ¥1170, 1¾ hours, two to four a day).

Getting Around

Buses to Hakodate airport depart frequently from near Hakodate station (¥300, 20 minutes).

A taxi from Hakodate station to the ferry terminal costs around ¥1500. City bus No 16 runs much more frequently between the ferry terminal and the Goryō-kaku-kōen-mae tram stop, from where you can catch a tram to Hakodate station.

Single-trip fares on trams are ¥200; on buses up to ¥250. One-day (¥1000) and two-day (¥1700) passes offering unlimited travel on city buses and trams are available at the tourist information offices or from drivers; bus services include the bus up Hakodate-yama.

MATSUMAE 松前
☎ 01394

As the furthest-flung outpost of the Tokugawa shōgunate, Matsumae was once the stronghold of the Matsumae clan and centre of Japanese political power on Hokkaidō. In the 19th century, the Tokugawa shōgunate, followed by the forces of the Meiji Restoration, gradually took over governmental functions and Matsumae's political importance faded. With its rich history, Matsumae is a reasonable day trip from Hakodate, or a pleasant detour en route from Honshū.

Matsumae-jō (☎ 2-2216; admission ¥350; open 9am-5pm daily mid-Apr–mid-Dec), Hokkaidō's only castle and the last one to be built in Japan, was completed in 1854 (the same year as Commodore Perry arrived) as a possible defence against Russian expansion down from Sakhalin. The restored castle houses typical feudal relics and a small collection of Ainu items. There is a small **tourist information office** (☎ 2-3868; open 9am-5pm daily Apr-Oct) near the castle. Further uphill is a 17th-

century temple district and the burial grounds of the Matsumae clan. Even further along is **Matsumae Hanyashiki** (admission ¥350; open 9am-5pm daily mid-Apr–mid-Dec), an interesting replica of an Edo-period village built using authentic materials and construction techniques.

To reach Matsumae from Hakodate, take the JR Esashi line to Kikonai (kaisoku ¥810, 45 minutes), which is also on the JR Tsugaru Kaikyō line for connections with Honshū. From Kikonai station there are direct buses to Matsumae; get off at the Matsumae-jō stop (¥1330, 90 minutes). Buses then continue to the Matsumae station across town, from where there are buses to Esashi between April and November (¥2720, two hours, four a day).

ESASHI 江差
☎ 01395

If Matsumae was Hokkaidō's Edo-period political centre, Esashi was the economic centre. It's still an important fishing town (herring – until stocks were depleted in the early 20th century – and other seafood now). Among the dozens of **nishingoten** (herring barons' homes) that once dominated the shoreline, **Yokoyama House** (☎ 2-0018; admission ¥300; open 9am-5pm daily mid-Apr–Nov, 9am-5pm Tues-Sun Nov–mid-Apr) and **Nakamura House** (☎ 2-1617; admission ¥200; open 9am-5pm daily late Apr-Oct, 9am-5pm Tues-Sun Nov–mid-Apr) remain well-preserved. You can hear performances of Esashi Oiwake, a nationally known music style, at 11am, 1pm and 2.30pm at the **Esashi Oiwake Museum** (☎ 2-0920; admission ¥300; open 9am-5pm daily 29 Apr-Oct, 9am-5pm Tues-Sun Nov-late Apr). Local information is also available here.

Esashi is renowned for its **annual festival** from 9 to 11 August, parading more than a dozen ornate floats in honour of Ubagami Dai-jingū, Hokkaidō's oldest shrine.

Esashi is also the most convenient gateway to **Okushiri-tō**, a sleepy island with small fishing villages, few foreign visitors, beautiful coastal scenery and some tourist sights cluttering the view.

Getting There & Away

There are infrequent local trains between Hakodate and Esashi (¥1790, 2½ hours).

From Esashi station, it's a 25-minute walk downhill to the tourist sights. Direct buses from Hakodate (¥1830, 2¼ hours, six a day) stop across the street from the terminal. From April to November buses run between Esashi and Matsumae (¥2720, two hours, four a day).

From Esashi ferry terminal, near the tourist sights, ferries depart twice daily for Okushiri-tō (¥2100, 2¼ hours), or once daily between January and March. Between late April and October, ferries also operate between Okushiri-tō and Setana, north along the coast.

Dō-ō (Central Hokkaidō) 道央

OTARU 小樽
☎ 0134 • pop 154,000

A popular day trip from Sapporo or a stop on the ferry from Honshū, Otaru played an important role in the early development of Hokkaidō and the herring industry. That legacy lives on in a collection of Western-style buildings, an attractive canal area and lingering signs of Russian trading influence.

Information

The **tourist information office** (☎ 29-1333; open 9am-6pm daily) is inside JR Otaru station. The *Otaru Tourist Guide* has several maps and details of sights, transport and accommodation. There are also **tourist information offices** near the Otaru Museum and at Asakusa-bashi in the canal area.

Things to See & Do

Otaru's best-known attraction is the **Otaru Unga** (Otaru Canal), which parallels the harbour and is lined with walkways and gas lamps – very romantic at dusk. Along the canal are several Meiji- and Taisho-era buildings; you'll find several more along **Nichigin-dori** (once known as the 'Wall Street of the North'), including the street's namesake Bank of Japan. Also rated highly are the **Former Nippon Yūsen Company building** (☎ 22-3316; admission ¥100; open 9.30am-5pm Tues-Sun) and the **Mitsui-Sumitomo Mitsui Banking Corporation** (SMBC; still in operation). Some have been beautifully renovated for other uses.

Hokkaidō's Top 10 Views

1 Mashū-ko on a clear day

2 Winter drift ice in the Sea of Okhotsk (Abashiri)

3 Whales, dolphins and porpoises during summer boat cruises from Muroran

4 Kuril seals basking below the cliffs at the cape Erimo-Misaki

5 The white peaks of Tokachidake mountains rising behind the lavender fields of Furano and Biei

6 Tōya-ko's frisky young volcanoes, and Usu-zan

7 Boats sailing in and out of Hakodate's harbour

8 Sapporo skyline from Moiwa-yama

9 Sunset over Momo-iwa on Rebun-tō

10 An ocean sunset while soaking in the warm pools of Kamuiwakka-no-taki

A few glass-blowing workshops are the source of Otaru's tenuous self-comparison with Venice. The interestingly named **K's Blowing** (☎ 31-5454; prices ¥1500-2200) offers 10-minute lessons (English OK) in making a cup or a bowl, which you keep. It's located in a lively area of craft shops. At **Yuzu Kōbo** (☎ 34-1314) you can make your own ring (¥1500) or glass bead (¥300).

Nearby, the **Otaru Museum** (☎ 33-2439; admission ¥100; open 9.30am-5pm daily) occupies a brick warehouse dating from 1893. It houses a tastefully presented collection on local history, including items from the herring industry and ceramics kilns; ask for the English-language explanation pages.

Otaru's most fascinating sight is **Nishin-goten** (Herring Mansion; ☎ 22-1038; admission ¥200; open 9am-5pm daily early Apr-late Nov), built in 1897 and relocated to the coast at Shukutsu in 1956. The original owners were herring industry barons during the Meiji and Taishō eras, and lived in this enormous complex along with seasonal labourers. To get there, take bus No 11 from Otaru station to the last stop at Otaru Suizokukan (Otaru Aquarium; bus ¥200, 25 minutes). From late April to mid-October you can also get to Shikotsu-kō port by **sightseeing boat** from Otaru's Pier 3 (¥1550, 85 minutes).

HOKKAIDŌ

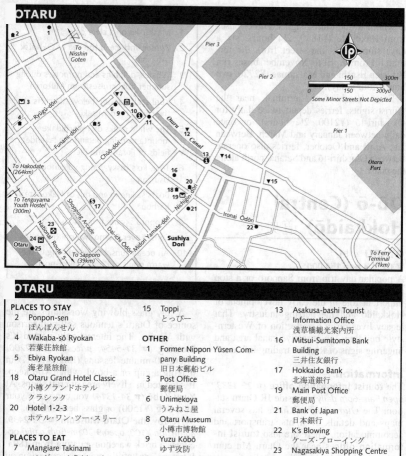

OTARU

OTARU

PLACES TO STAY	15	Toppi	13	Asakusa-bashi Tourist
2	Ponpon-sen		とっぴ		Information Office
	ぽんぽんせん				浅草橋観光案内所
4	Wakaba-sō Ryokan		**OTHER**	16	Mitsui-Sumitomo Bank
	若葉荘旅館	1	Former Nippon Yūsen Com-		Building
5	Ebiya Ryokan		pany Building		三井住友銀行
	海老屋旅館		旧日本郵船ビル	17	Hokkaido Bank
18	Otaru Grand Hotel Classic	3	Post Office		北海道銀行
	小樽グランドホテル		郵便局	19	Main Post Office
	クラシック	6	Unimekoya		郵便局
20	Hotel 1-2-3		うみねこ屋	21	Bank of Japan
	ホテル・ワン・ツー・スリー	8	Otaru Museum		日本銀行
			小樽市博物館	22	K's Blowing
PLACES TO EAT	9	Yuzu Kōbō		ケーズ・ブローイング
7	Mangiare Takinami		ゆず攻防	23	Nagasakiya Shopping Centre
	マンジャーレTakinami	10	Unga Plaza Tourist		長崎屋
12	Otaru Sōko No 1		Information Booth	24	Bus Station
	小樽倉庫 No 1		運河プラザ観光案内所		バスターミナル
14	Otaru Unga Shokudō	11	Unga Plaza	25	JR Rent-a-Cycle
	小樽運河食堂		運河プラザ		JRレンタサイクル

Places to Stay – Budget

The tourist information office can give you directions to any of several rider houses that are located around town – all cost from ¥1200 a night. A few are accessible by public transport.

Otaru Tengu-yama Youth Hostel (☎ 34-1474, fax 34-1475; Ⓦ www.tengu.co.jp; beds ¥2750) is close to the Tengu-yama cable car and ski area, which is a 20-minute bus ride southwest of Otaru station (¥200).

The Toho network **Ponpon-sen** (☎/fax 27-0866; Ⓔ VZY03353@nifty.ne.jp; dorm beds ¥3500) is a quirky place with guitars on the walls. It's in a residential neighbourhood northwest of the town centre (12 minutes on foot from the station), though there was talk that it might move. It's basically open in summer only.

Wakaba-sō Ryokan (☎/fax 27-3111; rooms per person summer/winter ¥3500/4000), on a sidestreet west of the centre, is small but well kept. Rates include a light breakfast.

Places to Stay – Mid-Range

Hotel 1-2-3 (say 'wan-tsū-surī'; ☎ 31-3939, fax 31-5995; w www.hyper-hotel.co.jp; singles/ doubles/triples ¥4900/5900/6900) is brand new and an amazing deal in a stylishly renovated former bank building. Western-style rooms have no phone, but rates include a light breakfast.

Ebiya Ryokan (☎ 22-2317; per person with breakfast/2 meals ¥5800/6500) is in a quiet area close to the canal. While the common areas are showing their age, Japanese-style rooms are handsomely decorated.

Places to Stay – Top End

Otaru Grand Hotel Classic (☎ 22-6500; singles/doubles peak ¥13,500/21,000, off-peak ¥7500/13,000), in another former bank, is its own slice of history, with fine Western-style rooms and very lovely leaded glass.

Places to Eat

The area along the canal has numerous little European-style cafés and restaurants.

Mangiare Takinami (☎ 33-3394; set lunches ¥780-880), one block off the canal, is a relaxing place with wooden rafters and excellent pasta and fish set lunches.

Uminekoya (☎ 32-2914; dishes ¥600-1400), nearby, in an atmospheric old brick warehouse, serves fish, chicken and pasta; at night it doubles as a pub.

Otaru Sōko No 1 (☎ 21-2323; most dishes ¥380-980) is one of a new breed of microbreweries throughout northern Japan. There's a German and Japanese menu to accompany its over-the-top Bavarian interior.

Otaru Unga Shokudō (☎ 24-8000; rāmen ¥700-1150), a food court, specialises in rāmen.

Sushi-ya Dori has numerous restaurants serving…you can guess; and although we generally avoid conveyor-belt sushi, locals swear that the fish at **Toppi** (☎ 0120-09-6000; per plate ¥120-220) is both cheap and delicious.

Or, you could munch on an ear of fresh, grilled corn from a street vendor for ¥300.

Getting There & Away

Otaru is 30 minutes from Sapporo by kaisoku or 50 minutes by futsū (ordinary train); fares for both cost ¥620. Special airport kaisoku trains run via Sapporo to New Chitose Airport (¥1740, 75 minutes).

Occasional local trains run south to Niseko (¥1410, two hours).

You can catch frequent buses to Sapporo (¥590, one hour), and less frequent ones to Niseko (¥1330, 1¾ hours).

Ferries run daily between Otaru and Maizuru (from ¥6700, 28½ hours), north of Kyoto, and almost daily to Niigata (¥5400, 17¾ hours). To get to the ferry terminal, take bus No 10 from in front of the station (¥200, 10 minutes). Tourist-loop buses also stop at the port a couple of times daily.

Getting Around

The main part of town is small enough to tackle on foot. Bicycle rental is available at the station through **JR Rent-A-Cycle** (☎ 24-6300; open May-Sept) starting at ¥800 for two hours (discounts for holders of student ID and certain rail passes).

Tourist buses loop through the city taking in most of the sights (¥200 a ride, ¥750 for a one-day pass). Buses leave approximately every 20 minutes from Otaru station between 9am and 6.30pm.

NISEKO ニセコ
☎ 0136

One of Hokkaidō's prime ski resorts during winter and a hiking base during summer and autumn, Niseko sprawls between the mountain Yōtei-zan to the east and Niseko Annupuri to the west. There are plenty of opportunities for canoeing, kayaking and river rafting in summer, and ice climbing, snowshoeing or even dog sledding in winter, and hot springs throughout the year.

The **Niseko Outdoor Centre** (☎ 44-1133) near the Annupuri ski ground and **Niseko Adventure Centre** (☎ 23-2093) in the village of Hirafu organise activities. At Niseko station is a **tourist information office** (☎ 44-2468; open 9am-7pm July & Aug, 9am-6pm Sept-June); information is available via the Internet at w www.niseko.gr.jp. Depending on where you're heading, it may make more sense to travel via one of two other stations serving the area, Hirafu and Kutchan.

Places to Stay

There are rider houses throughout the area. **Tourist Home** (☎ 44-2517; per person with own bedding ¥1000, including bedding & 2 meals ¥5000), in Niseko village, is a perennial favourite.

HOKKAIDŌ

Niseko Annupuri Youth Hostel (☎ 58-2084; Ⓦ www.annupuri-yh.com; *beds per person ¥3100*) is a four-star mountain lodge near the Annupuri ski ground. The hospitable owner is an excellent source of information about outdoor activities and can provide local hiking and cycling maps. Meals here are highly recommended. If you phone ahead, someone will pick you up at Niseko station.

Niseko Ambishiasu (*say 'ambitious';* ☎ 44-3011; per person with 2 meals winter ¥4800, rest of year ¥4500), a Toho network member, is popular and offers shared, Japanese-style rooms. The owners will pick you up from the station. Ski rental is also available.

Jam Garden (☎ 22-6676, fax 22-4506; *rooms per person peak/off-peak ¥6000/5000*), a short hop from the intersection at the foot of the Hirafu ski lifts, sits in a valley like a cosy farmhouse...if farmhouses had Jacuzzi and sauna (most rooms don't have private facilities). Rooms and meals are Western style. Phone ahead for pickup at Hirafu or Kutchan stations.

Niseko Hotel Nikko Annupuri (☎ 58-3311, fax 58-3317; Ⓦ www.nikko-annupuri .co.jp; *rooms per person with 2 meals from ¥13,000*), near the top of the mountain road, is top of the line. It's a professional operation with Western-style rooms, splendid valley views and easy bus access.

Getting There & Away

Unfortunately, in summer Niseko is not an easy place to reach without your own transport. There are a few direct *kaisoku* trains from Sapporo (¥3050, 2¼ hours); otherwise you'll have wait up to 1½ hours when changing trains at Otaru (¥1410, two hours). Alternatively, you could hop on a direct bus to Niseko outside Otaru station (¥1330, two hours). From June to September, there is a daily bus from New Chitose Airport to the Niseko Hotel Nikko Annupuri (¥2300, 2½ hours).

Winter is a different story: there are frequent direct buses to the area's ski resorts from Sapporo (three hours) and New Chitose Airport (3¼ hours); either costs ¥2190/3660 one way/return; trains run more frequently as well. During the ski season, there are shuttle buses between the train stations and major ski areas.

TŌYA-KO 洞爺湖
☎ 0142

Part of Shikotsu-Tōya National Park (983 sq km), Tōya-ko is a large and attractive lake, not too badly marred by some monolithic hotels in the town of Tōya-ko Onsen on the southern shore. However, most foreign visitors bypass the lake to concentrate on the nearby volcanoes. Fast and easy access from Sapporo or New Chitose Airport makes this area a favourite with those who have only a short time to spend in Hokkaidō. The **Tōya-ko Onsen tourist office** (☎ 75-2446; *open 9am-5pm daily*) is downhill from the bus station.

Volcanic sites

In 1943, after a series of earthquakes, **Shōwa Shin-zan** first emerged as an upstart bump in some vegetable fields southeast of Tōya-ko Onsen and then continued to surge upwards for two more years to reach its present height (407m). At the time, the Japanese government was keen to hush it up as it was thought the event might be misinterpreted as a bad omen and hamper the progress of WWII. Local authorities were urged to douse the volcanic flames (it didn't happen) so that enemy aircrews couldn't use them for orientation. Shōwa Shin-zan is still an awesome sight, hissing, issuing steam and keeping the locals guessing about its next move.

Its next-door neighbour, **Usu-zan** (729m and the force behind the creation of Shōwa Shin-zan), may hold some clues. On 31 March 2000, after a mere few days of rumbling, Usu-zan shot white, then black, smoke 2700m straight up, which then drifted and completely covered the lake, Tōya-ko. Although no lava flowed and locals were safely evacuated, massive flying rocks threatened to down news helicopters recording the event. In the end, some homes, crops, roads and businesses were lost, but there was far less fall-out than when 30cm of ash rained down on Tōya-ko Onsen during Usu-zan's previous eruption (1977).

The mountains share a large car park (cars ¥410) with some irritating tourist facilities. You can't climb the peaks, but a ropeway (cable-car; ☎ 75-2401), takes you up Usu-zan. It costs ¥1450 return, and is open 8.15am to 5.45pm May to mid-September; it's then open shorter hours from mid-September to April and closed in December.

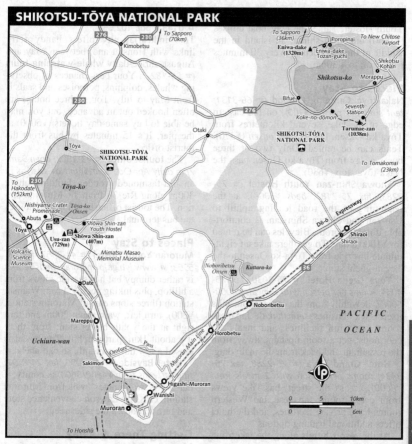

SHIKOTSU-TŌYA NATIONAL PARK

(map)

To Sapporo (70km)
Kimobetsu
To Sapporo (36km)
Poropinai
Eniwa-dake (1320m)
Eniwa-dake Tozan-guchi
To New Chitose Airport
Shikotsu Kohan
Morappu
Shikotsu-ko
Bifue
Seventh Station
Koke-no-dōmon
Tarumae-zan (1038m)
Otaki
SHIKOTSU-TŌYA NATIONAL PARK
To Tomakomai (23km)
Tōya
SHIKOTSU-TŌYA NATIONAL PARK
To Hakodate (152km)
Tōya-ko
Nishiyama Crater Promenade
Tōya-ko Onsen
Abuta
Tōya
Usu-zan (729m)
Shōwa Shin-zan Youth Hostel
Shōwa Shin-zan (407m)
Mimatsu Masao Memorial Museum
Dō-ō Expressway
Shiraoi
Shiraoi
Volcanic Science Museum
Date
Noboribetsu Onsen
Kuttara-ko
Mareppu
Noboribetsu
PACIFIC OCEAN
Uchiura-wan
Orofure Pass
Horobetsu
Muroran Main Line
Sakimori
Higashi-Muroran
Wanishi
Muroran
0   5   10km
0   3   6mi
To Honshū

HOKKAIDŌ

Behind the tourist shops, the small **Mimatsu Masao Memorial Museum** (☎ 75-2365; admission ¥300; open 8am-5pm daily Feb & Apr-Dec, irregular hours Jan & Mar) is devoted to the local postmaster, who purchased the volcano in 1946 (for a princely ¥28,000) and spent years diagramming its growth using an ingenious method, now a standard for vulcanologists. Note that there is only limited English signage.

More interesting – and creepy – is the **Nishiyama Crater Promenade** (Nishiyama Kakō Sansakurō; ☎ 72-1008; admission free; open 7am-6pm daily except during snow season), where you can stroll the site of some of the devastation caused by the 2000 eruption. Scorched trees and half-buried houses, utility poles and road signs sit amid

still-steaming vents and newly created ponds. It's up a hill about 2km southwest of Tōya-ko Onsen; buses cost ¥160, parking your own car is ¥300.

Not cratering yet? Above the Tōya-ko Onsen bus terminal is the **Volcanic Science Museum** (☎ 75-4400; admission ¥600; open 9am-5pm daily), including a film that allows you to experience the visual and aural fury of an eruption via ear-blowing speakers.

Tōya-ko Onsen 洞爺湖温泉

During the summer, the town offers **fireworks displays** every evening. Ambitious cyclists can take a 37km **cycling course** around the lake; bicycle rental is available at extortionate rates near the bus station or

more affordably at the **Shōwa Shin-zan Youth Hostel** (¥1660) out to **Ō-shima**, an island in the middle of the lake, depart every 30 minutes from 8am to 4.30pm.

Places to Stay
Naka-tōya Camping Ground (☎ 66-3131; *tent sites per person ¥300*), on the eastern edge of the lake, several kilometres from Tōya-ko Onsen, has its own *onsen* (¥370). Tents can be rented. Only two or three buses a day from Tōya-ko Onsen pass the Naka-tōya stop (¥630).

Shōwa Shin-zan Youth Hostel (☎ 75-2283, fax 75-2482; *beds ¥3000*), at the beginning of the road leading uphill to Usu-zan and Shōwa Shin-zan, is comfortable if unglamorous. Bicycles can be rented for ¥1000 a day. To get there take an eight-minute bus ride from Tōya-ko Onsen to the Tozan-guchi stop.

Tōya Green Hotel (☎ 75-3030, fax 75-4054; *rooms per person with 2 meals ¥4000-6000*), downhill from the bus station, bills itself as a 'business *minshuku*'. Japanese rooms have full facilities, and meals are enormous; get a room upstairs, away from the restaurant and back from the main drag.

Hotel Grand Tōya (☎ 75-2288, fax 75-3434; *rooms per person with 2 meals from ¥8000*), across the street, has lake views from every room. Japanese and Western rooms have private facilities, and the hotel offers additional bathing options.

At the **resort hotels** along the lakefront, you will find that per-person rates start at around ¥12,000.

Getting There & Away
Trains to Hakodate (¥4830, 1½ hours) or Sapporo (¥5250, 1¾ hours) stop at the town of Tōya, and buses run every 30 minutes between Tōya station and Tōya-ko Onsen (¥320, 25 minutes).

Less expensive are the frequent buses from Tōya-ko Onsen to Sapporo station (¥2700, 2¾ hours) and Muroran (¥1170, 1¾ hours).

Between late April and late November, there are also up to four buses a day via the scenic Orofure pass to Noboribetsu Onsen (¥1530, 1¼ hours), some of which continue to New Chitose Airport (¥2140, 2½ hours).

MURORAN 室蘭
☎ 0143 • pop 102,660
This industrial city offers handy ferry links with Honshū and, between May and August, thrice-daily **whale-watching tours** (☎ 26-1822). Your best chances of observing whales, dolphins, porpoises and seals is from May to July. Tours (three hours) are often booked out in advance, but you may be able to buy same-day tickets (¥6000) at the pier. It's 15 minutes by bus from the tourist office.

The **tourist office** (☎ 23-1002; *open 9am-7pm daily Apr-Oct, 9am-5pm Nov-Mar*) is in an old-fashioned wooden building about 300m along Rte 36 from JR Muroran station. The tourist office building also houses the bus terminal.

Places to Stay
Muroran Youth Hostel (☎ 44-3357, fax 45-5953; **w** www.jyh.gr.jp/muroran; *beds ¥2500*) is rather dumpy but has seaside views from a hilltop, plus hiking nearby. From Wanishi station (three stops east of Muroran station, ¥200), turn left, walk about 200m and turn right at the youth hostel sign; from there it's about 1km, partly uphill. The hostel is closed a few days a month, so call ahead.

Hotel Bayside (☎ 24-8090, fax 24-8092; *singles/twins from ¥4800/8600*) is comfy, if dated. It's two minutes' walk from Muroran station; cross by Lawson convenience store and turn left down the sidestreet.

Getting There & Away
Most long-distance trains depart from Higashi-Muroran station, three stops east of Muroran station; transfer to central Muroran is included in long-distance fares. Direct *tokkyū* trains run south to Hakodate (¥5670, two hours) and north to Sapporo (¥4170, 1¼ hours).

From the bus station there are fairly frequent departures for Sapporo (¥2000, 2¼ hours), Noboribetsu Onsen (¥710, 80 minutes) and Tōya-ko Onsen (¥1170, 1¾ hours).

Ferries from Muroran depart for Hachinohe (¥3970, eight hours, daily). There are overnight ferries to Aomori (¥3460, seven hours, daily) and Naoetsu (¥7030, 17 hours, three a week). The ferry terminal is about a 10-minute walk from Muroran station. Ring **Higashi Nihon Ferry** (☎ 22-1668) for details.

NOBORIBETSU ONSEN 登別鴛泉
☎ 0143

Noboribetsu Onsen is the most popular hot-springs resort in Hokkaidō, although way overdone as a tourist destination. Despite tacky hotels, tour groups and their buses clogging the narrow streets, there are some gems and interesting hikes.

A couple of minutes on foot uphill from the bus station, the **tourist association office** (☎ 84-2018) has helpful English guides and maps to accommodation and sights, most of which are accessible on foot from the main street.

Dai-Ichi Takimoto-kan (☎ 84-3322; admission ¥2000; open 9am-5pm daily) is a luxury hotel boasting one of Japan's largest bath complexes. To make the most of the steep admission, spend half a day or longer wandering from floor to floor trying out the mineral pools (very hot!), waterfalls, walking pools, cold pools (freezing!), steam room and swimming pool with waterslide.

A five-minute walk further uphill is **Jigokudani** (Hell Valley), with steaming, sulphurous vents and streams of hot water bubbling out of vividly coloured rocks. Bearing left up the valley you come to a lookout over **Ōyu-numa** (Boiling Water Swamp), where water bubbles violently on the pond's sickly coloured surface. The entire area is crisscrossed by a network of hiking trails.

Places to Stay

Kurofuku (☎ 85-2565, fax 84-2073; beds ¥2750) is the town's only youth hostel. It's damp, moulding and unpleasant. Consider yourself warned.

Ryokan Hanaya (☎ 84-2521, fax 84-2240; W www4.ocn.ne.jp/~k-hanaya; rooms per person ¥6000-7000), by contrast, is civilised, intimate and lovely. Japanese rooms (many overlooking the river) have private toilet and sink, and there are hot-spring baths and English-speaking staff.

Prices at the large tourist hotels begin at around ¥10,000 per person. Readers have written to recommend the lighted nighttime views of Jigokudani from **Dai-Ichi Takimoto-kan** (☎ 84-3322).

Getting There & Away

Noboribetsu Onsen is about 13 minutes by bus (¥330) from JR Noboribetsu station, with local train connections to Higashi-Muroran (¥350, 20 minutes), Shiraoi (¥350, 30 minutes) and Tomakomai (¥810, 45 minutes) for connections to Sapporo.

From Noboribetsu Onsen there are direct express buses to Sapporo (Eki-mae terminal; ¥1900, 1½ to 2¾ hours). There are also buses to New Chitose Airport (¥1330, 65 minutes, one to three times a day) and Muroran (¥710, 80 minutes, hourly). Between late April and late November, there are also up to four buses a day via the scenic Orofure pass to Tōya-ko Onsen (¥1530, 1¼ hours).

SHIKOTSU-KO 支笏湖
☎ 0123

Part of Shikotsu-Tōya National Park, Shikotsu-ko is a caldera lake surrounded by several volcanoes. It's Japan's second-deepest lake after Tazawa-ko in Akita-ken. The main centre for transport and information is poky **Shikotsu Kohan**, which consists of a bus station, a **visitors centre** (☎ 25-2404; open 9.30am-4.30pm daily), a pier for boat excursions, and assorted souvenir shops, restaurants and places to stay. The peaceful settlement of **Morappu**, a few kilometres south along the lake, also has some lodgings.

From Shikotsu Kohan's boat pier, rather tame 30-minute **sightseeing cruises** (☎ 25-2031) depart. An adult ticket costs ¥930, and they run from April to November. If you cross the bridge on your far left as you walk down to the lake, you can follow a nature trail for an hour to Morappu.

There's not much bus service around the lake, but you can cycle to various destinations or take on the full circuit (50km). The youth hostel rents bicycles for ¥400 an hour or ¥2000 a day (less for hostel guests).

Hiking

Mountain hikes are perhaps the most interesting things to do around Shikotsu-ko.

Eniwa-dake (1320m) lies on the northwestern side of the lake. The start of the mountain trail is about 10 minutes on foot from the Eniwa-dake Tozan-guchi bus stop near Poropinai. It takes about 3½ hours to hike to the summit, where there is a fine panorama. Avoid this hike if it rains. Buses from Shikotsu Kohan to Sapporo pass the Eniwa-dake Tozan-guchi stop (¥340).

Tarumae-zan (1038m) lies on the southern side of the lake. Here you can enjoy the rugged delights of wandering around the crater of an active volcano, though at the time of writing hikers were warned against climbing due to increased activity. The crater is an easy 40-minute hike from the seventh station, which can be reached from Shikotsu Kohan in three hours on foot (¥3500 by taxi). There is bus service as far as the turn-off from the main highway, but it's 12km from there to the seventh station; many people also hitchhike. Stay on the established routes, as other routes are said to harbour bears.

From the crater, you can follow a trail northwest down the mountain for 2½ hours to **Koke-no-dōmon** *(open 9am-5pm daily June-Oct)*, a spectacular mossy gorge. Between mid-July and mid-September, there are also buses twice a day (¥410) to/from Koke-no-dōmon from Shikotsu Kohan that allow you about 25 minutes to look around. If you miss the last bus you'll have to walk or hitch the 15km back to Shikotsu Kohan. The gorge is officially open during the dates shown and you cannot enter after 4pm.

Places to Stay
There are a dozen or so lodgings in Shikotsu Kohan.

Shikotsu-ko Youth Hostel *(☎ 25-2311, fax 25-2312; dorm beds ¥2900)*, across the car park from the bus station, is a friendly place with family rooms as well as the usual dormitory-style accommodation. Bicycle rental and a hot-springs bath are available.

Log Bear *(☎/fax 25-2738; w http://log bear.hoops.ne.jp; B&B per person ¥5000)*, in the town centre, is a intimate log cabin with a few rooms and a coffee shop. The owner speaks excellent English.

Shikotsu-sō *(☎ 25-2718, fax 25-2728; rooms per person with 2 meals ¥5800)*, just behind the bus station, is a cheerful *minshuku*.

Morappu Camping Ground *(☎ 25-2439; tent sites from ¥400; open late Apr-late Oct)*, in Morappu, is nicely situated by the lake.

Lapland *(☎/fax 25-2239; dorm beds with 2 meals ¥4900)*, a minute away, is a Toho network member. It's a great little log cabin with nice views of the lake and carpeted Japanese-style rooms. Private rooms, when available, cost ¥5900 per person. The owners will pick you up and take you back to the bus station or to mountain trailheads. Buses bound for Koke-no-dōmon from Shikotsu Kohan pass Morappu (¥240, 10 minutes).

Getting There & Away
Between mid-June and mid-October, there are three to four buses a day from Shikotsu Kohan to Sapporo station (¥1330, 80 minutes). Other buses run year round to New Chitose Airport (¥920, 55 minutes).

Dō-hoku (Northern Hokkaidō) 道北

ASAHIKAWA 旭川
☎ 0166 • pop 361,000
Asahikawa, Hokkaidō's second-largest city, features a compact, busy central area surrounded by unimpressive urban sprawl. For the traveller, its importance is largely as a transport hub: to the north, it's a long haul to Wakkanai; to the southeast is Daisetsuzan National Park, with Biei and Furano due south.

Historically, the area was one of the largest Ainu settlements in Hokkaidō. The present city had its origins in the Meiji period as a militia settlement and has since developed into a major industrial centre.

Information
There's a large **information counter** *(☎ 22-6704; open 8.30am-7pm daily July-Sept, 9am-5pm daily Oct-June)* inside Asahikawa station. Though only some staff speak English, they're knowledgeable about both the city and the region, and have some terrific English-language tourist literature. Elsewhere in the station, the **hotel booking desk** *(☎ 22-5139)* is known for excellent deals. There's also a **post office** – with ATM – in the station. Internet access is available at **Terako-ya** *(☎ 23-9789; ¥500/hr; open Mon-Sat)*, a couple of blocks from the station.

Things to See
The **Hokkaidō Folk Arts and Crafts Village** consists of three museums on a hill west of the city centre. Of them, the **International Dyeing and Weaving Art Museum** *(☎ 61-6161; admission ¥550; open 9am-5.30pm daily Apr-Nov)* has the most gravitas, with an extensive display of textiles from around Japan and the world, including embroidered traditional Ainu tree-bark cloth. Textilists should also enjoy the **Yukara Ori Folk Craft**

Museum (☎ 62-8811; admission ¥450; open 9am-5.30pm daily Apr-Nov, 9am-5pm Tues-Sun Dec-Mar), highlighting this distinctive local weaving style. The most interesting aspect about the **Snow Crystal Museum** (☎ 63-2211; admission ¥650; open 9am-5pm daily Feb-Mar, 9am-5.30pm daily Apr-Nov) is the walk-through gallery of huge freezers containing metres-long icicles; the rest is a little precious – a dainty concert hall looks like it was beamed in from Vienna. A combined ticket (¥1400) covers all three museums. Between May and October, free hourly shuttles depart between 10am and 4pm from bus stop No 11 near Asahikawa station.

Northwest of the city centre, the **Kawamura Kaneto Ainu Memorial Museum** (☎ 51-2461; admission ¥500; open 9am-5pm daily Sept-June, 8am-6pm daily July & Aug) has an interesting, if tiny, exhibition hall and some traditional wood-and-straw buildings.

The ticket office sells an English-language booklet, Living in the Ainu Moshir by Kawamura Shinrit Eoripak Ainu, the present curator and founder's son. Take bus No 24 from bus stop No 4 near Asahikawa station to the Ainu Kinenkan-mae stop (¥170, 15 minutes).

Sample one of Japan's most historic brands of sake at the **Otokoyama Sake Brewery Museum** (☎ 47-7080; admission free; open 9am-5pm daily). Exhibits demonstrate the production process and include an ukiyo-e (woodblock print) collection. Several city buses (¥280, 15 minutes) from the station area pass Otokoyama – ask the driver where to get off.

Special Events

The **Ainu Kotan Matsuri** (Ainu Village Festival) usually takes place in late September on the banks of Ishikari-gawa, south of the city. According to Ainu legend, a hero once defeated an evil deity here, throwing its severed head and its body into the river and turning them into two large rocks. During the festival you can see traditional dances, music, and kamui-nomi and inau-shiki prayer ceremonies offered to the deities of fire, river, kotan (village) and mountain.

At the beginning of February, you can see enormous ice sculptures during Asahikawa's own **Yuki Matsuri** (Snow Festival), the second-largest such festival in Hokkaidō after Sapporo's.

Places to Stay & Eat

Asahikawa Youth Hostel (☎ 61-2751, fax 61-8886; rooms per person ¥3200) is 15 minutes from station bus stop No 11; take bus No 444 or 550 to the Yūsu-hosuteru-mae stop (¥200). There are Japanese-style and two- or four-person bunk-bed rooms. The hostel is far from the city centre (though near a ski area) and can be deserted.

Tokiya Ryokan (☎ 23-2237, fax 26-3874; w www.tokiya.net/tokiyaryokan2.html; rooms per person with/without 2 meals ¥6000/4500), north of the station, is inviting and good value. Some staff speak English, and rooms with private facilities are available for a surcharge. Inquire about a possible re-opening of the city's longest-running inn, gracious **Echigoya Ryokan** (☎ 23-5131) down the block.

New Hokkai Hotel (☎ 24-3111, fax 22-3510; singles/doubles from ¥9500/17,000) is Asahikawa's Establishment choice, several blocks north of the station. It's a spacious place, and the 9th-floor breakfast buffet room affords calming views of distant mountains.

If Hokkaidō has a rāmen cult, one of its temples is **Santōka** (☎ 25-3401; rāmen ¥750-1050). The smaller of its two locations is a tiny counter with famous shio rāmen (rāmen in salt broth) and a perennial queue. **Boarders** (☎ 27-2399), around the corner, is a bar run by a friendly Australian snowboarder; it's a great place to collect local information.

Getting There & Away

Asahikawa has flights to Osaka, Nagoya, Tokyo and Niigata. Buses between the airport and Asahikawa station (¥570, 35 minutes) are timed to connect with flight arrivals and departures.

Trains link Asahikawa with Sapporo (tokkyū ¥3690, 1½ hours). You will find there are few afternoon kaisoku trains on the same route (¥2420, 2½ hours). S-kippu cost ¥4940.

Trains also run from Asahikawa via Biei (¥530, 30 minutes) to Furano (futsū ¥1040, 1¼ hours). Eastward, trains serve Kamikawa and Bihoro en route to Abashiri (¥7240, 3¾ hours). Tokkyū trains run north to Wakkanai three times a day (¥7560, four

HOKKAIDŌ

hours). For ¥6300 more, you can board the sleeper service.

Asahikawa station and surrounding streets comprise a bus hub, including buses serving Daisetsuzan National Park. Two or three buses a day serve Tenninkyō Onsen (65 minutes) and Asahidake Onsen (95 minutes); see the Asahidake Onsen section later in this chapter for information on seasonal free fares. From May to October, there are hourly buses to Sōunkyō Onsen (¥1900, 1¾ hours, last bus at 5.20pm); rail pass holders can save moolah by catching the same buses at Kamikawa.

Other bus services include Wakkanai (¥4350, 4½ hours, one a day), Furano (¥860, 1½ hours, last bus at 5pm) and Sapporo (¥2000, two hours, two or three an hour).

WAKKANAI 稚内
☎ 0162 • pop 43,300

While not of compelling interest itself, this windswept port on the northernmost fringe of Hokkaidō is the access point for the islands of Rishiri-tō and Rebun-tō, as well as Russia's Sakhalin Island. You'll see Russian streetsigns and souvenirs, and if you're around in late February, you might catch the **Japan Cup National Dogsled Races**. If nothing else 'Wakkanai' sounds like a contraction of *wakaranai* (I don't know), leading to Hokkaidō's favourite 'Who's on First?' joke.

Orientation & Information

Wakkanai station is steps from the bus terminal, or seven minutes' walk to the ferry terminal. Tourist information counters (☎ 22-2384; open 10am-6pm daily) are at Wakkanai station and the ferry terminal (open 6.30am-4pm daily June-Sept).

Things to See & Do

Wakkanai-kōen, atop a grassy hill a few blocks from the train station, offers a number of walking trails and the **Centennial Memorial Tower** (☎ 24-4019; admission ¥400; open 9am-5pm Tues-Sun late Apr–Oct, until 9pm daily June-Sep) with 360-degree views of northern Hokkaidō and, on clear days, Sakhalin. You can reach the park via a ropeway (☎ 22-0833; one way/return ¥180/240) or walk uphill. Also nearby are a number of eclectic monuments, including the **Gate to Ice and Snow**, a memorial to the

former Japanese settlements on Sakhalin, and **Monument to the Nine Ladies**, which commemorates postal workers on Sakhalin who committed suicide after Japan's defeat in WWII.

Wakkanai Onsen (☎ 28-1160; admission ¥600; open 10am-10pm daily, closed 1st Mon each month) is an 18-minute bus ride from the bus terminal.

About 30km east of Wakkanai is **Sōya-misaki**, Japan's northernmost point, just 43km from Sakhalin. Collectors of 'northernmosts' will want to visit, and there are a number of monuments of greater or lesser interest. The recorded Sōya-misaki song plays from a monument at the point, and several monuments sit atop the hill above the cape – one is dedicated to the victims of Korean Airlines flight 007, which was shot down by a Soviet fighter jet off the Sakhalin coast in 1983. Buses run four times a day between Wakkanai's bus terminal and Sōya-misaki (¥1350, 50 minutes).

Places to Stay & Eat

Wakkanai Moshiripa Youth Hostel (☎ 24-0180; beds ¥3100) is about a five-minute walk from Wakkanai station or eight minutes on foot from the port. Bicycles can be rented for ¥1500 a day. The hostel is also closed at times during the winter, so phone ahead.

Wakkanai Youth Hostel (☎ 23-7162, fax 23-7179; e komadori@gray.plala.or.jp; beds ¥2900) has received good reviews from travellers, though it's ageing. Most accommodation is in private rooms, and bicycle rental is ¥500/1000 per half/full day. The hostel is a 15-minute walk from Minami-Wakkanai station, one stop before the Wakkanai terminus. From Wakkanai station, fairly frequent buses bound for Midori-roku-chōme run past the Minami-shōgakkō-mae stop (¥210, 10 minutes). From there it's a 10-minute walk uphill (left) to the pale-green hostel.

Rider House Midori-yu (☎ 22-4275; beds ¥1000) offers spartan shared accommodation; you'll pass it on the way uphill from the same bus stop as for the youth hostel. It's to your left off of the main road, adjacent to a local *sentō* (public bath).

There are some **camping grounds** in town, but you should inquire as to which are bear-free. Some campers also squat at the **Wakkanai Dome** (a half-shell arcade near the ferry terminal), but the city is trying to discourage it.

Saihate Ryokan (☎ 23-3556; rooms per person from ¥4000), down the small street just to the right of the station, is simple though well maintained, with both Japanese- and Western-style rooms. Note for those sensitive to noise: it's near the ferry and bus terminals.

Hotel Okabe (☎ 22-3411, fax 22-3407; e ho-okabe@giga.ocn.ne.jp; rooms per person peak/off-peak ¥8000/6000) is brand new. It has pleasant, spacious, mostly Western-style rooms with harbour views and private facilities. There is also a nice Japanese bath. It's at the north end of the city centre, 10-minutes' walk from the station.

ANA Hotel Wakkanai (☎ 23-8111, toll-free 0120-029-501, fax 23-8112; rooms per person with 2 meals peak from ¥22,000, room only off-peak from ¥7400), right by the ferry terminal, is so sleek and contemporary that it looks almost out of place in Wakkanai. Ask about discounted rates.

In 2002 a fire destroyed the **Wakkanai Chūō Renbai**, a much-loved restaurant district known as the 'kitchen of Wakkanai'. As we went to press its future was uncertain, but for now your best bets are *rāmen* shops and *izakaya* in the station area.

Getting There & Away

Between Wakkanai and Sapporo, there is one flight a day to New Chitose Airport (50 minutes) and two to Okadama (one hour); both cost ¥19,500 during peak times. Wakkanai also has direct flights to Tokyo (¥37,000, 1¾ hours) and Kansai (¥44,500, 2½ hours). Buses to Wakkanai airport (35 minutes) cost ¥590.

There are a few *tokkyū* trains that travel between Wakkanai and Asahikawa (¥7560, four hours), most of which continue to Sapporo (¥9660, six hours). R-kippu cost ¥14,000 to Sapporo and S-kippu ¥9800 to Asahikawa. There is also a sleeper service (¥15,960) that leaves Sapporo at 11pm and arrives via Asahikawa in Wakkanai at 6am, in time for the early ferry to Rishiri-tō or Rebun-tō.

There are several daily buses to Sapporo (¥5750, six hours) and a daily bus to Asahikawa (¥4350, 4¾ hours). Discounted return tickets are available for either trip.

Ferry The **Higashi Nihonkai Ferry** (☎ 23-2870, fax 23-6730) sails from Wakkanai to Rishiri-tō, Rebun-tō and Russia's Sakhalin Island.

From Wakkanai it sails to Oshidomari, on Rishiri-tō, at least twice daily throughout the year, with four departures a day between May and September (¥1880, 1¾ hours), and also to Kutsugata on Rishiri-tō (¥2200).

From Wakkanai to Kafuka on Rebun-tō it departs two to five times a day (¥2100, two hours). Between Oshidomari and Kafuka there are two departures each way daily (¥730, 40 minutes); one departure each way in January and February. Between May and September there are also two ferries a day between Kutsugata and Kafuka (¥730).

Drivers will need deep pockets to take cars on the ferry, assuming you can get a reservation. One-way transport to Oshidomari starts at ¥9790. Parking at Wakkanai's ferry terminal is ¥1000 a night.

Ticket offices are inside the large building to the left of the pier.

From May to mid-October the ferry sails five to seven times a month between Wakkanai and Korsakov on Sakhalin Island. The cheapest 2nd-class fare is ¥20,000 one way, but 1st-class Japanese-style rooms cost only ¥5000 more. Return tickets start at ¥30,000. For details on Russian visa requirements, see the Getting There & Away section at the beginning of this chapter.

RISHIRI-REBUN-SAROBETSU NATIONAL PARK

利尻礼文Tロベツ国立公園

Rishiri-Rebun-Sarobetsu National Park is comprised mostly of the two islands, Rishiri-tō and Rebun-tō. It also includes Sarobetsu Gensei-kaen on Hokkaidō's mainland, a vast, swampy 27km coastal strip famous for its vistas of flowers – mainly rhododendrons, irises and lilies – which bloom in June and July.

Rishiri-tō 利尻島

☎ 01638

This island is dominated by the majestic volcanic peak Rishiri-zan (1721m), known locally as Rishiri-Fuji. The main activity for visitors is hiking the trails and lakes below the summit. Providing you have some warm clothes and proper footwear, the hike to the summit can be comfortably completed in a full day. A road encircles the island, and a bus service links the small fishing communities.

Oshidomari and Kutsugata are the island's main ports. At both ferry terminals, **information booths** (in Oshidomari, open 8am-5.30pm daily May-Oct; in Kutsugata, open 10am-4.30pm daily May-Sept) provide maps and details about transport, sights and hiking. Staff will also be able to book accommodation.

Hiking The two most reliable trails to the summit of Rishiri-zan start at Oshidomari and Kutsugata. Either trailhead is about 3km from town. There is limited bus service to the trailheads; otherwise you must either walk (just over an hour), hitch, take a taxi or arrange rides at lodgings.

Prepare properly for a mountain hike. Aim for an early start and allow at least 10 hours for the ascent and descent. The best time to hike is from late June to mid-September. Advice and maps with excellent hiking details and contour lines, mostly in

Japanese, are available from the information booths at the ports and at the youth hostel.

About two hours below the summit, just past the eighth station, is **Rishiri-dake Yamagoya**, an unstaffed mountain hut, which perches on the edge of a precipice and provides the bare minimum for a roof over your head (no water). If you're coming from Kutsugata, you'll have to head down the mountain for over an hour from where you meet up with the Oshidomari trail to reach the hut. Take your own food (purchase it from shops in the ports) and water. If you stay here, be warned that it's bloody cold at night and the wind contributes generously to the drop in temperature. If you can't sleep, the night views are absolutely amazing, and providing the clarity holds, the views during the day extend as far as Sakhalin. There is severe erosion on the sections between the mountain hut and the summit, especially around the ninth station, and rockslides sometimes occur after heavy rain, so hike with care.

If you don't feel like hiking to the summit, several enjoyable hikes are less strenuous.

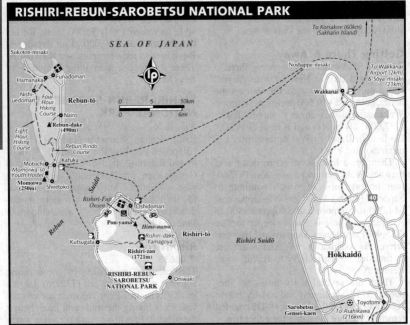

RISHIRI-REBUN-SAROBETSU NATIONAL PARK

One of these follows the trail from Oshidomari for an hour past the Hokuroku Camping Ground towards the summit, but veers left in thick forest, about 10 minutes after reaching a group of A-frame chalets at the end of a paved road. In 1¾ hours, this trail leads to Hime-numa, with the option of a 30-minute side trip to Pon-yama. From Hime-numa, it's 6km to Oshidomari along Rte 108.

Rishiri-Fuji Onsen (☎ 2-2388; admission ¥400; open 11am-9pm daily May-Oct, 11am-9.30pm daily July & Aug, noon-9pm daily Nov-Apr except 1st & 3rd Mon each month) makes the most of its plain building, with Jacuzzis, mountain-view rotemburo, saunas and indoor baths. The onsen is a 30-minute walk from Oshidomari en route to the camping ground and trailhead for Rishiri-zan. A couple of buses a day (¥150, 10 minutes) from Oshidomari also pass the onsen.

Places to Stay Most lodgings are in Oshidomari and Kutsugata. In July and August, it's wise to book well in advance.

Places to Stay – Budget Rishiri-tō has five **camping grounds**. All are open from approximately May to October and are free unless you rent a tent or cabin.

Hokuroku Camping Ground (☎ 2-2394; cabins ¥2500) is quite popular with hikers. It's near the trailhead for the Oshidomari route up to Rishiri-zan. From Rishiri-Fuji Onsen it's about a 45-minute walk.

Kutsugata-shinrin-kōen camping ground (☎ 4-2349; cabins ¥2300-2500) has also received good reviews. It's about 25 minutes' walk from the ferry terminal, through the town centre; turn right at the traffic light, and if you reach the fire station you've gone too far.

There's also a **camping ground** by the Kutsugata ferry terminal, but it's known for being unpleasantly windy.

Rishiri Green Hill Youth Hostel (☎ 2-2507, fax 2-2383; beds ¥2900; open Mar-Sept) is a about a 25-minute walk from Oshidomari-kō port, or a short bus ride (¥150) to the Gurīn-Hiru-Yūsu-Hosuterumae stop. The staff will be able to provide information on hiking Rishiri-zan, and you will find that bicycles are available for rent.

Places to Stay – Mid-Range On the dock across from the ferry pier is **Pension Misaki** (☎ 2-1659, fax 2-2176; rooms per person with 2 meals ¥7500) – turn right and go around the inlet, about five minutes. This informal place has harbour-view Japanese rooms and a Japanese bath.

Minshuku Kutsugata-sō (☎ 4-2038; rooms per person with 2 meals ¥7000), in Kutsugata, offers simple lodgings and honest value, under 10 minutes' walk from the ferry pier and near the town's traffic light.

Places to Stay – Top End Within sight of the Oshidomari ferry terminal, the new **Rishiri Fuji Kankō Hotel** (☎ 2-1531, fax 2-1897; rooms per person with 2 meals peak/off-peak ¥15,000/10,000) has Japanese rooms with private and onsen-fed common bath. It's often busy with bus tours, though at least you know it's the real deal.

Places to Eat Most lodgings specialise in seafood meals, and the stall **Aji-no-Ichiba** (☎ 2-1105; open end June–Aug) serves seafood straight from the local fishing boats to your mouth, sometimes without any cooking in between. Live uni (sea urchin) costs ¥500. You can obtain it from the small, nondescript building next to a warehouse; exit to the right from the Oshidomari ferry terminal.

Getting There & Away From Rishiri there are one or two flights a day to Wakkanai (¥8340, 20 minutes) and Sapporo (¥17,000, 50 minutes). The island bus runs by the airport only once a day from Oshidomari (¥310, 20 minutes) or Kutsugata-kō port (¥520, 25 minutes). A taxi from the airport to Oshidomari costs ¥1500.

For details of ferry services from Oshidomari and Kutsugata to Kafuka on Rebun-tō and Wakkanai, see the Wakkanai Getting There & Away section.

Getting Around Several buses a day run in both directions around the island's perimeter. Buses originating in Kutsugata (¥2200) complete a clockwise circuit in 1¾ hours. Counter-clockwise, the trip from Oshidomari to Kutsugata costs ¥730 and takes 30 to 50 minutes, depending on whether the bus stops at the onsen and/or the airport.

Cycling is a great way to get around the island, and bicycles can be rented at the youth hostel and shops near the Oshidomari ferry terminal. You can complete a leisurely circuit (56km) of the island in about five to seven hours. There is also a 29km cycling path running through woods and coastal plain from Oshidomari past Kutsugata.

Rebun-tō 礼文島
☎ 01638

In contrast to the conical height of its neighbour, Rebun-tō (82 sq km) is a low, arrow-shaped island that has one major road down its east coast. The main attractions of the island are the hiking trails. Its terrain is more varied than that of Rishiri, making Rebun a better place if you want to spend several days trying different hiking routes and distances. Between late May and early September, the island's alpine flowers – over 300 species – pull out all the stops for a floral extravaganza: a memorable experience. Unfortunately, almost every species of tour group seems to be on the island at this time as well.

Kafuka (also known locally as 'Kabuka') is the main community and port in southern Rebun. There is a **tourist information counter** (☎ 6-2655; open 8am-5pm daily Apr-mid-Oct; ☎ 6-1001 mid-Oct–Mar) at the Kafuka ferry terminal that can provide a few maps and help book accommodation. Other useful points on the island include Sukoton-misaki and Funadomari in the north, Momoiwa to the west and Shiretoko to the south.

Hiking The classic hike down the western coast is known as the **hachijikan haikingu kōsu** (eight-hour hiking course). It's a marvellous excursion across grassy cliff tops, fields of dwarf bamboo, forests of conifers, deserted, rocky beaches and remote harbours with clusters of fishing shacks and racks of seaweed.

There doesn't seem to be much sense in following the example of many Japanese hikers who turn it into an endurance race. If you have the extra day, it may be more enjoyable to break the hike into two sections.

The hike starts at Sukoton-misaki on the northwestern tip, heads generally southward and ends along the Rebun Rindo (Rebun forest road) course, northwest of Kafuka. Although the hike is not death-defying, it has some tricky stretches, mostly in the southern half, including steep slopes of loose scree and several kilometres of boulder-hopping along beaches, which can become very nasty or even shut down in the unpredictable weather of these northern regions. Much of the trail is several hours away from human habitation, and for the most part, those who slip off a cliff or twist an ankle will require rescue by boat; this is the reason group hiking is encouraged. Momoiwa-sō Youth Hostel martials hikers into groups.

A **yojikan haiking kōsu** (four-hour hiking course) also starts at Sukoton-misaki, runs south to Nishi-uedomari and then heads northeast to the bus stop at Hamanaka

You can follow the trails in either direction, but most people seem to hike from Sukoton-misaki. Momoiwa-sō Youth Hostel and other places to stay on the island can provide information on hiking and transport to trailheads.

Another popular hike is from Nairo, halfway down the east coast, to the top of Rebun-dake. The peak is a tiddler at 490m, but it's a pleasant 3½-hour return hike. Near the southern tip of the island, there is a trail starting near Kafuka, running by the Momo-iwa (Peach Rock, 249.5m) observation point and down to the lighthouse at Shiretoko-misaki.

Whichever hike you take, you'll need proper footwear, warm clothes and some form of raingear. Do *not* drink the water from the streams: during the 1930s, foxes were introduced from the Kurile Islands (Russia), and their faeces now contaminate the streams.

Places to Stay There are many *minshuku* and ryokan, a couple of hotels, a Toho inn and a youth hostel on the island. If you phone ahead, most of the more remote places will arrange for you to be picked up at the port.

Places to Stay – Budget There is a good **camping ground** (camp sites ¥300) in a pretty lakeside setting at Funadomari on the island's north side.

Momoiwa-sō Youth Hostel (☎/fax 6-1421; beds ¥2800; open June-Sept) has a hard-earned reputation as one of Japan's craziest youth hostels: group hiking by day and camp songs until lights-out at 10pm. It's close to some trailheads, with good views out to sea and of nearby Momo-iwa. There are crowded Japanese-style dorms and much nicer 2nd-floor bunks – which gender gets which depends on who is there in greater numbers. The staff always have someone waiting when ferries dock – call ahead for reservations and look out for the enthusiastic guys vigorously waving the Momoiwa-sō banner and screaming, *okaeri nasai* (Welcome home!). From Kafuka-kō there are also a few buses bound for Motochi that pass the Yūsu-mae stop after about 15 minutes. From there it's a seven-minute walk downhill to the hostel.

If you don't love the meals, a short walk away is **Ben and Joe** *(mains ¥500-680; open 7am-5pm daily)*, a funky, folksy café with cheesecake, real coffee and curry rice.

Places to Stay – Mid-Range A member of the Toho network, **Field Inn Seikan-sō** *(☎ 7-2818; dorm beds with 2 meals ¥5500; open May-Oct)* is a more peaceful alternative to Momoiwa-sō and gets good reviews from travellers. On the northern side of the island, it's next to one of the eight-hour hiking-course trailheads. Buses from Kafuka-kō stop right in front of the inn before continuing to Sukoton-misaki, but staff will come and pick you up at the port if you phone ahead.

Kaachan Yado *(☎ 6-1406, fax 6-2188; rooms per person with 2 meals ¥8000)*, meaning 'Mum's Place', receives enthusiastic reports from travellers for its warmth and, interestingly, its toilets. It's in Shiretoko.

Minshuku Shiretoko *(☎/fax 6-1335; rooms per person with 2 meals ¥8000)*, up the street, is a clean, friendly place; some rooms have great views across the water to Rishiri-zan.

Places to Stay – Top End In northern Kafuka, **Nature Inn Hanashin** *(☎ 6-1648, fax 6-1608; rooms per person with 2 meals ¥10,800)* is a popular, well-kept place in a former youth hostel – hence, most rooms do not have private facilities. It's about 25 minutes on foot from Kafuka-kō. You could also take a bus bound for Sukoton-misaki or Nishi-uedomari and get off after five minutes at another Yūsu-mae bus stop (not to be confused with the one by Momoiwa-sō Youth Hostel).

Getting There & Away From Wakkanai there are one or two flights a day to Rebun-tō (¥9930, 20 minutes). The closest bus stop to the airport is Kūkō-shita, about a 15-minute walk from the terminal. A taxi to Kafuka costs ¥5500.

For details of the boat service between Wakkanai, Kafuka, Oshidomari and Kutsugata, on Rishiri-tō, see the Wakkanai Getting There & Away section.

Getting Around Most of the time you'll be getting around the island on foot, though some lodgings will help with transport arrangements on arrival or departure. The main bus service follows the island's one major road from Kafuka in the south to Sukoton-misaki in the north (¥1180, 70 minutes). En route it passes the Kūkō-shita (airport) bus stop (¥830) and Funadomari (¥900).

Some buses turn off after Funadomari and head to Nishi-uedomari. Buses run on this route up to six times a day: four go to Sukoton-misaki, two to Nishi-uedomari.

There are also three to five buses a day from Kafuka to Shiretoko (¥300, 13 minutes) or Motochi via Yūsu-mae (¥440, 16 minutes).

All services are sharply reduced from November to April. Be sure to pick up a copy of the island's bus timetable from the information counter at the Kafuka ferry terminal.

Some lodgings rent bicycles, and scooters and cars can be rented near the Kafuka ferry terminal. As a last resort, some locals recommend hitchhiking.

Unusual Hokkaidō Events

- Sapporo's Yuki Matsuri (Snow Festival)
- The Women's Sumō National Championship (Onna-zumō Senshuken Taikai) in Kawayu Onsen
- Orochon-no-Hi (Fire Festival) in Abashiri
- Japan Cup National Dogsled Races in Wakkanai
- The Kyōkoku Hi Matsuri (Fire Festival) at Sōunkyō Onsen
- Heso Matsuri (Navel Festival) in Furano

HOKKAIDŌ

Daisetsuzan National Park & Environs

大雪山国立公園

Sometimes spelled 'Taisetsuzan', this park is Japan's largest national park (2309 sq km), consisting of several mountain groups, volcanoes, hot springs, lakes and forests. It also includes Asahi-dake, which at 2290m is Hokkaidō's highest peak. The park is spectacular hiking and skiing territory, but note that a few days are needed to get away from tourist areas. If you have limited time,

Asahidake Onsen is a good spot for a quick look at the park. Tokachidake Onsen is more remote and good for those wanting to escape the crowds (a key consideration in summer and early autumn). Only a couple of hikes on the more well-trodden trails have been mentioned here, but there are many more routes leading to more remote regions if you have several days, or even a week, to spare.

Buses run to the interior of the park from Asahikawa, Furano and Biei in the west, Kamikawa in the north, Kitami in the east and Obihiro in the south. Hiking and other information with some English-language text is available at tourist information offices in the larger towns and destinations. Also look for *Daisetsuzan Attack* (¥1200), a very detailed map of the park in Japanese.

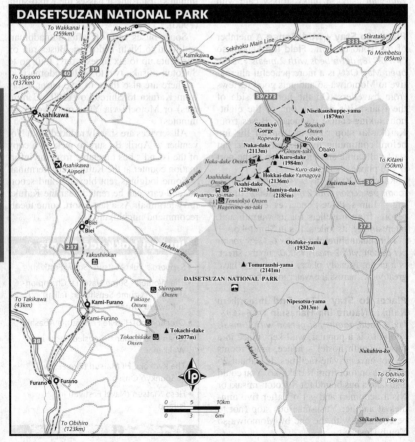

DAISETSUZAN NATIONAL PARK

FURANO 富良野
☏ 0167

The geographical centre of Hokkaidō, marked by, among other things, the **Heso Matsuri** (Navel Festival) in late July, Furano is an agricultural community surrounded by one of Japan's most famous ski resorts, with over a dozen ski lifts and excellent facilities for powder skiing.

Information

Outside Furano station are two **information offices** (☏ 23-3388; open 9am-6pm daily). Across from the station you can rent **bicycles** for ¥200 an hour.

Things to See & Do

If you're not hitting the slopes (or driving), the **Furano Wine Factory** (☏ 22-3242; open 9am-6pm daily June-Oct, 9am-4.30pm daily Nov-May), about 4km northwest of the station, offers a walk-through peek at the process; a **Grape Juice Factory** (☏ 23-3033; open 9am-5pm daily June-Sept) is about 1.5km away. Eager gourmands could also visit the **Furano Cheese Factory** (☏ 23-1156; open 9am-5pm daily May-Oct, 9am-4pm Tues-Sun Nov-Apr, closed 1st & 3rd Sat each month Nov-Apr) across town, which includes the **Ice Milk Factory** (open May-Oct). Admission to all factories is free, and – except at the ice milk factory – you get free samples. Signage at all factories is in Japanese only.

Between June and September buses run infrequently from the station to most local attractions, including the famous, busy lavender fields at **Farm Tomita** (☏ 39-3939; admission free; open 8.30am-6pm daily late Apr–Sept, hours vary Oct–late April), 10km from Furano near Naka-Furano station or the summer-only Lavender Field station; lavender-flavoured soft ice cream costs ¥250 a cone.

Places to Stay

There are plenty of *minshuku*, ryokan, hotels and pensions, but if you're planning a winter ski trip to Furano, it's best to make bookings through a travel agent, who will probably get you better rates for accommodation (and sometimes for train fares) than you would get if you booked directly.

Furano Youth Hostel (☏ 44-4441, fax 44-4521; w www4.ocn.ne.jp/~furanoyh; rooms per person ¥3200) is a rustic red contemporary farmhouse with a big deck. It's five minutes' walk from Naka-Furano station.

Rokugō Furarin Youth Hostel (☏ 29-2172; rooms per person ¥3200) has, according to some travellers, a real 'at home' atmosphere. From Furano station, it's a 15-minute bus ride to the terminus at Rokugō, but free pick-up is available from Furano station if you phone ahead.

Sumire Ryokan (☏ 23-4767; rooms per person with/without 2 meals ¥6000/4000) is an informal, traditional standby with cats and laundry machines, five minutes on foot from Furano station.

Getting There & Away

On the JR Furano line, *kaisoku* trains from Asahikawa reach Furano in 1¼ hours (¥1040), some continuing as far as Obihiro (¥2420) in another two hours. Frequent local trains along this line stop at Kami-Furano (¥350, 20 minutes) and Biei (¥620, 40 minutes). To Sapporo are direct *tokkyū* trains (¥4170), or you can pay ¥3520 instead if you change in Takikawa.

Fairly frequent buses connect Furano with Asahikawa (¥860, 1½ hours), via Biei, and Sapporo (¥2100, 2½ hours).

BIEI 美瑛
☏ 0166

With the dramatic Daisetsuzan mountains as a backdrop, this picturesque town is an artists' and nature-lovers' mecca. Distances among lodgings and attractions are so great – separated by expansive fields of lavender, poppies (attracting thousands of visitors in late June and early July) and produce (the rest of summer) – that you may wonder whether you've left Japan. Biei lends itself to lazy days cycling dirt roads, lingering at art galleries and coffee shops, or, in winter, cross-country skiing and snowshoeing.

Information

The **tourist information building** (☏ 92-4378; open 8.30am-7pm daily May-Oct, 8.30am-5pm daily Nov-Apr) is outside Biei station. Staff here and at the youth hostels can supply you with cycling maps and *Hokkaidō Town of Hills Biei*, which contains an English-language map and details of local sights, outdoor pursuits and art classes. Several shops around the station offer **bicycle rental** at reasonable prices. Be careful to keep to the dirt roads and paths and don't go trampling through the fields, as local farmers depend upon the crops.

Things to See

A highlight of any visit to Biei is **Takushinkan** (☎ 92-3355; open 9am-5pm daily May-Oct, 10am-4pm daily Nov-Apr) a lovely museum dedicated to the internationally known photographer Shinzō Maeda (1922–98). His arresting photos of the Tokachi area are famous for their vibrant and unusual colour and composition. The museum is a 10km ride from Biei in the direction of Bibaushi. Ask around for directions to other galleries.

Places to Stay

Many Biei lodgings are set amid idyllic farm fields with mountain views; they're far from public transport, but most will arrange for pick-up from Biei station with a day's notice (and reservation).

Biei Potato-no-Oka Youth Hostel (☎ 92-3255, fax 92-3254; e potato@dm.mbn.or.jp; dorm beds with/without 2 meals ¥4800/3200) has warm and friendly staff (some English-speaking). Accommodation is in comfortable four-person bunk-bed dorms, and meals are excellent. There are loads of activities, including nightly 'guidance' sessions for cyclists and hikers, star-gazing and cross-country skiing. Bikes are available for rent, too.

Hoshi-no-Anne (☎ 92-4993; dorm beds with 2 meals ¥5000; open late Apr-early Nov, late Dec-Feb) is a Toho network inn. It's like a cosy farmhouse with Western-style accommodation amid rolling fields. During off-peak times, private rooms may be available for ¥7000 per person. There are occasional mid-season closures, so reserve ahead.

Gardening House Ermitage (☎ 92-0991, fax 92-0990; e erumi@lilac.hokkai.net; rooms per person with 2 meals from ¥10,500) is in a similar setting, with private rooms and a more sophisticated atmosphere. Its Western-style rooms are lovely, and the aromas coming from the kitchen made us want to stay longer.

Bibaushi Liberty Youth Hostel (☎ 95-2141, fax 95-2142; e bibaushi@hokkai.or.jp; dorm beds ¥3200), visible from Bibaushi station, one stop south of Biei, is one place that *is* accessible by public transport. This attractive white house is set among cof-fee shops and galleries. In winter it offers cross-country skiing and snowshoeing.

Getting There & Away

Biei is on the JR Furano line between Asahikawa (futsū ¥530, 30 minutes) and Furano (¥620, 40 minutes). From near Biei station, there are frequent buses to Asahikawa (¥570, 50 minutes).

TOKACHIDAKE, FUKIAGE & SHIROGANE ONSENS

十勝岳・吹上温泉・白金温泉

Northeast of Furano, these remote hot-spring villages are good crowd-free bases for hiking and skiing. You can climb the peak **Tokachi-dake** (2077m) in a day; some trails extend as far as Tenninkyō Onsen or the peak Asahidake, though these require three or four days of hiking. About 3km from Tokachidake Onsen, on the road to Shirogane Onsen, Fukiage Onsen has a free, public *rotemburo* overlooking a gorge, though locals warn of theft from cars.

Places to Stay

Tokachidake Onsen has just a few lodgings, none particularly cheap.

Kamihoro-sō (☎ 0167-45-2970, fax 45-2226; rooms per person with 2 meals from ¥8800) has large Japanese-style rooms and pleasant hot-spring baths.

Hakugin-sō (☎ 0167-45-4126/3251, fax 0167-45-6634; dorm beds ¥2600) is crisp and clean, and offers dormitory-style accommodation and its own beautiful baths (¥600 without overnight stay; open 10am to 9pm). Kitchen facilities are available but no meals are served. Its camping ground charges ¥500 per tent. It's a few hundred metres from Fukiage Onsen's public *rotemburo*.

Kokuminshukusha Shirakaba-sō (☎ 0166-94-3344; rooms per person ¥2550), at Shirogane Onsen, is inexpensive, kind of down-trodden and serves no meals, though rates include access to the hot-spring bath.

Hoshi-no-Akari-ya (☎/fax 0166-94-3535; rooms per person with 2 meals peak/off-peak from ¥8000/7000), nearby, is a brand-new pension, with comfortable Japanese-style rooms and its own hot-spring bath.

Shirogane Onsen Hotel (☎ 0166-94-3333, fax 0166-94-3014; rooms per person with 2 meals from ¥10,000) is the area's up-scale choice, with generous Japanese-style rooms and hot-spring baths overlooking a gorge.

There are two **camping grounds** *(tent rental ¥350; open June-Oct)* at Shirogane Onsen. You can pitch your own tent for ¥250.

Getting There & Away
From Kami-Furano station, it's a 45-minute bus ride to Tokachidake Onsen (¥490, up to three a day). Buses to Shirogane Onsen leave from Biei up to five times a day (¥600, 30 minutes). There are also up to four direct buses a day to Shirogane Onsen from Asahikawa (¥1100, 1¼ hours).

ASAHIDAKE ONSEN 旭岳鴛泉
☎ 0166
This cosy, forested hot-springs resort consists of some 10 mostly small inns at the foot of **Asahi-dake** (2290m). At the end of the road, a cable car runs to within easy hiking distance of the peak. Though Asahidake Onsen is not overdeveloped, it can become quite crowded, particularly during autumn. Sometimes transport there is – get this – free.

Hiking
There are dozens of hiking options in this region. The **Asahidake Visitor Centre** *(☎ 97-2153; e visitor.center@town.higashikawa.Hokkaidō.jp; open 9am-5pm daily June-Oct, 10am-4pm Tues-Sun Nov-May)* has great contour maps that the helpful staff will mark with the latest trail conditions.

One popular hike follows trails from the Asahidake ropeway (cable car; ☎ 68-9111) via several peaks to **Sōunkyō Onsen** – allow seven to eight hours, plus 2½ hours if the ropeway is not in operation. Take warm clothing, appropriate footwear, and sufficient food and drink. Costs for adults are one way/return ¥1500/2800 from July to mid-October or ¥1000/1800 from mid-October to June; there's a special rates for skiers. It operates 6am to 7pm from late June to August; shorter hours for the rest of the year. It's closed late May, mid-November to early December and during high winds.

From the top of the ropeway, it takes 1½ hours to climb along a ridge overlooking steaming, volcanic vents to reach the peak of Asahi-dake. From there, it's a one-hour hike to the trail junction at Mamiya-dake

(2185m) for the northern and southern routes leading to Sōunkyō: the southern is more scenic, but the northern is usually recommended for less snow and better trails.

For the northern route, turn left at the junction and hike over Mamiya-dake and Naka-dake (2113m, two hours) to where the trail rejoins with the southern route at Kuro-dake Yamagoya (mountain hut). For the southern route, turn right at the original junction and continue via Hokkai-dake (2136m, 45 minutes) and **Kuro-dake Ishimuro** (another hour) until you come to Kuro-dake Yamagoya.

From the mountain hut, it's 30 minutes' walk to the peak of **Kuro-dake** (1984m), and then a steep descent (40 minutes) to the top station of the Sōunkyō Onsen chairlift. The lift takes 15 minutes to connect with a cable car that whisks you down to Sōunkyō Onsen in seven minutes.

There are *rotemburo* off the northern route at **Naka-dake Onsen**; branch left at Nakadake-bunki just before ascending Naka-dake. Do *not* enter Yudoku Onsen – it's poisonous.

From Asahidake Onsen there's also a 5.5km trail leading through the forest in about two hours to **Tenninkyō Onsen**, a small hot-springs resort with a scenic gorge and the beautiful **Hagoromo-no-taki** (Angels' Robe Waterfall).

The region is also popular for cross-country skiing.

Places to Stay
Daisetsuzan Shirakaba-sō *(☎ 97-2246, fax 97-2247; hostel beds ¥4800, hotel beds ¥6500, both with 2 meals)* is both youth hostel and ryokan. It is very handsome and features a large lodge and a small log cabin, with Japanese- and Western-style rooms and indoor and outdoor hot-springs baths. As well, you can save some money by preparing your own meals in the small kitchen.

Lodge Nutapukaushipe *(aka Lodge Nutapu; ☎/fax 97-2150; rooms per person with 2 meals ¥7000)*, next door, is cosy and hand-hewn from logs and stone, including the riverside indoor and outdoor baths (day use ¥500). Meals are wholesome, and the lodge is non smoking.

By bus from Asahikawa, get off at the Kyampu-jō-mae stop for these lodgings.

HOKKAIDŌ

Getting There & Away

It's hard to believe, but between 15 October and 15 June buses from Asahikawa to Tenninkyō Onsen and Asahidake Onsen are free. Even in high season, the ride up costs ¥1320, but if you spend more than ¥2000 at Asahidake Onsen (including lodging; save your receipts if you don't spend it all in one place), you can get a coupon for a free ride back. Buses run twice a day (three or four times a day from mid-June to October) from Asahikawa station bus stop No 4 and take one hour to Tenninkyō Onsen – another 30 minutes to Asahidake Onsen. The last bus from Asahikawa is at 3.10pm and the last bus leaves Asahidake Onsen at 5pm (first bus from Asahidake Onsen is at 9am). Between Asahidake Onsen and Tenninkyō Onsen, buses are always free.

SŌUNKYŌ ONSEN 層雲峡温泉
☎ 01658

Sōunkyō Onsen is a gateway for forays into the interior of the park as well as the gorge, Sōunkyō. Although the town once possessed a degree of charm, it has become an aggressive, cutesy, overpriced resort and many travellers leave disappointed; hikers may be better off starting at Asahidake Onsen.

The **tourist information office** (☎ 5-3350, fax 5-3841; open 10.30am-5pm daily), next to the bus station, has several maps and English-language pamphlets. Its booking service may be useful if you arrive at peak times. Just up the hill, **mountain-bike rental** is available for around ¥2000/day. Next to the ropeway (cable car) terminus, the park **visitor centre** (☎ 9-4400; open 9am-5pm Tues-Sun) can provide information on park conditions.

After a hard day of cycling or hiking, **Kurodake-no-yu** (admission ¥600; open 10am-6pm daily May-Oct, 10am-6pm Thur-Tues Nov-Apr) offers handsome hot-springs baths (including rotemburo), on the town's main pedestrian street. You can also soothe your aching dogs in the free **ashi-no-yu** (foot bath), next to the Ginsenkaku Hotel.

Sōunkyō 層雲峡

This rather tame gorge stretches for about 8km beyond Sōunkyō Onsen and is renowned for its waterfalls – **Ryūsei-no-taki** (Shooting Stars Falls) and **Ginga-no-taki** (Milky Way Falls) are the main ones – and for two sections of perpendicular rock columns that give an enclosed feeling – hence their names of **Ōbako** (Big Box) and **Kobako** (Little Box).

Until recently, it was possible to walk the entire 8km, but the riverside foot/bike path collapsed and may not be rebuilt. The view from the road, meanwhile, is restricted by several kilometres of tunnels through which biking is hazardous – emphatically not recommended. Ask at the tourist office for current status. One bus runs daily to Ōbako (¥350, 35 minutes) and returns about 30 minutes later.

Hiking

The combination of a ropeway (cable car; ☎ 5-3031) provides fast access to **Kuro-dake** for hikers and sightseers. One way/return on the ropeway costs ¥900/1650 and on the chairlift ¥400/600. Hours of operation vary seasonally (8am to 7pm in July and August, closed intermittently in winter).

In fair weather, one popular hike goes to **Asahi-dake** from either Sōunkyō Onsen or Asahidake Onsen – see the Asahidake Onsen section earlier for details. You can arrange to leave your baggage at either end and pick it up later or simply restrict your baggage to the minimum required for an overnight stay. Better yet, take advantage of the coin lockers inside Asahikawa station before heading into the park. You could also do simple day hikes from the top of the Sōunkyō lift station to nearby peaks.

There is one bus a day to the trailhead for **Aka-dake** (2078m) at Ginsen-dai. The bus leaves Sōunkyō Onsen at 7.35am and returns from Ginsen-dai at 2.15pm (¥800, one hour), leaving you plenty of time for your ascent and descent.

Special Events

In February and early March, the **Hyōbaku Matsuri** (Ice-Waterfall Festival), features ice sculptures, tunnels and domes, some lit up. On the last Saturday in July, the **Kyōkoku Hi Matsuri** (Kyōkoku Fire Festival) is meant to purify the hot springs and appease the mountain and fire deities. There are performances of traditional Ainu owl dances and drumming, climaxing with archers shooting flaming arrows into the gorge.

O-Akan-dake and Me-Akan-dake viewed from Daisetsuzan National Park, Hokkaidō

Rishiri-tō viewed from the Rebun-dake trail, Hokkaidō

Fields outside Biei, Hokkaidō

Fishing nets, Hokkaidō

Sōya-misaki, Wakkanai, Hokkaidō

Lavender farm, Kami-Furano, Hokkaidō

Places to Stay

Sōunkyō Youth Hostel (☎ 5-3418; beds ¥2800; open June-Oct) is dwarfed by the Prince and Taisetsuzan hotels, about a 10-minute walk uphill from the bus station. The hostel, with mostly bunk-bed accommodation, has information on trails in the park, organises hikes and rents out gear for braving the elements.

Minshuku Midori (☎ 5-3315; rooms per person with 2 meals ¥6500), on the main pedestrian street, is tiny and creaky. It has clean Japanese-style rooms and bathing a few doors down at Kurodake-no-yu.

Most of the high-end hotels are ugly and hulking, but across from Minshuku Midori is **Ginsenkaku** (☎ 5-3003, toll-free 0120-493-800, fax 5-3121; e info@ginsenkaku.com; rooms per person with 2 meals peak/off-peak from ¥15,000/8000). This is a very professional operation that has some English-speaking staff, Japanese-style rooms with full facilities, and nice common baths, including rotemburo.

Getting There & Away

Buses from Sōunkyō Onsen run approximately hourly via JR Kamikawa station to Asahikawa (¥1900, two hours) – rail pass holders can save money by transferring to the bus at Kamikawa (¥770). There are also up to four buses a day direct to Kitami (¥2500, two hours), where you can transfer for connections to Bihoro (¥530, 30 minutes) or Abashiri (¥1040, one hour). From May to October, there are up to three buses a day from Bihoro to Kawayu Onsen in Akan National Park (¥2690, two to 2¾ hours).

From Sōunkyō Onsen there are two buses a day to Kushiro (¥4790, five hours) via Akan Kohan (¥3260, 3¼ hours) in Akan National Park. There are also two buses a day to Obihiro (¥2200, 2¼ hours) that follow a scenic route via Nukabira-ko.

Dō-tō (Eastern Hokkaidō) 道東

ABASHIRI 網走
☎ 0152 • pop 43,000

Nestled against a mountain topped with several museums, Abashiri is a good hub for access to Shiretoko-hantō. Each winter ice

floes from Russia seal off Abashiri's harbour in late January or early February and expand until March when up to 80% of the sea is ice-clogged. During this time, the **Aurora icebreaker sightseeing boats** (☎ 43-6000) depart from Abashiri-kō port for one-hour cruises (¥3000) into the Sea of Okhotsk. Cruises depart four to six times a day.

Information

The **tourist information office** (☎ 44-5849; w www2s.biglobe.ne.jp/~abashiri/index.html; open 9am-5pm daily) outside Abashiri station has the excellent Okhotsk Abashiri Tourist Guide, maps and discount coupons for local attractions.

Things to See

Tento-zan, the mountain rising above central Abashiri, also doubles as a sprawling park with some smart museums. The **Abashiri Prison Museum** (☎ 45-2411; admission ¥1050; open 8am-6pm daily Apr-Oct, 9am-5pm Nov-Mar) is actually a Meiji-era prison, and is best known for its radial five-winged design and for a popular Japanese TV series set there.

Atop Tento-zan, there's a lookout point and the **Okhotsk Ryūhyō Museum** (Museum of Ice Floes), which you can safely skip. But don't miss the **Hokkaidō Museum of Northern Peoples** (☎ 45-3888; admission ¥300; open 9.30am-4.30pm Tues-Sun), a short walk downhill, which has fascinating exhibits and documentary videos on the culture of indigenous tribes of northern Eurasia and North America.

Special Events

On the last Saturday in July is **Orochon-no-Hi**, a fire festival derived from shamanistic ceremonial rites of the indigenous Gilyak people, who once lived in the Abashiri area.

Places to Stay

Abashiri Gensei-kaen Youth Hostel (☎/fax 46-2630; w http://sapporo/cool.ne.jp/genseikaen; beds ¥3050; open mid-Jan–mid-Nov, closed last part of April) is in the middle of a wildflower preserve. When the weather is good, it offers great views across the lake to Shari-dake and Shiretoko-hantō. The friendly staff rent bicycles and advise on outings. The hostel is 800m from Kitahama station, four stops east of Abashiri (¥230). Turn left outside the station, walk past the second stoplight and turn right at the 'Lake Toufutsu' sign, then follow the youth hostel signs.

Minshuku Hokui 44 (☎ 44-4325, fax 45-2682; beds ¥4300), a member of the Toho network, offers dormitory-style accommodation that's a bit cramped, but rates include two home-cooked meals and free admission (and a lift) to the nearby luxury *onsen* hotel. The inn is 20 minutes on foot west of the station, but if you phone ahead, a member of the family will pick you up. No English is spoken.

Hotel Shinbashi (☎ 43-4307, fax 45-2091; singles/twins ¥6000/10,000) is a classy place opposite Abashiri station, with both Japanese- and Western-style rooms (some without private facilities).

Places to Eat

Remontei (think 'lemon tea'; ☎ 44-4277; mains ¥700-1100) is a snug place only steps from the station. It serves pizza, curries, pilafs and spaghetti, and it's a good place to meet Japanese travellers.

Abashiri Beer Kan (☎ 45-5100; dishes ¥300-980) is a microbrewery with a rotating menu that includes both Western and Asian flavours. From the station it's about 10 minutes' walk to the right and across the street, overlooking the river.

Getting There & Away

Memanbetsu airport links Abashiri with Sapporo, Fukuoka, Nagoya, Osaka and Tokyo. Airport buses (¥750, 30 minutes) are approximately timed to flights and run from the bus station via Abashiri station (they're about 1km apart) to the airport.

Abashiri is the terminus for the JR Sekihoku main line, which runs across the centre of Hokkaidō to Asahikawa (*tokkyū* ¥7240, 3¾ hours). Local trains along the same route stop at Bihoro (¥530, 30 minutes) and Kitami (¥1040, 1¼ hours). From May to October, there are up to three buses a day from Bihoro to Kawayu Onsen in Akan National Park (¥2690, two to 2¾ hours). From Kitami you can catch buses to Sōunkyō Onsen in Daisetsuzan National Park (¥2500, two hours).

Abashiri is also the terminus for the JR Senmō main line, which runs east to Shiretoko-Shari station (*futsū*, ¥810, 45 minutes) then turns south to Kushiro. There is one direct bus a day from Abashiri station to Shari (¥1120, 65 minutes), though there are four other buses a day bound for 18-Sen that connect with onward buses to Shari.

Direct buses from Abashiri to Sapporo leave from the bus terminal, a 10-minute bus ride east of Abashiri station (¥6210, six hours). Between June and mid-October there are three buses from Memanbetsu airport via Abashiri to Utoro in Shiretoko National Park (¥2800, 2¼ hours).

Renting a car is recommended if you really want to explore Shiretoko and Akan national parks; there are car-rental offices in town and at the airport.

Getting Around

A convenient tourist loop bus (9am to 4pm, hourly) stops at the train station, the bus terminal and all the major sights on Tento-zan. A one-day pass costs ¥900 and entitles you to discounted admission to many of the sights.

Bicycles can be rented at the youth hostel and near Abashiri station.

AKAN NATIONAL PARK
阿寒国立公園

This large park (905 sq km) contains several volcanic peaks, some large caldera lakes and extensive forests. The gorgeous scenery attracts some 6.6 million visitors a year, but in late spring and early autumn the crowds thin out, giving you ample opportunity to actually commune with nature rather than tour groups. There aren't many extended hikes, but there are several interesting day-hike options.

The main gateways on the fringe of the park are Abashiri and Bihoro in the north and Kushiro in the south. The major centres inside the park are the towns of Kawayu Onsen in the northeast and Akan Kohan in the southwest. The small town of Teshikaga (aka Mashū Onsen) lies outside the park proper, but is a useful transport hub.

The only efficient transport in the park is provided by Akan Bus Company sightseeing buses. The running recorded commentary gets a bit tiresome, but the ride brings you past all the major sights and through beautiful scenery – on clear days there are outstanding views of the park's mountains and lakes. Abashiri would be a convenient place to rent a car, giving you the option of adding a side trip to Shiretoko National Park as well.

Kawayu Onsen 川湯温泉
☎ 01548

This pleasant little hot-springs resort, the sort of place where people walk around in their *yukata* (cotton robes) on warm nights, is a convenient base for visiting the nearby sights of Kusshero-ko, Iō-zan and Mashū-ko. The town itself is centred on a small park and surrounded by forest.

The **tourist information office** (☎ 3-2255, fax 3-2670; e kawayuonsen@8.dion.ne.jp; open 9am-6.30pm daily June-Sept, 9am-5pm daily Oct-May) is about 10 minutes on foot down the main street from the bus station. Staff have maps of the region, including the useful English-language *Teshikaga English Guide Map*. They can also help book accommodation. Note that some locations mentioned in this section are easier reached via Mashū station in Teshikaga, where there is also a small **information counter** (☎ 2-2642; open 9am-5pm daily).

The **Kawayu Eco-Museum Center** (☎ 3-4100; open 8am-5pm Thur-Tues May-Oct, 9am-4pm Thur-Tues Nov-Apr) is a five-minute walk through the park from the bus station. English-language pamphlets with basic information on the park, as well as more detailed hiking and nature guides in Japanese, are available.

Things to See & Do Sumō fanatics can visit the **Koki Taiho Sumō Memorial Hall** (☎ 2-2924; admission ¥310; open 6.30am-9pm daily June-Sept, 9am-5pm daily Oct-May), dedicated to hometown hero and 48th sumō grand champion Koki Taiho. There's little English signage, but there's a nice collection of memorabilia and some video clips from his heyday in the 1960s. In early September, the town hosts the **Women's Sumō National Championship** (Onna-zumō Senshuken Taikai). The grand prize is an aeroplane ticket and a horse, for which, according to the rules, contestants must bring their own pick-up truck. In case you're wondering, the contestants do not wear *fundōshi* loincloths – white T-shirts and denim shorts are the usual uniform.

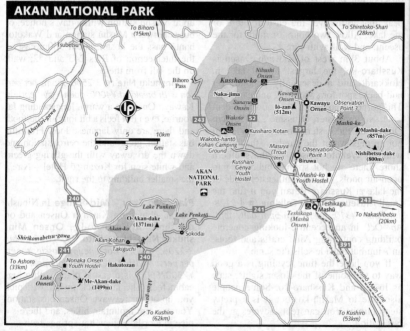

AKAN NATIONAL PARK

Just outside Kawayu Onsen is **Iō-zan** (512m), a mountain unmistakable for its distinctive smell and impressive hissing vents, billowing clouds of steam and bright yellow sulphur deposits. A beautiful nature trail leads from behind the bus station for 2.5km through dwarf pines to the mountain in about 50 minutes.

Often cited as Japan's most beautiful lake, **Mashū-ko** is about 15km southeast of Kawayu Onsen. The small isle in the centre of the lake (it's actually a lava hill rising from the lake bottom) is known to the Ainu as the Isle of the Gods, and there is certainly an unusual atmosphere to the whole lake, which is surrounded by steep rock walls that reach a height of 300m. Mashū-ko is legendary for fog, but if you are fortunate enough to visit when the lake is not wreathed in mist, the clarity of the water and its intense blue colour are quite startling – its transparency depth of over 35m was once a world record. Visitors view the lake from observation point Nos 1 (parking costs ¥410 per car) and 3 (parking free) – No 2 was eliminated during construction of the road now linking points 1 and 3. From observation point No 1 you can hike to **Mashū-dake** (857m), the craggy volcanic peak that lords over the eastern shore of the lake. Allow two hours or more for the ascent, and walk with care

About 3km west of Kawayu Onsen is **Kussharo-ko**, the largest inland lake in Hokkaidō and a deservedly popular, yet laid-back, spot for swimming and camping. This gorgeous lake even has its own resident Loch Ness monster, 'Kusshie'. At **Sunayu Onsen**, on the eastern shore, a few small hot springs warm the sand on the beach, while at **Wakoto Onsen**, on the southern shore, there are hot springs bubbling into open-air pools. On the southeastern side of the lake at **Kussharo Kotan** you'll find the small **Museum of Ainu Folklore** (☎ 4-2128; admission ¥310; open 9am-5pm daily mid-Apr–Oct) in an eccentric-looking concrete building containing Ainu crafts and tools; an Ainu hut outside sells the same.

If you have the time, cycling is a good way to see some of the closer sights, such as Iō-zan and Kussharo-ko. Some people also ride to Mashū-ko, but it is a pretty steep climb. You can rent bicycles at the bus station.

Places to Stay – Budget There are seven camping grounds in the area. **Wakoto-hantō Kohan Camping Ground** (☎ 4-2350; camp sites per person ¥400; open late Apr–mid-Oct), on the southern shore of Kussharo-ko, is one of the nicest. It has extremely basic cabins, and canoes and kayaks available for rent. Buses between Mashū station and Wakoto-hantō stop here, as do some buses from Bihoro and Kawayu Onsen.

There are two youth hostels in the area. **Mashū-ko Youth Hostel** (☎ 2-3098, fax 2-4875; ⓦ www.masyuko.co.jp; beds ¥3200; closed parts of Dec) sits like a handsome farmhouse about 5.5km south of Mashū-ko. From Mashū station, take a bus bound for Bihoro or Kawayu and get off after 10 minutes at the Yūsu-hosuteru-mae stop. If you arrive at Mashū station after 4pm, ring the hostel for a lift. The hostel organises free night hikes around the lake and has information on canoeing, dairy-farm 'school' and cross-country skiing.

The **Kussharo-Genya Youth Guesthouse** (☎/fax 4-2609; ⓦ www.gogogenya.com; beds from ¥3500; usually closed Nov, Dec & Apr) is a bit fancier than your average hostel, surrounded by farmland south of Kussharo-ko; you can rent bicycles. Staff will pick you up at Mashū station with a day's notice, or buses between Mashū station and Wakoto-hantō pass the hostel, about 500m east of the intersection of Rtes 243 and 52; walk up the hill from there.

Minshuku Nire (☎ 3-2506; rooms per person with breakfast ¥4000; open May-Sept), in Kawayu Onsen, is a warm, longstanding favourite, even if it feels a bit long-in-the-tooth and there are only Japanese loos. From the bus station, go around the petrol station and down the driveway with the glaring green-and-white sign for Kozan-sō Hotel – Nire's the smaller building to the right.

Places to Stay – Mid-Range In Nibushi Onsen, 4km from Kawayu Onsen and on the shore of Kussharo-ko, **Onsen Minshuku Nibushi-no-Sato** (☎ 3-2294, fax 3-2206; ⓦ www1.ocn.ne.jp/~kussie; rooms per person with 2 meals peak/off-peak from ¥7500/6500) is a casual place with a log-cabin feel. The laid-back owner will pick you up at the Kawayu Onsen bus station. You can rent mountain bikes, and there's a nice indoor lake-view hot-springs bath.

Masuya (aka Trout Inn; ☎ 2-5489; beds with 2 meals per person ¥5500) is located in an attractive wooden building off Rte 243, between Teshikaga and Kussharo-ko. It is a member of the Toho network, and the accommodation here is dormitory style – private rooms, when available, cost ¥6700 per person. You can go snowshoeing and cross-country skiing in winter. If you call ahead, staff will come to pick you up at Mashū station. Buses between Mashū station and Wakoto-hantō also pass nearby; you get off at the Sattomonai bus stop, and Masuya is about 10 minutes' walk down the dirt road.

Places to Stay – Top End Across from Kawayu Onsen's tourist office, **Misono Hotel** (☎ 3-2511, fax 3-2795; ⓦ www.sip.or .jp; rooms per person peak/off-peak from ¥12,000/8000) is recommended by locals, particularly for its hot-spring baths. Rooms are Japanese, Western or a combination of both, and all have in-room facilities.

Places to Eat In Kawayu Onsen, **Genpei** (☎ 3-3338; dishes ¥300-1000) is an atmospheric izakaya redolent with the aromas of robata-yaki (fresh grills) and rāmen.

Marukipune (☎ 4-2644; dishes ¥400-1500) restaurant is next door to the Museum of Ainu Folklore in Kussharo Kotan. Specialities include kotan-don (pork, egg and vegetables over rice) and howaitu rāmen ('white rāmen', noodles in milk broth); sashimi of parimomo (a local river fish) is so fresh that the head arrives in the centre of the plate – still moving. Live performances of Ainu music (¥3000) are given some Saturday nights; reservations are advised for performances.

The Great Bear (☎ 2-3830; breakfast ¥800, dinner ¥1000-1500) is the de facto dining hall for the Mashū-ko Youth Hostel, serving popular farm-fresh meals including steaks and curry rice.

Getting There & Away The JR Senmō main line runs north from Kawayu Onsen to Shiretoko-Shari (kaisoku, ¥900, 45 minutes) and south to Kushiro (kaisoku, ¥1790, 1½ hours) via Mashū station. Kawayu Onsen station is about a 10-minute bus ride from the town centre (¥280), where the bus station is located. Buses are timed to meet most trains, but you'll only have a minute or two to transfer.

From Kawayu Onsen bus station there are up to three buses a day to Bihoro (¥2690, two to 2¾ hours) and two buses a day to Kushiro (¥2810, 2½ hours). The Bihoro service runs via scenic Bihoro pass; some of these buses continue as far as Memanbestu airport. These buses also pass Nibushi, Sunayu and Wakoto Onsen en route.

Between May and October a sightseeing bus service operates four times a day from Kawayu Onsen bus station via the main sights in the park to Akan Kohan (¥3250, 2¼ hours). The bus makes stops of around 20 minutes each at Iō-zan and Mashū-ko observation point No 1. You can get off the bus at observation point No 3 after about 40 minutes (¥920), but then you'll have to wait for the next bus to continue onward. Between May and September there are also two buses to observation point No 1 from Mashū station (¥670, 25 minutes). Both services run past the stop for Mashū-ko Youth Hostel, south of the lake.

Buses between Kawayu Onsen and Mashū station cost ¥1720. Direct buses between Mashū station and Wakoto-hantō pass the turn-offs for the Trout Inn, Kussharo Genya Youth Guesthouse and the camping ground at Wakoto-hantō (¥880, 35 minutes).

Between Mashū station and Akan Kohan is a particularly scenic stretch on Rte 241, with an outstanding lookout at **Sokodai** that overlooks the lakes Penketō and Panketō.

Akan Kohan 阿寒湖畔
☎ 0154

Busy Akan Kohan has one of the largest Ainu kotan settlements on Hokkaidō, but unlike Kawayu Onsen, this somewhat garish hot-springs resort on the southern shore of pretty Akan-ko has done little to try to blend in with its surroundings.

The Ainu village is on the western side of town. At the top of the hill is the **Ainu Seikatsu Kinenkan** (☎ 67-2727; admission ¥300; open 10am-10pm daily May-Oct), basically a hut with a few Ainu items inside – not worth the price of admission if you've already visited Ainu museums elsewhere. Next door is **Onnechise** (admission ¥1000), a hall where 30-minute Ainu dance performances take place six times

HOKKAIDŌ

daily from April to October and at least once daily the rest of the year. A street of brash souvenir shops leads down toward the lake. If you're feeling overwhelmed, the nearby sedate **Akan Forest & Lake Culture Museum** (☎ 67-2001; admission ¥500; open 10am-5pm May-Oct), while not huge, has nice displays of traditional Ainu ways and the area's wildlife; congenial staff are usually on hand to explain the exhibits, run the slide show and offer you a cup of coffee.

Akan-ko itself is famous for **marimo**, fuzzballs of algae that many Japanese find irresistibly *kawaii* (cute). *Marimo* are said to take 200 years to grow to the size of a baseball. Ironically, *marimo* became endangered only after they were declared a National Treasure and tourists began to steal them as souvenirs. In response, the local Ainu community started the **Marimo Matsuri** (Marimo Festival), held in mid-October, led by an Ainu elder who ceremonially returns *marimo* to the lake, one by one. *Marimo* are also subject to natural disasters: a typhoon in October 2002 pushed 50% of the *marimo* out of the lake (they were quickly returned and expected to survive). You can safely skip the **boat trips** (☎ 67-2511) to the Marimo Exhibition and Observation Centre. These trips cost ¥1220 and operate from May to November. Preferable is the **Akan Kohan Eco-Museum Center** (☎ 67-4100; admission free; open 9am-7pm summer, 9am-5pm rest of year), on the eastern edge of town, which has *marimo* in tanks. There are also hiking maps and exhibits on the area's flora and fauna.

Behind the Eco-Museum is a scenic nature trail through the woods to **Bokke** (a collection of spluttering mud holes beside the lake), which returns via the lake shore to town (about 30 minutes return).

Back towards the centre of town, the **tourism information office** (☎ 67-3200; open 9am-6pm daily) has English-language pamphlets about the park, including excellent alpine trail guides with contour maps of O-Akan-dake and Me-Akan-dake.

Hiking About 6km east of Akan Kohan is **O-Akan-dake** (Male Mountain, 1371m). Buses to Kushiro pass the Takiguchi trail entrance five minutes out of Akan Kohan. The ascent takes a fairly arduous 3½ hours

and the descent takes about another 2½ hours. From the peak there are very fine views of the lakes **Penketō** and **Panketō**, and in summer the top is covered with alpine wildflowers. On clear days one can even see as far as Daisetsuzan National Park.

The highest mountain in the park, **Me-Akan-dake** (Female Mountain, 1499m), is an active volcano, but was closed to hikers at the time of writing. Ask at the tourist information office in Akan Kohan about current conditions. If you do climb this peak, watch out for the noxious effects of the sulphur fumes from the vents.

For an excellent short hike, the climb up to the observation platform on **Hakutō-zan** (650m) affords fine views of the lake and the surrounding peaks. The trail starts at the Akan Kohan skiing ground, about 2km south of town. The ascent from the ski ground takes about an hour, winding through birch and fir forests and past several groups of bubbling sulphur hot springs.

Places to Stay In a beautiful setting about 20km southwest of Akan-ko, **Nonaka Onsen Youth Hostel** (☎ 01562-9-7454; beds ¥2700) provides Japanese-style rooms, its own *onsen* and a base for climbing Me-Akan-dake. From July to mid-October, two daily buses from Akan Kohan bound for Lake Onnetō reach Me-Akan Onsen in about 20 minutes (¥970); from there it's a one-minute walk. The hostel is often fully booked and closes for a time around November, so phone ahead.

There are around a dozen *minshuku* in Akan Kohan, including two lovely ones on the western side of town:

Minshuku Kiri (☎/fax 67-2755; rooms per person with 2 meals ¥5500) is above a souvenir shop, opposite the Emerald Hotel on the road that runs alongside the lake: look for the woodblock print-style sign. It's famous for its hot-spring baths.

Yamaguchi (☎ 67-2555, fax 67-2506; rooms per person with 2 meals ¥5500), just out of the tourist fray, across the street and a minute's walk west, has clean rooms, home-style atmosphere, friendly staff and hot-spring baths.

Akan Kohan has numerous upmarket resort hotels. Per-person rates with two meals vary dramatically but start at ¥10,000 on weekdays in summer (¥2000 more on weekends), dropping as low as ¥8000 during winter.

Good choices include the old-line **Hotel Akanko-sō** (☎ 67-2231, fax 67-2593) and the flashier **New Akan Hotel Shangri-la** (☎ 67-2121, fax 67-3339).

Getting There & Away See the previous Kawayu Onsen Getting There & Away section for details of the park sightseeing bus service. From Akan Kohan bus centre there are several buses a day to Kitami (¥1800, 80 minutes) on the JR line to Abashiri for access to Shiretoko National Park. Buses to Asahikawa run via Sōunkyō Onsen in Daisetsuzan National Park (¥4580, five hours). There are also up to five buses a day to Kushiro (¥2650, 2¼ hours).

KUSHIRO SHITSUGEN NATIONAL PARK 釧路湿原国立公園
Also referred to as Kushiro Marshlands Park, this swampy area is famed for its flora and *tanchō-zuru* (red-crested white cranes), traditional symbols of Japan and longevity. From the Kushiro Marsh Observatory, wooden walkways thread their way for several kilometres through the reeds; your best chance of observing the over 600 resident cranes is during winter.

The park is most easily reached via the port city of Kushiro. From the bus station next to Kushiro station, frequent buses reach the observatory in 35 minutes (¥1320 return). Between late April and late October, several daily tour buses do a circuit of the park observation stations (¥2340 to ¥5600, 4½ to 6½ hours), and special large-windowed JR trains run two or three times a day into the park as far as Tōro station (¥530, 30 minutes). Kushiro has train connections with Shiretoko-Shari, Ikeda, Obihiro and Sapporo, and bus connections to Akan Kohan, Kawayu Onsen, Rausu and Asahikawa.

Places to Stay & Eat
Kushiro Shitsugen Tōro Youth Hostel (☎/fax 01548-7-2510; beds from ¥3150) is convenient to a few of the observation stations and has both Japanese- and Western-style accommodation. From Tōro station, it's a two-minute walk.

Kushiro Royal Inn (☎ 0154-31-2121, fax 0154-31-2122; singles/doubles from ¥5715/

8286), in Kushiro, is a plush business hotel just outside the station.

The restaurants and bars of Kushiro's Suehiro entertainment district are about seven blocks southeast of the station. Locals adore the conveyor-belt sushi at **Nagoyaka-Tei** (☎ 0154-24-2033; sushi from ¥120), though you'll probably need a taxi to get the closest location (about ¥1200).

SHARI 斜里
☎ 01522
Shari is the closest train stop to Shiretoko-hantō (an hour's bus ride away), but unless you miss the last bus there's no reason to stay in this slightly run-down town. Staff at the **tourist information office** (☎ 3-2424; open 10am-5pm daily mid-Apr–mid-Oct) by Shiretoko-Shari's train and bus stations can provide maps and book accommodation.

Places to Stay
Kurione (☎ 3-1889; camping for 1st person in tent ¥800, each additional person ¥400) is about 25 minutes' walk from the station (turn left, cross the bridge, turn left again and bear right at the fork). There's also a rider house (per person ¥1000). Prices include use of the adjacent *onsen*.

Shari Central Hotel (☎ 3-2355, 0120-801-144 toll free; rooms per person ¥6300) has well-maintained rooms, within sight of the station. **Ryokan Tanakaya** (☎ 3-3165, fax 3-0666; rooms per person with 2 meals ¥7000) is an attractive place around the corner.

Getting There & Away
Infrequent trains connect Shiretoko-Shari station with Abashiri (*futsū* ¥810, 45 minutes) and Kushiro (*kaisoku* ¥2730, two hours). Shari's bus centre is to the left as you exit Shiretoko-Shari station. There are between five and nine buses a day year-round to Utoro (¥1490), but there are only three buses between late April and October that continue as far as Iwaobetsu (¥1770, 70 minutes).

SHIRETOKO-HANTŌ 知床半島
☎ 01522
In Ainu, 'Shiretoko' means 'end of the world', and outside peak season it can live up to that name. Shiretoko National Park (386 sq km) covers most of this remote peninsula, with volcanic peaks leading out to

HOKKAIDŌ

the rugged cliffs around Shiretoko-misaki. The area has seen little development and remains one of Japan's most pristine wilderness areas. The main season for visitors is from mid-June to mid-September; most hikes are not recommended at other times. Roads run along each side of the peninsula, but they peter out well before the tip. Another road crosses the peninsula from Utoro to Rausu, the only towns of any size.

Utoro ウトロ

Utoro, on the peninsula's northern side, is the main gateway to Shiretoko National Park. The **tourist information office** (*☎ 4-2639; open 8am-7pm July-Aug, hours vary Sept-June*) at the bus centre can provide maps and timetables, as well as point out places to rent bicycles or motorcycles.

Two boat excursions operate from Utoro: one runs once a day out to the soaring cliffs of Shiretoko-misaki (¥6000, 3¾ hours, June to September) and the other runs up to six times a day for a short cruise along the coast as far as the waterfalls Kamuiwakka-no-taki (¥2700, 1½ hours, late April to late October). Short of hiking for several days, the longer boat cruise is the only way to catch a glimpse of the very tip of the peninsula. That said, your money might be better spent on bicycle rental or bus fares to more accessible attractions.

There are *minshuku* aplenty along the main road through town. Simple **Minshuku Taiyō** (*☎ 4-2939; rooms per person with 2 meals ¥4000*) is opposite the bus station. The owners say they haven't changed the price since they opened almost 25 years ago.

Bon's Home (*☎ 4-2271; rooms per person with/without 2 meals ¥4800/3500; open Feb-Oct*) – a member of the Toho network – is located just down the street, on the same side as the bus station. Accommodation is dormitory-style, and scooters and mountain bikes can be rented. **Minshuku Peleke** (*☎ 4-2236; rooms per person with 2 meals ¥7500*) has more upmarket rooms than next-door Minshuku Taiyō.

Shiretoko National Park
知床国立公園

About 5km from Utoro, **Shiretoko Nature Centre** (*☎ 4-2114; open 8am-5.40pm daily mid-Apr–mid-Oct, 9am-4pm daily mid-Oct–mid-Apr*) has hiking maps and a 20-minute slide show about the peninsula (¥500), which may be a worthwhile substitute if the weather is foul.

A few kilometres up the coast is the hamlet of **Iwaobetsu**, home of the riverside **Shiretoko Iwaobetsu Youth Hostel** (*☎ 4-2311, fax 4-2312; ⓔ shiretoko-ax@noah.ne.jp; beds ¥3045; open May-late Nov & late Dec-late Mar*). It deserves recommendation as a friendly and convenient base for exploring the peninsula, and runs 'briefing' sessions to outline hikes. It also rents mountain bikes.

Iwaobetsu Nature Lodge, on the premises, has slightly more expensive accommodation (¥3675).

Kinoshita-goya (*☎ 4-2824; beds ¥1500; open June-Sept*), nearby, at the trailhead for Rausu-dake, is a cheery mountain hut that offers extremely basic but clean accommodation. It is best to book ahead.

Bus services pass the nature centre and the youth hostel before reaching **Shiretoko Go-ko** (Shiretoko Five Lakes), where wooden walkways allow visitors to stroll around the lakes in an hour or so. The trails are sometimes closed due to bear sightings.

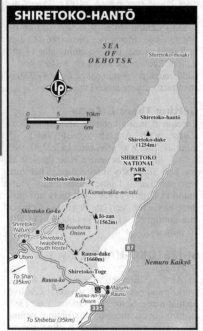

SHIRETOKO-HANTŌ

SEA OF OKHOTSK

Shiretoko-misaki

0 5 10km
0 3 6mi

Shiretoko-hantō

▲ Shiretoko-dake (1254m)

SHIRETOKO NATIONAL PARK

Shiretoko-ōhashi

Kamuiwakka-no-taki

Shiretoko Go-ko

▲ Iō-zan (1562m)

Shiretoko Nature Centre

Iwaobetsu Onsen

Shiretoko Iwaobetsu Youth Hostel

▲ Rausu-dake (1660m)

Utoro

To Shari (35km)

Shiretoko-Tōge

Rausu-ko

Nemuro Kaikyō

Marumi Rausu

Kuma-no-yu Onsen

To Shibetsu (35km)

Another 30 minutes' drive down the dirt road towards the tip of the peninsula takes you to the spectacular *rotemburo*-waterfall **Kamuiwakka-no-taki**. It takes about 25 minutes to climb up through water that gradually increases in temperature, until you reach cascades of hot water emptying into a succession of pools. Ocean panoramas here can be awesome. Unlike at other natural *onsen*, decorum here often dictates that bathers wear swimsuits, particularly at peak times.

Hiking There are several hikes on the peninsula. The nature centre and the youth hostel can provide detailed advice on routes, trail conditions and organising transport. Proper footwear and warm clothes are essential. Avoid all contact with the peninsula's foxes because they carry the parasite Echinococcosis.

A road almost opposite the youth hostel leads 4km uphill to Iwaobetsu Onsen, which lies at the start of a trail up **Rausu-dake** (1660m). There's only one bus a day, there and back, but the youth hostel may be able to give you a lift to the trailhead; allow four hours from there to reach the top at a comfortable pace. For an alternative approach to the mountain, see Rausu following this section.

Warning: Bear Activity

The peninsula, Shiretoko-hantō, is home to around 600 brown bears, one of the largest bear populations in Japan. Park pamphlets warn visitors that once they enter Shiretoko National Park, they should assume bears can appear at any time. Favourite bear haunts include Shiretoko Go-ko (Shiretoko Five Lakes) and the falls, Kamuiwakka-no-taki.

Hikers are strongly advised not to go into the forest in the early morning or at dusk, and to avoid hiking alone. Carrying a bell or some other noise-making device is also recommended (bears don't like surprises). If you're camping, tie up your food and do not bury your rubbish. Bear activity picks up noticeably during early autumn, when the creatures are actively foraging for food ahead of their winter hibernation. Visitors should be especially cautious at this time

There is also a much shorter hike to Rausu-ko, near **Shiretoko-Toge** pass. The trailhead is several kilometres south of the pass, on the way to Rausu. The hike takes about four hours there and back, and leads you through virtually untouched wilderness. Buses between Utoro and Rausu run via the pass, which on clear days offers great views of the mountains and Kunashiri-tō, the closest of Japan's 'northern territories', currently still in Russian hands.

Getting Around From late April to October buses run three times a day from Utoro (¥1080, 50 minutes) along the northern side of the peninsula, passing the nature centre, the youth hostel, Shiretoko Go-ko and Kamuiwakka-no-taki before terminating at Shiretoko-ōhashi. The rest of the year buses run only as far as the nature centre.

From mid-June to mid-October there are also buses twice a day to Rausu via the dramatic Shiretoko-Toge pass (¥1310, 55 minutes).

During the peak tourist season (late July to mid-August), the road beyond Shiretoko Go-ko is closed to private vehicles, and visitors *must* use buses (every 20 minutes from 7am to 6.30pm) from the nature centre or youth hostel, making all stops along the way. The one-way journey to Shiretoko-ōhashi takes 50 minutes, including breaks for gawking at deer, foxes and – just maybe – bears. A few buses a day continue to/from Utoro.

RAUSU 羅臼
☎ 01538

This small fishing village once grew wealthy on herring fishing, though there's not much reason to come here unless you're planning to hike around the peninsula or take an alternative approach to Rausu-dake.

A challenging but well-marked trailhead for Rausu-dake starts a few kilometres outside town towards Shiretoko-Toge, near the camping ground (free) at **Kuma-no-yu Onsen**.

Only genuinely experienced hikers should consider hiking up the eastern side of the peninsula to Shiretoko-misaki (one to three days).

Weather permitting, you could hire a local fishing boat for a ride back to the start of the trail at **Rider House Kuma-no-yado** at the end of Rte 87, 24km outside Rausu.

Be warned: this hike is *extremely* difficult, as the eroded trail sometimes crawls along steep cliffs or over slippery boulders. If you get hurt, there is no one to help until a fishing boat happens by. In some parts, swimming is often a preferable shortcut, but watch out for jellyfish. One traveller wrote:

I ended up walking on my hands and, in push-up fashion, letting my feet rest on the few inches of trail that were available, sometimes pushing them against the wall when the path disappeared. I suppose I looked somewhat like a crab inching its way along the shore...

Steve Maki

If you go, take plenty of food and water, as well as hiking boots with good ankle support, and keep an eye out for bears.

Marumi (☎ 8-1313, fax 8-2128; rooms per person from ¥8800), by the seaside, is a well-regarded ryokan with Japanese rooms (surcharge for private facilities), lovely seafood meals, *rotemburo* and sauna.

Getting There and Away

From mid-June to mid-October, there are two buses a day (¥1310, 55 minutes) that run between Utoro and Rausu via Shiretoko-Toge. From Rausu, buses run four times a day (¥4740, 3½ hours) year-round to Kushiro.

Tokachi 十勝

OBIHIRO 帯広

☎ 0155 • pop 174,000

This surprisingly up-to-date city is the hub of the Tokachi plain and it is squeezed between the Hidaka and Daisetsuzan mountain ranges. Although historically an Ainu stronghold, the modern city was founded in 1883 by the Banseisha, a group of 'land reclaimers' (colonial settlers) from Shizuoka.

For travellers, Obihiro is the southeastern back door to Daisetsuzan National Park; you may also find yourself passing through en route to Ikeda or Erimo-Misaki.

Information

Tokachi Tourist Information (☎ 23-6403; open 9am-7pm daily) is on the 2nd floor of the Esta shopping mall at the sparkling new Obihiro station. A **room-booking service** (☎ 25-1670; available 11am-6pm daily) is on the station's ground floor.

Places to Stay & Eat

Toipirka Youth Hostel (☎/fax 30-4165; W http://homepage1.nifty.com/TOIPIRKA; beds ¥3200) is in an attractive log house with Western-style beds and nightly 'tea time'. It's outside town, towards Tokachi-gawa Onsen. Buses from Obihiro station (¥470, 20 minutes, last at 7.15pm) pass the Shimoshihoro-shōgakkō-mae stop. From there it's a 12-minute walk to the hostel, but if you phone ahead the staff will pick you up at the bus stop.

In the station area, there is no shortage of reasonably priced accommodation. **Hotel Musashi** (☎ 25-1181; singles/twins weekend ¥4000/8000) is a business hotel and has special weekend rates (slightly more on weekdays).

The **Hotel Paco Obihiro** (☎ 23-8585, fax 23-0085; W www.paco.co.jp; singles/doubles from ¥7000/9000) has clean, contemporary rooms and its own *onsen* bath.

Obihiro's culinary speciality is *buta-donburi*, delicious barbecued pork on rice. **Panchō** (☎ 22-1974; dishes ¥850-1250), across from the station, is the place that started it all; *buta-donburi* is the only dish on the menu. Expect long queues during peak times.

Getting There & Away

Flights connect Obihiro with Tokyo-Haneda, Osaka-Kansai and Nagoya. Buses from in front of Obihiro station (¥1000, 40 minutes) are timed to meet flights.

Tokkyū trains run from Obihiro to New Chitose Airport (¥6200, 1¾ hours) and Sapporo (¥6510, 2¼ hours). S-Kippu to Sapporo cost ¥11,940. The JR Nemuro main line runs east to Ikeda (*kaisoku* ¥440, 30 minutes) and Kushiro (*tokkyū* ¥3690, 1½ hours).

From in front of the station, long-distance buses depart a few times a day for Sapporo (¥3670, 4½ hours), Kushiro (¥2240, 2½ hours) and Asahikawa (¥3150, 3¾ hours). Buses to Asahikawa run along two different routes through Daisetsuzan National Park, conveniently passing either Furano/Biei or Sōunkyō Onsen. Local buses to Ikeda (¥590) take about an hour.

IKEDA 池田
☎ 01557

In the eastern Tokachi plain, Ikeda is a small farming town that became famous when the municipal government began making wine there in the 1960s. It's a pleasant place to spend a lazy afternoon wandering fields and back roads. Town maps are available at the **tourist information desk** *(☎ 2-2025; open 10am-5pm daily Apr-Oct)* inside JR Ikeda station.

Wines are made at the **Wain-jō** *(wine castle; ☎ 2-2467; admission free; open 9am-5pm daily)*, on a hillside overlooking the town; head for the Ferris wheel. After observing the production process and partaking of free tastings, you can walk beside wheat fields and vineyards to **Happiness Dairy** *(☎ 2-2001; admission free; open 9.30am-5.30pm Mon-Fri, 9.30am-6pm Sat & Sun summer; 9.30am-5pm Mon-Fri, 9.30am-5.30pm Sat & Sun rest of year)*, where you can buy fresh cheese or home-made gelato (cones ¥250).

On the way back to town, you could detour to **Moon Face Gallery & Café** *(☎ 2-2198; admission free; open 10am-7pm Wed-Mon)*, which displays works by local artists, or swing by the wool weaving workshop at **Spinner's Farm** *(☎ 2-2848; admission free; open 10am-6pm Tues-Sun, closed 2nd Sat each month & Jan-Feb)*.

Ikeda Kita-no-kotan Youth Hostel *(☎ 2-3666; beds ¥2900)* is a treat, with friendly management and excellent dinners (¥1000, including a glass of wine). Bicycles can be rented. The hostel is five minutes on foot from Toshibetsu station, one stop west of Ikeda (¥200).

Ikeda is 30 minutes by local train from Obihiro (¥440). There are also frequent buses between Ikeda and Obihiro (¥590, 55 minutes). On the privately owned Furusato-Ginga line, there are four trains a day to Kitami (¥3410, 2¼ to three hours), from where you can catch buses to Sōunkyō Onsen in Daisetsuzan National Park or take the JR Sekihoku main line east to Bihoro and Abashiri.

ERIMO-MISAKI えりも岬
☎ 01466

This remote cape, with its windswept cliffs and dramatic ocean vistas, is something of an ecological miracle. Beginning in the Meiji Era, the hills surrounding this kelp-farming community were gradually deforested, so that by the 1950s it was nicknamed 'Erimo Desert'. Sand blew into the ocean, destroying the kelp, and the community faced a stark choice: reforest or leave. Thanks to some extremely persevering locals, the hills now boast a Japanese black pine forest.

At the cape are a lighthouse and a wind museum, **Kaze-no-Yakata** *(☎ 3-1133; admission ¥500; open 8.30am-7pm daily July-Aug, 8.30am-6pm May-Jun & Sept, 9am-5pm Oct-Apr)*, with weather-related films and exhibits; you can also be blasted by gale-force winds inside a man-made wind tunnel. During calm seas, Kuril seals lounge on the rocks below, while nearby fishing boats are back to harvesting kelp. The seals are called *zenigata-azarashi*, meaning 'money-shaped', because the white spots on their black bodies appear like old Japanese coins.

Erimo Misaki Youth Hostel *(☎ 3-1144, fax 3-1074; beds with 2 meals ¥4350)* is rustic and offers bunk-bed accommodation and seafood cuisine, 20 minutes' walk to the cape.

At the cape is the homey *minshuku* **Misaki-sō** *(☎ 3-1316; rooms per person with 2 meals ¥6000-8000)*. There is also a **camping ground** *(open May-Nov)* on the beach at Hyakunin-hama, 8km northeast of the cape.

Erimo-Misaki is so remote that getting here is a chore without your own transport. One daily bus from Sapporo (¥3500, four hours) arrives late and returns early, or you can catch a local train via Tomakomai to Samani (¥3150, 3½ hours), but there can be a long wait for a bus connection (¥1370, 35 minutes).

Shikoku 四国

In Japan's feudal past, the island of Shikoku (population 4,200,000) was divided into four regions – hence the name 'shi' (four) and 'koku' (region). The provinces of Awa, Tosa, Iyo and Sanuki became the modern day prefectures of Tokushima, Kōchi, Ehime and Kagawa. The old names are still in common use in their prefectures. Although Shikoku is Japan's fourth largest island, it's predominantly rural and remains well off the standard tourist track for most foreigners – which makes it all the more worthwhile to go there.

The island is home to Japan's best-known pilgrimage, which is essentially the country's oldest tourist trail. Pilgrims, or *henro* as they are known in Japanese, have been walking around the 88 Sacred Temples of Shikoku (see the boxed text '88 Sacred Temples of Shikoku') for over 1000 years, using a published guidebook since 1685. Modern *henro*, and even foreign visitors, can hike along age-old trails in that ever-elusive search for enlightenment – or just to experience that bit of Japan that seems to have disappeared in the urban areas.

There are countless attractions, both natural and otherwise, that make Shikoku a worthwhile excursion. The island is rugged and mountainous. The village of Monobe in Kōchi-ken claims to have the highest levels of rainfall in Japan, while in Kagawa-ken at the northern end of the island, the land is pock-marked with *tameike* (water collection ponds) as there isn't enough water.

SUGGESTED ITINERARIES

If you have the time and the inclination, the best way to see and experience Shikoku is to journey around the 88 Sacred Temples. Shikoku is a very special place, but a lot of people rush through and leave without really understanding what it has to offer. This is an opportunity to immerse yourself in Japan and experience something unique – to be a 'doer' rather than a 'looker'. The pilgrimage can be hiked, biked, hitch-hiked, done using public transport, a scooter, taxis or cars – walking can take anywhere from 30 to 60 days; other methods take less time. If you have a car and not much time, you can probably visit all the temples in four or five days,

Highlights

- Sense your accomplishment on completing the 88 Sacred Temples of Shikoku pilgrimage
- Make the hike up Shikoku's most sacred mountains, Tsurugi-san and Ishizuchi-san
- Enjoy paddling a sea kayak in the warm waters of the Inland Sea (Seto-nai-kai)
- Stroll through Takamatsu's exquisite garden, Ritsurin-kōen, or take in the spectacular views from Yashima plateau
- Trek up the 800-odd granite steps to pay homage at the sacred shrine Kompira-san in Kotohira
- Soak your bones in the ancient hot springs at Matsuyama's famed Dōgo Onsen
- Explore the deep gorges, abundant nature and vine suspension bridges in Tokushima-ken's secluded Iya Valley

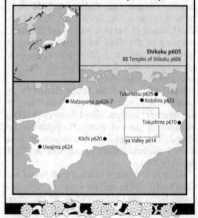

but that would defeat the purpose of the visit. The first temple is the Ryōzen-ji, just north of Tokushima city. The pilgrimage then travels clockwise around the island, moving into Kōchi, Ehime and Kagawa prefectures, before finishing back at the Ryōzen-ji.

For those wanting a shorter visit, one popular route involves arriving in Takamatsu or Tokushima, winding down through the Iya Valley, heading south to Kōchi, then around to the cape, Ashizuri-misaki, and up the coast toward Matsuyama.

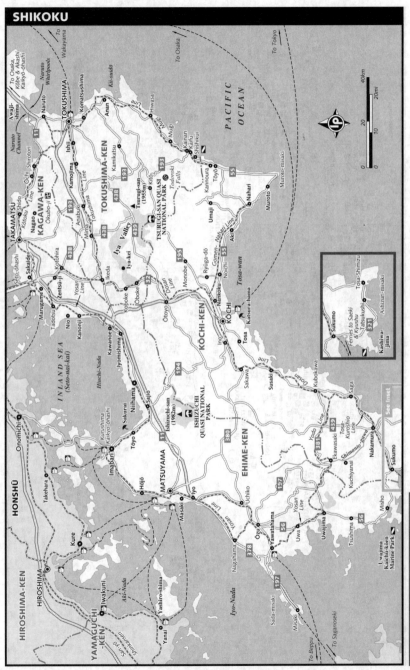

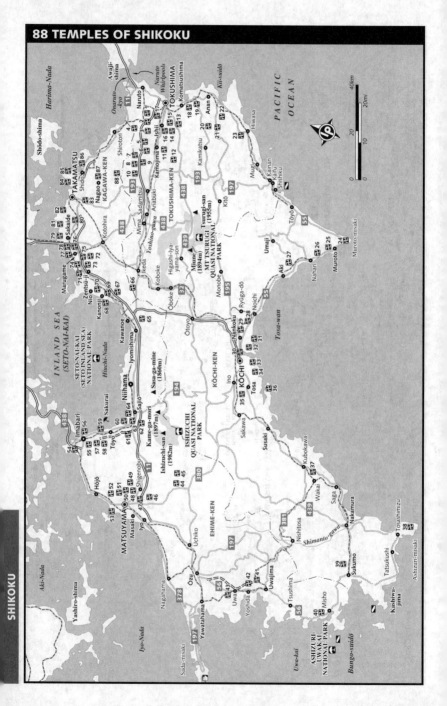

88 TEMPLES OF SHIKOKU

1 Ryōzen-ji 霊山寺	30 Zenraku-ji 善楽寺	60 Hōju-ji 宝寿寺
2 Gokuraku-ji 極楽寺	31 Zenjibu-ji 禅師峰寺	61 Kōon-ji 香園寺
3 Konsen-ji 金泉寺	32 Chikurin-ji 竹林寺	62 Yokomine-ji 横峰寺
4 Dainichi-ji 大日寺	33 Sekkei-ji 雪蹊寺	63 Maegami-ji 前神寺
5 Jizō-ji 地蔵寺	34 Tanema-ji 種間寺	64 Kisshō-ji 吉祥寺
6 Anraku-ji 安楽寺	35 Kiyotaki-ji 清滝寺	65 Sankaku-ji 三角寺
7 Juraku-ji 十楽寺	36 Shōryū-ji 青龍寺	66 Unpen-ji 雲辺寺
8 Kumadani-ji 熊谷寺	37 Iwamoto-ji 岩本寺	67 Daikō-ji 大興寺 (小松尾寺)
9 Hōrin-ji 法輪寺	38 Kongōfuku-ji 金剛福寺	68 Jinne-in 神恵院
10 Kirihata-ji 切幡寺	39 Enkō-ji 延光寺	69 Kanon-ji 観音寺
11 Fujii-dera 藤井寺	40 Kanjizai-ji 観自在寺	70 Motoyama-ji 本山寺
12 Shōzan-ji 焼山寺	41 Ryūkō-ji 龍光寺	71 Iyadani-ji 弥谷寺
13 Dainichi-ji 大日寺	42 Butsumoku-ji 仏木寺	72 Mandara-ji 曼陀羅寺
14 Jōraku-ji 常楽寺	43 Meiseki-ji 明石寺	73 Shusshaka-ji 出釈迦寺
15 Kokubun-ji 国分寺	44 Taihō-ji 大宝寺	74 Kōyama-ji 甲山寺
16 Kannon-ji 観音寺	45 Iwaya-ji 岩屋寺	75 Zentsū-ji 善通寺
17 Ido-ji 井戸寺	46 Jōruri-ji 浄瑠璃寺	76 Konzō-ji 金倉寺
18 Onzan-ji 恩山寺	47 Yasaka-ji 八坂寺	77 Dōryū-ji 道隆寺
19 Tatsue-ji 立江寺	48 Sairin-ji 西林寺	78 Gōshō-ji 郷照寺
20 Kakurin-ji 鶴林寺	49 Jōdo-ji 浄土寺	79 Kōshō-in 高照院 (天皇寺)
21 Tairyū-ji 太龍寺	50 Hanta-ji 繁多寺	80 Kokubun-ji 国分寺
22 Byōdō-ji 平等寺	51 Ishite-ji 石手寺	81 Shiramine-ji 白峰寺
23 Yakuō-ji 薬王寺	52 Taisan-ji 太山寺	82 Negoro-ji 根香寺
24 Hotsumisaki-ji 最御崎寺	53 Enmyō-ji 円明寺	83 Ichinomiya-ji 一宮寺
25 Shinshō-ji 津照寺	54 Enmei-ji 延命寺	84 Yashima-ji 屋島寺
26 Kongōchō-ji 金剛頂寺	55 Nankō-bō 南光坊	85 Yakuri-ji 八栗寺
27 Kōnomine-ji 神峯寺	56 Taisan-ji 泰山寺	86 Shido-ji 志度寺
28 Dainichi-ji 大日寺	57 Eifuku-ji 栄福寺	87 Nagao-ji 長尾寺
29 Kokubun-ji 国分寺	58 Senyū-ji 仙遊寺	88 Okubo-ji 大窪寺
	59 Kokubun-ji 国分寺	

SHIKOKU

88 Sacred Temples of Shikoku

Henro (pilgrims) have been walking clockwise around Shikoku for over 1000 years, following in the footsteps of the great Buddhist Saint Kōbō Daishi (774–835). Kōbō Daishi achieved enlightenment on Shikoku, the island of his birth, and by following in his path, a millennium of pilgrims have hoped to do the same.

Known as Kūkai (meaning 'the sky and the sea') during his lifetime, the great saint was awarded the title of Kōbō Daishi – *kōbō* means 'to spread widely the Buddhist teachings', and *daishi* means 'great teacher' or 'saint' – following his death. He was not the only *daishi*, but the Japanese have a saying that 'Kōbō stole the title of *daishi*,' and when anyone talks of 'the *daishi*', everyone knows who is being referred to.

Kōbō Daishi founded the Shingon sect of Buddhism, the only major sect that believes enlightenment can be achieved in this lifetime. It is commonly referred to as Esoteric Buddhism. He is also credited with, among other things, putting together the first Chinese-Japanese dictionary, and creating *hiragana*, the system of syllabic writing that made it easier for Japanese to put their language into writing. Kōbō Daishi is enshrined at the Kōya-san temple complex (see the Kansai chapter) in Wakayama-ken on Honshū, and it is a tradition that pilgrims start and end their journey at Kōya – asking for Kōbō Daishi's support and blessing for their upcoming journey, and thanking him for that support and their safety on their return. Pilgrims never walk alone; Kōbō Daishi is always by their side.

For 1000 years, the pilgrimage was an arduous task – the only way to make the journey was to walk the 1400km track, an incredible journey. Until 1685 there was no guidebook. There were no weather forecasts, no telephones for pilgrims to use to call home if they got homesick, no paramed-

CHAPTER ORGANISATION

This chapter is written in the same order that most of Shikoku's visitors have travelled around the island over the past thousand years – in a circle starting in Tokushima and moving through Kōchi, Ehime and Kagawa prefectures. Shikoku's only train connection with Honshū, however, is via the bridge Seto-ōhashi, so if you arrive by rail, your first prefecture will be Kagawa.

GETTING THERE & AWAY

Before 1986 Shikoku was considered much more remote, with access being mainly by ferry. There are now a total of three bridge systems linking Shikoku with Honshū. The Seto-ōhashi connects Okayama to Sakaide, which is west of Takamatsu. The Akashi Kaikyō-ōhashi is west of Kōbe and leads to Tokushima (via Awaji-shima). Finally, the Kurushima Kaikyō-ōhashi island-hops along the Shimanami Highway (Shimanami-kaidō) from Onomichi in Hiroshima-ken to Imabari in Ehime-ken.

Air services connect major cities in Shikoku with Tokyo, Osaka and other centres on Honshū.

Numerous ferries ply the waters of the Inland Sea (Seto-nai-kai), linking points on Shikoku with neighbouring islands and ports on the San-yō coast of Honshū.

There are frequent train services from Okayama to Shikoku via the Seto-ōhashi, as well as direct bus services from both Osaka and Tokyo.

GETTING AROUND

Over the last 1000 years, the majority of visitors to Shikoku have walked around the island. If that doesn't appeal, Shikoku is great for biking. It is also well accessed by public transport, though to reach remote mountain areas, private transport is a boon (cars can be rented in Shikoku's major cities and airports).

Tokushima-ken
徳島県

From the vivacious Awa Odori (Awa Dance Festival) and the mighty channel whirlpools of the Naruto-kaikyō, to the pristine scenery of Iya Valley and the surf beaches of the southern coast, Tokushima-ken offers an array of attractions to quench adventurous thirsts.

88 Sacred Temples of Shikoku

ics to pick them up if they fell ill. Many never made it. Those who did overcame great hardships. Nowadays, for most *henro*, hardship is not a factor. They buzz around in air-conditioned vehicles collecting the 88 temple stamps and give little thought to the past. There are still walkers, although they make up only a tiny percentage of those who make the pilgrimage. In recent years there has been a resurgence of Japanese who, disenchanted with the pace of modern life and looking for meaning and self-realisation, strike out on foot.

There is also the occasional *gaijin henro* (foreign pilgrim). If you're interested, all the gear you need is at Temple 1, the Ryōzen-ji, just north of Tokushima city. There's more information in each prefecture's section in this chapter. The pilgrimage is considered non-sectarian and some people out there aren't even Buddhists – just people in search of themselves. With the right attitude, the pilgrimage is as big an adventure today as it was in the past – and is definitely a way to immerse yourself in Japan. Allow 30 to 60 days if walking (depending on your fitness), two weeks to a month on a bicycle, less by motorised transport. One point to remember – there are actually 89 temples. All pilgrims should travel back from Temple 88 to Temple 1 and complete the circle – for a circle is never-ending, just like the search for enlightenment.

For more information pick up three English-language books – Oliver Statler's *Japanese Pilgrimage* is a classic academic work on the pilgrimage and its history; Ed Readicker-Henderson's *The Traveller's Guide to Japanese Pilgrimages* has information on each temple; and Craig McLachlan's *Tales of a Summer Henro* retells the adventures of a walking *gaijin henro*.

Always remember the words of Kōbō Daishi – 'Do not just walk in the footsteps of the men of old, seek what they sought'.

THE PILGRIMAGE IN TOKUSHIMA

Tokushima is known as Hosshin no dōjō – the place to determine to achieve enlightenment – and has the first 23 of the 88 temples. Funnily enough, it also has Temple 66, the Umpen-ji in its far western corner. Temple 1 is the Ryōzen-ji, a 10-minute walk from Bandō station on the JR Kōtoku line north of Tokushima city. The Ryōzen-ji is number one as through the centuries, it was the first temple on Shikoku that pilgrims reached after leaving Kōya-san in Wakayama-ken. The temple has a shop where you can buy what you need for the journey, including traditional gear if you want it. There are maps and guidebooks in Japanese. It also has a **shukubō** *(temple lodging;* ☎ *088-689-1111; room with 2 meals ¥6000).* Many of the temples provide accommodation for pilgrims at around that rate and there is information in the various guides on the temples.

The first 10 temples are more or less on an east–west line spanning about 25km on the north side of the Yoshino river valley. They were considered a mini-pilgrimage in days of old, and even if you're not doing the full 88-temple pilgrimage, you can get a feel for it by visiting the first few. It's only a 15-minute walk from the Ryōzen-ji to Temple 2, the Gokuraku-ji.

The walk from temples 11 to 12, in the mountains on the south side of the Yoshino River valley, is infamous among *henro* – it has the reputation of being the steepest and hardest climb on the pilgrimage, although it's possible to walk it in five hours. Temple 19, the Tatsue-ji is a barrier temple – only those who are 'pure of intention' can pass. After that, pilgrims are truly on the long road.

TOKUSHIMA 徳島
☎ 088 • pop 270,000

Tokushima is a bustling modern city known for its annual **Awa Odori Festival** in August, and traditional Awa puppet theatre.

Orientation & Information

Tokushima is neatly defined by two hills. One, with the castle ruins, rises up directly behind the train station. From in front of the station, Shinmachibashi-dōri heads southwest across the Shinmachi-gawa to the ropeway station at the base of the other hill, Bizan. The entertainment district and main shopping arcade are west of the river.

There's a **tourist information booth** outside JR Tokushima station, but the **Tokushima**

SHIKOKU

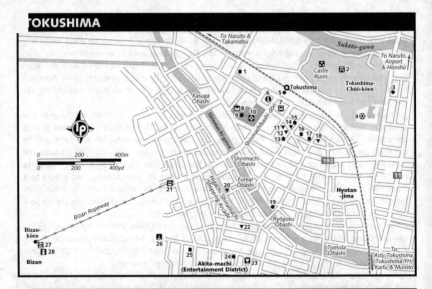

TOKUSHIMA

TOKUSHIMA

PLACES TO STAY
1 Grand Palace Hotel
ホテルグランドパレス徳島
9 Tōkyū Inn
東急イン
13 AWA Kankō Hotel
阿波観光ホテル
15 Station Hotel
ステーションホテル
16 Dai-Ichi Hotel
第一ホテル
17 Astoria Hotel
アストリアホテル
25 Washington Hotel
ワシントンホテル

PLACES TO EAT
11 Rokuemon Ichibanchō
ろくえもん
12 Copa
コパ
14 R's Café
R's カフェ

18 Big Brother's Sandwich
Shop
20 Vivash
22 Hashimoto
橋本

OTHER
2 Gokoku-jinja
護国神社
3 Akane-an Teahouse
茜庵
4 Senshūkaku-teien
旧徳島城表御殿庭園
5 JR Tokushima;
Clement Plaza;
Hotel Clement; Masala;
Tora Kaitenzushi
クレメントプラザ
6 Tourist Information Booth
観光案内所
7 Bus Station
バスターミナル

8 Post Office
徳島郵便局
10 Sogō Department
Store
そごう百貨店
19 Row Boat Rental
貸しボート
21 Cablecar Station; Awa
Odori Kaikan
眉山ケーブルカー駅;
阿波踊り会館
23 ACTY 21
24 Dancing Clock
阿波おどり時計
26 Zuigan-ji
端厳寺
27 Wenceslão de Morães
Museum
モラエス記念館
28 Peace Pagoda
平和塔

Prefecture International Exchange Association (Topia; ☎ 656-3303; open 10am-6pm daily) is a far better place to get started. There are helpful English-speaking staff, and facilities include a library, satellite TV, computers with Internet access and an information/message board. Staff can help with finding accommodation. To reach Topia from inside JR Tokushima station, take the elevator to the 6th floor of Clement Plaza.

Bizan 眉山
A broad avenue with a central parade of palm trees runs southwest from the station to the foot of Bizan. There's a ropeway, otherwise known as a cable car (¥600/1000 one way/return), to the 280m-high summit. From the top there are fine views over the city and sea. You can walk down in 15 minutes.

At the top, Bizan-kōen has a **Peace Pagoda**, erected in 1958 as a memorial to local

SHIKOKU

Dancing Fools

The streets of Tokushima, an otherwise placid city, play host to one of the premier good-time events in Japan, the Awa Odori (Awa Dance Festival). The event is the largest and most famous *'bon'* dance in Japan and attracts tens of thousands of people from 12 to 15 August every year.

Every night, over four days, the revelry continues as men, women and children don *yukata* (light cotton kimono) and take to the streets to dance to the samba-like rhythm of the theme song 'Yoshikono,' accompanied by the sounds of *shamisen* (three-stringed guitars), *taiko* (drums) and *fue* (flutes). Dancing and mayhem last into the wee hours of the morning!

As at Rio's Carnival or the Mardi Gras in New Orleans, the participants dance in *ren* (groups), waving their hands, shuffling their feet and chanting a phrase, which says it all:

> The dancing fools
> And the watching fools
> Are foolish the same
> So why not dance?

Some groups delight in having *gaijin* (foreigners) join their pack; staff at Tokushima Prefecture International Exchange Association (Topia) can provide details. And if you can't be there for the real thing in August, you can always try the dance at the local hall, the Awa Odori Kaikan (see the Bizan entry in this section).

soldiers who died in Burma (Myanmar) during WWII, and the **Wenceslão de Morães Museum** *(admission ¥200; open 9.30am-5pm daily, closed 2nd & 4th Wed each month)*. Morães, a Portuguese naval officer, lived in Japan from 1893 until his death in 1929, and produced a multi-volume study of Japan.

At the foot of the ropeway, the **Awa Odori Kaikan** *(☎ 611-1611; admission free; open 9am-5pm daily, closed 2nd & 4th Wed of month)* features extensive exhibits relating to the local dance, the *awa odori*.

Chūō-kōen 中央公園

Less than 500m northeast of the train station, the ruins of Tokushima-jō, built in 1586, stand in Chūō-kōen. In the park you will also find the attractively landscaped **Senshūkaku-teien** *(admission ¥50)*, a garden dating from the Momoyama period, and the **Tokushima Castle Museum** *(admission ¥300; open 9.30am-4.30pm Tues-Sun)*.

Just east of Chūō-kōen is **Akane-an**, an excellent place to experience an authentic Japanese **tea ceremony**. For a reasonable ¥1000, you'll be served fragrant *ko-sencha* (medium grade green tea), followed by *matcha* (powdered green tea), then a sweet *yuzu* (citron) fruit juice and finally standard *o-cha* (green tea). To arrange a formal tea ceremony *(o-temae)*, reservations are required (ask at Topia).

Awa Puppet Theatre 人形浄瑠璃

For hundreds of years, bunraku (puppet theatre), known in the region as *ningyō jōruri*, thrived in the farming communities in and around Tokushima as a popular form of amusement (while the wealthy were entertained with the likes of kabuki). Gradually the region's many puppet theatres dwindled and today one of the last remaining local puppet dramas can be seen at the **Awa no Jūrobei Yashiki** *(☎ 665-2202; admission ¥350)*.

This museum is the former residence of the samurai Jūrobei, whose tragic Edo-era life story forms the material for the drama *Keisei Awa no Naruto*. A section from this puppet drama is performed by local women. Shows take place at varying times, but generally at 3pm daily. Ask at the tourist information booth outside JR Tokushima for details – then take a bus from just outside to the Jūrobei Yashiki-mae bus stop (¥270; 15 minutes).

Next door is the **Awa Deko Ningyō Kaikan** *(Awa Puppet Hall; admission ¥400; open 8.30am-5pm daily)*, with puppet displays and demonstrations of their manufacture and use.

Other Attractions

Free **boat rides** (30 minutes) can be taken circling Hyotan-jima, the island forming

SHIKOKU

central Tokushima. Ask for a timetable at Topia. Departures are from the Ryogoku-bashi, south of JR Tokushima.

Just south of here near the entertainment district, Akita-machi, the **dancing clock** is a curious contraption featuring figurines that perform the local Awa Odori dance; they pop out of an otherwise ordinary bus stop five times a day.

ASTY Tokushima (☎ 624-5111; admission ¥910; open 9am-5pm daily), south of the city centre, has potted highlights of regional culture (including puppet drama and pottery) under one roof. At the 'arts village' **Kōgei-mura** (☎ 624-5000; open 9.30am-5pm Wed-Mon), which is the highlight of the complex, you can observe (and for a nominal fee partake in) a variety of traditional arts and crafts, including *aizome* (indigo dyeing), *washi* (paper-making) and pottery. Buses from JR Tokushima station reach ASTY in about 15 minutes.

Places to Stay – Budget

Tokushima Youth Hostel (☎ 663-1505; beds ¥2800; meals available) is near the sea, about 15 minutes by bus from the centre of town. It has a good reputation and friendly staff.

Dai-Ichi Hotel (☎ 655-5505; singles from ¥5000) is near the station.

Places to Stay – Mid-Range to Top End

Hotels near the train station include **Station Hotel** (☎ 652-8181; singles/doubles ¥6000/11,000) and **Astoria Hotel** (☎ 653-6151; singles/doubles ¥6000/11,000). There are more expensive places, such as the **AWA Kankō Hotel** (☎ 622-5161; singles/doubles from ¥7200/14,000); **Grand Palace Hotel** (☎ 626-1111; singles/doubles from ¥8400/15,000); and **Tōkyū Inn** (☎ 626-0109; singles/doubles from ¥6900/12,000).

Hotel Clement (☎ 656-3131; singles from ¥10,000) is part of the JR Tokushima complex. **Washington Hotel** (☎ 653-7111; singles/twins from ¥8000/17,000) is on the edge of the Akita-machi area.

Places to Eat & Drink

There is an expansive delicatessen area in the basement of Clement Plaza (inside JR Tokushima station) and a variety of eateries on the 5th floor. **Masala** offers good Indian food, while **Tora Kaitenzushi** lets you pick sushi as it comes around on a conveyor belt.

R's Café is a 2nd-storey eatery, about a two-minute walk from the station, that also has Internet terminals. Nearby, **Rokuemon Ichibanchō**, a basement *izakaya* (Japanese-style pub), has a decidedly country atmosphere. Also in the area is **Big Brother's Sandwich Shop**, which is run by expats.

Hashimoto, a popular *soba* (buckwheat noodles) eatery, has a couple of branches, one near the 'dancing clock'. Not far away is **Vivash**, serving bagels, salads and desserts.

Copa, a short stumble from JR Tokushima station, is a woodsy little pub, though if you're up for a night out, head to the Akita-machi area.

There's a variety of nightlife, but a good place to start is in the **ACTY 21** building, just down from the dancing clock.

Getting There & Away

Tokushima's airport is 8km north of the city and there are flights to all major cities. Buses from the airport to town cost ¥430.

Tokushima is less than 1½ hours from Takamatsu by *tokkyū* (limited express). There are also trains west to Ikeda on the JR Dosan line (which runs between Takamatsu and Kōchi) and south along the coast.

The city has bus connections to/from all Japan's main cities.

Ferry services are starting to dwindle, but there are still connections with Tokyo, Kitakyūshū and various smaller ports. **Nankai Ferry** (☎ 0120-732-156) has regular departures daily between Wakayama in Kansai and Tokushima.

Getting Around

It's easy to get around Tokushima on foot – from JR Tokushima station to the Bizan cable-car station it's less than 1km. Bicycles can be rented from the underground bicycle park in front of the JR Tokushima station.

NORTHERN TOKUSHIMA-KEN
徳島県北部

Naruto Whirlpools 鳴門のうず潮

At the change of tide, seawater whisks through the narrow Naruto-kaikyō (Naruto Channel) with such velocity that ferocious whirlpools are created. Boats venture out into the channel that separates Shikoku from nearby Awaji-shima, and travel under the Naruto-ōhashi to inspect the whirlpools close up. Brochures available at the JR Tokushima station tourist information booth outline tide times (ask for *naruto-no-uzu-shio*) and boat trips. The whirls generally occur four times a day, but at changing times. Get the timetable and don't go at the wrong time. There are views over the channel from **Naruto-kōen**. For a birds-eye view you can walk the **Uzu-no-michi** *(admission ¥500; open daily 9.30am-5.30pm Apr-Sept, 9.30am-4.30pm daily Oct-Mar)*, a walkway under the Naruto-ōhashi, 45m above the swirling water.

From Tokushima, take a train to JR Naruto station (¥330, 40 minutes) and a bus from there (¥310, 20 minutes, infrequent) to the bridge; or take a bus directly to Naruto-kōen from Tokushima bus station (the easiest option).

Also at Naruto-kōen is the new **Otsuka International Museum of Art** *(admission ¥3000; open 9.30am-5pm Fri-Wed)*, which is dedicated to the ceramic arts and has over 1000 exhibits from around the world.

WESTERN TOKUSHIMA-KEN
徳島県西部

Iya Valley 祖谷渓
☎ 0883

The remote Iya Valley is considered one of Japan's 'three hidden regions'. It was to here that Kyoto's defeated Heike clan fled from the rival Genji clan during the 12th-century civil wars. Iya is romanticised in Alex Kerr's award-winning book *Lost Japan*. In 1972, Kerr bought an 18th-century thatch-roofed farmhouse in Higashi Iya and has since been restoring it to its original brilliance (see the boxed text 'Chiiori – A Rural Retreat' below).

Iya draws a steady stream of travellers who come to cross the famed *kazura-bashi* (vine bridges) that span the deep river gorges. Rivers in Shikoku's mountainous interior were once commonly spanned by these perilous catwalks, which could conveniently be cut down to prevent enemy forces from crossing.

A good place to stay en route to Iya is the **Awa Ikeda Youth Hostel** *(☎ 72-5277; beds ¥2850)*, part of the Mitsugon-ji mountain temple complex. Book early and take advantage of their pick-up/drop-off service from/to JR Awa Ikeda station (last pick-up 6pm). The priest and his wife are very friendly. Other accommodation offerings in the Iya Valley itself are listed following.

Getting There & Around The entrance to the Iya Valley, Ōboke, is easy to reach by train via JR Ōboke station. Getting around the valley, however, involves some planning. Although there are bus services that can get you as far as the vine bridge in Nishi Iya, the best way to explore the region is with your own wheels (rental cars are available in most of Shikoku's major cities, including Ikeda).

Chiiori – A Rural Retreat

In Alex Kerr's *Lost Japan*, he writes of discovering a thatched-roof farmhouse in Iya Valley, which he bought in 1973 and named Chiiori (Cottage of the Flute) With its houses perched high on hillsides and its air of isolation, Iya has been dubbed the 'Tibet of Japan'. In 1997 I joined Alex in the job of maintaining the 300-year-old structure, and lately a steady stream of like-minded enthusiasts have rallied around the house. In 1998 we founded the Chiiori Project.

The goal of the project is to bring the house and the depopulated village around it back to life, and to offer visitors an experience like no other in Japan. With its *irori* hearths (indoor campfires), glistening wooden floorboards and soaring rafters, Chiiori is a window to a lost world.

The Chiiori experience is not for everyone – smoke and dust, damp summers and icy winters. During volunteer weekends people trade their sweat to learn about carpentry, farming or roof-thatching. Other visitors come for seminars or workshops ranging from Zen Buddhism to country cooking. In the evening, it's off to the local *onsen* (mineral hot-spring bath). Back at Chiiori, we sip sake, watch the smoke billow up into the rafters and chat until the wee hours. See Ｗ www.chiiori.org.

Mason Florence

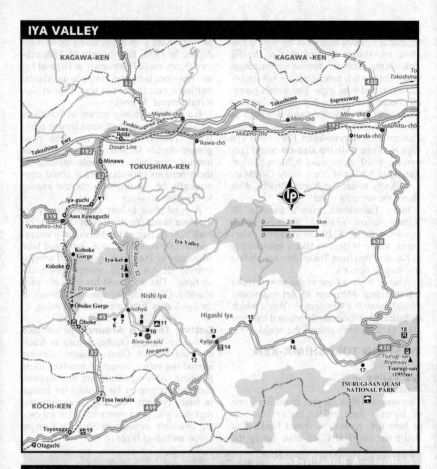

IYA VALLEY

PLACES TO STAY

3 Iya Onsen
   祖谷温泉
7 Hikyo-no-yu
   秘境の湯
8 Hotel Kazura-bashi
   ホテルかずら橋
9 Iya So Minshuku;
   Kazuraya
   Minshuku
   民宿いや荘;
   観光ホテルかずらや
11 Kazura-bashi
    Camping Village
    かずら橋キャンプ村
12 Mampu Lodge &
    Ryūgūgake-koen
    Park
    龍宮崖公園

16 Iya Shino Onsen
    Kyo
    いやしの温泉郷

PLACES TO EAT

1 Woody Rest
   渓流館
4 Restaurant
   Mannaka
   ホテルまんなか
6 Senkichi
   仙吉
15 Soba Dojo
    そば道場

OTHER

2 Peeing Boy
   Statue

小便小僧

5 Lapis Ōboke
   Museum
   ラピス大歩危
10 Kazura-bashi
    かずら橋
13 Buke Yashiki
    Samurai House
    武家屋敷喜多家
14 Higashi Iya Folk
    Museum
    東祖谷民族資料館
17 Oku Iya Kazura-bashi
    奥祖谷かずら橋
18 Ōtsurugi-jinja
    大剣神社
19 Jōfuku-ji
    定福寺

Ōboke & Koboke 大歩危・小歩危

The 8km stretch of the Yoshino-gawa gorge between Koboke and Ōboke is spectacular. From Restaurant Mannaka, there are 30-minute **boat rides** down the gentle river rapids (¥1000). More adventurous **rafting** and **kayaking trips** run from late April to the end of October. Costs average ¥15,000 for a day excursion. Contact **Tanken Club** (☎ 76-6672; **W** www.tanken-club.com), **Mont Bell Challenge** (☎ 75-0898; **W** www.montbell.com) or **Gekiryu** (**W** www.gekiryu.com).

Lapis Ōboke (admission ¥500; open 9am-5pm daily), north of JR Ōboke station, is a geology museum with a fine collection of precious stones.

If you're travelling south from Ikeda to Iya by private transport, there is stunning scenery in the deep canyons along old Rte 32. Turn east off the new Rte 32, over the blue bridge near JR Iya-guchi station. Just north of here, **Woody Rest** is a good lunch spot. Follow the narrow road through the gorge to Nishi Iya. Just beyond the curious 'peeing boy' statue, there are riverside **hot-spring baths** and accommodation at **Iya Onsen** (rooms per person with breakfast & dinner ¥15,000); admission to the baths is ¥1500 for nonguests.

Nishi Iya 西祖谷

Nishi Iya is best known for the famed **Kazura-bashi** (Vine Bridge). There's a charge of ¥500 to walk across the bridge. More adventurous travellers will want to head east to the remote Oku-Iya double vine bridges in Higashi Iya (see following).

The **Hikyu-no-yu** (☎ 87-2800; rooms ¥14,000) is a grand onsen complex featuring indoor and outdoor baths (nonguests ¥1000), a restaurant and plush hotel.

Up the road is **Senkichi** (☎ 87-2733; noodles ¥520; open 10.30am-7pm Fri-Wed) serves Iya soba noodles in a traditional farmhouse atmosphere and is decorated with a superb collection of antiques and local folk-crafts.

Hotel Kazura-bashi (☎ 87-2171; rooms per person with 2 meals ¥16,000) offers Japanese-style rooms with great mountain views. There are excellent hill-top hot-spring baths (nonguests ¥1000) here.

Other accommodation options in the vine bridge area include **Iya-So Minshuku** (☎ 87-2242; rooms per person with breakfast & dinner ¥6500) and the more upmarket **Kazuraya**

Minshuku (☎ 87-2831; rooms per person ¥12,000). **Kazura-bashi Camping Village** (camping ¥500, huts ¥5200) is a great campground upriver from the Kazura-bashi beyond **Biwa-no-taki**, a 50m-high waterfall.

By bus from JR Ōboke station, it's 12km to the bridge; buses are infrequent and take 45 minutes (¥880). More frequent buses from JR Awa Ikeda station take around 1¼ hours (¥1250).

From March to November, retro-style **'Bonnet Bus' tours** (☎ 72-1231) to Iya leave from JR Awa Ikeda station and cost ¥5200, including lunch.

Higashi Iya 東祖谷

To escape the throngs of Japanese tourists at the Nishi Iya Kazura-bashi, head 30km east to the remote **Oku Iya Kazura-bashi** (¥500) in Higashi Iya. Set in a pristine natural environment, the *fufu* (husband and wife) vine bridges hang side-by-side, high over the river gorge. There is also a free **camping ground** by the river's edge.

En route to the bridges is **Buke Yashiki** (admission ¥300; open 9am-5pm Wed-Mon), an enormous thatched-roof samurai house, and an interesting **folk craft museum** (admission ¥400) housed in the large red building in Kyōjo.

At the **Soba Dōjō** you can taste Iya soba and also try making your own.

Further toward Tsurugi-san, there are cabins for rent at **Iya Shino Onsen Kyo** (☎ 88-2975; cabins from ¥5000), part of a new hot-spring complex, and at **Mampu Lodge** (☎ 88-5001; cabins per person ¥4000) in Ryūgūgake-kōen.

Memme Juku (☎ 88-2170; **W** www.iya.jp/takumi) is a field studies school led by local villagers who offer 19 different courses related to traditional Iya arts, crafts, and customs. For a local's perspective of Higashi Iya, log onto **W** www.east-iya.com.

Tsurugi-san The mountain's name translates to Sword Peak, although it is actually gently rounded rather than sharp-edged. It is also known locally as 'Ken-zan'. At 1955m, it is the second highest mountain in Shikoku and provides excellent hiking opportunities. A chairlift can take you to a point from which it is a leisurely 40-minute walk to the summit, but many prefer to start from **Ōtsurugi-jinja**, the shrine near the car park. For detailed information on hiking Tsurugi-san pick up a copy of Lonely Planet's *Hiking in Japan*.

Jōfuku-ji 定福寺
Further south (in Kōchi-ken), tranquil Jōfuku-ji has a **Youth Hostel** (☎ 0887-74-0301; beds ¥3150; meals available), a 20-minute uphill walk from Toyonaga station.

SOUTHERN TOKUSHIMA-KEN
徳島県南部
Tokushima's spectacular southern coastline is well worth a visit. The JR Mugi line runs down the coast as far as **Kaifu**, just short of the border with Kōchi-ken. From there, the private Asa Kaigan railway runs two stops into Kōchi, but that's the end of the line. You can continue by bus or thumb to the cape at **Muroto-misaki** and on to Kōchi city.

Hiwasa 日和佐
If you're doing the pilgrimage, you'll be visiting the Yakuō-ji, Temple 23 and the last temple in Tokushima. The Yakuō-ji, in this fishing town, is a *yakuyoke-dera*, a temple specialising in warding off bad luck during unlucky years. Although there are a number of designated unlucky years, the unluckiest age for men is 42, while for women it is 33. The stairway up to the temple is split. The men's side has 42 steps, while the women's has 33. Pilgrims approach on the appropriate side and put a coin on each step – if you turn up at a busy time, the steps are virtually overflowing with money!

From May to late August, turtles come ashore to lay their eggs on beaches in the area. The Hiwasa **Sea Turtle Museum** (admission ¥600; open 8.30am-5pm daily) has all sorts of information, and turtles for up-close viewing.

The Yakuō-ji has accommodation in its **shukubō** (☎ 0884-77-1105), and the **Hiwasa Youth Hostel** (☎ 0884-77-0755; beds ¥2750; meals available) is just down from the temple.

Mugi 牟岐
The next town down the line is Mugi. It has a great **Seashell Museum** (admission ¥300; open 9am-4.30pm Tues-Sun) with over 6000 shells on display in a wooden building designed in the image of a seashell.

Not far from Sabase station, the next stop south, is **Ozuna beach**, popular in summer for swimming and snorkelling.

Kainan, Kaifu, Shishikui & Tōyō
海南・海部・宍喰・東洋
The next few towns are 'surf city' Japan. Kainan, Kaifu, Shishikui and Tōyō in neighbouring Kōchi-ken are where it's at in Japan for surfers. The coastline is spectacular, and there are superb beaches, colourful characters, tanned bodies and plenty of seafood. National and international surfing contests are held in the area. There is also great snorkelling and diving.

Visitors with private transport can head inland on Rte 193 from Kainan for about 25km to Shikoku's highest waterfall, the 55m Todoroki Falls. There is good **hiking** in the surrounding area.

Between Kaifu and Shishikui train stations on the main coast road is one of those rare little gems. The name says it all, **Da Hawaiian Kitchen**. Run by English-speaking Ten, the pint-sized restaurant has great views, free Internet access, Hawaiian music and the menu painted on a surfboard. Fill yourself with the *yokozuna* set for ¥900. Ten is on island time, as his kitchen is only open from 11am to 4pm April to November.

At Shishikui, take the Blue Marine **glass-bottomed boat cruise** to see the spectacular sea life. The cruise operates hourly from 9am to 4pm daily, and costs ¥1400. Also check out the new **Shishikui Onsen** complex. Fishing tours are also available.

For accommodation, there is the upmarket **Hotel Riviera Shishikui** (☎ 0884-6-3300; per person with meals from ¥12,000), the **Kokuminshukusha Mitoko-so** (☎ 0884-76-3510; per person with meals ¥6400), and a selection of ryokan and *minshuku*.

Kōchi-ken 高知県

The largest of Shikoku's four prefectures, Kōchi-ken (formerly the land of Tosa) spans the entire Pacific coastline from east of the cape at Muroto-misaki to west of Ashizuri-misaki. It is a popular domain for outdoor activities, from diving, surfing and whale-watching to canoeing, rafting, and camping along the Shimanto-gawa – the last undammed, naturally flowing river in Japan.

Looking at the Shikoku map, this Kōchi section follows on from the Tokushima-Kōchi border and moves southwest to Muroto-misaki, westwards around Tosa-wan (Tosa Bay) to Ashizuri-misaki, then on to the border with Ehime – the same basic route most visitors to Kōchi have taken over the last 1000 years.

THE PILGRIMAGE IN KŌCHI

Kōchi-ken is known as Shūgyō no dōjō – the place of practice – and has a reputation as the *henro*'s testing ground. The trip through Tosa makes up more than a third of the pilgrimage, but there are only 16 of the 88 temples in the province. Tosa was always considered wild and remote through Japanese history, cut off by a barrier of mountains. Consequently, the Tosa character is thought of as strong, independent and proud. While Tokushima nurtured puppet theatre, in Tosa they raised fighting dogs.

The tough work ahead is symbolised by the fact that there is fully 84km between the last temple in Tokushima, the Yakuō-ji in Hiwasa, and the first in Tosa at Muroto-misaki. Kōchi's first temple, however, marks the spot where Kōbō Daishi achieved enlightenment at the age of 19, and holds huge significance to pilgrims. The route then follows a wide arc around Tosa-wan; visits the nine temples in and around Kōchi city; then drops to the end of Shikoku's second great southern cape that juts out into the Pacific, Ashizuri-misaki. The distance from Temple 37 in Kubokawa to Temple 38 at Ashizuri-misaki is 87 km, the longest distance between temples on the pilgrimage. There are few places as remote in all Japan. Even then, there is still work to be done to get through Tosa, and the *henro* tends to breathe a sigh of relief on moving into Ehime-ken; the hard work has been done.

TOKUSHIMA TO MUROTO-MISAKI

If you've just come down the coast from Tokushima and Hiwasa, then you're literally at the end of the line at Kannoura as you pass into Kōchi-ken. That's the end of the train line, and if you want to carry on down to Muroto-misaki you'll either have to take the bus or use your thumb. The good news is that the coast and its beaches and rocky headlands are spectacular. In par-ticular, Shirahama and Ikumi beaches are popular with surfers.

There are a host of *minshuku* around, and the **White Beach Hotel** (☎ 0887-29-3344; with/without meals ¥7500/6000) is right beside Shirahama Beach. There's **camping** next door.

Minami Kaze (☎ 0887-29-3638; per person ¥3000), right on the beach at Ikumi, is popular with surfies. It has 10 rooms, and shared toilets and showers. Meals and draught beer are also available.

Halfway down the coast to Muroto-misaki, **whale-watching tours** (☎ 0887-27-2572) are available in Sakihama. Call for details as tours run irregularly.

The Kannoura to Muroto-misaki bus takes one hour and costs ¥1480. To Kōchi city it takes 2½ hours and costs ¥2770. For the last 40km to the cape, the road hugs the coast, hemmed in by mountains on one side and the sea on the other.

Muroto-misaki 室戸岬

Muroto-misaki is one of Shikoku's two great capes that jut out into the Pacific. In Japanese literature, Muroto is famed as one of the wildest spots in the nation and as the doorway to the land of the dead. To pilgrims, it is the place where Kōbō Daishi achieved enlightenment, and many come to try and do the same. On a calm day, the Pacific is like a millpond; in bad weather Muroto is pounded by huge waves and buffeted by the wind. Visitors can explore Kōbō Daishi's bathing hole among the rockpools, or the cave where he meditated.

Temple 24, **Hotsumisaki-ji** (also known as Higashi-dera), sits on top of the hill directly above the point. It has a **Youth Hostel** (☎ 0887-23-0024; beds ¥3200; meals available) that is part of the temple complex.

There are regular buses from Muroto to Kōchi station.

MUROTO-MISAKI TO KŌCHI

The coastline and towns between Muroto-misaki and Kōchi city have just become increasingly accessible thanks to a rare phenomena in Japan – a new train line. The country has lost plenty of uneconomic lines since the railways were privatised in 1987, and a new line is unusual. As of July 2002 the Gomen-Nahari line connects Kōchi city with Nahari, about 30km north of the cape.

SHIKOKU

Aki 安芸市

Aki is where Iwasaki Yatarō, founder of the giant Mitsubishi conglomerate, was born in 1834. His **thatched-roofed house** (☎ 0887-34-1111) is well preserved; call if you would like to visit it.

Aki is also home to the **Calligraphy Art Museum** (admission ¥300; open 9am-5pm Tues-Sun), with over 1000 examples of shodo on display.

Yasu 夜須

At Yasu, on the new train line, there is a good swimming at Tei beach and the **Yasu Cycling Terminal** (☎ 0887-54-3196), where you can rent bicycles and ride east along the coast on a 'cycling road' for bicycles only.

Ryūga-dō 龍河洞

Accessible by bus from Kōchi, Noicho on the new train line and Tosa-Yamada station on the JR Dosan line is the impressive limestone cave Ryūga-dō (admission ¥1000; open 8.30am-5pm daily). It has characteristic stalactites and stalagmites, and traces of prehistoric habitation. You can also see the famed long-tailed roosters here.

KŌCHI 高知

☎ 088 • pop 320,000

Kōchi was the castle town of what used to be Tosa province, and the small but original castle still stands. Like Kagoshima in Kyūshū and Hagi in western Honshū, this pleasant city lays claim to having played an important role in the Meiji Restoration.

Orientation

Kōchi city is inland. Harimayabashi-dōri, the main street, runs on a north–south axis, with a tram line down the centre. The street crosses the main shopping arcade and the other main street near Harimaya-bashi, a recently rebuilt replica of the original bridge.

The top festival is **Yosakoi** (held 9 to 12 August), immediately before Tokushima's Awa-ōdori festival.

Information

The **tourist information office** (☎ 882-7777; open 9am-8pm daily) is at JR Kōchi station. Staff can provide brochures in English, and also help to book accommodation. Scheduled day and half-day bus tours of the city's sights depart from JR Kōchi station at 8.30am and 1.50pm. To find out more or to make a booking, ask at this office.

Also well worth visiting for local information, maps and friendly advice is the **Kōchi International Association** (KIA; ☎ 875-0022; open 8.30am-5.15pm Mon-Sat), on the south side of the castle. There is free Internet access, a library and English newspapers.

Kōchi-jō 高知城

Kōchi's castle (admission ¥400; open 9am-4.30pm daily) is a real survivor, not a postwar concrete reconstruction, and the lovely grounds are great for a stroll. Although a building on the site dates back to the 14th century, the present castle was built between 1601 and 1611, burnt down in 1727 and rebuilt in 1753. By this time, the peace of the Tokugawa period was well established and castles were scarcely necessary, except as a symbol of a feudal lord's power. The Kōchi lord therefore rebuilt the castle with his kaitokukan (living quarters) on the ground floor, with doors opening into the garden. Kōchi-jō, therefore, is not a gloomy castle, unlike those that were strongly fortified against enemy attack. The castle offers fine views over the town.

At the bottom of the castle hill is the well-preserved gateway, **Ōte-mon**. Nearby the castle there is a **museum** with exhibits relating to Sakamoto Ryōma.

Godaisan-kōen & Chikurin-ji

五台山公園・竹林寺

The hilltop temple Chikurin-ji and Kōchi's botanical gardens, Godaisan-kōen (combined admission ¥400), are both in Godaisan, several kilometres from the town centre. The temple is No 31 on the 88 Sacred Temple Circuit, and there's an attractive five-storey pagoda at the top of the hill. The temple's Treasure House has an interesting collection of statues, some looking very Indian or Tantric.

On the other side of the car park is the **Makino Botanical Garden** and greenhouse (admission ¥500).

Katsura-hama 桂浜

Katsura-hama is a popular beach 13km south of central Kōchi. The Kōchi area is noted for its fighting dogs. These mastiff-like dogs are ranked like sumō wrestlers and even wear similar aprons. Dog-fight demonstrations are held in the **Tosa Tōken Centre** (*admission ¥2000; open 8.30am-6pm daily*) at Katsura-hama, but you may have to wait until sufficient spectators have gathered.

A five-minute walk west of Katsura-hama is the **Sakamoto Ryōma Memorial Museum** (*admission ¥400; open 9am-4.30pm daily*), which tells the local hero's life story in miniature dioramas. The **Katsura-hama Aquarium** (*admission ¥1100; open 8.30am-5.30pm daily*) features local *akame* fished from the bay, Tosa-wan. Local kids enjoy feeding the fish and resident sea turtles.

Buses make the run from Kōchi bus station to Katsura-hama hourly (¥610, 30 minutes).

Sunday Market

If you're in Kōchi on Sunday, don't miss the colourful street market along Phoenix-dōri, the road leading to the castle. The market, which has been going for some 300 years, has everything from fruit, vegetables and goldfish, to antiques, knives and large garden stones.

Roosters

Breeders have coaxed the long-tailed rooster (*onaga-dori*) to produce tail feathers up to 10m long! You can see them at the **Chōbikei Centre** (*admission ¥500; open 9am-4pm daily*) in Nankoku city, out towards Kōchi airport and also at the cave, Ryūga-dō.

Places to Stay – Budget

Tosa Bekkan (☎ 883-5685; *rooms per person ¥4000*) is the best deal, with Japanese-style rooms, air-conditioning and coin laundry. **Hotel Tosa** (☎ 825-3332; *rooms from ¥3900*) is not far from the Horizume tram stop. **Big 1** (☎ 883-9603; *capsules ¥3700*),

for men only, is a sauna and capsule hotel near the station.

Places to Stay – Mid-Range

Kōchi Green Kaikan (☎ 825-2701; *singles/twins ¥5700/10,600*) is just south of the Kencho-mae tram stop. **Kōchi Green Hotel** (☎ 822-1800; *singles/doubles/twins from ¥5500/10,300/10,300*) is another standard hotel that's not too far from the station. **Hotel Takasago** (☎ 822-1288; *singles/twins from ¥6300/12,600*) is also not far from the station.

Places to Stay – Top End

Sansuien Ryokan (☎ 822-0131; *per person from ¥15,000*), south of the castle, is a ryokan-style place and includes some old buildings from the grounds of the Kōchi *daimyō* (regional lord under the shōgun) and an *onsen*. Rates include meals. The *onsen* (*admission ¥900; open 10am-4pm daily*) is open to the public.

Places to Eat & Drink

Kōchi's best restaurants are clustered around the Daimaru department store, in and around the Obiyamachi shopping arcade. **Tsukasa**, a Japanese Tosa-ryōri (Tosa-cuisine) restaurant has two branches in Kōchi and displays plastic meals from *tempura* to sashimi. **Hakobe** offers excellent 'cook it yourself' *okonomiyaki*. **Ninniku-ya**, is for garlic lovers and has an all-garlic menu (illustrated and in English).

Jungri-la, a 2nd-floor *izakaya* with a jungle motif, serves out-of-the-ordinary dishes including alligator meat! **Hirome Market** boasts an interesting collection of shops and eateries that are well worth checking out.

Sakamoto Ryōma – Local Hero

Although it was the progressive samurai of Kagoshima and Hagi who played the major part in the dramatic events of the Meiji Restoration, the citizens of Kōchi claim it was their boy Sakamoto Ryōma who brought the two sides together.

Unhappy with the rigid class structure institutionalised under Tokugawa rule, Sakamoto sought exile in Nagasaki, where he ran a trading company and helped build the powerful alliances that prompted the collapse of the shōgunate.

His assassination in Kyoto in 1867, when he was just 32 years old, cemented his romantic albeit tragic image, and he appears, looking distinctly sour, on countless postcards and other tourist memorabilia in Kōchi. There's a notable statue of Sakamoto at Katsura-hama.

SHIKOKU

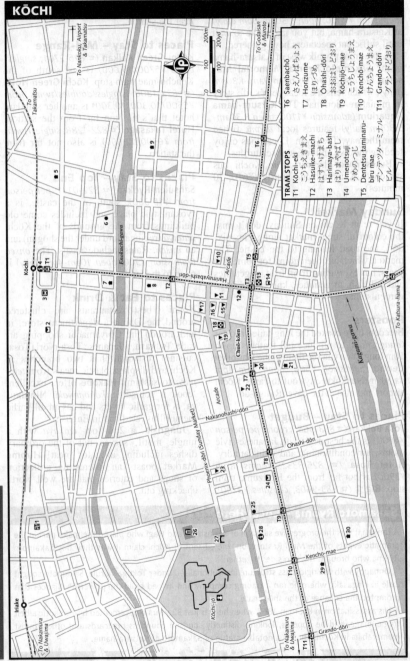

KŌCHI

To Takamatsu

To Nankoku, Airport & Takamatsu

To Godaisan & Muroto

Kōchi

Iriake

To Nakamura & Uwajima

To Nakamura & Uwajima

Enokuchi-gawa

Harimayabashi-dōri

Arcade

Arcade

Nakanohashi-dōri

Phoenix-dōri (Sunday Market)

Ohashi-dōri

Chuō-kōen

Kagami-gawa

To Katsura-hama

Kōchi-jō

Kenchō-mae

Grando-dōri

200m
200yd
0 100
0 100

KŌCHI

PLACES TO STAY		16	Irish Bar		6	Kagiyama Bicycle
5	Big 1		アイリッシュバー			Rental
7	Hotel Takasago	17	Hakobe			かぎやま自転車
	ホテル高砂		はこべ		12	Harimaya-bashi
8	Kōchi Green Hotel	19	Tsukasa			はりまや橋
	高知グリーンホテル		料亭司		13	Seibu Department
9	Tosa Bekkan	20	Jungri-la			Store
	とさ別館		ジャングリラ			西武デパート
21	Business Hotel	22	Ninniku-ya		14	Katsura-hama Bus Stop
	Tatsumi		にんにく屋			かつら浜バス停
	ビジネスホテルたつみ	23	Hirome Market		18	Daimaru Department
29	Kōchi Green Kaikan		ひろめマーケット			Store
	高知グリーン会館					大丸百貨店
30	Sansuien Ryokan;	OTHER			24	Post Office
	Onsen Hoteru	1	Anraku-ji			郵便局
	三翠園ホテル		安楽寺		25	NTT
		2	Main Post Office		26	Prefectural Museum-
PLACES TO EAT			高知中央郵便局			Kōchi History Museum
10	Get	3	Kōchi Bus Station			高知県立文学館
	ゲット		(to Matsuyama)		27	Ōte-mon
11	Tsukasa		バスターミナル		28	Kōchi International
	料亭司		(松山行き他)			Association (KIA)
15	Tsukasa	4	Tourist Information Office			高知インターナショナルアソ
	料亭司		観光案内所			シエーション

Irish Bar is just what you'd expect, right down to the Guinness on tap, while **Get** plays soul music.

Getting There & Away

Kōchi airport is about 10km east of the city and there are connections to all Japan's major cities. The bus between Kōchi station and the airport costs ¥700.

Kōchi is on the JR Dosan line, which runs from Takamatsu on the north coast of Shikoku via Kotohira. It takes 2½ hours by *tokkyū* from Takamatsu. From Kōchi, rail services continue westward to just beyond Kubokawa where the line splits southwest to Nakamura and west to Uwajima. From Uwajima, you can continue north to Matsuyama.

Long-distance buses run between Kōchi and the major cities. Travel between Kōchi and Matsuyama is faster by bus than by train (¥3300, 3¼ hours). To travel around the south coast, either west around Ashizuri-misaki to Uwajima or east around Muroto-misaki to Tokushima, you will have to spend some time on a bus as the train lines do not extend all the way.

Kōchi is connected by overnight ferry to Osaka (¥4610, nine hours).

Getting Around

The tram service (¥180) running north–south from the station intersects the east–west tram route at the Harimaya-bashi junction. Pay when you get off. Ask for a *norikaeken* (transfer ticket) if you have to transfer lines. You can easily reach the castle on foot, though to reach the town's other attractions you must take a bus. **Kagiyama Rental Cycle** (☎ 882-1585; ¥1200/day) is near the station.

KŌCHI TO ASHIZURI-MISAKI

There are all sorts of interesting things going on between Kōchi and Ashizuri-misaki, particularly the closer you get to the cape.

Kubokawa 窪川

Kubokawa, one hour south of Kōchi by the fastest train, is a sleepy little town with a very pleasant **youth hostel** (☎ 0880-22-0376; beds ¥3200; meals available) in the **Iwamoto-ji**, which is also Temple 37 of the 88. It's 10 minutes' walk south of the station. The next temple is at the cape, 87 km away, so if you're on the pilgrimage and walking, you may want to mentally prepare yourself.

The train lines part at Kubokawa and the JR Yodo line heads west through the mountains to Uwajima in Ehime-ken.

Along the way, but still in Kōchi, is the hard-to-get-to but often-raved-about **Shimanto-gawa Youth Hostel** (☎ 0880-54-1352; beds ¥3150; meals available). Get off at Ekawa-saki station, and take the bus for 30 minutes

SHIKOKU

to Kuchiyanai. The youth hostel is 4.5km away across the river, but the manager will come and pick you up if you call and ask nicely. You couldn't get much more away from it all in Japan. The hostel runs canoeing trips, with all tuition and gear included for ¥5500.

The Tosa Kuroshio-tetsudo Nakamura-Sukumo line heads south to Nakamura, then west to Sukumo. There are **whale-watching trips** on offer in Saga (☎ 0880-55-3131) and Ōgata (☎ 0880-43-1058) from spring to autumn, but you might want to call ahead to see if they are going. A three-hour trip costs ¥5000.

Nakamura 中村

Nakamura is on the Shimanto-gawa, and the point where the train line turns west to Sukumo. There are no trains south of here. From JR Nakamura station there is a regular bus service to Ashizuri-misaki (¥1970, one hour). You can continue around the cape and on to Sukumo and Uwajima by bus.

Nakamura is a good place to organise trips on the beautiful **Shimanto-gawa**, proudly hailed as the last free-flowing river in Japan. Staff at the **tourist information office** at JR Nakamura station can provide information on river-boat trips, camping and outdoor activities. You can also get to Kuchiyanai, close to the Shimanto-gawa Youth Hostel (see the previous Kubokawa entry), in 50 minutes by bus from here.

About 40 minutes south of Nakamura on the bus to Ashizuri-misaki is **Ōki-no-hama**, a 2km-long stretch of sandy white beach backed by pine trees that is likely to have you blinking in disbelief and reaching for your swimming gear.

ASHIZURI-MISAKI 足摺岬

Ashizuri-misaki, like Muroto-misaki, is a wild and picturesque promontory ending at a lighthouse, and it is a popular visitor destination. Ashizuri means 'foot stamping' and the cape got its name from the story of an old monk who stamped his foot in anguish when his young disciple set off looking for the promised land of Fudaraku in a boat. Fudaraku was believed to be the blessed realm of Kannon, goddess of mercy, and many set forth from the cape in their search of paradise in this lifetime, never to be heard from again. Centuries later, Ashizuri is famous for suicides, with stories such as that of a young geisha who danced off the edge onto the beckoning rocks below.

Manjirō the Hero

Nearly every corner of Shikoku boasts a local hero, but perhaps most extraordinary of them all is Kōchi-born John Manjirō.

His real name was Nakahama Manjirō. In 1841, while helping out on a fishing boat, a violent storm swept 14-year-old Manjirō and four others onto the desolate shores of Tori-shima, 600km off Tokyo Bay. Five months later they were rescued by a US whaler, and granted safe passage to Hawaii.

In Hawaii the ship's captain invited Manjirō to return to his home in Massachusetts, where the boy spent four years learning English, navigation and the ways of the West, before his skills took him back to sea and around the world. In 1851, 10 years after the shipwreck, Manjirō returned to Japan, where he was interrogated (Japan's National Seclusion policy forbade overseas travel), but allowed to return to Kōchi.

When Commodore Perry's 'black ships' arrived in 1853, Manjirō was summoned to Edo to advise the shōgun. He was later the chief translator for the Harris Treaty negotiations of 1858, and subsequently published Japan's first English-language phrase book, *Shortcut to Anglo-American Conversation.* He returned to the US in 1860 as part of a Japanese delegation, and after the Meiji Restoration in 1867 took up post at the Kaisei School for Western Learning (which later became part of Tokyo University).

Manjirō is remembered as a man whose destiny took him from the simple life of a teenage fisherman to becoming one of Japan's first true statesmen. On the cape at Ashizuri-misaki, a large statue stands in his honour, and there is a museum dedicated to his achievements. Manjirō's intrepid journey is recounted in Masuji Ibuse's *Castaways* (Kodansha International).

The **Kongōfuku-ji** is Temple 38 of the 88, but it doesn't have Ashizuri-misaki to itself. There are hotels, ryokan, tour buses and the **Ashizuri Youth Hostel** (☎ 0880-88-0324; beds ¥2900; meals available). There is a small **tourist information booth** with English maps of the area and a statue of local hero John Manjirō (see the boxed text 'Manjirō the Hero').

NORTHWEST TO SUKUMO & UWAJIMA

Tosa-Shimizu 土佐清水

Ferries operate to/from Osaka (¥6600) from Tosa-Shimizu at the northern end of the cape, via Kōchi. There are also **whale-watching tours** (☎ 0880-84-0723) on offer for ¥5000.

From Tosa-Shimizu, the road continues around the southern coast.

Tatsukushi 竜串

The scenery is particularly attractive through Tatsukushi, which means 'dragon's skewers' and got its name from spectacular rock pillars that protrude from the sea. There is a **coral museum** (admission ¥500; open 8am-5.30pm daily), which has a collection of local pink coral, and the **Ashizuri Submarine Lookout** (admission ¥800; open 9am-5pm daily), where you can view fish from an observation room below sea level. Sightseeing boats and glass-bottom boats operate from the town.

If you really want to get away from it all, the **Odo Sunset Youth Hostel** (☎ 0880-76-0222; beds ¥2750; meals available) is almost at the end of a 17km dead-end road at the end of a spiny peninsula with stunning scenery. The turn-off is about halfway between Tatsukushi and Sukumo. Using public transport, it's best accessed by catching the bus to Kashiwa-jima for an hour from Sukumo, and getting off at the Shin-Kashiwa-jima ōhashi stop. **Kashiwa-jima** is a popular diving site.

Sukumo 宿毛

Sukumo itself has a fine harbour and the **Sukumo Youth Hostel** (☎ 0880-64-0233; beds ¥2900; meals available). The hostel is 20 minutes out of town, but if you call and ask nicely staff will come and get you.

Sukumo is only half an hour by train from Nakamura, but much longer around the coast via the cape on the bus; travel on to Uwajima takes about two hours by bus. From Sukumo, ferries make the three-hour crossing several times daily to Saeki on Kyūshū.

There are several popular **dive sites** off islands in the area that are reached by boat from Sukumo – notably at Nishiumi and Oki-no-shima.

Ehime-ken 愛媛県

Occupying the northwestern region of Shikoku, the highlights of Ehime-ken include Matsuyama-jō and Dōgo Onsen, the sacred peak Ishizuchi-san (1982m), and the notorious Taga-jinja (Taga Shrine) and sex museum of Uwajima.

Looking at the Shikoku map, this section starts in the southwest corner of the prefecture for those who are following the circular route of the island. It then works its way north to Matsuyama, before turning east towards Kagawa-ken.

THE PILGRIMAGE IN EHIME

Ehime-ken is known as Bodai no dōjō – the place of attainment of wisdom – and has the largest number of pilgrimage temples, with 27 in this prefecture. The southern part of the prefecture was always considered, like Tosa, to be wild and remote – they still have bullfighting in Uwajima. Further north, there are two temples in the inland mountains, with the Iwaya-ji, Temple 45, well worth a visit, hanging on a cliff-side high above the valley floor. The place oozes sacredness. As *henro* approach Shikoku's largest city of Matsuyama and the eight temples in and around it, they know that the hard work of the pilgrimage has been done. There are another six temples in and around Imabari, where the new Shimanami-kaidō bridge system links Shikoku to Honshū, from where the trail turns east.

UWAJIMA 宇和島

☎ 0895 • pop 65,000

Uwajima is a relatively quiet and peaceful place with a small, unreconstructed castle and a notorious sex shrine! It makes a very interesting pause between Kōchi and Matsuyama.

SHIKOKU

Information

There is a **tourist information office** (☎ 22-3934; open 8.30am-5pm Mon-Fri, 9am-5pm Sat & Sun) across the road from JR Uwajima station. There is free Internet access (limit one hour) and the staff are extremely helpful. They will make accommodation bookings for you and may feign surprise when you ask the way to the sex museum. There are also bicycles for hire for ¥100 an hour.

Uwajima-jō 宇和島城

Dating from 1601, Uwajima-jō (admission ¥200; open 9am-4pm daily) is an interesting little three-storey structure. It once stood by the sea and, although land reclamation has moved the water well back, it still has good views over the town.

Inside the castle grounds there are photos of its recent restoration and of other castles in Japan and overseas. The surrounding park is open from sunrise to sunset.

Taga-jinja & Sex Museum
多賀神社

Once upon a time, many Shintō shrines had a connection to fertility rites, but this aspect was comprehensively purged when puritanism was imported from the West following the Meiji Restoration. Nevertheless, a handful of these shrines survived and Uwajima's Taga-jinja is one of them – it is totally dedicated to sex. There is a tree trunk phallus and various other statues and stone carvings found around the grounds, but the three-storey sex museum (admission ¥800; open 8am-5pm daily) is the major attraction.

Inside, the musuem is packed floor to ceiling with everything from explicit Peruvian pottery to Greek vases; from the illustrated *Kama Sutra* to Tibetan Tantric sculptures; from South Pacific fertility gods to a showcase full of leather S&M gear; and from early Japanese *shunga* (pornographic prints) to their European Victorian equivalents, not to mention modern porn magazines.

Watching the reactions of Japanese visitors here is almost as interesting as inspecting the intriguing exhibits.

Even if you're sick to death of temples and shrines, this is one to put on the 'to visit' list.

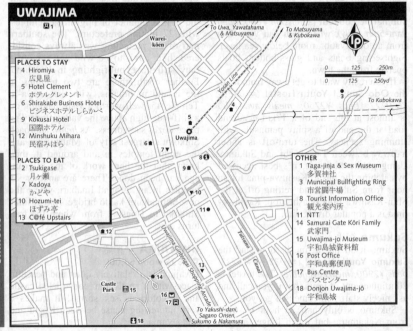

UWAJIMA

PLACES TO STAY
- 4 Hiromiya
  広見屋
- 5 Hotel Clement
  ホテルクレメント
- 6 Shirakabe Business Hotel
  ビジネスホテルしらかべ
- 9 Kokusai Hotel
  国際ホテル
- 12 Minshuku Mihara
  民宿みはら

PLACES TO EAT
- 2 Tsukigase
  月ヶ瀬
- 7 Kadoya
  かどや
- 10 Hozumi-tei
  ほづみ亭
- 13 C@fé Upstairs

OTHER
- 1 Taga-jinja & Sex Museum
  多賀神社
- 3 Municipal Bullfighting Ring
  市営闘牛場
- 8 Tourist Information Office
  観光案内所
- 11 NTT
- 14 Samurai Gate Kōri Family
  武家門
- 15 Uwajima-jo Museum
  宇和島城資料館
- 16 Post Office
  宇和島郵便局
- 17 Bus Centre
  バスセンター
- 18 Donjon Uwajima-jō
  宇和島城

Wareikōen

To Uwa, Yawatahama & Matsuyama

To Matsuyama & Kubokawa

Yosan Line

Uwajima

To Kubokawa

Uwajima Ginten-gai Shopping Arcade

Tatsuno Canal

Castle Park

To Yakushi-dani, Sagano Onsen, Sukumo & Nakamura

Small shrine, north coast of Shikoku

Bridge over the Shimanto-gawa, Kōchi-ken, Shikoku

Awa Odori dancer statue, Tokushima-ken

Lighthouse, Ashizuri-misaki, Shikoku

Koi Nobori flags, Yoshino-gawa gorge, Shikoku

Statue, Iya Valley gorge, Tokushima-ken

Temples & Shrines

In the southeastern part of town, a number of less exciting old temples and a shrine can be found by the canal. They include **Seigōzen-ji**, **Ryūgesan Tōkaku-ji**, **Kongōsan Dairyū-ji**, with its old tombs, and **Uwatsuhiko-jinja**.

Bullfights 市営闘牛場

Tōgyū is a sort of bovine sumō where one animal tries to shove the other out of the ring (actually, victory is achieved when one animal forces the other to its knees, or when one forces the other to turn and flee from the ring). Fights are held at Uwajima's municipal bullfighting ring. You might be lucky enough to hook up with a tour group that has paid for a special performance (ask at the information office); otherwise, fights (¥3000) are held on five dates each year: 2 January, the first Sunday of April, 24 July, 14 August and the second Sunday of November.

Other Attractions

East of Uwajima there is good hiking at Yakushi-dani; while the pleasant **Sagano Onsen** (☎ 27-3511; admission ¥680; open 10am-11pm daily) has a natural setting, with a riverside bath and a good restaurant. Ask at the tourist information office for the best way to get there.

Places to Stay

Uwajima Youth Hostel (☎ 22-7177; beds ¥3200; meals available) is a long walk south of the town centre and rather inconvenient. There are better options near the station. **Hiromiya** (☎ 22-2162; per person ¥3600) is satisfactory, though since it's next to the train line, you probably won't sleep in. **Minshuku Mihara** (☎ 25-5384; per person ¥6000) is a friendly place that's good value and includes two meals. **Shirakabe Business Hotel** (☎ 22-3585; singles ¥4800) has standard business hotel–type rooms.

Kokusai Hotel (☎ 25-0111; per person with meals from ¥13,000) has top-end Japanese-style rooms, while **Hotel Clement** (☎ 23-6111; singles/twins ¥6900/12,000) is part of the new station building.

Places to Eat

There's a **bakery** in the JR station, and the Uwajima Gitengai shopping arcade has various places to eat. **C@fe Upstairs** (¥350/ 30min) is an Internet café, and good for lunch. **Kadoya**, up the main road from the station, has the local delicacy *tai-meishi* (sea bream mixed with rice) on offer. **Hozumi-tei** is another good spot for seafood. **Tsukigase** (lunch sets from ¥1500), out by Warei-kōen, serves excellent *tempura* and local seafood.

Getting There & Away

You can reach Uwajima by train from Matsuyama via Uchiko and Ōzu by *tokkyū* (1¼ hours). From Kōchi, it takes three hours by the fastest trains via Kubokawa. To head to Ashizuri-misaki, you'll have to resort to buses.

There is no train line from Sukumo (Kōchi) to Uwajima, but there is a bus that makes the trip around the rugged coastline in a little under two hours (¥1750). The island-dotted coastal scenery is spectacular and rugged headlands often force the road inland. There are masses of white floats out in the sea where pearls are being grown.

UWAJIMA TO MATSUYAMA

If you've come from points south, then from Uwajima you're back in the land of trains. There's a choice of the JR Yodo line heading back to Kubokawa and Kōchi, or the JR Yosan line heading north to Matsuyama.

Yawatahama 八幡浜

Through the centuries, 88-Temple pilgrims from Kyūshū traditionally arrived in Yawatahama by ferry, and for them the Meiseki-ji near Uwa was their first temple. They would start and complete their circle there. There are still ferry services from Yawatahama to Beppu (¥1770, 2½ hours) and Usuki (¥1320, 2¼ hours) on Kyūshū. Yawatahama-kō port, is a 10-minute bus ride north of Yawatahama station.

Sada-misaki extends about 50km towards Kyūshū just north of Yawatahama, and from Misaki, near the end of the cape, car and passenger ferries (¥610) make the crossing to Saganoseki (near Oita and Beppu) in just over an hour.

Ōzu 大洲

On the Yosan line northeast of Yawatahama is Ōzu, where traditional cormorant riverfishing (*ukai*) takes place on the Hiji-kawa from 1 June to 20 September. From 6pm to

9pm each day, **sightseeing boats** *(yakata-bune* (☎ *0893-24-2029)* follow the fishing boats down the river as the cormorants catch fish – a ring around its neck stops the bird from swallowing the fish. Boat trips cost ¥3000 per person; reservations required.

Ōzu Kyōdokan Youth Hostel (☎ *0893-24-2258; beds ¥3200; meals available)* is in the southwest of town, near the Ōzu-jō ruins. It takes 30 minutes on foot from Ōzu station, or it's a seven-minute walk from Honmachi bus stop (an eight-minute ride from Ōzu station).

Uchiko 内子

This charming town has a photogenic street called **Yōkaichi**, lined with traditional buildings dating from the late Edo period and early years following the Meiji Restoration. At that time, Uchiko was an important centre for the production of the vegetable wax known as *rō*, and some of the houses along Yōkaichi belonged to merchants who made their fortunes from producing the wax. At the start of the street is the **Moribun Brewery**, where you can sample the local brew.

The **International Exchange Association** (☎ *0893-44-2111)* on the 3rd floor of the City Hall can provide an English pamphlet on local attractions. Yōkaichi is just over 1km from JR Uchiko station.

MATSUYAMA 松山
☎ 089 ● pop 470,000

Shikoku's largest city, Matsuyama, is a busy north-coast town and an important transport

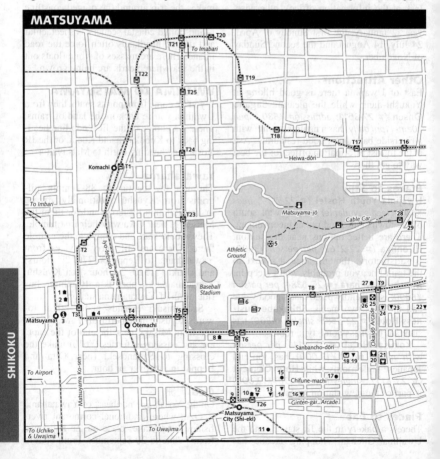

MATSUYAMA

hub. Matsuyama's major attractions are its castle, Matsutyama-jo – one of the finest survivors from the feudal era – and the Dōgo Onsen area, with its magnificent old public baths.

Orientation & Information

JR Matsuyama station is west of the castle. The town centre is immediately south of the castle and around Matsuyama City station (Shi-eki) on the private Iyo-tetsudō line. Dōgo Onsen is east of town, while the ferry port at Takahama is north of the town centre and the JR Matsuyama station.

There is an information counter at the ferry terminal for arrivals from Hiroshima, though the main **Tourist Information Center** (TIC; ☎ 931-3914; open 8.30am-8.30pm daily) is the JR Matsuyama station branch. The staff are very helpful, although English-speaking is likely to be minimal after 5.15pm. Dōgo Onsen also has a **tourist information office** near the tram terminus, at the entrance to the arcade leading to the famous public bath.

The **Ehime Prefectural International Centre** (EPIC; ☎ 943-6688; open 8.30am-5pm Mon-Sat) has friendly advice, free Internet access, English newspapers etc. It is near Tram stop T19, known as Minami-machi or Kenmin Bunkakaikan-mae. EPIC is set back off the main road and a little hard to find.

Both EPIC and the information centre at JR Matsuyama station have the **Seto Inland Sea Welcome Card**, which can get you

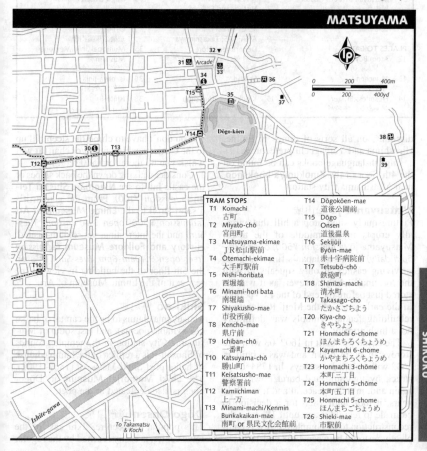

MATSUYAMA

TRAM STOPS			
T1	Komachi 古町	T14	Dōgokōen-mae 道後公園前
T2	Miyato-chō 宮田町	T15	Dōgo Onsen 道後温泉
T3	Matsuyama-ekimae JR松山駅前	T16	Sekijūji Byōin-mae 赤十字病院前
T4	Ōtemachi-ekimae 大手町駅前	T17	Tetsubō-chō 鉄砲町
T5	Nishi-horibata 西堀端	T18	Shimizu-machi 清水町
T6	Minami-hori bata 南堀端	T19	Takasago-cho たかさごちょう
T7	Shiyakusho-mae 市役所前	T20	Kiya-cho きやちょう
T8	Kenchō-mae 県庁前	T21	Honmachi 6-chome ほんまちろくちょうめ
T9	Ichiban-chō 一番町	T22	Kayamachi 6-chome かやまちろくちょうめ
T10	Katsuyama-chō 勝山町	T23	Honmachi 3-chōme 本町三丁目
T11	Keisatsusho-mae 警察署前	T24	Honmachi 5-chōme 本町五丁目
T12	Kamiichiman 上一万	T25	Honmachi 5-chome ほんまちごちょうめ
T13	Minami-machi/Kenmin Bunkakaikan-mae 南町 or 県民文化会館前	T26	Shieki-mae 市駅前

To Takamatsu & Kōchi

Ishite-gawa

SHIKOKU

MATSUYAMA

discounts on all sorts of things in Ehime, Hiroshima and Yamaguchi prefectures.

English-language books can be found on the 4th floor of the **Kinokuniya bookshop**, near Matsuyama City station.

Matsuyama-jō 松山城

Picturesquely sited atop a hill that virtually erupts in the middle of the town, Matsuyama-jō *(admission ¥500; open 9am-5pm daily)* is one of Japan's finest original surviving castles. It only squeaks in with the 'original' label, however, as it was restored just before the end of the Edo period. In the early years of the Meiji Restoration, rebuilding feudal symbols was definitely not a high priority.

The castle was built in 1602–03 with five storeys; it burnt down and was rebuilt in 1642 with only three storeys. In 1784 it was struck by lightning and burnt down once again and, in those peaceful and torpid Edo years, it took until 1820 for a decision to be made to rebuild it and until 1854 for the reconstruction to be completed! It was completely restored between 1968 and 1986.

You don't have to climb the steep hill up to the castle; a cable car and/or chairlift will whisk you up there for ¥500 return.

Consider walking down the back slopes of the castle hill to see **Ninomaru Shiseki Tei-en** *(admission ¥100)*. From the garden it's a short stroll to the **Ehime Museum of Art** *(admission ¥500; open 9.40am-6pm Tues-Sun)* and the interesting, yet seldom-visited, **History and Folklore Museum** *(admission free; open 9.40am-6pm Tues-Sun)*. It's on the 5th floor of the building in view of the rear exit of the Ehime Museum of Art.

Shiki-dō 子規堂

Matsuyama claims to be the capital of haiku (17-syllable poems), and just south of Matsuyama City station in the temple grounds of Shoshu-ji is a replica of the humble house of haiku poet Shiki Masaoka (1867–1902). The **Shiki Memorial Museum** in Dōgo-kōen is also dedicated to the poet.

Dōgo Onsen 道後温泉

This popular spa centre, 2km east of the town centre, is easily reached by the regular tram service; it terminates at the start of the spa's shopping arcade. The arcade leads to the front of Dōgo Onsen Honkan (Dōgo Spa Main Building).

Dōgo Onsen Honkan A high priority for any visitor to Matsuyama should be a bath at this rambling old public bath house *(open 6.30am-10pm daily)*. It's another place where the correct sequence of steps can be a little confusing. Pay your money outside: ¥300 for a basic bath, or ¥620 (the best overall value ticket) for a bath followed by tea and a snack, including a rental *yukata* (a light cotton kimono). For ¥980 to ¥1240 you get the *tama-no-yu* (Bath of the Spirits), followed by tea and *dango* (a sweet dumpling), and more private resting quarters.

Enter and leave your shoes in a locker. If you've paid ¥300, go to the *kami-no-yu* (Bath of the Gods) changing room (signposted in English).

If you've paid ¥620 or more, first go upstairs to get your *yukata*, then return to the appropriate changing room. You can leave valuables upstairs in the charge of the attendants who dispense the *yukata*. After your bath, those destined for upstairs can don their *yukata* and retire to the tatami mats and veranda to sip tea and gaze down on bath-hoppers clip-clopping by in *geta* (traditional wooden sandals).

The baths can get quite crowded, especially on weekends and holidays; dinner time is less crowded, as most Japanese tourists will be dining in their respective inns.

Tsubaki-no-yu Onsen One minute on foot from the Honkan (through the arcade) is Dōgo Onsen's **hot spring annexe** *(admission ¥300; open 6am-11pm daily)*. The baths are popular with locals.

Isaniwa-jinja 伊佐爾波神社
A few minutes' walk from the Dōgo Onsen bathhouse, a long flight of shrine steps leads up to the Hachiman Isaniwa-jinja, built in 1667.

Municipal Shiki Memorial Museum 市立子規記念博物館
This museum *(admission ¥300; open 9am-4.30pm Tues-Sun)* is dedicated to the memory of the local haiku master Shiki Masaoka.

Ishite-ji 石手寺
'Ishite' means 'stone hand', from a legend about a Matsuyama lord born with a stone in his hand. The Ishite-ji is 51 of the 88 Sacred Temples and is noted for its fine Kamakura architecture. It has a three-storey pagoda and is overlooked by a Buddha-figure high up on the hill. It's said to be the second busiest of the 88 temples after the Zentsū-ji in Kagawa, which was Kōbō Daishi's boyhood home. It's a 15-minute walk east from the Dōgo Onsen area to Ishite-ji. Matsuyama also has seven of the other 88 Sacred Temples.

Places to Stay
Matsuyama has three accommodation areas: around the JR Matsuyama station (business hotels); the city centre (business hotels and more top-end hotels); and atmospheric Dōgo Onsen (youth hostel, ryokan and Japanese-style hotels).

Places to Stay – Budget Dōgo Onsen, east of the town centre, makes a pleasant area to overnight. **Matsuyama Youth Hostel** *(☎ 933-6366; beds ¥3200; meals available)*, where Internet access is available, regularly tops the Japan youth hostel popularity poll.

Most Japanese-style hotels and ryokan in the Dōgo Onsen area are quite pricey. **Minshuku Miyoshi** *(☎ 977-2581; per person with/without 2 meals ¥7000/4000)*, behind the petrol station near Ishite-ji, is an exception and has friendly staff.

Matsuyama Downtown Youth Hostel *(☎ 986-8880; beds ¥3200; breakfast available)*, at the foot of the ropeway up to the castle, is new.

Grand Capsule *(☎ 945-7089; capsules ¥2600)* is a capsule hotel opposite Matsuyama City station. Men are on the 9th floor and women on the 6th floor.

Next to JR Matsuyama station are **Business Hotel Mimachi** *(☎ 921-6924; per person from ¥3000)* and **Business Hotel Dai-Ichi** *(☎ 946-2422; per person from ¥3300)*.

Places to Stay – Mid-Range to Top End The tourist office at JR Matsuyama station has a huge list of accommodation in the mid- to top-end bracket, and the staff are very helpful. Choices include **Hotel New Kajiwara** *(☎ 941-0402; singles/twins from ¥5250/8820)*, just down the main street from the station, and **Tokyo Dai Ichi Hotel** (☎ 947-4411; singles/doubles/twins from ¥6800/13,000/13,000), closer to Matsuyama City station.

ANA Hotel Matsuyama (☎ 933-5511; singles/twins from ¥10,500/17,500) is an upmarket place near the Ichiban-chō tram stop. **Matsuyama Tokyū Inn** (☎ 941-0109; singles/doubles/twins from ¥8600/16,000/16,000) is just across the road from the ANA Hotel.

Places to Eat & Drink

In and around the Ginten-gai and Okaidō shopping arcades in central Matsuyama are the best places to seek out interesting eating options.

Matsuyama is known for *goshiki somen*, thin noodles in five colours, and you can try them at **Goshiki**, next to the post office in the town centre. There are plastic models in the window and an illustrated menu showing the multi-coloured noodles.

Opposite Matsuyama City station are **Munchen**, a pseudo-German beer hall, and **Atom Boy Sushi**, an inexpensive *kaitenzushi* (conveyor-belt sushi) shop. Not far away is **Freshness Burger**, near the Kinokuniya bookshop, which whips up good burgers and sandwiches. Also close is **Charlie**, just off the Ginten-gai arcade, which has the cheapest *rāmen* in town (¥270).

Just off the Ōkaidō arcade is **Pound House Bakery**, near the **Murasaki** *robatayaki* (restaurant specialising in charcoal-grilled fish), which has a delicious selection of cakes. Further along is **Paradisen**, which has the bases covered with a pizzeria on one side of the street and a bar on the other.

For a night out, there are plenty of choices in and around the Okaidō arcade. **Déjà vu** is Matsuyama's most infamous *gaijin* dive, while **Piccadilly Circus**, a basement-level 'British antique bar', is decked out with all kinds of British paraphernalia.

Dōgo Biiru-kan, just across from the main bath-house in Dōgo Onsen, serves respectable micro-beer and pub grub. The arcade leading from the Dōgo Onsen tram stop to the main bath house also has a number of restaurants with plastic meal replicas.

Getting There & Away

Matsuyama airport is on the coast west of the city and has connections with all major cities. Buses to the JR Matsuyama station cost ¥330.

The JR Yosan line connects Matsuyama with Takamatsu, and there are also services across the Seto-ōhashi to Honshū. Trains also run southwest from Matsuyama to Uwajima and then east to Kōchi, though this is a rather circuitous route – it's faster to take a bus directly to Kōchi. There are also direct buses that run from Osaka and Tokyo.

There are frequent ferry and hydrofoil connections with Hiroshima. Take the Iyotetsudō private train line from Matsuyama City or Ōtemachi stations right to the end of the line at Takahama (¥360 from Ōtemachi). From Takahama, a connecting bus whisks you the remaining distance to the port, Matsuyama Kankō-kō.

Other boats operate to/from Matsuyama and Beppu, Kokura and Oita on Kyūshū, as well as Iwakuni, Kure, Mihara, Onomichi and Yanai on Honshū, but check which of the Matsuyama ports these services operate from.

Getting Around

Matsuyama has an excellent tram service costing a flat ¥150 (pay when you get off). A day ticket costs just ¥300 and can be bought at any of the major stops where there are staff available. There's a loop line and major terminus at Dōgo Onsen and outside Matsuyama City station. The Ichiban-chō stop outside the Mitsukoshi department store and ANA Hotel Matsuyama is a good central stopping point.

Lines 1 and 2 are loop lines, running clockwise/anticlockwise around Katsuyama (the mountain the castle is on); line 3 runs from Matsuyama City station to Dōgo Onsen; line 5 goes from JR Matsuyama station to Dōgo Onsen; and line 6 from Kiya-chō to Dōgo Onsen.

Bicycle rental (☎ 943-5002; open Mon-Sat) is available at the JR Matsuyama left-luggage counter for ¥600 a day.

NORTH & EAST OF MATSUYAMA

Kashima 鹿島

Kashima is a pleasant little island popular with locals, and makes an easy day trip from Matsuyama. It's so close that you could virtually swim there, but there is a return ferry for ¥300. The island has resident deer, an *onsen*, a nice beach, camping and *minshuku* if you plan to overnight. Trains from JR Matsuyama station reach Iyo-Hōjō station in 20 minutes; from here it's a short walk to the ferry (fashioned with a plastic deer on top).

If you're looking for somewhere quiet to stay, but close to Matsuyama, there's the **Hōjō Suigun Youth Hostel** (☎ 0899-92-4150; beds ¥3000; meals available) a five-minute walk from Iyo Hōjō station.

Imabari 今治

Imabari is an industrial port city at the southern end of the Shimanami-kaidō bridge system that island-hops to Onomichi in Hiroshima-ken. There are numerous ferry services connecting Imabari with ports on Honshū including Hiroshima, Kōbe, Mihara, Onomichi, Takehara and islands of the Inland Sea. There are also buses to Honshū. Imabari is noted for its tasty *yakitori*.

Saijo 西条

In Saijo is the new **Asahi Brewery** (☎ 0897 53-7770), where visitors can tour the factory and sample freshly brewed *Super Dry* for free. Reservations are required. There is a beer garden next door with all-you-can-eat barbecued mutton and beer.

The bus for hiking up Ishizuchi-san (see its entry in this section) leaves from JR Iyo-Saijō station.

Niihama 新居浜

Niihama sits sandwiched between the Inland Sea and a nearby mountain range. The area is known for its parks, waterfalls, and hiking opportunities around Besshi-yama, but most of all for the annual **Taiko Matsuri**, a drum festival held from 16 to 18 October. Niihama station, on the JR Yosan line, is a couple of kilometres from the middle of town.

Ishizuchi-san 石鎚山

At 1982m, Ishizuchi-san is the highest mountain in western Japan. It's a holy mountain and many pilgrim climbers make the hike, particularly during the July–August climbing season. In winter Ishizuchi boasts a ski-field from late December to late March. From Matsuyama, you can take a bus to Tsuchi-goya, southeast of the mountain, or you can take a bus from JR Iyo Saijō station on the Yosan line to the Nishi-no-kawa cable car station on the northern side. You

can climb up one way and down the other or even make a complete circuit from Nishi-no-kawa to the summit, down to Tsuchi-goya and then back to Nishi-no-kawa. Allow all day and an early start for the circuit.

For detailed information on hiking Ishizuchi-san, snap up a copy of Lonely Planet's *Hiking in Japan*.

Kagawa-ken 香川県

Formerly known as Sanuki, Kagawa-ken is the smallest of Shikoku's four island regions and the second smallest of the country's 47 prefectures. Kagawa is a major arrival point on Shikoku as the only rail link with Honshū is via the Seto-ōhashi to Okayama. Highlights include the beautiful gardens of Ritsurin-kōen at Takamatsu, sea kayaking off the northeast coast, the folk village of Shikoku-mura, near Yashima, and the celebrated shrine of Kompira-san at Kotohira.

This section continues the circle of Shikoku, starting in southwest Kagawa, then moving on to Kotohira and on to Takamatsu.

THE PILGRIMAGE IN KAGAWA

To *henro*, Kagawa-ken is known as Nehan no dōjō – the Place of Completion – and has the last 22 of Kōbō Daishi's 88 sacred temples. Its hospitable weather and welcoming people have always been of great comfort to *henro* as they complete their journey with both a sense of accomplishment and sadness that the pilgrimage/adventure is coming to an end. If you're doing it properly though, the pilgrimage is not quite over when you get to the Ōkubo-ji, Temple 88 – it's still a 40km journey back to Temple 1 in Tokushima to complete the circle. The pilgrimage route follows an arc in Kagawa, starting in the southwest of the prefecture, moving up to Takamatsu in the north and finishing in the mountains in the southeast.

NORTHEAST TO TAKAMATSU
Kanonji 観音寺

If you've come from Ehime-ken on the pilgrimage or on the train, the first town of consequence in Kagawa-ken is Kanonji, noted for having two of the 88 Temples at the same place, and for **Zenigata**, a 350m-diameter outline of a square-holed coin dating from the 1600s. The coin's outline and four kanji characters are formed by trenches, which it is said were dug by the local population as a warning to their feudal lord not to waste the taxes they were forced to pay him. The huge coin is beside the sea, at the foot of Kotohiki Hill in Kotohiki-kōen, 1½km northwest of Kanonji station.

Also in the park are temples 68 and 69 of the 88 Sacred Temples, **Jinne-in** and **Kannonji**, and a **World Coin Museum** (Sekai-no-koin-kan; admission ¥300; open 9am-5pm Tues-Sun). There is a good swimming **beach** on the far side of the park.

Tadotsu 多度津

Tadotsu is where the rail lines split. The JR Yosan line runs around the coast between Takamatsu and Matsuyama. At Tadotsu, the JR Dosan line splits off it and runs south to Zentsū-ji, Kotohira, through the Iya Valley (see the earlier Tokushima section) and eventually to Kōchi. Most trains for the Dosan line start in Takamatsu, can be joined in Tadotsu and end their journey at Kotohira – to continue south on the line will require a change of trains there.

Tadotsu is known throughout Japan for having the national headquarters for the martial art of **Shorinji-kempo**. If you're extremely keen to watch training, call ☎ 0877-33-1010 (in Japanese) and ask politely.

It is also the spot where you will end up if you take the Inland Sea get-away-from-it-all option detailed in the Western Honshū chapter (see the boxed text 'Taking it Easy in the Inland Sea' in the Inland Sea section in that chapter) and catch the ferry to Shikoku. There are also direct ferry connections with Fukuyama in Hiroshima-ken. The ferry terminal is about 15 minutes' walk from the station.

Marugame 丸亀

At Marugame, on the JR Yosan line and close to the southern end of the Seto-ōhashi, is **Marugame-jō** (admission ¥100; open 9am-4.30pm daily), dates from 1597 and has one of only 12 original wooden donjon remaining of more than 5000 castles in Japan. The stepped stone walls tower over 50m high.

At the **Uchiwa Museum** (admission free; open 9.30am-5pm Tues-Sun) there are displays and craft demonstrations of traditional Japanese uchiwa (paper fans). Marugame is responsible for about 90% of the country's paper fan output, making it a logical place to pick one up. There's a **tourist information office** (open 9.30am-6pm daily) at the station.

Zentsū-ji 善通寺

Zentsū-ji is Temple 75 of the 88 Sacred Temples and holds a special significance as the boyhood home of Kōbō Daishi. It is also the largest temple and most of the other 88 could fit in its carpark. The temple boasts a magnificent five-storey pagoda and giant camphor trees. To get into the Buddhist spirit, for ¥500 visitors can venture into the basement and traverse a 100m-long passageway in pitch darkness: by moving along with your left hand pressed to the wall (which is painted with mandalas, angels and lotus flowers) you are said to be safely following Buddha's way.

Zentsū-ji's other claim to fame is as the home of the cube watermelon, that ingenuous square-sided Japanese modification so that watermelons can fit into refrigerators more efficiently.

Zentsū-ji is one station north of Kotohira on the JR Dosan line.

KOTOHIRA 琴平
☎ 0877

The Kompira-san shrine at Kotohira is one of Shikoku's major attractions and is well known throughout Japan. If you say you've been there, everyone you meet in Japan will ask if you walked to the top.

Orientation & Information

Kotohira is small enough to make orientation quite straightforward. A few streets southeast of the two stations, the busy shopping arcade continues until it reaches the shrine entranceway, lined with the inevitable souvenir shops. Those seeking to truly immerse themselves in the Japanese experience might like to buy a walking stick at one of the shops for the trek up to the shrine.

There is a **Tourist Information Center** (☎ 75-3500; open 9.30am-8pm daily) along the main road between JR Kotohira station and Kotoden Kotohira station. Staff can provide an English-language brochure and accommodation information. They also rent

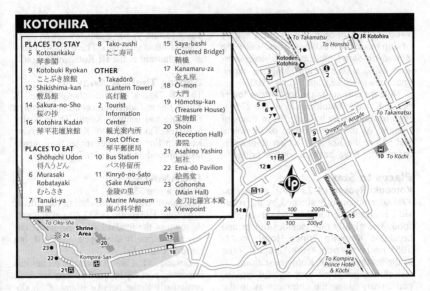

KOTOHIRA

PLACES TO STAY
5 Kotosankaku
琴参閣
9 Kotobuki Ryokan
ことぶき旅館
12 Shikishima-kan
敷島館
14 Sakura-no-Sho
桜の抄
16 Kotohira Kadan
琴平花壇旅館

PLACES TO EAT
4 Shōhachi Udon
将八うどん
6 Murasaki
Robatayaki
むらさき
7 Tanuki-ya
狸屋

8 Tako-zushi
たこ寿司

OTHER
1 Takadōrō
(Lantern Tower)
高灯籠
2 Tourist
Information
Center
観光案内所
3 Post Office
琴平郵便局
10 Bus Station
バス停留所
11 Kinryō-no-Sato
(Sake Museum)
金陵の里
13 Marine Museum
海の科学館

15 Saya-bashi
(Covered Bridge)
鞘橋
17 Kanamaru-za
金丸座
18 Ō-mon
大門
19 Hōmotsu-kan
(Treasure House)
宝物館
20 Shoin
(Reception Hall)
書院
21 Asahino Yashiro
旭社
22 Ema-dō Pavilion
絵馬堂
23 Gohonsha
(Main Hall)
金刀比羅宮本殿
24 Viewpoint

bikes (¥100/500 per hour/day), and hand out a discount book for the area's attractions.

Kompira-san 金刀比羅宮

Kompira-san or, more formally, Kotohira-gū, was originally a temple dedicated to the Guardian of Mariners but became a shrine after the Meiji Restoration. Its hilltop position delivers superb views over the surrounding countryside, and there are some interesting reminders of its maritime connections.

An enormous fuss is made about how strenuous the climb is to the top but, if you've got this far in Japan, you've probably completed a few long ascents to shrines already. If you really blanch at the thought of climbing all those steps (nearly 800 of them) you can dish out ¥6500 and be carried up and down in a palanquin.

The first notable landmark on the long climb is the **Ō-mon**, a stone gateway. Just to the right, beyond the gate, is the **Hōmotsu-kan** (*admission ¥300; open 8.30am-4.30pm daily*) treasure house. Nearby you will find five traditional sweets vendors at tables shaded by large white parasols. A symbol of ancient times, these Gonin Byakushō (Five Farmers) are the descendants of the original families permitted to trade within the grounds of the shrine. Further uphill is the **Shoin** (*admission ¥300; open 8.30am-*

4.30pm daily), a reception hall. Built in 1659, this National Treasure has some interesting screen paintings and a small garden.

Continuing the ascent, you eventually reach the large **Asahino Yashiro** (Shrine of the Rising Sun). The hall, built in 1837 and dedicated to the Sun Goddess Amaterasu, is noted for its ornate wood carving. From here, the short final ascent, which is the most beautiful leg of the walk, brings you to the **Gohonsha** (Gohon Hall) and the **Ema-dō** (Ema Pavilion); the latter is filled with maritime offerings. Exhibits range from pictures of ships to models, modern ship engines and a one-person solar sailboat hull donated to the shrine after its around-the-world navigation. The views from this level extend right down to the coast and over the Inland Sea. Incurable climbers can continue another 500-odd steps up to the **Oku-sha** (Inner Shrine).

Other Attractions

Kanamaru-za (*admission ¥300; open 9am-4pm Wed-Mon*) is Japan's oldest kabuki playhouse. It was built in 1835 and later became a cinema before being restored in 1976. Inside, you can wander backstage (delightfully unsupervised) and see the changing rooms and old wooden bath, and admire the revolving stage mechanism, basement trap doors and tunnel out to front-of-theatre.

SHIKOKU

There's a **Marine Museum** *(admission ¥400; open 9am-5pm daily)* with a variety of ship models and exhibits. There's also the **Kinryō-no-Sato** *(admission ¥310; open 9am-4pm daily)* sake museum along the shrine entranceway. Sake tasting costs ¥100.

Note the curious **Takadōrō lantern tower** beside Kotoden Kotohira station. The 27.6m-high tower was traditionally lit in times of trouble. At the southern end of the town, just before the Kotohira Kadan Ryokan, is the wooden **Saya-bashi**, a covered bridge.

Places to Stay
Kotobuki Ryokan *(☎ 73-3872; per person ¥7000)*, conveniently situated by the riverside, is clean, comfortable and serves good food. The nightly rate includes dinner and breakfast. **Kompira Prince Hotel** *(☎ 73-3051; per person from ¥5000)* is about 500m to the southeast of JR Kotohira station.

Kotohira has some very tasteful ryokan, particularly along the entranceway to the shrine steps. Costs per person include dinner and breakfast. **Shikishima-kan** *(☎ 75-5111; per person ¥12,000-20,000)* is a classic place. It dates back to 1624 and was popular with Shikoku samurai. **Kotohira Kadan** *(☎ 75-3232; per person from ¥15,000)* is just beyond the Saya-bashi.

Kotosankaku *(☎ 75-1000; per person ¥12,000)* is an elegant, Japanese-style place and features an excellent outdoor *onsen* (hot-spring spa bath). **Sakura-no-Sho** *(☎ 75-3218; per person ¥12,000-30,000)*, near the bottom of the steps up to the shrine, is upmarket and convenient.

Places to Eat
Many of the restaurants in Kotohira cater for day-trippers and, hence, close early. There are a couple of reasonably priced places serving *udon*, *katsudon* (pork cutlet served over rice) and so on across from the main post office, including **Shōhachi Udon**. **Tako-zushi**, (*tako* means 'octopus' in Japanese), just over the bridge at the end of the shopping arcade, is a quaint sushi shop that won't break the budget. Look for the big red octopus above the door. **Murasaki**, north of Tako-zushi, is a branch of the popular *robatayaki* chain. It has an illustrated menu.

Up near the entrance to the shrine, many of the souvenir shops serve *udon* lunches. They are a little expensive, but cheaper choices are available for under ¥1000. Tasty **Tanuki-ya** has a *sanuki-udon teishoku* (sanuki-udon set meal). There's also a simple **restaurant** at the JR Kotohira station.

Getting There & Away
The JR Dosan line branches off the JR Yosan line at Tadotsu and continues through Kotohira and south to Kōchi. There is also a direct Takamatsu to Kotohira private Kotoden line. By either route, the journey takes around an hour from Takamatsu.

TAKAMATSU 高松
☎ 087 • pop 330,000
Takamatsu was founded during the rule of Toyotomi Hideyoshi (1537–98) as the castle town of the feudal lord of Kagawa. The city was virtually destroyed in WWII, but rapidly rebounded.

Despite its rail link, Takamatsu remains an important port for Inland Sea ferry services, particularly to the popular island of Shōdo-shima (see the Western Honshū chapter). There are many day-trip possibilities around the city and prefecture, including Isamu Noguchi's extraordinary sculpture garden in Mure-chō; Marugame-jō, Zentsū-ji and Kotohira.

Orientation & Information
Takamatsu is surprisingly sprawling. It's a 2km walk to Ritsurin-kōen from JR Takamatsu station. Chūō-dōri, the main street through Takamatsu, extends south from Kotoden Chikkō train station. A busy shopping arcade area extends across Chūō-dōri and then runs parallel to it, passing through the entertainment district. The main shopping area is further south, near Kotoden Kawaramachi train station.

At the time of writing, there was major upheaval around JR Takamatsu station as the city makes way for Sunport Takamatsu, a massive reclaimed land project. The whole area is changing rapidly.

There's a **tourist information office** *(☎ 851-2009; open 9am-5pm daily)* outside the station where the helpful staff can provide useful leaflets and maps. They can also help with booking accommodation.

On the northwest corner of Chūō-kōen is the **Kagawa International Exchange** *(I-PAL Kagawa; ☎ 837-5901; open 9am-6pm Tues-Sun)*. This resource centre has a message board, foreign books and magazines,

SHIKOKU

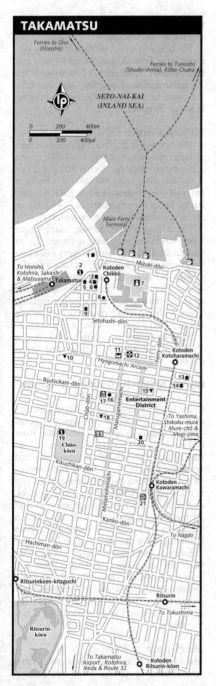

TAKAMATSU

PLACES TO STAY

1 ANA Hotel Clement
全日空ホテルクレメント高松

3 Station Hotel
ステーションホテル

4 Makiya
万喜屋

5 Pearl Hotel
高松パールホテル

9 Takamatsu Terminal Hotel
高松ターミナルホテル

13 New Grande Mimatsu
ニューグランデみまつ

14 Sakika Youth Hostel; Kanaya
さきかユースホステル；金屋

20 Royal Park Hotel
ロイヤルパークホテル

PLACES TO EAT

10 Tenkatsu
天勝本店

15 Kanaizumi
かな泉

18 Sea Dragon
シードラゴン

OTHER

2 Tourist Information Office
観光案内所

6 ANA
全日空

7 Takamatsu-jō; Tamamo-kōen
高松城；玉藻公園

8 JAL
日航

11 Post Office
高松郵便局

12 Mitsukoshi Department Store
三越百貨店

16 Miyawaki Shoten Bookstore
宮脇書店

17 Takamatsu City Museum of Art
高松市美術館

19 Kagawa International Exchange; TIC
アイパル香川

21 Queensbury Café

international phone and fax access, satellite TV and Internet access. **Queensbury Café**, next to Kotoden Kawaramachi station, also has Internet access available.

Visitors can pick up the free Kagawa Welcome Card at **Kagawa International Exchange** and the tourist information office (you'll need to show your passport). The card provides minor discounts around town, and comes with a mini-guidebook and fold-out city map.

The **Miyawaki Shoten bookshop** has a wide selection of English-language books and magazines on the 5th floor.

SHIKOKU

Ritsurin-kōen 栗林公園

Although not one of Japan's 'big three' gardens, Ritsurin-kōen (admission ¥350; open sunrise-sunset daily) could easily be a contender. The garden, dating from the mid-1600s, winds around a series of ponds with lookouts, tearooms, bridges and islands. It took more than a century to complete and was used as a villa garden for more than 200 years prior to the Meiji Restoration. In one direction, Shiun-zan forms a backdrop to the garden, but in the other direction there is some much less impressive 'borrowed scenery' in the form of dull modern buildings. (In Japanese garden design, 'borrowed scenery' refers to a view of distant scenery that is revealed at some place along the path.)

In the garden, the Sanuki Folkcraft Museum (admission free; open 8.45am-4.30pm daily) displays local crafts. The feudal-era Kikugetsu-tei teahouse, also known as the Chrysanthemum Moon Pavilion, offers Japanese tea and sweets. There are several other small teahouses inside the park, including the lovely thatched-roofed Higurashi-tei.

You can get there by Kotoden or JR train, but the easiest way is by bus (¥230) from JR Takamatsu station.

Takamatsu-jō 高松城

There's very little left of Takamatsu-jō, which is near Kotoden Chikkō station. The castle grounds today form a pleasant park, Tamamo-kōen (admission ¥200; open sunrise-sunset daily), yet are only one-ninth of their original size. When the castle was built in 1588, the moat was filled with seawater, with the sea itself forming the fourth side.

Yashima 屋島

The 292m-high tabletop plateau of Yashima is 5km east of the centre of Takamatsu. It's the locale of Yashima-ji (number 84 of the 88 temples), and offers fine views over the surrounding countryside and the Inland Sea.

In the 12th century it was the site of titanic struggles between the Genji and Heike clans. The temple's Treasure House collection relates to the battle. Just behind the treasure house is the Pond of Blood, where victorious warriors washed the blood from their swords, staining the water red.

A funicular railway runs to the top of Yashima from near a smaller shrine at the bottom (¥700/1300 one way/return). At the top you can rent a bicycle (¥500) to pedal around the attractions.

The best way to get to Yashima is by Kotoden train. From Kotoden Chikkō station it takes around 20 minutes (¥270) to Kotoden Yashima station. From here you can take the funicular railway to the top, or hike up in about 30 minutes.

Shikoku-mura 四国村

At the bottom of Yashima is this excellent village museum (admission ¥800; open 8.30am-5pm daily Apr-Oct, 8.30am-4.30pm daily Nov-Mar), with old buildings brought from all over Shikoku and neighbouring islands. There are explanations in English of the many buildings and their history.

The village's fine kabuki stage came from Shōdo-shima, which is famed for its traditional farmers' kabuki performances. Other interesting buildings include a border guardhouse from the Tokugawa era (a time when travel was tightly restricted) and a bark steaming-hut that was used in paper-making. There's also a water-powered rice-hulling machine and a fine old stone storehouse.

Shikoku-mura is north of Kotoden Yashima station and takes around seven minutes on foot.

Isamu Noguchi Garden Museum イサム・ノグチ庭園美術館

Consider an excursion out to Mure-chō, east of Takamatsu, to witness the legacy of noted sculptor Isamu Noguchi (1904–88). Born in Los Angeles to a Japanese poet and an American writer, Noguchi set up a studio and residence here in 1970. Today the complex (☎ 870-1500, fax 845-0505; admission ¥2000) is filled with hundreds of Noguchi's works, and holds its own as an impressive overall art installation. Inspiring sculptures are on display in the beautifully restored Japanese buildings and in the surrounding landscape.

Entry is decidedly worth it. One-hour tours are conducted at 10am, 1pm and 3pm on Tuesday, Thursday and Saturday; visitors should fax ahead for reservations – preferably two weeks in advance. Take the Kotoden train to Yakuri station and a taxi from there.

Megi-jima 女木島

Just offshore from Yashima is Megi-jima, also known as Oniga-shima or 'Demon

SHIKOKU

Island'. Several homes on the island are surrounded by ōte (high stone walls built to protect a house from waves, wind and ocean spray). It was here that Momotarō, the legendary 'Peach Boy' (see the boxed text 'Momotarō, the Peach Boy' under Okayama in the Western Honshū chapter), met and conquered the horrible demon. You can tour the caves where the demon was said to have hidden, but they've been a bit ruined by some fake demons put there to supposedly make it more realistic.

Boats run to Megi-jima from Takamatsu (¥340, 20 minutes). There are minshuku and campsites on the mountainous island.

Places to Stay – Budget

Sakika Youth Hostel (☎ 822-2111; beds ¥3900) is a hostel/business hotel run out of a ryokan. Near Kotoden Kataharamachi station, the hostel is actually run from the New Grande Mimatsu ryokan about 50m away. Go there first or you'll never find it. The hostel building has rooms like a business hotel, a beer machine and no curfew. The doors are open 24 hours and you're free to do as you please. It gets better. The ryokan has a great izakaya attached where guests can have a set-menu dinner for ¥1200 with a FREE beer. The place, called **Kanaya**, is quite unusual. It has authentic Japanese cuisine and atmosphere, but plays wicked jazz. If you want to stay in the ryokan, it costs ¥6000 with no meals, or ¥8000 with two meals. Breakfast is also served for ¥500. There's also a well-stocked supermarket over the road.

Makiya (☎ 822-3366; per person ¥3500) is near JR Takamatsu station.

Places to Stay – Mid-Range

There are several budget business hotels around JR Takamatsu station. **Pearl Hotel** (☎ 822-3382; singles/doubles from ¥5500/ 10,000) is small, clean and quite acceptable. **Station Hotel** (☎ 821-6989; singles/ doubles from ¥5500/11,000) is similar.

Takamatsu Terminal Hotel (☎ 822-3731; singles/twins from ¥6100/11,000), a few minutes' walk from the station, is a small, clean place.

Places to Stay – Top End

The **ANA Hotel Clement** (☎ 811-1111; singles from ¥11,550) is brand new and next to JR Takamatsu station. **Royal Park Hotel** (☎ 823-2222; singles/doubles from ¥12,700/ 15,000) is in the entertainment district.

Places to Eat

Takamatsu has no shortage of places to eat. There are countless choices in the covered arcades and entertainment district to the west side of the tracks between Kotoden Kataharamachi and Kawaramachi stations.

A trip to Takamatsu would not be complete without slurping back some of the region's prized sanuki udon. At **Kanaizumi** you may see it being made in the window. Udon places are everywhere, and you'll soon be able to recognise the characters for udon.

Tenkatsu is a few doors beyond the end of the Hyogo machi arcade west of Chūō-dōri, and is a seafood restaurant where you can see your order swimming about before it's prepared (see the boxed text 'Cruel Cuisine' below).

Sea Dragon is a popular bar, just off the Marugamemachi arcade, while **Queens-bury Café** near Kotoden Kawaramachi station has Internet access and serves drinks.

Kanaya (see Places to Stay earlier) is a friendly Japanese bar/restaurant, and if you're staying at the Sakika Youth Hostel, it's not far to stumble home.

Cruel Cuisine

Being cruel to your food is a Japanese tradition – you know the fish is fresh if it squeals when you eat it – and Takamatsu is certainly a centre for it. A prized dish here is sugata-zukuri – a sea bream sliced seconds before it's placed in front of you. If you're quick with the chopsticks you can get the first mouthfuls down before it dies. I ate at Tenkatsu one night, where the bar encloses a large tank of fish and other sea life. When a customer ordered octopus, the unfortunate creature was scooped out of the tank and four tentacles were hacked off. Then, still living, but less than complete, the octopus was tossed back into the tank to crawl forlornly into a corner.

Tony Wheeler

SHIKOKU

Sea Kayaking on the Inland Sea

For a bit of adventure, physical exertion and an enjoyable day out, you might like to try sea kayaking off the northeast coast of Kagawa-ken on the Inland Sea. **Noasobiya** *(toll-free ☎ 0077-784-011;* **W** *www.noasobiya.jp)* runs a thoroughly professional operation out of Ōchi, east of Takamatsu. Head guide Ryū holds New Zealand sea kayak-guiding qualifications and spends his off-seasons guiding in New Zealand's Abel Tasman National Park. Noasobiya has half-day (¥7000) and full-day (¥12,000) options, including all gear.

The operation is run out of a large log cabin that was once used as a rest house for Emperor Hirohito, and there are cabins next door where visitors can stay (¥16,000 for up to four people). There is also a hotel nearby with a large *onsen* for an after-trip soak. Tours can be run in English, and staff will pick you up at JR Sanbonmatsu station if you pre-request it. Trips run dependent on weather from April to November.

Getting There & Away

Takamatsu airport is 16km south of the city. Buses to/from JR Takamatsu station cost ¥740. There are flights to all the major cities.

The rail line crossing the Seto-ōhashi has brought Takamatsu much closer to the main island of Honshū. From Tokyo, you can take the *shinkansen* (bullet train) to Okayama, change trains and be in Takamatsu in five hours. The Okayama-Takamatsu trip takes around one hour. From Takamatsu, the JR Kōtoku line runs southeast to Tokushima and the JR Yosan line runs west to Matsuyama. The JR Yosan line branches off at Tadotsu and becomes the Dosan line, turning southwest to Kotohira and Kōchi. The private Kotoden line also runs direct to Kotohira.

Direct buses operate to/from Tokyo, Yokohama, Nagoya and Osaka.

Takamatsu has ferry services to various ports in the Inland Sea and Honshū, including Osaka, Kōbe, Uno (in Okayama) and Shōdo-shima. The tourist information office can provide details.

Getting Around

Takamatsu has local buses, but the major attractions are easily reached on the JR Kōtoku line or Kotoden line. The main Kotoden junction is Kotoden Kawaramachi, although the line ends at Kotoden Chikkō, near JR Takamatsu station.

ŌKUBO-JI 大窪寺

Temple 88, Ōkubo-ji, is the last of the sacred temples, and worth a visit even if you aren't doing the pilgrimage. It's devilishly hard to get to unless you are walking though, which

seems somewhat appropriate. The closest public transport will get you is Nagao, where Temple 87 is located. From Takamatsu it costs ¥460 by Kotoden train and the trip takes 35 minutes. It's either a taxi (around ¥3000 each way), your thumb or a 17km walk from there. Make sure you've got a decent map and sturdy footwear if you use your feet.

If you're hitching, go straight south on Rte 3 from Nagao, then left at the intersection with Rte 377. The temple is on your left after about 6km.

The walk follows Rte 3 for only about the first 5km, then turns off to the left. It is extremely interesting (if you like walking), though you've got to have your wits about you to make the right turns (and there are quite a few of them). Stone markers show the gravesites of *henro* who didn't make it, and the final climb takes you to nearly 800m above sea level before dropping over the other side into the mountain temple. Literally millions of *henro* must have made that same walk over the centuries.

The walls of the main hall are hung with crutches, braces, plaster casts and even a cripple's cart – testimony to those whose faith has seen them through over the last 1000 years. *Henro* traditionally leave their wooden staff here, and the temple has a fire ceremony each year to burn the accumulation. Holding pride of place is a stone pillar on which is written: The Place of Fulfillment of the Vow.

The temple doesn't have a *shukubō*, but the **Minshuku Yasukubo** (☎ *0879-56-2031)* is near the main gate. If you're heading back to Temple 1 in Tokushima you need to go south and out into the Yoshino river valley before turning east.

Kyūshū 九州

Kyūshū is the third-largest and southern-most of the four major islands of Japan. Its population numbers over 15 million. Although isolated from the Japanese mainstream on Honshū, it has been an important entry point for foreign influence and culture. During the long period of isolation from the West, the Dutch settlement at Nagasaki in Kyūshū was Japan's only legitimate connection to the outside world. Kyūshū is the closest island to Korea and China, and it was from Kyūshū that the Yamato tribe extended its power to Honshū. Some of the earliest evidence of Japanese civilisation can still be seen at the archaeological excavations around Miyazaki and at the many ancient stone carvings in the Usuki area.

In the north, the cosmopolitan city of Fukuoka/Hakata is a major international arrival point, and the terminus for the *shinkansen* (bullet train) line from Tokyo. In the centre of the island stands the massive volcanic caldera of Aso-san, while more volcanic activity can be witnessed in the south at Sakurajima. Cities like Kumamoto and Kagoshima offer fine gardens and magnificent castles, while Beppu is one of Japan's major hot-spring centres. There are also very good hiking opportunities, particularly along the Kirishima volcano chain.

The people of Kyūshū are reputedly hard drinkers (especially of *shōchū*, the preferred liquor) and outstandingly friendly – a visit to a local bar may provide proof of both theories.

SUGGESTED ITINERARIES

If time allows, it's worth exploring the backroads of Kyūshū. To do the island justice, at least seven days is advised, taking it slow and easy as the locals do. If not, at least check out Fukuoka, Nagasaki and Beppu. With an extra day take in Kagoshima and also perhaps the Shimabara peninsula, or a hike up to the Aso volcano caldera.

GETTING THERE & AWAY
Air

There are major airports at Fukuoka, Ōita (Beppu), Nagasaki, Kagoshima, Kumamoto and Miyazaki. There are also flights to is-

Highlights

- Soak in the hidden hot springs of *onsen*-crazed Beppu
- Hike around the world's most active volcano caldera at Aso-san
- Hang out in Fukuoka, a trendy Asia-aware metropolis with a thing for *rāmen* noodles
- Explore the city to which the West exported first Christianity, then nuclear holocaust – the festival-filled, easygoing Nagasaki
- Escape to the riverside baths and unspoiled, rural hot springs of Kurokawa Onsen
- Spend time in Kagoshima, so-called Naples of the East, a vibrant port city overlooked by the smoking cone of Sakurajima

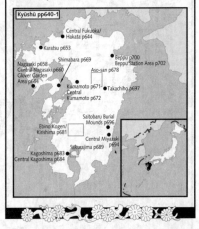

lands off the coast of Kyūshū and to the islands southwest of Kagoshima down to Okinawa.

Train

The *shinkansen* line from Tokyo and Osaka crosses to Kyūshū from Shimonoseki and terminates in Hakata (Fukuoka). Major cities in Kyūshū are connected by *tokkyū* (limited express) train, although an extension of the *shinkansen* line south to Kagoshima is underway.

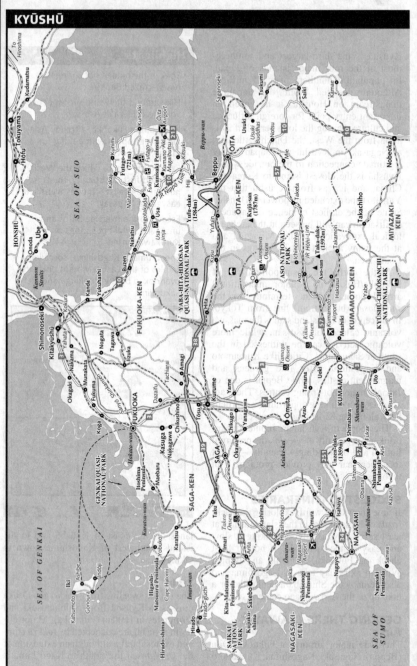

KYŪSHŪ

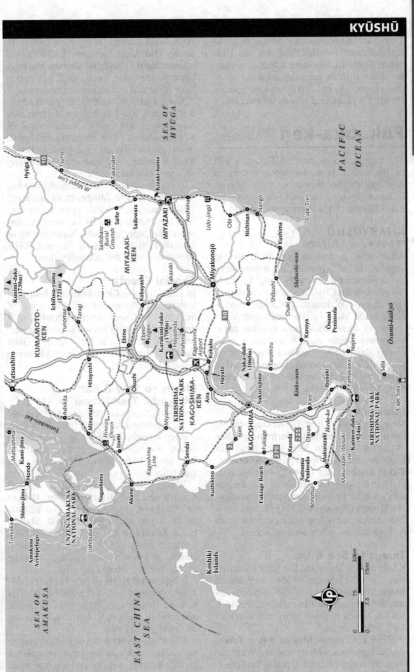

KYŪSHŪ

SEA OF HYUGA

PACIFIC OCEAN

SEA OF AMAKUSA

EAST CHINA SEA

Hyūga
Tsuno
JR Nippo Line
Takanabe
Kizaki-hama
Saito
Sadowara
Saitobaru Burial Grounds
MIYAZAKI
MIYAZAKI-KEN
Aoshima
Udo-jingū
Nichinan
Obi
Nango
Cape Toi
Kushima
Miyakonojō
Osumi
Shibushi
Shibushi-wan
Osaki
Ōsumi Peninsula
Kanoya
Nejime
Ōsumi-kaikyō
Cape Sata
Sata
Takazaki
Kobayashi
Ebino
Yunomae
Taragi
Kunimi-dake (1739m)
Ichifusa-yama (1721m)
KUMAMOTO-KEN
Yatsushiro
Ashikita
Hitoyoshi
Ōkuchi
Ebino-kōgen
Karakuni-dake (1700m)
Hayashida
Kirishima
KIRISHIMA NATIONAL PARK
Kagoshima Airport
Kokubu
Naka-dake (1066m)
Tarumizu
Kinkō-wan
Kokubu
Hayato
Aira
Sakurajima
KAGOSHIMA-KEN
Minamata
Miyanojo
Izumi
Hinagu Onsen
Kagoshima Line
Sendai
Kushikino
Akune
Nagashima
Kami-jima
Hondo
Shimo-jima
UNZEN-AMAKUSA NATIONAL PARK
Ushibuka
Tomioka
Amakusa Archipelago
Matsushima
Yatsushiro-kai
KAGOSHIMA
Ijūin
Fukiage
Fukiage Beach
Bōnotsu
Kaseda
Chiran
Makurazaki
Satsuma Peninsula
Makurazaki-Ibusuki Line
Ibusuki
Kaimon-dake (924m)
Ikeda-ko
Kure
Yamakawa
KIRISHIMA-YAKU NATIONAL PARK
Koshiki Islands

30km
15mi
0
7.5
15

Boat

There are numerous sea connections to Kyūshū from Honshū, Shikoku and Okinawa. Some of the more interesting ones are dealt with in the relevant sections of this chapter. Local ferry services operate between Kyūshū and islands off the coast.

Fukuoka-ken 福岡県

The northern prefecture of Fukuoka will be the arrival point for most visitors to Kyūshū, whether they cross over by road or tunnel from Shimonoseki or fly straight into Fukuoka city's international airport.

KITAKYŪSHŪ 北九州
☎ 093 • pop 1,027,000

Kitakyūshū is too industrialised to top anyone's list of favourites, but it does serve as an important transport link. Literally 'North Kyūshū City', it actually consists of five cities – Wakamatsu, Yahata, Tobata, Kokura and Moji – all merged together.

One of these would be a familiar name today worldwide were it not for a grey, cloudy day in 1945. Kokura was set to be the world's second atomic bomb target, but cloud obscured the city and the mission was diverted – to Nagasaki.

Information

Near the north exit at JR Kokura station, the downstairs **tourism information office** (☎ 541-4189; open 9am-6pm daily) has English-language maps and brochures. **Ticket Super** (open 10am-8pm daily), near Daiei in the shopping arcade outside the station's south exit, sells discounted train tickets. **Kinko's** (Heiwa-dōri; ¥200/10min; open 24hr daily), just a few minutes' walk from Kokura station, offers Internet access.

Things to See & Do

Kitakyūshū is trying hard to attract tourists, with the development of the much-touted **Space World** (admission ¥2500-5000), an amusement park built in collaboration with NASA, which at times sadly resembles an early Star Trek set.

More enticing is **Mojiko Retro Town**, the old port area, with its restored Western-style buildings. Located opposite the French Renaissance–style train station is the 1921 **Old Moji Mitsui Club**, where Einstein once slept. Walk over the suspension footbridge to the **Old Moji Customs Building** and **International Friendship Commemorative Library** (admission free), which has upper-floor historical and cultural exhibitions.

Kokura-jō (admission ¥350; open 9.30am-5.30pm daily Apr-Oct, 9.30am-4.30pm daily Nov-Mar) is about 600m southwest of JR Kokura station. The reconstructed castle is set attractively amongst gardens beside Yasaka shrine, and has some startlingly animated historical dioramas!

If you stay near Yahata, consider heading out to the **Kyūshū Mingei-mura** (Folkcraft Village; admission ¥500; open 10am-5pm Tues-Sun) for displays of lacquerware, furniture and paper products. Nishitetsu buses from JR Yahata station go to Jizō-mae (¥410, 35 minutes) near the folkcraft village.

Special Events

In late July, the **Gion Festivals** bring out lanterns and drumming. All five wards of the city join forces for the **Wasshoi Millions Festival**, with fireworks and parades, held near the castle in early August. Giant **Kunchi** festival floats are paraded between 2 and 4 November.

Places to Stay & Eat

Kitakyūshū Youth Hostel (☎ 681-8142; beds ¥2700; closed late Jan & mid-June) is a 25-minute hike uphill from JR Yahata station, straight out past the international centre and over the highway overpass. The hostel hides above Hobashira cable car station.

Western-style hotels cluster around Kokura station. **Nishitetsu Inn Kokura** (☎ 511-5454; singles/twins from ¥5700/8600) is just about the cheapest. **Station Hotel Kokura** (☎ 521-5031, fax 512-0345; singles/doubles ¥7800/14,000), both welcoming and modern, has cafés, a shopping arcade, health club and lap pool.

Rihga Royal Hotel (☎ 531-1121, fax 521-2068; singles/doubles ¥15,000/25,000) is Kokura's luxury spot, flush with restaurants and cocktail lounges. Rooms don't measure up to the grand lobby.

The small streets south of Kokura station are stacked with eateries. Local specialities include karashi mentai – cod roe marinated in spicy red pepper. Other restaurants are on the riverwalk east of the castle. **Shin Ye** *(lunch buffet ¥1000; open 11am-11pm daily)* has a breezy setting upstairs in the Kokura Riverside China building. **Espresso Bar Moon Beams** sometimes hosts live music – anything from gospel to funk.

Getting There & Away

Train The first train station on the Kita-kyūshū side of the Kanmon Straits is Moji, but Kokura is more central. From Kokura, frequent *tokkyū* trains head to Beppu (¥4290, 70 minutes). *Kaisoku* (rapid) trains go to Hakata (¥1250, 70 minutes) via Space World and Yahata (¥270, 15 minutes). *Futsū* (local) services connect to Mojikō station (¥270, 10 minutes).

Boat Overnight ferries to Matsuyama (¥3700, six hours) and Korea (Ulsan or Pusan) depart from Sunatsu Port, a five-minute walk north of JR Kokura station. Speedboats to Matsuyama depart from Moji-kō (¥7500, 2½ hours). Other domestic ferry services, for example to Tokyo (2nd class ¥12,600) or Osaka (¥6000) via Kobe, depart from Shin-Mojikō on the coast.

FUKUOKA/HAKATA 福岡・博多
☎ 092 • pop 1,366,000

Fukuoka/Hakata is the biggest city in Kyūshū. It was originally two separate towns – the lordly Fukuoka castle town to the west of the river, the Naka-gawa, and to the east, the common folks' Hakata. When the two merged in 1889, the label Fukuoka was applied to both towns, but subsequent development has mainly been in Hakata and many residents refer to the town that way. The airport is known as Fukuoka, the train station as Hakata.

Fukuoka has transformed itself over the last decade into one of Japan's most truly cosmopolitan and internationalised cities. The local government is keenly aware of the city's proximity to the rest of Asia, and encourages international exchange. Its sightseeing attractions are contemporary rather than traditional, but they are still very much worth seeing. Fukuoka/Hakata is also renowned as a culinary centre, and its nightlife, centred around the Nakasu and Tenjin districts, is vibrant.

Nationally the city is known for its 'Hakata *bijin*' (beautiful women), its feisty baseball team the Daiei Hawks, and, most of all, *rāmen* (Chinese-style egg noodles in broth).

Orientation

JR Hakata station is the transport centre for the city and is surrounded by hotels. Tenjin is the business and shopping centre – its focus is along Watanabe-dōri. Underneath this busy street is Tenjin Chikagai, a crowded underground shopping mall that extends for 400m. The Tenjin bus centre here is close to the terminus of the private Nishitetsu Ōmuta line.

Separating Hakata and Tenjin to the west is the Naka-gawa, site of the impressive Canal City and the island of Nakasu, the entertainment centre of the city. It's a maze of restaurants, strip clubs, hostess bars, cinemas, department stores and the famed *yatai* (food stalls).

Maps The widely available *Visitors Walking Maps* for Hakata, Nakasu, Tenjin and Momochi are invaluable, as they are written in both English and kanji, and are free.

Information

Tourist Offices The **tourist information desk** *(open 8am-8pm daily)* in JR Hakata station has limited information and maps in English. Ask for the free 'Fukuoka Welcome Card' entitling visitors to discounts at hotels, attractions, shops and restaurants.

The Fukuoka International Association's **Rainbow Plaza** *(☎ 733-2220; w www.rainbowfia.or.jp; 8th floor, IMS Bldg; open 10am-8pm daily)* in Tenjin has videos on Japan, books, magazines and a noticeboard for events, accommodation and job ads. Bilingual staff are extremely helpful.

ACROS Fukuoka *(☎ 725-9100; open 10am-7pm daily, closed 2nd & 4th Mon each month)*, on the 2nd floor of the cultural centre in Tenjin, has plenty of English-language information on the surrounding prefecture.

At Fukuoka airport, the **tourist information desk** *(☎ 473-2518)* is on the ground floor of the international terminal, beside a **reservations desk** *(☎ 483-7007; open 7am-9.30pm daily)* that can arrange hotel accommodation and car rentals.

Useful local English-language publications include *Fukuoka Now* (w www.fukuoka-now.com), a free monthly 'what's on'

KYŪSHŪ

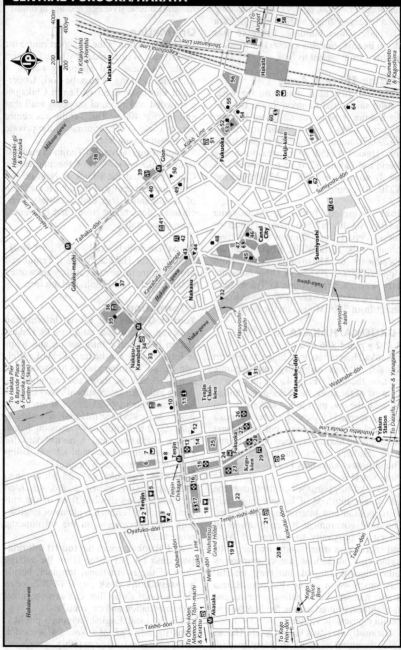

CENTRAL FUKUOKA/HAKATA

CENTRAL FUKUOKA/HAKATA

PLACES TO STAY

20 Lady's Hotel Petit Tenjin
レディースホテルプチ天神
31 Fukuoka Arty Inn
福岡アルティイン
33 Hotel Brave Inn Hakata
ホテルブレブイン博多
37 Amenity Hotel in Hakata
アメニティホテル博多
40 Kashima Honkan
鹿島本館
43 Hakata Riverside Hotel
博多リバーサイドホテル
45 Grand Hyatt Fukuoka
グランドハイアット福岡
48 Sauna Wellbe
サウナウェルビー
49 Hotel Sky Court Hakata
ホテルスカイコート博多
52 Hotel Cabinas Fukuoka
ホテルキャビナス福岡
57 Hotel Centraza Hakata;
ATM
ホテルセントラーザ；博多
58 JR Kyūshū Hotel Fukuoka
JR九州ホテル福岡
61 ANA Hotel Hakata
博多日空ホテル
62 Accord Hotel
アコードホテル
64 Super Hotel Hakata
スーパーホテル博多

PLACES TO EAT

4 Taiwan Yatai
台湾屋台
12 Ichiran
一蘭
32 Food Stalls
屋台
44 Menchan
めんちゃん

50 Uma-uma
うま馬
53 Cafe Serena; Hotel Nikko
Fukuoka
ホテル日航福岡

OTHER

1 Kinko's (Akasaka)
キンコーズ赤坂店
2 Crazy Cock
3 The Dark Room
5 Off Broadway; The Voodoo
Lounge; Club Vibe
6 Matsuya Ladies
松屋レディース
7 Central Post Office
福岡中央郵便局
8 ANA
9 Akarenga Bunka-kan
赤煉瓦文化館
10 JAL
11 ACROS Fukuoka;
Kokusai Hiroba
アクロス福岡；
国際ひろば
13 Fukuoka Building; Maruzen
福岡ビル；丸善
14 Tenjin Core
天神コア
15 Iwataya Department Store;
Nishitetsu Fukuoka Station
天神岩田屋；西鉄福岡駅
16 Shintenchō Plaza
新天町プラザ
17 International & Postal
ATMs
18 Blue Note
19 Happy Cock
21 Cybac Café
22 Iwataya Z-side; NTT
岩田屋ジーサイド
23 Solaria Plaza

24 Nishitetsu Tenjin Bus Centre
西鉄天神バスターミナル
25 IMS Building; Rainbow Plaza
イムズビル
26 El Gala
27 Daimaru Department Store
大丸
28 Mitsukoshi Department Store
福岡三越
29 Kego-Jinja
警固神社
30 Kinko's
キンコーズ
34 Media Café
35 Hakata Riverain
博多リバレイン
36 Fukuoka Asian Art Museum
福岡アジア美術館
38 Shōfuku-ji
聖福寺
39 Tōchō-ji
東長寺
41 Hakata Machiya
Furusato-kan
博多町家ふるさと館
42 Kushida-jinja; Hakata
Rekishi-kan
櫛田神社；博多歴史館
46 HIS No 1 Travel
47 ATM
51 Kinko's
キンコーズ
54 ANA
55 JAS
56 Kōtsū Bus Centre
福岡交通バスセンター
59 Hakata Post Office
博多郵便局
60 Fukuoka Ginkō
福岡銀行
63 Sumiyoshi-jinja; Rakusuien
住吉神社

guide; *Rainbow,* the Fukuoka International Association's current events newsletter; and *Fukuoka on Foot,* which describes walking courses throughout the city.

Travel Agents In the shopping arcade underneath Hakata station, **Ticket Fukuoka** *(open 9.30am-7pm Mon-Sat)* sells discount train tickets. **HIS No 1 Travel** *(☎ 761-0957; open Mon-Sat),* for cut-rate international airfares, has a branch beside Canal City.

Money There's a **Citibank ATM** *(open 6.30am-9.30pm daily)* on the 1st floor of the international arrivals terminal at Fukuoka airport. **Currency exchange counters** *(open 8.30am-9pm daily)* are upstairs.

Banks around Hakata station and Tenjin handle foreign exchange services.

There are international ATMs next to the post office upstairs on Shintenchō Minami-dōri; on the basement level of Canal City; and outside the Hotel Centraza Hakata on the east side of Hakata station.

Post The central post office, northeast of Tenjin subway station, has full services, including poste restante. There's another post office outside Hakata station's west exit.

Email & Internet Access Fukuoka is a wired city. **NTT** *(7th floor, Iwataya Z-side; open 10.30am-8pm Mon-Fri, 10am-8pm Sat & Sun)* offers free Internet browsing for

30 minutes (no email). **Rainbow Plaza** (see Tourist Offices earlier) offers 30 minutes of free Internet access, but expect to queue.

Cybac Café (membership fee ¥200; open 24hr) charges ¥480 for the first hour of Internet access. There's a branch near the Tenjin clubs. From 1am to 8am, unlimited Internet access with reclining chairs costs ¥1890. Local expats have been known to crash here after missing the last train home. **Media Café** (8th floor, Spoon Bldg; open 24hr), near Hakata Riverain, charges ¥300 per half-hour, but also offers good discount deals. **Kinko's** has 24-hour Internet access (¥200 per 10 minutes) at its locations around the city.

Bookshops An excellent selection of English-language books can be found at **Kinokuniya** (6th floor, Tenjin Core; open 10am-8pm daily). **Maruzen** (2nd & 3rd floors, Fukuoka Bldg; open 10am-8pm daily) also sells foreign-language titles.

Radio Broadcasting from Tenjin, Love 76.1FM offers programming in 10 languages. Cross 78.7FM has bilingual DJs and entertainment news.

Canal City – Hakata キャナルシティ

Is it a bird, is it a plane? Or is it a scheme to relieve you of all disposable income, and make you feel good about it? Fukuoka's six-building shopping mall and entertainment complex Canal City (☎ 282-2525) verges on the sexy. The central amphitheatre looks down onto an artificial canal with a fountain symphony. There are 13 cinema screens, a playhouse, two major hotels and innumerable boutiques, bars and bistros.

Canal City is 10 minutes' walk south of the Nakasu-Kawabata subway stop, or you can take one of many city buses to Canal City-mae.

Tenjin 天神

Shopping, or at least window shopping, in Tenjin's high-rise and underground labyrinthine complexes is a popular Hakata-ite pastime. Tenjin Core, Mitsukoshi, Iwataya Z-side, Daimaru, subterranean Tenjin Chikagai and IMS are all favourite spots. The latter gets bonus points for TVs in its lifts and a **rooftop terrace** (open 11am-9pm daily, weather-permitting).

Tenjin also has historic Western-style buildings, like the 1910 **Former Prefectural Hall & Official Guest House** in Tenjin Chūō-kōen. Copper-turreted **Akarenga Bunka-kan** (Akarenga Cultural Centre; admission free; open 9am-9pm Tues-Sun) has simple historical exhibits and a charming coffee shop.

Fukuoka Asian Art Museum
福岡アジア美術館

This user-friendly museum (☎ 263-1100; w http://faam.city.fukuoka.jp; 7th & 8th floors, Hakata Riverain; admission ¥200, special exhibitions from ¥1000; open 10am-7.30pm Thur-Tues) boasts some of the finest contemporary Asian art. Be sure to check out works by Mongolian artist Tserennadmidin Tsegmed and the rickshaw from Bangladesh. Cutting-edge shows by artists in residence are staged in the free upstairs gallery. The atrium coffee shop has skyline views.

Hakata Machiya Furusato-kan
博多町家ふるさと館

Near Kushida-jinja, this folk museum (admission ¥200; open 10am-5.30pm daily) features restored merchants' houses and has displays of traditional Hakata culture. You can even hear recordings of impenetrable Hakata dialect through antique telephones, or try your hand at weaving *Hakata-ori*. It's well worth a visit, despite a lack of English signage.

Shrines & Temples

Tochō-ji has impressively carved Kannon statues and upstairs, the largest wooden Buddha in Japan. **Shōfuku-ji** is a Zen temple originally founded in 1195 by Eisai, who introduced Zen and tea to Japan. Don't confuse it with Sōfuku-ji, once the temple of a feudal lord, with one gate taken from the original Fukuoka castle.

Kushida-jinja has displays of Hakata festival floats on the grounds, and a local **history museum** (admission ¥300; open 10am-4.30pm daily). Behind **Sumiyoshi-jinja**, a Shintō shrine, is tiny **Rakusuien** (admission ¥100; open 9am-5pm daily), a garden and teahouse built by a Meiji-era merchant.

Fukuoka-jō & Ōhori-kōen
福岡城・大濠公園

Only the walls of Fukuoka-jō remain in what is now Maizuru-kōen, but the castle's hilltop site provides fine views of the city.

Ōhori-kōen, adjacent to the castle grounds, has a traditional (though recently constructed) Japanese garden, **Nihon-teien** *(admission ¥240; open 9am-4.45pm Tues-Sun Sept-May, 9am-5.45pm Tues-Sun June-Aug)*.

Nearby, the **Fukuoka City Art Museum** (**w** *www.fukuoka-art-museum.jp; admission ¥200; open 9.30am-5pm Tues-Sun Sept-May, 9.30am-7pm Tues-Sat, 9.30am-5pm Sun July & Aug)* has ancient pottery and Buddhist guardians on one floor, with works by Andy Warhol and Salvador Dali upstairs. Take bus No 13 from Tenjin, or the subway to Ōhori-kōen station, then walk south along the pond for 10 minutes.

Momochi District
シーサイドももち海浜公園
Further out in the west of the city you'll find the overhyped **Fukuoka Tower** *(admission ¥800; open 9.30am-10pm daily Apr-Sept, 9.30am-9pm daily Oct-Mar)*. The 4th floor café Dart 234 (the tower is 234m tall) is a great place to view the city, especially at dusk. On the ground floor, there's a **traditional doll museum** *(admission ¥300)* for folkcraft enthusiasts.

Next to the tower is the park, **Momochi-kōen**, and its 2.5km artificial beach, a popular spot for swimming despite occasionally murky waters. Access is by subway to Nishijin station, then walk north toward the sea for 15 minutes.

On the way, you'll pass the amusing **Saibu Gas Museum** *(admission free; open 10am-5pm daily)*, worth a quick look for its natural gas 'phenomenart', and the **Fukuoka City Museum** *(admission ¥200; open 9.30am-5pm Tues-Sun)* with displays on local history and culture that make it obvious why Kyūshū residents have such fierce pride in their island. The most precious treasure is an ancient golden snake seal with an inscription proving Japan's historic ties to China.

Hawk's Town ホークスタウン
Hawk's Town is something of a seafront Canal City. Set on reclaimed land near Momochi-kōen, this entertainment and shopping complex is also the location of the luxury **Sea Hawk Hotel** and giant **Fukuoka Dome** (home to the local Daiei Hawks baseball team). The highlight is Sea Hawk's indoor jungle atrium, complete

with waterfalls and screeching tropical bird calls. Note that anyone can ride the hotel lifts up to the 35th floor for bird's-eye views of the city – for free!

Hawk's Town is 15 minutes' walk northwest of Tōjin-machi station. There are frequent direct buses to Fukuoka Dome from Tenjin.

Offshore Islands
Summer sightseeing cruises depart from Bayside Place. Ferries to delightfully rural **Shikanoshima**, where fresh seafood restaurants line the harbourside streets, depart every 40 minutes (¥650, 30 minutes). Shikanoshima also has a **fishing shrine** decorated with deer antlers and is famed for its *kyūdō* (Japanese archery) meets. Continuing clockwise around the island, you come to a popular **beach** after about 5km. Local buses are infrequent.

Nokoshima, famous for its flower fields, is only about 10km in circumference. There's a swimming **beach** and **campground** at the northern end of the island. Ferries depart from Marinoa City outlet mall, west of the city centre near Meinohama station (¥220, 10 minutes).

Special Events
On 3 January at the shrine, **Hakozaki-gū**, young men clad in loincloths engage in a primitive kind of soccer hooliganism, raucously chasing a wooden ball in the name of good fortune. The **Hakata Dontaku Matsuri** on 3 and 4 May rings to the unique percussive shock of rice servers being banged together, accompanied by *shamisen* (three-stringed instrument).

Further mayhem accompanies the city's main festival, **Hakata Yamagasa Matsuri**, held from 1 to 15 July. The climax starts at 4.59am on the morning of the 15th, when seven groups of men all converge at Kushida-jinja, just north of Canal City, and then race on a 5km course through the city carrying huge *mikoshi* (portable shrines). Participants supposedly follow a strict regimen beforehand, including sexual abstinence. According to legend, the festival originated after a 13th-century Buddhist priest was carried aloft, sprinkling holy water over victims of a plague.

The **Kyūshū Bashō sumō tournament** is held at the Fukuoka Kokusai Centre during mid-November. Limited same-day tickets *(tojitsu-ken)* are available starting at 8am, and people start lining up at dawn.

Places to Stay – Budget & Mid-Range

Hotel Sky Court Hakata *(☎ 262-4400, fax 262-8111; singles from ¥4500)* offers discounts to youth hostel members. Because these discount rates have limited availability, book ahead.

Sauna Wellbe *(☎ 291-1009; capsules ¥3800)* and **Hotel Cabinas Fukuoka** *(☎ 436-8880; capsules ¥3800-4300)* are great if you've always wanted to try a capsule hotel. Both accept male guests only. The posh Hotel Cabinas has a rooftop *rotemburo* (open-air bath).

Lady's Hotel Petit Tenjin *(☎ 713-2613, fax 713-4418; capsules ¥3000-3500, singles/twins from ¥5500/7000)* is for women only, offering on-site spa services and a sauna. It's eight minutes' walk southwest from Tenjin station. Reception is open 24 hours.

Hakata has dozens of cut-rate business hotels around the train station. Expect a surcharge on Saturday nights. **Super Hotel Hakata** *(☎ 474-9000; singles with continental breakfast buffet ¥4800)* has impeccably clean rooms and secure 24-hour access (reception closes at 11pm).

Hakata Riverside Hotel *(☎ 291-1455, 0120-20-8102; singles/twins from ¥4500/8000)*, in a Nakasu shopping arcade, gets good reviews. **Hotel Brave Inn Hakata** *(☎ 282-1111; singles ¥5000)* only charges ¥2000 for an extra person sharing a single room. **Amenity Hotel in Hakata** *(☎ 282-0041; rooms from ¥4900)* is on the outskirts of Tenjin.

Kashima Honkan *(☎ 291-0746; rooms per person with/without 2 meals ¥9000/6000)*, in the Gion district just northeast of Canal City, is a wholly unpretentious and traditional inn. It is built in Sukiya-zukuri style (architecture suggesting elements of the tea ceremony), has its own enclosed garden, and is pleasantly faded – you expect a Meiji-period novelist to pop up at any moment. The meals, featuring fresh seafood, are extraordinarily good value. The owner speaks English.

Fukuoka Arty Inn *(☎ 724-3511, fax 714-3200; singles/doubles ¥6400/8600)* is charmingly named and right in the centre of things, southeast of Tenjin station. Reception staff are unerringly helpful.

JR Kyūshū Hotel *(☎ 413-8787, fax 413-9746; e fukuoka@jrk-hotels.com; singles/twins from ¥7500/12,800)* is an oasis just a few steps from frenzied Hakata station. Ask about discounts on Sunday nights and holidays.

Places to Stay – Top End

Hotel Twins Momochi *(☎ 852-4800, fax 845-8637; rooms from ¥12,000)*, in the Momochi area, is refreshingly different. Spacious designer rooms have a spare, modernist feel, but also luxuries like king-sized beds. Guests share kitchenettes and coin laundry.

Sea Hawk Hotel & Resort *(☎ 844-8111; singles/doubles from ¥9000/18,000)*, in Hawk's Town, is lively. Whatever you do, don't get one of the garish 'European-style' rooms; the Japanese-style ones are far better.

ANA Hotel Hakata *(☎ 471-7111, 0120-02-9501, fax 472-7707; singles/doubles from ¥14,000/23,000)* especially caters to business travellers. Perks include a well-equipped business centre, a health club and swimming pool.

Grand Hyatt Fukuoka *(☎ 282-1234, 0120-51-2343, fax 282-2817; w http://fukuoka.grand.hyatt.com; singles/doubles from ¥17,000/22,000, Japanese-style suites ¥70,000)* is a lively hotel inside Canal City. The rooftop garden is traditional, but modern hotel rooms have hi-tech amenities. There's a health club, swimming pool and spa.

Places to Eat

To the vast majority of Japanese, Hakata means *rāmen*. In particular it means *tonkotsu-rāmen*, noodles in a distinctive, whitish broth distilled from pork bones. The telephone book lists 401 *rāmen* shops, and there are at least twice that many *yatai*, or food stalls, that are not listed. Discovering your own *rāmen* shop (and trusting the information only to one's nearest and dearest) is all part of the fun.

The majority of the *rāmen yatai* are on the streets around Tenjin station, especially where Oyafuko-dōri meets Shōwa-dōri, and along the riverbanks in Nakasu and in front of Canal City. Most open up as dusk approaches, and a bowl of noodles costs around ¥600.

Menchan *(open 7pm-4am Mon-Sat)*, across from Canal City, is a friendly place that topped the honours in an online 'Rāmen Freak' questionnaire. **Uma-uma** *(open 5.30pm-midnight Sun-Fri)*, next to a *pachinko* (pinball game) parlour, took second place.

Ichiran *(open 24hr daily)* has been serving noodles for 37 years. Unusually, customers eat at individual cubicles, and fill out forms requesting precisely how they want their noodles prepared. Flavour strength, fat content, noodle tenderness, quantity of 'secret sauce' and garlic content can all be regulated. Marvellously, an English-language request form is also available.

Many branches of this famous noodle shop can be found around town, including at **Rāmen Stadium** *(5th floor, Canal City)*, where noodle-lovers queue to slurp bowls of soup prepared in famous styles hailing from Hokkaidō all the way to southern Kyūshū. When *rāmen* palls (and it does), Canal City also has sleek Eurasian restaurants in the section inside the Grand Hyatt, where **CHI-NA** *(open daily)*, a Cantonese banquet hall, offers all-you-can-eat dim sum lunch (¥2800).

The IMS building in Tenjin has prime skyline views from its 12th- to 14th-floor restaurants, including **Pasta's Pietro** *(pasta plus salad bar ¥1500; open daily)* and **Asahi Beer Cruiser Pier 21** *(open daily)*, while down in the basement **Mrs Elizabeth Muffin** *(baked goods under ¥200; open daily)* sells sweet muffins with free unlimited refills on hot coffee!

Café Serena *(Hotel Nikko; lunch/dinner buffet ¥1700/2800; open daily)*, near Hakata station, has an unforgettable continental French buffet, serving succulent roast duck to tropical fruit sorbet.

Taiwan Yatai is a small but friendly place that does Taiwanese-Chinese food at very reasonable prices. It's a favourite with partygoers on Oyafuko-dōri. You'll find innovative upmarket **dining bars** a little off the beaten track in Kego. From the Kego police box, head either west on Kego Hon-dōri or north on Taishō-dōri toward Akasaka subway station, and pick one you like.

Over in Momochi, the **Sea Hawk Hotel & Resort** has a diverting Chinatown complex on the 35th floor. Experience the market-like frenzy of **Bunmei Ichijōgai** *(dishes*

from ¥550), where you can kick back with dim sum or a bowl of noodles, and enjoy the sweeping views.

Entertainment

Fukuoka-ites like to party, and the city is full of clubs, bars and pubs. Nakasu Island is one of the busiest entertainment districts in Japan, but you need to go with a Japanese regular unless you're prepared to spend a fortune. Tenjin, and especially Oyafuko-dōri, are a better bet for a night out.

Bōkairō *(35th floor, Sea Hawks Hotel; open nightly)* is a neo-Chinese cocktail lounge that has lipstick-red plush lounge seats and stellar night views. Cocktails start at ¥1000.

Blue Note *(☎ 715-6666)* will interest any jazz aficionados in Fukuoka. Ticket prices range from ¥5500 to ¥12,000 for international acts, but include food and drink coupons.

Generally, clubs have a cover charge at weekends of around ¥1500 to ¥2500, usually with a free drink or two. If you show up early in the evening, the cover may be waived.

Happy Cock *(☎ 734-2686; 9th floor, Neo Palace Bldg; open 6pm-1am Sun & Tues-Thurs, 6pm-4am Fri & Sat)* heaves with partygoers. It's usually busy right up until closing, with a mixture of '60s funk, '70s pop and '90s hip-hop. **Crazy Cock** *(☎ 722-3006; Oyafuko-dōri; open 9pm-3am Tues-Thur, 9pm-4am Fri-Sun)* is its close relative, and also a happening place.

The Dark Room *(☎ 725-2989; 8th floor, Bacchus-kan; open 6pm-midnight daily)* is mercifully cockless. Entertainingly hyperactive bar staff preside over a multi-level lounge space ideal for hipsters.

Voodoo Lounge *(☎ 732-4662; 3rd floor, Tenjin Centre Bldg; open 7pm-3am Sun, Mon, Wed & Thur, 7pm-4am Fri & Sat)* is a funky, chilled-out bar with varied live music acts. **Club Vibe** *(☎ 716-2030)*, the neighbouring hip-hop/house-playing club, has a throbbing dance floor. **Off Broadway** *(☎ 724-5383; 2nd floor, Tenjin Centre Bldg; open 7.30pm-2am Sun-Thur, 7.30pm-4am Fri & Sat)* has its quiet times, but still attracts a rowdy enough clientele. It's the kind of place where your feet adhere to the floor. Look for live acoustic shows by local expats.

Shopping

Clay Hakata dolls depicting women, children, samurai and geisha are a popular Fukuoka craft. Hakata obi, the silk sashes worn with a kimono, are another local product. Try Mitsukoshi or Daimaru department stores in Tenjin.

Getting There & Away

Air Fukuoka is a major international gateway with flights to and from South Korea, Hong Kong, China, the Philippines, Thailand, Malaysia, Indonesia, Taiwan and Honolulu.

There are also domestic flights to Tokyo's Haneda airport (¥27,900, more than 50 flights daily) and Narita international airport (four flights daily). Other domestic routes include Osaka (¥16,200) and Okinawa (Naha, ¥20,300, 1½ hours).

Japan's only independent cut-price carrier, **Skymark** (☎ 736-3131, in Tokyo ☎ 03-3433-7026) has daily flights to Tokyo's Haneda airport for ¥16,000.

Bus Long-distance buses depart from the Kōtsū bus centre near JR Hakata station and also from the Tenjin bus centre. Destinations include Tokyo (¥15,000, 14½ hours), Osaka (¥10,000, 9½ hours), Nagoya (¥10,500, 11 hours) and many other places around Kyūshū.

Train JR Hakata station is currently the western terminus of the 1175km Tokyo–Osaka–Hakata *shinkansen*. There are services to/from Tokyo (¥21,720, five to six hours), Osaka (¥14,590, 2½ to three hours) and Hiroshima (¥8700, one to two hours). Prices are slightly higher for the Nozomi *shinkansen*.

JR lines also fan out from Hakata to other parts of Kyūshū. The Nippō line runs through Beppu and Miyazaki; the Kagoshima line runs through Hakata, Kumamoto and Kagoshima; and both the Nagasaki and Sasebo lines run from Hakata to Saga and Sasebo or to Nagasaki. You can also travel by subway and JR train to Karatsu and continue from there to Nagasaki by train.

Boat There are ferry services from Hakata to Okinawa, and other islands off Kyūshū. An international high-speed hydrofoil service run by **JR Kyūshū** (reservations ☎ 281-2315) connects the city with Pusan in Korea, taking about three hours (¥13,000, two daily). The **Camellia line** (☎ 262-2323) has a regular daily ferry service to Pusan (¥9000, 14½ hours).

Getting Around

To/From the Airport Fukuoka airport is conveniently close to the city centre. The airport has three domestic terminals and an international terminal, all connected by a free shuttle bus.

The subway from the domestic terminals takes just five minutes to reach Hakata station (¥250) and 11 minutes to Tenjin (¥250). Buses run frequently between Hakata station and the international terminal.

Airport taxis cost around ¥1300 to Hakata and ¥1800 to Tenjin.

Bus City bus services operate from the Kōtsū bus centre in Hakata and the Tenjin bus centre. Nishitetsu bus has a flat ¥100 rate for city-centre rides.

From stand E opposite Hakata station, bus No 11 or 19 goes to Hakata Port's International Terminal (¥220), while No 47 or 48 reaches Bayside Place for ferries to islands.

Subway There are two subway lines in Fukuoka. The Kūkō (airport) line runs from Fukuoka domestic airport terminal to Meinohama via Hakata, Nakasu-Kawabata and Tenjin stations. The Hakozaki line runs from Nakasu-Kawabata station to Kaizuka. Fares around town start at ¥200; a one-day pass costs ¥600. Trains stop running around midnight.

DAZAIFU 太宰府
☎ 092 • pop 66,000

Dazaifu, once the governmental centre of Kyūshū, is an amiable enough place for a half-day visit, but once you've seen the shrine and several temples, it's deadsville. The **information office** (☎ 925-1880) at Nishitetsu-Dazaifu station has helpful staff and an excellent English-language brochure map that details outlying ruins, temples and minor sights.

Tenman-gū 天満宮

Poet and scholar Sugawara-no-Michizane was an important personage in the Kyoto court until he fell foul of political intrigue and was exiled to distant Dazaifu, where he died two years later. Subsequent disasters that struck Kyoto were blamed on his unfair dismissal and he became deified as Tenman Tenjin, the god of culture and scholars. Tenman-gū, his great shrine and burial place, attracts countless visitors.

The brightly painted orange shrine is entered via a picturesque arched bridge. The *honden* (main hall) was rebuilt in 1583. Behind it is the **Kankō Historical Museum** *(admission ¥200; open Wed-Mon)* with dioramas showing events in Tenjin's life. The **treasure house** *(admission ¥300; open 9am-4.30pm Tues-Sun)* has artefacts connected with his life and the history of the shrine.

Once a month the shrine hosts an *omoshiro-ichi* (literally, 'interesting market'), a giant flea market selling everything from antique kimono to Mickey Mouse telephones. Dates vary, so check with tourist information.

Kōmyōzen-ji 光明禅寺

Secreted away inside this small temple *(admission by ¥200 donation; usually open 9am-4.30pm daily)* is an exquisite jewel of a Zen garden. It's a peaceful contrast to the crowds at the nearby shrine.

Other Attractions

The musty **Kyūshū Historical Museum** *(admission free; open 9am-4pm Tues-Sun)* is not far beyond Kōmyōzen-ji.

Hidden out among the rice fields, **Kaidan-in** dates from 755 and was one of the most important ordination monasteries in Japan. Adjacent **Kanzeon-ji** dates from 746 but only the great bell, said to be the oldest in Japan, remains from the original construction. Its **treasure hall** *(admission ¥500; open 9am-4.30pm daily)* has an impressive collection of statuary, most of it wood, dating from the 10th to 12th centuries. The style of some of the pieces appears to be Indian or Tibetan.

Dazaifu Exhibition Hall *(admission ¥150; open 9am-4.30pm Tues-Sun)* displays finds from local archaeological excavations. Nearby are the **Tofurō ruins**, foundations of the ancient government buildings. **Enoki-sha** is where Sugawara-no-Michizane died. His body was transported from here to its burial place, now Tenman-gū, on the ox cart that appears in so many local depictions.

Places to Eat

Ume-no-Hana *(☎ 928-7787; meals ¥2300-6500; open 11am-3.30pm & 4.30pm-8pm daily)* demurely hides behind its own garden wall, a short curving walk east of the shrine. It's justifiably renowned for its tofu cuisine. Reservations are a good idea.

Getting There & Around

The private Nishitetsu line connects Tenjin with Dazaifu (¥390, 25 minutes), but a change of trains at Nishitetsu-Futsukaichi station is required.

Bicycles can be rented at Nishitetsu-Dazaifu station for ¥500 per day.

FUTSUKAICHI ONSEN 二日市温泉

Fifteen minutes' walk south of Nishitetsu-Futsukaichi Station, this small *onsen* town is unassuming. Its public baths are grouped together in the old main street. Favoured by traditionalists, **Gozen-yu** *(admission ¥200; closed 1st & 3rd Wed each month)* is the most characteristic. All are open 9am to 9pm daily. From JR Futsukaichi station, cross back over the tracks, then follow the road under the torii gate and across the stream.

TACHIARAI 大刀洗

Even locals don't know about **Tachiarai Heiwa Kinenkan** *(admission ¥500; open 9.30am-5pm daily)*, a tiny memorial museum established by ex-aviators and residents of Tachiarai, a small village set in farmland. The museum commemorates Japanese killed in WWII, including kamikaze pilots and Tachiarai locals who died when USAF B-52s bombed the area in 1945 (Tachiarai was the site of a military air base and aircraft factory). It's a strangely affecting place, with wartime memorabilia bundled together alongside speedometers from Phantom F-4s and Soviet MiG jets, and 24-year-old Toshihiro Watanabe's Zero-sen fighter, retrieved from the sea off Okinawa. Little is labelled in English.

Take the Nishitetsu private line to Ogōri by *kyūkō* (ordinary express, ¥500, 30 minutes) then change to the Amagi-tetsudō train line (¥280, 11 minutes). The museum is in front of Tachiarai station.

KURUME 久留米

The town of Kurume, south of Dazaifu, is noted for its crafts, including splash-dyed indigo textiles, paper making, lacquerware and bamboo work. Its rubber industry is responsible for *zashiki-tabi*, the floppy split-toed shoes worn by labourers all over Japan. Pottery is produced in nearby towns.

Narita-san *(admission ¥500; usually open 8am-5pm daily)*, a branch of the more famous temple outside Tokyo, is the town's biggest attraction, both literally and metaphorically speaking. Its 62m-high statue of the goddess of mercy, Kannon, stands beside a miniaturised replica of Borobudur. Inside the statue you can climb up past Buddhist treasures and religious dioramas right into the divine forehead.

It takes about 30 minutes to get to Kurume from Fukuoka, either on the JR Kagoshima line or the private Nishitetsu line (¥600, 30 minutes). Local buses to Kamitsu-machi (¥210, 20 minutes), near Narita-san, depart from stand No 1 downstairs.

Saga-ken 佐賀県

KARATSU 唐津
☎ 0955 • pop 80,000

Only 50km southwest of Fukuoka, the small castle town of Karatsu makes a good jumping-off point for visits to Iki island. Potters in Karatsu turn out primitive but well-respected pottery, with clear connections to the Korean techniques first introduced into Japan. At JR Karatsu station, the **information desk** *(☎ 72-4963; open 9am-6pm daily)* has a good English-language map booklet. Staff can book accommodation, but no English is spoken.

Things to See & Do
Although a modern reconstruction, **Karatsu-jō** *(admission ¥310; open 9am-4.40pm daily Sept-June, 9am-5.40pm daily July & Aug)* is picturesquely perched on a hill overlooking the sea. Inside are antique ceramics, samurai armour and archaeological displays.

The 14 floats used in the Karatsu Kunchi Matsuri are displayed in the **Hikiyama Festival Float Exhibition Hall** *(admission ¥200; open 9am-5pm daily)* beside Karatsu-jinja. The festival is believed to have started in 1592. Designs include the Aka-jishi (Red Lion), samurai helmets, a dragon and...a chicken.

Around town there are a number of **kilns** where you can see local potters at work, and there are also ceramic shops along the street between the train station and the town centre. The most famous kiln-gallery is that of **Nakazato Tarōemon** *(admission free)*. It's five minutes' walk southeast of Karatsu station.

A dirt cycling track cuts through the pine trees planted behind 5km-long **Niji-no-Matsubara Beach**. Each morning there is a busy *asa-ichi* (morning market) at the west end of the beach, from dawn until 9am.

Special Events
In late July and early August the *doyō-yoichi* (Saturday night market) is held in the town centre with much singing and dancing. The spectacular **Karatsu Kunchi Matsuri** takes place from 2 to 4 November.

Places to Stay & Eat
Hotel SOLA *(☎ 72-3003; singles ¥4900)* is a bright, modern business hotel. **Business Hotel Chitose** *(☎ 72-3361; singles/twins ¥4700/7800)* feels more traditional, and has very spacious rooms. It's off the end of the main shopping arcade.

Ryokan Yōyōkaku *(☎ 72-7181; rooms per person from ¥15,000)* is a beautiful Zen-like building that harks back to earlier centuries. The owners speak English. Exquisite seafood meals are available, but not included in the rates.

Niji-no-Matsubara Camp Site *(☎ 75-1785; sites per person ¥500, tent rental ¥2000; open July & Aug)* is right next to the highway, and kind of soggy. **Kokumin-shukusha Niji-no-Matsubara Hotel** *(☎ 73-9111, 0120-73-9100, fax 75-9991; singles/ twins ¥6000/10,000, Japanese-style rooms ¥14,500)* is typical of other overpriced beach accommodation.

Manbō *(☎ 75-1881; dishes from ¥500)*, inside the Karatsu station shopping arcade, offers tantalising seafood. Try the tempura *teishoku* (set meal, ¥1500), hot calamari or melt-in-your-mouth squid *shūmai*. Look for the blue *noren* (cloth) hanging over the entrance.

Entertainment
Dreadlock *(☎ 72-1207; open 7pm-2am Thur-Tues)* is a fun reggae bar run by Karatsu's resident Rastafarian, Nishimura Eiji, and is out near the beach. The English-speaking owner is a wealth of information about diving, surfing and ceramics.

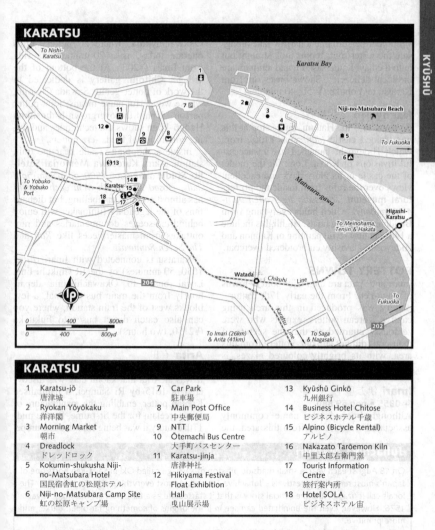

KARATSU

1	Karatsu-jō 唐津城	7	Car Park 駐車場	13	Kyūshū Ginkō 九州銀行
2	Ryokan Yōyōkaku 洋洋閣	8	Main Post Office 中央郵便局	14	Business Hotel Chitose ビジネスホテル千歳
3	Morning Market 朝市	9	NTT	15	Alpino (Bicycle Rental) アルピノ
4	Dreadlock ドレッドロック	10	Ōtemachi Bus Centre 大手町バスセンター	16	Nakazato Tarōemon Kiln 中里太郎右衛門窯
5	Kokumin-shukusha Niji- no-Matsubara Hotel 国民宿舎虹の松原ホテル	11	Karatsu-jinja 唐津神社	17	Tourist Information Centre 旅行案内所
6	Niji-no-Matsubara Camp Site 虹の松原キャンプ場	12	Hikiyama Festival Float Exhibition Hall 曳山展示場	18	Hotel SOLA ビジネスホテル宙

Getting There & Around

From Fukuoka, take the Kūkō subway line from Hakata or Tenjin to the end of the line, continuing on the JR Chikuhi line (¥1110, 80 minutes). Onwards to Nagasaki take the JR Karatsu line to Saga and the JR Nagasaki line from there.

From the Ōtemachi bus centre, highway buses depart for Tenjin (¥1000, 70 minutes) and Nagasaki (¥2000, two hours).

Tourists are able to borrow bicycles (for free!) from the **Alpino** building. For excursions around Saga-ken, **Eki-mae Rent-a-**

Car (☎ 74-6204) is located in front of Karatsu station.

HIGASHI-MATSUURA PENINSULA 東松浦半島

Karatsu is at the base of Higashi-Matsuura Peninsula with its dramatic coastline and little fishing ports.

Yobuko 呼子

This busy fishing port has a wonderful **morning market** for fish and produce; the main action is over by 8am. A series of modern concrete ryokan, charging from around ¥7000 per person, line a narrow lane alongside the waterfront; rooms look straight out onto the bay. Squid sashimi and tempura are the local delicacies. Shōwa buses run from Karatsu to Yobuko (¥750, 40 minutes).

Nagoya-jō 名古屋城

En route to Cape Hatomi, buses stop at this now ruined castle (admission ¥100), from which Hideyoshi launched his unsuccessful invasions of Korea. Look for the model of the castle in its glory days and excellent views over the ruins from inside the **prefectural museum** (admission free; open 9am-4.30pm daily), which holds everything from Buddhas to fishing boats. Highlights include a 14th-century scroll painting of Kannon and Hideyoshi's lavishly embroidered overcoat.

POTTERY TOWNS

Imari and Arita are the major pottery towns of Saga-ken. From the early 17th century, pottery was produced in this area using captive Korean potters, experts who were zealously guarded so that the secrets of their craft did not slip out. Pottery from this area, with its brightly coloured glazes, is still highly esteemed in Japan.

Imari 伊万里

☎ 0955 ● pop 59,880

Although Imari is the name commonly associated with pottery from this area, the pottery is actually produced outside town. **Ōkawachiyama**, where 20 pottery kilns operate today, is a 20-minute bus ride from Imari (¥200). At the bottom of the village, **Chitōjin** gallery is dedicated to the work of potter-genius Sawada Chitōjin, whose wonderful name means 'idiot potter person'. Uphill the overgrown **Nabeshima Hanyō-kōen** shows the techniques and living conditions of feudal-era potters.

Inside a shopping arcade near the train station, **Akira Kurosawa Memorial Satellite Studio** (admission ¥500; open 9am-5pm daily, closed 2nd & 4th Mon each month) has almost no English labelling, but diehard fans of the legendary filmmaker will enjoy behind-the-scenes documentaries and rare outtakes from masterpieces like Ran and The Seven Samurai.

Karatsu is connected with Imari (futsū ¥630, 50 minutes) by the JR Chikuhi line. Local buses to Ōkawachiyama depart hourly from the main bus terminal, a few blocks west of the train station, where you can also catch direct buses to Fukuoka (¥2150, two hours).

Arita 有田

☎ 0955 ● pop 17,800

It was at Arita that kaolin clay was discovered in 1615 by Ri Sampei, a naturalised Korean potter, enabling the manufacture of fine porcelain for the first time. By the mid-17th century it was being exported to Europe.

Juhachiya Matsuri

On 18 August each year, a small roadside pit-stop of a village called Ōki in Saga-ken hosts one of Japan's most remarkable festivals – Juhachiya Matsuri. Almost everything about it is unique. The locals call it 'izayoi', and the official story is that it started life as a farmers' rain-making festival in 1576. However, even the uninitiated can see in it the origins of something far older, darker and more primitive.

The proceedings begin as night falls, with Oki's 18-year-old males parading through the village, beating with gusto on a huge gong with metal hammers. Suspended on long bamboo poles above their heads are home-made miniflares, showering them in sulphurous sparks. Flautists and drummers add to the din and smoke – it sounds like Tom Waits' percussion section falling off a cliff. Yet this is small scale – there are only about 50 men and boys – and for that reason, it's all the more striking.

The action moves to the local temple, Ryusen-ji, where a sandy arena has been prepared. The entire village is waiting, ready to witness Ukitate Kenka, or the Floating-Standing Fight.

The gong is moved to one side of the ring, then all hell breaks loose. The youths rush to take possession of it. However, between them and their goal are the village 'elders' – blacksmiths, firemen, truck drivers, lumberjacks – none of whom look even remotely elderly. They put up a

The **tourist information desk** (☎ 42-4052; W www.arita.or.jp/index_e.html) inside Arita station can help orient visitors with maps and bus schedules. An annual pottery fair is held 29 April to 5 May.

Shops line the main street leading out from the station towards the **Kyūshū Ceramics Museum** (admission ¥200; open 9am-4.30pm Tues-Sun), well worth a visit if you want an overview of the development of ceramic arts in Kyūshū. Pottery connoisseurs are sure to find the **Imaizumi Imaemon Gallery** (open 9am-5pm Mon-Sat), **Sakaida Kakiemon Kiln** (open 8am-5pm daily) and **Genemon Kiln** (open 9am-4pm Mon-Sat) interesting, and there are dozens of other workshops to visit.

For the full treatment, join the Japanese package tours at **Arita Porcelain Park** (admission ¥500; open 10am-5pm daily Mar-Nov, 10am-4pm daily Dec-Feb), a 10-minute bus ride from the station, or **China on the Park** (open 9am-5pm daily), 5km west of town on Route 202, where you can watch the firing process. A taxi from Arita station costs ¥1000.

A short hop east of Arita, **Takeo Onsen** is a modern hot-springs town. The traditional baths are said to have refreshed the armies of Hideyoshi Toyotomi. Look for the lacquered Chinese-style gate, which was built without nails. **Takeo Onsen Youth Hostel** (☎ 0954-22-2490, fax 0954-20-1208; beds ¥2600; closed late May & early June) is an option, but the last bus to the hostel leaves Takeo Onsen station before 6pm.

From outside JR Arita station, private Matsuura-tetsudō trains depart for Arita (¥400, 25 minutes). JR limited express trains between Hakata (Fukuoka) and Nagasaki stop at Arita, and also Takeo Onsen, which is also connected to Arita by local trains (¥270, 15 minutes). Around town, community bus routes (¥150) cover most of the outlying sights, departing hourly from Arita station.

Northwest Islands

Five large and many smaller islands lie to the northwest of Kyūshū and are accessible from Fukuoka, Sasebo and Nagasaki, but reaching them is not cheap. These are strictly islands for those who want to get far away from it all. Some are part of Saga-ken, while other islands are part of Nagasaki-ken.

IKI 壱岐
☎ 09204 • pop 36,530

Attractive Iki, with an area of 138 sq km, lies closer to Karatsu than Fukuoka. In addition to fine beaches, it's also relatively flat and a decent place for cyclists. Toyotomi Hideyoshi fortified **Gonoura**, the busiest port and a base for exploring the island. **Ondakejinja**, north of Ashibe, features eroded

---

Juhachiya Matsuri

human barricade that could teach the American Football League a thing or two. Time after time the young men attack, only to be repelled or pushed face down into the sand. One youth nearly reaches the gong, only to be dealt a stabbing right-hand jab to the cheekbone by a wiry 'elder', and he's carried off to a waiting medical crew, bleeding profusely. No-one loses their temper. Finally, inevitably, the exhausted, battered youths withdraw, the gong remains in the hands of age and authority, and the temple officials rush in to set up the evening's finale, known as the *jamon*.

The *jamon* is a pyrotechnic catastrophe waiting to happen. All day, as the 18-year-olds have been psyching themselves up for the battle, their mothers, sisters and grandmothers have been hand-rolling miniature explosives and inserting them into the *jamon*, a wooden tower. At a given signal, the flame creeps slowly up the tower, the wind catches an ember, there's a glimmer of orange, and KABOOOOOOOOOOOOOOM!!!

And then it's over. The villagers melt away to party at home, the country darkness floods back in, and this observer is left sharing a ghostly dark station platform with an egregiously drunken civil servant who managed to get stuck here on his way back from the town office in Arita. He asks, in all innocence, 'What was all that noise?'.

John Ashburne

'monkey men', carved by a local lord, and cobwebs, plus fine views. **Yunomoto Onsen** on the west coast is the island's only hot spring. Other minor sights include burial mounds, Buddhist rock carvings and historic ruins. The gorgeous little **beach** near Katsumoto on the island's north side also has a **camping ground** nearby. At the hot springs, the *kokumin-shukusha* (people's lodge) **Ikishima-sō** (☎ 3-0124; rooms with 2 meals ¥6000) is good value. Cheerful **Tomioka Minshuku** (☎ 7-0011; rooms with 2 meals ¥5000) is in Gonoura. At Gonoura ferry terminal, the **information desk** can help book other *minshuku*, pension and ryokan accommodation around the island.

Between April and September, jetfoils go from Hakata to Gonoura or Ashibe (¥4680, 70 minutes) on Iki. Ordinary car ferry services take twice that long (¥1930). From Yobuko port near Karatsu, more frequent ferries go to Indōji (¥1310, 70 minutes). Although the port is only a five-minute ride from Yobuko town, infrequent local bus services are not timed to ferries. Express buses bound for Nagasaki sometimes meet ferries at Yobuko port.

On Iki, rental cars start at ¥3000 per three hours, costing ¥10,000 for two days. They can be rented at all of the ferry ports. Try friendly **Genkai Kotsū Rent-a-Car** (☎ 4-5658, 4-5827).

HIRADO-SHIMA 平戸島
☎ 0950 • pop 25,000

Blessed with sunshine and verdant tea fields, Hirado-shima's proximity to the mainland makes it easy – and cheap – to access. The island has interesting historical sights, beckoning white-sand beaches, two noteworthy festivals and a little-known collection of erotic drawings. The **tourist information booth** (☎ 0120-86-2015; open 8am-5.15pm daily), on the waterfront by the bus terminal, has excellent English-language brochures and can book accommodation.

The island, close to Sasebo and actually joined to Kyūshū by a toll bridge (¥100) from Hirado-guchi, has had an interesting European history. Portuguese ships first landed on Hirado-shima in 1549 and, a year later, St Francis Xavier paid a visit to the island (after his expulsion from Kagoshima). It was not until 1584 that the Portuguese formally established a trad-

ing post on the island, but they were soon followed by the Dutch and the British. Relations between the British and Dutch became so acrimonious that, in 1618, the Japanese had to restore law and order on the island. In 1621, the British abandoned Hirado-shima and Japan, and turned their full attention to India.

The main town is small enough to navigate on foot. The **Matsuura Historical Museum** (admission ¥500; open 8am-5.30pm daily) is housed in the residence of the Matsuura clan, who ruled the island from the 11th to the 19th centuries. Among the esteemed treasures is **Kanun-tei**, a *chanoyu* (tea ceremony) house for the unusual Chinshin-ryū warrior-style tea ceremony that is still practised on the island today. **Hirado Tourist Museum** (admission ¥300; open 8am-5pm daily Jan-Nov) displays some musty items relating to the island's history, including a Maria-Kannon statue that the 'hidden Christians' (see Religion in the Facts about Japan chapter) used in place of the Virgin Mary image.

Hirado-jō (admission ¥500; open 8.30am-5.30pm daily) presides over the town, with an enormous number of rebuilt structures. Inside you'll see traditional armour and clothing, and a few artefacts from the hidden Christian era. Not mentioned in the tourist literature is the rather more earthy **Issho-raku** (☎ 23-3434), a small private collection of erotic drawings dating back almost 400 years. Ask at tourist information to arrange a viewing. The owners don't speak English but are very friendly.

There are fine views over the islands of the Gotō-rettō from **Cape Shijiki**. About midway down the beautiful west coast of the island, **Neshiko Beach** is a lovely and long stretch of sand, while **Senri-ga-hama** is renowned for windsurfing. In the northern part of the island, **Kamisuki-no-sato** has pottery workshops and kiln ruins.

Jangara Matsuri, a folk festival held on 18 August, is particularly colourful. It is quite different to mainland festivals and is reminiscent of Okinawa or Korea. Arrive by late morning, if possible, for the afternoon events. From 24 to 27 October, the **Okunchi Matsuri** has dragon and lion dancing at Kameoka-jinja.

Over in Hirado-guchi, the closest mainland town, there's a campground and a **youth hostel** (☎ 57-1443; beds ¥3200).

Hirado-guchi (aka Tabira) is accessible by bus from Sasebo (¥1300, 80 minutes). Local buses cross the bridge to Hirado town (¥260, 10 minutes). Express buses run to the island from Hakata (¥2850, 3¾ hours). From Kashimae, half an hour by bus from Sasebo, regular boats operate to Hirado-shima via the islands, Kujuku-shima.

GOTŌ-RETTŌ 五島列島

The two main islands in the Gotō-rettō group are **Fukue-jima** and **Nakadōri-shima**, but there are three other medium-sized islands plus over 100 small islands and islets. At one time, these islands were a refuge for Japanese Christians fleeing the Edo government's anti-Christian repression; today the main attraction is their natural beauty.

Fukue, the fishing port on the island of the same name, is the main town in the group. The town's **Ishida-jō** was rebuilt in the 1860s. There's a street of samurai houses nearby. **Ondake**, a 40-minute walk from Fukue, is a cotyloid volcano (315m) covered by grass and an astronomical observatory. **Dozaki Tenshudō** (admission ¥300; usually open 9am-4.30pm daily) has exhibits of artefacts from the 'hidden Christian' era, and is the oldest church in the Gotō islands. It's a half-hour bus ride from Fukue. The island's most popular **beaches** are on the north central coast.

All Nippon Koku (ANK) has flights to Gotō-Fukue airport from Nagasaki (¥10,000) and Fukuoka (¥15,500). Jetfoils leave Nagasaki for Fukue up to five times daily (¥6080, 90 minutes); regular ferry services depart less frequently (¥2400, 3¾ hours). Bicycles and cars can be rented on Fukue-jima.

Nagasaki-ken 長崎県

NAGASAKI 長崎
☎ 095 • pop 423,160

Nagasaki is a vibrant city, but its unfortunate fate as the second atomic bomb target overshadows its early history of contact with the Portuguese and Dutch. Despite the image of Nagasaki as a modern city rising from an atomic wasteland, there are certainly many charming reminders of its fascinating, complex and multicultural history.

History

Nagasaki has the most varied history of any city in Japan, much of it tied up with the dramatic events of the 'Christian Century'. The accidental arrival of an off-course Portuguese ship in 1542 signalled the start of Nagasaki's long period as Japan's principal connection with the West.

The first visitors were soon followed by the missionary St Francis Xavier in 1560 and, although their visits were brief, these Portuguese contacts were to have far-reaching effects. The primitive guns introduced by the Portuguese soon revolutionised warfare in Japan, forcing the construction of new and stronger castles and bringing the anarchy and chaos of the 'Country at War' century to an end.

Among the first Japanese to be converted to Christianity by the visitors was a minor *daimyō* (regional lord), Ōmura Sumitada, in northwestern Kyūshū. Under Ōmura, Nagasaki, established in 1571, soon became the main arrival point for Portuguese trade ships. Although the Portuguese principally acted as intermediaries between China and Japan, the trade was mutually profitable, and Nagasaki quickly became a fashionable and wealthy city.

By 1587, Japanese authorities had begun to perceive the growing influence of Christianity as a threat. Jesuit missionaries were expelled and a policy of persecution was soon implemented. In 1597, 26 European and Japanese Christians were crucified in Nagasaki and in 1614 the religion was banned. Suspected Christians were rounded up, tortured and killed; the Japanese wives and children of foreigners were deported to Macau and Batavia; and the Catholic Portuguese and Spanish traders were expelled in favour of the Protestant Dutch, who were perceived as being more interested in trade and less in religion.

The Shimabara peasant uprising of 1637–38 – perceived as a Christian uprising at the time – was the final chapter in the events of the 'Christian Century'. All subsequent contact with foreigners was banned and no Japanese were allowed to travel overseas. One small loophole was the closely watched Dutch enclave on the island of Dejima near Nagasaki. Through this small outpost a trickle of Western science and culture continued to filter into Japan, and

KYŪSHŪ

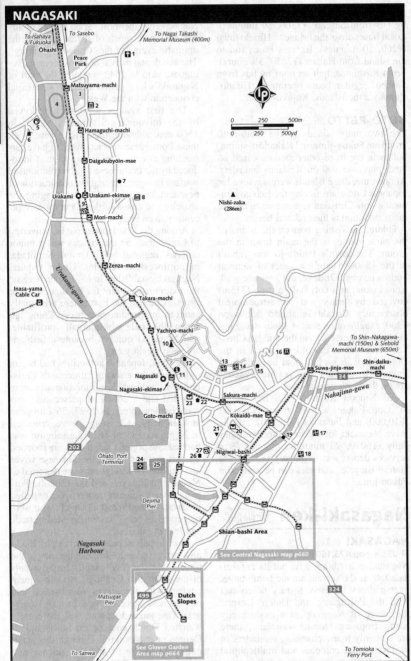

NAGASAKI

To Isahaya & Fukuoka

To Sasebo

To Nagai Takashi Memorial Museum (400m)

Ōhashi

Peace Park

Matsuyama-machi

Hamaguchi-machi

Daigakubyōin-mae

Urakami
Urakami-ekimae
Mori-machi

Inasa-yama Cable Car

Zenza-machi

Takara-machi

Yachiyo-machi

Nagasaki
Nagasaki-ekimae

Goto-machi

Ōhato Port Terminal

Nagasaki Harbour

Dejima Pier

Matsugae Pier

Nishi-zaka (286m)

To Shin-Nakagawa-machi (150m) & Siebold Memorial Museum (650m)

Suwa-jinja-mae
Shin-daiku-machi

Sakura-machi

Nakajima-gawa

Kōkaidō-mae

Nigiwai-bashi

Shian-bashi Area

See Central Nagasaki map p660

Dutch Slopes

See Glover Garden Area map p664

Urakami-gawa

To Sanwa

To Tomioka Ferry Port

0   250   500m
0   250   500yd

NAGASAKI

from 1720, when Dutch books were once again permitted to enter the country, Nagasaki became an important scientific and artistic centre. When Nagasaki reopened to the West in 1859, it quickly re-established itself as a major economic force, particularly in shipbuilding, the industry that made it a target on 9 August 1945.

Orientation

About a kilometre south of Nagasaki station, the Hamano-machi arcade and Shian-bashi entertainment area make up Nagasaki's central city area. Nagasaki is relatively compact and it's quite feasible to walk all the way south to the Dutch slopes and Glover Garden. The atomic bomb hypocentre is in the suburb of Urakami, about 2.5km north of JR Nagasaki station.

Information

The **tourist information office** (☎ 823-3631; open 8am-7pm daily) in Nagasaki station can assist with finding accommodation, although you may have to be a bit persistent – no English is spoken.

The **Nagasaki Prefectural Tourist Federation** (☎ 826-9407; open 9am-5.30pm Mon-Sat Sept-May, 9am-7pm Mon-Sat June-Aug) has detailed information on the city and extremely helpful English-speaking staff. Cross the pedestrian walkway to enter the prefectural building on the 2nd floor.

Chikyūkan (☎ 822-7966; open 10am-5pm Thur-Tues), a café in Oranda-zaka (the Dutch Slopes area), is aimed at long-term foreign residents and has limited information about the city and environs. Internet access costs ¥100 per 10 minutes.

Most **postal savings ATMs** accept internationally issued cards, and there's one inside Nagasaki station. Several branches of **18 Bank** handle foreign currency exchange.

Chikyū-shimin Hiroba (☎ 842-3783; 2nd floor, Nagasaki Brick Hall; open 9am-8pm daily) charges ¥100 per hour for Internet access. Beside JR Nagasaki station, **Kinko's** (¥200/10min) is open 24 hours; there's another branch in Shian-bashi. **Cybac Café** (membership fee ¥200, ¥480/1st hr) is also open 24 hours.

Near Ōhato ferry terminal, **Kinokuniya** (4th floor, Yume-saito Bldg) bookshop has a branch.

Urakami 浦上

A-Bomb Site Urakami, the hypocentre of the atomic explosion, is today a prosperous, peaceful suburb with modern shops, restaurants, cafés and even a couple of love hotels just a few steps from the hypocentre. Nuclear ruin seems comfortably far away.

Hypocentre Park has a black square stone column marking the exact point above which the bomb exploded. Nearby are bomb-blasted relics, including a section

KYŪSHŪ

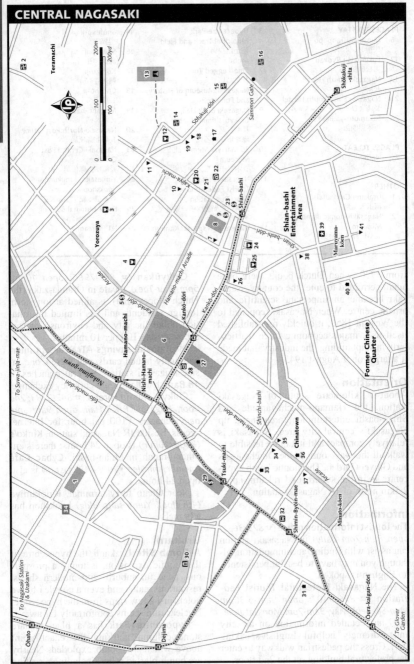

CENTRAL NAGASAKI

Teramachi

Shōkakuji-shita

Sofukuji-dōri

Sammon Gate

Shian-bashi
Entertainment
Area

Maruyama-kōen

Former Chinese
Quarter

Yorozuya

Hamano-machi Arcade

Kankō-dōri

Kankō-dōri

Shian-bashi-dōri

Shian-bashi

Kanko-dōri

Hamano-machi

Nishi-Hamano-
machi

To Suwa-jinja-mae

Nakajima-gawa

Edo-machi-dōri

Nishi-hama-dōri

Shinchi-bashi

Chinatown

Arcade

Tsuki-machi

Shimin-Byōin-mae

Minato-kōen

To Nagasaki Station
& Urakami

To Clover
Garden

Ohato

Dejima

Oura-kaigan-dōri

200m

200yd

CENTRAL NAGASAKI

PLACES TO STAY
17 Miyuki-sō
　三幸荘
27 Holiday Inn
　ホリデイイン長崎
31 Fukumoto Ryokan
　福本旅館
33 Nagasaki Washington
　Hotel
　長崎ワシントンホテル
36 Shinchi Business Hotel
　ビジネスホテル新地
40 Nishiki-sō
　にしき荘

PLACES TO EAT
7 Unryūtei
　雲龍亭
10 Hamakatsu
　浜勝
11 Ginrei
　銀嶺
18 Hamakatsu Restaurant
　浜勝
19 Wine Cellar Rosenthal
　ローゼンタル

21 Gyūkaku
　牛角
26 Unryū-tei
　雲龍亭
34 Kyōka-en
　京華園
35 Kairaku-en
　会楽園
37 Chūka-en
　中華園
38 Fukusaya Castella Cake Shop
　福砂屋本家
41 Kagetsu
　花月

OTHER
1 Nagasaki Grand Hotel
　長崎グランドホテル
2 Kōtai-ji
　皓喜寺
3 Ayer's Rock
4 Fan Fan
5 International ATM
6 Daimaru Department Store
　大丸
8 With Nagasaki

9 Shinwa Ginkō
　親和銀行
12 JB Trick
13 Daion-ji
　大音寺
14 Hosshin-ji
　発心寺
15 Daikō-ji
　大光寺
16 Sōfuku -ji
　崇福寺
20 Copen
22 Cybac Café
23 18 Bank
　十八銀行
24 Albert's Place
25 Moonshine
28 Kinko's
　キンコズ
29 18 Bank
　十八銀行
30 Dejima Museum
　出島資料館
32 Shinchi Bus Terminal
　新地バスターミナル
39 Police Post

of the wall of the Urakami Cathedral. The Matsuyama-machi tram stop on tram routes 1 or 3 is near the site.

Nagasaki Atomic Bomb Museum
As you descend a spiral stairway into the sobering Gembaku Shiryōkan *(A-Bomb Museum; admission ¥200, audio guide rental ¥150; open 8.30am-5pm daily)*, the parallels with a descent into hell are all too obvious. Exhibits begin with live footage of the bomb blast, then move excruciatingly through details of the city's destruction and loss of human life, as well as Japan's 15 years of military aggression prior to 1945. These riveting exhibitions end with an urgent report on the current status of nuclear weapons worldwide, with convincing video testimonials.

Peace Park North of Hypocentre Park is Heiwa-kōen (Peace Park), presided over by the Nagasaki Peace Statue, which – good intentions aside – is a monstrosity of immense proportions. At the time of the explosion, the park was the site of the Urakami Prison and every one of the prison's 134 occupants – prisoners and warders – was killed instantly. An annual antinuclear protest is held at the park on 9 August.

Urakami Cathedral The original Urakami Cathedral, the largest church in the east, was completed after three decades in 1914, then flattened in three seconds in 1945. The replacement cathedral was completed in 1959.

Nagai Takashi Memorial Museum The courage of Dr Nagai Takashi in the face of overwhelming adversity is the subject of this extraordinary little museum *(admission ¥100; open 9am-5pm daily)*. Already suffering from leukaemia, and having lost his wife during the atomic explosion, Dr Nagai devoted himself to the treatment of bomb victims until he died in 1951. Even after he became bed-ridden, Dr Nagai continued to write prolifically and secure donations for survivors and orphans from the international community.

The genius of this museum is its focus on the effects of the A-bomb on a single individual family, bringing into sharp relief the entire devastation on a human scale. Make time for the short documentary videos, available in several languages.

Next door, Dr Nagai's small hut **Nyokodō** is preserved as a memorial. Its name echoes the sentiment 'love thy neighbour as thyself', as both the doctor and his wife were Christians.

The Atomic Explosion

When the United States Air Force (USAF) B-29 bomber *Bock's Car* set off from Tinian in the Marianas on 9 August 1945 to drop the second atomic bomb on Japan, the target was Kokura on the northeastern coast of Kyūshū. Fortunately for Kokura it was a cloudy day and, despite flying over the city three times, the bomber's crew could not sight the target, so a course was set for the secondary target, Nagasaki.

The B-29 arrived over Nagasaki at 10.58am but again visibility was obscured by cloud. When a momentary gap appeared in the cloud cover, the Mitsubishi Arms Factory, not the intended Mitsubishi shipyard, was sighted and became the target. The 4.5-ton 'Fat Man' bomb had an explosive power equivalent to 21 kilotons of TNT, far more than the 13 kilotons of Hiroshima's 'Little Boy'.

The bomb actually missed its intended target and scored a near-direct hit on the largest Catholic church in Japan. The explosion took place at 11.02am, at an altitude of 500m, completely devastating the Urakami suburb of northern Nagasaki and killing 75,000 of Nagasaki's 240,000 population. Most victims were women, children and senior citizens, but those killed also included an estimated 13,000 conscripted Korean labourers and 200 allied POWs. Another 75,000 people were injured and it is estimated that as many people again have subsequently died as a result of the blast. Anybody out in the open within 2km of the epicentre suffered severe burns from the heat of the explosion; even at 3.5km away exposed bare skin was burnt. Everything within a 1km radius of the explosion was destroyed and after the resulting fires, a third of the city was wiped out.

Other Sights The 'One-legged Torii' (a torii is an entrance gate to a Shintō shrine) is southeast of the hypocentre. The blast knocked down one side of the entrance arch to the Sanno-jinja, but the other leg still stands to this day.

A short walk from the torii is the forgotten **Nagasaki Museum of History and Folklore** (*admission free; open 9am-4.30pm Tues-Sun*), which exhibits a miscellany of antiques upstairs.

Nagasaki Station Area

26 Martyrs Memorial A few minutes' walk from JR Nagasaki station on Nishizaka is a memorial wall with reliefs of the 26 Christians crucified in 1597. In this, Japan's most brutal crackdown on Christianity, six of those crucified were Spanish friars, the other 20 were Japanese and the two youngest were boys aged 12 and 13. Behind it is a simple **museum** (*admission ¥250; open 9am-5pm daily*) with displays about Christianity in the area.

Fukusai-ji Although Fukusai-ji (*admission ¥200; usually open 8am-4pm daily*) is not on any list of architectural or cultural gems, this unique construction, also known as Nagasaki Kannon Universal Temple, shouldn't be missed. In fact, you can't miss it, since the temple is in the form of a huge turtle

carrying an 18m-high figure of the goddess Kannon on its back. Inside, a Foucault pendulum (a device that demonstrates the rotation of the earth on its tilted axis) hangs from near the top of the hollow statue. Only St Petersburg and Paris have larger examples.

The original temple was built in 1628 but was completely burnt by the A-bomb fire. The replacement, totally unlike the original, was built in 1979. A bell tolls from the temple at 11.02am daily, the exact time of the explosion. If you're lucky, the caretaker will give you a personalised tour of the premises in her quirky English.

Shōfuku-ji This temple, not to be confused with Sōfuku-ji (see the Teramachi section later in this chapter), is a 10-minute walk from Nagasaki station. Its gardens are particularly pleasant and contain an arched stone gate dating from 1657. The main building, of typical Chinese style, was reconstructed in 1715.

Just west is another temple, **Kanzen-ji**, with the biggest camphor tree in Nagasaki.

Suwa-jinja 諏訪神社

Between 7 and 9 October, this enormous shrine comes to life with the dragon dance of **Okunchi Matsuri**, Nagasaki's most important annual celebration. Suwa-jinja was originally established in 1625 and its forested hilltop setting is meditative. Tram lines 3, 4 and 5 run to the Suwa-jinja-mae stop.

Teramachi (Temple Row) 寺町

Incongruously close to the Shian-bashi entertainment area, the path between Sōfuku-ji and Kōfuku-ji is lined with a series of smaller temples. It would be a wonderfully peaceful walk except for the taxis, cars and noisy trucks barrelling dangerously along its narrow streets.

An Ōbaku (the third-largest Zen sect after Rinzai and Sōtō) temple, and one of Nagasaki's most important, **Sōfuku-ji** (admission ¥300; open 8am-5pm daily) dates from 1635 and has a Ming-style gate. Inside the temple you can admire a great bell from 1647 and a huge cauldron that was used to prepare food for victims of a famine in 1680.

Just down the road from Sōfuku-ji, steep steps lead up to **Daikō-ji**. At almost the bottom of the road, turn right and take a few steps to the **Hosshin-ji bell**. Cast in 1438, it's the oldest temple bell in Nagasaki. Then climb the stairs to the large Kuroganemochi tree at the entrance to **Daion-ji** and follow the path that heads to the grave of Matsudaira Zushonokami. He had been magistrate of Nagasaki for a year when, in 1808, the British warship HMS *Phaeton* sailed into Nagasaki Harbour and seized two Dutch hostages. The British and Dutch were on opposite sides in the Napoleonic War at that time. Unable to oppose the British, Zushonokami capitulated to their demands for supplies, then promptly disembowelled himself.

A short distance further on, turn down the path to **Kōtai-ji**, a favourite with local artists; it has a notable bell dating from 1702. The final temple along the temple-row walk, **Kōfuku-ji** (admission ¥200; open 6am-6pm daily), dates from the 1620s and has always had strong Chinese connections. The temple is noted for its lawns and cycad palms and for the Chinese-influenced architecture of the main hall. Like Sōfuku-ji, it is an Ōbaku Zen temple – but this one is the oldest in Japan.

Megane-bashi Parallel to the temple row is the river, the Nakajima-gawa, which is crossed by a picturesque collection of stone bridges. At one time, each bridge was the distinct entranceway to a separate temple. The best-known is the double-arched Megane-bashi (Spectacles Bridge), so called because if the water is at the right height, the arches and their reflection in the water come together to create a 'spectacles' effect.

Shian-bashi Area 思案橋

The Shian-bashi tram stop marks the site of the bridge over which pleasure seekers would cross into the Shian-bashi quarter. The bridge and the elegant old brothels are long gone but this is still the entertainment area of Nagasaki. During Japan's long period of isolation from the West, the Dutch – cordoned off at their Dejima trading post – were only allowed contact with Japanese trading partners and courtesans. It's said that fortunes were made as much from smuggling as from the world's oldest profession.

In between the bars, restaurants and clubs, Shian-bashi still has a few reminders of those old days. A walk up from the southern tram stop on Shian-bashi-dōri to where the first road forks leads to the Fukusaya Castella Cake Shop. Turn left at this junction, pass the police post and you come to the driveway to Kagetsu, now an elegant and expensive restaurant, but at one time an even more elegant and expensive brothel.

Dejima Museum 出島

From the mid-17th century until 1855, this small isolated conclave of Dejima was Japan's only contact with the Western world, and fortunes were made by the Dutch traders through exchange of Japanese crafts for Western medicine and technology. Although the island was submerged during 19th-century land reclamation projects, attempts to reconstruct the trading post, now a national historic site, are moving ahead. The small **museum** (admission ¥300; open 9am-6.40pm daily) has exhibits on the Dutch and other foreign contact with Nagasaki, and free walking tour maps of the entire site.

Chinatown Area 中国街

Theoretically, during Japan's long period of seclusion, Chinese traders were just as circumscribed in their movements as the

Dutch, but in practice they were relatively free. Only a couple of buildings remain from the old area, but Nagasaki still has an energetic Chinese community that has had a great influence on the city's culture, festivals and cuisine.

Glover Garden Area
グラバー園周辺

Glover Garden At the southern end of Nagasaki, some former homes of the city's pioneering Meiji period European residents have been reassembled in this hillside garden *(admission ¥600; open 8am-9.30pm daily late July–mid-Oct, 8am-6pm daily rest of year)*. The series of moving stairways up the hill, along with the goldfish ponds, fountains and squawking public announcement system, give it the air of a cultural Disneyland, but the houses are appealing, the history is interesting and the views across Nagasaki are superb.

The garden takes its name from Thomas Glover (1838–1911), the best-known of the expat community. Glover's arms-importing operations played an important part in the Meiji Restoration; he built the first train line in Japan and he even helped establish the first modern shipyard from which Nagasaki's Mitsubishi shipyard is a direct descendant.

The best way to explore the hillside garden is to take the walkways to the top and then walk back downhill. At the top of the park is **Mitsubishi No 2 Dock building** with displays about the city's important shipyard. Going down the hill you come to **Walker House**, the **Ringer** and **Alt houses** and finally **Glover House**. Halfway down the hill, above Glover House, is the renowned **statue** of the Japanese opera singer Miura Tamaki, which is often referred to as Madame Butterfly. You exit the garden through the **Nagasaki Traditional Performing Arts Museum**, which has a display of dragons and floats used in the colourful Okunchi Matsuri.

Ōura Catholic Church Just below Glover Garden is this attractively situated church *(admission ¥300; open 8.30am-5pm daily winter, 8am-6pm daily rest of year)*, built in 1864 for Nagasaki's new foreign community. Soon after its opening, a group of Japanese came to the church and announced that Christianity had been maintained among the Urakami community throughout the 250

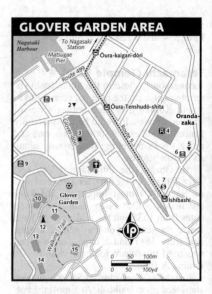

years it had been banned in Japan. Unfortunately, despite Japan's newly opened doors to the West, Christianity was still banned for Japanese people. When this news leaked out, thousands of Urakami residents were exiled to other parts of Japan, where many of them died before Christianity was legalised in 1873. The church is dedicated to the 26 Christians crucified in 1597.

Dutch Slopes The gently inclined flagstone streets known as Oranda-zaka (Dutch Slopes) were once lined with wooden Dutch houses. A few have been restored *(combined admission ¥200; open 9am-5pm Tues-Sun)*: **Maizō-shiryōkan**, displaying Edo-period archaeological finds and **Furushashin-shiryōkan**, with three houses holding galleries of old photographs – including a rare one of Meiji hero Sakamoto Ryoma.

Other Attractions Behind the jauntily coloured **Kōshi-byō**, a Confucian shrine, the **Historical Museum of China** *(admission ¥525; open 8.30am-5pm daily)* has exhibits on loan from Beijing. The original shrine dates from 1893, but was destroyed in the fires following the A-bomb explosion.

The historic **Hong Kong & Shanghai Bank Nagasaki Branch Museum** *(admission ¥100; open 9am-5pm daily)* is also worth a peek.

GLOVER GARDEN AREA

1	Hong Kong & Shanghai Bank Nagasaki Branch Museum 香港上海銀行長崎支店記念館	5	Chikyūkan 地球館	10	Glover House 旧グラバー住宅
2	Shikairō 四海楼	6	Furushashin-shiryōkan 古写真資料館	11	Walker House 旧ウォーカー住宅
3	ANA Hotel Nagasaki Glover Hill 長崎全日空ホテルグラバ ーヒル	7	18 Bank 十八銀行	12	Madame Butterfly Statue
		8	Ōura Catholic Church 大浦天主堂	13	Ringer House 旧リンガー住宅
4	Kōshi-byō; Historical Museum of China 孔子廟；中国歴史博物館	9	Nagasaki Traditional Performing Arts Museum 長崎伝統芸能館	14	Alt House 旧オルト住宅
				15	Mitsubishi No 2 Dock Building 旧三菱第2ドックハウス

Siebold Memorial Museum
シーボルト記念館

Not far from Shin-Nakagawamachi tram stop is the site of Dr Siebold's house *(admission ¥100; open 9am-4.30pm Tues-Sun)*, an imposing Western-style structure, set in a leafy residential neighbourhood. The doctor is credited with being an important force behind the introduction of Western medicine and scientific learning to Japan between 1823 and 1829 – that is, before he was expelled for trying to smuggle Japanese goods.

Inasa-yama Lookout 稲左山展望台

From the western side of the harbour, a cable car (¥1200 return, 9am to 10pm daily March to November, to 9pm 11 December to 28 February, every 20 minutes) ascends to the top of 333m-high Inasa-yama, offering superb views over Nagasaki, particularly at night. Bus Nos 3 and 4 leave from outside JR Nagasaki station; get off at the Ropeway-mae stop and walk up the stone steps through the grounds of Fuchi-jinja. You can also walk up in 15 minutes from the Takara-machi tram stop.

Special Events

Colourful **Peiron dragon boat races**, introduced by the Chinese in the mid-1600s and held to appease the god of the sea, still take place in Nagasaki Harbour in late July. On 15 August there's the beautiful **Shōrō-nagashi Matsuri**, where lantern-lit floats are carried down to the harbour. The best viewpoint is at Ōhato. The energetic **Okunchi Matsuri**, held between 7 and 9 October, features more Chinese dragons, this time dancing all around the city but especially at Suwa-jinja.

Places to Stay

Nagasaki has a wide range of accommodation possibilities, from the love hotels clustered around the A-bomb site to the upmarket hotels of the Glover Garden area.

Places to Stay – Budget

Nagasaki Ebisu Youth Hostel (☎ 824-3823; beds with/without meals ¥4300/2800) is run by a friendly family with years of experience helping travellers. Curfew isn't until 11pm.

Nagasaki Youth Hostel (☎ 823-5032; beds per person ¥2800) is also within walking distance of JR Nagasaki station and is often full. It's well signposted in English, but institutional and strict.

Nagasaki has a number of budget *minshuku* and ryokan, most containing basic rooms with shared bathrooms and paper-thin walls.

Fukumatsu Ryokan (☎ 823-3769; rooms ¥3500) is uphill behind Kenei bus station, near JR Nagasaki station, but off the main drag. This is among the cheapest in the area, but there are only a handful of rooms.

Minshuku Fumi (☎ 822-4962; rooms ¥3500) is in the side street behind Kenei bus station. Although rooms aren't exactly great, it's OK for crashing after a long journey.

Miyuki-sō Business Hotel (☎ 821-3487; singles ¥3500-4000, doubles ¥7000-7500), a five-minute walk northeast of the Shianbashi entertainment district, has Japanese- and Western-style rooms.

Places to Stay – Mid-Range & Top End

Central Nagasaki, the best place to be based, has a few affordable ryokan.

Nishiki-sō (*☎ 826-6371; rooms with bath ¥4000-4500*), the pick of the pack, is a delightful, creaky old building with fabulous views over Nagasaki. **Fukumoto Ryokan** (*☎ 821-0478; singles/doubles ¥4000/8000*) is also clean and friendly.

Minshuku Tanpopo (*☎ 861-6230; singles/ doubles/triples with shared bath ¥4000/ 7000/9000*), a Japanese Inn Group member, is north of JR Nagasaki station and near the A-bomb site. The common baths have mineral spring waters.

Shinchi Business Hotel (*☎ 827-1123; singles/doubles ¥5250/8450, Japanese-style rooms ¥9450*) is not only perfectly poised in the Chinatown shopping arcade, but also within striking distance of nightlife. This tidy hotel is a good deal.

JR Kyūshū Hotel Nagasaki (*☎ 832-8000, fax 832-8001; singles/twins ¥6500/12,000*), right in the Nagasaki station complex, has unusually large rooms. Check-in is from 2pm; check out by 11am.

Nagasaki Washington Hotel (*☎ 828-1211, fax 825-8023; singles/doubles from ¥6500/15,000*) is a rather more upmarket hotel, where the entertainment area merges into the Chinatown district.

Holiday Inn (*☎ 828-1234, 0120-381-489, fax 828-0178; singles/doubles from ¥6900/ 9000*), near the Shian-bashi entertainment area, is tastefully appointed and good value. It caters to business travellers.

ANA Hotel Nagasaki Glover Hill (*☎ 818-6601, 0120-02-9501, fax 818-6110; singles/ doubles from ¥11,000/20,000*), just below Glover Garden, is a renovated luxury hotel with spacious rooms.

Sakamoto-ya Bekkan (*☎ 826-8211; rooms per person with 2 meals from ¥15,000*) is an old and very well-kept ryokan, full of traditional touches.

Places to Eat
Like Yokohama and Kōbe, Nagasaki has the reputation of being a culinary crossroads. The city's diverse influences come together in *shippoku-ryōri*, a banquet-style offering (generally you need at least four diners) that rolls together Chinese, Japanese and Portuguese influences. *Champon*, the local *rāmen* speciality, is less expensive but overrated unless you're a fan of shredded cabbage. *Sara-udon* is the stir-fried equivalent.

Central Nagasaki A good area for ferreting out restaurants is the sidestreets off the Hamano-machi arcade.

Unryūtei (*open 3pm-late daily*), tucked away at the end of Shian-bashi Gourmet Street, only seats six and specialises in cheap and tasty *gyoza* (dumplings), which are excellent with a beer. There's another branch nearby.

Ginrei Restaurant (*☎ 821-2073; dishes from ¥800; open 10.30am-9.30pm daily*) is a well-known European-style restaurant (look for the ivy hanging outside) serving basic steaks, curries and so on. The quiet bar is intimate.

Wine Cellar Rosenthal (*mains ¥800-2500; open 5pm-10pm daily*) boasts an import list of vino to die for, and excellently priced fresh Italian bistro dishes.

Hamakatsu Restaurant (*☎ 826-8321; open daily*) serves the banquet-style *shippoku* cuisine from around ¥5000 per person. **Hamakatsu** (*Teramachi-dōri; open 11am-10pm daily*), around the corner from Hamakatsu Restaurant, is run by the same owners. It serves excellent *tonkatsu* (pork cutlets), has an illustrated menu and is far less expensive than it looks.

Kagetsu (*☎ 822-0191; lunch sets from ¥5200; open noon-2pm & 6pm-10pm Mon-Fri, 6pm-10pm Sat & Sun*) is a *shippoku* restaurant with a history that dates back to 1642. At one time it was a high-class brothel. Today it's still high class; count on ¥20,000 per person at dinner.

During Japan's long period of isolation from the West, Nagasaki was a conduit not only for Dutch trade and culture but also for the trade and culture of the Chinese, a history reflected in the city's restaurants. Popular Chinese restaurants cluster around the Nagasaki Washington Hotel, including **Kyōka-en**, **Chūka-en** and one famed for its *champon*, **Kairaku-en**.

Other Areas Beside JR Nagasaki station, **Amyu Plaza** has a surprisingly varied restaurant arcade up on the 5th floor. Set meals start at ¥650. **Dragon Deli** is an import grocery shop on the ground floor selling goodies from all across Asia and the West.

Harbin (*à la carte dishes ¥350-800, dinner mains ¥2000-5000; open daily*) specialises in Russian and French cuisine, worthy of connoisseurs. It's an atmospheric place, with white tablecloths, heavy cutlery and dark wood furniture. At lunch, you can select from a long menu offering a starter, main course, bread and tea or coffee, costing from ¥1800. Everything from smoked fish buckwheat crepes to peroshkis is delicious, but portions are small. Ask for the English-language menu.

Chikyūkan *(lunch ¥750; open noon-2pm Thur-Tues)*, in Oranda-zaka, is a casual café serving a different international cuisine each day, prepared by foreign residents of 49 countries so far.

Shikairō *(☎ 822-1296; open daily)*, an imposing Chinese-style restaurant near Glover Garden, claims to be the creator of *champon*. It has been in operation since 1899.

Entertainment

Nagasaki's nightlife is rather subdued for such a large city. **Moonshine** *(open daily)*, set above a *rāmen* shop, is a mellow, *gaijin*-friendly dining bar that feels somehow Dutch.

JB Trick *(☎ 824-9185; Sōfukuji-dōri; open 7pm-3am daily)* is a soul bar and a favourite place for an inexpensive beer. **Albert's Place**, run by a former English teacher, is about the size of a closet. **Fan Fan** *(☎ 827-3976; open 7.30pm-2am daily)* is a jazz freak's paradise.

Ayer's Rock *(☎ 828-0505; cover Fri & Sat ¥1000)* is a alternative place with good vibes, techno DJs, bongos and beers for ¥500. If you're curious about the local rave scene, ask here.

Shopping

There are displays of local crafts and products directly opposite JR Nagasaki station on the same floor as the Prefectural Tourist Federation. You'll also find lots of shops along the busy Hamano-machi shopping arcade.

For Japanese visitors, the Portuguese-influenced sponge cake, *kasutera*, is the present to take back from Nagasaki. **Fukusaya Castella Cake Shop** *(☎ 821-2938; open daily)* in Shian-bashi was established in 1624. It's in a charming traditional building, and sells its handmade cakes in gift-ready packaging.

Please ignore Nagasaki's tortoise-shell crafts: turtles need their shells more than humans do.

Getting There & Away

There are flights between Nagasaki and Tokyo (Haneda airport, ¥29,700), Osaka (¥19,400) and Naha (¥23,000, 1½ hours) in Okinawa, as well as flights to other Kyūshū cities.

From the Kenei bus station opposite JR Nagasaki station, buses depart for Unzen (¥1900, 1¾ hours), Sasebo (¥1450, 1½ hours), Fukuoka (¥2900, 2¾ hours), Kumamoto (¥3790, three hours) and Beppu (¥4500, 3½ hours). Night buses for Osaka (¥11,000) leave from both the Kenei bus station and the highway bus station next to the Irie-machi tram stop.

JR lines from Nagasaki head for Sasebo (*kaisoku* ¥2100, 1¾ hours) or Hakata (Fukuoka; *tokkyū* ¥4910, two hours).

There are ferries from a few places around Nagasaki, including Ōhato terminal, south of JR Nagasaki station.

Getting Around

To/From the Airport Nagasaki's airport is about 40km from the city. Airport buses (¥800, 45 minutes) operate from stand No 4 of the Kenei bus station opposite JR Nagasaki station.

Bus A greater area is covered by buses (reaching more of the sights directly) but the Japanese script is more difficult to decipher than the tram service.

Tram The best way of getting around Nagasaki is on the easy-to-use tram service. There are four colour-coded routes numbered 1, 3, 4 and 5 (there's no No 2 for some reason). Most stops are signposted in English. It costs ¥100 to travel anywhere in town, but you can only transfer to another line at the Tsuki-machi stop unless you have a ¥500 all-day pass for unlimited travel. These passes are available from the shop beside the station information counter, from the Prefectural Tourist Federation across the road or from major hotels. Most trams stop running before 11.30pm.

HUIS TEN BOSCH ハウステンボス

You'll see this 'virtual-Holland' theme-park *(☎ 0956-27-0001; w www.huistenbosch .co.jp)* advertised everywhere, but did you really come to Japan to spend ¥5000 to see a replica of another country?

Shimabara Peninsula 島原半島

A popular route between Nagasaki and Kumamoto is via this peninsula. Local bus services connect with ferries from Shimabara to the Kumamoto coast, and certain tour buses operating between Nagasaki and Kumamoto make stops around the peninsula.

It was the uprising on the Shimabara peninsula that led to the suppression of Christianity in Japan and the country's subsequent two centuries of seclusion from the West. The peasant rebels made their final valiant stand against overwhelming odds (37,000 versus 120,000) at Hara-jō, at almost the southern tip of the peninsula. The warlords even chartered a Dutch man-of-war to bombard the hapless rebels, who held out for 80 days but were eventually slaughtered.

In June 1991, the 1359m peak of Unzen-dake erupted after lying dormant for 199 years. Nearby villages were evacuated and the lava flow reached the outskirts of Shimabara. The explosion left at least 40 people dead.

UNZEN 雲仙
☎ 0957

Unzen is shrouded in mysterious, rather smelly gases – it is obviously a very active volcanic centre. Its walks and paths are clearly signposted and it's easy to spend hours wandering around the town. Meanwhile, the friendly staff at the Shimatetsu bus station will store your luggage for ¥100 per day.

The bubbling and spurting *jigoku* (hells) currently boil nothing more sinister than the popular wayside snack of eggs, known as *onsen tamago*; a few centuries ago the same fate was reserved for Christians. Today you can voluntarily boil yourself at any of the resort's luxury hotels, though budget travellers will likely prefer the three public baths, all within walking distance of the bus station: **Yunosato** (*admission ¥100; open 9am-10.30pm daily*), **Shin-yu** (*admission ¥100; open 9am-11pm daily*) and **Kojigoku** (*admission ¥400; open 9am-9pm daily*). The ultra-modern **Unzen Spa House** (*admission ¥800; open 9am-6pm daily*), opposite the post office, even has a glass-blowing workshop (lessons cost ¥2000 per 10 minutes).

From the town there are popular walks to Kinugasa, Takaiwa-san and Yadake, all situated within the Unzen-Amakusa National Park, Japan's oldest national park. The **national park visitors centre** (*☎ 73-2642; open 7am-6pm daily*), near the Shin-yu Hotel, has excellent displays on flora and fauna and plentiful information in English, especially about hiking trails. Around town, the screeching, geyser-like **Daikyōkan Jigoku** and the 1300-year-old temple, **Manmyō-ji**, are worth seeing.

Outside town, reached via Nita Pass, is **Fugen-dake** (1359m), part of the Unzen-dake range, with its popular hiking trail. The bus to Nita-tōge, the starting point for the Fugen-dake walk, operates regularly from the Unzen bus station (¥370, 25 minutes). A cable car (ropeway; ¥1220 return, 9am to 5.30pm daily) whisks you almost to the 1333m summit of **Myōken-dake**, from where the hike to Fugen-dake (1359m) via Kunimi-wakare takes just under two hours return. The views of the lava flow from the summit are incredible. For a longer excursion, you can detour to Kunimi-dake (1347m) or walk back to Nita via the village and valley of Azami-dani in about 70 minutes. The last bus back to Unzen usually leaves around 5pm.

Places to Stay

Unzen has numerous hotels, *minshuku* and ryokan (most very pricey) with nightly rates from around ¥7000, including dinner and breakfast. You can easily visit as a day-tripper, but staying overnight makes for a refreshing stop between Nagasaki and Kumamoto. On Saturday nights and holidays, expect to pay a hefty surcharge.

Shirakumo-no-ike camp ground (*☎ 73-2642; sites from ¥300*) is a 10-minute walk downhill from the post office, and tent hire is available.

Kokumin-shukusha Seiun-sō (*☎ 73-3273; fax 73-2698; rooms per person with 2 meals ¥7400-9400*) is also quite a steep walk, but an affordable option and has enormous communal baths.

Ryokan Kaseya (*☎ 73-3321; fax 73-3322; rooms per person ¥6800-9980*) is a smart-looking choice. On the grounds are a small garden and, naturally, a hot-springs bath.

Yumoto Hotel (*☎ 73-3259, fax 73-2126; rooms per person ¥10,000*), a hive of activity in the town centre, has a sauna, *rotemburo* and traditional Japanese garden. Anyone can use their *ashi-yu* (foot bath) outside the front lobby for free.

Unzen Kankō Hotel (☎ 73-3263, fax 73-3419; ⓦ www.unzenkankohotel.com; Japanese- or Western-style singles/doubles/twins from ¥8000/12,000/14,000) dates back to the 1930s, when it was a summer retreat for expat *gaijin*. Overall its ambience is like a European mountain lodge. Meals are available at the hotel restaurant.

Getting There & Away

Direct buses between Nagasaki and Unzen take almost two hours (¥1900). Buses run more frequently from the town of Isahaya, which is 35 minutes by *kaisoku* train (¥450) from Nagasaki. From Isahaya to Unzen, buses take another 80 minutes (¥1300). Onward buses from Unzen to Shimabara (¥820, 50 minutes) stop at the port and castle before arriving at Shimabara train station.

SHIMABARA 島原
☎ 0957 • pop 41,000

Shimabara is the port for ferries to nearby Kumamoto. Its castle and reclining Buddha are the town's main attractions. **Shimabara-jō** (open 9am-5pm daily), originally built in 1624, played a part in the Shimabara Rebellion and was rebuilt in 1964 during Japan's nationwide spate of castle reconstruction. It houses a few minor museums (combined admission ¥520): one displaying items relating to the Christian uprising, another detailing Fugen-dake's pyrotechnic exploits (including the colossal explosion of 1792 in which 15,000 people died) and a third dedicated to the artwork of Seibō Kitamura, who sculpted the Nagasaki Peace Statue. Another small **folk museum** (admission free) is stuffed with antiques from the Edo, Meiji and Shōwa periods.

In the Teppo-chō area, northwest of the castle, is a *buke-yashiki,* or collection of **samurai houses**. Just south of the town centre, near the Shimatetsu bus station, are **carp streams** with lots of colourful fish. At Kōtō-ji is the rather beautiful **Nehan-zō**, or 'Nirvana Statue'. It's the longest reclining Buddha statue in Japan, though by Thai or Burmese reclining-Buddha standards, it's a bit of a shorty.

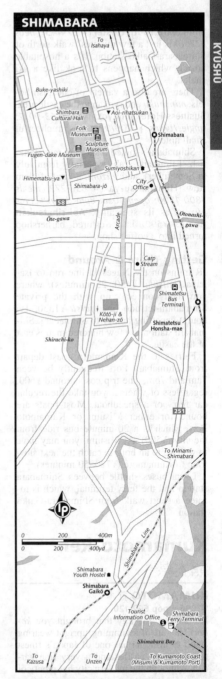

SHIMABARA

Places to Stay & Eat

Shimabara Youth Hostel (☎ 62-4451; beds ¥2750) is just a few minutes' walk north of Shimabara-Gaikō station. It's a hospitable hostel, which happens to look like a ski chalet.

There are also a variety of cheapish hotels, *minshuku* and ryokan in the castle area. **Business Hotel Sumiyoshikan** (☎ 63-0032; singles/twins ¥5700/9000) is a cheerful small hotel.

Shimabara's famed dishes are raw stonefish, Taira-gane crab (especially from July to September), and *gūzoni*, a kind of clam stew. **Himematsu-ya** (☎ 63-7272; meals ¥800-1800; open 10am-8pm daily) serves *gūzoni* as its speciality. **Aoi-rihatsukan** (snacks ¥500) is a restored barbershop turned into a coffee shop.

Getting There & Around

JR trains on the Nagasaki line run to Isahaya (*kaisoku* ¥450, 25 minutes), where you then connect up with the private Shimabara-tetsudō line (*futsū* ¥1330, 1¼ hours) departing hourly to Shimabara. Shimabara station is a few hundred metres east of the castle.

Ferries to the Kumamoto coast depart from Shimabara Port frequently between 7am and 7pm. The trip costs around ¥600, regardless of whether you take the regular car ferry or a speedboat. Most boats are bound for either Misumi or Kumamoto Port, which is a 30-minute bus ride from the city (¥500). At Misumi, you may have to wait up to an hour to catch the next slow train to Kumamoto (¥720, 50 minutes).

Local buses shuttle between Shimabara station and the ferry terminal, which is located a short walk from Shimabara-Gaikō station.

Kumamoto-ken
熊本県

KUMAMOTO 熊本
☎ 096 • pop 662,120

Kumamoto, the city that brought you *kobori* (the art of swimming upright wearing a suit of armour) has one of Japan's finest reconstructed castles and a very fine garden. Although the modern city has plenty of concrete, its brash vitality, ample nightlife and convenient location (whether you're travelling up, down or across the island) make it worth a look.

Orientation & Information

The JR station is some distance southwest of Kumamoto's city centre, which is where you'll find banks, hotels, restaurants, the bus centre and the entertainment area, along with the castle and other attractions.

Inside JR Kumamoto station, the **tourist information office** (☎ 352-3743; open 9am-1pm & 2pm-5.30pm daily) has a helpful English-speaking assistant. South of Kumamoto-jō, **NTT Dream Plaza** (open 11am-6.30pm daily) offers free Internet access. **Kumamoto City International Centre** (☎ 359-2121; open 9am-8pm Mon-Fri, 9am-7pm Sat, 9am-7pm 1st & 3rd Sun each month) has CNN news and English-language magazines.

On the northeast side of Kumamoto station is an **international ATM** (open 8am-9pm Mon-Fri, 9am-7pm Sat & Sun) that accepts Visa, MasterCard and Cirrus, and a **postal savings ATM**. Central **Higo Bank** has currency exchange facilities. **Kinokuniya** bookshop stocks foreign-language titles.

Kumamoto-jō 熊本城

Kumamoto's castle (admission ¥500; open 8.30am-5.30pm daily Apr-Oct, 8.30am-4.30pm daily Nov-Mar) dominates the centre of town. A modern reproduction, its sheer size and numerous exhibits make it visit-worthy.

Built between 1601 and 1607, it was once one of the great castles of feudal Japan. Its architect, Katō Kiyomasa, was a master of castle design and some of his ingenious engineering, including slots for dropping stones and other missiles onto attackers, can be seen in the reconstruction.

Nevertheless, in 1877, during the turmoil of the Satsuma Rebellion (a postscript to the Meiji Restoration) the castle was besieged and burnt in one of the final stands made by samurai warriors against the new order. The rebel samurai held out for 50 days before finally being overcome. For more on the rebellion and its leader, Saigō Takamori, see the Kagoshima-ken section later in this chapter.

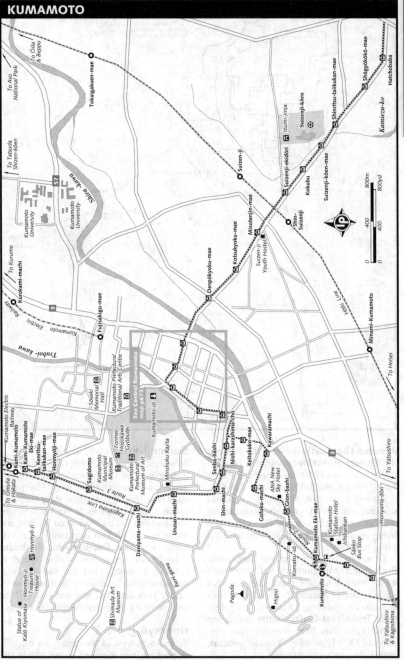

KUMAMOTO

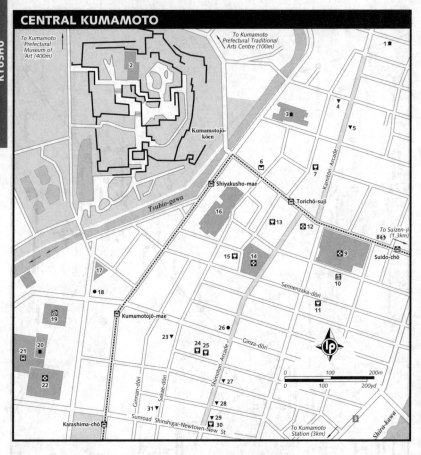

CENTRAL KUMAMOTO

To Kumamoto Prefectural Museum of Art (400m)

To Kumamoto Prefectural Traditional Arts Centre (100m)

Kumamotojō-kōen

Kamitōri Arcade

Shiyakusho-mae

Tsubio-gawa

Torichō-suji

To Suizen-ji (1.3km)

Suido-chō

Sannenzaka-dōri

Kumamotojō-mae

Ginza-dōri

Shimotōri Arcade

Ginnan-dōri

Sakae-dōri

Sunroad Shinshigai-Newtown-New St

Karashima-chō

To Kumamoto Station (3km)

Shira-kawa

0   100   200m
0   100   200yd

Around the Castle Beyond the castle is the **Former Hosokawa Gyōbutei** (☎ 352-6522; admission ¥300, combined with castle ¥640; open 8.30am-5.30pm daily Apr-Oct, 8.30am-4.30pm daily Nov-Mar), a spacious samurai villa with grounds pleasant for wandering. The Hosokawa clan came into being around 1632 and held sway until the Meiji restoration.

Closer to the main road, the **Kumamoto Prefectural Museum of Art** (admission ¥260; open 9.30am-4.30pm Tues-Sun) has a mixed bag of ancient Buddhist sculptures and modern paintings. **Kumamoto Prefectural Traditional Crafts Centre** (admission ¥200; open 9am-5pm Tues-Sun) has displays of local Higo inlay, Yamaga lanterns, porcelains and woodcarving.

Suizenji-kōen 水前寺公園
Southeast of the city centre, originating with a temple in 1632, this extensive strolling garden (admission ¥360; open 7.30am-6pm daily Mar-Nov, 8.30am-5pm daily Dec-Feb) imitates the 53 stations of the Tōkaidō (the old road that linked Tokyo and Kyoto), and the miniature Mt Fuji is instantly recognisable. The **Kokin Denju-no-Ma Teahouse** (The Passing on of Knowledge Space) is somewhat shoddy, but the views across the ornamental lake show the garden at its finest. Turn the other way and you will see only souvenir stalls and relentless crowds.

Honmyō-ji 本妙寺
To the northwest of the centre, on the hills sloping up from the river, is the temple and

CENTRAL KUMAMOTO

PLACES TO STAY		31	Higokko Robatayaki 肥後っ子	15	The Sharp
1	Maruko Hotel 丸小ホテル			16	City Hall 市役所
3	Kumamoto Castle Hotel 熊本ホテルキャッスル	**OTHER** 2	Kumamoto-jō 熊本城	17	Kumamoto City International Centre 国際交流会館
20	Kumamoto Kōtsū Center Hotel 熊本交通センターホテル	6	Post Office 郵便局	18	JAS
		7	Rock Balloon	19	NTT Dream Plaza NTT夢プラザ
PLACES TO EAT		8	Higo Bank 肥後銀行	21	Kumamoto Kōtsū Bus Centre 熊本交通バスセンター
4	Chinese Café Anding	9	Tsuruya Department Store 鶴屋	22	Iwataya Department Store 岩田屋
5	Chai Shop	10	Lafcadio Hearn House		
	Shankar G	11	Shark Attack	24	Days デイズ
23	Jang Jang Go ジャンジャンゴー	12	Parco Department Store; The Body Shop パルコ	25	Sanctuary
27	Kōrantei 香蘭亭	13	Bar Jail	26	Kinokuniya Bookshop 紀伊国屋書店
28	Seibi-ya 青美屋	14	Daiei ダイエー	30	DJ's Café 15
29	Dynamic Kitchen				

mausoleum of Katō Kiyomasa, the architect of Kumamoto's great castle. A steep flight of steps leads up to the mausoleum that was designed to be at the same height as the castle's donjon. There's also a **treasure house** *(admission ¥300; open 9am-4.30pm Tues-Sun).*

Writers' Homes

Right in the centre of town, behind the Tsuruya department store, is the former home of writer Lafcadio Hearn, known to the Japanese as Koizumi Yakumo *(admission ¥200; open 9am-4.30pm daily)*. It's not as interesting as his first Japanese residence in Matsue (see the Western Honshū chapter).

The former home of the Meiji-era novelist Sōseki Natsume is preserved as the **Sōseki Memorial Hall** *(admission ¥200; open 9.30am-4.30pm Tues-Sun)*. Sōseki lived here as an English teacher, but only for a few years.

Other Attractions

Continue north up the hill beyond the cheap ryokan and *minshuku* near JR Kumamoto station, past the love hotels and you eventually reach the **pagoda** topping the hill. The effort of the climb is rewarded with superb views over the town.

The delightful **Shimada Art Museum** *(admission ¥500; open 9am-5pm Thur-Tues)* collects works pertaining to Miyamoto Musashi, mainly calligraphy and scrolls. It's within walking distance of Honmyō-ji.

Northeast of the town centre, **Tatsuda Shizen-kōen** *(Tatsuda Nature Park; admission ¥200; open 8.30am-4.30pm daily)* contains the 1646 Taishō-ji and a famous teahouse once used by Hosokawa lords. The grave of Hosokawa Gracia (1563–1600) is in the temple grounds. She was an early convert to Christianity but her husband arranged her death to prevent his enemies from capturing her. To get there, take a Musashigaoka-kita line bus from platform 28 at Kumamoto Kōtsū bus centre (¥190, 25 minutes).

Special Events

On the first Saturday of August, you can catch torchlight **Takigi Nō** performances at Suizenji-kōen. In mid-August, the **Hi-no-kuni Matsuri** (Land of Fire Festival) lights up Kumamoto with fireworks and dancing. Kumamoto-jō has its grand **autumn festival**, with *taiko* drumming and cultural events, from mid-October to early November.

Places to Stay

Suizen-ji Youth Hostel *(☎ 371-9193; dorm beds ¥2800)* is a clean, but typically strict place, located out toward Suizenji-kōen.

Higoji *(☎/fax 352-7860; rooms per person from ¥3000)*, on the hill above the station, is Kumamoto's best-value traditional-style accommodation. It's a small *minshuku* run by a friendly elderly gentleman. He'll pick you up from the station if you call first. English is spoken, and the night view is superb.

Komatsu-sō *(rooms per person ¥3500)*, north of the station (look for the English sign), is another good place, but the older lady who runs it doesn't answer the phone!

Minshuku Kajita *(☎/fax 353-1546; singles/doubles ¥4000/7500)*, the Japanese Inn group's representative in Kumamoto, is adequate. Rooms are Japanese-style and don't have bathrooms. From Kumamoto station, take a bus to the Shin-machi stop; from there it's a five-minute walk.

Kumamoto Station Hotel *(☎ 325-2001; singles/doubles ¥6000/10,600)* and **Ichiban-kan** *(singles/doubles from ¥3500/5500)* are ten minutes' walk from the station, just across the first small river. Both have Japanese- and Western-style rooms.

Kumamoto Kōtsū Center Hotel *(☎ 326-8828, 354-1111; singles/doubles/triples from ¥5700/13,000/16,500)* is above the bus terminal; reception is on the 3rd floor.

Maruko Hotel *(☎ 353-1241, fax 353-1217; doubles ¥12,000-27,000)* is a century-old Japanese inn in the town centre. From Kumamoto station, take a Route 2 tram to Tetori-Honchō, then look for signs inside the covered arcade.

Kumamoto Castle Hotel *(☎ 326-3311, fax 326-3324; singles/twins from ¥8900/ 16,000, Japanese-style rooms ¥30,000)*, overlooking the castle, is an elegant Japanese hotel with women in kimonos flitting about.

Places to Eat

Gourmands will want to try a bite of *basashi* (raw horsemeat), *karashi-renkon* (fried lotus root with mustard) or *Higo-gyū* (Higo beef).

Most of Kumamoto's restaurants are tucked into shopping arcades.

Chai Shop Shankar G *(meals ¥500-780; open 11am-3pm & 4pm-11pm daily, sometimes closed Thur)* has great curry, samosas and *chai* (Indian tea) sets. The upstairs dining room has a reggae beat, rattan chairs and an outdoor deck.

Higokko Robatayaki *(items ¥300-500; open daily)*, just off the Shinshigai arcade, lets you sit at the bar and select from a wide range of *kushi* (assorted meat, fish and vegetables grilled on skewers). The chef grills them right in front of you and passes them over the counter on a long paddle.

Kōran-tei *(open daily)*, back down the Shimotori arcade, is a Chinese restaurant

with some good *teishoku* deals at lunchtime. Try the *chashū men* (roast-pork noodle soup) for ¥600.

Seibi-ya *(meals from ¥750; open daily)* cooks up savoury pancakes, anything from Kansai-style *okonomiyaki* to Tokyo's *monja-yaki* (and Hiroshima's *modan-yaki*, too).

Chinese Café Anding *(lunch under ¥1000; open 11.30am-10.30pm Mon-Sat)* serves simple noodle dishes complemented by pan-Asian sweets, teas and Vietnamese coffee. It's up on the 4th floor.

Jang Jang Go *(☎ 323-1121; open 5.30pm-2am daily)* is a trendy place serving neo-Chinese cuisine in a mock-Colonial-style building. For couples it's Kumamoto's most popular date spot. Expect to spend at least ¥2500 per person.

Dynamic Kitchen *(☎ 212-5551; multi-course dinner ¥3500-4500; open 5pm-midnight daily)*, with bamboo and lanterns on the stairs, is like walking inside a futuristic Buddhist temple. Á la carte dishes, from dim-sum to Japanese seafood, are delectable.

Entertainment

Kumamoto has a sprinkling of *gaijin* haunts if you are in need of a few drinks and some conversation

The Sharp *(☎ 322-5445; open 7.30pm-1am Sun-Thur, 7.30pm-4am Fri & Sat)* is a long-running place behind Daiei that regularly has live bands. Beers cost from ¥500. **Sanctuary** *(☎ 325-5634)* and **Days** *(☎ 323-7110)* are both hip haunts.

Bar Jail *(☎ 359-1814; open 7pm-3am daily)* is a peculiarly narrow place, with a shoebox downstairs for dancing in. **Rock Balloon** *(☎ 354-6888; DJ events per person ¥2000-2500)* is a grungy establishment – graffiti and lots of noise. Draught beers cost ¥500 and there's often no cover charge.

Shark Attack *(8th floor, Anty Rashon Bldg)* is worth finding for something unusual. It's the only bar we've come across that has sand (the stuff you usually find on beaches). **DJ's Cafè 15** *(☎ 356-1687)* has vinyl records stacked on the walls and a retro groove.

At more traditional pubs, ask for *aka-zake*, Kumamoto's reddish sake.

Shopping

Higo-zōgan, black steel with silver and gold inlaid patterns wrought into a chrysanthemum-like shape, is a renowned local craft that used to adorn swords. Another curious local product is *obake-no-Kinta,* a tiny red ghost head that sticks out its little red tongue when you pull its string, the whole affair topped with a black dunce's cap – don't travel without one.

Getting There & Away

Although there are flights to Kumamoto from Tokyo, Osaka and Naha (Okinawa), most visitors by train from elsewhere around Kyūshū. The JR Kagoshima line runs north to Hakata (*tokkyū* ¥3430, 1½ hours) and south to Nishi-Kagoshima station (¥5250, 2½ hours), while the JR Hōhi line goes to Beppu (¥5330, three hours).

Highway buses depart from the Kumamoto Kōtsū bus centre for almost every major destination in Kyūshū, including Hakata/Fukuoka (¥2000, two hours).

See the earlier Shimabara Peninsula section for details on travel to Nagasaki via Shimabara and Unzen. Kumamoto is a popular gateway to Aso-san, from where you can travel across the island to Beppu.

Getting Around

To/From the Airport Buses to and from the airport (¥670, 50 minutes) stop at the Kumamoto Kōtsū bus centre and JR Kumamoto station.

Tram Kumamoto's tram service allows access to all the major sights. On boarding the tram, take a ticket with your starting tram stop number. When you finish your trip a display panel at the front of the tram indicates the fare for each starting point (under ¥200). A one-day pass (¥500) allows unlimited travel, and can be bought on the trams, or in front of Kumamoto station.

Route 2 starts near JR Kumamoto station, runs through the town centre and out past Suizenji-kōen. Route 3 starts to the north, near Kami-Kumamoto station and merges with Route 2 just before the centre. Mysteriously, there is no Route 1.

Bus One-day tram passes are valid for travel on green-coloured Shiei buses (but not any other city buses), which are handy for connecting between the tram and outlying sights, for example Honmyō-ji and the Shimada Art Museum, or zooming between Kumamoto station and the bus centre.

The Castle Loop Bus (¥130) connects the bus centre with all the sights in the castle area every half-hour or better, between 8.30am and 5pm daily. A one-day loop pass costs ¥300.

YAMAGA & KIKUCHI ONSEN
山鹿温泉・菊池温泉
☎ 0968

These hot-springs towns are both nice enough, but there's really no special reason to visit except during the spectacular **Yamaga Chōchin Matsuri** held on 15 and 16 August. The whole region seems to converge on Yamaga Onsen for these two nights, when the women of the town, clad in summer kimono, dance through the streets to the sound of *shamisen,* wearing lanterns on their heads. Though the sound is wholly 'Japanese', visually this is more like China or Okinawa – a reminder of Kyūshū's historical remove from 'mainland' Japan.

Outside Kikuchi Onsen, named for the lords who once ruled all of Kyūshū, **Kikuchi Gorge** *(open mid-Apr–Nov)* has walking trails and refreshingly cool waters. Back in town, the hot-springs ryokan, *minshuku* and hotels are all clustered together on a quiet maze of streets, just downhill from an impressive **statue** of a feudal lord on horseback.

Yamaga Cycling Terminal *(☎ 43-1136; shared rooms per person with 2 meals ¥5200),* on a 35km cycling route from Kumamoto, has large communal tatami rooms and a huge bath. It's a 10-minute taxi ride from the centre of Yamaga Onsen. Don't try to walk back post-festival unless you've got infrared night vision – the terminal is set invisibly above pitch-black rice fields.

The **Kikuchi Onsen Ryokan Tourism Association** *(☎ 25-2926, fax 24-4690)* can book accommodation with two meals from ¥8000. **Kikuchi Kankō Hotel** *(☎ 25-2111, fax 24-0473; doubles ¥14,000-22,000)* has rooms with mountain views and a *rotemburo.*

Getting There & Around

From Kumamoto station or the Kumamoto Kōtsū bus centre, there are frequent buses to either Yamaga Onsen (¥860, 1¼ hours) or Kikuchi Onsen (¥880, 1½ hours). Inconveniently, there are only a few buses per day between them (¥430, 30 minutes).

ASO-SAN AREA 阿蘇山
☎ 0967

In the centre of Kyūshū, halfway from Ku-mamoto to Beppu, is the gigantic Aso-san volcano caldera. There have been a series of eruptions over the past 30 million years but the explosion that formed the outer crater about 100,000 years ago must have been a big one – the crater has a 128km circum-ference and accommodates towns, villages and trains.

It's still the largest active caldera in the world – in 1979 an eruption of Naka-dake killed a woman on her honeymoon. The last major blast was in 1993, but the summit is regularly declared off limits due to toxic gas emissions. Check with the tourist informa-tion office for daily updates around 9am.

Orientation & Information

Routes 57, 265 and 325 make a circuit of the outer caldera, and the JR Hōhi line runs across the northern section. Aso is the main town in the crater but there are other towns, including Takamori, on the southern side. All the roads running into the centre of the crater and to the five 'modern' peaks within the one huge, ancient outer peak are toll roads.

At JR Aso station, there's an informative **tourist office** (☎ 34-0751; open 9am-5pm Thur-Tues) offering free hiking maps. Coin lockers are available.

Aso-gogaku 阿蘇五岳

The Five Mountains of Aso are the five smaller mountains within the outer rim. They are Eboshi-dake (1337m), Kijima-dake (1321m), Naka-dake (1506m), Neko-dake (1408m) and Taka-dake (1592m). Naka-dake is currently the active volcano in this group. Neko-dake, furthest to the east, is instantly recognisable by its craggy peak but Taka-dake, between Neko-dake and Naka-dake, is the highest.

Aso Volcanic Museum
阿蘇火山博物館

Despite the usual shortage of English-language labelling, this museum (admission ¥840, with cable-car return ¥1480; open 9am-5pm daily) has great live footage taken inside the active crater. An entertaining se-lection of big-screen videos shows various volcanoes from around the world strutting their stuff.

Kusasenri & Kome-zuka
草千里・米塚

Opposite the volcanic museum is Kusas-enri (literally, '1000km of grass'), a grassy meadow with two lakes in the flattened crater of an ancient volcano.

Just off the road that runs from the museum down to the town of Aso is the perfectly shaped small cone of Kome-zuka, another extinct volcano. The name means 'rice mound'.

Naka-dake 中岳

Naka-dake has been very active in recent years. The cable car to the summit was closed from August 1989 to March 1990 due to eruptions, and it had only been opened for a few weeks when the volcano erupted again in April 1990, spewing dust and ash over a large area to the north.

In 1958, when a totally unexpected erup-tion killed 12 onlookers, concrete 'bomb shelters' were built around the rim for sightseers to take shelter in, in an emer-gency. Nevertheless, an eruption in 1979 killed three visitors over a kilometre from the cone, in an area that was thought to be safe. This eruption destroyed a cable car that used to run up the northeastern slope of the cone.

From the museum, it's 3km up to the cable car station. When Naka-dake is not misbehaving, the cable car (¥410, 8.30am to 5pm daily) whisks you up to the summit in just four minutes. The walk to the top takes less than half an hour. The 100m-deep crater varies in width from 400m to 1100m and there's a walk around the southern edge of the crater rim. Ascending the heights early in the morning you can see a sea of clouds hovering inside the crater, with Kujū-san on the horizon.

Activities

From the top of the cable-car run you can walk around the crater rim to the peak of Naka-dake and on to the top of Taka-dake. From there you can descend to Sensui Gorge (Sensui-kyō), which blooms with azaleas in mid-May, or to the road that runs between Taka-dake and Neko-dake. Either way will then take you to Miyaji, the next train station east of Aso. The direct descent to Sensui-kyō is very steep, so it's easier to continue back from Taka-dake to the Naka-dake rim and then follow the old cable car route down to Sensui-kyō. Allow four or five hours from the Aso-nishi cable car station walking uphill to Sensui-kyō, then another 1½ hours for the descent.

Shorter walks include the interesting ascent of Kijima-dake from the Aso Volcanic Museum. From the top of Kijima-dake you can descend to the top of the ski lift, used for both snow skiing and summer grass skiing. You can also climb to the top of Eboshi-dake. Any of the peaks offer superb views over the whole Aso area. The outer rim of the ancient crater also has great views. Shiro-yama Tembōdai, a lookout on the Yamanami Hwy as it leaves the crater, is one good point; Daikanbō, near Uchinomaki Onsen, is another.

Special Events
On a Saturday in early March (dates vary), **Aso-jinja** is the scene of esoteric dances and a spectacular, highly photogenic fire festival. The shrine is a 15-minute walk north of JR Miyaji station.

Places to Stay & Eat
There are over 50 places to stay around Aso-san, including a collection of places at Aso town, Uchinomaki Onsen and Takamori village. Most other accommodation is spread out, and difficult to get to by public transport. Bookings are essential.

Aso Village A 20-minute walk from JR Aso station uphill toward the mountain is **Aso Youth Hostel** (☎ 34-0804; beds ¥2450). Buses up to the cable car station stop outside.

There are also a few campgrounds on the mountain, including **Bōchū Kyampu-jo** (☎ 34-0351; sites per person ¥310), reached via a path that veers off the highway below the youth hostel.

Kokumin-shukusha Aso (☎ 34-0111; rooms per person with 2 meals ¥6300) is opposite JR Aso station. Its small hot-springs bath, Yume-no-yu, is available to non-guests (admission ¥400).

Aso-no-Fumoto (☎ 32-0624; rooms per person with/without meals ¥6200/4200) is a good minshuku, conveniently close to the station. The owner will pick you up.

Coffee Plaza East (meals ¥750-1000; open 9am-10.40pm Fri-Wed) has filling, if less than memorable, meals and an illustrated menu. It's just about the only place in town open after dark. **Wild Cats Pizza** is out among the noodle shops and takeaway joints on Rte 57, a 10-minute walk west.

Around the Crater A 25-minute walk west of JR Akamizu station, across the river, is **Kumamoto YMCA Aso Camp** (☎ 35-0124; beds ¥3000-3200). The youth hostel has newly renovated cabins.

Murataya Ryokan Youth Hostel (☎ 09676-2-0066; beds ¥2700-2900), in Takamori town, is quite pleasant. It's best to book ahead in the summer months. From the train station, walk straight out past the bus terminal and post office, then turn left at the pharmacy corner and walk to the end of the block.

Deer To House (meals from ¥800; open 11am-8pm daily) is a charming family-run eatery close to Takamori station. The chef turns out hearty Western-style meals and homemade apple pie. The handwritten English menu is charmingly descriptive.

Bluegrass (☎ 09676-2-3366, fax 09676-2-3022; rooms per person with/without 2 meals ¥6900/5000) offers accommodation in a rustic ranch house. Its Western-style cookhouse (meals from ¥1500; open 11am-8pm Wed-Mon) serves steaks and barbecued cuisine.

There are a few other places on the outskirts of Takamori town, but you'll need your own transport.

Kokumin-kyūkamura Minami-Aso (☎ 09 676-2-2111; rooms per person from ¥5500), a national vacation village, is crowded in July and August.

Beyond it is a pension mura (pension village) charging rates of around ¥8000 per person, with two meals. Try **Wonderland** (☎ 09676-2-3040), **Cream House** (☎ 09676-2-3090) or **Flower Garden** (☎ 09676-2-3021).

Dengaku-no-Sato (open 11am-7pm daily; teishoku from ¥1800) is not too far away. At this old farmhouse restaurant, you cook your own kebab-like dengaku (hardened mochi rice dipped in miso) on individual hibachi (barbecues).

Getting There & Around
Aso is on the JR Hōhi line between Kumamoto (tokkyū ¥2180, one hour, three daily)

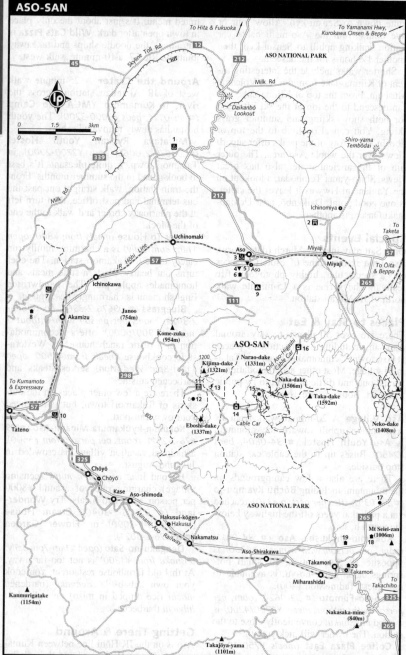

ASO-SAN

ASO-SAN

1	Uchinomaki Onsen 内牧温泉	8	Kumamoto YMCA Aso Camp 熊本YMCA阿蘇キャンプ
2	Aso-jinja 阿蘇神社	9	Bōchū Kyampu-jo 防虫キャンプ場
3	Kokumin-shukusha Aso; Yume-no-yu Onsen 国民宿舎阿蘇；夢の湯温泉	10	Tochinoki Onsen 栃木温泉
4	Wild Cats Pizza	11	Aso Volcanic Museum 阿蘇火山博物館
5	Coffee Plaza East 東	12	Kusasenri Meadow 草千里
6	Aso Youth Hostel 阿蘇ユースホステル	13	Ski Field スキー場
7	Akamizu Onsen 赤水温泉	14	Aso-nishi Cable Car Station 阿蘇西ロープウエイ乗り場

15	Naka-dake Crater 中岳
16	Sensui-kyo 仙酔峡
17	Takamori Pension Mura 高森ペンション村
18	Kokumin-kyūkamura Minami-Aso 国民休暇村南阿蘇
19	Bluegrass 青い草
20	Murataya Ryokan Youth Hostel ユースホステル村田屋旅館

and Ōita (*tokkyū* ¥3940, two hours). From March to November the *SL Aso Boy* (¥1960, 2¼ hours) steam train makes a daily run from Kumamoto to Aso, terminating at Miyaji station. Buses from Beppu (¥3800, 2¾ hours) may continue to the Aso-nishi cable car station (an extra ¥1550).

To get to Takamori on the southern side of the crater, transfer from the JR Hōhi line at Tateno (¥360, 30 minutes) to the scenic Minami-Aso private line, which terminates at Takamori (¥470, 30 minutes). Buses from Takamori continue southeast to the mountain resort of Takachiho (¥1280, 70 minutes, three daily).

Buses operate approximately every 90 minutes from JR Aso station via the youth hostel and volcano museum to Aso-nishi cable car station (¥470, 30 minutes). The first bus up leaves around 8.30am, with the last return trip down from the cable car station around 5pm.

KUROKAWA ONSEN 黒川温泉
☎ 0967 • pop 400

This hot spring is a real treasure. A few dozen ryokan lie along a steep-sided valley beside the Kurokawa, some 6km west of the Yamanami Hwy. Though it is touristed, the development has been well done, with not a karaoke bar or *pachinko* parlour in sight.

The enlightened Onsen Association has also made it affordable. You can buy a ticket (¥1200) from the **tourist information desk** (☎ 44-0076; open 9am-6pm daily) that allows you access to three ryokan baths of your choice (8.30am to 9pm). Kurokawa is especially famous for its 23 *rotemburo*. Yamamizuki, Kurokawa-sō and the magnificent Shimmei-kan, with

its cave baths and riverside *rotemburo*, are among local favourites. Most places offer *konyoku* (mixed bathing) and separate male and female baths.

Places to Stay
The *onsen* ryokan are well worth splashing out on. **Kyuhō-kan** (☎ 44-0651; rooms per person from ¥10,000) and **Ryokan Nishimura** (☎ 44-0753; rooms ¥10,000-15,000) are among the cheapest. Both offer two meals in the rates.

Aso Senomoto Youth Hostel (☎ 44-0157; beds ¥2300) is one of Kyūshū's best. It has lots of information and the friendly English-speaking manager will pick you up if you call in advance. It's a good base for attacking Kujū-san, a massif of several volcanoes including the highest peaks in Kyūshū.

Getting There & Away
There's a late-morning bus around 10.30am from Aso to Senomoto and Kurokawa (¥940, one hour), but the only return bus leaves the *onsen* less than two hours later. The only solution is to take a taxi out to the Yamanami Hwy (¥1000) and take a bus from the Senomoto bus stop. There's a final bus in the late afternoon to Kumamoto around 4.15pm, and another to Beppu around 4.45pm.

There are four buses daily to Senomoto from JR Miyaji station (¥1150, 30 minutes).

SOUTH OF KUMAMOTO
The port of **Minamata** became infamous in the late '60s and early '70s when it was discovered that the high incidence of illness and birth defects in the town were caused by mercury poisoning. A local factory had

dumped waste containing high levels of mercury into the sea and this had contaminated the fish eaten by local residents. The company's ruthless efforts to suppress the story, and W Eugene Smith's heart-rending documentary photos, focused worldwide attention on the town.

Further south along the coast at **Hinagu Onsen**, there are fine views out towards the Amakusa archipelago. Most of the hot-springs ryokan charge ¥9000 per person with two meals.

AMAKUSA ARCHIPELAGO
天草諸島
☎ 0969
South of the Shimabara peninsula are the islands of the Amakusa-shotō. The islands were a stronghold of Christianity during Japan's 'Christian Century' and the grinding poverty here was a major factor in the Shimabara Rebellion of 1637–38. It's still one of the least developed regions of Japan.

Around the islands, there are opportunities for diving and dolphin-watching cruises. **Hondo** is the main town and has exhibition halls relating to the Christian era. **Amakusa Youth Hostel** (☎ 22-3085; beds ¥2650) is a 15-minute walk uphill from the bus terminal. Tomioka, where Nagasaki ferries berth, has castle ruins; this west coast area is particularly interesting.

Getting to the islands usually involves a ferry from various places in Nagasaki-ken or along the Kumamoto coast. Amakusa Five Bridges link the island directly with Misumi, southwest of Kumamoto.

Kagoshima-ken
鹿児島県

Kyūshū's southernmost prefecture has the city of Kagoshima, overlooked by the ominous volcano of Sakurajima across the bay. To the south is the Satsuma Peninsula, while the north has Kirishima National Park with its superb volcanoes and hiking.

KIRISHIMA NATIONAL PARK
霧島
The day walk from Ebino-kōgen (Ebino Plateau, not to be confused with the town of Ebino down on the plains) to the summits

of a string of volcanoes is one of the finest volcanic hikes in Japan. It's 15km from the summit of Karakuni-dake to the summit of Takachiho-no-mine and there's superb scenery – if the peaks aren't being lashed by thunderstorms or shrouded in fog! There are shorter walks, such as a lake stroll on the plateau or up and down Karakuni-dake or Takachiho-no-mine. The area is known for its spring wildflowers, hot springs and the impressive 75m waterfall, **Senriga-taki**.

Orientation & Information
There are **visitors centres** with maps and information in Ebino-kōgen village and at Takachiho-gawara, the two ends of the volcano walk. Ebino-kōgen has most of the hotels, restaurants and camping facilities.

The **Eco-Museum Centre** (☎ 0984-33-3002; open 9am-5pm daily) has displays on local wildlife and geology, plus an indoor rest area with hot drink–vending machines. Staff sell topographic hiking maps, and dispense local advice for free.

Ebino Plateau Walks
The Ebino-kōgen lake circuit is a relaxed stroll around a series of volcanic lakes – **Rokkannon Mi-ike** has the most intense colour. Across the road from the lake, Fudō-ike, at the base of Karakuni-dake, is a steaming *jigoku*. The stiff climb to the 1700m summit of **Karakuni-dake** skirts the edge of the volcano's deep crater before arriving at the high point on the eastern side. The panoramic view to the south is superb, taking in the perfectly circular caldera lake of Ōnami-ike, rounded Shinmoe-dake and the perfect cone of Takachiho-no-mine. On a clear day, you can see right down to Kagoshima and the smoking cone of Sakurajima.

Longer Walks
The view across the almost lunar landscape from any of the volcano summits is other-worldly. If you have six hours or so, you can continue from Karakuni-dake to Shishiko-dake, Shinmoe-dake, Naka-dake and Takachiho-gawara, from where you can make the ascent of Takachiho-no-mine. Close up, Takachiho is a decidedly ugly volcano with a huge, gaping crater. Legends relate that Ninigi-no-mikoto, a descendant of the sun goddess, arrived in Japan on the summit of this mountain.

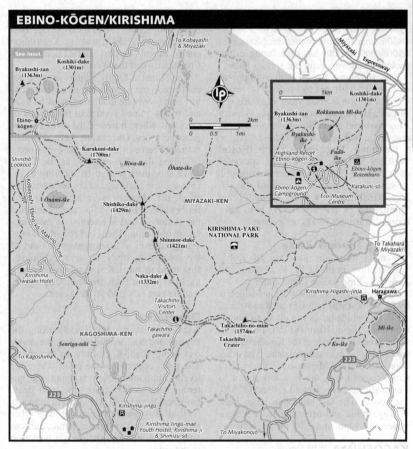

EBINO-KŌGEN/KIRISHIMA

If you miss the late afternoon bus from Takachiho-gawara to Kirishima-jingū, it's a 7km walk down to the village around the shrine.

Kirishima-jingū 霧島神社

Bright-orange Kirishima-jingū is beautifully situated, offering fine views down towards Kagoshima and Sakurajima. Though it dates from the 6th century, the present shrine was built in 1715. It is dedicated to Ninigi-no-mikoto, who made his legendary landing in Japan on the Takachiho-no-mine's summit.

The shrine can be visited en route to the national park. It is accessible by bus (¥240, 15 minutes) from JR Kirishima-jingū station. The festivals of **Saitan-sai** on 1 January, **Ota-ue-sai** in mid-March and the lantern festival of **Kontō-sai** on 5 August are all worth seeing.

Places to Stay & Eat

Ebino-kōgen village has a reasonable choice of accommodation.

Ebino-kōgen Campground (☎ 0984-33-0800; sites/cabins from ¥800/1250) is a 10-minute walk from the visitors centre. Tent and blanket hire are available.

Ebino-kōgen Rotemburo (☎ 0984-33-0800; basic tatami hut per adult ¥1670, futon rental ¥810) is a 20-minute walk downhill from the bus terminal and visitors centre. It has a popular series of open-air hot-spring baths (bring a torch for a night bath). Check-in is until 6pm, with reservations advised in summer.

Karakuni-sō (☎ 0984-33-0650, fax 0984-33-4928; rooms per person with 2 meals ¥8600, annexe house singles/doubles/triples ¥5000/8000/9000) has deer lazing in the backyard and wonderful hot-springs baths.

The **Highland Resort Ebino-kōgen-sō** (☎ 0984-33-0161, fax 0984-33-0114; rooms per person with 2 meals from ¥12,000) is a surprisingly elegant kokumin-shukusha with rotemburo and sauna. Stop by its good-value restaurant, **Nokaidō** (lunch ¥600-1200).

Kirishima Jingū-mae Youth Hostel (☎ 0995-57-1188; beds ¥2500), southeast of Kirishima-jingū, is basic. Among the cluster of minshuku at the top of the village, **Kirishima-ji** (☎ 0995-57-0272) and **Shimizu-sō** (☎ 0955-57-0111) both have rooms for around ¥6000 per person.

Getting There & Away

The main train junctions are JR Kobayashi station, north of Ebino Plateau, and Kirishima-jinja station to the south.

However, a direct bus to Ebino-kōgen is by far the best way to go. From Kagoshima, some Hayashida buses run direct to Ebino-kōgen starting at 10am (¥1550, 1¾ hours). Other buses terminate at the Kirishima Iwasaki Hotel, far below the plateau. The other approach is from Miyazaki. From Miyakō City bus terminal, the first bus direct to Ebino-kōgen leaves around 8.40am (¥2620, 2¼ hours). The last afternoon buses back to Kagoshima and Miyazaki leave Ebino-kōgen at 1.30pm and 2.10pm, respectively.

KAGOSHIMA 鹿児島

☎ 099 • pop 552,100

Known as the Naples of Japan, Kagoshima is the southernmost major city in Kyūshū and a warm, sunny and relaxed place – at least as long as Kagoshima's very own Vesuvius, Sakurajima, just a stone's throw across Kinkō-wan, is behaving itself. 'Dustfall' brings out the umbrellas in Kagoshima as frequently as rainfall in other parts of the world.

History

Kagoshima's history has been dominated by a single family, the Shimazu clan, who held sway there for 29 generations (nearly 700 years) until the Meiji Restoration. The Kagoshima region, known as Satsuma, was always receptive to outside contact and for

many years was an important centre for trade with China. St Francis Xavier first arrived here in 1549, making Kagoshima one of Japan's earliest contact points with Christianity and the West.

The Shimazu family's interests were not confined to trade, however. In the 16th century its power extended throughout Kyūshū and it also gained control of the islands of Okinawa, where it treated the people so oppressively that Okinawans have regarded mainland Japan with suspicion ever since.

During the 19th century, as the Tokugawa shōgunate proved its inability to respond to the challenge of the industrialised West, the Shimazu were already looking further afield. In the 1850s they established the country's first Western-style manufacturing operation. Then, in 1865, the family smuggled over a dozen young men out of the country to study Western technology first-hand in the UK. In conjunction with the Mori clan of Hagi, the Shimazu played a leading part in the Meiji Restoration.

Orientation

Kagoshima sprawls north–south along the bayside and has two JR stations, the major one being Nishi-Kagoshima to the south. The town centre is at the point where the lively Tenmonkan-dōri shopping and entertainment arcade crosses the tram lines. Iso-teien, the town's principal attraction, is north of Kagoshima station but most other things to do are around the centre, particularly on the hillside that forms a backdrop to the city.

Information

The **tourist information office** (☎ 253-2500; open 8.30am-6pm daily) outside Nishi-Kagoshima station has information in English, and can help book accommodation. The quieter Kagoshima station branch (☎ 222-2500; open 8.30am-5pm daily) is also helpful.

In Tenmonkan, the **International Exchange Plaza** (☎ 225-3279; 11th floor, I'm Bldg; open 9am-5.30pm Mon-Sat) offers a free half-hour of Internet access. It also has magazines and books for browsing. **Update Visitor Centre** (☎ 224-8011; W www .synapse.ne.jp/update; 2nd floor, Hiratabashi Bldg; open 9.30am-5pm Mon-Fri, 9.30am-4pm Sat) has an excellent website.

KAGOSHIMA

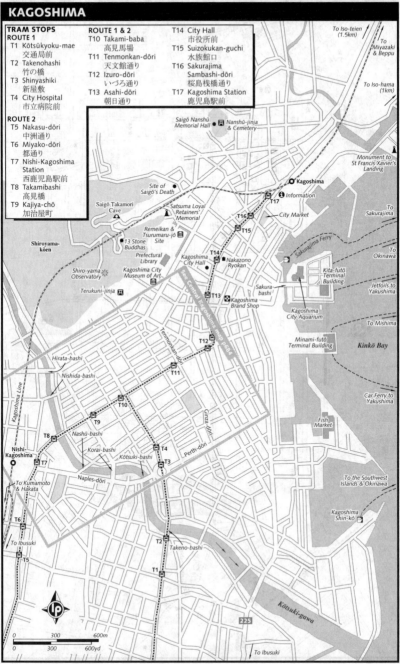

TRAM STOPS
ROUTE 1
T1 Kōtsūkyoku-mae
    交通局前
T2 Takenohashi
    竹の橋
T3 Shinyashiki
    新屋敷
T4 City Hospital
    市立病院前

ROUTE 2
T5 Nakasu-dōri
    中洲通り
T6 Miyako-dōri
    都通り
T7 Nishi-Kagoshima
    Station
    西鹿児島駅前
T8 Takamibashi
    高見橋
T9 Kajiya-chō
    加治屋町

ROUTE 1 & 2
T10 Takami-baba
    高見馬場
T11 Tenmonkan-dōri
    天文館通り
T12 Izuro-dōri
    いづろ通り
T13 Asahi-dōri
    朝日通り

T14 City Hall
    市役所前
T15 Suizokukan-guchi
    水族館口
T16 Sakurajima
    Sambashi-dōri
    桜島桟橋通り
T17 Kagoshima Station
    鹿児島駅前

To Iso-teien
(1.5km)

To Miyazaki
& Beppu

To Iso-hama
(1km)

Monument to
St Francis Xavier's
Landing

Saigō Nanshū
Memorial Hall ● ■ Nanshū-jinja
& Cemetery

Kagoshima

i Information

T17

Site of
Saigō's Death

Saigō Takamori
Cave

Satsuma Loyal
Retainers'
Memorial

T16 City Market

To
Sakurajima

Remeikan &
Tsurumaru-jō Site ■

T15

Shiroyama-
kōen

● 13 Stone
Buddhas

Prefectural
Library

Kagoshima
City Hall T14

Sakurajima Ferry

Shiro-yama
Observatory

Kagoshima City
Museum of Art

Nakazono
Ryokan

To
Okinawa

Kita-futō
Terminal
Building

Terukuni-jinja ■

Sakura-
bashi

Jetfoils to
Yakushima

T13 Kagoshima
     Brand Shop

Kagoshima
City Aquarium

To Mishima

Hirata-bashi

Tenmonkan-dōri

T12

Minami-futō
Terminal Building

Kinkō Bay

Nishida-bashi

T11

Car Ferry to
Yakushima

Kagoshima Line

Ginza-dōri

T10

Fish
Market

T9

Nashū-bashi

T8

Korai-bashi

Kōtsuki-bashi T4

Nishi-
Kagoshima

T7

Perth-dōri

To Kumamoto
& Hakata

Naples-dōri

T6

To the Southwest
Islands & Okinawa

Kagoshima
Shin-kō

To Ibusuki

T5

T2

Takeno-bashi

T1

Kōtsuki-gawa

225

To Ibusuki

LP

0   300   600m
0   300   600yd

KYŪSHŪ

CENTRAL KAGOSHIMA

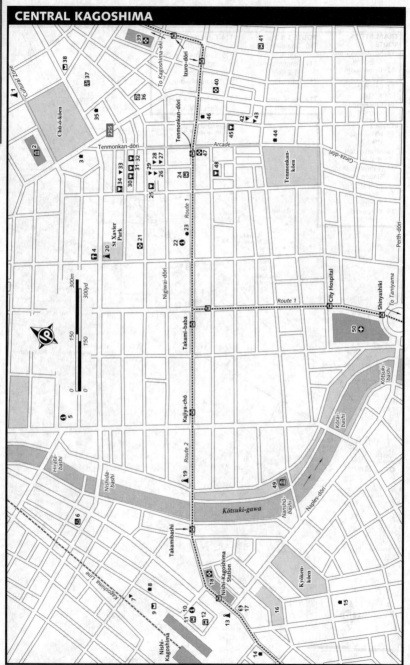

CENTRAL KAGOSHIMA

PLACES TO STAY

3　Onsen Hotel Nakahara Bessō
　　中原別荘
8　Hotel Ishibara-sō
　　ホテル石原荘
14　Business Hotel Suzuya
　　ビジネスホテルすずや
15　Silk Inn Kagoshima
　　シルクイン鹿児島
35　Nanshū-kan Hotel
　　南州館
44　Hotel New Nishino
　　ホテルニュウにしの
46　Business Hotel Paris;
　　Master's Kitchen
　　ビジネスホテル巴里（パリ）；
　　レストランマスターの台所

PLACES TO EAT

7　Xiang Xiang
　　香香
26　Wakasa Honten
　　吾愛人本店
27　Komurasaki
　　こむらさき
28　Wadaya
　　和田屋
29　Kuroiwa
　　くろいわラーメン
33　Kumasotei
　　熊襲亭
42　Yakushima
　　屋久島
43　Moon Garden
　　月の八し

OTHER

1　Saigō Takamori Statue
　　西郷隆盛銅像
2　Kagoshima Prefectural
　　Museum
　　鹿児島県立博物館
4　St Francis Xavier Church
　　ザビエル教会
5　Update Visitor Centre
6　Nishida Onsen
　　西田温泉
9　Central Post Office
　　中央郵便局
10　Tourist Information
　　Office
　　観光案内所
11　Kagoshima Kōtsū
　　(Sightseeing Buses)
　　鹿児島交通（観光バス）
12　Bus Stops
　　バスのりば
13　17 Young Pioneers Statues
　　若き鹿児島の群像
16　Morning Market
　　朝市
17　Kagoshima Bank
　　鹿児島銀行
18　Daiei
　　ダイエイ
19　Statue of Ōkubo
　　Toshimichi
　　大久保利通銅像
20　St Francis Xavier Memorial
　　ザビエル記念碑
21　Caparvo

22　International Exchange Plaza;
　　I'm Building
　　国際交流プラザ；アイムビル
23　JAL
　　日本航空
24　Hayashida Bus
　　林田バス
25　Namaste; Bar Soul Dimension
30　Kanejyō
　　かねじょう
31　Sur Bar
32　Jazz Club Pannonica
　　パノニカ
34　Speakeasy
36　Internet & Comics Space
　　Create
37　Nishi-Honganji
　　西本願寺
38　Kagoshima East Post Office
　　鹿児島東郵便局
39　Yamakataya Department
　　Store; Bus Station
　　山形屋；バスセンター
40　Mitsukoshi Department Store
　　三越
41　Izuro Kōsoku Bus Centre
　　いづろ高速バスのりば
45　Doggy Bar
47　Taka-Pla; Tower Records
48　De'Nile
49　Museum of the Meiji
　　Restoration
　　維新ふるさと館
50　Shiritsu-byōin
　　市立病院

The **postal savings ATM** at the main post office near Nishi-Kagoshima station accepts internationally issued cards.

Internet & Comics Space Create *(membership fee ¥300, ¥360-480/hr; open 24hr)* has reclining chairs, unlimited soft drinks and billiards tables.

Iso-teien (Sengan-en) 磯庭園

Starting in 1658, the 19th Shimazu lord laid out this beautiful bayside garden *(admission ¥1000, with guided villa tour & tea ceremony ¥1500; open 8.30am-5.15pm daily)*, incorporating one of the most impressive pieces of 'borrowed scenery' to be found anywhere in Japan – the fuming peak of Sakurajima. Look for the stream where the 21st Shimazu lord once held poetry parties – the participants had to compose a poem before the next cup of sake floated down the stream to them. The villa, **Shimazu-ke**, was once the family home of the omnipotent Shimazu clan. Women in elegant kimonos

guide you through the villa, after which you are served traditional tea and sweets.

Other tea shops around the garden sell *jambo* (pounded rice cakes on a stick).

Shōko Shūseikan Adjacent to Iso-teien, this museum *(admission free with garden ticket; open 8.30am-5.15pm daily)* is housed in Japan's first factory, built in the 1850s. Exhibits relate to the Shimazu family – in fact, most of the 10,000 items are precious heirlooms, including ancient scrolls, military goods and pottery. The art of *kiriko* (cut glass) has been revived at an on-site workshop.

Other Museums

The **Kagoshima City Museum of Art** *(admission ¥200; open 9.30am-6pm Tues-Sun)* has a small, permanent collection of local works, including some 16th-century porcelains and woodblock prints. Its collection of Sakurajima paintings is most distinctive.

Saigō Takamori

Although the Great Saigō had played a leading part in the Meiji Restoration in 1868, in 1877 he changed his mind – possibly because he felt the curtailment of samurai power and status had gone too far – and this led to the ill-fated Satsuma or Seinan Rebellion. Kumamoto's magnificent castle was burnt down during the rebellion but when defeat became inevitable, Saigō eventually retreated to Kagoshima and committed *seppuku* (ritual suicide by disembowelment).

Despite his mixed status as both a hero and villain of the restoration, Saigō is still a towering figure in the history of Japan. His square-headed features and bulky stature are instantly recognisable, and Kagoshima has a famous Saigō statue (and a spooky Saigō hologram), as does Ueno-kōen in Tokyo.

Reimeikan (*Kagoshima Prefectural Museum of Culture; admission ¥300; open 9am-4.30pm Tues-Sun*) is also on the former site of Tsurumaru-jō – the walls and the impressive moat are all that remain of the 1602 castle. Inside, the museum's three floors showcase very interesting exhibits on Satsuma history, festivals and folklore. Don't miss the model of the castle or ancient swordmaking displays.

The quirky **Museum of the Meiji Restoration** (*admission ¥300; open 9am-5.30pm daily 15 Jul-31 Aug, 9am-4.30pm rest of year*) has hourly performances by robotic Meiji reformers, including a downright spooky-looking Saigō. Exhibits and historical dioramas, labelled mostly in Japanese, laud Kagoshima firsts (Japan's first telegraph, first gas lighting etc), along with Satsuma culture and the daunting local dialect.

Saigō Takamori 高森西郷

There are numerous reminders of Saigō Takamori's importance in Kagoshima, including a large statue of him near the City Art Museum. The cave where he hid and the place where he eventually committed suicide are on Shiro-yama. Further north are Nanshū-jinja; the **Saigō Nanshū Memorial Hall** (*admission ¥100; open 9am-5pm Tues-Sun*), where displays tell of the failed rebel-

lion; and Nanshū-bochi (cemetery), which contains the graves of more than 2000 of Saigō's followers.

Other Attractions

Terukuni-jinja is dedicated to Shimazu Nari-akira, the 28th Shimazu lord who was responsible for building Japan's first factory and introducing modern Western technology. He also designed Japan's still-controversial *hinomaru* – the rising sun flag. Continue up the hillside behind the shrine and you'll eventually reach the **observatory** in Shiroyama-kōen.

Kagoshima boasts no less than 50 public *onsen* baths. Local favourite **Shin-tosō Onsen** (☎ 255-4826) has a good view of Sakurajima. Take city bus No 25 from Nishi-Kagoshima station to Toso (15 minutes). **Nishida Onsen** is just a few minutes' walk from Nishi-Kagoshima station.

Kagoshima City Aquarium (*adult/child ¥1500/750; open 9am-5pm daily*) is well done, not least the examples of local marine life, giving glimpses of spectacular diving in the Southwest Islands. **Iso-hama**, the city's popular summer beach getaway, has a cordoned off area for swimming and splashing about.

Ask at tourist information for the free *Kagoshima City* guide booklet, which has detailed information on visiting local pottery kilns, silk-weaving workshops, *shōchū* distilleries and even a Satsuma fish paste factory!

Special Events

One of Kagoshima's more unusual events is the late July **Sogadon-no-Kasayaki** (Umbrella Burning Festival). Boys burn umbrellas on the banks of Kōtsuki-gawa in honour of the Soga brothers, though why they do this isn't exactly clear. Other events include the **Isle of Fire Festival** in late July on Sakurajima and the **Ohara Festival** in early November, featuring folk-dancing in the streets.

Places to Stay

Kagoshima Shiroyama Youth Hostel (☎ 223-2648; beds ¥3100) is a homely place with a kitchen and small garden. Call the English-speaking owners to ask for directions – it's hidden up in the hills, a 10-minute bus ride from Nishi-Kagoshima station.

Nakazono Ryokan (☎ 226-5125, fax 226-5126; e shindon@satsuma.ne.jp; singles/doubles/triples ¥4000/8000/11,400), part of the Japanese Inn Group, is a superb place to be based. It's a particularly friendly *minshuku*, used to dealing with the vagaries of *gaijin* clients. The ryokan is close to both Kagoshima station and the Sakurajima pier, and there's a mineral-water *sentō* (public bath house) nearby. The ryokan is tucked down an alley behind a temple, near the Shiyakusho-mae (City Hall) tram stop.

Business Hotel Suzuya (☎ 258-2385; rooms per person ¥3500-4500) is the cheapest place around Nishi-Kagoshima station. **Business Hotel Ishibara-sō** (☎ 254-4181; singles/doubles ¥4500/8500), quite a step up, serves Satsuma cuisine in its restaurants. **Silk Inn Kagoshima** (☎ 258-1221; singles/doubles ¥5800/9500) has its own hot spring.

Hotel New Nishino (☎ 224-3232; singles/twins ¥5400/9600, Japanese-style rooms from ¥9600) reserves its 4th-floor sauna complex for men only.

Nanshū-kan (☎ 226-8188, fax 226-9383; singles/doubles from ¥6000/8000), although slightly faded, is convenient. The water pressure in the showers is enough to knock over a horse. Ask about car rental packages.

JR Kyūshū Hotel Kagoshima (☎ 213-8000, fax 213-8029; e kagoshima@jrk-ho tels.com; singles/twins ¥6500/12,000), an upmarket hotel attached to Nishi-Kagoshima station, has only a dozen twin rooms (as compared to over 100 singles). Check-in is anytime after 2pm, check-out is by 11am

Onsen Hotel Nakahara Bessō (☎ 225-2800, fax 226-3688; rooms per person with/without 2 meals ¥10,000/8000) has mostly Japanese-style accommodation, with its own Satsuma cuisine restaurant and a *rotemburo*. It's close to sightseeing and nightlife.

Places to Eat

Side streets around Nishi-Kagoshima station have an abundance of eateries.

Xiang Xiang (dishes ¥700-1100; open 11am-2pm & 6pm-10pm Mon-Sat) should be your first choice, where gracious servers in traditional *ao dai* serve fresh Vietnamese fare. The owner speaks impeccable English.

There's something of a *rāmen* battle going on in Tenmonkan. With its stone

facade and wooden horseshoe-shaped bar, **Komurasaki** (open 11am-9pm Fri-Wed) is good but pricey; **Kuroiwa** (open 10.30am-9pm daily) – plain but tasty; and **Wadaya** (open 11am-1.50am daily) – 'striking'.

Kumasotei (☎ 222-6356; meals from ¥1400; open 11am-3pm & 5pm-10pm daily) is a favourite for Satsuma cuisine. The ¥3000 dinner gives you a taste of all the most popular specialities. **Wakasa Honten** (☎ 222-5559; dishes around ¥700; open 5.30pm-11.15pm daily) has much of the same, but is rather cheaper.

Moon Garden (open 5pm-11pm Mon-Fri, 5pm-1am Sat) is a beautiful and rambunctious dining bar. Its English-language drinks menu lists regional sake and *shōchū* varieties.

Yakushima (open 5pm-11pm Mon-Sat), a few doors north (look for the jolly *obasan* painted on the sign), is a rustic place for island seafood cuisine.

Entertainment

There's a lot happening in Tenmonkan – shot bars, discos, bunny bars, peep shows, karaoke boxes and retro coffee shops.

Kanejyō (☎ 223-0487; open to midnight daily) is an atmospheric jazz café and bar. **Jazz Bar Pannonica** (cover ¥500-1000; open nightly) has live vocalists. **Namaste** (open 8am-3pm daily) is a basement reggae bar. **Bar Soul Dimension**

(☎ 219-1618) plays soul music all the time, but it's open pretty random hours.

Most dance clubs don't get going until around 11pm. **Sur Bar** *(☎ 222-0902; cover ¥500)* has a small basement dance space suffused by white lights and incense. Look for bongos in the corner. **De'Nile** *(☎ 222-4970; cover with 2 free drinks weekend ¥1000-3000)* is another subterranean dance spot with different DJs every night. **Doggy Bar** *(4th floor; cover ¥1500-3000)* calls the hip-hop and reggae crowd, especially for live events.

Shopping

Satsuma specialities include a variation on the *ningyō (Japanese doll), kiriko (cut glass)* and cards printed with inks produced from Sakurajima volcanic ash. Satsuma-yaki porcelain is also highly valued, but not as much as Kagoshima's pride and joy – *imo shōchū* (potato liquor). You can shop for quality goods at Iso-teien and **Kagoshima Brand Shop** *(Kagoshima-ken Bussan-kaikan; open 9am-5pm daily)* in Tenmonkan.

Kagoshima's **asa ichi** *(morning market; open 6am-noon Mon-Sat)* is just south of Nishi-Kagoshima station. It's a raucous, lively event. There's another morning market at the main Kagoshima station.

Getting There & Away

Air Kagoshima's airport has international connections with Hong Kong, Shanghai and Seoul, as well as domestic flights to Tokyo, Osaka and other Kyūshū destinations. Kagoshima is also the major jumping-off point for flights to the Southwest Islands and Okinawa.

Skymark *(☎ 223-0123)* is Japan's only cut-rate carrier, offering flights to Tokyo (Haneda, ¥24,500). Book at the office in Tenmonkan.

Bus There are a few bus centres and a myriad of highway bus stops, mostly found around Nishi-Kagoshima station and in Tenmonkan.

Typical fares include ¥2700 to Miyazaki (2¾ hours), ¥3600 to Kumamoto (3½ hours), ¥5300 to Fukuoka (four hours) and ¥10,800 to Osaka (12½ hours).

Hayashida buses to Ebino-kōgen (¥1550, 1¾ hours) depart from opposite Taka-Pla department store.

Train Most trains arrive and depart from Nishi-Kagoshima station. The JR Kagoshima line heads north to Kumamoto *(tokkyū ¥5750, 2½ hours)* and Hakata (Fukuoka; ¥8270, four hours). Also stopping at Kagoshima station, the JR Nippō line goes to Miyazaki *(tokkyū ¥4690, two hours)* and Beppu (¥10,460, six hours).

Trains also run south from Kagoshima to the popular hot-spring resort of Ibusuki and continue partway around the Satsuma Peninsula.

Boat Ferries shuttle across the bay to Sakurajima, and from the Kita-futō terminal further afield to Okinawa (¥14,200, 19 hours) and by jetfoil to Yakushima. Regular ferries to Yakushima depart from Minamifutō pier just 10 minutes' walk south. For details on ferry services to Yakushima, see the Okinawa & the Southwest Islands chapter.

From Kagoshima New Port (Kagoshima Shin-kō), **Queen Coral Marix Line** *(☎ 225-1551)* has ferries to Naha (Okinawa) via the Amami archipelago (¥13,200, 25½ hours).

Getting Around

To/From the Airport Frequent airport buses depart from Nishi-Kagoshima station, Tenmonkan and various other stops around the city (¥1200, one hour).

Bus There's a comprehensive city bus network, though trams are usually simpler.

For tourists, the City View Bus (¥180) does a loop of all the major sights, departing every 30 minutes throughout the day, from 9.30am to 5pm daily. A one-day pass costs ¥600, and is also valid on trams.

Tram The tram service in Kagoshima is easy to understand and operates frequently. Route 1 starts from Kagoshima station, goes through the centre and on into the suburbs. Route 2 diverges at Takami-baba to Nishi-Kagoshima station and terminates at Korimoto. Either pay the flat fare (¥160) or buy a one-day travel pass (¥600) from tourist information offices.

SAKURAJIMA 桜島
☎ 099

Dominating the skyline from Kagoshima is the brooding cone of this decidedly hyperactive volcano. In fact, Sakurajima is so active that the Japanese differentiate between its mere eruptions (since 1955 there has been an almost continuous stream of smoke and ash) and real explosions. The most violent was in 1914, when the volcano poured out over three billion tonnes of lava, overwhelming numerous villages and converting the island to a peninsula.

Sakurajima has three peaks, but at present only Minami-dake (1040m) is active. Although visitors are not permitted to climb the volcano, there are several good lookout points with walkways across a small corner of the immense lava flow. While some parts of Sakurajima are covered in deep volcanic ash or crumbling lava, other places have exceptionally fertile soil. Huge *daikon* (radishes) weighing up to 35kg and tiny oranges, only 3cm in diameter but ¥500 each, are locally grown.

Sakurajima Visitors Centre

The visitors centre (☎ 293-2443; open 9am-5pm Tues-Sun) is located near the ferry terminal and has a variety of exhibits and videos about the volcano, its eruptions and its natural history. A working model showing the volcano's growth over the years is the visitors centre's main attraction. There's a short lava field paved walkway nearby that leads along the coast toward a lookout.

Other Attractions

South of the visitors centre is **Buried Tori-shima**, where the 1914 lava flow totally engulfed the small island that had been half a kilometre offshore. On the way down the mountainside the lava swallowed three villages, destroying over 1000 homes.

Continuing anticlockwise around the island, you come to a **monument** to writer Hayashi Fumiko, and the hot springs at **Furusato Onsen**. Furusato Kankō hotel has a pool-sized cliffside **rotemburo** (admission ¥1050, rental locker & towel ¥410; closed Mon & Thur morning). As it is also a shrine, you'll have to wear a *yukata* (light kimono for summer or indoor use) as you soak.

At **Kurokami Buried Torii**, only the top of a torii emerges from the volcanic ash. On the north coast you can soak in the muddy waters of **Shirahama Onsen Centre** (admission ¥300; open 10am-9pm daily).

Organised Tours

Sightseeing bus tours leave from the ferry terminal (¥1700, three hours, 9.30am and 1.30pm daily). JR Kyūshū also runs tours of Sakurajima, leaving from Nishi-Kagoshima station at 8.45am (¥4000, 6¼ hours).

Places to Stay

There's a **campground** across the road from the visitors centre.

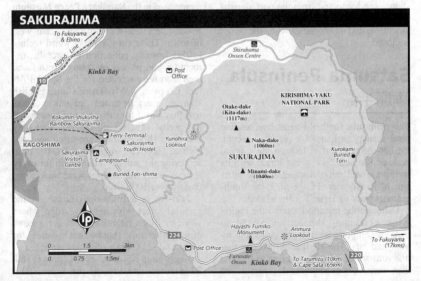

SAKURAJIMA

Sakurajima Youth Hostel (☎/fax 293-2150; beds with/without 2 meals ¥3870/2650) is faded, but friendly. It's a 15-minute walk from the ferry terminal. In order to arrive before reception closes, you must catch the 8.30pm ferry from Kagoshima.

Kokumin-shukusha Rainbow Sakurajima (☎ 293-2323; rooms per person with 2 meals ¥8000) is also near the ferry terminal.

Getting There & Around

A 24-hour passenger and car ferry service shuttles frequently back and forth between Kagoshima and Sakurajima (¥150, 15 minutes). Pay at the Sakurajima end.

The Sakurajima ferry terminal is a short bus ride from Nishi-Kagoshima station. Take the **City View Bus** or any bus bound for the aquarium and get off at Suizokukan-mae (¥180, half-hourly).

Getting around Sakurajima without your own transport can be difficult. Bicycles can be rented near the ferry terminal but a complete circuit of the volcano (36km) would be quite a push, even without the climbs to the various lookouts.

Local buses run regularly around the island until around 8pm daily. JR buses from the ferry terminal run past Furusato Onsen (¥290) and up to the Arimura lookout. Otherwise, the Furusato Kankō Hotel at Furusato Onsen offers a limited free shuttle service to and from the port, departing roughly every half-hour except during lunchtime and on mornings when the *onsen* is closed.

Satsuma Peninsula
薩摩半島

This peninsula, south of Kagoshima, has fine rural scenery, a kamikaze pilots' museum, the hot-spring resort of Ibusuki, the conical peak of Kaimon-dake, and Chiran, with its well-preserved samurai street. On the other side of Kinkō-wan is Cape Sata, the southernmost point of Japan's main islands.

Using public transport around the region is time-consuming, although it is possible to make a complete loop of the peninsula by train and bus. The JR Ibusuki-Makurazaki line runs south from Kagoshima to Ibusuki then turns west to Makurazaki, from where

you can eventually make your way by local bus back to Kagoshima.

Renting a car can be useful. There are also daily bus tours to Ibusuki and Chiran from Nishi-Kagoshima station. For a sample of what's on offer, a daily sightseeing bus (¥4550) heads off to Chiran at 8.50am, whizzes you around the sights and then does the same thing in Ibusuki, ending the day with a soak in a hot spring.

CHIRAN 知覧
☎ 0993 • pop 13,886

South of Kagoshima, Chiran is a detour en route to or from Ibusuki. The town has a fine collection of samurai houses and gardens, plus a fascinating memorial and museum to WWII's kamikaze pilots. Chiran was one of the major bases from which the hapless pilots made their suicidal and less than totally successful attacks on Allied ships.

All seven of the residences along Chiran's **samurai street** (admission ¥500; open 9am-5pm daily) dating from the mid-Edo period are noted for their gardens. Look for the use of 'borrowed scenery', particularly in No 6. Water is usually symbolised by sand or gravel. Along the main road, parallel to the samurai street, is a well-stocked **carp stream**.

A modern version of the samurai is commemorated in the **Kamikaze Peace Museum** (Chiran Tokkō Heiwa-Kaikan; admission ¥500; open 9am-4.30pm daily), 2km west of town. There's a distinctly weird feeling to this fawning collection of aircraft, mementoes and photos of young, fresh-faced men who were selected for the Special Attack Corps in WWII. There's little English signage, apart from the dubious message that they did it for the dream of 'peace and prosperity'. There's no mention that they had little choice, and were often sent out high on Hiropon – amphetamines. Far from achieving the aim of 'a battleship for every aircraft', only minor ships were sunk at the cost of over 1000 lives.

Taki-An is a traditional house on the samurai street with a nice garden where you can sit on tatami mats to eat a bowl of upmarket *soba* (buckwheat noodles) for ¥600, and sip Chiran's famous green tea.

Kagoshima Kōtsū buses to Chiran (¥860, 80 minutes) and Ibusuki run from Nishi-

Kagoshima station and the Yamakataya bus station in Tenmonkan. From Chiran, there are only a few buses per day to Ibusuki (¥900, one hour), leaving from stops along the highway.

IBUSUKI 指宿
☎ 0993 • pop 30,640

At the southeastern end of the Satsuma Peninsula, 50km from Kagoshima, is the hotspring resort of Ibusuki. It's pretty rundown, and unless you want to stay overnight here before exploring the peninsula, it's best to make a day trip from Kagoshima. At Ibusuki station, the **information desk** (☎ 22-2111; open 9am-6pm daily) has basic maps.

On the beachfront is Ibusuki's *raison d'etre*, the **Tennen Sunamushi Kaikan Saraku sand baths** (admission ¥900; open 8.30am-noon & 1pm-9pm daily). You pay at the entrance (the fee includes a *yukata* and towel), change downstairs, and wander down to the beach where the burial ladies are waiting, shovel in hand, to cover you in red-hot black volcanic sand. The weight and heat feel very odd, and it takes iron-clad willpower to endure the full 15-minute treatment, but as you rinse off the sand in the showers afterwards, you feel unusually energised. The sand baths are a 20-minute walk or a short bus ride (¥130) southeast of Ibusuki station.

Places to Stay & Eat
Yunosato Youth Hostel (☎ 22-5680; beds with/without 2 meals ¥4600/3000) has its own hot spring and rents bicycles. It's 800m northeast of the station.

Tamaya Youth Hostel (☎ 22-3553; beds with/without 2 meals ¥3950/2600), like most accommodation in Ibusuki, is just a stone's throw from the sand baths.

Minshuku Marutomi (☎ 22-5579, fax 22-3993; rooms with 2 meals from ¥7000) is a small but very popular inn, famous for its fresh seafood.

Ryokan Ginshō (☎ 22-3231, fax 22-2219; rooms per person with 2 meals from ¥12,500) has been in operation for over 50 years. It has a lovely garden, with smart-looking staff waiting to welcome you out front. Its seaside *rotemburo* has romantic lantern-lit shower stalls.

Ibusuki is short of decent places to eat. There are a few restaurants on the street leading out from the station and along the beach road. In summer, the **Iwasaki Hotel** has a beer garden.

Getting There & Away
Ibusuki is less than two hours from Kagoshima by bus (¥850); see the Chiran section earlier for details. Trains also operate from Nishi-Kagoshima station (*kaisoku* ¥970, 80 minutes).

AROUND THE PENINSULA
West of Ibusuki, **Ikeda-ko** is a beautiful volcanic caldera lake, inhabited by giant eels that grow up to 2m long. West along the coast, you come to **Cape Nagasakibana**, from where offshore islands can be seen on a clear day. There's a **campground** near the flower gardens. The beautifully symmetrical 922m cone of **Kaimon-dake** can be climbed in two hours from the Kaimon-dake bus stop, or also from JR Kaimon station. Start as early as possible and you'll be rewarded with views of Sakurajima, Cape Sata and tropical islands, Yakushima and Tanegashima.

At the southwestern end of the peninsula is **Makurazaki**, a busy fishing port and the terminus for the train line from Kagoshima. Just beyond Makurazaki is **Bōnotsu**, a pretty little fishing village that was an unofficial trading link with the outside world via Okinawa during Japan's two centuries of seclusion. North of Bōnotsu is **Fukiage Beach**. A 15-minute walk from JR Ijūin station, **Fukiage-hama Youth Hostel** (☎/fax 292-3455; beds ¥2750) has just a dozen beds.

The southernmost point on the main islands of Japan, **Cape Sata**, is marked by the oldest lighthouse in Japan. You can reach the cape from the Kagoshima side of Kinkō-wan by taking the ferry from Yamakawa, one stop south of Ibusuki, to Nejime. However, public transport onward is nearly impossible. An 8km bicycle track leads down to the end of the cape.

Miyazaki-ken 宮崎県

Rte 222 from Miyakonojō to Obi and Nichinan on the coast is a superb road, twisting and winding as it climbs over the hills along the sea. Along this rugged coastline south of Miyazaki, the usual approach is by train or bus.

KYŪSHŪ

AOSHIMA 青島
☎ 0985

This touristy beach resort is famed for the small island covered in betel palms, fringed by washboard rock formations and connected to the mainland by a causeway. Due to the prevailing warm currents, the only place you'll find warmer water in Japan is much further south in Okinawa. On the island, a short walk east of Aoshima station, is photogenic **Aoshima-jinja**, reputedly good for match-making, and the scene of two exciting festivals. On the second Monday in January, loincloth-wearing locals dive into the ocean, while on 17 June there's another aquatic twist when *mikoshi* are carried through the shallows to the shrine.

Aoshima is on the JR Nichinan line from Miyazaki (¥360, 30 minutes). Buses from Miyazaki station stop at Aoshima (¥670, 40 minutes, hourly) en route to Udo-jingū.

UDO-JINGŪ 鵜戸神宮
If you walk through this brightly painted coastal shrine to the end of the path, you'll find yourself in an open cavern overlooking some rock formations at the ocean's edge. A popular sport is to buy five *undama* (luck stones) and try to get them into a shallow depression on top of one of the turtle-shaped rocks (men, throw with your right hand; women, use your left). Succeeding at this task is supposed to make your wish come true. Wishes are usually related to marriage and childbirth, most likely because the boulders in front of the cave are said to represent Emperor Jimmu's mother's breasts!

Frequent buses from Aoshima (¥990, 40 minutes) and Miyazaki (¥1440, 90 minutes) stop on the highway, downhill from the shrine. There are few onward buses to Obi (¥820, 45 minutes).

OBI 飫肥
From 1587, the wealthy Ito clan ruled this town from the castle for 14 generations, surviving the 'one kingdom, one castle' ruling in 1615. The clan eventually moved out in 1869 after the Meiji Restoration ended the feudal period.

Things to See & Do
Although only the walls of the actual castle remain, the grounds of **Obi-jō** contain a number of interesting buildings (*combined admission ¥600; open 9.30am-4.30pm daily*). The castle **museum** has a collection relating to the Ito clan's long rule over Obi, everything from weapons and armour to traditional clothes and household equipment. **Matsuo-no-Maru**, the lord's private residence, has been reconstructed. When the lord visited the toilet at the far end of the house, he was accompanied by three pages – one to lead the way, one to carry water for the lord to wash his hands and one to fan him during the summer months!

When the Obi lord was forced to abandon his castle after the Meiji Restoration, he moved down the hill to **Yōshōkan**, formerly the residence of the clan's chief retainer. It stands just outside the castle entrance and has a large garden incorporating Atago-san as 'borrowed scenery'. Beyond this house you enter the castle proper through the impressive gate, **Ōte-mon**.

The hall, **Shintōku-dō**, adjacent to the castle, was established as a samurai school in 1831. Up the hill behind Shintōku-dō is **Tanoue Hachiman-jinja**; the shrine is shrouded by trees and reached by a steep flight of steps.

On the western side of the river, **Ioshi-jinja** has a pleasant garden and the Ito family mausoleum.

Getting There & Around
The JR Nichinan line connects Obi with Miyazaki (*kaisoku* ¥910, 65 minutes) via Aoshima. From Obi station, it's a short bus ride (¥220) or a 15-minute walk to the castle, reached by turning left outside the station. Buses from Miyazaki (¥1990, 2¼ hours, last return bus 4pm) stop along the main road below the castle entrance.

NICHINAN-KAIGAN & CAPE TOI
日南海岸・都井岬

The beautiful 50km stretch of coast from Nichinan to Miyazaki offers stunning views, pretty little coves, interesting stretches of 'washboard' rocks and, at holiday times, heavy traffic. Like Cape Sata, the views over the ocean from Cape Toi are superb. On the last weekend in September, Cape Toi hosts a dramatic fire festival. The cape is also famed for its herds of wild horses, although the word 'wild' has to be treated with some suspicion in Japan. There's a good beach at **Ishinami-kaigan** where, during the summer only, you can stay in old farmhouse *min-shuku*. The tiny island of **Kō-jima**, just off the coast, has a group of monkeys that were the focus for some interesting anthropological discoveries. **Toi-misaki Youth Hostel** (☎ 76-1397; beds ¥2500) is a five-minute walk from the Toi-misaki Kankō Hotel bus stop, reached via buses from Miyazaki's Miyakō City bus terminal (¥1500, 1½ hours)

MIYAZAKI 宮崎
☎ 0985 • pop 306,000

Due to the warm offshore currents, the city of Miyazaki has a balmy climate (much touted in tourist literature) and some world-class surfing, particularly at Kizaki-hama and other beaches further north toward Hyūga. The area around Miyazaki played an important part in early Japanese civilisation and some interesting excavations can be seen at Saitobaru.

Information

At the **tourist information office** (☎ 22-6469; open 9am-6.30pm daily) inside Miyazaki station, some English is spoken. Make sure you pick up the excellent *Discovering Miyazaki: A Travel Guide* or *Let's Go Miyazaki City* guidebook and pull-out map.

The **Miyazaki Prefectural International Centre** (☎ 32-8457; 6th floor, Higashi-bekkan; open 8.30am-5.15pm Mon-Fri) has CNN and English-language newspapers, but no Internet access.

There's an **ATM** that accepts Visa, MasterCard and Cirrus in the Fresta shopping complex at Miyazaki station. At Miyakō City bus terminal, the **postal savings ATM** (open 8am-9pm Mon-Fri, 10am-9pm Sat, 10am-7pm Sun) accepts internationally issued cards.

There's a 24-hour **Internet café** above Cafe Lanai charging ¥480 for the first hour, or ¥1980 for unlimited Internet access between midnight and 8am, including soft drinks.

Miyazaki Science Centre
宮崎科学技術館

A short walk from Miyazaki station, this hi-tech science museum (admission with sky show ¥730; open 9am-4pm Tues-Sun) topped by a gleaming silver dome boasts the world's largest planetarium. English-language pamphlets are available.

Miyazaki-jingū & Museum
宮崎神宮

Miyazaki-jingū, 3km north of the town centre, is dedicated to the Emperor Jimmu, the semimythical first emperor of Japan and founder of the Yamoto court. There are wisteria trees said to be 600 years old covering the thickly forested grounds.

Outside the northern end of the shrine grounds, the **Miyazaki Prefectural Museum of Nature & History** (admission ¥300; open 9am-4.30pm Tues-Sun) has kid-oriented exhibits on local history, archaeological finds, festivals and folkcrafts. Behind the museum is **Minka-en** (admission free; open Tues-Sun), with its four traditional-style Kyūshū farmhouses.

The shrine is located a 15-minute walk from Miyazaki-jingū station, one stop north of Miyazaki. Several buses from Miyazaki station and Tachibana-dōri run directly to the shrine (¥200, 10 minutes).

Heiwadai-kōen 平和台公園

The centrepiece of Heiwadai-kōen (Peace Park) is a 37m-high tower constructed in 1940, a time when peace in Japan was about to disappear. Standing in front of the tower and clapping your hands produces a strange echo.

Haniwa Garden, which is in the park, is dotted with reproductions of the curious clay *haniwa* (tomb guardians) that have been excavated from Saitobaru burial mounds.

Haniwa Garden is about 1.5km north of Miyazaki-jingū, but only a few buses per day go there from Miyazaki station (¥290, 20 minutes). More frequent services depart from along Tachibana-dōri.

Seagaia シーガイヤ

About 10km north of town at Seagaia resort, the **Ocean Dome** (☎ 0985-21-1177; adult/child ¥2000/10000; open from 10am daily) is a miraculous thing – a kind of *Brave New World* water amusement park, with a mock volcano and body-boarding on artificial waves. It is certainly not, as the hype puts it, a 'paradise within a paradise', but the idea of putting a 140m white-sand beach and a splash of ocean under a huge dome is mind-boggling. Is putting it next to the *real* ocean a beautiful stroke of irony or a bitter reflection of our times?

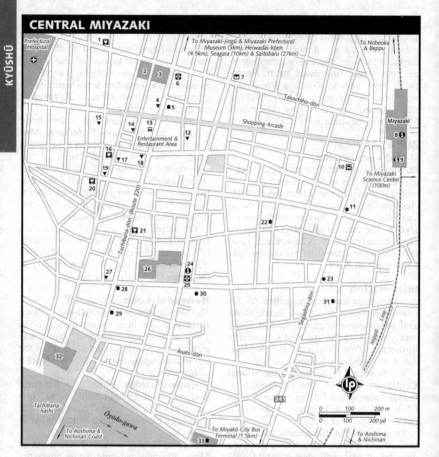

CENTRAL MIYAZAKI

Prefectural Hospital

To Miyazaki-jingū & Miyazaki Prefectural Museum (3km), Heiwadai-kōen (4.5km), Seagaia (10km) & Saitobaru (27km)

To Nobeoka & Beppu

Takachiho-dōri

Shopping Arcade

Entertainment & Restaurant Area

Miyazaki

To Miyazaki Science Center (100m)

Tachibana-dōri (Route 220)

Segashira-dōri

Nippō Line

Asahi-dōri

Tachibana-hashi

Ōyodo-gawa

To Aoshima & Nichinan Coast

To Miyakō City Bus Terminal (1.5km)

To Aoshima & Nichinan

0   100   200 m
0   100   200 yd

Buses run to Seagaia from JR Miyazaki station along Tachibana-dōri every 30 minutes (¥470, 25 minutes).

Special Events

On 2 and 3 April there's *yabusame* (samurai-style horseback archery) at Miyazaki-jingū. Mid-April's **Furusato Matsuri** has around 10,000 participants in traditional attire dancing to local folk songs on Tachibana-dōri. **Miyazaki-jingū Grand Festival**, in late October, is similar with *mikoshi* being carried through the streets. Miyazaki is host to Kyūshū's largest fireworks show in late July.

Places to Stay

Most accommodation in Miyazaki fills up quickly, so book ahead.

Fujin-kaikan Youth Hostel (☎ 24-5785; *beds ¥2500*), a typically institutional place with an early curfew, is 15 minutes' walk from Miyazaki station.

Business Family Hotel Miyako (☎ 27-9991, fax 27-0023; *Japanese- or Western-style rooms with bath per person ¥3500*) is on a quiet side street, about midway between the station and Tachibana-dōri. Reception is welcoming, but the doors are locked at midnight.

Hotel Crane (☎ 27-2111; *singles/twins from ¥4200/7500*) is the pick of business hotels around Tachibana-dōri. **Hotel Crane-bashi** (☎ 27-6868; *singles/doubles from ¥4900/7000, Japanese-style singles/doubles ¥4760/6760*) is slightly older, but rates include breakfast.

CENTRAL MIYAZAKI

Business Hotel Royal (☎ 25-5221; *singles/twins from ¥4500/7000*) may not be anything special, but it's much closer to Miyazaki station.

Hotel Kensington (☎ 20-5500, fax 32-7700; **w** *www.face.ne.jp/kensington in Japanese*; *singles/doubles ¥6300/10,000*) is a cut above the average business hotel. Its British-style atmosphere is nevertheless charming. Discounts are available for online bookings, but note that the website is in Japanese.

On the riverside are Miyazaki's top-end hotels. **Miyazaki Kankō Hotel** (☎ 32-5920, fax 25-8748; *singles/doubles from ¥7000/14,000, Japanese-style rooms ¥15,000-22,000*) has its own hot-springs baths.

Places to Eat

Hiya-jiru is a cold summer soup made from baked tofu, fish, miso paste and cucumbers, which you pour over a bowl of rice. Miyazaki station is known for its *shiitake ekiben*, a boxed lunch featuring mushrooms.

La Dish Gourmet & Deli (*open 11am-3am Mon-Sat, 6pm-1am Sun*) is an import grocery store amid the hustle of the entertainment district that sells both cold and hot deli items, plus a good selection of wines, cheeses and desserts.

Bon Belta department store has an 8th-floor restaurant arcade (lunch sets under ¥1000) and a bewildering variety of take-away options available from its basement

marketplace. Don't miss the *onigiri* counter. The ground-floor café at the nearby **Hotel Kensington** does reasonable breakfast and lunch sets (¥750).

Sai-en (☎ 28-5638; *teishoku ¥700; open 11.30am-2.30pm & 5pm-9pm daily*) serves organic vegetarian cuisine, and there's an English-language menu. It's up on the 2nd floor, above a boutique.

Suginoko (☎ 22-5798; *lunch dishes from ¥800, multicourse dinners from ¥4000*) specialises in Miyazaki cuisine, by reservation only. An abbreviated menu is available in English.

Den Den Den is a boisterous restaurant specialising in *kushiage* (deep-fried seafood on skewers). **Izakaya Seoul** (*1st floor, Dai-ichi Yoshino Bldg*) is a bustling, no-nonsense Korean restaurant not far away.

Beware that many attractive-looking eateries in the entertainment district discreetly tack on a 'table charge' of at least a few hundred yen per person.

Restaurant-Bar De-meté-r (*dishes ¥450-1100, pizzas ¥600-1300; open 6pm-late daily*) has an endless bilingual menu, draught beers and no cover charge.

Rojak Restaurant & Bar (☎ 29-4020; *2nd floor, Daisan Miwa Bldg; dishes ¥600-1400; open 6pm-midnight daily*) has Buddhas and lanterns illuminating the staircase. The ¥200 table charge is worth it, both for Eurasian fare and sleek ambience.

APAS *(☎ 31-8929; set meals ¥2200-3600; open 11am-3pm & 5pm-10pm daily)* specialises in *Miyazaki-gyū* (Miyazaki beef). It's not especially atmospheric or cheap, but the steaks are the real thing.

Park Avenue Café *(☎ 31-7090; dishes ¥1000-1800; open lunch & dinner Mon-Sat)* is an upscale bistro along the riverside. Plates of fresh seafood and pasta in tropically inspired sauces are accompanied by an excellent wine list.

Entertainment
Locals claim that Miyazaki has some 3500 bars. In summer, Bon Belta department store has a rooftop **beer garden**.

Suntory Shot Bar *(open daily)* is good for a quiet, inexpensive beer; the master-san speaks some English – ask him for his 'special'. **Cafe Lanai** *(usually open 11am-10pm daily)* has a Hawaiian surf-and-aloha groove.

Cross Over Space CUBE *(☎ 60-2127; cover ¥500-3500)* is a dance space; DJs spin anything from soul to trance, bossa nova to hip-hop. Schedules are posted outside.

Beat Clap *(cover ¥1000-3500)* is a barn-like dance club that fills to the rafters on a Saturday night.

Shopping
The **Miyazaki Prefectural Products Promotion Exhibition Hall** *(open 9.30am-7pm Tues-Fri, 10am-6.30pm Sat & Sun)* sells hand-woven textiles, *haniwa* figures and Igo (go) chess boards.

Getting There & Away
Air Miyazaki is connected by air with Tokyo (¥27,900), Osaka (¥17,600) and Okinawa (¥22,500), as well as other cities around Kyūshū.

Bus Most long-distance buses originate at the Miyakō City bus terminal south of the river, near JR Minami-Miyazaki station, including to Kagoshima (¥4900, 2¾ hours), Ebino-kōgen in Kirishima National Park (¥2450, 2¼ hours), Kumamoto (¥4500, 3¼ hours) and Fukuoka (¥6000, four hours).

Many buses run along Tachibana-dōri, but if you don't read Japanese you may be better off heading down to the southern bus station. There is another regional bus station opposite Miyazaki station.

Train The JR Nippō line runs down to Kagoshima (*tokkyū* ¥4690, two hours) and up to Beppu (*tokkyū* ¥6270, three hours). The JR Nichinan line runs slowly along the coast south to Aoshima and Obi.

Boat There are ferry services linking Miyazaki with Osaka (2nd class ¥8380, 12½ hours) and Kawasaki (¥12,640, 21 hours). For reservations contact **Marine Express** *(in Kyūshū ☎ 0982-55-9090, in Osaka ☎ 06-6616-4661)*.

Getting Around
Miyazaki's airport is connected to the city centre by bus (¥400, 30 minutes) or train (¥510, 10 minutes) from JR Miyazaki station.

Although most bus services start and finish at the Miyakō City bus terminal, many run along Tachibana-dōri in the centre. Only a few depart from outside Miyazaki station. There are several car rental companies around Miyazaki station and at the airport.

AROUND MIYAZAKI 宮崎周辺
Saitobaru 西都原
☎ 0983

If the *haniwa* pottery figures in Miyazaki piqued your interest in the region's archaeology, then you should head north 27km to the **Saitobaru Burial Mounds Park**, where

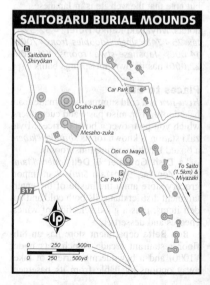

SAITOBARU BURIAL MOUNDS

several square kilometres of fields and forest are dotted with over 300 *kofun* (burial mounds). The mounds, dating from 300 to 600, range from insignificant little bumps to hillocks large enough to appear as natural creations. They also vary in shape, as do burial mounds in Korea, although Japanese scholars are reluctant to admit it.

An interesting small **museum** (*Saitobaru Shiryōkan; admission ¥200; open 9am-4.30pm Tues-Sun*) has displays about archaeological finds that have been made, including ancient swords, armour, jewellery, *haniwa* pottery figures and much more. Another exhibit showcases items from the Edo period.

The park area is always open. Buses run frequently to Saitobaru from along Tachibana-dōri in Miyazaki and also from Miyakō City bus terminal (¥1040, one hour). You'll need your own transport if you want to explore the mound-dotted countryside, or you should plan to walk a lot.

Saitobaru is just outside the town of Saito, where the unique **Usudaiko** dance festival, with drummers wearing odd pole-like headgear, takes place in early September. The equally bizarre and mysterious **Shiromi Kagura** performances are on 14 and 15 December.

TAKACHIHO 高千穂
☎ 0982 • pop 15,840

The mountain resort town of Takachiho is about midway between Nobeoka on the coast and Aso-san in the centre of Kyūshū. There's a **tourist information counter** (*☎ 72-4680; open 8.30am-5pm daily*) by the tiny train station (which was disastrously inept when we visited). Ask for the English-language *Guide to Takachiho*, also available from the stationmaster's office up the steps.

Takachiho-kyō 高千穂峡
Takachiho's beautiful gorge, with its waterfalls, overhanging rocks and sheer walls, is the town's major attraction. There's a 1km walk alongside the gorge, or you can inspect it from below in a rowboat, usually available until 4.30pm (¥1100 for 40 minutes). The gorge is about 2km from the centre. You can walk it in just over half an hour.

Takachiho-jinja 高千穂神社
Takachiho-jinja, close to the train and bus stations, is set in a grove of cryptomeria

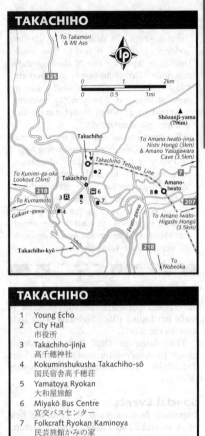

TAKACHIHO

TAKACHIHO

1	Young Echo
2	City Hall 市役所
3	Takachiho-jinja 高千穂神社
4	Kokuminshukusha Takachiho-sō 国民宿舎高千穂荘
5	Yamatoya Ryokan 大和屋旅館
6	Miyakō Bus Centre 宮交バスセンター
7	Folkcraft Ryokan Kaminoya 民芸旅館かみの家
8	Takachiho Youth Hostel 高千穂ユースホステル

pines. The local *iwato kagura* dances (see the Takachiho Legends boxed text in this section) are performed for an hour each evening from 8pm (tickets ¥500).

Amano Iwato-jinja 天岩戸神
The Iwato-gawa splits Amano Iwato-jinja into two parts. The main shrine, Nishi Hongū, is on the west bank of the river while on the east bank is Higashi Hongū, at the actual cave where the sun goddess hid and was lured out by the first performance of the *iwato kagura* dance.

A beautiful short walk from the Amano Iwato-jinja beside a picture-postcard stream takes you to the **Amano Yasugawara** cave.

Takachiho Legends

Ninigi-no-mikoto, a descendant of the sun goddess Amaterasu, is said to have made landfall in Japan on top of the legendary mountain Takachiho-yama in southern Kyūshū. Or at least that's what's said in most of Japan; in Takachiho the residents insist that it was in their hamlet that the sun goddess' grandson arrived.

Residents also lay claim to a few other important mythological events, including Amano-Iwato, or the boulder door of heaven. Here Amaterasu hid night and day fell across the world. To lure her out, another goddess performed a dance so comically lewd that the sun goddess was soon forced to emerge from hiding to find out what the merriment was about. That dance, the *iwato kagura*, is still performed in Takachiho today.

Here, it is said, the gods conferred on how they could persuade the sun goddess to leave her hiding place and thus bring light back to the world.

The shrine is 8km from Takachiho, closer to Awato-jinja station. Buses from Takachiho bus station depart hourly (¥370).

Special Events

Important *iwato kagura* festivals are held on or around 2 and 3 May, 21 to 23 September and 3 November at the Amano Iwato-jinja. There are also all-night performances in farmhouses from the end of November to early February and a visit can be arranged by inquiring at the shrine.

Places to Stay & Eat

Takachiho has three dozen hotels, ryokan, *minshuku* and pensions. Every place in town can be booked out during peak holiday periods.

Takachiho Youth Hostel (*☎/fax 72-3021; beds ¥2700*) is 2km from the centre, near Amano-Iwato station.

Folkcraft Ryokan Kaminoya (*☎ 72-2111, fax 72-5040; rooms with 2 meals from ¥9500*) is just downhill from the bus station, right in the centre of Takachiho.

Yamatoya Ryokan (*☎ 72-2243, fax 72-6868; rooms per person with 2 meals from*

¥8000) is easy to recognise by the masked *kagura* dancer painted on the front.

Many visitors just eat at their ryokan or *minshuku*, but Takachiho has plenty of restaurants, including a preponderance of *yakitori-ya* where you can order *kappo-zake*, local sake heated in bamboo stalks.

Young Echo (*dishes from ¥500; open 8am-11pm daily*) coffee shop functions like a second waiting room for the train station. Its mod furnishings are beyond comfortable. The outdoor summer **beer garden** stays open until 2am.

Getting There & Around

The private Takachiho-tetsudō train line runs inland from Nobeoka on the coast (¥1470, 1¼ hours).

From Takachiho bus station, a 10-minute walk downhill from the train station, there are buses to Takamori (¥1280, 70 minutes, three daily), near Aso-san, and Kumamoto (¥2300, 2¾ hours).

Although you can walk to the gorge and Takachiho-jinja, the other sites are some distance from town and public transport is a problem. Regular tours leave from the bus station: the 'A Course' (¥1660) covers everything, while the 'B Course' (¥1150) misses Amano Iwato-jinja.

Ōita-ken 大分県

Ōita-ken offers Japanese *onsen* mania, Beppu and the town of Yufuin. The region also bears some traces of Japan's earliest civilisations, particularly on the Kunisaki Peninsula.

USUKI 臼杵
☎ 0982

About 5km from Usuki is a collection of some superb 10th- to 13th-century **Buddha images** (*admission ¥550; open 8.30am-sunset daily*). More than 60 images lie in a series of niches in a ravine. Some are complete statues, whereas others have only the heads remaining, but many are in wonderful condition, even with paintwork still intact. The **Dainichi Buddha head** is the most impressive and important. There are various other stone Buddha images at sites around Ōita-ken, but the Usuki images are the most numerous and most interesting.

Usuki also has some interesting temples and well-preserved traditional houses. On the last Saturday in August, the town hosts a **fire festival**, and there are other festivities throughout the year. Ask for details at the **tourist information office** (☎ 65-3300; open 8.30am-5pm daily). Local restaurants boast the best *fugu* (blowfish) in Japan; expect to pay ¥3000 to ¥5000 for dinner.

The town of Usuki is about 40km southeast of Beppu. Take the JR Nippō line to Usuki station (*futsū*, ¥1430, 85 minutes), from where it's a short bus ride to the ravine site. Alternatively, you could walk the few kilometres from Kami-Usuki station.

BEPPU 別府
☎ 0977 • pop 126,500

At first glance, Beppu seems to be the Las Vegas of spa resort towns, a place where bad taste is almost a requisite. The secret, just as in Las Vegas, is to enjoy the kitsch and have a good time – and then get down to the serious business of bathing, with a sand bath to rival Ibusuki's and, hidden around the city, several wonderful springs that tourists have yet to discover.

Orientation & Information

Beppu is a sprawling town and the hot-spring areas are spread out, often some distance from the town centre. The adjacent town of Ōita is virtually contiguous with Beppu, although it lacks any notable attractions.

In the northeast corner of JR Beppu station, housed in a department store specialising in tourist goodies, is the **Foreign Tourist Information Office** (☎ 23-1119; open 9am-5pm daily). The helpful English-speaking personnel have assembled an arsenal of English-language information on Beppu and its environs, and will happily recommend accommodation, itineraries and more.

Ōita International Centre (☎ 097-538-5161; open 9am-5pm Mon-Fri, 9am-12.30pm Sat) is a local resource for foreigners in Ōita city. To get there walk straight out from JR Ōita station for about 20 minutes to the Shinkawa intersection.

Back in Beppu, the **Kitahama post office** near the **Cosmopia shopping centre** has an ATM accepting international cards. The **Ōita Bank** next door handles foreign exchange services.

Hot Springs

Beppu has two types of hot springs, and they pump out more than 100 million litres of hot water every day. *Jigoku* (hells) are hot springs for looking at. *Onsen* are hot springs for bathing in.

The Hells Beppu's most hyped attraction is the 'hells' or *jigoku*, a collection of hot springs (open 8am-5pm daily) where the water bubbles forth from underground, often with unusual results. Admission to each hell costs ¥400 (a ¥2000 coupon covers all except one). Unless you like overflowing car parks and psychotically enthusiastic flag-waving tour guides, you won't want to see them all.

The hells are in two groups – seven at Kannawa, over 4km northwest of Beppu station, and two more several kilometres away. In the Kannawa group, **Umi Jigoku** (Sea Hell), with its large expanse of gently steaming blue water, and **Shiraike Jigoku** (White Pond Hell) may be worth a look. **Kinryū Jigoku** (Golden Dragon Hell) and **Kamado Jigoku** (Oven Hell) have dragon and demon figures overlooking the pond. Skip the **Oni-yama Jigoku** (Devil's Mountain Hell), where crocodiles are kept in miserably cramped concrete pens, and **Yama Jigoku** (Mountain Hell), where a variety of animals are kept under shamefully bad conditions.

The smaller pair has **Chi-no-ike Jigoku** (Blood Pool Hell), with its photogenically red water, and **Tatsumaki Jigoku** (Waterspout Hell), where a geyser performs regularly. The former is worth a visit, but the latter can be skipped (too much concrete, too little natural beauty). The final hell, and the one not included in the group's admission ticket, is **Bōzu Jigoku** (Monk's Hell). It has a collection of hiccupping and belching hot-mud pools up the long hill from the main group of hells.

From the bus stop at JR Beppu station, bus Nos 16 and 17 go to the main group of hells at Kannawa. There are half a dozen buses an hour but the round trip costs virtually the same as an unlimited travel day pass. The No 26 bus continues to the smaller Chi-no-ike/Tatsumaki pair and returns to the station in a loop. Bus No 41 and 43 go directly to Bōzu Jigoku.

Jigoku tour buses regularly depart from the JR Beppu station (¥4500, including admission).

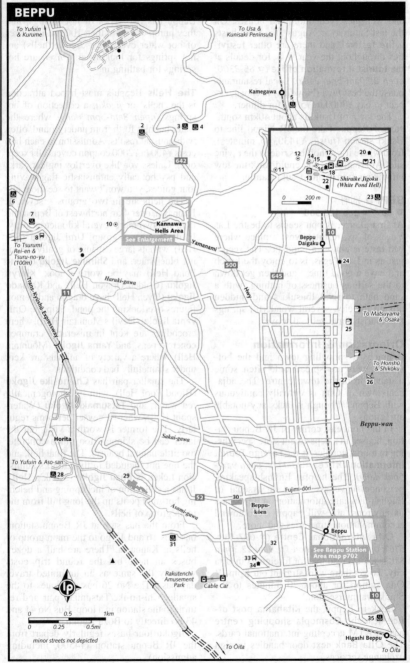

BEPPU

BEPPU

PLACES TO STAY

16 Hotel Ashiya
ホテルあしや

17 Rakuraku-en Ryokan
楽々園旅館

20 Minshuku Sakae-ya
民宿サカエヤ

22 Ōishi Hotel
大石ホテル

34 Beppu Youth Hostel
別府ユースホステル

OTHER

1 Ritsumeikan Asia-Pacific
University
立命館アジア太平洋大学

2 Shibaseki Onsen Area
柴石温泉

3 Chi-no-ike Jigoku
(Blood Pool Hell)
血の池地獄

4 Tatsumaki Jigoku
(Waterspout Hell)
竜巻地獄

5 Kamegawa Onsen Area
亀川温泉

6 Myōban Onsen Area
明礬温泉

7 Onsen Hoyōland
温泉保養ランド

8 Tsurumi Rei-en Bus Stop
鶴見霊園バス停

9 Bōzu Jigoku
坊主地獄

10 Umi Jigoku (Sea Hell)
海地獄

11 Yama Jigoku (Mountain Hell)
山地獄

12 Kamado Jigoku
(Oven Hell)
かまど地獄

13 Hihōkan Sex Museum
別府秘宝館

14 Oni-yama Jigoku
(Devil's Mountain Hell)
鬼山地獄

15 Kinryū Jigoku
(Golden Dragon Hell)
金龍地獄

18 Kamenoi Bus Station
(Buses to Chi-no-ike Jigoku)
亀の井バスターミナル
(至血の池地獄)

19 Kamenoi Bus Station
(Buses to Beppu Station)
亀の井バスターミナル
(至別府駅)

21 Post Office
郵便局

23 Hyōtan Onsen
ひょうたん温泉

24 Shōnin-ga-hama
Sand Bath
上人ヶ浜

25 Harbour Terminal
ハーバーターミナル

26 SS Oriana

27 Main Post
Office
中央郵便局

28 Mugen-no-sato
夢幻の里

29 Suginoi Palace
杉乃井パレス

30 B-Con Plaza
ビーコンプラザ

31 Ichinoide Kaikan

32 Baseball Stadium
野球場

33 Yakyū-jō-mae
Bus Stop
野球場前バス亭

35 Hamawaki Onsen
Area
浜脇温泉

Onsen The Hells, though mildly interesting, shouldn't distract you from the *real* hot springs. Scattered around the town are eight *onsen* areas. *Onsen* enthusiasts spend their time in Beppu moving from one bath to another – experts consider at least three baths a day 'de rigeur'. Costs range from ¥60 to ¥600, though many (and two of the best) are free. Bring your own soap and towel. There's an *onsen* festival during the first weekend in April.

Near JR Beppu station, **Takegawara Onsen** *(admission ¥100, sand bath ¥780; open 6.30am-10.30pm daily, sand bath 8am-9.30pm daily)* dates from the Meiji era and has a relaxing sand bath where no *yukata* is necessary. You lie down in a shallow trench and are buried up to your neck in heated sand. There's a good English-language pamphlet.

North of the town, in the **Kannawa onsen area**, near the major group of hells, is the quaint **Mushi-yu steam bath** *(admission ¥150; open 6.30am-8pm daily)*. **Hyōtan Onsen** *(admission ¥700; open 8am-9pm daily)* has a *rotemburo* and also offers sand baths *(yukata rental ¥200)*. Many ryokan and *minshuku* also have public baths.

Newly rebuilt **Shibaseki onsen** is near the smaller pair of hells. In addition to its communal baths *(admission ¥210; open 7am-8pm daily)*, you can rent a private *kazoku-buro* (family bath/couples bath) for ¥1310 (one hour). Also north of JR Beppu station is the **Kamegawa onsen area**. The **Shōnin-ga-hama sand bath** *(admission ¥780; open 8.30am-5pm daily, weather permitting)* is 2km south of the Kamegawa *onsen* area, on the beach.

In the hills northwest of the town centre is the **Myōban onsen area**. Nearby, **Onsen Hoyōland** *(admission ¥1050; open 9am-7.30pm daily)* has wonderful giant mud baths, as well as mixed and open-air bathing. In the southeastern part of town, almost on the road to Ōita, is the **Hamawaki onsen area**.

Hidden Baths

Tsuru-no-yu & Hebi-no-yu Beppu has a number of wonderful baths, tucked away out of the public eye. Locals built and maintain Tsuru-no-yu, a lovely free *rotemburo* up on the edge of Ogi-yama. During July and August, a natural stream emerges to form the milky blue bath. Take a

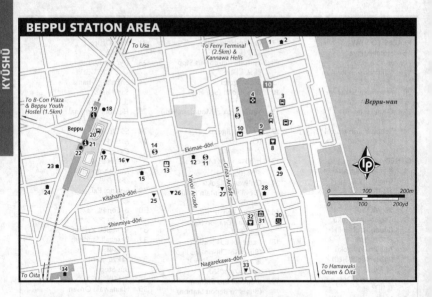

BEPPU STATION AREA

bus to Tsurumi Rei-en bus stop (40 minutes northwest from Beppu station). Turn left by the small flower shop and hike uphill till you come to the cemetery. Walk up the small road that hugs the right side of the graveyard until the road ends. Dive into the bushes to your left, and there's the bath. Higher in the mountain greenery is another free *rotemburo*, the 'Snake Bath', Hebi-no-yu. It's impossible to describe the trail up from Tsuru-no-yu; ask another bather.

Mugen-no-Sato This is a collection of privately available small *rotemburo* – ideal for a romantic, secluded dip. Ask for a **kazoku-buro** *(admission ¥600; open 9am-10pm daily)*. Take a bus up past Suginoi Palace Hotel to Horita. Mugen-no-sato is five minutes' walk west.

Ichinoide Kaikan This must be a first – a bath in a *bentō* shop! The owner of **Ichinoide Kaikan** *(☎ 21-4728)* is a commercial caterer, but he's also an *onsen* fanatic, so much so that he built three pool-sized *rotemburo* in his back yard. You can swim lengths, and the view, overlooking Beppu and the bay, is the city's finest. Bathing is free when you order a *bentō* (¥1000). The chefs prepare it while you swim. To get there, take a bus to Yakyū-jō-mae, walk 100m further along the main road until you reach the Joyful 24-hour

restaurant. Take the narrow road on the right of the restaurant and walk up, and up…and up, for about thirty minutes. A taxi (about ¥1000) might be a good investment.

Hihōkan Sex Museum 別府秘宝館
Given all that sybaritic bathing, a sex museum *(admission ¥1000; open 9am-10pm daily)* seems just the thing for Beppu. It's in among the Kannawa hells. Inside you'll find a bizarre collection ranging from 'positions' models and illustrations to a large collection of wooden phalluses (some very large indeed). Erotic art on display ranges from Papua New Guinean fertility figures to Tibetan Tantric figures. As you exit through a sex shop, the sales ladies (not one of them under 70) rather disconcertingly peddle the latest in vibrator technology.

Other Attractions
Near Takegawara Onsen, the **Hirano Library** *(admission free; open daily)* is a private institution with historical exhibits and photographs of the Beppu area.

The hands-on **Traditional Bamboo Crafts Centre** *(☎ 23-1072)* displays masterpieces dating from the Edo period. From Beppu station, take Kamenoi bus No 1, 22 or 25 to Minami-baru.

The Kyoto-based **Ritsumeikan Asia-Pacific University** *(☎ 78-1114)* has opened

BEPPU STATION AREA

PLACES TO STAY	OTHER	
2 Takenoi Hotel 竹の井ホテル	1 Beppu Tower 別府タワー	11 Fukuoka City Bank 福岡シティ銀行
12 Ekimae Kōtō Onsen 駅前こうとう温泉	3 Kamenoi Bus Station (Sightseeing Buses) 亀の井バスセンター	13 Bluebird Cinema シネマブルーバード
15 Minshuku Kokage 民宿こかげ	4 Cosmopia Shopping	14 Iyo Bank 伊予銀行
23 Business Hotel Star	Centre; Tokiwa	17 Family Mart
24 Business Hotel Kagetsu ビジネスホテル花月	Department Store コスモピア	18 Car Rental Office 駅レンタカー
28 Nogami Honkan 野上本館	5 Ōita Bank 大分銀行	19 Foreign Tourist Information Office 外国人旅行者観光案内所
34 Kamenoi Hotel 亀の井ホテル	6 Airport Bus Stop 空港バス停	20 Beppu Station Bus Stop 別府駅バス停
PLACES TO EAT	7 Kitahama Bus Station (Sightseeing Buses & Buses to Fukuoka) 北浜バスセンター	21 Tourist Information Counter 観光案内所
16 Jūtoku-ya 十徳屋	8 Robata & Beer Pub	22 Daie ダイエイ
25 Ureshi-ya うれしや	9 Bus Stop for Kannawa Onsen	29 JTB
26 Kuishinbō くいしん坊	鉄輪温泉行きバス亭	30 Takegawara Onsen 竹瓦温泉
27 Natsume Kissa なつめ喫茶	10 Kitahama Post Office	31 Hirano Library
33 Shingai Coffee Shop	別府北浜郵便局	32 Speakeasy

its landmark college in Beppu, with about half its undergraduates drawn from other parts of Asia – a unique situation in Japan. The campus overlooks the city in Jumonji-baru, a 35-minute bus trip from Beppu station.

Places to Stay
Beppu's most basic accommodation is found at **Ekimae Kōtō Onsen** (☎ 21-0541; *shared/private tatami rooms per person from ¥1500/2500*), a bathhouse close to the station. Shared rooms are male-only.

Beppu Youth Hostel (☎ 23-4116; *beds ¥3000*) is only a 15-minute walk from JR Beppu station. It has its own small hot-springs bath.

Minshuku Kokage (☎ 23-1753, fax 23-3895; *singles/doubles/triples with bath ¥4000/7000/10,500*), a member of the Japanese Inn group, is just a few minutes' walk from Beppu station. There's a hot-springs bath downstairs.

Business Hotel Star (☎ 25-1188; *singles/doubles ¥4000/7000*), behind the station, has very basic rooms. **Business Hotel Kagetsu** (☎ 24-2355; *rooms per person ¥3500*), a slightly down-at-heel *minshuku*, is around the corner.

Nogami Honkan (☎ 22-1334; *rooms per person with/without 2 meals ¥8000/4500*) is located near Takegawara *onsen*, and has

a *rotemburo*. English is spoken and there's free Internet access.

Kamenoi Hotel (☎ 22-3301, fax 21-1232; *singles/doubles/twins from ¥5800/8800/9800*) is far more comfortable than the average business hotel and has good-value restaurants, a *rotemburo* and sauna.

Takenoi Hotel (☎ 23-3261, fax 25-3800; *doubles from ¥12,500*) is a lavish traditional-looking hotel, down near Beppu Tower and the beach.

There are a number of *minshuku* and ryokan around Kannawa hot springs.

Rakuraku-en Ryokan (☎ 67-2682; *rooms per person with 2 meals ¥7500*) has a mixed and a women-only *rotemburo*.

Minshuku Sakae-ya (☎ 66-6234; *rooms per person with 2 meals ¥6500*) is downhill from the *jigoku*. This popular traditional *minshuku* uses the heat from the local hot spring to prepare meals.

Places to Eat
Beppu is renowned for its freshwater fish, for its *fugu* (globefish) and for the wild vegetables grown in the mountains further inland. Also look out for *dango-jiru*, a miso soup with vegetables and dumplings. **Fugu Matsu** (*open 11am-9pm daily*) is the place to try *fugu* in style, if you're game. Expect to pay from ¥3000.

Jūtoku-ya *(open daily) izakaya* is close to the station and has an enormous range of dishes on its illustrated menu, all at reasonable prices. The area around Min-shuku Kokage also has some cheap *yakitori* restaurants.

Ureshi-ya *(open 5.30pm-2am Sat-Thur)* is a very popular *shokudō* (budget eatery) with *donburi* and noodles for around ¥700. Fresh vegetable and meat dishes are displayed in the window.

Kuishinbō *(dishes from ¥600; open 5pm-midnight daily)* is a cheerful *izakaya* serving unusual tofu and *daikon* steaks, and *chawan-mushi* custard.

Entertainment
Speakeasy *(☎ 21-8116; open 8.30pm-3am Wed-Mon)*, a friendly shot-bar down a back alley near Takegawara *onsen*, is where Beppu's cool crowd hang out. Beers and stronger stuff cost from ¥500. **Robata & Beer Pub** *(open 5pm-11.30pm daily)* has a flashing neon fish sign.

Beppu hides some one-of-a-kind coffee shops in the central shopping arcades. **Natsume Kissa** makes its own mellow *onsen kōhī* (¥500), coffee made with hot-springs water. **Shingai Coffee Shop** *(open daily)* displays antique maps and photographs.

West of the station towards Suginoi Palace, the enormous **B-Con Plaza**, a convention centre marked by the 125m Global Tower, is the place for concerts and mega-events.

Getting There & Away
There are flights to Ōita airport from Tokyo (¥27,000), Osaka (¥16,000), Okinawa (¥24,500) and cities around Kyūshū. It's even possible to fly direct to Seoul.

Beppu to Aso-san takes about three hours by bus and costs around ¥4000 (note the exact routing affects the price). It's another hour from Aso-san to Kumamoto.

The JR Nippō line runs from Hakata (Fukuoka) to Beppu (*tokkyū* ¥5250, 2¼ hours) via Kitakyūshū, continuing down the coast to Miyazaki (¥5770, 2½ hours). The JR Hōhi line connects Beppu with Kumamoto (¥5330, three hours) via Aso-san (¥3940, 1½ hours).

Boat The **Kansai Kisen ferry service** *(☎ 22-1311)* does a daily run between Beppu and Osaka (¥7400, 13½ hours), stopping en route at Matsuyama (4½ hours) and Kōbe (10 hours). Late evening boats to western Honshū pass through the Inland Sea during daylight hours the next morning. For the port, take Bus No 19 from Beppu station's west exit.

Getting Around
To/From the Airport Hovercraft (☎ 097-558-7180, 0120-81-4080) run from JR Ōita station to Ōita airport (¥2750, 25 minutes), located around the bay from Beppu on the Kunisaki peninsula.

From Beppu, airport buses from Beppu stop outside the Cosmopia shopping centre (¥1450, 45 minutes, twice hourly) and sometimes also JR Beppu station.

Bus There are few local bus companies, of which **Kamenoi** *(☎ 23-5170)* is the largest. Most buses are numbered. An unlimited 'My Beppu Free' travel pass for Kamenoi buses comes in two varieties: the 'mini pass' (¥900), which covers all the local attractions, including the hells; and the 'wide pass' (¥1600/2400 for one/two days), which goes further afield to Yufuin. Passes are available from near the foreign tourist information office and at various lodgings around town.

YUFUIN 湯布院
☎ 0977 • pop 11,407
About 25km inland from Beppu, beautiful and quietly rustic Yufuin has suffered in the last few years from tourist development. It's still very much worth a stop en route to Aso, but avoid weekends and holidays.

The **tourist information office** *(☎ 84-2446; open 9am-7pm daily Sept-July, 9am-8pm daily Aug)* inside the train station has English-language information in English, including an excellent detailed map showing galleries, museums and *onsen*. Make sure you change money in Beppu, as there's no place to do it readily in Yufuin.

As in Beppu, making a pilgrimage from one *onsen* to another is a popular activity in Yufuin. **Shitan-yu** *(admission ¥100; open 10am-5pm daily)* is a thatched bathhouse on the northern shore of Kirin-ko, a lake fed by hot springs, so it's warm(ish) all year round. Yufuin is noted for its high-quality handicrafts. The town also has a few interesting temples and shrines.

Udo-jingū, Miyazaki-ken, Kyūshū

Fishing boats, Shimabara, Kyūshū

Shrine, Takachiho-no-mine summit, Kyūshū

Kōmyōzen-ji, Dazaifu, Kyūshū

Hot springs, Beppu, Kyūshū

The double-peaked, 1584m **Yufu-dake** volcano overlooks Yufuin and takes about one hour to climb. A few buses between Beppu and Yufuin stop at the trailhead, Yufudake-tozan-guchi.

Places to Stay & Eat

Yufuin has many *minshuku*, ryokan and pensions; most are high-class, with rates to match.

Yufuin Youth Hostel (☎ 84-3734; beds ¥3100) is almost 2.5km northeast of the train station. This peaceful hostel is set on a forested hillside with breathtaking views, but buses to the nearby Kuso-no-mori stop are infrequent.

Pension Yufuin (☎ 85-3311; B&B rooms from ¥7000), a popular 'rural Western' guesthouse fantasy, is on the riverside. The very hospitable owner does her best to speak English.

Makiba-no-yado (☎ 84-2138, fax 85-4045; rooms per person with 2 meals ¥8000-13,000) offers accommodation in a series of thatched-roof huts around its large open-air *rotemburo*. The garden restaurant, filled with antiques, does bear and wild-boar *teishoku* (around ¥1800)!

Getting There & Away

Local trains on the JR Kyūdai line connect Ōita with Yufuin (¥910, one hour). Only limited express trains originate in Beppu.

Buses depart JR Beppu station for Yufuin every few hours (¥900). Continuing beyond Yufuin is not always easy. Buses go to Aso and Kumamoto but not year round. There are also direct buses to Fukuoka (¥2800).

YUFUIN TO ASO-SAN

The picturesque Yamanami Hwy extends 63km from the Aso-san region to near Yufuin; from there, the Ōita Expressway runs to Beppu on the east coast. There's a steep toll to drive along this scenic road, however, and tour buses operating between Kumamoto, Aso and Beppu also use this route. The road crosses a high plateau and passes numerous mountain peaks, including **Kujū-san** (1787m), the highest point in Kyūshū.

Taketa 竹田

South of Yufuin, near the town of Taketa, are the **Oka-jō ruins**, which have a truly magnificent ridge-top position. The ruins are over 2km from JR Bungo-Taketa station. Taketa has some interesting reminders of the Christian period, as well as some atmospheric temples and well-preserved traditional houses. **Hanamizuki Onsen** (admission ¥500; open 9am-8.30pm daily) is a short walk from the station. It sells lemonade and liquor made from local citrus varieties, including *kabosu* and *yuzu*.

From Aso-san, it takes just under an hour by train on the JR Hōhi line to Bungo-Taketa (*futsū* ¥820); from there it's just over an hour by train to Ōita (¥1250) – a little longer by bus.

KUNISAKI PENINSULA 国東半島

Immediately north of Beppu, Kunisaki-hantō bulges eastwards from the Kyūshū coast. The region is noted for its early Buddhist influence, including some rock-carved images related to more famous images at Usuki.

Usa 宇佐

In the early post-WWII era, when 'Made in Japan' was no recommendation at all, it's said that companies would register in Usa so they could proclaim that their goods were 'Made in USA'! **Usa-jinja** (admission ¥300), the original of which dates back over 1000 years, is connected with the warrior-god Hachiman, a favourite deity of Japan's right wing. It's a 10-minute bus ride from Usa station on the JR Nippō line from Beppu (*tokkyū* ¥1880, 35 minutes).

Other Attractions

The Kunisaki Peninsula is said to have more than half of all the stone Buddhas in Japan. The 11th-century **Fuki-ji** (admission ¥300) in Bungotakada is the oldest wooden structure in Kyūshū and one of the oldest wooden temples in Japan. Ōita Kōtsū buses from Usa station go to Fuki-ji (¥770, 30 minutes).

Right in the centre of the peninsula, near the summit of Futago-san, is **Futago-ji** (admission ¥200), dedicated to Fudō-Myō-o, the ferocious, fire-enshrouded, sword-wielding deity who ensures all good Buddhists learn their Scriptures. It's difficult to get there by public transport.

Carved into a cliff behind Taizo-ji, 2km south of **Maki Ōdō** temple, are two

8th-century Buddha images; a 6m-high figure of the Dainichi Buddha and an 8m-high figure of Fudō-Myō-o. These are known as the **Kumano Magaibutsu** and are the largest Buddhist images of this type in Japan. Other stone statues, thought to be from the Heian period, can be seen in Maki Ōdō. You can get there via the bus to Fuki-ji from Usa station (¥1000, 70 minutes).

Getting Around

Beppu's Ōita airport is on the peninsula, about 40km from Beppu. Ōita Kōtsū buses from Usa station do a loop around the main attractions of the peninsula, with tour buses departing from either Beppu or Ōita (reservations ☎ 097-534-7455). Otherwise try **Eki Rent-a-Car** (☎ 0977-24-4428) outside JR Beppu station.

Okinawa & the Southwest Islands 沖縄・南西諸島

The Nansei-shotō, or Southwest Islands, usually referred to collectively as 'Okinawa', meander for more than 1000km from the southern tip of Kyūshū to Yonaguni-jima, a little over 100km from the east coast of Taiwan.

Okinawa-hontō, the ancient Ryūkyū capital, is the hub of the island chain and its key role as tragic battleground in the closing months of WWII holds a continuing fascination for visitors. But for natural beauty and insights into Okinawan culture, head for the *rito* (outer islands). Iheya-jima and Izena-jima, are famous for their unspoilt beauty; Taketomi-jima is a tiny island with a picture-postcard village; and rugged Iriomote-jima is cloaked in dense tropical jungle.

Despite centuries of mainland exploitation, the horrific destruction during the closing months of WWII and, more recently, the increasing number of tourists, many of the traditional ways of these islands live on. A tropical climate, some pristine beaches, excellent snorkelling and diving, and traces of the old Ryūkyū kingdom are all star attractions.

But don't think of these islands as forgotten backwaters with a mere handful of visitors – both All Nippon Airlines (ANA) and Japan Airlines (JAL) fly tourists to Okinawa from 'mainland' Japan by the 747-load, and even the local flights from Okinawa to other islands in the chain are by 737.

SUGGESTED ITINERARIES

Except when travelling to Yakushima, which is best approached from Kagoshima (southern Kyūshū), most visitors use Naha as a point of arrival in Okinawa-ken. From here you can briefly explore Okinawa-hontō before heading to the outer islands.

Time permitting, one popular route is to take the ferry south from Naha via Miyako-jima to the Yaeyama-shotō, where you can make jaunts from Ishigaki-jima over to Taketomi-jima, Iriomote-jima and other beautiful islands. From Ishigaki there are

Highlights

- Trek to the millennia-old giant cedar trees and revered mountain peaks of Yakushima
- Visit Shuri-jō, near Naha, a beautifully executed re-creation of the traditional seat of Ryūkyū power
- Dive off Ishigaki-jima and its sun-drenched neighbouring islands, offering pristine beaches and lazy cycling trails
- Explore Iriomote-jima, Japan's only pocket of jungle wilderness, on foot or by kayak

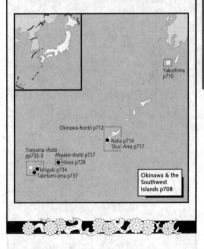

Yakushima p710

Okinawa-hontō p712
Naha p714
Shuri Area p717

Yaeyama-shotō pp732-3
Miyako-shotō p727
Hirara p728
Ishigaki p734
Taketomi-jima p737

Okinawa & the Southwest Islands p708

regular flights back to Naha and, for a price, even direct to Tokyo.

WHEN TO GO

The climate of the Nansei-shotō is much warmer than mainland Japan, and Okinawa is virtually a tropical getaway. Although the winter months (November to March) are somewhat cooler, they are considered the best season to travel, since crowds are smaller, accommodation is less expensive and underwater visibility for divers is at its best. May and June can bring heavy rain, July to August is not only very hot but also very crowded, and September to October is the typhoon season.

707

OKINAWA & THE SOUTHWEST ISLANDS

KYŪSHŪ

PACIFIC OCEAN

KAGOSHIMA

Tanegashima   ŌSUMI-SHOTŌ

Kuro-shima

Kuchino-
Erabu-jima   Yakushima

Kuchino-shima
Nakano-shima
Gaja-jima   Suanose-jima   TOKARA-
SHOTŌ
Taira-shima   Akuseki-jima

Takara-jima   Kikai-jima
KAGOSHIMA-KEN

Naze   Amami-
Ōshima

Kakeroma-jima
Yoro-shima   Uke-jima
AMAMI-SHOTŌ

Tokuno-shima
EAST   Yokoate-jima
CHINA
SEA   Okino-Erabu-jima

Yoron-tō

Iheya-jima
Izena-jima
OKINAWA-   Nago
SHOTŌ   Ie-jima
Okinawa City   Okinawa-
hontō
Aguni-jima   NAHA
Zamami-jima   Tokashiki-
jima
Kume-jima   Kerama-rettō
OKINAWA-KEN   Tonaki-shima

| 0 | 100 | 200km |
| 0 | 50 | 100mi |

Hirara
MIYAKO-   Miyako-jima
SHOTŌ   Irabu-jima
Shimoji-jima
Tarama-jima
YAEYAMA-
SHOTŌ   Ishigaki-jima
Ishigaki   Taketomi-jima
Iriomote-jima   Kuro-shima
Kohama-jima
Yonaguni-jima   Hateruma-jima

HISTORY

The islands of the Nansei-shotō chain, like stepping stones between Japan and Taiwan, have long been a bridge between Japanese and Chinese culture. For centuries, the islands formed a border zone of trade squeezed between Chinese and Japanese suzerainty, which often placed unfortunate residents of the islands under pressure from both sides.

For centuries the islands were ruled by *anji* (local chieftains), who battled for control of small fiefdoms and built *gusuku* (castles) of which so many ruins can be seen today.

In 1372, the Chūzan king of the middle kingdom on Okinawa-hontō initiated tributes to the Chinese court, a practice that was quickly matched by his northern and southern rivals and was to continue for 500 years. In the 15th century, the island was united under the rule of the Shō dynasty and the capital of the Ryūkyū kingdom shifted from Urasoe to Shuri, where it was to remain until the early years of the Meiji Restoration (1868–1912).

The period from 1477 to 1525 is remembered as a golden age of Okinawan history. Spurred by an influx of Chinese culture brought across the seas by ambassadors from the emperor at Peking, Okinawan classical music and dance, literature, ceramics and other arts flourished. Under Chinese sanction, Okinawan trading power reached into the far corners of Asia, bringing wealth to an archipelago poor in natural resources.

By the 17th century, however, Japanese power was on the ascendancy. Okinawans found themselves under a new ruler when the Satsuma kingdom of southern Kyūshū invaded in 1609. From this time the islands were controlled with an iron fist and taxed and exploited greedily. In 1879 the islands were formally made a Japanese prefecture under Meiji rule. Treated as foreign subjects by the Japanese emperor just as they had been by the Satsuma regime, Okinawans were subsequently pushed to become 'real' Japanese, as their native language and elements of traditional Ryūkyūan culture were forbidden.

Okinawan islanders paid a heavy price for their new citizenship in the closing stages of WWII, when they were trapped between the relentless US hammer and the fanatically resistant Japanese anvil.

Okinawan Cuisine

One of the real treats of visiting the southern islands is all the fine cuisine. The exceptionally long average life-span of the Okinawan people may in fact be attributed to their balanced diet, with an abundance of healthy *konbu* (kelp) imported from Hokkaidō.

As well as an abundance of fresh produce and seafood, prize beefsteak cows are raised in Okinawa. Pork is also widely enjoyed, particularly in *sōki soba*, bowls of hot noodles with thick slices of tender marinated pork. *Rafute* (pork stewed in ginger, brown sugar, *shōyu* and *awamori*) is a dish once served at the Ryūkyū court.

Thick Okinawan *soba* is justifiably famous, in particular the local varieties found in the Miyako and Yaeyama island groups. Another must-try Okinawan dish is *champuru*, a mixed stir-fry that can be made with a variety of ingredients such as *goya* (bitter melon), *fū* (gluten), papaya, etc. For those with strong stomachs, look for stamina-inducing *hījā-jiru* (goat soup) or chewy *mimigā* (pig's ears, sliced and marinated in vinegar).

If you fancy spirits, *awamori*, the local firewater made from rice, has an alcohol content of 30% to 60%. A tonic version even comes with a small habu snake coiled in the bottom of the bottle.

US bombing started in October 1944. On 1 April 1945, US troops landed on the island. The Japanese made an all-out stand. It took 82 horrendous days for the island to be captured. Not until 23 June was the conquest complete, by which time 12,500 US soldiers and an estimated quarter of a million Japanese had died.

Almost half of the Japanese casualties were Okinawan civilians. There are terrible tales of mass suicides by leaping from clifftops, often after coercion by Japanese military personnel. Other civilians became caught in the crossfire when Japanese soldiers evicted them from the limestone caves and family tombs in which they had taken refuge.

The Japanese commanders committed seppuku (ritual suicide), but a final horror remained. The underground naval headquarters were so well hidden they were not discovered until three weeks after the US victory. The underground corridors contained the bodies of 4000 naval officers and men, all of whom had committed suicide.

Okinawa-hontō became a major US military base during the Cold War, and today a strong US military presence persists on the island.

GETTING THERE & AROUND

There are numerous flights and ferry services to Naha, the main city on Okinawa-hontō, from Kagoshima at the southern tip of Kyūshū and also from many other cities on the Japanese mainland, including Tokyo.

When discounts airfares are available, flying direct may be just as cheap as taking the slow boat.

There are connecting flights and ferries between many of the islands in the Nansei-shotō. Ferry schedules are particularly vulnerable to change; check before you plan to use these services. Around most of the islands, rental bicycles, motor scooters, motorcycles and cars are available. Advance reservations are usually only necessary for cars.

Ōsumi-shotō
大隈諸島

The northernmost island group of the Nansei-shotō, less than 100km from Kagoshima, is the Ōsumi-shotō. The two main islands are Yakushima, an extraordinary nature-lovers' paradise, and Tanegashima, known for its surf and Japan's rocket-launch facility.

YAKUSHIMA 屋久島
☎ 09974

Just 25km in diameter, Yakushima is one of Japan's most remarkable travel destinations, justifiably designated a Unesco World Heritage site (Japan's first) in 1993.

Over 75% of the island is covered with thickly forested mountains. Yakushima's towering terrain catches every inbound rain cloud, giving the island one of the wettest climates in Japan. While the high peaks

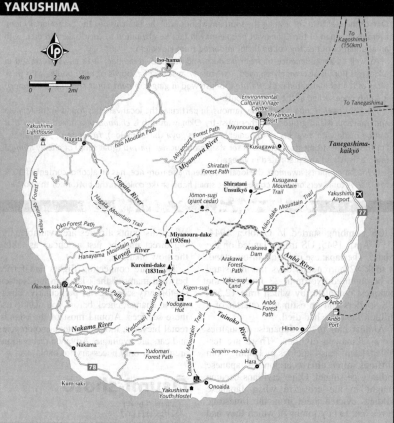

YAKUSHIMA

are snowcapped in winter, the flat land around the coastline remains subtropical. Its beaches are favoured as nesting grounds by sea turtles.

Yakushima is the farthest place north that mangroves grow in Japan. Other indigenous plants have been utilised by herbologists for centuries; in fact, the old kanji (Chinese characters) for Yakushima meant 'Medicine Island.' Plants still harvested for digestive medicines include *gajutsu*, a type of native ginger.

Orientation & Information

Miyanoura, on the northeast coast, is the main port. A road runs around the perimeter of the island, passing through the hotsprings town of Onoaida in the south.

On the west coast the road narrows to just one paved lane, taking an hour to drive through the jungle (there's no bus service here). Watch out for monkeys and falling rocks.

Both ferry terminals have **information desks** (*Miyanoura* ☎ 2-1019, *Anbō* ☎ 6-2333) that can help find accommodation and sell topographic hiking maps.

In Miyanoura, the **Environmental Cultural Village Centre** (☎ 2-2900; *museum admission & film ¥500; open 9am-5pm Tues-Sun*) is at the corner of the ferry-terminal road. It has a worthwhile little museum with bilingual exhibits about the island's natural history and traditions. Subtitles are available upon request in several foreign languages for screenings of an inspiring 25-

minute IMAX film. Staff at the centre can also recommend guided ecotour operators around the island, charging around ¥15,000 for full-day outings, which may include kayaking, snorkelling and diving.

Activities
The island offers superb hiking through ancient forests of giant *yaku-sugi (Cryptomeria japonica)*, a local cedar species. Choose from a day-long outing to the 1935m summit of **Miyanoura-dake**, the highest point in southern Japan, or to the 2600-year-old cedar tree, **Jōmon-sugi**. For the latter, allow at least five hours return from the trailhead, Arakawa-tozan-guchi. Alternatively, plan a two- or three-day trek across several mountain peaks. For the complete scoop on the island's hikes, pick up a copy of Lonely Planet's *Hiking in Japan*.

Yaku-sugi Land (*admission ¥300; open 9am-5pm daily*) offers shorter hiking courses over wooden boardwalks, and longer treks deep into the millennia-old cedar forest. Its 80-minute hiking course passes by the 1800-year-old **Buddha Cedar**. The preserve is a 30-minute drive inland from Anbō. **Kigen-sugi**, another giant cedar tree, is 6km further up the road. There are also a few waterfalls and beaches around the island. **Isso-hama** is a short but lovely stretch of white sand, good for swimming and sunsets. On the northern side of the island, **Shiratani Gorge** also has hiking paths into the ancient cedar forest.

Places to Stay & Eat
There is **camping** along the coast, as well as in the highland interior, plus an established system of mountain huts along the summit trail.

Yakushima Youth Hostel (*☎ 7-3751, fax 7-2477; beds with/without two meals ¥4400/2800*) is an impeccably run mountain lodge. Bicycles can be rented for trips to nearby waterfalls and hot springs. It's a short walk south of the Yahata-shōgakkō-mae bus stop.

Tabitoyado Chinryū-an (*☎/fax 7-3900; e chinryu@sa.uno.ne.jp; rooms per person with/without two meals ¥5630/3980*) is a woodsy place in Onoaida. The friendly young couple here speak English well, and can provide information on hiking and other attractions on the island.

Shiki-no-yado Onoaida (*☎ 7-3377; rooms per person with 2 meals ¥7000*) is another Onoaida inn with mountain views.

There are plenty of *minshuku*, ryokan and *pension* in the port towns of Miyanoura and Anbō. Rates start at ¥6000 per person with two meals. **Lodge Yaedake-yamasō** (*☎ 2-2552*) offers Japanese-style rooms in riverside cabins, all connected by wooden walkways, and its own hot-springs bath.

Forum Cafe (*lunch ¥600-1000; open 9am-4pm Tues-Sun*), inside the Environmental Cultural Village Centre, serves generously sized seafood salads, pasta and noodle dishes.

Getting There & Around
Japan Air System (JAS) affiliated flights connect Kagoshima with the two main islands, but most visitors prefer the scenic ferry route to Miyanoura (¥5200, 3¾ hours, once daily). **Toppy** (*☎ 099-255-7888*) speedboats from Kagoshima go to Miyanoura and Anbō (¥7000, 1½ hours). Keep in mind that these jet foils stop running at the slightest hint of inclement weather.

Local buses travel the coastal road partway around Yakushima roughly every hour, but a scant few go into the island's interior. Between March and November, a bus departs Miyanoura around 5am and goes to Arakawa-tozan-guchi (¥1380, 90 minutes), returning around 5pm. Other buses go to Shiratani gorge at 9am and 1pm (¥530, 40 minutes), with the last return bus at 2.40pm.

Okinawa-hontō
沖縄本島

☎ 098
Okinawa-hontō is the largest island in the Nansei-shotō. Its cultural differences with mainland Japan were once most evident in its architecture, of which almost all traces were obliterated in WWII.

The USA retained control of Okinawa after the war, handing it back to Japan in 1972 only after widespread Okinawan protests over continuing civil rights violations by the occupying forces. Okinawa still has the biggest US military base in Japan, with 50,000 military and civilian personnel and dependents.

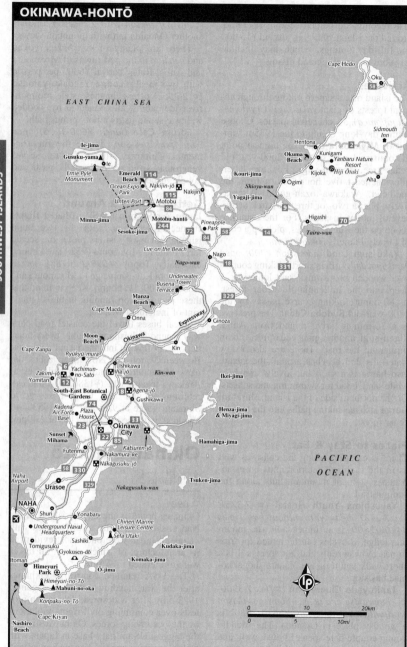

OKINAWA-HONTŌ

EAST CHINA SEA

Cape Hedo

Oku
58

Sidmouth
Inn

Ie-jima
Gusuku-yama
Ernie Pyle
Monument
Ie

Hentona

Okuma
Beach

Kunigami
Yanbaru Nature
Resort
Hiji Ōtaki

2

Emerald
Beach
114

Ocean Expo
Park

Nakijin-jō
115

Nakijin

Kouri-jima

Kijoka

Aha

Unten Port

Motobu
84

Minna-jima

Motobu-hantō
244

Sesoko-jima

72

Pineapple
Park

84
58

Shioya-wan
Yagaji-jima

Ōgimi

9

Higashi

14

Taira-wan

70

Lue on the Beach

Nago-wan

Nago

18

331

Underwater
Tower
Busena
Terrace

329

Manza
Beach

Cape Maeda

Onna

Expressway

Ginoza

Moon
Beach

Okinawa

Cape Zanpa

Ryūkyū-mura

Kin

Kin-wan

Ikei-jima

Zakimi-jō
Yomitan

6
12

Yachimun-
no-Sato

Ishikawa
Iha-jō

75

South-East Botanical
Gardens

74

8

Agena-jō
Gushikawa

Henza-jima
& Miyagi-jima

Kadena
Air Force
Base

Plaza
House

23

33

Okinawa
City

Hamahiga-jima

Sunset
Mihama

22

85

Katsuren-jō

PACIFIC
OCEAN

Futenma

Nakamura-ke
Nakagusuku-jō

58
330

Naha
Airport

329

Urasoe

Nakagusuku-wan

Tsuken-jima

NAHA

Shuri

Yonabaru

Underground Naval
Headquarters

Chinen Marine
Leisure Centre
Seta Utaki

Tomigusuku

Sashiki

Gyokusen-dō

Kudaka-jima

Itoman

Himeyuri
Park

Ō-jima

Komaka-jima

Himeyuri-no-Tō
Mabuni-no-oka

Konpaku-no-Tō

Cape Kiyan

Nashiro
Beach

0   10   20km
0   5   10mi

The American Problem

Okinawa-hontō is tiny, amounting to just 0.6% of Japan's total landmass. It is curious then that 75% of the nation's US military bases should be crowded onto the island. Military bases occupy over 20% of Okinawa's land, and have a heavy hand in sustaining the local economy.

Okinawan resentment at being a de facto US colony came to a head in September 1995, when three US soldiers abducted a 12-year-old girl, drove her to a field in a rented car and raped her. Sentencing of the soldiers to jail terms of seven years was widely seen as inadequate and did little to quell public anger. A protest rally in October 1995 drew a crowd of 85,000 people. US promises to return some 20% of military-owned land were received with weak enthusiasm when the USA refused to lower the number of troops stationed on Okinawa.

Okinawan anger is directed not just at the USA but also at 'mainland' Japan, which many Okinawans claim habitually deals out losing hands to the Ryūkyū islanders. Some islanders wonder whether greater autonomy, or even complete independence, isn't the best way forward.

The issue of US bases has perhaps hastened a political awakening in a part of Japan that many see as experiencing a 'renaissance'. Okinawan music has made inroads into the Japanese pop music industry, and many younger Japanese are moving to Okinawa, where they find life is more relaxed and relationships more intimate. It is with new-found confidence that Okinawans are asking the central government in Tokyo to share some of the burden if the US bases are to remain in Japan.

OKINAWA & SOUTHWEST ISLANDS

Twenty-six years of US occupation did an effective job of wiping out what remained of the old Okinawan ways, but for good measure the Japanese transformed the island into a major tourist resort. A day spent around Naha is all you need to cover the major sights. War memorials are clustered in the south of the island, while the central area has ruins and a few cultural attractions. If you're keen on snorkelling and diving, head straight to the Motobu Peninsula and its beautiful off-shore islands. The farther north you go, the more rural things become.

NAHA 那覇

☎ 098 • pop 316,000

Naha, the capital of Okinawa, was flattened in WWII and little remains of the old Ryūkyū culture.

Today the city is chiefly a gateway to other places. Kokusai-dōri (International Blvd), Naha's colourful, energetic main drag, is 1.6 kilometres of hotels, souvenir shops, restaurants and bars. A short distance east is Shuri, the erstwhile Okinawan capital and the site of renovated ruins.

Information

For information and news in English, you can quickly get your fill of the US forces radio on 648 kHz AM – the homegrown ads are amazingly awful.

Keep an eye out for the weekly *Japan Update* (w www.japanupdate.com). Though targeted mainly at US military personnel, this English-language newspaper is excellent for covering local events. Also check out the Okinawa Tourism & Convention Bureau's website (w www.ocvb.or.jp).

The city **tourist information office** (☎ 868-4887; Kokusai-dōri; open 8.30am-8pm Mon-Fri, 10am-8pm Sat & Sun) has free maps and staff speak some English. The **airport information desk** (☎ 857-6884; open 9am-9pm daily) can help book accommodation and provide maps.

Most **postal savings ATMs** around Naha, including on Kokusai-dōri and at the airport, accept internationally issued cards on major networks like VISA or Cirrus. Several banks handle foreign currency exchange, but usually only on weekdays.

Net Cafe (Kokusai-dōri; open 10am-midnight daily) charges ¥480 for the first hour of Internet access, including free soft drinks and snacks.

There are heaps of travel agencies around Kokusai-dōri. **Nice Ticket** (☎ 866-8988; open 10am-7pm Mon-Fri, 10am-5pm Sat) sells discounted airline tickets.

Central Naha 那覇中心街

Kokusai-dōri makes a colourful walk, day or night. Turning south opposite Mitsukoshi

NAHA

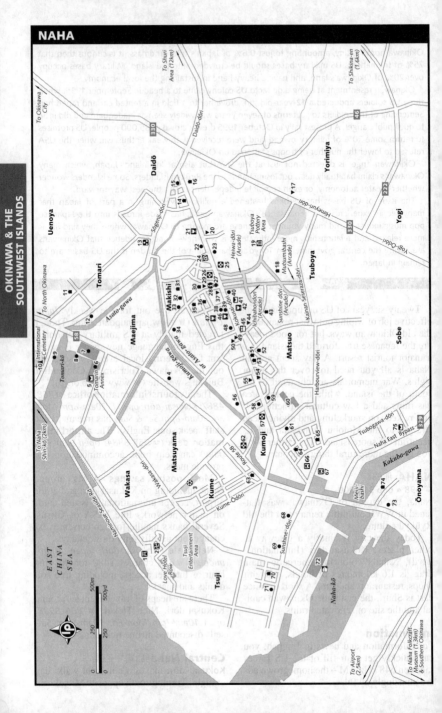

To Shuri Area (12km)

To Okinawa City

To Shikina-en (1.6km)

Daidō-dōri

Daidō

Yorimiya

Yogi

Uenoya

Sōgenji-dōri

Himeyun-dōri

Tsuboya Pottery Area

Heiwa-dōri (Arcade)

Matsumibashi (Arcade)

Tsuboya

Tomari

Makishi

Maejima

Asato-gawa

Kumoji-gawa or Asato-gawa

International Cemetery

Tomari-kō

Tomari Annex

EAST CHINA SEA

To Naha Shin-kō (2km)

Numinoue Seaside Rd

Matsuyama

Wakasa

Kume-Ōdōri

Kume

Matsuo

Sunshine-dōri (Arcade)

Kainan Sekerza-dōri

Ichibahondori

Kokusai-dōri

Sobe

Harbourview-dōri

Kumoji

Route 58

Tsubogawa-dōri

Naha East Bypass

Kokuba-gawa

Ōnoyama

Meiji-bashi

Tsuji Entertainment Area

Love Hotel Row

Tsuji

Sunshine-dōri

Naha-kō

To Airport (2.5km)

To Naha Folkcraft Museum (1.3km) & Southern Okinawa

NAHA

PLACES TO STAY
11 Harumi Youth Hostel
    晴海荘ユースホステル
14 Hotel Seibu Orion
    ホテル西武オリオン
16 Capsule Inn Okinawa
    キャプセルイン沖縄
18 Domitory Okinawa
    ドミトリー沖縄
30 Business Hotel Sankyō
    サンキョービジネスホテル
31 Narumi Ryokan
    なるみ旅館
32 Community House; Straw
    Bale Cafe
    ストロベールカフェ
35 Moonlight Guesthouse
    月光荘
36 Taetake Guesthouse; Smile
    Guesthouse
    タエ竹ゲストハウス；
    スマイルの宿
43 Shinkinichi Ryokan; African
    Pub Baobab
    新金一旅館；バオバブ
51 Hotel Kokusai Plaza
    ホテル国際プラザ
52 Naha Grand Hotel
    那覇グランドホテル
53 Hotel New Okinawa
    ホテルニュー沖縄
63 Okinawa Oceanview Hotel
    沖縄オーシャンビューホテル
64 Business Hotel Yagi
    ホテルやぎ
65 Hotel Route Inn Izumizaki
    ホテルルートイン泉崎
70 Okinawa Guesthouse
    沖縄ゲストハウス
74 Okinawa International Youth
    Hostel
    沖縄国際ユースホステル

PLACES TO EAT
17 McDonald's
20 Rawhide
    ローハイド
29 Modem
    モデム
37 Sams Maui
    サムズマウイ
44 About Cafe; Ukushima
49 Ryūkyū Kissakan
    琉球喫茶館

50 Teida
    ていだ
54 Wa-no-Ichi
    和の市
55 Café Fish Pool
    カフェフィッシュプール

OTHER
1   Naminoue-gū
    波上宮
2   Gokoku-ji
    護国寺
3   Fukushū-en
    福州園
4   Nissan Rent-a-Car
    日産レンタカー
5   Post Office
    郵便局
6   Primart Supermarket
    プリマート
7   Tomarin (Ferry Ticket
    Offices)
    トマリン
8   Ferry to Zamami-jima &
    Aka-jima
9   Speedboats to Zamami-jima
    & Aka-jima
10 Commodore Perry
    Memorial; International
    Cemetery
    ペルリ提督上陸記念碑
12 Family Mart
13 Sōgen-ji Gates
    崇元寺石門
15 Orion Rent-a-Car
    オリオンレンタカー
19 Tsuboya Pottery Museum
    壺屋焼物博物館
21 Kams Jazz; Soul Brothers
    Club
    カムズ；ソウルブラザーズ
    クラブ
22 Kudaka
    久田カ
23 Rock in Okinawa
    ロックインオキナワ
24 Net Cafe; Mr Donuts
    ネットカフェ；ミスタドーナッツ
25 Kokusai Shopping Center
    国際ショッピングセンター
26 Mitsukoshi Department
    Store; Naha Tower; Zavares
    三越百貨店；那覇タワー
27 Starbuck's

28 City Tourist Information
    Office
    観光案内所
33 Nice Ticket
    ナイスチケット
34 Daie
    ダイエ
38 Earthnic
    アースニック
39 Seattle's Best Coffee
40 OPA; Tower Records;
    Club Cran Berry Double
    オパ
41 Post Office; Tacos-ya
    郵便局；タコス屋
42 Be-Green
45 Kokueikan Cinema
    国映館
46 Helios Craft Beer Pub
47 Bagues
    バグースくりものバー
48 Chakura
    チャクラ
56 JAL
    日本航空
57 Ryū Bō; Palette Kumoji
    デパトリュウボウ；パレット
    くもじ
58 JAS
    日本エアシステム
59 Best Denki Building; Club
    Cielo
    ベスト電器ビル
60 Okinawa Prefectural Office
    沖縄県庁
61 Naha City Office
    那覇市役所
62 ANA
    全日空
66 Bus Station
    那覇バスターミナル
67 Bus Stop
    バス亭
68 Japaren Rent-a-Car
    (AVIS)
    ジャパレンレンタカー
69 Nippon Rent-a-Car
    ニッポンレンタカー
71 Lawson's
72 Ferry Terminal Building
73 OTS Rent-a-Car
75 Main Post Office
    中央郵便局

department stores leads you down **Heiwa-dōri** shopping arcade, which has the distinct flavour of an Asian market.

If you take the left fork at the first major junction, a short walk beyond the shopping arcade brings you to the **Tsuboya pottery area**. Over a dozen traditional potteries still

operate in this compact neighbourhood, a centre of ceramic production since 1682, when Ryūkyūan kilns were consolidated here by royal decree. Most shops sell all the same popular Okinawan ceramics, such as *shiisā* (lion roof guardians) and containers for serving *awamori*, the local firewater.

The **Tsuboya Pottery Museum** (*Tsuboya-yakimono Hakubutsukan; admission ¥315; open 10am-5.30pm Tues-Sun*) contains some masterpieces. Although there is no English labelling, you can inspect potters' wheels and appreciate *arayachi* (unglazed) and *jōyachi* (glazed) pieces displayed inside a model of a traditional Okinawan house.

At the eastern end of Kokusai-dōri, a right turn takes you towards Shuri, while turning left eventually brings you to the reconstructed gates of **Sōgen-ji**. The original stone gates once led to the 16th-century temple of the Ryūkyū kings, but, like almost everything else in Naha, it was destroyed in WWII.

Much farther along, almost at the waterfront, is the **Commodore Perry Memorial** commemorating Perry's landing in Naha. The US naval officer subsequently used Okinawa as a base while he forced the Tokugawa shōgunate to finally open Japanese ports to the West in 1853.

The **Tsuji entertainment area**, once a brothel quarter, now features ubiquitous clubs and bars, a collection of love hotels and US-style steakhouses. As Japanese red-light areas go, it's decidedly lacking in atmosphere. The hilltop shrine **Naminoue-gū**, Buddhist temple **Gokoku-ji** and Confucian shrine **Kōshi-byō** overlook the sea, but the buildings are unexceptional modern reconstructions.

Garden fans should take a stroll through Chinese-style **Fukushū-en** (*admission free; open 9am-6pm Thur-Tues*). All materials were brought from Fuzhou, Naha's sister city in China, including the pagoda that sits atop a small waterfall.

Shuri Area 首里

Prior to the Meiji Restoration, Shuri was the capital of Okinawa (that title was surrendered to Naha in 1879). Shuri's temples, shrines, tombs and castle were all destroyed in WWII, although some impressive reconstructions and repairs have been made.

Several buses from Kokusai-dōri and Naha bus terminal run to Shurijō-kōen-iriguchi, the entrance to the park containing most of what's left of the old Ryūkyū royal capital. Bus No 1, 12, 13, 14 and 17 (¥200) are all convenient.

Shurijō-kōen The reconstructed old residence of the Okinawan royal family, **Shuri-jō**

(*admission ¥800; open 9am-5.30pm daily Mar-Nov, 9am-5pm daily Dec-Feb*), invites comparison to China's Forbidden City, although admittedly on a much smaller scale.

The original castle was destroyed during the WWII Battle of Okinawa. Reconstruction has been carried out with meticulous attention to detail. Inside are several worthwhile exhibition halls, with historical displays and royal treasures. Classical court dances are occasionally held.

The castle's walls have numerous gates of minor interest. The pick is the Chinese-influenced **Shurei-no-mon**, which appears on Japan's ¥2000 bank note. As the ceremonial entrance to the castle, the gate was originally constructed some 500 years ago, then rebuilt after the war in 1958. It's considered to be *the* symbol of Okinawa, so there's a constant stream of tour groups and school parties lining up to be photographed in front of it. Women in traditional Okinawan costume stand ready to make guest appearances in the photos, for a suitable fee.

The nearby **Sumuikan** (*admission free*) complex has interesting historical exhibits and an Okinawan restaurant.

There are a couple of temples on the park grounds, but don't expect too much. **Bezaiten-dō**, in the middle of a pond, was first destroyed in the early 17th century, then rebuilt again after WWII. Across the road are the rather bedraggled remnants of **Enkaku-ji**. This temple dates from 1492, but it too was destroyed in the Battle of Okinawa. All that remains is the outer gate, a bridge (note the masterful stone carvings) leading over a lotus pond, and steps beyond the pond leading to the main gate.

The wartime destruction also did not spare **Tama-udun** (*admission ¥200; open 9am-5.30pm daily*). These 16th-century royal tombs have recently been restored. Traditionally, bodies were first placed in the central chamber. When the flesh had decayed, the bones were removed, cleaned and permanently interred: kings and queens to the left, princes and princesses to the right.

Other Attractions The displays in the **Okinawa Prefectural Museum** (*admission ¥200; open 9am-6.30pm daily*) are connected with Okinawan lifestyle and culture and include exhibits on the Battle of Okinawa and a large model of Shuri-jō.

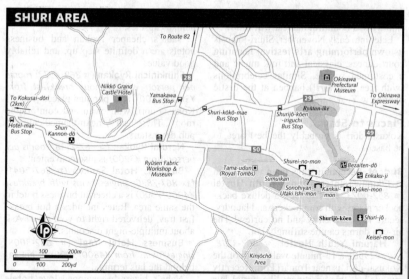

SHURI AREA

To Route 82

Nikkō Grand
Castle Hotel

To Kokusai-dōri
(2km)

Yamakawa
Bus Stop

Okinawa
Prefectural
Museum

To Okinawa
Expressway

Hotel-mae
Bus Stop

Shuri
Kannon-dō

Shuri-kōkō-mae
Bus Stop

Shurijō-kōen
-iriguchi
Bus Stop

Ryūtan-ike

Ryūsen Fabric
Workshop &
Museum

Tama-udun
(Royal Tombs)

Sumuikan

Shurei-no-mon

Bezaiten-dō

Enkaku-ji

Sonohiyan
Utaki Ishi-mon

Kankai-
mon

Kyūkei-mon

Shurijō-kōen

Shuri-jō

Keisei-mon

Kinjōchō
Area

0   100   200m
0   100   200yd

OKINAWA &
SOUTHWEST ISLANDS

Ryūtan-ike, across the road, was built in 1427 and was used for dragon-boat races.

There are a number of factories in the Shuri area producing traditional *bingata* (stencil-dyed) fabrics. The **Ryūsen Fabric Workshop & Museum** *(admission free; open 9am-6pm daily)* specialises in *ryūsen*, an expensive material similar to *bingata*. Upstairs are simple weaving displays and authentic-looking Okinawan props from an NHK television drama.

At one time, **Kinjōchō-no-Ishidatami-michi**, a 15th-century stone street, ran for 10km to Naha port. Now there's just one stretch of a couple of hundred metres, plus a few side lanes, but the steep and narrow path, with its old stone walls and ornate gateways, is very picturesque.

AROUND NAHA 那覇周辺
Shikina-en 四季名園

This garden *(admission ¥300; open 9am-5pm Thur-Tues)* contains stone bridges, a Chinese-style viewing pavilion and a villa that belonged to the Ryūkyū royal family. Everything had to be painstakingly rebuilt following WWII. Its extensive collection of native plants almost qualifies it as a botanical garden.

From Naha bus terminal, take bus No 1 or 5 to the Shikinaen-mae stop (¥200, 20 minutes).

Naha Folkcraft Museum
那覇市伝統工芸間

Often overrun by Japanese tour groups, this small museum *(Naha-shi Dentō-kōgeikan; admission ¥300; open 9am-5.30pm Wed-Mon)* has an exquisite collection of traditional Okinawan crafts. Staff are on hand to demonstrate glass-blowing, weaving and pottery-making in the workshops.

From the stop opposite Naha bus terminal, take Itoman-bound bus No 89 to the Kukōzō-mae stop (¥200, 10 minutes), which is a short walk from the museum.

Special Events

Naha is a festive city. Most famous are Okinawa's version of summer Obon dances, called Eisa.

Dragon-boat races are held in early May, particularly in Itoman and Naha. With Chinese origins dating back several centuries, these races – called *hari* – bless the luck and prosperity of fishing families.

In October, the **Dai-Ryūkyū Matsuri** brings together over a dozen festivals and special events celebrating Okinawan culture. The Tsunahiki festival takes place in various locations around the island, notably in Naha on the 10th, when huge teams compete in a tug-of-war using a gigantic 1m-thick rope weighing over 40 tons. The two halves of the rope symbolise male and female parts, and traditionally if the female side wins, a bountiful harvest will follow.

Later into early November, Shuri-jō hosts its own **performing arts festival** featuring court dances, classical and folk music and a costumed parade. Similar celebrations (with free *awamori*!) happen at the castle over New Year's.

Places to Stay

Kokusai-dōri is probably the best area to be based.

Budget Reception stays open until 11pm at **Okinawa International Youth Hostel** (☎ 857-0073; beds ¥3150), a deluxe backpacker resort with coin lockers and laundry, secure key-card entry and no curfew! The air-con dorms can be stiflingly hot.

Harumi Youth Hostel (☎ 867-3218; beds ¥2950), a 15-minute walk north of the Kokusai-dōri, is near Tomari Port. Recently remodelled, this apartment-like hostel lets guests borrow bicycles for free.

Budget guesthouses are cheap as dirt, but many are practically falling apart. A few good ones offer amenities like air-con or Internet access.

Okinawa Guesthouse (☎ 090-9782-9696; beds ¥1500) is within walking distance of Naha port, and has plenty of alternative characters hanging out.

Dormitory Okinawa (☎ 090-9780-1935; beds ¥1500) is in the busier Tsuboya area. From the Kainan bus stop, walk up Sunrise-dōri arcade, turn right into the small lane between Okinawa Bank and an optometry shop, and look for the dormitory on the right.

Many, many other guesthouses are signposted off Kokusai-dōri.

Community House (☎ 867-9999; dorm beds ¥2200, rooms per person ¥3500) is another bohemian crash pad. Check-in and complimentary breakfast are at the vegetarian-friendly **Earthnic** café, located a few blocks away.

Taetake Guest House (☎ 090-1947-5064; singles/doubles ¥2000/3500), **Smile Guest House** (☎ 090-7150-1745) and **Moonlight Guest House** (☎ 862-5328) charge ¥1500 per dorm bed. All offer weekly and monthly discounts.

Capsule Inn Okinawa (☎ 867-6017; 2nd floor, Urban Kohatsu Bldg; standard/deluxe capsules ¥3300/4300) is at the far end of Kokusai-dōri. Women only pay ¥3500 for deluxe capsules.

Naha's cheaper ryokan and business hotels are a definite step up, and reliably good value.

Shinkinichi Ryokan (☎ 869-4973; rooms per person with/without breakfast from ¥3600/3000) is a popular place, just off Kokusai-dōri, with clean and comfortable rooms. There's an African-themed café and pub downstairs.

Narumi Ryokan (☎ 867-2138; rooms per person from ¥3200) is also convenient.

Business Hotel Sankyō (☎ 867-5041, fax 867-7826; singles/twins with breakfast ¥4000/7500) is a cheerful business hotel in the same area. Rates includes a hot breakfast tray, delivered right to your door! Ask about multiple-night discounts.

Business Hotel Yagi (☎ 862-3008; singles/twins from ¥4800/9000) is not far behind the bus terminal.

Naha's bizarrely-fashioned **love hotels** (overnight from ¥4200) are found running parallel to the waterfront road in the old entertainment district.

Mid-Range & Top End A fairly new place, **Hotel Route Inn Izumizaki** (☎ 860-8311, fax 860-8010; singles/doubles ¥6500/11,500) is convenient to the bus station.

Hotel Kokusai Plaza (☎ 862-4243; singles/twins ¥6000/9600) and **Hotel New Okinawa** (☎ 867-7200; singles/twins from ¥6000/9800) are two old stand-bys on Kokusai-dōri. **Naha Grand Hotel** (☎ 862-6161; singles/doubles from ¥6500/10,000) is quieter.

Hotel Seibu Orion (☎ 866-5533, fax 862-9039; e seibu@ryukyu.ne.jp; singles/twins from ¥8500/12,000) is a luxury oasis at the north end of Kokusai-dōri.

Okinawa Oceanview Hotel (☎ 853-2112, fax 862-6112; singles/twins from ¥9700/14,000) is a very posh high-rise hotel, close to the bus station and ferry terminals.

Places to Eat

The thing to do if you're a Japanese tourist in Naha is dine out on steak and seafood. **Rawhide** and **Sam's Maui** on Kokusai-dōri are long runners, where chefs prepare grill items made to order, right in front of you at your table. Set meals start from under ¥3000.

If you're on a budget, try browsing along the shopping arcade **Heiwa-dōri**, where you can buy anything from fresh seafood to *andagi* (Okinawan deep-fried doughnuts) to unique local citrus. **Mitsukoshi** department store has a basement food market with takeaway. Keep an eye out for fuchsia-coloured dragonfruit at the fresh juice bar.

Tacos-ya *(items from ¥150)* is a tiny place that puts an Okinawan twist on Mexican food: deep-fried tacos! Surprisingly, they're pretty tasty, and come with fresh salsa.

Modem *(dishes ¥350-600)* is a streetfront food stall serving Okinawa *soba* (buckwheat noodles) and *okonomiyaki* (cabbage pancakes). After dark, a hip crowd shows up for cheap beers and conversation.

Wa-no-Ichi *(open 11am-midnight daily; dishes ¥300-1000)* is a rustic-looking *izakaya* (Japanese-style pub) with a fantastic selection of Okinawan dishes and an artfully illustrated English menu. You shouldn't mind the long queue, especially when there's live music almost nightly. *Awamori* by the glass costs ¥210.

Teida *(dishes from ¥500)*, an Okinawan *izakaya*, whips up superb vegetable *soba* and various other traditional specialities.

Ryūkyū Kissakan *(drinks ¥500, dishes from ¥800)* is a soothing café, full of rustic pottery and antiques and serving Okinawan *bukubuku-cha* (frothy tea) and coffee.

Ukushima *(dishes ¥350-550; open 6pm-3am daily)* is where Okinawan cuisine gets funky, with anything from *goya* (bitter gourd) chips to *hirayāchi* (Okinawan-style *okonomiyaki*). Look for the starlight terrace up on the third floor behind the cinema.

Café Fish Pool *(lunch ¥750-950, dinner mains ¥800-2000; open 11.30am-11pm daily)* is a bright and trendy 2nd-storey Italian bistro. Seafood is a specialty, and there's decadent caramel-and-chocolate-chip gelato for dessert.

Entertainment

Day or night, a stroll along bustling Kokusai-dōri should be enough to keep anybody entertained. It seems every little side street harbours a couple of hidden-away drinking spots. Most are friendly, but due to the overwhelming US military presence don't be surprised to find certain bars and clubs unwelcoming to *gaijin* (foreigners).

Rock in Okinawa *(☎ 861-6394; cover ¥500-1500)* is one place you won't have a problem entering. Its posted schedule of live events covers everything from Okinawan pop to hard rock to reggae and ska.

Chakura *(☎ 869-0283; cover ¥3000; open 7pm-1am daily)* is a celebrated 'live house' run by local music maverick Kina Shōkichi. Kina-san and his band, Champloose, perform here nightly (when not touring) starting at 8pm.

Soul Brothers Club *(cover around ¥500)* may not attract many of true African descent, but for Motown music look no further. There's a sign announcing 'Black Harlem' outside the 6th floor. **Kam's Jazz** *(☎ 863-3651; cover around ¥1000)* has excellent live acts downstairs.

Helios Craft Beer Pub *(open 11.30am-11pm daily)* serves commendable microbrews and light food. Try the sampler: four beer shots for ¥700. **About Cafe** *(open 8pm daily)* is just one among dozens of nearby ¥500 food-and-drink bars to choose from.

Bagues *(open 7pm daily)*, an Indonesian-style reggae bar, has carved-wood furniture and flickering candles. **African Pub Baobab** is worth finding in the backstreets off Kokusai-dōri. It's downstairs in the same building as Shinkinichi Ryokan.

Dance clubs wax and wane in popularity. When we were in town, red-hot **Be-Green** *(cover ¥1500-2500)* was one of a few subterranean dance spots. Otherwise look for flyers at the **OPA** building on Kokusai-dōri, which has a **Tower Records** *(6th floor)* and its own **Club Cran Berry Double** *(7th floor; open 9pm-midnight daily)*.

Jun Plaza, another shopping complex, often has DJ events at **Zavares** *(6th floor)* and at **Club Cafe Air** *(5th floor; cover ¥1500-3000; open 9pm-midnight)*, which might spin anything from house or trance to hip-hop and R&B.

Club Cielo *(☎ 861-9955; 6th floor, Best Denki Bldg; cover ¥1500-2500)* is a posh penthouse club, with an enforceable dress code to match.

Shopping

Okinawa is renowned for its colourful Ryūkyū glassware, a relatively modern folk art that originated after WWII by recycling soda pop and juice bottles used by US occupation forces.

OKINAWA & SOUTHWEST ISLANDS

Okinawa also has its own distinctive textiles, particularly the brightly coloured *bingata* and *ryūsen* fabrics made in Shuri. Other fabrics include Bashōfu, plaid Kasuri and Tsumugi silks from Kume-jima.

Much of the Tsuboya pottery is in the form of storage vessels, but look for *shiisā*, the guardian lion-figures that can be seen perched on the rooftops of many traditional Okinawan buildings.

Kudaka (☎ 861-6690; open 10am-10pm daily) stands out among the bargain-basement souvenir shops among Kokusai-dōri. Its carefully chosen wares are all high quality, including unique ceramics, textiles and jewellery. Look for its emblem, a white *shiisā* on a blood-red circle background.

Getting There & Away

Air There are direct flights to Okinawa from Seoul, Hong Kong, Shanghai and Taiwan. Connections to the Japanese mainland include Kagoshima (¥21,000), Nagasaki (¥23,000) and Fukuoka/Hakata (¥28,500), as well as Osaka (¥29,100), and Tokyo (¥25,700).

Boat Various operators have ferry services to Naha from Tokyo, Nagoya, Osaka, Kōbe, Kagoshima and other ports. The schedules are complex (and subject to weather delays), and there is a wide variety of fares. In general, spending an extra ¥500 or ¥1000 for a Western-style berth guarantees more comfort and privacy than a 2nd-class tatami-mat room. Be sure to bring enough food with you.

There are three ports in Naha, and this can be confusing. From Naha Port (Naha-kō), ferries head north to Fukuoka/Hakata and Kagoshima, while Naha New Port (Naha Shin-kō) has ferries to Nagoya, Kōbe, Osaka and Tokyo. Ferries to Miyako-jima and Ishigaki-jima may depart from either place. Meanwhile from Tomari Port (Tomari-kō) on Route 58, ferries operate to a number of the smaller islands around Okinawa-hontō, including Zamami-jima and Aka-jima.

Arimura Sangyō (☎ 869-1980) operates a weekly ferry service that runs between Naha New Port and Taiwan (2nd class ¥18,000, 22 hours), stopping at Miyako-jima and Ishigaki-jima only on the outbound journey.

Getting Around

To/From the Airport Naha Airport is only 3km from the town centre. If traffic isn't snarled, it takes 15 minutes by taxi (¥1500) or slightly longer by bus (¥200).

Bus Nos 13, 120, 124 and 125 from the airport stop at Naha bus terminal before heading along Kokusai-dōri.

To/From the Ferry Terminals For Naha port (Naha-kō), walk for 15 minutes from Naha bus terminal or take a taxi (¥450).

Dozens of city buses along Route 58 pass by Tomari Port (Tomari-kō). Bus No 101 from Naha bus terminal heads further north to Naha New Port (Naha Shin-kō). A taxi to Kokusai-dōri from either costs around ¥550, depending on traffic.

Bus When riding on local town buses, simply dump ¥200 into the slot next to the driver as you enter. For longer trips, collect a ticket showing your starting point as you board and pay the appropriate fare as you disembark.

Buses run from Naha to destinations all over the island. There are also bus tours around the island, particularly to the war sites in the south. Try any travel agent on Kokusai-dōri.

Car & Motorcycle Okinawa-hontō is a good place to get around in a rented vehicle, although traffic can be heavy, except in the northern part of the island, which is lightly populated and also has poor public transport. Beware: road signs are not always clearly labelled.

Numerous car-rental agencies around Naha charge from around ¥5000 per day. **Orion Rent-A-Car** (☎ 867-0082, 0120-178-002), **Nippon Rent-a-Car** (☎ 868-4554), **Japaren Rent-a-Car** (☎ 861-3900) and **Toyota Rent-a-Car** (☎ 857-0100) all have branches at the airport.

Ask around at the guesthouses or youth hostels about renting bicycles, motor scooters or motorcycles.

SOUTHERN OKINAWA-HONTŌ
沖縄本島の南部
☎ 098
The area south of Naha was the scene of some of the heaviest fighting during the closing days of the Battle of Okinawa. There

Suna-yama Beach, Miyako-jima

Butterfly, Iriomote-jima, Yaeyama-shotō

Statue of the Iriomote *yamaneko* (wildcat)

Kayaking, Iriomote-jima, Yaeyama-shotō

Limestone cave, Okinawa

Ryūkūan village market, Okinawa

Replica of Shuri-jō, Shuri, Okinawa

are a number of reminders of those terrible days, as well as some other places of interest in this densely populated part of the island.

The initial US landing on Okinawa took place north of Naha at Kadena and Chatan on 1 April 1945. By 20 April, US forces had captured the northern part of the island and as far south of their landing place as Naha. The rest of the island was not captured until 21 June.

Underground Naval Headquarters 旧海軍司令部壕

Directly south of Naha in Kaigungo-kōen is the underground naval headquarters, where 4000 men committed suicide as the battle for Okinawa drew to its prolonged and bloody conclusion.

Of the **tunnels** (admission ¥420; open 8.30am-5pm daily), only 250m are open, but you can wander through the maze of corridors, see the commander's final words on the wall of his room and inspect the holes and scars in other walls from the grenade blasts that killed many of the men.

To get to Kaigungo-kōen, take bus No 33 or 46 from opposite Naha bus station to the Tomigusuku-kōen-mae stop (¥230, 20 minutes). From there it's a 10-minute walk.

Other War Sites

The ruins of Gushikawa-jō at **Cape Kiyan** are popular with hang-gliding enthusiasts, but in the closing days of the Battle of Okinawa many civilians jumped to their death from the cliffs.

On 19 June 1945 at **Himeyuri-no-Tō**, 200 Okinawan schoolgirls and their teachers who had been conscripted by Japanese troops as field nurses and trench-diggers were abruptly demobilised. After being evicted from the sheltering caves, many were killed by American bullets and gas shells, while others committed suicide in the school grounds rather than fall into the hands of the US military, whom they had been led to believe were barbarians.

Directly south on the coast is **Konpaku-no-Tō**, a memorial to 35,000 unknown victims of the fighting whose dead bodies lay neglected on the beach for months after the war ended.

At **Mabuni-no-oka**, the remaining Japanese forces were virtually pushed into the sea. In their underground hideaway the commanders committed seppuku on 23 June 1945, while above ground the US forces already had complete control of the island. Memorials from every prefecture in Japan dot the hillside. The **Cornerstone of Peace** is inscribed with the names of everyone who died in the Battle of Okinawa, controversially listing Okinawan civilians and foreign military personnel right alongside Japanese military commanders.

The **Okinawa Peace Memorial Museum** (Okinawa-ken Heiwa Kinenkan; admission ¥300; open 9am-4.30pm Tues-Sun) should not be missed. It tells the gruesome story of the 90-day 'typhoon of steel' during the American invasion. The focus is on Okinawan suffering at the hands of both the Japanese military and subsequent US occupation authorities.

Bus No 32 or 89 from opposite Naha bus terminal goes to Itoman (¥550, one hour), from where you transfer to bus No 82, which goes to Himeyuri-no-tō (¥270, 20 minutes, hourly) and the peace park, Heiwa Kinen-kōen (¥400, 25 minutes).

Other Attractions

Beyond Mabuni-no-oka, turn east on Route 76 to reach **Tomori-no-Ojishi**, where a large (1.4m high) stone shiisā overlooks a reservoir. This particular shiisā dates back to at least 1689 and is carved of coral stone; a popular image from the Battle of Okinawa shows a US soldier sheltering behind it while watching with binoculars.

Tiny **Ō-jima** is linked to the main island by bridge and has good beaches, as does **Niibaru**. The latter is popular with Japanese tourists for its glass-bottomed-boat cruises (¥1500). Bus No 53 from Naha bus station goes direct to Ōjima (¥600, one hour).

For centuries, **Sefa Utaki** (admission free; open until sunset daily) was the central shrine for Okinawan religious rites. An utaki refers to any sacred grove of trees, a reflection of Okinawans' traditional animistic beliefs. After being confirmed here, royal priestesses once went on to exercise as much secular power as the Ryūkyūan kings who were their brothers, fathers or uncles. Formerly men could only enter the shrine if they dressed in drag. The main altar lies past the sacred spring, inside a limestone cave with natural views out to sea and Kudaka-jima.

One stop farther north is **Chinen Marine Leisure Centre**, where day-trippers hire boats (¥2500 per person) to *mujin-shima* (uninhabited islands), including **Kudaka-jima** and minute **Komaka-jima**, both encircled by fine beaches.

Bus No 38 from Naha bus station passes by the leisure centre first (¥750, 1¼ hours). For the shrine, get off at Taiiku-sentā-mae and walk for five minutes up the hill behind the post office, past the teahouse.

CENTRAL OKINAWA-HONTŌ
沖縄本島の中部
☎ 098

Around this heavily populated stretch of Okinawa are an amazing number of artificial tourist attractions where many thousands of yen could be squandered on entry fees. The US military bases are principally in the southern part of central Okinawa-hontō, and the resorts are in the northern part.

Urasoe 浦添

Urasoe, 8km north of Naha, was the early capital of the Ryūkyū kingdom. Today the park, Jōseki-kōen, contains the restored 13th-century **Urasoe Yōdore** (Urasoe Royal Tombs) and the original castle ruins. Bus No 56 runs from Naha bus station to the park (¥350).

Nakagusuku-jō 中城城

In an enviable position overlooking the coast, these castle ruins *(admission ¥300; open 8.30am-5pm daily)* predated stone

Bullfighting

Battles between bulls, where one tries to push the other out of the ring (rather like *sumō* wrestling), are known as *tōgyū* in Japan. The sport is found in a long sweep of islands all the way from Indonesia to Japan. There are over a dozen *tōgyū* stadiums in Okinawa, the most important ones in Gushikawa and Okinawa City. Prominent fights are held on the second Sunday of May and November, but they take place a couple of times a month year round. The bulls for Okinawa *tōgyū* are bred on Kuro-shima, near Iriomote-jima.

construction of this type on the mainland by at least 80 years. The castle was destroyed in 1458 in a bizarre episode of feudal manoeuvring known as the Amawari Rebellion. When Gosamaru, the Nakagusuku lord, heard that Amawari, another Okinawan lord, was plotting a rebellion against the king, he mobilised his troops in the king's defence. The scheming Amawari then convinced the king that it was Gosamaru who was planning to revolt, so the hapless Nakagusuku ruler committed suicide.

To get here from Naha, take a bus to Futenma, then transfer to bus No 59. If you've got time, it's a five-minute walk from the bus stop in Futenma to **Futenma Utaki**, a shrine dating back over 500 years, which has a limestone cave holding fertility stones.

Nakamura-ke 中村家

Probably the best-preserved traditional Okinawan house on the island is Nakamura-ke *(admission ¥300; open 9am-5.30pm daily)*. The Nakamura family's origins in the area can be traced back to the 15th century, but the foundations date only from around 1720. Originally the roof would've been thatched. Notice the substantial stone pig pens, elevated storage area to deter rats and trees grown as typhoon windbreaks. It's a 10-minute walk uphill from Nakagusuku-jō; bus No 59 passes by.

OKINAWA CITY 沖縄市

Okinawa City is the US military centre on Okinawa-hontō, focused around Kadena Air Force Base. What was a village before the war has mushroomed to over 120,000 people and has all the hallmarks of US influence, from pizzerias to army surplus stores.

Tuttle Bookstore *(Plaza House mall; open 10am-7pm daily)* is the best English-language bookshop on Okinawa. A few kilometres west in Chatan, the US-style **Sunset Mihama** complex has movie theatres, family-style restaurants, shopping and bars, plus a beachfront Ferris wheel.

Attractions around Okinawa City, some decidedly artificial, are minor. **Southeast Botanical Gardens** *(Nantō Shokubutsu-surakuen; admission ¥1000; open 9am-6pm daily Mar-Oct, 9am-5pm Nov-Feb)* have hundreds of varieties of palm trees. **Moromi Folkcraft Museum** *(admission ¥300;*

open 9.30am-5.30pm daily), hidden in the backstreets off Route 330, is a fascinating repository of musty WWII-era memorabilia and Okinawan antiques.

There are buses to Okinawa City from Naha (¥800, 80 minutes).

OKINAWA CITY TO NAGO

Castle-ruin enthusiasts can visit **Iha-jō**, near Ishikawa. **Zakimi-jō** *(admission ¥200; open 9am-4.30pm Tues-Sun)* on the west coast has the oldest arched stone gates left standing in Okinawa. In Yomitan village, on the very edge of Kadena Air Force Base, **Yachimun-no-Sato** has pottery workshops and an outdoor climbing kiln.

The Okinawan resort strip starts from **Zampa Beach**. The touristy **Ryūkyū-mura** *(admission ¥840; open 8.30am-5.30pm daily)* offers another re-creation of Okinawan farming life and yet another snake park, where, for the amusement of tourists, those 'deadly' habu lose out to those plucky mongooses (see the 'Habu Snakes' boxed text). It may be worth visiting for the folkcraft demonstrations and live music and dance shows.

More beach life can be found at Moon Beach and Manza Beach. As well as the expensive resort hotels along this coast, **Cape Maeda Divers House** *(☎ 964-2497; beds ¥2000)* has dormitories inside a former youth hostel. Call for directions.

Busena Terrace *(☎ 51-1333, fax 51-1331; rooms peak/off-peak from ¥45,000/30,000)* looks as manicured as a golf course. This luxury hotel hosted the 2000 G8 summit and offers water sports and an **underwater tower** *(admission ¥1000; open 9am-6pm daily)* for viewing marine life.

Bus No 20 from Naha runs along the west coast past all these sites to Nago. It takes about one hour to get to Ryūkyū-mura, one hour and 20 minutes to get to Moon Beach and two hours to the Busena Terrace resort.

NAGO 名護

☎ 0980 • pop 55,900

Nago is about two-thirds of the way up the island. There are fine views over the town and the coast from the hilltop on the east side of town, and although very little remains of the old castle, in spring the cherry blossoms are famous.

Habu Snakes

Any discussion of the Nansei-shotō eventually gets around to 'deadly' habu snakes. Perhaps it's a reflection of Japan's severe shortage of real dangers, but you could easily get the impression that the poor habu is the world's most dangerous snake and that there's one waiting behind every tree, shrub, bush and bar stool on the islands. They're hardly so prolific – the most likely place to see one is at a mongoose-versus-habu fight put on for tourists. Nevertheless, it's probably not a good idea to go barefoot when stomping through the bushes. Do stomp though – the vibrations will scare any snakes away.

A fine old banyan tree, Himpun Gajumara, is a useful landmark in the centre of town. A few blocks north is Nago Crossroads, the main intersection. The **tourist information office** *(☎ 53-7755; open 8.30am-5.30pm Mon-Fri, 10am-5pm Sat & Sun)*, just south of the crossroads, has English-language maps and information.

You can find out all about traditional farming, fishing and Okinawan cuisine at the child-friendly **Nago Museum** *(☎ 53-1342; admission ¥150; open 10am-6pm Tues-Sun)*, south of the banyan tree, which has eye-catching snakeskin *jamisen* (three-stringed Japanese banjo) and old photographs of traditional *hejichi* (women's tattooing). Just east, **Orion Brewery** *(☎ 52-2137; open to public 9am-11am & 1pm-4pm Mon-Fri)* offers Japanese-language tours, for which advance reservations are required.

Places to Stay & Eat

Nago's accommodation isn't particularly cheap or appealing.

Yamada-sō *(☎ 52-2272)*, **Nago Business Hotel** *(☎ 54-5557)* and **Hotel Tōwa** *(☎ 52-3793)* are low-key business hotels, just southeast of the crossroads.

Hotel Yugaf Inn Okinawa *(☎ 53-0031, 0120-48-9875; singles/doubles with breakfast ¥7000/12,000)* is near the bus station. **Hotel 21st Century** *(☎ 53-2655, 0120-21-7515; singles/twins/triples ¥6000/10,000/13,500)* lies further north on Route 58.

Shinzan Shokudō *(dishes ¥500-800)* is a famous Nago *soba* shop that has been

OKINAWA & SOUTHWEST ISLANDS

running for more than 60 years. It's around the corner from Yamada-sō.

Izakaya Hottarakashi *(dishes ¥500-1000; open dinner Fri-Wed)*, a few blocks to the west, offers authentic Okinawan fare, like *hījā-jiru* and fresh seafood.

Entertainment

Nago's entertainment area has the usual plethora of snack bars. On weekends, military personnel driving up from Kadena have fuelled a proliferation of American-style bars. **Bar 77**, just south of the crossroads, has live music and billiards.

Getting There & Away

Nago is the junction town for buses to northern Okinawa or the Motobu Peninsula. From Naha, take the hourly airport express bus (¥2020, 1¾ hours). Slower, cheaper services include bus No 20 and 120 (two hours) or No 21 and 77 (2½ hours).

MOTOBU-HONTŌ 本部半島
☎ 0980

Jutting out to the northwest of Nago, hilly Motobu-hantō has several points of interest and ferry services to nearby islands. There is a **tourist information office** (☎ 47-3641) just north of Motobu town, on the west side of the highway after the overpass. Staff speak a little English and can book accommodation.

From Nago frequent bus services cover the peninsula, including circular routes No 66 (anticlockwise) and No 65 (clockwise). Speedboats to Motobu leave from Naha's Tomari Port (¥3500, one hour, twice daily).

Ocean Expo Park 海洋博公園
The site of the 1975 International Ocean Exposition, this park *(admission free; open 9.30am-7pm Fri-Wed summer, 9.30am-5.30pm Fri-Wed rest of year)* boasts lovely (if crowded) **Emerald Beach**. Most individual attractions charge entry fees and close 30 minutes earlier than the park.

Worthwhile sights include the rebuilt 10,000-ton **aquarium** *(admission ¥670)*; **Oceanic Culture Museum** *(admission ¥170)*, with fascinating cultural artefacts drawn from all over Polynesia, Melanesia, Micronesia and Southeast Asia; and a **Native Okinawan Village** *(admission free)* of traditional houses and indigenous plants.

From Nago, bus No 70 runs directly to the park (¥790). Both peninsula loop lines stop outside, as do buses from Naha.

Nakijin-jō 今帰仁城
Winding over a hilltop, the 14th-century walls of Nakijin-jō *(admission ¥150; open 8.30am-6pm daily)* look especially wonderful when the cherry trees bloom. The ruins were once visited by Commodore Perry, who compared its stone gate to ancient Egyptian architecture. In the past, this was the head castle of the unruly Hokuzan kings and contained shrines and sacred houses for *noro* (hereditary priestesses). From the summit of the hill, there are superb views out to sea.

Around the corner, **Nakijin Cultural Centre** *(admission ¥200; open 9am-4.30pm Tues-Sun)* contains 14th-century Ming pottery from Okinawan trading missions to China and many other wonders. Ask for the encyclopaedic English pamphlet.

Bus No 66 from Nago (¥910) or No 65 from Ocean Expo Park pass nearby.

Other Attractions
Touristy **Pineapple Park** has little pineapple-shaped electric cars that take visitors out into pineapple fields, originally planted in the early 20th century. **Garden Cafe Nanraidō** *(drinks & snacks ¥500; open 10am-5pm daily)*, with its Thai-style teak buildings, is just down the road. Both are a 15-minute ride from Nago on bus No 70.

The stretch of highway from Nago to Motobu is fairly undeveloped. **Lue on the Beach** *(☎ 47-3535, fax 47-5686; singles/twins/condos peak ¥7000/11,000/14,000, off-peak ¥5000/8000/12,000)* is a mini-hotel and PADI dive shop. Its laidback beachfront restaurant *(dishes under ¥1000; open 11.30am-9pm daily)* serves Okinawan seafood cuisine. Beware of highway noise and karaoke!

Connected to the peninsula by a bridge south of Motobu, **Sesoko-jima** has good beaches and camping facilities. Bus No 76 goes direct from Nago terminal (¥650, one hour, four daily). From the terminus it's around a 20-minute walk to the west-side beaches (the island is only 8 sq km).

Tiny **Minna-jima**, only half a square kilometre, has fabulous beaches and diving spots and is further west. **Minshuku Ōjō** *(☎ 47-3646)* and **Coral Reef** *(☎ 47-5688)* provide simple overnight accommodation. Ferries from Motobu town run to the island up to a dozen times daily (¥750, 15 minutes).

Ie-jima 伊江島

Northwest of the peninsula, this island offers wonderful views from the top of **Gusuku-yama**, a 45-minute walk from the ferry. Around ten minutes' walk west of the pier is a **monument** to the US war correspondent Ernie Pyle, who was killed on the island during the early days of the Battle of Okinawa.

Those planning a longer stay on the island can camp on the coast at **Ie-jima Seishōnen Ryokō-mura** (*Young Men's Tourist Village;* ☎ *49-5247; camp sites ¥300, tent hire ¥1500*), which also rents bicycles. **Hotel Spinnaker Iejima** (☎ *49-3012, fax 49-5918; doubles/triples/quads ¥7000/9000/10,000*) is even closer to the beach.

Marco Polo Pension (☎ *49-5242; rooms with 2 meals per person from ¥6500*) is about 300m north of the pier.

Ferries make the trip to the island from Motobu port, just south of the Sesoko-jima bridge, four times daily (¥580, 30 minutes). Buses around the 8km-by-3km island are irregular, but bicycles and scooters can be rented at the pier.

NORTHERN OKINAWA-HONTŌ
沖縄本島の北部
☎ 0980

The northern part of Okinawa-hontō is lightly populated and comparatively wild and rugged. A road runs around the coast.

West Coast 西海岸

The village of **Kijoka** is noted for its traditional houses and production of *Bashōfu*, a very rare cloth made from a banana plant. Call ahead if you want to visit the **weaving workshop** (☎ *44-3033; call ahead for hrs*). **JAL Private Resort** (☎ *41-2222, 0120-58-2586, fax 41-2234; cottages with breakfast per person peak/off-peak ¥28,000/11,000*) at lovely **Okuma Beach** offers diving excursions, wakeboarding and sunset cruises.

Detouring inland at Kunigami brings you to **Hiji Ōtaki** (*admission ¥200; last entry 4pm*), a waterfall reached via a gentle path from the camping ground. Nearby **Yanbaru Nature Resort** (*admission free; open 10am-4.30pm Tues-Sun*) offers walking trails and bird watching.

The town of **Hentona** has shops, a morning fish market, *minshuku* (Japanese B&B-style inns) and other basic facilities. **Cape Hedo** marks the northern end of Okinawa. The point is an incredibly scenic spot backed by hills, with rocks rising from the dense greenery.

From Nago, bus No 67 travels along the coast to Hentona (¥960, one hour), but you have to continue north on infrequent bus No 69 (¥670, 45 minutes).

East Coast 東海岸

From Cape Hedo, the road continues to **Oku**, the termination point for buses travelling up the west coast.

For the next 15km the road stays very close to the coastline, with more fine-looking beaches but frequent warnings of current and tide dangers for swimmers, divers and snorkellers. **Sidmouth Inn** (☎ *41-7070, fax 41-7050; rooms from ¥5700*) is a colonial Vietnamese-style mansion, with highly recommended meals.

Aha is a picturesque village that still has some traditional thatched-roof houses, a rare glimpse of what Okinawa looked like before WWII.

ISLANDS AROUND OKINAWA-HONTŌ

Apart from the islands just a stone's throw from the Okinawan coast (see the Motobu Peninsula section earlier), there are other islands a little farther away.

Iheya-jima & Izena-jima
伊平屋島・伊是名島

North of Okinawa, these islands have good beaches and snorkelling, a number of *minshuku* and ties to ancient Ryūkyū. Covered in sugar-cane fields, Izena-jima was ruled by *noro* well into the 19th century, longer than any other island. Iheya-jima was the royal birthplace of the king Shō En.

Twice-daily ferries runs from Unten Port, north of Motobu town, to Izena-jima (¥1760, one hour) and Iheya-jima (¥2380, 80 minutes).

Kerama-rettō 慶良間列島
☎ 098

There are about 20 islands in this group west of Okinawa-hontō, only four of which are inhabited. Many dive operators

Diving in Okinawa

Visitors interested in exploring Okinawa from a submarine perspective will find numerous opportunities to dive deep and get friendly with the outstanding variety of fish and coral species that inhabit the tropical Kushiro Straits. The Yaeyama island group boasts Japan's largest reef, stretching some 20km from Ishigaki-jima to Iriomote-jima, and plentiful manta rays.

Whether you're a beginner or an old hand wanting to dive from a boat or from the shore, chances are there's an operator to suit you. Little English is spoken at most of the dive outfits on the islands, which is something those who don't speak Japanese might want to consider.

One exception is **Fathoms Diving** (☎ 090-8766-0868, fax 956-6191; **W** www.fathoms.net), which is based on Okinawa-hontō and is run by *gaijin*. It offers classes from beginner to instructor level, rental equipment and professional guided shore and boat dives.

If you're confident of your ability to go diving and speak Japanese at the same time, you'll find operator information in this chapter's Kerama-rettō, Miyako-jima, Ishigaki-jima and Iriomote-jima sections.

on Okinawa-hontō run day trips around the Kerama (see the 'Diving in Okinawa' boxed text above).

Zamami-jima and **Aka-jima** have recently started to develop facilities to cater to the waves of tourists seeking a glimpse of the humpback whales that have recently returned to these waters. During February and March, whale-watching **cruises** (☎ 896-4141) depart from Zamami-jima (¥5000).

On Zamami-jima, white-sand **Furuzamami Beach** has a roped-off area for swimming and snorkelling. Rockier **Ama Beach** offers camping. Ask at the harbour **tourist information office** (☎ 987-2277) for English-language maps. Shuttle buses to the beaches depart outside. You can also hire boats at the harbour to deserted islands, costing from ¥2000.

More rugged Aka-jima sees fewer daytrippers. There's a shallow beach west of the ferry terminal; at the far end, **Cafe-Bar Loco Motion** rents snorkel gear, arranges diving trips and has live music at night. Otherwise, walk east up over the hill to **Nishibama Beach**, where snorkel and dive boats anchor. You can also head south over several bridges to explore smaller islands.

Shirahama Islands Resort (☎ 987-3111, fax 987-2655; rooms per person with 2 meals from ¥8500), on Zamami-jima, is an eight-minute walk from the port. This friendly mini-hotel offers café fare, scooter rental and a dive shop, **Kerama Islands Club** (☎ 098-987-2336). Joy Joy (☎ 987-2245) is a *minshuku* and diving operation on the other side of Zamami-jima's only town.

Unzun (open 6pm-midnight Mon-Sat) is a boisterous *izakaya* across the street from the resort. **Marumiya** (open 11am-1.45pm & 6pm-11pm Thur-Tues; meals ¥500-1000) has a bilingual menu of unexciting, yet filling Okinawan food. It's nearby Joy Joy.

Resort Aka-jima Sea Do Run (☎ 098-987-2341; rooms per person with 2 meals from ¥9000), on Aka-jima, is a five-minute walk from the port. **Saesir** (☎ 0120-10-2737) is another popular dive-and-stay operation on the island. Both offer pick-ups at the ferry terminal.

From Naha (Tomari Port), regular ferries (¥2250, two hours) and speedboats (¥2750, one hour) depart for Zamami-jima and Aka-jima. Motorboats zip between the islands (¥300, 15 minutes, five daily).

Miyako-shotō
宮古諸島

☎ 09807
About 300km southwest of Okinawa, directly en route to the Yaeyama-shotō, is the eight-island Miyako group, comprising Miyako-jima and, a few kilometres to the west, Irabu-jima and Shimoji-jima, plus a scattering of smaller islands.

MIYAKO-JIMA 宮古島
Covered in sugar-cane plantations, Miyako-jima offers fine beaches and diving. Over 1500 triathletes flock to the island each year in April for the Strongman All-Japan

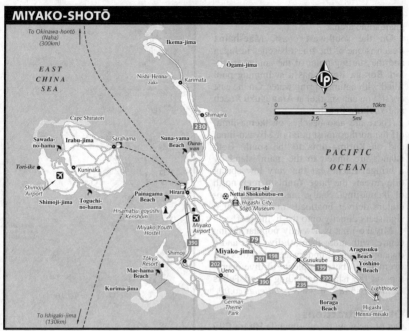

MIYAKO-SHOTŌ

Triathlon. The traditional Miyako Festival is held in July.

Hirara 平良
pop 32,100

Spread-out Hirara, the main town on Miyako-jima, isn't easy to navigate. There are a few minor attractions here, but the operative word is indeed 'minor'.

The **tourist information office** (☎ 3-1881; 4th floor, Ferry Terminal Bldg; open 8.30am-5.30pm daily) has an English-language Okinawa Miyako Islands Guide that it distributes. On the ground floor, **Eco-Guide Cafe** (open 8.30am daily) offers maps of nearby islands, diving advice and free Internet access; closing time varies wildly. The nearby **postal savings ATM** (open 9am-7pm Mon-Fri, 9am-5pm Sat & Sun) accepts foreign cards.

Harimizu Utaki is a shrine devoted to local gods. Other sights include the **Hakuai (Kaiser Wilhelm) Monument**, presented as a gesture of gratitude for the rescue of the crew of a typhoon-wrecked German merchant ship in 1873. (Further capitalising on this historical connection is a highly kitsch **German Theme Park** out on the southern coast of the island.)

Near the waterfront is the **mausoleum** of Nakasone Tōimiya, the 15th-century hero who not only conquered the Yaeyama-shotō, but prevented an invasion from the north. There's another impressive mausoleum cut into the hillside beyond it.

Continuing north along the coast road, the **Nintōzeiseki** (Tax Stone) is a 1.4m-high stone, more or less plonked down in someone's front garden. During the heavy-handed rule of the Satsuma kingdom (which invaded from southern Kyūshū), anyone taller than this stone was required to pay taxes using jōfu, a textile of woven hemp.

Miyako Traditional Arts & Crafts Centre (open daily) displays jōfu and ceramics. Eccentric **Keiko Art Museum** (admission ¥500; open noon-7pm Tues-Wed & Fri-Sun) shows contemporary art.

Beaches & Diving

Miyako-jima has its share of good beaches, surf and diving spots. North of Hirara is lovely **Suna-yama Beach** (literally, 'Sand Mountain'), where after clambering over a dune, you can watch the sunset through a giant stone arch.

On the southwest coast, **Mae-hama Beach** is one of the finest beaches in Japan and the starting point of the annual triathlon. **Boraga Beach** has a swimming pool filled with natural-spring water. On the east coast, you can snorkel at **Aragusuku Beach** and **Yoshino Beach**.

There are also beaches on **Ikema-jima**, off the northernmost point of Miyako-jima, and on **Kurima-jima** to the south. Both islands are linked to the main island by a bridge. Each year the very low spring tide reveals the huge **Yaebishi reef**, north of Ikema-jima. Sadly, misguided tour operators deliver boatloads of heavy-footed sightseers directly onto the living reef!

Miyako-jima is a wildly popular diving centre, with more than 50 dive sites and a dynamic range of underwater drop-offs and overhangs. There are plenty of dive operators on the island, including **Good Fellas Club** (☎ 3-5483; W www.goodfellas.co.jp).

Other Attractions

Out of the way, the worthwhile **Hirara City Sōgō Museum** (*Higashi-shi Sōgō Haku-bustukan; admission ¥300; open 9am-4pm Tues-Sun*) shows documentary videos of fast-disappearing Okinawan religious rites and traditional island festivals.

At **Cape Higashi-Henna**, a long, narrow and quite spectacular peninsula ends with a picturesquely placed lighthouse overlooking the rocky coastline.

Places to Stay

There are **camping grounds** at many beaches, including Mae-hama, Boraga and Aragusuku.

Miyako Youth Hostel (☎ 3-7700; *beds ¥3000*) has super-clean air-con dorms. Curfew is relaxed. It's a 30-minute hike from the ferry terminal. Once you reach the Okinawa Denki intersection, turn right and take the first side road on your left. A taxi costs under ¥1000.

Other budget guesthouses often advertise with flyers inside the ferry terminal.

Guesthouse Miyako-jima (☎/fax 6-2330; e yonaha233@beach.ocn.ne.jp; *beds ¥3000*) is en route to Mae-hama Beach. All basic rooms have air-con and share a kitchen. Call ahead for free pick-ups from

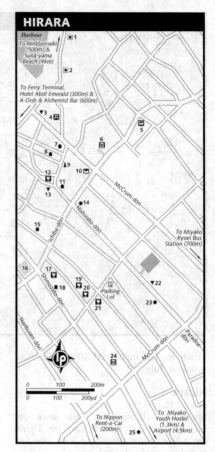

HIRARA

the airport or ferry terminal. Guests can borrow bicycles and 50cc motorbikes for free.

Migration (☎ 5-2480; *beds ¥2500*), on Ikema-jima, can arrange diving and snorkelling. **Guesthouse Only One** (☎/fax 4-4001; *beds ¥3000*) is out toward Cape Higashi-Henna.

Hirara is chock-a-block with drab, concrete *minshuku*. Rates average ¥6000 with two meals thrown in. **Ryokan Uruma-sō** (☎ 2-3113) is up near the harbour terminal. **Ryokan Tsurumi-sō** (☎ 3-9314; *dorm beds ¥2000, rooms per person ¥2500*) rents bicycles and snorkel gear.

The **Pension Star** (☎ 3-1239, fax 2-9922; *singles/doubles/triples with breakfast ¥5500/10,000/13,500*), its neon star flash-

HIRARA

PLACES TO STAY
7   Ryokan Uruma-sō
    旅館うるま荘
8   Ryokan Tsurumi-sō
    旅館つるみ荘
11 Petit Hotel Premier
    プチホテルプレミア
15 Hotel Island Coral
    ホテルアイランドコーラル
18 Pension Star;
    A&W
    ペンションスター

PLACES TO EAT
3   Banana Kitchen
    バナナ台所
13 Koja Honten
    古謝本店
22 Kintarō
    金太楼寿司

OTHER
1   Chirimara Tōimiya
    Mausoleum
    和利真良豊見親之墓
2   Nakasone Tōimiya
    Mausoleum
    仲宗根豊見親之墓
4   Harimizu Utaki
    張水御獄
5   Yachiyo Bus Station
    八千代バスターミナル
6   Miyako Traditional
    Arts & Crafts
    Centre
    宮古伝統民芸品センター
9   Hakuai (Kaiser Wilhelm)
    Monument
    博愛記念碑
10 Post Office
    郵便局

12 ISLA
14 Yamako Supermarket
16 Hirara Public Market
    平良市公設市場
17 Gakagoya Roadhouse
    がかごや
19 Temps
    テンプス
20 Soul Bar Marvin
    マービン
21 New York, New York
    ニューヨークニューヨーク
23 Tomihama
    (Motorcycle Rental)
    富浜
24 Keiko Art Museum
    惠子美術館
25 Marutama
    (Motorcycle Rental)
    丸玉

OKINAWA & SOUTHWEST ISLANDS

ing above the entertainment district, has a rooftop deck. Reception is on the 4th floor.

Petit Hotel Premier (☎ 3-8162; singles/ twins ¥4800/8600) is at the edge of the entertainment district. Rooms are standard, but still worth the money. **Hotel Island Coral** (☎/fax 3-2345; singles/twins/triples with breakfast ¥5550/6700/10,200) is another business hotel.

Raza Cosmica Tourist Home (☎/fax 5-2020; ⓦ www.raza-cosmica.com; rooms per person ¥10,000), located on Ikema-jima, has peace and quiet in truly beautiful surroundings. Run by a friendly young couple, this charmingly eclectic inn sits above a secluded little beach cove. Rates include two vegetarian meals.

Places to Eat
Miyako-jima is known for its local soba. **Koja Honten**, in central Hirara, is as cheap and good as any other.

Banana Kitchen (dishes ¥250-500; open 11.30am-11pm daily) has lazy ceiling fans and a photo-illustrated menu of cheap, filling Okinawan cuisine, including jīmami-dōfu (creamy tofu) with peanut dipping sauce.

Kintarō (open 5pm-10.30pm daily), near the entertainment district, serves fresh sushi and sashimi.

Santa Fe (1st floor, Hotel Atoll Emerald; lunch sets ¥880; open 11.30am-2pm & 5.30pm-9pm daily), next to the ferry terminal, has sea views and gourmet fare,

including daily Chinese, Japanese and Western lunch specials.

A-Dish (☎ 2-7114; dishes ¥500-1500; open 6pm-11pm Tues-Sat, 5pm-10pm Sun), a 10-minute walk southwest of the ferry terminal, offers hip atmosphere. Its tempting pastas feature fresh local ingredients.

Entertainment
Alchemist (closed Mon) is a funky bar upstairs from A-Dish.

ISLA (open from 8pm nightly) is a funky Jamaica-inspired reggae bar in central Hirara. **Gakagoya Roadhouse** (open 10pm-4am Thur-Tues; cover ¥1000) is a rustic place with live music.

Soul Bar Marvin (open from 9pm nightly) plays Soul Train videos and Motown music. Nearby **Temps** (as in The Temptations) is Miyako-jima's long-running dance spot. **New York, New York** (open from 9pm nightly) has billiards, and graffiti on the walls.

Getting There & Away
Air Direct flights on JTA, an affiliate of JAL, go to Ishigaki-jima (¥9500), Naha (¥14,500), Osaka (KIX; ¥42,000) and Tokyo (Narita; ¥46,800).

Boat Overnight ferries from Naha (2nd class ¥4500, nine hours) usually continue on to Ishigaki-jima (¥2070, 5½ hours). Since departures are not daily, check the latest schedules posted in the ferry terminal building. Then buy tickets in advance from

The 'Communication Drink'

The friendly people of Miyako-jima have earned a reputation for drinking, and the Izato entertainment area in the town of Hirara is said to have more bars relative to its population than any other town in Japan.

Miyako even has its unique local drinking custom, called *otori*. This group ritual involves making a speech, filling your own glass (usually with potent *awamori*, the local liquor) and then filling the glasses of all in the room. Everyone drinks up, the leader makes a short closing speech and picks the next victim, and the routine starts all over again.

Miyako's *otori* is so notorious that even hard-livered Okinawans from neighbouring islands are said to fear the ritual. If you happen to end up lured into an otori and want to sneak out before getting plastered, one local veteran boozer advises, 'Never say goodbye. Just head for the toilet and don't come back!'

the main companies, **RKK Line** (☎ 2-2046) or **Arimura Sangyō** (☎ 098-868-1126).

Getting Around

A taxi into central Hirara costs about ¥1000 from the airport and ¥500 from the ferry terminal.

Miyako-jima has a sporadic bus network. Buses run from Yachiyo bus station in Hirara to the north of the island, including to Ikema-jima (35 minutes). Buses from Miyako Kyōei terminal head south toward Mae-hama and Higashi-Henna-misaki (50 minutes). Services run every couple of hours.

Car hire starts at ¥5000 per day. Try **Nippon Rent-a-Car** (☎ 2-0919, 0120-17-0919), **OTS Rent-a-Car** (☎ 3-0008, 0120-34-3732) or **Kūkō Rent-a-Car** (☎ 3-1516), near the airport. Advance reservations are necessary, especially for pick-ups from the airport or ferry terminal.

Motor scooters rent for around ¥3000 a day and motorcycles for ¥6500 per day. Try the two **Honda** dealers shown on the Hirara map (Tomihama and Marutama).

IRABU-JIMA & SHIMOJI-JIMA
伊良部島・下地島

If you fly over Shimoji-jima (between Okinawa and Ishigaki-jima), have a look at the airport runway. It seems to be out of all proportion to the size of the island. This is because airlines use it for 747 touch-and-go training.

Irabu-jima and Shimoji-jima, linked by six small bridges, are pleasantly rural islands with fields of sugar cane. **Sawada-no-hama** and **Toguchi-no-hama** are two good beaches on Irabu-jima, both with

camping grounds. On Shimoji-jima, **Tōri-ike** are linked to the sea by hidden tunnels (a great dive site!).

The islands are best visited as a day trip from Hirara. Speedboats depart for Irabu-jima (¥410, 10 minutes) every half an hour. There are two agencies in the Hirara ferry terminal selling tickets for boats, each with different schedules. On Irabu-jima, bicycles can be rented.

Yaeyama-shotō
八重山諸島

At the far southwestern end of the Nansei-shotō are the islands of the Yaeyama group, consisting of two main islands (Ishigaki-jima and Iriomote-jima) and a scattering of smaller isles between and beyond. Most visitors to these islands, which have excellent dive sites, are day-trippers.

ISHIGAKI-JIMA 石垣島
☎ 09808

Ishigaki-jima is the major flight destination in the Yaeyama-shotō, and boat services fan out from its harbour to the other islands. Like Miyako-jima, Ishigaki hosts an international triathlon every spring.

Orientation & Information

The town of Ishigaki centres on its harbour. You can stroll around the rest in an hour. Parallel to the main street are two covered shopping arcades.

The **tourist information office** (☎ 2-2809; open 8.30am-5pm Mon-Sat) has

English-language maps and diving guides for the entire Yaeyama-shotō.

Ishigaki-jima access is available at **Ishigaki Net Cafe** *(¥300/hr; open 11am-3am daily)* and **Yaima World** *(¥100/hr; open noon-6.30pm daily)*.

Things to See & Do
Nearby the harbour, the modest **Yaeyama Museum** *(admission ¥100; open 9am-4.30pm Tues-Sun)* displays coffin palanquins, dugout canoes, island textiles and festival photographs.

Although the Nansei-shotō never really had samurai, **Miyara Dōnchi** *(admission ¥200; open Wed-Mon)* is essentially a samurai-style house. Worth strolling over to see, it dates from 1819 and is the only one left in the whole island chain.

Founded in 1614, the Zen temple of **Tōrin-ji** has 18th-century statues of Deva kings (said to be the guardian deities of the islands) that can be seen in the dim interiors. Immediately adjacent to the temple is **Gongen-dō**. The original shrine was built in 1614, but destroyed by a tsunami in 1771. Although it is private, you should be able to see the nearby 19th-century garden, **Ishigaki-ke-Teien**, if the wooden gate is open and you ask politely.

Beaches & Diving
There are a number of beaches around the island for snorkelling and diving.

If you walk out over an expanse of dead coral at **Yonehara Beach**, there's good snorkelling at the reef's edge. On the southeast coast, from the village of **Shiraho**, snorkelling boats at high tide cross the off-shore reef, which has unusual species of coral. Expect to pay ¥2000 per person.

Famed **Kabira-wan** is a sheltered bay with fine sand, glass-bottomed-boat tours and a cultured black-pearl industry. Entering the water here is not permitted. Instead walk over to **Sukuji Beach**.

There are a number of dive shops on Ishigaki-jima, including **Tom Sawyer** *(☎ 3-4677)* in Ishigaki town. Manta rays can be spotted from late spring to early autumn. Popular dive spots include the maze-like tunnels at Kabira-wan and reefs off Yonehara Beach and Cape Hirakubo lighthouse. Boat-dive trips with lunch included cost around ¥12,000.

Hikes & Other Attractions
Dating from 1742, **Fusaki Kannon-dō** is about 6km northwest of the town. Further north is **Tōjin-baka**, a Chinese cemetery with colourful mausoleums. It commemorates those Chinese labourers who sought refuge on Ishigaki-jima after escaping from British and American taskmasters during their voyage to California.

Banna-dake (230m) has fine views from along its skyline approach road. Below a botanical garden **Banna-dake-kōen** *(admission free)* has over 2500 species of tropical flora.

Omoto-dake (524m) is the highest point in Okinawa-ken, with good views from the large boulder at the top. Better hiking exists on **Nosoko-māpe**, the eroded core of a volcano, where a steep 45-minute trek takes you to the summit. To get to the trailhead, turn off Hwy 79 north of Nosoko Primary School.

Near Kabira-wan, **Mae-dake** has a moister, jungle feel and, like Nosoko-māpe, is steep at the top with great views. North of the Kabira town post office, a small shows visitors about the making of Okinawa's firewater. Tastings are free.

A little over halfway up the east coast of Ishigaki-jima is **Tamatorizaki-tenbōdai**. The viewing platform provides great coastal views and is a short walk from some untouched beaches. Buses go there from the Ishigaki bus station; get off at the Tamatori stop (¥800, one hour).

Places to Stay
Ishigaki is a compact little town and there are plenty of places to stay within walking distance of the harbour.

For camping, head for Yonehara Beach or coastal **Minami-no-yume Raku-en** *(☎ 3-5199; camp sites per person ¥500)*, an 800m walk from Tōjin-baka. It has hot showers and tent hire is available.

Yashima Ryokan Youth Hostel *(☎ 2-3157; beds ¥2600)* is close to Ishigaki's town centre, a few minutes' walk north of the Yaeyama Museum.

Other places with shared accommodation are even more basic. **Panari Yanbu Zeena** *(☎ 3-3011; beds ¥1800)* is a family-run guesthouse, set in a quiet spot opposite Miyura Dōnchi. **Minshuku Paipati Rōma** *(☎ 090-7926-3436; beds ¥1500)* and **Ryō-no-yado** *(☎ 2-8038; beds ¥1500)* are closer to the harbour.

YAEYAMA–SHOTŌ

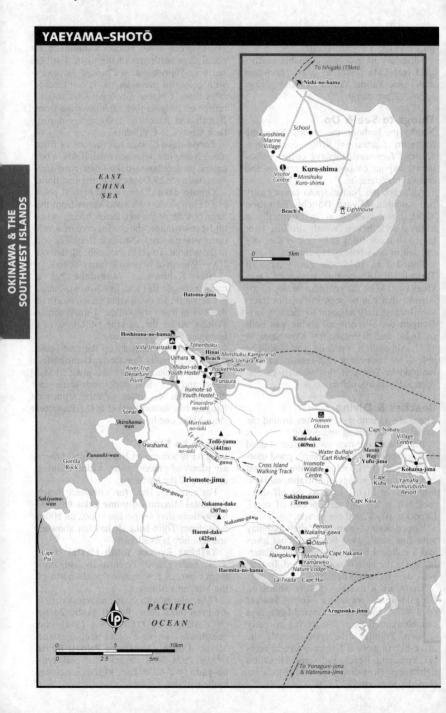

OKINAWA & THE
SOUTHWEST ISLANDS

EAST
CHINA
SEA

To Ishigaki (15km)
Nishi-no-hama

Kuroshima
Marine
Village

School

Visitor
Centre

Kuro-shima

**Minshuku
Kuro-shima**

Beach

Lighthouse

0   1km

Hatoma-jima

Hoshisuna-no-hama
Villa Unarizaki
Tōhenboku
**Hinai
Beach**
Minshuku Kampira-sō
& Uehara-Kan
Uehara
River Trip
Departure
Point
Midori-sō
Youth Hostel
Pocket House
Funaura
Irumote-sō
Youth Hostel
Pinaisāra-
no-taki

Iriomote
Onsen

Komi-dake
(469m)

Water Buffalo
Cart Rides

Cape Nobaru

Village
Centre

Mana
Way
Yufu-jima

Iriomote
Wildlife
Centre

Cape
Kuba

Kōhama-jima

Yamaha
Haimurubushi
Resort

Sonai

Shirahama-
wan

Shirahama

Mariyudō-
no-taki

Tedō-yama
(441m)

Kampire-
no-taki

Urauchi-gawa

Cross Island
Walking Track

Iriomote-jima

Nakama-dake
(307m)

**Sakishimasuo
Trees**

Cape Kasa

Gorilla
Rock

Funauki-wan

Nakama-gawa

Nakama-gawa

Haemi-dake
(425m)

Sakiyama-
wan

Pension
Nakama-gawa

Ōtomi

Ōhara

Cape Nakama

Cape Pai

Nangoku
Nature Lodge
La Teada

Minshuku
Yamaneko

Haemita-no-hama

Cape Hai

Aragusuku-jima

PACIFIC
OCEAN

0   5   10km
0   2.5   5mi

To Yonaguni-jima
& Hateruma-jima

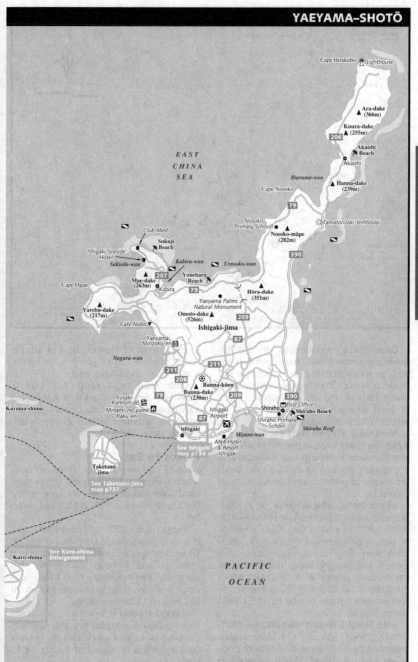

YAEYAMA–SHOTŌ

Cape Hirakubo ☀ *Lighthouse*

▲ Ara-dake
(366m)

206

Kuura-dake
▲ (255m)

Akaishi
Beach

● Akaishi

*EAST
CHINA
SEA*

Ibaruma-wan

Cape Nosoko

▲ Hanna-dake
(239m)

79

*Nosoko
Primary School* ●

☀ *Tamatorizaki-tembōdai*

Nosoko-mápe
(282m)

390

Club Med

Sukuji
Beach

*Ishigaki Seaside
Hotel*

Sakieda-wan

Kabira-wan

Urasoko-wan

Cape Ogan

Mae-dake
(263m) ▲

207

● Kabira

Yonehara
Beach

79

▲ Hōra-dake
(351m)

▼ Yarebu-dake
(217m)

*Yaeyama Palms
Natural Monument*

Omoto-dake ▲
(526m)

209

Ishigaki-jima

Cafe Nūbo ▼

*Yaeyama
Minzoku-en* ▥

87

Nagura-wan

211

211

208

✿ **Banna-kōen**

Kaya-ma-shima

*Fusaki
Kannon-dō* ☖

79

▲ Banna-dake
(230m)

209

Shiraho ●

390

☑ *Post Office*

☖ Shiraho Beach

*Minami-no-yume
Raku-en* ⌂

● Ishigaki

*Ishigaki
Airport*
✈

*Shiraho Primary
School*

Shiraho Reef

See Ishigaki
map p734

ANA Hotel
& Resort
Ishigaki

Miyara-wan

**Taketomi-
jima**

See Taketomi-jima
map p737

*PACIFIC

OCEAN*

Kuro-shima

See Kuro-shima
Enlargement

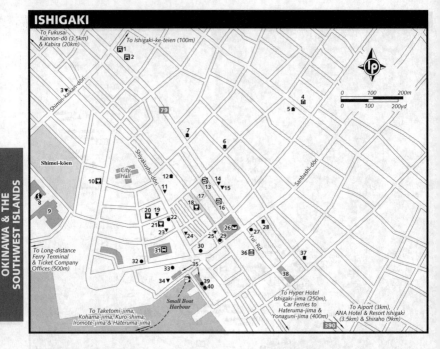

ISHIGAKI

Guesthouse Rakutenya (☎ 3-8713; rooms per person ¥3000) has non-dormitory budget accommodation in a rickety, old wooden house. The friendly couple here speak English and are a fantastic source of local information. Book ahead and be prepared for mosquitoes.

Minshuku Ishigaki-jima (☎ 2-6066, 2-4353, fax 3-0637; rooms per person ¥6000), just next door to Guesthouse Rakutenya, is a charming place. You can trust the food: the owner has written cookbooks on local cuisine!

Hyper Hotel Ishigaki-jima (☎ 2-2000; singles/doubles/triples with breakfast ¥4900/ 5900/6900) is a hotel that offers all kinds of perks, including extra-wide beds, complimentary English-language maps, coin lockers and laundry. Super Hotel Ishigaki (☎ 3-9000; singles with breakfast Mon-Fri ¥5800, Sat & Sun ¥4000) has single rooms only. Both hotels have 24-hour secure access.

ANA Hotel & Resort Ishigaki (☎ 8-7111, 0120-02-9501, fax 2-7904; rooms with breakfast peak/off-peak ¥46,000/22,000) is out near the airport. This tropical resort is reminiscent of Hawaii. Best of all, the beach offers a full range of water sports, plus a jungly swimming pool.

Club Med (☎ 4-4600, fax 8-2600; Ⓦ www.clubmed.com), north of Kabira, has a swallowed up one of the island's prettiest beaches. Activities include diving, windsurfing and mountain-biking.

Places to Eat

Ishigaki has several little bohemian cafés worth seeking out. Yūkunumi serves great local soba and desserts – try kohii zenzai (¥400), shaved ice with coffee and sweet beans.

Yaoya (dishes ¥200-800; open late daily) is a delicious yakitori shop that dishes up Okinawan specialties, like nigana (bitter spinach), and Ishigaki microbrews. It's open late. Beijing (dishes from ¥700; open lunch & dinner daily) has tatami-mat rooms and refined Chinese cooking.

Izakaya Hanaki is worth a try if you can brave a Japanese menu. It's a delightfully cluttered place that specialises in 'country cooking' but it is celebrated locally for its sushi.

OKINAWA & THE SOUTHWEST ISLANDS

ISHIGAKI

PLACES TO STAY		
5	Panari Yanbu Zeena パナリヤンブジーナ	
6	Guesthouse Rakutenya; Minshuku Ishigaki-jima 民宿楽天屋；民宿石垣島	
7	Super Hotel Ishigaki スーパーホテル石垣	
12	Minshuku Paipati Rōma 民宿パイパティローマ	
28	Ryo-no-yado 旅の宿	
37	Yashima Ryokan Youth Hostel やしま旅館ユースホステル	

PLACES TO EAT		
3	Sushi Bar Tatsu たつ	
11	Izakaya Hanaki 居酒屋はなき	
14	Mori-no-Kokage 森のこかげ	
15	Asian Kitchen KAPI	
19	Beijing 北京	
23	Yaoya 八百屋	

24	A&W Burger
25	Yūkunumi ゆうくぬみ
34	Fish Market

OTHER	
1	Tōrin-ji 桃林寺
2	Gongen-dō 権現堂
4	Miyara Dōnchi 宮良殿内
8	Tourist Information Office 観光協会案内所
9	Ishigaki City Library 石垣市図書館
10	Golden Misaki; Beer Garden ゴールデン美崎；ビアガーデン
13	Ishigaki Net Cafe 石垣ネットキャフェ
16	Yaima World やいまワールド
17	Public Market; Ishigaki City Special Products Centre 公設市場；石垣市 特産品販売センター

18	Jazz Scarecrow
20	In Yan; Rocket Records インヤン
21	Blue Café
22	Hot Spar
26	Yaeyama Post Office 八重山郵便局
27	Ai Ai あいあい
29	Tom Sawyer Dive Shop
30	ANK エアーニッポン
31	Bus Station バスターミナル
32	Nissan Rent-a-Car 日産レンタカー
33	Sanpo さんぽ
35	Ferry Company Offices フェリー事務所
36	Yaeyama Museum 八重山博物館
38	OTS Rent-a-Car
39	Yaeyama Kankō 八重山観光
40	Anei Kankō 案栄観光

Mori-no-Kokage (dishes ¥500-1000; open 5pm-midnight Tues-Sun) is a bustling Okinawan izakaya, serving champuru and sashimi salads. Its exterior forest facade is fantastical.

Iso (meals from ¥750; open 11am-10.30pm daily), like Mori-no-Kokage, also fixes a traditional Okinawan menu. This place looks far more expensive than it actually is.

Asian Kitchen KAPI (dishes ¥650-1000; open 11.20am-2pm & 5.30pm-11pm Tues-Sun) does pan-Asian fare, from curries to spring rolls.

Sushi Bar Tatsu (set menus from ¥980; open 6pm-late Mon-Sat) is run by a Japanese sushi chef who once lived in Hawaii. An enthusiastic welcome is guaranteed, and the menu lists both traditional and fusion sushi. On Saturday night, all sushi is half-price!

Cafe Nūbō (open 11am-6pm Fri-Wed; seafood curry ¥650-750), is located en route to Yonehara Beach, and looks as if it was airlifted straight out of Brazil. This is a good place to relax with a cold beer on the outdoor deck, from where the seaside views are magnificent.

Entertainment
Ishigaki's reggae bars, **Blue Café** (open from 9pm daily) and **In Yan** (open from 8pm daily), are both open nightly. A few doors over from In Yan, groovy **Rocket Records** has flyers for club events.

Jazz Scarecrow (open 6pm-1am daily), a chilled-out basement lounge, occasionally has live shows.

The **Golden Misaki building** has a rooftop beer garden. It's on the edge of the entertainment district, stacked with snack bars.

Shopping
In the main shopping arcade, the **public market** is a sight. **Ishigaki City Special Products Centre** (open 10am-7pm daily) upstairs lets visitors sample traditional herbal teas, and browse textiles and pearl jewellery.

Minsā Kōgeikan (open 9am-5pm daily), a weaving workshop and showroom, has exhibits upstairs on Yaeyama-shotō textiles. Airport buses stop outside.

Getting There & Away
Air Direct flights on JTA (a JAL affiliate) go to Tokyo (Narita; ¥50,200) and Osaka (KIX; ¥41,500).

JTA/ANK have more than a dozen flights a day between Naha and Ishigaki-jima (¥19,000), but only a few to Miyako-jima (¥9500). JTA also flies to the tiny Yonaguni-jima (¥10,000) and Hateruma-jima.

Boat Ishigaki-jima is the centre for all the Yaeyama-shotō ferries and its small boat harbour is a hive of activity. The two main ferry operators are **Yaeyama Kankō** (☎ 2-5010) and **Anei Kankō** (☎ 3-0055). There are often several other ticket agencies servicing a given destination at varying prices.

Regular car ferries to Yonaguni-jima and Hateruma-jima depart from just east of the harbour. Long-distance ferries to Miyako-jima (¥2070, five hours) and Naha (¥5900, 10½ hours) depart from a terminal west of the harbour (a 15-minute walk). These services are not daily – exact prices and travel times vary depending on the company.

The Okinawa-Taiwan ferry service occasionally operates via Ishigaki (see Getting There & Away under Naha for details).

Getting Around
The bus station is across the road from the harbour in Ishigaki town. Buses to the airport (¥200, 15 minutes) are timed to flights. Infrequent services head north to Kabira-wan (¥580, 40 minutes) and Yonehara Beach (¥720, one hour), or to Shiraho (¥350, 30 minutes) and up the east coast to the island's northern tip.

OTS Rent-a-Car (☎ 2-4323, 0120-34-3732), **Nissan Rent-a-Car** (☎ 3-0024) and **Nippon Rent-a-Car** (☎ 2-3629) have offices in town and at the airport.

Affordable and friendly **Ai Ai** (☎ 3-9530; open 9am-7pm daily) rents bicycles and motorbikes, as does **Sanpo** (☎ 2-8883) nearer the harbour.

TAKETOMI-JIMA 竹富島
☎ 09808
A 10-minute boat ride from Ishigaki is the popular but relaxed little island, Taketomi-jima. It's got some strong traces of Ryūkyū culture and plenty of traditional architecture (even the post office was built Okinawan-style!). Mostly dirt roads fan out from the flower-bedecked village in the centre to various places around the island's coast. The **visitors centre** has a coral-and-shell display.

The concrete lookout, **Nagomi-no-dai**, on tiny Akayama-oka is atop an even tinier hillock, but on this otherwise pancake-flat island it offers good views over the red-tiled roofs. Look for walls of coral and rock and angry-looking *shiisā* on the rooftops. The other observation point is **Unbufuru Lookout** (*Unbufuru-tembōdai; admission ¥100*), at the southern end of the village (on top of someone's house).

Nishitō Utaki is a shrine dedicated to a 16th-century ruler of the Yaeyama-shotō. **Kihōin** (*admission ¥300*) has a private collection of diverse folk artefacts. **Taketomi Mingei-kan** (*admission free*) is where the island's woven Minsā belts and other textiles are produced.

Most of the island is fringed with beach, but usually very shallow water. At **Kondoi Beach** you'll find the best swimming on the island, and at the next beach south, the main *hoshi-suna* (star sand) hunting grounds. Although you are requested not to souvenir more than a few grains (which are actually the dried skeletons of tiny creatures), it's sold by the bucketful at local shops.

Dive boats from Ishigaki-jima usually visit an **underwater hot spring** on the east coast, where there's a spouting geyser and ambient water temperature of almost 50°C, plus kaleidoscopic coral.

Places to Stay & Eat
Many of the traditional houses around the island are Japanese-style inns. Two meals are usually included in the rates. Book ahead.

Takana Ryokan Youth Hostel (☎ 5-2151; beds ¥2500) is opposite the tiny post office.

Minshuku Izumiya (☎ 5-2250) is known for its gardens. **Nohara-sō** (☎ 5-5252; rooms per person ¥5000) and **Nitta-sō** (☎ 5-2201) offers similar standards and rates.

Takenoko and **Yarabo** are woodsy little cafés that serve good Yaeyama *soba* and *kaki-kōri* (shaved ice). **Chirorin-mura** is a rustic café-pub.

Getting There & Around
Ferries from Ishigaki-jima (¥580, 10 minutes) are fast and frequent.

The island is small enough for you to be able to get around on foot if the weather isn't too muggy. Otherwise, rental bicycles are great for exploring the sandy roads. You can also hire motor scooters.

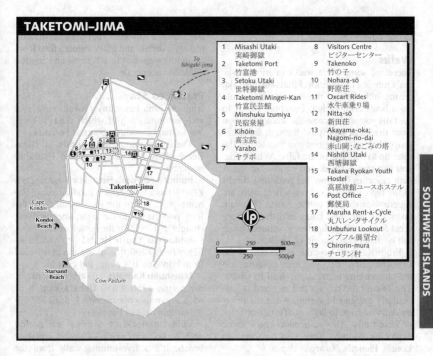

TAKETOMI-JIMA

1	Misashi Utaki 実崎御嶽	8	Visitors Centre ビジターセンター
2	Taketomi Port 竹富港	9	Takenoko 竹の子
3	Setoku Utaki 世特御嶽	10	Nohara-sō 野原荘
4	Taketomi Mingei-Kan 竹富民芸館	11	Oxcart Rides 水牛車乗り場
5	Minshuku Izumiya 民宿泉屋	12	Nitta-sō 新田荘
6	Kihōin 喜宝院	13	Akayama-oka; Nagomi-no-dai 赤山岡；なごみの塔
7	Yarabo ヤラボ	14	Nishitō Utaki 西塘御嶽
		15	Takana Ryokan Youth Hostel 高那旅館ユースホステル
		16	Post Office 郵便局
		17	Maruha Rent-a-Cycle 丸八レンタサイクル
		18	Unbufuru Lookout ンブフル展望台
		19	Chirorin-mura チロリン村

For Japanese visitors, a popular activity is taking a 30-minute tour (¥1000) of the island in a cart drawn by water buffalo.

IRIOMOTE-JIMA 西表島
☎ 09808

Dense jungle blankets much of Iriomote-jima, an island that could well qualify as Japan's last frontier. Trekking through the interior, you may find leeches, which in Japan is probably good enough to merit the 'wilderness' tag.

The island's major attractions are beaches, rivers and waterfalls, and the Iriomote *yamaneko* (wildcat). Similar in size and appearance to a domestic cat, the wildcat is nocturnal and rarely seen. Road signs alerting drivers to its possible presence are common.

Much easier to find are the curious *sakishimasuo* trees, with their twisting, ribbon-like root buttresses. You'll find them all over the island, but particularly along the coast north of Ōhara.

Orientation

Iriomote-jima has several small towns and a perimeter road that runs about halfway around the coast. No roads run into the interior, which is virtually untouched.

River Trips

Iriomote's number-one attraction is a trip up the Urauchi-gawa, a winding brown river that's a lot like a tiny stretch of the Amazon. From where the boats stop, it's a half-hour walk to the spectacular waterfalls, **Mariyudō-no-taki**, and long, rapids-like **Kampirē-no-taki**. There are some good swimming holes around the falls. Boats operate from approximately 9am to 4pm, charging ¥1500 per person (minimum four passengers). There is less waiting around if you arrive in the morning, when most of the day-trippers turn up.

From close to the Ōhara docks it is possible to take hour-long cruises (¥1200) up Iriomote's second-largest river, the **Nakama-gawa**, passing through lush, jungle-like vegetation.

Self-propelled travellers can also rent canoes and kayaks near boat departure points, or join one of several ecotour operators for an upriver excursion. **MaYaGuSuKu** (*☎/fax 5-6288*) has experienced guides and a variety of courses lasting from six hours to two days.

Walks

There are some great walks in Iriomote-jima's jungle-clad interior. **Pinaisāra-no-taki**, on the hills behind the lagoon, are visible from boats coming into Funaura. To get to the falls you wade across the shallow lagoon from the causeway, plod through the mangroves behind the lagoon and then follow the river up to the base of the falls. At high tide, you can rent a kayak and paddle across. A path branches off from the river and climbs to the top of the falls, from where there are superb views down to the coast. The walk takes less than two hours and the falls are great for a cooling dip, but in summer bring salt or matches to get rid of leeches.

From Kampirē-no-taki, at the end of the Urauchi-gawa trip, you can continue on the challenging cross-island trail to Ōhara. The 18km hike takes a full day and is particularly popular in spring, when the many trekkers manage to lay a confusing network of false trails. All you need to know about exploring Iriomote-jima can be found in Lonely Planet's *Hiking in Japan*.

Beaches & Diving

Most of the island's scenic beaches are rocky and have shallow waters. **Hoshisuna-no-hama** has star sand. From Shirahama, at the western end of the coast road, boats to **Funauki Beach** depart three times a day (¥400).

Diving around Iriomote-jima certainly isn't cheap, but there are some fine sites, like the famed *Manta Way* in the straits between Iriomote-jima and Kohama-jima, where you are almost certain to come across manta rays, especially in late spring and early summer.

Local operators include **Mr Sakana Diving Service** (☎ 5-6472) and **Diving Team Unarizaki** (☎ 5-6142). Both are in Uehara, and very little English is spoken at either.

Other Attractions

Iriomote Onsen (*admission ¥1200; open 11am-9pm daily*) has a *rotemburo* and hot-rock sauna. Further south, carts drawn by water buffalo (¥1300 per person) roll through the shallow shoreline waters over to **Yufu-jima**, a botanical islet off the coast.

Iriomote Wildlife Centre (*admission free; open 10am-4pm Tues-Sun*) has natural history exhibits and a live camera feed from an outdoor enclosure where ill and injured wildcats recuperate.

Places to Stay

Iriomote-jima has many ryokan, *minshuku* and *pensions*, each of which sends a minibus to meet incoming boats at Funaura.

There are **camping grounds** at Hinai Beach, Hoshisuna-no-hama and Haemita-no-hama.

Irumote-sō Youth Hostel (*☎ 5-6255; beds ¥2900*) has a great hilltop location above Funaura port. Where the road uphill from the ferry port curves to the right, keep walking straight and look for the hostel signs.

Midori-sō Youth Hostel (*☎ 5-6526, 6-6253; beds ¥2500*) is along the coast road from Funaura. It's plain, but central.

Minshuku Kampira-sō (*☎ 5-6526; rooms per person ¥3500*) and **Uehara-kan** (*☎ 5-6516; rooms per person with 2 meals ¥5500*) are simple inns in Funaura.

Villa Unarizaki (*☎ 5-6464; per person with breakfast from ¥9000*) is on a private beach. It's a five-minute walk from the Sumiyoshi bus stop.

Minshuku Yamaneko (*☎ 5-5242; beds ¥2000*) offers shared accommodation in Ōhara.

Pension Nakama-gawa (*☎ 85-5407; per person with 2 meals ¥7500*) serves local cuisine. It's near the Ōtomi bus stop, north of Ōhara.

Nature Lodge La Teada (*☎ 5-5555; fax 5-5988; standard/deluxe twins ¥10,500/ 13,500, cottages per person ¥12,000*) is off the coastal road, past Ōhara. Rates include two meals.

Places to Eat

Tōhenboku (*☎ 5-6050; open noon-3pm & 6pm-9pm Wed-Mon*), near the beach at Tsuki-ga-hama, serves Okinawan fare in beautiful garden surroundings.

Nangoku (*dishes ¥650-1000; open 9.30am-10pm daily*) is near the Ōhara bus terminal. Service may be slow, but filling meals include *hirayāchi* (an Okinawan savoury pancake) and wild bear *teishoku* (¥1800).

Pocket House (*dishes ¥500, meals from ¥1200*) is a hilltop house above Funaura. The menu includes Okinawan snacks and beers.

Getting There & Around

Boats from Ishigaki-jima either dock at Funaura (¥2000) – which is the place to get the Urauchi-gawa cruise – or remote Ōhara (¥1540). The trip typically takes under an hour.

Many *minshuku* and both youth hostels rent bicycles, motor scooters and cars. **Yamaneko Rent-a-Car** (☎ *5-5111, 5-6111*) charges ¥5000 per day and has offices in Funaura and Ōhara.

There's at least twice-daily bus service between Ōhara and Shirahama (¥1040, 1¼ hours), at the two ends of the island's 58km road. The trip from Funaura port to Urauchi-gawa costs ¥260.

ISLANDS AROUND IRIOMOTE-JIMA
☎ 09808

Directly north of Iriomote-jima and clearly visible from Funaura, tiny **Hatoma-jima** has some very fine beaches and snorkelling. It's accessible by charter boat.

Close to the east coast of Iriomote-jima, the small island of **Kohama-jima** has a sprinkling of *minshuku* and superb diving, particularly in Manta Way (there are boats there from Ishigaki-jima). Isolated Cape Kuba has a fishing village and end-of-the-world **Guesthouse Pana Pana** (☎ *5-3239*). Other *minshuku* are clustered together in the centre of the island, charging around ¥4500 with two meals included. Try traditional **Kohagura-sō** (☎ *5-3626*), **Kiyomi-sō** (☎ *5-3152*) or **Nagata-sō** (☎ *5-3250*). Boats from Ishigaki-jima depart hourly (¥1030, 25 minutes). Rental bikes are available at the pier.

Smaller **Kuro-shima**, directly south of Kohama-jima, is renowned as the place where bulls are raised for Okinawa's *tōgyū*. The island also has superb diving, quiet country roads for cycling, several shrines and a couple of beaches. **Minshuku Kuroshima** (☎ *5-4251; rooms per person with 2 meals ¥4500*) and **Kuro-shima Marine Village** (☎ *5-4126*) arrange diving trips. Ferries leave from Ishigaki-jima (¥1130, 30 minutes, five daily).

HATERUMA-JIMA 波照間島

Directly south of Iriomote-jima is tiny Hateruma-jima, only 5km long. A half-hour walk from the ferry terminal, **Nishi-no-hama** has azure waters, good snorkelling,

showers and toilets, and a beachfront camping ground. Of interest mainly to Japanese tourists is a rock carved with an inscription proclaiming it the southernmost point of Japan. Also on the south coast is an **observatory** (*admission ¥300; open Tues-Sun*).

There are a few *minshuku* on the island, but you can easily visit as a day-tripper. There are three speedboats daily between Ishigaki-jima and Hateruma-jima (¥3050, one hour). Slower ferries (¥2080, two hours) run once a day on Tuesday, Thursday and Saturday. Rental bicycles and motor scooters can be arranged.

YONAGUNI-JIMA 与那国島
☎ 09808

Yonaguni-jima is just 110km from Taiwan. The island is renowned for its strong sake and *yonagunisan* (jumbo-sized moths). In the spirit of the southernmost rock on Hateruma-jima, Yonaguni-jima sports a **westernmost rock**.

The coastline is marked with some great rock formations, much like those on the east coast of Taiwan. The most famous of these are **Tachigami-iwa** (literally, Standing-God Rock) and **Sanninu-dai** (Gunkan-iwa), evocative of virility. There are fine views from atop Urabu-dake (231m).

There's not a lot else to see on this small island, but it has a reputation as being a mysterious place. Some **underwater ruins** resembling an ancient pyramid were only discovered in the 1980s and now are a popular dive spot.

Yonaguni's airport is about 10 minutes by taxi from the main town of Sonai. There's not a great deal of interest in town, but you could check out the **folk museum** (*Yonaguni Minzoku Shiryōkan; admission free; open 8.30am-5pm daily*), with its cluttered history displays, or the **traditional crafts centre**.

Places to Stay

There are a few hotels, ryokan and *minshuku* in Sonai and a couple of places over near Japan's westernmost rock.

Minshuku Omoro (☎ *7-2419; rooms per person with 2 meals ¥4500*) makes an interesting choice, both for economy and atmosphere. It's just south of the museum.

Hotel Irifune (☎ *7-2311; rooms per person with 2 meals ¥7000*) is just up the road and sports a picture of a rampant marlin outside. The owners organise dive trips.

Getting There & Around

JTA flies to Yonaguni-jima from Ishigaki (¥10,000, 30 minutes, twice daily). On Wednesday and Saturday, the **Fukuyama ferry service** (☎ 7-2555, on Ishigaki-jima ☎ 09808-2-4962) has boats running from Ishigaki-jima to Yonaguni-jima (¥3640,

4½ hours). The boats return to Ishigaki-jima on Monday and Thursday. Check the schedule before you leave, as it's vulnerable to change.

Beihama Rent-a-Car (☎ 7-2148) has an office at the airport and in Sonai. **Yonaguni Honda** (☎ 7-2376) rents motor scooters and bicycles. Buses run infrequently along the coastal road between Kubura (the rock) and Sonai (the port).

Language

Japanese is the language spoken across all of Japan. While standard Japanese, or *hyōjungo,* is understood by almost all Japanese, whether educated or not, many Japanese, particularly in rural areas speak strong local dialects (known as *ben,* as in the famous dialect of Kansai, *Kansai-ben*). These dialects can be quite impenetrable, even for Japanese from other parts of the country. Luckily, you can always get your point across in hyōjungo (understanding the answer may be another issue).

In this section, we present a selection of useful Japanese words and phrases. See also the sample menus in the Japanese Cuisine special section (p113–28) for help with ordering food in Japanese. And for terms specific to train travel, see the Train Vocabulary box in the Getting Around chapter (p136).

Grammar

To English speakers, Japanese language patterns often seem to be back to front and lacking in essential information. For example, where an English speaker would say 'I'm going to the shop' a Japanese speaker would say 'shop to going', omitting the subject pronoun (I) altogether and putting the verb at the end of the sentence. To make matters worse, many moods which are indicated at the beginning of a sentence in English occur at the end of a sentence in Japanese, as in the Japanese sentence 'Japan to going if' – 'if you're going to Japan'.

Fortunately for visitors to Japan, it's not all bad news. Unlike other languages in the region (Chinese, Vietnamese and Thai among others), the Japanese pronunciation system is fairly easy to master. In fact, with a little effort, getting together a repertoire of travellers' phrases should be no trouble – the only problem will be understanding the replies you get.

Written Japanese

Japanese has one of the most complex writing systems in the world, using three different scripts (four if you include the increasingly used Roman script *romaji*). The most difficult of the three, for foreigners and Japanese alike, is *kanji,* the ideo-

Japanese and English

Visitors to Japan should be warned that many Japanese do not speak or understand much English. Although English is a required subject in both junior high school and high school, and many students go on to study more of it in university, several factors conspire to prevent many Japanese from acquiring usable English. These include the nature of the English educational system, which uses outdated methods like translation; the extreme difference between English and Japanese pronunciation and grammar; and the typical reticence of the Japanese, who may be shy to speak a language that they haven't mastered.

There are several ways to facilitate communication with Japanese who may not have a mastery of spoken English:

- Always start with a smile to set your opposite party at ease.
- Speak very slowly and clearly.
- When asking for information, choose people of university age or thereabouts, as these people are most likely to speak some English. Also, Japanese women tend to speak and understand English much better than Japanese men.
- If necessary, write down your question – Japanese are often able to understand written English even when they can't understand spoken English.
- Use the sample phrases in this chapter (if necessary, point to the Japanese phrase in question).

graphic script developed by the Chinese. Not only do you have to learn a couple of thousand of them, but unlike Chinese many Japanese kanji have wildly variant pronunciations depending on context.

Due to the differences between Chinese and Japanese grammar, kanji had to be supplemented with a 'syllabary' (an alphabet of syllables), known as *hiragana*. And there is yet another syllabary that is used largely for representing foreign-loan words such as *terebi* (TV) and *biiru* (beer); this script is known as *katakana*. If you're serious about learning to read Japanese you'll have to set aside several years.

If you're thinking of tackling the Japanese writing system before you go or while you're in Japan, your best bet would be to start with hiragana or katakana. Both these syllabaries have 48 characters each, and can be learned within a week, although it'll take at least a month to consolidate them. Once in the country, you can practise your katakana on restaurant menus, where such things as *kōhii* (coffee) and *kēiki* (cake) are frequently found. Practise your hiragana on train journeys, as station names are usually indicated in hiragana (in addition to English and kanji). If you fancy continuing on to learn the kanji, be warned that it will take a few years – perhaps more time than you'd be willing to invest for one simple vacation!

Romanisation

The romaji used in this book follows the Hepburn system of romanisation. Macrons are used to indicate long vowels. In this book, common Japanese nouns like *ji* or *tera* (temple) and *jinja* or *jingū* (shrine) are written without an English translation.

Language Guides

Lonely Planet's *Japanese phrasebook* offers a convenient collection of survival words and phrases for your trip to Japan, plus a section on grammar and pronunciation. If you'd like to delve deeper into the intricacies of the language, we recommend *Japanese for Busy People* (Kodansha) for beginners, *Introduction to Intermediate Japanese* (Mizutani Nobuko, Bojinsha) for intermediate students, and *Kanji in Context* (Nishiguchi Koichi and Kono Tamaki, Japan Times) for more advanced students. One of the best guides to the written language, for both study and reference, is *Kanji & Kana* (Wolfgang Hadamizky and Mark Spahn, Tuttle).

The following selection of Japanese phrases will see you through some of the more common situations experienced by travellers to Japan.

Pronunciation

Unlike Chinese, Vietnamese and Thai, among others, Japanese is not tonal and the pronunciation system is fairly easy to master.

The following examples reflect British pronunciation:

a	as in 'father'
e	as in 'get'
i	as in 'macaroni'
o	as in 'bone'
u	as in 'flu'

Vowels appearing in this book with a macron (or bar) over them (ā, ē, ō, ū) are pronounced in the same way as standard vowels except that the sound is held twice as long. You need to take care with this as vowel length can change the meaning of a word, eg, *yuki* means 'snow', while *yūki* means 'bravery'.

Consonants are generally pronounced as in English, with the following exceptions:

f	this sound is produced by pursing the lips and blowing lightly
g	as in 'get' at the start of word; and nasalised as the 'ng' in 'sing' in the middle of a word
r	more like an 'l' than an 'r'

Greetings & Civilities

The all-purpose title **san** is used after a name as an honorific and is the equivalent of Mr, Miss, Mrs and Ms.

Good morning.
   ohayō gozaimasu
   おはようございます。
Good afternoon.
   konnichiwa
   こんにちは。
Good evening.
   kombanwa
   こんばんは。
Goodbye.
   sayōnara
   さようなら。
See you later.
   dewa mata
   ではまた。
Please/Go ahead. (when offering)
   dōzo
   どうぞ。
Please. (when asking)
   onegai shimasu
   お願いします。
Thanks. (informal)
   dōmo
   どうも。

Thank you.
dōmo arigatō
どうもありがとう。

Thank you very much.
dōmo arigatō gozaimasu
どうもありがとうございます。

Thanks for having me.
(when leaving)
o-sewa ni narimashita
お世話になりました。

You're welcome.
dō itashimasite
どういたしまして。

No, thank you.
iie, kekkō desu
いいえ、けっこうです。

Excuse me/Pardon.
sumimasen
すみません。

Excuse me. (when entering a room)
o-jama shimasu/shitsurei shimasu
おじゃまします。／失礼します。

I'm sorry.
gomen nasai
ごめんなさい。

What's your name?
o-namae wa nan desu ka?
お名前は何ですか？

My name is ...
watashi wa ... desu
私は…です。

This is Mr/Mrs/Ms (Smith).
kochira wa (Sumisu) san desu
こちらは（スミス）さんです。

Pleased to meet you.
dōzo yoroshiku
どうぞよろしく。

Pleased to meet you too.
*hajimemashite, kochira koso dōzo
yoroshiku*
はじめまして、こちらこそどうぞよろしく。

Where are you from?
dochira no kata desu ka?
どちらのかたですか？

How are you?
o-genki desu ka?
お元気ですか？

Fine.
genki desu
元気です。

Is it OK to take a photo?
shashin o totte mo ii desu ka?
写真を撮ってもいいですか？

Cheers!
kampai!
乾杯！

Basics

Yes.
hai
はい。

No.
iie
いいえ。

No. (for indicating disagreement)
chigaimasu
違います。

No. (for indicating disagreement; less
emphatic)
chotto chigaimasu
ちょっと違います。

OK.
daijōbu (desu)/ōke
だいじょうぶ（です）。／オーケー。

What?
nani? なに？

When?
itsu? いつ？

Where?
doko? どこ？

Who?
dare? だれ？

Requests

Please give me this/that.
kore/sore o kudasai
（これ／それ）をください。

Please give me a (cup of tea).
(o-cha) o kudasai
（お茶）をください。

Please wait (a while).
(shōshō) o-machi kudasai
（少々）お待ちください。

Please show me the (ticket).
(kippu) o misete kudasai
（切符）を見せてください。

Language Difficulties

Do you understand English/Japanese?
ei-go/nihon-go wa wakarimasu ka?
（英語／日本語）はわかりますか？

I don't understand.
wakarimasen
わかりません。

Do you speak English?
eigo ga hanasemasu ka?
英語が話せますか？

I can't speak Japanese.
nihongo wa dekimasen
日本語はできません。

How do you say ... in Japanese?
nihongo de ... wa nan to iimasu ka?
日本語で…何といいますか？

What does ... mean?
... wa donna imi desu ka?
…はどんな意味ですか?

What is this called?
kore wa nan to iimasu ka?
これは何といいますか?

Please write in Japanese/English.
nihongo/eigo de kaite kudasai
（日本語／英語）で書いてください。

Please speak more slowly.
mō chotto yukkuri itte kudasai
もうちょっとゆっくり言ってください。

Please say it again more slowly.
mō ichidō, yukkuri itte kudasai
もう一度、ゆっくり言ってください。

What is this called?
kore wa nan to iimasu ka?
これは何といいますか?

Getting Around

What time does the next ... leave?
tsugi no ... wa nanji ni demasu ka?
次の…は何時に出ますか?

What time does the next ... arrive?
tsugi no ... wa nanji ni tsukimasu ka?
次の…は何時に着きますか?

boat
bōto/fune ボート／船

bus (city)
shibasu 市バス

bus (intercity)
chōkyoribasu 長距離バス

bus stop
basutei バス停

tram
romen densha 路面電車

train
densha 電車

subway
chikatetsu 地下鉄

station
eki 駅

ticket
kippu 切符

ticket office
kippu uriba 切符売り場

timetable
jikokuhyō 時刻表

taxi
takushī タクシー

entrance
iriguchi 入口

exit
deguchi 出口

Signs	
Information	
annaijo	案内所
Open	
eigyōchū	営業中
Closed	
junbichū	準備中
Toilets	
o-tearai/toire	お手洗い／トイレ
Men	
otoko	男
Women	
onna	女

left-luggage office
nimotsu azukarijo 荷物預かり所

one way
katamichi 片道

return
ōfuku 往復

non-smoking seat
kin'en seki 禁煙席

Where is the ...?
... wa doko desu ka?
…はどこですか?

How much is the fare to ...?
... made ikura desu ka?
…までいくらですか?

Does this (train, bus, etc) go to ...?
kore wa ... e ikimasu ka?
これは…へ行きますか?

Is the next station ...?
tsugi no eki wa ... desu ka?
次の駅は…ですか?

Please tell me when we get to ...
... ni tsuitara oshiete kudasai
…に着いたら教えてください。

Where is the ... exit?
... deguchi wa doko desu ka?
…出口はどこですか?

How far is it to walk?
aruite dono kurai kakarimasu ka?
歩いてどのくらいかかりますか?

I'd like to hire a ...
... o karitai no desu ga.
…を借りたいのですが。

I'd like to go to ...
... ni ikitai desu
…に行きたいです。

Please stop here.
koko de tomete kudasai
ここで停めてください。

How do I get to ...?
... e wa dono yō ni ikeba ii desu ka?
…へはどのように行けばいいですか?

Where is this address please?
kono jūsho wa doko desu ka?
この住所はどこですか？
Could you write down the address for me?
jūsho o kaite itadakemasen ka?
住所を書いていただけませんか？
Go straight ahead.
massugu itte まっすぐ行って。
Turn left/right.
hidari/migi e magatte
（左／右）へ曲がって。
near/far
chikai/tōi 近い／遠い

Around Town
bank
ginkō 銀行
embassy
taishi-kan 大使館
post office
yūbin kyoku 郵便局
market
ichiba 市場
a public telephone
kōshū denwa 公衆電話
toilet
o-tearai/toire お手洗い／トイレ
the tourist office
kankō annaijo 観光案内所

What time does it open/close?
nanji ni akimasu/shimarimasu ka
何時に（開きます／閉まります）か？

Accommodation
I'm looking for a ...
... o sagashite imasu
…を探しています。
hotel
hoteru ホテル
guesthouse
gesuto hausu ゲストハウス
inn
ryokan 旅館
youth hostel
yūsu hosuteru ユースホステル
camping ground
kyampu-jō キャンプ場
Japanese-style inn
ryokan 旅館
family-style inn
minshuku 民宿

Do you have any vacancies?
aki-beya wa arimasu ka?
空き部屋はありますか？

I don't have a reservation.
yoyaku wa shiteimasen
予約はしていません。

single room
shinguru rūmu シングルルーム
double room
daburu rūmu ダブルルーム
twin room
tsuin rūmu ツインルーム
Japanese-style room
washitsu 和室
Western-style room
yōshitsu 洋室
Japanese-style bath
o-furo お風呂

room with a (Western-style) bath
basu tsuki no heya
バス付きの部屋
How much is it per night/per person?
ippaku/hitori ikura de suka?
（一泊／一人）いくらですか？
Does it include breakfast/a meal?
chōshoku/shokuji wa tsuite imasu ka?
（朝食／食事）は付いていますか？
I'm going to stay for one night/two nights.
hito-ban/futa-ban tomarimasu
（一晩／二晩）泊まります。
Can I leave my luggage here?
nimotsu o azukatte itadakemasen ka?
荷物を預かっていただけませんか？

Shopping
I'd like to buy ...
... o kaitai desu
…を買いたいです。
How much is it?
ikura desu ka?
いくらですか？
I'm just looking.
miteiru dake desu
見ているだけです。
It's cheap.
yasui desu
安いです。
It's too expensive.
taka-sugi masu
高すぎます。
I'll take this one.
kore o kudasai
これをください。
Can I have a receipt?
ryōshūsho o itadakemasen ka?
領収書をいただけませんか？

Emergencies

Help!
tasukete!
助けて！

Call a doctor!
isha o yonde kudasai!
医者を呼んでください！

Call the police!
keisatsu o yonde kudasai!
警察を呼んでください！

I'm lost.
michi ni mayoi mashita
道に迷いました。

Go away!
hanarero!
離れろ！

big
   ōkii   大きい
small
   chiisai   小さい
shop
   mise   店
supermarket
   sūpā   スーパー
bookshop
   hon ya   本屋
camera shop
   shashin ya   写真屋
department store
   depāto   デパート

Food

breakfast
   chōshoku/asa gohan 朝食／朝ご飯
lunch
   ranchi/chūshoku/   ランチ／昼食／
   hiru gohan   昼ご飯
dinner
   yūshoku/ban gohan 夕食／晩ご飯

I'm a vegetarian.
   watashi wa bejitarian desu
   私はベジタリアンです。
Do you have any vegetarian meals?
   bejitarian-ryōri wa arimasu ka?
   ベジタリアン料理はありますか？
What do you recommend?
   o-susume wa nan desu ka?
   おすすめは何ですか？
Do you have an English menu?
   eigo no menyū wa arimasu ka?
   英語のメニューはありますか？

I'd like the set menu please.
   setto menyū o o-negai shimasu
   セットメニューをお願いします。
Please bring the bill.
   o-kanjō o onegai shimasu
   お勘定をお願いします。
This is delicious.
   oishii desu
   おいしいです。

Health

I need a doctor.
   isha ga hitsuyō desu
   医者が必要です。
How do you feel?
   kibun wa ikaga desu ka?
   気分はいかがですか？
I'm ill.
   kibun ga warui desu
   気分が悪いです。
It hurts here.
   koko ga itai desu
   ここが痛いです。
I have diarrhoea.
   geri o shiteimasu
   下痢をしています。
I have a toothache.
   ha ga itamimasu
   歯が痛みます。

I'm ...
   watashi wa ...   私は…
diabetic
   tōnyōbyō desu   糖尿病です。
epileptic
   tenkan desu   てんかんです。
asthmatic
   zensoku desu   喘息です。
I'm allergic to antibiotics/penicillin.
   kōsei-busshitsu/penishirin ni arerugii ga
   arimasu
   （抗生物質／ペニシリン）に
   アレルギーがあります。

antiseptic
   shōdokuyaku   消毒薬
aspirin
   asupirin   アスピリン
condoms
   kondōmu   コンドーム
contraceptive
   hinin yō piru   避妊用ピル
dentist
   ha-isha   歯医者

Glossary of Useful Terms

Geography

-dake/take	岳	peak
-dani/tani	谷	valley
-gawa/kawa	川	river
-hama	浜	beach
-hantō	半島	peninsula
-jima/shima	島	island
-kaikyō	海峡	channel/strait
-ko	湖	lake
-kō	港	port
-kōen	公園	park
-kōgen	高原	plateau
kokutei kōen	国定公園	quasi-national park
kokuritsu kōen	国立公園	national park
-kyō	峡	gorge
-minato	港	harbour
-misaki	岬	cape
...no-yu	…の湯	hot spring
-oka	丘	hill
onsen	温泉	hot spring
-san/zan	山	mountain
-shima/jima	島	island
shokubutsu-en	植物園	botanic garden
-shotō	諸島	archipelago
-take/dake	岳	peak
-taki	滝	waterfall
-tani/dani	谷	valley
-tō	島	island
-wan	湾	bay
-yama	山	mountain
-yu	湯	hot spring

-zaki/misaki	岬	cape
-zan/san	山	mountain

Regions

-shi	市	city
-chō	町	neighbourhood or village/s
-mura	村	village
-ken	県	prefecture
-gun	郡	county
-ku	区	ward

Sights

-dera/tera	寺	temple
-dō	堂	temple or hall of a temple
-en	園	garden
-in	院	temple or hall of a temple
-gū	宮	shrine
-ji	寺	temple
-jō	城	castle
-kōen	公園	park
-mon	門	gate
shokubutsu-en	植物園	botanical garden
-hori/bori	堀	moat
-jingū	神宮	shrine
-jinja	神社	shrine
-taisha	大社	shrine
-teien	庭園	garden
-tera/dera	寺	temple
-torii	鳥居	shrine gate

doctor		
isha	医者	
hospital		
byōin	病院	
medicine		
kusuri	薬	
pharmacy		
yakkyoku	薬局	
tampons		
tampon	タンポン	
(a) cold		
kaze	風邪	
diarrhoea		
geri	下痢	
fever		
hatsunetsu	発熱	
food poisoning		
shoku chūdoku	食中毒	
migraine		
henzutsū	偏頭痛	

Time, Days & Numbers

What time is it?
ima nan-ji desu ka?
今何時ですか？

today		
kyō	今日	
tomorrow		
ashita	明日	
yesterday		
kinō	きのう	
morning/afternoon		
asa/hiru	朝／昼	
Monday		
getsuyōbi	月曜日	
Tuesday		
kayōbi	火曜日	
Wednesday		
suiyōbi	水曜日	

Thursday			8	*hachi*	八
mokuyōbi	木曜日		9	*kyū/ku*	九
Friday			10	*jū*	十
kinyōbi	金曜日		11	*jūichi*	十一
Saturday			12	*jūni*	十二
doyōbi	土曜日		13	*jūsan*	十三
Sunday			14	*jūyon/ jūshi*	十四
nichiyōbi	日曜日		20	*nijū*	二十
			21	*nijūichi*	二十一

Numbers

			30	*sanjū*	三十
0	*zero/rei*	ゼロ／零	100	*hyaku*	百
1	*ichi*	一	200	*nihyaku*	二百
2	*ni*	二	1000	*sen*	千
3	*san*	三	5000	*gosen*	五千
4	*yon/shi*	四	10,000	*ichiman*	一万
5	*go*	五	20,000	*niman*	二万
6	*roku*	六	100,000	*jūman*	十万
7	*nana/shichi*	七	one million	*hyakuman*	百万

Glossary

aimai – ambiguous and unclear

Ainu – indigenous people of Hokkaidō and parts of northern Honshū

aka-chōchin – red lantern; a working man's pub marked by red lanterns outside

akirame – to relinquish; resignation

ama – women divers

Amaterasu – sun goddess and link to the imperial throne

ANA – All Nippon Airlines

ANK – All Nippon Koku

annai-sho – information office

arubaito – from the German *arbeit*, meaning 'to work', adapted into Japanese to refer to part-time work; often contracted to *baito*

asa-ichi – morning market

awamori – local alcohol of Okinawa

ayu – sweetfish caught during *ukai* (cormorant fishing)

baito – a part-time job (from *arbeit*, the German word meaning 'to work')

bangasa – rain umbrella made from oiled paper

banzai – 'hurrah' or 'hurray'; in the West this exclamation is, for the most part, associated with WWII, although its more modern usage is quite peaceful; literally '10,000 years'

bashō – sumō wrestling tournament

basho-gara – fitting to the particular conditions or circumstances; literally 'the character of a place'

bentō – boxed lunch, usually of rice, with a main dish and pickles or salad

bonsai – the art of growing miniature trees by careful pruning of branches and roots

boso-zoku – 'hot-car' or motorcycle gangs, usually noisy but harmless

bottle-keep – system whereby you buy a whole bottle of liquor in a bar, which is kept for you to drink on subsequent visits

bugaku – dance pieces played by court orchestras in ancient Japan

buke yashiki – samurai residence

bunraku – classical puppet theatre using huge puppets to portray dramas similar to *kabuki*

burakumin – traditionally outcasts associated with lowly occupations such as leather work; literally 'village people'

bushidō – a set of values followed by the samurai; literally 'the way of the warrior'

butsudan – Buddhist altar in Japanese homes

champuru – stir-fry with mixed ingredients such as *goya* and *fū*

chanelah – fashionable young woman with a predilection for name brands, in particular Chanel products

chaniwa – tea garden

chanoyu – tea ceremony

charm – small dish of peanuts or other snack food served with a drink at a bar – it's often not requested but is still added to your bill

chimpira – *yakuza* understudy; usually used pejoratively of a male with *yakuza* aspirations

chizu – map

chō – city area (for large cities) between a *ku* (ward) and *chōme* in size; also a street

chōchin – paper lantern

chōme – city area of a few blocks

chōnan – oldest son

chu – loyalty

daibutsu – Great Buddha

daifuku – sticky rice cakes filled with red bean paste and eaten on festive occasions; literally 'great happiness'

daimyō – regional lords under the shōguns

daira – plain

danchi – public apartments

dantai – a group

dashi – festival floats

donko – name for local trains in country areas

eboshi – black, triangular samurai hat

eki – train station

ekiben – *bentō* lunch box bought at a train station

ema – small votive plaques hung in shrine precincts as petitions for assistance from the resident deities

engawa – traditional veranda of a Japanese house overlooking the garden

enka – often described as the Japanese equivalent of country and western music, these are folk ballads about love and human suffering that are popular among the older generation

enryō – individual restraint and reserve

ero-guro – erotic and grotesque *manga*

fu – urban prefecture

fū – gluten

fude – brush used for calligraphy

fugu – poisonous blowfish or pufferfish

fundoshi – loincloth or breechcloth; a traditional male garment consisting of a wide belt and a cloth drawn over the genitals and between the buttocks. Usually seen only at festivals or on sumō wrestlers

furigana – Japanese script used to aid pronunciation of *kanji*

furii-kippu – one-day open ticket

fusuma – sliding screen

futon – traditional quilt-like mattress that is rolled up and stowed away during the day

futsū – a local train; literally 'ordinary'

gagaku – music of the imperial court

gaijin – foreigners; literally 'outside people'

gaijin house – cheap accommodation for long-term foreign residents

gajutsu – native ginger

gaman – to endure

gasshō-zukuri – an architectural style; literally 'hands in prayer'

gei-no-kai – the 'world of art and talent'; usually refers to TV

geisha – woman versed in arts and dramas who entertains guests; not a prostitute

genkan – foyer area where shoes are removed or replaced when entering or leaving a building

geta – traditional wooden sandals

giri – social obligations

giri-ninjō – combination of social obligations and personal values; the two are often in conflict

gekijō – theatre

go – board game; players alternately place white and black counters down, with the object to surround the opponent and make further moves impossible; probably originated in China, where it's known as *weiqi*

goya – bitter melon

habu – a venomous snake found in Okinawa

hachimaki – headband worn as a symbol of resolve; *kamikaze* pilots wore them in WWII, students wear them to exams

haiku – 17-syllable poems

hanami – blossom viewing (usually cherry blossoms)

haniwa – earthenware figures found in Kōfun-period tombs

hanko – stamp or seal used to authenticate any document; in Japan your *hanko* carries much more weight than your signature

hara – marshlands

hara-kiri – belly cutting; common name for *seppuku* or ritual suicide

hara-kyū – acupuncture

hari – dragon-boat races

hashi – chopsticks

heiwa – peace

henrō – pilgrims on the Shikoku 88 Temple Circuit

higasa – sunshade umbrella

Hikari – express *shinkansen*

hiragana – phonetic syllabary used to write Japanese words

honsen – main rail line

ichi-go – square wooden sake 'cups' holding 180ml

IDC – International Digital Communications

ike-ike onna – young Japanese woman who favours dyed brown hair, a boutique suntan and bright lipstick; literally 'go-go girl'

ijime – bullying or teasing; a problem in Japanese schools

ikebana – art of flower arrangement

irezumi – a tattoo or the art of tattooing

irori – hearth or fireplace

itadakimasu – an expression used before meals; literally 'I will receive'

ITJ – International Telecom Japan

ittaikan – feeling of unity, of being one type

izakaya – Japanese version of a pub; beer and *sake* and lots of snacks available in a rustic, boisterous setting

JAC – Japan Air Commuter

JAF – Japan Automobile Federation

JAL – Japan Airlines

JAS – Japan Air System

jiage-ya – specialists used by developers to persuade recalcitrant landowners to sell up

jigoku – boiling mineral hot springs, which are definitely not for bathing in; literally 'hells'

jika-tabi – split-toe boots traditionally worn by Japanese carpenters and builders

jikokuhyō – timetable or book of timetables

jinja – shrine

jitensha – bicycle

jizō – small stone statues of the Buddhist protector of travellers and children

JNTO – Japan National Tourist Organization

JR – Japan Railways

JTB – Japan Travel Bureau

jujitsu – martial art from which *judō* was derived

juku – after-school 'cram' schools

JYHA – Japan Youth Hostel Association

kabuki – a form of Japanese theatre based on popular legends, which is characterised by elaborate costumes, stylised acting and the use of male actors for all roles

kaikan – hotel-style accommodation sponsored by government; literally 'meeting hall'

kaiseki – Japanese cuisine which obeys very strict rules of etiquette for every detail of the meal, including the setting

kaisha – a company, firm

kaisoku – rapid train

kaisū-ken – a book of tickets

kaiten-zushi – sushi served at a conveyor-belt restaurant (also the name of such a restaurant)

kakizome – New Year's resolutions

kami – Shintō gods; spirits of natural phenomena

kamidana – Shintō altar in Japanese homes

kamikaze – typhoon that sunk Kublai Khan's 13th-century invasion fleet and the name adopted by suicide pilots in the waning days of WWII; literally 'divine wind'

kampai – 'Cheers!'

kampō – Chinese herbal medicines that were dominant in Japan until the 19th century, when Western pharmaceuticals were introduced

kana – the two phonetic syllabaries, *hiragana* and *katakana*

kanji – Chinese ideographic script used for writing Japanese; literally 'Chinese script'

Kannon – Buddhist goddess of mercy (Sanskrit: Avalokiteshvara)

kannushi – chief priest of a Shintō shrine

karakuri – mechanical puppets

karakasa – oiled paper umbrella

karaoke – bars where you sing along with taped music; literally 'empty orchestra'

kasa – umbrella

katakana – phonetic syllabary used to write foreign words

katamichi – one-way ticket

katana – Japanese sword

KDD – Kokusai Denshin Denwa (International Telephone & Telegraph)

keigo – honorific language used to show respect to elders or those of high rank

ken – prefecture

kendō – oldest martial art; literally 'the way of the sword'

ki – life force, will

kimono – brightly coloured, robe-like traditional outer garment

kin'en-sha – nonsmoking carriage

kissaten – coffee shop

kōban – police box

kōgen – general area, plain

koi – carp; considered to be a brave, tenacious and vigorous fish. Many towns and villages have carp ponds or channels teeming with colourful ornamental *nishiki-goi* carp.

koinobori – carp banners and windsocks; the colourful fish pennants that are flown in honour of sons whom it is hoped will inherit a carp's virtues. These wave over countless homes in Japan in late April and early May are for Boys' Day, the final holiday of Golden Week. These days, Boys' Day has become Children's Day and the windsocks don't necessarily simply fly in honour of the household's sons.

kokki – Japanese national flag

kūkō – airport

kokumin-shukusha – peoples' lodges; an inexpensive form of accommodation

kokutetsu – Japanese word for Japan Railways (JR)

Komeitō – Clean Government Party; third-largest political party

kotatsu – heated table with a quilt or cover over it to keep the legs and lower body warm

koto – 13-stringed instrument that is played flat on the floor

kuidaore – eat until you drop (Kansai)

kura – mud-walled storehouses

kyakuma – drawing room of a home, where guests are met

kyōiku mama – a woman who pushes her kids through the Japanese education system; literally 'education mother'

kyūkō – ordinary express train (faster than a *futsū*, only stopping at certain stations)

live house – nightclub or bar where live music is performed

machi – city area (for large cities) between a *ku* (ward) and *chōme* (area of a few blocks) in size; also street or area

maiko – apprentice *geisha*

mama-san – woman who manages a bar or club

maneki-neko – beckoning cat figure frequently seen in restaurants and bars; it's supposed to attract customers and trade

manga – Japanese comics

matsuri – festival

meinichi – the 'deathday' or anniversary of someone's death

meishi – business card

mentsu – face

miai-kekkon – arranged marriage

mibun – social rank

miko – shrine maidens

mikoshi – portable shrines carried during festivals

minshuku – the Japanese equivalent of a B&B; family-run budget accommodation

miso-shiru – bean-paste soup

MITI – Ministry of International Trade & Industry

mitsubachi – accommodation for motorcycle tourers

mizu-shōbai – entertainment, bars, prostitution, etc

mochi – pounded rice made into cakes and eaten at festive occasions

mōfu – blanket

morning service – *mōningu sābisu*; a light breakfast served until 10am in many *kissaten*

mura – village

nagashi-somen – flowing noodles

nengajō – New Year cards

N'EX – Narita Express

NHK – Nihon Hōsō Kyōkai (Japan Broadcasting Corporation)

Nihon or Nippon – Japanese word for Japan; literally 'source of the sun'

nihonga – term for Japanese-style painting

ningyō – Japanese doll

ninja – practitioners of *ninjutsu*

ninjutsu – 'the art of stealth'

nō – classical Japanese drama performed on a bare stage

noren – cloth hung as a sunshade, typically carrying the name of the shop or premises; indicates that a restaurant is open for business

norikae – to change buses or trains; make a connection

norikae-ken – transfer ticket (trams and buses)

NTT – Nippon Telegraph & Telephone Corporation

o- – prefix used to show respect to anything it is applied to; see *san*

o-bāsan – grandmotherly type; an old woman

obi – sash or belt worn with a kimono

o-cha – tea

ofuku – return ticket

o-furo – traditional Japanese bath

o-jōsan – young college-age woman of conservative taste and aspirations

okonomiyaki – cabbage pancakes

OL – 'office lady'; female employee of a large firm; usually a clerical worker – pronounced '*ō-eru*'

o-miai – arranged marriage

o-miyage – souvenir

on – favour

onnagata – male actor playing a woman's role (usually in *kabuki*)

onsen – mineral hot-spring spa area, usually with accommodation

origami – art of paper folding

o-shibori – hot towels provided in restaurants

o-tsumami – bar snacks or *charms*

oyabun/kobun – teacher/pupil or senior/junior relationship

oyaki – wheat buns filled with pickles, squash, radish and red-bean paste

pachinko – vertical pinball game which is a Japanese craze (estimated to take in over ¥6 trillion a year) and a major source of tax evasion, *yakuza* funds, etc

puripeido kādo – 'prepaid card'; a sort of reverse credit card: you buy a magnetically coded card for a given amount and it can be used for certain purchases until spent. The prepaid phonecards are the most widespread but there are many others such as Prepaid Highway Cards for use on toll roads

rakugo – Japanese raconteurs, stand-up comics

reien – cemetery

reisen – cold mineral spring

Rinzai – school of Zen Buddhism which places an emphasis on *kōan* (riddles)

robatayaki – *yakitori-ya* with a deliberately rustic, friendly, homey atmosphere; see also *izakaya*

romaji – Japanese roman script

rō – vegetable wax

rōnin – students who must resit university entrance exams; literally 'masterless samurai'

ropeway – Japanese word for a cable car or tramway

rotemburo – open-air baths

ryokan – traditional Japanese inn

sadō – tea ceremony; literally 'way of tea'

saisen-bako – offering box at Shintō shrines

sakazuki – *sake* cups

sakoku – Japan's period of national seclusion prior to the Meiji Restoration

sakura – cherry blossoms

salaryman – standard male employee of a large firm

sama – even more respectful suffix than *san* (see below); used in instances such as *o-kyaku-sama* – the 'honoured guest'

samurai – warrior class

san – suffix which shows respect to the person it is applied to; see also *o*, the equivalent honorific. Both can occasionally be used together as *o-kyaku-san*, where *kyaku* is the word for guest or customer.

sansai – mountain vegetables

san-sō – mountain cottage

satori – Zen concept of enlightenment

seku-hara – sexual harassment

sembei – flavoured rice crackers often sold in tourist areas

sempai – one's elder or senior at school or work

sensei – generally translates as 'teacher' but has wider reference

sentō – public baths

seppuku – ritual suicide by disembowelment

setto – set meal

seza – a kneeling position

shamisen – three-stringed instrument

shi – city (to distinguish cities with prefectures of the same name, eg, Kyoto-shi)

shiken-jigoku – the enormously important and stressful entrance exams to various levels of the Japanese education system; literally 'examination hell'

shikki – lacquerware

shinkansen – ultra fast 'bullet' trains; literally 'new trunk line', since new train lines were laid for the high speed trains

shitamachi – traditionally the low-lying, less affluent parts of Tokyo

shodō – Japanese calligraphy; literally the 'way of writing'

shōgi – a version of chess in which each player has 20 pieces and the object is to capture the opponent's king

shōgun – former military ruler of Japan

shogekijō – small theatre

shōji – sliding rice-paper screens

shōjin ryōri – vegetarian meals (especially at temple lodgings)

shūji – a lesser form of *shodō*; literally 'the practice of letters'

shukubō – temple lodgings

shunga – explicit erotic prints; literally 'spring pictures', the season of spring being a popular Chinese and Japanese euphemism for sexuality

Shugendō – offbeat Buddhist school, which incorporates ancient Shamanistic rites, Shintō beliefs and ascetic Buddhist traditions

shuntō – spring labour offensive; an annual 'strike'

shūyū-ken – excursion train ticket

soapland – Japanese euphemism for bathhouses that offer sexual services

soba – buckwheat noodles

soroban – abacus

Sōtō – a school of Zen Buddhism which places emphasis on *zazen*

sukebe – lewd in thought and deed; can be a compliment in the right context (eg, among male drinking partners), but generally shouldn't be used lightly; the English equivalent would be 'sleaze bag'

sukiyaki – thin slices of beef cooked in *sake*, soy and vinegar broth

sumi-e – black-ink brush paintings

sumō – Japanese wrestling

tabi – split-toed Japanese socks used when wearing *geta*

tadaima – a traditional greeting called out upon returning home; literally 'now' or 'present'

tako – kite

tanin – outsider, stranger, someone not connected with the current situation

tanka – poems of 31 syllables

tanuki – racoon or dog-like folklore character frequently represented in ceramic figures

tarento – 'talent'; generally refers to musical performers

tatami – tightly woven floor matting on which shoes are never worn. Traditionally, room size is defined by the number of tatami mats

tatemae – 'face'; how you act in public, your public position

TCAT – Tokyo City Air Terminal

teiki-ken – discount commuter passes

teishoku – set meal

tekitō – suitable or appropriate

tennō – heavenly king, the emperor

TIC – Tourist Information Center

to – metropolis, eg, Tokyo-to

tosu – toilet

tokkuri – *sake* flask

tokkyū – limited express; faster than an ordinary express *(kyūkō)* train

tokonoma – alcove in a house in which flowers may be displayed or a scroll hung

torii – entrance gate to a Shintō shrine

tsukiai – after-work socialising among salarymen

tsunami – huge tidal waves caused by an earthquake

tsuru – cranes; a symbol of longevity often reproduced in *origami* and represented in traditional gardens

uchi – has meanings relating to 'belonging' and 'being part of'; literally 'one's own house'

uchiwa – paper fan

ukai – fishing using trained cormorants

ukiyo-e – wood-block prints; literally 'pictures of the floating world'

umeboshi – pickled plums thought to aid digestion; often served with rice in *bentō* sets

wa – harmony, team spirit; also the old *kanji* used to denote Japan, and still used in Chinese and Japanese as a prefix to indicate things of Japanese origin; see *wafuku*

wabi – enjoyment of peace and tranquillity

wafuku – Japanese-style clothing

waka – 31-syllable poem

wanko – lacquerware bowls

waribashi – disposable wooden chopsticks

warikan – custom of sharing the bill (among good friends)

wasabi – Japanese horseradish

washi – Japanese handmade paper

yabusame – horseback archery

yakitori – charcoal-broiled chicken and other meats or vegetables, cooked on skewers

yakitori-ya – restaurant specialising in *yakitori*

yaku-sugi – Japanese mafia

yakuza – Japanese mafia

yamabushi – mountain priests (Shugendō Buddhism practitioners)

yama-goya – mountain huts

yamato – a term of much debated origins that refers to the Japanese world

yamato damashii – Japanese spirit, a term with parallels to the German *Volksgeist*; it was harnessed by the militarist government of the 1930s and 1940s and was identified with unquestioning loyalty to the emperor

yamato-e – traditional Japanese painting

yanqui – tastelessly dressed male, with dyed hair and a cellular phone

yatai – festival floats/hawker stalls

YCAT – Yokohama City Air Terminal

yōfuku – Western-style clothing

yukata – light cotton summer kimono, worn for lounging or casual use; standard issue when staying at a ryokan

zabuton – small cushions for sitting on (used in *tatami* rooms)

zaibatsu – industrial conglomerates; the term arose prior to WWII but the Japanese economy is still dominated by huge firms like Mitsui, Marubeni and Mitsubishi, which are involved in many different industries

zazen – seated meditation emphasised in the Sōtō school of Zen Buddhism

Zen – introduced to Japan in the 12th century from China, this offshoot of Buddhism emphasises a direct, intuitive approach to enlightenment rather than rational analysis

Thanks

Many thanks to the travellers who used the last edition and wrote to us with helpful hints, useful advice and interesting anecdotes:

Nikolay Kolesnikov, Linda (Anika) Bade, Husain Akbar, Jack Alexander, Jennifer Alker, Barbara Anderson, Erica Anderson, Peter Andersson, Justin Andrews, Mark Andrews, Vanessa Angell, Yuriko Aoki, Wiebke Arndt, Jun Asakura, Keiko Awaji, Berkay Aydogan, Mohd Sallehhudin Abd Aziz, Tanja Baar, Michael Bade, Rachel Bagenal, Rowland Bailey, Chris Bain, Caroline Baker, John Baker, Shems Baker-Jud, John Bament, Russell Banks, Kelly Banz, Ronald Barca, Steven Bardy, Judy Barnsley, Dr Paul Barret, Jacquie Barrett, Rosanna Barson, Geoff Barton, Gordon Bartram, Darren Bauer, Angela Beard, David Beattie, Simon Beck, Claus Behn, Steve Bein, Tony Bennett, Joachim Bergmann, Brian Berryman, Walter Bertschinger, James Best, Frédéric Billy, Roland Binet, Heidi Birkbeck, Rupert Blackstone, Jose Antonio Blanco, Inge Bley-Hiersemenzel, Julien Bodart, Jeroen Bok, Patrick Bommarito, Lea Bonnington, Tom Booij, Dianne Boothroyd, Jorn Borup, Jean-Pierre Boudrias, Gerard Bousquet, Kate Bowley, Jim Boyden, Kim Bradford-Watts, Yomi Braester, Andrea Brandle, Colleen Brandrick, Martin Brauen, Tanya Breau, Rosemarie Brickley, Ben Brock, Andrea Broglia, Douglas Brooks, Jan Brown, Chilla Bulbeck, Jonathan Bulut, Joel Bumgardner, Javier Burgos, Glen Burns, Mark Burton, Joseph Caldarera, Adrian Callender, Rod Campbell, Carianne Carleo-Evangelist, Lenora Carlson, Bonnie Carpenter, Bryan Carr, Ian Chamberlin, A Chan, Sui-Fung Chan, Mike Chang, Hubert Chanson, Dr Ronald Allan Charles, Agnes Chen, Christian Chester, Krishna Kishore Chilukuri, Anthony Shun Fung Chiu, John Julian Chodacki Karen Chou, Wendy Chouinard, Phil Chow, Heather Clapham, Grant Clark, Jim Clark, Ron Clark, Andrew Clarke, Helen Clarke, Emma Claxton, Amandine Clement, Leonard Cogan, Susan Cole, Yvonne & Brendan Colley, Micheal Collins, Steve Collins, Miriam Colwell, Shlomo Conforti, Bobbie Connor, Tom Cooper, Katrina Corcoran, Erin Corry, Helen Coulson, Laura Coulter, Jérome Courtois, Dean Cracknell, Holly Crisson, John Crocker, Janet Croft, Asher Crossman, B Cudal, Stephen Cullis, Felix Dahm, Adam Dangoor, Jez Darr, Shobha Rani Dash, Fereshteh Dastani, Elaine Davis, J de Jong, Erwin de Kock, Pamela De Mark, Jose Teles De Menezes, Coline de Valence, Hannah Deacon, Mike Dean, Gustavo Delgado, Leroy W Demery, David Deng, Pete Deuart, Cole Diamond, Jennifer Dickinson, Julian Diggle, Regina Dinneen, Francesco Diodato, Dan Dixon, Thomas Doggett, Lynne Donaldson, Alan Dorin, David Dougherty, Ian

Douglas, Daniel Dourneau, M & P Dowling, Mark Doyle, Haley Drake, Prunella Dunn, Carl Durdan, Mark Eberst, Dianne Edlington, David Edwards, Frazer Egerton, Pierre Elias, Carol Elk, Charles Elkington, Troy Ellis, James Embry, Blake Engelhard, Alexander Engelhardt, John Erskine Banta, Hayley Every, Tim Eyre, Gaynor Fairchild, Rita Farkas, Alireza Fatehi, Ian Fenwick, Gerard Ferlin, Macdara Ferris, Debra Filippin, Joachim Finkler, Megan Fisher, Tony Fitzcarl, Brian Fitzgerald, Birger Fjallman, Marc Flynn, Pernille & Kennet Foh, Del Ford, Suzanne France, Diodato Francesco, Kevin Friesen, Louise Frost, Cecilia Fujishima, Helene Gagnon, Amy Gaines, Mike Galvin, June Garbutt, Mark Garrity, Sean Geiger, Doriann Geller, Christine Gemon, Marianna Gentilin, Simon & Georgie, GP Gervat, John Gibb, Terry Gibbs, Dave Gifford, Steve Gill, Bruce Gilsen, Fleur Sophie Gittinger, Rachel Godet, Tim Gomersall, Andrew Goodwillie, Bob Gordon, Donna Goslin, Prof Ian Gough, Stephen Gowdy, Cameron Graham, Arne Granholm, Melissa Graves, A Grazina, M Greenwood, Scott Greenwood, David Greig, V Griffiths, Xavier Gros, Juli Gudehus, Frederic Guizot, Willie Gunn, John Gurskey, Shirley Hackam, Matt Haine, Kojin Hako, Hazel Hall, Jackie Hall, Kirsty Hall, Tracy Halmos, Rose Hampel, Mattew Hamrick, Karen Hanami, Brian Harding, Angela Harris, Victoria Hart, Fumiko Hattori, David Haugh, JV Haviland, Michael Havlik, Karla Hawke, J Hawksley, John & Vicki Hearnshaw, Stacey Hector, Josef Heiler, Birgit Heilig, Narelle Heinrich, Anthony Helies, Tamara Hellgren, Susan Henderson, Riann Henkel, R Henry, Francisco Hernandes, Fred Herriot, Charles Heydt, Jayne Hibbard, Andrew Hinchley, Louise Hirasawa, Taichi Hirose, Nitani Hirotaka, Lisa Hirst, Karina Ho, Tara Hoffman, Joy Hogley, Racahel Holmes, Thng Hui Hong, Clifton Hood, Martin Hopley, Damien Horigan, Jacqueline Horne, Tim Hornyak, James Howard, H Matthew Howarth, David Howells, Diane Hoxmeier, Brenda Huges, Keith Hughes, Rhidian Hughes, Steven Hunter, Tapani Huovinen, Tan Hwee Meing, Shawna Hyland, Michiko I, Suzana Ikiri, Otto Insam, Csilla-Sakura Istok, Lilla Ito-Hongo, Alene Ivey, Musashi Iwamoto, A Jackson, Jessica Jacob, Eelco Jacobs, Seth Jacoby, Sandro Jakoska, Joy Jarman-Wash, Wlad Jarnick, Richard Jarrott, Mike Javanmard, Rob Jimmieson, Bethan Jinkinson, Eishin Joel-Gerst, Jacob Johansen, Ake Johansson, Peter Johansson, Nic Johnson, Zachary Johnsrud, Mika & Eliah Jordan, John Kafka, KC Kan, Miyuki Kanda, Rachel Kane, Argo Kangro, Nicolas Karman, Makoto Kato, Masayuki Kato, Peter Kearney, Phil Kearse, Jackie Keating, George Kechagiouglou, Geordie Keefe, Ivo Keel, Peter Keightley, Michelle Kelner, Brendan Kiley, Robert King, Simon King, Nola Kirkpatrick, Leigh

Kirwan, Lucas Klamert, Carina Knoll, Cynthia M Knowles, Hisashi Wesley Kobayashi, Christian Kober, Selene Koh, Ralf Kohl, Michael Kohn, Anke Konietzka, Mathew Kroth, Bernd Kruyt, Jan Krynski, Robert Kulp, Ravi A Kumar, Kohei Kurimoto, Raj Ladher, Ian Laidlaw, Kate Lake, Cedric LaMar Joyner, Mark Lane, Thomas Laude, Bryce James Leavitt, Nancy Lee, L Lees, Peter Leichliter, Sophie Leighton, Brian Lennox, Manfred Lenten, Shane Leonard, Jason Lewis, Loretta Lewis, Keri Lim, Kerrie & Caris Lim, Joseph Limoli, Jenny Lin, Paul Lincoln, Kai Lingemann, Caroline Liou, Brian Little, Tanya Livingston, David Long, Eduardo Lopez Salas, Artur Loza, Jennifer Lui, Hoi Yan Lung, Christine Lutz, Roger Lyman, Ann Lyons, Connie Lyons, Melissa Macias, Ian Mackay, Gerrard MacKinnon, Sarah Macklin, Kylie Macpherson, Kathleen Maguire, Stephen Maidment, Alexander Mair, Ryu Makoto, Megan Mann, Michel Martin, Toni Martin, Kristian Martinsen, Mayumi Masing, Mayumi & Christian Masing, David Mason, Robert Mason, John Massy, Lee Ann Matsuda, Tetsuya Matsuguchi, Hitoshi Matsushima, Aki Matsuura, Gerald Matthe, Guido Mauchle, Corey Don McDaniel, Derry McDonell, Mike Mcgee, Terry McGlynn, Lynn McKee, Henley McKegg, Hamish McLean, Brian & Mon McNamara, Jodie McQueen, Blanca Melguizo, David Melhuish, James P Menath, Ryan Mentzos, J Keith Mercer, Simon Merry, Ira-Raphaela Meudt, Eric Meulien, Gavin Milligan, Josh Mink, Paul Minza, Manuel miseur, Heather Mitchell, Ken Mitchell, Hiroshi Mochizuki, Brian Moeran, Andrew G Moncrieff, Mario Moore, Simon Moore, John Moorhead, Jeanette Morehouse, Andrew Morgan, Leah Morgan, Yoshiharu Morohashi, Angela Morris, Katherine Morton, Brendon Moss, Heather Mulcahy, Gail Murayama, Patrick Murphy, Andrew Murray, Marco Mwaniki, Greg Naglis, Shinji Nakajima, Shinichi Nakazono, Monty Navarro, Sonja Neudörfer, Treasa Ni Mhiochain, Alan Nicholls, Francine Nicholson, Gordon Nisbet, Hideki Nitata, Mike Nolan, Josh Norton, Suzanne Nottage, Rip Noyes, Janet Nussmann, Steve Oades, John O'Connell, John O'Doherty, Robin O'Donoghue, Carl Oliver, Mike O'Loughlin, Balazs Oroszlany, Eugene & Maumi Orwell, Phyllis Oster, Susan Oster, Carrie Ottsen, Jude Page, Julie Page, Aristea Parissi, Woo Sok Park, Howell Parry, Todd Patola, Janice Paton, Trent Paton, Stacey Pearl, Jerry Peek, Marion Penaud, Karene Perkins, Jan Petermann, Y Petersen, Charles Petran, Steven Pickles, Lisa Pirrie, Hennie Platerink, Joe Poconto, Douglas Poole, Semin Poonja, Yves Prescott, Kenneth Pechter, Mitch Pryor, Aaron Quigley, Sarah Jane Quinnell, Patrick Raitt, Allison Ralph, M Ralph, Alexander W Rauscher, Ossie Ravid, Etienne Raynaud, Lawrence Redfern, Howard Reed, Fitzcarl Reid, Dan Rempel, Drew Richardson, Liisa Richardson, Darren Riches, F Rickword, Michael Ridpath, Matthew A Rifkin, Jess Ripper, Dale Riva, Paul Rivers, Kim Roberts, Bill Robertson, Eduardo Robinovich, Gardner Robinson, Bernd Oliver Rose, Karen Rosenblum, Sandra Roth, Nick Rowan, Kristoffer Roxbergh, Jo Rumble, Julie Russell, Vanessa Ryan, Tianna Salmond, Darren Salter, Sue Salvano, Jon Salz, Claire Sampson, Damien Sams, Phil Sandahl, Jessica Sanders, Cynthia Sandler, Karen Sandness, Victor Sarmiento, Jo Saunders, Stuart Schechter, Travis Schedler, Jeana Schieffer, Nick Schilov, Peter Schinkelshoek, Jochen Schmaehling, Andrea Schnell, Scott Schocker, James Schumann, Sara Sclaroff, Mark Scott, Patti Scott, William Seager, Roy Sedgwick, Don Seekins, Dave Seibert, Erik Selmer, Lorenza Severi, James Shafto, Paul Sharkey, Vincent Shields, Pamela Shore, Mitch Siemens Rhodes, Laura Sikstrom, Mark Silverberg, Molly Simpson, Justin Sinodinos, Bryn Skilbeck, Zdenek Slanina, Donnie & Stephen Smalley, Sheldon Smart, Roger Smith, Russell Smith, Mike Smithies, Brent Soo Hoo, Chris Sorochin, Eduardo Spaccasassi, Greg Sparke, Tomas Speight, Tomaz Sporn, Karin Stadtlander, Wilhelm Staudt, Mike Steane, Joshua Steiner, Eeva Stene, Giorgio Stenner, Erik Stern, Harry Stiles, Scott Stiller, Jessica Stone, Andreas Strohm, Beverly Suderman, Sean Sullivan, Fei-Pong Sun, Cyril Suszckiewicz, Kumiko Suzuki, Gote Svanholm, Glenn Sweitzer, Ann Tait, Joseph Tan, Yvonne Tan, Huihong Tang, Leigh Taylor, David Tejadilla, Judy Terry, Mizuno Tetsuyuki, Mathilde Teuben, Anita Teufel, Clare Thomas, Ned & Cherlyn Thomas, Rachael Thomas, Stephanie Thomas, Michael Thompson, Brian Thorburn, Brian & Janice Thorburn, Rawbie Thring, Stanley Tick, Jean Timberlake, Simon Tipping, Anne Tischlinger, Jason Titus, David Todd, Lily Toh, Derek Tokashiki, Kristin Torgerson, Nguu v Tran, Anna Trloar, Franky Tseng, Shinichi Tsuyuki, Robert Tu, William Twaddell, Justine Ullmann, Laura Upton, Leon D Urbain, Stephen Uther, Rodrigo Valades, Marianna & Jean-Philippe Vallauri-Zana, Hans van der Veen, Matt van Pelt, Lyn Veall, Louise Vella, Glenn Vickery, Iris Vogel, Isabelle & Ulrich von Arx, Narumol Vongthanasunthorn, Jaco Vos, Liz Wade, Nick Wagner, Lek Wai Mun, Clare Wainwright, John A Wakimoto, Shuichi Wakumoto, M Waldron, Hooky Walker, NA Walker, Tim Walker, Bill Walter, Jennifer Wang, Jill Warneke, Hidekazu Watanabe, Kazunori Watanabe, Michiko Watanabe-Merry, Jill Waters, Emma Watson, Gavin Watson, Stefanie Weber, Guangping Wei, Florian Weig, Reinier & Welmoet Wels, Stephanie Weng, Mario Westphal, Jamie Wheeler, Gary White, Niels Wiedenhof, Hans Wieler, Carole Wilkinson, Laurie Williams, Martin Williams, Tim Williams, Kate Williamson, Nora Wilson, Stella Wood, Andy Woodcock, David Woodhouse, Tim Woodward, Jan & Nick Wooller, Brian Wopershall, C Wrentmore, Cornelius Wuelker, Kaoru Yamamoto, Hoi Yan Lung, Elena Yap, Tomoko Yasue, Sylvia Yau, Gary David Yngve, Tomoko Yoshida, Andrew Young, Kuramasu Yutaka, Martee Zaccirey, Jitka Zelenkova, Andre Zimmermann

Index

Abbreviations

Text

Bold indicates maps.